Macroeconomics

ELEVENTH EDITION

GLOBAL EDITION

Andrew B. Abel
The Wharton School of the University of Pennsylvania

Ben S. Bernanke
Brookings Institution

Dean Croushore
Robins School of Business University of Richmond

Pearson

Harlow, England • London • New York • Boston • San Francisco • Toronto • Sydney • Dubai • Singapore • Hong Kong
Tokyo • Seoul • Taipei • New Delhi • Cape Town • São Paulo • Mexico City • Madrid • Amsterdam • Munich • Paris • Milan

Content Production: Abhilasha Watsa
Product Management: Yajnaseni Das, Paromita Banerjee, Daniel J.N. Luiz, and Ratul Ghosh
Product Marketing: Joanne Dieguez
Rights and Permissions: Anjali Singh and Ashish Vyas
Cover Image: NESPIX/Shutterstock

Pearson Education Limited
KAO Two
KAO Park
Hockham Way
Harlow
Essex
CM17 9SR
United Kingdom

and Associated Companies throughout the world

Visit us on the World Wide Web at: www.pearson.com

ISBN 10: 1-292-44612-9
ISBN 13: 978-1-292-44612-7

British Library Cataloguing-in-Publication Data
A catalogue record for this book is available from the British Library

10 9 8 7 6 5 4 3 2

Typeset in Palatino LT Pro by Straive
Printed and bound by CPI Group (UK) Ltd, Croydon, CR0 4YY

Pearson's Commitment to Diversity, Equity, and Inclusion

Pearson is dedicated to creating bias-free content that reflects the diversity, depth, and breadth of all learners' lived experiences.

We embrace the many dimensions of diversity, including but not limited to race, ethnicity, gender, sex, sexual orientation, socioeconomic status, ability, age, and religious or political beliefs.

Education is a powerful force for equity and change in our world. It has the potential to deliver opportunities that improve lives and enable economic mobility. As we work with authors to create content for every product and service, we acknowledge our responsibility to demonstrate inclusivity and incorporate diverse scholarship so that everyone can achieve their potential through learning. As the world's leading learning company, we have a duty to help drive change and live up to our purpose to help more people create a better life for themselves and to create a better world.

Our ambition is to purposefully contribute to a world where:

- Everyone has an equitable and lifelong opportunity to succeed through learning.
- Our educational content accurately reflects the histories and lived experiences of the learners we serve.
- Our educational products and services are inclusive and represent the rich diversity of learners.
- Our educational content prompts deeper discussions with students and motivates them to expand their own learning (and worldview).

Accessibility

We are also committed to providing products that are fully accessible to all learners. As per Pearson's guidelines for accessible educational Web media, we test and retest the capabilities of our products against the highest standards for every release, following the WCAG guidelines in developing new products for copyright year 2022 and beyond.

You can learn more about Pearson's commitment to accessibility at **https://www.pearson.com/uk/accessibility.html**

Pearson

Contact Us

While we work hard to present unbiased, fully accessible content, we want to hear from you about any concerns or needs with this Pearson product so that we can investigate and address them.

Please contact us with concerns about any potential bias at **https://www.pearson.com/report-bias.html**

For accessibility-related issues, such as using assistive technology with Pearson products, alternative text requests, or accessibility documentation, email the Pearson Disability Support team at **disability.support@pearson.com**

About the Authors

Andrew B. Abel

The Wharton School of the University of Pennsylvania

Ronald A. Rosenfeld Professor of Finance at The Wharton School and professor of economics at the University of Pennsylvania, Andrew Abel received his A.B. *summa cum laude* from Princeton University and his Ph.D. from the Massachusetts Institute of Technology.

He began his teaching career at the University of Chicago and Harvard University and has held visiting appointments at both Tel Aviv University and The Hebrew University of Jerusalem.

A prolific researcher, Abel has published extensively on fiscal policy, capital formation, monetary policy, asset pricing, and Social Security—as well as serving on the editorial boards of numerous journals. He has been honored as an Alfred P. Sloan Fellow, a Fellow of the Econometric Society, and a recipient of the John Kenneth Galbraith Award for teaching excellence. Abel has served as a visiting scholar at the Federal Reserve Bank of Philadelphia, as a member of the Panel of Economic Advisers at the Congressional Budget Office, and as a member of the Technical Advisory Panel on Assumptions and Methods for the Social Security Advisory Board. He is also a Research Associate of the National Bureau of Economic Research and a member of the Advisory Board of the Carnegie-Rochester–NYU Conference Series.

Ben S. Bernanke

Brookings Institution

Ben Bernanke is currently Distinguished Fellow in Residence with the Economic Studies Program at the Brookings Institution. From February 2006 to January 2014, he was Chairman of the Board of Governors of the Federal Reserve System. Before that, he served as Chair of the President's Council of Economic Advisors from June 2005 to January 2006 and was a Governor of the Federal Reserve System from August 2002 to June 2005. Prior to his work in public service, he was the Howard Harrison and Gabrielle Snyder Beck Professor of Economics and Public Affairs at Princeton University. He received his B.A. in economics from Harvard University *summa cum laude*—capturing both the Allyn Young Prize for best Harvard undergraduate economics thesis and the John H. Williams prize for outstanding senior in the Economics Department. Like coauthor Abel, he holds a Ph.D. from the Massachusetts Institute of Technology.

Bernanke began his career at the Stanford Graduate School of Business in 1979. In 1985, he moved to Princeton University, where he served as chair of the Economics Department from 1995 to 2002. He has twice been visiting professor at MIT and once at New York University, and has taught in undergraduate, M.B.A., M.P.A., and Ph.D. programs. He has authored more than 60 publications in macroeconomics, macroeconomic history, and finance.

Bernanke has served as a visiting scholar and advisor to the Federal Reserve System. He is a Guggenheim Fellow and a Fellow of the Econometric Society. He has also been variously honored as an Alfred P. Sloan Research Fellow, a Hoover Institution National Fellow, a National Science Foundation Graduate Fellow, and a Research Associate of the National Bureau of Economic Research. In 2022, he was one of the winners of the Nobel Prize in Economics for his research on banks and financial crises, which helped lay the foundations for financial market regulation. He has served as editor of the *American Economic Review*.

Dean Croushore

Robins School of Business, University of Richmond

Dean Croushore is professor of economics and Rigsby Fellow at the University of Richmond. He received his A.B. from Ohio University and his Ph.D. from Ohio State University.

Croushore began his career at Pennsylvania State University in 1984. After teaching for 5 years, he moved to the Federal Reserve Bank of Philadelphia, where he was vice president and economist. His duties during his 14 years at the Philadelphia Fed included heading the macroeconomics section, briefing the bank's president and board of directors on the state of the economy and advising them about formulating monetary policy, writing articles about the economy, administering two national surveys of forecasters, and researching current issues in monetary policy. In his role at the Fed, he created the Survey of Professional Forecasters (taking over the defunct ASA/NBER survey and revitalizing it) and developed the Real-Time Data Set for Macroeconomists.

Croushore returned to academia at the University of Richmond in 2003. The focus of his research in recent years has been on forecasting and how data revisions affect monetary policy, forecasting, and macroeconomic research. Croushore's publications include articles in many leading economics journals and a textbook on money and banking. He is associate editor of several journals and a visiting scholar at the Federal Reserve Bank of Philadelphia and an adjunct associate professor in the business school at Columbia University.

Brief Contents

Detailed Contents

Summary Tables

Key Diagrams

Applying Macroeconomics to the Real World

Applications

In Touch with Data and Research

Symbols Used in This Book

A	productivity
B	government debt
$BASE$	monetary base
C	consumption
CA	current account balance
CU	currency held by nonbank public
DEP	bank deposits
E	worker effort
FA	financial account balance
G	government purchases
I	investment
INT	net interest payments
K	capital stock
M	money supply
MC	marginal cost
MPK	marginal product of capital
MPN	marginal product of labor
$MRPN$	marginal revenue product of labor
N	employment, labor
$\bar{N}$	full-employment level of employment
NFP	net factor payments
NM	nonmonetary assets
NX	net exports
P	price level
P^e	expected price level
P_{sr}	short-run price level
R	real seignorage revenue
RES	bank reserves
S	national saving
S_{pvt}	private saving
S_{govt}	government saving
T	taxes
TR	transfers
V	velocity
W	nominal wage
Y	total income or output
$\bar{Y}$	full-employment output
a	individual wealth or assets
c	individual consumption; consumption per worker
cu	currency–deposit ratio
d	depreciation rate
e	real exchange rate
e_{nom}	nominal exchange rate
$\bar{e}_{\text{nom}}$	official value of nominal exchange rate
i	nominal interest rate
i^m	nominal interest rate on money
k	capital–labor ratio
n	growth rate of labor force
pK	price of capital goods
r	expected real interest rate
r^w	world real interest rate
$r_{\text{a-t}}$	expected real after-tax interest rate
res	reserve–deposit ratio
s	individual saving; saving rate
t	income tax rate
u	unemployment rate
$\bar{u}$	natural unemployment rate
uc	user cost of capital
w	real wage
y	individual labor income; output per worker
π	inflation rate
π^e	expected inflation rate
η_Y	income elasticity of money demand
τ	tax rate on firm revenues

Preface

New to This Edition

Listed below is a summary of the changes made in this textbook for the eleventh edition. See the following section for further details on these changes.

- Added material on changes in private saving in the pandemic (Chapter 2)
- More details on developments of the gig economy (Chapter 3)
- Comparison of pandemic versus financial crisis affecting U-3 and U-6 measures of unemployment rate (Chapter 3)
- New applications on the production function and changes in productivity in the European Union, the gig economy in the ASEAN nations, unemployment during the European debt crisis, and recent trends in labor supply and a box on labor market data (Chapter 3)
- New applications on investors' responses to tax incentives and the impact of the pandemic on consumption (Chapter 4)
- New application on income distribution trends in South Africa (Chapter 6)
- Discussion of the changes made to the definition of M1 in 2021 (Chapter 7)
- New application on measuring inflation expectations (Chapter 7)
- Eliminated discussion of M1 velocity due to non-comparability of series over time (Chapter 7)
- Discussion of the unusual nature of the pandemic recession in 2020 (Chapter 8)
- Added discussion of the Fed's new policy in 2020 of flexible inflation targeting, and the increase in the inflation rate that followed (Chapter 12)
- Eliminated discussion of the money multiplier (Chapter 14)
- Deleted application on the money multiplier in severe financial crises (Chapter 14)
- Eliminated discussion of vault cash (Chapter 14)
- Added material on monetary policy in the pandemic (Chapter 14)
- Added discussion of the Fed's new operating procedures with abundant reserves (Chapter 14)
- New applications on the lender of last resort, zero lower bound, global financial crisis of 2008, and inflation targeting (Chapter 14)
- Deleted application on quantitative easing and inflation (Chapter 15)
- New applications on supply-side economics and social security in the United Kingdom and a box on the impact of government purchases (Chapter 15)

New and Updated Coverage

What is taught in intermediate macroeconomics courses—and how it is taught—has changed substantially in recent years. Previous editions of *Macroeconomics* played a major role in these developments. The eleventh edition provides lively coverage of a broad spectrum of macroeconomic issues and ideas, including a variety of new and updated topics:

- *Long-term economic growth.* Because the rate of economic growth plays a central role in determining living standards, we devote much of Part 2 to growth and related issues. We first discuss factors contributing to growth, such as productivity (Chapter 3) and rates of saving and investment (Chapter 4); then in Chapter 6 we turn to a full-fledged analysis of the growth process, using tools such as growth accounting and the Solow model. Growth-related topics covered include the factors that determine long-run living standards and the productivity rebound of the 1990s.
  New coverage: A discussion of the pandemic of 2020 and its impact on saving (Chapter 2), on labor supply and the unemployment rate (Chapter 3), and on consumption spending (Chapter 4).
- *Business cycles.* Our analysis of business cycles begins with facts rather than theories. In Chapter 8 we give a history of U.S. business cycles and then describe the observed cyclical behavior of a variety of important economic variables (the "business cycle facts"). In Chapters 9–11 we evaluate alternative classical and Keynesian theories of the cycle by how well they explain the facts.

  New coverage: The text discusses the pandemic recession of 2020 and its aftermath compared with other recessions (Chapter 8).
- *Monetary and fiscal policy.* The effects of macroeconomic policies are considered in nearly every chapter, in both theory and applications. We present classical (Chapter 10), Keynesian (Chapter 11), and monetarist (Chapter 14) views on the appropriate use of policy.

  New or substantially revised coverage: We discuss the Fed's new flexible inflation-targeting strategy (Chapter 12). We change Chapter 14 substantially to describe the Fed's new model of monetary policy with abundant reserves and discuss new tools for monetary policy used in the pandemic.
- *Labor market issues.* We pay close attention to issues relating to employment, unemployment, and real wages. We introduce the basic supply–demand model of the labor market, as well as unemployment, early, in Chapter 3. We discuss unemployment more extensively in Chapter 12, which covers the inflation–unemployment trade-off, the costs of unemployment, and government policies for reducing unemployment. Other labor market topics include efficiency wages (Chapter 11) and the effects of marginal and average tax rate changes on labor supply (Chapter 15).

  New coverage: The text discusses recent trends in the labor force participation rate in the aftermath of the pandemic in 2020 (Chapter 3).
- *Data use.* Throughout the text, we emphasize macroeconomic data and how to use it and analyze it. Numerous boxes called In Touch with Data and Research provide descriptions of macroeconomic data. At the end of almost every chapter, problems in the Working with Macroeconomic Data section give students hands-on experience with manipulating data to help them understand macroeconomic theory and how it applies to the world.

  New coverage: This edition includes coverage of the gig economy in the ASEAN nations and the Fed's redefinition of the M1 measure of the money supply and how that affects analysis of the effects of money on the economy (Chapter 7).

- *Modeling.* The central theme of the textbook is to develop a complete macroeconomic model that students can use to understand the world's economies. We build the model in pieces in Part 2, Chapters 3–7, and put the pieces together in Part 3, Chapters 8–11.

  New material: We add a discussion of the Fed's new model of the reserves market when reserves are abundant and the role played by the interest rate on bank reserve balances (Chapter 14).
- *Enhanced Pearson eTextbook: A New Way of Learning.* The Pearson eTextbook gives students access to their textbook anytime, anywhere. In addition to notetaking, highlighting, and bookmarking, the Pearson eTextbook offers interactive and sharing features. Students actively read and learn, through embedded and auto-graded practice, real-time data-graphs, animations, author videos, and more. Instructors can share comments or highlights, and students can add their own, for a tight community of learners in any class.

Program Introduction

From February 2006 to January 2014, Ben Bernanke was chairman of the Board of Governors of the Federal Reserve System. Federal ethics rules prohibited him from working on the sixth, seventh, and eighth editions, but he has returned to make substantive contributions to the most recent ninth, tenth, and eleventh editions.

In preparing the eleventh edition, we viewed our main objective to keep the book fresh and up-to-date, especially in light of the worldwide pandemic and the many new tools used by the Federal Reserve in response to it. In addition, the empirical problems at the end of most chapters direct students to appropriate data in the FRED database on the website of the Federal Reserve Bank of St. Louis. Because this database is frequently updated and is available free of charge, students will develop familiarity and facility with a current data source that they can continue to use after completing the course.

To improve student results, we recommend pairing the text content with **MyLab Economics**, which is the teaching and learning platform that empowers you to reach every student. By combining trusted author content with digital tools and a flexible platform, MyLab personalizes the learning experience and will help your students learn and retain key course concepts while developing skills that future employers are seeking in their candidates. From **Animated Graphs to Real-time Data Analysis Exercises**, MyLab Economics helps you teach your course, your way. Learn more at *www.pearson.com/mylab/economics*.

Solving Teaching and Learning Challenges

The eleventh edition builds on the strengths that underlie the book's lasting ability to help solve teaching and learning challenges for instructors and students alike, including:

- *Real-world applications.* A perennial challenge for instructors is to help students make active use of the economic ideas developed in the text. The rich variety of applications in this book shows by example how economic concepts can be put to work in explaining real-world issues such as the housing crisis of 2007–2011 and the financial crisis of 2008, the slowdown and revival in productivity growth, the challenges facing the UK Social Security system, the impact of globalization on the U.S. economy, and new approaches to making monetary policy that were used in response to the financial crisis in 2008 and the pandemic in 2020. The eleventh edition offers new applications as well as updates of the best applications and analyses of previous editions.

- *Broad modern coverage.* From its inception, *Macroeconomics* has responded to students' desires to investigate and understand a wider range of macroeconomic issues than is permitted by the course's traditional emphasis on short-run fluctuations and stabilization policy. This book provides a modern treatment of these traditional topics but also gives in-depth coverage of other important macroeconomic issues such as the determinants of long-run economic growth, the trade balance and financial flows, labor markets, and the institutional framework of policymaking.
- *Innovative pedagogy.* The eleventh edition, like its predecessors, provides a variety of useful tools to help students study, understand, and retain the material. Features such as detailed full-color graphs that use color to demonstrate the shifts in curves, worked numerical problems at the end of selected chapters, real-world data that is regularly fed in from FRED, and end-of-chapter review and self-test material help encourage better comprehension and retention of the material.
- *Reliance on a set of core economic ideas.* Although we cover a wide range of topics, we avoid developing a new model or theory for each issue. Instead we emphasize the broad applicability of a set of core economic ideas (such as the production function, the trade-off between consuming today and saving for tomorrow, and supply–demand analysis). Using these core ideas, we build a theoretical framework that encompasses all the macroeconomic analyses presented in the book: long-run and short-run, open-economy and closed-economy, and classical and Keynesian.
- *A balanced presentation.* Macroeconomics is full of controversies, which can make it difficult to determine the best method of presentation. Sometimes the controversies overshadow the broad common ground shared by both the classicals and Keynesians (of the old, new, and neo-varieties). We emphasize that common ground. First, we pay greater attention to long-run issues (on which classicals and Keynesians have less disagreement). Second, we develop the classical and Keynesian analyses of short-run fluctuations within a single overall framework, in which we show that the two approaches differ principally in their assumptions about how quickly wages and prices adjust. Where differences in viewpoint remain—for example, in the search versus efficiency-wage interpretations of unemployment—we present and critique both perspectives. This balanced approach exposes students to all the best ideas in modern macroeconomics. At the same time, an instructor of either classical or Keynesian inclination can easily base a course on this book.

Developing Employability Skills

For students to succeed in a rapidly changing job market, they should be aware of their career options and how to go about developing a variety of skills. With *Macroeconomics,* eleventh edition and MyLab Economics, we focus on developing these skills in the following ways:

- *Working with Macroeconomic Data.* In nearly every chapter of *Macroeconomics,* eleventh edition, end-of-chapter questions ask students to download data from macroeconomic databases and to manipulate the data to illustrate theoretical ideas.

These questions give students the opportunity to get hands-on experience with data while doing a variety of empirical exercises, which provides experience that employers find valuable. In addition, MyLab Economics provides Real-Time Data Analysis Exercises, which use current macro data to help students understand the impact of changes in economic variables. Real-Time Data Analysis Exercises communicate directly with the Federal Reserve Bank of St. Louis FRED® site and update automatically as new data become available.

- *Applications.* Applications in each chapter show students how they can use theory to understand an important episode or issue. Examples of topics covered in Applications include the increase in the duration of unemployment in the European Debt Crisis (Chapter 3), the macroeconomic consequences of the boom and bust in stock prices (Chapter 4), how investors respond to tax incentives (Chapter 4), the United States as international debtor (Chapter 5), the recent surge in U.S. productivity growth (Chapter 6), the 2008 oil price shock (Chapter 9), calibrating the business cycle (Chapter 10), inflation targeting, the lender of last resort, and whether there is a zero lower bound on nominal interest rates (Chapter 14), and supply-side economics (Chapter 15).
- *In Touch with Data and Research.* These boxes give the reader further insight into new developments in economic research as well as a guide to keeping abreast of new developments in the economy. Research topics in these boxes include discussions of biases in inflation measurement (Chapter 2), alternative measures of unemployment (Chapter 3), the link between capital investment and the stock market (Chapter 4), flows of U.S. dollars abroad (Chapter 7), DSGE models and the classical–Keynesian debate (Chapter 10), the Lucas critique (Chapter 12), and the impact on the economy of fiscal stimulus packages (Chapter 15). Keeping abreast of the economy requires an understanding of what data are available, as well as their strengths and shortcomings. We provide a series of boxes to show where to find key macroeconomic data—such as labor market data (Chapter 3), balance of payments data (Chapter 5), and exchange rates (Chapter 13)—and how to interpret them.

A Flexible Organization

The eleventh edition maintains the flexible structure of earlier editions. In Part 1 (Chapters 1–2), we introduce the field of macroeconomics and discuss issues of economic measurement. In Part 2 (Chapters 3–7), we focus on long-run issues, including productivity, saving, investment, the trade balance, growth, and inflation. We devote Part 3 (Chapters 8–11) to the study of short-run economic fluctuations and stabilization policy. Finally, in Part 4 (Chapters 12–15), we take a closer look at issues and institutions of policymaking. Appendix A at the end of the book reviews useful algebraic and graphical tools.

Instructors of intermediate macroeconomics have different preferences as to course content, and their choices are often constrained by their students' backgrounds and the length of the term. The structure of *Macroeconomics* accommodates various needs. In planning how to use the book, instructors might find it useful to consider the following points:

- *Core chapters.* We recommend that every course include these six chapters:

  Chapter 1 Introduction to Macroeconomics

  Chapter 2 The Measurement and Structure of the National Economy

Chapter 3 Productivity, Output, and Employment
Chapter 4 Consumption, Saving, and Investment
Chapter 7 The Asset Market, Money, and Prices
Chapter 9 The *IS–LM/AD–AS* Model: A General Framework for Macroeconomic Analysis

Chapters 1 and 2 provide an introduction to macroeconomics, including national income accounting. The next four chapters in the list make up the analytical core of the book: Chapter 3 examines the labor market, Chapters 3 and 4 together develop the goods market, Chapter 7 discusses the asset market, and Chapter 9 combines the three markets into a general equilibrium model usable for short-run analysis (in either a classical or Keynesian mode).

- *Suggested additions.* To a syllabus containing these six chapters, instructors can add various combinations of the other chapters, depending on the course focus. The following are some possible choices:

Short-run focus. Instructors who prefer to emphasize short-run issues (business cycle fluctuations and stabilization policy) may omit Chapters 5 and 6 without loss of continuity. They could also go directly from Chapters 1 and 2 to Chapters 8 and 9, which introduce business cycles and the *IS–LM/AD–AS* framework. Although the presentation in Chapters 8 and 9 is self-contained, it will be helpful for instructors who skip Chapters 3–7 to provide some background and motivation for the various behavioral relationships and equilibrium conditions.

Classical emphasis. For instructors who want to teach the course with a modern classical emphasis, we recommend assigning all the chapters in Part 2. In Part 3, Chapters 8–10 provide a self-contained presentation of classical business cycle theory. Other material of interest includes the Friedman–Phelps interpretation of the Phillips curve (Chapter 12), the role of credibility in monetary policy (Chapter 14), and Ricardian equivalence with multiple generations (Chapter 15).

Keynesian emphasis. Instructors who prefer a Keynesian emphasis may choose to omit Chapter 10 (classical business cycle analysis). As noted, if a short-run focus is preferred, Chapter 5 (full-employment analysis of the open economy) and Chapter 6 (long-run economic growth) may also be omitted without loss of continuity.

International focus. Chapter 5 discusses saving, investment, and the trade balance in an open economy with full employment. Chapter 13 considers exchange rate determination and macroeconomic policy in an open-economy model in which short-run deviations from full employment are possible. (Chapter 5 is a useful but not essential prerequisite for Chapter 13.) Both chapters may be omitted for a course focusing on the domestic economy.

Instructor Teaching Resources

This program comes with the following teaching resources.

Supplements available to instructors at www.pearson.com/en-gb.html	**Features of the Supplement**
Instructor's Manual authored by Dean Croushore from University of Richmond	• Chapter-by-chapter summaries • Teaching outlines • Suggested topics for class discussion • Solutions to end-of-chapter questions and problems in the book
Test Bank authored by Dean Croushore from University of Richmond	Over 1,600 multiple-choice, true/false, short- answer, and graphing questions with these annotations: • Difficulty level (1 for straight recall, 2 for some analysis, 3 for complex analysis) • Type (Multiple-choice and short-answer) • Topic (The section that covers the term or concept being tested) • Learning outcome
Computerized TestGen	TestGen allow instructors to: • Customize, save, and generate classroom tests • Edit, add, or delete questions from the Test Item Files • Analyze test results • Organize a database of tests and student results
PowerPoints authored by Dean Croushore from University of Richmond	Slides include all key text material including graphs, tables, and equations in the textbook. These PowerPoints meet accessibility standards for students with disabilities. Features include, but not limited to: • Keyboard and Screen Reader access • Alternative text for images • High color contrast between background and foreground colors

Acknowledgments

A textbook isn't the lonely venture of its author or coauthors but rather is the joint project of dozens of skilled and dedicated people. We extend special thanks to Carrie Sharp, Senior Content Producer, for her superb work on the eleventh edition as well as Thomas Hayword, Senior Content Analyst, for guiding this edition from beginning to end. For their efforts, care, and craft, we also thank Kelly Murphy, project manager from Straive, and Noel Lotz, digital content team lead.

We also appreciate the contributions of the reviewers and colleagues who have offered valuable comments on succeeding drafts of the book in all eleven editions thus far:

Ugur Aker, *Hiram College*
Krishna Akkina, *Kansas State University*
Terence J. Alexander, *Iowa State University*
Edward Allen, *University of Houston*
Richard G. Anderson, *Lindenwood University*
David Aschauer, *Bates College*
Martin A. Asher, *The Wharton School, University of Pennsylvania*
David Backus, *New York University*
Daniel Barbezat, *Amherst College*
Reza Bavafa, *University of Southern California*
Parantap Basu, *Durham University*
Valerie R. Bencivenga, *University of Texas*

Haskel Benishay, *Kellogg Graduate School of Management, Northwestern University*
Charles A. Bennett, *Gannon University*
John F. Berdell, *DePaul University*
Joydeep Bhattacharya, *Iowa State University*
David Black, *University of Toledo*
Robert A. Blewett, *Saint Lawrence University*
Scott Bloom, *Missouri State University*
Bruce R. Bolnick, *Nathan Associates*
David Brasfield, *Murray State University*
Viacheslav Breusov, *Alliance Bernstein*
Audie Brewton, *Northeastern Illinois University*
Stacey Brook, *University of Iowa*
Nancy Burnett, *University of Wisconsin, Oshkosh*
Maureen Burton, *California Polytechnic University, Pomona*
John Campbell, *Harvard University*
Kevin Carey, *The World Bank*
J. Lon Carlson, *Illinois State University*
Wayne Carroll, *University of Wisconsin, Eau Claire*
Arthur Schiller Casimir, *Western New England University*
Stephen Cecchetti, *Brandeis University*
Paul Chambers, *University of Central Missouri*
Anthony Chan, *JPMorgan Chase*
Leo Chan, *Utah Valley University*
S. Chandrasekhar, *Indira Gandhi Institute of Development Research*
Henry Chappell, *American University of Sharjah*
Jen–Chi Cheng, *Wichita State University*
Menzie Chinn, *University of Wisconsin*
K. A. Chopra, *State University of New York, Oneonta*
Nan-Ting Chou, *University of Louisville*
Jens Christiansen, *Mount Holyoke College*
Reid W. Click, *George Washington University*
John P. Cochran, *Metropolitan State College of Denver*
Juan Carlos Cordoba, *Iowa State University*
Steven R. Cunningham, *University of Connecticut*
Waclaw Dajnowiec, *Ryerson University, Chang School*
Bruce R. Dalgaard, *Carleton College*
Betty C. Daniel, *University at Albany—SUNY*
Joe Daniels, *Marquette University*
Edward Day, *University of Central Florida*
Luis De Araujo, *Michigan State University*
Robert Dekle, *University of Southern California*
Greg Delemeester, *Marietta College*
Wouter J. Den Haan, *London School of Economics*
Johan Deprez, *Texas Tech University*
James Devine, *Loyola Marymount University*
Wael William Diab, *Broadcom*
Peter Dohlman, *International Monetary Fund*
Patrick Dolenc, *Keene State College*
David Doorn, *West Chester University of Pennsylvania*
Allan Drazen, *University of Maryland*
Robert Driskill, *Vanderbilt University*
Bill Dupor, *Federal Reserve Bank of St Louis*
Donald H. Dutkowsky, *Syracuse University*
James E. Eaton, *Bridgewater College*
Janice C. Eberly, *Northwestern University*
Andrew Economopoulos, *Ursinus College*
Alejandra Cox Edwards, *California State University, Long Beach*
Martin Eichenbaum, *Northwestern University*
Carlos G. Elias, *Radford University*
Kirk Elwood, *James Madison University*
Abel Embaye, *University of Arkansas*
Sharon J. Erenburg, *Eastern Michigan University*
Christopher Erickson, *New Mexico State University*
James Fackler, *University of Kentucky*
Steven Fazzari, *Washington University*
J. Peter Ferderer, *Macalester College*
Abdollah Ferdowsi, *Ferris State University*
David W. Findlay, *Colby College*
Thomas J. Finn, *Wayne State University*
Charles C. Fischer, *Pittsburg State University*
John A. Flanders, *Central Methodist College*
Juergen Fleck, *Hollins College*
Adrian Fleissig, *California State University, Fullerton*
R. N. Folsom, *San Jose State University*
Kevin Foster, *City University of New York*
J. E. Fredland, *U.S. Naval Academy*
James R. Gale, *Michigan Technological University*
Edward N. Gamber, *Congressional Budget Office*
William T. Ganley, *Buffalo State College*
Charles B. Garrison, *University of Tennessee, Knoxville*
Kathie Gilbert, *Mississippi State University*
Roger Goldberg, *Ohio Northern University*
Joao Gomes, *The Wharton School, University of Pennsylvania*
Fred C. Graham, *Federal Housing Finance Agency*
John W. Graham, *Rutgers University*
Stephen A. Greenlaw, *University of Mary Washington*
Alan F. Gummerson, *Florida International University*
A. R. Gutowsky, *California State University, Sacramento*
David R. Hakes, *University of Northern Iowa*
Michael Haliassos, *Goethe University Frankfurt*
George J. Hall, *Brandeis University*
John C. Haltiwanger, *University of Maryland*
James Hamilton, *University of California, San Diego*
David Hammes, *University of Hawaii*
Reza Hamzaee, *Missouri Western State University*
Robert Stanley Herren, *North Dakota University*
Charles Himmelberg, *Goldman Sachs*
Barney F. Hope, *California State University, Chico*
Fenn Horton, *Naval Postgraduate School*
Christopher House, *University of Michigan*
E. Philip Howrey, *University of Michigan*
John Huizinga, *University of Chicago*
Nayyer Hussain, *Rockland Community College*
Syed Muhammad Hussain, *Virginia Commonwealth University*
Steven Husted, *University of Pittsburgh*
Matthew Hyle, *Winona State University*
Matteo Iacoviello, *Boston College*
Selo Imrohoroglu, *University of Southern California*
Kenneth Inman, *Neustar College*

Liana Jacobi, *University of Melbourne*
Zuzana Janko, *San Francisco State University*
Philip N. Jefferson, *Swarthmore College*
Urban Jermann, *The Wharton School, University of Pennsylvania*
Charles W. Johnston, *Baker College*
Barry E. Jones, *Binghamton University*
Paul Junk, *University of Minnesota*
James Kahn, *Yeshiva University*
George Karras, *University of Illinois, Chicago*
Roger Kaufman, *Smith College*
Adrienne Kearney, *University of Maine*
James Keeler, *Kenyon College*
Patrick R. Kelso, *West Texas State University*
Kusum Ketkar, *Seton Hall University*
F. Khan, *University of Wisconsin, Parkside*
Jinill Kim, *Korea University*
Robert King, *Boston University*
Ruby P. Kishan, *Texas State University*
Milka S. Kirova, *Saint Louis University*
Nobuhiro Kiyotaki, *Princeton University*
Michael Klein, *Tufts University*
Peter Klenow, *Stanford University*
Kenneth Koelln, *University of North Texas*
Douglas Koritz, *Buffalo State College*
Eugene Kroch, *Villanova University*
Corinne Krupp, *University of North Carolina, Chapel Hill*
Kishore Kulkarni, *Metropolitan State College of Denver*
Krishna B. Kumar, *University of Southern California*
Andre Kurmann, *Drexel University*
Maureen Lage, *Miami University*
John S. Lapp, *North Carolina State University*
G. Paul Larson, *University of North Dakota*
Sven R. Larson, *Skidmore College*
James Lee, *Fort Hays State University*
Junsoo Lee, *University of Alabama*
Keith J. Leggett, *Davis and Elkins College*
Carol Scotese Lehr, *Virginia Commonwealth University*
John Leyes, *Florida International University*
Xuan Liu, *East Carolina University*
Ming Chien Lo, *University of Virginia*
Mary Lorely, *Syracuse University*
Cara Lown, *Federal Reserve Bank of New York*
Richard MacDonald, *St. Cloud State University*
Thampy Mammen, *St. Norbert College*
Linda M. Manning, *University of Missouri*
Michael Marlow, *California Polytechnic State University*
Kathryn G. Marshall, *Cal Poly San Luis Obispo*
Patrick Mason, *Florida State University*
Ben Matta, *New Mexico State University*
Stephen McCafferty, *Ohio State University*
J. Harold McClure, Jr., *Thomson Reuters*
Ken McCormick, *University of Northern Iowa*
John McDermott, *University of South Carolina*
Michael B. McElroy, *North Carolina State University*
Randolph McGee, *University of Kentucky*
Michael McPherson, *University of North Texas*
William Melick, *Kenyon University*
Stephen M. Miller, *University of Nevada, Las Vegas*
Tim Miller, *Denison University*
Bruce Mizrach, *Rutgers University*
Tommaso Monacelli, *Bocconi University*
Basil Moore, *Wesleyan University*
W. Douglas Morgan, *University of California, Santa Barbara*
Jon Nadenichek, *California State University, Northridge*
K. R. Nair, *West Virginia Wesleyan College*
Emi Nakamura, *Columbia University*
Aimee Narcisenfeld, *The Bullis School*
John Neri, *University of Maryland*
Alexandra Nica, *University of Iowa*
Jeffrey Nugent, *University of Southern California*
Maurice Obstfeld, *University of California, Berkeley*
Stephen A. O'Connell, *Swarthmore College*
William P. O'Dea, *State University of New York, Oneonta*
Heather O'Neill, *Ursinus College*
Athanasios Orphanides, *Massachusetts Institute of Technology*
Spencer Pack, *Connecticut College*
Walter Park, *American University*
Randall Parker, *East Carolina University*
Allen Parkman, *University of New Mexico*
David Parsley, *Vanderbilt University*
James E. Payne, *University of New Orleans*
Rowena Pecchenino, *National University of Ireland Maynooth*
Peter Pedroni, *Williams College*
Mark Pernecky, *St. Olaf College*
Christopher Phelan, *University of Minnesota*
Kerk Phillips, *Brigham Young University*
Paul Pieper, *University of Illinois, Chicago*
Andrew J. Policano, *University of California, Irvine*
Richard Pollock, *University of Hawaii, Manoa*
Jay B. Prag, *Claremont McKenna College*
Kojo Quartey, *Monroe County Community College*
Vaman Rao, *Western Illinois University*
Neil Raymon, *University of Missouri, Columbia*
Colin Read, *SUNY Plattsburgh*
Michael Redfearn, *Citigroup*
Robert R. Reed, *University of Alabama*
Charles Revier, *Colorado State University*
Patricia Reynolds, *International Monetary Fund*
Jack Rezelman, *State University of New York, Potsdam*
Robert Rich, *Federal Reserve Bank of New York*
Libby Rittenberg, *Colorado College*
Helen Roberts, *University of Illinois, Chicago*
Kenneth Rogoff, *Harvard University*
Rosemary Rossiter, *Ohio University*
Glenn Rudebusch, *Federal Reserve Bank of San Francisco*
Benjamin Russo, *University of North Carolina, Charlotte*
Heajin Heidi Ryoo, *La Trobe University*
Plutarchos Sakellaris, *Athens University of Economics and Business*
Christine Sauer, *University of New Mexico*
Perihan Saygin, *University of Florida*
Edward Schmidt, *Randolph–Macon College*
Stacey Schreft, *Scout Investments*
Scott Schuh, *West Virginia University*
Daria Sevastianova, *University of Southern Indiana*
William Seyfried, *Rollins College*
Tayyeb Shabbir, *Wharton School, University of Pennsylvania*
Andrei Shevchenko, *Michigan State University*
Virginia Shingleton, *Valparaiso University*

Dorothy Siden, *Salem State University*

Scott Simkins, *North Carolina A&T State University*

Tara Sinclair, *George Washington University*

Abdol Soofi, *University of Wisconsin, Platteville*

Nicholas Souleles, *The Wharton School, University of Pennsylvania*

David E. Spencer, *Brigham Young University*

Don Stabile, *St. Mary's College*

Richard Startz, *University of California, Santa Barbara*

Gabriel Talmain, *University of Glasgow*

Bryan Taylor, *Global Financial Data*

Susan Washburn Taylor, *Millsaps College*

M. Dek Terrell, *Louisiana State University*

Henry S. Terrell, *University of Maryland*

Willem Thorbecke, *George Mason University*

Stephen J. Turnovsky, *University of Washington*

Michael Twomey, *University of Michigan, Dearborn*

Michael Ulan, *U.S. Department of State*

Victor Valcarcel, *Texas Tech University*

Dietrich Vollrath, *University of Houston*

Ronald Warren, *University of Georgia*

Chong K. Yip, *Chinese University of Hong Kong*

Carlos Zarazaga, *Southern Methodist University*

We thank John Haltiwanger of the University of Maryland for supplying data on job creation and destruction used in Chapter 10 and Shigeru Fujita of the Federal Reserve Bank of Philadelphia for data on the rates of job loss and job finding used in Chapter 8. We would also like to thank the late Robert H. Rasche, former research director at the Federal Reserve Bank of St. Louis, for assisting us in our use of the FRED database cited at the end of each chapter in the Working with Macroeconomic Data exercises.

Finally, we thank Mark Gertler, Rick Mishkin, and Steve Zeldes for valuable assistance with the first edition. Also, we are grateful to several cohorts of students at the University of Pennsylvania, Princeton University, and the University of Richmond who—not entirely of their own free will but nonetheless very graciously—assisted us in the development of this textbook. Last and most important, we thank our families for their patience and support. We dedicate this book to them.

A. B. A.
Wynnewood, PA

B. S. B.
Washington, DC

D. C.
Richmond, VA

Global Edition Acknowledgments

Pearson would like to thank the following people for their work on the Global Edition:

Contributors

Monal Abdel-Baki, *Durban University of Technology*

Mduduzi Biyase, *University of Johannesburg*

Simeon Coleman, *Loughborough University*

Rabi'ah Abd. Rahman, *Taylor's University*

Patrick Terroir, *Sciences Po, France*

Reviewers

Ahmad Hassan Ahmad, *Loughborough University*

Natalie Chen, *University of Warwick*

Sara Eugeni, *Durham University*

Richard Farkas, *University of Pécs*

Gregory William Whitten, *Lingnan University*

1

Introduction to Macroeconomics

1.1 What Macroeconomics Is About

Summarize the primary issues addressed in macroeconomics.

Macroeconomics is the study of the structure and performance of national economies and of the policies that governments use to try to affect economic performance. The issues that macroeconomists address include the following:

- *What determines a nation's long-run economic growth?* In 1870, income per capita was smaller in Norway than in Argentina. But today, income per capita is four times as high in Norway as in Argentina. Why do some nations' economies grow quickly, providing their citizens with rapidly improving living standards, whereas other nations' economies are relatively stagnant?
- *What causes a nation's economic activity to fluctuate?* Following a deep recession from the end of 2007 to mid-2009, the U.S. economy enjoyed the longest period of uninterrupted economic growth in U.S. economic history, until the COVID pandemic hit the entire world economy in early 2020. In the second quarter of 2020, output declined by more than 31%, the largest decline in U.S. history. But output grew more than 33% in the third quarter, which is the largest increase in the nation's history. Why do economies sometimes experience sharp short-run fluctuations, lurching between periods of prosperity and periods of hard times?
- *What causes unemployment?* During the 1930s, one-quarter of the work force in the United States was unemployed. A decade later, during World War II, less than 2% of the work force was unemployed. Why does unemployment sometimes reach very high levels? Why, even during times of relative prosperity, is a significant fraction of the work force unemployed?
- *What causes prices to rise?* The rate of inflation in the United States crept steadily upward during the 1970s, and exceeded 10% per year in the early 1980s, before dropping to less than 4% per year in the mid-1980s and dropping even further to less than 2% per year in the late 1990s. Germany's inflation experience has been much more extreme: Although Germany has earned a reputation for low inflation in recent decades, following its defeat in World War I, Germany experienced an 18-month period (July 1922–December 1923) during which prices rose by a factor of several billion! What causes inflation, and what can be done about it?
- *How does being part of a global economic system affect nations' economies?* In the late 1990s, the U.S. economy was the engine of worldwide economic growth. From 2007 to 2009, when the U.S. economy fell into a deep decline,

Learning Objectives

1.1 Summarize the primary issues addressed in macroeconomics.

1.2 Describe the activities and objectives of macroeconomists.

1.3 Differentiate between the classical and Keynesian approaches to macroeconomics.

most of the rest of the world followed. How do economic links among nations, such as international trade and borrowing, affect the performance of individual economies and the world economy as a whole?

- *Can government policies be used to improve a nation's economic performance?* In the 1980s and 1990s, the U.S. economy's output, unemployment rate, and inflation rate fluctuated much less than in the 1960s and 1970s. Some economists credit good government policy for the improvement in economic performance. In the financial crisis of 2008, the Federal Reserve and the federal government used extraordinary measures to keep banks and other financial institutions from failing. But some economists criticized these measures for going too far in trying to stabilize the economy, at the expense of creating incentives for increased risk taking by financial firms. Other economists criticized the Federal Reserve for not going far enough because the unemployment rate remained persistently high for years after the end of the recession in 2009. How should economic policy be conducted to keep the economy as prosperous and stable as possible?

Macroeconomics seeks to offer answers to such questions, which are of great practical importance and are constantly debated by politicians, the press, and the public. In the rest of this section, we consider these key macroeconomic issues in more detail.

Long-Run Economic Growth

If you have ever traveled in a developing country, you could not help but observe the difference in living standards relative to those of countries such as the United States. The problems of inadequate food, shelter, and health care experienced by citizens of rich nations who are the poorest often represent the average situation for the people of a developing country. From a macroeconomic perspective, the difference between rich nations and developing nations may be summarized by saying that rich nations have at some point in their history experienced extended periods of rapid economic growth but that the poorer nations either have never experienced sustained growth or have had periods of growth offset by periods of economic decline.

Figure 1.1 summarizes the growth in output of the U.S. economy since 1869.[1] The record is an impressive one: Over the past 152 years, the annual output of U.S. goods and services has increased by more than 150 times. The performance of the U.S. economy is not unique, however; other industrial nations have had similar, and in some cases higher, rates of growth over the same period of time. This massive increase in the output of industrial economies is one of the central facts of modern history and has had enormous political, military, social, and even cultural implications.

In part, the long-term growth of the U.S. economy is the result of a rising population, which has meant a steady increase in the number of available workers. But another significant factor is the increase in the amount of output that can be

[1]Output is measured in Fig. 1.1 by two very similar concepts, real gross national product (real GNP) prior to 1929 and real gross domestic product (real GDP) since 1929, both of which measure the inflation-adjusted amount of production in each year. We discuss the measurement of output in detail in Chapter 2.

FIGURE 1.1

Output of the U.S. economy, 1869–2021

In this graph the output of the U.S. economy is measured by real gross domestic product (real GDP) for the period 1929–2021 and by real gross national product (real GNP) for the period prior to 1929, with goods and services valued at their 2012 prices in both cases (see Chapter 2). Note the strong upward trend in output over time, as well as sharp fluctuations during the Great Depression (1929–1940), World War II (1941–1945), and the recessions of 1973–1975, 1981–1982, 1990–1991, 2001, 2007–2009, and 2020.

Sources: Real GNP 1869–1928 from Christina D. Romer, "The Prewar Business Cycle Reconsidered: New Estimates of Gross National Product, 1869–1908," *Journal of Political Economy*, 97, 1 (February 1989), pp. 22–23; real GDP 1929 onward from FRED database, Federal Reserve Bank of St. Louis, *fred.stlouisfed.org/series/GDPCA*. Data from Romer were rescaled to 2012 prices.

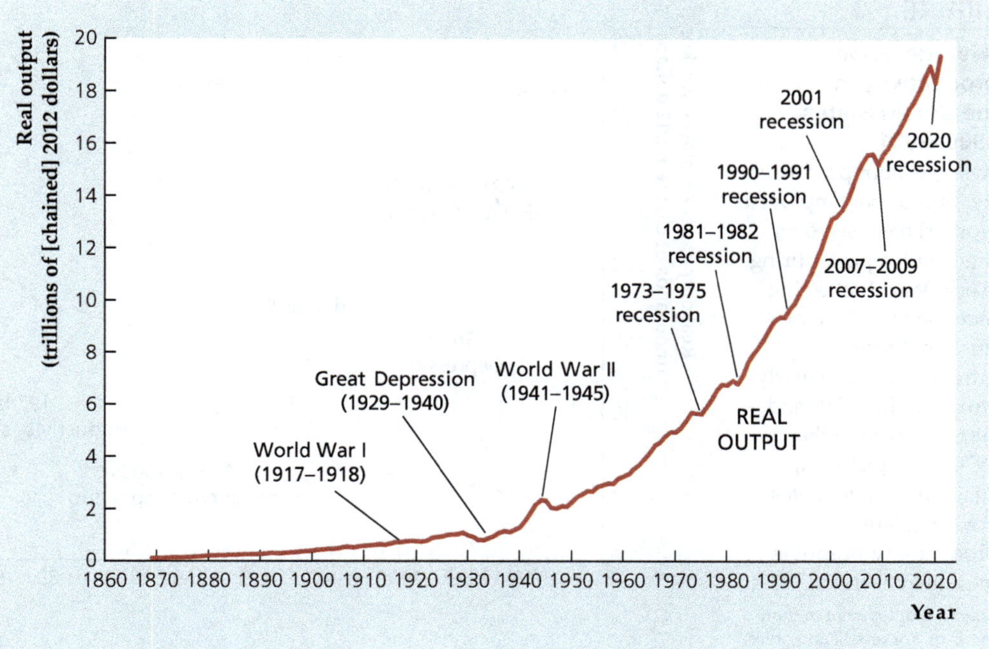

produced with a given amount of labor. The amount of output produced per unit of labor input—for example, per worker or per hour of work—is called **average labor productivity**. Figure 1.2 shows how average labor productivity, defined in this case as output per employed worker, has changed since 1900. In 2021, the average worker in the United States produced more than eight times as much output as the average worker at the beginning of the twentieth century, despite working fewer hours over the course of the year. Because today's typical worker is so much more productive, Americans enjoy a significantly higher standard of living than would have been possible a century ago.

Although the long-term record of productivity growth in the U.S. economy is excellent, productivity growth varies significantly over time. Output per worker grew about 2.6% per year from 1949 to 1973, but only 1.1% per year from 1973 to 1995. More recently, from 1995 to 2007, output per worker increased 1.9% per year, but grew only 1.3% per year from 2007 to 2021.

Because the rates of growth of output and, particularly, of output per worker ultimately determine whether a nation will be rich or poor, understanding what determines growth is one of the most important goals of macroeconomics. Unfortunately, explaining why economies grow is not easy. Why, for example, did resource-poor Japan and South Korea experience growth rates that transformed them in a generation or two from war-torn nations into industrial powers, whereas several resource-rich nations of Latin America, such as Venezuela, have had erratic or even negative growth in recent decades? Although macroeconomists have nothing close to a complete answer to the question of what determines rates of economic growth, they do have some ideas to offer. For example, as we discuss in some detail in this book, most macroeconomists believe that rates of saving and investment are important for growth. Another key determinant of growth we discuss is the rate at which technological change and other factors help increase the productivity of machines and workers.

FIGURE 1.2

Average labor productivity in the United States, 1900–2021

Average labor productivity (output per employed worker) has risen over time, with a peak during World War II reflecting increased wartime production. Productivity growth was particularly strong in the 1950s and 1960s, slowed in the 1970s, and picked up again in the mid-1990s. For the calculation of productivity, output is measured as in Fig. 1.1.

Sources: Employment in thousands of workers 14 and older for 1900–1947 from *Historical Statistics of the United States, Colonial Times to 1970,* p. 126; workers 16 and older for 1948 onward from FRED database, Federal Reserve Bank of St. Louis, *fred.stlouisfed.org/series/CE16OV*. Average labor productivity is output divided by employment, where output is from Fig. 1.1.

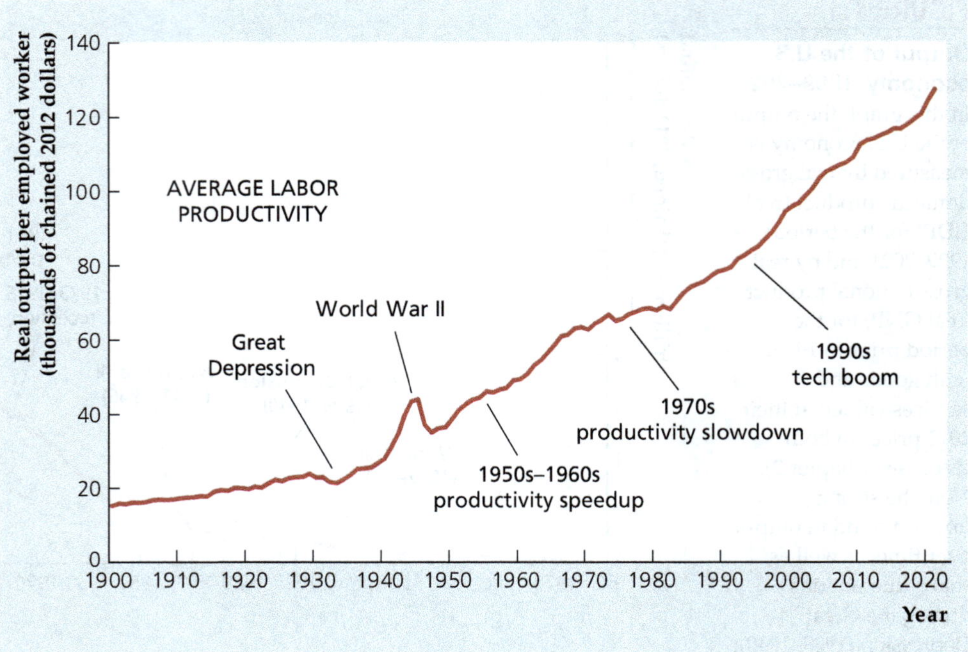

Business Cycles

If you look at the history of U.S. output in Fig. 1.1, you will notice that the growth of output isn't always smooth but has hills and valleys. Most striking is the period between 1929 and 1945, which spans the Great Depression and World War II. During the 1929–1933 economic collapse that marked the first major phase of the Great Depression, the output of the U.S. economy fell by nearly 30%. Over the period 1939–1944, as the United States entered World War II and expanded production of armaments, output nearly doubled. No fluctuations in U.S. output since 1945 have been as severe as those of the 1929–1945 period. However, during the postwar era there have been periods of unusually rapid economic growth, such as during the 1960s and 1990s, and times during which output actually declined from one year to the next, as in 1973–1975, 1981–1982, 1990–1991, 2007–2009, and 2020.

Macroeconomists use the term *business cycle* to describe short-run, but sometimes sharp, contractions and expansions in economic activity.[2] The downward phase of a business cycle, during which national output may be falling or perhaps growing only very slowly, is called a *recession*. Even when they are relatively mild, recessions mean hard economic times for many people. Recessions are also a major political concern because almost every politician wants to be reelected and the chances of reelection are better if the nation's economy is expanding rather than contracting. Macroeconomists put a lot of effort into trying to figure out what causes business cycles and deciding what can or should be done about them. In this book, we describe a variety of features of business cycles, compare alternative explanations for cyclical fluctuations, and evaluate the policy options that are available for affecting the course of the cycle.

---

[2]A more exact definition is given in Chapter 8. Business cycles do not include fluctuations lasting only a few months, such as the increase in activity that occurs around Christmas.

FIGURE 1.3

The U.S. unemployment rate, 1890–2021
The figure shows the percentage of the civilian labor force (excluding people in the military) that was unemployed in each year since 1890. Unemployment peaked during the depression of the 1890s and the Great Depression of the 1930s, and reached low points in 1920 and during World War II. Since World War II, the highest unemployment rates occurred during the 1981–1982, 2007–2009, and 2020 recessions.

Sources: Civilian unemployment rate (people aged 14 and older until 1947, aged 16 and older after 1947) for 1890–1947 from *Historical Statistics of the United States, Colonial Times to 1970,* p. 135; for 1948 onward from FRED database, Federal Reserve Bank of St. Louis, *fred.stlouisfed.org/series/UNRATE.*

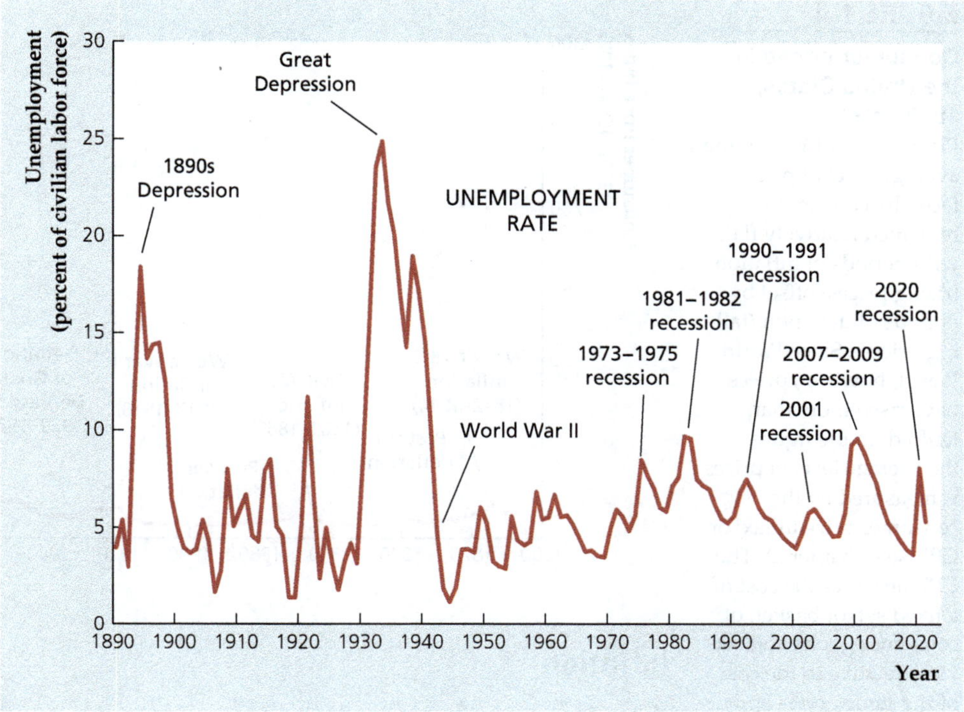

Unemployment

One important aspect of recessions is that they usually are accompanied by an increase in **unemployment**, or the number of people who are available for work and are actively seeking work but cannot find jobs. Along with growth and business cycles, the problem of unemployment is a third major issue in macroeconomics.

The best-known measure of unemployment is the unemployment rate, which is the number of unemployed divided by the total labor force (the number of people either working or seeking work). Figure 1.3 shows the unemployment rate in the United States over the past century and a quarter. The highest and most prolonged period of unemployment occurred during the Great Depression of the 1930s. In 1933, the unemployment rate was 24.9%, indicating that about one of every four potential workers was unable to find a job. In contrast, the tremendous increase in economic activity that occurred during World War II significantly reduced unemployment. In 1944, at the peak of the wartime boom, the unemployment rate was 1.2%.

Recessions have led to significant increases in unemployment in the postwar period. For example, during the 1981–1982 recession the U.S. unemployment rate reached 10.8%, during the 2007–2009 recession it rose to 10.0%, and during the 2020 pandemic recession it reached 14.7%.[3] Even during periods of economic expansion, however, the unemployment rate remains well above zero, as you can see from Fig. 1.3. In February 2020, after more than 10 years of economic growth with no recession, the unemployment rate was still about 3.5% Why the unemployment rate can remain fairly high even when the economy as a whole is doing well is another important question in macroeconomics.

[3]The unemployment rate was 14.7% in April 2020. The unemployment rate plotted in Fig. 1.3 is not this high because the graph only shows annual data—the average unemployment rate over the 12 months of each year—which was 8.1% in 2020.

FIGURE 1.4

Consumer prices in the United States, 1800–2021

Prior to World War II, the average level of prices faced by consumers remained relatively flat, with periods of inflation (rising prices) offset by periods of deflation (falling prices). Since World War II, however, prices have risen more than tenfold. In the figure, the average level of prices is measured by the consumer price index, or CPI (see Chapter 2). The CPI measures the cost of a fixed set, or basket, of consumer goods and services relative to the cost of the same goods and services in a base period—in this case, 1982–1984. Thus a CPI of 271 in 2021 means that a basket of consumer goods and services that cost $100 in 1982–1984 would cost $271 in 2021.

Sources: Consumer price index, 1800–1946 (1967 = 100) from *Historical Statistics of the United States, Colonial Times to 1970,* pp. 210–211; 1947 onward (1982–1984 = 100) from FRED database, Federal Reserve Bank of St. Louis, *fred.stlouisfed.org/series/CPIAUCSL.* Data prior to 1947 were rescaled to a base with 1982–1984 = 100.

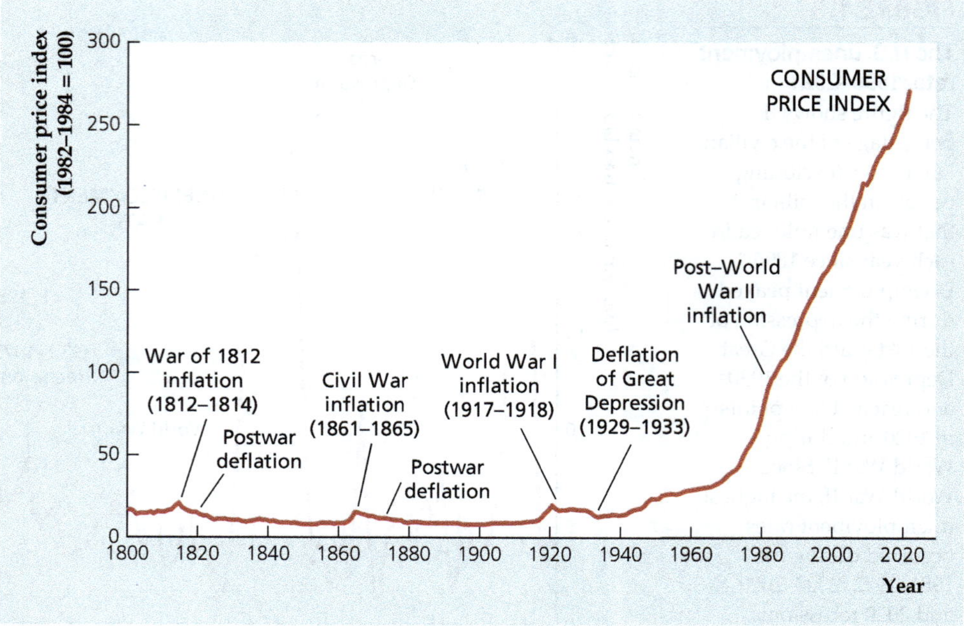

Inflation

When the prices of most goods and services are rising over time, the economy is said to be experiencing **inflation**. Figure 1.4 shows a measure of the average level of prices faced by consumers in the United States over the past two centuries.[4] Note that prior to World War II inflation usually occurred only during wartime, such as during the War of 1812, the Civil War, and World War I. These wartime periods of inflation were followed by periods of **deflation**, during which the prices of most goods and services fell. The result of these offsetting periods of inflation and deflation was that, over the long run, the level of prices was fairly constant. For example, prices at the end of World War I (1918) stood at about the same level as in 1800, more than a century earlier.

The last significant deflation in the United States occurred during 1929–1933, the initial phase of the Great Depression. Since then, inflation, without offsetting deflation, has become the normal state of affairs, although inflation was fairly low in the 1990s and 2000s. Figure 1.4 shows that consumer prices have risen significantly since World War II, with the measure of prices shown increasing tenfold.

The percentage increase in the average level of prices over some period, often a year, is called the *inflation rate.* If the inflation rate in consumer prices is 10% per year, for example, then on average the prices of items that consumers buy are rising by 10% per year. Rates of inflation may vary dramatically both over time and by country, from 1 or 2% per year in low-inflation countries (such as Switzerland) to 1000% per year or more in countries (such as a number of the former Soviet republics in the early 1990s; like Turkmenistan, Kazakhstan, Georgia, and Krygyzstan) that are experiencing hyperinflations, or extreme inflations. When

[4]This measure is called the consumer price index, or CPI, which is discussed in Chapter 2. Conceptually, the CPI is intended to measure the cost of buying a certain fixed set, or "basket," of consumer goods and services. However, the construction of a consumer price index over a period as long as two centuries involves many compromises. For instance, the basket of goods and services priced by the CPI is not literally the same over the entire period shown in Fig. 1.4 but is changed from time to time to reflect the different mix of consumer goods and services available at different times.

the inflation rate reaches an extremely high level, with prices changing daily or hourly, the economy tends to function poorly. High inflation also means that the purchasing power of money erodes quickly. This situation forces people to scramble to spend their money almost as soon as they receive it.

The International Economy

Today every major economy is an **open economy**, or one that has extensive trading and financial relationships with other national economies. (In contrast, a **closed economy** doesn't interact economically with the rest of the world.) Macroeconomists study patterns of international trade and borrowing to understand better the links among national economies. For example, an important topic in macroeconomics is how international trade and borrowing relationships can help transmit business cycles from country to country.

Another issue for which international considerations are central is trade imbalances. Figure 1.5 shows the historical behavior of the imports and exports of

FIGURE 1.5

U.S. exports and imports, 1869–2021

The figure shows U.S. exports (black) and U.S. imports (red), each expressed as a percentage of total output. Exports and imports need not be equal in each year: U.S. exports exceeded imports (shaded gray) during much of the twentieth century. During the 1980s, 1990s, and 2000s, however, U.S. exports were smaller than U.S. imports (shaded pink).

Sources: Imports and exports of goods and services: 1869–1959 from *Historical Statistics of the United States, Colonial Times to 1970*, pp. 864–865; 1960 onward from International Transactions Accounts, U.S. Bureau of Economic Analysis, *bea.gov/iTable/index_ita.cfm*, Table 1.1; nominal output: 1869–1928 from Christina D. Romer, "The Prewar Business Cycle Reconsidered: New Estimates of Gross National Product, 1869–1908," *Journal of Political Economy*, 97, 1 (February 1989), pp. 22–23; 1929 onward from FRED database, *fred.stlouisfed.org/series/GDPA*.

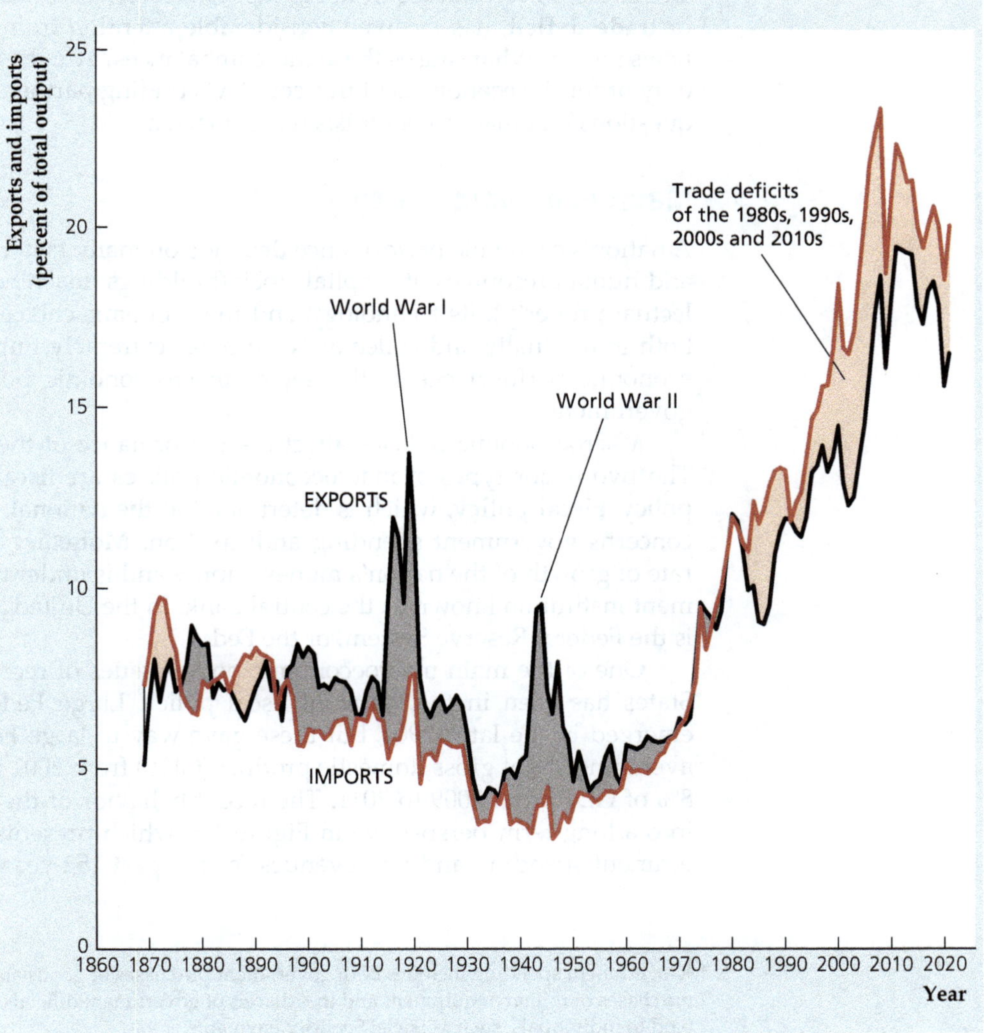

goods and services by the United States. U.S. imports are goods and services produced abroad and purchased by people in the United States; U.S. exports are goods and services produced in the United States and sold to people in other countries. To give you a sense of the relative importance of international trade, Fig. 1.5 expresses exports and imports as percentages of total U.S. output. Currently, both exports and imports are larger fractions of U.S. output than they were during the 1950s and 1960s, reflecting both the recovery of trade from the disruptions of the Great Depression and World War II and the trend toward greater economic interdependence among nations. Note, though, that a century ago exports and imports already were important relative to the size of the overall economy.

Figure 1.5 demonstrates that exports and imports need not be equal in each year. For example, following World War I and World War II, U.S. exports outstripped U.S. imports because the country was sending large quantities of supplies to countries whose economies had been damaged by war. When exports exceed imports, a **trade surplus** exists. In the 1980s, however, U.S. exports declined sharply relative to imports, a situation that has persisted through the 1990s, 2000s, and 2010s, as you can see from Fig. 1.5. This recent excess of imports over exports, or **trade deficit**, has received considerable attention from policymakers and the news media. What causes these trade imbalances? Are they bad for the U.S. economy or for the economies of this country's trading partners? These are among the questions that macroeconomists try to answer.

Macroeconomic Policy

A nation's economic performance depends on many factors, including its natural and human resources, its capital stock (buildings, machines, software, and intellectual property), its technology, and the economic choices made by its citizens, both individually and collectively. Another extremely important factor affecting economic performance is the set of macroeconomic policies pursued by the government.

Macroeconomic policies affect the performance of the economy as a whole. The two major types of macroeconomic policies are fiscal policy and monetary policy. **Fiscal policy**, which is determined at the national, state, and local levels, concerns government spending and taxation. **Monetary policy** determines the rate of growth of the nation's money supply and is under the control of a government institution known as the central bank. In the United States, the central bank is the Federal Reserve System, or the Fed.

One of the main macroeconomic policy issues of recent years in the United States has been in the realm of fiscal policy. Large Federal budget surpluses emerged in the late 1990s, but these gave way to large Federal budget deficits, averaging 2% of gross domestic product (GDP) from 2001 to 2008, and more than 8% of GDP from 2009 to 2011. The recent behavior of the Federal budget is put into a long-term perspective in Figure 1.6, which presents data on Federal government spending and tax revenues for the past 152 years.[5] Again, so that their

[5]Government spending includes both government purchases of goods and services, such as purchases of military equipment and the salaries of government officials, and government benefits paid to individuals, such as Social Security payments.

FIGURE 1.6

U.S. Federal government spending and tax collections, 1869–2021

U.S. Federal government spending (red) and U.S. Federal government tax collections (black) are shown as a percentage of total output. Deficits (excesses of spending over tax collections) are shaded pink, and surpluses (excesses of taxes over spending) are shaded gray. The government sector's share of the economy has grown since World War II. Large deficits occurred during the two world wars, the Great Depression, and during most of the period since the mid-1970s, except for 1998–2001, when the government ran large surpluses and during the pandemic recession of 2020.

Sources: Federal spending and receipts for 1869–1929 from *Historical Statistics of the United States, Colonial Times to 1970*, p. 1104; nominal output, 1869–1929: same as in Fig. 1.5; Federal spending and receipts as percentage of output, 1930–2017 from *Historical Tables, Budget of the U.S. Government*, Table 1.2, *www.whitehouse.gov/omb/historical-tables*.

importance relative to the economy as a whole is indicated, spending, tax collections, and government budget deficits and surpluses are expressed as percentages of total output.

Two obvious features of Fig. 1.6 are the peaks in government spending and deficits that resulted from military buildups in World War I and World War II. At its high point during World War II, Federal government spending exceeded 43% of total output. Significant deficits also occurred during the Great Depression of the 1930s because the government increased its spending on various programs designed to help the economy, such as government-financed jobs programs. Also shown clearly is the increase in the size of the government sector since World War II, an increase reflected in the major upward shift in government spending and in tax collections relative to national output that occurred in about 1940 as well as the mild upward trend in both variables that has occurred since then. Figure 1.6 also illustrates the huge increase in the deficit in 2020, as the government sought to mitigate the impact of the pandemic recession.

The large and persistent Federal budget deficits of the 1980s and early and mid-1990s were historically unusual in that they occurred during a period of peace and relative prosperity. The emergence of large Federal deficits in the 1980s coincided with the emergence of large trade deficits (see Fig. 1.5). Indeed, the Federal budget deficit and the trade deficit have been called the "twin deficits." Are these deficits related? If so, what can be done about them? These questions also fall within the purview of macroeconomics.

The possible link between the government's budget deficit and the trade imbalance illustrates an important aspect of macroeconomics: Macroeconomic issues and problems are frequently interconnected. For this reason, studying one macroeconomic question, such as the effects of the government budget deficit, in isolation generally is not sufficient. Instead, macroeconomists usually study the economy as a complete system, recognizing that changes in one sector or market may affect the behavior of the entire economy.

Aggregation

Macroeconomics is one of two broad areas within the field of economics; the other is microeconomics. Macroeconomics and microeconomics have many basic economic ideas and methods in common; the difference between them is the level at which the economy is studied. Microeconomists focus on individual consumers, workers, and firms, each of which is too small to have an impact on the national economy. Macroeconomists ignore the fine distinctions among the many different kinds of goods, firms, and markets that exist in the economy and instead focus on national totals. For example, in their analyses macroeconomists do not care whether consumers are buying Microsoft Xboxes or Sony PlayStations, beef or chicken, Pepsi or Coke. Instead, they add consumer expenditures on all goods and services to get an overall total called *aggregate consumption*. The process of summing individual economic variables to obtain economy-wide totals is called **aggregation**. The use of aggregation and the emphasis on aggregate quantities such as aggregate consumption, aggregate investment, and aggregate output are the primary factors that distinguish macroeconomics from microeconomics.

1.2 What Macroeconomists Do

Describe the activities and objectives of macroeconomists.

How do macroeconomists use their skills, and what do they do with all the data they gather and the theories they develop? Besides teaching economics, macroeconomists engage in a wide variety of activities, including forecasting, macroeconomic analysis, basic research, and data development for government, nonprofit organizations, and private businesses.

Macroeconomic Forecasting

Many people believe that economists spend most of their time trying to forecast the performance of the economy. In fact, except for a relatively small number of forecasting specialists, forecasting is a minor part of what macroeconomists do. One reason macroeconomists don't emphasize forecasting is that on the whole they are not terribly good at it! Forecasting is difficult not only because our understanding of how the economy works is imperfect, but also because it is impossible to take into account *all* the factors—many of them not strictly economic—that might affect future economic trends. Here are some questions that a forecaster, in trying to project the course of the economy, might have to try to answer: How will events abroad affect congressional authorizations for military spending over the next few years? Will there be a severe drought in agricultural regions, with effects on global markets for commodities? Will productivity rise as rapidly in the future as it did in the late 1990s and early 2000s as businesses increasingly adopted computer technology? Because answers to such questions are highly uncertain, macroeconomic forecasters rarely offer a single prediction. Instead, they usually combine a "most likely" forecast with "optimistic" and "pessimistic" alternative scenarios.

Does the fact that macroeconomics can't be used to make highly accurate forecasts of economic activity mean that it is a pointless field of study? Some people may think so, but that's really an unreasonable standard. Meteorology is an example of a field in which forecasting is difficult (will it *definitely* be sunny this weekend?) but in which there is also a lot of useful knowledge (meteorologists helped discover the depletion of the earth's ozone layer and pointed out its dangers). Similarly, cardiologists usually can't predict if or when a patient will have a heart attack—they can only talk about probabilities. Like meteorologists and doctors, economists deal with a system whose complexity makes gaining a thorough understanding difficult and forecasting the system's behavior even more difficult. Rather than predicting what will happen, most macroeconomists are engaged in analyzing and interpreting events as they happen (macroeconomic analysis) or in trying to understand the structure of the economy in general (macroeconomic research).

Macroeconomic Analysis

Macroeconomic analysts monitor the economy and think about the implications of current economic events. Many analysts are employed in the private sector, such as in banks or large corporations. Private-sector analysts try to determine how general economic trends will affect their employers' financial investments, their opportunities for expansion, the demand for their products, and so on. Some private firms specialize in macroeconomic analysis and assist clients on a fee-for-service basis.

The public sector, which includes national and regional governments and international agencies such as the World Bank and the International Monetary Fund, also employs many macroeconomic analysts. The main function of public-sector analysts is to assist in policymaking—for example, by writing reports that assess various macroeconomic problems and by identifying and evaluating possible policy options. Among U.S. policymakers, the officials who set monetary policy may call on the aid of several hundred Ph.D. economists employed within the Federal Reserve System, and the President has the advice of the Council of Economic Advisers and the professional staffs of numerous departments and agencies. For members of Congress, a frequent source of macroeconomic analysis is the Congressional Budget Office. Economic policymakers also often go outside the government to seek the advice of macroeconomists from business or academia.

Macroeconomic Research

Macroeconomic research takes an amazing variety of forms, from abstract mathematical analysis to psychological experimentation to simulation projects in which computers are used to generate random numbers that represent the randomness of day-to-day economic activity. Nevertheless, the goal of all macroeconomic research is to make general statements about how the economy works. The general insights about the economy gained from successful research form the basis for the analyses of specific economic problems, policies, or situations.

To see why research is important, imagine that you are an economist with the International Monetary Fund whose task is to help Zimbabwe control its high rate of inflation. On what basis can you offer advice? Basically, you should know what inflation-fighting policies other countries have used in the past, what the results have been, how the results have depended on the characteristics of the country employing the policy, and so on. Particularly if the situation you are analyzing is not identical to any of the previous cases, having some theoretical principles would also help you identify and understand the main factors contributing to that country's inflation. Analyzing the historical cases and working out the theoretical principles by yourself from scratch might involve many years' effort. The value of ongoing research activities is that many of the results and ideas that you need will already be available in books or professional journals or circulated in unpublished form. Because it forms the basis for activities such as economic analysis and forecasting, macroeconomic research is the engine that pulls the whole enterprise of macroeconomics behind it.

Macroeconomic research takes place primarily in colleges and universities, in nonprofit institutions (such as the National Bureau of Economic Research, the Brookings Institution, and the American Enterprise Institute), and in the public sector (the government and international agencies). Particularly in the public sector, the line between economic analysis and macroeconomic research is much fuzzier than we have drawn it here. The reason is that many economists move back and forth between analysis of specific problems (such as Zimbabwe's inflation problem) and more basic macroeconomic research (such as an analysis of inflation in general).

Economic Theory. How is macroeconomic research carried out? As in many other fields, macroeconomic research proceeds primarily through the formulation and testing of theories. An **economic theory** is a set of ideas about the economy that has been organized in a logical framework. Most economic theories are developed in terms of an **economic model**, which is a simplified description of some aspect of the economy, usually expressed in mathematical form. Economists evaluate an economic model or theory by applying four criteria:

1. Are its assumptions reasonable and realistic?
2. Is it understandable and manageable enough to be used in studying real problems?
3. Does it have implications that can be tested by **empirical analysis**? That is, can its implications be evaluated by comparing them with data obtained in the real world?
4. When the implications and the data are compared, are the implications of the theory consistent with the data?

For a theory or model—of any type, not just economic—to be useful, the answer to each of these questions must be "yes." Unfortunately, though, economists may not always agree in their evaluation of a particular model, with the result that controversies sometimes persist about the best way to model a given economic situation.

We present a summary of the main steps in developing and testing an economic theory or model in "In Touch with Data and Research: Developing and Testing an Economic Theory."

Data Development

The collection of economic data is a vital part of macroeconomics, and many economists are involved in the data development process. In the United States as well as all other major countries, data on thousands of economic variables are collected and analyzed. We have already presented some important macroeconomic data

In Touch with Data and Research

Developing and Testing an Economic Theory

To illustrate the process of developing and testing an economic theory, suppose that we want to develop a theory that explains the routes that people take when they commute from home to work and back. Such a theory would be useful, for example, to a traffic planner who is concerned about how a proposed housing development will affect traffic patterns. Here are the steps we would take.

Step 1. State the research question.

Example: What determines traffic flows in the city during rush hours?

Step 2. Make provisional assumptions that describe the economic setting and the behavior of the economic actors. These assumptions should be simple yet capture the most important aspects of the problem.

Example: The setting is described by the map of the city. The assumption about behavior is that commuters choose routes that minimize driving time.

Step 3. Work out the implications of the theory.

Example: Use the map of the city to plot a route that minimizes driving time between home and place of work.

Step 4. Conduct an *empirical analysis* to compare the implications of the theory with the data.

Example: Conduct a survey of commuters to identify (1) home locations, (2) work locations, and (3) routes taken to work. Then determine whether the routes predicted by the model are generally the same as those reported in the commuter survey.

Step 5. Evaluate the results of your comparisons.

If the theory fits the data well: Use the theory to predict what would happen if the economic setting or economic policies change.

Example: Use the minimum-driving-time assumption to evaluate the traffic effects of a new housing development by figuring out which routes the residents of the development are likely to take.

If the theory fits the data poorly: Start from scratch with a new model. Repeat Steps 2–5.

Example: Change the provisional behavioral assumption to the following: Commuters choose the route that minimizes the *distance* they must drive (not the time they spend driving).

If the theory fits the data moderately well: Either make do with a partially successful theory or modify the model with additional assumptions and then repeat Steps 3–5.

Example: A possible modification of the minimum-driving-time assumption is that commuters will choose more scenic over less scenic routes, if driving time is not increased by more than a certain number of minutes. To test the model with this modified assumption, you must determine which routes are more scenic (those that pass a lake) and which are less scenic (those that pass a dump).

series, such as measures of output and the price level, and we will look at these and others in more detail in Chapter 2. Macroeconomists use economic data to assess the current state of the economy, make forecasts, analyze policy alternatives, and test macroeconomic theories.

Most economic data are collected and published by the Federal government—for example, by agencies such as the Bureau of the Census, the Bureau of Labor Statistics, and the Bureau of Economic Analysis in the United States, and by central banks such as the Federal Reserve. To an increasing degree, however, these activities also take place in the private sector. For example, marketing firms and private economic forecasting companies are important collectors, users, and sellers of economic data. In this book, many of the boxes called "In Touch with Data and Research" describe major macroeconomic data series and tell you how they are collected and where to find them; other "In Touch with Data and Research" boxes describe topics and issues in macroeconomic research.

Much of the data collection and preparation process is routine. However, because providers of data want their numbers to be as useful as possible while keeping costs down, the organization of major data collection projects is typically the joint effort of many skilled professionals. Providers of data must decide what types of data should be collected on the basis of who is expected to use the data and how. They must take care that measures of economic activity correspond to abstract concepts (such as "capital" and "labor") that are suggested by economic theory. In addition, data providers must guarantee the confidentiality of data that may reveal information about individual firms and people in the economy. In a large data-gathering organization such as the Bureau of the Census, each of these issues is exhaustively analyzed by economists and statisticians before data collection begins.[6]

1.3 Why Macroeconomists Disagree

Differentiate between the classical and Keynesian approaches to macroeconomics.

Over the years, the efforts of thousands of analysts, data collectors, and researchers have greatly enhanced the understanding of macroeconomic phenomena. Yet no matter what the macroeconomic issue, the news media seemingly can find an economist to argue either side of it. Why do macroeconomists appear to disagree so much?[7]

To a certain extent, the amount of disagreement among macroeconomists is exaggerated by the tendency of the public and the media to focus on the most difficult and controversial issues. In addition, the fact that economic policy and performance are of such broad interest and concern contributes to the intensity of debate: More than controversies in many other fields, debates in macroeconomics tend to take place in public, rather than in the seminar room or the laboratory. Although important disagreements among macroeconomists certainly exist, there also are many areas of substantial agreement in macroeconomics.

We can provide an insight into why macroeconomists disagree by drawing the important distinction between positive and normative analyses of economic

---

[6]For a readable discussion of issues that face statistical agencies, see Keith Hall, former Commissioner of the Bureau of Labor Statistics, "The Challenges of Producing Economic Data for the 21st Century," testimony before Congress, June 12, 2012, available online at: *www.mercatus.org/publication/challenges-producing-economic-data-21st-century*.

[7]Not only do macroeconomists often seem to disagree with one another, but they also sometimes are accused of not being able to agree with themselves. President Harry Truman expressed the frustration of many policymakers when he said he wanted a one-handed economist—one who wouldn't always say, "On the one hand, . . . ; on the other hand. . . ."

policy. A **positive analysis** of an economic policy examines the economic consequences of a policy but doesn't address the question of whether those consequences are desirable. A **normative analysis** of policy tries to determine whether a certain policy *should* be used. For example, if an economist is asked to evaluate the effects on the economy of a 5% reduction in the income tax, the response involves a positive analysis. But if asked whether the income tax *should* be reduced by 5%, the economist's response requires a normative analysis. This normative analysis will involve not only the economist's objective, scientific understanding of how the economy works but also personal value judgments—for example, about the appropriate size of the government sector or the amount of income redistribution that is desirable.

Economists may agree on the positive analysis of a question yet disagree on the normative part because of differences in values. Value differences also are common in other fields: Physicists may be in general agreement about the consequences of a meltdown of a nuclear reactor (a positive analysis). Yet there might be extensive disagreement among these physicists about whether a new nuclear power plant should be built (a normative question).

Disagreement may occur on positive issues, however, and these differences are important in economics. In macroeconomics there always have been many schools of thought, each with a somewhat different perspective on how the economy works. Examples include monetarism and supply-side economics, both of which we discuss in this book. However, the most important—and enduring—disagreements on positive issues in macroeconomics involve the two leading schools of thought: the classical approach and the Keynesian approach.

Classicals Versus Keynesians

The classical approach and the Keynesian approach are the two major intellectual traditions in macroeconomics. We discuss the differences between the two approaches briefly here and in much greater detail later in the book.

The Classical Approach. The origins of the classical approach go back more than two centuries, at least to the famous Scottish economist Adam Smith. In 1776 Smith published his classic, *The Wealth of Nations,* in which he proposed the concept of the "invisible hand." The idea of the **invisible hand** is that if there are free markets and individuals conduct their economic affairs in their own best interests, the overall economy will work well. As Smith put it, in a market economy, individuals pursuing their own self-interests seem to be led by an invisible hand to maximize the general welfare of everyone in the economy.

However, we must not overstate what Smith claimed: To say that an invisible hand is at work does *not* mean that no one in a market economy will be hungry or dissatisfied; free markets cannot insulate a nation from the effects of drought, war, or political instability. Nor does the invisible hand rule out the existence of great inequalities between the rich and the poor because in Smith's analysis, he took the initial distribution of wealth among people as given. Rather, the invisible-hand idea says that given a country's resources (natural, human, and technological) and its initial distribution of wealth, the use of free markets will make people as economically well off as possible.

Validity of the invisible-hand idea depends on a key assumption: The various markets in the economy, including financial markets, labor markets, and markets for goods and services, must function smoothly and without impediments such as minimum wages and interest rate ceilings. In particular, wages and prices must adjust rapidly to equate quantities demanded and supplied. In a market in which there are no impediments, equating quantities demanded and supplied will bring the market into **equilibrium**—a situation in which there is no pressure for wages or prices to change. In markets where quantity demanded exceeds quantity supplied, prices must rise to bring the market into equilibrium. In markets where more of a good is available than people want to buy, prices must fall to bring the market into equilibrium.

Wage and price flexibility is crucial to the invisible-hand idea because in a free-market system, changes in wages and prices are the signals that coordinate the actions of people in the economy. To illustrate, suppose that war abroad disrupts oil imports. This drop in supply will drive up the price of oil. A higher oil price will make it profitable for domestic oil suppliers to pump more oil and to drill more wells. The higher price will also induce domestic consumers to conserve oil and to switch to alternative sources of energy. Increased demand for alternative energy sources will raise their prices and stimulate *their* production, and so on. Thus, in the absence of impediments such as government price controls, the adjustment of prices helps the free-market economy respond in a constructive and coordinated way to the initial disruption of supplies.

The **classical approach** to macroeconomics builds on Smith's basic assumptions that people pursue their own economic self-interests and that prices adjust reasonably quickly to achieve equilibrium in all markets. With these two assumptions as a basis, followers of the classical approach attempt to construct models of the macroeconomy that are consistent with the data and that can be used to answer the questions raised at the beginning of this chapter.

The use of the classical approach carries with it some strong policy implications. Because the classical assumptions imply that the invisible hand works well, classical economists often argue (as a normative proposition) that the government should have, *at most*, a limited role in the economy. As a positive proposition, classical economists also often argue that government policies will be ineffective or counterproductive at achieving their stated goals. Thus, for example, most classicals believe that the government should not try actively to eliminate business cycles.

The Keynesian Approach. Compared with the classical approach, the **Keynesian approach** is relatively recent. The book that introduced it, *The General Theory of Employment, Interest, and Money* by British economist John Maynard Keynes, appeared in 1936—160 years after Adam Smith's *The Wealth of Nations.* In 1936 the world was suffering through the Great Depression: Unprecedentedly high rates of unemployment had afflicted most of the world's economies for years, and the invisible hand of free markets seemed completely ineffective. From the viewpoint of 1936, the classical theory appeared to be seriously inconsistent with the data, creating a need for a new macroeconomic theory. Keynes provided this theory.

In his book, Keynes offered an explanation of persistently high unemployment.[8] He based this explanation on an assumption about wage and price adjustment that was fundamentally different from the classical assumption. Instead of

[8]Actually, Keynes presented a number of explanations of unemployment in his book, and debate continues about "what Keynes really meant." Our interpretation of what Keynes meant is the one adopted by his major followers.

assuming that wages and prices adjust rapidly to equate quantities demanded and supplied in each market, as in the classical tradition, Keynes assumed that wages and prices adjust slowly. Slow wage and price adjustment meant that quantities demanded might not equal quantities supplied for long periods of time. In the Keynesian theory, unemployment can persist because wages and prices don't adjust to equalize the number of people that firms want to employ with the number of people who want to work.

Keynes's proposed solution to high unemployment was to have the government increase its purchases of goods and services, thus raising the demand for output. Keynes argued that this policy would reduce unemployment because, to meet the higher demands for their products, businesses would have to employ more workers. In addition, Keynes suggested, the newly hired workers would have more income to spend, creating another source of demand for output that would raise employment further. More generally, in contrast to classicals, Keynesians tend to be skeptical about the invisible hand and thus are more willing to advocate a role for government in improving macroeconomic performance.

The Evolution of the Classical–Keynesian Debate. Because the Great Depression so strongly shook many economists' faith in the classical approach, the Keynesian approach dominated macroeconomic theory and policy from World War II until about 1970. At the height of Keynesian influence, economists widely believed that, through the skillful use of macroeconomic policies, the government could promote economic growth while avoiding inflation or recession. The main problems of macroeconomics apparently had been solved, with only some details to be filled in.

However, in the 1970s the United States suffered from both high unemployment and high inflation—called **stagflation**, or stagnation plus inflation. This experience weakened economists' and policymakers' confidence in the traditional Keynesian approach, much as the Great Depression had undermined the traditional classical approach. In addition, the Keynesian assumption that prices and wages adjust slowly was criticized as being without sound theoretical foundations. While the Keynesian approach was coming under attack, developments in economic theory made classical macroeconomics look more interesting and attractive to many economists. Starting in the early 1970s, a modernized classical approach enjoyed a major resurgence among macroeconomic researchers, although classical macroeconomics did not achieve the dominance that Keynesianism had enjoyed in the early postwar years.

In the past three decades, advocates of both approaches have reworked them extensively to repair their weaknesses. Economists working in the classical tradition have improved their explanations of business cycles and unemployment. Keynesians have worked on the development of sound theoretical foundations for the slow adjustment of wages and prices, and Keynesian models can now accommodate stagflation. Currently, excellent research is being conducted with both approaches, and substantial communication and cross-fertilization are occurring between them.

A Unified Approach to Macroeconomics

In writing this book, we needed a strategy to deal with the fact that there are two major macroeconomic schools of thought. One strategy would have been to emphasize one of the two schools of thought and to treat the other only briefly.

The problem with that strategy is that it would not expose you to the full range of ideas and insights that compose modern macroeconomics. Alternatively, we might have presented the two approaches separately and then compared and contrasted their conclusions—but you would have missed the opportunity to explore the large common ground shared by the two schools of thought.

Our choice was to take an approach to macroeconomics that is as balanced and unified as possible. In keeping with this unified approach, all our analyses in this book—whether of economic growth, business cycles, inflation, or policy, and whether classical or Keynesian in spirit—are based on a *single economic model*, or on components or extensions of the basic model. This economic model, which draws heavily from both the classical and Keynesian traditions, has the following characteristics.

1. *Individuals, firms, and the government interact in goods markets, asset markets, and labor markets.* We have already discussed the need for aggregation in macroeconomics. In the economic model of this book, we follow standard macroeconomic practice and aggregate all the markets in the economy into three major markets: the market for goods and services, the asset market (in which assets such as money, stocks, bonds, and real estate are traded), and the labor market. We show how participants in the economy interact in each of these three markets and how these markets relate to one another and to the economy as a whole.
2. *The model's macroeconomic analysis is based on the analysis of individual behavior.* Macroeconomic behavior reflects the behaviors of many individuals and firms interacting in markets. To understand how individuals and firms behave, we take a "bottom-up" approach and focus our analysis at the level of individual decision making (as in "In Touch with Data and Research: Developing and Testing an Economic Theory," where we discuss a model of individual choices about the route to take to work). The insights gained are then used for studying the economy as a whole.

   The guiding principle in analyzing the behavior of individuals and firms is the assumption that they *try to maximize their own economic satisfaction, given their needs, desires, opportunities, and resources.* Although the founder of classical economics, Adam Smith, emphasized this assumption, it is generally accepted by Keynesians and classicals alike, and it is used in virtually all modern macroeconomic research.
3. Although Keynesians reject the classical assumption that wages and prices quickly adjust in the short run, *Keynesians and classicals both agree that, in the long run, prices and wages fully adjust to achieve equilibrium in the markets for goods, assets, and labor.* Because complete flexibility of wages and prices in the long run is not controversial, we examine the long-term behavior of the economy (Chapters 3–7) before discussing short-run issues associated with business cycles (Chapters 8–13).
4. *The basic model that we present may be used with either the classical assumption that wages and prices are flexible or the Keynesian assumption that wages and prices are slow to adjust.* This aspect of the model allows us to compare classical and Keynesian conclusions and policy recommendations within a common theoretical framework.

CHAPTER SUMMARY

1. Macroeconomics is the study of the structure and performance of national economies and the policies that governments use to try to affect economic performance. Important topics in macroeconomics include the determinants of long-run economic growth, business cycles, unemployment, inflation, international trade and lending, and macroeconomic policy.
2. Because macroeconomics covers the economy as a whole, macroeconomists ignore the fine distinctions among different kinds of goods, firms, or markets and focus on national totals such as aggregate consumption. The process of adding individual economic variables to obtain economywide totals is called *aggregation*.
3. The activities engaged in by macroeconomists include (in addition to teaching) forecasting, macroeconomic analysis, macroeconomic research, and data development.
4. The goal of macroeconomic research is to make general statements about how the economy works. Macroeconomic research makes progress toward this goal by developing economic theories and testing them empirically—that is, by seeing whether they are consistent with data obtained from the real world. A useful economic theory is based on reasonable and realistic assumptions, is easy to use, has implications that can be tested in the real world, and is consistent with the data and the observed behavior of the real-world economy.
5. A positive analysis of an economic policy examines the economic consequences of the policy but does not address the question of whether those consequences are desirable. A normative analysis of a policy tries to determine whether the policy *should* be used. Disagreements among macroeconomists may arise because of differences in normative conclusions, as the result of differences in personal values and beliefs, and because of differences in the positive analysis of a policy proposal.
6. The classical approach to macroeconomics is based on the assumptions that individuals and firms act in their own best interests and that wages and prices adjust quickly to achieve equilibrium in all markets. Under these assumptions the invisible hand of the free-market economy works well, with only a limited scope for government intervention in the economy.
7. The Keynesian approach to macroeconomics assumes that wages and prices do not adjust rapidly and thus the invisible hand may not work well. Keynesians argue that, because of slow wage and price adjustment, unemployment may remain high for a long time. Keynesians are usually more inclined than classicals to believe that government intervention in the economy may help improve economic performance.

KEY TERMS

aggregation, p. 40
average labor productivity, p. 33
classical approach, p. 46
closed economy, p. 37
deflation, p. 36
economic model, p. 42
economic theory, p. 42
empirical analysis, p. 42
equilibrium, p. 46
fiscal policy, p. 38
inflation, p. 36
invisible hand, p. 45
Keynesian approach, p. 46
macroeconomics, p. 31
monetary policy, p. 38
normative analysis, p. 45
open economy, p. 37
positive analysis, p. 45
stagflation, p. 47
trade deficit, p. 38
trade surplus, p. 38
unemployment, p. 35

REVIEW QUESTIONS

1. How have total output and output per worker changed over time in the United States? How have these changes affected the lives of typical people?
2. What is a business cycle? How does the unemployment rate behave over the course of a business cycle? Does the unemployment rate ever reach zero?
3. Define *inflation* and *deflation*. Compare the behavior of consumer prices in the United States in the years before and after World War II.
4. Historically, when has the Federal government been most likely to run budget deficits? What has been the recent experience?

5. Define *trade deficit* and *trade surplus*. In recent years, has the U.S. economy had trade deficits or trade surpluses? What was the U.S. experience from 1900 to 1970?
6. List the principal professional activities of macroeconomists. What role does macroeconomic research play in each of these activities?
7. What steps are involved in developing and testing an economic theory or model? What are the criteria for a useful theory or model?
8. Might two economists agree about the effects of a particular economic policy but disagree about the desirability of implementing the policy? Explain your answer.
9. Compare the classical and Keynesian views on the speed of wage and price adjustment. What are the important consequences of the differences in their views?
10. What was stagflation, and when did it occur? How did it change economists' views about macroeconomics?

NUMERICAL PROBLEMS

1. Here are some macroeconomic data for Canada for the years 2019 and 2020.

	2019	2020
Output (constant dollar GDP)	$527 billion	$500 billion
Employment	23.1 million workers	22.4 million workers
Unemployed	1.4 million workers	2.2 million workers
Total labor force	24.5 million workers	24.6 million workers
Consumer Price Index	106.73	108.33

Canada's output is real GDP measured in constant Canadian dollars. Data are from the Federal Reserve Bank of St. Louis FRED database. Calculate each of the following macroeconomic variables for Canada, being sure to give units.

a. Average labor productivity in 2019 and 2020.

b. The growth rate of average labor productivity between 2019 and 2020.

c. The unemployment rate in 2019 and 2020.

d. The inflation rate between 2019 and 2020.

2. In the FRED database, find data on nominal gross domestic product (a measure of total output), nominal exports, nominal imports, the Federal government's current receipts, and Federal government current expenditures for the past three calendar years.

a. Calculate the ratio of exports to GDP, the ratio of imports to GDP, and the ratio of the trade imbalance to GDP for the most recent three years. Is there any trend apparent in the data?

b. Calculate the ratio of Federal government receipts to GDP, the ratio of Federal government expenditures to GDP, and the ratio of the budget deficit to GDP, for the most recent three years. Is there any trend apparent in the data?

ANALYTICAL PROBLEMS

1. Can average labor productivity fall even though total output is rising? Can the unemployment rate rise even though total output is rising?
2. Prices were much higher in the United States in 2022 than in 1890. Does this fact mean that people were economically better off in 1890? Why or why not?
3. State a theory for why people vote Republican or Democratic that potentially could satisfy the criteria for a useful theory given in the text. How would you go about testing your theory?
4. Which of the following statements are positive in nature and which are normative?

a. A tax cut will raise interest rates.

b. A reduction in the payroll tax would primarily benefit poor and middle-class workers.

c. Payroll taxes are too high.

d. A cut in the payroll tax would improve the President's popularity ratings.

e. Payroll taxes should not be cut unless capital gains taxes are also cut.

5. In 2002, President George W. Bush imposed tariffs on certain types of imported steel. He argued that foreign steel producers were dumping their steel on the U.S. market at low prices. The foreign steel producers were able to sell steel cheaply because they received subsidies from their governments. The Bush administration argued that the influx of steel was disrupting the U.S. economy, harming the domestic steel industry, and causing unemployment among U.S. steel workers. What might a classical economist say in response to these claims? Would a Keynesian economist be more or less sympathetic to the imposition of tariffs? Why?

WORKING WITH MACROECONOMIC DATA

For data to use in these exercises, go to the Federal Reserve Bank of St. Louis FRED database at fred.stlouisfed.org.

1. *a.* Calculate the total percentage growth in average labor productivity in the U.S. economy for the 1950s, 1960s, 1970s, 1980s, 1990s, 2000s, and 2010s. To do this, calculate average labor productivity in the last year of each decade beginning in 1949 as real gross domestic product in the last quarter of the year divided by non-farm payroll employment in the last month of the year. In which decades did average labor productivity grow the most quickly overall? The most slowly? Express the growth rates for each decade in annualized terms by using the formula

$$(1 + g)^{10} = 1 + G$$

where g is the annual growth rate, expressed as a decimal (for example, 0.05 for 5%), and G is the growth rate for the decade (the change in productivity during the decade divided by the initial productivity level). For each of the seven decades, use your calculated values for G and the formula above to solve for g.

b. Calculate annual labor productivity growth rates for each year since 2020 for which data are available. (Define average labor productivity for each year as real gross domestic product in the last quarter of the year divided by non-farm payroll employment in the last month of the year.) How do the recent growth rates compare with those of the seven previous decades?

2. Graph the behavior of the civilian unemployment rate from 1961 until the present using monthly data. Vertical gray bars in FRED indicate periods of recession. In terms of the unemployment rate, how does the severity of the recession of 2020 compare with the recessions of 1969–1970, 1973–1975, 1980, 1981–1982, 1990–1991, 2001, and 2007–2009? How does the behavior of the unemployment rate over the 2000s and 2010s compare to its behavior in the 1960s, 1970s, 1980s, and 1990s?

3. Using monthly data on the consumer price index (CPI) for all urban consumers, calculate and graph the U.S. inflation rate as the percentage change in the price index from one year ago for each year since 1948. In which periods within the postwar era did the United States experience the highest inflation rates? In which periods was the inflation rate the most stable (that is, roughly constant from one year to the next)?

4. In FRED, find data for GDP for the United States, Japan, and Mexico. Calculate the annual average growth rate of GDP for the last five years for which the data are available. How do the growth rates compare to each other? Which country grew the fastest over the past five years? Which country grew the slowest?

5. Plot the FRED data on gross federal debt held by the public as a percent of GDP for the United States. In which periods within the postwar era did the United States experience prolonged declines in the ratio of federal debt relative to GDP? In which periods did the ratio of federal debt to GDP rise rapidly? Can you explain the main causes of the increases in the ratio of federal debt to GDP?

2

The Measurement and Structure of the National Economy

Learning Objectives

2.1 Differentiate among the three approaches to national income accounting.

2.2 Explain how GDP is measured.

2.3 Discuss the measurement of aggregate saving and its relation to wealth.

2.4 Explain the calculation of real GDP, price indexes, and inflation.

2.5 Define real and nominal interest rates.

Measurement is a crucial part of scientific study. Accurate measurement is essential for making new discoveries, evaluating competing theories, and predicting future events or trends. During the first half of the twentieth century, painstaking research by economists such as Nobel Prize winner Simon Kuznets (the first person to obtain comprehensive measures of national output) and the team of Arthur Burns and Wesley Mitchell (who performed detailed measurements of the stages of the business cycle) showed that careful economic measurement is not only possible but also necessary for any serious understanding of the economy. Their work, and the efforts of many other researchers, transformed economics from a field in which scholars relied on informal observations and broad generalizations to one in which numbers and statistical analysis play an essential role.

In this chapter we present some of the conceptual and practical issues involved in measuring the macroeconomy. We focus on the national income accounts, a framework for measuring economic activity that is widely used by economic researchers and analysts. Learning about the national income accounts will familiarize you with some useful economic data. In addition, because the national income accounts are set up in a logical way that mirrors the structure of the economy, working through these accounts is an important first step toward understanding how the macroeconomy works. When you finish this chapter, you will have a clearer understanding of the relationships that exist among key macroeconomic variables and among the different sectors of the economy.

2.1 National Income Accounting: The Measurement of Production, Income, and Expenditure

Differentiate among the three approaches to national income accounting.

The **national income accounts** are an accounting framework used in measuring current economic activity. Almost all countries have some form of official national income accounts. (For background information on the Malaysian national income accounts, see "In Touch with Data and Research: The National Income and Product Accounts in Malaysia.")

The national income accounts are based on the idea that the amount of economic activity that occurs during a period of time can be measured in terms of

1. the amount of output produced, excluding output used up in intermediate stages of production (the product approach);
2. the incomes received by the producers of output (the income approach); and
3. the amount of spending by the ultimate purchasers of output (the expenditure approach).

Each approach gives a different perspective on the economy. However, the fundamental principle underlying national income accounting is that, except for problems such as incomplete or misreported data, *all three approaches give identical measurements of the amount of current economic activity.*

We can illustrate why these three approaches are equivalent by an example. Imagine an economy with only two businesses, called OrangeInc and JuiceInc. OrangeInc owns and operates orange groves. It sells some of its oranges directly to the public. It sells the rest of its oranges to JuiceInc, which produces and sells orange juice. The following table shows the transactions of each business during a year.

OrangeInc Transactions	
Wages paid to OrangeInc employees	$15,000
Taxes paid to government	5,000
Revenue received from sale of oranges	35,000
Oranges sold to public	10,000
Oranges sold to JuiceInc	25,000
JuiceInc Transactions	
Wages paid to JuiceInc employees	$10,000
Taxes paid to government	2,000
Oranges purchased from OrangeInc	25,000
Revenue received from sale of orange juice	40,000

OrangeInc pays $15,000 per year in wages to workers to pick oranges, and it sells these oranges for $35,000 ($10,000 worth of oranges to households and $25,000 worth of oranges to JuiceInc). Thus OrangeInc's profit before taxes is $\$35,000 - \$15,000 = \$20,000$. Because OrangeInc pays taxes of $5000, its after-tax profit is $15,000.

JuiceInc buys $25,000 of oranges from OrangeInc and pays wages of $10,000 to workers to process the oranges into orange juice. It sells the orange juice for $40,000, so its profit before taxes is $5000 ($\$40,000 - \$25,000 - \$10,000$). After paying taxes of $2000, its after-tax profit is $3000.

What is the total value, measured in dollars, of the economic activity generated by these two businesses? The product approach, income approach, and expenditure approach are three different ways of arriving at the answer to this question; all yield the same answer.

1. The **product approach** measures economic activity by adding the market values of goods and services produced, excluding any goods and services used

up in intermediate stages of production. This approach makes use of the value-added concept. The **value added** of any producer is the value of its output minus the value of the inputs it purchases from other producers. The product approach computes economic activity by summing the value added by all producers.

In our example, OrangeInc produces output worth $35,000 and JuiceInc produces output worth $40,000. However, measuring overall economic activity by simply adding $35,000 and $40,000 would "double count" the $25,000 of oranges that JuiceInc purchased from OrangeInc and processed into juice. To avoid this double counting, we sum value added rather than output: Because JuiceInc processed oranges worth $25,000 into a product worth $40,000, JuiceInc's value added is $15,000 ($40,000 – $25,000).

In Touch with Data and Research

The National Income and Product Accounts in Malaysia

In Malaysia, the national income accounts are officially compiled, produced, and disseminated by the National Accounts Statistics Division in the Department of Statistics Malaysia (DOSM), which operates under the Prime Minister's Department.

Established in 1949 as the Bureau of Statistics, the DOSM produced statistics limited to only external trade and estate agriculture. However, since 1965, its functions have expanded to also include data on the economy and social areas. Currently, national accounts statistics are compiled quarterly and annually based on types of economic activity, while expenditure on GDP is compiled based on type of expenditure at current and constant prices. On the production side, the data is compiled based on industry, and on the expenditure side, based on the type of final consumption. The DOSM also compiles and produces other national accounts statistics such as national income, national income per capita, consumption, savings, and other economic variables.

In the past, most of the statistical data were disseminated in printed form. Since 1955, the DOSM has compiled and published national accounts statistics at current prices on an annual basis. The annual national income data are also available in the economic report published by the Ministry of Finance. This report is released in conjunction with the national budget in September every year. In addition, the Economic Planning Unit (EPU) of the Prime Minister's Department has a summary of GDP tables for annual series and quarterly series (from 2000). Reports are released two months after each quarter end and are available through the DOSM and Bank Negara Malaysia (BNM).

National income data is now also available and accessible online. The DOSM home page at www.statistics.gov.my provides access to current and historical data. Data on national income accounts are also disseminated through the websites of other agencies, such as the Malaysian National News Agency, EPU, and BNM, and through international statistical agency websites such as the United Nations Statistics Division and the ASEAN Secretariat.

OrangeInc doesn't use any inputs purchased from other businesses, so its value added equals its revenue of \$35,000. Thus total value added in the economy is $\$35,000 + \$15,000 = \$50,000$.

2. The **income approach** measures economic activity by adding all income received by producers of output, including wages received by workers and profits received by owners of firms. As you have seen, the (before-tax) profits of OrangeInc equal its revenues of \$35,000 minus its wage costs of \$15,000, or \$20,000. The profits of JuiceInc equal its revenues of \$40,000 minus the \$25,000 the company paid to buy oranges and the \$10,000 in wages paid to its employees, or \$5000. Adding the \$20,000 profit of OrangeInc, the \$5000 profit of JuiceInc, and the \$25,000 in wage income received by the employees of the two companies, we get a total of \$50,000, the same amount determined by the product approach.

   In this calculation we added the before-tax incomes of workers and firm owners. Equivalently, we could have added the after-tax incomes of producers of output and the taxes received by the government. Recall that, when taxes are subtracted, OrangeInc's after-tax profits are \$15,000 and JuiceInc's after-tax profits are \$3000. Adding the two firms' after-tax profits of \$18,000, total wage income of \$25,000 (we assumed that workers pay no taxes), and the \$7000 in taxes received by the government, we again obtain \$50,000 as the measure of economic activity

3. Finally, the **expenditure approach** measures activity by adding the amount spent by all ultimate users of output. In this example, households are ultimate users of oranges. JuiceInc is not an ultimate user of oranges because it sells the oranges (in processed, liquid form) to households. Thus ultimate users purchase \$10,000 of oranges from OrangeInc and \$40,000 of orange juice from JuiceInc for a total of \$50,000, the same amount computed in both the product and the income approaches.[1]

Why the Three Approaches Are Equivalent

That the product, income, and expenditure approaches all give the same answer is no accident. The logic of these three approaches is such that they must *always* give the same answer.

To see why, first observe that the market value of goods and services produced in a given period is *by definition* equal to the amount that buyers must spend to purchase them. JuiceInc's orange juice has a market value of \$40,000 only because that is what people are willing to spend to buy it. The market value of a good or service and the spending on that good or service are always the same, so the product approach (which measures market values) and the expenditure approach (which measures spending) must give the same measure of economic activity.[2]

[1]In the example, each business also purchases labor services from employees, but because these services are used in production, they aren't counted as services purchased by ultimate users.

[2]Our explanation implicitly assumes that everything produced is sold. What if a firm produces some goods that it can't sell? As we discuss shortly, the national income accounts treat unsold goods as though they were purchased by the firm from itself; that is, accumulation of unsold goods in inventory is treated as part of expenditure. Thus expenditure and production remain equal even if some goods remain unsold.

Next, observe that what the seller receives must equal what the buyers spend. The seller's receipts in turn equal the total income generated by the economic activity, including the incomes paid to workers and suppliers, taxes paid to the government, and profits (whatever is left over). Thus total expenditure must equal total income generated, implying that the expenditure and income approaches must also produce the same answer. Finally, as both product value and income equal expenditure, they also must be equal.

Because of the equivalence of the three approaches, over any specified time period

$$\text{total production} = \text{total income} = \text{total expenditure}, \qquad \textbf{(2.1)}$$

where production, income, and expenditure all are measured in the same units (for example, in dollars). Equation (2.1) is called the **fundamental identity of national income accounting** and forms the basis for national income accounting. (An identity is an equation that is true by definition.) In Section 2.2, we show how this fundamental identity is used in measuring current economic activity for the economy as a whole.

2.2 Gross Domestic Product

Explain how GDP is measured.

The broadest measure of aggregate economic activity, as well as the best-known and most often used, is gross domestic product, or GDP. As in the example in Section 2.1, a country's GDP may be measured by the product approach, the expenditure approach, or the income approach. Although the three approaches arrive at the same value for GDP, each views GDP differently. Using all three approaches gives a more complete picture of an economy's structure than any single approach could.

The Product Approach to Measuring GDP

The product approach defines a nation's **gross domestic product (GDP)** as the market value of final goods and services newly produced within a nation during a fixed period of time. In working through the various parts of this definition, we discuss some practical issues that arise in measuring GDP.

Market Value. Goods and services are counted in GDP at their market values—that is, at the prices at which they are sold. The advantage of using market values is that it allows adding the production of different goods and services. Imagine, for example, that you want to measure the total output of an economy that produces 7 cars and 100 pairs of shoes. Adding the number of cars and the number of pairs of shoes to get a total output of 107 wouldn't make much sense because cars and shoes aren't of equal economic value. But suppose that each car sells for \$20,000 and each pair of shoes sells for \$80. Taking these market-determined prices as measures of relative economic values, you can calculate the value of cars produced as $\$140,000$ ($7 \times \$20,000$) and the value of shoes produced as $\$8000$ ($100 \times \$80$). The total market value of production, or GDP, is $\$140,000 + \$8000 = \$148,000$. Using market values to measure production makes sense because it takes into account differences in the relative economic importance of different goods and services.

A problem with using market values to measure GDP is that some useful goods and services are not sold in formal markets. Ideally, GDP should be adjusted upward to reflect the existence of these goods and services. However, because of the difficulty of obtaining reliable measures, some nonmarket goods and services simply are ignored in the calculation of GDP. Household production and child-rearing services performed within the household without pay, for example, are not included in GDP, although household production and child care that are provided for pay (for example, by professional housecleaners or by private day-care centers) are included. Similarly, because the benefits of clean air and water aren't bought and sold in markets, actions to reduce pollution or otherwise improve environmental quality usually are not reflected in GDP (see "In Touch with Data and Research: Natural Resources, the Environment, and the National Income Accounts.").

Some nonmarket goods and services are partially incorporated in official GDP measures. An example is activities in the so-called underground economy. The **underground economy** includes both legal activities hidden from government record keepers (to avoid payment of taxes or compliance with regulations, for example) and illegal activities such as drug dealing, prostitution, and (in some places) gambling. Some might argue that activities such as drug dealing are "bads" rather than "goods" and shouldn't be included in GDP anyway—although a consistent application of this argument might rule out many goods and services currently included in GDP, such as cigarette production. Clearly, though, the services of a housepainter who is paid in cash to avoid taxes should be included in GDP. Government statisticians are unable to reliably adjust GDP figures to include estimates of the underground economy's size, but they do make some adjustments for underreported income.[3]

A particularly important component of economic activity that does not pass through markets is the value of the services provided by government, such as defense, public education, and the building and maintenance of roads and bridges. The fact that most government services are not sold in markets implies a lack of market values to use when calculating the government's contribution to GDP. In this case, the solution that has been adopted is to value government services at their cost of production. Thus the contribution of national defense to GDP equals the government's cost of providing defense: the salaries of service and civilian personnel, the costs of building and maintaining weapons and bases, and so on. Similarly, the contribution of public education to GDP is measured by the cost of teachers' salaries, new schools and equipment, and so on.

Newly Produced Goods and Services. As a measure of current economic activity, GDP includes only goods or services that are newly produced within the current period. GDP excludes purchases or sales of goods that were produced in previous periods. Thus, although the market price paid for a newly constructed house would be included in GDP, the price paid in the sale of a used house is not counted in GDP. (The value of the used house would have been included in GDP for the year

[3]Discussion of NIPA adjustments for the underground economy is given in "Taking the Pulse of the Economy: Measuring GDP" by J. Steven Landefeld, Eugene P. Seskin, and Barbara M. Fraumeni, *Journal of Economic Perspectives* 22 (Spring 2008), pp. 193–216. On estimating the size of the underground economy, see Edgar Feige, "Measuring Underground (Unobserved, Non-observed, Unrecorded) Economies in Transition Countries: Can We Trust GDP?" *Journal of Comparative Economics* 36 (June 2008), pp. 287–306.

it was built.) However, the value of the services of the real estate agent involved in the sale of the used house is part of GDP, because those services are provided in the current period.

Final Goods and Services. Goods and services produced during a period of time may be classified as either intermediate goods and services or final goods and services. **Intermediate goods and services** are those used up in the production of other goods and services *in the same period that they themselves were produced.* For example, flour that is produced and then used to make bread in the same year is an intermediate good. The trucking company that delivers the flour to the bakery provides an intermediate service.

Final goods and services are those goods and services that are not intermediate. Final goods and services are the end products of a process. For example, bread produced by the bakery is a final good, and a shopper's bus ride home from the bakery is a final service. Because the purpose of economic activity is the production of final goods and services, with intermediate goods being but a step along the way, only final goods and services are counted in GDP.

Sometimes the distinction between intermediate goods and final goods is subtle. For example, is a new lathe sold to a furniture manufacturer an intermediate good or a final good? Although the lathe is used to produce other goods, it is not used up during the year. Hence it is not an intermediate good; it is a final good. In particular, the lathe is an example of a type of final good called a *capital good.* Other more general examples of capital goods include factories, office buildings, equipment, software, and intellectual property, such as copyrights. A **capital good** is a good that is itself produced (which rules out natural resources such as land) and is used to produce other goods; however, unlike an intermediate good, a capital good is not used up in the same period that it is produced. The preparers of the national income accounts decided to classify capital goods as final goods and thus to include their production in GDP. Their reasoning was that the addition to productive capacity from new capital goods represents economic activity.

Another subtle distinction between intermediate and final goods arises in the treatment of inventory investment. **Inventories** are stocks of unsold finished goods, goods in process, and raw materials held by firms. Inventory investment is the amount by which inventories increase during the year.[4] For example, suppose that a baker began the year with $1000 worth of flour in her storeroom and that at the end of the year she is holding $1100 worth of flour. The difference between her beginning and ending stocks, or $100 worth of flour, equals the baker's inventory investment during the year. Even though the ultimate purpose of the baker's flour is for making bread, her increase in inventory represents production of flour that is not used up during the year.[5] As in the case of capital goods, inventory investment is treated as a final good and thus part of GDP because increased inventories on hand imply greater productive capacity in the future.

In the OrangeInc–JuiceInc example, we showed that total economic activity could be measured by summing the value added (value of output minus value of

---

[4]When inventories decline during the year, inventory investment is negative.

[5]Inventory investment is the change in the physical quantity of goods in inventory multiplied by their price. Changes in the valuation of inventories arising from price changes (capital gains or losses) are not considered inventory investment.

purchased inputs) for each producer. The advantage of the value-added technique is that it automatically includes final goods and excludes intermediate goods from the measure of total output. If you go back to that example, you will see that, by summing the value added of the two companies, we obtained a measure of economic activity that included the value of final sales of the two businesses to the public but excluded the intermediate goods (unprocessed oranges) sold to JuiceInc by OrangeInc.

GNP Versus GDP. Until 1991, most economists working with U.S. data focused on a measure of economic activity known as gross national product rather than on GDP. However, in 1991, primarily to conform with national income accounting practices in other major industrialized countries, the Department of Commerce began to use GDP as its basic measure of economic activity. The difference between GNP and GDP lies in the treatment of output produced by capital and labor working outside their home (domestic) country. Specifically, **gross national product (GNP)** is the market value of final goods and services newly produced *by domestic factors of production* during the current period, whereas GDP is production taking place within a country.

In Touch with Data and Research

Natural Resources, the Environment, and the National Income Accounts

Much of any country's economic well-being flows from natural, rather than human-made, assets—land, rivers and oceans, natural resources (such as oil and timber), and indeed the air that everyone breathes. Ideally, for the purposes of economic and environmental planning, the use and misuse of natural resources and the environment should be appropriately measured in the national income accounts. Unfortunately, they are not. There are at least two important conceptual problems with the way the national income accounts currently handle the economic use of natural resources and the environment.

1. *Natural resource depletion.* When an oil driller pumps oil from an underground field, the value of the oil produced is counted as part of the nation's GDP; there is no offsetting deduction to account for the fact that nonrenewable resources are being depleted. In principle, the draining of the oil field can be thought of as a type of negative inventory investment because in a sense it reduces the inventory of oil. If it were included in the national income accounts, this negative inventory investment would reduce the computed value of GDP.

2. *The costs and benefits of pollution control.* Imagine that a company has the following choices: It can produce $100 million worth of output and in the process pollute the local river by dumping its wastes; alternatively, by using 10% of its workers to dispose properly of its wastes, it can avoid polluting but will get only $90 million of output. Under current national income accounting rules, if the firm chooses to pollute rather than not to pollute, its contribution to GDP will be larger ($100 million rather than $90 million) because the national income accounts attach no explicit value to a clean river. In an ideal accounting system, the economic costs

(continued)

of environmental degradation would be subtracted in the calculation of a firm's contribution to output, and activities that improve the environment—because they provide real economic benefits—would be added to output.

Discussing the national income accounting implications of resource depletion and pollution may seem to trivialize these important problems. Actually, because GDP and related statistics are used frequently in policy analyses, abstract questions of measurement often may turn out to have significant real effects. For example, economic development experts have expressed concern that some poor countries, in attempting to raise measured GDP as quickly as possible, have done so in part by overexploiting their natural resources and harming the environment. Conceivably, explicitly incorporating "hidden" resource and environmental costs into official measures of economic growth might cause these policies to be modified. Similarly, in industrialized countries, political debates about the environment at times have emphasized the impact on conventionally measured GDP of proposed pollution control measures, rather than their impact on overall economic welfare. Better accounting for environmental quality might serve to refocus these debates to the more relevant question of whether, for any particular environmental proposal, the benefits (economic and noneconomic) exceed the costs.

When U.S. capital and labor—also called factors of production—are used abroad, they produce output and earn income. This output and income are included in U.S. GNP but not in U.S. GDP because they don't represent production taking place within the United States. So, for example, the value of roads built by a U.S. construction company in Saudi Arabia, as measured by the fees that the construction company receives from the Saudi government, is counted in U.S. GNP but not in U.S. GDP. Similarly, when foreign capital or labor is used in the United States, the output produced and the income earned are part of U.S. GDP (because the production occurs within the United States) but not of U.S. GNP (they are counted in the foreign country's GNP instead). For example, the portion of the value of Japanese cars built in the United States that is attributable to Japanese capital and management counts in Japanese GNP and U.S. GDP, but not in U.S. GNP.

We define **net factor payments from abroad (NFP)** to be income paid to domestic factors of production by the rest of the world minus income paid to foreign factors of production by the domestic economy. Using this concept, we express the relationship between GDP and GNP as

$$\text{GDP} = \text{GNP} - \text{NFP}. \qquad \textbf{(2.2)}$$

For the United States, GDP and GNP give similar measures of economic activity. For example, in 2021 the U.S. GDP was $22,996.1 billion and the U.S. GNP was $23,248.5 billion, a difference of just over 1%. The distinction between GNP and GDP is more important for countries such as Egypt and Turkey that have many citizens working abroad. The reason is that income earned by workers abroad is part of a country's GNP but not its GDP.

The Expenditure Approach to Measuring GDP

A different perspective on the components of GDP is obtained by looking at the expenditure side of the national income accounts. The expenditure approach measures GDP as total spending on final goods and services produced within a nation during a specified period of time. Four major categories of spending are added to get GDP: consumption, investment, government purchases of goods and services, and net exports of goods and services. In symbols,

$$\begin{aligned} Y = \text{GDP} &= \text{total production (or output)} \\ &= \text{total income} \\ &= \text{total expenditure}; \end{aligned}$$

$$\begin{aligned} C &= \text{consumption}; \\ I &= \text{investment}; \\ G &= \text{government purchases of goods and services}; \\ NX &= \text{net exports of goods and services.} \end{aligned}$$

With these symbols, we express the expenditure approach to measuring GDP as

$$Y = C + I + G + NX. \tag{2.3}$$

TABLE 2.1

Expenditure Approach to Measuring GDP in the United States, 2021

	Billions of dollars	Percent of GDP
Personal consumption expenditures (C)	**15,750**	**68.5**
Consumer durables	2025	8.8
Nondurable goods	3457	15.0
Services	10,269	44.7
Gross private domestic investment (I)	**4108**	**17.9**
Business fixed investment	3051	13.3
Nonresidential structures	579	2.5
Equipment	1273	5.5
Intellectual property products	1200	5.2
Residential investment	1083	4.7
Inventory investment	−26	−0.1
Government purchases of goods and services (G)	**4052**	**17.6**
Federal	1565	6.8
National defense	905	3.9
Nondefense	660	2.9
State and local	2487	10.8
Net exports (NX)	**−916**	**−4.0**
Exports	2480	10.8
Imports	3396	14.8
Total (equals GDP) (Y)	**22,994**	**100.0**

Note: Numbers may not add to totals shown owing to rounding.
Source: Bureau of Economic Analysis website, *www.bea.gov*, NIPA Table 1.1.5, January 27, 2022.

Equation (2.3), like Eq. (2.1), is one of the basic relationships in macroeconomics. Equation (2.3) is called the **income–expenditure identity** because it states that income, Y, equals total expenditure, $C + I + G + NX$. Recent U.S. data for the four categories of spending, along with some major subcategories, are given in Table 2.1. As you read the rest of this section, you should look at Table 2.1 to get a feel for the relative sizes of different components of spending in the U.S. economy.

Consumption. **Consumption** is spending by domestic households on final goods and services, including those produced abroad.[6] It is the largest component of expenditure, usually accounting for a little more than two-thirds of GDP in the United States. Consumption expenditures are grouped into three categories:

1. *consumer durables*, which are long-lived consumer items, such as cars, televisions, furniture, and major appliances (but not houses, which are classified under investment);
2. *nondurable goods*, which are shorter-lived items, such as food, clothing, and fuel; and
3. *services*, such as education, health care, financial services, and transportation.

Investment. **Investment** includes both spending for new capital goods, called *fixed investment*, and increases in firms' inventory holdings, called *inventory investment*. Fixed investment in turn has two major components:

1. *business fixed investment*, which is spending by businesses on structures (factories, warehouses, and office buildings, for example), equipment (such as machines, vehicles, computers, and furniture), and intellectual property products (such as software, investment in research and development, and literary, entertainment, and artistic originals); and
2. *residential investment*, which is spending on the construction of new houses and apartment buildings. Houses and apartment buildings are treated as capital goods because they provide a service (shelter) over a long period of time.

Like consumption, investment includes spending on foreign-produced goods. Fixed investment in the United States is volatile, ranging from about 13% to almost 20% of GDP.

As we have mentioned, increases in inventories are included in investment spending, regardless of why inventories rose. In particular, if a firm produces goods that it can't sell, the resulting rise in inventories counts as investment by the firm. For the purposes of national income accounting, the firm has, in effect, purchased the unsold goods from itself. This accounting rule is useful because it guarantees that production and expenditure will always be equal in the national income accounts. Anything that is produced must, by definition, either be bought by a customer or "purchased" by the firm itself.

Government Purchases of Goods and Services. **Government purchases** of goods and services, which include any expenditure by the government for a

[6]Later, we subtract imports from total expenditures and add exports to calculate total spending on the goods and services produced by the domestic economy.

currently produced good or service, foreign or domestic, is the third major component of spending. Government purchases in the United States recently have been about one-sixth of GDP. Note in Table 2.1 that in the United States the majority of government purchases are made by state and local governments, not the Federal government.

Not all the checks written by the government are for purchases of current goods and services. **Transfers**, a category that includes government payments for Social Security and Medicare benefits,[7] unemployment insurance, Temporary Assistance for Needy Families (TANF) payments, and so on, are payments (primarily to individuals) by the government that are not made in exchange for current goods or services. As a result, they are excluded from the government purchases category and are not counted in GDP as calculated by the expenditure approach. Similarly, interest payments on the national debt are not counted as part of government purchases.

Much like the distinction between private-sector consumption and investment, some part of government purchases goes toward current needs (such as employee salaries) and some is devoted to acquiring capital goods (such as office buildings). In the U.S. national income and product accounts, government spending on capital goods (buildings, equipment, software, and intellectual property) is often reported separately from other government purchases. Investment by the government is fairly sizable—more than $600 billion annually in recent years, or about one-fifth of the amount invested annually by the private sector. When we speak of "investment" in the national income accounts, however, we are generally referring to investment by the private sector, I; for simplicity, we include government investment as part of government purchases of goods and services, G.

Net Exports. **Net exports** are exports minus imports. As discussed in Chapter 1, exports are the goods and services produced within a country that are purchased by foreigners; imports are the goods and services produced abroad that are purchased by a country's residents. Net exports are positive if exports are greater than imports and negative if imports exceed exports.

Exports are added to total spending because they represent spending (by foreigners) on final goods and services produced in a country.[8] Imports are subtracted from total spending because consumption, investment, and government purchases are defined to include imported goods and services. Subtracting imports ensures that total spending, $C + I + G + NX$, reflects spending only on output produced in the country. For example, an increase in imports may mean that Americans are buying Japanese cars instead of American cars. For fixed total spending by domestic residents, therefore, an increase in imports lowers spending on domestic production.

---

[7]Although it might seem that Medicare benefits are a current expenditure by the government and not a transfer, in the NIPAs the medical expenditure is considered consumption spending by households, and the government payment to cover the medical expenditure is a transfer payment from the government to the household.

[8]Exports include intermediate goods, as well as final goods, that are sold abroad because the remaining process to turn them into final goods will not occur in the United States; hence these intermediate goods will not be "double-counted" in U.S. GDP. Similarly, imports include intermediate goods, which are subtracted from GDP, so that only the part of the final goods that is produced in the United States will be counted in GDP.

The Income Approach to Measuring GDP

The third and final way to measure GDP is the income approach. It calculates GDP by adding the incomes received by producers, including profits, and taxes paid to the government. A key part of the income approach is a concept known as national income. **National income** is the sum of eight types of income (see Table 2.2 for recent U.S. data).

1. *Compensation of employees.* Compensation of employees is the income of workers (excluding the self-employed) and includes wages, salaries, employee benefits (including contributions by employers to pension plans), and employer contributions to Social Security. As you can see from Table 2.2, compensation of employees is the largest component of national income, accounting for 54.4% of GDP, on average, in the past 25 years.
2. *Proprietors' income.* Proprietors' income is the income of the nonincorporated self-employed. Because many self-employed people own some capital (examples are a farmer's tractor or a dentist's X-ray machine), proprietors' income includes both labor income and capital income. Proprietors' income has averaged about 7.6% of GDP over the past 25 years.
3. *Rental income of persons.* Rental income of persons, a small item, is the income earned by individuals who own land or structures that they rent to others. Some miscellaneous types of income, such as royalty income paid to authors,

TABLE 2.2

Income Approach to Measuring GDP in the United States, 2021

	Billions of dollars	Percent of GDP
Compensation of employees	12,581	54.7
Proprietor's income	1822	7.9
Rental income of persons	726	3.2
Corporate profits	2806	12.2
Net interest	686	3.0
Taxes on production and imports	1148	5.0
Business current transfer payments	164	0.7
Current surplus of government enterprises	−13	−0.1
Total (equals **National Income**)	**19,920**	**86.6**
Plus Statistical discrepancy	−520	−2.3
Equals **Net National Product**	**19,401**	**84.4**
Plus Consumption of fixed capital	3848	16.7
Equals **Gross National Product** (GNP)	**23,249**	**101.1**
Less Factor income received from rest of world	1145	5.0
Plus Payments of factor income to rest of world	893	3.9
Equals **Gross Domestic Product** (GDP)	**22,996**	**100.0**

Note: Numbers may not add to totals shown owing to rounding.
Source: Bureau of Economic Analysis website, *www.bea.gov*, NIPA Tables 1.7.5 and 1.12, March 30, 2022.

recording artists, and others, also are included in this category. Rental income of persons averaged 2.5% of GDP over the past 25 years.[9]

4. *Corporate profits.* Corporate profits are the profits earned by corporations and represent the remainder of corporate revenue after wages, interest, rents, and other costs have been paid. Corporate profits are used to pay taxes levied on corporations, such as the corporate income tax, and to pay dividends to shareholders. The rest of corporate profits after taxes and dividends, called *retained earnings*, are kept by the corporations. Corporate profits have averaged a bit over 10% of GDP over the past 25 years, but the amount of profits earned by corporations may change dramatically from year to year or even from quarter to quarter. Table 2.2 shows that corporate profits were 12.2% of GDP in 2021, somewhat higher than the 25-year average.
5. *Net interest.* Net interest is interest earned by individuals from businesses and foreign sources minus interest paid by individuals. Net interest has varied from 2.6% to 5.3% of GDP each year over the past 25 years, averaging 3.7% of GDP.
6. *Taxes on production and imports.* Taxes on production and imports include indirect business taxes, such as sales and excise taxes, that are paid by businesses to Federal, state, and local governments, as well as customs duties and taxes on residential real estate and motor vehicle licenses paid by households. These taxes have averaged about 6.5% of GDP for the past 25 years.
7. *Business current transfer payments (net).* Business current transfer payments are payments made by businesses to individuals or governments or foreigners, but not for wages or taxes or as payment for services. Instead, such transactions as charitable donations, insurance payments, FDIC insurance premiums paid by banks, and legal settlements are covered by this category of income. Business current transfer payments have been between 0.6% and 0.9% of GDP each year for the past 25 years.
8. *Current surplus of government enterprises.* Current surplus of government enterprises is essentially the profit of businesses that are owned by governments, such as water, electric, and sewer companies; trash companies; mass transit firms; and housing firms. Current surplus of government enterprises is often negative when the firms suffer losses, as has occurred in each of the past 17 years, though the losses have never been more than 0.2% of GDP.

In addition to the eight components of national income just described, three other items need to be accounted for to obtain GDP:

- statistical discrepancy;
- depreciation; and
- net factor payments from abroad.

Statistical discrepancy arises because data on income are compiled from different sources than data on production; the production measure minus the income measure equals the statistical discrepancy. Thus, a positive statistical discrepancy means that the income measure adds up to less than the production measure.

[9]Rental income of persons is a tiny fraction of GDP because it represents net rental income, or rents received minus the cost of replacing worn-out or depreciated structures. Also, rental income of persons does not include all rents paid in the economy because it excludes rents received by corporations.

National income plus the statistical discrepancy equals **net national product (NNP)**, as indicated in Table 2.2.

Depreciation (also known as consumption of fixed capital) is the value of the capital that wears out during the period over which economic activity is being measured.[10] In the calculation of the components of national income (specifically, proprietors' income, corporate profits, and rental income), depreciation is subtracted from total, or gross, income. Thus, to compute the total or gross amount of income, we must add back in depreciation. The sum of net national product and depreciation is gross national product (GNP). Gross national product and gross domestic product are called gross because they measure the nation's total production or equivalently output of goods and services without subtracting depreciation.

As we discussed earlier, to go from GNP to GDP we have to subtract net factor payments from abroad, NFP (see Eq. 2.2). As we have already mentioned and as you can see from Table 2.2, for the United States net factor payments are relatively small and so GDP and GNP are very close.

Private Sector and Government Sector Income. In this section we have measured economic activity as the sum of all the incomes received in an economy. Sometimes, however, economists need to know how much of total income was received by the private sector (households and businesses) and how much accrues to the government sector, which in the United States consists of Federal, state, and local governments. For example, in trying to predict the demand for consumer goods, focusing on the income available to the private sector might be more useful than focusing on the income of the economy as a whole.

The income of the private sector, known as **private disposable income**, measures the amount of income the private sector has available to spend. In general, as for a household, the disposable income of the private sector as a whole equals income received from private-sector activities, plus payments received by the private sector from the government, minus taxes paid to the government. The precise definition is

$$\text{private disposable income} = Y + NFP + TR + INT - T, \qquad \textbf{(2.4)}$$

where

$$\begin{aligned} Y &= \text{gross domestic product (GDP);} \\ NFP &= \text{net factor payments from abroad;} \\ TR &= \text{transfers received from the government;} \\ INT &= \text{interest on government debt;} \\ T &= \text{taxes.} \end{aligned}$$

As you can see from Eq. (2.4), private disposable income equals private sector income earned at home (GDP) and abroad (net factor payments from abroad, NFP);[11] plus payments to the private sector from the government sector (transfers, TR, and interest on government debt, INT);[12] minus taxes paid to the government, T.

[10]Depreciation (consumption of fixed capital) includes both capital that physically wears out and capital that is scrapped because it is no longer economically useful. For instance, still-functioning computers that are scrapped because they have been made obsolete by newer models would be included in depreciation.

[11]Note that the sum of incomes earned at home and abroad, GDP + NFP, equals GNP.

[12]Some of interest on government debt is paid to foreign investors, businesses and governments. These interest payments should be deducted from INT in calculating private disposable income.

The part of GDP that is not at the disposal of the private sector is the net income of the government sector. **Net government income** equals taxes paid by the private sector, T, minus payments from the government to the private sector (transfers, TR, and interest on government debt, INT):

$$\text{net government income} = T - TR - INT. \tag{2.5}$$

Adding Eqs. (2.4) and (2.5) yields the sum of private disposable income and net government income, $Y + NFP$, which is gross national product.

2.3 Saving and Wealth

Discuss the measurement of aggregate saving and its relation to wealth.

If you wanted to assess the economic situation of a household, the current income of the household would be an important piece of information. However, someone with a high current income isn't necessarily better off economically than someone with a low current income. For example, a retired plumber who has no current earnings but owns real estate worth $5 million probably is economically better off than his daughter who is a newly graduated doctor with a high salary but heavy debts left over from medical school. To determine how well off a household is, in addition to knowing current income, you also need to know what the household owns (its assets) and owes (its liabilities). The value of assets minus the value of liabilities is called **wealth**.

As for a household, the economic well-being of a country depends not only on its income but also on its wealth. The wealth of an entire nation is called **national wealth**.

An important determinant of wealth is the rate of saving: A person who puts aside a quarter of its income each month will accumulate wealth much more quickly than one with the same income who saves only 2% of its income. Similarly, the rate at which national wealth increases depends on the rate at which individuals, businesses, and governments in the economy save. Thus rates of saving and wealth accumulation are closely related.

In this section we present some concepts of aggregate saving and wealth and examine the relationships among them. Our main interest here is measurement. Questions such as what determines the rate of saving in a country are covered in later chapters.

Measures of Aggregate Saving

In general, the **saving** of any economic unit is the unit's current income minus its spending on current needs. The saving *rate* of an economic unit is its saving divided by its income. From a macroeconomic perspective, three important measures of saving are private saving, government saving, and national saving. Summary table 1 outlines the definitions of each measure.

Private Saving. The saving of the private sector, known as **private saving**, equals private disposable income minus consumption. Using the definition of private disposable income from Eq. (2.4), we have

$$\begin{aligned} S_{pvt} &= \text{private disposable income} - \text{consumption} \\ &= (Y + NFP + TR + INT - T) - C, \end{aligned} \tag{2.6}$$

where S_{pvt} is private saving. Consumption is subtracted from private disposable income to obtain private saving because consumption represents the private sector's spending to meet current needs. Investment, although part of private sector spending, is not subtracted from private disposable income because capital goods are purchased to enhance future productive capacity rather than to satisfy current needs. The private saving *rate* is private saving divided by private disposable income.

Government Saving. **Government saving** is defined as net government income, Eq. (2.5), less government purchases of goods and services. Using S_{govt} for government saving, we write this definition of government saving as

$$S_{govt} = \text{net government income} - \text{government purchases} \\ = (T - TR - INT) - G. \quad \textbf{(2.7)}$$

Equation (2.7) treats total government purchases, G, as the government's spending to meet current needs. Thus the definition of government saving fits the general definition of saving as income less spending on current needs.

However, as we discussed earlier, not all government purchases are in fact devoted to satisfying current needs; some part of G is devoted to the acquisition of long-lived capital, such as schools, highways, and dams. The national income and product accounts break total government purchases into the portion devoted to current needs (referred to as *government consumption*) and the portion spent on long-lived capital goods (referred to as *government investment*). Under this breakdown, government saving could be defined as net government income less government consumption only, rather than net government income less all government purchases. This alternative approach would increase the amount of measured saving and investment in the U.S. economy by the amount of government investment, an amount exceeding $600 billion per year in most recent years.[13]

SUMMARY 1

Measures of Aggregate Saving

Saving measure	Definition and formula
Private saving	Private disposable income less consumption $S_{pvt} = (Y + NFP + TR + INT - T) - C$
Government saving	Net government income - government purchases $S_{govt} = (T - TR - INT) - G$
National saving	Private saving plus government saving; also GNP ($Y + NFP$) less consumption and government purchases $S = S_{pvt} + S_{govt}$ $= Y + NFP - C - G$

[13]Note that, by similar reasoning, household spending on cars and other long-lived consumer durables should not be subtracted from private disposable income in the calculation of private saving; however, in practice they are subtracted.

Although the alternative definition of government saving is conceptually more correct, for most analyses in this book, keeping track of government consumption and government investment separately is an unnecessary complication. To keep things simple, we usually ignore government investment, assuming that government purchases are made up entirely of government consumption. With this assumption, we can use the traditional definition of government saving, Eq. (2.7). When considering issues such as the government budget deficit, however, keep in mind that, in fact, some government spending is devoted to building or acquiring long-lived capital goods.

Another, probably more familiar, name for government saving is the government budget surplus. The government **budget surplus** equals government receipts minus government outlays. **Government receipts** equal tax revenue, T. **Government outlays** are the sum of government purchases of goods and services, G, transfers, TR, and interest payments on government debt, INT. Thus the government budget surplus equals $T - (G + TR + INT)$, which, as you can see from Eq. (2.7), is the same as government saving.

When government receipts are less than government outlays, the difference between outlays and receipts is known as the government **budget deficit**. Thus, when the government runs a budget deficit, with its outlays greater than its receipts, government saving is negative.

National Saving. **National saving**, or the saving of the economy as a whole, equals private saving plus government saving. Using the definitions of private and government saving, Eqs. (2.6) and (2.7), we obtain national saving, S:

$$\begin{aligned} S &= S_{\text{pvt}} + S_{\text{govt}} \qquad \textbf{(2.8)} \\ &= (Y + NFP + TR + INT - C - T) + (T - TR - INT - G) \\ &= Y + NFP - C - G. \end{aligned}$$

Equation (2.8) shows that national saving equals the total income of the economy, $Y + NFP$ (which equals GNP), minus spending to satisfy current needs (consumption, C, and government purchases, G).

Figure 2.1 shows national saving, government saving, and private saving in the United States since 1960—all expressed as percentages of GDP. Government saving averaged -5.4% of GDP so that national saving fell short of private saving by an average of 5.4% of GDP.[14]

The Uses of Private Saving

How is private saving in an economy put to use? Private saving is used to fund new capital investment, provide the resources the government needs to finance its budget deficits, and acquire assets from or lend to foreigners.

[14]The correlation between national saving and government saving had been high until the pandemic began in 2020. But the pandemic years of 2020 and 2021 changed the correlations of the three saving variables with each other, as Fig. 2.1 suggests.

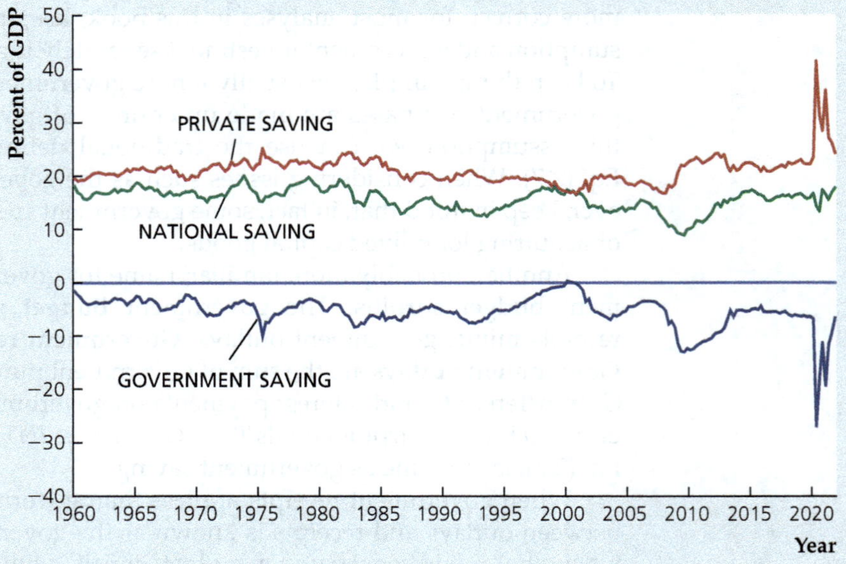

FIGURE 2.1

U.S. saving measures as a percentage of GDP, 1960Q1–2021Q4

National saving has fluctuated in a relatively narrow range since 1960. Movements in national saving mirrored movements in government saving until the pandemic in 2020 and 2021.

Sources: Bureau of Economic Analysis, National Income and Product Accounts, downloaded from Federal Reserve Bank of St. Louis, FRED database, *fred.stlouisfed.org/*. Private saving: FRED series *GPSAVE*. Government saving: FRED series *GGSAVE* (gross government saving, ignoring gross government investment as a component of outlays) minus *A782RC1Q027SBEA* (gross government investment). National saving: sum of private and government saving. GDP: FRED series *GDP*.

To derive an important identity that illustrates the uses of private saving, we first use the income–expenditure identity (Eq. 2.3) and substitute $C + I + G + NX$ for Y in the expression for national saving (Eq. 2.8):

$$S = (C + I + G + NX) + NFP - C - G.$$

Simplifying this expression, we obtain

$$S = I + (NX + NFP). \qquad \textbf{(2.9)}$$

The expression for national saving in Eq. (2.9) contains the term $NX + NFP$, which is the sum of net exports and net factor payments, and is called the current account balance, CA.[15] The **current account balance** equals payments received from abroad in exchange for currently produced goods and services (including factor services), minus the analogous payments made to foreigners by the domestic economy. Substituting CA for $NX + NFP$ in Eq. (2.9), we obtain

$$S = I + CA. \qquad \textbf{(2.10)}$$

We now have an expression for national saving, S; our goal is an expression for private saving, S_{pvt}. Equation (2.8) shows that private saving, S_{pvt}, equals national saving, S, minus government saving, S_{govt}. Then, subtracting S_{govt} from both sides of Eq. (2.10), we get

$$S_{pvt} = I + (-S_{govt}) + CA, \qquad \textbf{(2.11)}$$

where $-S_{govt}$ is the government budget deficit.

[15]Actually, the current account balance also includes the term *net unilateral transfers*, which measures transfers between countries such as private gifts or official foreign aid (see Chapter 5). In our analysis we generally ignore this term.

Equation (2.11) is another important macroeconomic identity, called the **uses-of-saving identity**. It states that an economy's private saving is used in three ways.

1. *Investment* (I). Firms borrow from private savers to finance the construction and purchase of new capital (including residential capital) and inventory investment.
2. *The government budget deficit* $(-S_{govt})$. When the government runs a budget deficit (so that S_{govt} is negative and $-S_{govt}$ is positive), it must borrow from private savers to cover the difference between outlays and receipts.
3. *The current account balance* (CA). When the U.S. current account balance is positive, foreigners' receipts of payments from the United States are not sufficient to cover the payments they make to the United States. To make up the difference, foreigners must either borrow from U.S. private savers or sell to U.S. savers some of their assets, such as land, factories, stocks, and bonds. Thus financing the current account balance is a use of a country's private saving.

   In contrast, when the U.S. current account balance is negative, as it was during most of the 1980s, 1990s, and 2000s, U.S. receipts of payments from foreigners are not sufficient to cover U.S. payments to foreigners. To offset this excess of payments over receipts, the United States must borrow from foreigners or sell to foreigners some U.S. assets. In this case, foreigners use their saving to lend to the United States or to acquire U.S. assets.[16]

Figure 2.2 shows private saving, investment, the government budget deficit, and the current account balance in the United States since 1960—all expressed as percentages of GDP. Since the early 1990s, the current account balance has been negative, so that foreigners have been buying U.S. assets, providing financing for U.S. investment, and the government budget deficit. In some crisis periods, such as 1975 and 2008–2010, we observe large increases in the government budget deficit accompanied by sharp declines in gross private domestic investment and increases in private saving. In periods of strong growth, such as the late 1990s, we observe a decline in private saving and the government budget deficit, along with a rise in investment.

Relating Saving and Wealth

Saving is a key economic variable because it is closely related to the rate of wealth accumulation. In the rest of this section we discuss the relationship between saving and wealth. To do so, however, we must first introduce the concept of stocks versus flows.

Stocks and Flows. The economic variables we have discussed so far in this chapter—such as GDP and the various types of expenditure, income, and saving—are measured per unit of time (for example, per quarter or per year). For instance,

---

[16]The current account and its relationship to international borrowing and lending are discussed in greater detail in Chapter 5.

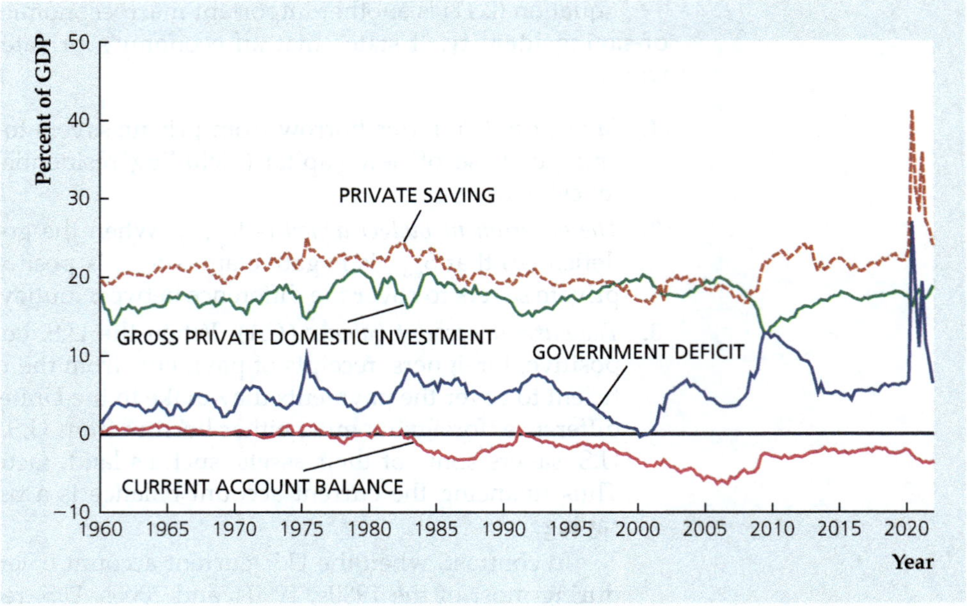

FIGURE 2.2

Components of the U.S. uses-of-saving identity, 1960Q1–2021Q4

Private saving equals the sum of gross private domestic investment, the government budget deficit, and the current account balance. The current account balance has been negative since the early 1990s, which means that foreigners have been providing funds for U.S. investment and the government budget deficit.

Sources: Bureau of Economic Analysis, National Income and Product Accounts, downloaded from Federal Reserve Bank of St. Louis FRED database at *fred.stlouisfed.org*. Private saving and government deficit: same as in Fig. 2.1. Investment: FRED series *GPDI*. Current account balance: FRED series *NETFI*. GDP: FRED series *GDP*.

annual GDP figures measure the economy's production per year. Variables that are measured per unit of time are called **flow variables**.

In contrast, some economic variables, called **stock variables**, are defined at a point in time. Examples of stock variables include the amount of money in your bank account on September 15 of this year and the total value of all houses in the United States on January 1, 2023.

In many applications, a flow variable is the rate of change in a stock variable. A classic example is a bathtub with water flowing in from a faucet. The amount of water in the tub at any moment is a stock variable. The units of a stock variable (gallons, in this case) don't have a time dimension. The rate at which water enters the tub is a flow variable; its units (gallons per minute) have a time dimension. In this case the flow equals the rate of change of the stock.

Wealth and Saving as Stock and Flow. Saving and wealth are related to each other in much the same way that the flow and stock of water in a bathtub are related. The wealth of any economic unit (a household, firm, or government), also called *net worth*, is its assets (the things that it owns, including IOUs from other economic units) minus its liabilities (what it owes to other units). Wealth is measured in dollars at a point in time and is a stock variable. Saving is measured in dollars per unit time and is a flow variable. Because saving takes the form of an accumulation of assets or a reduction in liabilities (for example, if saving is used to pay off debts), it adds to wealth just as water flowing into a bathtub adds to the stock of water.

National Wealth. National wealth is the total wealth of the residents of a country. National wealth consists of two parts: (1) the country's domestic physical assets, such as its stock of capital goods and land;[17] and (2) its net foreign assets. The **net foreign assets** of a country equal the country's foreign assets (foreign stocks, bonds, and factories owned by domestic residents) minus its foreign liabilities (domestic physical and financial assets owned by foreigners). Net foreign assets are part of national wealth because they represent claims on foreigners that are not offset by foreigners' claims on the domestic economy.

Domestic financial assets held by domestic residents are not part of national wealth because the value of any domestic financial asset is offset by a domestic financial liability. For example, a checking account of a U.S. resident in a U.S. bank is an asset for the depositor but a liability for the bank; it thus does not represent wealth for the economy as a whole. In contrast, a U.S. resident's checking account in a foreign bank has no corresponding domestic liability (it is a liability of a foreigner) and so is part of U.S. national wealth.

National wealth can change in two ways over time. First, the value of the existing assets or liabilities that make up national wealth may change. For example, the dramatic increase in the stock market during the 1990s increased U.S. national wealth. The wearing out or depreciation of physical assets, which corresponds to a drop in the value of those assets, reduces national wealth.

The second way that national wealth can change is through national saving. Over any particular period of time, with the value of existing assets and liabilities held constant, each extra dollar of national saving adds a dollar to national wealth. That is,

$$S = I + CA,$$

which you will recognize as Eq. (2.10). This equation shows that national saving has two uses: (1) to increase the stock of domestic physical capital through investment, I; and (2) to increase the nation's stock of net foreign assets by lending to foreigners or acquiring foreign assets in an amount equal to the current account balance, CA. But each dollar increase in domestic physical assets or net foreign assets is a one-dollar increase in national wealth. Thus, over a given period of time, an increase in national saving increases national wealth dollar for dollar. As in the example of water flowing into a bathtub, the more rapid the flow of national saving, the more quickly the stock of national wealth will rise.

How do national saving and investment in the United States compare to that in other countries? The United States is a relatively low-saving country, compared with other industrialized nations. Investment is also relatively low in the United States, according to the official statistics.[18] However, investment rates in the United States are generally higher than saving rates. Using the relationship $S = I + CA$, we see that, if investment, I, is greater than national saving, S, then the current account balance, CA, must be negative. As we mentioned earlier, the U.S. current

[17] In principle, national wealth should also include the value of the skills and training of the country's residents—what economists call *human capital*. In practice, because of measurement problems, human capital is not usually included in measures of national wealth.

[18] Some economists have suggested that the low U.S. saving and investment rates reflect various measurement problems as much as fundamental differences in behavior. See, for example, Milton Marquis, "What's Behind the Low U.S. Personal Saving Rate?" Federal Reserve Bank of San Francisco *Economic Letter* 2002–09, March 2002, and Rudolph Penner, "Measuring Personal Saving: A Tale of American Profligacy," Urban Institute, Retirement Policy Program Brief No. 21, May 2008.

account has indeed been in deficit nearly every year since 1980. In contrast, high-saving countries such as China have typically had investment rates lower than their saving rates, resulting in consistently positive current account balances for those countries.

2.4 Real GDP, Price Indexes, and Inflation

Explain the calculation of real GDP, price indexes, and inflation.

All of the key macroeconomic variables that we have discussed so far in this chapter—GDP, the components of expenditure and income, national wealth, and saving—are measured in terms of current market values. Such variables are called **nominal variables**. The advantage of using market values to measure economic activity is that it allows summing of different types of goods and services.

However, a problem with measuring economic activity in nominal terms arises if you want to compare the values of an economic variable—GDP, for example—at two different points in time. If the current market value of the goods and services included in GDP changes over time, you can't tell whether this change reflects changes in the quantities of goods and services produced, changes in the prices of goods and services, or a combination of these factors. For example, a large increase in the current market value of GDP might mean that a country has greatly expanded its production of goods and services, or it might mean that the country has experienced inflation, which raised the prices of goods and services.

Real GDP

Economists have devised methods for breaking down changes in nominal variables into the part owing to changes in physical quantities and the part owing to changes in prices. Consider the numerical example in Table 2.3, which gives production and price data for an economy that produces two types of goods: computers and bicycles. The data are presented for two different years. In year 1, the value of GDP is $46,000 (5 computers worth $1200 each and 200 bicycles worth

TABLE 2.3

Production and Price Data

	Year 1	Year 2	Percent change from year 1 to year 2
Product (quantity)			
Computers	5	10	+100%
Bicycles	200	250	+25%
Price			
Computers	$1200/computer	$600/computer	−50%
Bicycles	$200/bicycle	$240/bicycle	+20%
Value			
Computers	$6000	$6000	0
Bicycles	$40,000	$60,000	+50%
Total	**$46,000**	**$66,000**	**+43.5%**

$200 each). In year 2, the value of GDP is $66,000 (10 computers worth $600 each and 250 bicycles worth $240 each), which is 43.5% higher than the value of GDP in year 1. This 43.5% increase in nominal GDP does not reflect either a 43.5% increase in physical output or a 43.5% increase in prices. Instead, it reflects changes in both physical output and prices.

How much of the 43.5% increase in nominal output is attributable to an increase in physical output? A simple way to remove the effects of price changes, and thus to focus on changes in quantities of output, is to measure the value of production in each year by using the prices from some base year. For this example, let's choose year 1 as the base year. Using the prices from year 1 ($1200 per computer and $200 per bicycle) to value the production in year 2 (10 computers and 250 bicycles) yields a value of $62,000, as shown in Table 2.4. We say that $62,000 is the value of *real* GDP in year 2, measured using the prices of year 1.

In general, an economic variable that is measured by the prices of a base year is called a **real variable.** Real economic variables measure the physical quantity of economic activity. Specifically, **real GDP**, also called *constant-dollar GDP*, measures the physical volume of an economy's final production using the prices of a

TABLE 2.4

Calculation of Real Output with Alternative Base Years

Calculation of real output with base year = Year 1					
	Current quantities		**Base-year prices**		
Year 1					
Computers	5	×	$1200	=	$6000
Bicycles	200	×	$200	=	$40,000
				Total =	**$46,000**
Year 2					
Computers	10	×	$1200	=	$12,000
Bicycles	250	×	$200	=	$50,000
				Total =	**$62,000**
Percentage growth of real GDP = ($62,000 − $46,000)/$46,000 = 34.8%					
Calculation of real output with base year = Year 2					
	Current quantities		**Base-year prices**		
Year 1					
Computers	5	×	$600	=	$3000
Bicycles	200	×	$240	=	$48,000
				Total =	**$51,000**
Year 2					
Computers	10	×	$600	=	$6000
Bicycles	250	×	$240	=	$60,000
				Total =	**$66,000**
Percentage growth of real GDP = ($66,000 − $51,000)/$51,000 = 29.4%					

base year. **Nominal GDP**, also called *current-dollar GDP*, is the dollar value of an economy's final output measured at current market prices. Thus nominal GDP in year 2 for our example is \$66,000, which we computed earlier using current (that is, year 2) prices to value output.

What is the value of real GDP in year 1? Continuing to treat year 1 as the base year, use the prices of year 1 (\$1200 per computer and \$200 per bicycle) to value production. The production of 5 computers and 200 bicycles has a value of \$46,000. Thus the value of real GDP in year 1 is the same as the value of nominal GDP in year 1. This result is a general one: Because current prices and base-year prices are the same in the base year, real and nominal values are always the same in the base year. Specifically, real GDP and nominal GDP are equal in the base year.

Now we are prepared to calculate the increase in the physical production from year 1 to year 2. Real GDP is designed to measure the physical quantity of production. Because real GDP in year 2 is \$62,000, and real GDP in year 1 is \$46,000, output, as measured by real GDP, is 34.8% higher in year 2 than in year 1.

GDP Growth. The discussion above focused on measuring the level of GDP. Economists are typically more interested in how fast real GDP grows over time rather than the level of real GDP. For example, when a new release of the NIPA data occurs, economists will focus on the growth rate of real GDP, on whether it is positive or negative, and on how it compares with the growth rate from the previous quarter and year. Here is how the growth rate is calculated.

Real GDP growth is sometimes calculated over a calendar quarter and is sometimes calculated over a year. To facilitate comparison of these alternative calculations, we "annualize" the quarterly growth rates—that is, we ask the question: If real GDP were to grow at the same rate for the whole year as it did in the quarter, what would the annual growth rate be? To do this, we use the formula:

$$\frac{\Delta Y}{Y} = \left(\frac{Y(t)}{Y(t-1)}\right)^4 - 1, \tag{2.12}$$

where $Y(t)$ is the level of real GDP in quarter t. The resulting number is called the annualized quarterly growth rate of GDP. The ratio of the levels of real GDP is raised to the fourth power to allow for compounding. For example, suppose the ratio of output in quarter t to output in quarter $t - 1$ is 1.01. Then at the end of four quarters, the level of output would be $1.01 \times 1.01 \times 1.01 \times 1.01 = 1.01^4$ times higher than at the start of the year.

For example, in the first data release for the fourth quarter of 2021 (which was announced in January 2022), GDP for that quarter was reported as 19,805.962 (all numbers are in billions of constant dollars). GDP for the third quarter had been 19,478.893. So, we calculate the annualized quarterly growth rate as

$$\frac{\Delta Y}{Y} = \left(\frac{19{,}805.962}{19{,}478.893}\right)^4 - 1 = 0.069 = 6.9\%.$$

In this case, we say that the annualized quarterly growth rate of GDP in the fourth quarter of 2021 was 0.069 or 6.9%. Note that we can discuss growth rates in decimal terms (0.069) or in growth rates (6.9%), where we can convert a decimal to a percent by multiplying by 100.

If you have annual data, then you would use the same general format as in Eq. (2.12), but you would not raise the ratio of the levels of GDP in Eq. (2.12) to the fourth power because the levels of GDP are for the whole year and so are already annualized. (If you had monthly data, you would raise the ratio in Eq. (2.12) to the 12th power because there are 12 months in a year.) For example, when the GDP growth rate for 2021Q4 of 6.9% was released, the government also released data for the year as a whole. The ratio of real GDP for 2021 to real GDP for 2020 was 1.057, so the growth rate for the year was 0.057 or 5.7%. Thus the fourth quarter growth rate (6.9%) was slightly higher than the growth rate for the year as a whole (5.7%), and the convention of annualizing the growth rate allows a direct comparison.

The convention in the United States is to annualize growth rates of quarterly data. So, when you read in the news that the growth rate of real GDP was 6.9% in the fourth quarter of 2021, you need to realize that it is an annualized growth rate. However, in many other countries, the government statistical agencies do not follow the same convention. So, if the same numbers were reported in Europe, for example, the GDP growth rate would be reported as 0.017 or 1.7%. The number they report is not annualized, so in Eq. (2.12), the government agency did not raise the ratio to the fourth power.

A second convention for U.S. data is that the government statistical agencies report data that are seasonally adjusted, that is, the data are modified to account for normal seasonal variation. The statistical agencies do this to make it easier for users to compare data over the course of a year. For example, many people take long vacations during the summer, so real GDP is lower in the summer months. Many firms gear up production for holiday shopping in November and December, so real GDP in the fall is higher. Some activities such as construction are curtailed in the cold winter months, so real GDP in January and February is lower. Because these seasonal variations are fairly predictable, the statistical agencies seasonally adjust the data to pull out the predictable part of real GDP fluctuations that arise because of these seasonal effects. Similar seasonal adjustment is the norm in other countries, too, but sometimes a country does not seasonally adjust the data because doing so requires a long history so that the statistical agency can accurately detect the seasonal pattern in the data and remove it.

Both the annualization of the data and seasonal adjustment of it are often described by saying the data are "SAAR," which means "seasonally adjusted at an annual rate." So, the next time you hear about a government data report, pay attention to see if it is SAAR, SA and not AR, AR and not SA, or neither.

Growth rates of real GDP vary considerably over time. When the economy enters a recession, the annualized quarterly real GDP growth rate is usually negative. Coming out of a recession, real GDP growth is often very high. To see this, Figure 2.3 shows the SAAR growth rate of real GDP for the United States from 1960Q1 to 2021Q4. Note that the annualized quarterly growth rate is quite volatile. It is easy to pick out periods of recession (shown by green shaded bars), when real GDP growth is often negative.

Price Indexes

We have seen how to calculate the portion of the change in nominal GDP owing to a change in physical quantities. Now we turn our attention to the change in prices by using price indexes. A **price index** is a measure of the average level of prices for some specified set of goods and services, relative to the prices in a specified base year. For example, the **GDP deflator** is a price index that measures the overall level of prices of goods and services included in GDP, and is defined by the formula

$$\text{real GDP} = \text{nominal GDP}/(\text{GDP deflator}/100).$$

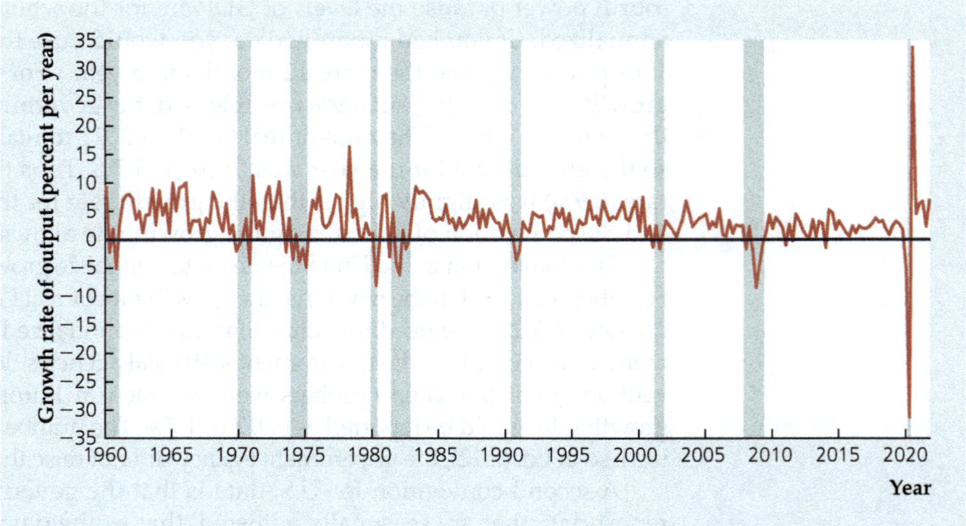

FIGURE 2.3

The annualized quarterly growth rate of U.S. real GDP, 1960Q1–2021Q4

The quarterly growth rate of U.S. real GDP is annualized by convention to make comparisons between quarterly and annual data easier. The annualized quarterly growth rate is highly volatile and is frequently negative during recessions (shown by green shaded bars).

Source: Bureau of Economic Analysis, National Income and Product Accounts, downloaded from FRED database *fred.stlouisfed.org/series/GDPC1*.

The GDP deflator (divided by 100) is the amount by which nominal GDP must be divided, or "deflated," to obtain real GDP. In our example, we have already computed nominal GDP and real GDP, so we can now calculate the GDP deflator by rewriting the preceding formula as

$$\text{GDP deflator} = 100 \times \text{nominal GDP/real GDP}.$$

In year 1 (the base year in our example), nominal GDP and real GDP are equal, so the GDP deflator equals 100. This result is an example of the general principle that the GDP deflator always equals 100 in the base year. In year 2, nominal GDP is $66,000 (see Table 2.3) and real GDP is $62,000 (see Table 2.4), so the GDP deflator in year 2 is $100 \times \$66{,}000/\$62{,}000 = 106.5$, which is 6.5% higher than the value of the GDP deflator in year 1. Thus the overall level of prices, as measured by the GDP deflator, is 6.5% higher in year 2 than in year 1.

The measurement of real GDP and the GDP deflator depends on the choice of a base year. "In Touch with Data and Research: The Computer Revolution and Chain-Weighted GDP" demonstrates that the choice of a base year can have important effects on the calculated growth of real output, which in turn affects the calculated change in the price level.

In Touch with Data and Research

The Computer Revolution and Chain-Weighted GDP

The widespread use of computers has revolutionized business, education, and leisure throughout much of the developed world. The fraction of the real spending in the United States devoted to computers began to take off in the mid-1980s and continued into the 2000s, while prices of computers fell steadily throughout that period. The sharp increase in the real quantity of computers and the sharp decline in computer prices highlight the problem of choosing a base year in calculating the growth of real GDP.

We can use the example in Tables 2.3 and 2.4, which includes a large increase in the quantity of computers coupled with a sharp decrease in computer prices, to illustrate the problem. We have shown that, when we treat year 1 as the base year, real output increases by 34.8% from year 1 to year 2. However, as we will see in this box using Table 2.4, we get a substantially different measure of real output growth if we treat year 2 as the base year. Treating year 2 as the base year means that we use the prices of year 2 to value output. Specifically, each computer is valued at $600 and each bicycle is valued at $240. Thus the real value of the 5 computers and 200 bicycles produced in year 1 is $51,000. If we continue to treat year 2 as the base year, the real value of output in year 2 is the same as the nominal value of output, which we have already calculated to be $66,000. Thus, by treating year 2 as the base year, we see real output grow from $51,000 in year 1 to $66,000 in year 2, an increase of 29.4%.

Let's summarize our calculations so far. Using year 1 as the base year, the calculated growth of output is 34.8%, but using year 2 as the base year, the calculated growth of output is only 29.4%. Why does this difference arise? In this example, the quantity of computers grows by 100% (from 5 to 10) and the quantity of bicycles grows by 25% (from 200 to 250) from year 1 to year 2. The computed growth of overall output—34.8% using year 1 as the base year or 29.4% using year 2 as the base year—is between the growth rates of the two individual goods. The overall growth rate is a sort of weighted average of the growth rates of the individual goods. When year 1 is the base year, we use year 1 prices to value output, and in year 1 computers are much more expensive than bicycles. Thus the growth of overall output is closer to the very high growth rate of computers than when the growth rate is computed using year 2 as the base year.

Which base year is the "right" one to use? There is no clear reason to prefer one over the other. To deal with this problem, in 1996 the Bureau of Economic Analysis introduced chain-weighted indexes to measure real GDP. Chain-weighted real GDP represents a mathematical compromise between using year 1 and using year 2 as the base year. The growth rate of real GDP computed using chain-weighted real GDP is a sort of average of the growth rate computed using year 1 as the base year and the growth rate computed using year 2 as the base year. (In this example, the growth rate of real GDP using chain-weighting is 32.1%, but we will not go through the details of that calculation here.)[19]

Before the Bureau of Economic Analysis adopted chain-weighting, it used 1987 as the base year to compute real GDP. As time passed, it became necessary to update the base year so that the prices used to compute real GDP would reflect the true values of various goods being produced. Every time the base year was changed, the Bureau of Economic Analysis had to calculate new historical data for real GDP. Chain-weighting effectively updates the base year automatically. The annual growth rate for a given year is computed using that year and the preceding year as base years. As time goes on, there is no need to recompute historical growth rates of real GDP using new base years. Nevertheless, chain-weighted real GDP has a

[19]For discussions of chain-weighting, see Charles Steindel, "Chain-Weighting: The New Approach to Measuring GDP," *Current Issues in Economics and Finance*, New York: Federal Reserve Bank of New York, December 1995, and "A Guide to the NIPAs," on the website of the Bureau of Economic Analysis, *www.bea.gov/national/pdf/nipaguid.pdf*.

(*continued*)

peculiar feature. Although the income–expenditure identity, $Y = C + I + G + NX$, always holds exactly in nominal terms, for technical reasons, this relationship need not hold exactly when GDP and its components are measured in real terms when chain-weighting is used. Because the discrepancy is usually small, we assume in this book that the income–expenditure identity holds in both real and nominal terms.

Chain-weighting was introduced to resolve the problem of choosing a given year as a base year in calculating real GDP. How large a difference does chain-weighting make in the face of the rapidly increasing production of computers and plummeting computer prices? Using 1987 as the base year, real GDP in the fourth quarter of 1994 was computed to be growing at a 5.1% annual rate. Using chain-weighting, real GDP growth during that quarter was a less impressive 4.0%. The Bureau of Economic Analysis estimates that computers account for about three-fifths of the difference between these two growth rates.[20]

[20]These figures are from p. 36 of J. Steven Landefeld and Robert P. Parker, "Preview of the Comprehensive Revision of the National Income and Product Accounts: BEA's New Featured Measures of Output and Prices," *Survey of Current Business*, July 1995, pp. 31–38.

The Consumer Price Index. The GDP deflator measures the average level of prices of goods and services included in GDP. The **consumer price index**, or CPI, measures the prices of consumer goods. Unlike the GDP deflator, which is calculated quarterly, the CPI is available monthly. The Bureau of Labor Statistics constructs the CPI by sending people out each month to find the current prices of a fixed list, or "basket," of consumer goods and services, including many specific items of food, clothing, housing, and fuel. The CPI for that month is then calculated as 100 times the current cost of the basket of consumer items divided by the cost of the same basket of items in the reference base period.

The calculation of the CPI requires the use of a reference base period, for comparing prices over time, and an expenditure base period, for determining the basket of goods used in the index. Currently the reference base period is 1982–1984, which means that the CPI is constructed so it averages 100 for the three-year period from January 1982 to December 1984. So, if the CPI averages 271 in 2021, that means the average level of consumer prices is 171% higher than it was in the 1982–1984 period.

The expenditure base period for the CPI is the period on which the Bureau of Labor Statistics bases the basket of goods, which is currently 2019–2020. A survey of consumers' expenditure patterns over the years 2019–2020 is used to weight the goods and services for constructing the CPI. Currently the reference base period differs from the expenditure base period. The government updates the expenditure base period every few years and does not want to recalculate the past values of the index by changing the reference base period. Even though the government updates the expenditure base period every few years, there is reason to think that the CPI inflation rate is biased upward, as discussed in "In Touch with Data and Research: Does CPI Inflation Overstate Increases in the Cost of Living?"

In Touch with Data and Research

Does CPI Inflation Overstate Increases in the Cost of Living?

In 1995–1996 a government commission, headed by Michael Boskin of Stanford University, prepared a report on the accuracy of official inflation measures. The commission concluded that inflation as measured by the CPI may overstate true increases in the cost of living by as much as 1–2 percentage points per year. In other words, if the official inflation rate is 3% per year, the "true" inflation rate may well be only 1%–2% per year.

Why might increases in the CPI overstate the actual rate at which the cost of living rises? One reason is the difficulty that government statisticians face in trying to measure changes in the quality of goods. For example, if the design of an air conditioner is improved so that it can put out 10% more cold air without an increased use of electricity, then a 10% increase in the price of the air conditioner should not be considered inflation; although paying 10% more, the consumer is also receiving 10% more cooling capacity. However, if government statisticians fail to account for the improved quality of the air conditioner and simply note its 10% increase in price, the price change will be incorrectly interpreted as inflation.

Although measuring the output of an air conditioner isn't difficult, for some products (especially services) quality change is hard to measure. For example, by what percentage does the availability of online bill-paying services improve the quality of banking services? To the extent that the CPI fails to account for quality improvements in the goods and services people use, inflation will be overstated. This overstatement is called the *quality adjustment bias*.

Another problem with CPI inflation as a measure of cost-of-living increases can be illustrated by the following example. Suppose that consumers like chicken and turkey about equally well and in the base year consume equal amounts of each. But then for some reason the price of chicken rises sharply, leading consumers to switch to eating turkey almost exclusively. Because consumers are about equally satisfied with chicken and turkey, this switch doesn't make them significantly worse off; their true cost of living has not been affected much by the rise in the price of chicken. However, the official CPI, which measures the cost of buying the base-year basket of goods and services, will register a significant increase when the price of chicken skyrockets. Thus the rise in the CPI exaggerates the true increase in the cost of living. The problem is that the CPI is based on the assumption that consumers purchase a basket of goods and services that is fixed over time, ignoring the fact that consumers can (and do) substitute cheaper goods or services for more expensive ones. This source of overstatement of the true increase in the cost of living is called the *substitution bias*.

If official inflation measures do, in fact, overstate true inflation, there are important implications. First, if increases in the cost of living are overstated, then increases in important quantities such as real household income (the purchasing power of a typical household's income) are correspondingly understated. As a result, the bias in the CPI may lead to too gloomy a view of how well the U.S. economy has done over the past few decades. Second, many government payments and taxes are tied, or indexed, to the CPI. Social Security benefits, for example, automatically increase each year by the same percentage as the CPI. If CPI inflation overstates true inflation, then Social Security recipients have been receiving greater benefit increases than necessary to compensate them for increases in the cost of living. If Social Security and other transfer program payments were set to increase at the rate of "true" inflation, rather than at the CPI inflation rate, the Federal government would save billions of dollars each year.

(*continued*)

In response to the Boskin Commission's report, the Bureau of Labor Statistics (BLS) made several technical changes in the way it constructs the CPI to reduce substitution bias. These changes have reduced the overstatement of the "true" inflation rate by 0.2 to 0.4 percentage points per year. However, the substitution bias was originally larger than the Boskin Commission's estimate, so the bias in the inflation rate is still 1% per year or perhaps even higher.

Note: For a detailed discussion of biases in the CPI, see David Lebow and Jeremy Rudd, "Measurement Error in the Consumer Price Index: Where Do We Stand?" *Journal of Economic Literature*, March 2003, pp. 159–201; and Robert J. Gordon, "The Boskin Commission Report: A Retrospective One Decade Later," NBER Working Paper No. 12311, June 2006.

Inflation. An important variable that is measured with price indexes is the inflation rate. The inflation rate equals the percentage rate of increase in the price index per period. Thus, if the GDP deflator rises from 100 in one year to 105 the next, the inflation rate between the two years is $(105 - 100)/100 = 5/100 = 0.05 = 5\%$ per year. If in the third year the GDP deflator is 112, the inflation rate between the second and third years is $(112 - 105)/105 = 7/105 = 0.0667 = 6.67\%$ per year. More generally, if *Pt* is the price level in period t and P_{t+1} is the price level in period $t + 1$, the inflation rate between t and $t + 1$, or π_{t+1}, is

$$\pi_{t+1} = \frac{P_{t+1} - P_t}{P_t} = \frac{\Delta P_{t+1}}{P_t},$$

where ΔP_{t+1}, or $P_{t+1} - P_t$, represents the change in the price level from period t to period $t + 1$.

Figure 2.4 shows the U.S. inflation rate for 1960–2021, based on the GDP deflator as the measure of the price level. Inflation rose during the 1960s and 1970s, fell from the early 1980s through the 1990s, and has neither trended upward nor downward since then.

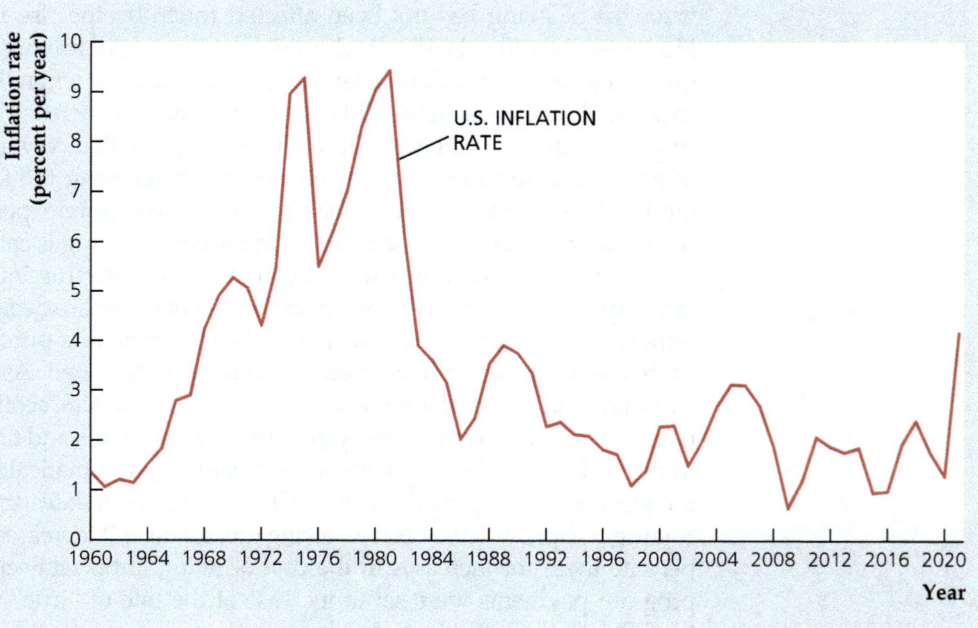

FIGURE 2.4

The inflation rate in the United States, 1960–2021

Here, inflation is measured as the annual percentage change in the GDP deflator. Inflation rose during the 1960s and 1970s, fell from the early 1980s through the 1990s, and has neither trended upward nor downward since then.

Source: Implicit price deflator for GDP, U.S. Bureau of Economic Analysis, downloaded from FRED database, Federal Reserve Bank of St. Louis, *fred.stlouisfed.org/series/GDPCTPI.*

Application

The Federal Reserve's Preferred Inflation Measures

Our discussion of price indexes describes the GDP deflator and the consumer price index (CPI). But the Federal Reserve (the Fed, for short), in reporting its forecasts of the economy, focuses on a different measure of prices: the personal consumption expenditures (PCE) price index, which is the measure of consumer prices in the national income and product accounts. The Fed announced in November 2007 that it would forecast inflation and other variables four times each year (instead of twice each year as it had done before). It also said that it would forecast both the overall inflation rate in the PCE price index and the core inflation rate of the same index, which excludes food and energy prices.

In the 1990s, the Fed provided forecasts of the inflation rate based on the CPI. But the Boskin Commission's finding (see "In Touch with Data and Research: Does CPI Inflation Overstate Increases in the Cost of Living?") that the CPI measure of inflation substantially overstates increases in the cost of living caused the Fed to move away from focusing on the CPI and to pay more attention to the PCE price index.[21] Because the PCE price index is based on actual household expenditures on various goods and services, it avoids the substitution bias inherent in the CPI.[22] In addition, the Fed suggested that the PCE measure of consumption spending is broader than the CPI, and the PCE measure has the advantage of being revised when better data are available, whereas the CPI is not revised.

Other differences between the CPI and PCE price index include differences in the formulas used to calculate the index, the coverage of different items, and the weights given to different items.[23] The CPI is an index with a given base year whereas the PCE price index is a chain-weighted index, as discussed in "In Touch with Data and Research: The Computer Revolution and Chain-Weighted GDP." The PCE price index covers more types of goods and services, as the CPI is based on the average spending habits of people who live in urban areas, whereas the PCE price index covers all spending on consumer goods in the economy. The weights on different spending categories differ as well; for example, homeownership costs are about 20% of the CPI but only about 11% of the PCE price index.

The Fed used the rate of change of the PCE price index as its main measure of inflation beginning in 2000. Because short-term shocks to food and energy prices can cause sharp, but usually temporary, fluctuations in the inflation rate, the Fed also pays attention to the PCE price index excluding food and energy prices. The inflation rate using this index is called the *core* PCE inflation rate and the inflation rate that includes inflation in food and energy is called the *overall* PCE inflation rate. In explaining its use of the core PCE inflation rate, the Fed said that it was a better measure of "underlying inflation trends."[24] Since November 2007 the Fed has provided public forecasts of both core and overall PCE inflation.

[21]See the Federal Reserve Board of *Governors, Monetary Policy Report to the Congress*, February 2000, p. 4.

[22]The PCE price measure may still suffer from some of the other problems, such as quality adjustment bias, that plague the CPI.

[23]For more details, see the article by Todd E. Clark, "A Comparison of the CPI and the PCE Price Index," Federal Reserve Bank of Kansas City *Economic Review*, Third Quarter 1999, pp. 15–29.

[24]See the Federal Reserve Board of Governors, *Monetary Policy Report to the Congress*, July 2004, p. 3.

(*continued*)

Figure 2.5 shows how overall PCE inflation differs from core PCE inflation. The figure shows the inflation rates from January 1960 to May 2018.[25] You can see in the figure that overall PCE inflation and core PCE inflation differed from each other substantially in many years. Large increases in the price of oil in the mid-1970s and again in the late 1970s caused the overall PCE inflation rate to be above the core PCE inflation rate during these episodes. However, as the relative price of oil declined in the 1980s, the overall PCE inflation rate was less than the core PCE inflation rate from 1982 to 1987. After that, the core PCE inflation rate has not varied as much as the overall PCE inflation rate. Generally, the overall PCE inflation rate tends to revert to the core PCE inflation rate after several years of being above it or below it.

FIGURE 2.5

Overall PCE inflation rate and core PCE inflation rate, January 1960 to December 2021

The overall PCE inflation rate usually differs from the core PCE inflation rate. However, the overall PCE inflation rate tends to revert to the core PCE inflation rate.

Source: Bureau of Economic Analysis; data downloaded from Federal Reserve Bank of St. Louis FRED database at *fred.stlouisfed.org/series/PCEPI* and *PCEPILFE*. Inflation rates are calculated as the percent change in the price index from 12 months earlier.

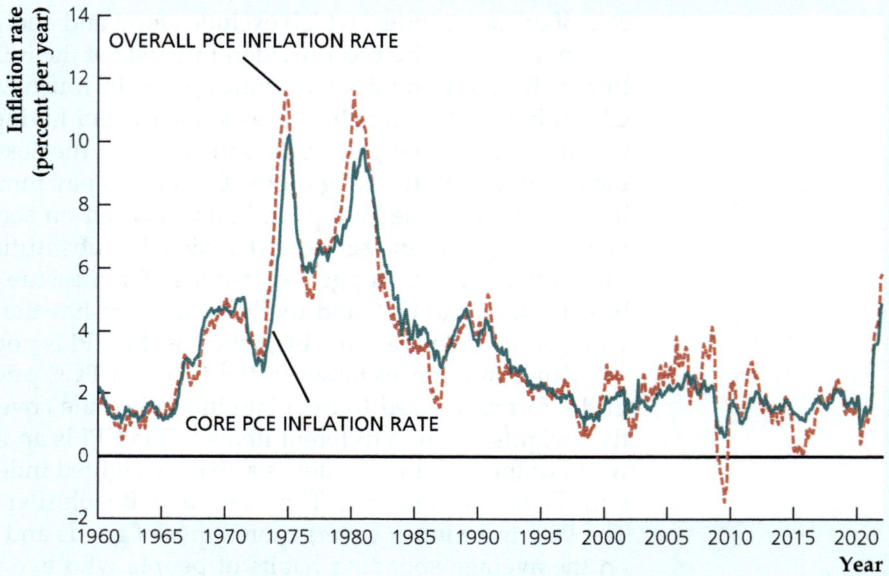

[25]The data plotted in Fig. 2.5 are the inflation rates between a given month and the same month one year earlier. The inflation rate is calculated by dividing the price index for a particular month by the value twelve months earlier, then subtracting 1 and multiplying by 100 to put the result in percentage points. That is, the inflation rate is $\pi_t = \left[\left(\frac{P_t}{P_{t-12}}\right) - 1\right] \times 100$ where P_t is the price index in month t.

2.5 Interest Rates

Define real and nominal interest rates.

Interest rates are another important—and familiar—type of economic variable. An **interest rate** is a rate of return promised by a borrower to a lender. If, for example, the interest rate on a $100, one-year loan is 8%, the borrower has promised to repay the lender $108 one year from now, or $8 interest plus repayment of the $100 borrowed.

As we discuss in more detail in Chapter 4, there are many different interest rates in the economy. Interest rates vary according to who is doing the borrowing, how long the funds are borrowed for, and other factors (see "In Touch with Data and Research: Interest Rates"). There are also many assets in the economy, such as shares of corporate stock, that do not pay a specified interest rate but do pay their holders a return; for shares of stock, the return comes in the form of dividends and capital gains (increases in the stock's market price). The existence of so many different assets, each with its own rate of return, has the potential to complicate greatly the study of macroeconomics. Fortunately, however, most interest rates and other rates of return tend to move up and down together. For purposes of macroeconomic analysis we usually speak of "the" interest rate, as if there were only one. If we say that a certain policy causes "the" interest rate to rise, for example, we mean that interest rates and rates of return in general are likely to rise.

Real Versus Nominal Interest Rates. Interest rates and other rates of return share a measurement problem with nominal GDP: An interest rate indicates how quickly the nominal, or dollar, value of an interest-bearing asset increases over time, but it does not reveal how quickly the value of the asset changes in real, or purchasing-power, terms. Consider, for example, a savings account with an interest rate of 4% per year that has $300 in it at the beginning of the year. At the end of the year the savings account is worth $312, which is a relatively good deal for the depositor if inflation is zero; with no inflation the price level is unchanged over the year, and $312 buys 4% more goods and services in real terms than the initial $300 did one year earlier. If inflation is 4% per year, however, what cost $300 one year earlier now costs $312, and in real terms the savings account is worth no more today than it was a year ago.

To distinguish changes in the real value of assets from changes in nominal value, economists frequently use the concept of the real interest rate. The **real interest rate** (or real rate of return) on an asset is the rate at which the real value or purchasing power of the asset increases over time. We refer to conventionally measured interest rates, such as those reported in the media, as nominal interest rates, to distinguish them from real interest rates. The **nominal interest rate** (or nominal rate of return) is the rate at which the nominal value of an asset increases over time. The symbol for the nominal interest rate is i.

The real interest rate is related to the nominal interest rate and the inflation rate as follows:

$$\begin{aligned}\text{real interest rate} &= \text{nominal interest rate} - \text{inflation rate} \\ &= i - \pi.\end{aligned} \tag{2.13}$$

We derive and discuss Eq. (2.13) further at the end of the book in Appendix A, Section A.7.[26] For now, consider again the savings account paying 4% interest. If the inflation rate is zero, the real interest rate on that savings account is the 4% nominal interest rate minus the 0% inflation rate, which equals 4%. A 4% real interest rate on the account means that the depositor will be able to buy 4% more goods and services at the end of the year than at the beginning. But if inflation is 4%, the real interest rate on the savings account is the 4% nominal interest rate minus the 4% inflation rate, which equals 0%. In this case, the purchasing power of the account is no greater at the end of the year than at the beginning.

Nominal and real interest rates for the United States for 1960–2021 are shown in Figure 2.6. The real interest rate was unusually low in the mid-1970s; indeed, it was negative, which means that the real values of interest-bearing assets actually were declining over time. Both nominal and real interest rates rose to record highs in the early 1980s before returning to more normal levels in the 1990s. But the real interest rate turned negative in the early 2000s and again beginning in 2010.

---

[26]Equation (2.13) is an approximation rather than an exact relationship. This approximation holds most closely when interest rates and inflation rates are not too high.

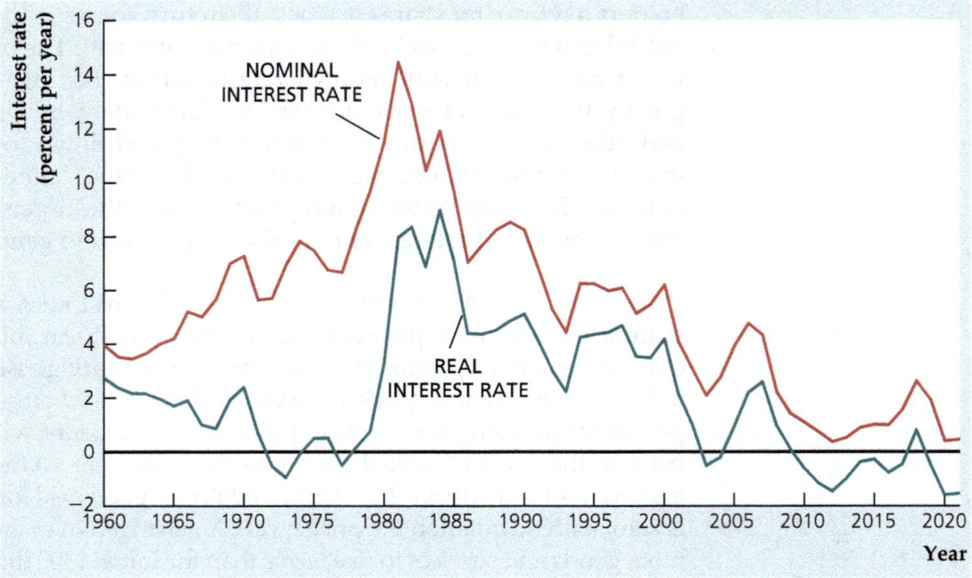

FIGURE 2.6

Nominal and real interest rates in the United States, 1960–2021

The nominal interest rate shown is the interest rate on three-year Treasury securities. The real interest rate is measured as the nominal interest rate minus the average inflation rate (using the GDP deflator) over the current and subsequent two years. The real interest rate was unusually low (actually negative) in the mid-1970s. In the early 1980s, both the nominal and real interest rates were very high. Nominal and real interest rates returned to more normal levels in the 1990s and then fell sharply, with real interest rates becoming negative again in the early 2000s and 2010s.

Source: The implicit price deflator for GDP is the same as for Fig. 2.4. Inflation rates for 2022 and 2023 are assumed to be 2%. The nominal interest rate on three-year Treasury securities is from the Board of Governors of the Federal Reserve System, Statistical Release H15, *www.federalreserve.gov/releases*.

The Expected Real Interest Rate. When you borrow, lend, or make a bank deposit, the nominal interest rate is specified in advance. But what about the real interest rate? For any nominal interest rate, Eq. (2.13) states that the real interest rate depends on the rate of inflation over the period of the loan or deposit—say, one year. However, the rate of inflation during the year generally can't be determined until the year is over. Thus, at the time that a loan or deposit is made, the real interest rate that will be received is uncertain.

Because borrowers, lenders, and depositors don't know what the actual real interest rate will be, they must make their decisions about how much to borrow, lend, or deposit on the basis of the real interest rate they expect to prevail. They know the nominal interest rate in advance, so the real interest rate they expect depends on what they think inflation will be. The **expected real interest rate** is the nominal interest rate minus the expected rate of inflation, or

$$r = i - \pi^e, \qquad \textbf{(2.14)}$$

where r is the expected real interest rate and π^e is the expected rate of inflation.

Comparing Eqs. (2.13) and (2.14), you can see that if people are correct in their expectations—so that expected inflation and actual inflation turn out to be the same—the expected real interest rate and the real interest rate actually received will be the same.

The expected real interest rate is the correct interest rate to use for studying most types of economic decisions, such as people's decisions about how much to borrow or lend. However, a problem in measuring the expected real interest rate is that economists generally don't know exactly what the public's expected rate of inflation is. Economists use various means to measure expected inflation. One approach is to survey the public and simply ask what rate of inflation people expect. A second method is to assume that the public's expectations of inflation are the same as publicly announced government or private forecasts. A third possibility is to assume that people's inflation expectations are an extrapolation of recently observed rates of inflation. Unfortunately, none of these methods is perfect, so the measurement of the expected real interest rate always contains some error.

CHAPTER SUMMARY

1. The national income accounts are an accounting framework used in measuring current economic activity. The national income accounts measure activity in three ways: the product approach, the expenditure approach, and the income approach. Although each gives the same value for current economic activity, all three approaches are used because each gives a different perspective on the economy.
2. Gross domestic product (GDP) is the broadest measure of aggregate economic activity occurring during a specified period of time. The product approach measures GDP by adding the market values of final goods and services newly produced in an economy; this approach sums the value added by all producers. The expenditure approach measures GDP by adding the four categories of spending: consumption, investment, government purchases, and net exports. The income approach measures GDP by adding all the incomes, including taxes and profits, generated by economic activity.
3. The income of the private sector (domestic households and businesses) is called *private disposable income*. Private disposable income equals income received from private-sector activities (GDP plus net factor payments from abroad, or GNP) plus payments received from the government (transfers and interest on government debt) minus taxes paid to the government. The net income of the government sector equals taxes collected minus transfer payments and interest paid on government debt. Private disposable income and net government income sum to GNP.
4. Saving is the portion of an economic unit's current income that it doesn't spend to meet current needs. Saving by the private sector, called *private saving*, equals private disposable income minus consumption. Government saving, which is the same as the government budget surplus, equals the government's net income minus its purchases of goods and services (assuming that government purchases are devoted solely to government consumption rather than partially to government investment). Equivalently, government saving equals government receipts minus government outlays. National saving is the sum of private saving and government saving; it equals GDP plus net factor payments from abroad minus consumption and government purchases.
5. The uses-of-saving identity states that private saving equals the sum of investment, the government budget deficit, and the current account balance. Equivalently, national saving equals the sum of investment and the current account balance.
6. The national wealth of a country equals its physical assets, such as capital, plus its net foreign assets. National wealth increases in two ways: through changes in the value of existing assets and through national saving. National saving adds to national wealth because national saving is used either for investment, thus adding to physical capital, or for lending to foreigners an amount that equals the current account balance, which increases the country's net foreign assets.
7. Nominal GDP is the value of an economy's final output measured at current market prices. Real GDP is a measure of the economy's final output valued in terms of prices in a base year. Real GDP equals nominal GDP divided by the GDP deflator/100.
8. A price index is a measure of the current price level relative to a base year. The GDP deflator measures the overall price level of goods and services included in GDP. The consumer price index (CPI) measures the price level of a basket of consumer goods. The rate of inflation is the percentage rate of change of the price level, as measured by percentage rate of change of a price index such as the GDP deflator or the CPI.
9. An interest rate is a rate of return promised by a borrower to a lender. The nominal interest rate is the rate at which the nominal value of an interest-bearing asset increases over time. The real interest rate, or the nominal interest rate minus the rate of inflation, is the rate at which the value of an asset grows in real, or purchasing-power, terms. Borrowing and lending decisions are based on the expected real interest rate, which is the nominal interest rate less the expected rate of inflation.

KEY TERMS

KEY EQUATIONS

$$\text{total production} = \text{total income} = \text{total expenditure} \tag{2.1}$$

The *fundamental identity of national income accounting* states that the same value of total economic activity is obtained whether activity is measured by the production of final goods and services, the amount of income generated by the economic activity, or the expenditure on final goods and services.

$$Y = C + I + G + NX \tag{2.3}$$

According to the *income-expenditure identity*, total income or product or output, Y, equals the sum of the four types of expenditure: consumption, C, investment, I, government purchases, G, and net exports, NX.

$$S_{pvt} = (Y + NFP + TR + INT - T) - C \tag{2.6}$$

Private saving equals private disposable income less consumption, C. Private disposable income equals gross domestic product, Y, plus net factor payments from abroad, NFP, plus transfers, TR, and interest, INT, received from the government, less taxes paid, T.

$$S_{govt} = (T - TR - INT) - G \tag{2.7}$$

Government saving equals government receipts from taxes, T, less outlays for transfers, TR, interest on government debt, INT, and government purchases, G. Government saving is the same as the government budget surplus and is the negative of the government budget deficit.

$$S = S_{pvt} + S_{govt} = Y + NFP - C - G \tag{2.8}$$

National saving, S, is the sum of private saving and government saving. Equivalently, national saving equals gross domestic product, Y, plus net factor payments from abroad, NFP, less consumption, C, and government purchases, G.

$$S = I + CA \tag{2.10}$$

National saving, S, has two uses: to finance investment, I, and to lend to foreigners (or to acquire foreign assets) an amount that equals the current account balance, CA. The current account balance equals the increase in net foreign assets.

$$S_{pvt} = I + (-S_{govt}) + CA \tag{2.11}$$

According to the *uses-of-saving identity*, private saving is used to finance investment spending, I, to provide the government with the funds it needs to cover its budget deficit, $-S_{govt}$, and to lend to foreigners (or to acquire foreign assets) an amount that equals the current account balance, CA.

$$r = i - \pi^e \tag{2.14}$$

The expected real interest rate, r, equals the nominal interest rate, i, minus expected inflation π^e.

REVIEW QUESTIONS

1. What are the three approaches to measuring economic activity? Why do they give the same answer?
2. Why are goods and services counted in GDP at market value? Are there any disadvantages or problems in using market values to measure production?
3. What is the difference between intermediate and final goods? In which of these categories do capital goods, such as factories and machines, fall? Why is the distinction between intermediate and final goods important for measuring GDP?
4. How does GDP differ from GNP? If a country employs many foreign workers, which is likely to be higher: GDP or GNP?
5. List the four components of total spending. Why are imports subtracted when GDP is calculated in the expenditure approach?
6. Define private saving. How is private saving used in the economy? What is the relationship between private saving and national saving?
7. Describe the three approaches to measuring the volume of economic activity that occurs during a period of time and explain why they all lead to identical measurements.
8. What is the most significant difference between GDP and GNP for countries that have many citizens who work abroad?
9. How are net exports, net factor payments from abroad, and the current account balance related?
10. Explain the differences among the nominal interest rate, the real interest rate, and the expected real interest rate. Which interest rate concept is the most important for the decisions made by borrowers and lenders? Why?

NUMERICAL PROBLEMS

1. In the country of Kwaki, people produce canoes, fish for salmon, and grow corn. In one year, they produced 5000 canoes using only labor and natural materials but sold only 4000 as the economy had entered a recession. The cost of producing each canoe was \$1000, but the ones that sold were priced at \$1250. They fished \$30 million worth of salmon. They used \$3 million worth of the salmon as fertilizer for corn. They grew and consumed \$55 million worth of corn. What was Kwaki's GDP for the year?
2. In one year in the country of Countem, workers earned \$4150, the proprietor's income was \$392, rental income was \$20, corporate profits were \$683, net interest was \$228, taxes on production and imports were \$329, business current transfer payments were \$12, the current surplus of government enterprises was \$3, statistical discrepancy was \$28, consumption of fixed capital was \$882, factor income received from the rest of the world was \$331, and payments of factor income to the rest of the world was \$623. Compute the national income, net national product, gross national product, and gross domestic product.
3. ABC Computer Company has a ₹1.4 billion (Indian rupees) factory in Bangalore, India. During the current year, ABC builds ₹140 million worth of computer components. ABC's costs for labor are ₹70 million; interest on debt, ₹7 million; and taxes, ₹14 million.

   ABC sells all its output to XYZ Supercomputer. Using ABC's components, XYZ builds four supercomputers at a cost of ₹56 million each (components worth ₹35 million, labor costs of ₹14 million, and ₹7 million in taxes per computer). XYZ has a ₹2.1 billion factory.

   XYZ sells three of the supercomputers for ₹70 million each. At year's end, it had not sold the fourth. The unsold computer is carried on XYZ's books as a ₹56 million increase in inventory.

   a. Calculate the contributions to GDP of these transactions, showing that all three approaches give the same answer.

   b. Repeat part (*a*), but now assume that, in addition to its other costs, ABC paid ₹35 million for imported computer chips.
4. For each of the following transactions, determine the contribution to the current year's GDP. Explain the effects on the product, income, and expenditure accounts.

   a. On January 1, you purchase 10 liters of gasoline at €1.80 per liter. The gas station had purchased the gasoline the previous week at the wholesale price (transportation included) of €1.60 per liter.

   b. Jorge Santiago purchases a Victorian mansion for \$1,000,000. The broker's fee is 6%.

c. A homemaker enters the workforce in London, taking a job that will pay £40,000 over the course of the year. He incurs £16,000 during the same period for professional child care services.

d. A Japanese company builds an auto plant in Europe for €100,000,000 using only local labor and materials. (*Hint*: The auto plant is a capital good produced by the European workers and purchased by the Japanese company.)

e. You are informed that you have won R3,000,000 (South African rand) in a lottery, to be paid to you in total immediately.

f. The state government pays you a fee of $5000 to appear in a TV commercial publicizing the state lottery.

g. Rent-a-Car replaces its rental fleet by buying $100,000,000 worth of new cars from Toyota. It sells its old fleet to a consortium of used-car dealers for $40,000,000. The consortium resells the used cars to the public for a total of $60,000,000.

5. You are given the following information about an economy:

Gross private domestic investment = 40
Government purchases of goods and services = 30
Gross national product (GNP) = 200
Current account balance = −20
Taxes = 60
Government transfer payments to the domestic private sector = 25
Interest payments from the government to the domestic private sector = 15 (Assume all interest payments by the government go to domestic households.)
Factor income received from rest of world = 7
Factor payments made to rest of world = 9

Find the following, assuming that government investment is zero:

a. Consumption
b. Net exports
c. GDP
d. Net factor payments from abroad
e. Private saving
f. Government saving
g. National saving

6. Consider an economy that produces only three types of fruit: apples, oranges, and bananas. In the base year (a few years ago), the production and price data were as follows:

Fruit	Quantity	Price
Apples	3000 bags	$2 per bag
Bananas	6000 bunches	$3 per bunch
Oranges	8000 bags	$4 per bag

In the current year the production and price data are as follows:

Fruit	Quantity	Price
Apples	4000 bags	$3 per bag
Bananas	14,000 bunches	$2 per bunch
Oranges	32,000 bags	$5 per bag

a. Find nominal GDP in the current year and in the base year. What is the percentage increase since the base year?

b. Find real GDP in the current year and in the base year. By what percentage does real GDP increase from the base year to the current year?

c. Find the GDP deflator for the current year and the base year. By what percentage does the price level change from the base year to the current year?

d. Would you say that the percentage increase in nominal GDP in this economy since the base year is due more to increases in prices or increases in the physical volume of output?

7. Use the following FRED data for the consumer price index in the United Kingdom from 1929 to 1933 and calculate the rate of inflation for each year from 1930 to 1933. What is unusual about this period, relative to recent experience?

Year	1929	1930	1931	1932	1933	1934	1935
CPI (base year 2015)	2.31	2.25	2.15	2.10	2.05	2.05	2.07

8. Loretta agrees to lend Ted $500,000 to buy computers for his consulting firm. They agree to a nominal interest rate of 8%. Both expect the inflation rate to be 2%.

a. Calculate the expected real interest rate.

b. If inflation turns out to be 3% over the life of the loan, what is the real interest rate? Who gains from unexpectedly high inflation, Loretta or Ted?

c. If inflation turns out to be 1% over the life of the loan, what is the real interest rate? Who gains from unexpectedly low inflation, Loretta or Ted?

9. The GDP deflator in Econoland is 200 on January 1, 2021. The deflator rises to 242 by January 1, 2023, and to 266.2 by January 1, 2024.

a. What is the annual rate of inflation over the two-year period between January 1, 2021, and January 1, 2023? In other words, what constant yearly rate of inflation would lead to the price rise observed over those two years?

b. What is the annual rate of inflation over the three-year period from January 1, 2021, to January 1, 2024?

c. In general, if P_0 is the price level at the beginning of an n-year period, and Pn is the price level at the end of that period, show that the annual rate of inflation π over that period satisfies the equation

$$(1 + \pi)^n = P_n/P_0.$$

ANALYTICAL PROBLEMS

1. A reputable study shows that a particular new workplace safety regulation will reduce the growth of real GDP. Is this an argument against implementing the regulation? Explain.

2. Consider a closed economy with a single telephone company, Calls-R-Us. The residents of the country make 2 million phone calls per year and pay $3 per phone call. One day a new phone company, CheapCall, enters the market and charges only $2 per phone call. All of the residents immediately stop using Calls-R-Us and switch to CheapCall. They still make 2 million phone calls per year. The executives of CheapCall are proud of their market share. Moreover, they post billboards stating, "Our country has increased its national saving by $2 million per year by switching to CheapCall." Comment on the accuracy of the statement on the billboards.

3. Economists have tried to measure the GDPs of virtually all the world's nations. This problem asks you to think about some practical issues that arise in that effort.

a. Before the fall of communism, the economies of the Soviet Union and Eastern Europe were centrally planned. One aspect of central planning is that most prices are set by the government. A government-set price may be too low, in that people want to buy more of the good at the fixed price than there are supplies available; or the price may be too high, so that large stocks of the good sit unsold on store shelves.

What problem does government control of prices create for economists attempting to measure a country's GDP? Suggest a strategy for dealing with this problem.

b. In very poor, agricultural countries, many people grow their own food, make their own clothes, and provide services for one another within a kin or village group. Official GDP estimates for these countries are often extremely low, perhaps just a few hundred dollars per person per year. Some economists have argued that the official GDP figures underestimate these nations' actual GDPs. Why might this be so? Again, can you suggest a strategy for dealing with this measurement problem?

4. We showed in Eq. (2.10) that $S = I + CA$, where S is national saving, I is investment, and CA is the current account balance. Calculations of national saving and investment depend on the treatment of government investment. In the text, we treated government purchases, G, as if they were consumption expenditures. Therefore, Eq. (2.7) states that government saving is $S_{govt} = (T - TR - INT) - G$, so that (1) national saving in Eq. (2.8) is $S = Y + NFP - C - G$, and (2) I in Eq. (2.10) is gross private domestic investment $GPDI$.

As mentioned in the text, a more detailed treatment recognizes that government purchases comprise consumption expenditures, which we will call GCE, and government investment, which we will call GI, so $G = GCE + GI$. Now define government saving as $(T - TR - INT) - GCE$. With this alternative definition of government saving, show that private saving plus government saving $= I + CA$, where investment (I) is the sum of $GPDI$ and GI.

Table 5.1, titled "Saving and Investment by Sector," in the National Income and Product Accounts (found online at *www.bea.gov*) uses this more detailed treatment. For the most recent quarter for which all data in Table 5.1 are available, what are the values of gross saving, gross domestic investment (gross private domestic investment plus gross government investment), and the current account balance (shown in Table 5.1 as "Net lending or net borrowing")? Does the identity hold true? If not, how can the entries for capital account transactions and statistical discrepancy in Table 5.1 help?

WORKING WITH MACROECONOMIC DATA

For data to use in these exercises, go to the Federal Reserve Bank of St. Louis FRED database at fred.stlouisfed.org.

1. Graph the main expenditure components of GDP (consumption, investment, government consumption expenditures and gross investment, exports, and imports), in real terms, since the first quarter of 1947. Also graph the expenditure components as a share of total real GDP. Do you see any significant trends?
2. Graph South Africa's national saving and investment as fractions of GDP from 2004 to the present. (Note that national saving is called gross saving and gross investment is called capital formation in the FRED database.) Comment on the behavior of these variables. Explain how investment can exceed national saving.
3. Graph the annual CPI inflation rate and the annual GDP deflator inflation rate for Indonesia since 2000. What are the conceptual differences between these two measures of inflation? Judging from your graph, would you say that the two measures give similar or different estimates of the rate of inflation in the economy?
4. If the real interest rate were approximately constant, then in periods in which inflation is high, the nominal interest rate should be relatively high (because the nominal interest rate equals the real interest rate plus the inflation rate). Using annual data since 1948, graph the three-month Treasury bill interest rate (FRED variable *TB3MS*, 3-Month Treasury Bill: Secondary Market Rate) and the CPI inflation rate for the U.S. economy. (Take annual averages of monthly interest rates and measure annual inflation rates as the change in the CPI from December to December.) Is it generally true that nominal interest rates rise with inflation? Does the relationship appear to be one-for-one (so that each additional percentage point of inflation raises the nominal interest rate by one percentage point), as would be the case if the real interest rate were constant? Calculate the real interest rate and graph its behavior since 1948.
5. In theory, in the national income and product accounts, income should equal expenditures. However, when we add up income from various sources, it differs from expenditures, in part because the government statisticians are unable to count all income and all expenditures precisely. The difference between the two measures is the "statistical discrepancy." To see how important the statistical discrepancy is, plot the annualized quarterly growth rates of GDP and GDI (gross domestic income) in one graph. Over the past five years, what is the average difference in the growth rates of GDP and GDI?
6. Plot the growth rate of real GDP from 1960 to last year in three different ways: (1) annualized quarterly growth rates, (2) quarterly data using the percent change from a year ago, and (3) quarterly data using the percent change from the previous quarter. How do the three series differ? Which measure is least volatile? Which measure is the most volatile?

3

Productivity, Output, and Employment

In Chapter 2, we discussed the measurement of several economic variables used to gauge the economy's health. The measurement of economic performance is a prelude to the main objective of macroeconomics: *to understand how the economy works.* Understanding how the economy works requires a shift from economic *measurement* to economic *analysis*.

In Part 2 of this book, which begins with this chapter, we have two main goals. The first is to analyze the factors that affect the longer-term performance of the economy, including the rate of economic growth, productivity and living standards, the long-run levels of employment and unemployment, saving and capital formation, and the rate of inflation, among others.

The second goal is to develop a theoretical model of the macroeconomy that you can use to analyze the economic issues covered in this book and others that you may encounter in the future. As outlined in Chapter 1, our model is based on the assumption that individuals, firms, and the government interact in three aggregate markets: the labor market (covered in this chapter), the goods market (Chapter 4), and the asset market (Chapter 7). In developing and using this model in Part 2, we generally assume that the economy is at full employment, with quantities supplied and demanded being equal in the three major markets. As we are focusing on the long-term behavior of the economy, this assumption is a reasonable one. In Part 3, in which we explore business cycles, we allow for the possibility that quantities supplied and demanded may not be equal in the short run.

In this chapter, we begin the discussion of how the economy works with what is perhaps the most fundamental determinant of economic well-being in a society: the economy's productive capacity. Everything else being equal, the greater the quantity of goods and services an economy can produce, the more people will be able to consume in the present and the more they will be able to save and invest for the future.

In the first section of the chapter, we show that the amount of output an economy produces depends on two factors: (1) the quantities of inputs (such as labor, capital, and raw materials) utilized in the production process and (2) the **productivity** of the inputs—that is, the effectiveness with which they are used. As discussed in Chapter 1, an economy's productivity is basic to determining living standards. In this chapter, we show how productivity affects people's incomes by helping to determine how many workers are employed and how much they receive in wages.

Learning Objectives

3.1 Discuss production function properties and changes.

3.2 Discuss factors that affect the demand for labor.

3.3 Discuss factors that affect the supply of labor.

3.4 Identify factors that affect labor market equilibrium.

3.5 Explain how the unemployment rate is measured and describe changes in employment status.

3.6 Explain the significance of Okun's law.

Of the various inputs to production, the most important (as measured by share of total cost) is labor. For this reason, we spend most of the chapter analyzing the labor market, using the tools of supply and demand. We first consider the factors that affect the quantity of labor demanded by employers and supplied by workers and then look at the forces that bring the labor market into equilibrium. Equilibrium in the labor market determines wages and employment; in turn, the level of employment, together with the quantities of other inputs (such as capital) and the level of productivity, determines how much output an economy produces.

Our basic model of the labor market rests on the assumption that the quantities of labor supplied and demanded are equal so that all labor resources are fully utilized. In reality, however, there are always some unemployed workers. In the latter part of the chapter, we introduce unemployment and look at the relationship between the unemployment rate and the amount of output produced in the economy.

3.1 How Much Does the Economy Produce? The Production Function

Discuss production function properties and changes.

Every day the business news reports many economic variables that influence the economy's performance—the rate of consumer spending, the value of the dollar, the gyrations of the stock market, the growth rate of the money supply, and so on. All of these variables are important. However, no determinant of economic performance and living standards is more basic than the economy's physical capacity to produce goods and services. If an economy's factories, farms, and other businesses all shut down for some reason, other economic factors wouldn't mean much.

What determines the quantity of goods and services that an economy can produce? A key factor is the quantity of inputs—such as capital goods, labor, raw materials, land, and energy—that producers in the economy use. Economists refer to inputs to the production process as **factors of production**. All else being equal, the greater the quantities of factors of production used, the more goods and services are produced.

Of the various factors of production, the two most important are capital (factories, machines, software, and intellectual property, for example) and labor (workers). Hence we focus on these two factors in discussing an economy's capacity to produce goods and services. In modern economies, however, output often responds strongly to changes in the supply of other factors, such as energy or raw materials. Later in this chapter, the Application "Output, Employment, and the Real Wage During Oil Price Shocks," discusses the effects of a disruption in oil supplies on the economy.

The quantities of capital and labor (and other inputs) used in production don't completely determine the amount of output produced. Equally important is how effectively these factors are used. For the same stocks of capital and labor, an economy with superior technologies and management practices, for example, will produce a greater amount of output than an economy without those strengths.

The effectiveness with which capital and labor are used may be summarized by a relationship called the production function. The **production function** is a mathematical expression relating the amount of output produced to quantities of capital and labor utilized. A convenient way to write the production function is

$$Y = AF(K, N), \tag{3.1}$$

where

Y = real output produced in a given period of time;
A = a number measuring overall productivity;
K = the capital stock, or quantity of capital used in the period;
N = the number of workers employed in the period;
F = a function relating output Y to capital K and labor N.

The production function in Eq. (3.1) applies both to an economy as a whole (where Y, K, and N refer to the economy's output, capital stock, and number of workers, respectively) and to an individual firm, in which case Y, K, and N refer to the firm's output, capital, and number of workers, respectively.

According to Eq. (3.1), the amount of output Y that an economy (or firm) can produce during any period of time depends on the size of the capital stock K and the number of workers N. The symbol A in Eq. (3.1), which multiplies the function $F(K, N)$, is a measure of the overall effectiveness with which capital and labor are used. We refer to A as **total factor productivity**, or simply productivity. Note that, for any values of capital and labor, an increase in productivity of, say, 10% implies a 10% increase in the amount of output that can be produced. Thus increases in productivity, A, correspond to improvements in production technology or to any other change in the economy that allows capital and labor to be utilized more effectively.

Application

The Production Function and Changes in Productivity in the European Union

GDP growth is a summary indicator of the economy's capacity to generate real growth and eliminate cyclical slowdowns. To policymakers, the severity of the global financial crisis and the subsequent emergence of the European debt crisis clearly indicate the importance of the production function approach to illustrate policy options during boom–bust episodes. As such, the Economic Policy Committee of the European Union has recently elected to use the production function approach for budgetary surveillance purposes in prudently reviewing and assessing the past and future evolution of GDP growth in the European Union.[1]

[1]More details about the production function methodology used by the EU are available at Francesca D'Auria et al., "The Production Function Methodology for Calculating Potential Growth Rates & Output Gaps," Economic Paper No. 420, European Commission, Directorate-General for Economic and Financial Affairs Publications, 2010, Belgium, *http://ec.europa.eu/economy_finance/publications/economic_paper/2010/pdf/ecp420_en.pdf*.

(continued)

TABLE 3.1

The Production Function of the EU-28, 2005–2014

Year	(1) Real GDP (*Y*) in 2010 prices Million EUR	(2) Real Capital Stock (*K*) in 2010 prices Million EUR	(3) Labor, *N* (millions of workers)	(4) $A = Y/(K^{0.33}N^{0.67})$	(5) Growth in *A* (% change in *A*)
2005	12,230	2660	208	25.35	—
2006	12,647	2848	212	25.32	0.12%
2007	13,037	3031	216	25.55	0.91%
2008	13,103	2980	218	25.36	−0.74%
2009	12,527	2478	214	26.1	2.92%
2010	12,789	2613	212	26.33	0.88%
2011	13,011	2696	212	26.51	0.68%
2012	12,943	2539	211	26.99	1.8%
2013	12,956	2513	210	27.19	0.74%
2014	13,127	2576	213	27.08	−0.40%

Source: Real GDP, capital stock, and labor force figures are from the Eurostat Database website, *http://ec.europa.eu/eurostat/data/database.*

Researchers of the EU Economic Policy Committee empirically describe the relationship between output and inputs in the European Union through the following production function:[2]

$$Y = AK^{0.33}N^{0.67}. \tag{3.2}$$

The production function in Eq. (3.2) is a specific example of the general production function in Eq. (3.1), in which we set the general function $F(K, N)$ equal to $K^{0.33}N^{0.67}$ (Note that this production function contains exponents; if you need to review the properties of exponents, see Appendix A, Section A.6.) Equation (3.2) shows how output, Y, relates to the use of factors of production, capital, K, and labor, N, and to productivity, A, in the European Union.

Table 3.1 shows data on these variables for the 28 EU nations from 2005 to 2014. Columns (1), (2), and (3) show real output or GDP, capital stock, and labor for each year. Real GDP and the capital stock are measured in millions of 2010 euros, and labor is measured in millions of employed workers. Column (4) shows the EU-28 growth rates for production during the same period. It is obtained using the following formula derived from Eq. (3.2): $A = Y/(K^{0.33}N^{0.67})$. In 2005, for example, $Y = 12,230$, $K = 2660$, and $N = 208$; therefore, the value of A for 2005 is $12,230/[(2660)^{0.33}(208)^{0.67}]$ or $A = 25.35$. Column (5) shows the year-to-year growth rates of the productivity measures. Between 2009 and 2010, for example, the change in A or $\Delta A = [(26.33 - 26.1)/26.1] \times 100 = 0.88\%$.

[2]This is called a Cobb–Douglas production function. Cobb–Douglas production functions take the form $Y = AK^{a}N^{1-a}$. The parameters a and $1 - a$ in the Cobb–Douglas production function correspond to the production factor elasticity of labor and capital, respectively. Observing the actual shares of income received by capital and labor provides a way of estimating the parameter a.

An examination of the productivity growth rates (A) in Table 3.1 shows that growth can vary substantially over different periods. As a result of the global financial crisis, productivity took a deep dive in 2008 but showed significant signs of recovery in 2009. Again, the European debt crisis left its marks on productivity in 2014, where A declined by 0.4%. This may indicate that productivity declines during times of recession and rises during times of economic recovery. But this premise is quite controversial. We return to this issue in Part 3 of this book. The main reason for gauging productivity growth is because it impacts GDP per capita and, hence, standards of living. Chapter 6 details the relationship between productivity and living standards.

The Shape of the Production Function

The production function in Eq. (3.1) can be shown graphically. The easiest way to graph it is to hold both total factor productivity and one of the two factors of production, either capital or labor, constant and then graph the relationship between output and the other factor.[3] Suppose that we use the U.S. production function for the year 2020 and hold labor N at its actual 2020 value of 157.5 million workers (see Table 3.1). We also use the actual 2020 value of 25.99 for A. The production function Eq. (3.2) becomes

$$Y = AK^{0.3}N^{0.7} = (25.99)(K^{0.3})(157.5^{0.7}) = 897.228K^{0.3}.$$

This relationship is graphed in Figure 3.1, with capital stock K on the horizontal axis and output Y on the vertical axis. With labor and productivity held at their 2020 values, the graph shows the amount of output that could have been produced in that year for any value of the capital stock. Point A on the graph shows the situation that actually occurred in 2020: The value of the capital stock ($23,539 billion) appears on the horizontal axis, and the value of real GDP ($18,385 billion) appears on the vertical axis.

The U.S. production function graphed in Fig. 3.1 shares two properties with most production functions:

1. *The production function slopes upward from left to right.* The slope of the production function reveals that, as the capital stock increases, more output can be produced.
2. *The slope of the production function becomes flatter from left to right.* This property implies that although more capital always leads to more output, it does so at a decreasing rate.

Before discussing the economics behind the second property of the production function, we can illustrate it numerically, using Fig. 3.1. Suppose that we are initially at point B, where the capital stock is $2000 billion. Adding $1000 billion in capital moves us to point C, where the capital stock is $3000 billion. How much extra output has this expansion in capital provided? The difference in output between points B and C is $1135 billion ($9909 billion output at C minus

[3]To show the relationship among output and both factors of production simultaneously would require a three-dimensional graph.

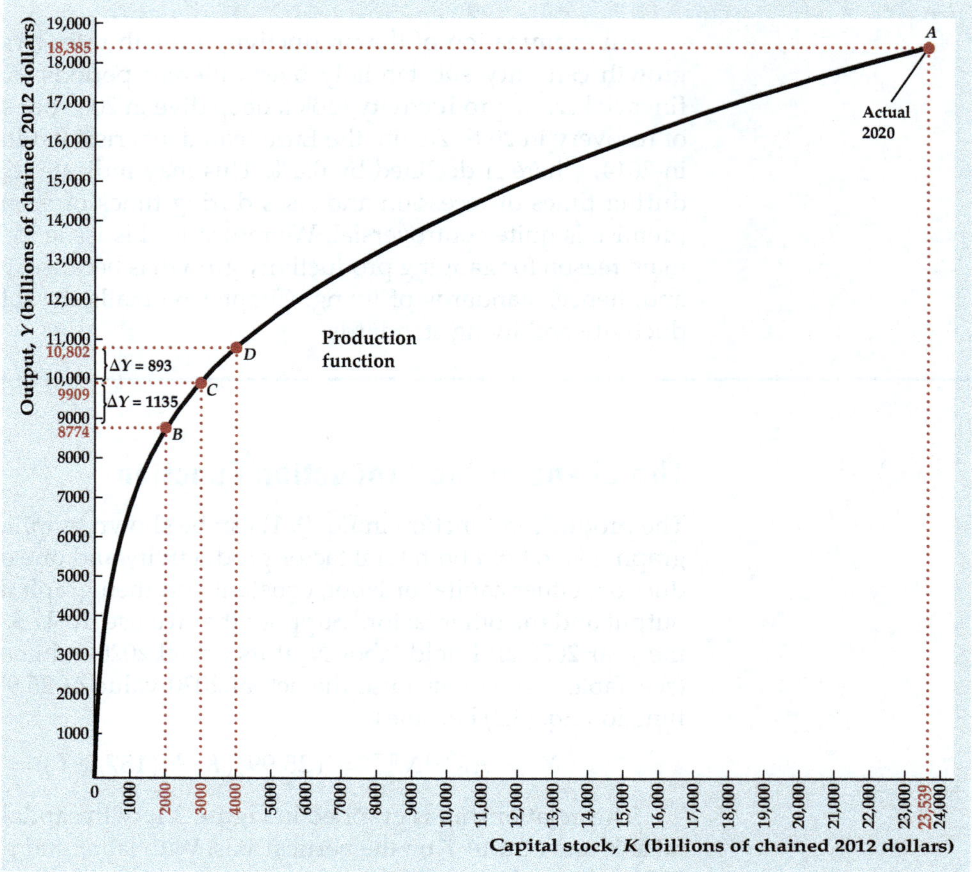

FIGURE 3.1

The production function relating output and capital

This production function shows how much output the U.S. economy could produce for each level of U.S. capital stock, holding U.S. labor and productivity at 2020 levels. Point *A* corresponds to the actual 2020 output and capital stock. The production function has diminishing marginal productivity of capital: Raising the capital stock by \$1000 billion to move from point *B* to point *C* raises output by \$1135 billion, but adding another \$1000 billion in capital to go from point *C* to point *D* increases output by only \$893 billion.

\$8774 billion output at *B*). This extra \$1135 billion in output is the benefit from raising the capital stock from \$2000 billion to \$3000 billion, with productivity and employment held constant.

Now suppose that, starting at *C*, we add another \$1000 billion of capital. This new addition of capital takes us to *D*, where the capital stock is \$4000 billion. The difference in output between *C* and *D* is only \$893 billion (\$10,802 billion output at *D* minus \$9909 billion output at *C*), which is less than the \$1135 billion increase in output between *B* and *C*. Thus, although the second \$1000 billion of extra capital raises total output, it does so by less than did the first \$1000 billion of extra capital. This result illustrates that the production function rises less steeply between points *C* and *D* than between points *B* and *C*.

The Marginal Product of Capital

The two properties of the production function are closely related to a concept known as the marginal product of capital. To understand this concept, we can start from some given capital stock, K, and increase the capital stock by some amount, ΔK (other factors held constant). This increase in capital would cause output, Y, to increase by some amount, ΔY. The **marginal product of capital (*MPK*)** is the increase in output produced that results from a one-unit increase in the capital stock. Because ΔK additional units of capital permit the production of ΔY additional units of output, the amount of additional output produced per additional unit of capital is $\Delta Y/\Delta K$. Thus the marginal product of capital is $\Delta Y/\Delta K$.

The marginal product of capital, $\Delta Y/\Delta K$, is the change in the variable on the vertical axis of the production function graph, ΔY, divided by the change in the variable on the horizontal axis, ΔK, which you might recognize as a slope.[4] For small increases in the capital stock, the *MPK* can be measured by the slope of a line drawn tangent to the production function. Figure 3.2 illustrates this way of measuring the *MPK*. When the capital stock is 2000, for example, the *MPK* equals the slope of the line tangent to the production function at point *B*.[5] We can use the concept of the marginal product of capital to restate the two properties of production functions listed earlier.

1. *The marginal product of capital is positive.* Whenever the capital stock is increased, more output can be produced. Because the marginal product of capital is positive, the production function slopes upward from left to right.

FIGURE 3.2

The marginal product of capital

The marginal product of capital (*MPK*) at any point can be measured as the slope of the line tangent to the production function at that point. Because the slope of the line tangent to the production function at point *B* is greater than the slope of the line tangent to the production function at point *D*, we know that the *MPK* is greater at *B* than at *D*. At higher levels of capital stock, the *MPK* is lower, reflecting diminishing marginal productivity of capital.

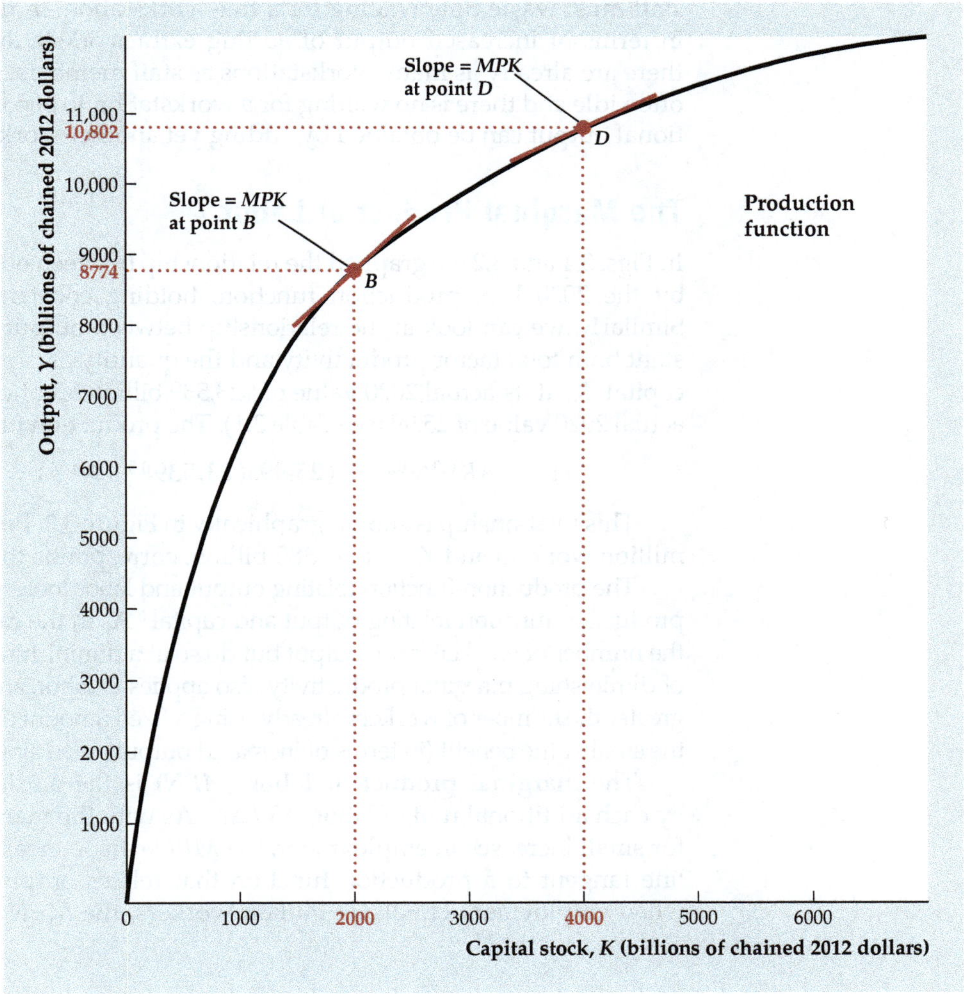

[4]For definitions and a discussion of slopes of lines and curves, see Appendix A, Section A.2.

[5]We often refer to the slope of the line tangent to the production function at a given point as simply the slope of the production function at that point, for short.

2. *The marginal product of capital declines as the capital stock is increased.* Because the marginal product of capital is the slope of the production function, the slope of the production function decreases as the capital stock is increased. As Fig. 3.2 shows, the slope of the production function at point D, where the capital stock is 4000, is smaller than the slope at point B, where the capital stock is 2000. Thus the production function becomes flatter from left to right.

The tendency for the marginal product of capital to decline as the amount of capital in use increases is called the **diminishing marginal productivity** of capital. The economic reason for diminishing marginal productivity of capital is as follows: When the capital stock is low, there are many workers for each machine, and the benefits of increasing capital further are great; but when the capital stock is high, workers already have plenty of capital to work with, and little benefit is to be gained from expanding capital further. For example, in a business firm's call center in which there are many more staff members than workstations (phones and computer terminals), each workstation is constantly being utilized, and the staff must waste time waiting for a free workstation. In this situation, the benefit in terms of increased output of adding extra workstations is high. However, if there are already as many workstations as staff members, so that workstations are often idle and there is no waiting for a workstation to become available, little additional output can be obtained by adding yet another workstation.

The Marginal Product of Labor

In Figs. 3.1 and 3.2 we graphed the relationship between output and capital implied by the 2020 U.S. production function, holding constant the amount of labor. Similarly, we can look at the relationship between output and labor, holding constant both total factor productivity and the quantity of capital. Suppose that we fix capital, K, at its actual 2020 value of \$23,539 billion and hold productivity, A, at its actual 2020 value of 25.99 (see Table 3.1). The production function Eq. (3.2) becomes

$$Y = AK^{0.3}N^{0.7} = (25.99)(23{,}539^{0.3})(N^{0.7}) = 532.528N^{0.7}.$$

This relationship is shown graphically in Figure 3.3. Point A, where $N = 157.5$ million workers and $Y = \$18{,}385$ billion, corresponds to the actual 2020 values.

The production function relating output and labor looks generally the same as the production function relating output and capital.[6] As in the case of capital, increases in the number of workers raise output but do so at a diminishing rate. Thus the principle of diminishing marginal productivity also applies to labor, and for similar reasons: the greater the number of workers already using a fixed amount of capital and other inputs, the smaller the benefit (in terms of increased output) of adding even more workers.

The **marginal product of labor (*MPN*)** is the additional output produced by each additional unit of labor, $\Delta Y/\Delta N$. As with the marginal product of capital, for small increases in employment, the MPN can be measured by the slope of the line tangent to a production function that relates output and labor. In Fig. 3.3, when employment equals 30 million workers, the MPN equals the slope of the

[6]Because N is raised to the power of 0.7 but K is raised to the power of 0.3, the production function relating output and labor is not as sharply bowed as the production function relating output and capital. The closer the power is to 1, the closer the production function will be to a straight line.

FIGURE 3.3

The production function relating output and labor
This production function shows how much output the U.S. economy could produce at each level of employment (labor input), holding productivity and the capital stock constant at 2020 levels. Point *A* corresponds to actual 2020 output and employment. The marginal product of labor (*MPN*) at any point is measured as the slope of the line tangent to the production function at that point. The *MPN* is lower at higher levels of employment, reflecting diminishing marginal productivity of labor.

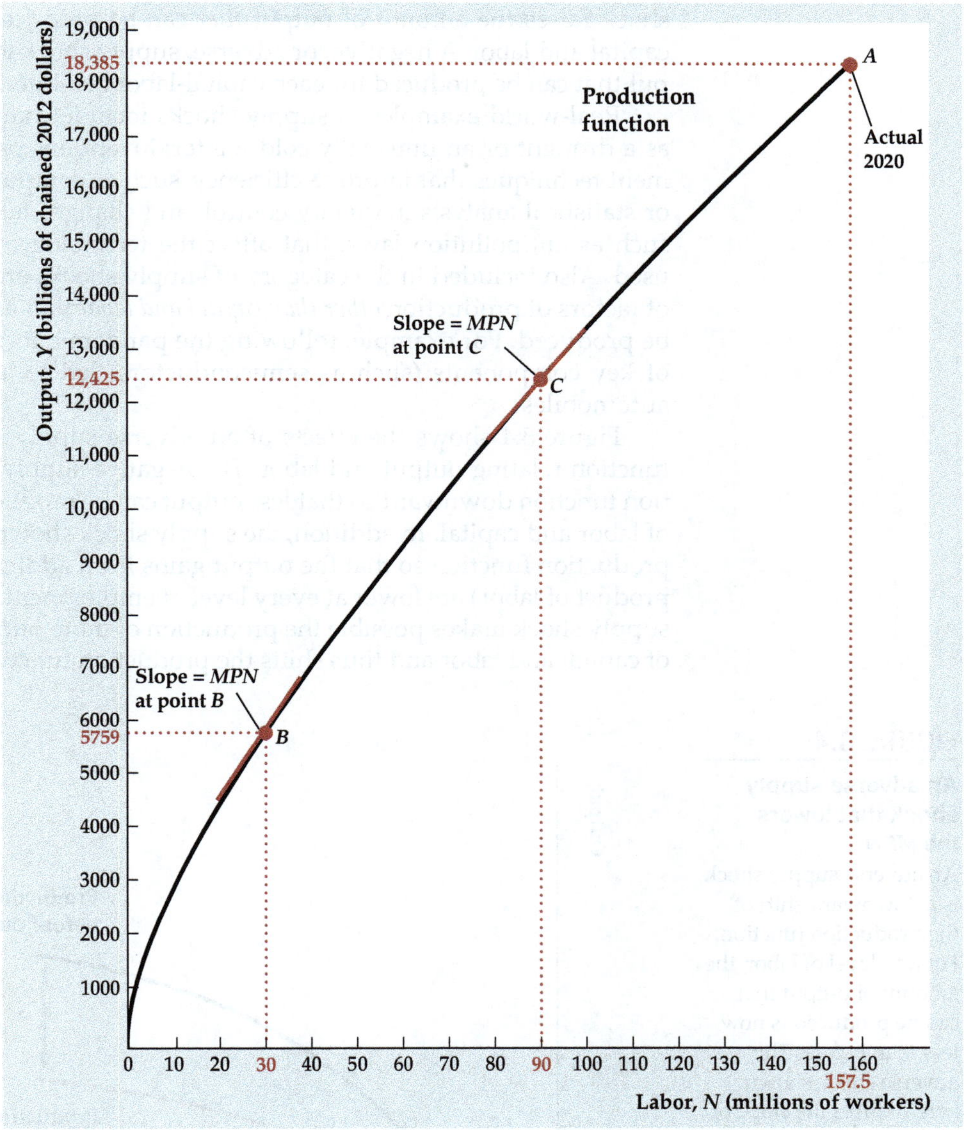

line tangent to the production function at point *B;* when employment is 90 million workers, the *MPN* is the slope of the line that touches the production function at point C. Because of the diminishing marginal productivity of labor, the slope of the production function relating output to labor is greater at *B* than at C, and the production function flattens from left to right.

Supply Shocks

The production function of an economy doesn't usually remain fixed over time. Economists use the term **supply shock**—or, sometimes, *productivity shock*—to refer to a change in an economy's production function.[7] A positive, or beneficial, supply

[7]The term *shock* is a slight misnomer. Not all changes in the production function are sharp or unpredictable, although many are.

shock raises the amount of output that can be produced for given quantities of capital and labor. A negative, or adverse, supply shock lowers the amount of output that can be produced for each capital-labor combination.

Real-world examples of supply shocks include changes in the weather, such as a drought or an unusually cold winter; inventions or innovations in management techniques that improve efficiency, such as computerized inventory control or statistical analysis in quality control; and changes in government regulations, such as antipollution laws, that affect the technologies or production methods used. Also included in the category of supply shocks are changes in the supplies of factors of production *other than capital and labor* that affect the amount that can be produced. For example, following the pandemic recession of 2020, shortages of key components (such as semiconductors) led to a shortfall in supplies of automobiles.

Figure 3.4 shows the effects of an adverse supply shock on the production function relating output and labor. The negative supply shock shifts the production function downward so that less output can be produced for specific quantities of labor and capital. In addition, the supply shock shown reduces the slope of the production function so that the output gains from adding a worker (the marginal product of labor) are lower at every level of employment.[8] Conversely, a beneficial supply shock makes possible the production of more output with given quantities of capital and labor and thus shifts the production function upward.[9]

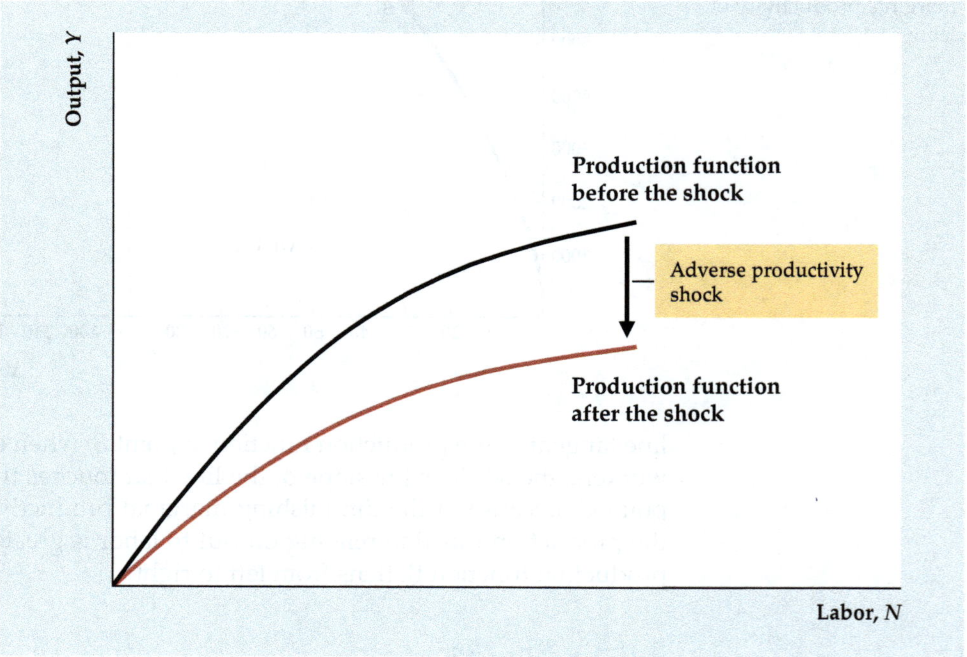

FIGURE 3.4

An adverse supply shock that lowers the *MPN*

An adverse supply shock is a downward shift of the production function. For any level of labor, the amount of output that can be produced is now less than before. The adverse shock shown here reduces the slope of the production function at every level of employment.

[8]Logically, an adverse supply shock need not always reduce the marginal products of labor and capital; for example, the production function could make a parallel downward shift. However, it is reasonable to think of an adverse supply shock reducing marginal products as being the normal case. A shift of the production function like that shown in Fig. 3.4 would occur if there were a decline in total factor productivity, A, for example.

[9]The effects of supply shocks on the production function relating output and capital would be similar.

3.2 The Demand for Labor

Discuss factors that affect the demand for labor.

We have shown that the amount of output produced by a country, or by a firm, depends both on productivity and the quantities of inputs used in the production process. In Section 3.1 our focus was on productivity—its measurement and factors such as supply shocks that cause it to change. In this section, we examine what determines the quantities of inputs that producers use.

Recall that the two most important inputs are capital and labor. The capital stock in an economy changes over time as a result of investment by firms and the scrapping of worn-out or obsolete capital. However, because the capital stock is long-lived and has been built up over many years, new investment and the scrapping of old capital only slowly have a significant effect on the overall quantity of capital available. Thus, for analyses spanning only a few quarters or years, economists often treat the economy's capital stock as fixed. For now we follow this practice and assume a fixed capital stock. In taking up long-term economic growth in Chapter 6, we drop this assumption and examine how the capital stock evolves over time.

In contrast to the amount of capital, the amount of labor employed in the economy can change fairly quickly. For example, firms may lay off workers or ask them to work overtime without much notice. Workers may quit or decide to enter the work force quickly. Thus year-to-year changes in production often can be traced to changes in employment. To explain why employment changes, for the remainder of this chapter we focus on how the labor market works, using a supply and demand approach. In this section we look at labor demand, and in Section 3.3 we discuss factors affecting labor supply.

As a step toward understanding the overall demand for labor in the economy, we consider how an individual firm decides how many workers to employ. To keep things simple for the time being, we make the following assumptions:

1. *Workers are all alike.* We ignore differences in workers' aptitudes, skills, ambitions, and so on.
2. *Firms view the wages of the workers they hire as being determined in a competitive labor market and not set by the firms themselves.* For example, a competitive firm in Cleveland that wants to hire machinists knows that it must pay the going local wage for machinists if it wants to attract qualified workers. The firm then decides how many machinists to employ.
3. *In making the decision about how many workers to employ, a firm's goal is to earn the highest possible level of profit* (the value of its output minus its costs of production, including taxes). The firm will demand the amount of labor that maximizes its profit.

To figure out the profit-maximizing amount of labor, the firm must compare the costs and benefits of hiring each additional worker. The cost of an extra worker is the worker's wage, and the benefit of an extra worker is the value of the additional goods or services the worker produces. As long as the benefits of additional labor exceed the costs, hiring more labor will increase the firm's profits. The firm will continue to hire additional labor until the benefit of an extra worker (the value of extra goods or services produced) equals the cost (the wage).

The Marginal Product of Labor and Labor Demand: An Example

Let's make the discussion of labor demand more concrete by looking at The Clip Joint, a small business that grooms dogs. The Clip Joint uses both capital, such as clippers, tubs, and brushes, and labor to produce its output of groomed dogs.

The production function that applies to The Clip Joint appears in Table 3.2. For given levels of productivity and the capital stock, it shows how The Clip Joint's daily output of groomed dogs, column (2), depends on the number of workers employed, column (1). The more workers The Clip Joint has, the greater its daily output.

The *MPN* of each worker at The Clip Joint is shown in column (3). Employing the first worker raises The Clip Joint's output from 0 to 11, so the *MPN* of the first worker is 11. Employing the second worker raises The Clip Joint's output from 11 to 20, an increase of 9, so the *MPN* of the second worker is 9; and so on. Column (3) also shows that, as the number of workers at The Clip Joint increases, the *MPN* falls so that labor at The Clip Joint has diminishing marginal productivity. The more workers there are on the job, the more they must share the fixed amount of capital (tubs, clippers, brushes), and the less benefit there is to adding yet another worker.

The marginal product of labor measures the benefit of employing an additional worker in terms of the extra *output* produced. A related concept, the **marginal revenue product of labor (*MRPN*)** measures the benefit of employing an additional worker in terms of the extra *revenue* produced. To calculate the *MRPN*, we need to know the price of the firm's output. If The Clip Joint receives $30 for each dog it grooms, the *MRPN* of the first worker is $330 per day (11 additional dogs groomed per day at $30 per grooming). More generally, the marginal revenue product of an additional worker equals the price of the firm's output, *P*, times the extra output gained by adding the worker, *MPN:*

$$MRPN = P \times MPN. \tag{3.3}$$

TABLE 3.2

The Clip Joint's Production Function

(1) Number of workers, *N*	(2) Number of dogs groomed, *Y*	(3) Marginal product of labor, *MPN*	(4) Marginal revenue product of labor, *MRPN* = *MPN* × *P* (when *P* = $30 per grooming)
0	0		
		11	$330
1	11		
		9	$270
2	20		
		7	$210
3	27		
		5	$150
4	32		
		3	$90
5	35		
		1	$30
6	36		

At The Clip Joint the price of output, P, is \$30 per grooming, so the *MRPN* of each worker, column (4), equals the *MPN* of the worker, column (3), multiplied by \$30.

Now suppose that the wage, W, that The Clip Joint must pay to attract qualified workers is \$240 per day. (We refer to the wage, W, when measured in the conventional way in terms of today's dollars, as the *nominal wage.*) How many workers should The Clip Joint employ to maximize its profits? To answer this question, The Clip Joint compares the benefits and costs of employing each additional worker. The benefit of employing an additional worker, in dollars per day, is the worker's marginal revenue product, *MRPN.* The cost of an additional worker, in dollars per day, is the nominal daily wage, W.

Table 3.2 shows that the *MRPN* of the first worker is \$330 per day, which exceeds the daily wage of \$240, so employing the first worker is profitable for The Clip Joint. Adding a second worker increases The Clip Joint's profit as well because the *MRPN* of the second worker (\$270 per day) also exceeds the daily wage. However, employing a third worker reduces The Clip Joint's profit because the third worker's *MRPN* of \$210 per day is less than the \$240 daily wage. Therefore, The Clip Joint's profit-maximizing level of employment at \$240/day—equivalently, the quantity of labor demanded by The Clip Joint—is two workers.

In finding the quantity of labor demanded by The Clip Joint, we measured the benefits and costs of an extra worker in nominal, or dollar, terms. If we measure the benefits and costs of an extra worker in real terms, the results would be the same. In real terms the benefit to The Clip Joint of an extra worker is the number of extra groomings that the extra worker provides, which is the marginal product of labor, *MPN*. The real cost of adding another worker is the **real wage**, which is the wage measured in terms of units of output. Algebraically, the real wage, w, equals the nominal wage, W, divided by the price of output, P.

In this example the nominal wage, W, is \$240 per day and the price of output, P, is \$30 per grooming, so the real wage, w, equals (\$240 per day)/(\$30 per grooming), or 8 groomings per day. To find the profit-maximizing level of employment, The Clip Joint compares this real cost of an additional worker with the real benefit of an additional worker, the *MPN*. The *MPN* of the first worker is 11 groomings per day, which exceeds the real wage of 8 groomings per day, so employing this worker is profitable. The second worker also should be hired, as the second worker's *MPN* of 9 groomings per day also exceeds the real wage of 8 groomings per day. However, a third worker should not be hired because the third worker's *MPN* of 7 groomings per day is less than the real wage. The quantity of labor demanded by The Clip Joint is therefore two workers, which is the same result we got when we compared costs and benefits in nominal terms.

This example shows that, when the benefit of an additional worker exceeds the cost of an additional worker, the firm should increase employment so as to maximize profits. Similarly, if at the firm's current employment level the benefit of the last worker employed is less than the cost of the worker, the firm should reduce employment. For example, if The Clip Joint currently employed three workers, the *MRPN* of the third worker is \$210, which is less than the nominal wage of \$240, so the firm should fire one worker. Summary table 2 compares benefits and costs of additional labor in both real and nominal terms. In the choice of the profit-maximizing level of employment, a comparison of benefits and costs in either real or nominal terms is equally valid.

A Change in the Wage

The Clip Joint's decision to employ two workers was based on a nominal wage of \$240 per day. Now suppose that for some reason the nominal wage needed to attract qualified workers drops to \$180 per day. How will the reduction in the nominal wage affect the number of workers that The Clip Joint wants to employ?

To find the answer, we can compare costs and benefits in either nominal or real terms. Let's make the comparison in real terms. If the nominal wage drops to \$180 per day while the price of groomings remains at \$30, the real wage falls to (\$180 per day)/(\$30 per grooming), or 6 groomings per day. Column (3) of Table 3.2 shows that the *MPN* of the third worker is 7 groomings per day, which is now greater than the real wage. Thus, at the lower wage, expanding the quantity of labor demanded from two to three workers is profitable for The Clip Joint. However, the firm will not hire a fourth worker because the *MPN* of the fourth worker (5 groomings per day) is less than the new real wage (6 groomings per day).

This example illustrates a general point about the effect of the real wage on labor demand: All else being equal, *a decrease in the real wage raises the amount of labor demanded.* Similarly, *an increase in the real wage decreases the amount of labor demanded.*

The Marginal Product of Labor and the Labor Demand Curve

Using The Clip Joint as an example, we showed the negative relationship between the real wage and the quantity of labor that a firm demands. Figure 3.5 shows in more general terms how the link between the real wage and the quantity of labor demanded is determined. The amount of labor, *N*, is on the horizontal axis. The *MPN* and the real wage, both of which are measured in goods per unit of labor, are on the vertical axis. The downward-sloping curve is

SUMMARY 2

Comparing the Benefits and Costs of Changing the Amount of Labor

To maximize profits, the firm should:	Increase employment if, for an additional worker	Decrease employment if, for the last worker employed
Real terms	$MPN > w$ $(MPN > W/P)$	$MPN < w$ $(MPN < W/P)$
Nominal terms	$P \times MPN > W$ $(MRPN > W)$	$P \times MPN < W$ $(MRPN < W)$

MPN = marginal product of labor
P = price of output
$MRPN$ = marginal revenue product of labor = $P \times MPN$
W = nominal wage
w = real wage = W/P

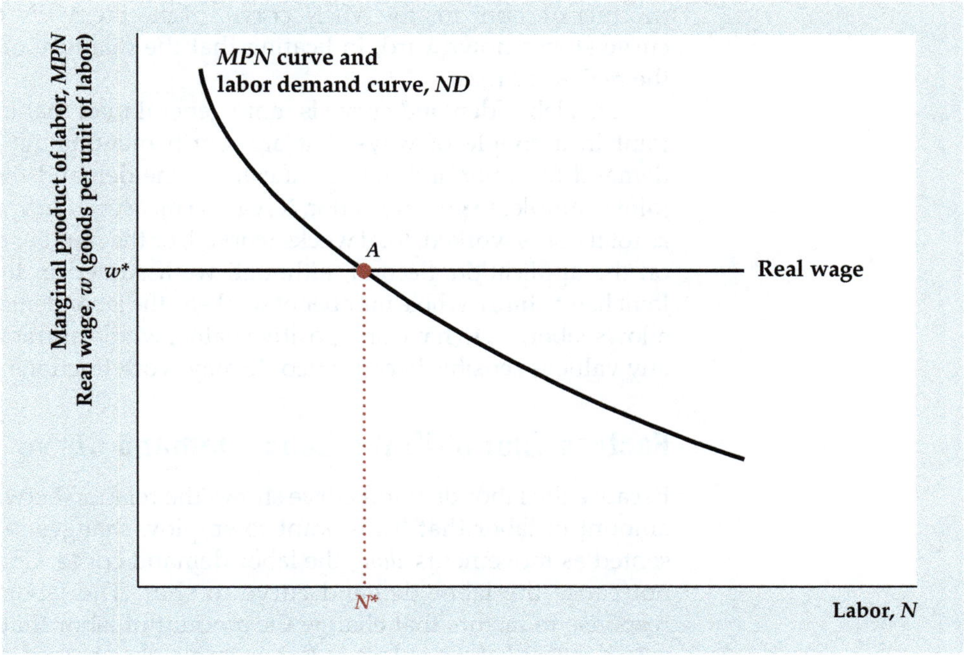

FIGURE 3.5

The determination of labor demand

The amount of labor demanded is determined by locating the point on the *MPN* curve at which the *MPN* equals the real wage rate; the amount of labor corresponding to that point is the amount of labor demanded. For example, when the real wage is w^*, the *MPN* equals the real wage at point *A* and the quantity of labor demanded is N^*. The labor demand curve, *ND*, shows the amount of labor demanded at each level of the real wage. The labor demand curve is identical to the *MPN* curve.

the *MPN* curve; it relates the marginal product of labor, *MPN*, to the amount of labor employed by the firm, *N*. The *MPN* curve slopes downward because of the diminishing marginal productivity of labor. The horizontal line represents the real wage firms face in the labor market, which the firms take as given. Here, the real wage is w^*.

For any real wage, w^*, the amount of labor that yields the highest profit (and therefore the amount of labor demanded) is determined at point *A*, the intersection of the real-wage line and the *MPN* curve. At *A* the quantity of labor demanded is N^*. Why is N^* a firm's profit-maximizing level of labor input? At employment levels less than N^*, the marginal product of labor exceeds the real wage (the *MPN* curve lies above the real-wage line); thus, if the firm's employment is initially less than N^*, it can increase its profit by expanding the amount of labor it uses. Similarly, if the firm's employment is initially greater than N^*, the marginal product of labor is less than the real wage ($MPN < w^*$) and the firm can raise profits by reducing employment. Only when employment equals N^* will the firm be satisfied with the number of workers it has. More generally, for any real wage, the profit-maximizing amount of labor input—labor demanded—corresponds to the point at which the *MPN* curve and the real-wage line intersect.

The graph of the relationship between the amount of labor demanded by a firm and the real wage that the firm faces is called the *labor demand curve.* Because the *MPN* curve also shows the amount of labor demanded at any real wage, *the labor demand curve is the same as the MPN curve,* except that the vertical axis measures the real wage for the labor demand curve and measures the marginal product of labor for the *MPN* curve.[10] Like the *MPN* curve, the labor demand curve slopes downward, indicating that the quantity of labor demanded falls as the real wage rises.

This labor demand curve is more general than that in the example of The Clip Joint in a couple of ways that are worth mentioning. First, we referred to the demand for labor and not specifically to the demand for workers, as in The Clip Joint example. In general, labor, N, can be measured in various ways—for example, as total hours worked, total weeks worked, or the number of employees—depending on the application. Second, although we assumed in the example that The Clip Joint had to hire a whole number of workers, the labor demand curve shown in Fig. 3.5 allows labor, N, to have any positive value, whole or fractional. Allowing N to take any value is sensible because people may work fractions of an hour.

Factors That Shift the Labor Demand Curve

Because the labor demand curve shows the relation between the real wage and the amount of labor that firms want to employ, changes in the real wage are represented as movements *along* the labor demand curve. Changes in the real wage do not cause the labor demand curve to shift. The labor demand curve shifts in response to factors that change the amount of labor that firms want to employ *at any given level of the real wage.* For example, we showed earlier in this chapter that beneficial, or positive, supply shocks are likely to increase the *MPN* at all levels of labor input and that adverse, or negative, supply shocks are likely to reduce the *MPN* at all levels of labor input. Thus a beneficial supply shock shifts the *MPN* curve upward and to the right and raises the quantity of labor demanded at any given real wage; an adverse supply shock does the reverse.

The effect of a supply shock on The Clip Joint's demand for labor can be illustrated by imagining that the proprietor of The Clip Joint discovers that playing classical music soothes the dogs. It makes them more cooperative and doubles the number of groomings per day that the same number of workers can produce. This technological improvement gives The Clip Joint a new production function, as described in Table 3.3. Note that doubling total output doubles the *MPN* at each employment level.

The Clip Joint demanded two workers when faced with the original production function (Table 3.2) and a real wage of 8 groomings per day. Table 3.3 shows that the productivity improvement increases The Clip Joint's labor demand at the given real wage to four workers, because the *MPN* of the fourth worker (10 groomings per day) now exceeds the real wage. The Clip Joint will not hire a fifth worker, however, because this worker's *MPN* (6 groomings per day) is less than the real wage.

The effect of a beneficial supply shock on the labor demand curve is shown in Figure 3.6. The shock causes the *MPN* to increase at any level of labor input, so the *MPN* curve shifts upward and to the right. Because the *MPN* and labor demand curves are identical, the labor demand curve also shifts upward and to the right, from ND^1 to ND^2 in Fig. 3.6. When the labor demand curve is ND^2, the firm hires more workers at any real wage level than when the labor demand curve is ND^1. Thus worker productivity and the amount of labor demanded are closely linked.

---

[10]Recall that the real wage and the *MPN* are measured in the same units, goods per unit of labor.

TABLE 3.3

The Clip Joint's Production Function After a Beneficial Productivity Shock

(1) Number of workers, N	(2) Number of dogs groomed, Y	(3) Marginal product of labor, MPN	(4) Marginal revenue product of labor, $MRPN = MPN \times P$ (when $P = \$30$ per grooming)
0	0		
		22	$660
1	22		
		18	$540
2	40		
		14	$420
3	54		
		10	$300
4	64		
		6	$180
5	70		
		2	$60
6	72		

Another factor that may affect labor demand is the size of the capital stock. Generally, an increase in the capital stock, K—by giving each worker more machines or equipment to work with—raises workers' productivity and increases the MPN at any level of labor. Hence an increase in the capital stock will cause the

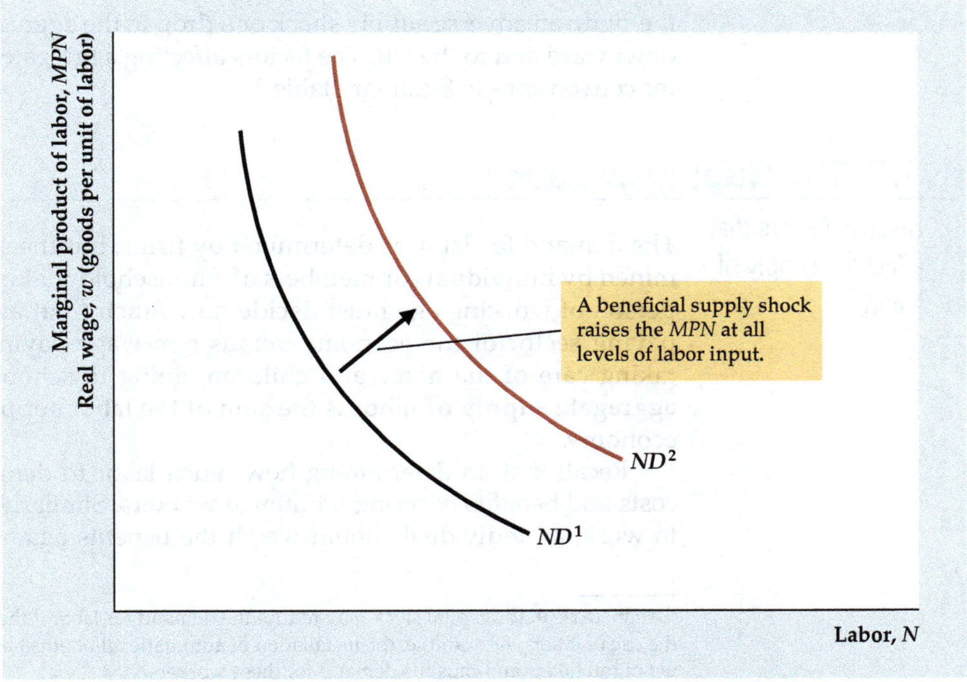

FIGURE 3.6

The effect of a beneficial supply shock on labor demand

A beneficial supply shock that raises the MPN at every level of labor shifts the MPN curve upward and to the right. Because the labor demand curve is identical to the MPN curve, the labor demand curve shifts upward and to the right from ND^1 to ND^2. For any real wage, firms demand more labor after a beneficial supply shock.

SUMMARY 3

Factors That Shift the Aggregate Labor Demand Curve

An increase in	Causes the labor demand curve to shift	Reason
Productivity	Right	Beneficial supply shock increases MPN and shifts MPN curve up and to the right.
Capital stock	Right	Higher capital stock increases MPN and shifts MPN curve up and to the right.

labor demand curve to shift upward and to the right, raising the amount of labor that a firm demands at any particular real wage.[11]

Aggregate Labor Demand

So far we have focused on the demand for labor by an individual firm, such as The Clip Joint. For macroeconomic analysis, however, we usually work with the concept of the **aggregate demand for labor**, or the sum of the labor demands of all the firms in an economy.

Because the aggregate demand for labor is the sum of firms' labor demands, the factors that determine the aggregate demand for labor are the same as those for an individual firm. Thus the aggregate labor demand curve looks the same as the labor demand curve for an individual firm (Fig. 3.5). Like the firm's labor demand curve, the aggregate labor demand curve slopes downward, showing that an increase in the economywide real wage reduces the total amount of labor that firms want to use. Similarly, a beneficial supply shock or an increase in the aggregate capital stock shifts the aggregate labor demand curve upward and to the right; an adverse supply shock or a drop in the aggregate capital stock shifts it downward and to the left. The factors affecting aggregate labor demand are listed for convenience in Summary table 3.

3.3 The Supply of Labor

Discuss factors that affect the supply of labor.

The demand for labor is determined by firms, but the supply of labor is determined by individuals or members of a household making a joint decision. Each person of working age must decide how much (if at all) to work in the wage-paying sector of the economy versus non-wage-paying alternatives, such as taking care of the home and children, going to school, or being retired. The **aggregate supply of labor** is the sum of the labor supplied by everyone in the economy.

Recall that, in determining how much labor to demand, firms compare the costs and benefits of hiring additional workers. Similarly, in deciding how much to work, an individual should weigh the benefits against the costs of working.

[11] An increase in the capital stock may reduce the demand for labor if the new capital substitutes for the use of labor. For example, the installation of automatic tollbooths has reduced the marginal product of toll takers and thus the demand for these workers.

Beyond any psychological satisfaction gained from having a job, the principal benefit of working is the income earned, which can be used to buy necessities and luxuries. The principal cost of working is that it involves time and effort that are no longer available for other activities. Economists use the term **leisure**[12] for all off-the-job activities, including eating, sleeping, working around the house, spending time with family and friends, and so on. To make themselves as well off as possible, individuals should choose to supply labor up to the point at which the income obtained from working an extra hour just makes up for the extra hour of leisure they have to forgo.

The Income–Leisure Trade-Off

To illustrate how the trade-off between income and leisure affects the labor supply decision, let's look at an example. Consider a tennis instructor named Ace who offers tennis lessons. After paying taxes and job-related expenses, Ace can earn $60 per hour, which we will call his (after-tax) nominal wage rate. Ace enjoys a reputation as an outstanding tennis instructor and could work as many hours per year as he chooses. He is reluctant to work too much, however, because every day he spends teaching tennis means one less day available to devote to his real passion, skydiving. The decision Ace faces is how many hours to work this year—or, in other words, how much labor to supply.

Ace approaches this question by asking himself: Economically speaking, what really makes me happy? After a little reflection, Ace concludes that his level of happiness, or *utility*, depends on the amount of goods and services he consumes and on the amount of leisure time he has available to jump out of airplanes. His question can therefore be recast as follows: How much should I work this year so as to obtain the highest possible level of utility?

To find the level of labor supply that maximizes his utility, Ace must compare the costs and benefits of working an extra hour. The cost of an extra hour of work is the loss of an hour of leisure; this cost can be measured as the loss in utility that Ace experiences when he must work for an hour instead of skydive. The benefit of working an extra hour is an increase of $60 in income, which allows Ace to enjoy more consumption.

If the benefit of working an extra hour (the utility gained from extra income) exceeds the cost (the utility lost by reducing leisure), Ace should work the extra hour. In fact, he should continue to increase his time at work until the utility he receives from the additional income of $60 just equals the loss of utility associated with missing an hour of leisure. Ace's labor supply at that point is the one that maximizes his utility.[13] Using the idea that the labor supply decision results from a trade-off of leisure against income, we can discuss factors that influence the amount of labor supplied by Ace.

---

[12]The term *leisure* does not imply that all off-the-job activities (housework or schoolwork, for example) are "leisurely"!

[13]Not everyone can choose their labor supply as flexibly as Ace; for example, some jobs are available for 40 hours a week or not at all. Nevertheless, by choosing to work overtime, part-time, or at a second job or by varying the number of family members who are working, households do have a significant amount of latitude over how much labor to supply.

Real Wages and Labor Supply

The real wage is the amount of real income that a worker receives in exchange for giving up a unit of leisure (an hour, a day, or a week, for example) for work. It is an important determinant of the quantity of labor that is supplied.

Generally, an increase in the real wage affects the labor supply decision in two ways. First, an increase in the real wage raises the benefit (in terms of additional real income) of working an additional hour and thus tends to make the worker want to supply more labor. The tendency of workers to supply more labor in response to a higher reward for working is called the **substitution effect of a higher real wage** on the quantity of labor supplied.

Second, an increase in the real wage makes workers effectively wealthier because for the same amount of work they now earn a higher real income. Someone who is wealthier will be better able to afford additional leisure and, as a result, will supply less labor. The tendency of workers to supply less labor in response to becoming wealthier is called the **income effect of a higher real wage** on the quantity of labor supplied. Note that the substitution and income effects of a higher real wage operate in opposite directions, with the substitution effect tending to raise the quantity of labor supplied and the income effect tending to reduce it.

A Pure Substitution Effect: A One-Day Rise in the Real Wage. We can illustrate the substitution effect by supposing that, after some consideration, Ace decides to work 48 hours per week, by working eight hours per day for six days each week. He leaves every Wednesday free to go skydiving. Although Ace could work and earn $60 per hour each Wednesday, his highest utility is obtained by taking leisure on that day instead.

Now imagine that one Tuesday, an eccentric tennis player calls Ace and requests a lesson on Wednesday to help him prepare for a weekend amateur tournament. He offers Ace his regular wage of $60 per hour, but Ace declines, explaining that he plans to go skydiving on Wednesday. Not willing to take "no" for an answer, the tennis player then offers to pay Ace $600 per hour for an all-day lesson on Wednesday. When Ace hears this offer to work for 10 times his usual wage rate, he thinks: "I don't get offers like this one every day. I'll go skydiving some other day, but this Wednesday I'm going to work."

Ace's decision to work rather than skydive (that is, to substitute labor for leisure) on this particular Wednesday represents a response to a very high reward, in terms of additional income, that each additional hour of work on that day will bring. His decision to work the extra day results from the substitution effect. Because receiving a very high wage for only one day doesn't make Ace substantially wealthier, the income effect of the one-day wage increase is negligible. Thus the effect of a one-day increase in the real wage on the quantity of labor supplied by Ace is an almost pure example of the substitution effect.

A Pure Income Effect: Winning the Lottery. In addition to skydiving, Ace enjoys playing the state lottery. As luck would have it, a week after spending the Wednesday teaching the eccentric tennis player, Ace wins $300,000 in the state lottery. Ace's response is to reduce his workweek from six to five days, because the additional $300,000 of wealth enables him to afford to take more time off from work—and so he does. Because the lottery prize has made him wealthier, he reduces his labor supply. As the lottery prize does not affect the current reward for giving up an hour of leisure to work—Ace's wage is still $60 per hour—there is no substitution effect. Thus, winning the lottery is an example of a pure income effect.

Another example of a pure income effect is an increase in the expected future real wage. Suppose that the aging tennis pro at the posh country club in Ace's community announces that he will retire the following year, and the country club agrees to hire Ace beginning one year from now. Ace will earn $100 per hour (after taxes) for as many hours as he wants to teach tennis.[14] Ace recognizes that this increase in his future wage has effectively made him wealthier by increasing the future income he will receive for any given amount of labor supplied in the future. Looking at his lifetime income, Ace realizes that he is better able to afford leisure today. That is, the increase in the future real wage has an income effect that leads Ace to reduce his current labor supply. Because this increase in the future wage does not change Ace's current wage, and thus does not affect the current reward for giving up an hour of leisure to work an additional hour, there is no substitution effect on Ace's current labor supply. Thus the increase in the future real wage has a pure income effect on Ace's labor supply.

The Substitution Effect and the Income Effect Together: A Long-Term Increase in the Real Wage. The aging tennis pro at the country club quits suddenly, and the country club asks Ace to start work immediately. Ace accepts the offer and earns $100 per hour (after taxes) for as many hours as he wants to teach tennis.

On his new job, will Ace work more hours or fewer hours than he did before? In this case, the two effects work in opposite directions. On the one hand, because the reward for working is greater, Ace will be tempted to work more than he did previously. This tendency to increase labor supply in response to a higher real wage is the substitution effect. On the other hand, at his new, higher wage, Ace can pay for food, rent, and skydiving expenses by working only three or four days each week, so he is tempted to work less and spend more time skydiving. This tendency to reduce labor supply because he is wealthier is the income effect.

Which effect wins? One factor that will influence Ace's decision is the length of time he expects his new, higher wage to last. The longer the higher wage is expected to last, the larger its impact on Ace's lifetime resources is, and the stronger the income effect is. Thus, if Ace expects to hold the new job until he retires, the income effect is strong (he is much wealthier) and he is more likely to reduce the amount of time that he works. In contrast, if Ace believes that the job may not last very long, the income effect is weak (the increase in his lifetime resources is small) and he may choose to work more so as to take advantage of the higher wage while he can. In general, the longer an increase in the real wage is expected to last, the larger the income effect is and the more likely it is that the quantity of labor supplied will be reduced.

Empirical Evidence on Real Wages and Labor Supply. Because of conflicting income and substitution effects, some ambiguity exists regarding how a change in the real wage will affect labor supply. What is the empirical evidence?

Research on labor supply generally shows that the aggregate amount of labor supplied rises in response to a temporary increase in the real wage but falls in

[14] We assume that zero inflation is expected over the next year, so the $100 per hour wage rate in the following year is an increase in Ace's real wage rate as well as an increase in his nominal wage rate.

Application

The Gig Economy in the ASEAN Nations

The term *gig economy* describes an economy where firms prefer to recruit independent contractors for short-term commitments or positions. Gig workers, on-call workers, and freelancers have often been associated with such "short-term" or task-based jobs. According to the International Labour Organisation, the criteria for being considered a gig worker is to be engaged in work independently at least once a week.[15] Though the gig economy offers greater flexibility with which to accommodate workers' needs and goals, it may not be able to solve the long-term growth target of an economy, as this type of job is highly uncertain by nature and depends on the demand for the service performed.

In surveys of employment and earnings, gig workers are not easily identified. Singapore, Vietnam, and Indonesia, for instance, use "self-employed" as a proxy to identify gig workers, while Malaysia lists them as "own-account workers." The prevalence of gig workers in Vietnam and Indonesia were recorded at 59.6% and 50.9% respectively. Singapore has the lowest percentage of self-employed workers in the Association of Southeast Asian Nations (ASEAN) group, at only 10%. In terms of earnings, the Philippines has the sixth fastest-growing gig economy in the world.[16]

Several explanations have been put forward for the rising trend in the gig economy: Vietnam, for example, reported that 53% of their graduates and intellectuals choose freelancing jobs because of the flexibility in working hours and location, while Indonesia attributes the trend to the rise of digitalization.[17]

[15]Luis Pinedo Caro, Niall O'Higgins, and Janine Berg 2021, "Young People and the Gig Economy," May 7, 2021, *https://www.ilo.org/wcmsp5/groups/public/---ed_emp/documents/publication/wcms_790117.pdf*.

[16]Payoneer, "Global Gig-Economy Index: Q2 2019," *https://explore.payoneer.com/q2_global_freelancing_index/*.

[17]Fairwork, "Fairwork Indonesia Ratings 2021: Labour Standards in the Gig Economy," Yogyakarta, Indonesia; Oxford, United Kingdom, 2021, *https://fair.work/wp-content/uploads/sites/17/2021/12/211209_Fairwork_Report_Indonesia-2021.pdf*.

response to a permanent increase in the real wage.[18] The finding that a temporary increase in the real wage raises the amount of labor supplied confirms the substitution effect: If the reward for working rises for a short period, people will take advantage of the opportunity to work more. The result that a permanent increase in the real wage lowers the aggregate amount of labor supplied indicates that for long-lived increases in the real wage, the income effect outweighs the substitution effect: If permanently higher wages make workers much better off, they will choose to work less. The size of these effects depends on a person's family situation (married or not and whether the person or couple has children or is

[18]For a detailed review of research on labor supply, see the article by Richard Blundell and Thomas MaCurdy, "Labor Supply: A Review of Alternative Approaches," in O. Ashenfelter and D. Card, eds., *Handbook of Labor Economics*, volume 3 (Amsterdam: North-Holland, 1999), pp. 1559–1695. For more information about key areas of recent research, see the articles by Michael Keane and Richard Rogerson, "Micro and Macro Labor Supply Elasticities: A Reassessment of Conventional Wisdom," *Journal of Economic Literature*, June 2012, pp. 464–476; and Michael P. Keane, "Labor Supply and Taxes: A Survey," *Journal of Economic Literature*, December 2011, pp. 961–1075. Recently, prime-age participation rates have been declining, as we discuss in the Application: Recent Trends in Labor Supply, on p. 129.

caring for an aging parent) and the tax rate (which determines how much income can be kept after taxes are paid).

The Labor Supply Curve

We have discussed how the amount of labor supplied by an individual depends on the current and expected future real wage rates. The *labor supply curve* of an individual relates the amount of labor supplied to the current real wage rate, holding constant all other factors (including the expected future real wage rate) that affect the amount of labor supplied. Figure 3.7 presents a graph of a typical labor supply curve. The current real wage is measured on the vertical axis, and the amount of labor supplied is measured on the horizontal axis. The labor supply curve slopes upward because an increase in the current real wage (holding constant the expected future real wage) leads to an increase in the amount of labor supplied.

Factors That Shift the Labor Supply Curve. Any factor that changes the amount of labor supplied at a given level of the current real wage shifts the labor supply curve. Specifically, any factor that increases the amount of labor supplied at a given level of the real wage shifts the labor supply curve to the right, and any factor that decreases the amount of labor supplied at a given real wage shifts the labor supply curve to the left. We have already discussed how an increase in wealth (say, from winning the lottery) has a pure income effect that reduces the amount of labor supplied at a given real wage. Thus, as shown in Figure 3.8, an increase in wealth shifts the labor supply curve to the left. We have also discussed how an increase in the expected future real wage has a pure income effect that reduces the amount of labor supplied at a given real wage. Figure 3.8 also depicts the response of the labor supply curve to an increase in the expected future real wage.

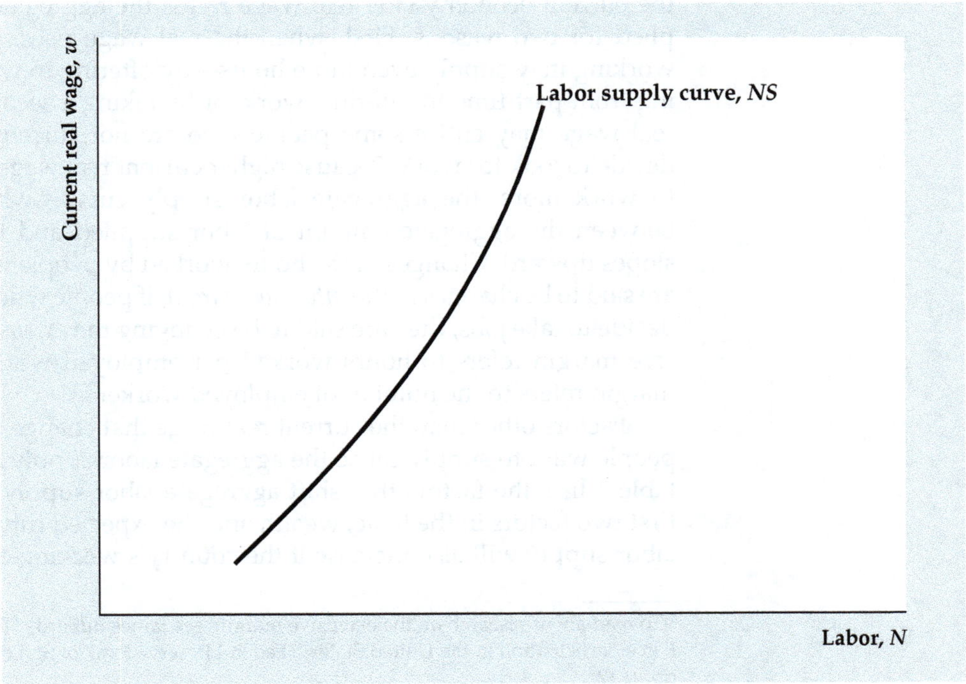

FIGURE 3.7

The labor supply curve of an individual worker
The horizontal axis shows the amount of labor that a worker will supply for any given current real wage on the vertical axis. The labor supply curve slopes upward, indicating that—with other factors, including the expected future real wage, held constant—an increase in the current real wage raises the amount of labor supplied.

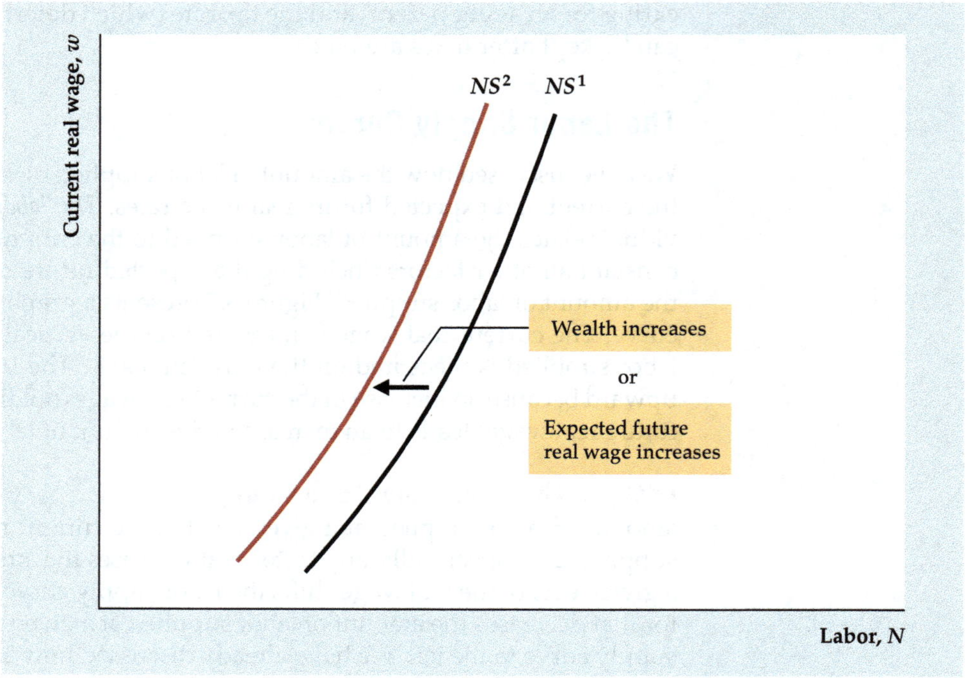

FIGURE 3.8

The effect on labor supply of an increase in wealth

An increase in wealth reduces the amount of labor supplied at any real wage. Therefore an increase in wealth causes the labor supply curve to shift to the left. Similarly, an increase in the expected future real wage, which has the effect of making the worker wealthier, reduces the amount of labor supplied at any given current real wage and shifts the labor supply curve to the left.

Aggregate Labor Supply

As we mentioned earlier, the aggregate supply of labor is the total amount of labor supplied by everyone in the economy. Just as the quantity of labor supplied by an individual rises when the person's current real wage rises, the aggregate quantity of labor supplied increases when the economywide real wage rises. An increase in the current economywide real wage raises the aggregate quantity of labor supplied for two reasons. First, when the real wage rises, people who are already working may supply even more hours—by offering to work overtime, by changing from part-time to full-time work, or by taking a second job. Second, a higher real wage may entice some people who are not currently in the labor force to decide to look for work. Because higher current real wages induce people to want to work more, the aggregate labor supply curve—which shows the relation between the aggregate amount of labor supplied and the current real wage—slopes upward. Changes in the hours worked by people who are already working are said to be changes in the *intensive margin*; if people who had not been employed decide to take jobs, they are said to be changing the *extensive margin*. So, the intensive margin refers to hours worked per employed worker, while the extensive margin refers to the number of employed workers.[19]

Factors other than the current real wage that change the amount of labor that people want to supply cause the aggregate labor supply curve to shift. Summary table 4 lists the factors that shift aggregate labor supply. We have discussed the first two factors in the table, wealth and the expected future real wage. Aggregate labor supply will also increase if the country's working-age population increases

[19]To read about research on the extensive margin, see James Bullard, "The Rise and Fall of Labor Force Participation in the United States," Federal Reserve Bank of St. Louis *Review*, First Quarter 2014, pp. 1–12.

SUMMARY 4

Factors That Shift the Aggregate Labor Supply Curve

An increase in	Causes the labor supply curve to shift	Reason
Wealth	Left	Increase in wealth increases amount of leisure workers can afford.
Expected future real wage	Left	Increase in expected future real wage increases amount of leisure workers can afford.
Working-age population	Right	Increased number of potential workers increases amount of labor supplied.
Participation rate	Right	Increased number of people wanting to work increases amount of labor supplied.

(for example, because of an increased birth rate or immigration), or if changes in the social or legal environment cause a greater proportion of the working-age population to enter the labor force (increased labor force participation). For example, evolving attitudes about the role of women in society contributed to a large increase in the number of women in the U.S. labor market from the late 1960s to the mid-1990s; and the elimination of mandatory retirement in many fields may increase the participation rates of older workers.

3.4 Labor Market Equilibrium

Identify factors that affect labor market equilibrium.

Equilibrium in the labor market requires that the aggregate quantity of labor demanded equal the aggregate quantity of labor supplied. The basic supply–demand model of the labor market introduced here (called the *classical model of the labor market*) is based on the assumption that the real wage adjusts reasonably quickly to equate labor supply and labor demand. Thus, if labor supply is less than labor demand, firms competing for scarce workers bid up the real wage, whereas if many workers are competing for relatively few jobs, the real wage will tend to fall.

Labor market equilibrium is represented graphically by the intersection of the aggregate labor demand curve and the aggregate labor supply curve at point E in Figure 3.9. The equilibrium level of employment, achieved after the complete adjustment of wages and prices, is known as the **full-employment level of employment**, $\bar{N}$. The corresponding market-clearing real wage is $\bar{w}$.

Factors that shift either the aggregate labor demand curve or the aggregate labor supply curve affect both the equilibrium real wage and the full-employment level of employment. An example of such a factor is a temporary adverse supply shock. A temporary adverse supply shock—because of, say, a spell of unusually bad weather—decreases the marginal product of labor at every level of employment. As Figure 3.10 shows, this decrease causes the labor demand curve to shift to the left, from ND^1 to ND^2. Because the supply shock is temporary, however, it is not expected to affect future marginal products or the future real wage, so the labor supply curve

FIGURE 3.9

Labor market equilibrium
The quantity of labor demanded equals the quantity of labor supplied at point *E*. The equilibrium real wage is $\bar{w}$, and the corresponding equilibrium level of employment is $\bar{N}$, the full-employment level of employment.

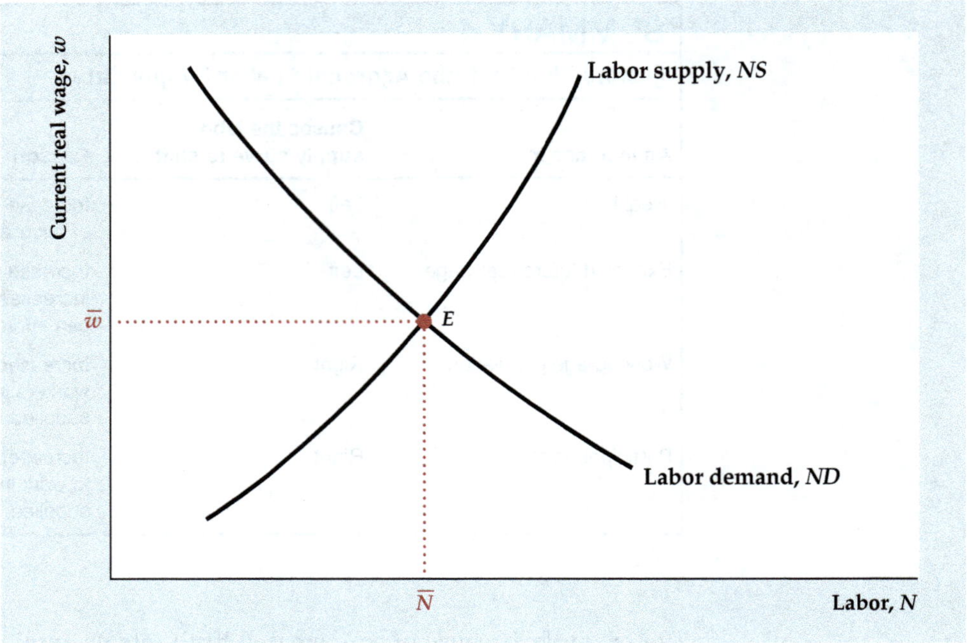

doesn't shift. Equilibrium in the labor market moves from point *A* to point *B*. Thus the model predicts that a temporary supply shock will lower both the current real wage (from $\bar{w}_1$ to $\bar{w}_2$) and the full-employment level of employment (from $\bar{N}_1$ to $\bar{N}_2$).

The classical supply–demand model of the labor market has the virtue of simplicity and is quite useful for studying how economic disturbances or changes in economic policy affect employment and the real wage. However, a significant

FIGURE 3.10

Effects of a temporary adverse supply shock on the labor market
An adverse supply shock that lowers the marginal product of labor (see Fig. 3.4) reduces the quantity of labor demanded at any real wage level. Thus the labor demand curve shifts left, from ND^1 to ND^2, and the labor market equilibrium moves from point *A* to point *B*. The adverse supply shock causes the real wage to fall from $\bar{w}_1$ to $\bar{w}_2$ and reduces the full-employment level of employment from $\bar{N}_1$ to $\bar{N}_2$.

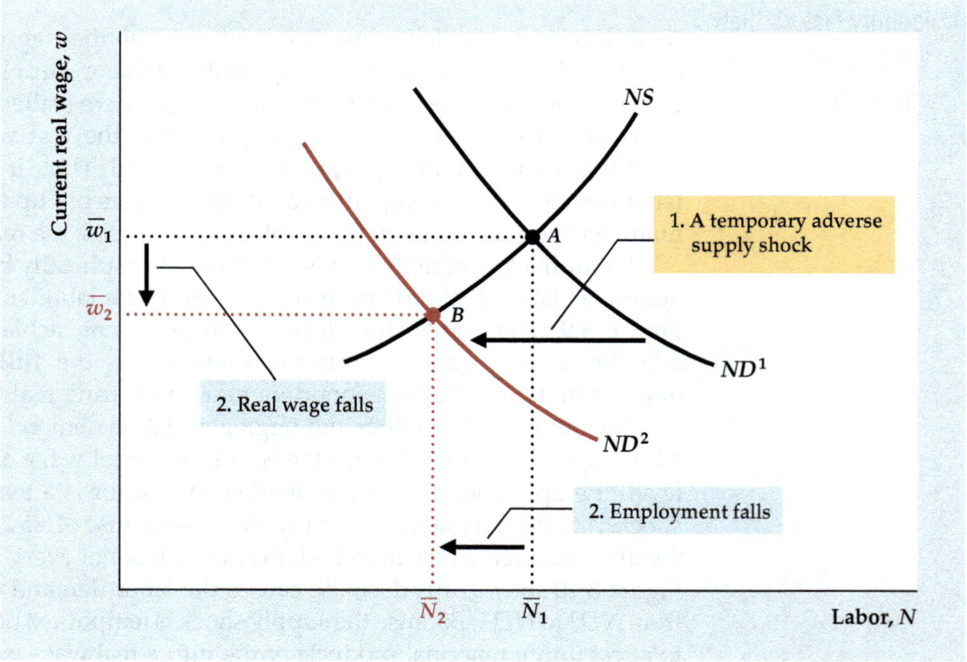

drawback of this basic model is that it cannot be used to study unemployment. Because it assumes that any worker who wants to work at the equilibrium real wage can find a job, the model implies zero unemployment, which never occurs. We discuss unemployment later in this chapter, but in the meantime we will continue to use the classical supply–demand model of the labor market.

Full-Employment Output

By combining labor market equilibrium and the production function, we can determine the amount of output that firms want to supply. **Full-employment output**, $\bar{Y}$, sometimes called *potential output,* is the level of output that firms in the economy supply when wages and prices have fully adjusted. Equivalently, full-employment output is the level of output supplied when aggregate employment equals its full-employment level, $\bar{N}$. Algebraically, we define full-employment output, $\bar{Y}$, by using the production function Eq. (3.1):

$$\bar{Y} = AF(K, \bar{N}). \tag{3.4}$$

Equation (3.4) shows that, for constant capital stock, K, full-employment output is determined by two general factors: the full-employment level of employment, $\bar{N}$, and the production function relating output to employment.

Anything that changes either the full-employment level of employment, $\bar{N}$, or the production function will change full-employment output, $\bar{Y}$. For example, a temporary adverse supply shock that reduces the *MPN* (Fig. 3.10) works in two distinct ways to lower full-employment output:

1. The adverse supply shock lowers output directly, by reducing the quantity of output that can be produced with any fixed amounts of capital and labor. This direct effect can be thought of as a reduction in the productivity measure A in Eq. (3.4).
2. The adverse supply shock reduces the demand for labor and thus lowers the full-employment level of employment $\bar{N}$, as Fig. 3.10 shows. A reduction in $\bar{N}$ also reduces full-employment output, $\bar{Y}$, as Eq. (3.4) confirms.

Application

Output, Employment, and the Real Wage During Oil Price Shocks

Among the most severe supply shocks hitting the U.S. and world economies since World War II were sharp increases in the prices of oil and other energy products. Figure 3.11 shows how the price of energy paid by firms, measured relative to the GDP deflator (the general price level of all output), varied during the period 1960–2017. Three adverse oil price shocks stand out: one in 1973–1974, when the Organization of Petroleum Exporting Countries (OPEC) first imposed an oil embargo and then greatly increased crude oil prices; a second in 1979–1980, after the Iranian revolution disrupted oil supplies; and a third in 2003–2008, when surging demand for oil by large rapidly developing countries such as China and India, combined with weak supply (because of insufficient production capacity, hurricanes that damaged Gulf of Mexico production, and geopolitical concerns in the Middle

(continued)

FIGURE 3.11

Relative price of energy, 1960–2021

The figure shows the producer price index of fuels and related products and power (an index of energy prices paid by producers) relative to the GDP deflator. Note the impact of the 1973–1974, 1979–1980, and 2003–2008 oil shocks and the decline in energy prices in the first half of the 1980s.

Sources: Bureau of Economic Analysis, downloaded from FRED database at *fred.stlouisfed.org.* Producer price index for fuels and related products and power: FRED series *PPIENG;* GDP deflator: FRED series *GDPDEF.* Data were scaled so that the relative price of energy equals 100 in year 2000.

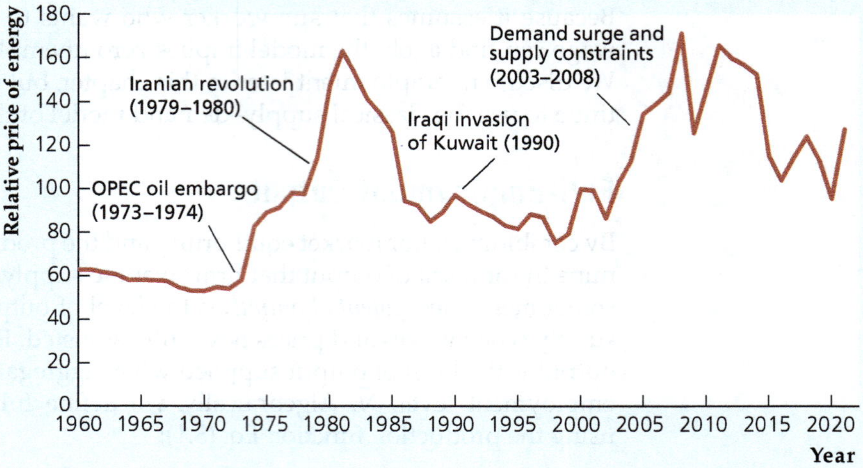

East, Russia, Venezuela, and Nigeria) caused the price of oil to rise sharply. The 1979–1980 oil price shock turned out to be temporary, as energy prices subsequently fell. The increase in oil prices following Iraq's invasion of Kuwait in August 1990 had less of an impact on overall energy prices than the three oil price shocks mentioned above and thus doesn't appear as much more than a blip in Fig. 3.11.

When a reduction or disruption in the supply of oil causes energy prices to rise, firms cut back on energy use, implying that less output is produced at any particular levels of capital and labor, which is an adverse supply shock. How large is the effect on GDP from an oil price shock? It is difficult to disentangle everything else going on in the economy when such a shock occurs and the outcome depends on the government's policy response. But empirical research suggests that an increase of 10% in the price of oil reduces GDP by about 0.4 percentage points.[20] Thus the 96% increase in oil prices from 2002 to 2008 led GDP to be about 3.8% lower than it would have been in the absence of the increase in oil prices.

Our analysis predicts that an adverse supply shock will lower labor demand, reducing employment and the real wage, as well as reducing the supply of output. In fact, the economy went into recession, with negative GDP growth, following the increases in oil prices resulting from restrictions in the supply of oil in 1973–1974, 1979–1980, and 1990. In each case, employment and the real wage fell. Care must be taken in interpreting these results because macroeconomic policies and other factors were changing at the same time; however, our model appears to account for the response of the economy to these major oil price increases.

[20]See Charles T. Carlstrom and Timothy S. Fuerst, "Oil Prices, Monetary Policy, and the Macroeconomy," Federal Reserve Bank of Cleveland, *Economic Commentary* (July 2005), and John Fernald and Bharat Trehan, "Why Hasn't the Jump in Oil Prices Led to a Recession?" Federal Reserve Bank of San Francisco, *Economic Letter*, Number 2005-31, November 18, 2005.

3.5 Unemployment

Explain how the unemployment rate is measured and describe changes in employment status.

Our classical model of the labor market, which relies on supply–demand analysis, is useful for studying the wage rate and the level of employment in an economy and for showing how these variables are linked to output and productivity. However, this model of the labor market is based on the strong assumption that, when the labor market is in equilibrium, all workers who are willing to work at the prevailing wage are able to find jobs. In reality, of course, not everyone who would like to work has a job; there is always some unemployment. The existence of unemployment implies that, at any time, not all of society's labor resources are actively involved in producing goods and services.

We discuss the problem of unemployment several times in this book, notably in Chapter 12. Here we introduce the topic by presenting some basic facts about unemployment and then turning to a preliminary economic analysis of it.

Measuring Unemployment

To estimate the unemployment rate in the United States, each month the Bureau of Labor Statistics (BLS) surveys about 60,000 households. Each person 16 years of age and older in the surveyed households is assigned to one of three categories:

1. *employed*, if the person worked full-time or part-time during the past week (or was on sick leave or vacation from a job);
2. *unemployed*, if the person didn't work during the past week but looked for work during the past four weeks; or
3. *not in the labor force*, if the person didn't work during the past week and didn't look for work during the past four weeks (examples are full-time students, homemakers, and retirees).

Table 3.4 shows the number of people in each category in January 2022. (Good sources for these and other data about the labor market are described in "In Touch with Data and Research: "Labor Market Data in Kazakhstan.") In that month there were 157.2 million

TABLE 3.4

Employment Status of the U.S. Adult Population, January 2022

Category	Number (millions)	Share of labor force (percent)	Share of adult population (percent)
Employed workers	157.2	96.0	59.7 (employment ratio)
Unemployed workers	6.5	4.0 (unemployment rate)	2.5
Labor force (employed + unemployed workers)	163.7	100.0	62.2 (participation rate)
Not in labor force	99.5		37.8
Adult population (labor force + not in labor force)	263.2		100.0

Note: Figures may not add up because of rounding.

Source: The Employment Situation, January 2022, Table A-1.

employed and 6.5 million unemployed workers. The **labor force** consists of all employed and unemployed workers, so in January 2022 it totaled 163.7 million workers (157.2 million employed plus 6.5 million unemployed). The adult (age 16 and older) population in January 2022 was 263.2 million, which leaves 99.5 million adults not in the labor force (total population of 263.2 million less 163.7 million in the labor force).

Some useful measures of the labor market are the unemployment rate, the participation rate, and the employment ratio. The **unemployment rate** is the fraction of the labor force that is unemployed. In January 2022, the unemployment rate was 4.0% (6.5 million unemployed divided by 163.7 million in the labor force). Figure 1.3 shows the U.S. unemployment rate for the period since 1890.

The fraction of the adult population in the labor force is the **participation rate**. Of the 263.2 million adults in the United States in January 2022, 163.7 million were in the labor force, so the participation rate was 62.2% (because $163.7/263.2 = 0.622 = 62.2\%$).

The **employment ratio** is the employed fraction of the adult population. In January 2022 the employment ratio was 59.7% (157.2 million employed divided by the adult population of 263.2 million). With an employment ratio of 59.7%, 40.3% of the adult population was not employed in January 2022. Of this 40.3%, 2.5% reflected unemployment and the remaining 37.8% reflected people not in the labor force.[21] Thus a large majority of adults who are not employed at any given time are not in the labor force rather than unemployed.

Changes in Employment Status

The labor market is in a constant state of flux. Even when the unemployment rate remains unchanged from one month to the next, during the month hundreds of thousands of U.S. workers become unemployed and hundreds of thousands become employed.

In Touch with Data and Research

Labor Market Data in Kazakhstan

The Agency of Statistics of the Republic of Kazakhstan (ASRK) is the governmental body responsible for collection and distribution of statistical data, including data pertaining to the labor market. A useful summary of labor market data can be found in the reports *Number and Wages of Employees by Types of Economic Activities*, published monthly and quarterly, and *Basic Indicators of Labor Market*, published quarterly.[22] The former report, which has been published since 2000, includes monthly and quarterly data on the number of hired workers, the payroll fund, average monthly wages, real wage indexes, actual time worked by hired workers per week, and the number of open vacancies; the data are presented for various categories of enterprises based on type of economic activity, region, and size. The latter report, published since 2001, includes quarterly data on employment, unemployment, and hours worked each week for various

[21] There is a small rounding difference here.

[22] Both are available online at *www.stat.kz/publishing/Pages/trud_2012_god.aspx*.

categories of workers based on age, gender, occupation, level of educational attainment, and region.

The data in the *Number and Wages of Employees by Types of Economic Activities* are obtained from monthly and quarterly establishment surveys (known as the *Report on Labor 1T*). The monthly establishment survey is obtained from the responses of all large and medium enterprises within the territory of Kazakhstan about their employment, hours worked, employee earnings, and categories of employees. Small enterprises and organizations are surveyed only quarterly.[23] The data in the *Basic Indicators of Labor Market* are obtained from quarterly household surveys and are used to calculate the employment and unemployment rate. The household surveys started in 2001. Every quarter, the ASRK surveys 21,000 households, which represent 0.5 percent of the total population.[24]

[23]Agency of Statistics of the Republic of Kazakhstan, *Methodological Guidelines on Statistics*, third edition, supplemented, Astana 2009, p. 99. Retrieved on November 12, 2012, from *http://www.stat.kz/metod/standart_ARKS/Documents/MEtod_rus.indd.pdf.*

[24]Ibid., pp. 70–71.

Figure 3.12 shows how workers change their employment status (that is, whether they are employed, unemployed, or not in the labor force) in a typical month (the numbers are from January 2022). The arrows between each pair of boxes represent changes from one employment status to another, and the number on each arrow shows the fraction of the people in one status that switch to the other status in a typical month.[25] For example, the arrow from the employed box to the unemployed box has the label 1%, indicating that 1% of employed workers will become unemployed by the following month.

What are the employment prospects of a person who is unemployed? Figure 3.12 shows that 30% of the unemployed people in a typical month will be employed the following month and that 25% of the unemployed people will be out of the labor force the next month. The remaining 45% of the unemployed people will still be unemployed the following month. Of the 25% of the unemployed who leave the labor force each month, some are **discouraged workers**, or people who have become so discouraged by lack of success at finding a job that they stop searching. Other unemployed workers leave the labor force to engage in some activity outside the labor market, focusing on household duties such caring for a young child or an elderly parent, or going to school.

How Long Are People Unemployed?

Of the 45% of those unemployed in a typical month who remain unemployed the following month, some may remain unemployed for a considerable period of time. The period of time that an individual is continuously unemployed is called an **unemployment spell**. The length of time that an unemployment spell lasts is called its **duration**. The duration of an unemployment spell determines in large part the degree of hardship suffered by an unemployed worker. At one extreme, a

[25]Figure 3.12 makes use of data on transition rates between employment, unemployment, and not-in-the-labor-force status. The rates are from the Bureau of Labor Statistics research series on labor force status flows from the Current Population Survey, *www.bls.gov/cps/cps_flows.htm*.

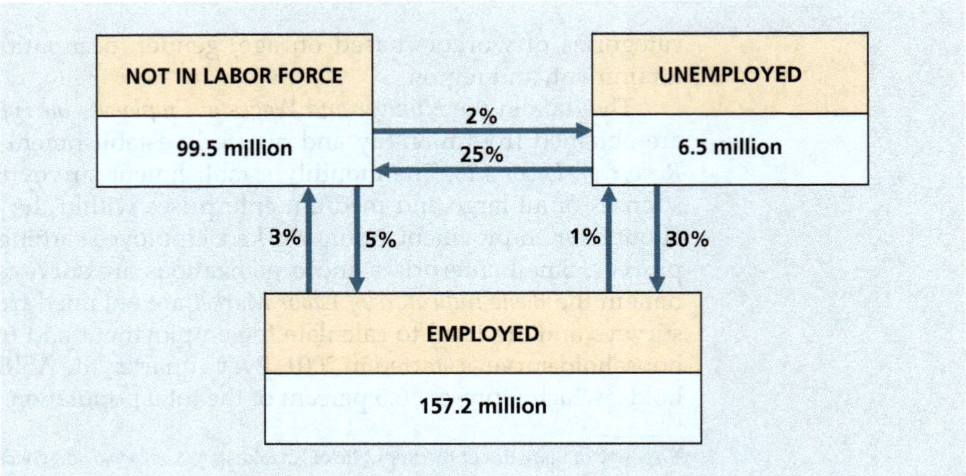

FIGURE 3.12

Changes in employment status in a typical month

The arrows between two boxes represent changes from one employment status to another; the labels on the arrows show the fraction of the people in one status who switch to the other status in a typical month. For example, the arrow from the unemployed box to the employed box indicates that 30% of unemployed workers become employed the following month; the arrow from the employed box to the unemployed box indicates that 1% of employed workers become unemployed the following month. The numbers of people in each employment status are from January 2022.
Source: Labor Statistics from the Current Population Survey, Bureau of Labor Statistics, available at BLS website at *www.bls.gov/cps/cps_flows.htm.*

one-week unemployment spell will cost a worker a week's pay but probably will not seriously affect the worker's standard of living. At the other extreme, an unemployment spell that lasts for several months may force an unemployed worker to exhaust their life savings or to sell a car or house.

The duration of unemployment spells in the United States is characterized by two seemingly contradictory statements:

1. Most unemployment spells are of short duration, about two months or less.
2. Most people who are unemployed on a given date are experiencing unemployment spells with long duration.

To understand how both of these statements can be true, consider an economy with 100 people in the labor force. Suppose that at the beginning of every month, two workers become unemployed and remain unemployed for one month before finding new jobs. In addition, at the beginning of every year four workers become unemployed and remain unemployed for the entire year.

In this example, there are 28 spells of unemployment during a year: 24 spells that last one month, and four spells that last one year. Thus 24 of 28, or 86%, of the spells last only one month, which is consistent with the first statement: Most spells are short.

How many people are unemployed on a given day—say, on May 15? There are six unemployed workers on May 15: two unemployed workers who began one-month spells of unemployment on May 1, and four unemployed workers who began one-year spells of unemployment on January 1. Thus, four of six, or 67%, of the workers unemployed on May 15 are experiencing one-year spells of unemployment, which is consistent with the second statement: Most people who are unemployed on a given date are experiencing long spells of unemployment.

So far we have focused on completed spells of unemployment. A completed spell begins when someone becomes unemployed and ends when that person is no longer unemployed, either by becoming employed or by leaving the labor force. However, a common measure of the duration of unemployment focuses on ongoing, or *incomplete*, spells of unemployment, which are spells that have not yet ended. On any given day, all of the unemployed are experiencing incomplete spells of unemployment because they have not yet become employed or left the labor force. The measured duration of an incomplete spell of unemployment is the length of time the person has been continuously unemployed up to the current date. The average length of ongoing, incomplete spells of unemployment is called the mean duration of unemployment. In the example in the preceding few paragraphs, six people are unemployed on May 15. Two of them have been unemployed for 0.5 month (since May 1) and four of them have been unemployed for 4.5 months (since January 1). Therefore, the mean duration of unemployment on May 15 is $(2 \times 0.5 + 4 \times 4.5)/6 = 3.17$ months.

Application

Unemployment During the European Debt Crisis

Unemployment is considered a lagging indicator, meaning it takes two or three quarters to adapt to changes in the business cycle. This is why it might continue to rise even after the economy has started to recover from a recession.

The impact of the 2007–2009 recession extended beyond the United States and was felt throughout Europe in GDP growth and employment. Greece, Spain, and Italy were among the countries that were most severely affected, and they found it increasingly difficult to continue to bail out financial institutions, refinance government deficits, and repay sovereign debt. This led to the European debt crisis as the fiscal positions and debt levels of a number of eurozone countries became unsustainable. These nations had no choice but to seek loans and bailouts from the European Central Bank (ECB), the International Monetary Fund (IMF), and the European Financial Stability Facility (EFSF).[26] As part of the bailout packages they received, these countries had to adopt a number of austerity measures by cutting public spending and increasing taxes. This caused further economic contraction, investment slowdown, and unemployment.

As Figure 3.13 shows, unemployment rates started to increase as each of these two crises hit the euro area and continued to increase till the end of the later crisis.

A study by economists from the European Central Bank (ECB) and the national central banks of the EU countries explains this trend.[27] During the 2007–2009 recession, most employers chose to steeply cut wages. As the recession continued, they began to lay off employees and reduced the working hours of the ones that remained. However, consecutive shocks forced the governments to ease employment protection legislations and wage bargaining. Therefore, by the time the debt crisis peaked in 2010, firms were able to reduce employment and cut wages and hours *simultaneously*.

As the affected economies started to show signs of recovery, firms responded by hiring more people rather than increasing the number hours worked. As a result, governments of these nations began reverting to stricter labor legislation, with Greece and Spain increasing the minimum wage in 2019.

[26]The EFSF was a temporary crisis resolution measure created by the EU in 2010 following the sovereign debt crisis. It provided financial assistance to the affected nations.

[27]Thomas Y. Mathä et al., "Shocks and Labour Cost Adjustment: Evidence from a Survey of European Firms," 2019, ECB Working Paper Series, No. 2269, European Central Bank, April 2019.

(continued)

FIGURE 3.13

Unemployment rates during the Great Recession and the European sovereign debt crisis

Steep reductions in wages during the 2007–2009 recession were followed by layoffs. As governments had reduced employment protection during this time, employment, wages, and hours reduced simultaneously.

Source: Eurostat, "Unemployment by Sex and Age—Annual Average, 2019, *https://ec.europa.eu/eurostat/web/products-datasets/-/UNE_RT_A.*

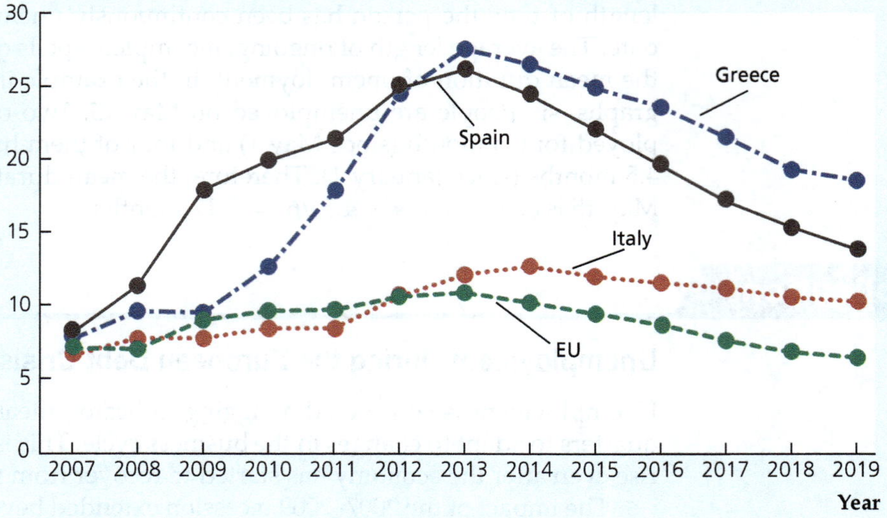

Why There Always Are Unemployed People

Even when the economy is growing vigorously and many new jobs are being created, some people remain unemployed. Why is unemployment apparently a permanent feature of the economy? Here we discuss frictional unemployment and structural unemployment, two types of unemployment that always exist in the labor market and thus prevent the unemployment rate from ever reaching zero.

Frictional Unemployment. The labor market is characterized by a great deal of searching by both workers and firms. Unemployed workers search for suitable jobs, and firms with vacancies search for suitable workers. If all workers were identical and all jobs were identical, these searches would be short and easy: Unemployed workers would simply have to find firms that had vacancies and they would immediately be hired. The problem, of course, is that neither jobs nor workers are identical. Workers vary in their talents, skills, experience, goals, geographic location (and willingness to move), and amount of time and energy they are willing to commit to their job. Similarly, jobs vary in the skills and experience required, working conditions, location, hours, and pay. Because of these differences, an unemployed worker may search for several weeks or more before finding a suitable job; similarly, a firm may search for a considerable time before it is able to hire a suitable worker.

The unemployment that arises as workers search for suitable jobs and firms search for suitable workers is called **frictional unemployment**. Because the economy is dynamic, with jobs continually being created and destroyed and workers continually entering and exiting the labor force, there is always some frictional unemployment as workers are matched with appropriate jobs.

Structural Unemployment. In addition to those suffering long spells of unemployment, many people are chronically unemployed. Although their unemployment spells may be broken by brief periods of employment or being out of the labor force, workers who are **chronically unemployed** are unemployed a large part of the time. Long spells of unemployment and chronic unemployment can't be attributed primarily to the matching process. People in these situations don't seem to search for work very intensively and don't generally find stable employment. The long-term and chronic unemployment that exists even when the economy is not in a recession is called **structural unemployment**.

Structural unemployment occurs for two primary reasons. First, workers who are unskilled or low-skilled often are unable to obtain desirable, long-term jobs. The jobs available to them typically offer relatively low wages and little chance for training or advancement. Most directly related to the issue of structural unemployment is the fact that jobs held by workers with low-skills often don't last long. After a few months the job may end, or the worker may quit or be fired, thus entering another spell of unemployment. Some workers with low skill levels eventually get enough training or experience to obtain more secure, long-term jobs. Because of factors such as inadequate education, discrimination, and language barriers, however, some workers who are unskilled never make the transition to long-term employment and remain chronically unemployed.

The second source of structural unemployment is the reallocation of labor from industries that are shrinking, or regions that are depressed, to areas that are growing. When industries find that their products are no longer in demand (for example, home builders from 2008 to 2012 following the housing crisis) or that they are no longer competitive (for example, U.S. producers of color television sets that lost much of the market to producers in Asia), workers in these industries lose their jobs. At the same time, some industries will be growing (for example, health care providers and computer software developers). To prevent unemployment from rising requires that workers who lose jobs in declining industries be matched somehow with jobs in growing industries. This matching may involve a long period of unemployment, especially if workers need to relocate or be trained for a new job.

The Natural Rate of Unemployment. Because of the combination of frictional and structural unemployment, an economy's unemployment rate is never zero, even when the economy is at its full-employment level. The rate of unemployment that prevails when output and employment are at their full-employment levels is called the **natural rate of unemployment**, $\bar{u}$. The natural rate of unemployment reflects unemployment owing to frictional and structural causes. Although there is no single official measure of the natural rate of unemployment, many economists believe that the natural rate was about 4% or 5% during the 1950s and increased gradually to about 6% in the 1980s. As of 2021, Federal Reserve policymakers estimated the natural rate to be close to 4.0%. In Chapter 12 we discuss the reasons for the variations in the natural rate.

As output fluctuates around its full-employment level, the unemployment rate fluctuates around the natural rate. The difference between the actual unemployment rate and the natural rate of unemployment is called **cyclical unemployment**.

Specifically, cyclical unemployment $= u - \bar{u}$, where u is the actual unemployment rate and $\bar{u}$ is the natural rate. Cyclical unemployment is positive whenever the economy's output and employment are below full-employment levels; it is negative when output and employment exceed full-employment levels.

In Touch with Data and Research

Alternative Measures of the Unemployment Rate

The official unemployment rate is the fraction of the civilian labor force that is unemployed. But there are reasonable alternative definitions of who should be counted as unemployed or in the labor force. So, the Bureau of Labor Statistics compiles other measures of the unemployment rate that reflect some of these factors. The alternative measures are as follows:

U-1: Only counts people as unemployed if they have been unemployed 15 weeks or more

U-2: Only counts people as unemployed if they are job losers or persons who completed temporary jobs, so it does not count people who have quit their jobs

U-3: The official unemployment rate; counts people as unemployed if they do not have a job and are looking for a job

U-4: Adds discouraged workers to both the number of unemployed and the civilian labor force; discouraged workers are those who say they are not looking for work because they do not think they can find a job

U-5: Adds both discouraged workers and marginally attached workers to both the number of unemployed and the civilian labor force; marginally attached workers are those who say they are not looking for work but indicate that they want and are available for a job and have looked for work sometime in the past 12 months

U-6: Similar to U-5, but adds persons who are employed part time for economic reasons to the number of unemployed; persons employed part time for economic reasons are those who want and are available for full-time work but have had to settle for a part-time schedule

The U-1 measure shows the lowest unemployment rate, and each successive measure shows a higher unemployment rate at each point in time. Although these measures generally move together over time, sometimes the differences in the measures illuminate an aspect of labor-market conditions that may be important for economists and policymakers. For example, Figure 3.14 shows monthly U-3 and U-6 since 1994, and also shows the average values of U-3 and U-6 from January 1994 to December 2007, when the recession of 2007–2009 began. You can see that both U-3 and U-6 increased sharply following the onset of this recession and later fell below their respective average values that prevailed before the recession. But the U-6 measure took nearly two years longer to return to its pre-recession average level than the U-3 measure did, showing that the U-3 measure understated the weakness in the labor market. Following the most recent recession in 2020, both the U-3 and the U-6 measures returned to their pre-recession levels more quickly than in the 2007–2009 recession.

FIGURE 3.14

Alternative Measures of Unemployment, 1994–2021

Following the recession of 2007 to 2009, the various measures of the unemployment rate declined. But the U-6 measure remained elevated for several years after the U-3 measure had returned to its long-run average level.

Sources: Bureau of Labor Statistics, downloaded from FRED database, *fred.stlouisfed.org*; U-3: FRED series *UNRATE*; U-6 FRED series *U6RATE*.

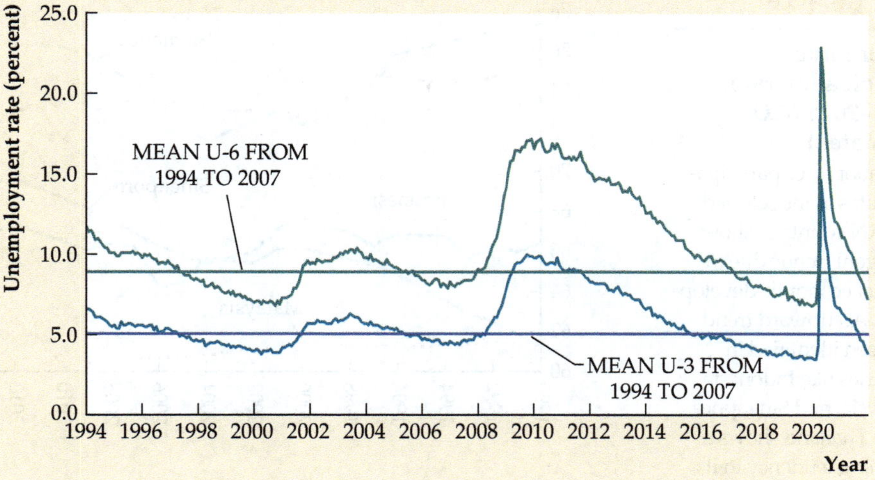

Application

Recent Trends in Labor Supply

The labor force participation rate (LFPR) in the ASEAN countries shows divergent trajectories, which is plausible given the distinctive economic development of each nation. In general, the trend has been attributed to female participation in the labor force; that is, the ratio of women who are paid for work or searching for it. Based on Figure 3.15, Malaysia recorded an overall labor force participation rate of between 63% and 67%, while Vietnam recorded a higher rate of between 71% and 77%.[28]

Figure 3.15 shows a descending trend in Malaysia's LFPR until 2010. One of the reasons for the declining trend is the inclination of the younger population to pursue higher education along with higher potential income. More recent research, however, reveals a more disturbing reason for the fall in the LFPR among the youth. A high unemployment rate in this demographic, 15.6% at its peak, has been attributed to structural problems such as deficiencies in education quality, mismatch of skills, and low-quality jobs.[29] However, after 2010, the trend levelled off and steadily soared to a participation rate of 65% in 2021. This is attributed to female LFPR, which has risen from about 43% in 2010 to 51.74% in 2019, suggesting that women choose to stay in the labor force longer due to more flexible working arrangements and greater job opportunities.

Vietnam offers a unique reason for its relatively high LFPR compared to its counterparts in the region. With a recorded average of 78% female labor force participation since 1990, there is considerable evidence that the Vietnam War was

[28]Source: data/worldbank.org/indicator

[29]See Lee Hwok Aun, "Unemployment among Malaysia's Youth: Structural Trends and Current Challenges," *ISEAS Perspective*, no. 65, June 18, 2020.

(continued)

FIGURE 3.15

Labor force participation rate, 1990–2021 (ILO estimates)

The labor force participation rates in the selected ASEAN countries show divergent trends due to distinct economic development. An upward trend has been identified in countries like Indonesia, Malaysia, and Singapore, while Thailand shows a declining tendency in its labor supply.

Source: https://data.worldbank.org/indicator/SL.TLF.CACT.ZS?locations=MY-SG-VN-TH-ID

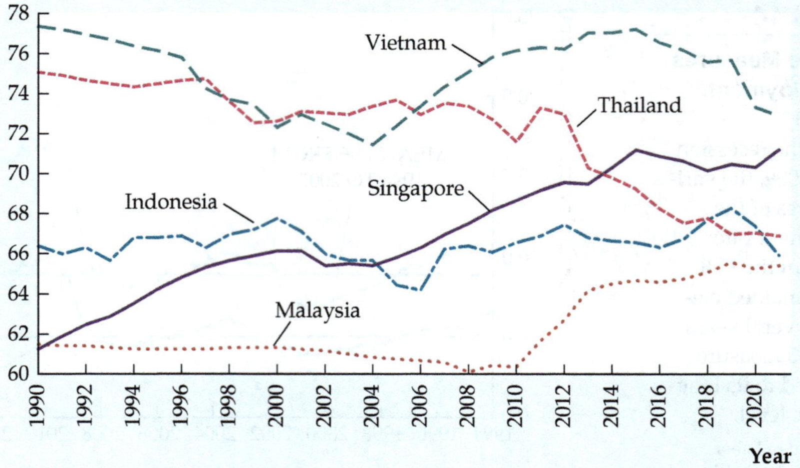

the leading cause for this trend.[30] The rise in female LFPR has been attributed to the effects of "missing men" because of war-related mobilization and casualties. Vietnam's female labor participation has received a further boost from government policy promoting more gender equality in education.

While female participation in the labor force is key to explaining the rising trend in the overall LFPR for Malaysia and Vietnam, Thailand observed a steady decline, as only about 67% of its population participated in the labor market. This is attributed to its aging population; Thailand has the second-highest percentage of elderly people among the ASEAN countries, trailing only behind Singapore. The proportion of elderly people in Thailand was reported to have increased from 5.5% in 1980 to 13% in 2020. Research found that older Thai people with pensions and poor health conditions are less likely to participate in the labor force.[31] Singapore, on the other hand, has extended their re-employment age from 65 to 67, emphasizing the value of learning from, and growing with, its aging workforce.[32]

[30]Merle Kreibaum and Stephan Klasen, "Missing Men: Differential Effects of War and Socialism on Female Labour Force Participation in Vietnam," *Courant Research Centre: Poverty, Equity and Growth—Discussion Papers*, no. 181, 2015, Courant Research Centre PEG.

[31]The World Bank Group, "Aging and the Labor Market in Thailand," June 22, 2021, *https://www.worldbank.org/en/country/thailand/publication/aging-and-the-labor-market-in-thailand.*

[32]Ministry of Finance, Singapore, "The Big Shift from Young to Ageing Workforce," July 23, 2016, *https://www.mof.gov.sg/news-publications/media-articles/The-Big-Shift-from-Young-to-Ageing-Workforce.*

3.6 Relating Output and Unemployment: Okun's Law

Explain the significance of Okun's law.

Earlier in this chapter we said that many short-run output fluctuations result from changes in employment. When employment falls and unemployment rises, the reduction in the number of people working leads to a decline in the quantity of goods and services produced. We can use the concept of cyclical unemployment to provide a more precise link between the state of the labor market and aggregate output.

The quantitative impact on aggregate output of a change in the unemployment rate is described by Okun's law, a rule of thumb (rather than a "law") first stated by Arthur Okun, chairman of the Council of Economic Advisers in the 1960s during the Johnson administration. According to **Okun's law**, the gap between an economy's full-employment output and its actual level of output increases by 2 percentage points for each percentage point the unemployment rate increases.[33, 34] We express Okun's law algebraically as

$$\frac{\bar{Y} - Y}{\bar{Y}} = 2(u - \bar{u}). \tag{3.5}$$

The left side of Eq. (3.5) equals the amount by which actual output, Y, falls short of full-employment output, $\bar{Y}$, expressed as a percentage of $\bar{Y}$. Thus Eq. (3.5) says that the percentage gap between potential and actual output equals 2 times the cyclical unemployment rate.

Let's apply Okun's law by supposing that the natural rate of unemployment is 4% and that the full-employment level of output is \$20,000 billion. If the actual unemployment rate is 5%, or 1 percentage point above the natural rate, cyclical unemployment, $u - \bar{u}$, equals 1%. If cyclical unemployment is 1%, Okun's law predicts that actual output, Y, will be 2% (2 times 1%) lower than full-employment output, $\bar{Y}$. Because $\bar{Y}$ equals \$20,000 billion, Okun's law says that actual output will be \$400 billion below the full-employment level (2% times \$20,000 billion).

You may wonder why a 1 percentage point increase in the unemployment rate, which reduces employment by about 1%, leads (according to Okun's law) to a drop in output that is about twice as large in percentage terms. The reason is that when cyclical unemployment increases, other factors that determine output—the number of people in the labor force, the number of hours each worker works per week, the average productivity of labor—also fall, which magnifies the effect of the increase in unemployment. Numerical Problem 10 at the end of this chapter illustrates this point.

Sometimes we express Okun's law in a slightly different form:

$$\frac{\Delta Y}{Y} = 3 - 2\Delta u, \tag{3.6}$$

where $\Delta Y/Y$ is the percentage growth rate of output and Δu is the change in the actual unemployment rate from one year to the next. Equation (3.6) says that when unemployment is rising ($\Delta u > 0$), actual output, Y, is growing more slowly than 3% per year, which is the average growth rate of full-employment output in the United States. Equation (3.6), which requires the assumption that the natural rate of unemployment is constant, is called the growth rate form of Okun's law. See Appendix 3.A at the end of this chapter for a derivation of Eq. (3.6).

Figure 3.16 illustrates the growth rate form of Okun's law. The figure shows the relation between the annual change in the unemployment rate (measured on the horizontal axis) and the annual growth rate of U.S. output (measured on the vertical axis) for the period 1951–2021. Line OL in this figure represents Okun's law. Its slope is -2, indicating that a 1 percentage point increase in the unemployment rate is

---

[33]When the unemployment rate increases, for example, from 6% to 9%, we say that it increases by 3 percentage points (9%–6%) or that it increases by 50% (3% is 50% of 6%).

[34]In Okun's original work ("Potential GNP: Its Measurement and Significance," reprinted in Arthur Okun, *The Political Economy of Prosperity*, Washington, DC: Brookings Institution, 1970, pp. 132–145), the "Okun's law coefficient" was about 3 rather than 2, so each percentage point of cyclical unemployment was associated with a difference between actual output and full-employment output of 3 percentage points. Current estimates put the Okun's law coefficient closer to 2.

FIGURE 3.16

Okun's law in the United States: 1951–2021

This figure shows the relation between the growth rate of real GDP (vertical axis) and the change in the unemployment rate (horizontal axis). Line OL is a graph of Okun's law Eq. (3.6). The slope of this line is −2, indicating that a 1 percentage point change in the unemployment rate changes the growth rate of output by 2 percentage points in the opposite direction. The horizontal line at 3% shows the approximate average growth rate of full-employment output, equaling the rate at which actual output would grow if there were no change in the unemployment rate ($\Delta u = 0$).

Sources: Real GDP growth rate from Bureau of Economic Analysis, downloaded from the Federal Reserve Bank of St. Louis FRED database, *fred.stlouisfed.org/series/GDPCA*. Civilian unemployment rate for all civilian workers from Bureau of Labor Statistics, downloaded from FRED database, series *UNRATE*.

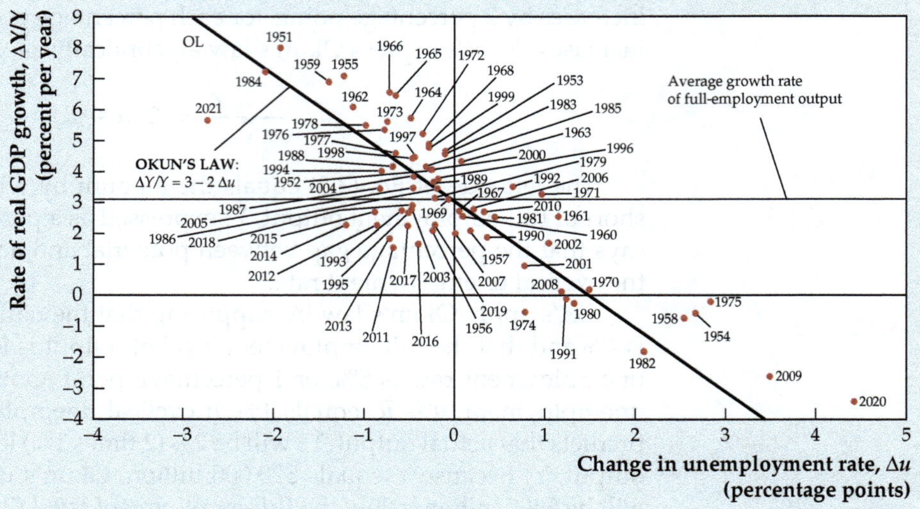

associated with a 2% drop in output. The vertical line rising from 0 on the horizontal axis intersects OL at 3%. This intercept indicates that, when no change occurs in the unemployment rate, the growth rate of actual output is 3%, or the approximate average growth rate of full-employment output in the United States.

In Fig. 3.16, the points representing every year from 2011 to 2019 all lie below the straight line showing Okun's law. The unemployment rate fell and real GDP grew in all of these years, but the growth in output in each year was smaller than would be expected from Okun's law and the actual unemployment rate. Put differently, the economy's recovery after the financial crisis of 2008 looked stronger when measured by the fall in the unemployment rate than when measured by GDP growth. Because of this, some economists doubt that Okun's law is useful in modern times.

CHAPTER SUMMARY

1. The production function tells us the amount of output that can be produced with any given quantities of capital and labor. It can be graphed as a relationship between output and capital, holding labor fixed, or as a relationship between output and labor, holding capital fixed. In either case, the production function slopes upward, implying that greater use of capital or labor leads to more output. A shift in the production function, which indicates a change in the amount of output that can be produced with given amounts of capital and labor, is called a supply shock.
2. The extra output that can be produced when the capital stock is increased by one unit, with labor held constant, is called the marginal product of capital (MPK). In a graph of the production function relating output to capital, the MPK can be measured as the slope of the production function. The MPK falls as the capital stock increases, reflecting the diminishing marginal productivity of capital. Similarly, the marginal product of labor (MPN) is the extra output that can be produced when labor increases by one unit, with capital held constant. The MPN—which can be measured as the slope of the production function relating output to labor—falls as employment rises, indicating that labor also has diminishing marginal productivity.
3. To maximize profits, firms demand labor to the point that the marginal revenue product of labor ($MRPN$) equals the nominal wage, W; or, equivalently, to the point that the MPN equals the real wage, w.
4. The labor demand curve is identical to the MPN curve. Because an increase in the real wage causes firms to demand less labor, the labor demand curve slopes downward. Factors that increase the amount of labor demanded at any real wage, such as a beneficial supply shock or an increase in the capital stock, shift the labor demand curve to the right. Aggregate labor demand is the sum of the labor demands of firms in the economy.
5. An individual's decision about how much labor to supply reflects a comparison of the benefit and cost of working an additional hour. The benefit of working an additional hour is the additional real income earned, which can be used to increase consumption. The cost of working an extra hour is the loss of an hour's leisure. An individual's happiness, or utility, is maximized by supplying labor to the point where the cost of working an extra hour (the utility lost because of reduced leisure) equals the benefit (the utility gained because of increased income).
6. An increase in the real wage has competing substitution and income effects on the amount of labor supplied. The substitution effect of a higher real wage increases the amount of labor supplied, as the worker responds to the increased reward for working. The income effect reduces the amount of labor supplied, as the higher real wage makes the worker wealthier and thus able to afford a greater amount of leisure. The longer an increase in the real wage is expected to last, the stronger the income effect is. Thus a temporary increase in the real wage will increase the amount of labor supplied. A permanent increase in the real wage will increase the amount of labor supplied by a smaller amount than a temporary increase in the real wage of the same size, however, and may even lead to a decrease in the amount of labor supplied.
7. The labor supply curve relates the amount of labor supplied to the current real wage. The labor supply curve slopes upward, indicating that an increase in the current real wage—with other factors, including the expected future real wage, held fixed—raises the amount of labor supplied. Factors that decrease the quantity of labor supplied at the current real wage, and thus shift the labor supply curve to the left, include an increase in wealth and an increase in the expected future real wage. Aggregate labor supply, which is the sum of labor supplies of the individuals in the economy, is also influenced by changes in the adult population and social or legal factors that affect the number of people participating in the labor market.
8. The classical supply–demand model of the labor market is based on the assumption that the real wage adjusts relatively quickly to equalize the quantities of labor demanded and supplied. The equilibrium level of employment, which arises when wages and prices in the economy have fully adjusted, is called the *full-employment level of employment.* Fluctuations in employment and the real wage result from factors that shift the labor supply curve and/or the labor demand curve.
9. Full-employment output, or potential output, is the amount of output produced when employment is at its full-employment level. Increases in the full-employment level of employment or beneficial supply shocks increase the full-employment level of output.
10. Adults without jobs are classified as unemployed if they looked for work during the preceding four weeks; they are classified as not in the labor force if they haven't been looking for work. The labor force consists of all employed workers plus all unemployed workers. The unemployment rate is the fraction of the labor force that is unemployed.

11. Frictional unemployment reflects the time required for potential workers to find suitable jobs and for firms with vacancies to find suitable workers. Structural unemployment—long-term and chronic unemployment that exists even when the economy isn't in recession—occurs because some workers don't have the skills needed to obtain long-term employment, or because of delays as workers relocate from economically depressed areas to those that are growing. Frictional and structural unemployment together account for the natural rate of unemployment, which is the unemployment rate that exists when employment is at its full-employment level. Cyclical unemployment is the excess of the actual unemployment rate over the natural rate of unemployment.

12. According to Okun's law, a 1 percentage point increase in the rate of cyclical unemployment reduces output by 2%.

KEY DIAGRAM 1

The production function

The production function indicates how much output an economy or a firm can produce with any given quantities of capital and labor.

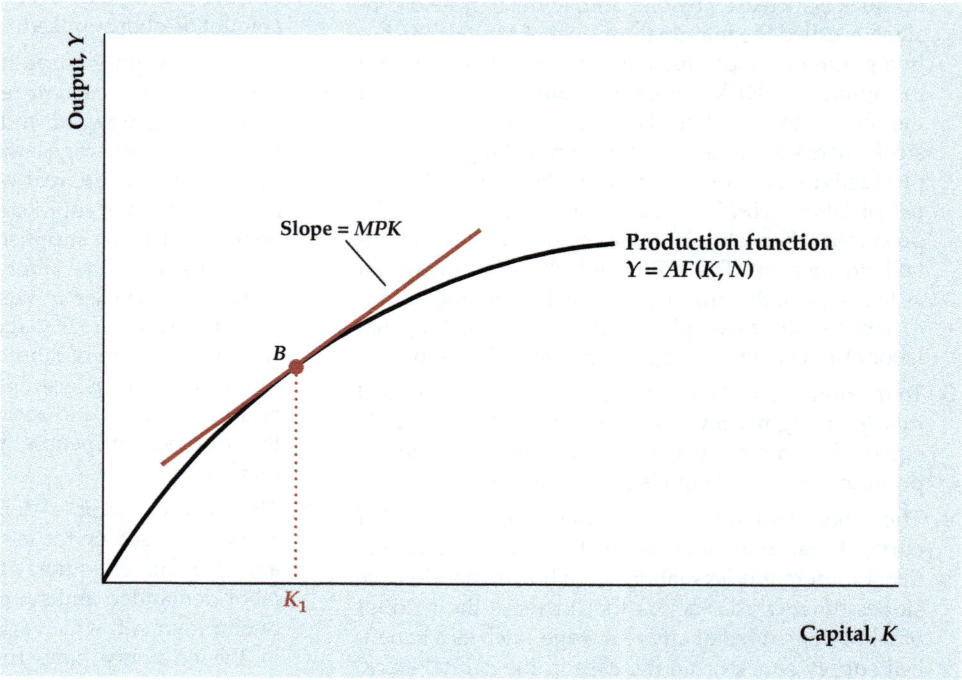

Diagram Elements

- The production function graphed here has the amount of output produced, Y, on the vertical axis and the quantity of capital used, K, on the horizontal axis, with labor, N, held constant. It can also be drawn as a relationship between output and labor, with capital held constant. The production function relating output to labor looks like the graph shown here.
- The equation for the production function is $Y = AF(K, N)$, where A (total factor productivity, or simply productivity) measures how effectively the economy uses capital and labor.

Analysis

- The production function slopes upward, reflecting the fact that an increase in the quantity of capital will allow more output to be produced.
- The production function becomes flatter from left to right, implying that the larger the capital stock already is, the less extra output is gained by adding another unit of capital. The fact that extra capital becomes less productive as the capital stock grows is called diminishing marginal productivity of capital.
- With labor held constant, if an increase in capital of ΔK leads to an increase in output of ΔY, then

$\Delta Y/\Delta K$ is called the marginal product of capital, or *MPK*. The *MPK* is measured graphically by the slope of the line tangent to the production function. For example, in the diagram the *MPK* when the capital stock is K_1 equals the slope of the line tangent to the production function at point *B*.

Factors That Shift the Curve

- Any change that allows more output to be produced for given quantities of capital and labor—a beneficial supply shock—shifts the production function upward. Examples of beneficial supply shocks include new inventions and improved management techniques.
- Any change that reduces the amount of output that can be produced for given quantities of capital and labor—an adverse supply shock—shifts the production function downward. Examples of adverse supply shocks include bad weather and the depletion of natural resources.

▶ KEY DIAGRAM 2

The labor market
An economy's level of employment and the real wage are determined in the labor market.

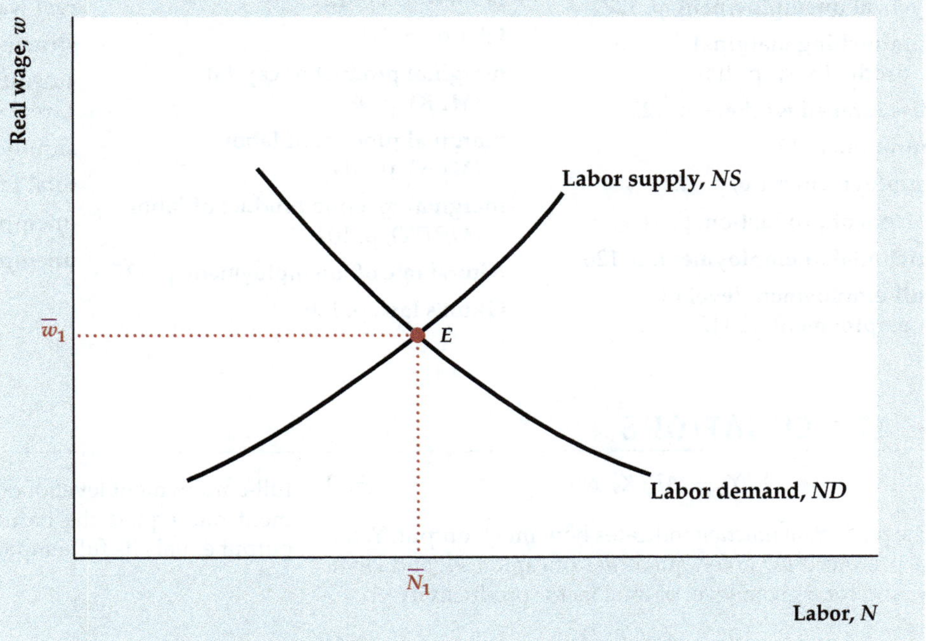

Diagram Elements

- The current real wage, w, is on the vertical axis, and the level of employment, N, is on the horizontal axis. The variable N may also represent alternative measures of labor, such as total hours worked.
- The labor demand curve, *ND*, shows the amount of labor that firms want to employ at each current real wage. The labor demand curve slopes downward because firms find hiring more labor profitable when the real wage falls. The labor demand curve for an individual firm is the same as the *MPN* curve, which shows the marginal product of labor at each level of employment.
- The labor supply curve, *NS*, shows the amount of labor offered by workers at each current real wage. The labor supply curve slopes upward because an increase in the current real wage, with other factors held constant, increases the amount of labor supplied.

Analysis

- Equilibrium in the labor market occurs when the quantity of labor demanded equals the quantity of labor supplied. In the figure, equilibrium employment is $\bar{N}_1$ and the equilibrium real wage is $\bar{w}_1$. The equilibrium level of employment, which occurs after wages and prices have fully adjusted, is called the *full-employment level of employment*.

Factors That Shift Curves

- Any factor that increases the amount of labor demanded at a given current real wage shifts the labor demand curve to the right. Such factors include an increase in productivity that increases the marginal product of labor and an increase in the capital stock. See Summary table 3.
- Any factor that increases the amount of labor supplied at a given current real wage shifts the labor supply curve to the right. Such factors include a decline in wealth, a drop in the expected future real wage, an increase in the adult population, and an increase in labor force participation. See Summary table 4.

KEY TERMS

aggregate demand for labor, p. 110
aggregate supply of labor, p. 110
chronically unemployed, p. 127
cyclical unemployment, p. 127
diminishing marginal productivity, p. 100
discouraged workers, p. 123
duration, p. 123
employment ratio, p. 122
factors of production, p. 94
frictional unemployment, p. 126
full-employment level of employment, p. 117
full-employment output, p. 119
income effect of a higher real wage, p. 112
labor force, p. 122
leisure, p. 111
marginal product of capital (*MPK*), p. 98
marginal product of labor (*MPN*), p. 100
marginal revenue product of labor (*MRPN*), p. 104
natural rate of unemployment, p. 127
Okun's law, p. 130
participation rate, p. 122
production function, p. 94
productivity, p. 93
real wage, p. 105
structural unemployment, p. 127
substitution effect of a higher real wage, p. 112
supply shock, p. 101
total factor productivity, p. 95
unemployment rate, p. 122
unemployment spell, p. 123

KEY EQUATIONS

$$Y = AF(K, N) \quad (3.1)$$

The *production function* indicates how much output, Y, can be produced for given quantities of capital, K, and labor, N, and for a given level of total factor productivity, A.

$$\bar{Y} = AF(K, \bar{N}) \quad (3.4)$$

Full-employment output, $\bar{Y}$, is the quantity of output supplied by firms when wages and prices have fully adjusted, and employment equals its equilibrium value, $\bar{N}$.

$$\frac{\bar{Y} - Y}{\bar{Y}} = 2(u - \bar{u}) \quad (3.5)$$

Okun's law states that a 1 percentage point increase in the unemployment rate, u, reduces output, Y, by 2% of the full-employment level of output, $\bar{Y}$. When the unemployment rate equals the natural rate of unemployment, $\bar{u}$, output equals its full-employment level.

$$\frac{\Delta Y}{Y} = 3 - 2\Delta u \quad (3.6)$$

The growth rate form of Okun's law relates the growth rate of output, $\Delta Y/Y$, to the average growth rate of full-employment output in the United States, 3%, and the change in the unemployment rate, Δu. According to Eq. (3.6), output grows more slowly than full-employment output when unemployment is rising and more quickly than full-employment output when unemployment is falling. This version of Okun's law is based on the assumption that the natural rate of unemployment is constant.

REVIEW QUESTIONS

1. What is a production function? What are some factors that can cause a nation's production function to shift over time? What do you have to know besides an economy's production function to know how much output the economy can produce?
2. The production function slopes upward, but its slope declines from left to right. Give an economic interpretation of each of these properties of the production function.
3. Define *marginal product of capital,* or *MPK.* How can the *MPK* be shown graphically?
4. Explain why the profit-maximizing level of employment for a firm occurs when the marginal revenue product of labor equals the nominal wage. How can this profit-maximizing condition be expressed in real terms?
5. What is the *MPN* curve? How is the *MPN* curve related to the production function? How is it related to labor demand?
6. Use the concepts of income effect and substitution effect to explain why a temporary increase in the real wage increases the amount of labor supplied, but a permanent increase in the real wage may decrease the quantity of labor supplied.
7. What two variables are related by the aggregate labor supply curve? What are some factors that cause the aggregate labor supply curve to shift?
8. Define *full-employment output.* How is full-employment output affected by an increase in the participation rate? By a beneficial supply shock?
9. Why is the classical model of the labor market discussed in this chapter not very useful for studying unemployment?
10. Define the following: *labor force, unemployment rate, participation rate,* and *employment ratio.*
11. Define *unemployment spell* and *duration.* What are the two seemingly contradictory facts about unemployment spells? Why are the two facts not actually contradictory?
12. What is frictional unemployment? Why is a certain amount of frictional unemployment probably necessary in a well-functioning economy?
13. What is structural unemployment? What are the two principal sources of structural unemployment?
14. Define the *natural rate of unemployment* and *cyclical unemployment.* What does negative cyclical unemployment mean?
15. What is Okun's law? If the unemployment rate increases by 2 percentage points between this year and next year, by how much will output change during the same period? Assume that the natural unemployment rate and full-employment output are constant. Use the form of Okun's law in Eq. (3.6).

NUMERICAL PROBLEMS

1. The following data give real GDP, Y, capital, *K*, and labor, *N*, for the U.S. economy in various years.

Year	Y	K	N
1960	3262	3821	65
1970	4954	5767	78
1980	6764	8293	99
1990	9371	11,298	117
2000	13,138	15,887	134
2010	15,649	19,373	140
2020	18,385	23,539	158

Units and sources are the same as in Table 3.1. Assume that the production function is $Y = AK^{0.3}N^{0.7}$.

a. By what percentage did U.S. total factor productivity grow in each decade?

b. What happened to the marginal product of labor between 1960 and 2020? Calculate the marginal product numerically as the extra output gained by adding 1 million workers in each of the two years. (The data for employment, *N*, are measured in millions of workers, so an increase of 1 million workers is an increase of 1.0.)

2. Suppose the production function is $Y = AK^{0.3}N^{0.7}$ and that in 2000, $K = 1000$, $N = 100$, and $Y = 199.5$. In 2010, capital, labor, and output have doubled, so $K = 2000$, $N = 200$, and $Y = 399$.

a. By what percentage did productivity grow from 2000 to 2010?

b. If output had risen to 798 instead of 399 and capital and labor had doubled, by what percentage would productivity have grown from 2000 to 2010?

3. Acme Widget, Inc. has the following production function.

Number of Workers	Number of Widgets Produced
0	0
1	8
2	15
3	21
4	26
5	30
6	33

a. Find the *MPN* for each level of employment.

b. Acme can get $5 for each widget it produces. How many workers will it hire if the nominal wage is $38? If it is $27? If it is $22?

c. Graph the relationship between Acme's labor demand and the nominal wage. How does this graph differ from a labor demand curve? Graph Acme's labor demand curve.

d. With the nominal wage fixed at $38, the price of widgets doubles from $5 each to $10 each. What happens to Acme's labor demand and production?

e. With the nominal wage fixed at $38 and the price of widgets fixed at $5, the introduction of a new automatic widget maker doubles the number of widgets that the same number of workers can produce. What happens to labor demand and production?

f. What is the relationship between your answers to part (*d*) and part (*e*)? Explain.

4. The marginal product of labor (measured in units of output) for a certain firm is

$$MPN = A(100 - N),$$

where A measures productivity and N is the number of labor hours used in production. The price of output is $2.00 per unit.

a. If $A = 1.0$, what will be the demand for labor if the nominal wage is $10? If it is $20? Graph the demand curve for labor. What is the equilibrium real wage if the supply of labor is fixed at 95?

b. Repeat part (*a*) for $A = 2.0$.

5. Consider an economy in which the marginal product of labor *MPN* is $MPN = 309 - 2N$, where N is the amount of labor used. The amount of labor supplied, *NS*, is given by $NS = 22 + 12w + 2T$, where w is the real wage and T is a lump-sum tax levied on individuals.

a. Use the concepts of income effect and substitution effect to explain why an increase in lump-sum taxes will increase the amount of labor supplied.

b. Suppose that $T = 35$. What are the equilibrium values of employment and the real wage?

c. With T remaining equal to 35, the government passes minimum-wage legislation that requires firms to pay a real wage greater than or equal to 7. What are the resulting values of employment and the real wage?

6. Suppose that the production function is $Y = 9K^{0.5}N^{0.5}$. With this production function, the marginal product of labor is $MPN = 4.5K^{0.5}N^{-0.5}$. The capital stock is $K = 25$. The labor supply curve is $NS = 100[(1 - t)w]^2$, where w is the real wage rate, t is the tax rate on labor income, and hence $(1 - t)w$ is the after-tax real wage rate.

a. Assume that the tax rate on labor income, t, equals zero. Find the equation of the labor demand curve. Calculate the equilibrium levels of the real wage and employment, the level of full-employment output, and the total after-tax wage income of workers.

b. Repeat part (*a*) under the assumption that the tax rate on labor income, t, equals 0.6.

c. Suppose that a minimum wage of $w = 2$ is imposed. If the tax rate on labor income, t, equals zero, what are the resulting values of employment and the real wage? Does the introduction of the minimum wage increase the total income of workers, taken as a group?

7. Consider an economy with 500 people in the labor force. At the beginning of every month, 5 people lose their jobs and remain unemployed for exactly one month; one month later, they find new jobs and become employed. In addition, on January 1 of each year, 20 people lose their jobs and remain unemployed for six months before finding new jobs. Finally, on July 1 of each year, 20 people lose their jobs and remain unemployed for six months before finding new jobs.

a. What is the unemployment rate in this economy in a typical month?

b. What fraction of unemployment spells last for one month? What fraction last for six months?

c. What is the average duration of a completed spell of unemployment?

d. On any particular date, what fraction of the unemployed are suffering a long spell (six months) of unemployment?

8. Suppose the economy's production function is $Y = AK^{0.3}N^{0.7}$ and that $K = 200$, $N = 2000$, and $A = 1$. Calculate the marginal products of labor and capital.

9. You are given the following data on the unemployment rate and output in France.

Year	1	2	3	4
Unemployment rate	8%	7%	9%	10%
Output	39,000	41,500	40,600	42,000

a. Assume that the natural rate of unemployment is 8% and that $(\bar{Y} - Y)/\bar{Y} = 2(u - \bar{u})$. Find the full employment level of output in each year

b. Calculate the growth rate of full-employment output in years 2, 3, and 4 in two different ways. First, calculate the growth rates by using the values for full-employment output that you found in part (*a*). Then calculate the growth rate of full-employment output by using only the change in the unemployment rate, the growth rate of output, and the growth rate version of Okun's law, $\Delta Y/Y = \Delta\bar{Y}/\bar{Y} - 2\Delta u$, which is similar to Eq. (3.6)—except where $\Delta\bar{Y}/\bar{Y} = 3$ for the United States in Eq. (3.6), for this economy, $\Delta\bar{Y}/\bar{Y}$ could differ from 3. Compare your answers from the two sets of calculations.

10. Consider an economy that initially has a labor force of 2000 workers. Of these workers, 1900 are employed and each works 40 hours per week. Ten units of output are produced by each hour of labor.

a. What is the total number of hours worked per week in the economy? What is the total output per week in the economy? What is the unemployment rate?

b. The economy enters a recession. Employment falls by 4%, and the number of hours per week worked by each employed worker falls by 2.5%. In addition, 0.2% of the labor force becomes discouraged at the prospect of finding a job and leaves the labor force. Finally, suppose that whenever total hours fall by 1%, total output falls by 1.4%.

After the recession begins, what is the size of the labor force? How many workers are unemployed and what is the unemployment rate? What is the total output per week in the economy?

By what percentage has total output fallen relative to the initial situation? What is the value of the Okun's law coefficient relating the loss of output to the increase in the unemployment rate?

ANALYTICAL PROBLEMS

1. *a.* A technological breakthrough raises a country's total factor productivity A by 10%. Show how this change affects the graphs of both the production function relating output to capital and the production function relating output to labor.

b. Show that a 10% increase in A also increases the MPK and the MPN by 10% at any level of capital and labor. (*Hint:* What happens to ΔY for any increase in capital, ΔK, or for any increase in labor, ΔN?)

c. Can a beneficial supply shock leave the MPK and MPN unaffected? Show your answer graphically.

2. How would each of the following affect the current level of full-employment output? Explain.

a. A large number of immigrants enter the country.

b. Energy supplies become depleted.

c. New teaching techniques improve the educational performance of high school seniors.

d. A new law mandates the shutdown of some unsafe forms of capital.

3. During the 1980s and 1990s the average rate of unemployment in Europe was high. Some economists claimed that this rate was in part the result of "real-wage rigidity," a situation in which unions kept real wages above their market-clearing levels.

a. Accepting for the sake of argument that real wages were too high in Europe in the 1980s and 1990s, show how this situation would lead to unemployment (a situation where people who would like to work at the going wage cannot find jobs).

b. What is the effect of real-wage rigidity on the output actually supplied by firms, relative to the output they would supply if there were no real-wage rigidity?

4. How would each of the following affect Helena Handbasket's supply of labor?

a. The value of Helena's home triples in an unexpectedly hot real estate market.

b. Originally an unskilled worker, Helena acquires skills that give her access to a higher-paying job. Assume that her preferences about leisure are not affected by the change in jobs.

c. A temporary income tax surcharge raises the percentage of her income that she must pay in taxes, for the current year only. (Taxes are proportional to income in Helena's country.)

5. Suppose that under a new law all businesses must pay a tax equal to 6% of their sales revenue. Assume that this tax is not passed on to consumers. Instead, consumers pay the same prices after the tax is imposed as they did before. What is the effect of this tax on labor demand? If the labor supply curve is unchanged, what will be the effect of the tax on employment and the real wage?

6. Can the unemployment rate and the employment ratio rise during the same month? Can the participation rate fall at the same time that the employment ratio rises? Explain.

7. Self-employed workers in the United States must pay Social Security taxes equal to 12.4% of any income up to $147,000 in 2022. This income level of $147,000 is known as the "cap." Income in excess of the cap is not subject to Social Security tax, so self-employed workers with incomes exceeding $147,000 pay $\$147{,}000 \times 0.124 = \$18{,}228$. Now consider two proposals designed to increase Social Security tax revenue. Proposal A increases the cap to $177,822.60 so that Social Security taxes equal 12.4% of income up to $177,822.60. Proposal B increases the Social Security tax rate to 15%, but leaves the cap unchanged at $147,000. For people with income that always exceeds the cap, the amount of Social Security tax is the same under Proposal A ($\$177{,}822.60 \times 0.124 = \$22{,}050$) as under Proposal B ($\$147{,}000 \times 0.15 = \$22{,}050$). There are no planned changes in future Social Security benefits anticipated by current workers.

   a. Sally is self-employed and earns $200,000 per year. What are the effects of Proposal A and Proposal B on Sally's labor supply? Under which proposal would she supply a greater amount of labor? Explain your answers using the concepts of income effect and substitution effect.

   b. Fred is self-employed and earns $50,000 per year. What are the effects of Proposal A and Proposal B on Fred's labor supply? Under which proposal would he supply a greater amount of labor? Explain your answers using the concepts of income effect and substitution effect.

WORKING WITH MACROECONOMIC DATA

For data to use in these exercises, go to the Federal Reserve Bank of St. Louis FRED database at fred.stlouisfed.org.

1. Calculate and graph the growth rate of total factor productivity since 1960 using FRED series MFPNFBS. (Note that this series is not the same as used in Table 3.1, but is similar.). How would you characterize the movements in productivity since 1960? How do recessions affect the growth rate of productivity? How was productivity affected by the oil shocks of 1973–1975, 1979–1980, 1990, and 2003–2008?

2. Using monthly seasonally adjusted data from 1960 to the present, calculate and graph the total working-age population (called the civilian noninstitutional population), the number of employed workers, the number of unemployed workers, and the number of workers in the labor force.

   At the website of the Bureau of Labor Statistics, *www.bls.gov/cps/cpsatabs.htm*, find seasonally adjusted data since 1960 and graph the labor force participation rate for the overall working-age population aged 20 and older, and graph the labor force participation rates for males aged 20 and older and for females aged 20 and older. What are the major changes in these variables that have occurred since 1960?

3. Plot a graph of quarterly data for real GDP and full-employment GDP from 1970 to the present. (In the FRED database, full-employment GDP is called Real Potential GDP.) Which variable is "smoother"? How would you characterize the volatility of real GDP before 1980 compared with after 1980? From 1950 to 2020, how would you characterize the overall movements in the growth rate of real full-employment GDP?

4. Figure 3.11 shows the relative price of energy. In this exercise, we derive the series plotted in that figure and examine recent data. First, find data on the producer price index for fuels and related products and power, and plot the growth rate in the index from one year earlier. What is the growth rate of energy prices over the most recent 12 months?

   Note, however, that this series represents the inflation rate in energy prices but does not tell you how that inflation rate compares with other producer prices, so you do not know if there is an increase in energy prices relative to overall prices. To remedy that, next go back to the energy price index level (rather than the growth rate). Then find data on overall producer prices and divide the energy price series by the overall producer price series. Now find (and plot) the growth rate of this relative energy price series from one year earlier. What is the growth rate of relative energy prices over the most recent 12 months?

   What do the differences in the two series you have plotted tell you about the relative price of energy? What does the difference in the two values over the most recent 12 months tell you about recent movements of energy prices compared with other producer prices?

Appendix
3.A

The Growth Rate Form of Okun's Law

To derive the growth rate form of Okun's law, Eq. (3.6), we start with the basic form of Okun's law, Eq. (3.5):

$$\frac{\bar{Y} - Y}{\bar{Y}} = 2(u - \bar{u}). \tag{3.5}$$

After multiplying by -1, we rewrite Eq. (3.5) as

$$-1 + \frac{Y}{\bar{Y}} = -2u + 2\bar{u}.$$

We now calculate the change from the previous year to the current year for each side of this equation. Setting the change on the left side equal to the change on the right side, and assuming that $\bar{u}$ is constant (so that $\Delta \bar{u} = 0$), we get

$$\Delta(Y/\bar{Y}) = -2\Delta u. \tag{3.6}$$

Using the formula that states that the growth rate of a ratio is approximately the growth rate of the numerator minus the growth rate of the denominator (Appendix A, Section A.7), we can write $\frac{\Delta(Y/\bar{Y})}{Y/\bar{Y}} = \frac{\Delta Y}{Y} - \frac{\Delta \bar{Y}}{\bar{Y}}$. Since $\frac{Y}{\bar{Y}}$ is approximately equal to one, we can write (approximately)

$$\Delta \frac{Y}{\bar{Y}} = \frac{\Delta Y}{Y} - \frac{\Delta \bar{Y}}{\bar{Y}}. \tag{3.7}$$

Then, since the left-hand side of Eq. (3.7) is the same as the left-hand side of Eq. (3.6), we can equate the right-hand sides of the two equations to get

$$\frac{\Delta Y}{Y} - \frac{\Delta \bar{Y}}{\bar{Y}} = -2\Delta u.$$

In the United States, the average growth rate of full-employment output is 3% per year. Substituting 3% into this equation and rearranging gives the growth rate form of Okun's law, Eq. (3.6).

4

Consumption, Saving, and Investment

Learning Objectives

4.1 Discuss the factors that affect consumption and saving decisions.

4.2 Discuss the factors that affect the investment behavior of firms.

4.3 Explain the factors affecting goods market equilibrium.

In Chapter 3 we focused on some of the factors determining the amount of output produced, or *supplied*, in the economy. In this chapter we consider the factors that underlie the economywide *demand* for goods and services. In other words, we move from examining how much is produced to examining how that production is used.

Recall from Chapter 2 that aggregate demand (spending) in the economy has four components: the demand for consumer goods and services by households (consumption), the demand for new capital goods by firms and new homes by households (investment), government purchases of goods and services, and the net demand for domestic goods by foreigners (net exports). Because the level of government purchases is determined primarily by the political process, macroeconomic analysis usually treats that component of spending as given. For this chapter we also assume that the economy is closed so that net exports are zero (we drop the closed-economy assumption in Chapter 5). That leaves two major components of spending—consumption and investment—to be discussed in this chapter. In Section 4.1 we present the factors that determine how much households choose to consume, and in Section 4.2 we look at the decision by firms about how much to invest.

We have said that this chapter is about the aggregate demand for goods and services. However, we could just as easily say that it is about a seemingly very different (but equally important) topic: the determination of saving and capital formation. Studying the aggregate demand for goods and services is the same as studying the factors that determine saving and capital formation for the following reasons. First, saving is simply what is left after an economic unit (say, a household) decides how much of its income to consume. Thus the decision about how much to consume is the same as the decision about how much to save. Second, investment spending is part of the aggregate demand for goods and services, but it also represents the acquisition of new capital goods by firms. In studying investment spending, we therefore are also looking at the factors that lead an economy to acquire new factories, machines, and housing. In effect, we do two things at once in this chapter:

- We explore the determinants of the aggregate demand for goods, which prepares you for future discussions of topics such as the role of spending fluctuations in business cycles.

- While exploring aggregate demand we also examine the factors affecting saving and capital formation, which prepares you for future discussions of the sources of economic growth and other issues.

In making many economic decisions, including those we consider in this chapter, people must trade off the present against the future. In deciding how much to consume and save, for example, the people in a household must weigh the benefits of enjoying more consumption today against the benefits of putting aside some of its income as saving for the future. Similarly, in deciding how much to invest, a firm's manager must determine how much to spend today so as to increase the firm's productive capacity one, five, or even twenty years from now. In making these trade-offs, households and firms must take into account their expectations about the future of the economy, including expectations about government policy.

In Chapter 3 we asked, What forces act to bring the labor market into equilibrium? We close this chapter by asking the same question for the goods market. The goods market is in equilibrium when the quantity of goods and services that producers want to supply (discussed in Chapter 3) equals the quantity of goods and services demanded by households, firms, and the government (discussed in this chapter). Equivalently, the goods market is in equilibrium when desired saving in the economy equals desired investment. We show that the real interest rate plays a key role in bringing the goods market into equilibrium.

4.1 Consumption and Saving

Discuss the factors that affect consumption and saving decisions.

We begin consideration of the demand for goods and services by discussing the factors that affect consumer spending. Because consumption spending by households is by far the largest component of the demand for goods and services—accounting for more than two-thirds of total spending in the United States—changes in consumers' willingness to spend have major implications for the behavior of the economy.

Besides the sheer size of consumption spending, another reason to study consumption is that the individual's or household's decision about how much to consume is closely linked to another important economic decision, the decision about how much to save. Indeed, for given levels of disposable income, the decision about how much to consume and the decision about how much to save are really the same decision. For example, Evelyn Yamaguchi, a college student with a part-time job that pays $8000 per year after taxes might decide to spend $7400 per year on clothes, food, entertainment, and other consumption. If she does consume this amount, her saving will automatically be $600 ($8000 minus $7400) per year. Equivalently, she might decide to save $600 per year. If she succeeds in saving $600, her consumption automatically is $7400 ($8000 minus $600) per year. Because the decision about how much to consume and the decision about how much to save actually are two sides of the same coin, we analyze them together.

From a macroeconomic perspective, we are interested in the aggregate, or national, levels of consumption and saving. We define the national level of *desired consumption*, C^d, as the aggregate quantity of goods and services that households want to consume, given income and other factors that determine households' economic opportunities. We will analyze desired consumption and its response to various factors, such as income and interest rates, by examining the consumption decisions of individual households. The aggregate level of desired consumption, C^d, is obtained by adding up the desired consumption of all households. Thus any factor that increases the desired consumption of individual households will increase C^d, and any factor that decreases the desired consumption of individual households will decrease C^d.

Just as a household's consumption decision and saving decision are closely linked, a country's desired consumption is closely linked to its desired national saving. Specifically, *desired national saving*, S^d, is the level of national saving that occurs when aggregate consumption is at its desired level.[1] Recall from Chapter 2 (Eq. 2.8) that if net factor payments from abroad *(NFP)* equal zero (as must be true in a closed economy), national saving, S, equals $Y - C - G$, where Y is output, C is consumption, and G is government purchases. Because desired national saving, S^d, is the level of national saving that occurs when consumption equals its desired level, we obtain an expression for desired national saving by substituting desired consumption, C^d, for consumption, C, in the definition of national saving. This substitution yields

$$S^d = Y - C^d - G. \quad \textbf{(4.1)}$$

We can gain insight into the factors that affect consumption and saving at the national level by considering how consumption and saving decisions are made at the individual level. Appendix 4.A provides a more formal analysis of this decision-making process.

The Consumption and Saving Decision of an Individual

Let's consider the case of Prudence, a bookkeeper for the Spectacular Eyeglasses Company. Prudence earns \$60,000 per year after taxes. Hence she could, if she chose, consume \$60,000 worth of goods and services every year. Prudence, however, has two other options.

First, she can save by consuming less than \$60,000 per year. Why should Prudence consume less than her income allows? The reason is that she is thinking about the future. By consuming less than her current income, she will accumulate savings that will allow her, at some time in the future, to consume more than her income. For example, Prudence may expect her income to be very low when she retires; by saving during her working life, she will be able to consume more than her income during retirement. Indeed, the desire to provide for retirement is an important motivation for saving in the real world.

Alternatively, Prudence could consume more than her current income by borrowing or by drawing down previously accumulated savings. If she borrows \$5000 from a bank, for example, she could consume as much as \$65,000 worth of goods and services this year even though her income is only \$60,000. Consuming more than her income is enjoyable for Prudence, but the cost to her is that at some future time, when she must repay the loan, she will have to consume less than her income.

If Prudence consumes less today, she will be able to consume more in the future, and vice versa. In other words, she faces a *trade-off* between current consumption and future consumption. The rate at which Prudence trades off current and future consumption depends on the real interest rate prevailing in the economy. Suppose that Prudence can earn a real interest rate of r per year on her saving and, for simplicity, suppose that if she borrows, she must pay the same real interest rate r on the loan. These assumptions imply that Prudence can trade one unit of

[1]Note that the term *saving* refers to a flow of funds that is the amount not consumed out of income. We use the term *savings* to refer to a stock of funds that represents the accumulated amount of net saving over time.

current (this year's) consumption for $1 + r$ units of future (next year's) consumption. For example, suppose Prudence reduces her consumption today by one dollar, thereby increasing her saving by one dollar. Because she earns a real interest rate of r on her saving, the dollar she saves today will be worth $1 + r$ dollars one year from now.[2] Under the assumption that Prudence uses the extra $1 + r$ dollars to increase her next year's consumption, she has effectively traded one dollar's worth of consumption today for $1 + r$ dollars of consumption a year from now.

Similarly, Prudence can trade $1 + r$ real dollars of future consumption for one extra dollar of consumption today. She does so by borrowing and spending an extra dollar today. In a year she will have to repay the loan with interest, a total of $1 + r$ dollars. Because she has to repay $1 + r$ dollars next year, her consumption next year will be $1 + r$ dollars less than it would be otherwise. So the "price" to Prudence of one dollar's worth of extra consumption today is $1 + r$ dollars' worth of consumption in the future.

The real interest rate r determines the relative price of current consumption and future consumption. Given this relative price, how should Prudence choose between consuming today and consuming in the future? One extreme possibility would be for her to borrow heavily and consume much more than her income today. The problem with this strategy is that, after repaying her loan, Prudence would be able to consume almost nothing in the future. The opposite, but equally extreme, approach would be for Prudence to save nearly all of her current income. This strategy would allow her to consume a great deal in the future, but at the cost of near-starvation today.

Realistically, most people would choose neither of those extreme strategies but would instead try to avoid sharp fluctuations in consumption. The desire to have a relatively even pattern of consumption over time—avoiding periods of very high or very low consumption—is known as the **consumption-smoothing motive**. Because of her consumption-smoothing motive, Prudence will try to spread her consumption spending more or less evenly over time, rather than bingeing in one period and starving in another.

Next, we will see how the consumption-smoothing motive guides Prudence's behavior when changes occur in some important determinants of her economic well-being, including her current income, her expected future income, and her wealth. As we consider each of these changes, we will hold constant the real interest rate r and, hence, the relative price of current consumption and future consumption. Later, we will discuss what happens if the real interest rate changes.

Effect of Changes in Current Income

Current income is an important factor affecting consumption and saving decisions. To illustrate, suppose that Prudence receives a one-time bonus of \$6000 at work, which increases her current year's income by \$6000. (We ignore income taxes; equivalently, we can assume that the bonus is actually larger than \$6000 but that, after paying her taxes, Prudence finds that her current income has increased by \$6000.) What will she do with this extra income? Prudence could splurge and spend the entire bonus on a trip to Hawaii. If she spends the entire bonus, her current consumption will increase by \$6000, but because she has not increased her saving, her future consumption will be unchanged. Alternatively, she could save the entire bonus, leaving her current

[2] We are assuming that there is zero inflation over the coming year, so that \$1 purchases the same amount of real goods in each period. Alternatively, we could say that since the real interest rate is r, each *real* dollar Prudence saves today will be worth $1 + r$ *real* dollars one year from now.

consumption unchanged but using the bonus plus the interest it earns to increase her consumption in the future. Because of the consumption-smoothing motive, however, Prudence is unlikely to follow either of these extreme strategies. Instead, she will spend part of the bonus (increasing current consumption) and save the rest (enabling her to increase future consumption as well).

The portion of her bonus that Prudence spends will depend on factors such as her willingness to defer gratification and her assessment of her current and future needs. We define Prudence's **marginal propensity to consume (*MPC*)** as the fraction of additional current income that she consumes in the current period. Because Prudence consumes some but not all of her extra income, her *MPC* will be between zero and one. Suppose, for example that Prudence has an *MPC* equal to 0.4, so that she consumes 0.4, or 40%, of an increase in current income. Then, when she receives a \$6000 bonus, Prudence will increase her current consumption by $0.4 \times \$6000 = \$2400$. Because the part of income that is not consumed is saved, her saving also increases by the amount of $\$6000 - \$2400 = \$3600$.

The marginal propensity to consume also applies to *declines* in current income. For example, if Prudence were temporarily laid off from her bookkeeping job so that her current year's income decreased by \$8000, she would reduce both her consumption and her saving. If we assume that her marginal propensity to consume remains 0.4, she would reduce her consumption by $0.4 \times \$8000 = \$3200$, and her saving would therefore have to diminish by $\$8000 - \$3200 = \$4800$.

Aggregate income and consumption reflect the decisions of millions of individuals and households, so that the lessons we learned from thinking about the case of Prudence also apply at the macroeconomic level. Just as an increase in Prudence's income caused her to consume more, we would expect an increase in aggregate output (income) Y to lead to an increase in aggregate desired consumption, C^d, as well. Because marginal propensities to consume are less than 1, however, the increase in C^d will be less than the increase in Y. As not all of the increase in Y is spent, desired national saving S^d will also rise when Y rises.

Effect of Changes in Expected Future Income

Today's consumption decisions may depend not only on current income but also on the income that one expects to earn in the future. For example, an individual who is currently not employed but who has a contract to begin a high-paying job in three months will probably consume more today than a similar individual who is currently not employed but has no prospects for a job in the near future.

To illustrate the effect of changes in expected future income, suppose that instead of receiving the \$6000 bonus during the current year, Prudence learns that she will receive a \$6000 bonus (after taxes) next year. The promise of the bonus is legally binding, and Prudence has no doubt that she will receive the extra income next year. How will this information affect Prudence's consumption and saving in the current year?

Because her current income is unaffected, Prudence could leave her current consumption and saving unchanged, waiting until she actually receives the bonus to increase her consumption. If her decisions are guided by a consumption-smoothing motive, however, she will prefer to use the bonus to increase her current consumption as well as her future consumption. She can increase her current consumption, despite the fact that her current income remains unchanged, by reducing her current saving (she could even "dissave," or have negative current saving, with current consumption exceeding current income, by using her accumulated assets or by borrowing). Suppose, for example, that Prudence decides to consume $1000 more this year. Because her current income is unchanged, Prudence's $1000 increase in current consumption is equivalent to a $1000 reduction in current saving.

The $1000 reduction in current saving will reduce Prudence's available resources in the next year, relative to the situation in which her saving is unchanged, by $\$1000 \times (1 + r)$. For example, if the real interest rate is 0.05 per year, cutting current saving by $1000 reduces Prudence's available resources next year by $\$1000 \times 1.05 = \$1050$. Overall, her available resources next year will increase by $6000 because of the bonus but will decrease by $1050 because of reduced current saving, giving a net increase in resources of $\$6000 - \$1050 = \$4950$, which can be used to increase consumption next year or in the following years. Effectively, Prudence can use the increase in her expected future income to increase consumption both in the present and in the future.

To summarize, an increase in an individual's expected future income is likely to lead that person to increase current consumption and decrease current saving. The same result applies at the macroeconomic level: If people expect that aggregate output and income, Y, will be higher in the future, current desired consumption, C^d, should increase and current desired national saving, S^d, should decrease. Consumption and saving can also be affected by other shocks, as we discuss in the Application "The Impact of the Pandemic Recession of 2020 on Consumption."

Application

The Impact of the Pandemic Recession of 2020 on Consumption

In March 2020, a global pandemic affected the world's economies in significant ways. Governments throughout the world shut down portions of their economies so that people would not come in close contact with each other until a vaccine could be developed. The result was a sharp decline in economic activity that caused a deep recession, much deeper than any recession since the Great Depression in the 1930s and far worse than in the Global Financial Crisis in 2008, as Figure 4.1

FIGURE 4.1

Real GDP Growth Rate, 1980Q1–2021Q4

The quarterly, annualized growth rate of real GDP had its biggest decline in history in the second quarter of 2020 followed by the largest increase in history in the third quarter of 2020. The pandemic recession of 2020 was the shortest recession in history as well.

Source: FRED database, Federal Reserve Bank of St. Louis, *fred.stlouisfed.org/series/GDPC1.*

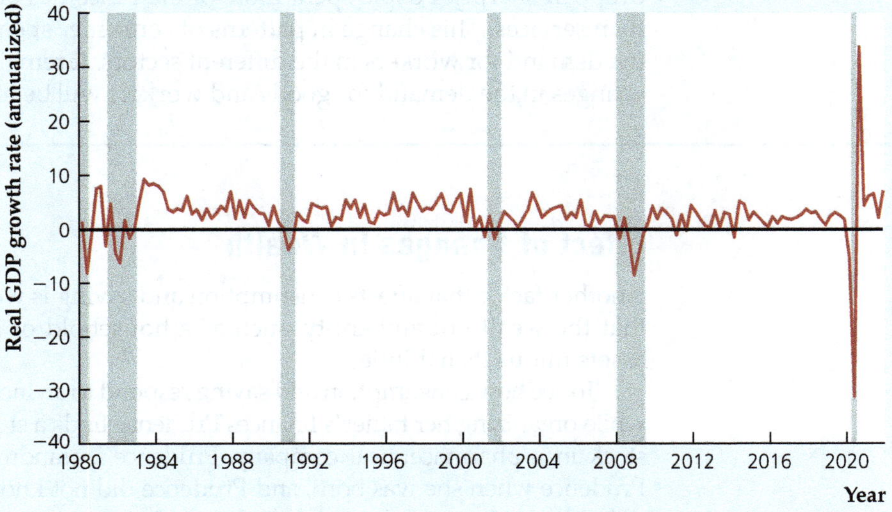

(continued)

FIGURE 4.2

Income, Consumption, and Saving, January 2002–December 2021

Monthly income, consumption, and saving showed dramatic changes during and following the pandemic recession. Income spiked up because of government programs, while consumption declined because people avoided contact with each other. As a result, saving rose substantially for more than a year.

Source: FRED database, Federal Reserve Bank of St. Louis, *fred.stlouisfed.org*. Income is real disposable personal income, series *DSPIC96*. Consumption is real personal consumption expenditures, series *PCEC96*. Saving is income minus consumption.

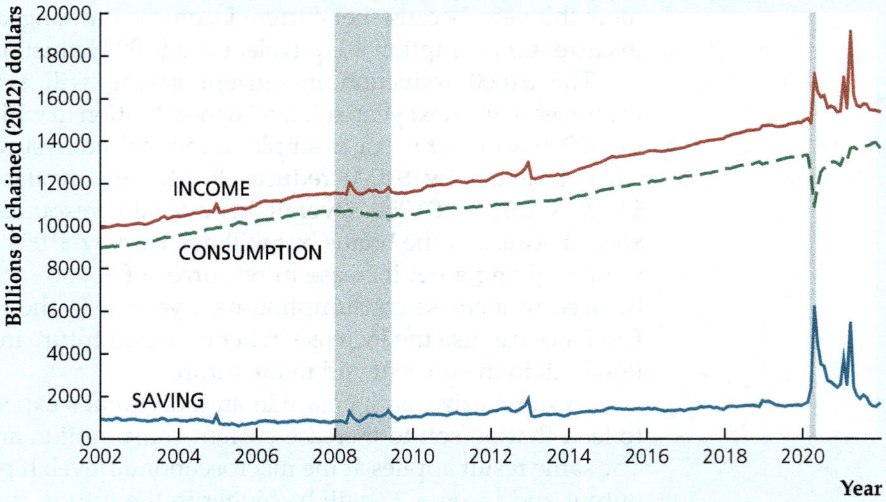

illustrates. However, because of its unusual source, the recession was also the shortest in history, lasting only two months.

The sudden drop in income for many people led governments to provide support to help replace lost incomes. For example, in the United States, the Federal government greatly increased the unemployment insurance program and sent cash directly to many people whose incomes were below a certain level, in addition to other programs. As a result, the level of after-tax disposable income actually increased, rather than declining, during the recession and for some time after it was over. Nonetheless, overall consumer spending declined sharply, as people avoided spending activities that involved direct contact, especially on travel and dining. The increase in incomes and decline in consumer spending led to an increase in saving, as Figure 4.2 shows.

People's spending patterns also changed. Because of the need to avoid close contact with other people, spending on entertainment services, travel, and dining all dropped sharply. People spent more of their incomes on purchases of goods rather than services. This change in patterns of consumer spending then led to changes in the demand for workers in the different sectors. It remains to be seen whether these changes in the demand for goods and workers will be temporary or permanent.

Effect of Changes in Wealth

Another factor that affects consumption and saving is wealth. Recall from Chapter 2 that the wealth of any entity, such as a household or an entire nation, equals its assets minus its liabilities.

To see how consumption and saving respond to an increase in wealth, suppose that while organizing her father's finances Prudence finds a stock certificate for 50 shares of stock in a pharmaceutical company. Prudence's grandmother bought this stock for Prudence when she was born, and Prudence did not know about it. She immediately calls her broker and learns that the stock is now worth \$6000. This unexpected \$6000 increase in Prudence's wealth has the same effect on her available resources as the

$6000 increase in current income that we examined earlier. As in the case involving an increase in her current income, Prudence will use her increase in wealth to increase her current consumption by an amount smaller than $6000 so that she can use some of the additional $6000 to increase her future consumption. Because Prudence's current income is not affected by finding the stock certificate, the increase in her current consumption is matched by a decrease in current saving of the same size. In this way, an increase in wealth increases current consumption and reduces current saving. The same line of reasoning leads to the conclusion that a decrease in wealth reduces current consumption and increases saving.

The ups and downs in the stock market are an important source of changes in wealth, and the effects on consumption of changes in the stock market are explored in the Application "Macroeconomic Consequences of the Boom and Bust in Stock Prices."

Effect of Changes in the Real Interest Rate

We have seen that the real interest rate is the price of current consumption in terms of future consumption. We held the real interest rate fixed when we examined the effects of changes in current income, expected future income, and wealth. Now we let the real interest rate vary, examining the effect of changes in the real interest rate on current consumption and saving.

How would Prudence's consumption and saving change in response to an increase in the real interest rate? Her response to such an increase reflects two opposing tendencies. On the one hand, because each real dollar of saving in the current year grows to $1 + r$ real dollars next year, an increase in the real interest rate means that each dollar of current saving will have a higher payoff in terms of increased future consumption. This increased reward for current saving tends to increase saving.

On the other hand, a higher real interest rate means that Prudence can achieve any future savings target with a smaller amount of current saving. For example, suppose that she is trying to accumulate $1400 to buy a new laptop computer next year. An increase in the real interest rate means that any current saving will grow to a larger amount by next year, so the amount that she needs to save this year to reach her goal of $1400 is lower. Because she needs to save less to reach her goal, she can increase her current consumption and thus reduce her saving.

The two opposing effects described above are known as the substitution effect and the income effect of an increase in the real interest rate. The **substitution effect of the real interest rate on saving** reflects the tendency to reduce current consumption and increase future consumption as the price of current consumption, $1 + r$, increases. In response to an increase in the price of current consumption, consumers *substitute* away from current consumption, which has become relatively more expensive, toward future consumption, which has become relatively less expensive. The reduction in current consumption implies that current saving increases. Thus the substitution effect implies that current saving increases in response to an increase in the real interest rate.

The **income effect of the real interest rate on saving** reflects the change in current consumption that results when a higher real interest rate makes a consumer richer or poorer. For example, if Prudence has a savings account and has not borrowed any funds, she is a recipient of interest payments. She therefore benefits from an increase in the real interest rate because her interest income increases.

With a higher interest rate, she can afford to have the same levels of current and future consumption as before the interest rate change, and she would have some additional resources to spend. These extra resources are effectively the same as an increase in her wealth, so she will increase both her current and her future consumption. Thus, for a saver, who is a recipient of interest payments, the income effect of an increase in the real interest rate is to increase current consumption and reduce current saving. Therefore, for a saver, the income and substitution effects of an increase in the real interest rate work in opposite directions, with the income effect reducing saving and the substitution effect increasing saving.

The income effect of an increase in the real interest rate is different for a payer of interest, such as a borrower. An increase in the real interest rate increases the amount of interest payments that a borrower must make, thereby making the borrower unable to afford the same levels of current and future consumption as before the increase in the real interest rate. The borrower has effectively suffered a loss of wealth as a result of the increase in the real interest rate and responds to this decline in wealth by reducing both current consumption and future consumption. The reduction in current consumption means that current saving increases (that is, borrowing decreases). Hence, for a borrower, the income effect of an increase in the real interest rate is to increase saving. Thus both the substitution effect and the income effect of an increase in the real interest rate increase the saving of a borrower.

Let's summarize the effect of an increase in the real interest rate. For a saver, who is a recipient of interest, an increase in the real interest rate tends to increase saving through the substitution effect but to reduce saving through the income effect. Without additional information, we cannot say which of these two opposing effects is larger. For a borrower, who is a payer of interest, both the substitution effect and the income effect operate to increase saving. Consequently, the saving of a borrower unambiguously increases.

What is the effect of an increase in the real interest rate on national saving? Because the national economy is composed of both borrowers and savers, and because, in principle, savers could either increase or decrease their saving in response to an increase in the real interest rate, economic theory cannot answer this question. Because economic theory does not indicate whether national saving increases or decreases in response to an increase in the real interest rate, we must rely on empirical studies that examine this relationship using actual data. Unfortunately, interpretation of the empirical evidence from the many studies done continues to inspire debate. The most widely accepted conclusion seems to be that an increase in the real interest rate reduces current consumption and increases saving, but this effect isn't very strong.

Taxes and the Real Return to Saving. In discussing the real return that savers earn, we have not yet mentioned an important practical consideration: Interest earnings (and other returns on savings) are taxed. Because part of interest earnings must be paid as taxes, the real return earned by savers is actually less than the difference between the nominal interest rate and expected inflation.

A useful measure of the returns received by savers that recognizes the effects of taxes is the *expected real after-tax interest rate*. To define this concept, we let i represent the nominal interest rate and t the rate at which interest income is taxed. In the United States, for example, most interest earnings are taxed as ordinary income, so t is the income tax rate. Savers retain a fraction $(1 - t)$ of total interest earned so that the nominal after-tax interest rate, received by savers after payment of taxes, is $(1 - t)i$. The **expected real after-tax interest rate**, r_{a-t}, is the after-tax nominal interest rate minus the expected inflation rate, π^e, or

$$r_{a-t} = (1 - t)i - \pi^e. \quad \textbf{(4.2)}$$

The expected real after-tax interest rate is the appropriate interest rate for consumers to use in making consumption and saving decisions because it measures the increase in the purchasing power of their saving after payment of taxes.

Table 4.1 shows how to calculate the nominal after-tax interest rate and the expected real after-tax interest rate. Note that, given the nominal interest rate and expected inflation, a reduction in the tax rate on interest income increases the nominal and real after-tax rates of return that a saver receives. Thus, by reducing the rate at which it taxes interest, the government can increase the real rate of return earned by savers and (possibly) increase the rate of saving in the economy.

The stimulation of saving is the motivation for tax provisions, such as individual retirement accounts (IRAs), that allow savers to shelter part of their interest earnings from taxes and thus earn higher after-tax rates of return. Unfortunately, because economists disagree about the effect of higher real interest rates on saving, the effectiveness of IRAs and similar tax breaks for saving also is in dispute.

Fiscal Policy

We've just demonstrated how government tax policies can affect the real return earned by savers and thus, perhaps, the saving rate. However, even when government fiscal policies—decisions about spending and taxes—aren't intentionally directed at affecting the saving rate, these policies have important implications for the amount of consumption and saving that takes place in the economy. Although understanding the links between fiscal policy and consumer behavior requires some difficult economic reasoning, these links are so important that we introduce them here. Later we discuss several of these issues further, particularly in Chapter 15.

To make the discussion of fiscal policy effects as straightforward as possible, we take the economy's aggregate output, Y, as a given. That is, we ignore the possibility that the changes in fiscal policy that we consider could affect the aggregate supply of goods and services. This assumption is valid if the economy is at full employment (as we are assuming throughout Part 2 of this book) and if the fiscal

TABLE 4.1

Calculating After-Tax Interest Rates

i = nominal interest rate = 5% per year
π^e = expected inflation rate = 2% per year

Example 1
t = tax rate on interest income = 30%
Nominal after-tax interest rate = $(1 - t)i$ = $(1 - 0.30)5\%$ = 3.5%
Expected real after-tax interest rate = $(1 - t)i - \pi^e$ = $(1 - 0.30)5\% - 2\%$ = 1.5%

Example 2
t = tax rate on interest income = 20%
Nominal after-tax interest rate = $(1 - t)i$ = $(1 - 0.20)5\%$ = 4%
Expected real after-tax interest rate = $(1 - t)i - \pi^e$ = $(1 - 0.20)5\% - 2\%$ = 2%

policy changes don't significantly affect the capital stock or employment. Later we relax the fixed-output assumption and discuss both the classical and Keynesian views about how fiscal policy changes can affect output.

In general, fiscal policy affects *desired consumption*, C^d, primarily by affecting households' current and expected future incomes. More specifically, fiscal changes that increase the tax burden on the private sector, either by raising current taxes or by leading people to expect that taxes will be higher in the future, will cause people to consume less.

For a given level of output, Y, government fiscal policies affect *desired national saving*, S^d, or $Y - C^d - G$, in two basic ways. First, as we just noted, fiscal policy can influence desired consumption: For any levels of output, Y, and government purchases, G, a fiscal policy change that reduces desired consumption, C^d, by one dollar will at the same time raise desired national saving, S^d, by one dollar. Second, for any levels of output and desired consumption, increases in government purchases directly lower desired national saving, as is apparent from the definition of desired national saving, $S^d = Y - C^d - G$.

To illustrate these general points, we consider how desired consumption and desired national saving would be affected by two specific fiscal policy changes: an increase in government purchases and a tax cut.

In Touch with Data and Research

Interest Rates

Although in our theoretical discussions we refer to "the" interest rate, as if there were only one, actually there are many different interest rates, each of which depends on the identity of the borrower and the terms of the loan. Shown here are some interest rates that appeared in Federal Reserve statistical release H.15 on February 23, 2021, and February 23, 2022.

	February 23, 2022	February 23, 2021
Prime rate	3.25%	3.25%
Federal funds	0.08%	0.07%
3-month Treasury bills	0.36%	0.04%
6-month Treasury bills	0.74%	0.05%
10-year Treasury notes	1.99%	1.37%
30-year Treasury bonds	2.29%	2.21%

The prime rate is the basic rate that banks charge on loans to their best customers. The federal funds rate is the rate at which banks make overnight loans to one another. Treasury bills, notes, and bonds are debts of the U.S. government. With the exception of the prime rate, these interest rates vary continuously as financial market conditions change. The prime rate is an average of lending rates set by major banks and changes less frequently.

The interest rates charged on these different types of loans need not be the same. One reason for this variation is differences in the risk of nonrepayment, or default. Federal government debt is believed to be free from default risk, but there is always a chance that a business or bank may not be able to repay what it borrowed. Lenders charge risky borrowers extra interest to compensate themselves for the risk of default. Thus the prime rate and the federal funds rate are higher than they would be if there were no default risk.

A second factor affecting interest rates is the length of time for which the funds are borrowed. The relationship between the life of a bond (its *maturity*) and the interest rate it pays is called the *yield curve*. The accompanying figure shows the yield curve in February 2022 and the yield curve one year earlier. Because longer maturity bonds typically pay higher interest rates than shorter maturity bonds, the yield curve generally slopes upward. We will discuss how interest rates relate to the maturity of a bond in the section "Time to Maturity" in Chapter 7.

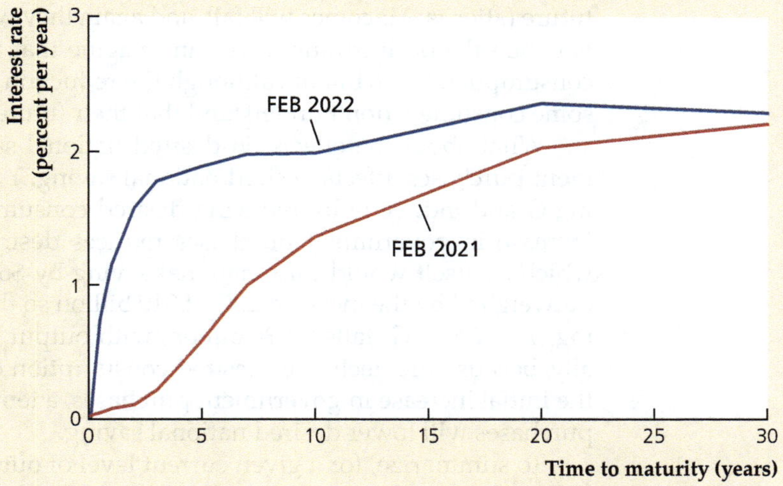

Although the levels of the various interest rates are quite different, interest rates go up and down together most of the time. As the graph shows, from February 2021 to February 2022, all of the interest rates rose, with the short-term rates rising generally more than the long-term rates. We will discuss a theory about that in Chapter 7, in Section 7.2, when we discuss the term structure of interest rates. As a general rule, interest rates tend to move together, so in our economic analyses we usually refer to "the" interest rate, as if there were only one.

Government Purchases. Suppose that current government purchases, G, increase by \$10 billion, perhaps because the government increases military spending. Assume that this increase in G is temporary so that plans for future government purchases are unchanged. (Analytical Problem 5 at the end of this chapter looks at the case of a permanent increase in government purchases.) For any fixed level of output, Y, how will this change in fiscal policy affect desired consumption and desired national saving in the economy?

Let's start by finding the effect of the increased government purchases on consumption. As already mentioned, changes in government purchases affect consumption because they affect private-sector tax burdens. Suppose for example that the government pays for the extra \$10 billion in military spending by raising current taxes by \$10 billion. For a given total (before-tax) output, Y, this tax increase implies a \$10 billion decline in consumers' current (after-tax) incomes.

We know that consumers respond to a decline in their current incomes by reducing consumption, although by less than the decline in current income.[3] So, in response to the $10 billion tax increase, consumers might, for example, reduce their current consumption by $6 billion.

What happens to consumption if the government doesn't increase current taxes when it increases its purchases? The analysis in this case is more subtle. If the government doesn't increase current taxes, it will have to borrow the $10 billion to pay for the extra spending. The government will have to repay the $10 billion it borrows, plus interest, sometime in the future, implying that future taxes will have to rise. If taxpayers are clever enough to understand that increased government purchases today mean higher taxes in the future, households' expected future (after-tax) incomes will fall, and again they will reduce desired consumption. For the sake of illustration, we can imagine that they again reduce their current consumption by $6 billion, although the reduction in consumption might be less if some consumers don't understand that their future taxes are likely to rise.

What about the effects on desired national saving? The increase in government purchases affects desired national saving, $Y - C^d - G$, directly by increasing G and indirectly by reducing desired consumption, C^d. In our example, the increase in government purchases reduces desired consumption by $6 billion, which by itself would raise national saving by $6 billion. However, this effect is outweighed by the increase in G of $10 billion so that overall desired national saving, $Y - C^d - G$, falls by $4 billion, with output, Y, held constant.[4] More generally, because the decline in desired consumption can be expected to be less than the initial increase in government purchases, a temporary increase in government purchases will lower desired national saving.

To summarize, for a given current level of output, Y, we conclude that a temporary increase in government purchases reduces both desired consumption and desired national saving.

Taxes. Now suppose that government purchases, G, remain constant but that the government reduces current taxes, T, by $10 billion. To keep things as simple as possible, we suppose that each taxpayer receives the same amount (think of the country's 100 million taxpayers receiving $100 each). We call this a **lump-sum tax cut**. With government purchases, G, and output, Y, held constant, desired national saving, $Y - C^d - G$, will change only if desired consumption, C^d, changes. So the question is, How will desired consumption respond to such a lump-sum tax cut?

Again the key issue is, How does the tax cut affect people's current and expected future incomes? The $10 billion current tax cut directly increases current (after-tax) incomes by $10 billion, so the tax cut should increase desired consumption (by somewhat less than $10 billion). However, the $10 billion current tax cut also should lead people to expect *lower* after-tax incomes in the future. The reason is that, because the government hasn't changed its spending, to cut taxes by $10 billion today the government must also increase its current borrowing by $10 billion. Because the extra $10 billion of government debt will have to be repaid with interest in the future, future taxes will have to be higher, which in turn implies lower future

[3]Recall that the marginal propensity to consume out of current income is positive but less than 1.

[4]Note that national saving would fall by even more than $4 billion if consumers ignored the prospect of future tax increases and thus didn't reduce their current consumption.

disposable incomes for households. All else being equal, the decline in expected future incomes will cause people to consume less today, offsetting the positive effect of increased current income on desired consumption. Thus, in principle, a current tax cut—which raises current incomes but lowers expected future incomes—could either raise or lower current desired consumption.

Interestingly, some economists argue that the positive effect of increased current income and the negative effect of decreased future income on desired consumption should exactly cancel so that the overall effect of a current tax cut on consumption is zero! The idea that tax cuts do not affect desired consumption and (therefore) also do not affect desired national saving,[5] is called the **Ricardian equivalence proposition.**[6]

The Ricardian equivalence idea can be briefly explained as follows (see Chapter 15 for a more detailed discussion). In the long run, all government purchases must be paid for by taxes. Thus, if the government's current and planned purchases do not change, a cut in current taxes can affect the *timing* of tax collections but (advocates of Ricardian equivalence emphasize) not the ultimate tax burden borne by consumers. A current tax cut with no change in government purchases doesn't really make consumers any better off (any reduction in taxes today is balanced by tax increases in the future), so they have no reason to respond to the tax cut by changing their desired consumption.

SUMMARY 5

Determinants of Desired National Saving

An increase in	Causes desired national saving to	Reason
Current output, Y	Rise	Part of the extra income is saved to provide for future consumption.
Expected future output	Fall	Anticipation of future income raises current desired consumption, lowering current desired saving.
Wealth	Fall	Some of the extra wealth is consumed, which reduces saving for given income.
Expected real interest rate, r	Probably rise	An increased return makes saving more attractive, probably outweighing the fact that less must be saved to reach a specific savings target.
Government purchases, G	Fall	Higher government purchases directly lower desired national saving.
Taxes, T	Remain unchanged or rise	Saving doesn't change if consumers take into account an offsetting future tax cut; saving rises if consumers don't take into account a future tax cut and thus reduce current consumption.

[5]In this example, private disposable income rises by $10 billion, so if desired consumption doesn't change, desired private saving rises by $10 billion. However, the government deficit also rises by $10 billion because of the tax cut, so government saving falls by $10 billion. Therefore desired national saving—private saving plus government saving—doesn't change.

[6]The argument was first advanced by the nineteenth-century economist David Ricardo, although he expressed some reservations about its applicability to real-world situations. The word *equivalence* refers to the idea that, if Ricardian equivalence is true, taxes and government borrowing have equivalent effects on the economy.

Although the logic of the Ricardian equivalence proposition is sound, many economists question whether it makes sense in practice. Most of these skeptics argue that, even though the proposition predicts that consumers will not increase consumption when taxes are cut, in reality lower current taxes likely will lead to increased desired consumption and thus reduced desired national saving. One reason that consumption may rise after a tax cut is that many—perhaps most—consumers do not understand that increased government borrowing today is likely to lead to higher taxes in the future. Thus consumers may simply respond to the current tax cut, as they would to any other increase in current income, by increasing their desired consumption.

The effects of a tax cut on consumption and saving may be summarized as follows: According to the Ricardian equivalence proposition, with no change in current or planned government purchases, a tax cut doesn't change desired consumption and desired national saving. However, the Ricardian equivalence proposition may not apply if consumers fail to take account of possible future tax increases in their planning; in that case, a tax cut will increase desired consumption and reduce desired national saving.

The factors that affect consumption and saving are listed in Summary table 5.

Application

How Investors Respond to Tax Incentives

Any tax policy involves trade-offs between economic stimulation and raising revenue to finance public expenditure. When a government's prime goal is to solve a fiscal budget deficit or to finance public goods and services, it may raise taxes. Governments of emerging market economies (EMEs) focusing on social justice issues are even more pressed to collect higher taxes for the sake of expanding social programs. On the other hand, when the fiscal agent is more concerned about stimulating macroeconomic growth and additional productive investment, it will resort to tax incentives.

Investment tax incentives are fiscal measures employed with the prime aim of attracting private investment capital to certain economic sectors and/or regions of the country. They can be classified into six distinct categories: tax holidays, sectoral or targeted tax reliefs, tax credits, tax reductions, tax deferrals, and tax-free economic zones. Each of these tax incentives is likely to affect investment decisions favorably; in fact, the positive impacts of investment tax incentives on enhancing returns on investment in many OECD nations have tempted many EMEs to follow suit. However, the overall benefits may not always outweigh the disadvantages.

If properly targeted and effectively fine-tuned, tax incentives may offer many advantages in fostering growth. Most developed nations that provide incentives consider their political advantages over costly expenditure programs needed to stimulate private production and investment. Moreover, investment tax incentives are especially justified by positive externalities and linkage effects. A firm creates forward linkages when it encourages further investments in subsequent stages of production and backward linkages when it encourages investment in existing facilities in earlier stages of production. Granting tax incentives to firms with high forward and backward linkages can indirectly help raise further fiscal revenue and stimulate employment.

In a world of globalized capital mobility, many governments in EMEs use tax incentives to signal openness to private investment and to respond to tax competition from other jurisdictions. Other EMEs use investment tax incentives to compensate for possible deficiencies in the investment climate and to counterbalance investment disincentives. Examples of the investment disadvantages that investors may face are poor infrastructure, obsolete laws, corruption, poor regulatory frameworks, bureaucratic complexities, and weak administrative systems.

We may be inclined to think that it is best to address the problem at its roots by reforming the legal framework, building administrative capacities, and enhancing the infrastructure. However, these solutions are quite costly and enduring, and tax incentives may provide short-term relief until the more fundamental structural remedies are carried out. Investors also need incentives to help compensate for inherent foreign exchange, political, credit, and legislative risk factors. Lastly, incentives could be carefully directed to sectors of economic activity that the government wishes to develop.

Against all of these benefits, tax incentives have costs and disadvantages that go beyond immediate loss of potential revenue. Advocates of the Ricardian equivalence proposition extend their argument from consumer to investor behavior, rendering them the strongest critics of investment tax incentives. They argue that in many instances investment spending would not increase much in response to a tax incentive, especially in EMEs where the poor investment environment, tax complexity, and the exposure to risk factors outweigh potential investment gains.[7] For example, it takes Nigerian companies approximately 908 hours each year to prepare, file, and pay their taxes, ranking Nigeria 179th in tax payment, according to the World Bank's Doing Business 2015 report. Further, the results of surveying 14,000 business executives in 148 economies by the World Economic Forum's 2014 Executive Opinion Survey reveal that financing and political stability are more important than tax considerations.

Moreover, preferential treatment of firms qualifying for tax incentives distorts efficient market equilibrium. As investors benefiting from incentives could possibly crowd out other investments, the aggregate investment capital stock may not increase, but simply move from one sector to the other. In addition to foregone revenue losses, the introduction of these tax incentives further complicates tax regulations, raising the administrative costs needed to collect taxes and to prevent fraudulent abuse of the incentive schemes.[8]

A study by the IMF[9] also reveals that tax incentives are not without social costs. They often lead to unfavorable cross-border tax competition, with the final result of providing private investors with windfall incomes at the expense of public expenditure and social benefits. Second, the desire to benefit from these preferential investment schemes can increase rent-seeking activities by individuals and businesses and may even increase corruption levels. The IMF study also notes

---

[7]Nick Huber, 2015, "The Growth Paradox," *EY Tax Insights for Business Leaders*, no. 13, 2015, pp. 38–41.

[8]Many agencies are created to build capacity and to enhance expertise among tax authorities in EMEs. Examples are the African Tax Administration Forum (ATAF), with 36 African countries; the Study Group on Asian Tax Administration and Research (SGATAR), with 16 Asia-Pacific nations; and the Centro Interamericano de Administraciones Tributarias (CIAT), with 31 nations from the Americas and 9 non-American nations.

[9]IMF Working Paper, "Fiscal Affairs Department Causes, Benefits, and Risks of Business Tax Incentives," prepared by Alexander Klemm and authorized for distribution by Victoria Perry, January 2009, available at *https://www.imf.org/external/pubs/ft/wp/2009/wp0921.pdf*.

(*continued*)

that since the capital stock may move toward larger or multinational firms, especially those operating within mobile sectors, the repercussions on employment and growth would be substantial for self-employed and small and medium enterprises, which have proved to be active engines of job creation.

In conclusion, investment tax incentives that are widely used by emerging market economies to attract private investment have had mixed effects. They only prove beneficial if the pertinent pre-conditions are met and the correct type of incentive is employed. In order to introduce rational tax policy tools, policymakers should first carefully weigh the costs and benefits of the incentives. For example, before introducing sector-specific incentives, revenue gains from additional employment taxes or taxes on inputs should be carefully weighed against the crowding out of other investments that may be more highly productive, job-generating, and taxable.

4.2 Investment

Discuss the factors that affect the investment behavior of firms.

Let's now turn to a second major component of spending: investment spending by firms. Like consumption and saving decisions, the decision about how much to invest depends largely on expectations about the economy's future. Investment also shares in common with saving and consumption the idea of a trade-off between the present and the future. In making a capital investment, a firm commits its current resources (which could otherwise be used, for example, to pay increased dividends to shareholders) to increasing its capacity to produce and earn profits in the future.

Recall from Chapter 2 that investment refers to the purchase or construction of capital goods, including buildings, equipment, software, and intellectual property products used in production, and additions to inventory stocks. From a macroeconomic perspective, there are two main reasons to study investment behavior. First, more so than the other components of aggregate spending, investment spending fluctuates sharply over the business cycle, falling in recessions and rising in booms. Even though investment is only about one-sixth of GDP, in the typical recession half or more of the total decline in spending is reduced investment spending. Hence explaining the behavior of investment is important for understanding the business cycle, which we explore further in Part 3.

The second reason for studying investment behavior is that investment plays a crucial role in determining the long-run productive capacity of the economy. Because investment creates new capital goods, a high rate of investment means that the capital stock is growing quickly. As discussed in Chapter 3, capital is one of the two most important factors of production (the other is labor). All else being equal, output will be higher in an economy that has invested rapidly and thus built up a large capital stock than in an economy that hasn't acquired much capital.

The Desired Capital Stock

To understand what determines the amount of investment, we must consider how firms decide how much capital they want. If firms attempt to maximize profit, as we assume, a firm's **desired capital stock** is the amount of capital that allows the firm to earn the largest expected profit. Managers can determine the profit-maximizing level of the capital stock by comparing the costs and benefits of using additional capital—a new machine, for example. If the benefits outweigh the costs, expanding the capital stock will raise profits. But if the costs outweigh the benefits, the firm shouldn't increase its planned capital stock and may even want to reduce it. As you might infer from this brief description, the economic logic underlying a firm's decision about how much capital to use is similar to the logic underlying its decision about how many workers to employ, discussed in Chapter 3.

In real terms, the benefit to a firm of having an additional unit of capital is the marginal product of capital, *MPK*. Recall from Chapter 3 that the *MPK* is the increase in output that a firm can obtain by adding a unit of capital, holding constant the firm's work force and other factors of production. Because lags occur in obtaining and installing new capital, the expected *future* marginal product of capital, MPK^f, is the benefit from increasing investment today by one unit of capital. This expected future benefit must be compared to the expected cost of using that extra unit of capital, or the user cost of capital.

The User Cost of Capital. To make the discussion of the user cost of capital more concrete, let's consider the case of Kyle's Bakery, Inc., a company that produces specialty cookies. Kyle, the bakery's owner-manager, is considering investing in a new solar-powered oven that will allow him to produce more cookies in the future. If he decides to buy such an oven, he must also determine its size. In making this decision, Kyle has the following information:

1. A new oven can be purchased in any size at a price of $100 per cubic foot, measured in real (base-year) dollars.
2. Because the oven is solar powered, using it does not involve energy costs. The oven also does not require maintenance expenditures.[10] However, the oven becomes less efficient as it ages: With each year that passes, the oven produces 10% fewer cookies. Because of this depreciation, the real value of an oven falls 10% per year. For example, after one year of use, the real value of the oven is $90 per cubic foot.
3. Kyle can borrow (from a bank) or lend (to the government, by buying a one-year government bond) at the prevailing expected real interest rate of 8% per year.

In calculating the user cost of capital, we use the following symbols (the numerical values are from the example of Kyle's Bakery):

$$\begin{aligned} p_K &= \text{real price of capital goods (\$100 per cubic foot);} \\ d &= \text{rate at which capital depreciates (10\% per year);} \\ r &= \text{expected real interest rate (8\% per year).} \end{aligned}$$

The **user cost of capital** is the expected real cost of using a unit of capital for a specified period of time. For Kyle's Bakery, we consider the expected costs of purchasing a new oven, using it for a year, and then selling it. The cost of using the oven has two components: depreciation and interest.

In general, the depreciation cost of using capital is the value lost as the capital wears out. Because of depreciation, after one year the oven for which Kyle pays $100 per cubic foot when new will be worth only $90 per cubic foot. The $10-per-cubic-foot loss that Kyle suffers over the year is the depreciation cost of using the oven. Even if Kyle doesn't sell the oven at the end of a year, he suffers this loss because at the end of the year the asset's (the oven's) economic value will be 10% less.

[10]These assumptions simplify the example. If there were operating costs, such as fuel and maintenance costs, we would subtract them from the expected future marginal product of capital when calculating the benefit of using the oven.

The interest cost of using capital equals the expected real interest rate times the price of the capital. As the expected real interest rate is 8% per year, Kyle's interest cost of using the oven for a year is 8% of $100 per cubic foot, or $8 per cubic foot. To see why the interest cost is a cost of using capital, imagine first that Kyle must borrow the funds necessary to buy the oven; in this case, the interest cost of $8 per cubic foot is the interest he pays on the loan, which is obviously part of the total cost of using the oven. Alternatively, if Kyle uses profits from the business to buy the oven, he gives up the opportunity to use those funds to buy an interest-bearing asset, such as a government bond. For every $100 that Kyle puts into the oven, he is sacrificing $8 in interest that he would have earned by purchasing a $100 government bond. This forgone interest is a cost to Kyle of using the oven. Thus the interest cost is part of the true economic cost of using capital, whether the capital's purchase is financed with borrowed funds or with the firm's own retained profits.

The user cost of capital is the sum of the depreciation cost and the interest cost. The interest cost is rp_K, the depreciation cost is dp_K, and the user cost of capital, uc, is

$$uc = rp_K + dp_K = (r + d)p_K. \tag{4.3}$$

In the case of Kyle's Bakery,

$$\begin{aligned} uc &= (0.08 \text{ per year} \times \$100 \text{ per cubic foot}) \\ &\quad + (0.10 \text{ per year} \times \$100 \text{ per cubic foot}) \\ &= \$18 \text{ per cubic foot per year}. \end{aligned}$$

Thus Kyle's user cost of capital is $18 per cubic foot per year.

Determining the Desired Capital Stock. Now we can find a firm's profit-maximizing capital stock, or desired capital stock. A firm's desired capital stock is the capital stock at which the expected future marginal product of capital equals the user cost of capital.

Figure 4.3 shows the determination of the desired capital stock for Kyle's Bakery. The capital stock, K, expressed as cubic feet of oven capacity, is measured along the horizontal axis. Both the MPK^f and the user cost of capital are measured along the vertical axis.

The downward-sloping curve shows the value of the MPK^f for different sizes of the capital stock, K; at each level of K, the MPK^f equals the expected real value of the extra cookies that could be produced per year if oven capacity were expanded an additional cubic foot. The MPK^f curve slopes downward because the marginal product of capital falls as the capital stock is increased (we discussed reasons for the diminishing marginal productivity of capital in Chapter 3). The user cost (equal to $18 per cubic foot per year in the example) doesn't depend on the amount of capital and is represented by a horizontal line.

The amount of capital that maximizes the expected profit of Kyle's Bakery is 5000 cubic feet, represented by point A in Fig. 4.3. At A, the expected benefit of an additional unit of capital, MPK^f, equals the user cost, uc. For any amount of oven capacity less than 5000 cubic feet, Kyle's Bakery could increase its expected profit by increasing oven capacity. For example, Fig. 4.3 shows that at a planned capacity of 4000 cubic feet the MPK^f of an additional cubic foot is $20 worth of cookies per year, which exceeds the $18 per year expected cost of using the additional cubic foot of capacity. Starting from a planned capacity

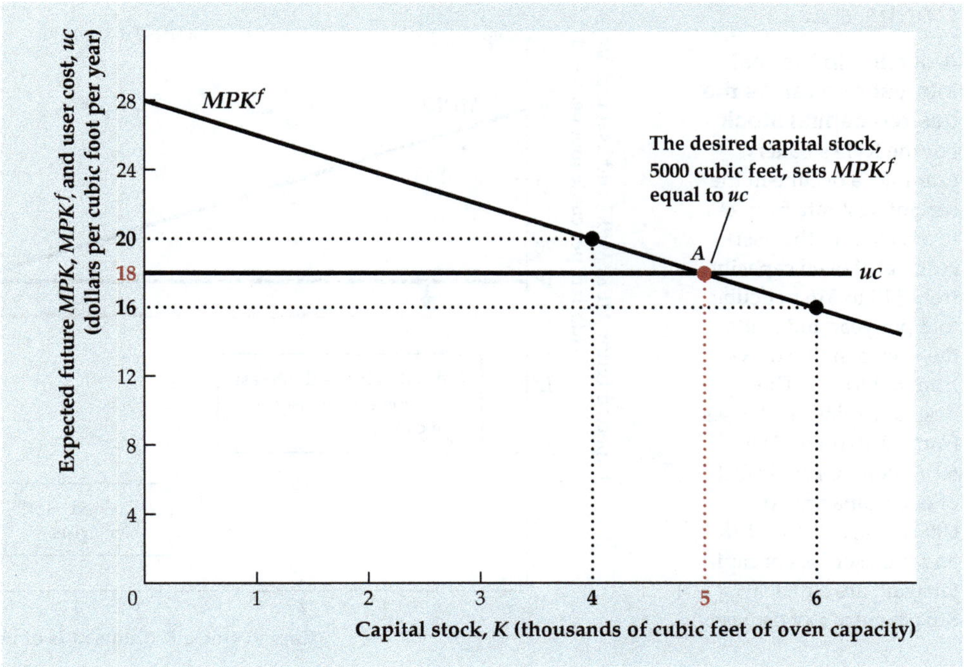

FIGURE 4.3

Determination of the desired capital stock
The desired capital stock (5000 cubic feet of oven capacity in this example) is the capital stock that maximizes profits. When the capital stock is 5000 cubic feet, the expected future marginal product of capital, MPK^f, is equal to the user cost of capital, uc. If the MPK^f is larger than uc, as it is when the capital stock is 4000 cubic feet, the benefit of extra capital exceeds the cost, and the firm should increase its capital stock. If the MPK^f is smaller than uc, as it is at 6000 cubic feet, the cost of extra capital exceeds the benefit, and the firm should reduce its capital stock.

of 4000 cubic feet, if Kyle adds an extra cubic foot of capacity, he will gain an additional \$20 worth of future output per year while incurring only \$18 per year in expected future costs. Thus expanding beyond 4000 cubic feet is profitable for Kyle. Similarly, Fig. 4.3 shows that at an oven capacity of more than 5000 cubic feet the expected future marginal product of capital, MPK^f, is less than the user cost, uc; in this case Kyle's Bakery could increase expected profit by reducing its capital stock. Only when $MPK^f = uc$ will the capital stock be at the level that maximizes expected profit.

As mentioned earlier, the determination of the desired capital stock is similar to the determination of the firm's labor demand, described in Chapter 3. Recall that the firm's profit-maximizing level of employment is the level at which the marginal product of labor equals the wage. Analogously, the firm's profit-maximizing level of capital is the level at which the expected future marginal product of capital equals the user cost, which can be thought of as the "wage" of capital (the cost of using capital for one period).

Changes in the Desired Capital Stock

Any factor that shifts the MPK^f curve or changes the user cost of capital changes the firm's desired capital stock. For Kyle's Bakery, suppose that the real interest rate falls from 8% per year to 6% per year. If the real interest rate, r, is 0.06 per year and the depreciation rate, d, and the price of capital, p_K, remain at 0.10 per year and \$100 per cubic foot, respectively, the decline in the real interest rate reduces the user cost of capital, $(r + d)p_K$, from \$18 per cubic foot per year to $(0.06 + 0.10)\$100$ per cubic foot per year, or \$16 per cubic foot per year.

This decline in the user cost is shown as a downward shift of the user cost line, from uc^1 to uc^2 in Figure 4.4. After that shift, the MPK^f at the original desired capital stock of 5000 cubic feet (point A), or \$18 per cubic foot per year,

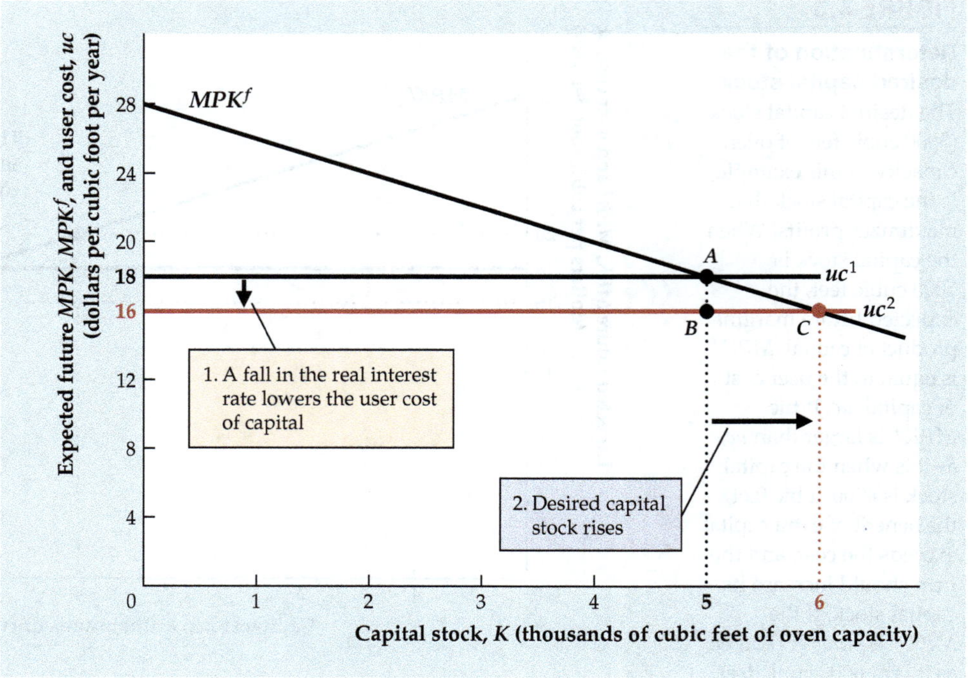

FIGURE 4.4

A decline in the real interest rate raises the desired capital stock

For the Kyle's Bakery example, a decline in the real interest rate from 8% to 6% reduces the user cost, *uc*, of oven capacity from \$18 to \$16 per cubic foot per year and shifts the user-cost line down from uc^1 to uc^2. The desired capital stock rises from 5000 (point *A*) to 6000 (point *C*) cubic feet of oven capacity. At 6000 cubic feet the MPK^f and the user cost of capital again are equal, at \$16 per cubic foot per year.

exceeds the user cost of capital, now \$16 per cubic foot per year (point *B*). Kyle's Bakery can increase its profit by raising planned oven capacity to 6000 cubic feet, where the MPK^f equals the user cost of \$16 per cubic foot per year (point *C*). This example illustrates that a decrease in the expected real interest rate—or any other change that lowers the user cost of capital—increases the desired capital stock.

Technological changes that affect the MPK^f curve also affect the desired stock of capital. Suppose that Kyle invents a new type of cookie dough that requires less baking time, allowing 12.5% more cookies to be baked daily. Such a technological advance would cause the MPK^f curve for ovens to shift upward by 12.5% at each value of the capital stock. Figure 4.5 shows this effect as a shift of the MPK^f curve from MPK_1^f to MPK_2^f. If the user cost remains at \$18 per cubic foot per year, the technological advance causes Kyle's desired capital stock to rise from 5000 to 6000 cubic feet. At 6000 cubic feet (point *D*) the MPK^f again equals the user cost of capital. In general, with the user cost of capital held constant, an increase in the expected future marginal product of capital at any level of capital raises the desired capital stock.

Taxes and the Desired Capital Stock. So far we have ignored the role of taxes in the investment decision. But Kyle is interested in maximizing the profit his firm gets to keep after paying taxes. Thus he must take into account taxes in evaluating the desirability of an additional unit of capital.

Suppose that Kyle's Bakery pays 20% of its revenues in taxes. In this case, extra oven capacity that increases the firm's future revenues by, say, \$20 will raise Kyle's after-tax revenue by only \$16, with \$4 going to the government. To decide whether to add this extra capacity, Kyle should compare the after-tax MPK^f of \$16 per cubic foot per year—not the before-tax MPK^f of \$20 per cubic

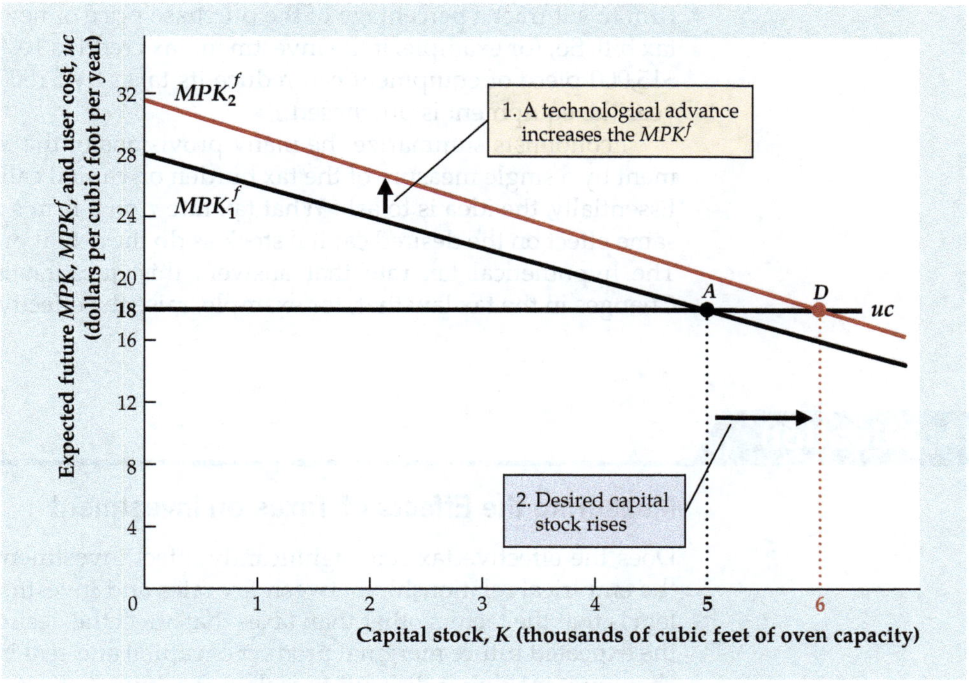

FIGURE 4.5

An increase in the expected future MPK raises the desired capital stock

A technological advance raises the expected future marginal product of capital, MPK^f, shifting the MPK^f curve upward from MPK_1^f to MPK_2^f. The desired capital stock increases from 5000 (point *A*) to 6000 (point *D*) cubic feet of oven capacity. At 6000 cubic feet the MPK^f equals the user cost of capital *uc* at \$18 per cubic foot per year.

foot per year—with the user cost. In general, if τ is the tax rate on firm revenues, the after-tax future marginal product of capital is $(1 - \tau)MPK^f$. The desired capital stock is the one for which the after-tax future marginal product equals the user cost, or

$$(1 - \tau)MPK^f = uc.$$

Dividing both sides of this equation by $1 - \tau$, we obtain

$$MPK^f = \frac{uc}{1 - \tau} = \frac{(r + d)p_K}{1 - \tau}. \qquad \textbf{(4.4)}$$

In Eq. (4.4), the term $uc/(1 - \tau)$ is called the tax-adjusted user cost of capital. The **tax-adjusted user cost of capital** shows how large the before-tax future marginal product of capital must be for a firm to willingly add another unit of capital. An increase in the tax rate τ raises the tax-adjusted user cost and thus reduces the desired stock of capital.

To derive the tax-adjusted user cost, we assumed that taxes are levied as a proportion of firms' revenues. However, actual corporate taxes in the United States and other countries are much more complicated. Firms generally pay taxes on their profits rather than on their revenues, and the part of profit that is considered taxable may depend on how much the firm invests. For example, when a firm purchases some capital, it is allowed to deduct part of the purchase price of the capital from its taxable profit in both the year of purchase and in subsequent years. By reducing the amount of profit to be taxed, these deductions, known as *depreciation allowances*, allow the firm to reduce its total tax payment.

Another important tax provision, which has been used at various times in the United States, is the *investment tax credit*. An investment tax credit permits the firm to subtract a percentage of the purchase price of new capital directly from its tax bill. So, for example, if the investment tax credit is 10%, a firm that purchases a $15,000 piece of equipment can reduce its taxes by $1500 (10% of $15,000) in the year the equipment is purchased.

Economists summarize the many provisions of the tax code affecting investment by a single measure of the tax burden on capital called the **effective tax rate**. Essentially, the idea is to ask: What tax rate τ on a firm's revenue would have the same effect on the desired capital stock as do the actual provisions of the tax code? The hypothetical tax rate that answers this question is the effective tax rate. Changes in the tax law that, for example, raise the effective tax rate are equivalent

Application

Measuring the Effects of Taxes on Investment

Does the effective tax rate significantly affect investment patterns? Determining the empirical relationship between tax rates and investment isn't easy. One problem is that the factors other than taxes that affect the desired capital stock—such as the expected future marginal product of capital and real interest rates—are always changing, making it difficult to isolate the "pure" effects of tax changes. Another problem is that changes in the tax code don't happen randomly but reflect the government's assessment of economic conditions. For example, Congress is likely to reduce taxes on investment when investment spending is expected to be unusually low so as to boost spending. But if Congress does so, low taxes on capital will tend to be associated with periods of low investment, and an econometrician might mistakenly conclude that tax cuts reduce rather than increase investment spending. For example, Congress passed an economic stimulus plan in early 2002 designed to increase investment by allowing firms to depreciate capital for tax purposes faster than the true depreciation on the capital, effectively reducing the tax rate on the capital. But gross private domestic investment had already declined from 19.8% of GDP in 2000 to 18.2% in 2001, and it fell to 17.5% in 2002 despite the tax cut. More recently, the stimulus package passed by Congress in early 2009 provided an $8000 tax credit for qualified first-time homebuyers, which reduces the tax-adjusted user cost of housing for recipients of the credit, and was intended to stimulate residential investment. But by the first quarter of 2009 residential investment had fallen to 2.8% of GDP from 5.3% of GDP in the first quarter of 2007, and 3.9% of GDP in the first quarter of 2008. Unfortunately, residential investment slipped to 2.6% of GDP in the second quarter of 2009 and remained below 3.0% of GDP for the subsequent three years.

An interesting study that attempted to solve both of these problems was carried out by Jason Cummins of Brevan Howard, Inc., R. Glenn Hubbard of Columbia University, and Kevin Hassett of the American Enterprise Institute.[11]

[11]"A Reconsideration of Investment Behavior Using Tax Reforms as Natural Experiments," *Brookings Papers on Economic Activity*, 1994:2, pp. 1–59. For a survey of work on taxation and investment, see Kevin Hassett and R. Glenn Hubbard, "Tax Policy and Investment," in A. J. Auerbach, ed., *Fiscal Policy: Lessons from Economic Research*, Cambridge, MA: MIT Press, 1997.

To get around the problem that factors other than taxes are always changing, Cummins, Hubbard, and Hassett focused on the periods around 13 major tax reforms, beginning with the investment tax credit initiated by President John F. Kennedy in 1962 and ending with the major tax reform of 1986, passed under President Ronald Reagan. The authors' idea was that, by looking at occasions when the tax code changed significantly in a short period of time, they could reasonably assume that most of the ensuing change in investment was the result of the tax change rather than other factors. To get around the second problem, that tax cuts tend to take place when aggregate investment is low, Cummins, Hubbard, and Hassett didn't look at the behavior of aggregate investment; instead, they compared the investment responses of a large number of individual corporations to each tax reform. Because the tax laws treat different types of capital differently (for example, a machine and a factory are taxed differently) and because companies use capital in different combinations, the authors argued that observing how different companies changed their investment after each tax reform would provide information on the effects of the tax changes. For example, if a tax reform cuts taxes on machines relative to taxes on factories and taxes are an important determinant of investment, companies whose investment is concentrated in machinery should respond relatively more strongly to the tax change than companies who invest primarily in factories.

Cummins, Hubbard, and Hassett found considerably stronger effects of tax changes on investment than reported in previous studies, possibly because the earlier studies didn't deal effectively with the two problems that we identified. These authors found an empirical elasticity of about −0.66. That is, according to their estimates, a tax change that lowers the user cost of capital by 10% would raise aggregate investment by about 6.6%, a significant amount. Thus, the effective tax rate significantly affects investment.

to an increased tax on firm revenue and a rise in the tax-adjusted user cost of capital. Thus, all else being equal, an increase in the effective tax rate lowers the desired capital stock.

Table 4.2 shows effective tax rates on capital for countries in the Organisation for Economic Co-operation and Development (OECD) in 2019. The effective tax rate on capital ranges from −42.4% in Italy to 23.9% in Chile. In the table, the effective tax rate is −2.7% for the United States because of a change in the tax code that allows firms to fully expense the purchase of some types of capital immediately rather than to use depreciation allowances that are spread out over a number of years.[12] Also shown are the ratios of gross investment to GDP in each of these countries. Because an increase in the effective tax rate on capital increases the tax-adjusted user cost of capital, we would expect countries with high effective tax rates on capital to have low rates of investment, all else being equal. However, all else is not equal in the various countries in Table 4.2, and, in fact, there is little statistical relationship between the effective tax rate and investment in this group of countries. In the Application "Measuring the Effects of Taxes on Investment," we describe a successful approach to measuring the impact of taxes on investment.

[12]In 2017, the United States enacted a tax cut called the Tax Cut and Jobs Act, which decreased the statutory corporate tax rate to 21% to 35% and allowed for immediate expensing of expenditures to purchase some types of new capital.

TABLE 4.2

Effective Tax Rate on Capital, 2019

	ETR	*I/GDP*		*ETR*	*I/GDP*
Australia	14.9	22.3	Japan	23.4	25.5
Austria	16.7	25.4	Korea (Rep. of)	13.7	30.1
Belgium	−19.1	25.2	Luxembourg	11.9	18.0
Canada	7.1	21.9	Mexico	15.7	19.9
Chile	23.9	22.2	Netherlands	14.2	22.3
Czech Republic	10.3	28.1	New Zealand	23.5	24.9
Denmark	8.4	21.8	Norway	10.3	29.8
Finland	16.3	23.0	Poland	−5.8	20.2
France	9.9	24.3	Portugal	−24.8	18.0
Germany	16.9	21.3	Slovak Republic	8.6	24.0
Greece	15.3	12.3	Slovenia	7.9	20.3
Hungary	4.7	27.6	Spain	11.8	20.6
Iceland	12.5	21.1	Sweden	13.1	24.9
Ireland	10.5	54.7	Switzerland	12.1	24.7
Israel	12.1	22.3	Turkey	−5	0.0
Italy	−42.4	18.3	United Kingdom	3.7	17.9
			United States	−2.7	21.9

Note: ETR is effective tax rate on capital in 2019, in percent. *I/GDP* is the ratio of gross capital formation to GDP, in percent, for 2019.

Sources: ETR from OECD.Stat, *https://stats.oecd.org/index.aspx?DataSetCode=CTS_ETR I/GDP from OECD.* Stat, *https://stats.oecd.org/index.aspx?DataSetCode=SNA_TABLE1* variables P5: gross capital formation and B1_GA: GDP (output approach)

From the Desired Capital Stock to Investment

Now let's look at the link between a firm's desired capital stock and the amount it invests. In general, the capital stock (of a firm or of a country) changes over time through two opposing channels. First, the purchase or construction of new capital goods increases the capital stock. We've been calling the total purchase or construction of new capital goods that takes place each year "investment," but its precise name is **gross investment**. Second, the capital stock depreciates or wears out, which reduces the capital stock.

Whether the capital stock increases or decreases over the course of a year depends on whether gross investment is greater or less than depreciation during the year; when gross investment exceeds depreciation, the capital stock grows. The change in the capital stock over the year—or, equivalently, the difference between gross investment and depreciation—is **net investment**.

We express these concepts symbolically as

$$I_t = \text{gross investment during year } t,$$

$$K_t = \text{capital stock at the beginning of year } t, \text{ and}$$

$$K_{t+1} = \text{capital stock at the beginning of year } t+1$$

$$(\text{equivalently, at the end of year } t).$$

Net investment, the change in the capital stock during period t, equals $K_{t+1} - K_t$. The amount of depreciation during year t is dK_t, where d is the fraction of capital that depreciates each year. The relationship between net and gross investment is

$$\text{net investment} = \text{gross investment} - \text{depreciation}; \qquad \textbf{(4.5)}$$
$$K_{t+1} - K_t = I_t - dK_t.$$

In most but not all years, gross investment is larger than depreciation so that net investment is positive and the capital stock increases. Figure 4.6 shows the behavior since 1929 of gross and net investment in the United States, expressed as percentages of GDP; the difference between gross and net investment is depreciation. Note the occasional large swings in both gross and net investment and the negative rates of net investment that occurred in some years during the Great Depression of the 1930s and World War II (1941–1945). Net investment was very low from 2009 to 2011 in the aftermath of the financial crisis.

We use Eq. (4.5) to illustrate the relationship between the desired capital stock and investment. First, rewriting Eq. (4.5) gives

$$I_t = K_{t+1} - K_t + dK_t,$$

which states that gross investment equals net investment plus depreciation.[13]

Now suppose that firms use information available at the beginning of year t about the expected future marginal product of capital and the user cost of capital and determine the desired capital stock, K^*, they want by the end of year t (the beginning of year $t + 1$). For the moment, suppose also that capital is easily

FIGURE 4.6

Gross and net investment, 1929–2021
Gross and net investment in the United States since 1929 are shown as percentages of GDP. During some years of the Great Depression and World War II net investment was negative, implying that the capital stock was shrinking.

Sources: GDP, gross private domestic investment, and net private domestic investment from Bureau of Economic Analysis, downloaded from Federal Reserve Bank of St. Louis FRED database, *fred.stlouisfed.org*, series *GDPA*, *GPDIA*, and *A557RC1A027NBEA*.

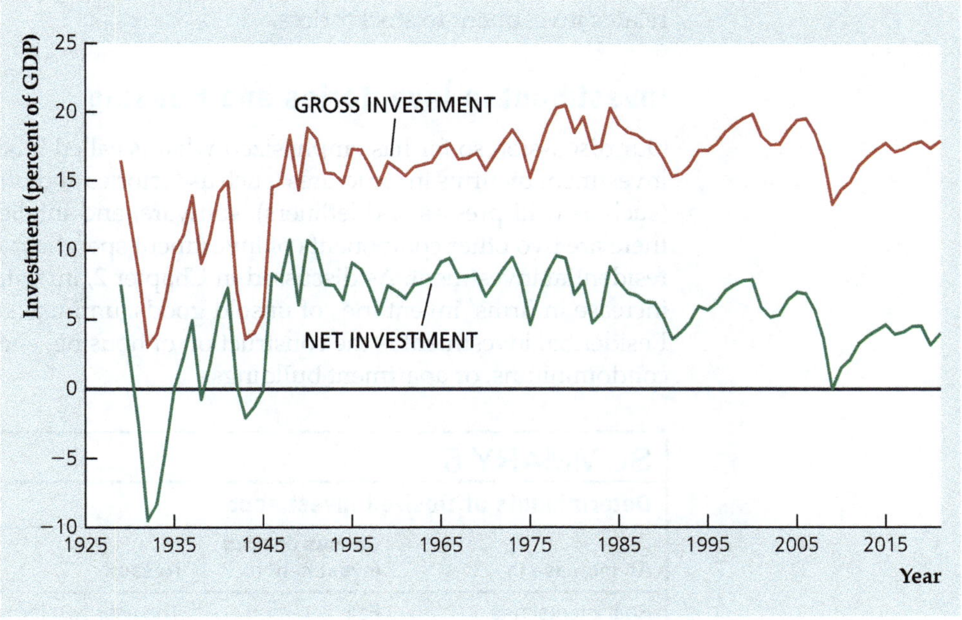

[13]In this equation, we are implicitly assuming that the relative price of capital is constant and equal to 1. More generally, the price of capital could be different from 1, in which case the equation would be:

$$I_t = p_K(K_{t+1} - K_t + dK_t).$$

obtainable so that firms can match the actual capital stock at the end of year t, K_{t+1}, with the desired capital stock, K^*. Substituting K^* for K_{t+1} in the preceding equation yields

$$I_t = K^* - K_t + dK_t. \quad \textbf{(4.6)}$$

Equation (4.6) shows that firms' gross investment, I_t, during a year has two parts: (1) the desired net increase in the capital stock over the year, $K^* - K_t$; and (2) the investment needed to replace worn-out or depreciated capital, dK_t. The amount of depreciation that occurs during a year is determined by the depreciation rate and the initial capital stock. However, the desired net increase in the capital stock over the year depends on the factors—such as taxes, interest rates, and the expected future marginal product of capital—that affect the desired capital stock. Indeed, Eq. (4.6) shows that any factor that leads to a change in the desired capital stock, K^*, results in an equal change in gross investment, I_t.

Lags and Investment. The assumption just made—that firms can obtain capital quickly enough to match actual capital stocks with desired levels each year—isn't realistic in all cases. Although most types of equipment are readily available, a skyscraper or a nuclear power plant may take years to construct. Thus, in practice, a \$1 million increase in a firm's desired capital stock may not translate into a \$1 million increase in gross investment within the year; instead, the extra investment may be spread over several years as planning and construction proceed. Despite this qualification, factors that increase firms' desired capital stocks also tend to increase the current rate of investment. Summary table 6 brings together the factors that affect investment. In "In Touch with Data and Research: Investment and the Stock Market," we discuss an alternative approach to investment, which relates investment to stock prices.

Investment in Inventories and Housing

Our discussion so far has emphasized what is called business fixed investment, or investment by firms in structures (such as factories and office buildings), equipment (such as drill presses and jetliners), software, and intellectual property. However, there are two other components of investment spending: inventory investment and residential investment. As discussed in Chapter 2, inventory investment equals the increase in firms' inventories of unsold goods, unfinished goods, or raw materials. Residential investment is the construction of housing, such as single-family homes, condominiums, or apartment buildings.

SUMMARY 6

Determinants of Desired Investment

An increase in	Causes desired investment to	Reason
Real interest rate, r	Fall	The user cost increases, which reduces desired capital stock.
Effective tax rate, τ	Fall	The tax-adjusted user cost increases, which reduces desired capital stock.
Expected future *MPK*	Rise	The desired capital stock increases.

Fortunately, the concepts of future marginal product and the user cost of capital, which we used to examine business fixed investment, apply equally well to inventory investment and residential investment. Consider, for example, Patricia, a new-car dealer trying to decide whether to increase the number of cars she normally keeps on her lot from 100 to 150—that is, whether to make an inventory investment of 50 cars. The benefit of having more cars to show is that potential car buyers will have a greater variety of models from which to select and may not have to wait for delivery, enabling the car dealer to sell more cars. The increase in sales commissions the car dealer expects to make, measured in real terms and with the same sales force, is the expected future marginal product of the increased inventory. The cost of holding more cars reflects (1) depreciation of the cars sitting on the lot and (2) the interest the car dealer must pay on the loan obtained to finance the higher inventory. The car dealer will make the inventory investment if the expected benefits of increasing her inventory, in terms of increased sales commissions, are at least as great as the interest and depreciation costs of adding 50 cars. This principle is the same one that applies to business fixed investment.

In Touch with Data and Research

Investment and the Stock Market

Fluctuations in the stock market can have important macroeconomic effects. Changes in stock prices may cause households to change how much they consume and save (see the Application "Macroeconomic Consequences of the Boom and Bust in Stock Prices"). Similarly, economic theory suggests that rises and falls in the stock market should lead firms to change their rates of capital investment in the same direction. The relationship between stock prices and firms' investment in physical capital is captured by the "q theory of investment," developed by James Tobin, who was a Nobel laureate at Yale University.

Tobin argued that the rate of investment in any particular type of capital can be predicted by looking at the ratio of the capital's market value to its replacement cost. When this ratio, often called "Tobin's q," is greater than 1, it is profitable to acquire additional capital because the value of capital exceeds the cost of acquiring it. Similarly, when Tobin's q is smaller than 1, the value of capital is less than the cost of acquiring it, so it is not profitable to invest in additional capital.[14]

Because much of the value of firms comes from the capital they own, we can use the stock market value of a firm as a measure of the market value of the firm's capital stock. If we let V be the stock market value of a firm, K be the amount of capital the firm owns, and p_K be the price of new capital goods, then for an individual firm

$$\text{Tobin's } q = \frac{V}{p_K K}$$

where $p_K K$ is the replacement cost of the firm's capital stock. If the replacement cost of capital isn't changing much, a boom in the stock market (an increase in V)

[14]Why is investment positive when q is less than one? Even when q for the aggregate economy is less than one, many firms will have q greater than one and will undertake gross investment.

(continued)

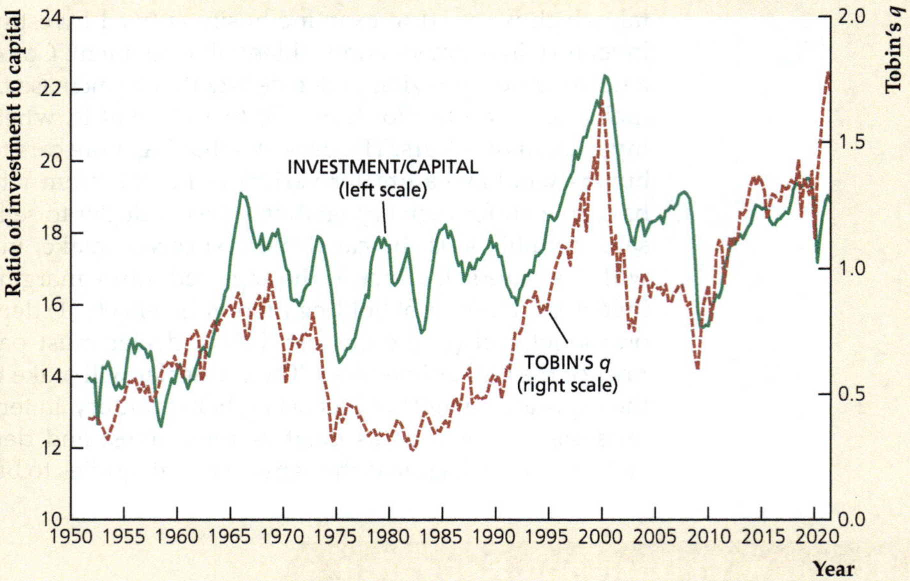

FIGURE 4.7

Ratio of Investment to Capital and Tobin's *q*, 1951Q4–2021Q3

The graph shows the ratio of investment to the capital stock on the left axis and the value of Tobin's *q* on the right axis. Note that the investment/capital ratio and Tobin's *q* usually move together, rising or falling at about the same time.

Source: Investment is nonfinancial fixed investment from Bureau of Economic Analysis, downloaded from St. Louis Fed website at *fred.stlouisfed.org* series *PNFI*; capital is sum of nonfinancial corporate sector equipment and structures, FRED series *RCSNNWMVBSNNCB* and *ESABSNNCB*; Tobin's *q* is the ratio of nonfinancial corporate sector equities value, FRED series *MVEONWMVBSNNCB*, to net worth, FRED series *TNWMVBSNNCB*.

will cause Tobin's q to rise for most firms, leading to increased rates of investment. Essentially, when the stock market is high, firms find it profitable to expand.

Figure 4.7 shows quarterly data on Tobin's q and the ratio of investment to capital. Consistent with the theory, the two are closely related; Tobin's q and investment rose together in the 1950s, 1960s, and 2010s, and then both fell sharply in 2000 and 2008. However, from 1975 to 1995, Tobin's q and the ratio of investment to capital are less closely related.

Although it may seem different, the q theory of investment is similar to the theory of investment discussed in this chapter. In the theory developed in this chapter we identified three main factors affecting the desired capital stock: the expected future marginal product of capital, MPK^f; the real interest rate, r; and the purchase price of new capital, p_K. Each of these factors also affects Tobin's q: (1) An increase in the expected marginal product of capital tends to increase the expected future earnings of the firm, which raises the stock market value of the firm and thus increases q; (2) a reduction in the real interest rate also tends to raise stock prices (and hence q), as financial investors substitute away from low-yielding bonds and bank deposits and buy stocks instead; and (3) a decrease in the purchase price of capital reduces the denominator of the q ratio and thus increases q. Because all three types of change increase Tobin's q, they also increase the desired capital stock and investment, as predicted by our analysis in this chapter.

We can also use this same approach to analyze residential investment. The expected future marginal product of an apartment building, for example, is the real value of rents that can be collected from the tenants, minus taxes and operating costs. The user cost of capital for an apartment building during a year is its depreciation, or loss of value from wear and tear, plus the interest cost (reflected in mortgage payments, for example). As for other types of capital, constructing an apartment building is profitable only if its expected future marginal product is at least as great as its user cost.

4.3 Goods Market Equilibrium

Explain the factors affecting goods market equilibrium.

In Chapter 3 we showed that the quantity of goods and services supplied in an economy depends on the level of productivity—as determined, for example, by the technology used—and on the quantity of inputs, such as the capital and labor used. In this chapter we have discussed the factors that affect the demand for goods and services, particularly the demand for consumption goods by households and the demand for investment goods by firms. But how do we know that the amount of goods and services that consumers and investors want to buy will be the same as the amount that producers are willing to provide? Putting the question another way, What economic forces bring the goods market into equilibrium, with quantities demanded equal to quantities supplied? In this section, we show that the real interest rate is the key economic variable whose adjustments help bring the quantities of goods supplied and demanded into balance; thus a benefit of our analysis is an explanation of what determines interest rates. Another benefit is that, by adding the analysis of goods market equilibrium to the analysis of labor market equilibrium in Chapter 3, we take another large step toward constructing a complete model of the macroeconomy.

The goods market is in equilibrium when the aggregate quantity of goods supplied equals the aggregate quantity of goods demanded. (For brevity, we refer only to "goods" rather than to "goods and services," but services always are included.) Algebraically, this condition is

$$Y = C^d + I^d + G. \quad \textbf{(4.7)}$$

The left side of Eq. (4.7) is the quantity of goods, Y, supplied by firms, which is determined by the factors discussed in Chapter 3. The right side of Eq. (4.7) is the aggregate demand for goods. If we continue to assume no foreign sector, so that net exports are zero, the quantity of goods demanded is the sum of desired consumption by households, C^d, desired investment by firms, I^d, and government purchases, G.[15] Equation (4.7) is called the *goods market equilibrium condition.*

The goods market equilibrium condition is different in an important way from the income–expenditure identity for a closed economy, $Y = C + I + G$ (this identity is Eq. 2.3, with $NX = 0$). The income–expenditure identity is a relationship between actual income (output) and actual spending, which, by definition, is always satisfied. In contrast, the goods market equilibrium condition does not always have to be satisfied. For example, firms may produce output faster than consumers want to buy it so that undesired inventories pile up in firms' warehouses. In this situation, the income–expenditure identity is still satisfied (because the undesired additions to firms' inventories are counted as part of total spending—see Chapter 2), but the goods market wouldn't be in equilibrium because production exceeds *desired* spending (which does *not* include the

[15]We assume that G always equals the level desired by the government and so we don't distinguish between desired and actual G.

undesired increases in inventories). Although in principle the goods market equilibrium condition need not always hold, strong forces act to bring the goods market into equilibrium fairly quickly.

A different, but equivalent, way to write the goods market equilibrium condition emphasizes the relationship between desired saving and desired investment. To obtain this alternative form of the goods market equilibrium condition, we first subtract $C^d + G$ from both sides of Eq. (4.7):

$$Y - C^d - G = I^d.$$

The left side of this equation, $Y - C^d - G$, is desired national saving, S^d (see Eq. 4.1). Thus the goods market equilibrium condition becomes

$$S^d = I^d. \qquad \textbf{(4.8)}$$

This alternative way of writing the goods market equilibrium condition says that the goods market is in equilibrium when desired national saving equals desired investment.

Because saving and investment are central to many issues we present in this book and because the desired-saving-equals-desired-investment form of the goods market equilibrium condition often is easier to work with, we use Eq. (4.8) in most of our analyses. However, we emphasize once again that Eq. (4.8) is equivalent to the condition that the supply of goods equals the demand for goods, Eq. (4.7).

The Saving–Investment Diagram

For the goods market to be in equilibrium, then, the aggregate supply of goods must equal the aggregate demand for goods, or equivalently, desired national saving must equal desired investment. We demonstrate in this section that adjustments of the real interest rate allow the goods market to attain equilibrium.[16]

The determination of goods market equilibrium can be shown graphically with a saving–investment diagram (Figure 4.8), which shows the amount of funds supplied by savers and the amount of funds demanded by firms for investment. The real interest rate is measured along the vertical axis, and national saving and investment are measured along the horizontal axis. The saving curve, S, shows the relationship between desired national saving and the real interest rate. The upward slope of the saving curve reflects the empirical finding (Section 4.1) that a higher real interest rate raises desired national saving. The investment curve, I, shows the relationship between desired investment and the real interest rate. The investment curve slopes downward because a higher real interest rate increases the user cost of capital and thus reduces desired investment.

Goods market equilibrium is represented by point E, at which desired national saving equals desired investment, as required by Eq. (4.8). The real interest rate corresponding to E (6% in this example) is the only real interest rate that clears the goods market. When the real interest rate is 6%, both desired national saving and desired investment equal 1000.

How does the goods market come to equilibrium at E, where the real interest rate is 6%? Suppose instead that the real interest rate is 3%. As Fig. 4.8 shows, when the real interest rate is 3%, the amount of investment that firms want to

[16]Strictly speaking, we should refer to the expected real interest rate rather than simply the real interest rate. The two are the same if expected inflation and actual inflation are equal.

FIGURE 4.8

Goods market equilibrium

Goods market equilibrium occurs when desired national saving equals desired investment. In the figure, equilibrium occurs when the real interest rate is 6% and both desired national saving and desired investment equal 1000. If the real interest rate were, say, 3%, desired investment (1500) would not equal desired national saving (850), and the goods market would not be in equilibrium. Competition among borrowers for funds would then cause the real interest rate to rise until it reaches 6%.

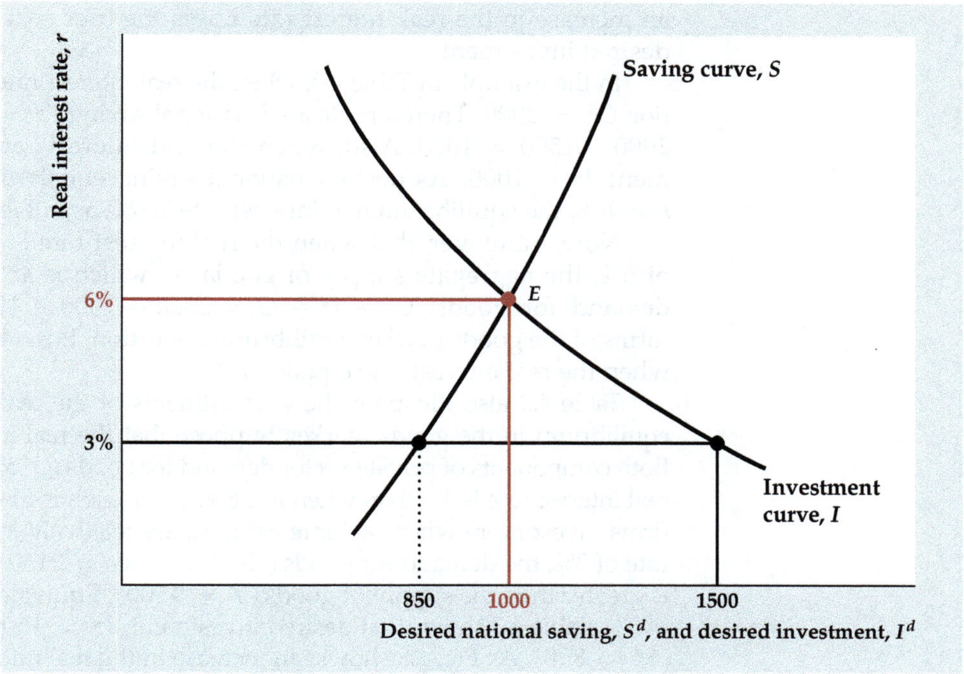

undertake (1500) exceeds desired national saving (850). With investors wanting to borrow more than savers want to lend, the "price" of funds—the real interest rate that lenders receive—will be bid up. The return to savers will rise until it reaches 6%, and desired national saving and desired investment are equal. Similarly, if the real interest rate exceeds 6%, the amount that savers want to lend will exceed what investors want to borrow, and the real return paid to savers will be bid down. Thus adjustments of the real interest rate, in response to an excess supply or excess demand for funds, bring the goods market into equilibrium.

Although Fig. 4.8 shows goods market equilibrium in terms of equal saving and investment, keep in mind that an equivalent way to express goods market equilibrium is that the supply of goods, Y, equals the demand for goods, $C^d + I^d + G$ (Eq. 4.7). Table 4.3 illustrates this point with a numerical example consistent with the values shown in Fig. 4.8. Here the assumption is that output, Y, and government purchases, G, are fixed at values of 4500 and 1500, respectively. Desired consumption, C^d, and desired investment, I^d, depend on the real interest rate. Desired consumption depends on the real interest rate because a higher real interest rate raises desired saving, which necessarily reduces desired consumption. Desired investment depends on the real interest rate because

TABLE 4.3

Components of Aggregate Demand for Goods (An Example)

Real Interest Rate, r	Output, Y	Desired Consumption, C^d	Desired Investment, I^d	Government Purchases, G	Desired National Saving, $S^d = Y - C^d - G$	Aggregate Demand for Goods, $C^d + I^d + G$
3%	4500	2150	1500	1500	850	5150
6%	4500	2000	1000	1500	1000	4500

an increase in the real interest rate raises the user cost of capital, which lowers desired investment.

In the example in Table 4.3, when the real interest rate is 6%, desired consumption $C^d = 2000$. Therefore desired national saving $S^d = Y - C^d - G = 4500 - 2000 - 1500 = 1000$. Also, when the real interest rate is 6%, desired investment $I^d = 1000$. As desired national saving equals desired investment when $r = 6\%$, the equilibrium real interest rate is 6%, as in Fig. 4.8.

Note, moreover, that when the real interest rate is at the equilibrium value of 6%, the aggregate supply of goods, Y, which is 4500, equals the aggregate demand for goods, $C^d + I^d + G = 2000 + 1000 + 1500 = 4500$. Thus, both forms of the goods market equilibrium condition, Eqs. (4.7) and (4.8), are satisfied when the real interest rate equals 6%.

Table 4.3 also illustrates how adjustments of the real interest rate bring about equilibrium in the goods market. Suppose that the real interest rate initially is 3%. Both components of private-sector demand for goods (C^d and I^d) are higher when the real interest rate is 3% than when it is 6%. The reason is that consumers save less and firms invest more when real interest rates are relatively low. Thus, at a real interest rate of 3%, the demand for goods $(C^d + I^d + G = 2150 + 1500 + 1500 = 5150)$ is greater than the supply of goods $(Y = 4500)$. Equivalently, at a real interest rate of 3%, Table 4.3 shows that desired investment $(I^d = 1500)$ exceeds desired saving $(S^d = 850)$. As Fig. 4.8 shows, an increase in the real interest rate to 6% eliminates the disequilibrium in the goods market by reducing desired investment and increasing desired national saving. An alternative explanation is that the increase in the real interest rate eliminates the excess of the demand for goods over the supply of goods by reducing both consumption demand and investment demand.

Shifts of the Saving Curve. For any real interest rate, a change in the economy that raises desired national saving shifts the saving curve to the right, and a change that reduces desired national saving shifts the saving curve to the left. (Summary table 5 lists the factors affecting desired national saving.)

A shift of the saving curve leads to a new goods market equilibrium with a different real interest rate and different amounts of saving and investment. Figure 4.9 illustrates the effects of a decrease in desired national saving—resulting, for example, from a temporary increase in current government purchases. The initial equilibrium point is at E, where (as in Fig. 4.8) the real interest rate is 6% and desired national saving and desired investment both equal 1000. When current government purchases increase, the resulting decrease in desired national saving causes the saving curve to shift to the left, from S^1 to S^2. At the new goods market equilibrium point, F, the real interest rate is 7%, reflecting the fact that at the initial real interest rate of 6% the demand for funds by investors now exceeds the supply of saving.

Figure 4.9 also shows that, in response to the increase in government purchases, national saving and investment both fall, from 1000 to 850. Saving falls because of the initial decrease in desired saving, which is only partially offset by the increase in the real interest rate. Investment falls because the higher real interest rate raises the user cost of capital that firms face. When increased government purchases cause investment to decline, economists say that investment has been *crowded out*. The crowding out of investment by increased government purchases occurs, in effect, because the government is using more real resources, some of which would otherwise have gone into investment.

FIGURE 4.9

A decline in desired saving

A change that reduces desired national saving, such as a temporary increase in current government purchases, shifts the saving curve to the left, from S^1 to S^2. The goods market equilibrium point moves from *E* to *F*. The decline in desired saving raises the real interest rate, from 6% to 7%, and lowers saving and investment, from 1000 to 850.

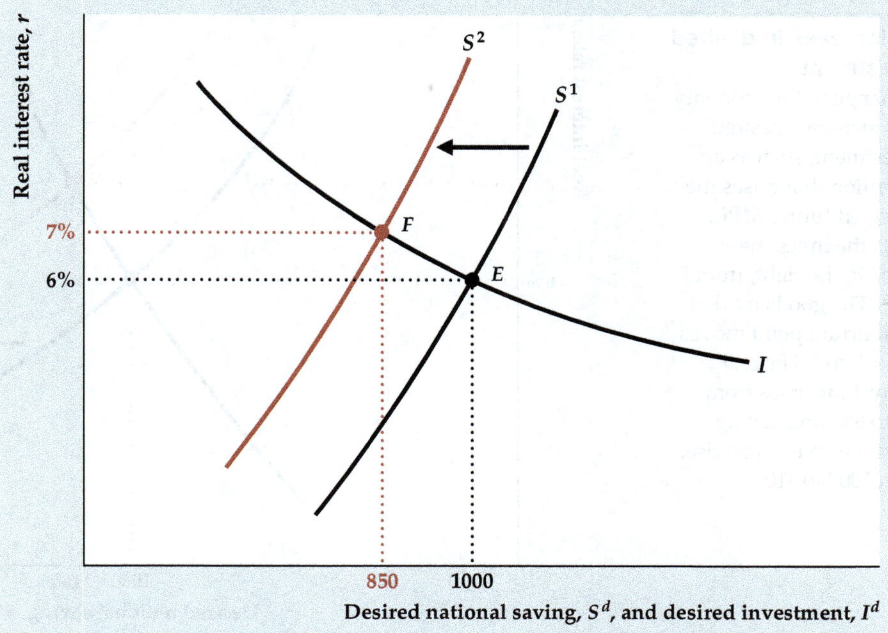

Shifts of the Investment Curve. Like the saving curve, the investment curve can shift. For any real interest rate, a change in the economy that raises desired investment shifts the investment curve to the right, and a change that lowers desired investment shifts the investment curve to the left. (See Summary table 6 for the factors affecting desired investment.)

The effects on goods market equilibrium of an increase in desired investment—as from an invention that raises the expected future marginal product of capital—are shown in Figure 4.10. The increase in desired investment shifts the investment curve to the right, from I^1 to I^2, changing the goods market equilibrium point from *E* to *G*. The real interest rate rises from 6% to 8% because the increased demand for investment funds causes the real interest rate to be bid up. Saving and investment also increase, from 1000 to 1100, with the higher saving reflecting the willingness of savers to save more when the real interest rate rises.

In these last two chapters, we have presented supply–demand analyses of the labor and goods markets and developed tools needed to understand the behavior of various macroeconomic variables, including employment, the real wage, output, saving, investment, and the real interest rate. These concepts—and a few more developed in the study of asset markets in Chapter 7—form the basis for the economic analysis presented in the rest of this book. In Chapter 5, we use the concepts developed so far to examine the determinants of trade flows and international borrowing and lending. In Chapter 6, we use them to tackle the fundamental question of why some countries' economies grow more quickly than others.

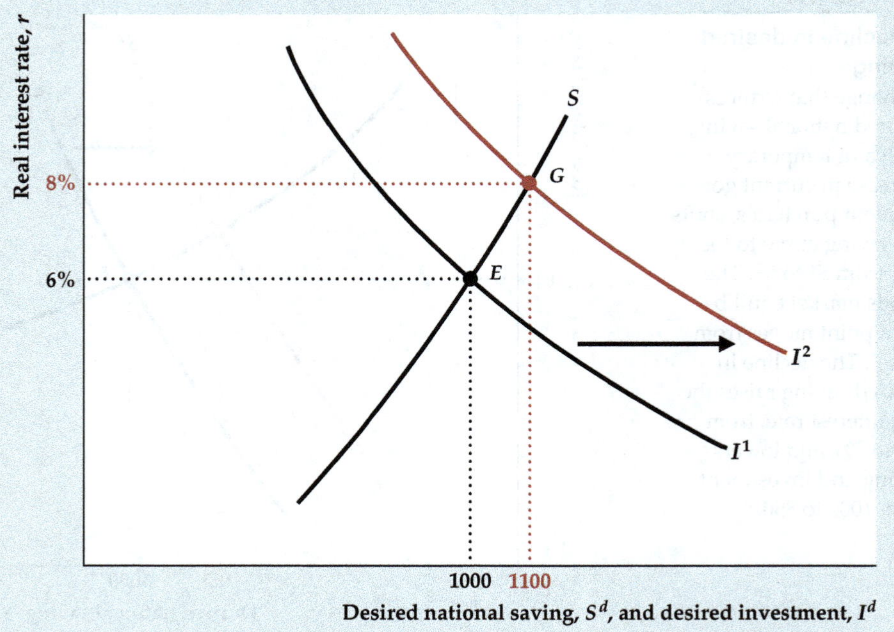

FIGURE 4.10

An increase in desired investment

A change in the economy that increases desired investment, such as an invention that raises the expected future *MPK*, shifts the investment curve to the right, from I^1 to I^2. The goods market equilibrium point moves from *E* to *G*. The real interest rate rises from 6% to 8%, and saving and investment also rise, from 1000 to 1100.

Application

Macroeconomic Consequences of the Boom and Bust in Stock Prices

On October 19, 1987, stock prices took their biggest-ever one-day plunge. The Wilshire 5000 stock price index dropped 18% that day, after having fallen by 15% from the market's peak in August of the same year. About $1 trillion of financial wealth was eliminated by the decline in stock prices on that single day.

Stock prices in the United States soared during the 1990s, especially during the second half of the decade, but then tumbled sharply early in the first year of the new century. Stock prices continued to fall for several years, and stockholders lost wealth of about $5 trillion, an amount equal to about half of a year's GDP. After rising from 2003 to 2007, stock prices plunged during the financial crisis of 2008, with stocks losing 48% of their value in real terms. By the first quarter of 2009, real stock prices were at their lowest level since 1995. After that, however, stock prices more than tripled from 2009 to 2018.

What are the macroeconomic effects of such booms and busts in stock prices? We have emphasized two major macroeconomic channels for stock prices: a wealth effect on consumption and an effect on capital investment through Tobin's *q*. Let's see how each of those effects worked after the stock market crash of 1987, the increase in stock values in the 1990s, the decline in stock market wealth in the early 2000s, and the financial crisis of 2008.

The *wealth effect* on consumption arises because stocks are a component of households' financial assets. Because a stock market boom makes households better off financially, they should respond by consuming more, and likewise, a bust in

FIGURE 4.11

Real U.S. stock prices and the ratio of consumption to GDP, 1987Q1–2021Q4

The graph shows the values of the real (inflation-adjusted) Wilshire 5000 stock price index, which covers all U.S. corporations with available market prices, and the ratio of consumption spending to GDP from 1987 to the fourth quarter of 2021. The variables move together in some episodes and in opposite directions in other episodes.

Source: Wilshire 5000 index from Wilshire Associates, downloaded from Federal Reserve Bank of St. Louis FRED database at *fred.stlouisfed.org/WILL5000PR*; real stock prices calculated as Wilshire 5000 divided by GDP deflator; GDP deflator, consumption spending, and GDP from Bureau of Economic Analysis, downloaded from FRED database, series *GDPDEF, PCEC,* and *GDP*, respectively.

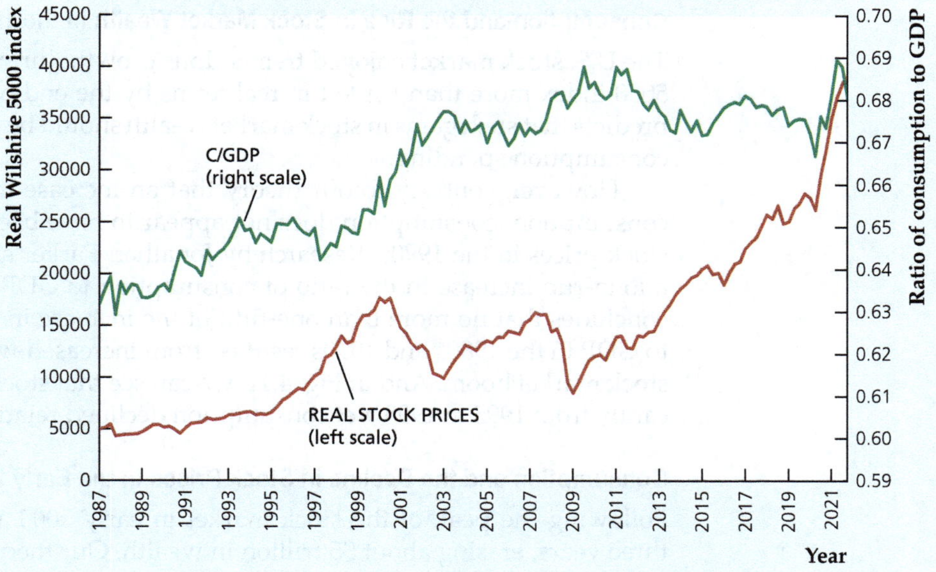

the stock market reduces household wealth and should reduce consumption. To show how consumption and stock prices are related, Figure 4.11 plots the value of the Wilshire 5000 index, adjusted for inflation, along with the ratio of consumption spending to GDP.

Consumption and the 1987 Crash

We would expect that following the 1987 stock market crash, consumers would reduce spending, but the decline in consumption should have been much smaller than the $1 trillion decline in wealth because consumers would spread the effects of their losses over a long period of time by reducing planned future consumption as well as current consumption. If consumers spread changes in their wealth over 25 years, then we might guess that current consumption spending would decline by about $40 billion (assuming the real interest rate is near zero). However, consumers might also worry that the stock market crash would lead to a recession, so they might cut consumption further; such a scenario suggests that consumption should decline by more than $40 billion. However, economists who estimated the actual decline in consumption suggest that it fell less than $40 billion.[17] Why did consumption decline less than economic theory suggests? Perhaps the reason is that the rise in stock prices had been very recent—stock prices had risen 39% in the 8 months preceding the crash. Because the increase in stock prices occurred so rapidly, it is possible that by August 1987, stockholders had not yet fully adjusted their consumption to reflect the higher level of wealth. Thus, when the market fell, consumption did not have to decline by very much to fall back into line with wealth.[18]

[17]See C. Alan Garner, "Has the Stock Market Crash Reduced Consumer Spending?" *Economic Review*, Federal Reserve Bank of Kansas City, April 1988, pp. 3–6; and David Runkle, "Why No Crunch from the Crash?" *Quarterly Review*, Federal Reserve Bank of Minneapolis, Winter 1988, pp. 2–7.

[18]In "Consumption, Aggregate Wealth, and Expected Stock Returns," *Journal of Finance*, June 2001, pp. 815–849, Martin Lettau and Sydney Ludvigson noted that, prior to the crash, aggregate consumption was unusually low relative to stock market wealth. Their analysis indicates that this behavior reflected consumers' expectations of a decline in the stock market.

(*continued*)

Consumption and the Rise in Stock Market Wealth in the 1990s

The U.S. stock market enjoyed tremendous growth during the 1990s. The Wilshire 5000 index more than tripled in real terms by the end of the decade. Our theory predicts that such gains in stock market wealth should be associated with increased consumption spending.

However, contrary to our theory that an increase in wealth should increase consumption, consumption does not appear to have been closely correlated with stock prices in the 1990s. Research by Jonathan Parker shows that there has been a long-run increase in the ratio of consumption to GDP that began in 1979.[19] He concludes that no more than one-fifth of the increase in the ratio of consumption to GDP in the 1980s and 1990s resulted from increased wealth associated with the stock market boom. And in Fig. 4.11, we can see that stock prices increased significantly from 1995 to 1998, yet consumption declined relative to GDP in that period.

Consumption and the Decline in Stock Prices in the Early 2000s

Following the peak of the stock market in early 2000, stock prices declined for three years, erasing about $5 trillion in wealth. Our theory suggests that consumers should respond by reducing their consumption spending. Yet Fig. 4.11 shows that, in fact, consumption spending increased significantly relative to GDP during that period, rising from 65% of GDP in 1999 to 67% in 2002. Several reasons may explain why consumption did not decline after stock prices fell: (1) the reduction in people's wealth is spread throughout their lifetimes, so there is not a large immediate impact on consumption; (2) at the same time stock prices declined, home prices rose, so many people who lost wealth in the stock market gained it back in real estate; and (3) people may have just viewed their gains in the late 1990s as "paper profits" that were lost in the early 2000s, so neither the gains nor the losses affected consumption.

Investment and the Declines in the Stock Market in the 2000s

As we have seen in Fig. 4.11, the stock market fell precipitously in 2000 and 2008. The large declines in the stock market led to large declines in Tobin's q, the ratio of the market value of firms to the replacement cost of their capital, as you can see in Fig. 4.7 in "In Touch with Data and Research: Investment and the Stock Market." This figure also shows very sharp declines in real investment beginning shortly after the stock market and Tobin's q began to fall in 2000 and again in 2008. The slight delay in the fall in investment, relative to the fall in the stock market, reflects the lags in the process of making investment decisions, planning capital formation, and implementing the plans. But despite these lags, the declines in investment following large declines in the stock market are quite evident.

The Financial Crisis of 2008

During the financial crisis of 2008, stock prices plunged rapidly. In the six months from August 2008 to February 2009, U.S. stock prices declined in nominal terms

[19]"Spendthrift in America? On Two Decades of Decline in the U.S. Saving Rate," in B. Bernanke and J. Rotemberg, eds., *NBER Macroeconomics Annual, 1999*, Cambridge, MA: MIT Press, 1999.

by 43%, one of the fastest declines in stock prices on record. Investors feared that a depression was possible because of a meltdown in the financial sector, which had taken excessive risks, especially in real-estate markets. The recession that had begun in December 2007 became much worse, and the unemployment rate increased dramatically. In this case, unlike the episode in the early 2000s, home prices also declined, and the simultaneous decline in housing prices and stock values translated into a nearly 20% decline in household net wealth, which fell from $66.7 trillion at the end of 2007 to $55.0 trillion by the end of March 2009. Yet the ratio of consumption to GDP declined by less than 1 percentage point in 2008, as Fig. 4.11 shows, and then it rebounded in early 2009.

The Stock Market Boom Since 2009

After bottoming out in early 2009, the stock market bounced back strongly in the following 12 years, increasing in real terms by more than 300% (from its low point in 2009 to the end of 2021). Consumption spending remained at a high and fairly constant level of about 68% of GDP, but both GDP growth and consumption growth rates were lower than they had been before the financial crisis.

CHAPTER SUMMARY

1. Because saving equals income minus consumption, a household's decisions about how much to consume and how much to save are really the same decision. Individuals and households save because they value both future consumption and current consumption; for the same amount of income, an increase in current saving reduces current consumption but increases the amount that the individual or household will be able to consume in the future.

2. For an individual or household, an increase in current income raises both desired consumption and desired saving. Analogously, at the national level, an increase in current output raises both desired consumption and desired national saving. At both the household and national levels, an increase in expected future income or in wealth raises desired consumption; however, because these changes raise desired consumption without affecting current income or output, they cause desired saving to fall.

3. An increase in the real interest rate has two potentially offsetting effects on saving. First, a higher real interest rate increases the price of current consumption relative to future consumption (each unit of current consumption costs $1 + r$ units of forgone future consumption). In response to the increased relative price of current consumption, people substitute future consumption for current consumption by saving more today. This tendency to increase saving in response to an increase in the relative price of current consumption is called the *substitution effect* of the real interest rate on saving. Second, a higher real interest rate increases the wealth of savers by increasing the interest payments they receive, while reducing the wealth of borrowers by increasing the amount of interest they must pay. By making savers wealthier, an increase in the real interest rate leads savers to consume more and reduce their saving; however, because it makes borrowers poorer, an increase in the real interest rate causes borrowers to reduce their consumption and increase their saving. The change in current consumption that results because a consumer is made richer or poorer by an increase in the real interest rate is called the income effect of the real interest rate on saving.

   For a saver, the substitution effect of an increase in the real interest rate (which tends to boost saving) and the income effect (which tends to reduce saving) work in opposite directions, so that the overall effect is ambiguous. For a borrower, both the substitution effect and the income effect of a higher real interest rate act to increase saving. Overall, empirical studies suggest that an increase in the real interest rate increases desired national saving and reduces desired consumption, but not by very much.

   The real interest rate that is relevant to saving decisions is the expected real after-tax interest rate, which is the real return that savers expect to earn after paying a portion of the interest they receive in taxes.

4. With total output held constant, a temporary increase in government purchases reduces desired consumption. The reason is that higher government purchases imply increases in present or future taxes, which makes consumers feel poorer. However, the decrease in desired consumption is smaller than the increase in government purchases, so that desired national saving, $Y - C^d - G$, falls as a result of a temporary increase in government purchases.

5. According to the Ricardian equivalence proposition, a current lump-sum tax cut should have no effect on desired consumption or desired national saving. The reason is that, if no change occurs in current or planned government purchases, a tax cut that increases current income must be offset by future tax increases that lower expected future income. If consumers do not take into account expected future tax changes, however, the Ricardian equivalence proposition will not hold and a tax cut is likely to raise desired consumption and lower desired national saving.

6. The desired capital stock is the level of capital that maximizes expected profits. At the desired capital stock, the expected future marginal product of capital equals the user cost of capital. The user cost of capital is the expected real cost of using a unit of capital for a period of time; it is the sum of the depreciation cost (the loss in value because the capital wears out) and the interest cost (the interest rate times the price of the capital good).

7. Any change that reduces the user cost of capital or increases the expected future marginal product of capital increases the desired capital stock. A reduction in the taxation of capital, as measured by the effective tax rate, also increases the desired capital stock.

8. Gross investment is spending on new capital goods. Gross investment minus depreciation (worn-out or scrapped capital) equals net investment, or the change in the capital stock. Firms invest so as to achieve their desired level of capital stock; when the desired capital stock increases, firms invest more.

9. The goods market is in equilibrium when the aggregate quantity of goods supplied equals the aggregate quantity of goods demanded, which (in a closed economy) is the sum of desired consumption, desired investment, and government purchases of goods and services.

Equivalently, the goods market is in equilibrium when desired national saving equals desired investment. For any given level of output, the goods market is brought into equilibrium by changes in the real interest rate.

10. The determination of goods market equilibrium, for any fixed supply of output, Y, is represented graphically by the saving–investment diagram. The saving curve slopes upward because empirical evidence suggests that a higher real interest rate raises desired saving. The investment curve slopes downward because a higher real interest rate raises the user cost of capital, which lowers firms' desired capital stocks and thus the amount of investment they do. Changes in variables that affect desired saving or investment shift the saving or investment curves and change the real interest rate that clears the goods market.

KEY DIAGRAM 3

The saving–investment diagram

In an economy with no foreign trade, the goods market is in equilibrium when desired national saving equals desired investment. Equivalently, the goods market is in equilibrium when the aggregate quantity of goods supplied equals the aggregate quantity of goods demanded.

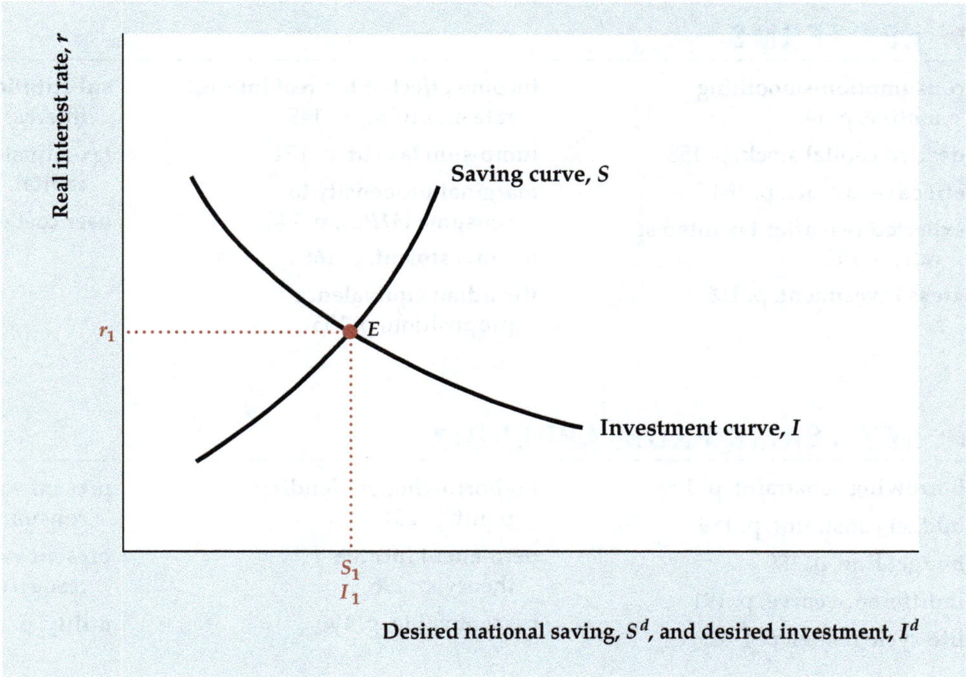

Diagram Elements

- The real interest rate, r, is on the vertical axis; desired national saving, S^d, and desired investment, I^d, are on the horizontal axis.
- The saving curve, S, shows the level of desired national saving at each real interest rate. The saving curve slopes upward because a higher real interest rate increases the reward for saving and causes households to save more. (Empirically, this effect outweighs the tendency of a higher real interest rate to lower saving by reducing the amount of saving necessary to reach any specified target.) Desired national saving is defined as $S^d = Y - C^d - G$, where Y is output, C^d is desired consumption, and G is government purchases.
- The investment curve, I, shows the amount that firms want to invest in new capital goods at each real interest rate. The investment curve slopes downward because a higher real interest rate raises the user cost of capital and thus lowers the amount of capital that firms want to use.

Analysis

- Goods market equilibrium requires that desired national saving equal desired investment, or $S^d = I^d$.
- Goods market equilibrium occurs in the diagram at point E, where the saving curve and investment curve intersect. At E, desired national saving equals S_1, desired investment equals I_1, and $S_1 = I_1$. The real interest rate at E, r_1, is the real interest rate that clears the goods market.

- An alternative way to express the goods market equilibrium condition is as follows: The quantity of goods supplied, Y, equals the quantity of goods demanded by households, C^d, firms, I^d, and the government, G, or $Y = C^d + I^d + G$. As $S^d = Y - C^d - G$, this condition is equivalent to $S^d = I^d$.

Factors That Shift the Curves

- Any factor that raises desired national saving at a given real interest rate shifts the saving curve to the right; similarly, any factor that lowers desired national saving shifts the saving curve to the left. Factors that affect desired national saving are listed in Summary table 5. Similarly, factors that change desired investment for a given real interest rate shift the investment curve; see Summary table 6, for factors that affect desired investment. Shifts of either curve change the goods market equilibrium point and thus change national saving, investment, and the real interest rate.

KEY TERMS

consumption-smoothing motive, p. 145

desired capital stock, p. 158

effective tax rate, p. 164

expected real after-tax interest rate, p. 151

gross investment, p. 166

income effect of the real interest rate on saving, p. 149

lump-sum tax cut, p. 154

marginal propensity to consume (*MPC*), p. 146

net investment, p. 166

Ricardian equivalence proposition, p. 155

substitution effect of the real interest rate on saving, p. 149

tax-adjusted user cost of capital, p. 163

user cost of capital, p. 159

KEY TERMS FROM APPENDIX

borrowing constraint, p. 199

budget constraint, p. 189

budget line, p. 189

indifference curve, p. 191

life-cycle model, p. 197

no-borrowing, no-lending point, p. 201

permanent income theory, p. 196

present value, p. 190

present value of lifetime consumption (*PVLC*), p. 191

present value of lifetime resources (*PVLR*), p. 190

utility, p. 191

KEY EQUATIONS

$$S^d = Y - C^d - G \qquad (4.1)$$

Desired national saving, S^d, is the level of national saving that occurs when consumption is at its desired level. Equation (4.1) is obtained by substituting desired consumption, C^d, for actual consumption, C, in the definition of national saving.

$$r_{a-t} = (1 - t)i - \pi^e \qquad (4.2)$$

The expected real after-tax interest rate, r_{a-t}, is the after-tax nominal interest rate, $(1 - t)i$, minus the expected rate of inflation, π^e. The expected real after-tax interest rate is the real return expected by a saver when a portion, t, of interest income must be paid as taxes.

$$uc = rp_K + dp_K = (r + d)p_K \qquad (4.3)$$

The user cost of capital, uc, is the sum of the interest cost, rp_K, and the depreciation cost, dp_K, where d is the depreciation rate and p_K is the price of a capital good.

$$MPK^f = \frac{uc}{1 - \tau} = \frac{(r + d)p_K}{1 - \tau} \qquad (4.4)$$

The desired capital stock, or the capital stock that maximizes the firm's expected profits, is the capital stock for which the expected future marginal product of capital, MPK^f, equals the tax-adjusted user cost of capital, $uc/(1 - \tau)$, where τ is the tax rate on the firm's revenues (equivalently, the effective tax rate).

$$Y = C^d + I^d + G \quad (4.7)$$

The *goods market equilibrium condition* in a closed economy says that the goods market is in equilibrium when the aggregate quantity of goods supplied, Y, equals the aggregate quantity of goods demanded, $C^d + I^d + G$.

$$S^d = I^d \quad (4.8)$$

Another way of stating the goods market equilibrium condition is that desired national saving, S^d, must equal desired investment, I^d. This equation is equivalent to Eq. (4.7).

REVIEW QUESTIONS

1. Given income, how are consumption and saving linked? What is the basic motivation for saving?
2. How are desired consumption and desired saving affected by increases in current income, expected future income, and wealth?
3. Use the concepts of income effect and substitution effect to explain why the effect on desired saving of an increase in the expected real interest rate is potentially ambiguous.
4. Define the expected real after-tax interest rate. If the tax rate on interest income declines, what happens to the expected real after-tax interest rate?
5. What effect does a temporary increase in government purchases—for example, to fight a war—have on desired consumption and desired national saving, for a constant level of output? What is the effect on desired national saving of a lump-sum tax increase? Why is the effect of a lump-sum tax increase controversial?
6. What are the two components of the user cost of capital? Explain why each is a cost of using a capital good.
7. What is the desired capital stock? How does it depend on the expected future marginal product of capital, the user cost of capital, and the effective tax rate?
8. What is the difference between gross investment and net investment? Can gross investment be positive when net investment is negative?
9. Give two equivalent ways of describing equilibrium in the goods market. Use a diagram to show how goods market equilibrium is attained.
10. Explain why the saving curve slopes upward and the investment curve slopes downward in the saving–investment diagram. Give two examples of changes that would shift the saving curve to the right, and two examples of changes that would shift the investment curve to the right.

NUMERICAL PROBLEMS

1. Julia is making saving plans for this year and next. She knows her real income after taxes will be \$50,000 in both years. Any part of her income saved this year will earn a real interest rate of 10% between this year and next year. Currently, the consumer has no wealth (no money in the bank or other financial assets, and no debts). There is no uncertainty about the future.

   The consumer wants to save an amount this year that will allow her to (1) make college tuition payments next year equal to \$16,800 in real terms; (2) enjoy exactly the same amount of consumption this year and next year, not counting tuition payments as part of next year's consumption; and (3) have neither assets nor debts at the end of next year.

   a. How much should the consumer save this year? How much should she consume?

   How are the amounts that the consumer should save and consume affected by each of the following changes (taken one at a time, with other variables held at their original values)?

   b. Her current income rises from \$50,000 to \$54,200.

   c. The income she expects to receive next year rises from \$50,000 to \$54,200.

   d. During the current year she receives an inheritance of \$1050 (an increase in wealth, not income).

   e. The expected tuition payment for next year rises from \$16,800 to \$18,900 in real terms.

   f. The real interest rate rises from 10% to 24%.
2. Hula hoop fabricators cost \$100 each. Kai, the CFO of the Hi-Ho Hula Hoop Company is trying to decide how many of these machines to buy. HHHHC expects to produce the following number of hoops each year for each level of capital stock shown.

Number of Fabricators	Number of Hoops Produced per Year
0	0
1	100
2	150
3	180
4	195
5	205
6	210

Hula hoops have a real value of $1 each. HHHHC has no other costs besides the cost of fabricators.

a. Find the expected future marginal product of capital (in terms of dollars) for each level of capital. The MPK^f for the third fabricator, for example, is the real value of the extra output obtained when the third fabricator is added.

b. If the real interest rate is 12% per year and the depreciation rate of capital is 20% per year, find the user cost of capital (in dollars per fabricator per year). How many fabricators should Kai buy?

c. Repeat part (*b*) for a real interest rate of 8% per year.

d. Repeat part (*b*) for a 40% tax on HHHHC's sales revenues.

e. A technical innovation doubles the number of hoops a fabricator can produce. How many fabricators should Kai buy when the real interest rate is 12% per year? 8% per year? Assume that there are no taxes and that the depreciation rate is still 20% per year.

3. You have just taken a job that requires you to move to a new city. In relocating, you face the decision of whether to buy or rent a house. A suitable house costs $300,000 and you have saved enough for the down payment. The (nominal) mortgage interest rate is 10% per year, and you can also earn 10% per year on savings. Mortgage interest payments are tax deductible, interest earnings on savings are taxable, and you are in a 30% tax bracket. Interest is paid or received, and taxes are paid, on the last day of the year. The expected inflation rate is 5% per year.

The cost of maintaining the house (replacing worn-out roofing, painting, and so on) is 6% of the value of the house. Assume that these expenses also are paid entirely on the last day of the year. If the maintenance is done, the house retains its full real value. There are no other relevant costs or expenses.

a. What is the expected real after-tax interest rate on the home mortgage?

b. What is the user cost of the house?

c. If all you care about is minimizing your living expenses, at what (annual) rent level would you be just indifferent between buying a house and renting a house of comparable quality? Rent is also paid on the last day of the year.

4. Huxley, the owner of the Missing Link Chain-Link Fence Company is trying to determine how many chain-link fabricating machines to buy for its factory. If we define a chain-link fence of some specified length to be equal to one unit of output, the price of a new fabricating machine is 60 units of output, and the price of a one-year-old machine is 51 units of output. These relative prices are expected to be the same in the future. The expected future marginal product of fabricating machines, measured in units of output, is $165 - 2K$, where K is the number of machines in use. There are no taxes of any sort. The real interest rate is 10% per year.

a. What is the user cost of capital? Specify the units in which your answer is measured.

b. Determine the number of machines that will allow Missing Link to maximize its profit.

c. Suppose that Missing Link must pay a tax equal to 40% of its gross revenue. What is the optimal number of machines for the company?

d. Suppose that in addition to the 40% tax on revenue described in part (*c*), the firm can take advantage of a 20% investment tax credit, which allows it to reduce its taxes paid by 20% of the cost of any new machines purchased. What is Missing Link's desired capital stock now? (*Hint:* An investment tax credit effectively reduces the price of capital to the firm.)

5. An economy has full-employment output of 9000, and government purchases are 2000. Desired consumption and desired investment are as follows:

Real Interest Rate (%)	Desired Consumption	Desired Investment
2	6100	1500
3	6000	1400
4	5900	1300
5	5800	1200
6	5700	1100

a. Why do desired consumption and desired investment fall as the real interest rate rises?

b. Find desired national saving for each value of the real interest rate.

c. If the goods market is in equilibrium, what are the values of the real interest rate, desired national saving, and desired investment? Show that both forms of the goods market equilibrium condition,

Eqs. (4.7) and (4.8), are satisfied at the equilibrium. Assume that output is fixed at its full-employment level.

d. Repeat part (*c*) for the case in which government purchases fall to 1600. Assume that the amount people desire to consume at each real interest rate is unchanged.

6. An economy has full-employment output of 6000. Government purchases, G, are 1200. Desired consumption and desired investment are

$$C^d = 3600 - 2000r + 0.10Y, \text{ and}$$
$$I^d = 1200 - 4000r,$$

where Y is output and r is the real interest rate.

a. Find an equation relating desired national saving, S^d, to r and Y.

b. Using both versions of the goods market equilibrium condition, Eqs. (4.7) and (4.8), find the real interest rate that clears the goods market. Assume that output equals full-employment output.

c. Government purchases rise to 1440. How does this increase change the equation describing desired national saving? Show the change graphically. What happens to the market-clearing real interest rate?

7. Suppose that the economywide expected future marginal product of capital is $MPK^f = 20 - 0.02K$, where K is the future capital stock. The depreciation rate of capital, d, is 20% per period. The current capital stock is 900 units of capital. The price of a unit of capital is 1 unit of output. Firms pay taxes equal to 15% of their output. The consumption function in the economy is $C = 100 + 0.5Y - 200r$, where C is consumption, Y is output, and r is the real interest rate. Government purchases equal 200, and full-employment output is 1000.

a. Suppose that the real interest rate is 10% per period. What are the values of the tax-adjusted user cost of capital, the desired future capital stock, and the desired level of investment?

b. Now consider the real interest rate determined by goods market equilibrium. This part of the problem will guide you to this interest rate.

i. Write the tax-adjusted user cost of capital as a function of the real interest rate r. Also write the desired future capital stock and desired investment as functions of r.

ii. Use the investment function derived in part (i) along with the consumption function and government purchases, to calculate the real interest rate that clears the goods market. What are the goods market-clearing values of consumption, saving, and investment? What are the tax-adjusted user cost of capital and the desired capital stock in this equilibrium?

8. (Appendix 4.A) A consumer has initial real wealth of 20, current real income of 90, and future real income of 110. The real interest rate is 10% per period.

a. Find the consumer's *PVLR*.

b. Write the equation for the consumer's budget constraint (using the given numerical values) and graph the budget line.

Suppose that the consumer's goal is to smooth consumption completely. That is, he wants to have the same level of consumption in both the current and the future period.

c. How much will he save and consume in the current period?

d. How will his current saving and consumption be affected by an increase of 11 in current income?

e. How will his current saving and consumption be affected by an increase of 11 in future income?

f. How will his current saving and consumption be affected by an increase of 11 in his initial wealth?

9. (Appendix 4.A) A consumer lives three periods, called the learning period, the working period, and the retirement period. Her income is 200 during the learning period, 800 during the working period, and 200 again during the retirement period. The consumer's initial assets are 300. The real interest rate is zero. The consumer desires perfectly smooth consumption over her lifetime.

a. What are consumption and saving in each period, assuming no borrowing constraints? What happens if the consumer faces a borrowing constraint that prevents her from borrowing?

b. Assume that the consumer's initial wealth is zero instead of 300. Repeat part (*a*). Does being borrowing-constrained mean that consumption is lower in all three periods of the consumer's life than it would be if no borrowing constraints applied?

ANALYTICAL PROBLEMS

1. Use the saving–investment diagram to analyze the effects of the following on national saving, investment, and the real interest rate. Explain your reasoning.
   a. Consumers become more future-oriented and thus decide to save more.
   b. The government announces a large, one-time bonus payment to veterans returning from a war. The bonus will be financed by additional taxes levied on the general population over the next five years.
   c. The government introduces an investment tax credit (offset by other types of taxes, so total tax collections remain unchanged).
   d. A large number of accessible oil deposits are discovered, which increases the expected future marginal product of oil rigs and pipelines. It also causes an increase in expected future income.

2. A country loses much of its capital stock to a war.
   a. What effects should this event have on the country's current employment, output, and real wage?
   b. What effect will the loss of capital have on desired investment?
   c. Assume that the desired saving function doesn't change. What effect does the loss of capital have on the country's real interest rate and the quantity of investment?

3. *a.* Analyze the effects of a temporary increase in the price of oil (a temporary adverse supply shock) on current output, employment, the real wage, national saving, investment, and the real interest rate. Because the supply shock is temporary, you should assume that the expected future *MPK* and households' expected future incomes are unchanged. Assume throughout that output and employment remain at full-employment levels (which may change).
   b. Analyze the effects of a permanent increase in the price of oil (a permanent adverse supply shock) on current output, employment, the real wage, national saving, investment, and the real interest rate. Show that in this case, unlike the case of a temporary supply shock, the real interest rate need not change. (*Hint:* A permanent adverse supply shock lowers the current productivity of capital and labor, just as a temporary supply shock does. In addition, a permanent supply shock lowers both the expected future *MPK* and households' expected future incomes.)

4. Economists often argue that a temporary increase in government purchases—say, for military purposes—will crowd out private investment. Use the saving–investment diagram to illustrate this point, explaining why the curve(s) shift. Does it matter whether the temporary increase in military spending is funded by taxes or by borrowing?

   Alternatively, suppose that the temporary increase in government purchases is for infrastructure (roads, sewers, bridges) rather than for military purposes. The government spending on infrastructure makes private investment more productive, increasing the expected future *MPK* at each level of the capital stock. Use the saving–investment diagram to analyze the effects of government infrastructure spending on current consumption, national saving, investment, and the real interest rate. Does investment by private firms get crowded out by this kind of government investment? If not, what kind of spending, if any, does get crowded out? Assume that there is no change in current productivity or current output and assume (for simplicity) that households do not expect a change in their future incomes.

5. "A permanent increase in government purchases has a larger effect than a temporary increase of the same amount." Use the saving–investment diagram to evaluate this statement, focusing on effects on consumption, investment, and the real interest rate for a fixed level of output. (*Hint:* The permanent increase in government purchases implies larger increases in current and future taxes.)

6. (Appendix 4.A) Draw a budget line and indifference curves for a consumer who initially is a borrower. Be sure to indicate the no-borrowing, no-lending point and the optimal consumption point. Then show the effect on the budget line and the consumer's optimal consumption of an increase in the real interest rate. Using an intermediate budget line, show the income effect and the substitution effect. Do they work in the same direction or in opposite directions? Explain your answer.

7. (Appendix 4.A) Consumers typically pay a higher real interest rate to borrow than they receive when they lend (by making bank deposits, for example). Draw a consumer's budget line under the assumption that the real interest rate earned on funds lent, r_l is lower than the real interest rate paid to borrow, r_b. Show how the budget line is affected by an increase in r_l, an increase in r_b, or an increase in the consumer's initial wealth.

   Show that changes in r_l and r_b may leave current and future consumption unchanged. (*Hint:* Draw the consumer's indifference curves so that the consumer initially chooses the no-borrowing, no-lending point.)

WORKING WITH MACROECONOMIC DATA

For data to use in these exercises, go to the Federal Reserve Bank of St. Louis FRED database at fred.stlouisfed.org.

1. Graph the index of consumer sentiment, using quarterly data since 1965. Construct scatter plots relating the consumer sentiment index to the growth rate of real consumption expenditures, using quarterly data since 1965. Generally speaking, does consumption grow more quickly when consumers are more optimistic? Do the same exercise for consumer sentiment and real consumption expenditures on durable goods since 1999.

2. The Wilshire 5000 stock market index measures the total dollar value of a large set of stocks traded on the stock market. The real value of the Wilshire 5000 index, which measures the real value of the wealth represented by that set of stocks, is obtained by dividing the index by a measure of the price level, such as the CPI. (To obtain monthly data on the Wilshire 5000, use *WILL5000PR* in the FRED database.)

   Using monthly data for the period since 1971, graph the real value of the Wilshire 5000 stock market index. What striking difference do you see in comparing the values in the 1970s with the values in the rest of the period? According to the theory, what effect should the behavior of stock market wealth during the 1970s have had on the household saving rate during that period, relative to the 1980s and 1990s? Plot net private saving of households and institutions as a percentage of GDP since 1960. Would you say that the prediction is borne out? Discuss. How did the stock market change during the financial crisis in 2008 and 2009, and what happened to the saving rate in response?

3. This problem asks you to calculate the actual (as opposed to the expected) real after-tax interest rate using annual data from 1961 to the present. The formula for the actual real after-tax interest rate is $(1 - t)i - \pi$, where i is the nominal interest rate, t is the tax rate, and π is the inflation rate.

   Use the average for each year of the three-month Treasury bill interest rate for the nominal interest rate i and measure annual inflation π by the CPI inflation rate from December to December. Take the tax rate t to be the ratio of total (Federal plus state and local) government receipts to nominal GDP in the fourth quarter of each year. In what periods was the real after-tax interest rate positive? In what periods was it negative?

4. Using quarterly data from 1947 to the present, graph residential fixed investment relative to GDP.

   a. Compare the graph of residential fixed investment relative to GDP to a graph of the civilian unemployment rate. What happens to residential investment during recessions? In this respect, is residential investment similar to or different from other types of investment?

   b. During the two decades after World War II, there was an upsurge in population growth and household formation known as the "baby boom." The baby boom was followed by a "baby bust" during which population growth slowed. How are these demographic trends connected to the behavior of residential investment relative to GDP shown in your graph?

5. The chapter claims that interest rates tend to move together. Using monthly data since 1975, graph the interest rate on three-month Treasury bills, the yield on high-grade corporate bonds, the 30-year conventional mortgage rate, the prime rate charged by banks, and the yield on ten-year Treasury bonds. Which interest rates tend to be highest? Lowest? Explain. Which interest rates tend to move together? Explain.

6. Graph real private nonresidential fixed investment in (a) structures, (b) equipment, and (c) intellectual property products since 1999. How has the relative emphasis on the three types of investment changed? Can you think of an explanation?

Appendix 4.A

A Formal Model of Consumption and Saving

This appendix analyzes more formally the decision about how much to consume and how much to save. We focus on the decisions of a consumer named Penelope. To help keep the analysis manageable, we make three simplifying assumptions:

1. The time horizon over which Penelope makes plans consists of only two periods: the present, or current, period and the future period. The current period might represent Penelope's working years and the future period might represent her retirement years, for example.
2. Penelope takes her current income, future income, and wealth as given.
3. Penelope faces a given real interest rate and can choose how much to borrow or save at that rate.

How Much Can the Consumer Afford? The Budget Constraint

To analyze Penelope's decision about how much to consume and save, we first examine the choices available to her. To have some specific numbers to analyze, let's suppose that Penelope receives a fixed after-tax income, measured in real terms,[1] of 42,000 in the current period and expects to receive a real income of 33,000 in the future period. In addition, she begins the current period with real wealth of 18,000 in a savings account, and she can borrow or lend at a real interest rate of 10% per period.

Next, we list the symbols used to represent Penelope's situation:

y = Penelope's current real income (42,000);
y^f = Penelope's future real income (33,000)[2];
a = Penelope's real wealth (assets) at the beginning of the current period (18,000);
r = real interest rate (10%);
c = Penelope's current real consumption (not yet determined);
c^f = Penelope's future real consumption (not yet determined).

In general, any amount of current consumption, c, that Penelope chooses will determine the amount of future consumption, c^f, that she will be able to afford. To work out this relationship, note that the funds that Penelope has on hand in the current period are her current income, y, and her initial wealth, a. If her current consumption is c, then at the end of the current period she has $y + a - c$ left.

[1]The units in which Penelope's income is measured are base-year dollars.

[2]We do not include in future income y^f, the interest that Penelope earns on her saving. Future income, y^f, includes only labor income or transfers received, such as Social Security payments.

Penelope can put these leftover current resources, $y + a - c$, in the bank to earn interest. If the real interest rate that she can earn on her deposit is r, the real value of her bank account (principal plus interest) in the future period will be $(y + a - c)(1 + r)$. In addition to the real value of her bank account in the future period, Penelope receives income of y^f, so her total resources in the future period equal $(y + a - c)(1 + r) + y^f$. Because the future period is the last period of Penelope's life, she spends all of her remaining resources on consumption.[3] Thus Penelope's future consumption, c^f, is

$$c^f = (y + a - c)(1 + r) + y^f. \qquad \textbf{(4.A.1)}$$

Equation (4A.1) is called the **budget constraint**. It shows for any level of current consumption, c, how much future consumption, c^f, Penelope can afford based on her current and future income and initial wealth.[4] The budget constraint in Eq (4.A.1) is represented graphically by the **budget line**, which shows the combinations of current and future consumption that Penelope can afford, based on her current and future income, her initial level of wealth, and the real interest rate. Figure 4.A.1 depicts Penelope's budget line, with current consumption, c, on the horizontal axis and future consumption, c^f, on the vertical axis.

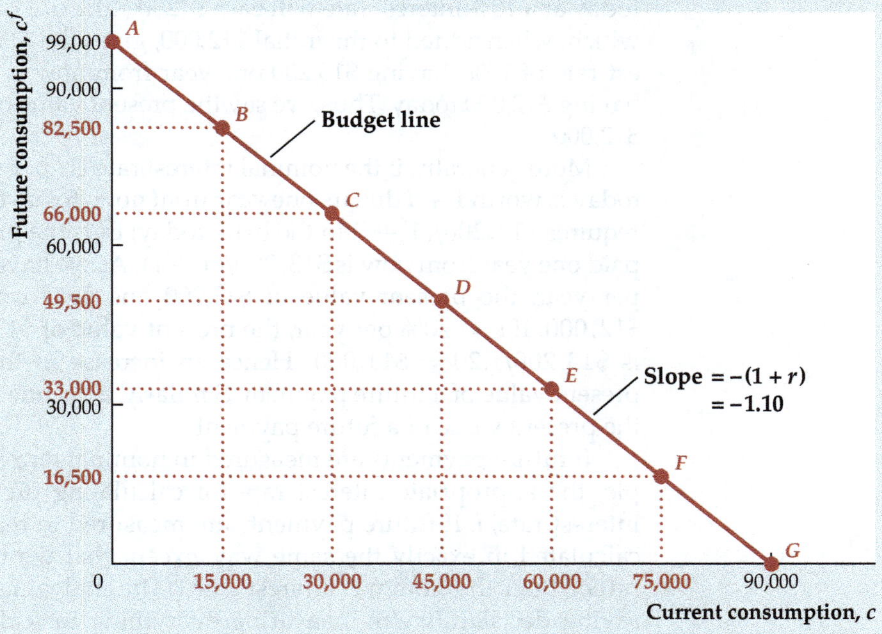

FIGURE 4.A.1

The budget line
The budget line shows the combinations of current and future consumption, c and c^f, available to Penelope. The slope of the budget line is $-(1 + r) = -1.10$. The horizontal intercept is at $c = 90{,}000$, which equals *PVLR* as defined in Eq. (4.A.2); the vertical intercept is at $c^f = 99{,}000$. You can verify that the combinations of current and future consumption at each of the lettered points (as well as any point on the budget line) satisfies the equation $c + c^f/(1 + r) = 90{,}000$, which equals *PVLR* as defined in Eq. (4.A.2).

[3]Here we assume that Penelope does not want to leave a bequest to anyone. Later we will briefly examine the effect of bequests on saving decisions.

[4]In our derivation of Eq (4.A.1), we assumed that Penelope's current consumption was less than her total current resources so that she had some resources left to deposit in the bank. However, the budget constraint, Eq (4.A.1), still works if Penelope's current consumption exceeds her total current resources so that she must borrow from the bank. Note that this works as long as y^f is at least as large as $[c - (y + a)] \times (1 + r)$, so that $c^f \geq 0$.

The budget line slopes downward, reflecting the trade-off between current and future consumption. If Penelope increases her current consumption by one unit, her saving falls by one unit. Because saving earns interest at rate r, a one-unit decline in saving today implies that Penelope's future resources—and thus her future consumption—will be lower by $1 + r$ units. Because a one-unit increase in current consumption lowers future consumption by $1 + r$ units, the slope of the budget line is $-(1 + r)$. In our numerical example, the real interest rate is 10%, so the slope of the budget line in Fig. 4.A.1 is -1.10.

Present Values

We can conveniently represent Penelope's budget constraint by using the concept of **present value**. The present value measures the value of payments to be made in the future in terms of today's dollars or goods. To illustrate this concept, suppose you must make a payment of $13,200 one year from now. How much money would you have to put aside today so you could make that future payment? The answer to this question is called the present value.

The present value of a future payment depends on the interest rate. If the current nominal interest rate, i, is 10% per year, the present value of $13,200 to be paid one year from now is $12,000. The reason is that $12,000 deposited in the bank today at a 10% interest rate will earn $1200 (10% of $12,000) of interest in one year, which, when added to the initial $12,000, gives the $13,200. Therefore, at an interest rate of 10%, having $13,200 one year from now is economically equivalent to having $12,000 today. Thus, we say the present value of $13,200 in one year equals $12,000.

More generally, if the nominal interest rate is i per year, each dollar in the bank today is worth $1 + i$ dollars one year from now. To have $13,200 one year from now requires $\$13,200/(1 + i)$ in the bank today; thus the present value of $13,200 to be paid one year from now is $\$13,200/(1 + i)$. As we have already shown, if $i = 10\%$ per year, the present value of $13,200 one year from now is $\$13,200/1.10 = \$12,000$. If $i = 20\%$ per year, the present value of $13,200 one year in the future is $\$13,200/1.20 = \$11,000$. Hence an increase in the interest rate reduces the present value of a future payment. Similarly, a decline in the interest rate increases the present value of a future payment.

If future payments are measured in nominal terms, as in the preceding example, the appropriate interest rate for calculating present values is the nominal interest rate, i. If future payments are measured in real terms, present values are calculated in exactly the same way, except that we use the real interest rate, r, rather than the nominal interest rate, i. In analyzing Penelope's consumption–saving decision, we're measuring everything in real terms, so we use the real interest rate, r, to calculate the present values of Penelope's future income and consumption.

Present Value and the Budget Constraint

We define the **present value of lifetime resources (*PVLR*)** as the present value of the income that a consumer expects to receive in current and future periods plus initial wealth. In the two-period case, the present value of lifetime resources is

$$PVLR = a + y + y^f/(1 + r), \qquad \textbf{(4.A.2)}$$

which is the sum of current wealth, a, current income, y,[5] and the present value of future income, $y^f/(1 + r)$. In our example, Penelope has $PVLR = 18{,}000 + 42{,}000 + (33{,}000/1.10) = 90{,}000$.

Next, we divide both sides of Eq (4.A.1) by $(1 + r)$ and then add c to both sides to get

$$\begin{aligned} c + c^f/(1 + r) &= a + y + y^f/(1 + r) \\ PVLC &= PVLR. \end{aligned} \qquad \textbf{(4.A.3)}$$

The left side of Eq. (4.A.3) is the present value of lifetime consumption, $c + c^f/(1 + r)$, which we denote *PVLC*. The budget constraint in Eq. (4.A.3) states that the **present value of lifetime consumption (*PVLC*)** equals the present value of lifetime resources *PVLR*.

In terms of Fig. 4.A.1, and indeed for any graph of the budget line, *PVLR* equals the value of current consumption, c, at the horizontal intercept of the budget line because the horizontal intercept is the point on the budget line at which future consumption, c^f, equals zero. Setting future consumption, c^f, to zero in Eq. (4.A.3) yields current consumption, c, on the left side of the equation, which must equal *PVLR* on the right side. Thus $c = PVLR$ at the horizontal intercept of the budget line.

What Does the Consumer Want? Consumer Preferences

The budget constraint, represented graphically as the budget line, shows the combinations of current and future consumption *available* to Penelope. To determine which of the many possible consumption combinations Penelope will choose, we need to know something about Penelope's preferences for current versus future consumption.

Economists use the term **utility** to describe the satisfaction or well-being of an individual. Preferences about current versus future consumption are summarized by how much utility a consumer obtains from each combination of current and future consumption. We can graphically represent Penelope's preferences for current versus future consumption through **indifference curves**, which represent all combinations of current and future consumption that yield the same level of utility. Because Penelope is equally happy with all consumption combinations on an indifference curve, she doesn't care (that is, she is indifferent to) which combination she actually gets. Figure 4.A.2 shows two of Penelope's indifference curves. Because the consumption combinations corresponding to points X, Y, and Z all are on the same indifference curve, IC^1, Penelope would obtain the same level of utility at X, Y, and Z.

Indifference curves have three important properties, each of which has an economic interpretation and each of which appears in Fig. 4.A.2:

1. *Indifference curves slope downward from left to right.* To understand why, let's suppose that Penelope has selected the consumption combination at point Y, where $c = 45{,}000$ and $c^f = 45{,}000$.[6] Now suppose that Penelope must reduce her

[5]The present value of current wealth is simply current wealth and the present value of current income is simply current income.

[6]Point Y lies below Penelope's budget line, shown in Fig. 4.A.1, which means that not only could Penelope afford this consumption combination, but she would have resources left over at the end of the future period. Unless she wants to leave a bequest, she would not actually choose such a combination for the resources shown in Fig. 4.A.1.

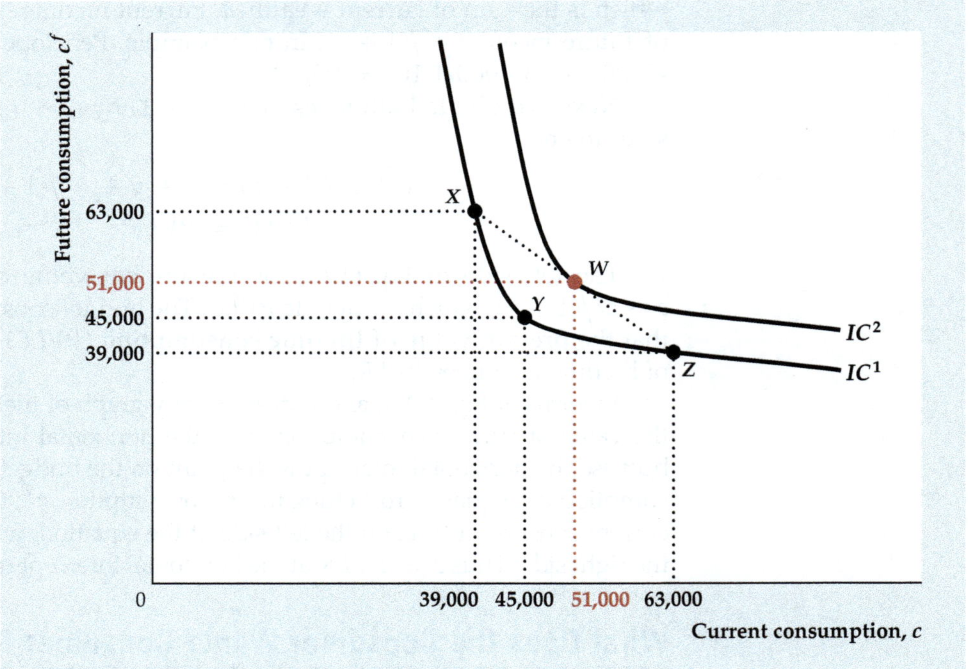

FIGURE 4.A.2

Indifference curves

All points on an indifference curve represent consumption combinations that yield the same level of utility. Indifference curves slope downward because a consumer can be compensated for a reduction in current consumption by an appropriate increase in future consumption. All points on IC^2 represent consumption combinations that are preferred to all consumption combinations represented by points on IC^1. Indifference curves are bowed toward the origin to reflect the consumption-smoothing motive. Penelope prefers the consumption combination at point W, which is an average of the combinations at points X and Z, to the consumption combinations at either X or Z because W represents a smoother pattern of consumption. Thus the indifference curve containing W (IC^2) lies above and to the right of the indifference curve containing X, Y, and Z (IC^1).

current consumption to $c = 39{,}000$. Clearly, if she reduces current consumption while maintaining future consumption at 45,000, she will suffer a reduction in utility. However, Penelope can be compensated for this reduction in current consumption by additional future consumption. Suppose that, if she increases her future consumption to $c^f = 63{,}000$ when her current consumption falls to $c = 39{,}000$, so that she moves to point X, her level of utility remains unchanged. In such a case, she is indifferent between the consumption combinations at X and Y, and points X and Y must lie on the same indifference curve. In general, any change in the level of current consumption must be accompanied by a change in the *opposite* direction in the level of future consumption so as to keep Penelope's level of utility unchanged. Thus indifference curves, which represent consumption combinations with equal levels of utility, must slope downward from left to right.

2. *Indifference curves that are farther up and to the right represent higher levels of utility.* Consider for example point W, which lies above and to the right of point Y in Fig. 4.A.2. Both current consumption and future consumption are higher at W than at Y. Because Penelope obtains utility from both current and future consumption, W offers a higher level of utility than does Y; that is, Penelope prefers W to Y. In fact, as all points on the indifference curve IC^1 yield the same level of utility as Y, Penelope prefers W to all points on the indifference curve IC^1. Furthermore, as all points on indifference curve IC^2 yield the same level of utility as W, Penelope prefers all points on IC^2 to all points on IC^1. In general, for any two indifference curves, consumers prefer consumption combinations on an indifference curve that is above and to the right of the other indifference curve.
3. *Indifference curves are bowed toward the origin.* This characteristic shape of indifference curves captures the consumption-smoothing motive, discussed in Chapter 4. Under the consumption-smoothing motive, consumers prefer a relatively smooth pattern of consumption over time to having large amounts of consumption in one period and small amounts in another period.

We can illustrate the link between the shape of indifference curves and the consumption-smoothing motive by considering the following three consumption combinations in Fig. 4.A.2: point $X(c = 39{,}000; c^f = 63{,}000)$, point $W(c = 51{,}000; c^f = 51{,}000)$ and point $Z(c = 63{,}000; c^f = 39{,}000)$. Note that W corresponds to complete consumption smoothing, with equal consumption occurring in both periods. In contrast, X and Z represent consumption combinations with large changes in consumption between the first period and the second period. In addition, note that W represents a consumption combination that is the average of the consumption combinations at X and Z: Current consumption at W, 51,000, is the average of current consumption at X and Z, 39,000 and 63,000, respectively; similarly, future consumption at W, also 51,000, is the average of future consumption at X and Z, 63,000 and 39,000, respectively.

Even though point W essentially is an average of points X and Z, and Penelope is indifferent between X and Z, she prefers W to X and Z because W represents much "smoother" (more even) consumption. Graphically, her preference for W over X and Z is indicated by W's position above and to the right of indifference curve IC^1 (which runs through X and Z). Note that W lies on a straight line drawn between X and Z. The only way that W can lie above and to the right of IC^1 is if IC^1 bows toward the origin, as depicted in Fig. 4.A.2. Thus the bowed shape of the indifference curve reflects the consumption-smoothing motive.

The Optimal Level of Consumption

Combining Penelope's budget line (which describes her available consumption combinations) and her indifference curves (which describe her preferences for current versus future consumption), we can find the levels of current consumption and saving that make her happiest. This best available, or *optimal*, level of current consumption and saving is represented graphically by the point at which Penelope's budget line is tangent to an indifference curve, shown as point D in Figure 4.A.3.

To see why Penelope achieves her highest possible level of satisfaction, or utility, at point D, first note that D lies on indifference curve IC^*, which means that all consumption combinations on IC^* yield the same level of utility as D. All points on Penelope's budget line other than point D—points such as B and E, for example—lie on indifference curves that are below and to the left of IC^*. Thus the consumption combinations represented by all of these other points yield a lower level of utility than the consumption combination at D. Penelope would prefer the consumption combination represented by a point such as T in Fig. 4.A.3 to the consumption combination represented by D because T lies on an indifference curve above and to the right of IC^*; because T also lies above the budget line, however, Penelope can't afford the consumption combination represented by that point. With her budget constraint, Penelope can't do any better than D.

We conclude that Penelope's utility-maximizing consumption and saving choice is represented by point D, where her budget line is tangent to an indifference curve. Here, her optimal level of current consumption is 45,000, and her optimal level of future consumption is 49,500. Penelope's choice of current consumption automatically determines her current saving, s, which equals her current income minus her optimal current consumption:

$$s = y - c = 42{,}000 - 45{,}000 = -3000.$$

Thus Penelope chooses to dissave (decrease her initial assets) by 3000.

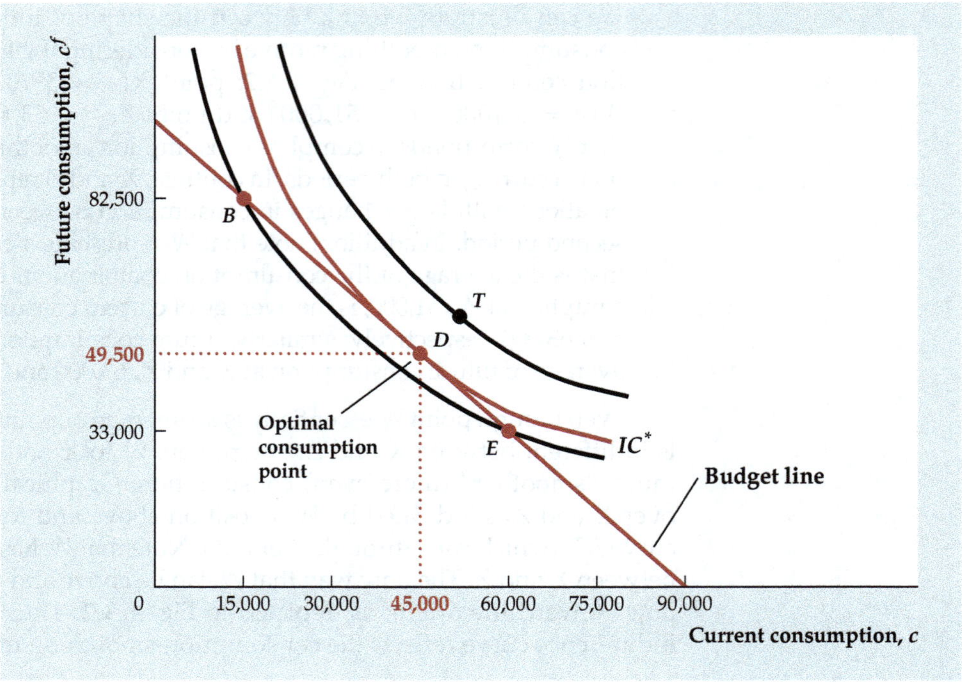

FIGURE 4.A.3

The optimal consumption combination

The optimal (highest utility) combination of current and future consumption is represented by the point of tangency between the budget line and an indifference curve (point *D*). All other points on the budget line, such as *B* and *E*, lie on indifference curves below and to the left of indifference curve IC^* and thus yield lower utility than the consumption combination at *D*, which lies on IC^*. Penelope would prefer the consumption combination at point *T* to the one at *D*, but as *T* lies above the budget line she can't afford the consumption combination that *T* represents.

The Effects of Changes in Income and Wealth on Consumption and Saving

The formal model developed in this appendix provides a helpful insight: *The effect on consumption of a change in current income, expected future income, or wealth depends only on how that change affects the consumer's present value of lifetime resources,* PVLR.

An Increase in Current Income

Suppose that Penelope receives a bonus at work of 12,000, which raises her current real income from 42,000 to 54,000. Her initial assets (18,000), future income (33,000), and the real interest rate (10%) remain unchanged; hence the increase of 12,000 in current income implies an equal increase in Penelope's present value of lifetime resources, or *PVLR*. If she hasn't yet committed herself to her original consumption–saving plan, how might Penelope revise that plan in light of her increased current income?

We use the graph in Figure 4.A.4 to answer this question. In Fig. 4.A.4, BL^1 is Penelope's original budget line, and point *D*, where $c = 45{,}000$ and $c^f = 49{,}500$ represents Penelope's original, pre-bonus consumption plan. Penelope's bonus will allow her to consume more, both now and in the future, so the increase in her income causes her budget line to shift. To see exactly how it shifts, note that the increase of 12,000 in Penelope's current income implies that her *PVLR* also increases by 12,000. Because the horizontal intercept of the budget line occurs at $c = PVLR$, the bonus shifts the horizontal intercept to the right by 12,000. The slope of the budget line, $-(1 + r) = -1.10$, remains unchanged because the real interest rate *r* is unchanged. Thus the increase in current income of 12,000 causes a parallel shift of the budget line to the right by 12,000, from BL^1 to BL^2.

FIGURE 4.A.4

An increase in income or wealth

An increase in current income, future income, and/or initial wealth that raises Penelope's *PVLR* by 12,000 causes the budget line to make a parallel shift to the right by 12,000, from BL^1 to BL^2. If Penelope's original consumption plan was to consume at point *D*, she could move to point *H* by spending all the increase on future consumption and none on current consumption; or she could move to point *K* by spending all the increase on current consumption and none on future consumption. However, if Penelope has a consumption-smoothing motive she will move to point *J*, which has both higher current consumption and higher future consumption than *D*. Point *J* is optimal because it lies where the new budget line BL^2 is tangent to an indifference curve, IC^{**}.

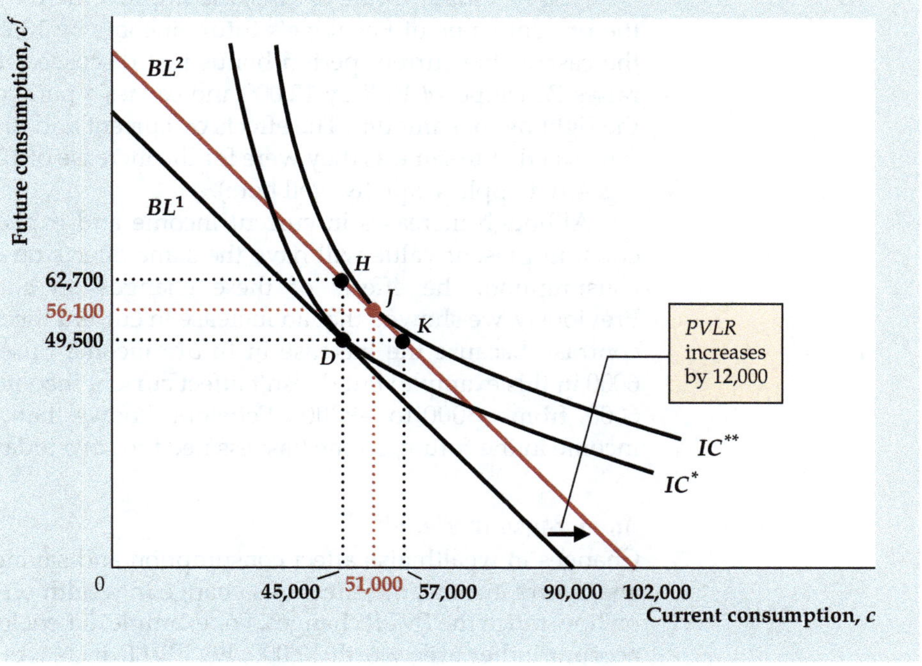

That shift demonstrates graphically that, after receiving her bonus, Penelope can enjoy greater current and future consumption. One strategy for Penelope, represented by point *K* on the new budget line BL^2, is to use the entire bonus to increase her current consumption by 12,000 while leaving her future consumption unchanged. Another strategy, represented by point *H* on BL^2, is to save all of her bonus while keeping her current consumption unchanged, and then use both the bonus and the interest of 1,200 earned on the bonus to increase her future consumption by 13,200.

If Penelope operates under a consumption-smoothing motive, she will use her bonus to increase *both* her current consumption and (by saving part of her bonus) her future consumption, thereby choosing a point on BL^2 between point *K* (consume the entire bonus) and point *H* (save the entire bonus). If her indifference curves are as shown in Fig. 4.A.4, she will move to *J*, where her new budget line, BL^2, is tangent to the indifference curve IC^{**}. At *J*, current consumption, *c*, is 51,000, future consumption, c^f, is 56,100, and saving, *s*, is $54{,}000 - 51{,}000 = 3000$. Both current and future consumption are higher at *J* than at *D* (where $c = 45{,}000$ and $c^f = 49{,}500$). Penelope's current saving of 3000 at *J* is higher than her saving was at *D* (where she dissaved by 3000) because the increase in her current consumption of 6000 is less than the increase in her current income of 12,000. This example illustrates that an increase in current income raises both current consumption and current saving.

An Increase in Future Income

Suppose that Penelope doesn't receive her bonus of 12,000 in the current period, so that her current income, *y*, remains at its initial level of 42,000. Instead, because of an improved company pension plan, she learns that her future income will increase by 13,200, so y^f rises from 33,000 to 46,200. How will this good news affect Penelope's current consumption and saving?

At a real interest rate of 10%, the improvement in the pension plan increases the present value of Penelope's future income by 13,200/1.10, or 12,000. So, as in the case of the current-period bonus just discussed, the improved pension plan raises Penelope's *PVLR* by 12,000 and causes a parallel shift of the budget line to the right by that amount. The effects on current and future consumption are therefore exactly the same as they were for the increase of 12,000 in current income (and Fig. 4.A.4 applies equally well here).

Although increases in current income and expected future income that are equal in present value will have the same effects on current and planned future consumption, the effects of these changes on current saving are different. Previously, we showed that an increase in current income raises current saving. In contrast, because the increase in future income raises current consumption (by 6000 in this example) but doesn't affect current income, it causes saving to fall (by 6000, from −3000 to −9000). Penelope knows that she will be receiving more income in the future, so she has less need to save today.

An Increase in Wealth

Changes in wealth also affect consumption and saving. As in the cases of current and future income, the effect of a change in wealth on consumption depends only on how much the *PVLR* changes. For example, if Penelope finds a passbook savings account in her attic worth 12,000, her *PVLR* increases by 12,000. To illustrate this situation, we use Fig. 4.A.4 again. Penelope's increase in wealth raises her *PVLR* by 12,000 and thus shifts the budget line to the right by 12,000, from BL^1 to BL^2. As before, her optimal consumption choice goes from point *D* (before she finds the passbook) to point *J* (after her increase in wealth). Because the increase in wealth raises current consumption (from 45,000 at *D* to 51,000 at *J*) but leaves current income (42,000) unchanged, it results in a decline in current saving (from –3000 at *D* to –9000 at *J*). Being wealthier, Penelope does not have to save as much of her current income (actually, she is increasing her dissaving) to provide for the future.

The preceding analyses show that changes in current income, future income, and initial wealth all lead to parallel shifts of the budget line by the amount that they change the *PVLR*. Economists use the term *income effect* to describe the impact of any change that causes a parallel shift of the budget line.

The Permanent Income Theory

In terms of our model, a temporary increase in income represents a rise in current income, y, with future income, y^f, held constant. A permanent increase in income raises *both* current income, y, *and* future income, y^f. Therefore a permanent one-unit increase in income leads to a larger increase in *PVLR* than does a temporary one-unit increase in income. Because income changes affect consumption only to the extent that they lead to changes in *PVLR*, our theory predicts that a permanent one-unit increase in income will raise current and future consumption more than a temporary one-unit increase in income will.

This distinction between the effects of permanent and temporary income changes is emphasized in the **permanent income theory** of consumption and saving, developed in the 1950s by Nobel laureate Milton Friedman. He pointed out that income should affect consumption only through the *PVLR* in a many-period version of the model we present here. Thus permanent changes in income, because they last for many periods, may have much larger effects on consumption than temporary changes in income. As a result, temporary income increases would be mostly saved, and permanent income increases would be mostly consumed.[7]

Consumption and Saving over Many Periods: The Life-Cycle Model

The two-period model suggests that a significant part of saving is intended to pay for retirement. However, it doesn't reflect other important aspects of a consumer's lifetime income and consumption patterns. For example, income typically rises over most of a person's working life, and people save for reasons other than retirement. The **life-cycle model** of consumption and saving, originated in the 1950s by Nobel laureate Franco Modigliani and his associates, extends the model from two periods to many periods and focuses on the patterns of income, consumption, and saving throughout an individual's life.

The essence of the life-cycle model is shown in Figure 4.A.5. In Fig. 4.A.5(a), the typical consumer's patterns of income and consumption are plotted against the consumer's age, from age 20 (the approximate age of economic independence) to age 90 (the approximate age of death). Two aspects of Fig. 4.A.5(a) are significant.

First, the average worker experiences steadily rising real income, with peak earnings typically occurring between the ages of 50 and 60. After retirement, income (excluding interest earned from previous saving) drops sharply.

Second, the lifetime pattern of consumption is much smoother than the pattern of income over time, which is consistent with the consumption-smoothing motive discussed earlier. Although shown as perfectly flat in Fig. 4.A.5(a), consumption, in reality, varies somewhat by age; for example, it will be higher during years of high child-rearing expenses. An advantage of using the life-cycle model to study consumption and saving is that it may be easily modified to allow for various patterns of lifetime income and consumption.

The lifetime pattern of saving, shown in Fig. 4.A.5(b), is the difference between the income and consumption curves in Fig. 4.A.5(a). This overall hump-shaped pattern has been confirmed empirically. Saving is minimal or even negative during the early working years, when income is low. Maximum saving occurs when the worker is between ages 50 and 60, when income is highest. Finally, dissaving occurs during retirement as the consumer draws down accumulated wealth to meet living expenses.

An important implication of the hump-shaped pattern of saving is that national saving rates depend on the age distribution of a country's population. Countries with unusually young or unusually old populations have low saving rates, and countries with relatively more people in their middle years have higher saving rates.

Bequests and Saving

We have assumed that the consumer plans to spend all of his or her wealth and income during his or her lifetime, leaving nothing to heirs. In reality, many people leave bequests, or inheritances, to children, charities, and others. To the extent that

[7]Friedman also provided some of the first empirical evidence for this theory. For example, he found that the consumption of farm families, on average, responded less to changes in income than the consumption of non-farm families. Friedman's explanation was that, because farm incomes depend heavily on weather and crop prices, both of which are volatile, changes in farm incomes are much more likely to be temporary than are changes in non-farm incomes. Current changes in farm incomes have a smaller effect on the *PVLR* and therefore have a smaller effect on current consumption.

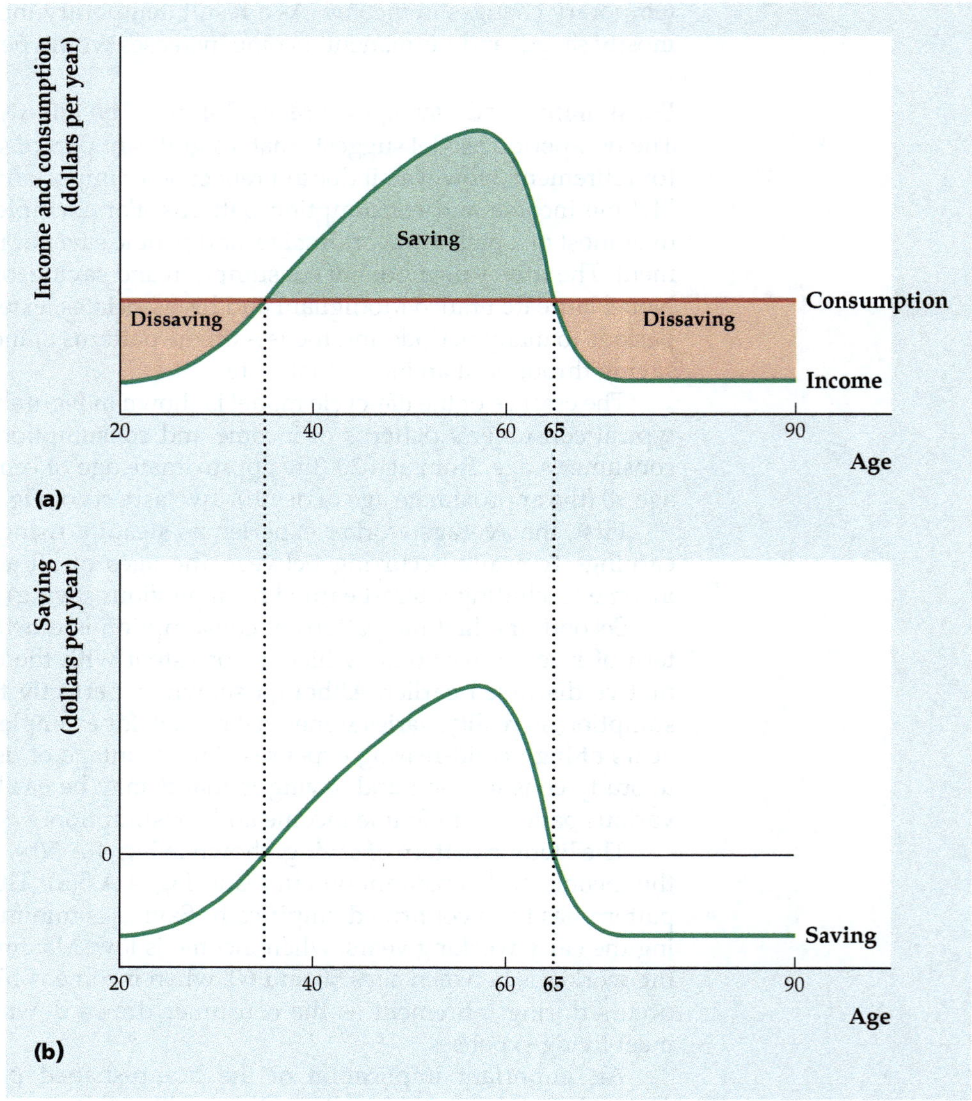

FIGURE 4.A.5

Life-cycle consumption, income, and saving

(a) Income and consumption are plotted against age. Income typically rises gradually throughout most of a person's working life and peaks shortly before retirement. The desire for a smooth pattern of consumption means that consumption varies less than income over the life cycle. Consumption here is constant. **(b)** Saving is the difference between income and consumption; the saving pattern is hump-shaped. Early in a person's working life consumption is larger than income, so saving is negative. In the middle years saving is positive; the excess of income over consumption is used to repay debts incurred earlier in life and to provide for retirement. During retirement people dissave.

consumers desire to leave bequests, they will consume less and save more than when they simply consume all their resources during their lifetimes.

Ricardian Equivalence

One of the most significant results of analyzing our model is that changes in income or wealth affect desired consumption only to the extent that they affect the consumer's *PVLR*. The point made by advocates of Ricardian equivalence, discussed in Chapter 4, is that, holding current and future government purchases constant, *a change in current taxes does not affect the consumer's* PVLR *and thus should not affect desired consumption,* C^d, *or desired national saving,* $Y - C^d - G$.

To illustrate this idea, suppose that the government cuts Penelope's current taxes by 300. This tax reduction increases Penelope's current income by 300, which (all else being equal) would cause her to consume more. Because the government's revenue has been reduced by 300 and its expenditures have not changed, however, the government must increase its current borrowing from the public by 300 (per taxpayer). Furthermore, the government must pay interest on its borrowings. For example, if the real interest rate that the government must pay on its debt is 10%, in the future period the government's outstanding debt will be 330 greater than it would have been without the tax cut.

As a taxpayer, Penelope is ultimately responsible for the government's debts. Suppose that the government decides to repay its borrowings and accumulated interest in the future period. (Chapter 15 discusses what happens if the government's debt is left for Penelope's descendants to repay.) To repay its debt plus interest, the government must raise taxes in the future period by 330, so Penelope's expected future income falls by 330. Overall, then, the government's tax program has raised Penelope's current income by 300 but reduced her future income by 330. At a real interest rate of 10%, the present value of the future income change is –300, which cancels out the increase in current income of 300. Thus Penelope's *PVLR* is unchanged by the tax cut, and (as the Ricardian equivalence proposition implies) she should not change her current consumption.

Excess Sensitivity and Borrowing Constraints

A variety of studies have confirmed that consumption is affected by current income, expected future income, and wealth, and that permanent income changes have larger effects on consumption than temporary income changes—all of which are outcomes implied by the model. Nevertheless, some studies show that the response of consumption to a change in current income is greater than would be expected on the basis of the effect of the current income change on *PVLR*. This tendency of consumption to respond to current income more strongly than the model predicts is called the *excess sensitivity* of consumption to current income.

One explanation for excess sensitivity is that people are more short-sighted than assumed in our model and thus consume a larger portion of an increase in current income than predicted by it. Another explanation, which is more in the spirit of the model, is that the amount that people can borrow is limited. A restriction imposed by lenders on the amount that someone can borrow against future income is called a **borrowing constraint**.

The effect of a borrowing constraint on the consumption–saving decision depends on whether the consumer would want to borrow in the absence of a borrowing constraint. If the consumer wouldn't want to borrow even if borrowing were possible, the borrowing constraint is said to be *nonbinding*. When a consumer wants to borrow but is prevented from doing so, the borrowing constraint is said to be *binding*. A consumer who faces a binding borrowing constraint will spend all available current income and wealth on current consumption so as to come as close as possible to the consumption combination desired in the absence of borrowing constraints. Such a consumer would consume the entire amount of an increase in current income. Thus the effect of an increase in current income on current consumption is greater for a consumer who faces a binding borrowing constraint than is predicted by our simple model without borrowing constraints. In macroeconomic terms, this result implies that—if a significant number of consumers face binding borrowing constraints—the response of aggregate consumption to an increase in aggregate income will be greater than implied by the basic theory in the absence of borrowing constraints. In other words, if borrowing constraints exist, consumption may be excessively sensitive to current income.[8]

The Real Interest Rate and the Consumption–Saving Decision

To explore the effects of a change in the real interest rate on consumption and saving, let's return to the two-period model and Penelope's situation. Recall that Penelope initially has current real income, y, of 42,000, future income, y^f, of 33,000, initial wealth, a, of 18,000, and that she faces a real interest rate, r, of 10%. Her budget line, which is the same as in Fig. 4.A.1, is shown in Figure 4.A.6 as BL^1. Now let's see what happens when for some reason the real interest rate jumps from 10% to 76%.[9]

FIGURE 4.A.6

The effect of an increase in the real interest rate on the budget line

The figure shows the effect on Penelope's budget line of an increase in the real interest rate, r, from 10% to 76%. Because the slope of a budget line is $-(1 + r)$ and the initial real interest is 10%, the slope of Penelope's initial budget line, BL^1, is -1.10. The initial budget line, BL^1, also passes through the no-borrowing, no-lending point, E, which represents the consumption combination that Penelope obtains by spending all her current income and wealth on current consumption. Because E can still be obtained when the real interest rate rises, it also lies on the new budget line, BL^2. However, the slope of BL^2 is -1.76, reflecting the rise in the real interest rate to 76%. Thus the higher real interest rate causes the budget line to pivot clockwise around the no-borrowing, no-lending point.

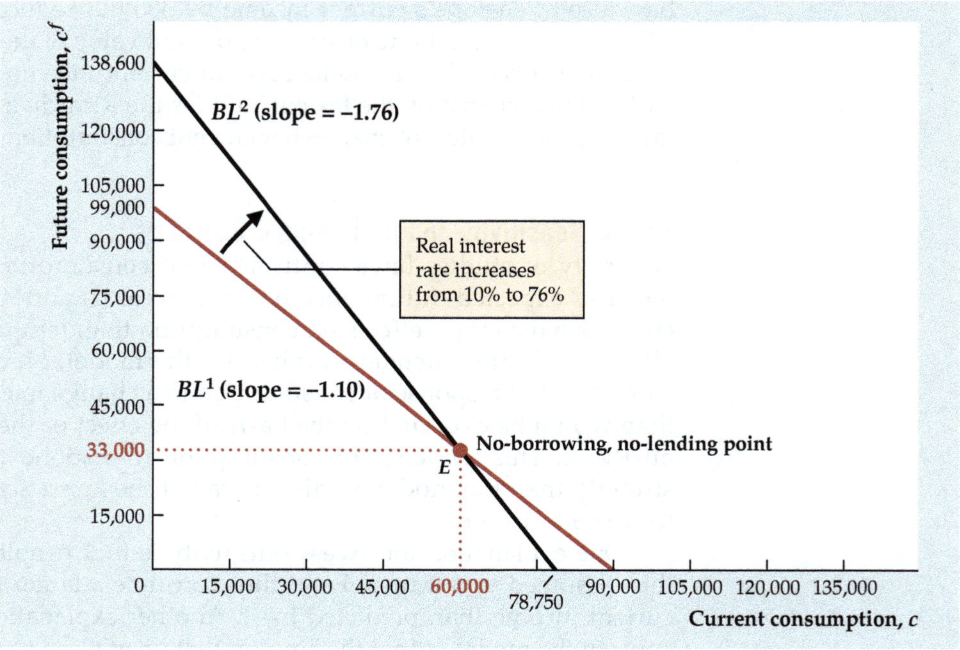

The Real Interest Rate and the Budget Line

To see how Penelope's budget line is affected when the real interest rate rises, let's first consider point E on the budget line BL^1. Point E is special in that it is the only point on the budget line at which current consumption equals current income plus initial wealth ($c = y + a = 60{,}000$) and future consumption equals future income ($c^f = y^f = 33{,}000$). If Penelope chooses this consumption combination, she doesn't need to borrow (her current income and initial wealth are just sufficient

[8]Although we have no direct way of counting how many consumers are constrained from borrowing, several studies estimate that to account for the observed relationship between consumption and current income, during any year some 20% to 50% of U.S. consumers face binding borrowing constraints. See, for example, John Y. Campbell and N. Gregory Mankiw, "Consumption, Income, and Interest Rates: Reinterpreting the Time Series Evidence," in O. Blanchard and S. Fischer, eds., *NBER Macroeconomics Annual*, Cambridge, MA: MIT Press, 1989; and Robert E. Hall and Frederic S. Mishkin, "The Sensitivity of Consumption to Transitory Income: Estimates from Panel Data on Households," *Econometrica*, March 1982, pp. 461–481.

[9]A real interest rate of 76% per period seems unrealistically high if a period is 1 year. But if a period is one-half of an adult lifetime, as in the two-period model, then 76% per period seems quite realistic.

to pay for her current consumption), nor does she have any current resources left to deposit in (lend to) the bank. Thus E is the **no-borrowing, no-lending point**. Because E involves neither borrowing nor lending, the consumption combination it represents is available to Penelope regardless of the real interest rate. Thus the no-borrowing, no-lending point remains on the budget line when the real interest rate changes.

Next, recall that the budget line's slope is $-(1 + r)$. When the real interest rate, r, jumps from 10% to 76%, the slope of the budget line changes from -1.10 to -1.76; that is, the new budget line becomes steeper. Because the budget line becomes steeper but still passes through the no-borrowing, no-lending point, E, it pivots clockwise around point E.

The Substitution Effect

As we discussed in Chapter 4, the price of current consumption in terms of future consumption is $1 + r$ because if Penelope increases her consumption by one unit today, thereby reducing her saving by one unit, she will have to reduce her future consumption by $1 + r$ units. When the real interest rate increases, current consumption becomes more expensive relative to future consumption. In response to this increase in the relative price of current consumption, Penelope substitutes away from current consumption toward future consumption by increasing her saving. This increase in saving reflects *the substitution effect of the real interest rate on saving*, introduced in Chapter 4.

The substitution effect is illustrated graphically in Figure 4.A.7. Initially, the real interest rate is 10% and the budget line is BL^1. Suppose for now that Penelope's preferences are such that BL^1 is tangent to an indifference curve, IC^1, at the no-borrowing, no-lending point, E.[10] At a real interest rate of 10%, Penelope chooses the consumption combination at E.

When the real interest rate rises from 10% to 76%, the budget line pivots clockwise to BL^2. Because Penelope's original consumption point—the no-borrowing, no-lending point, E—also lies on the new budget line, BL^2, she has the option of remaining at E and enjoying the same combination of current and future consumption after the real interest rate rises. Points along BL^2 immediately above and to the left of E lie above and to the right of IC^1, however. These points represent consumption combinations that are available to Penelope and yield a higher level of utility than the consumption combination at E. Penelope can attain the highest level of utility along BL^2 at point V, where indifference curve IC^2 is tangent to BL^2. In response to the increase in the relative price of current consumption, Penelope reduces her current consumption, from 60,000 to 51,000, and moves from E to V on BL^2. Her reduction of 9000 in current consumption between E and V is equivalent to an increase of 9000 in saving. The increase in saving between E and V reflects the substitution effect on saving of a higher real interest rate.

The Income Effect

If Penelope's current consumption initially equals her current resources (current income plus initial wealth) so that she is neither a lender nor a borrower, a change in the real interest rate has only a substitution effect on her saving, as shown in Fig. 4.A.7. If her current consumption initially is not equal to her current resources,

---

[10]Note that Penelope's indifference curves in Fig. 4.A.7 are different from those in Fig. 4.A.4.

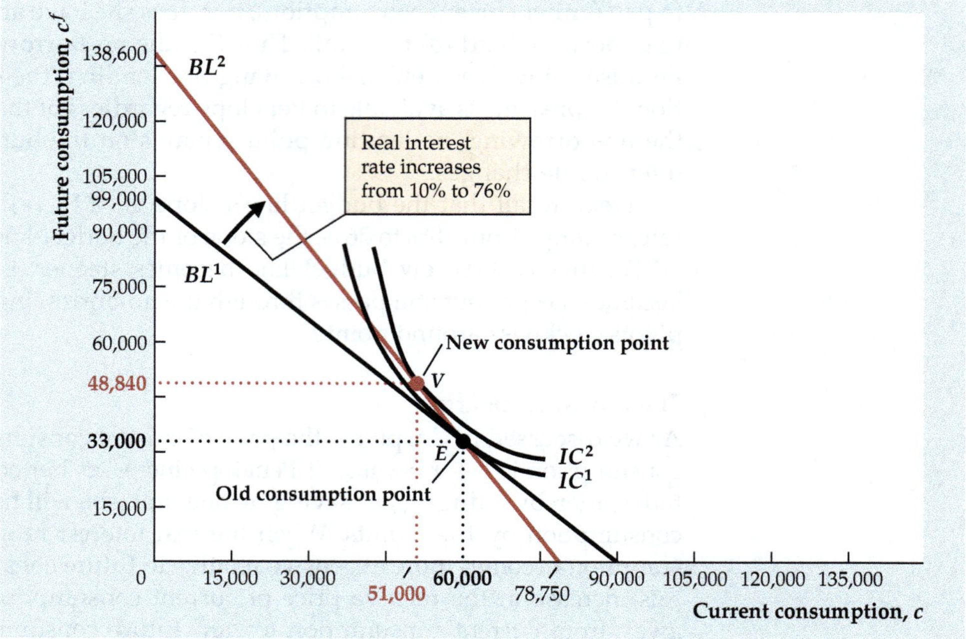

FIGURE 4.A.7

The substitution effect of an increase in the real interest rate

We assume that Penelope's preferences are such that when the real interest rate is 10%, she chooses the consumption combination at the no-borrowing, no-lending point, *E*, on the initial budget line BL^1. Point *E* lies on the indifference curve IC^1. An increase in the real interest rate to 76% causes the budget line to pivot clockwise from BL^1 to BL^2, as in Fig. 4.A.6. By substituting future consumption for current consumption along the new budget line, BL^2, Penelope can reach points that lie above and to the right of IC^1; these points represent consumption combinations that yield higher utility than the consumption combination at *E*. Her highest utility is achieved by moving to point *V*, where the new budget line, BL^2, is tangent to indifference curve IC^2. The drop in current consumption (by 9000) and the resulting equal rise in saving that occur in moving from *E* to *V* reflect the substitution effect of the increase in the real interest rate.

however, then an increase in the real interest rate also has an income effect. As we discussed in Chapter 4, if Penelope is initially a saver (equivalently, a lender), with current consumption less than her current resources (current income plus initial wealth), an increase in the real interest rate makes her financially better off by increasing the future interest payments that she will receive. In response to this increase in future interest income, she increases her current consumption and reduces her current saving. On the other hand, if Penelope is initially a borrower, with current consumption exceeding her current resources, an increase in the real interest rate increases the interest she will have to pay in the future. Having to make higher interest payments in the future makes Penelope financially worse off overall, leading her to reduce her current consumption. Thus, for a borrower, the income effect of an increase in the real interest rate leads to reduced current consumption and increased saving.

The Substitution Effect and the Income Effect Together

Figure 4.A.8 illustrates the full impact of an increase in the real interest rate on Penelope's saving, including the substitution and income effects—assuming that Penelope initially is a lender. As before, Penelope's original budget line is BL^1 when the real interest rate is 10%. We now assume that Penelope's preferences are such that BL^1 is tangent to an indifference curve, IC^1, at point *D*. Thus, at a 10% real interest rate, Penelope plans current consumption of 45,000 and future consumption of 49,500. Her current resources equal 60,000 (current income of 42,000 plus initial assets of 18,000), so if she enjoys current consumption of 45,000 she will have resources of 15,000 to lend. Her chosen point, *D*, is located to the left of the no-borrowing, no-lending point, *E* (current consumption is lower at *D* than at *E*), showing that Penelope is a lender.

The increase in the real interest rate from 10% to 76% causes Penelope's budget line to pivot clockwise through the no-borrowing, no-lending point, *E*, ending

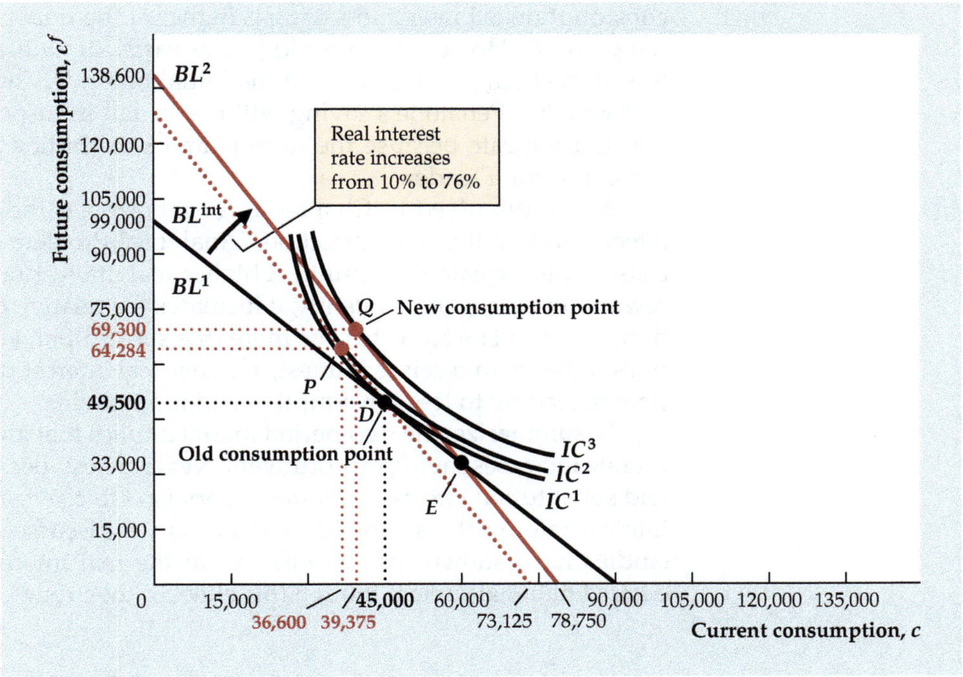

FIGURE 4.A.8

An increase in the real interest rate with both an income effect and a substitution effect

We assume that Penelope initially consumes at point *D* on the original budget line, BL^1. An increase in the real interest rate from 10% to 76% causes the budget line to pivot clockwise, from BL^1 to the new budget line, BL^2. We break the overall shift of the budget line into two parts: (1) a pivot around the original consumption point, *D*, to yield an intermediate budget line, BL^{int}, and (2) a parallel shift from BL^{int} to the final budget line, BL^2. The substitution effect is measured by the movement from the original consumption point, *D*, to point *P* on BL^{int}, and the income effect is measured by the movement from *P* to *Q* on BL^2. As drawn, the substitution effect is larger than the income effect so that the overall effect is for current consumption to fall and saving to rise.

at BL^2 as before. To separate the substitution and income effects of the increase in the real interest rate, think of the movement of the budget line from BL^1 to BL^2 as taking place in two steps.

First, imagine that the original budget line, BL^1, pivots clockwise around Penelope's original consumption combination, point *D*, until it is parallel to the new budget line, BL^2 (that is, its slope is -1.76). The resulting intermediate budget line is the dotted line, BL^{int}. Second, imagine that BL^{int} makes a parallel shift to the right to BL^2.

The response of Penelope's saving and current consumption to the increase in the real interest rate can also be broken into two steps. First, consider her response to the pivot of the budget line through point *D*, from BL^1 to BL^{int}. If this change were the only one in Penelope's budget line, she would move from *D* to *P* ($c = 36{,}600$ and $c^f = 64{,}284$) on BL^{int}. At *P*, she would save more and enjoy less current consumption than at *D*. The increase in saving between *D* and *P*, similar to Penelope's shift from *E* to *V* in Fig. 4.A.7, measures the substitution effect on Penelope's saving of the increase in the real interest rate.

Second, consider the effect of the parallel shift from BL^{int} to BL^2. The new budget line, BL^2, is tangent to an indifference curve, IC^3, at point *Q*, so Penelope will choose the consumption combination at *Q*. Current and future consumption are higher, and saving is lower, at *Q* than at *P*. The increase in current consumption and the decrease in saving between *P* and *Q* reflect the income effect of the increase in the real interest rate. Thus, as discussed earlier, income effects occur when a change in some variable causes a parallel shift of the budget line.

The total change in Penelope's consumption and saving resulting from the rise in the real interest rate is depicted in Fig. 4.A.8 as the change in saving between point *D* and point *Q*. This change is the sum of the substitution effect, measured by the increase in saving in moving from *D* to *P*, and the income effect, measured by the decline in saving in moving from *P* to *Q*. In Fig. 4.A.8, current consumption is lower and saving is higher at the final point, Q, than at the original point, D. However, we could just as easily draw the curves so that saving is less at the final point, Q, than at the initial point, D. Thus the theory fails to predict whether Penelope's saving will rise or fall in response to an increase in the real interest rate because the income and substitution effects work in opposite directions for a lender.

As we discussed in Chapter 4, for a borrower the income and substitution effects work in the same direction. (Analytical Problem 6 at the end of Chapter 4 asks you to explain this result.) A higher real interest rate increases a borrower's reward for saving (equivalently, it increases the relative price of current consumption), so he or she tends to save more (the substitution effect); because a borrower pays rather than receives interest, a higher real interest rate also makes him or her poorer, leading to less consumption and more saving.

To summarize, the two-period model implies that an increase in the real interest rate increases saving by borrowers. Nevertheless, because of conflicting income and substitution effects, economic theory isn't decisive about the effect of the real interest rate on the saving of lenders. As we discussed in Chapter 4, empirical studies have shown that an increase in the real interest rate tends to increase desired national saving, though this effect is not strong.

5

Saving and Investment in the Open Economy

Learning Objectives

5.1 Explain how the balance of payments is calculated.

5.2 Discuss goods market equilibrium in an open economy.

5.3 Discuss the factors that affect saving and investment and determine the current account balance in a small open economy.

5.4 Discuss the factors that affect saving and investment and determine the current account balance in a large open economy.

5.5 Analyze the relationship between the government budget deficit and the current account deficit.

With virtually no exceptions, modern economies are open economies, which means that they engage in international trade of goods and services and in international borrowing and lending. Economic openness is of tremendous benefit to the average person. Because the United States is an open economy, U.S. consumers can enjoy products from around the world (Japanese MP3 players, Italian shoes, Irish woolens) and U.S. businesses can find new markets abroad for their products (computers, beef, financial services). Similarly, the internationalization of financial markets means that U.S. savers have the opportunity to purchase German government bonds or shares in Taiwanese companies as well as domestic assets, and U.S. firms that want to finance investment projects can borrow in London or Tokyo as well as in New York.

Beyond the economic diversity and opportunity it creates, economic openness carries another important implication: In an open economy, *a country's spending need not equal its production in every period,* as would be required in a closed economy with no foreign trade and no international borrowing and lending. In particular, by importing more than they export and borrowing from abroad to pay for the difference, the residents of an open economy can temporarily spend more than they produce.

The ability of an open economy to spend more than it produces is both an opportunity and a potential problem. For example, by borrowing abroad (and by selling off U.S.-owned assets to foreign investors), the United States was able to finance a large excess of imports over exports beginning in the 1980s. As a result, U.S. citizens enjoyed higher levels of consumption, investment, and government purchases than they could have otherwise. At the same time, however, they incurred foreign debts that may be a future burden to the U.S. economy.

Why do countries sometimes borrow abroad to pay for an excess of imports over exports but at other times export more than they import and lend the difference to other countries? Why doesn't each country just balance its books and import as much as it exports each year? As we explain in this chapter, the fundamental determinants of a country's trade position are the country's saving and investment decisions. Thus although the issues of trade balances and international lending introduced here may seem at first to be unrelated to the topics covered in Chapter 4, the two sets of questions actually are closely related.

To explore how desired national saving and desired investment help determine patterns of international trade and lending, we extend the idea of goods market equilibrium, described by the saving–investment diagram, to include a foreign sector. We show that, unlike the situation in a closed economy, in an open economy desired national saving and desired investment don't have to be equal. Instead, we show that, when a country's desired national saving exceeds its desired investment, the country will be a lender in the international capital market and will have a current account surplus. Similarly, when a country's desired national saving is less than its desired investment, the country will be an international borrower and will have a current account deficit.

By emphasizing saving and investment, we develop an important theme of this part of the book. However, to focus on the role of saving and investment, we ignore some other factors that also influence international trade and lending. The most important of these factors is the exchange rate, or the rate at which domestic currency can be exchanged for foreign currency. We fully discuss exchange rates and their role in the open economy in Chapter 13.

5.1 Balance of Payments Accounting

Explain how the balance of payments is calculated.

Examining the factors that affect international trade and lending first requires an understanding of the basics of balance of payments accounting. The **balance of payments accounts**, which are part of the national income accounts discussed in Chapter 2, are the record of a country's international transactions. As you read this section, you should refer to Table 5.1, which presents U.S. balance of payments data for 2021.

The Current Account

The **current account** measures a country's trade in currently produced goods and services, along with unilateral transfers between countries. For convenience we divide the current account into three separate components: (1) net exports of goods and services, (2) net income from abroad, and (3) net unilateral transfers.

Net Exports of Goods and Services. We discussed the concept of net exports, NX, or exports minus imports, as part of the expenditure approach to measuring GDP in Chapter 2. Here we point out that net exports often are broken into two categories: goods and services.

Examples of internationally traded goods include U.S. soybeans, French perfume, Brazilian coffee, and Japanese cars. When a U.S. consumer buys a Japanese car, for example, the transaction is recorded as an import of goods for the United States and an export of goods for Japan.

Internationally traded services include tourism, insurance, education, and financial services. The Application "The Impact of Globalization on the U.S. Economy," discusses trade in business services. When a group of friends from the United States spends a week's vacation in Mexico, for example, the friends' expenditures for accommodations, food, sightseeing tours, and so on, are in the U.S. current account as an import of tourism services. The friends' expenditures are an export of tourism services for Mexico. Similarly, when foreign students attend college in the United States, their tuition payments are exports of services for the United States and imports of services for their home countries.

TABLE 5.1

Balance of Payments Accounts of the United States, 2021 (Billions of Dollars)

Current Account				
Net exports of goods and services (NX)			**−861.4**	
Exports of goods and services		2532.9		
Goods	1761.7			
Services	771.2			
less Imports of goods and services		3394.3		
Goods	2853.1			
Services	541.2			
Net income from abroad (NFP)			**174.9**	
Income receipts from abroad		1090.8		
less Income payments to residents of other countries		915.9		
Net unilateral transfers*			**−137.5**	
Current Account Balance (CA)				**−824.0**
Financial Account				
Financial Account				
Net financial flows			**645.5**	
Increase in foreign-owned assets in U.S. (financial inflow)		1858.8		
Foreign official assets	266.2			
Other foreign-owned assets	1592.6			
less Increase in U.S.-owned assets abroad (financial outflow)		1213.3		
U.S. official reserve assets	114.0			
Other U.S.-owned assets abroad	1099.3			
Financial Derivatives, Net**			**41.7**	
Financial Account Balance (FA)				**687.2**
Statistical Discrepancy				**137.0**
Memoranda:				
Balance on goods and services (trade balance)				−861.4
Balance on goods, services, and income				−686.5
Balance of payments = Increase in U.S. official reserve assets minus increase in foreign official assets = 114.0 − 266.2				−152.2

Note: Numbers may not add to totals shown owing to rounding.

*Net unilateral transfers includes the balance on secondary income (transfers of income) and the capital account (transfers of assets). The capital account is usually very small.

**The sign has been reversed from BEA Table 1 so that a positive number is a net increase in foreign-owned assets in U.S. (an inflow).

Source: "U.S. International Transactions: Fourth Quarter and Year 2021," Table 1, BEA news release downloaded from *www.bea.gov/sites/default/files/2022-03/intinv421.pdf*, and International Transactions Accounts, Table 9.1, downloaded from *https://www.bea.gov/data/intl-trade-investment/international-transactions.*

Table 5.1 shows that in 2021, U.S. exports of goods were more than twice as large as exports of services. Imports of goods were over five times as large as imports of services. Note also that exports of goods were much smaller than imports of goods but the reverse is true for services—U.S. firms export more services to other countries than are imported into the United States.

Net Income from Abroad. Net income from abroad equals income receipts from abroad minus income payments to residents of other countries. It is almost equal to net factor payments from abroad, *NFP*, discussed in Chapter 2.[1] We will ignore the difference between *NFP* and net income from abroad and treat the two as equivalent concepts.

The income receipts flowing into a country consist of compensation received by residents working abroad plus investment income from assets abroad. Investment income from assets abroad includes interest payments, dividends, royalties, and other returns that residents of a country receive from assets (such as bonds, stocks, and patents) that they own in other countries. An example is

In Touch with Data and Research

The Balance of Payments Accounts in Malaysia

We continue the example of Malaysia from Chapter 2 in this case. The Malaysian balance of payments statistics are governed by the Statistics Act of 1965 (revised in 1989). Generally, all data sources are on a quarterly basis, and updates of survey coverage are performed on a quarterly basis as well. Balance of payments estimates are compiled in millions of ringgits and are, as much as possible, in accordance with the international standards recommended by the International Monetary Fund (IMF). The Department of Statistics Malaysia (DOSM) is an official compiler of balance of payments estimates for Malaysia on a quarterly basis. It releases the official estimates for the previous year in the September of the following year, while the Central Bank of Malaysia releases preliminary balance of payments (BOP) estimates for the previous year in the March of the following year. Projections for the following year are made available by the Ministry of Finance (MOF) in the October of the current year.

The DOSM obtains data from various sources including surveys, Bank Negara Malaysia (BNM), government agencies such as Royal Malaysia Customs and the Pilgrimage Fund Board, and other administrative sources.

The data are published in the DOSM's *Quarterly Balance of Payments* reports and BNM's *Quarterly Bulletin*. The DOSM also reports the data published in the *Quarterly Balance of Payments* to the IMF. Any errors detected are announced in the current or next publication or dissemination. Select government agencies, such as the MOF, BNM, and the Economic Planning Unit of the Prime Minister's Department, have access to the data one week before release to the public. Statistical discrepancies and other problems are resolved at a quarterly technical meeting held with BNM. Revisions of quarterly BOP for the previous year are published together with data for the first quarter of the current year. If there are major changes regarding methodology, source data, and statistical techniques, an announcement is made by the DOSM through the department's website as well as its publication.[2]

[1]Net factor payments from abroad are presented in the national income and product accounts (NIPA), and net income from abroad is presented in the balance of payments accounts (BPA). The Bureau of Economic Analysis publishes a "reconciliation table" (in the Appendix section of BEA Current and Historical Data in *Survey of Current Business*) to account for the relatively minor differences between the NIPA and BPA accounts.

[2]Balance of payments data can also be obtained online by visiting the DOSM's website at *http://www.statistics.gov.my/portal/index.php?lang=en* and clicking on "Statistical Releases" under the heading "Products & Services." In addition, the data can also be accessed via BNM's "Rates & Statistics" page at *http://www.bnm.gov.my/index.php?ch=statistic&lang=en*.

interest received by a U.S. saver who owns a French government bond. Another example is the profits earned by a U.S. company from its foreign subsidiary. In both examples, the income is recorded as income receipts from abroad.

The income payments flowing out of a country consist of compensation paid to foreign residents working in the country plus payments to foreign owners of assets in the country. For example, the wages paid by a U.S. company to a Swedish engineer who is temporarily residing in the United States, or the dividends paid by a U.S. automobile company to a Mexican owner of stock in the company, are both income payments to residents of other countries.

Net Unilateral Transfers. **Unilateral transfers** are payments from one country to another that do not correspond to the purchase of any good, service, or asset. Examples are official foreign aid (a payment from one government to another) or a remittance of money from a resident of one country to family members living in another country. A country's net unilateral transfers equal unilateral transfers received by the country minus unilateral transfers flowing out of the country. The negative value of net unilateral transfers in Table 5.1 shows that the United States is a net donor to other countries.

Current Account Balance. Adding net exports of goods and services, net income from abroad, and net unilateral transfers yields a number called the **current account balance**. If the current account balance is positive, the country has a current account surplus. If the current account balance is negative, the country has a current account deficit. As Table 5.1 shows, in 2021 the United States had a \$824.0 billion current account deficit, equal to the sum of net exports of goods and services ($NX = -\$861.4$ billion), net income from abroad ($NFP = \$174.9$ billion), and net unilateral transfers ($-\$137.5$ billion).

The Financial Account

International transactions involving assets, either real or financial, are recorded in the **financial account**. When a U.S. firm or resident sells an asset to another country, for example, if a U.S. hotel is sold to Italian investors, the transaction is recorded as an increase in foreign-owned assets in the United States, which is a **financial inflow**, because funds flow into the United States to pay for the asset. Similarly, when the home country buys an asset from abroad—say a U.S. resident opens a Swiss bank account—the transaction involves a **financial outflow** from the United States and is recorded as an increase in U.S.-owned assets abroad.

The **financial account balance** equals the value of financial inflows minus the value of financial outflows plus the net increase in foreign-owned derivatives (which are financial assets whose value is based on, or "derived" from, the values of other assets) in the United States. When residents of a country sell more assets to foreigners than they buy from foreigners, the financial account balance is positive, creating a financial account surplus. When residents of the home country purchase more assets from foreigners than they sell, the financial account balance is negative, creating a financial account deficit. Table 5.1 shows that in 2021, U.S. residents increased their holdings of foreign assets (ignoring financial derivatives and unilaterally transferred assets) by \$1213.3 billion while foreigners increased their holdings of U.S. assets by \$1858.8 billion. Thus the United States had net financial flows of \$645.5 billion in 2021 ($1858.8 billion minus $1213.3 billion). Adding the net change in financial derivatives, the financial account balance in 2021 was $687.2 billion.

The Balance of Payments. In Table 5.1 one set of financial flows—transactions in official reserve assets—has been broken out separately. These transactions differ from other financial account transactions in that they are conducted by central banks (such as the Federal Reserve in the United States), which are the official institutions that determine national money supplies. Held by central banks, **official reserve assets** are assets, other than domestic money or securities, that can be used in making international payments. Historically, gold was the primary official reserve asset, but now the official reserves of central banks also include government securities of major industrialized economies, foreign bank deposits, and special assets created by the International Monetary Fund.

Central banks can change the quantity of official reserve assets they hold by buying or selling reserve assets on open markets. For example, the Federal Reserve could increase its reserve assets by using dollars to buy gold. According to Table 5.1 (see the line "U.S. official reserve assets"), in 2021 the U.S. central bank acquired $114.0 billion of official reserve assets. In the same year foreign central banks increased their holdings of dollar-denominated reserve assets by $266.2 billion (see the line "Foreign official assets"). The **balance of payments** is the net increase (domestic less foreign) in a country's official reserve assets. A country that increases its net holdings of reserve assets during a year has a balance of payments surplus, and a country that reduces its net holdings of reserve assets has a balance of payments deficit. For the United States in 2021 the balance of payments was −$152.2 billion (equal to the $114.0 billion increase in U.S. reserve assets minus the $266.2 billion increase in foreign dollar-denominated reserve assets). Thus the United States had a balance of payments deficit of $152.2 billion in 2021.

For the issues we discuss in this chapter, the balances on current account and on financial account play a much larger role than the balance of payments. We explain the macroeconomic significance of the balance of payments in Chapter 13 when we discuss the determination of exchange rates.

The Relationship Between the Current Account and the Financial Account

The logic of balance of payments accounting implies a close relationship between the current account and the financial account. Except for errors arising from problems of measurement, *in each period the current account balance and the financial account balance must sum to zero.* That is, if

$$CA = \text{current account balance and}$$
$$FA = \text{financial account balance,}$$

then

$$CA + FA = 0. \quad \textbf{(5.1)}$$

The reason that Eq. (5.1) holds is that every international transaction involves a swap of goods, services, or assets between countries. The two sides of the swap always have offsetting effects on the sum of the current account and the financial account balances, $CA + FA$. Thus the sum of the current account and the financial account balances must equal zero.

Table 5.2 helps clarify this point. Suppose that a U.S. consumer buys an imported British sweater, paying \$75 for it. This transaction is an import of goods to the United States and thus reduces the U.S. current account balance by \$75. However, the British exporter who sold the sweater now holds \$75. What will he do with it? There are several possibilities, any of which will offset the effect of the purchase of the sweater on the sum of the current account and the financial account balances.

The Briton may use the \$75 to buy a U.S. product—say, a computer game. This purchase is a \$75 export for the United States. This U.S. export, together with the original import of the sweater into the United States, results in no net change in the U.S. current account balance *CA*. The U.S. financial account balance *FA* hasn't changed, as no assets have been traded. Thus the sum of *CA* and *FA* remains the same.

A second possibility is that the Briton will use the \$75 to buy a U.S. asset—say, a bond issued by a U.S. corporation. The purchase of this bond is a financial inflow to the United States. This \$75 increase in the U.S. financial account offsets the \$75 reduction in the U.S. current account caused by the original import of the sweater. Again, the sum of the current account and the financial account balances, $CA + FA$, is unaffected by the combination of transactions.

TABLE 5.2

Why the Current Account Balance and the Financial Account Balance Sum to Zero: An Example (Balance of Payments Data Refer to the United States)

***Case I:* United States Imports \$75 Sweater from Britain; Britain Imports \$75 Computer Game from United States**	
Current Account	
Exports	\$75
less Imports	\$75
Current account balance, *CA*	0
Financial Account	
No transaction	
Financial account balance, *FA*	0
Sum of current and financial account balances, $CA + FA$	0
***Case II:* United States Imports \$75 Sweater from Britain; Britain Buys \$75 Bond from United States**	
Current Account	
less Imports	\$75
Current account balance, *CA*	−\$75
Financial Account	
Financial inflow	\$75
Financial account balance, *FA*	\$75
Sum of current and financial account balances, $CA + FA$	0
***Case III:* United States Imports \$75 Sweater from Britain; Federal Reserve Sells \$75 of British Pounds to British Bank**	
Current Account	
less Imports	\$75
Current account balance, *CA*	−\$75
Financial Account	
Financial inflow (reduction in U.S. official reserve assets)	\$75
Financial account balance, *FA*	+\$75
Sum of current and financial account balances, $CA + FA$	0

Finally, the Briton may decide to go to his bank and trade his dollars for British pounds. If the bank sells these dollars to another Briton for the purpose of buying U.S. exports or assets, or if it buys U.S. assets itself, one of the previous two cases is repeated. Alternatively, the bank may sell the dollars to the Federal Reserve in exchange for pounds. But in giving up $75 worth of British pounds, the Federal Reserve reduces its holdings of official reserve assets by $75, which counts as a financial inflow. As in the previous case, the financial account balance rises by $75, offsetting the decline in the current account balance caused by the import of the sweater.[3]

This example shows why, conceptually, the current account balance and the financial account balance must always sum to zero. In practice, problems in measuring international transactions prevent this relationship from holding exactly. The amount that would have to be added to the sum of the current account and the financial account balances for this sum to reach its theoretical value of zero is called the **statistical discrepancy**. As Table 5.1 shows, in 2017 the statistical discrepancy was $92.5 billion.

When you examine the data on the current account across countries, you see that for most of the past decade, the advanced economies of the world together ran a large current account deficit, while emerging and developing economies around the world ran a very large current account surplus. This means the emerging and developing economies have invested some of their saving in developed countries. See the Application "Recent Trends in the U.S. Current Account Deficit," for some reasons why this may have occurred.

Net Foreign Assets and the Balance of Payments Accounts

In Chapter 2 we defined the net foreign assets of a country as the foreign assets held by the country's residents (including, for example, foreign stocks, bonds, or real estate) minus the country's foreign liabilities (domestic physical and financial assets owned by foreigners). Net foreign assets are part of a country's national wealth, along with the country's domestic physical assets, such as land and the capital stock. The total value of a country's net foreign assets can change in two ways: (1) the value of existing foreign assets and foreign liabilities can change, as when stock held by a U.S. citizen in a foreign corporation increases in value or the value of U.S. farmland owned by a foreigner declines; and (2) the country can acquire new foreign assets or incur new foreign liabilities.

What determines the quantity of new foreign assets that a country can acquire? In any period *the net amount of new foreign assets that a country acquires equals its current account surplus.* For example, suppose a country exports $10 billion more in goods and services than it imports and thus runs a $10 billion current account surplus (assuming that net factor payments from abroad, *NFP*, and net unilateral transfers both are zero). The country must then use this $10 billion to acquire foreign assets or reduce foreign liabilities. In this case we say that the country has undertaken net foreign lending of $10 billion.

Similarly, if a country has a $10 billion current account deficit, it must cover this deficit either by selling assets to foreigners or by borrowing from foreigners. Either

[3]In this case, the balance of payments falls by $75, reflecting the Fed's loss of official reserves. We didn't consider the possibility that the Briton would just hold $75 in U.S. currency. As dollars are an obligation of the United States (in particular, of the Federal Reserve), the Briton's acquisition of dollars would appear in the financial account as an increase in foreign-owned assets in the United States, which is a financial inflow. This financial inflow would offset the reduction in the U.S. current account resulting from the import of the sweater.

SUMMARY 7
Equivalent Measures of a Country's International Trade and Lending
Each Item Describes the Same Situation
A current account surplus of $10 billion
A financial account deficit of $10 billion
Net acquisition of foreign assets of $10 billion
Net foreign lending of $10 billion
Net exports of $10 billion (if net factor payments, *NFP*, and net unilateral transfers equal zero)

action reduces the country's net foreign assets by $10 billion. We describe this situation by saying that the country has engaged in net foreign borrowing of $10 billion.

One important way in which a country borrows from foreigners occurs when a foreign business firm buys or builds capital goods; this is known as **foreign direct investment**. For example, when the Honda Motor Company from Japan builds a new auto production facility in Ohio, it engages in foreign direct investment. Because the facility is built in the United States but is financed by Japanese funds, foreign-owned assets in the United States increase, so the financial account balance increases. Foreign direct investment is different from portfolio investment, in which a foreigner acquires securities sold by a U.S. firm or investor. An example of portfolio investment occurs when a French investor buys shares of stock in Microsoft Corporation. This transaction also increases the financial account balance, as it represents an increase in foreign-owned assets in the United States.

Equation (5.1) emphasizes the link between the current account and the acquisition of foreign assets. Because $CA + FA = 0$, if a country has a current account surplus, it must have an equal financial account deficit. In turn, a financial account deficit implies that the country is increasing its net holdings of foreign assets. Similarly, a current account deficit implies a financial account surplus and a decline in the country's net holdings of foreign assets. Summary table 7 presents some equivalent ways of describing a country's current account balance and its acquisition of foreign assets.

Application

The United States as International Debtor

From about World War I until the 1980s, the United States was a net creditor internationally; that is, it had more foreign assets than liabilities. Since the early 1980s, however, the United States has consistently run large annual current account deficits. These current account deficits have had to be financed by net foreign borrowing (which we define broadly to include the sale of U.S.-owned assets to foreigners as well as the incurring of new foreign debts).

The accumulation of foreign debts and the sale of U.S. assets to foreigners have, over time, changed the United States from a net creditor internationally to a net debtor. Figure 5.1 shows the U.S. ownership of foreign assets and foreign ownership of U.S. assets, both measured as a percent of U.S. GDP, since 1982. As you can see, foreign ownership of U.S. assets overtook the U.S. ownership of foreign

(continued)

FIGURE 5.1

International ownership of assets relative to U.S. GDP, 1982–2021

The chart shows annual values for ownership of foreign assets by U.S. residents and ownership of U.S. assets by foreigners, each as a percentage of U.S. GDP for the period 1982 to 2021.

Sources: International ownership of assets: Bureau of Economic Analysis, International Economic Accounts, International Investment Position, Table 1.1, available at *apps.bea.gov/iTable/index_ita.cfm*. GDP: Bureau of Economic Analysis, National Income and Product Accounts, available at *fred.stlouisfed.org/series/GDPA*.

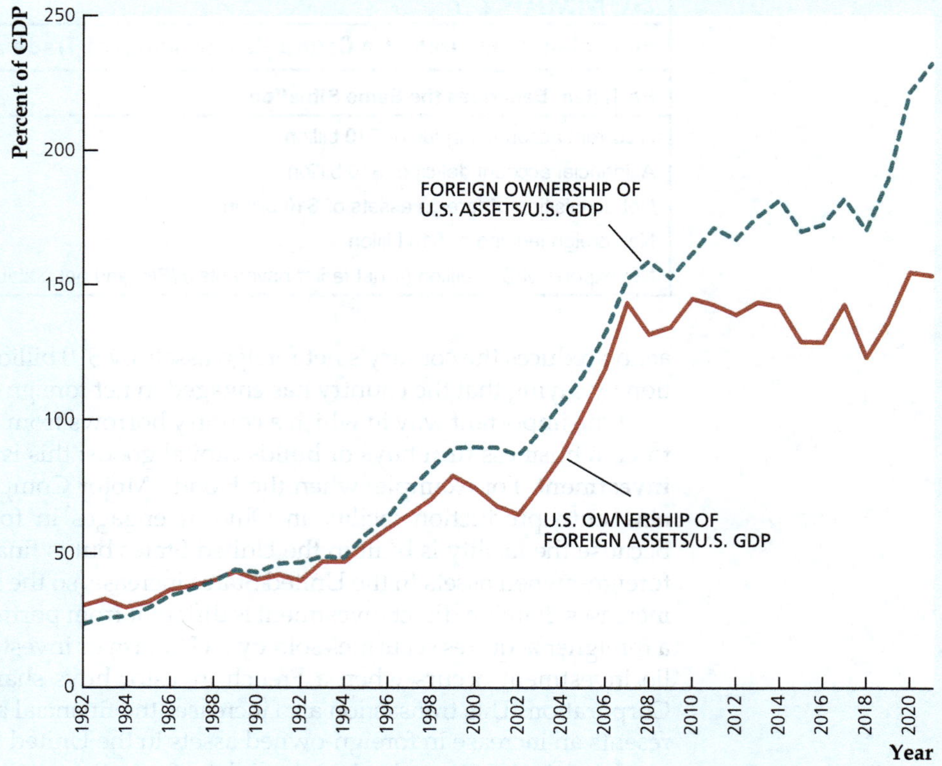

assets in the late 1980s and the gap between the two has grown substantially since then. According to estimates by the Bureau of Economic Analysis, at the end of 2021 the United States had net foreign assets of −$18.1 trillion, measured at current market prices. Equivalently, we could say that the United States had net foreign debt of $18.1 trillion.[4] This international obligation of more than $18 trillion is larger than that of any other country, making the United States the world's largest international debtor. This figure represents an increase of indebtedness of $4.1 trillion from yearend 2020. The U.S. current account deficit in 2021 was $824 billion. But the net debt of the United States increased by more because changes in the prices of stocks, bonds, and other assets caused increases in the value of foreign-owned assets in the United States relative to the value of U.S.-owned assets abroad.

Although the international debt of the United States is large, the numbers need to be put in perspective. First, the economic burden created by any debt depends not on the absolute size of the debt but on its size relative to the debtor's economic resources. Even at $18.1 trillion, the U.S. international debt is only about 79% of one year's GDP (U.S. GDP in 2021 was $20,894 billion). By contrast, some countries, especially certain developing countries, have ratios of net foreign debt to annual GDP that exceed 100%. Second, the large negative net foreign asset position of the United

[4]These and other data in this application are from BEA News Release, "U.S. International Investment Position: Fourth Quarter and Year 2021," *www.bea.gov/sites/default/files/2022-03/intinv421.pdf*.

States doesn't imply that it is being "bought up" or "controlled" by foreigners. If we focus on foreign direct investment, in which a resident of one country has ownership in a business in another country and has influence over the management of that business, it appears that the United States has a slightly smaller presence in other countries than they do in the United States. At the end of 2020, the market value of U.S. direct investment in foreign countries was $11,035 billion, and the market value of foreign direct investment in the United States was $14,840 billion.[5]

In evaluating the economic significance of a country's foreign debt, keep in mind that net foreign assets are only part of a country's wealth; the much greater part of wealth is a country's physical capital stock and (though it isn't included in the official national income accounts) its "human capital"—the economically valuable skills of its population. Thus, if a country borrows abroad but uses the proceeds of that borrowing to increase its physical and human capital, the foreign borrowing is of less concern than when a country borrows purely to finance current consumption spending. Unfortunately, the deterioration of the U.S. net foreign asset position doesn't appear to have been accompanied by any significant increase in the rates of physical investment or human capital formation in the United States. In that respect, the continued high rate of U.S. borrowing abroad is worrisome but unlikely to create a crisis in the near term.

[5]Incidentally, the largest direct investor in the United States is Japan. Japan is also the country that receives the most direct investment from the United States. For data on the distribution of U.S. direct investment abroad and foreign direct investment in the United States, see "Direct Investment by Country and Industry, 2020," Bureau of Economics Analysis website at *www.bea.gov/news/2021/direct-investment-country-and-industry-2020*, July 2021.

5.2 Goods Market Equilibrium in an Open Economy

Discuss goods market equilibrium in an open economy.

We are now ready to investigate the economic forces that determine international trade and borrowing. In the remainder of this chapter we demonstrate that a country's current account balance and foreign lending are closely linked to its domestic spending and production decisions. Understanding these links first requires developing the open-economy version of the goods market equilibrium condition.

In Chapter 4 we derived the goods market equilibrium condition for a closed economy. We showed that this condition can be expressed either as desired national saving equals desired investment or, equivalently, as the aggregate supply of goods equals the aggregate demand for goods. With some modification, we can use these same two conditions to describe goods market equilibrium in an open economy.

Let's begin with the open-economy version of the condition that desired national saving equals desired investment. In Chapter 2 we derived the national income accounting identity (Eq. 2.9):

$$S = I + CA = I + (NX + NFP). \quad \textbf{(5.2)}$$

Equation (5.2) is a version of the uses-of-saving identity. It states that national saving, S, has two uses: (1) to increase the nation's stock of capital by funding investment, I; and (2) to increase the nation's stock of net foreign assets by lending to foreigners (recall that the current account balance, CA, equals the amount of funds that the country has available for net foreign lending). Equation (5.2) also reminds us that (assuming no net unilateral transfers) the current account, CA, is the sum of net exports, NX, and net factor payments from abroad, NFP.

Because Eq. (5.2) is an identity, it must always hold (by definition). For the economy to be in goods market equilibrium, actual national saving and investment must also equal their desired levels. If actual and desired levels are equal, Eq. (5.2) becomes

$$S^d = I^d + CA = I^d + (NX + NFP), \tag{5.3}$$

where S^d and I^d represent desired national saving and desired investment, respectively. Equation (5.3) is the goods market equilibrium condition for an open economy, in which the current account balance, CA, equals net lending to foreigners, or financial outflows. Hence Eq. (5.3) states that *in goods market equilibrium in an open economy, the desired amount of national saving, S^d, must equal the desired amount of domestic investment, I^d, plus the amount lent abroad, CA.* Note that the closed-economy equilibrium condition is a special case of Eq. (5.3), with $CA = 0$.

If for simplicity we assume that net factor payments, NFP, are zero, the current account equals net exports and the goods market equilibrium condition, Eq. (5.3), becomes

$$S^d = I^d + NX. \tag{5.4}$$

Equation (5.4) is the form of the goods market equilibrium condition that we will work with. Under the assumption that net factor payments are zero, we can refer to the term NX interchangeably as net exports or as the current account balance.

As for the closed economy, we can also write the goods market equilibrium condition for the open economy in terms of the aggregate supply and aggregate demand for goods. In an open economy, where net exports, NX, are part of the aggregate demand for goods, this alternative condition for goods market equilibrium is

$$Y = C^d + I^d + G + NX, \tag{5.5}$$

where Y is output, C^d is desired consumption spending, and G is government purchases. This way of writing the goods market equilibrium condition is equivalent to the condition in Eq. (5.4).[6]

We can rewrite Eq. (5.5) as

$$NX = Y - (C^d + I^d + G). \tag{5.6}$$

Equation (5.6) states that in goods market equilibrium the amount of net exports a country sends abroad equals the country's total output (gross domestic product), Y, less total desired spending by domestic residents, $C^d + I^d + G$. Total spending by domestic residents is called **absorption**. Thus Eq. (5.6) states that an economy in which output exceeds absorption will send goods abroad ($NX > 0$) and have a current account surplus and that an economy that absorbs more than it produces will be a net importer ($NX < 0$), with a current account deficit.

---

[6]To see that Eq. (5.5) is equivalent to Eq. (5.4), subtract $C^d + G$ from both sides of Eq. (5.5) to obtain $Y - C^d - G = I^d + NX$. The left side of this equation equals desired national saving, S^d, so Eq. (5.5) is the same as Eq. (5.4).

5.3 Saving and Investment in a Small Open Economy

Discuss the factors that affect saving and investment and determine the current account balance in a small open economy.

To show how saving and investment are related to international trade and lending, we first present the case of a small open economy. A **small open economy** is an economy that is too small to affect the world real interest rate. The **world real interest rate** is the real interest rate that prevails in the international capital market—that is, the market in which individuals, businesses, and governments borrow and lend across national borders. Because changes in saving and investment in the small open economy aren't large enough to affect the world real interest rate, this interest rate is fixed in our analysis, which is a convenient simplification. Later in this chapter we consider the case of an open economy, such as the U.S. economy, that is large enough to affect the world real interest rate.

As with the closed economy, we can describe the goods market equilibrium in a small open economy by using the saving–investment diagram. The important new assumption that we make is that residents of the economy can borrow or lend in the international capital market at the (expected) world real interest rate, r^w, which for now we assume is fixed. If the world real interest rate is r^w, the domestic real interest rate must be r^w as well, as no domestic borrower with access to the international capital market would pay more than r^w to borrow, and no domestic saver with access to the international capital market would accept less than r^w to lend.[7]

Figure 5.2 shows the saving and investment curves for a small open economy. In a closed economy, goods market equilibrium would be represented by point E, the intersection of the curves. The equilibrium real interest rate in the closed

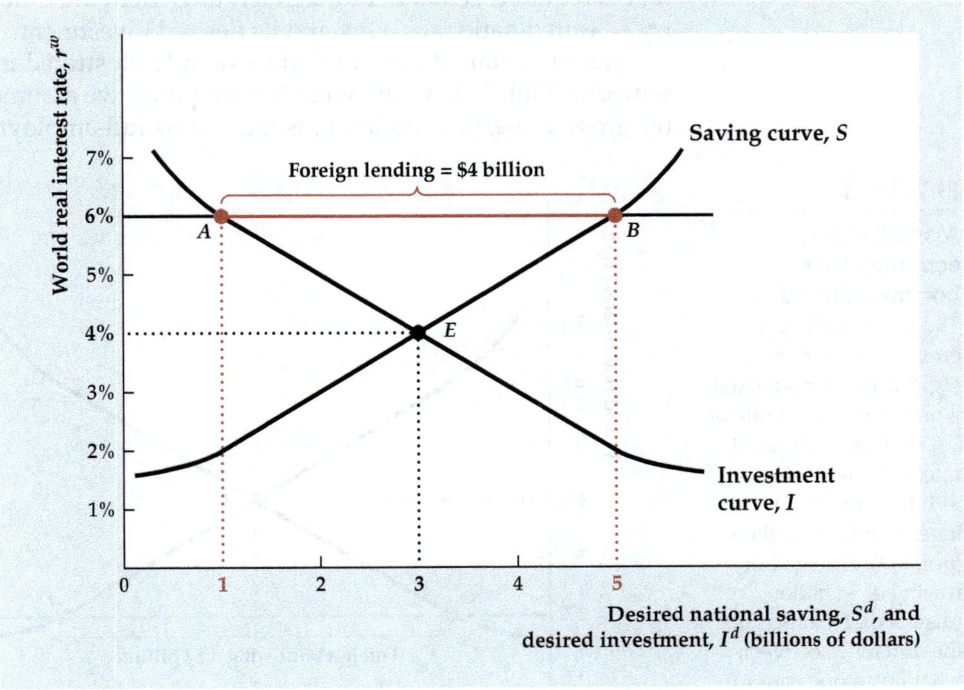

FIGURE 5.2

A small open economy that lends abroad

The graph shows the saving–investment diagram for a small open economy. The country faces a fixed world real interest rate of 6%. At this real interest rate, national saving is $5 billion (point *B*) and investment is $1 billion (point *A*). The part of national saving not used for investment is lent abroad, so foreign lending is $4 billion (distance *AB*).

[7]For simplicity, we ignore factors such as differences in risk or taxes that might cause the domestic real interest rate to differ from the world rate. We also assume that there are no legal barriers to international borrowing and lending (when they exist, such barriers are referred to as *capital controls*).

economy would be 4% (per year), and national saving and investment would be \$3 billion (per year). In an open economy, however, desired national saving need not equal desired investment. If the small open economy faces a fixed world real interest rate, r^w, higher than 4%, desired national saving will be greater than desired investment. For example, if r^w is 6%, desired national saving is \$5 billion and desired investment is \$1 billion, so desired national saving exceeds desired investment by \$4 billion.

Can the economy be in equilibrium when desired national saving exceeds desired investment by \$4 billion? In a closed economy it couldn't. The excess saving would have no place to go, and the real interest rate would have to fall to bring desired saving and desired investment into balance. However, in the open economy the excess \$4 billion of saving can be used to buy foreign assets. This financial outflow uses up the excess national saving so that there is no disequilibrium. Instead, the goods market is in equilibrium with desired national saving of \$5 billion, desired investment of \$1 billion, and net foreign lending of \$4 billion (see Eq. 5.4 and recall that net exports, NX, and net foreign lending are equal).

Alternatively, suppose that the world real interest rate, r^w, is 2% instead of 6%. As Figure 5.3 shows, in this case desired national saving is \$1 billion and desired investment is \$5 billion so that desired investment exceeds desired saving by \$4 billion. Now firms desiring to invest will have to borrow \$4 billion in the international capital market. Is this also a goods market equilibrium? Yes it is, because desired national saving (\$1 billion) again equals desired investment (\$5 billion) plus net foreign lending (minus \$4 billion). Indeed, a small open economy can achieve goods market equilibrium for any value of the world real interest rate. All that is required is that net foreign lending equal the difference between the country's desired national saving and its desired investment.

A more detailed version of the example illustrated in Figs. 5.2 and 5.3 is presented in Table 5.3. As shown in the top panel, we assume that in this small country gross domestic product, Y, is fixed at its full-employment value of \$20 billion

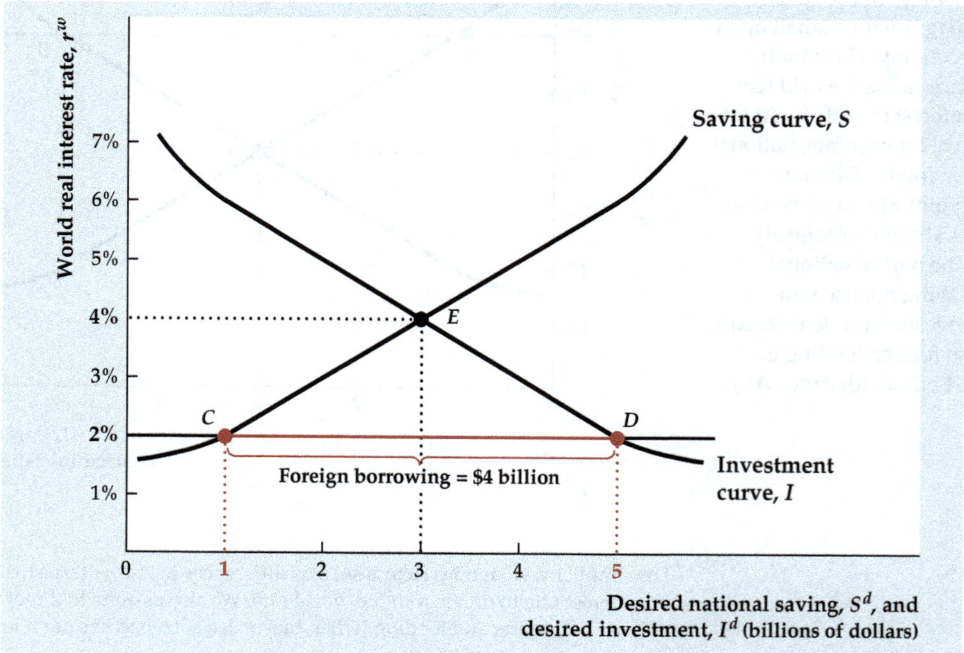

FIGURE 5.3

A small open economy that borrows abroad

The same small open economy shown in Fig. 5.2 now faces a fixed world real interest rate of 2%. At this real interest rate, national saving is \$1 billion (point C) and investment is \$5 billion (point D). Foreign borrowing of \$4 billion (distance CD) makes up the difference between what investors want to borrow and what domestic savers want to lend.

TABLE 5.3

Goods Market Equilibrium in a Small Open Economy: An Example (Billions of Dollars)

Given			
Gross domestic product, Y	20		
Government purchases, G	4		
Effect of real interest rate on desired consumption and investment			
	(1)	**(2)**	**(3)**
(1) World real interest rate, r^w (%)	2	4	6
(2) Desired consumption, C^d	15	13	11
(3) Desired investment, I^d	5	3	1
Results			
(4) Desired absorption, $C^d + I^d + G$	24	20	16
(5) Desired national saving, $S^d = Y - C^d - G$	1	3	5
(6) Net exports, $NX = Y -$ *desired absorption*	−4	0	4
(7) Desired foreign lending, $S^d - I^d$	−4	0	4

Note: We assume that net factor payments, *NFP*, and net unilateral transfers equal zero.

and government purchases, G, are fixed at \$4 billion. The middle panel shows three possible values for the world real interest rate, r^w, and the assumed levels of desired consumption and desired investment at each of these values of the real interest rate. Note that higher values of the world real interest rate imply lower levels of desired consumption (because people choose to save more) and lower desired investment. The bottom panel shows the values of various economic quantities implied by the assumed values in the top two panels.

The equilibrium in this example depends on the value of the world real interest rate, r^w. Suppose that $r^w = 6\%$, as shown in Fig. 5.2. Column (3) of Table 5.3 shows that, if $r^w = 6\%$, desired consumption, C^d, is \$11 billion (row 2) and that desired investment, I^d, is \$1 billion (row 3). With C^d at \$11 billion, desired national saving, $Y - C^d - G$, is \$5 billion (row 5). Desired net foreign lending, $S^d - I^d$, is \$4 billion (row 7)—the same result illustrated in Fig. 5.2.

If $r^w = 2\%$, as in Fig. 5.3, column (1) of Table 5.3 shows that desired national saving is \$1 billion (row 5) and that desired investment is \$5 billion (row 3). Thus desired foreign lending, $S^d - I^d$, equals −\$4 billion (row 7)—that is, foreign borrowing totals \$4 billion. Again, the result is the same as illustrated in Fig. 5.3.

An advantage of working through the numerical example in Table 5.3 is that we can also use it to demonstrate how the goods market equilibrium, which we've been interpreting in terms of desired saving and investment, can be interpreted in terms of output and absorption. Suppose again that $r^w = 6\%$, giving a desired consumption, C^d, of \$11 billion and a desired investment, I^d, of \$1 billion. Government purchases, G, are fixed at \$4 billion. Thus when r^w is 6%, desired absorption (the desired spending by domestic residents), $C^d + I^d + G$, totals \$16 billion (row 4, column 3).

In goods market equilibrium a country's net exports—the net quantity of goods and services that it sends abroad—equal gross domestic product, Y, minus desired absorption (Eq. 5.6). When r^w is 6%, Y is \$20 billion and desired absorption is \$16 billion so that net exports, NX, are \$4 billion. Net exports of \$4 billion imply that the country is lending \$4 billion abroad, as shown in Fig. 5.2. If the world real interest rate drops to 2%, desired absorption rises (because people

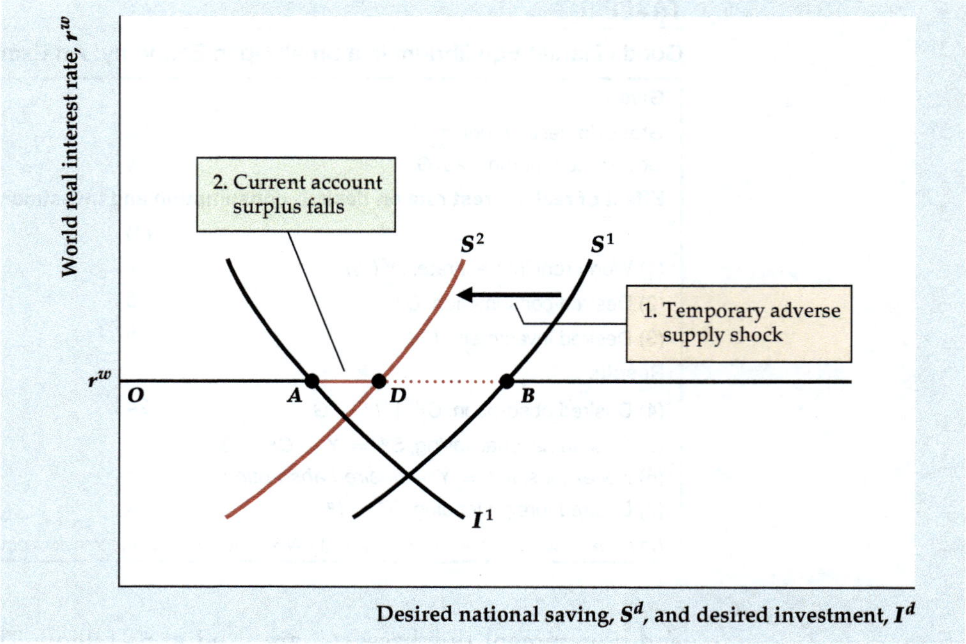

FIGURE 5.4

A temporary adverse supply shock in a small open economy
Curve S^1 is the initial saving curve, and curve I^1 is the initial investment curve of a small open economy. With a fixed world real interest rate of r^w, national saving equals the distance *OB* and investment equals distance *OA*. The current account surplus (equivalently, net foreign lending) is the difference between national saving and investment, shown as distance *AB*. A temporary adverse supply shock lowers current output and causes consumers to save less at any real interest rate, which shifts the saving curve left, from S^1 to S^2. National saving decreases to distance *OD*, and the current account surplus decreases to distance *AD*.

want to consume more and invest more) from \$16 billion to \$24 billion (row 4, column 1). Because in this case absorption (\$24 billion) exceeds domestic production (\$20 billion), the country has to import goods and services from abroad ($NX = -\$4$ billion). Note that desired net imports of \$4 billion imply net foreign borrowing of \$4 billion, as shown in Fig. 5.3.

The Effects of Economic Shocks in a Small Open Economy

The saving–investment diagram can be used to determine the effects of various types of economic disturbances in a small open economy. Briefly, any change that increases desired national saving relative to desired investment at a given world real interest rate will increase net foreign lending, the current account balance, and net exports, which are all equivalent under our assumption that net factor payments from abroad and net unilateral transfers are zero. A decline in desired national saving relative to desired investment reduces those quantities. Let's look at an example.

Suppose that a small open economy is hit with a severe drought—an adverse supply shock—that temporarily lowers output. The effects of the drought on the nation's saving, investment, and current account are shown in Figure 5.4. The initial saving and investment curves are S^1 and I^1, respectively. For the world real interest rate, r^w, initial net foreign lending (equivalently, net exports or the current account balance) is distance *AB*.

The drought brings with it a temporary decline in income. A drop in current income causes people to reduce their saving at any prevailing real interest rate, so the saving curve shifts left, from S^1 to S^2. If the supply shock is temporary, as we have assumed, the expected future marginal product of capital is unchanged. As a result, desired investment at any real interest rate is unchanged, and the investment curve does not shift. The world real interest rate is given and does not change.

In the new equilibrium, net foreign lending and the current account have shrunk to distance *AD*. The current account shrinks because the country saves less and thus is not able to lend abroad as much as before.

In this example, we assumed that the country started with a current account surplus, which is reduced by the drought. If, instead, the country had begun with a current account deficit, the drought would have made the deficit larger. In either case the drought reduces (in the algebraic sense) net foreign lending and the current account balance.

5.4 Saving and Investment in Large Open Economies

Discuss the factors that affect saving and investment and determine the current account balance in a large open economy.

Although the model of a small open economy facing a fixed real interest rate is appropriate for studying many of the countries in the world, it isn't the right model to use for analyzing the world's major developed economies. The problem is that significant changes in the saving and investment of a major economy can and do affect the world real interest rate, which violates the assumption made for the small open economy that the world real interest rate is fixed. Fortunately, we can readily adapt the analysis of the small open economy to the case of a **large open economy**, that is, an economy large enough to affect the world real interest rate.

To begin, let's think of the world as comprising only two large economies: (1) the home, or domestic economy, and (2) the foreign economy (representing the economies of the rest of the world combined). Figure 5.5 shows the saving–investment diagram that applies to this case. Figure 5.5(a) shows the saving curve, S, and the investment curve, I, of the home economy. Figure 5.5(b) displays the saving curve, S_{For}, and the investment curve, I_{For}, of the foreign economy. These saving and investment curves are just like those for the small open economy.

Instead of taking the world real interest rate as given, as we did in the model of a small open economy, we determine the world real interest rate within the model for a large open economy. What determines the value of the world real interest rate? Remember that for the closed economy the real interest rate was set by the condition that the amount that savers want to lend must equal the amount that investors want to borrow. Analogously, in the case of two large open economies, *the world real interest rate will be such that desired international lending by one country equals desired international borrowing by the other country.*

To illustrate the determination of the equilibrium world real interest rate, we return to Fig. 5.5. Suppose, arbitrarily, that the world real interest rate, r^w, is 6%. Does this rate result in a goods market equilibrium? Figure 5.5(a) shows that, at a 6% real interest rate, in the home country desired national saving is \$450 billion and desired investment is \$150 billion. Because desired national saving exceeds desired investment by \$300 billion, the amount that the home country would like to lend abroad is \$300 billion.

To find how much the foreign country wants to borrow, we turn to Fig. 5.5(b). When the real interest rate is 6%, desired national saving is \$550 billion and desired investment is \$650 billion in the foreign country. Thus at a 6% real interest rate the foreign country wants to borrow \$100 billion (\$650 billion less \$550 billion) in the international capital market. Because this amount is less than the \$300 billion the home country wants to lend, 6% is *not* the real interest rate that is consistent with equilibrium in the international capital market.

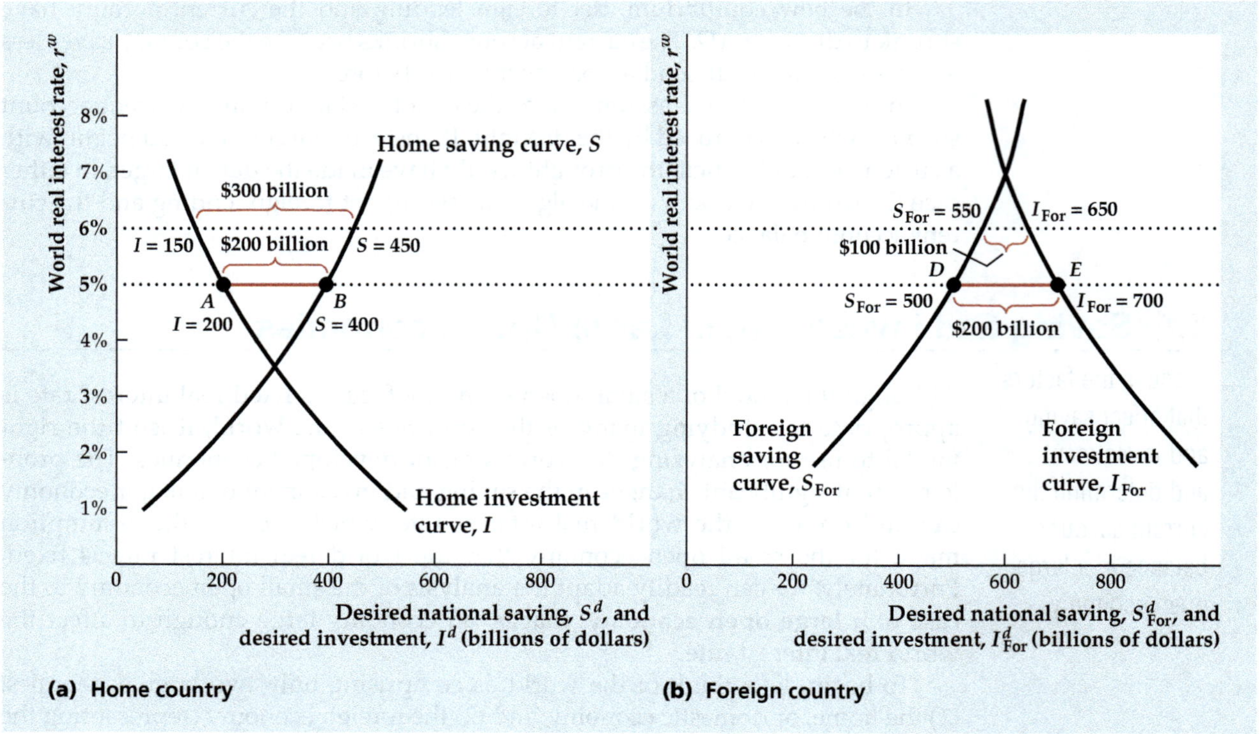

FIGURE 5.5

The determination of the world real interest rate with two large open economies

The equilibrium world real interest rate is the real interest rate at which desired international lending by one country equals desired international borrowing by the other country. In the figure, when the world real interest rate is 5%, desired international lending by the home country is \$200 billion (\$400 billion desired national saving less \$200 billion desired investment, or distance *AB*), which equals the foreign country's desired international borrowing of \$200 billion (\$700 billion desired investment less \$500 billion desired national saving, or distance *DE*). Thus 5% is the equilibrium world real interest rate. Equivalently, when the interest rate is 5%, the current account surplus of the home country equals the current account deficit of the foreign country (both are \$200 billion).

At a real interest rate of 6%, desired international lending exceeds desired international borrowing, so the equilibrium world real interest rate must be less than 6%. Let's try a real interest rate of 5%. Figure 5.5(a) shows that at that interest rate desired national saving is \$400 billion and desired investment is \$200 billion in the home country, so the home country wants to lend \$200 billion abroad. In Fig. 5.5(b), when the real interest rate is 5%, desired national saving in the foreign country is \$500 billion and desired investment is \$700 billion, so the foreign country's desired international borrowing is \$200 billion. At a 5% real interest rate, desired international borrowing and desired international lending are equal (both are \$200 billion), so the equilibrium world real interest rate is 5% in this example.

Graphically, the home country's desired lending when r^w equals 5% is distance *AB* in Fig. 5.5(a), and the foreign country's desired borrowing is distance *DE* in Fig. 5.5(b). Because distance *AB* equals distance *DE*, desired international lending and borrowing are equal when the world real interest rate is 5%.

We defined international equilibrium in terms of desired international lending and borrowing. Equivalently, we can define equilibrium in terms of international flows of goods and services. The amount the lending country desires to lend (distance AB in Fig. 5.5a) is the same as its current account surplus. The amount the borrowing country wants to borrow (distance DE in Fig. 5.5b) equals its current account deficit. Thus saying that desired international lending must equal desired international borrowing is the same as saying that the desired net outflow of goods and services from the lending country (its current account surplus) must equal the desired net inflow of goods and services to the borrowing country (its current account deficit).

In summary, for a large open economy the equilibrium world real interest rate is the rate at which the desired international lending by one country equals the desired international borrowing of the other country. Equivalently, it is the real interest rate at which the lending country's current account surplus equals the borrowing country's current account deficit.

Unlike the situation in a small open economy, for large open economies the world real interest rate is not fixed but will change when desired national saving or desired investment changes in either country. Generally, any factor that increases desired international lending relative to desired international borrowing at the initial world real interest rate causes the world real interest rate to fall. Similarly, a change that reduces desired international lending relative to desired international borrowing at the initial world real interest rate will cause the world real interest rate to rise.

Application

The Impact of Globalization on the U.S. Economy

Section 5.1, "Balance of Payments Accounting," showed how the international balance of payments accounts keep track of international trade and investment. These accounts reveal that the world's economies have become increasingly interdependent, as the volume of trade in goods and services has increased and as people in one country have increased their investment in other countries. This globalization is not without its consequences, and some people have argued that the United States needs to rein in the degree of globalization, restricting trade or international investment. To evaluate such proposals, we need to examine the facts about globalization, including how it has affected U.S. trade with other countries, how trade in services has changed, and how international investment has been altered.

To begin, let's look at how U.S. trade with other countries has changed over time. If we examine exports of goods and services as a percentage of our GDP, we can see the relative importance of exports in the economy; similarly for imports. Figure 5.6 shows both statistics from 1929 to 2021. After World War II, both exports and imports rose gradually relative to GDP until the mid 1980s, when both began growing more rapidly. From the mid 1980s to 2006, imports generally outpaced exports, thereby leading to a trade deficit that peaked at about 6.0% of GDP. The recession from 2007 to 2009 led to a reduction in imports relative to GDP, reducing the trade deficit to about 3%. Since 2014, the trade deficit rose, reaching over 6% of GDP by 2021.

In addition to increased trade in goods and services, investors have also increased their investments in foreign countries since the mid 1980s. As we saw in Fig. 5.1 in the Application "The United States as International Debtor," ownership of foreign assets by U.S. investors has increased rapidly, and ownership of U.S. assets by foreign investors has increased even more rapidly, so that the

(continued)

FIGURE 5.6

Exports and imports of goods and services as a percent of GDP, 1929–2021

The chart shows annual values for exports of goods and services from the United States and imports into the United States for the period 1929 to 2021.

Sources: Exports and imports: Bureau of Economic Analysis, Trade in Goods and Services, available at *fred.stlouisfed.org/series/EXPGSCA* and *IMPGSCA*. GDP: Bureau of Economic Analysis, National Income and Product Accounts, available at *fred.stlouisfed.org/series/GDPCA*.

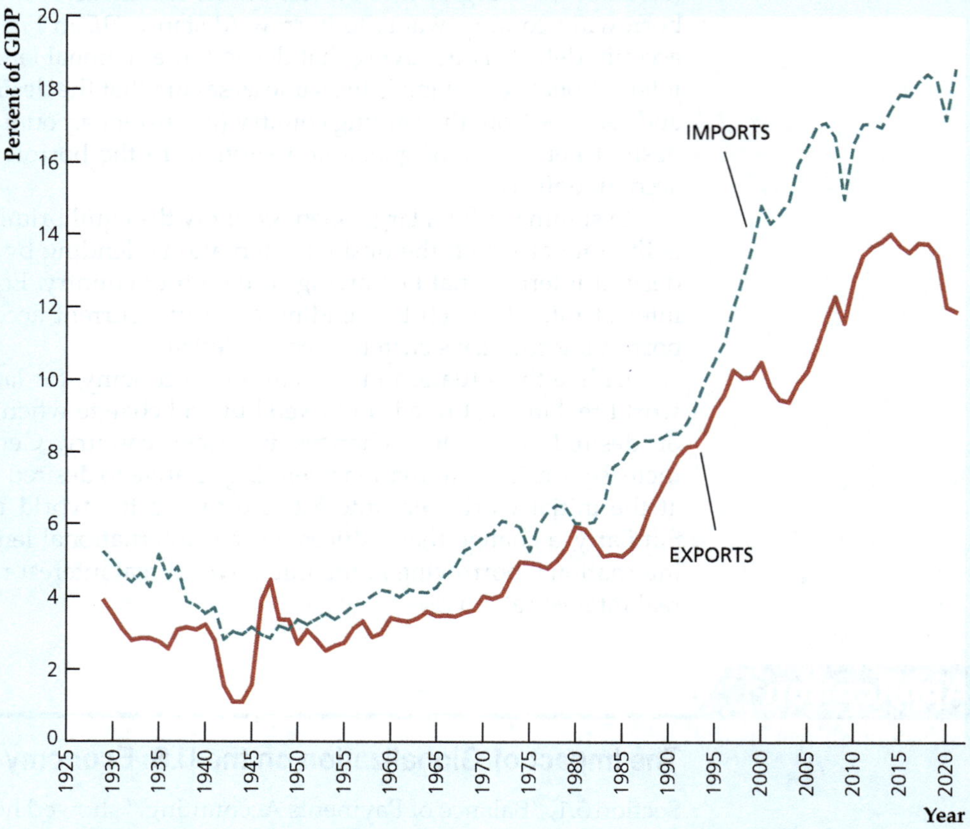

United States has gone from being a net international creditor prior to the mid 1980s (with U.S. ownership of foreign assets exceeding foreign ownership of U.S. assets) to a net international debtor (with U.S. ownership of foreign assets being less than foreign ownership of U.S. assets) today.

As the U.S. economy has become more interdependent with other economies, there have been some costs and complaints. Increased openness means that jobs in some sectors of the U.S. economy may be eliminated, as a particular good is produced by workers in another country. Often workers complain that they have lost their jobs to foreign workers. And there have been instances, widely reported in the U.S. business press, in which a company shuts down a facility in the United States and opens one to do the same work in a foreign country. There are costs in foreign countries as well. In the fourth quarter of 2008, U.S. GDP declined at an annualized rate of about 8% because of the financial crisis and recession. But countries in Asia that produced many goods that they export to the United States suffered declines of 12% (at an annualized growth rate) and more in their GDPs, as U.S. demand for their products declined dramatically.

Some people conclude that international trade destroys jobs. But international trade also creates jobs. Generally, the gains from increasing trade between countries exceed the costs. But the adjustment period can be painful in areas where jobs have been lost. A possible role for the government could be to help people adjust, for example, by helping them retrain to find new jobs. Otherwise, there may be people who lose from increased trade.

Research by David H. Autor of MIT, David Dorn of CEMFI, and Gordon H. Hansen of the University of California, San Diego, analyzed the impact of imports from China on U.S. labor markets from 1990 to 2007.[8] They found that imports from China into the United States led to increased unemployment, lower wages for workers, and reduced labor force participation in many local labor markets that produced goods that were directly exposed to competition from Chinese imports. Compared with the past, the shock to local labor markets was much larger and more abrupt. As a result, transfer payments in the form of unemployment benefits and disability payments to displaced workers were substantial. Although trade with other countries brings benefits, there are significant costs that governments should understand.

[8]"The China Syndrome: Local Labor Market Effects of Import Competition in the United States," *American Economic Review*, October 2013, pp. 2121–2168.

Application

Recent Trends in the U.S. Current Account Deficit

The United States has a very large current account deficit, as discussed in Section 5.1, "Balance of Payments Accounting." But the current account deficit shrank from 2007 to 2009, thanks to the U.S. recession, which reduced demand for imported goods.

Figure 5.7 shows how the current account balance has changed since 1960. The figure shows that the current account balance was generally positive in the 1960s, bounced up and down around zero in the 1970s, and then fell sharply to about −3% of GDP by the mid 1980s. In the second half of the 1980s, the current account balance improved, becoming positive again in 1991. From 1991 to 2005, it deteriorated markedly, falling to −6.2% of GDP by the end of 2005. The housing downturn of 2006 and the recession from 2007 to 2009 helped the current account balance improve to about −5% of GDP by mid 2008, as U.S. consumers bought fewer imported goods and services than before. When the financial crisis hit in late 2008, U.S. imports fell sharply and the current account balance improved to about −2.5% of GDP by mid 2009. As the U.S. economy improved slowly from 2009 to 2018, the current account balance remained higher than it was before the financial crisis at −2% to −3%. In the pandemic recession of 2020, the current account balance got even more negative, falling below −3%.

A major reason for the increase in the current account deficit from 1998 to 2005 was a change in the saving behavior of developing countries.[9] Developing nations that had borrowed from abroad in past decades began lending abroad, especially to the United States. In part, this change in behavior occurred as a result of past financial crises, such as Mexico experienced in 1994 and the countries of East Asia experienced in 1997–1998. Those crises were exacerbated by the fact that those countries had borrowed substantially from foreign countries. To prevent such crises from happening again, the countries increased their saving, built

[9]For an analysis of this view, see Ben S. Bernanke, "The Global Saving Glut and the U.S. Current Account Deficit," Sandridge Lecture, Virginia Association of Economists, Richmond, Virginia, March 10, 2005. Available at *www.federalreserve.gov/boarddocs/speeches/2005*.

(continued)

FIGURE 5.7

Current account balance as a percent of GDP, 1960Q1–2021Q4

The chart shows quarterly values for the current account balance as a percent of GDP for the period from the first quarter of 1960 to the fourth quarter of 2021.

Sources: Balance on current account: Bureau of Economic Analysis, available online at *fred.stlouisfed.org/series/NETFI.* GDP: Bureau of Economic Analysis, available at *fred.stlouisfed.org/series/GDP.*

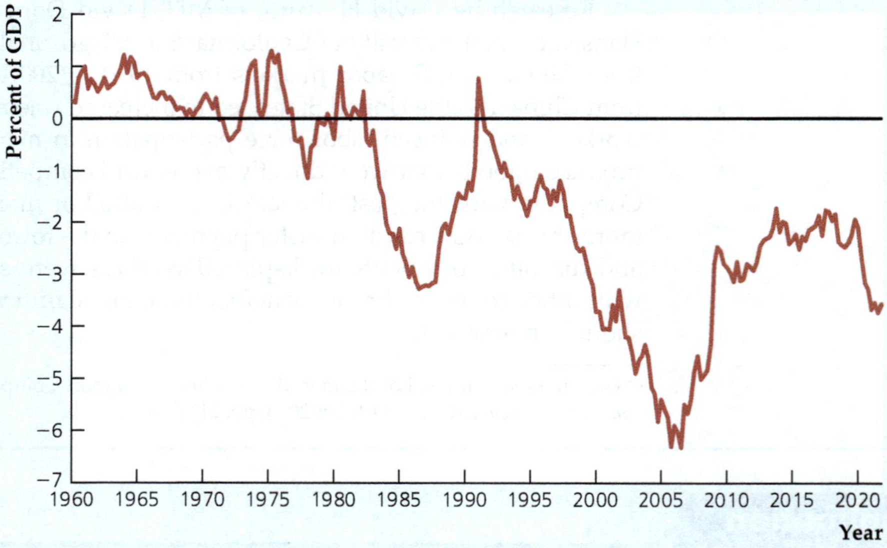

up foreign exchange reserves, and became net lenders to foreign countries instead of net borrowers.

After 2005, other developments contributed to a continuation of the global increase in saving, including an increase in the current account balances of Germany and other countries in Europe. The consequence has been low global interest rates. Those rates may begin to rise when the reasons for the increased saving diminish in the future.

A country can have a current account deficit overall but have bilateral current account surpluses with some countries and current account deficits with other countries. Those bilateral balances reflect the specific nature of trade between the countries. For example, suppose a country like China has many manual laborers with low wages. Firms bring many unfinished goods to China from other countries and assemble them into final products in China. Because U.S. consumers buy many manufactured goods and because China is the final assembly point for many such goods, the United States runs a large bilateral trade deficit with China. That bilateral trade deficit thus mainly arises because U.S. consumers desire manufactured goods. The size of the bilateral trade deficit is exacerbated by the fact that in the international trade statistics, the entire value of the final manufactured good is counted as an import into the United States from China, even though many of the component parts may have come from other countries. Thus the bilateral trade balance is a misleading indicator of the value of U.S. trade with China.

Here is a simple example of how this works and why the U.S. bilateral trade deficit with China is not something we should worry about. Consider a hair stylist who produces haircuts and a butcher who produces meat in a grocery. The stylist buys meat from the butcher and thus has a trade deficit with the stylist. But the stylist sells haircuts to many other people and uses the income from those haircuts to pay for the meat from the butcher. Thus the stylist's trade surpluses with others covers the bilateral trade deficit with the butcher.

What might happen if a country imposes restrictions, such as tariffs, on imported goods? The demand for the goods with tariffs will decline because they will become more expensive. But, most likely, the other country will retaliate with tariffs of its own. As a result, tariffs are unlikely to reduce the bilateral trade balance or the overall trade balance. Most likely, both countries will produce less total output, as the gains from *comparative advantage* will be lost.[10] Thus both countries will be worse off, and the trade balances are unlikely to change significantly.

[10]Comparative advantage is the idea that some countries are relatively good at producing certain goods, while other countries are relatively good at producing other goods. Ideally, each country produces the goods that it is relatively better at producing and trades with other countries, and thus the total output of the world economy is higher.

5.5 Fiscal Policy and the Current Account

Analyze the relationship between the government budget deficit and the current account deficit.

During the 1980s and 1990s the United States often had both large government budget deficits and large current account deficits. Are these two phenomena related? Many economists and other commentators argue that they are, suggesting that in fact the budget deficit is the primary cause of the current account deficit. Those supporting this view often use the phrase "twin deficits" to convey the idea that the government budget deficit and the current account deficit are closely linked. Not all economists agree with this interpretation, however; some argue that the two deficits are largely unrelated. In this section we briefly discuss what the theory has to say about this issue and then turn to the evidence.

The Critical Factor: The Response of National Saving

In theory, the issue of whether a link exists between the government budget deficit and the current account deficit revolves around the following proposition: *An increase in the government budget deficit will raise the current account deficit only if the increase in the budget deficit reduces desired national saving.*

Let's first look at why the link to national saving is crucial. Figure 5.8 shows the case of the small open economy. The world real interest rate is fixed at r^w. We draw the initial saving and investment curves, S^1 and I, so that, at the world real interest rate, r^w, the country is running a current account surplus, represented by distance AB. Now suppose that the government budget deficit rises. For simplicity, we assume throughout this section that the change in fiscal policy doesn't affect the tax treatment of investment so that the investment curve doesn't shift. Hence as Fig. 5.8 shows, the government deficit increase will change the current account balance only if it affects desired national saving.

The usual claim made by supporters of the twin-deficits idea is that an increase in the government budget deficit reduces desired national saving. If it does, the increase in the government deficit shifts the desired national saving curve to the left, from S^1 to S^2. The country still has a current account surplus, now equal to distance AC, but it is less than the original surplus, AB.

We conclude that in a small open economy an increase in the government budget deficit reduces the current account balance by the same amount that it reduces desired national saving. By reducing saving, the increased budget deficit reduces the amount that domestic residents want to lend abroad at the world real interest rate, thus lowering financial outflows. Equivalently, reduced national

FIGURE 5.8

The government budget deficit and the current account in a small open economy An increase in the government budget deficit affects the current account only if the increased budget deficit reduces national saving. Initially, the saving curve is S^1 and the current account surplus is distance AB. If an increase in the government deficit reduces national saving, the saving curve shifts to the left, from S^1 to S^2. With no change in the effective tax rate on capital, the investment curve, I, doesn't move. Thus the increase in the budget deficit causes the current account surplus to decrease from distance AB to distance AC. In contrast, if the increase in the budget deficit has no effect on national saving, the current account also is unaffected and remains equal to distance AB.

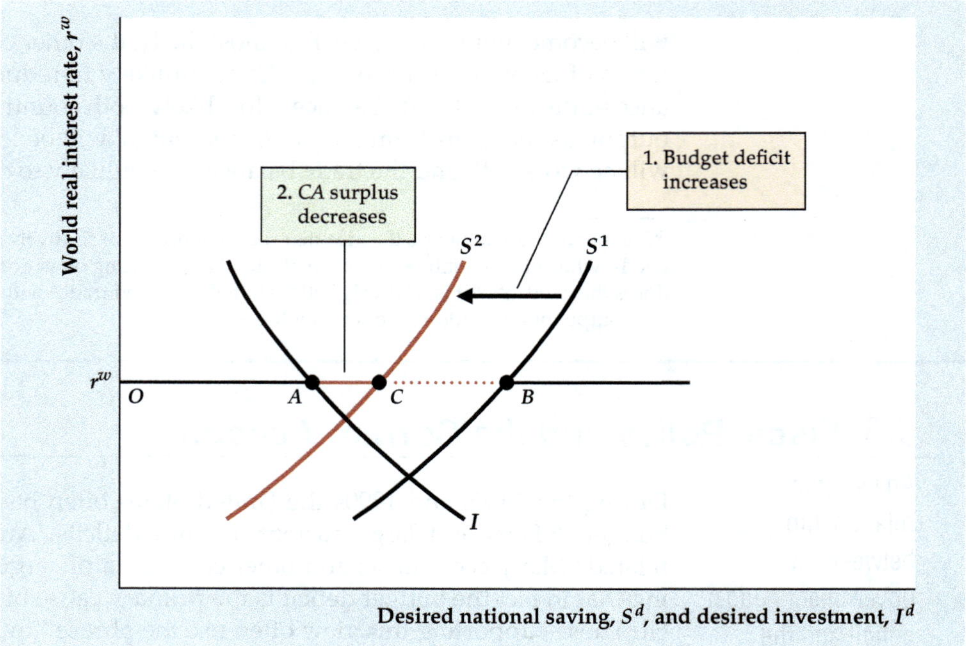

saving means that a greater part of domestic output is absorbed at home; with less output to send abroad, the country's current account balance falls. Similar results hold for the large open economy (you are asked to work out this case in Analytical Problem 4 at the end of the chapter).

The Government Budget Deficit and National Saving

Let's now turn to the link between the budget deficit and saving and consider two cases: a budget deficit arising from an increase in government purchases and a deficit originating from a cut in taxes.

A Deficit Caused by Increased Government Purchases. Suppose that the source of the government budget deficit is a temporary increase in government purchases, perhaps owing to a military buildup. In this case there is no controversy: Recall (Chapter 4) that with output, Y, held constant at its full-employment level, an increase in government purchases, G, directly reduces desired national saving, $S^d = Y - C^d - G$.[11,12] Because economists agree that a deficit owing to increased government purchases reduces desired national saving, they also agree that a deficit resulting from increased government purchases reduces the nation's current account balance.

A Deficit Resulting from a Tax Cut. Suppose instead that the government budget deficit is the result of a cut in current taxes, with current and planned future

[11]Because the increase in government purchases also means that taxes may be raised in the future, lowering consumers' expected future income, desired consumption, C^d, may fall. However, because the increase in G is temporary so that the future tax increase need not be too large, this drop in C^d should not completely offset the effect of increased G on desired national saving.

[12]In general, in an open economy $S^d = Y + NFP - C^d - G$, but we are assuming that $NFP = 0$ so that $S^d = Y - C^d - G$.

government purchases unchanged. With government purchases, G, unchanged and with output, Y, held constant at its full-employment level, the tax cut will cause desired national saving, $S^d = Y - C^d - G$, to fall only if it causes desired consumption, C^d, to rise.

Will a tax cut cause people to consume more? As we discussed in Chapter 4, believers in the Ricardian equivalence proposition argue that a lump-sum tax change (with current and future government purchases held constant) won't affect desired consumption or desired national saving. These economists point out that a cut in taxes today forces the government to borrow more to pay for its current purchases; when this extra borrowing plus interest is repaid in the future, future taxes will have to rise. Thus, although a tax cut raises consumers' current after-tax incomes, the tax cut creates the need for higher future taxes and lowers the after-tax incomes that consumers can expect to receive in the future. Overall, according to this argument, a tax cut doesn't benefit consumers and thus won't increase their desired consumption.

If the Ricardian equivalence proposition is true, a budget deficit resulting from a tax cut will have no effect on the current account because it doesn't affect desired national saving. However, as we noted in Chapter 4, many economists argue that—despite the logic of Ricardian equivalence—in practice many consumers do respond to a current tax cut by consuming more. For example, consumers simply may not understand that a higher deficit today makes higher taxes tomorrow more likely. Or some consumers may face binding borrowing constraints, so that a current tax cut allows them to spend more today, which they find desirable. If for any reason consumers do respond to a tax cut by consuming more, the deficit resulting from a tax cut will reduce national saving and thus also will reduce the current account balance.

Application

The Twin Deficits

The relationship between the U.S. government budget and the U.S. current account for the period 1960–2021 is illustrated in Figure 5.9. This figure shows government purchases and net government income (taxes less transfers and interest) for the Federal government alone as well as for the combined Federal, state, and local governments, all measured as a percentage of GDP. Our discussion of the current account balance as the excess of national saving over investment leads us to focus on the broadest level of government, which includes state and local government in addition to the Federal government. We also present data on the purchases and net income of the Federal government alone because Federal budget deficits and surpluses are often the focus of public attention. In addition, as shown in Fig. 5.9, much of the movement in purchases and net income of the combined Federal, state, and local government reflects movement in the corresponding components of the Federal budget.

The excess of government purchases over net income is the government budget deficit, shown in beige.[13] Negative values of the current account balance indicate a current account deficit, also shown in beige. Large deficits—both government and current account—occurred during the 1980s and much of the 1990s.

[13]Government purchases are current expenditures minus transfer payments and interest. Thus government investment is not included in government purchases. The budget deficit is the current deficit; see Chapter 15 for a further discussion of this concept.

(continued)

FIGURE 5.9

The government budget deficit and the current account in the United States, 1960–2021

Shown are government purchases, net government income (taxes less transfers and interest), and the current account balance for the United States for 1960–2021. All data series are measured as a percentage of GDP. The government deficit (beige) is the excess of government purchases over net government income. The simultaneous appearance of the government budget deficit and the current account deficit in the 1980s and early 1990s is the twin-deficits phenomenon.

Sources: Total government and Federal government receipts, current expenditures, interest, and transfers: BEA website, *www.bea.gov*, NIPA Tables 3.1 and 3.2. GDP: BEA website, NIPA Table 1.1.5. Current account balance: BEA website, International transactions accounts Table 1.1.

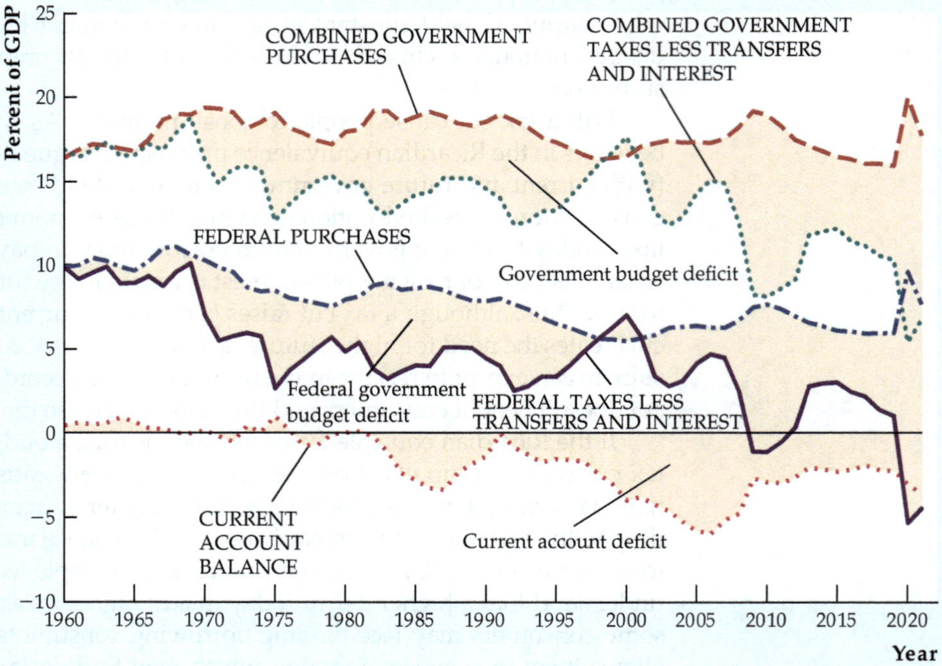

The apparently close relationship between the U.S. government budget deficit and the current account deficit in the 1980s and the first half of the 1990s is consistent with the twin-deficits idea that budget deficits cause current account deficits. Because the rise in budget deficits primarily reflected tax cuts (or increases in transfers and interest payments, which reduced net government income) rather than increased government purchases, this behavior of the two deficits also seems to contradict the Ricardian equivalence proposition, which says that tax cuts should have no effect on saving or the current account.

Even though the U.S. experience during the 1980s and first half of the 1990s seems to confirm the link between government budget and the current account, evidence from other episodes is less supportive of the twin-deficits idea. For example, the United States simultaneously ran large government budget deficits and large current account surpluses in the periods around World War I and II (compare Figs. 1.5 and 1.6). In the late 1990s, the Federal government budget and the combined government budget were both in surplus, yet the U.S. current account balance remained deeply in deficit because private saving fell and investment rose as a share of GDP at the same time. And from 2008 to 2011, the government budget deficit grew substantially as the government increased spending to stimulate the economy, but the current account deficit fell considerably as consumers cut back on their purchases of imported goods and services.

The evidence from other countries on the relationship between government budget and current account deficits is also mixed. The International Monetary Fund (IMF) conducted a systematic analysis of the twin deficits in a group of 17 countries over the period 1978–2009.[14] Almost two-thirds of the 291 changes in fiscal policy in this sample of countries were reductions in the government budget

[14]International Monetary Fund, *World Economic Outlook: Slowing Growth, Rising Risks*, Chapter 4: Separated at Birth? The Twin Budget and Trade Balances, September 2011, pp. 135–160.

deficit. The IMF found that a change in fiscal policy that reduces the government budget deficit by 1% of GDP typically reduces the current account deficit by a little more than 0.5% of GDP. Nevertheless, a good deal of disagreement persists among economists about the relationship between government budget deficits and current account deficits.[15] We can say for sure (because it is implied by the uses-of-saving identity, Eq. [2.11]) that if an increase in the government budget deficit is not offset by an equal increase in private saving, the result must be a decline in domestic investment, a rise in the current account deficit, or both.

[15]For a review of research on twin deficits, see Michele Cavallo, "Understanding the Twin Deficits: New Approaches, New Results," Federal Reserve Bank of San Francisco, *Economic Letter*, No. 2005–16, July 22, 2005.

CHAPTER SUMMARY

1. The balance of payments accounts consist of the current account and the financial account. The current account records trade in currently produced goods and services, income from abroad, and transfers between countries. The financial account records trade in existing assets, both real and financial.

2. The current account balance, *CA*, equals the sum of net exports of goods and services, net income from abroad, and net unilateral transfers. Ignoring net income from abroad and net unilateral transfers, the current account balance is the same as net exports, *NX*. The financial account balance, *FA*, is the value of assets sold to foreigners (financial inflows) minus the value of assets purchased from foreigners (financial outflows) plus net unilateral transfers of assets.

3. In each period, except for measurement errors, the current account balance, *CA*, and the financial account balance, *FA*, must sum to zero. The reason is that any international transaction amounts to a swap of goods, services, or assets between countries; the two sides of the swap always have offsetting effects on the sum of the current account and financial account balances.

4. In an open economy, goods market equilibrium requires that the desired amount of national saving equal the desired amount of domestic investment plus the amount the country lends abroad. Equivalently, net exports must equal the country's output (gross domestic product) less desired total spending by domestic residents (absorption).

5. A small open economy faces a fixed real interest rate in the international capital market. In goods market equilibrium in a small open economy, national saving and investment equal their desired levels at the prevailing world real interest rate; foreign lending, net exports, and the current account balance all equal the excess of national saving over investment. Any factor that increases desired national saving or reduces desired investment at the world real interest rate will increase the small open economy's foreign lending (equivalently, its current account balance).

6. The levels of saving and investment of a large open economy affect the world real interest rate. In a model of two large open economies, the equilibrium real interest rate in the international capital market is the rate at which desired international lending by one country equals desired international borrowing by the other country. Equivalently, it is the rate at which the lending country's current account surplus equals the borrowing country's current account deficit. Any factor that increases desired national saving or reduces desired investment at the initial interest rate for either large country will increase the supply of international loans relative to the demand and cause the world real interest rate to fall.

7. According to the twin-deficits hypothesis, the large U.S. government budget deficits of the 1980s and the first half of the 1990s helped cause the sharply increased U.S. current account deficits of that period. Whether budget deficits cause current account deficits is the subject of disagreement. In theory, and if we assume no change in the tax treatment of investment, an increase in the government budget deficit will raise the current account deficit only if it reduces national saving. Economists generally agree that an increase in the budget deficit caused by a temporary increase in government purchases will reduce national saving, but whether an increase in the budget deficit caused by a tax cut reduces national saving remains controversial.

▶ KEY DIAGRAM 4

National saving and investment in a small open economy

This open-economy version of the saving–investment diagram shows the determination of national saving, investment, and the current account balance in a small open economy that takes the world real interest rate as given.

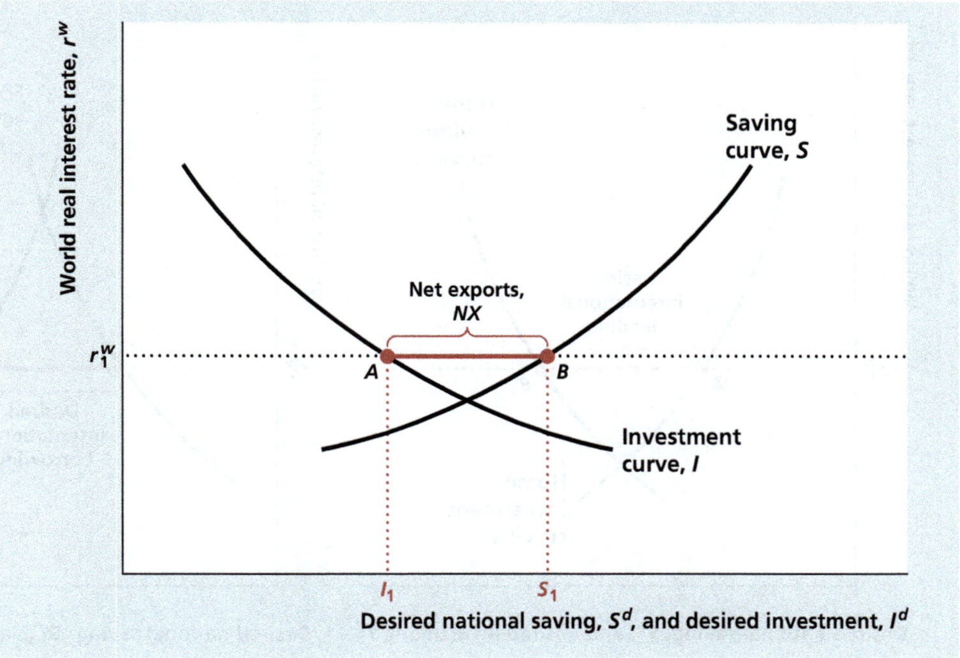

Diagram Elements

- The world real interest rate is measured on the vertical axis, and the small open economy's desired national saving, S^d, and desired investment, I^d, are measured on the horizontal axis.
- The world real interest rate, r^w, is fixed, as indicated by the horizontal line.
- The saving curve, S, and the investment curve, I, are the same as in the closed-economy saving–investment diagram, Key Diagram 3.

Analysis

- Goods market equilibrium in a small open economy requires that desired national saving equal desired investment plus net exports (Eq. 5.4). In the diagram when the world real interest rate is r_1^w, desired national saving is S_1 and desired investment is I_1. The country's net exports, NX, and current account balance, CA, or $S_1 - I_1$, is distance AB. Equivalently, distance AB, the excess of desired national saving over desired investment, is the amount that the small open economy is lending abroad, or its financial account deficit, $-FA$.

Factors That Shift the Curves

- Anything that increases desired national saving in the small open economy, for a fixed value of the world real interest rate, shifts the saving curve to the right. Factors that shift the saving curve to the right (see Summary table 5 in Chapter 4) include

  an increase in current output, Y,
  a decrease in expected future output,
  a decrease in wealth,

  a decrease in current government purchases, G, and (if Ricardian equivalence doesn't hold and taxes affect saving) an increase in current taxes, T.
- Anything that increases desired investment at the prevailing real interest rate shifts the investment curve to the right. Factors that shift the investment curve to the right (see Summary table 6) include an increase in the expected future marginal product of capital, MPK^f, and a decrease in the effective tax rate on capital.
- An increase in desired national saving shifts the saving curve to the right and raises net exports and the current account balance, CA. Equivalently, an increase in desired national saving raises the country's net foreign lending, which equals its financial account deficit, $-FA$. Similarly, an increase in desired investment shifts the investment curve to the right and lowers net exports, the current account balance, net foreign lending, and the financial account deficit.
- An increase in the world real interest rate, r^w, raises the horizontal line in the diagram. Because an increase in the world real interest rate increases national saving and reduces investment, it raises net foreign lending, net exports, the current account surplus, and the financial account deficit.

KEY DIAGRAM 5

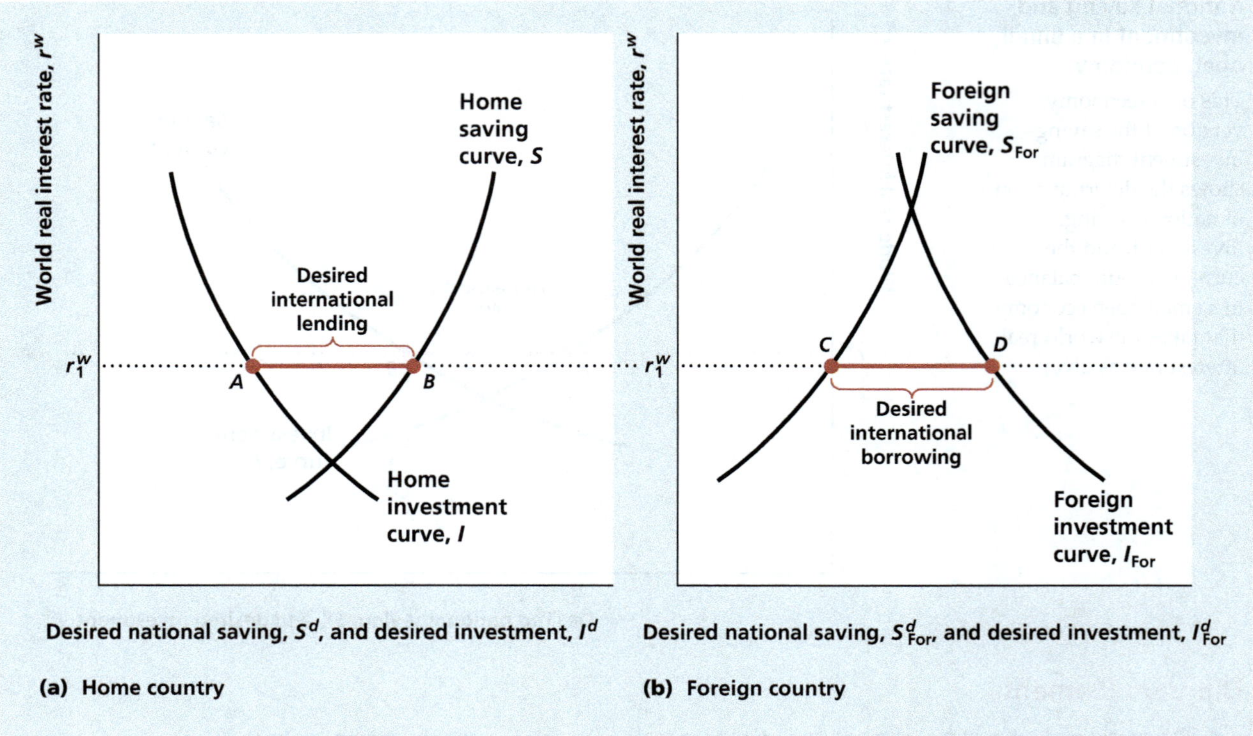

National saving and investment in large open economies

This diagram shows the determination of national saving, investment, and the current account balance in large open economies—that is, economies large enough to affect the world real interest rate.

Diagram Elements

- The figure consists of two saving–investment diagrams, one for the home country and one for the foreign country (representing the rest of the world).
- The world real interest rate, r^w, measured on the vertical axis, is the real interest rate faced by both countries in the international capital market.
- The saving and investment curves in the home country (S and I) and in the foreign country (S_{For} and I_{For}) are the same as the saving and investment curves presented before (Key Diagram 3 and Key Diagram 4).

Analysis

- This case differs from the case of the small open economy (Key Diagram 4) in that the world real interest rate, r^w, is determined within the model, not given.
- Goods market equilibrium for large open economies requires that the desired international lending of one country equal the desired international borrowing of the other. Equivalently, because a country's international lending equals its current account balance, goods market equilibrium requires that one country's current account surplus equal the other country's current account deficit.
- The world real interest rate adjusts to achieve goods market equilibrium. In the diagram r_1^w is the equilibrium world real interest rate, because at that interest rate the home country's desired international lending (its desired national saving less desired investment, or distance AB) equals the foreign country's desired international borrowing (its desired investment less desired national saving, or distance CD).

Factors That Shift the Curves

- The saving and investment curves in the two countries are shifted by the same factors as in Key Diagram 3 in Chapter 4 and Key Diagram 4.
- The world real interest rate changes when desired national saving or desired investment changes in either

country. Any change that increases desired international lending relative to desired international borrowing at the initial world real interest rate will cause the world real interest rate to fall to restore equilibrium in the international capital market. Changes that increase desired international lending relative to desired international borrowing include an increase in desired national saving or a decrease in desired investment in either country. Similarly, a decrease in desired national saving or an increase in desired investment in either country reduces desired international lending relative to desired international borrowing and raises the world real interest rate.

KEY TERMS

absorption, p. 216
balance of payments, p. 210
balance of payments accounts, p. 206
current account, p. 206
current account balance, p. 209
financial account, p. 209
financial account balance, p. 209
financial inflow, p. 209
financial outflow, p. 209
foreign direct investment, p. 213
large open economy, p. 221
official reserve assets, p. 210
small open economy, p. 217
statistical discrepancy, p. 212
unilateral transfers, p. 209
world real interest rate, p. 217

KEY EQUATIONS

$$CA + FA = 0 \tag{5.1}$$

Except for problems of measurement, the current account balance, CA, and the financial account balance, FA, always sum to zero. The reason is that every international transaction involves a swap of goods, services, or assets; the two sides of the swap always have offsetting effects on $CA + FA$.

$$S^d = I^d + NX \tag{5.4}$$

The goods market equilibrium condition in an open economy is that desired national saving, S^d, must equal desired investment, I^d, plus the amount lent abroad. The amount lent abroad equals the current account balance, which (if we assume that net factor payments and unilateral transfers are zero) also equals net exports, NX.

$$NX = Y - (C^d + I^d + G) \tag{5.6}$$

An alternative way of writing the goods market equilibrium condition, this equation states that net exports must equal the country's output, Y, less its desired absorption, $C^d + I^d + G$.

REVIEW QUESTIONS

1. List the categories of transactions that appear in a country's current account. What is the current account balance? What is the relationship between the current account balance and net exports?
2. What is the key difference that determines whether an international transaction appears in the current account or the financial account?
3. A U.S. publisher sells $200 worth of books to a resident of Brazil. By itself, this item increases the U.S. current account balance. Describe some offsetting transactions that could ensure that the U.S. current account and financial account balances would continue to sum to zero.
4. How do a country's current account and financial account balances affect its net foreign assets? If country A has greater net foreign assets per citizen than does country B, is country A necessarily better off than country B?
5. Explain why, in a small open economy, (a) national saving does not have to equal investment, and (b) output does not have to equal absorption.
6. Generally, what types of changes in desired saving and desired investment lead to large current account deficits in a small open economy? What factors lead to these changes in desired saving and desired investment?
7. In a world with two large open economies, what determines the world real interest rate? What relationship between the current accounts of the two countries is satisfied when the world real interest rate is at its equilibrium value?
8. How does an increase in desired national saving in a large open economy affect the world real interest rate? How does an increase in desired investment affect it? Why do changes in desired saving or investment in large open economies affect the world real

interest rate but changes in desired saving or investment in small open economies do not?

9. Under what circumstances will an increase in the government budget deficit affect the current account balance in a small open economy? In the cases in which the current account balance changes, by how much does it change? What is the connection between the government budget deficit and the current account balance?

10. In what periods has the United States had twin deficits? In what periods did the deficits move in opposite directions?

NUMERICAL PROBLEMS

1. Here are some balance of payments data:

   Exports of goods, 100

   Imports of goods, 125

   Exports of services, 90

   Imports of services, 80

   Income receipts from abroad, 110

   Income payments to foreigners, 150

   Increase in home country's ownership of assets abroad, 160

   Increase in foreign ownership of assets in home country, 200

   Increase in home reserve assets, 30

   Increase in foreign reserve assets, 35

   Assuming that unilateral transfers equal zero, find net exports, the current account balance, the financial account balance, the balance of payments, and the statistical discrepancy. (*Note:* The increase in home reserve assets of 30 is included in the increase in the home country's ownership of assets abroad of 160, and the increase in foreign reserve assets of 35 is included in the increase in foreign ownership of assets in the home country of 200.)

2. In a small open economy, output (gross domestic product) is $25 billion, government purchases are $6 billion, and net factor payments from abroad are zero. Desired consumption and desired investment are related to the world real interest rate in the following manner:

World Real Interest Rate	Desired Consumption	Desired Investment
5%	$12 billion	$3 billion
4%	$13 billion	$4 billion
3%	$14 billion	$5 billion
2%	$15 billion	$6 billion

   For each value of the world real interest rate, find national saving, foreign lending, and absorption. Calculate net exports as the difference between output and absorption. What is the relationship between net exports and foreign lending?

3. In a small open economy,

$$\text{desired national saving, } S^d = \$10 \text{ billion} + (\$100 \text{ billion})r^w;$$

$$\text{desired investment, } I^d = \$15 \text{ billion} - (\$100 \text{ billion})r^w;$$

$$\text{output, } Y = \$50 \text{ billion};$$

$$\text{government purchases, } G = \$10 \text{ billion};$$

$$\text{world real interest rate, } r^w = 0.03.$$

   a. Find the economy's national saving, investment, current account surplus, net exports, desired consumption, and absorption.

   b. Owing to a technological innovation that increases future productivity, the country's desired investment rises by $2 billion at each level of the world real interest rate. Repeat Part (a) with this new information.

4. Consider two large open economies, the home economy and the foreign economy. In the home country the following relationships hold:

$$\text{desired consumption, } C^d = 320 + 0.4(Y - T) - 200r^w;$$

$$\text{desired investment, } I^d = 150 - 200r^w;$$

$$\text{output, } Y = 1000;$$

$$\text{taxes, } T = 200;$$

$$\text{government purchases, } G = 275.$$

   In the foreign country the following relationships hold:

$$\text{desired consumption, } C^d_{For} = 480 + 0.4(Y_{For} - T_{For}) - 300r^w;$$

$$\text{desired investment, } I^d_{For} = 225 - 300r^w;$$

$$\text{output, } Y_{For} = 1500;$$

$$\text{taxes, } T_{For} = 300;$$

$$\text{government purchases, } G_{For} = 300.$$

   a. What is the equilibrium interest rate in the international capital market? What are the equilibrium values of consumption, national saving, investment, and the current account balance in each country?

b. Suppose that in the home country government purchases increase by 50 to 325. Taxes also increase by 50 to keep the deficit from increasing. What is the new equilibrium interest rate in the international capital market? What are the new equilibrium values of consumption, national saving, investment, and the current account balance in each country?

5. Consider a world with only two countries, which are designated the home country (H) and the foreign country (F). Output equals its full-employment level in each country. You are given the following information about each country:

Home Country

Consumption: $C_H = 100 + 0.5Y_H - 500r^w$

Investment: $I_H = 300 - 500r^w$

Government Purchases: $G_H = 155$

Full-employment Output: $\bar{Y}_H = 1000$

Foreign Country

Consumption: $C_F = 225 + 0.7Y_F - 600r^w$

Investment: $I_F = 250 - 200r^w$

Government Purchases: $G_F = 190$

Full-employment Output: $\bar{Y}_F = 1200$

a. Write national saving in the home country and in the foreign country as functions of the world real interest rate r^w.

b. What is the equilibrium value of the world real interest rate?

c. What are the equilibrium values of consumption, national saving, investment, the current account balance, and absorption in each country?

6. A small island nation is endowed with indestructible coconut trees. These trees live forever and no new trees can be planted. Every year $1 million worth of coconuts fall off the trees and can be eaten locally or exported to other countries. In past years the island nation ran current account surpluses and financial account deficits, acquiring foreign bonds. It now owns $500,000 of foreign bonds. The interest rate on these bonds is 5% per year. The residents of the island nation consume $1,025,000 per year. What are the values of investment, national saving, the current account balance, the financial account balance, net exports, GDP, and GNP in this country?

ANALYTICAL PROBLEMS

1. Explain how each of the following transactions would enter the U.S. balance of payments accounts. Discuss only the transactions described. Do not be concerned with possible offsetting transactions.

a. The U.S. government sells F–16 fighter planes to a foreign government.

b. A London bank sells yen to and buys dollars from a Swiss bank.

c. The Federal Reserve sells yen to and buys dollars from a Swiss bank.

d. A New York bank receives the interest on its loans to Brazil.

e. A U.S. collector buys some ancient artifacts from a collection in Egypt.

f. A U.S. oil company buys insurance from a Canadian insurance company to insure its oil rigs in the Gulf of Mexico.

g. A U.S. company borrows from a British bank.

2. For each transaction described in Analytical Problem 1 that by itself changes the sum of the U.S. current account balance, *CA*, and the U.S. financial account balance, *FA*, give an example of an offsetting transaction that would leave $CA + FA$ unchanged.

3. A large country imposes capital controls that prohibit foreign borrowing and lending by domestic residents. Analyze the effects on the country's current account balance, national saving, and investment, and on domestic and world real interest rates. Assume that, before the capital controls were imposed, the large country was running a financial account surplus.

4. The text showed, for a small open economy, that an increase in the government budget deficit raises the current account deficit only if it affects desired national saving in the home country. Show that this result is also true for a large open economy. Then assume that an increase in the government budget deficit does affect desired national saving in the home country. What effects will the increased budget deficit have on the foreign country's current account, investment in both countries, and the world real interest rate?

5. How would each of the following affect national saving, investment, the current account balance, and the real interest rate in a large open economy?

a. An increase in the domestic willingness to save (which raises desired national saving at any given real interest rate).

b. An increase in the willingness of foreigners to save.

c. A temporary increase in foreign government purchases.

d. An increase in foreign taxes (consider both the case in which Ricardian equivalence holds and the case in which it doesn't hold).

6. Analyze the effects on a large open economy of a temporary adverse supply shock that hits only the foreign economy. Discuss the impact on the home country's national saving, investment, and current account balance—and on the world real interest rate. How does your answer differ if the adverse supply shock is worldwide?

7. The chief economic advisor of a small open economy made the following announcement: "We have good news and bad news: The good news is that we have just had a temporary beneficial productivity shock that will increase output; the bad news is that the increase in output and income will lead domestic consumers to buy more imported goods, and our current account balance will fall." Analyze this statement, taking as given that a beneficial productivity shock has indeed occurred.

8. The world is made up of only two large countries: Eastland and Westland. Westland is running a large current account deficit and often appeals to Eastland for help in reducing this current account deficit. Currently, the government of Eastland purchases $10 billion of goods and services, and all of these goods and services are produced in Eastland. The finance minister of Eastland proposes that the government purchase half of its goods from Westland. Specifically, the government of Eastland will continue to purchase $10 billion of goods, but $5 billion will be from Eastland and $5 billion will be from Westland. The finance minister gives the following rationale: "Both countries produce identical goods so it does not really matter to us which country produced the goods we purchase. Moreover, this change in purchasing policy will help reduce Westland's large current account deficit." What are the effects of this change in purchasing policy on the current account balance in each country and on the world real interest rate? (*Hint:* What happens to net exports by the private sector in each country after the government of Eastland changes its purchasing policy?)

WORKING WITH MACROECONOMIC DATA

For data to use in these exercises, go to the Federal Reserve Bank of St. Louis FRED database at fred.stlouisfed.org.

1. A popular measure of a country's "openness" to international trade is an index computed as the sum of the country's exports and imports divided by its GDP. Calculate and graph the openness index for the United States using quarterly data since 1947. What has been the postwar trend? Can you think of any factors that might help explain this trend? (*Hint:* Be careful with the data, as some databases record imports with a negative sign and then add them to exports to get net exports. If that is the case with your data, take the absolute value of imports before adding it to exports, because we are interested in the total volume of trade, not the balance of trade.) What usually happens to the openness index in recessions?

2. Using quarterly data since 1960, graph output and absorption (both in real terms) in the same figure. In another figure, graph real investment, national saving, and the current account balance for the same period. (Use real GNP, which includes net factor payments, as the measure of output and/or income.) What is the relationship between the two figures?

3. Using quarterly data since 1960, graph the following four series, expressing each as a percent of GDP: exports of goods (sometimes called merchandise), exports of services, imports of goods (sometimes called merchandise), and imports of services. What trends do you notice in U.S. exports and imports of goods and services? How has the interdependence of the U.S. economy with the rest of the world's economies changed over time? (*Note:* When computing the percentage of GDP, you should note that quarterly data on exports and imports often are not expressed at annual rates, but the data on GDP are expressed at annual rates; if this is the case with your data, multiply your data on imports and exports by 4 to get the appropriate ratio relative to GDP.)

4. In FRED, find and plot data on the ratio of outstanding total international debt to GDP for (a) the Euro area, (b) the United States, and (c) Japan. These amounts represent the international indebtedness of each region to the rest of the world. Which region has the highest international debt relative to GDP? Which region has the lowest international debt relative to GDP? Describe how all three ratios have changed over the past five years.

6

Long-Run Economic Growth

Learning Objectives

6.1 Discuss the sources of economic growth and the fundamentals of growth accounting.

6.2 Explain the factors affecting long-run living standards in the Solow model.

6.3 Summarize endogenous growth theory.

6.4 Discuss government policies for raising long-run living standards.

A nation's ability to provide improving standards of living for its people depends crucially on its long-run rate of economic growth. Over a long period of time, even an apparently small difference in the rate of economic growth can translate into a large difference in the income of the average person.[1]

Compare, for example, the historical experiences of the United Kingdom and Japan. In 1870, real GDP per person was almost four times as large in the United Kingdom as in Japan, as the data on national growth performances in Table 6.1 show. The UK economy did not stand still after 1870. Over the next 148 years, UK real GDP per person grew by 1.3% per year so that by 2018 the real income of the average Briton was more than six times as great as it had been in 1870. However, during the same period, Japanese real GDP per person grew at a rate of 2.2% per year, reaching a level in 2018 that was more than 20 times as large as it had been in 1870.

The Japanese growth rate of 2.2% per year may not seem dramatically greater than the UK growth rate of 1.3% per year. Yet by 1980, Japan, which had been far poorer than the United Kingdom a century earlier, had surpassed the United Kingdom in per capita GDP, and the gap between the two countries continued to grow until 1992, when the Japan's per capita GDP exceeded that in the United Kingdom by more than 20%. However, sluggish growth in Japan in the 1990s allowed the United Kingdom to retake the lead by 2002, and they have had similar per capita GDP levels since then. We can draw other, similar comparisons from Table 6.1; compare, for example, the long-term growth performance of the United Kingdom against that of Canada or Sweden. Note, however, that even those countries that grew relatively slowly have dramatically increased their output per person during the past 148 years.

Although the comparisons highlighted by Table 6.1 span a long period of time, a change in the rate of economic growth can have important effects over even a decade or two. For example, since about 1973 the United States and other industrialized countries have experienced a sustained slowdown in their rates of growth. Between 1947 and 1973, total (not per capita) real GDP in the United States grew by 4.0% per year, but between 1973 and 2021 U.S. real GDP grew by only 2.6% per year. To appreciate the significance of this slowdown,

[1]The income of the average person is a common measure of the standard of living but it ignores any inequality in the standard of living among people in a given country. The Application "Trends in Income Distribution in South Africa," describes the measurement and behavior of income inequality in South Africa.

TABLE 6.1

Economic Growth in Eight Major Countries, 1870–2018

	Levels of real GDP per capita				
Country	**1870**	**1913**	**1950**	**2018**	**Annual growth rate 1870–2018**
Australia	5217	8220	11,815	49,831	1.5
Canada	2702	7088	11,622	44,869	1.9
France	2990	5555	8266	38,516	1.7
Germany	2931	5815	6186	46,178	1.9
Japan	1580	2431	3062	38,674	2.2
Sweden	2144	4581	10,742	45,542	2.1
United Kingdom	5829	8212	11,061	38,058	1.3
United States	4803	10,108	15,240	55,335	1.7

Note: Figures are in U.S. dollars at 2011 prices, adjusted for differences in the purchasing power of the various national currencies.

Source: Data from the Maddison-Project, *www.ggdc.net/maddison/maddison-project/home.htm*, 2020 version.

imagine that the 1947–1973 growth trend had continued—that is, suppose that real GDP in the United States had continued to grow at 4.0% per year instead of at the 2.6% per year rate actually achieved. Then in 2021 U.S. real GDP would have been more than 92% higher than its actual value—a bonus of about $18 trillion, or almost $64,000 per person (in 2021 dollars).

No one understands completely why economies grow, and no one has a magic formula for inducing rapid growth. Indeed, if such a formula existed, there would be no poor nations. Nevertheless, economists have gained useful insights about the growth process. In this chapter we identify the forces that determine the growth rate of an economy over long periods of time and examine various policies that governments may use to try to influence the rate of growth. Once again, saving and investment decisions play a central role in the analysis. Along with changes in productivity, the rates at which a nation saves and invests—and thus the rate at which it accumulates capital goods—are important factors in determining the standard of living that the nation's people can attain.

6.1 The Sources of Economic Growth

Discuss the sources of economic growth and the fundamentals of growth accounting.

An economy's output of goods and services depends on the quantities of available inputs, such as capital and labor, and on the productivity of those inputs. The relationship between output and inputs is described by the production function, introduced in Chapter 3:

$$Y = AF(K,N). \tag{6.1}$$

Equation (6.1) relates total output, Y, to the economy's use of capital, K, and labor, N, and to productivity, A.

If inputs and productivity are constant, the production function states that output also will be constant—there will be no economic growth. For the quantity of output to grow, either the quantity of inputs must grow or productivity must improve, or both. The relationship between the rate of output growth and the rates of input growth and productivity growth is

$$\frac{\Delta Y}{Y} = \frac{\Delta A}{A} + a_K\frac{\Delta K}{K} + a_N\frac{\Delta N}{N}, \quad \textbf{(6.2)}$$

where

$$\frac{\Delta Y}{Y} = \text{rate of output growth;}$$
$$\frac{\Delta A}{A} = \text{rate of productivity growth;}$$
$$\frac{\Delta K}{K} = \text{rate of capital growth;}$$
$$\frac{\Delta N}{N} = \text{rate of labor growth;}$$
$$a_K = \text{elasticity of output with respect to capital;}$$
$$a_N = \text{elasticity of output with respect to labor.}$$

In Eq. (6.2) the elasticity of output with respect to capital, a_K, is the percentage increase in output resulting from a 1% increase in the capital stock, and the elasticity of output with respect to labor, a_N, is the percentage increase in output resulting from a 1% increase in the amount of labor used. The elasticities a_K and a_N both are numbers between 0 and 1 that must be estimated from historical data.[2]

Equation (6.2), called the **growth accounting equation**, is the production function (Eq. 6.1) written in growth rate form. Some examples will be helpful for understanding the growth accounting equation.

Suppose a new invention allows firms to produce 10% more output for the same amount of capital and labor. In terms of the production function, Eq. (6.1), for constant capital and labor inputs, a 10% increase in productivity, A, raises output, Y, by 10%. Similarly, from the growth accounting equation, Eq. (6.2), if productivity growth, $\Delta A/A$, equals 10% and capital and labor growth are zero, output growth, $\Delta Y/Y$, will be 10%. Thus the production function and the growth accounting equation give the same result, as they should.

Now suppose that firms' investments cause the economy's capital stock to rise by 10% ($\Delta K/K = 10\%$) while labor input and productivity remain unchanged. What will happen to output? The production function shows that, if the capital stock grows, output will increase. However, because of the diminishing marginal productivity of capital (see Chapter 3), the extra capital will be less productive than that used previously, so the increase in output will be less than 10%. Diminishing marginal productivity of capital is the reason that the growth rate of capital, $\Delta K/K$, is multiplied by a factor less than 1 in the growth accounting equation. For the United States this factor, a_K, the elasticity of output with respect to capital, is about 0.3. Thus the growth accounting equation, Eq. (6.2), indicates that a 10% increase in the capital stock, with labor and productivity held constant, will increase U.S. output by about 3%, or $0.3 \times 10\%$.

[2]Elasticities and growth rate formulas such as Eq. (6.2) are discussed further in Appendix A, Sections A.3 and A.7.

Similarly, the elasticity of output with respect to labor, a_N, is about 0.7 in the United States. Thus, according to Eq. (6.2), a 10% increase in the amount of labor used ($\Delta N/N = 10\%$), with no change in capital or productivity, will raise U.S. output by about 7%, or $0.7 \times 10\%$.[3]

Growth Accounting

According to Eq. (6.2), output growth, $\Delta Y/Y$, can be broken into three parts:

1. that resulting from productivity growth, $\Delta A/A$,
2. that resulting from increased capital inputs, $a_K \Delta K/K$, and
3. that resulting from increased labor inputs, $a_N \Delta N/N$.

Growth accounting measures empirically the relative importance of these three sources of output growth. A typical growth accounting analysis involves the following four steps (see Table 6.2 for a summary and numerical example):

- *Step 1.* Obtain measures of the growth rates of output, $\Delta Y/Y$, capital, $\Delta K/K$, and labor, $\Delta N/N$, for the economy over any period of time. In the calculation of growth rates for capital and labor, more sophisticated analyses make adjustments for changing quality as well as quantity of inputs. For example, to obtain a quality-adjusted measure of N, an hour of work by a skilled worker is counted as more labor than an hour of work by an unskilled worker. Similarly, to obtain a quality-adjusted measure of K, a machine that can turn fifty bolts per minute is treated as being more capital than a machine that can turn only thirty bolts per minute.
- *Step 2.* Estimate values for the elasticities a_K and a_N from historical data. Keep in mind the estimates for the United States of 0.3 for a_K and 0.7 for a_N.
- *Step 3.* Calculate the contribution of capital to economic growth as $a_K \Delta K/K$ and the contribution of labor to economic growth as $a_N \Delta N/N$.
- *Step 4.* The part of economic growth assignable to neither capital growth nor labor growth is attributed to improvements in total factor productivity, A. The rate of productivity change, $\Delta A/A$, is calculated from the formula

$$\frac{\Delta A}{A} = \frac{\Delta Y}{Y} - a_K \frac{\Delta K}{K} - a_N \frac{\Delta N}{N},$$

which is the growth accounting equation, Eq. (6.2), rewritten with $\Delta A/A$ on the left side. Thus the growth accounting technique treats productivity change as a residual—that is, the portion of growth not otherwise explained.[4]

[3]In Chapter 3 we examined the production function for the U.S. economy, $Y = AK^{0.3}N^{0.7}$. In that production function, called a Cobb-Douglas production function, the exponent on the capital stock, K, 0.3, equals the elasticity of output with respect to capital, and the exponent on the quantity of labor input, N, 0.7, equals the elasticity of output with respect to labor. See Appendix A, Section A.6.

[4]The growth accounting method for calculating productivity growth is similar to the method we used to find productivity growth in Section 3.1, where we also determined productivity growth as the part of output growth not explained by increases in capital and labor. The differences are that growth accounting uses the growth accounting equation, which is the production function in growth rate form, instead of using the production function directly, as we did in Chapter 3; and growth accounting analyses usually adjust measures of capital and labor for changes in quality, which we did not do in Chapter 3.

TABLE 6.2

The Steps of Growth Accounting: A Numerical Example

Step 1. Obtain measures of output growth, capital growth, and labor growth over the period to be studied.

Example:

$$\text{output growth} = \frac{\Delta Y}{Y} = 40\%;$$

$$\text{capital growth} = \frac{\Delta K}{K} = 20\%;$$

$$\text{labor growth} = \frac{\Delta N}{N} = 30\%.$$

Step 2. Using historical data, obtain estimates of the elasticities of output with respect to capital and labor, a_K and a_N.

Example:

$$a_K = 0.3 \quad \text{and} \quad a_N = 0.7.$$

Step 3. Find the contributions to growth of capital and labor.

Example:

$$\text{contribution to output growth of growth in capital} = a_K \frac{\Delta K}{K} = 0.3 \times 20\% = 6\%;$$

$$\text{contribution to output growth of growth in labor} = a_N \frac{\Delta N}{N} = 0.7 \times 30\% = 21\%.$$

Step 4. Find productivity growth as the residual (the part of output growth not explained by capital or labor).

Example:

$$\text{productivity growth} = \frac{\Delta A}{A} = \frac{\Delta Y}{Y} - a_K \frac{\Delta K}{K} - a_N \frac{\Delta N}{N}$$

$$= 40\% - 6\% - 21\% = 13\%.$$

Growth Accounting and Productivity Trends. What does growth accounting say about the sources of U.S. economic growth? Among the best-known research using the growth accounting framework was done at the Brookings Institution by Edward Denison. Table 6.3 summarizes Denison's findings for the period 1929–1982 and provides more recent data from the Bureau of Labor Statistics covering the period 1982–2020.

The last entry in column (4) shows that, over the 1929–1982 period, output grew at an average rate of 2.92% per year. According to Denison's measurements (column 4), the growth of labor accounted for output growth of 1.34% per year. The growth of labor in turn resulted primarily from an increase in population, an increase in the percentage of the population in the labor force, and higher educational levels, which raised workers' skills. (Offsetting these trends to a degree was a decline in the number of hours worked per person.) According to Denison, the growth of the capital stock accounted for output growth of 0.56% per year. So, taken together, labor and capital growth contributed 1.90% to the annual growth rate of output.

The difference between total growth (2.92%) and the amount of growth attributed to capital and labor growth (1.90%) is 1.02%. By the growth accounting method, this remaining 1.02% per year of growth is attributed to increases in productivity. Thus, according to Denison, increased quantities of factors of production

TABLE 6.3

Sources of Economic Growth in the United States (Percent per Year)

	(1) 1929–1948	(2) 1948–1973	(3) 1973–1982	(4) 1929–1982	(5) 1982–2020
Source of Growth					
Labor growth	1.42	1.40	1.13	1.34	0.94
Capital growth	0.11	0.77	0.69	0.56	1.23
Total input growth	1.53	2.17	1.82	1.90	2.18
Productivity growth	1.01	1.53	−0.27	1.02	0.85
Total output growth	**2.54**	**3.70**	**1.55**	**2.92**	**3.02**

Sources: Columns (1)–(4) from Edward F. Denison, *Trends in American Economic Growth, 1929–1982*, Washington, DC: The Brookings Institution, 1985, Table 8.1, p. 111. Column (5) from Bureau of Labor Statistics website, Total Factor Productivity Trends, available at *www.bls.gov/productivity/tables/total-factor-productivity-major-sectors-historical.xlsx*.

and improvements in the effectiveness with which those factors were used both played an important role in U.S. growth after 1929.

Data for three shorter periods are given in columns (1)–(3) of Table 6.3. This breakdown highlights a striking conclusion: Productivity growth during 1973–1982 was negative (fourth entry in column 3). In other words, Denison estimated that any combination of capital and labor would have produced less output in 1982 than it could have in 1973! (See the Application "Waves of Productivity Growth over Time," for various hypotheses to explain this drop in productivity.) Comparing columns (2) and (3) reveals that the decline in U.S. productivity growth between the 1948–1973 and 1973–1982 periods of 1.80 percentage points (1.53 minus –0.27) accounts for the bulk of the overall slowdown in output growth between those periods of 2.15 percentage points (3.70 minus 1.55).

The slowdown in productivity growth after 1973 reported by Denison was confirmed by other studies, both for the United States and for other industrialized countries. This slowdown generated widespread concern, because a sustained reduction in the rate of productivity growth would have an adverse effect on future real wages and living standards. In addition, to the extent that future Social Security benefits will be paid by taxing the wage income of future workers, a long-term productivity slowdown would threaten the future of the Social Security system. But will the productivity slowdown continue? To shed light on this question, the final column of Table 6.3 extends Denison's calculations by adding 38 years of more recent data. During the period 1982–2020, productivity grew at an average annual rate of 0.85%. Although the return to a positive rate of productivity growth was a welcome development, the 0.85% growth rate was less than two-thirds of the productivity growth rate seen during the 25-year period preceding the 1973 slowdown. But beginning in the second half of the 1990s, productivity growth increased. From 1995 to 2007 (before the financial crisis), it averaged 1.33% per year, which is only 0.20 percentage points lower than it was from 1948 to 1973. For more details, see the Application "The Rebound in U.S. Productivity Growth."

Although advances in information technology continue, gains in total factor productivity since 2007 have been meager (only 0.27% per year from 2007 to 2020, according to the Bureau of Labor Statistics (BLS), as compared to 1.33% per year from 1995 through 2007). What's going on? It's too soon to know for sure, but it may be that the financial crisis from 2008 to 2009 and the pandemic recession in 2020 hampered productivity growth. For example, with credit tight in the years after the crisis, firms were less inclined to invest in research and development or to upgrade their plant and equipment. There were also many fewer new firms starting up, which impeded the introduction of new products and production techniques. Moreover, high rates of unemployment may have caused the skills of some workers to deteriorate. Each of these factors could lead to slower growth in productivity, at least for a time.

Application

Waves of Productivity Growth over Time

We have seen in Table 6.3 that productivity growth in the United States has averaged a bit under 1% per year from 1929 to 2020, but in waves. Productivity grew faster than average from 1948 to 1973, but then declined from 1973 to 1982. After 1982, productivity growth was slightly below 1% again, though the period in the late 1990s was marked by rapid growth of productivity.

Waves in productivity growth have been going on for some time.[5] In the early 1800s, the development of water power, textiles, and iron led to rapid improvements in the standard of living. Another wave of innovation came in the mid- to late 1800s in the form of steel, steam, and railroads. The next wave began in the early 1900s with the internal combustion engine, electrification, and the use of chemicals. The 1950s and 1960s brought commercial aviation, electronics, and petrochemicals. Finally, the late 1990s and early 2000s saw the development of the Internet and cell phones. Today, we think that artificial intelligence and self-driving cars are likely to be part of the future, but studies of past innovations suggest that it might take a couple of decades before productivity growth rises significantly as a result of those innovations.

Will improved productivity and the next wave of innovation destroy jobs and lead to poverty? Some analysts think that self-driving cars and robotics could replace much human work activity. As a result, some have called for governments to provide a guaranteed income for workers who are displaced and might never work again. As the labor-market theory in Chapter 3 notes, improved technology normally increases the marginal product of labor. For example, artificial-intelligence programs are being developed that can help doctors make more accurate diagnoses, and robots on the assembly line allow a given number of workers to produce more cars with fewer defects. Increases in the marginal product of labor brought about by better technologies imply that labor demand and wages should rise, not fall. Indeed, as Joel Mokyr of Northwestern University, Chris Vickers of Auburn University, and Nicolas L. Ziebarth of the University of Iowa note, people have worried about technology disrupting their lives for generations.[6] Generally, predictions about the demise of the labor force and falling wages have been incorrect and misguided. Could this time be different?

---

[5] For an early discussion, see Nikolai D. Kondratieff, "The Long Waves in Economic Life," *Review of Economics and Statistics*, November 1935, pp. 105–115.

[6] "The History of Technological Anxiety and the Future of Economic Growth: Is This Time Different?" *Journal of Economic Perspectives*, Summer 2015, pp. 31–50.

Application

The Rebound in U.S. Productivity Growth

Our discussion of productivity growth in Table 6.3 showed that although productivity growth slowed in the period from 1973 to 1982 (indeed total factor productivity growth was negative), it began to grow more rapidly after 1982. In the late 1990s, labor productivity grew far more rapidly than it had for the preceding 20 years. Since then, labor productivity (output per hour in the nonfarm business sector) and total factor productivity (*A* in Eq. 6.1) have continued to grow, and economists have developed new explanations for that growth.

Figure 6.1 shows that both labor productivity and total factor productivity grew fairly steadily since bottoming out in 1982, until the financial crisis began in 2008, when the economy slowed abruptly along with total factor productivity. Labor productivity has grown somewhat faster than total factor productivity. (Note that both of the variables are indexed to have a value of 100 in year 2012. So, the levels of the indexes themselves have no inherent meaning.)

Figure 6.2 shows the growth rates of the productivity measures and illustrates a widening gap between labor productivity growth and total factor productivity growth from 1995 to 2008. After 2008, productivity growth slowed substantially for both productivity measures. To understand the relationship between the growth rates of total factor productivity and average labor productivity, recall Eq. (6.2), which is

$$\frac{\Delta Y}{Y} = \frac{\Delta A}{A} + a_K \frac{\Delta K}{K} + a_N \frac{\Delta N}{N}.$$

FIGURE 6.1

Productivity levels, 1948–2020

The chart shows annual values for labor productivity (output per hour in the nonfarm business sector) and total factor productivity (variable *A* in Eq. 6.1) for the period 1948–2020.

Sources: Labor productivity: Bureau of Labor Statistics, Nonfarm Business Sector: Output Per Hour of All Persons, available at *fred.stlouisfed.org/series/OPHNFB*. Total factor productivity: Bureau of Labor Statistics, Total Factor Productivity Trends, available at *www.bls.gov/productivity/tables/total-factor-productivity-major-sectors.xlsx*.

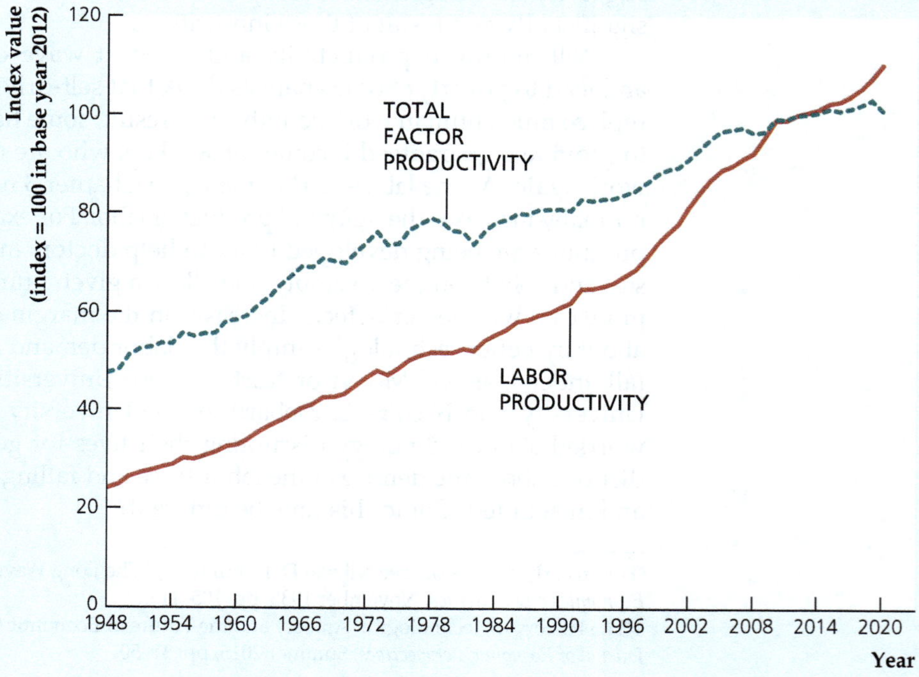

FIGURE 6.2

Productivity growth, 1949–2020

The chart shows annual values of labor productivity growth and total factor productivity growth for the period 1949–2020.

Sources: Same as Fig. 6.1.

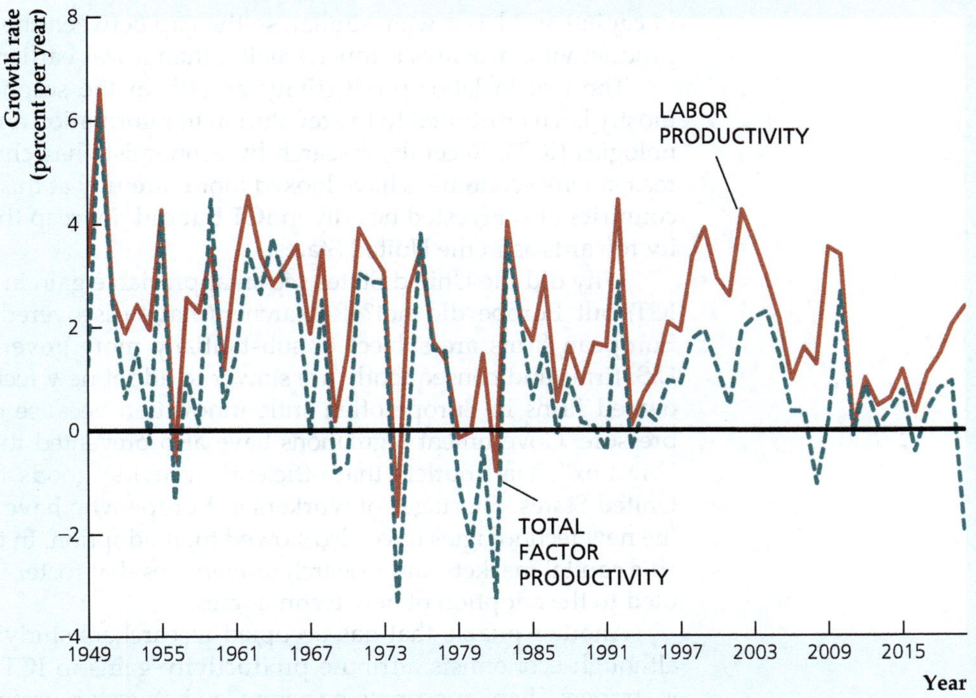

Empirically, the elasticity of output with respect to capital, a_K, plus the elasticity of output with respect to labor, a_N, equals one, so that $a_N = 1 - a_K$. Substituting $1 - a_K$ for a_N in Eq. (6.2) yields

$$\frac{\Delta Y}{Y} = \frac{\Delta A}{A} + a_K\frac{\Delta K}{K} + (1 - a_K)\frac{\Delta N}{N}.$$

Finally, subtracting the growth rate of labor, $\Delta N/N$, from both sides of this equation yields

$$\frac{\Delta Y}{Y} - \frac{\Delta N}{N} = \frac{\Delta A}{A} + a_K\left(\frac{\Delta K}{K} - \frac{\Delta N}{N}\right). \qquad \textbf{(6.3)}$$

Notice that the left-hand side of Eq. (6.3), $\frac{\Delta Y}{Y} - \frac{\Delta N}{N}$, is the growth rate of Y/N, that is, it is the growth rate of average labor productivity. The amount of capital per unit of labor, K/N, grows at the rate $\frac{\Delta K}{K} - \frac{\Delta N}{N}$. Thus, Eq. (6.3) states that the growth rate of average labor productivity equals the growth rate of total factor productivity, $\Delta A/A$, plus a_K times the growth rate of capital per unit of labor. As shown in Fig. 6.2, because capital per unit of labor generally grows, so that $\frac{\Delta K}{K} - \frac{\Delta N}{N} > 0$, the growth rate of average labor productivity is generally higher than the growth rate of total factor productivity. Figure 6.2 also shows that the excess of average labor productivity growth over total factor productivity growth was unusually large from 1995 to 2008, which is consistent with a higher growth rate of capital per unit of labor during this time. From 2008 to 2020, the growth rates

(*continued*)

of capital and labor were similar, so the gap between the growth rates of the two productivity measures is much smaller than it was earlier.

The rise in labor productivity growth in the second half of the 1990s has mostly been attributed to the revolution in information and communications technologies (ICT). Recently, research by economists has challenged that view. One reason why economists have looked more carefully at this issue is that many other countries also invested heavily in ICT but did not reap the same labor productivity rewards as in the United States.

Why did the United States see an appreciable gain in labor productivity from ICT, but Europe did not? Researchers have discovered a number of reasons.[7] European firms are subject to substantially more government regulations than U.S. firms and consequently are slower to adopt new technologies. Government-owned firms in Europe often stifle innovation because of a lack of competitive pressure. Government regulations have also prevented the existence in Europe of "big box" retail outlets that efficiently provide goods to consumers, as in the United States. Shortages of workers in Europe who have the skills needed to use the new technologies have also slowed their adoption. In the United States, adaptable capital markets and research universities that foster innovation have contributed to the adoption of new technologies.

Another puzzle that has occupied researchers studying productivity is that, although economists attribute productivity gains to ICT investment, the timing is strange: There appears to be a long lag between investment in ICT and a rise in productivity. U.S. firms invested heavily in computers in the 1980s, but productivity growth did not rise very much—not nearly as much as it has since 1995. In addition, ICT investment fell sharply in 2000, but productivity growth remained strong. As we discussed in the Application "Waves of Productivity Growth over Time," this weak link in timing between ICT investment and productivity improvements may arise because the use of ICT requires more than just buying computers—it takes research and development expenditures, reorganization of the firm, and training of workers. These activities, which economists call investment in intangible capital, take time and may temporarily cause a firm's output to decline rather than to rise. Thus, investment in intangible capital can help explain the lag between increases in ICT investment and productivity growth.

Is the increase in productivity from 1995 to 2008 unique in U.S. history? Not at all. In fact, researchers have identified three similar periods in our past: 1873 to 1890, following the Civil War; 1917 to 1927, following World War I; and 1948 to 1973, following World War II.[8] In each of these episodes, productivity improvements led to a substantial increase in the U.S. standard of living. New technologies included steam power, railroad transportation, and communication by telegraph in the late 1800s; electrification in factories after World War I; and the transistor

[7]For a readable summary of this research with references to original sources, see Ben S. Bernanke, "Productivity," Remarks at the Peter C. McColough Roundtable Series on International Economics at the University of Arkansas at Little Rock, February 24, 2005. Available at *www.federalreserve.gov/boarddocs/speeches/2005*.

[8]For details, see Roger W. Ferguson, Jr., and William L. Wascher, "Lessons from Past Productivity Booms," *Journal of Economic Perspectives* 18 (Spring 2004), pp. 3–28.

after World War II. Each of these periods was characterized not only by new technology but also by changes in how business firms were organized and by investments in workers (education and training).

Beginning around 2008, productivity growth slowed. Economists have debated the causes of this slowdown, with three main explanations: measurement issues, a lack of important technological innovations, and firms failing to keep up with technology. First, government statisticians may have trouble keeping up with technology, especially accounting properly for intangible investment.[9] Second, major technology improvements may have been exhausted, so the economy is in a phase with low productivity growth.[10] Third, firms may simply be unable or unwilling to keep up with technological change, perhaps because of a lack of competition between firms.[11]

In the Internet age, the apps on our smartphones certainly make it seem that we are in a new era of enhanced productivity. But the benefits of technology may help people in ways that do not show up in the GDP or productivity statistics. As David M. Byrne of the Federal Reserve Board, John G. Fernald of the Federal Reserve Bank of San Francisco, and Marshall B. Reinsdorf of the International Monetary Fund note, "Consumers are more productive in using their nonmarket time to produce services they value. These benefits raise consumer well-being but do not imply that market sector production functions are shifting out more rapidly than measured."[12] Thus, the reasons for the slowdown in productivity growth are less about mismeasurement than just a change in the structure of the goods and services that consumers use.

The lesson from history is that productivity growth varies over time, as innovations and the ability of U.S. firms to adapt and use new technology changes. Though comparisons to historical periods suggest that productivity growth has been very slow since 2008, consumer welfare may actually be improving substantially.

[9]See Carol A. Corrado and Charles R. Hulten, "How Do You Measure a 'Technological Revolution'?" *American Economic Review*, May 2010, pp. 99–104.

[10]See Robert J. Gordon, 2016. *The Rise and Fall of American Growth*. Princeton: Princeton University Press.

[11]See Martin Neil Baily and Nicholas Montalbano, "Why Is U.S. Productivity Growth So Slow? Possible Explanations and Policy Responses," The Brookings Institution, Hutchins Center Working Paper #22, September 2016.

[12]"Does the United States Have a Productivity Slowdown or a Measurement Problem?" *Brookings Papers on Economic Activity*, Spring 2019, pp. 109–182.

6.2 Long-Run Growth: The Solow Model

Explain the factors affecting long-run living standards in the Solow model.

Although growth accounting provides useful information about the sources of economic growth, it doesn't completely explain a country's growth performance. Because growth accounting takes the economy's rates of input growth as given, it can't explain why capital and labor grow at the rates that they do. The growth of the capital stock in particular is the result of the myriad saving and investment decisions of households and firms. By taking the growth of the capital stock as given, the growth accounting method leaves out an important part of the story.

In this section we take a closer look at the dynamics of economic growth, or how the growth process evolves over time. In doing so, we drop the assumption made in Chapter 3 that the capital stock is fixed and study the factors that cause the economy's stock of capital to grow. Our analysis is based on a famous model of economic growth developed in the late 1950s by Nobel laureate Robert Solow[13] of MIT, a model that has become the basic framework for most subsequent research on growth. Besides clarifying how capital accumulation and economic growth are interrelated, the Solow model is useful for examining two basic questions about growth:

1. What is the relationship between a nation's long-run standard of living and fundamental factors such as its saving rate, its population growth rate, and its rate of technical progress?
2. How does a nation's rate of economic growth evolve over time? Will economic growth stabilize, accelerate, or stop?

Setup of the Solow Model

The Solow model examines an economy as it evolves over time. To analyze the effects of labor force growth as well as changes in capital, we assume that the population is growing and that at any particular time a fixed share of the population is of working age. For any year, t,

$$N_t = \text{the number of workers available.}$$

We assume that the population and work force both grow at fixed rate n. So, if $n = 0.01$, the number of workers in any year is 1% greater than in the previous year.

At the beginning of each year, t, the economy has available a capital stock, K_t. (We demonstrate shortly how this capital stock is determined.) During each year, t, capital, K_t, and labor, N_t, are used to produce the economy's total output, Y_t. Part of the output produced each year is invested in new capital or in replacing worn-out capital. We further assume that the economy is closed and that there are no government purchases,[14] so the uninvested part of output is consumed by the population. If

$$\begin{aligned} Y_t &= \text{output produced in year } t, \\ I_t &= \text{gross (total) investment in year } t\text{, and} \\ C_t &= \text{consumption in year } t, \end{aligned}$$

the relationship among consumption, output, and investment in each year is

$$C_t = Y_t - I_t. \tag{6.4}$$

Equation (6.4) states that the uninvested part of the economy's output is consumed.

[13]The original article is Robert M. Solow, "A Contribution to the Theory of Economic Growth," *Quarterly Journal of Economics*, February 1956, pp. 65–94.

[14]Analytical Problem 3 at the end of this chapter adds government purchases to the model.

Because the population and the labor force are growing in this economy, focusing on output, consumption, and the capital stock *per worker* is convenient. Hence we use the following notation:

$$y_t = \frac{Y_t}{N_t} = \text{output per worker in year } t;$$

$$c_t = \frac{C_t}{N_t} = \text{consumption per worker in year } t;$$

$$k_t = \frac{K_t}{N_t} = \text{capital stock per worker in year } t.$$

The capital stock per worker, k_t, is also called the **capital–labor ratio**. An important goal of the model is to understand how output per worker, consumption per worker, and the capital–labor ratio change over time.[15]

The Per-Worker Production Function. In general, the amount of output that can be produced by specific quantities of inputs is determined by the production function. Until now we have written the production function as a relationship between total output, Y, and the total quantities of capital and labor inputs, K and N. However, we can also write the production function in per-worker terms as

$$y_t = f(k_t). \quad \textbf{(6.5)}$$

Equation (6.5) indicates that, in each year t, output per worker, y_t, depends on the amount of available capital per worker, k_t.[16] Here we use a lower case f instead of an upper case F for the production function to emphasize that the measurement of output and capital is in *per-worker* terms. For the time being we focus on the role of the capital stock in the growth process by assuming no productivity growth and thus leaving the productivity term out of the production function, Eq. (6.5).[17] We bring productivity growth back into the model later.

The per-worker production function is graphed in Figure 6.3. The capital–labor ratio (the amount of capital per worker), k_t, is measured on the horizontal axis, and output per worker, y_t, is measured on the vertical axis. The production function slopes upward from left to right because an increase in the amount of capital per worker allows each worker to produce more output. As with the standard production function, the bowed shape of the per-worker production function reflects the diminishing marginal productivity of capital. Thus when the capital–labor ratio is already high, an increase in the capital–labor ratio has a relatively small effect on output per worker.

---

[15]For purposes of analysis, discussing output and consumption per worker is more convenient than discussing output and consumption per member of the population as a whole. Under the assumption that the labor force is a fixed fraction of the population and is fully employed, anything we say about the growth rate of output or consumption per worker also will be true of the growth rate of output or consumption per member of the population.

[16]To write the production function in the form of Eq. (6.5) requires the assumption of constant returns to scale, which means that an equal percentage increase in both capital and labor inputs results in the same percentage increase in total output. So, for example, with constant returns to scale, a 10% increase in both capital and labor raises output by 10%. In terms of the growth accounting equation, Eq. (6.2), constant returns to scale requires that $a_K + a_N = 1$. See Analytical Problem 6 at the end of this chapter.

[17]More precisely, we set the total factor productivity term A equal to 1.

FIGURE 6.3

The per-worker production function

The per-worker production function, $y_t = f(k_t)$, relates the amount of output produced per worker, y_t, to the capital–labor ratio, k_t. For example, when the capital–labor ratio is k_1, output per worker is y_1. The per-worker production function slopes upward from left to right because an increase in the capital–labor ratio raises the amount of output produced per worker. The bowed shape of the production function reflects the diminishing marginal productivity of capital.

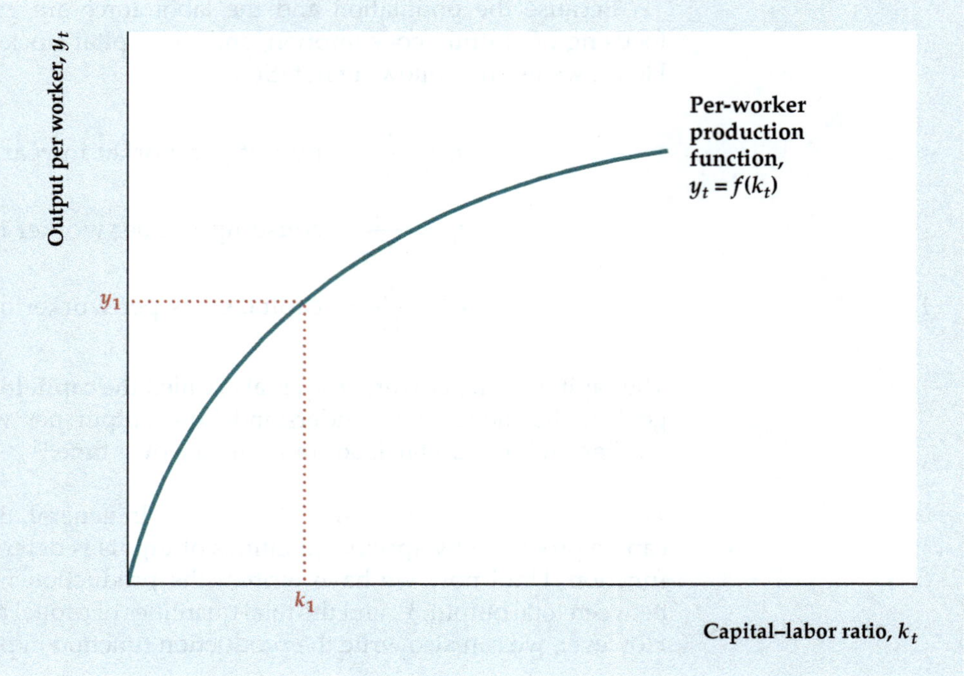

Steady States. One of the most striking conclusions obtained from the Solow model is that in the absence of productivity growth the economy reaches a steady state in the long run. A **steady state** is a situation in which the economy's output per worker, consumption per worker, and capital stock per worker are constant—that is, in the steady state, y_t, c_t, and k_t don't change over time.[18] To explain how the Solow model works, we first examine the characteristics of a steady state and then discuss how the economy might attain it.

Let's begin by looking at investment in a steady state. In general, gross (total) investment in year t, I_t, is devoted to two purposes: (1) replacing worn-out or depreciated capital, and (2) expanding the size of the capital stock. If d is the capital depreciation rate, or the fraction of capital that wears out each year, the total amount of depreciation in year t is dK_t. The amount by which the capital stock is increased is net investment. What is net investment in a steady state? Because capital per worker, K_t/N_t, is constant in a steady state, the total capital stock grows at the same rate as the labor force—that is, at rate n. Net investment is therefore nK_t in a steady state.[19] To obtain steady-state gross investment, we add steady-state net investment nK_t and depreciation dK_t:

$$I_t = (n + d)K_t \quad \text{(in a steady state).} \tag{6.6}$$

[18]Note that if output, consumption, and capital per worker are constant, then total output, consumption, and capital all are growing at rate n, the rate of growth of the work force.

[19]Algebraically, net investment in year t is $K_{t+1} - K_t$. If total capital grows at rate n, then $K_{t+1} = (1 + n)K_t$. Substituting for K_{t+1} in the definition of net investment, we find that net investment $= (1 + n)K_t - K_t = nK_t$ in a steady state.

To obtain steady-state consumption (output less investment), we substitute Eq. (6.6) into Eq. (6.4):

$$C_t = Y_t - (n + d)K_t \quad \text{(in a steady state).} \tag{6.7}$$

Equation (6.7) measures consumption, output, and capital as economywide totals rather than in per-worker terms. To put them in per-worker terms, we divide both sides of Eq. (6.7) by the number of workers, N_t, recalling that $c_t = C_t/N_t$, $y_t = Y_t/N_t$, and $k_t = K_t/N_t$. Then we use the per-worker production function, Eq. (6.5), to replace y_t with $f(k_t)$ and obtain

$$c = f(k) - (n + d)k \quad \text{(in a steady state).} \tag{6.8}$$

Equation (6.8) shows the relationship between consumption per worker, c, and the capital–labor ratio, k, in the steady state. Because consumption per worker and the capital–labor ratio are constant in the steady state, we dropped the time subscripts, t.

Equation (6.8) shows that an increase in the steady-state capital–labor ratio, k, has two opposing effects on steady-state consumption per worker, c. First, an increase in the steady-state capital–labor ratio raises the amount of output each worker can produce, $f(k)$. Second, an increase in the steady-state capital–labor ratio increases the amount of output per worker that must be devoted to investment, $(n + d)k$. More goods devoted to investment leaves fewer goods to consume.

Figure 6.4 shows the trade-off between these two effects. In Fig. 6.4(a) different possible values of the steady-state capital–labor ratio, k, are measured on the horizontal axis. The curve is the per-worker production function, $y = f(k)$, as in Fig. 6.3. The straight line shows steady-state investment per worker, $(n + d)k$. Equation (6.8) indicates that steady-state consumption per worker, c, equals the height of the curve, $f(k)$, minus the height of the straight line, $(n + d)k$. Thus consumption per worker is the height of the shaded area.

The relationship between consumption per worker and the capital–labor ratio in the steady state is shown more explicitly in Fig. 6.4(b). For each value of the steady-state capital–labor ratio, k, steady-state consumption, c, is the difference between the production function and investment in Fig. 6.4(a). Note that, starting from low and medium values of k (values less than k_G in Fig. 6.4(b)), increases in the steady-state capital–labor ratio lead to greater steady-state consumption per worker. The level of the capital–labor ratio that maximizes consumption per worker in the steady state, shown as k_G in Fig. 6.4, is known as the **Golden Rule capital–labor ratio**, so-called because it maximizes the economic welfare of future generations.[20]

However, for high values of k (values greater than the Golden Rule capital–labor ratio, k_G), increases in the steady-state capital–labor ratio actually result in lower steady-state consumption per worker because so much investment is needed to maintain the high level of capital per worker. In the extreme case, where $k = k_{\text{max}}$ in Fig. 6.4, all output has to be devoted to replacing and expanding the capital stock, with nothing left to consume!

Policymakers often try to improve long-run living standards with policies aimed at increasing the capital–labor ratio by stimulating saving and investment. Figure 6.4 shows the limits to this strategy. A country with a low amount of capital per worker may hope to improve long-run (steady-state) living standards

[20]Readers familiar with calculus might try to use Eq. (6.8) to show that, at the Golden Rule capital-labor ratio, the marginal product of capital equals $n + d$.

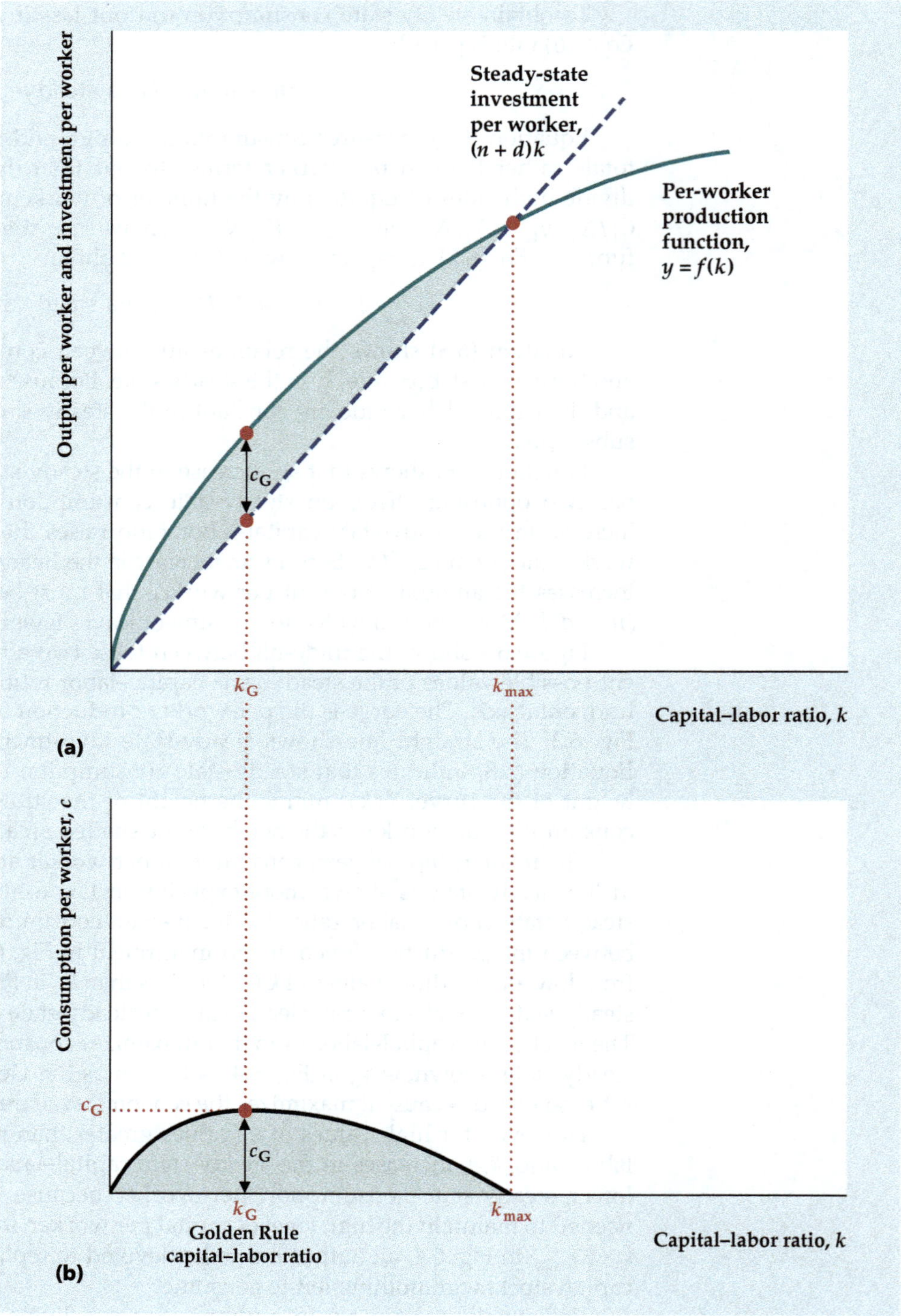

FIGURE 6.4

The relationship of consumption per worker to the capital–labor ratio in the steady state

(a) For each value of the capital–labor ratio, k, steady-state output per worker, y, is given by the per-worker production function, $f(k)$. Steady-state investment per worker, $(n + d)k$, is a straight line with slope $n + d$. Steady-state consumption per worker, c, is the difference between output per worker and investment per worker (the shaded area). For example, if the capital–labor ratio is k_G, steady-state consumption per worker is c_G. **(b)** For each value of the steady-state capital–labor ratio, k, steady-state consumption per worker, c, is derived in **(a)** as the difference between output per worker and investment per worker. Thus the shaded area in **(b)** corresponds to the shaded area in **(a)**. Note that, starting from a low value of the capital–labor ratio, an increase in the capital–labor ratio raises steady-state consumption per worker. However, starting from a capital–labor ratio greater than the Golden Rule level, k_G, an increase in the capital–labor ratio actually lowers consumption per worker. When the capital–labor ratio equals k_{max}, all output is devoted to investment, and steady-state consumption per worker is zero.

substantially by increasing its capital–labor ratio. However, a country that already has a high level of capital per worker may find that further increases in the capital–labor ratio fail to raise steady-state consumption much. The fundamental reason for this outcome is the diminishing marginal productivity of capital—that is, the larger the capital stock already is, the smaller the benefit from expanding the capital stock further. Indeed, Fig. 6.4 shows that, theoretically, capital per worker can be so high that further increases will actually *lower* steady-state consumption per worker.

In any economy in the world, could a higher capital stock lead to less consumption in the long run? An empirical study of seven advanced industrial countries concluded that the answer is "no." Even for high-saving Germany, further increases in capital per worker would lead to higher steady-state consumption per worker.[21] Thus in our analysis we will always assume that an increase in the steady-state capital–labor ratio raises steady-state consumption per worker.

Reaching the Steady State. Our discussion of steady states leaves two loose ends. First, we need to say something about why an economy like the one we describe here eventually will reach a steady state, as we claimed earlier. Second, we have not yet shown *which* steady state the economy will reach; that is, we would like to know the steady-state level of consumption per worker and the steady-state capital–labor ratio that the economy will eventually attain.

To tie up these loose ends, we need one more piece of information: the rate at which people save. To keep things as simple as possible, suppose that saving in this economy is proportional to current income:

$$S_t = sY_t, \qquad \textbf{(6.9)}$$

where S_t is national saving[22] in year t and s is the saving rate, which we assume to be constant. Because a \$1 increase in current income raises saving, but by less than \$1 (see Chapter 4), we take s to be a number between 0 and 1. Equation (6.9) ignores some other determinants of saving discussed in earlier chapters, such as the real interest rate. However, including these other factors wouldn't change our basic conclusions, so for simplicity we omit them.

In every year, national saving, S_t, equals investment, I_t. Therefore

$$sY_t = (n + d)K_t \text{ (in a steady state)}, \qquad \textbf{(6.10)}$$

where the left side of Eq. (6.10) is saving (see Eq. 6.9) and the right side of Eq. (6.10) is steady-state investment (see Eq. 6.6).

Equation (6.10) shows the relation between total output, Y_t, and the total capital stock, K_t, that holds in the steady state. To determine steady-state capital per worker, we divide both sides of Eq. (6.10) by N_t. We then use the production function, Eq. (6.5), to replace y_t with $f(k_t)$:

$$sf(k) = (n + d)k \text{ (in the steady state)}. \qquad \textbf{(6.11)}$$

Equation (6.11) indicates that saving per worker, $sf(k)$, equals steady-state investment per worker, $(n + d)k$. Because the capital–labor ratio, k, is constant in the steady state, we again drop the subscripts, t, from the equation.

With Eq. (6.11) we can now determine the steady-state capital–labor ratio that the economy will attain, as shown in Figure 6.5. The capital–labor ratio is measured along the horizontal axis. Saving per worker and investment per worker are measured on the vertical axis.

[21] See Andrew B. Abel, N. Gregory Mankiw, Lawrence H. Summers, and Richard J. Zeckhauser, "Assessing Dynamic Efficiency: Theory and Evidence," *Review of Economic Studies*, January 1989, pp. 1–20.

[22] With no government in this model, national saving and private saving are the same.

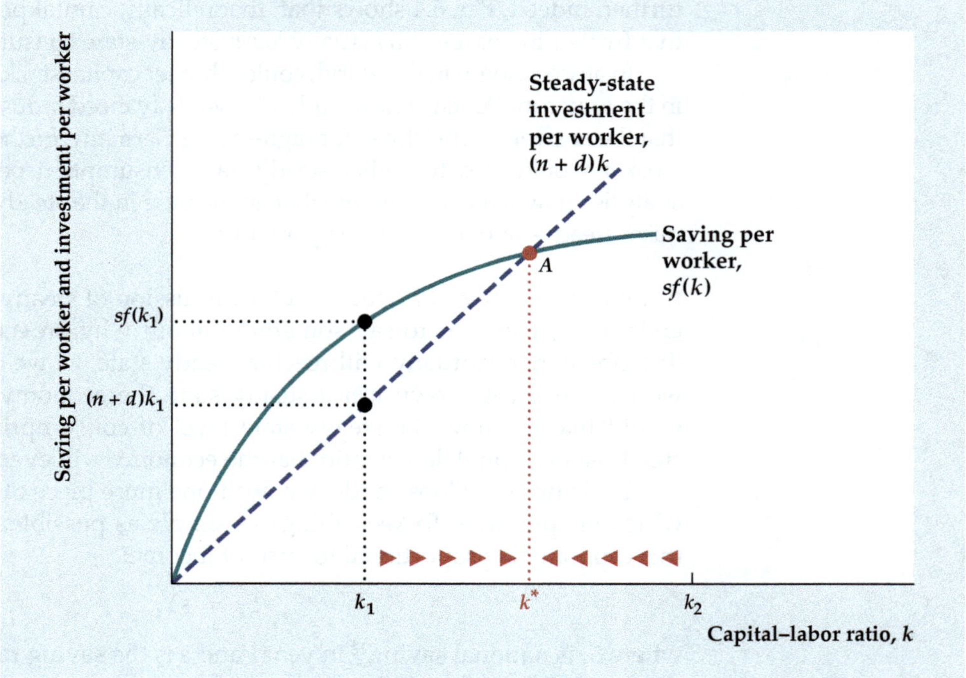

FIGURE 6.5

Determining the capital–labor ratio in the steady state

The steady-state capital–labor ratio, k^*, is determined by the condition that saving per worker, $sf(k)$, equals steady-state investment per worker, $(n + d)k$. The steady-state capital–labor ratio, k^*, corresponds to point A, where the saving curve and the steady-state investment line cross. From any starting point, eventually the capital–labor ratio reaches k^*. If the capital–labor ratio happens to be below k^* (say, at k_1), saving per worker, $sf(k_1)$, exceeds the investment per worker, $(n + d)k_1$, needed to maintain the capital–labor ratio at k_1. As this extra saving is converted into capital, the capital–labor ratio will rise, as indicated by the arrows. Similarly, if the capital–labor ratio is greater than k^* (say, at k_2), saving is too low to maintain the capital–labor ratio, and the capital–labor ratio will fall over time.

The bowed curve shows how the amount of saving per worker, $sf(k)$, is related to the capital–labor ratio. This curve slopes upward because an increase in the capital–labor ratio implies higher output per worker and thus more saving per worker. The saving-per-worker curve has the same general shape as the per-worker production function, because saving per worker equals the per-worker production function, $f(k)$, multiplied by the fixed saving rate, s.

The line in Fig. 6.5 represents steady-state investment per worker, $(n + d)k$. The steady-state investment line slopes upward because, as the capital–labor ratio rises, more investment per worker is required to replace depreciating capital and equip new workers with the same high level of capital.

According to Eq. (6.11), the steady-state capital–labor ratio must ensure that saving per worker and steady-state investment per worker are equal. The one level of the capital–labor ratio for which this condition is satisfied is shown in Fig. 6.5 as k^*, the value of k at which the saving curve and the steady-state investment line cross. For any other value of k, saving and steady-state investment won't be equal. Thus k^* is the only possible steady-state capital–labor ratio for this economy.[23]

With the unique steady-state capital–labor ratio, k^*, we can also find steady-state output and consumption per worker. From the per-worker production function, Eq. (6.5), if the steady-state capital–labor ratio is k^*, steady-state output per worker, y^*, is

$$y^* = f(k^*).$$

[23]Actually, there is also a steady state at the point $k = 0$, at which the capital stock, output, and consumption are zero forever. However, as long as the economy starts out with a positive amount of capital, it will never reach the zero-capital steady state.

From Eq. (6.8) steady-state consumption per worker, c^*, equals steady-state output per worker, $f(k^*)$, minus steady-state investment per worker, $(n + d)k^*$:

$$c^* = f(k^*) - (n + d)k^*.$$

Recall that, in the empirically realistic case, a higher value of the steady-state capital–labor ratio, k^*, implies greater steady-state consumption per worker, c^*.

Using the condition that in a steady state, national saving equals steady-state investment, we found the steady-state capital–labor ratio, k^*. When capital per worker is k^*, the amount that people choose to save will just equal the amount of investment necessary to keep capital per worker at k^*. Thus, when the economy's capital–labor ratio reaches k^*, it will remain there forever.

But is there any reason to believe that the capital–labor ratio will ever reach k^* if it starts at some other value? Yes, there is. Suppose that the capital–labor ratio happens to be less than k^*; for example, it equals k_1 in Fig. 6.5. When capital per worker is k_1, the amount of saving per worker, $sf(k_1)$, is greater than the amount of investment needed to keep the capital–labor ratio constant, $(n + d)k_1$. When this extra saving is invested to create new capital, the capital–labor ratio will rise. As indicated by the arrows on the horizontal axis, the capital–labor ratio will increase from k_1 toward k^*.

If capital per worker is initially greater than k^*—for example, if k equals k_2 in Fig. 6.5—the explanation of why the economy converges to a steady state is similar. If the capital–labor ratio exceeds k^*, the amount of saving that is done will be less than the amount of investment that is necessary to keep the capital–labor ratio constant. (In Fig. 6.5, when k equals k_2, the saving curve lies below the steady-state investment line.) Thus the capital–labor ratio will fall over time from k_2 toward k^*, as indicated by the arrows. Output per worker will also fall until it reaches its steady-state value.

To summarize, if we assume no productivity growth, the economy must eventually reach a steady state. In this steady state the capital–labor ratio, output per worker, and consumption per worker remain constant over time. (However, total capital, output, and consumption grow at rate n, the rate of growth of the labor force.) This conclusion might seem gloomy because it implies that living standards must eventually stop improving. However, that conclusion can be avoided if, in fact, productivity continually increases.

The Fundamental Determinants of Long-Run Living Standards

What determines how well off the average person in an economy will be in the long run? If we measure long-run well-being by the steady-state level of consumption per worker, we can use the Solow model to answer this question (keeping in mind that we are assuming that an increase in the steady-state capital-labor ratio will increase steady-state consumption per worker). Here, we discuss three factors that affect long-run living standards: the saving rate, population growth, and productivity growth (see Summary table 8).

The Saving Rate. According to the Solow model, a higher saving rate implies higher living standards in the long run, as illustrated in Figure 6.6. Suppose that the economy's initial saving rate is s_1 so that saving per worker is $s_1 f(k)$. The saving curve when the saving rate is s_1 is labeled "Initial saving per worker." The initial steady-state capital–labor ratio, k_1^*, is the capital–labor ratio at which the initial saving curve and the investment line cross (point A).

SUMMARY 8

The Fundamental Determinants of Long-Run Living Standards

An increase in	Causes long-run output, consumption, and capital per worker to	Reason
The saving rate, s	Rise	Higher saving allows for more investment and a larger capital stock.
The rate of population growth, n	Fall	With higher population growth more output must be used to equip new workers with capital, leaving less output available for consumption or to increase capital per worker.
Productivity	Rise	Higher productivity directly increases output; by raising incomes, it also raises saving and the capital stock.

Suppose now that the government introduces policies that strengthen the incentives for saving, causing the country's saving rate to rise from s_1 to s_2. The increased saving rate raises saving at every level of the capital–labor ratio. Graphically, the saving curve shifts upward from $s_1f(k)$ to $s_2f(k)$. The new steady-state capital–labor ratio, k_2^*, corresponds to the intersection of the new saving curve and the investment line (point B). Because k_2^* is larger than k_1^*, the higher saving rate has increased the steady-state capital–labor ratio. Gradually, this economy will move to the higher steady-state capital–labor ratio, as indicated by the arrows on the horizontal axis. In the new steady state, output per worker and consumption per worker will be higher than in the original steady state.

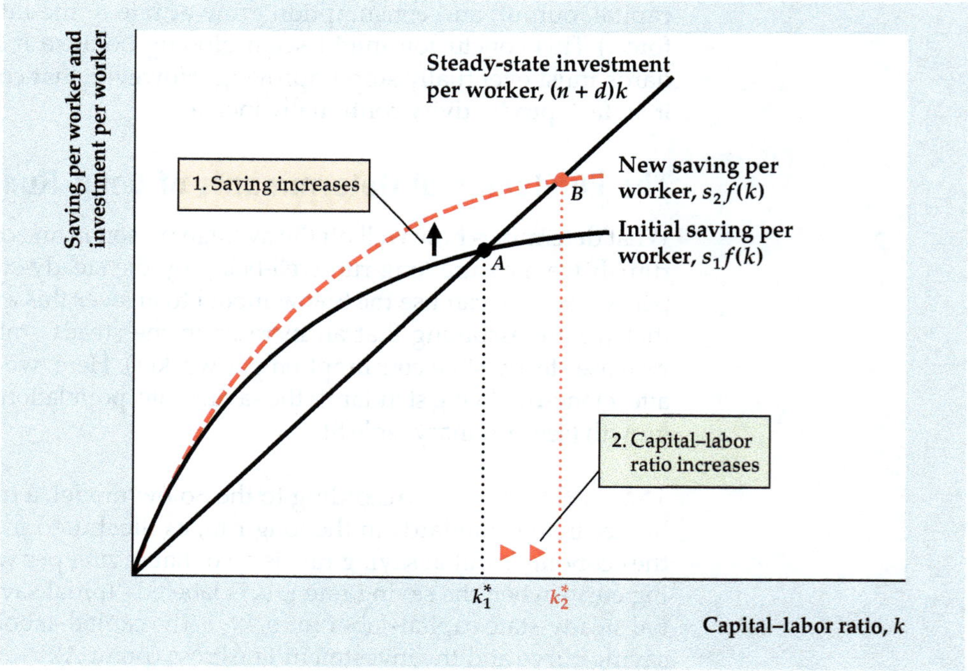

FIGURE 6.6

The effect of an increased saving rate on the steady-state capital–labor ratio

An increase in the saving rate from s_1 to s_2 raises the saving curve from $s_1f(k)$ to $s_2f(k)$. The point where saving per worker equals steady-state investment per worker moves from point A to point B, and the corresponding capital–labor ratio rises from k_1^* to k_2^*. Thus a higher saving rate raises the steady-state capital–labor ratio.

An increased saving rate leads to higher output, consumption, and capital per worker in the long run, so it might seem that a policy goal should be to make the country's saving rate as high as possible. However, this conclusion isn't necessarily correct: Although a higher saving rate raises consumption per worker in the long run, an increase in the saving rate initially causes consumption to fall. This decline occurs because, at the initial level of output, increases in saving and investment leave less available for current consumption. Thus higher future consumption has a cost in terms of lower present consumption. Society's choice of a saving rate should take into account this trade-off between current and future consumption. Beyond a certain point the cost of reduced consumption today will outweigh the long-run benefits of a higher saving rate.

Population Growth. In many developing countries a high rate of population growth is considered a major problem, and reducing it is a primary policy goal. What is the relationship between population growth and a country's level of development, as measured by output, consumption, and capital per worker?

The Solow model's answer to this question is shown in Figure 6.7. An initial steady-state capital–labor ratio, k_1^*, corresponds to the intersection of the steady-state investment line and the saving curve at point *A*. Now suppose that the rate of population growth, which is the same as the rate of labor force growth, rises from an initial level of n_1 to n_2. What happens?

An increase in the population growth rate means that workers are entering the labor force more rapidly than before. These new workers must be equipped with capital. Thus, to maintain the same steady-state capital–labor ratio, the amount of investment per current member of the work force must rise. Algebraically, the rise in n increases steady-state investment per worker from $(n_1 + d)k$ to $(n_2 + d)k$. This

FIGURE 6.7

The effect of a higher population growth rate on the steady-state capital–labor ratio

An increase in the population growth rate from n_1 to n_2 increases steady-state investment per worker from $(n_1 + d)k$ to $(n_2 + d)k$. The steady-state investment line pivots up and to the left as its slope rises from $n_1 + d$ to $n_2 + d$. The point where saving per worker equals steady-state investment per worker shifts from point *A* to point *B*, and the corresponding capital–labor ratio falls from k_1^* to k_2^*. A higher population growth rate therefore causes the steady-state capital–labor ratio to fall.

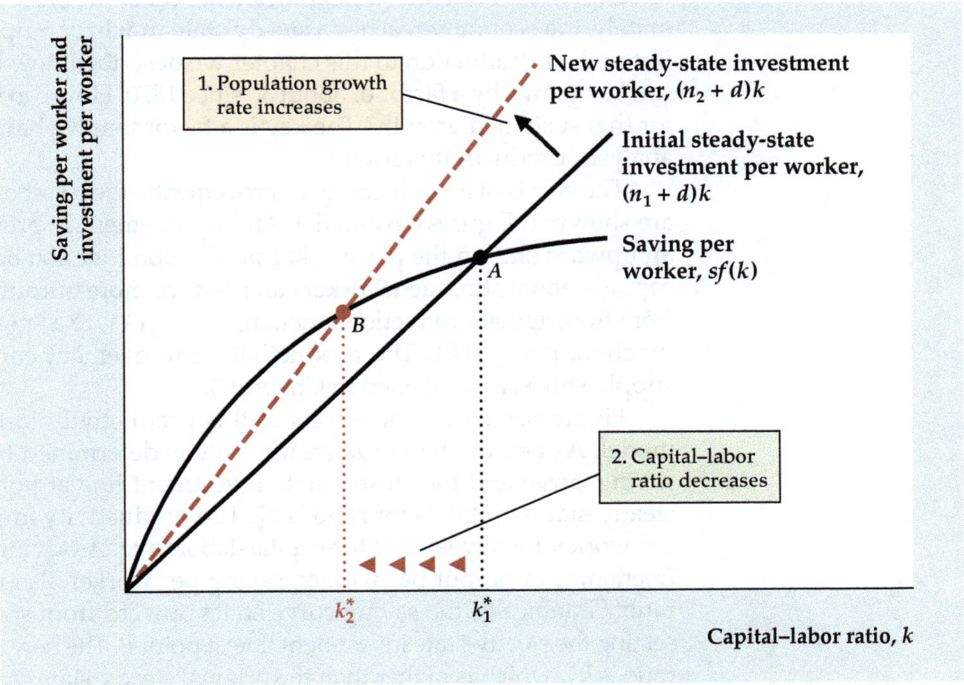

increase in the population growth rate causes the steady-state investment line to pivot up and to the left, as its slope rises from $(n_1 + d)$ to $(n_2 + d)$.

After the pivot of the steady-state investment line, the new steady state is at point *B*. The new steady-state capital–labor ratio is k_2^*, which is lower than the original capital–labor ratio, k_1^*. Because the new steady-state capital–labor ratio is lower, the new steady-state output per worker and consumption per worker will be lower as well.

Thus the Solow model implies that increased population growth will lower living standards. The basic problem is that when the work force is growing rapidly, a large part of current output must be devoted just to providing capital for the new workers to use. This result suggests that policies to limit population growth will indeed improve living standards.

There are some counterarguments to the conclusion that policy should aim to reduce population growth. First, although a reduction in the rate of population growth n raises consumption *per worker,* it also reduces the growth rate of *total* output and consumption, which grow at rate n in the steady state. Having fewer people means more for each person but also less total productive capacity. For some purposes (military, political) a country may care about its total output as well as output per person. Thus, for example, some European countries are concerned about projections that their populations will actually shrink in the coming decades, possibly reducing their ability to defend themselves or influence world events.

Second, an assumption in the Solow model is that the proportion of the total population that is of working age is fixed. When the population growth rate changes dramatically, this assumption may not hold. For example, declining birth rates in the United States imply that the ratio of working-age people to retirees will decline in the twenty-first century, a development that may cause problems for Social Security funding and other areas such as health care.

Productivity Growth. A significant aspect of the basic Solow model is that, ultimately, the economy reaches a steady state in which output per capita is constant. But in the introduction to this chapter we described how Japanese output per person has grown by a factor of about 30 since 1870! How can the Solow model account for that sustained growth? The key is a factor that we haven't yet made part of the analysis: productivity growth.

The effects of a productivity improvement—the result of, say, a new technology—are shown in Figures 6.8 and 6.9. An improvement in productivity corresponds to an upward shift in the per-worker production function because, at any prevailing capital–labor ratio, each worker can produce more output. Figure 6.8 shows a shift from the original production function, $y = f_1(k)$, to a "new, improved" production function, $y = f_2(k)$. The productivity improvement corresponds to a beneficial supply shock, as explained in Chapter 3.

Figure 6.9 shows the effects of this productivity improvement in the Solow model. As before, the initial steady state is determined by the intersection of the saving curve and the steady-state investment line at point A; the corresponding steady-state capital–labor ratio is k_1^*. The productivity improvement raises output per worker for any level of the capital–labor ratio. As saving per worker is a constant fraction, s, of output per worker, saving per worker also rises at any capital–labor ratio. Graphically, the saving curve shifts upward from $sf_1(k)$ to $sf_2(k)$, now intersecting the steady-state investment line at point B. The new steady-state capital–labor ratio is k_2^*, which is higher than the original steady-state capital–labor ratio, k_1^*.

FIGURE 6.8

An improvement in productivity

An improvement in productivity shifts the per-worker production function upward from the initial production function, $y = f_1(k)$, to the new production function, $y = f_2(k)$. After the productivity improvement, more output per worker, y, can be produced at any capital–labor ratio, k.

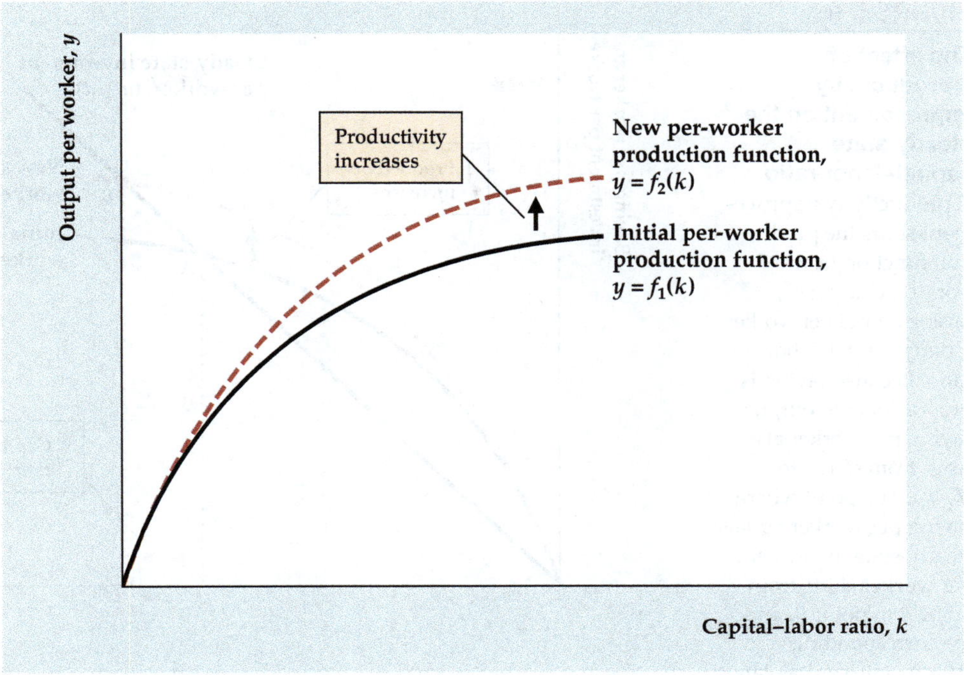

Overall, a productivity improvement raises steady-state output and consumption per worker in two ways. First, it directly increases the amount that can be produced at any capital–labor ratio. Second, as Fig. 6.9 shows, by raising the supply of saving, a productivity improvement causes the long-run capital–labor ratio to rise. Thus a productivity improvement has a doubly beneficial impact on the standard of living.

Like a one-time increase in the saving rate or decrease in the population growth rate, a one-time productivity improvement shifts the economy only from one steady state to a higher one. When the economy reaches the new steady state, consumption per worker once again becomes constant. Is there some way to keep consumption per worker growing indefinitely?

In reality, there are limits to how high the saving rate can rise (it certainly can't exceed 100%!) or how low the population growth rate can fall. Thus higher saving rates or slower population growth aren't likely sources of continually higher living standards. However, since the Industrial Revolution, if not before, people have shown remarkable ingenuity in becoming more and more productive. In the very long run, according to the Solow model, only these continuing increases in productivity hold the promise of perpetually better living standards. Thus we conclude that, *in the long run, the rate of productivity improvement is the dominant factor determining how quickly living standards rise.*

Economic Models, Endogenous Variables, and Exogenous Variables

The Solow model provides a useful framework for analyzing growth and illustrates several features of many different types of economic models—equilibrium conditions, endogenous variables, and exogenous variables.

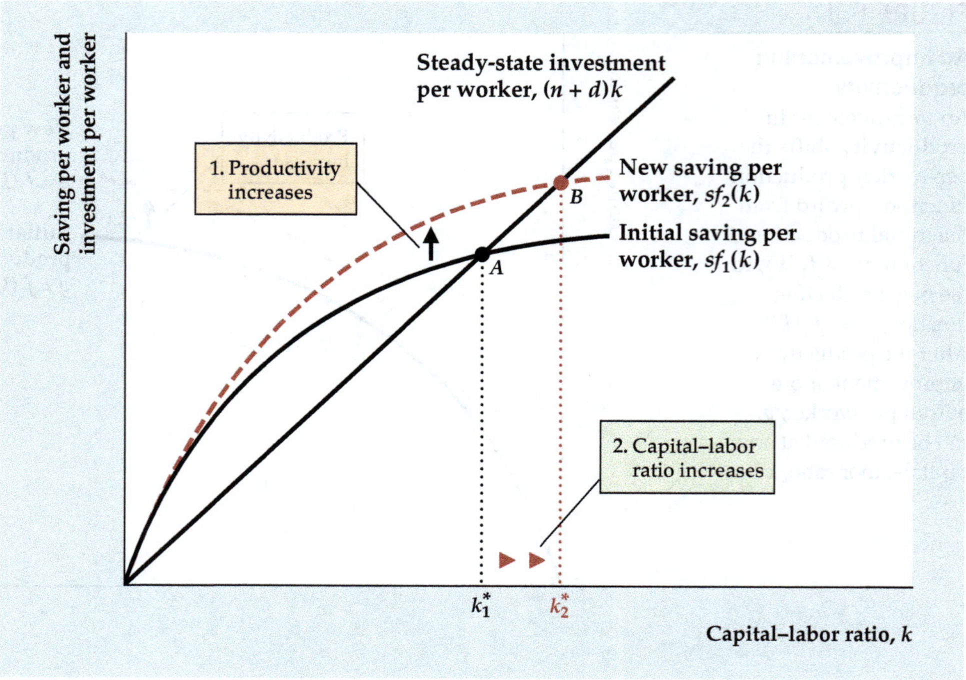

FIGURE 6.9

The effect of a productivity improvement on the steady-state capital–labor ratio

A productivity improvement shifts the production function upward from $f_1(k)$ to $f_2(k)$, raising output per worker for any capital–labor ratio. Because saving is proportional to output, saving per worker also rises, from $sf_1(k)$ to $sf_2(k)$. The point where saving per worker equals steady-state investment per worker shifts from point A to point B, and the corresponding steady-state capital–labor ratio rises from k_1^* to k_2^*. Thus a productivity improvement raises the steady-state capital–labor ratio.

Equilibrium Conditions. Economists solve models by finding a point of equilibrium. In the Solow model, the steady-state equilibrium occurs where in Fig. 6.5 the two lines cross, depicting the level of steady-state capital per worker at which steady-state investment per worker equals saving per worker. The graph shows the one point that satisfies Eq. (6.11), so we call that equation the **equilibrium condition.** Much of theoretical economic analysis involves developing a model that explains an economic situation and finding the equilibrium condition or conditions.

Exogenous Versus Endogenous Variables. No economic model can develop an equilibrium condition for every possible variable. Instead, some variables are taken as given, and the values of other variables are determined by the equilibrium of the model. A variable that is taken as given is called an **exogenous variable.** A variable that is determined by the equilibrium in the model is called an **endogenous variable.** For example, in the Solow model, we take the values of the variables n, s, and d as given. The model does not determine these variables, so they are exogenous variables. However, given the values of n, s, and d and knowledge of the production function, f, we can determine the values of variables k, y, and c, so those variables are endogenous. To see this, note that Fig. 6.5 and thus Eq. (6.11) determine the value of n. Then we can use Eq. (6.5) to determine y and use Eq. (6.8) to determine c.

When economists analyze an economic model, the most common type of question they can answer is: How does a change in an exogenous variable affect all the endogenous variables? For example, the analysis shown in Fig. 6.6 shows how a higher saving rate (an exogenous variable) affects the steady-state value of k (an endogenous variable). Then Eqs. (6.5) and (6.8) can be used to show how the steady-state values of y and c change because of the higher saving rate. Similarly, Fig. 6.7 shows the impact of a higher population growth rate. In a similar vein, because we took the production function, f, as given, we can analyze the impact of a change in productivity, as in Fig. 6.9, on the endogenous variables.

Some types of questions posed in analyses of economic models are not well posed or meaningful. For example, it is meaningless to ask how an endogenous variable affects an exogenous variable. So, suppose someone were to ask you: How does a higher steady-state capital stock affect the rate of population growth? Your answer would be: I cannot answer the question with the Solow model because the rate of population growth is an exogenous variable in the model. To answer that question, you would need a different model in which population growth is endogenous rather than exogenous. Developing a model with a good choice of exogenous and endogenous variables is one of the most important jobs of research economists.

Another meaningless question is to ask how one endogenous variable affects another one. You cannot answer the question: How does a change in steady-state consumption per person, c, affect steady-state capital per person, k, in the Solow model? Because both c and k and endogenous, you should first examine what change in an exogenous variable caused the change in c. The ultimate cause of a change in c must be some change in an exogenous variable or in the production function, which is also taken as given.

In subsequent models in the textbook, identifying which variables are exogenous and which are endogenous, along with finding the equilibrium conditions, will be a major part of the analysis.

Application

The Growth of China

China has experienced soaring growth rates in recent years. Because of its size (population of 1.4 billion), China could become the next great world economic power. Although it has grown rapidly in the past few decades, China started from such a low level of GDP per capita that the country has a long way to go before its GDP per capita catches up to GDP per capita in advanced economies.

Table 6.4 shows that China's GDP per capita compares poorly with other countries. Moreover, real GDP per capita in China was actually lower in 1950 than it had been 80 years earlier in 1870. As recently as 2000, China's real GDP per

TABLE 6.4

Economic Growth in China, Japan, and the United States

	Levels of real GDP per capita				
Country	**1870**	**1913**	**1950**	**2018**	**Annual growth rate 1870–2018**
China	945	985	799	13,102	1.8
Japan	1580	2431	3062	38,674	2.2
United States	4803	10,108	15,240	55,335	1.7

Note: Figures are in U.S. dollars at 2011 prices, adjusted for differences in the purchasing power of the various national currencies.

Source: Data from The Maddison-Project, *www.ggdc.net/maddison/maddison-project/home.htm*, 2020 version.

(continued)

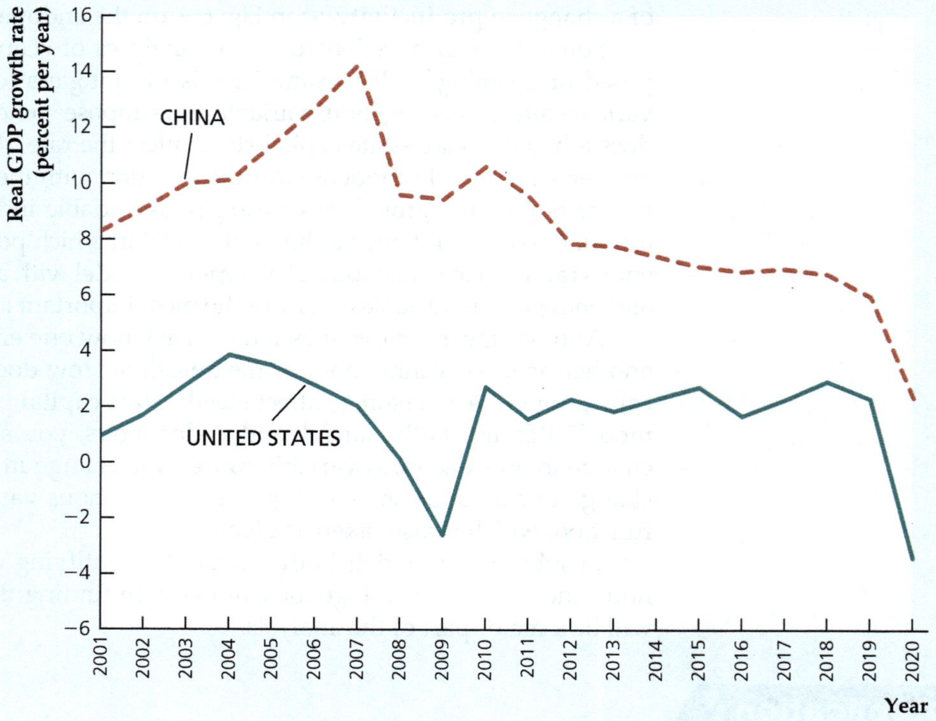

FIGURE 6.10

Real GDP growth in China and the United States, 2001–2020

The chart shows annual values for real GDP growth for both China and the United States for the period 2001–2020.

Source: Data from International Monetary Fund, World Economic Outlook, available at *www.imf.org/en/Publications/WEO/weo-database/2021/October.*

capita was only about 13% of Japan's, even though China's real GDP per capita was 65% of Japan's real GDP per capita in 1870.

In recent years, real GDP growth in China has been quite rapid. Figure 6.10 shows the growth rate of GDP in China compared with that in the United States. Over the period 2001–2020, China's GDP growth rate averaged 8.7% per year, whereas the U.S. GDP growth rate averaged just 1.7% per year. Analysts have attributed the rapid growth rate in China to a tremendous increase in capital investment, fast productivity growth that has arisen in part from the transition from a centrally planned economy to a market economy, and increased trade with other countries.

Will China be able to maintain its extremely high growth rate of GDP? The experience of many other countries suggests that periods of rapid economic growth by developing economies are often followed by substantial slowdowns in economic growth.[24] In the early stages of economic development, developing countries like China often grow much faster than advanced economies like the United States. This rapid growth arises as developing economies make more effective use of underemployed resources, such as labor, take advantage of more advanced technology developed elsewhere, or make important economic transitions such as from a centrally planned economy to a market economy with protection of property rights. But as economic growth progresses in a developing economy, underemployed resources are not as plentiful, technology has moved closer to the level in advanced economies, and the benefits of moving to an improved economic system have been largely exhausted. At that point, economic growth inevitably slows down. Looking forward, we cannot say when China's growth will slow down, nor by how much. However, we can say that if, starting from the levels of GDP per capita in 2018, China somehow managed to increase its GDP per capita by 10% per year while GDP per capita in the United States grows by only 1% per year, it would take about 17 years for China's GDP per capita to catch up with that in the United States. But if China's growth rate of GDP per capita were to average only 5% per year (still a very impressive growth rate) while U.S. GDP per capita grows 1% per year, it would take 37 years for GDP per capita in China to catch up to the level in the United States.

[24]See Barry Eichengreen, Donghyun Park, and Kwanho Shin, "When Fast Growing Economies Slow Down: International Evidence and Implications for China," *Asian Economic Papers, Winter/Spring* 2012, pp. 42–87.

6.3 Endogenous Growth Theory

Summarize endogenous growth theory.

The traditional Solow model of economic growth has proved quite useful, but it nevertheless has at least one serious shortcoming as a model of economic growth. According to the Solow model, productivity growth is the only source of long-run growth of output per capita, so a full explanation of long-run economic growth requires an explanation of productivity growth. The model, however, simply takes the rate of productivity growth as given, rather than trying to explain how it is determined. That is, the Solow model *assumes*, rather than *explains*, the behavior of the crucial determinant of the long-run growth rate of output per capita. In other words, in the Solow model, productivity is an exogenous variable.

In response to this shortcoming of the Solow model, a newer branch of growth theory, **endogenous growth theory**, has been developed to try to explain productivity growth—and hence the growth rate of output—*endogenously*, or *within the model*.[25] As we will see, an important implication of endogenous growth theory is that a country's long-run growth rate depends on its rate of saving and investment, not only on exogenous productivity growth (as implied by the Solow model).

Here we present a simple endogenous growth model in which the number of workers remains constant, a condition implying that the growth rate of output per worker is simply equal to the growth rate of output. Our simple endogenous growth model is based on the aggregate production function

$$Y = AK, \quad \textbf{(6.12)}$$

where Y is aggregate output and K is the aggregate capital stock. The parameter A in Eq. (6.12) is a positive constant. According to the production function in Eq. (6.12), each additional unit of capital increases output by A units, regardless of how many units of capital are used in production. Because the marginal product

[25]Two important early articles in endogenous growth theory are Paul Romer, "Increasing Returns and Long-Run Growth," *Journal of Political Economy*, October 1986, pp. 1002–1037; and Robert E. Lucas, Jr., "On the Mechanics of Economic Development," *Journal of Monetary Economics*, July 1988, pp. 3–42. A more accessible description of endogenous growth theory is in Paul Romer, "The Origins of Endogenous Growth," *Journal of Economic Perspectives*, Winter 1994, pp. 3–22.

of capital, equal to A, does not depend on the size of the capital stock K, the production function in Eq. (6.12) does not imply diminishing marginal productivity of capital. The assumption that the marginal productivity is constant, rather than diminishing, is a key departure from the Solow growth model.

Endogenous growth theorists have provided a number of reasons to explain why, for the economy as a whole, the marginal productivity of capital may not be diminishing. One explanation emphasizes the role of **human capital**, the economists' term for the knowledge, skills, and training of individuals. As economies accumulate capital and become richer, they devote more resources to "investing in people," through improved nutrition, schooling, health care, and on-the-job training. This investment in people increases the country's human capital, which in turn raises productivity. If the physical capital stock increases while the stock of human capital remains fixed, there will be diminishing marginal productivity of physical capital, as each unit of physical capital effectively works with a smaller amount of human capital. Endogenous growth theory argues that, as an economy's physical capital stock increases, its human capital stock tends to increase in the same proportion. Thus, when the physical capital stock increases, each unit of physical capital effectively works with the same amount of human capital, so the marginal productivity of capital need not decrease.

A second rationalization of a constant marginal productivity of capital is based on the observation that, in a growing economy, firms have incentives to undertake research and development (R&D) activities. These activities increase the stock of commercially valuable knowledge, including new products and production techniques. According to this R&D-focused explanation, increases in capital and output tend to generate increases in technical know-how, and the resulting productivity gains offset any tendency for the marginal productivity of capital to decline.

Having examined why a production function like Eq. (6.12) might be a reasonable description of the economy as a whole, once factors such as increased human capital and research and development are taken into account, let's work out the implications of this equation. As in the Solow model, let's assume that national saving, S, is a constant fraction s of aggregate output, AK, so that $S = sAK$. In a closed economy, investment must equal saving. Recall that total investment equals net investment (the net increase in the capital stock) plus depreciation, or $I = \Delta K + dK$. Therefore, setting investment equal to saving, we have

$$\Delta K + dK = sAK. \tag{6.13}$$

Next, we divide both sides of Eq. (6.13) by K and then subtract d from both sides of the resulting equation to obtain the growth rate of the capital stock.

$$\frac{\Delta K}{K} = sA - d. \tag{6.14}$$

Because output is proportional to the capital stock, the growth rate of output, $\frac{\Delta Y}{Y}$, equals the growth rate of the capital stock, $\frac{\Delta K}{K}$. Therefore, Eq. (6.14) implies

$$\frac{\Delta Y}{Y} = sA - d. \tag{6.15}$$

Equation (6.15) shows that, in the endogenous growth model, the growth rate of output depends on the saving rate s. As we are assuming that the number of workers remains constant over time, the growth rate of output per worker equals the growth rate of output given in Eq. (6.15), and thus depends on the saving rate s. The result that the saving rate affects the long-run growth rate of output stands in sharp contrast to the results of the Solow model, in which the saving rate does not affect the long-run growth rate. Saving affects long-run growth in the endogenous growth framework because, in that framework, higher rates of saving and capital formation stimulate greater investment in human capital and R&D. The resulting increases in productivity help to spur long-run growth. In summary, in comparison to the Solow model, the endogenous growth model places greater emphasis on saving, human capital formation, and R&D as sources of long-run growth.

The endogenous growth theory approach appears promising in at least two dimensions. First, this theory attempts to explain, rather than assumes, the economy's rate of productivity growth. Second, it shows how the long-run growth rate of output may depend on factors, such as the country's saving rate, that can be affected by government policies. Many economists working in this area are optimistic that endogenous growth theory will yield further insights into the creative processes underlying productivity growth, while providing lessons that might be applied to help the poorest nations of the world achieve substantially higher standards of living.

6.4 Government Policies to Raise Long-Run Living Standards

Discuss government policies for raising long-run living standards.

Increased growth and a higher standard of living in the long run often are cited by political leaders as primary policy goals. Let's take a closer look at government policies that may be useful in raising a country's long-run standard of living.

Policies to Affect the Saving Rate

The Solow model suggests that the rate of national saving is a principal determinant of long-run living standards. However, this conclusion doesn't necessarily mean that policymakers should try to force the saving rate upward, because more saving means less consumption in the short run. Indeed, if the "invisible hand" of free markets is working well, the saving rate freely chosen by individuals should be the one that optimally balances the benefit of saving more (higher future living standards) against the cost of saving more (less present consumption).

Despite the argument that saving decisions are best left to private individuals and the free market, some people claim that U.S. residents save too little and that U.S. policy should aim at raising the saving rate. One possible justification for this claim is that existing tax laws discriminate against saving by taxing away part of the returns to saving; a "pro-saving" policy thus is necessary to offset this bias. Another view is that people in the United States are just too shortsighted in their saving decisions and must be encouraged to save more.

What policies can be used to increase saving? If saving were highly responsive to the real interest rate, tax breaks that increase the real return that savers receive would be effective. For example, some economists advocate taxing households on how much they consume rather than on how much they earn, thereby exempting from taxation the income that is saved. But, as we noted in Chapter 4, although saving appears to increase when the expected real return available to savers rises, most studies find this response to be small.

An alternative and perhaps more direct way to increase the national saving rate is by increasing the amount that the government saves; in other words, the government should try to reduce its deficit or increase its surplus. Our analysis of the twin deficits debate (Chapter 5) indicated that reducing the deficit by reducing government purchases will lead to more national saving. Many economists also argue that raising taxes to reduce the deficit or increase the surplus will also increase national saving by leading people to consume less. However, believers in Ricardian equivalence contend that tax increases without changes in current or planned government purchases won't affect consumption or national saving.

Policies to Raise the Rate of Productivity Growth

Of the factors affecting long-run living standards, the rate of productivity growth may well be the most important in that—according to the Solow model—only ongoing productivity growth can lead to continuing improvement in output and consumption per worker. Government policy can attempt to increase productivity in several ways.[26]

Improving Infrastructure. Some research findings suggest a significant link between productivity and the quality of a nation's infrastructure—its highways, bridges, utilities, dams, airports, and other publicly owned capital.[27] The construction of the interstate highway system in the United States, for example, significantly reduced the cost of transporting goods and stimulated tourism and other industries. In the past decade the rate of U.S. government investment in infrastructure has fallen, leading to a decline in the quality and quantity of public capital.[28] Reversing this trend, some economists argue, might help achieve higher productivity. However, not everyone agrees that more infrastructure investment is needed. For example, some critics have pointed out that the links between productivity growth and infrastructure aren't clear. If rich countries are more likely to build roads and hospitals, perhaps higher productivity growth leads to more infrastructure, rather than vice versa. Others worry that infrastructure investments by the government may involve political considerations (for example, favoring the districts of powerful members of Congress) more than promoting economic efficiency.

Building Human Capital. Recent research findings point to a strong connection between productivity growth and human capital. The government affects human capital development through educational policies, worker training or relocation programs, health programs, and in other ways. Specific programs should be examined carefully to see whether benefits exceed costs, but a case may be made for greater commitment to human capital formation as a way to boost productivity growth.

---

[26]According to endogenous growth theory, an increase in the saving rate will increase the rate of productivity growth and hence increase the growth rates of output and consumption per worker. Thus, in addition to the policies discussed here, government may attempt to increase productivity growth by trying to increase the saving rate.

[27]See, for example, John G. Fernald, "Roads to Prosperity: Assessing the Link Between Public Capital and Productivity," *American Economic Review* 89 (June 1999), pp. 619–638.

[28]For data and discussion, see "Trends in Public Spending on Transportation and Water Infrastructure, 1956 to 2014," Congressional Budget Office, March 2015, available at *www.cbo.gov/sites/default/files/cbofiles/attachments/49910-Infrastructure.pdf*.

One crucial form of human capital, which we haven't yet mentioned, is entrepreneurial skill. People with the ability to build a successful new business or to bring a new product to market play a key role in economic growth. Productivity growth may increase if the government were to remove unnecessary barriers to entrepreneurial activity (such as excessive red tape) and give people with entrepreneurial skills greater incentives to use those skills productively.[29]

Encouraging Research and Development. The government also may be able to stimulate productivity growth by affecting rates of scientific and technical progress. The U.S. government directly supports much basic scientific research (through the National Science Foundation, for example). The rationale for such support comes from the fact that it is often difficult for inventors to profit from their inventions, even when such inventions greatly benefit society.[30] So, in the absence of government support, the private sector will engage in less research and development than is socially optimal. Examples of government support for research and development that have proved to be beneficial for society include hybrid seed corn, genetic engineering, the lithium-ion battery, and research on cancer.

The government can support research and development through a variety of mechanisms: funding government research facilities, providing grants to researchers, engaging private-sector contractors for particular projects, or giving tax incentives. It is important to keep in mind that government-supported research and development is a long-term investment that aims to improve the standard of living many years in the future, rather than an investment that will have a quick payoff. For example, the basics of the Internet came from research in the 1970s and 1980s, even though the Internet didn't get widespread use until the 1990s. Finally, the government can support research and development through education policies; for example, the government could encourage students to become scientists and engineers.

Application

Trends in Income Distribution in South Africa

The aim of this chapter is to shed light on how and why some countries grow faster than others and what kind of policies, if any, can be used to increase the national income for countries performing below expectations. While GDP per capita is used as a measure for economic growth and provides useful information concerning the amount of goods and services produced in an economy over time, it does not provide sufficient data about the incomes of citizens. To understand how national income is divided among a country's residents, economists use

(continued)

[29]For a discussion of entrepreneurial activity and how it affects productivity, see Douglas Holtz-Eakin and Chihwa Kao, "Entrepreneurship and Economic Growth: The Proof Is in the Productivity," Center for Policy Research working paper 50, Syracuse University, February 2003.

[30]The discussion in this section is based on a speech by Fed Chairman Ben S. Bernanke, "New Building Blocks for Jobs and Economic Growth," speech at Georgetown University, May 16, 2011, available online at *www.federalreserve.gov/newsevents/speech/bernanke20110516a.htm*.

FIGURE 6.11

Figure 6.11 Lorenz curves showing nominal income for 2015 and 2017

Lorenz curves for 2015 and 2017 illustrate the distribution of income in those years, plotting the cumulative share of the population ranked from those with lowest income to those with the highest and their share of total income. The curve is more bowed out in 2017 than in 2015, indicating a less-equal income distribution in 2017.

Source: DataFirst, National Income Dynamics Study 2015 and 2017, *https://www.datafirst.uct.ac.za/dataportal/index.php/catalog/?page=1&sk=nids&sort_by=title&sort_order=asc&ps=15;* Southern Africa Labour and Development Research Unit, "National Income Dynamics Study 2017," Version 1.0.0, Pretoria: Department of Planning, Monitoring, and Evaluation, Cape Town: Southern Africa Labour and Development Research Unit, 2018, Cape Town: DataFirst, 2018, DOI: *https://doi.org/10.25828/fw3h-v708.*

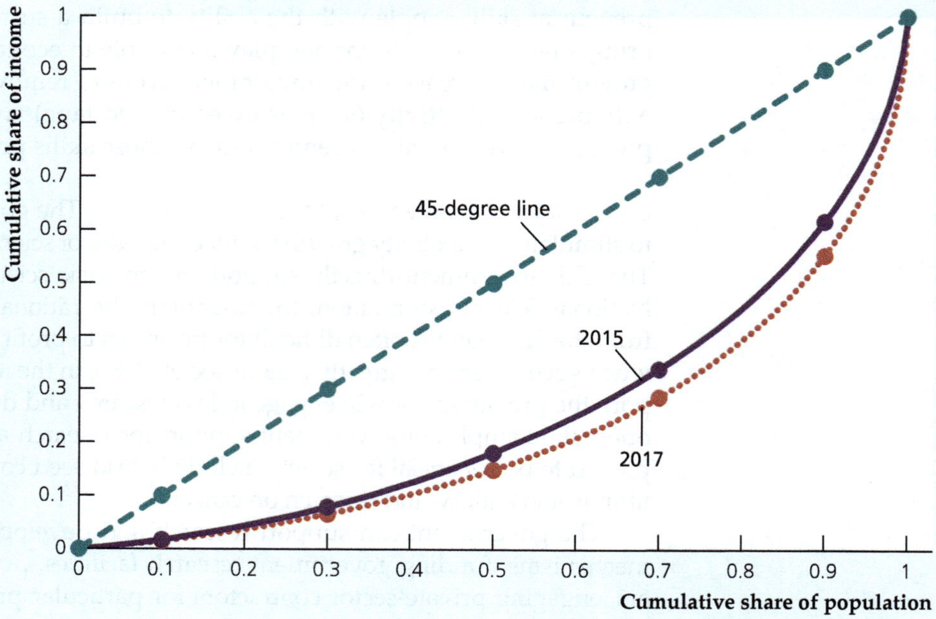

income distribution as a statistical measure. To illustrate this concept, let's assume that South Africa's income per head is R855,357 (the rand, R, is the official currency of South Africa). Although South Africa's income seems higher than that of other countries in the continent, it does not mean that the income is distributed fairly among its residents. What does the income distribution look like in South Africa, and how has it changed over time?

The *Lorenz curve* is a graphical representation of income distribution as displayed in Figure 6.11. It shows trends in percentiles of the population on the horizontal axis and the income cumulative share of the population on the vertical axis for the period 2008 to 2017. What stands out in Figure 6.11 is that, although income inequality was already high in 2008, it increased further in 2017.

Perhaps the most frequently used measure of income distribution by economists is the Gini coefficient, also called the Gini index or Gini ratio. The Gini coefficient can be calculated from the Lorenz curve in Figure 6.11 through the area between the Lorenz curve and the line of equality (or the 45-degree line), which is then expressed as a percentage of the area under the line of equality; that is, the 45-degree line. If income was equally distributed, then the Lorenz curve and the 45-degree line would be the same; that is, the Gini coefficient would be zero.

The Gini coefficient ranges from 0 to 1, with 0 signifying perfect equality and 1 demonstrating perfect inequality. For example, if all individuals in South Africa were to earn the same income, then the Gini coefficient would be 0. Similarly, if one individual in South Africa earned all the income while everyone else earned nothing, then the Gini coefficient would be 1.

A natural question to ask is, how does inequality manifest itself and affect the economy? In his keynote address, Vimal Ranchhod, an associate professor at the

FIGURE 6.12

Evolution of the Gini coefficient from 1980 to 2017 for South Africa

We observe that, by and large, the Gini coefficient increased between 1980 and 2008–2009 but has diminished since.

Source: Frederick Solt, "The Standardized World Income Inequality Database, Versions 8–9," 2019, *https://doi.org/10.7910/DVN/LM4OWF*

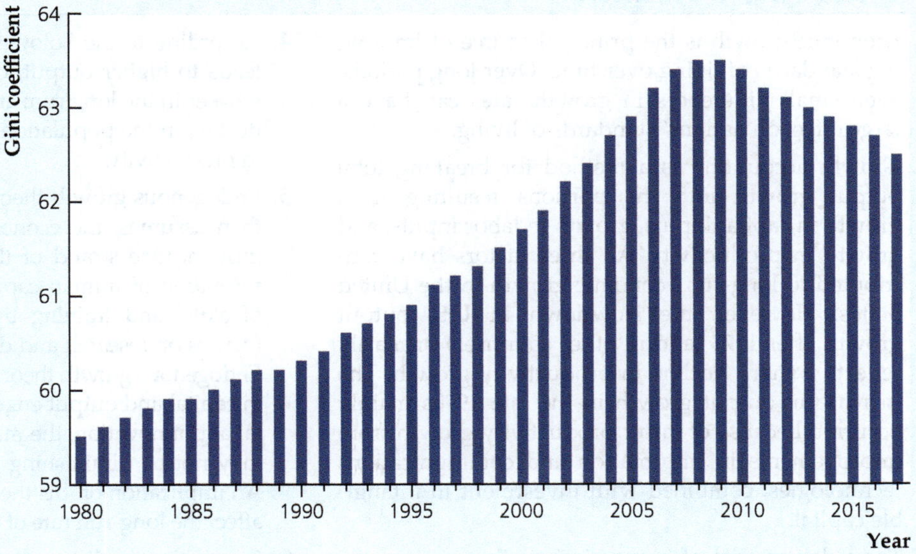

Southern Africa Labour and Development Research Unit (SALDRU), highlighted various ways through which inequality manifests itself, such as rural–urban, gender, educational, and racial inequalities. By way of example, he noted that educational inequalities mean that some children will never get an opportunity to attain the same skills as others. Consequently, only a portion of the youth entering the labor market will have the same high levels of secondary and tertiary education.

CHAPTER SUMMARY

1. Economic growth is the principal source of improving standards of living over time. Over long periods, even small differences in growth rates can have a large effect on nations' standards of living.
2. Growth accounting is a method for breaking total output growth into the portions resulting from growth in capital inputs, growth in labor inputs, and growth in productivity. All three factors have contributed to long-run economic growth in the United States. However, the slowdown in U.S. output growth after 1973 (and in other countries) primarily reflects a sharp decline in productivity growth. The increase in output growth in the late 1990s mainly occurred because of faster productivity growth from improvements in information and communications technologies, combined with investment in intangible capital.
3. The Solow model of economic growth examines the interaction of growth, saving, and capital accumulation over time. It predicts that in the absence of productivity growth the economy will reach a steady state in which output, consumption, and capital per worker are constant.
4. According to the Solow model, each of the following leads to higher output, consumption, and capital per worker in the long run: an increase in the saving rate, a decline in the population growth rate, and an increase in productivity.
5. Endogenous growth theory attempts to explain, rather than assumes, the economywide rate of productivity growth. One strand of this approach emphasizes the formation of human capital, including the acquisition of skills and training by workers. A second strand focuses on research and development activity by firms. Endogenous growth theorists argue that, because growth in capital and output engenders increased human capital and innovation, the marginal productivity of capital may not be diminishing for the economy as a whole. An implication of this theory is that the saving rate can affect the long-run rate of economic growth.
6. Government policies to raise long-run living standards include raising the rate of saving and increasing productivity. Possible ways of increasing productivity involve investing in public capital (infrastructure), encouraging the formation of human capital, and increasing research and development.

KEY TERMS

capital–labor ratio, p. 251
endogenous growth theory, p. 265
endogenous variable, p. 262
equilibrium condition, p. 262
exogenous variable, p. 262
Golden Rule capital–labor ratio, p. 253
growth accounting, p. 242
growth accounting equation, p. 241
human capital, p. 266
steady state, p. 252

KEY EQUATIONS

$$\frac{\Delta Y}{Y} = \frac{\Delta A}{A} + a_K\frac{\Delta K}{K} + a_N\frac{\Delta N}{N} \quad \textbf{(6.2)}$$

The growth accounting equation states that output growth, $\Delta Y/Y$, depends on the growth rate of productivity, $\Delta A/A$, the growth rate of capital, $\Delta K/K$, and the growth rate of labor, $\Delta N/N$. The elasticity of output with respect to capital, a_K, gives the percentage increase in output that results when capital increases by 1%. The elasticity of output with respect to labor, a_N, gives the percentage increase in output that results when labor increases by 1%.

$$y_t = f(k_t) \quad \textbf{(6.5)}$$

For any year, t, the per-worker production function relates output per worker, y_t, to capital per worker (also called the capital–labor ratio), k_t.

$$c = f(k) - (n + d)k \quad \textbf{(6.8)}$$

Steady-state consumption per worker, c, equals steady-state output per worker, $f(k)$, minus steady-state investment per worker, $(n + d)k$. Steady-state output per worker is determined by per-worker production, $f(k)$, where k is the steady-state capital–labor ratio. Steady-state investment per worker has two parts: equipping new workers with the per-worker capital stock, nk, and replacing worn-out or depreciated capital, dk.

$$sf(k) = (n + d)k \quad \textbf{(6.11)}$$

The steady state is determined by the condition that saving per worker, $sf(k)$, equals steady-state investment per worker, $(n + d)k$. Saving per worker equals the saving rate s times output per worker, $f(k)$.

$$Y = AK \quad \textbf{(6.12)}$$

Endogenous growth theory replaces the assumption of diminishing marginal productivity of capital with the assumption that the marginal productivity of capital is independent of the level of the capital stock. In the production function relating aggregate output Y to the aggregate capital stock K in Eq. (6.12), the marginal product of capital is constant and equal to the parameter A.

$$\frac{\Delta Y}{Y} = sA - d \quad \textbf{(6.15)}$$

In an endogenous growth model, the growth rate of output, $\frac{\Delta Y}{Y}$, is determined endogenously by the saving rate, s. An increase in the saving rate increases the growth rate of output.

REVIEW QUESTIONS

1. According to the growth accounting approach, what are the three sources of economic growth? From what basic economic relationship is the growth accounting approach derived?
2. Of the three sources of growth identified by growth accounting, which one is primarily responsible for the slowdown in U.S. economic growth after 1973? What explanations have been given for the decline in this source of growth?
3. How did technology increase U.S. economic growth in the 1990s?
4. Explain what is meant by a steady state. In the Solow model, which variables are constant in a steady state?
5. What types of government policies can increase long-run living standards?
6. Describe the main ideas of endogenous growth theory. What does it say about the role of government in economic growth?
7. What effect should each of the following have on long-run living standards, according to the Solow model?
   a. An increase in the saving rate.
   b. An increase in the population growth rate.
   c. A one-time improvement in productivity.
8. What two explanations of productivity growth does endogenous growth theory offer? How does the production function in an endogenous growth model differ from the production function in the Solow model?
9. What types of policies are available to a government that wants to promote economic growth? For each type of policy you identify, explain briefly how the policy is supposed to work and list its costs or disadvantages. How does endogenous growth theory possibly change our thinking about the effectiveness of various pro-growth policies, such as increasing the saving rate?

NUMERICAL PROBLEMS

1. Two economies, Hare and Tortoise, each start with a real GDP per person of $5000 in 1950. Real GDP per person grows 3% per year in Hare and 1% per year in Tortoise. In the year 2020, what will be real GDP per person in each economy? Make a guess first; then use a calculator to get the answer.
2. Over the past 20 years an economy's total output has grown from 1000 to 1300, its capital stock has risen from 2500 to 3250, and its labor force has increased from 500 to 575. All measurements are in real terms. Calculate the contributions to economic growth of growth in capital, labor, and productivity:
   a. assuming that $a_K = 0.3$ and $a_N = 0.7$.
   b. assuming that $a_K = 0.5$ and $a_N = 0.5$.
3. For a particular economy, the following capital input K and labor input N were reported in four different years:

Year	K	N
1	200	1000
2	250	1000
3	250	1250
4	300	1200

   The production function in this economy is

   $$Y = K^{0.3}N^{0.7},$$

   where Y is total output.

a. Find total output, the capital–labor ratio, and output per worker in each year. Compare year 1 with year 3 and year 2 with year 4. Can this production function be written in per-worker form? If so, write algebraically the per-worker form of the production function.

b. Repeat Part (*a*) but assume now that the production function is $Y = K^{0.3}N^{0.8}$.

4. Use the data from Table 6.1 to calculate annual growth rates of GDP per capita for each country listed over the period 1950–2018. [*Note:* The annual growth rate *z* will satisfy the equation $(1 + z)^{68} = \text{GDP}_{2018}/\text{GDP}_{1950}$. To solve this equation for *z* using a calculator, take logs of both sides of the equation.] You will find that Germany and Japan, two countries that suffered extensive damage in World War II, had the two highest growth rates after 1950. Give a reason, based on the analysis of the Solow model, for these countries' particularly fast growth during this period.

5. An economy has the per-worker production function

$$y_t = 3k_t^{0.5}$$

where y_t is output per worker and k_t is the capital–labor ratio. The depreciation rate is 0.1, and the population growth rate is 0.05. Saving is

$$S_t = 0.3Y_t,$$

where S_t is total national saving and Y_t is total output.

a. What are the steady-state values of the capital–labor ratio, output per worker, and consumption per worker?

The rest of the problem shows the effects of changes in the three fundamental determinants of long-run living standards.

b. Repeat Part (*a*) for a saving rate of 0.4 instead of 0.3.

c. Repeat Part (*a*) for a population growth rate of 0.08 (with a saving rate of 0.3).

d. Repeat Part (*a*) for a production function of

$$y_t = 4k_t^{0.5}.$$

Assume that the saving rate and population growth rate are at their original values.

6. Consider a closed economy in which the population grows at the rate of 1% per year. The per-worker production function is $y = 6\sqrt{k}$, where y is output per worker and k is capital per worker. The depreciation rate of capital is 14% per year.

a. Households consume 90% of income and save the remaining 10% of income. There is no government. What are the steady-state values of capital per worker, output per worker, consumption per worker, and investment per worker?

b. Suppose that the country wants to increase its steady-state value of output per worker. What steady-state value of the capital–labor ratio is needed to double the steady-state value of output per capita? What fraction of income would households have to save to achieve a steady-state level of output per worker that is twice as high as in Part (*a*)?

7. Both population and the work force grow at the rate of $n = 0.01$ per year in a closed economy. Consumption is $C = 0.5(1 - t)Y$, where t is the tax rate on income and Y is total output. The per-worker production function is $y = 8\sqrt{k}$, where y is output per worker and k is the capital–labor ratio. The depreciation rate of capital is $d = 0.09$ per year. Suppose for now that there are no government purchases and the tax rate on income is $t = 0$.

a. Find expressions for national saving per worker and the steady-state level of investment per worker as functions of the capital–labor ratio, k. In the steady state, what are the values of the capital–labor ratio, output per worker, consumption per worker, and investment per worker?

b. Suppose that the government purchases goods each year and pays for these purchases using taxes on income. The government runs a balanced budget in each period and the tax rate on income is $t = 0.5$. Repeat Part (*a*) and compare your results.

ANALYTICAL PROBLEMS

1. According to the Solow model, how would each of the following affect consumption per worker in the long run (that is, in the steady state)? Explain.

a. The destruction of a portion of the nation's capital stock in a war.

b. A permanent increase in the rate of immigration (which raises the overall population growth rate).

c. A permanent increase in energy prices.

d. A temporary rise in the saving rate.

e. A permanent increase in the fraction of the population in the labor force (the population growth rate is unchanged).

2. An economy is in a steady state with no productivity change. Because of an increase in acid rain, the rate of capital depreciation rises permanently.

a. According to the Solow model, what are the effects on steady-state capital per worker, output per worker, consumption per worker, and the long-run growth rate of the total capital stock?

b. In an endogenous growth model, what are the effects on the growth rates of output, capital, and consumption of an increase in the depreciation rate of capital?

3. This problem adds the government to the Solow model. Suppose that a government purchases goods in the amount of g per worker every year; with N_t workers in year t, total government purchases are gN_t. The government has a balanced budget so that its tax revenue in year t, T_t, equals total government purchases. Total national saving, S_t, is

$$S_t = s(Y_t - T_t),$$

where Y_t is total output and s is the saving rate.

a. Graphically show the steady state for the initial level of government purchases per worker.

b. Suppose that the government permanently increases its purchases per worker. What are the effects on the steady-state levels of capital per worker, output per worker, and consumption per worker? Does your result imply that the optimal level of government purchases is zero?

4. In a Solow-type economy, total national saving, S_t, is

$$S_t = sY_t - hK_t.$$

The extra term, $-hK_t$, reflects the idea that when wealth (as measured by the capital stock) is higher, saving is lower. (Wealthier people have less need to save for the future.)

Find the steady-state values of per-worker capital, output, and consumption. What is the effect on the steady state of an increase in h?

5. Two countries are identical in every way except that one has a much higher capital–labor ratio than the other. According to the Solow model, which country's total output will grow more quickly? Does your answer depend on whether one country or the other is in a steady state? In general terms, how will your answer be affected if the two countries are allowed to trade with each other?

6. Suppose that total capital and labor both increase by the same percentage amount, so that the amount of capital per worker, k, doesn't change. Writing the production function in per-worker terms, $y = f(k)$, requires that this increase in capital and labor must not change the amount of output produced per worker, y. Use the growth accounting equation to show that equal percentage increases in capital and labor will leave output per worker unaffected only if $a_K + a_N = 1$.

7. An economy has a per-capita production function $y = Ak^a h^{1-a}$, where A and a are fixed parameters, y is per-worker output, k is the capital–labor ratio, and h is human capital per worker, a measure of the skills and training of the average worker. The production function implies that, for a given capital–labor ratio, increases in average human capital raise output per worker.

The economy's saving rate is s, and all saving is used to create physical capital, which depreciates at rate d. Workers acquire skills on the job by working with capital; the more capital with which they have to work, the more skills they acquire. We capture this idea by assuming that human capital per worker is always proportional to the amount of physical capital per worker, or $h = Bk$, where B is a fixed parameter.

Find the long-run growth rates of physical capital, human capital, and output in this economy.

WORKING WITH MACROECONOMIC DATA

For data to use in these exercises, go to the Federal Reserve Bank of St. Louis FRED database at fred.stlouisfed.org.

1. This problem asks you to do your own growth accounting exercise. Using data since 1960, make a table of annual growth rates of real GDP, the capital stock (private fixed assets from the Fixed Assets section of the BEA website, *www.bea.gov*, Table 6.2), and civilian employment. Assuming $a_K = 0.3$ and $a_N = 0.7$, find the productivity growth rate for each year.

a. Graph the contributions to overall economic growth of capital growth, labor growth, and productivity growth for the period since 1960. Contrast the behavior of each of these variables in the post–1973 period to their behavior in the earlier period.

b. Compare the post–1973 behavior of productivity growth with the graph of the relative price of energy, shown in Fig. 3.11. To what extent do you think the productivity slowdown can be blamed on higher energy prices?

2. Graph the U.S. capital–labor ratio since 1960 (use private fixed assets from the Fixed Assets section of the BEA website, *www.bea.gov*, Table 6.2 as the measure of capital, and civilian employment as the measure of labor). Do you see evidence of convergence to a steady state during the postwar period? Now graph real output per worker and real consumption per worker for the same period. According to the Solow model, what are the two basic explanations for the upward trends in these two variables? Can output per worker and consumption per worker continue to grow even if the capital–labor ratio stops rising?

3. According to the Solow model, if countries differed primarily in terms of their capital–labor ratios, with rich countries having high capital–labor ratios and poor countries having low capital–labor ratios, then countries that have a lower real GDP per capita income should grow faster than countries with a higher real GDP per capita. (This prediction of the Solow model assumes that countries have similar saving rates, population growth rates, and production functions.) You can test this idea using the Penn World Tables at *www.rug.nl/ggdc/productivity/pwt/*. Pick a group of 10 countries and examine their initial levels of real GDP per capita in a year long ago, such as 1960. Then calculate the average growth rate of real GDP per capita since that initial year. Do your results suggest that countries that initially have lower real GDP per capita indeed grow faster than countries that initially have a higher real GDP per capita?

4. In FRED, get data on the levels of real GDP per capita for both the United States and China for the most recent year that such data are available for both countries. By what percentage does real GDP per capita in the United States exceed real GDP per capita in China? Next, calculate and report the average growth rate of real GDP per capita for the past 25 years for both countries. Which country is growing faster? If these growth rates for the past 25 years were to continue into the future, how many years will it be before China's real GDP per capita exceeds U.S. real GDP per capita?

7

The Asset Market, Money, and Prices

In Chapters 3 and 4 we discussed the labor market and the goods market, two of the three markets in our model of the macroeconomy. In this chapter we consider the third market, the asset market. By *asset market* we mean the entire set of markets in which people buy and sell real and financial assets, including, for example, gold, houses, stocks, and bonds.

A type of asset that has long been believed to have special macroeconomic significance is money. Money is the economist's term for assets that can be used in making payments, such as cash and checking accounts. One reason that money is important is that most prices are expressed in units of money, such as dollars, yen, and euros. Because prices are measured in money terms, understanding the role of money in the economy is basic to studying issues related to the price level, such as inflation and its causes. In addition, many economists believe that the amount of money in the economy affects real economic variables, such as output and employment. If it does, then it may be possible to use monetary policy to promote stable output growth and fight unemployment, as we discuss in Part 3.

Because money is such an important asset, it is the focus of our discussion of the asset market. In the first part of the chapter we explain what money is and why people choose to hold it. We show that a person's decision about how much money to hold (their money demand) is part of a broader decision about how to allocate wealth among the various assets that are available. We then bring together the demand for money and the supply of money (which is determined by the central bank) to analyze equilibrium in the asset market. This analysis demonstrates that the price level in an economy is closely related to the amount of money in the economy. Thus high rates of inflation—that is, rapid increases in prices—are likely when the money supply is growing rapidly.

Learning Objectives

7.1 Define money, discuss its functions, and describe how it is measured in the United States.

7.2 Discuss the factors that affect how people choose which assets they own.

7.3 Examine macroeconomic variables that affect the demand for money.

7.4 Discuss the fundamentals of asset market equilibrium.

7.5 Discuss the relationship between money growth and inflation.

7.1 What Is Money?

Define money, discuss its functions, and describe how it is measured in the United States.

In economics the meaning of the term *money* is different from its everyday meaning. People often say *money* when they mean *income* or *wealth,* as in "that job pays good money" or "their family has a lot of money." In economics, however, **money** refers specifically to assets that are widely used and accepted as payment. Historically, the forms of money have ranged from beads and shells to gold and silver—and even to cigarettes (see "In Touch with Data and Research: Money in a Prisoner-of-War Camp"). In modern economies the most familiar forms of money are coins and paper money, or **currency**. Another common form of money is checkable deposits, or bank accounts on which checks can be written for making payments.

In Touch with Data and Research

Money in a Prisoner-of-War Camp

Among the Allied soldiers liberated from German prisoner-of-war (POW) camps at the end of World War II was a young man named R. A. Radford. Radford had been trained in economics, and shortly after his return home he published an article titled "The Economic Organisation of a POW Camp."[1] This article, a minor classic in the economics literature, is a fascinating account of the daily lives of soldiers in several POW camps. It focuses particularly on the primitive "economies" that grew up spontaneously in the camps.

The scope for economic behavior in a POW camp might seem severely limited, and to a degree that's so. There was little production of goods within the camps, although there was some trade in services, such as laundry or tailoring services and even portraiture. However, prisoners were allowed to move around freely within the compound, and they actively traded goods obtained from the Red Cross, the Germans, and other sources. Among the commodities exchanged were tinned milk, jam, butter, biscuits, chocolate, sugar, clothing, and toilet articles. In one particular camp, which at various times had up to 50,000 prisoners of many nationalities, active trading centers were run entirely by the prisoners.

A key practical issue was how to organize the trading. At first, the camp economies used barter, but it proved to be slow and inefficient. Then the prisoners hit on the idea of using cigarettes as money. Soon prices of all goods were quoted in terms of cigarettes, and cigarettes were accepted as payment for any good or service. Even nonsmoking prisoners would happily accept cigarettes as payment because they knew that they could easily trade the cigarettes for other things they wanted. The use of cigarette money greatly simplified the problem of making trades and helped the camp economy function much more smoothly.

Why were cigarettes, rather than some other commodity, used as money by the POWs? Cigarettes satisfied a number of criteria for a good money: A cigarette is a fairly standardized commodity whose value was easy for both buyers and

[1] *Economica*, November 1945, pp. 189–201.

sellers to ascertain. An individual cigarette is low enough in value that making "change" wasn't a problem. Cigarettes are portable, are easily passed from hand to hand, and don't spoil quickly.

A drawback was that, as a commodity money (a form of money with an alternative use), cigarette money had a resource cost: Cigarettes that were being used as money could not simultaneously be smoked. In the same way, the traditional use of gold and silver as money was costly in that it diverted these metals from alternative uses.

The use of cigarettes as money isn't restricted to POW camps. Just before the collapse of communism in Eastern Europe, cigarette money reportedly was used in Romania and other countries instead of the nearly worthless official money.

The Functions of Money

Since the earliest times almost all societies—from the most primitive to the most sophisticated and with many types of political and economic systems—have used money. Money has three useful functions in an economy: It is a medium of exchange, a unit of account, and a store of value.

Medium of Exchange. In an economy with no money, trading takes the form of barter, or the direct exchange of certain goods for other goods. Even today some people belong to barter clubs, in which members swap goods and services among themselves. Generally, though, barter is an inefficient way to trade because finding someone who has the item you want and is willing to exchange that item for something you have is both difficult and time-consuming. In a barter system, if one of the authors of this book wanted a restaurant meal, he would first have to find a restaurateur willing to trade his blue-plate special for an economics lecture—which might not be easy to do.

Money makes searching for the perfect trading partner unnecessary. In an economy that uses money, the economics professor doesn't have to find a restaurant owner who is hungry for knowledge. Instead, he can first exchange his economics lecture to students for money and then use the money to buy a meal. In functioning as a **medium of exchange**, or a device for making transactions, money permits people to trade at less cost in time and effort. Having a medium of exchange also raises productivity by allowing people to specialize in economic activities at which they are most skilled. In an economy with money, specialized producers have no problem trading their goods or services for the things they need. In a barter economy, though, the difficulty of trading would leave people no choice but to produce most of their own food, clothing, and shelter. Thus in a barter economy the opportunity to specialize is greatly reduced.

Unit of Account. As a **unit of account**, money is the basic unit for measuring economic value. In the United States, for example, virtually all prices, wages, asset values, and debts are expressed in dollars. Having a single, uniform measure of value is convenient. For example, pricing all goods in the United States in dollars—instead of some goods being priced in yen, some in gold, and some in Microsoft shares—simplifies comparison among different goods.

The medium-of-exchange and unit-of-account functions of money are closely linked. Because goods and services are most often exchanged for money (the medium-of-exchange function), expressing economic values in money terms (the unit-of-account function) is natural. Otherwise, we could just as well express economic values in terms of, say, bushels of wheat. However, the medium of exchange and the unit of account aren't always the same. In countries with high and erratic inflation, for example, fluctuating currency value makes money a poor unit of account because prices must be changed frequently. In such cases, economic values are commonly stated in terms of a more stable unit of account, such as dollars or ounces of gold, even though transactions may continue to be carried out in the local currency.

Store of Value. As a **store of value**, money is a way of holding wealth. An extreme example is a miser who keeps his life's savings in cash under the mattress. But even someone who spends his cash wages 15 minutes after receiving them is using money as a store of value for that short period.

In most cases, only money functions as a medium of exchange or a unit of account, but any asset—for example, stocks, bonds, or real estate—can be a store of value. As these other types of assets normally pay the holder a higher return than money does, why do people use money as a store of value? The answer is that money's usefulness as a medium of exchange makes it worthwhile to hold, even though its return is relatively low.

Measuring Money: The Monetary Aggregates. Money is defined as those assets that are widely used and accepted in payment. This definition suggests a hard-and-fast line between assets that should be counted as money and those that should not. Actually, the distinction between monetary assets and nonmonetary assets isn't so clear.

Consider, for example, money-market mutual funds (MMMFs), which first became popular in the late 1970s. MMMFs are organizations that sell shares to the public and invest the proceeds in short-term government and corporate debt. MMMFs strive to earn a high return for their shareholders. At the same time, they typically allow their shareholders to write a small number of checks each month against their accounts, perhaps for a fee. Thus, although MMMF shares can be used to make payments, they are not as convenient as cash or regular checking accounts for this purpose. Should MMMF shares be counted as money? There is no definitive answer to this question.

Because assets differ in their "moneyness," no single measure of the amount of money in the economy—or the money stock, as it is often called—is likely to be completely satisfactory. For this reason, in most countries economists and policymakers use several different measures of the money stock. These official measures are known as **monetary aggregates**. The various monetary aggregates differ in how narrowly they define the concept of money. In the United States the two monetary aggregates are called M1 and M2. Summary definitions and data for these two aggregates are given in Table 7.1. Information about where to find data on the monetary aggregates is presented in "In Touch with Data and Research: The Monetary Aggregates."

TABLE 7.1

U.S. Monetary Aggregates (December 2021)

	Amounts in billions of dollars
M1	**20,600.1**
Currency	2129.1
Liquid deposits	18,471.1
M2	**21,724.0**
Components of M1	20,600.1
Small-denomination time deposits	93.2
Retail money-market funds	1030.7

Note: Numbers may not add to totals shown owing to rounding.
Source: Federal Reserve Statistical Release H.6, March 22, 2022.
Data are not seasonally adjusted.

The M1 Monetary Aggregate. The most narrowly defined official money measure, **M1**, consists primarily of currency and balances held in checking accounts and savings accounts. More precisely, M1 is made up of currency (including U.S. currency circulating outside the United States; see "In Touch with Data and Research: Where Have All the Dollars Gone?") and liquid deposits, which include transaction accounts that allow depositors to write checks and savings accounts. Note that savings accounts were added to liquid deposits in M1 in early 2021 after the Fed stopped distinguishing between savings deposits and transaction deposits. As a result of no longer being able to make that distinction, the Fed moved savings deposits into the M1 measure, causing it to increase substantially.

In Touch with Data and Research

The Monetary Aggregates

The official monetary aggregates—M1 and M2—are compiled and reported by the Board of Governors of the Federal Reserve System (Fed) in Washington. Only data for M1 were reported until 1971, when the Fed introduced M2 and M3. Since then the definitions of the monetary aggregates have changed several times, reflecting the evolution of the financial system. In 2006, the Fed stopped reporting M3. In early 2021, the Fed moved savings deposits from M2 into M1, retroactive to May 2020, which resulted in a break in the M1 series.

The Fed reports estimates of the aggregates both weekly and monthly, using data supplied by banks, the Treasury, money-market mutual funds, foreign central banks, and other sources. Each Thursday at 4:30 p.m. Eastern time the Fed announces figures for M1 and M2 for the week ending the Monday of the previous week. Historical data are available in the *Federal Reserve Bulletin,* the Federal Reserve Bank of St. Louis FRED database at *fred.stlouisfed.org*, the *Economic Report of the President,* and on the Federal Reserve System's website at *www.federalreserve.gov/releases/h6/current/default.htm.* Monetary data are revised frequently, reflecting the receipt of new data by the Federal Reserve or changes in the definitions of monetary aggregates.

Publication of the monetary aggregates helps keep the public and Congress informed about how the Fed is changing the nation's money supply.

In Touch with Data and Research

Where Have All the Dollars Gone?

In December 2021 the stock of U.S. currency was $2225.3 billion, or almost $6700 for every man, woman, and child in the United States. This figure is surprisingly high. After all, how many people actually have $6700 of cash on hand at any given time, and how many families of four hold $26,800 in cash?

Businesses, especially retailers, hold currency for making transactions, but the amount of currency held by U.S. businesses appears to account for a small fraction of the "missing" dollars. Currency also is extensively used in the underground economy, either to conduct illegal transactions (such as trade in illegal drugs) or to hide legal transactions from tax collectors. Studies have found that a substantial portion of the "missing" U.S. currency—amounting to 50% or more of currency outstanding—is held abroad.[2]

Why would people in other countries want to hold U.S. dollars? Even though the dollar may not serve as the medium of exchange or as a unit of account in a country, it can be a relatively attractive store of value, especially in countries that are economically or politically unstable. For example, in countries with high rates of inflation, the local currency is a particularly poor store of value because the real value (purchasing power) of the local currency decreases at the rate of inflation. In high-inflation countries the dollar, which has had a relatively stable purchasing power, may be much more attractive than local currency as a means of holding wealth. Political instability in a country might also induce residents to demand U.S. dollars because, if political upheaval forces people to flee the country, carrying dollars out may be the easiest way for them to take some of their wealth with them. About half the U.S. currency sent overseas between 1988 and 1995 went to Europe, much of it to Russia and other nations of Eastern Europe, which experienced substantial economic and political instability during that time (see the Application "Money Growth and Inflation in European Countries in Transition").

Because much currency is held abroad, events abroad that change the foreign demand for U.S. dollars can cause substantial changes in measured U.S. monetary aggregates. Since 1947, many of the months with the fastest growth in U.S. currency holdings were months in which a foreign crisis occurred. For example, U.S. currency growth was rapid in the months after Iraq invaded Kuwait in 1990. And several of the months with the fastest growth occurred in late 2008 and early 2009 during the worldwide financial crisis, where many foreigners traded their own currency for the safety of U.S. dollars.[3] These large increases in U.S. currency outstanding were driven by foreign concerns about political, military, and financial instability rather than by domestic factors determining money demand in the U.S. economy.

[2]See Ruth Judson, "Crisis and Calm: Demand for U.S. Currency at Home and Abroad from the Fall of the Berlin Wall to 2011," Federal Reserve Board of Governors, International Finance Discussion Paper 1058, November 2012.

[3]The month with the highest (seasonally adjusted) currency growth rate was December 1999, when businesses and individuals sharply increased their demand for cash in preparation for the century rollover, known at the time as Y2K.

Although foreign holdings of U.S. dollars reduce the reliability of measured monetary aggregates as indicators of conditions in the U.S. economy, the United States gets an important benefit from the foreign holdings of its currency. U.S. currency is a liability of the Federal Reserve System and thus represents a loan to the Federal Reserve System (and ultimately to the U.S. government, to which most Federal Reserve profits go). However, currency pays no interest, so this loan being provided by foreign holders of U.S. currency to the United States is interest-free! The interest savings associated with this interest-free loan to the U.S. government amount to many billions of dollars each year.

The M2 Monetary Aggregate. Everything in M1 plus other assets that are somewhat less "moneylike" compose **M2**. The main additional assets in M2 include small-denomination (under $100,000) time deposits and noninstitutional holdings of money-market mutual funds (MMMFs). Both of these accounts have limits on the number of checks or other transfers that can be written each month. Time deposits are interest-bearing deposits with a fixed term (early withdrawal usually involves a penalty). As mentioned, MMMFs invest their shareholders' funds in short-term securities, pay market-based interest rates, and allow holders to write a limited number of checks.

The Money Supply. The **money supply** is the amount of money available in an economy.[4] In modern economies the money supply is determined by the central bank—in the United States, the Federal Reserve System.

A detailed explanation of how central banks control the money supply raises issues that would take us too far afield at this point, so we defer that discussion to Chapter 14. To grasp the basic idea, however, let's consider the simple hypothetical situation in which the only form of money is currency. In this case, to increase the money supply the central bank needs only to increase the amount of currency in circulation. How can it do so?

One way—which is close to what happens in practice—is for the central bank to use newly minted currency to buy financial assets, such as government bonds, from the public. In making this swap, the public increases its holdings of money, and the amount of money in circulation rises. When the central bank uses money to purchase government bonds from the public, thus raising the money supply, it is said to have conducted an *open-market purchase*.

To reduce the money supply, the central bank can make this trade in reverse, selling government bonds that it holds to the public in exchange for currency. After the central bank removes this currency from circulation, the money supply

[4]The terms *money supply* and *money stock* are used interchangeably.

is lower. When the central bank sells government bonds to the public to reduce the money supply, the transaction is an *open-market sale*. Open-market purchases and sales together are called **open-market operations**.

In addition to buying government bonds from the public, the central bank can also increase the money supply by buying newly issued government bonds directly from the government itself. For example, if a country's treasury needs \$1 billion to pay for some new fighter planes, it might give an IOU for \$1 billion (government bonds) to the central bank in exchange for \$1 billion in newly printed currency. The treasury then gives the \$1 billion of currency to the manufacturer of the fighter planes. After the treasury has distributed this currency, the amount of money in circulation—the money supply—will be higher by \$1 billion. Effectively, this second way of increasing the money supply amounts to the government financing its expenditures by printing money.[5] This practice is most common in poor countries or in countries wracked by war or natural disaster, in which government spending often greatly exceeds the amount that can be raised through taxes.[6]

For the rest of this chapter, we assume that the economy has a money supply of M dollars, which is determined by the central bank. The term M may represent M1, M2, or some other measure of money. For the purpose of developing the theoretical model, which measure of money M refers to doesn't matter.

7.2 Portfolio Allocation and the Demand for Assets

Discuss the factors that affect how people choose which assets they own.

Our next goal is to understand how people determine the amount of money they choose to hold. We begin by considering the broader question of how people allocate their wealth among the many different assets that are available, of which money is only one example.

A consumer, a business, a pension fund, a university, or any other holder of wealth must decide how to distribute that wealth among many types of assets. The set of assets that a holder of wealth chooses to own is called a *portfolio*. The decision about which assets and how much of each asset to hold is called the **portfolio allocation decision**.

The portfolio allocation decision can be complex. Many people make their living by giving financial advice to holders of wealth, and a major branch of economics, called financial economics, is devoted largely to the study of the portfolio allocation decision. But, fundamentally, only four characteristics of assets matter for the portfolio allocation decision: expected return, risk, liquidity, and time to maturity.

Expected Return

The rate of return to an asset is the rate of increase in its value per unit of time. For example, the return on a bank account is the interest rate on the account. The return on a share of stock is the dividend paid by the stock plus any increase in

[5]In Chapter 2 we said that the portion of government outlays not covered by taxes had to be borrowed from the private sector. Is this still true when the government has the option of paying for its outlays by printing money? Yes; for national income accounting purposes, the Federal Reserve is treated as part of the private sector. So when the Treasury sells government bonds to the Federal Reserve in exchange for currency, it is still technically borrowing from the private sector.

[6]The financing of government spending through money creation is discussed further in Chapter 15.

the stock's price. Clearly, a high return is a desirable feature for an asset to have: All else being equal, the higher the return a wealth holder's portfolio provides, the more consumption she can enjoy in the future for any given amount of saving done today.

Of course, the return on an asset is not always known in advance. Stock prices may go up or down, for example. Thus holders of wealth must base their portfolio allocation decisions on **expected returns**, or their best guesses about returns on assets. Everything else being equal, the higher an asset's expected return (after subtracting taxes and fees such as brokers' commissions), the more desirable the asset is and the more of it holders of wealth will want to own.[7]

Risk

The uncertainty about the return an asset will earn relates to the second important characteristic of assets—riskiness. An asset or a portfolio of assets has high **risk** if there is a significant chance that the actual return received will be very different from the expected return. An example of a risky asset is a share in a start-up Internet company that will be worthless if the company fails but will grow in value by a factor of 10 if the company succeeds. Because most people don't like risk, they hold risky assets only if the expected return is higher than that on relatively safe assets, such as government bonds. The **risk premium** is the amount by which the expected return on a risky asset exceeds the return on an otherwise comparable safe asset.

Liquidity

Besides risk and return a third characteristic, liquidity, affects the desirability of assets. The **liquidity** of an asset is the ease and quickness with which it can be exchanged for goods, services, or other assets. Because it is accepted directly in payment, money is a highly liquid asset. An example of an illiquid asset is your automobile: Time and effort are required to exchange a used car for other goods and services; you must find someone interested in buying the car and arrange legal transfer of ownership. Between liquid money and illiquid autos are many assets, such as stocks and bonds, of intermediate liquidity. A share of stock, for example, can't be used directly to pay for groceries as cash can, but stock can be transformed into cash with a short delay and at the cost of a broker's fee.

In addition to making transactions easier and cheaper, liquidity provides flexibility to the holder of wealth. A liquid asset can easily be disposed of if there is an emergency need for funds or if an unexpectedly good financial investment opportunity arises. Thus, everything else being equal, the more liquid an asset is, the more attractive it will be to holders of wealth.

Time to Maturity

Financial securities have a fourth and final key characteristic, which is their time to maturity. **Time to maturity** is the amount of time until a financial security matures and the investor is repaid his or her principal. Considering time to

[7]For the purpose of comparing expected returns among assets, returns may be expressed in either real or nominal terms. For any expected rate of inflation, if asset A's nominal return is 1% higher than asset B's nominal return, asset A's expected real return (its nominal return minus expected inflation) will also be 1% higher than asset B's expected real return.

maturity is especially relevant for all types of bonds, as an investor can purchase bonds that will mature at any time—in one day, one week, one month, one year, or thirty years.

Let's consider Tim and Nathan, a couple that wants to buy bonds and keep their money invested for two years. They could choose one of two plans: Plan A is simply to buy a two-year bond today; Plan B calls for buying a one-year bond today and another one-year bond when that one matures one year from today. Ignoring, for the moment, any differences in the risk between Plan A and Plan B, the investors would choose the plan that they expect to give them the highest return over the two years. For example, if today's interest rate on the two-year bond is 7% per year, today's interest rate on a one-year bond is 5% per year, and if they expect the interest rate on a one-year bond to be 6% per year one year from now, then their return from Plan A (buying the two-year bond) is 7% per year and the return they expect from Plan B is 5.5% per year, which is the average of the 5% per year return on the one-year bond purchased today and the expected 6% per year return expected on the bond to be bought one year from today. So the investors are likely to choose Plan A; that is, they are likely to buy the two-year bond today.

The idea that investors compare the returns on bonds with differing times to maturity to see which is expected to give them the highest return underlies the **expectations theory of the term structure** of interest rates. "Term structure" refers to the fact that the theory explains why bonds that are similar in all respects except their terms to maturity have different rates of return. In equilibrium, according to the expectations theory, Plans A and B, which involve holding bonds with different terms to maturity over the same two-year period, should yield the same expected return; that is, the interest rate on a two-year bond should equal the average interest rate expected on two successive one-year bonds, so that an investor does not prefer one investment over another. More generally, the expected rate of return on an N-year bond should equal the average of the expected rates of return on one-year bonds during the current year and the $N-1$ succeeding years.

Although the expectations theory of the term structure of interest rates is a useful starting point, it cannot explain why, on average, we observe that the interest rates on long-term bonds generally exceed the interest rates on short-term bonds. (See the graph of the yield curve in Chapter 4, "In Touch with Data and Research: Interest Rates," which illustrates the term structure of interest rates.) When short-term interest rates are expected to be higher in the future than the current short-term rate, the expectations theory predicts that the long-term interest rate will exceed the short-term interest rate. However, when short-term interest rates are expected to be lower in the future than the current short-term interest rate, the expectations theory predicts that the long-term interest rate will be lower than the short-term interest rate. To see why long-term interest rates usually exceed short-term interest rates, we need to take account of the fact that longer-term bonds are riskier than shorter-term bonds because the prices of long-term bonds are more sensitive than the prices of short-term bonds are to changes in the interest rate. Because investors do not like risk, they must be compensated for holding longer-term bonds. The result is a **term premium**: an interest rate on long-term bonds that is somewhat higher than the expectations theory would suggest.

If we add the term premium to the expectations theory, we have a more complete theory of how interest rates vary with time to maturity. For example, suppose the interest rate on a one-year bond today is 5% per year, the interest rate on a one-year bond one year from now is expected to be 6% per year, and the term premium on a two-year bond is 0.75% per year. Then, in equilibrium, the interest rate on a two-year bond should equal the average interest rate on the one-year bonds, which equals $(5\% + 6\%)/2 = 5.5\%$, plus the term premium, 0.75%, or 6.25%.

Types of Assets and Their Characteristics

What types of assets do people hold, and how do the characteristics of those assets differ? Though there are many different assets, we will consider a few that are the most popular: money, bonds, stocks, houses, and consumer durable goods.

We have already seen in Section 7.1 that there are different types of money. All types of money usually have a low expected rate of return compared with other assets. Money usually does not have much risk, although there is always some risk that inflation will be higher than expected, so that the real return to holding money might turn out to be lower than expected. But money is very liquid compared with the other assets; indeed, its liquidity is generally the defining characteristic of what we call money. Because of its liquidity, money's time to maturity is generally very short. However, some assets included in M2, such as small time deposits, may have a longer time to maturity and are not very liquid.

Bonds are financial securities that are sometimes called *fixed-income securities* because they promise to pay bondholders specific amounts on specific dates. People often choose to own bonds issued by the U.S. government because these bonds have little risk of default. Bonds issued by corporations are similar, but there is always some chance that a corporation will go bankrupt and fail to pay the interest or repay the principal it owes to its bondholders. Thus bonds offer a higher expected return than money, but the return is riskier. Many bonds, especially those sold by the U.S. government, are very liquid because an investor can easily sell his or her bond quickly and with low transactions costs. However, some corporate bonds are not very liquid, especially in bad economic times, and it may be difficult to sell them without a high cost. Bonds are issued in a variety of times to maturity, generally ranging from 3 months to 30 years.

Stocks represent ownership in a company. Most stocks pay periodic dividends to the shareholders, but the dividend payments are not guaranteed. When the economy is weak and the company is not doing well, it may even stop paying dividends altogether for a time. Prices of stocks rise and fall every day, so the overall return to a shareholder consists of the dividends received plus any capital gain resulting from an increase in the value of the stock less any capital loss resulting from a decrease in the value of the stock. Because dividends and, especially, stock prices can change unpredictably, stocks are subject to a substantial amount of risk. Stocks in large companies are sold in very liquid markets, but when you buy or sell a stock there is a delay of several days for the transaction to clear and payment to be made. Most stocks do not have maturity dates, so the time to maturity is infinite.

Although most large companies are owned by shareholders who can readily buy and sell shares of stock in organized stock exchanges, such as the New York Stock Exchange, many small businesses are directly owned by one or a few people. These businesses, which are directly owned by their proprietors, are not incorporated and do not issue stock that can be traded on exchanges. Because there are no marketable shares of stock in these companies, it is difficult for the owners to quickly sell ownership in the companies, so this ownership is not very liquid. Indeed, because there are no marketable shares, it is difficult to measure accurately the value of the ownership stake in these companies. The return to the owners of the company takes the form of profits earned by the company plus the opportunity that they may someday sell the company.

For most homeowners, housing is their largest asset. The returns to owning a house come in two forms: (1) the benefits to the household in terms of shelter net of maintenance costs and property taxes and (2) the change in the value of the house (or the land it sits on) over time. For a time in the 2000s, many people seemed to think that there was no risk to investing in housing, and the United States and many other countries went through a tremendous boom in which millions of homes were built and it was very easy for home purchasers to get mortgage loans. But the risk turned out to be much higher than investors thought, and an unexpected downturn in housing prices led to a financial crisis, as we discuss in "In Touch with Data and Research: The Housing Crisis of 2007 to 2011." Compared with other assets, housing is very illiquid—it may take months or years for a household to sell its home, especially in a recession. However, the availability of home equity loans and home equity lines of credit permit households to quickly borrow money against a portion of the value of their house. There is, of course, no specified time to maturity on housing, as it is not a financial security.

Households also hold some of their assets in the form of consumer durable goods, such as automobiles and furniture. As in the case of housing, durable goods provide services (such as transportation) over a period of time but may also require maintenance expenditures and can depreciate over time. There is some risk to the value of consumer durables, and it may be difficult and costly to sell them, as the market for used consumer durables is not as well developed as the market for stocks and bonds. Thus, consumer durables are not very liquid, and, like housing, have no specified time to maturity.

Households must determine what mix of these various assets is ideal for them. Wealthier households generally purchase more financial assets (stocks and bonds) as a percentage of their total wealth than poorer households. Many households will also put aside funds for retirement by holding assets in pension funds, which hold stocks, bonds, and types of money (such as money-market mutual funds). Of course, their mix of different assets may change when market conditions change. For example, the housing crisis of 2007 to 2011 and the financial crisis of 2008 dramatically reduced the value of housing and stock holdings, as Table 7.2 indicates. The table shows the amounts of each type of asset that households (and nonprofit organizations) held at the end of 2006, at the end of the first quarter of 2009, and at the end of the fourth quarter of 2021. Note that the amount of currency and checkable deposits is far less than the amounts listed in Table 7.1 under M1 because much currency is held overseas (see "In Touch with Data and Research: Where Have All the Dollars Gone?") and because business firms have substantial holdings of currency and checkable deposits. The table also reports how much of each type of asset households held as a percentage of their total assets, so you can get a sense of how the relative amounts of each type of asset changed between 2006, 2009, and 2021.

TABLE 7.2

Household Assets, 2006, 2009, and 2021

	Amounts in trillions of dollars			Percentages of total assets		
	2006Q4	2009Q1	2021Q4	2006Q4	2009Q1	2021Q4
Real estate	26.5	22.7	42.4	32.3	30.7	25.1
Consumer durables	4.3	4.6	7.3	5.2	6.2	4.3
Currency and checkable deposits	0.3	0.5	4.1	0.4	0.6	2.4
Time, savings, and other deposits	6.8	8.2	14.0	8.3	11.1	8.3
Bonds	3.8	5.2	4.3	4.7	7.0	2.5
Stocks	13.9	7.8	45.1	16.9	10.5	26.7
Proprietors' investment in unincorporated businesses	8.3	6.8	15.1	10.1	9.2	9.0
Pension funds	15.5	15.4	31.8	19.0	20.8	18.8
Other assets	2.6	2.9	4.6	3.1	3.9	2.8
Total assets	81.9	73.9	168.6	100.0	100.0	100.0

Note: Numbers may not add to totals owing to rounding.
Source: Federal Reserve Financial Accounts of the United States, Statistical Release Z.1, March 10, 2022.

In Touch with Data and Research

The Housing Crisis of 2007 to 2011

U.S. households gained a tremendous amount of wealth in their houses throughout the late 1990s and early 2000s. The housing market was booming and the homeownership rate rose to a record level of 68.6 percent of households by 2007. But as people became more and more convinced that housing was a "can't miss" investment and housing prices spiraled ever upwards, mortgage lenders and homeowners began to make some serious mistakes, which would lead to a major financial crisis.

As housing prices moved higher and higher in the early 2000s, many people found themselves unable to afford to buy a home because the monthly mortgage payments would have been too high relative to their monthly incomes. Specifically, the lending standards of mortgage lenders required that borrowers have sufficient monthly income so that the monthly mortgage payment would not exceed a specified percentage of monthly income. But as housing prices increased rapidly, mortgage lenders began making loans to people who did not meet the lending standards. These people were known as *subprime borrowers*. The subprime mortgage market grew rapidly. To compensate the lenders for the additional risk and potential costs of lending to subprime borrowers, the interest rate on subprime mortgages was higher than the interest rate on conventional or prime mortgages. In many cases, subprime lenders even dispensed with the usual income verification of borrowers, thereby further subjecting themselves to the risk that the borrowers would not be able to repay. In addition, some loans had creative features that gave the appearance that the borrower could afford to make the monthly payments—at least for a while. For instance, most subprime loans were

(continued)

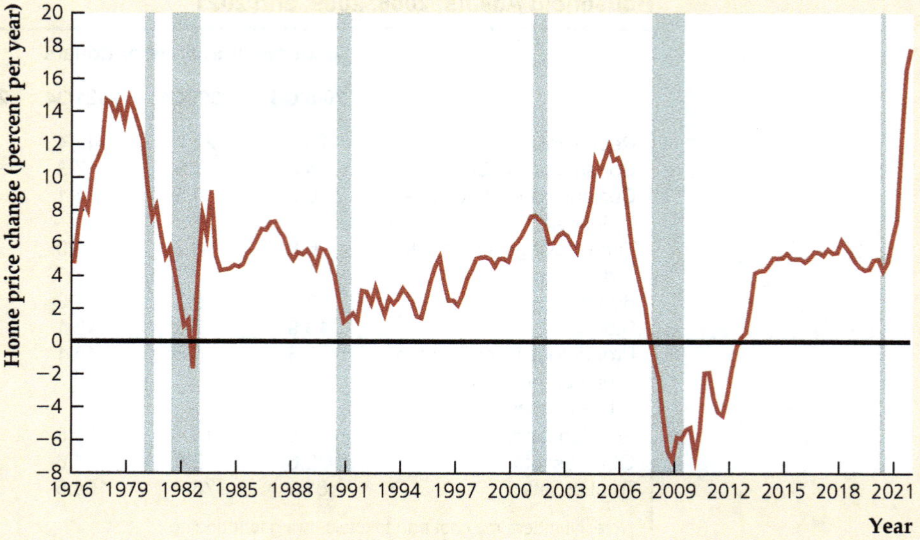

FIGURE 7.1

Increase in home prices from one year earlier, 1976Q1–2021Q4

The chart shows quarterly data on the percent increase in home prices from one year earlier, averaged across the United States, from the first quarter of 1976 to the fourth quarter of 2021. The appreciation in home prices averaged 4.7% per year over the entire period but exceeded 10% per year from early 2004 to early 2006. In 2007, the growth rate of home prices fell sharply, and in 2008, home prices began to decline, causing a crisis in mortgage markets. In 2021, following the pandemic recession, home prices rose almost 18%.

Source: Federal Housing Finance Agency, downloaded from Federal Reserve Bank of St. Louis FRED database, *fred.stlouisfed.org/series/USSTHPI.*

adjustable-rate loans with a low initial interest rate that would increase after two or three years in a process known as *mortgage reset.*

Why were lenders willing to offer these risky loans to subprime borrowers, and why were borrowers willing to take on these risky obligations? To a large degree, the answer is that they expected house prices to continue to rise rapidly for the foreseeable future. As long as house prices kept rising substantially, a borrower who might otherwise have trouble making mortgage payments in the future could either sell the house for a profit and pay off the mortgage or could borrow against the house's equity value, which would be higher as house prices increased further. So, both borrowers and lenders thought they were insulated from risk.

The problem with subprime mortgages is that the borrower and lender are insulated from risk only as long as house prices continue to rise substantially. In 2005, as mortgage interest rates across the country began to rise, the rate of increase of house prices began to slow. In 2006, defaults on subprime mortgages began to increase, as borrowers who had counted on rapidly rising house prices to bail them out found that their houses were not worth as much as they expected. In addition, as mortgage resets began to set in at higher interest rates, more and more borrowers could no longer make their monthly mortgage payments and began to default on their mortgages. And as defaults began to occur in increasing numbers, banks started to tighten their lending standards, so that by mid-2007, they were making few if any subprime mortgage loans. But that, in turn, reduced the demand for houses, thus causing the increase in housing prices to be even smaller. House prices even began to decline in some areas of the country in 2007 and by 2008 began to fall for the nation as a whole, as shown in Figure 7.1.

Falling house prices caused a variety of problems, at both the micro level and macro level. Thousands of households that had bought houses with subprime mortgages lost their homes through foreclosure when they could not make their mortgage payments. Homeowners often found themselves owning homes whose value had fallen far below the amount they owed on their mortgage loans (a situation that came to be known as "underwater"), giving them the incentive to stop making mortgage payments and allow their homes to be repossessed. Financial institutions lost billions of dollars on such deals because they owned the rights to the mortgage payments, which would no longer occur. Because house prices had fallen, whoever came to own the house, usually a bank, would usually have to sell it for much less than the outstanding mortgage balance.

But what surprised many people about the problems in the mortgage market is that the impact was felt even more broadly. It turns out that most banks had sold bundles of their mortgages in the form of mortgage-backed securities (MBSs), and investors in MBSs suffered large losses. Once the losses began to materialize, investors all at once tried to bail out of such investments, driving their prices to very low levels. This, in turn, led to the financial crisis of 2008, when investors began to realize that many financial institutions had lost hundreds of billions of dollars through mortgage-related securities. Panic ensued, stock prices fell dramatically, especially for financial firms, and the government and Federal Reserve bailed out many financial firms, as we describe in more detail in the Application "Macroeconomic Consequences of the Boom and Bust in Stock Prices," in Chapter 4.

At the end of 2006, households had over $80 trillion in assets, with $26.5 trillion worth of real estate and about $14 trillion in stocks, as well as about $15.5 trillion in pension fund assets. The steep declines in house prices and stock prices and the drop in proprietors' investment in unincorporated businesses reduced household wealth by about $8 trillion by the first quarter of 2009. The value of real estate holdings declined by 14%, and the value of stock holdings fell by about 44% from the end of 2006 to early 2009. Over this period of time, households reallocated their portfolios, putting more of their wealth in the form of money (time and savings deposits) and bonds (especially government bonds with little default risk). By mid-2016, the value of real estate had surpassed its 2006 level, and households' wealth in stocks and pension funds was substantially higher than it was before the housing crisis.

Asset Demands

Typically, there is a trade-off among the four characteristics that make an asset desirable: a high expected return, safety (low risk), liquidity, and short time to maturity. For example, a safe and liquid asset with a short time to maturity, such as a checking account, is likely to have a low expected return. The essence of the portfolio allocation decision is determining which assets, taken together, achieve the wealth holder's preferred combination of expected return, safety, liquidity, and time to maturity. In addition to the risk of each asset separately, the investor should also consider **diversification**, the idea that spreading out his or her investment in different assets with different characteristics can reduce overall risk because when one asset has a low return, another may have a high return.

The amount of each particular asset that a holder of wealth desires to include in their portfolio is their demand for that asset. Because all wealth must be held as some type of asset, the sum of a wealth holder's asset demands must equal their total wealth. For example, suppose that you have wealth of $10,000 and decide to hold $5000 in stock, $3000 in short-term bonds, $1000 in long-term bonds, and $1000 in cash. The sum of your four asset demands must equal your total wealth of $10,000.

7.3 The Demand for Money

Examine macroeconomic variables that affect the demand for money.

The **demand for money** is the quantity of monetary assets, such as cash and checking accounts, that people choose to hold in their portfolios. Choosing how much money to demand is thus a part of the broader portfolio allocation decision. In general, the demand for money—like the demand for any other asset—will depend on the expected return, risk, liquidity, and time to maturity of money and other assets.

In practice, two features of money are particularly important. First, money is the most liquid asset. This liquidity is the primary benefit of holding money.[8] Second, money pays a low return (indeed, currency pays a zero nominal return). The low return earned by money, relative to other assets, is the major cost of holding money. People's demand for money is determined by how they trade off their desire for liquidity against the cost of a lower return.

In this section we look at how some key macroeconomic variables affect the demand for money. Although we primarily consider the aggregate, or total, demand for money, the same economic arguments apply to individual money demands. This relationship is to be expected, as the aggregate demand for money is the sum of all individual money demands.

The macroeconomic variables that have the greatest effects on money demand are the price level, real income, and interest rates. Higher prices or incomes increase people's need for liquidity and thus raise the demand for money. Interest rates affect money demand through the expected return channel: The higher the interest rate on money, the more money people will demand; however, the higher the interest rate paid on alternative assets to money, the more people will want to switch from money to those alternative assets.

The Price Level

The higher the general level of prices, the more dollars people need to conduct transactions and thus the more dollars people will want to hold. For example, 65 years ago the price level in the United States was about one-tenth of its level today. Because less money was needed for transactions, the number of dollars that people held in the form of currency or checking accounts—their nominal demand for money—was probably much smaller than the amount of money you hold today. The general conclusion is that a higher price level, by raising the need for liquidity, increases the nominal demand for money. In fact, because prices are ten times higher today than they were in 1950, an identical transaction takes ten times as many dollars today as it did back then. Thus, everything else being equal, the nominal demand for money is *proportional* to the price level.

[8]Money also has low risk, but many alternative assets (such as short-term government bonds) are not much riskier than money and pay a higher return.

Real Income

The more transactions that individuals or businesses conduct, the more liquidity they need and the greater is their demand for money. An important factor determining the number of transactions is real income. For example, a large, high-volume supermarket has to deal with a larger number of customers and suppliers and pay more employees than does a corner grocery. Similarly, a high-income individual makes more and larger purchases than a low-income individual. Because higher real income means more transactions and a greater need for liquidity, the amount of money demanded should increase when real income increases.

Unlike the response of money demand to changes in the price level, the increase in money demand need not be proportional to an increase in real income. Actually, a 1% increase in real income usually leads to less than a 1% increase in money demand. One reason that money demand grows more slowly than income is that higher-income individuals and firms typically use their money more efficiently. For example, a high-income individual may open a special cash management account in which money not needed for current transactions is automatically invested in nonmonetary assets paying a higher return. Because of minimum-balance requirements and fees, such an account might not be worthwhile for a lower-income individual.

Another reason that money demand grows more slowly than income is that a nation's financial sophistication tends to increase as national income grows. In poor countries people may hold much of their saving in the form of money, for lack of anything better; in richer countries people have many attractive alternatives to money. Money substitutes such as credit cards also become more common as a country becomes richer, again causing aggregate money demand to grow more slowly than income.

Interest Rates

The theory of portfolio allocation implies that, with risk and liquidity held constant, the demand for money depends on the expected returns of both money and alternative, nonmonetary assets. An increase in the expected return on money increases the demand for money, and an increase in the expected return on alternative assets causes holders of wealth to switch from money to higher-return alternatives, thus lowering the demand for money.

For example, suppose that, of your total wealth of $10,000, you have $8000 in government bonds earning 8% interest and $2000 in an interest-bearing checking account earning 3%. You are willing to hold the checking account at a lower return because of the liquidity it provides. But if the interest rate on bonds rises to 10%, and the checking account interest rate remains unchanged, you may decide to switch $1000 from the checking account into bonds. In making this switch, you reduce your holding of money (your money demand) from $2000 to $1000. Effectively, you have chosen to trade some liquidity for the higher return offered by bonds.

Similarly, if the interest rate paid on money rises, holders of wealth will choose to hold more money. In the example, if the checking account begins paying 5% instead of 3%, with bonds still at 8%, you may sell $1000 of your bonds, lowering your holdings of bonds to $7000 and increasing your checking account to $3000. The sacrifice in return associated with holding money is less than before, so you increase your checking account balance and enjoy the flexibility and other benefits of extra liquidity. Thus a higher interest rate on money makes the demand for money rise.

In principle, the interest rate on each of the many alternatives to money should affect money demand. However, as previously noted (see Chapter 4, "In Touch with Data and Research: Interest Rates"), the many interest rates in the economy generally tend to move up and down together. For the purposes of macroeconomic analysis, therefore, assuming that there is just one nominal interest rate, i, which measures the nominal return on nonmonetary assets, is simpler and not too misleading. The nominal interest rate, i, minus the expected inflation rate, π^e, gives the expected real interest rate, r, that is relevant to saving and investment decisions, as discussed in Chapter 4.

Also, in reality, various interest rates are paid on money. For example, currency pays zero interest, but different types of checkable accounts pay varying rates. Again for simplicity, let's assume that there is just one nominal interest rate for money, i^m. The key conclusions are that an increase in the interest rate on nonmonetary assets, i, reduces the amount of money demanded and that an increase in the interest rate on money, i^m, raises the amount of money demanded.

The Money Demand Function

We express the effects of the price level, real income, and interest rates on money demand as

$$M^d = P \times L(Y, i), \tag{7.1}$$

where

M^d = the aggregate demand for money, in nominal terms;
P = the price level;
Y = real income or output;
i = the nominal interest rate earned by alternative, nonmonetary assets;
L = a function relating money demand to real income and the nominal interest rate.

Equation (7.1) holds that nominal money demand, M^d, is proportional to the price level, P. Hence, if the price level, P, doubles (and real income and interest rates don't change), nominal money demand, M^d, also will double, reflecting the fact that twice as much money is needed to conduct the same real transactions. Equation (7.1) also indicates that, for any price level, P, money demand depends (through the function L) on real income, Y, and the nominal interest rate on nonmonetary assets, i. An increase in real income, Y, raises the demand for liquidity and thus increases money demand. An increase in the nominal interest rate, i, makes nonmonetary assets more attractive, which reduces money demand.

We could have included the nominal interest rate on money, i^m, in Eq. (7.1) because an increase in the interest rate on money makes people more willing to hold money and thus increases money demand. Historically, however, the nominal interest rate on money has varied much less than the nominal interest rate on nonmonetary assets (for example, currency and a portion of checking accounts always have paid zero interest) and thus has been ignored by many statistical studies of Eq. (7.1). Thus for simplicity we do not explicitly include i^m in the equation.

An equivalent way of writing the demand for money expresses the nominal interest rate, i, in terms of the expected real interest rate and the expected rate of inflation. Recall from Eq. (2.14) that the expected real interest rate, r, equals the nominal interest rate, i, minus the expected rate of inflation, π^e. Therefore the nominal interest rate, i, equals $r + \pi^e$. Substituting $r + \pi^e$ for i in Eq. (7.1) yields

$$M^d = P \times L(Y, r + \pi^e). \quad \textbf{(7.2)}$$

Equation (7.2) shows that, for any expected rate of inflation, π^e, an increase in the real interest rate increases the nominal interest rate and reduces the demand for money. Similarly, for any real interest rate, an increase in the expected rate of inflation increases the nominal interest rate and reduces the demand for money.

Nominal money demand, M^d, measures the demand for money in terms of dollars (or yen or euros). But, sometimes, measuring money demand in real terms is more convenient. If we divide both sides of Eq. (7.2) by the price level, P, we get

$$\frac{M^d}{P} = L(Y, r + \pi^e). \quad \textbf{(7.3)}$$

The expression on the left side of Eq. (7.3), M^d/P, is called real money demand or, sometimes, the demand for **real balances**. Real money demand is the amount of money demanded in terms of the goods it can buy. Equation (7.3) states that real money demand, M^d/P, depends on real income (or output), Y, and on the nominal interest rate, which is the sum of the real interest rate, r, and expected inflation, π^e. The function L that relates real money demand to output and interest rates in Eq. (7.3) is called the **money demand function**.

Other Factors Affecting Money Demand

The money demand function in Eq. (7.3) captures the main macroeconomic determinants of money demand, but some other factors should be mentioned. Besides the nominal interest rate on money, which we have already discussed, additional factors influencing money demand include wealth, risk, liquidity of alternative assets, and payment technologies. Summary table 9 contains a comprehensive list of variables that affect the demand for money.

Wealth. When wealth increases, part of the extra wealth may be held as money, increasing total money demand. However, with income and the level of transactions held constant, a holder of wealth has little incentive to keep extra wealth in money rather than in higher-return alternative assets. Thus the effect of an increase in wealth on money demand is likely to be small.

Risk. Money usually pays a fixed nominal interest rate (zero in the case of cash), so holding money itself usually isn't risky. However, if the risk of alternative assets such as stocks and real estate increases greatly, people may demand safer assets, including money. Thus increased riskiness in the economy may increase money demand.[9]

---

[9]For some evidence that this effect occurred in the early 1980s, see James M. McGibany and Farrokh Nourzad, "Interest Rate Volatility and the Demand for Money," *Quarterly Review of Economics and Business,* Autumn 1986, pp. 73–83.

SUMMARY 9

Macroeconomic Determinants of the Demand for Money

An increase in	Causes money demand to	Reason
Price level, P	Rise proportionally	A doubling of the price level doubles the number of dollars needed for transactions.
Real income, Y	Rise less than proportionally	Higher real income implies more transactions and thus a greater demand for liquidity.
Real interest rate, r	Fall	Higher real interest rate means a higher return on alternative assets and thus a switch away from money.
Expected inflation, π^e	Fall	Higher expected inflation means a lower real return on money and thus a switch away from money.
Nominal interest rate on nonmonetary assets, i	Fall	Higher return on nonmonetary assets makes people less willing to hold money
Nominal interest rate on money, i^m	Rise	Higher return on money makes people more willing to hold money.
Wealth	Rise	Part of an increase in wealth may be held in the form of money.
Risk	Rise, if risk of alternative asset increases	Higher risk of alternative asset makes money more attractive.
	Fall, if risk of money increases	Higher risk of money makes it less attractive.
Liquidity of alternative assets	Fall	Higher liquidity of alternative assets makes these assets more attractive.
Efficiency of payments technologies	Fall	People can operate with less money.

However, money doesn't always carry a low risk. In a period of erratic inflation, even if the nominal return on money is fixed, the real return on money (the nominal return minus inflation) may become quite uncertain, making money risky. Money demand then will fall as people switch to inflation hedges (assets whose real returns are less likely to be affected by erratic inflation) such as gold, consumer durable goods, and real estate.

Liquidity of Alternative Assets. The more quickly and easily alternative assets can be converted into cash, the less need there is to hold money. In recent years the joint impact of deregulation, competition, and innovation in financial markets has made alternatives to money more liquid. For example, with a home equity line of credit, a person can now make investments or purchases that are backed by the value of their home. We have mentioned individual cash management accounts whose introduction allowed individuals to switch wealth easily between high-return assets, such as stocks, and more liquid forms. As alternative assets become more liquid, the demand for money declines.

Payment Technologies. Money demand also is affected by the technologies available for making and receiving payments. For example, the introduction of credit cards allowed people to make transactions without money—at least until the end of the month, when payment must be made on the credit card bill. Automatic teller machines (ATMs) probably have reduced the demand for cash because people know that they can obtain cash quickly whenever they need it. In the mid-2000s, check clearing became more efficient, thanks to the Check 21 law, which allowed for electronic clearing of images of checks. This process greatly reduces the costs of clearing checks and allows them to clear much more quickly than before. In the future more innovations in payment technologies, such as the ability to deposit checks and pay for transactions using your phone, undoubtedly will help people operate with less and less cash.[10] Some experts even predict that ultimately we will live in a "cashless society," in which almost all payments will be made through immediately accessible computerized accounting systems and that the demand for cash will be close to zero. The tremendous interest in Bitcoin and other cryptocurrencies in recent years suggests that we are getting closer to a cashless society, though many obstacles remain, especially safety and security issues. See the Application "Bitcoin and Cryptocurrencies."

Application

Bitcoin and Cryptocurrencies

Traditionally, money in the form of currency and coins has been issued by a country's government. Recently, however, a number of cryptocurrencies have been in use, in which money is created by entities other than a government. The most prominent of these is called Bitcoin.

A cryptocurrency does not exist in a physical form but rather is a claim to resources that is recorded in a computer system. Bitcoin, for example, uses a technology called blockchain to record who owns how many units of bitcoins. A person can buy or sell bitcoins using currency, such as dollars, through an exchange that provides such a service; demand and supply determine the exchange rate between bitcoins and dollars.

One feature of Bitcoin and other cryptocurrencies is that they allow anonymous transactions. When you use a bitcoin to buy something, no one knows who you are. You have credentials to an account that keeps track of how many bitcoins you own, but no one can figure out your identity. For this reason, cryptocurrencies such as Bitcoin are prone to being used by people who don't want their transactions to be visible, including tax evaders and criminals.

Bitcoin uses blockchain to verify accounts and transactions. Each transaction between two people is verified by other people and their computer systems. A public record is made of the transaction, and it is replicated by many computers within the system. As a result, it would be nearly impossible to engage in a fraudulent transaction. Although blockchain's initial use was for Bitcoin, it has many

(continued)

[10]In 2003, the number of electronic payments exceeded the number of check payments in the United States for the first time. The pace of change is accelerating so that just three years later, the number of electronic payments was twice the number of check payments. For more, see "The Federal Reserve Payments Study 2016: Recent Developments in Consumer and Business Payment Choices" by the staff of the Federal Reserve Board of Governors, available at *www.federalreserve.gov/newsevents/pressreleases/files/2016-payments-study-recent-developments-20170630.pdf*.

other potential uses in the business world, including "peer-to-peer lending, document verification, ride-sharing and crowdfunding, among other applications."[11]

Are Bitcoin and other cryptocurrencies likely to replace dollars for use in transactions? It may be possible someday, but cryptocurrencies are missing some features of money that people find useful. For something to be useful as money, it needs to serve as a medium of exchange and a store of value. In its medium-of-exchange function, an item that is money should be easy to use to buy things. Originally, Bitcoin seemed to fit that role and a number of merchants agreed to sell their goods in exchange for bitcoins. However, costs of making and validating a Bitcoin transaction are now higher than other payments methods, such as credit cards, so Bitcoin is unlikely to be used for small-value transactions. Also, the security of Bitcoin transactions has not prevented Bitcoin users from suffering large losses, including to hackers and lost password information. In its store-of-value role, for something to be useful as money, its value should be stable. However, Bitcoin's value has risen and fallen dramatically over time, with five days in 2017 in which it fell in value by 20% or more.[12] These fluctuations have led new financial firms to develop another class of cryptocurrency called "stablecoins," which have the goal of creating a cryptocurrency whose value is less volatile and could potentially be used as money.

Someday, we might all use a cryptocurrency in place of dollars. However, there are many obstacles to overcome before that happens. A useful cryptocurrency would have to serve as both a medium of exchange and a store of value, and no cryptocurrency yet does both well.

[11] See Christopher Koch and Gina C. Pieters, "Blockchain Technology Disrupting Traditional Records Systems," *Financial Insights*, Federal Reserve Bank of Dallas, Second Quarter 2017.

[12] See Scott Wolla, "Bitcoin: Money or Financial Investment?" Federal Reserve Bank of St. Louis *Page One Economics*, March 2018.

Elasticities of Money Demand. The theory of portfolio allocation helps economists identify factors that should affect the aggregate demand for money. However, for many purposes—such as forecasting and quantitative analyses of the economy—economists need to know not just which factors affect money demand but also how strong the various effects are. This information can be obtained only through statistical analysis of the data.

Over the past five decades, economists have performed hundreds of statistical studies of the money demand function. The results of these studies often are expressed in terms of elasticities, which measure the change in money demand resulting from changes in factors affecting the demand for money. Specifically, the **income elasticity of money demand** is the percentage change in money demand resulting from a 1% increase in real income. Thus, for example, if the income elasticity of money demand is 2/3, a 3% increase in real income will increase money demand by 2% ($2/3 \times 3\% = 2\%$). Similarly, the **interest elasticity of money demand** is the percentage change in money demand resulting from a 1% increase in the interest rate.

When we work with the interest elasticity of money demand, some care is needed to avoid a potential pitfall. To illustrate, suppose that the interest rate increases from 5% per year to 6% per year. To describe this increase in the interest rate as a 1% increase in the interest rate is tempting (but incorrect). In fact, it is a 20% increase in the interest rate because 6 is 20% larger than 5.[13] If the interest elasticity of money demand is -0.1, for example, an increase in the interest rate from 5% to 6% reduces money demand by 2% ($-0.1 \times 20\% = -2\%$). Note that, if the interest elasticity of money demand is negative, as in this example, an increase in the interest rate reduces money demand.

What are the actual values of the income elasticity and interest elasticity of money demand? Although the many statistical studies of money demand provide a range of answers, some common results emerge. First, there is widespread agreement that the income elasticity of money demand is positive. For example, in his classic 1973 study of M1 money demand, which established the framework for many later studies, Stephen Goldfeld of Princeton University found this elasticity to be about 2/3.[14] A positive income elasticity of money demand implies that money demand rises when income rises, as predicted by our theory. Goldfeld's finding that the income elasticity of money demand is less than 1.0 is similar to that of many other empirical analyses, although some studies have found values for this elasticity as large as 1.0. An income elasticity of money demand smaller than 1.0 implies that money demand rises less than proportionally with income. Earlier in the chapter we discussed some reasons why, as an individual or nation has higher income, the demand for money might be expected to grow more slowly than income.

Second, for the interest elasticity of money demand, most studies find a small negative value. For example, Goldfeld found the interest elasticity of money demand to be about -0.1 or -0.2. A negative value for the interest elasticity of money demand implies that when interest rates on nonmonetary assets rise, people reduce their holdings of money, again as predicted by the theory.

Finally, Goldfeld's study and others have confirmed empirically that the nominal demand for money is proportional to the price level. Again, this result is consistent with the theory, as reflected in the money demand equation, Eq. (7.3).

Velocity and the Quantity Theory of Money

A concept related to money demand, which at times is used in discussions of monetary policy, is velocity. It measures how often the money stock "turns over" each period. Specifically, **velocity** is nominal GDP (the price level, P, times real output, Y) divided by the nominal money stock, M. If we let V represent velocity,

$$V = \frac{\text{nominal GDP}}{\text{nominal money stock}} = \frac{PY}{M}. \tag{7.4}$$

If velocity rises, each dollar of the money stock is being used in a greater dollar volume of transactions in each period, if we assume that the volume of transactions is proportional to GDP. Figure 7.2 shows the velocity of M2 for the United States from 1959 through the fourth quarter of 2021.

[13]The change from 5% to 6% can be described as "a one *percentage point* increase" or as "a twenty *percent* increase."

[14]"The Demand for Money Revisited," *Brookings Papers on Economic Activity*, 1973:4, pp. 577–638. Goldfeld reported elasticities of money demand that applied to the short run and the long run. The figures we present here are long-run elasticities.

FIGURE 7.2

Velocity of M2, 1959Q1–2021Q4

M2 velocity is nominal GDP divided by M2. M2 velocity has trended down since the late 1990s.

Source: Board of Governors of the Federal Reserve System, downloaded from FRED database of the Federal Reserve Bank of St. Louis, *fred.stlouisfed.org*, series *M2SL* and *GDP*.

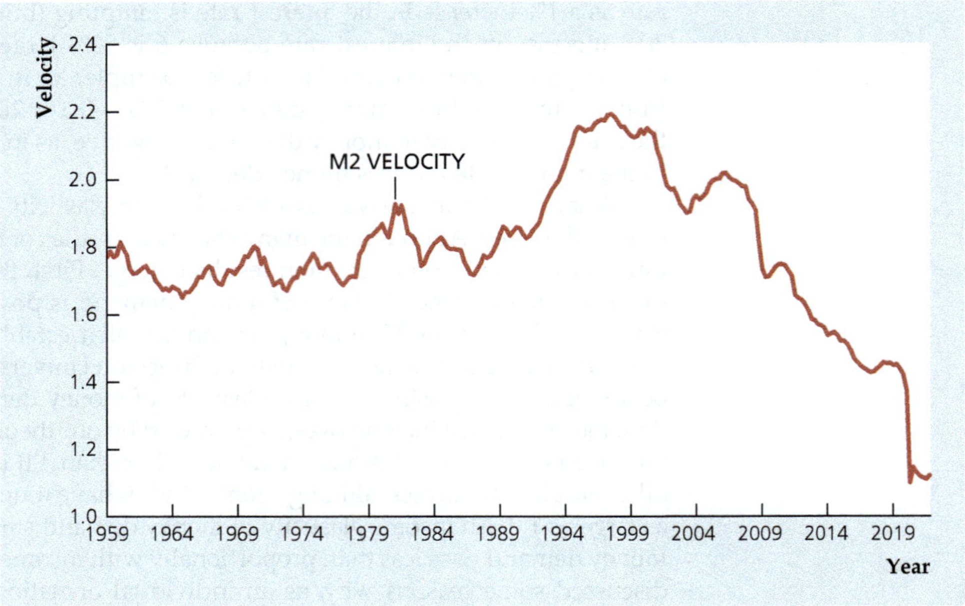

The concept of velocity comes from one of the earliest theories of money demand, the quantity theory of money.[15] The **quantity theory of money** asserts that real money demand is proportional to real income, or

$$\frac{M^d}{P} = kY, \tag{7.5}$$

where M^d/P is real money demand, Y is real income, and k is a constant. In Eq. (7.5) the real money demand function, $L(Y, r + \pi^e)$, takes the simple form kY. This way of writing money demand is based on the strong assumption that velocity is a constant, $1/k$, and doesn't depend on income or interest rates.[16]

But is velocity actually constant? As Fig. 7.2 shows, M2 velocity has been unpredictable over short periods and has trended down since reaching a peak in 1998. Throughout the 1990s, people began investing their savings in a broader variety of financial assets than they had before, pulling funds out of bank accounts (which are included in M2) and investing in bonds and stocks (which are not in M2). As a result, demand for M2 at any level of GDP was reduced, raising M2 velocity. Further, when the housing market was booming from the late 1990s to the mid-2000s, funds from refinancing of mortgages were temporarily parked in M2 accounts, leading to increased M2 and lower velocity. Following the pandemic recession, velocity plummeted, as people held increased balances in M2 accounts.

[15]The quantity theory of money was developed by several classical economists, notably Irving Fisher, in the late nineteenth and early twentieth centuries. A famous statement of the theory is contained in Fisher's book *The Purchasing Power of Money* (New York: Macmillan, 1911).

[16]To derive velocity under the quantity theory, we must assume that nominal money demand, M^d, equals the actual money stock, M, an assumption that we justify later in the chapter. Under this assumption, you should verify that $V = 1/k$.

FIGURE 7.3

Growth rates of M2 and nominal GDP, 1960Q1–2021Q4

The growth rates of M2 and nominal GDP plotted here show the percentage increase in both variables from their levels one year earlier, using quarterly data. Growth of M2 has fluctuated considerably because of financial innovations and foreign demand for currency. When the growth rate of the nominal money supply exceeds the growth rate of nominal GDP, velocity declines.

Source: Same as for Fig. 7.2.

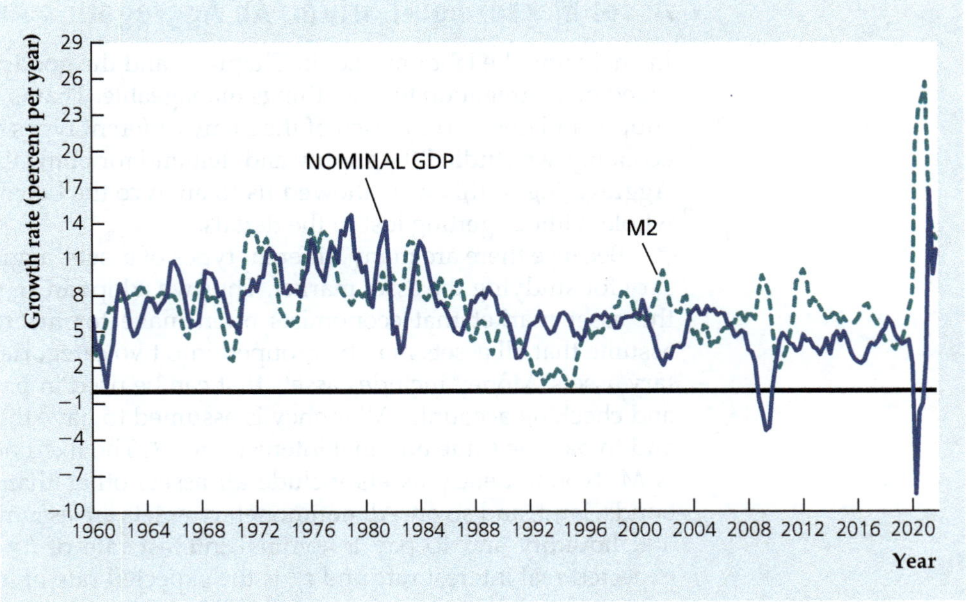

Because velocity is the ratio of nominal GDP to the nominal money supply, the growth rate of velocity equals the growth rate of nominal GDP minus the growth rate of the nominal money supply. Thus when the growth rate of the nominal money supply is lower than the growth rate of nominal GDP, the growth rate of velocity is positive, that is, velocity is rising. Of course when the growth rate of the nominal money supply is higher than the growth rate of nominal GDP, velocity is falling. Figure 7.3 shows the growth rate of nominal GDP as well as the growth rate of nominal M2. As you can see in this figure, the growth rate of M2 has generally exceeded that of nominal GDP since 1998; as a consequence, M2 velocity declined during this period, as shown in Fig. 7.2. The growth rate of nominal M2 was very high following the pandemic recession, far exceeding nominal GDP growth, so M2 velocity fell substantially.

7.4 Asset Market Equilibrium

Discuss the fundamentals of asset market equilibrium.

Recall that the asset market actually is a set of markets in which real and financial assets are traded. The demand for any asset (say, government bonds) is the quantity of the asset that holders of wealth want in their portfolios. The demand for each asset depends on its expected return, risk, liquidity, and time to maturity relative to other assets. The supply of each asset is the quantity of that asset that is available. At any particular time the supplies of individual assets are typically fixed, although over time asset supplies change (the government may issue more bonds, firms may issue new shares, more gold may be mined, and so on).

The asset market is in equilibrium when the quantity of each asset that holders of wealth demand equals the (fixed) available supply of that asset. In this section we examine asset market equilibrium, focusing on the role of money. We then show how asset market equilibrium is linked to the price level.

Asset Market Equilibrium: An Aggregation Assumption

In analyzing the labor market in Chapter 3 and the goods market in Chapter 4, we relied on aggregation to keep things manageable. That is, instead of looking at the supply and demand for each of the many different types of labor and goods in the economy, we studied the supply and demand for both labor and goods in general. Aggregating in this way allowed us to analyze the behavior of the economy as a whole without getting lost in the details.

Because there are many different types of assets, aggregation is equally necessary for studying the asset market. Thus we adopt an aggregation assumption for the asset market that economists often make for macroeconomic analysis: We assume that all assets may be grouped into two categories, money and nonmonetary assets. Money includes assets that can be used in payment, such as currency and checking accounts. All money is assumed to have the same risk and liquidity and to pay the same nominal interest rate, i^m. The fixed nominal supply of money is M. Nonmonetary assets include all assets other than money, such as stocks, bonds, land, and so on. All nonmonetary assets are assumed to have the same risk and liquidity and to pay a nominal interest rate of $i = r + \pi^e$, where r is the expected real interest rate and π^e is the expected rate of inflation. The fixed nominal supply of nonmonetary assets is NM.

Although the assumption that assets can be aggregated into two types ignores many interesting differences among assets, it greatly simplifies our analysis and has proved to be very useful. One immediate benefit of making this assumption is that, if we allow for only two types of assets, *asset market equilibrium reduces to the condition that the quantity of money supplied equals the quantity of money demanded.*

To demonstrate this point, let's look at the portfolio allocation decision of an individual named Ed. Ed has a fixed amount of wealth that he allocates between money and nonmonetary assets. If m^d is the nominal amount of money and nm^d is the nominal amount of nonmonetary assets that Ed wants to hold, the sum of Ed's desired money holdings and his desired holdings of nonmonetary assets must be his total wealth, or

$$m^d + nm^d = \text{Ed's total nominal wealth.}$$

This equation has to be true for every holder of wealth in the economy.

Suppose that we sum this equation across all holders of wealth in the economy. Then the sum of all individual money demands, m^d, equals the aggregate demand for money, M^d. The sum of all individual demands for nonmonetary assets is the aggregate demand for nonmonetary assets, NM^d. Finally, adding nominal wealth for all holders of wealth gives the aggregate nominal wealth of the economy, or

$$M^d + NM^d = \text{aggregate nominal wealth.} \qquad \textbf{(7.6)}$$

Equation (7.6) states that the total demand for money in the economy plus the total demand for nonmonetary assets must equal the economy's total nominal wealth.

Next, we relate the total supplies of money and nonmonetary assets to aggregate wealth. Because money and nonmonetary assets are the only assets in the economy, aggregate nominal wealth equals the supply of money, M, plus the supply of nonmonetary assets, NM, or

$$M + NM = \text{aggregate nominal wealth.} \qquad \textbf{(7.7)}$$

Finally, we subtract Eq. (7.7) from Eq. (7.6) to obtain

$$(M^d - M) + (NM^d - NM) = 0. \quad \textbf{(7.8)}$$

The term $M^d - M$ in Eq. (7.8) is the *excess demand for money,* or the amount by which the total amount of money demanded exceeds the money supply. Similarly, the term $NM^d - NM$ in Eq. (7.8) is the *excess demand for nonmonetary assets.*

Now suppose that the demand for money, M^d, equals the money supply, M, so that the excess demand for money, $M^d - M$, is zero. Equation (7.8) shows that, if $M^d - M$ is zero, $NM^d - NM$ must also be zero; that is, if the amounts of money supplied and demanded are equal, the amounts of nonmonetary assets supplied and demanded also must be equal. By definition, if quantities supplied and demanded are equal for each type of asset, the asset market is in equilibrium.

If we make the simplifying assumption that assets can be lumped into monetary and nonmonetary categories, the asset market is in equilibrium if the quantity of money supplied equals the quantity of money demanded. This result is convenient because it means that in studying asset market equilibrium we have to look at only the supply and demand for money and can ignore nonmonetary assets. As long as the amounts of money supplied and demanded are equal, the entire asset market will be in equilibrium.

The Asset Market Equilibrium Condition

Equilibrium in the asset market occurs when the quantity of money supplied equals the quantity of money demanded. This condition is valid whether money supply and demand are expressed in nominal terms or real terms. We work with this condition in real terms, or

$$\frac{M}{P} = L(Y, r + \pi^e). \quad \textbf{(7.9)}$$

The left side of Eq. (7.9) is the nominal supply of money, M, divided by the price level, P, which is the supply of money measured in real terms. The right side of the equation is the same as the real demand for money, M^d/P, as in Eq. (7.3). Equation (7.9), which states that the real quantity of money supplied equals the real quantity of money demanded, is called the asset market equilibrium condition.

The *asset market equilibrium condition* involves five variables: the nominal money supply, M; the price level, P; real income, Y; the real interest rate, r; and the expected rate of inflation, π^e. The nominal money supply, M, is determined by the central bank through its open-market operations. For now, we treat the expected rate of inflation, π^e, as fixed and thus exogenous (we return to the determination of expected inflation later in the chapter). That leaves three variables in the asset market equilibrium condition whose values we haven't yet specified: output, Y; the real interest rate, r; and the price level, P.

In this part of the book we have made the assumption that the economy is at full employment or, equivalently, that all markets are in equilibrium. Both classical and Keynesian economists agree that the full-employment assumption is reasonable for analyzing the long-term behavior of the economy. If we continue to assume full employment,[17] we can use the analysis from previous chapters to describe how

[17]We relax this assumption in Part 3 when we discuss short-run economic fluctuations.

output and the real interest rate are determined. Recall from Chapter 3 that, if the labor market is in equilibrium—with employment at its full-employment level—output equals full-employment output, $\bar{Y}$. In Chapter 4 we showed that, for any level of output, the real interest rate in a closed economy must take the value that makes desired national saving and desired investment equal (the goods market equilibrium condition).

With the values of output and the real interest rate established (endogenously) by equilibrium in the labor and goods markets, the only variable left to be determined by the asset market equilibrium condition is the price level, *P*. To emphasize that the price level is the variable determined by asset market equilibrium, we multiply both sides of Eq. (7.9) by *P* and divide both sides by real money demand, $L(Y, r + \pi^e)$, to obtain

$$P = \frac{M}{L(Y, r + \pi^e)}. \tag{7.10}$$

According to Eq. (7.10), the economy's price level, *P*, equals the ratio of the nominal money supply, *M*, to the real demand for money, $L(Y, r + \pi^e)$. For given values of real output, *Y*, the real interest rate, *r*, and the expected rate of inflation, π^e, the real demand for money, $L(Y, r + \pi^e)$, is fixed. Thus Eq. (7.10) states that the price level is proportional to the nominal money supply. A doubling of the nominal money supply, *M*, for instance, would double the price level, *P*, with other factors held constant. The existence of a close link between the price level and the money supply in an economy is one of the oldest and most reliable conclusions about macroeconomic behavior, having been recognized in some form for hundreds if not thousands of years. We discuss the empirical support for this link in Section 7.5.

What forces lead the price level to its equilibrium value shown in Eq. (7.10)? A complete description of how the price level adjusts to its equilibrium value involves an analysis of the goods market as well as the asset market; we leave this task until Chapter 9, where we discuss the links among the three main markets of the economy in more detail. Briefly, in Chapter 9 we show that an increase in the money supply leads people to increase their nominal spending on goods and services; this increased nominal demand for output leads prices to rise. Prices continue to rise until people are content to hold the increased nominal quantity of money in their portfolios, satisfying the asset market equilibrium condition (rewritten as Eq. 7.10).

7.5 Money Growth and Inflation

Discuss the relationship between money growth and inflation.

In Section 7.4 we established that, when the markets for labor, goods, and assets are all in equilibrium, the price level, *P*, is proportional to the nominal money supply, *M*. However, the price level itself generally is of less concern to policymakers and the public than is the rate of inflation, or the percentage rate of increase of the price level. In this section we extend our analysis of the price level to show how inflation is determined. We conclude that the inflation rate, which is the growth rate of the price level, is closely related to the growth rate of the nominal money supply.

To obtain an equation for the rate of inflation, we set the growth rate of the left side of Eq. (7.10) equal to the growth rate of its right side to obtain

$$\frac{\Delta P}{P} = \frac{\Delta M}{M} - \frac{\Delta L(Y, r + \pi^e)}{L(Y, r + \pi^e)}, \tag{7.11}$$

where the symbol Δ indicates the change in a variable from one year to the next. The left side of Eq. (7.11) is the growth rate of the price level, $\Delta P/P$, which is the same as the inflation rate, π. The right side of Eq. (7.11) expresses the growth rate of the ratio on the right side of Eq. (7.10) as the growth rate of the numerator, M, minus the growth rate of the denominator, $L(Y, r + \pi^e)$. (In Appendix A, Section A.7, we provide some useful formulas for calculating growth rates.) Equation (7.11) shows that, if the asset market is in equilibrium, *the rate of inflation equals the growth rate of the nominal money supply minus the growth rate of real money demand.*

Equation (7.11) highlights the point that the rate of inflation is closely related to the rate of growth of the nominal money supply. However, to use Eq. (7.11) to predict the behavior of inflation, we must also know how quickly real money demand is growing. The money demand function, Eq. (7.3), focused on two macroeconomic variables with significant effects on real money demand: income (or output), Y, and the nominal interest rate, $r + \pi^e$. The income elasticity of money demand is the percentage change in money demand resulting from a 1% increase in real income. If $\Delta Y/Y$ is the percentage change in real income from one year to the next and η_Y is the income elasticity of money demand, $\eta_Y \Delta Y/Y$ is the resulting percentage increase in the real demand for money, with the nominal interest rate and other factors affecting money demand held constant.[18] Substituting π for $\Delta P/P$ and $\eta_Y \Delta Y/Y$ for the growth rate of real money demand in Eq. (7.11) yields

$$\pi = \frac{\Delta M}{M} - \eta_Y \frac{\Delta Y}{Y}. \tag{7.12}$$

Equation (7.12) is a useful simple expression for the rate of inflation. According to Eq. (7.12), the rate of inflation equals the growth rate of the nominal money supply minus an adjustment for the growth rate of real money demand arising from growth in real output. For example, suppose that nominal money supply growth is 10% per year, real income is growing by 3% per year, and the income elasticity of money demand is 2/3. Then Eq. (7.12) predicts that the inflation rate will be 10% − (2/3)(3%), or 8% per year.

Application

Money Growth and Inflation in European Countries in Transition

The fall of communism in Eastern Europe and the breakup of the Soviet Union led to economic, political, and social upheaval. All of these countries, to varying degrees, introduced reforms intended to make their economies more market-oriented, and many (particularly the new countries formed from the breakup of the Soviet Union) introduced new currencies. However, Russia and many of the

(continued)

[18]The assumption that the nominal interest rate is constant is consistent with a long-run equilibrium with constant $\Delta Y/Y$, $\Delta M/M$, η_Y and real interest rate r because the inflation rate π would be constant and it would be reasonable that the expected inflation rate π^e would be constant and equal to π. Therefore, the nominal interest rate, $i = r + \pi^e$ would be constant.

Eastern European economies continued to face serious problems, including very high rates of inflation. The main reason for the high inflation rates is the rapid rates of money growth in these countries.

In general, both the growth of the nominal money supply and the growth of real money demand (resulting from real income growth, for example) affect the rate of inflation (see Eq. 7.12). In countries with high inflation, however, the growth of the nominal money supply usually is the much more important of these two factors. To illustrate, if the income elasticity of money demand in a country is 2/3, and real output were to grow at the stunning rate of 15% per year, then in Eq. (7.12) real money demand would grow at 10% per year ($2/3 \times 15\%$) in that country. If a second country also has an income elasticity of 2/3, but its income is falling at the painful rate of 15% per year, the rate of growth of real money demand is -10% per year. Thus even with these radically different income growth rates, the difference in the growth rates of real money demand is only 20 percentage points per year.

In contrast to the relatively modest differences among countries in the growth rates of real money demand, rates of growth of nominal money supplies may vary among countries by hundreds of percentage points per year. Thus large differences in inflation rates among countries almost always are the result of large differences in rates of money growth.

The link between the money growth rate and the inflation rate is illustrated in Figure 7.4, which shows the average annual values of these rates during the period 1995–2001 for the European countries designated by the International Monetary Fund as "countries in transition." Most of these countries were in

FIGURE 7.4

The relationship between money growth and inflation

Nominal money growth and inflation during the period 1995–2001 are plotted for the European countries in transition for which complete data are available. There is a strong relationship between money growth rates and inflation rates, with countries having money growth rates in excess of 80% per year also having inflation rates in excess of 80% per year.

Source: Based on money growth rates and consumer price inflation from *International Financial Statistics,* February 2003, International Monetary Fund. Figure shows European countries in transition for which there are complete data.

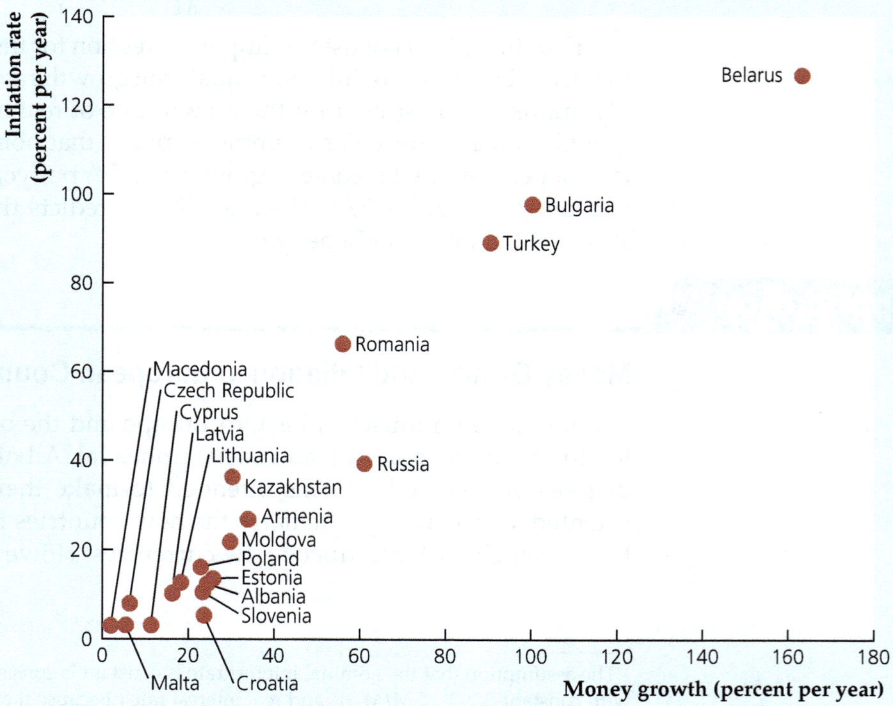

the process of moving from communism to free-market capitalism. The three countries that had inflation rates that averaged more than 80% per year during this period—Belarus, Turkey, and Bulgaria—also had money growth rates that averaged more than 80% per year. Whether we compare inflation rates among these three countries or compare the high inflation rates of these three countries with the relatively low inflation rates of the remaining 16 countries, large differences in inflation rates clearly are associated with large differences in rates of money growth.

If rapid money growth causes inflation, why do countries allow their money supplies to grow so quickly? As we discussed earlier, governments sometimes find that printing money (borrowing from the central bank) is the only way that they can finance their expenditures. This situation is most likely to occur in poor countries or countries that undergo economic upheavals associated with war, natural disaster, or (as in the case of the European countries in transition) major political and economic change. Unfortunately, the almost inevitable result of financing government expenditures in this way is increased inflation.

The Inflation Rate and the Nominal Interest Rate

The public's expected rate of inflation is not directly observable, except perhaps through surveys. (See the Application "Measuring Inflation Expectations.") However, it is apparent from Eq. (7.11) that if the growth rate of the nominal money supply and the factors that affect the growth rate of money demand, such as real income growth, are expected not to change much from their current values, then the rate of inflation will not be expected to change much from its current value. That is, π^e is approximately equal to π. Therefore, the nominal interest rate, $i = r + \pi^e$, is approximately equal to $r + \pi$. If, in addition, the real interest rate, r, is constant, the nominal interest will move one for one with the actual inflation rate, π.

The historical relationship between nominal interest rates and inflation is illustrated by Figure 7.5, which shows monthly data on the nominal interest rate on one-year Treasury bills and the twelve-month inflation rate measured by the consumer price index in the United States from January 1960 to December 2021. The nominal interest rate and the inflation rate have tended to move together, rising during the 1960s and 1970s and then falling sharply after reaching a peak in the early 1980s. However, movements in the inflation rate aren't perfectly matched by movements in the nominal interest rate because the real interest rate hasn't been constant over this period. In particular, during the late 1970s and early 1980s, the rise in the nominal interest rate was much greater than the rise in the inflation rate, reflecting an increase in the real interest rate from a negative value in the mid-1970s to much higher, positive values in the 1980s. Also, following the financial crisis of 2008, the real interest rate was negative, as the nominal interest rate was near zero and the inflation rate was 1 to 2% per year. (See Fig. 2.6 for a graph of the real interest rate.) In 2021, with the nominal interest rate remaining near zero, the inflation rate began rising sharply, as the economy recovered from the pandemic.

FIGURE 7.5

Inflation and the nominal interest rate in the United States, 1960–2021

The figure shows the nominal interest rate on one-year Treasury bills and the twelve-month rate of inflation as measured by the consumer price index. The nominal interest rate tends to move with inflation, although there are periods, such as the period since 2008, when the two variables do not move together.

Source: Interest rate from Board of Governors of the Federal Reserve System, downloaded from FRED database of the Federal Reserve Bank of St. Louis, *fred.stlouisfed.org/series/GS1*; CPI from Bureau of Labor Statistics, downloaded from FRED, series *CPIAUCNS*.

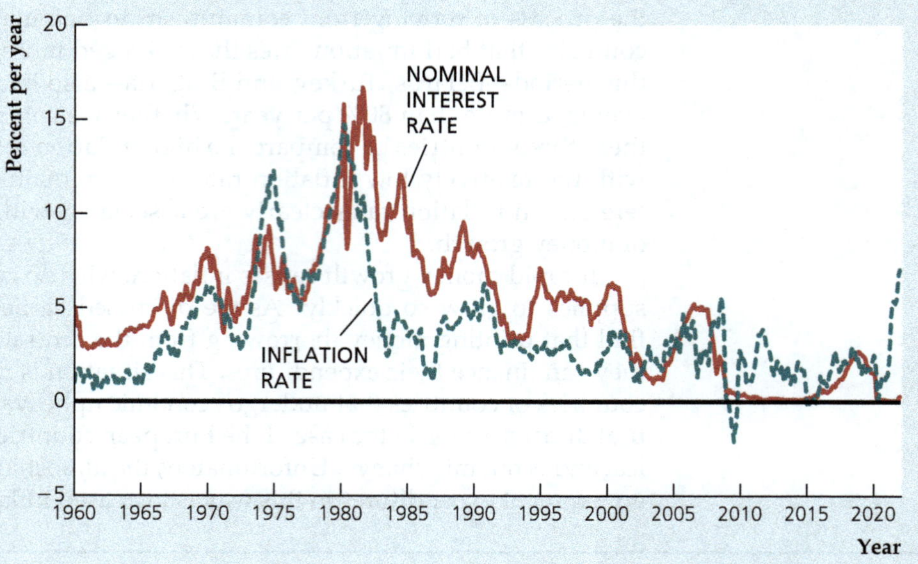

Application

Measuring Inflation Expectations

One of the factors that affect equilibrium in the asset market is people's expectations of future inflation rates. For this reason, various surveys are conducted by government research institutions and private specialized professional institutions (such as YouGov UK) to gather information about people's long-term inflation expectations. As they affect overall patterns of national spending and saving, gauging these future inflation expectations is important for policymakers and businesses alike. Moreover, future inflation expectations are important for pensioners and bond holders because a hike in prices is likely to lower their purchasing power and impact their real earnings on investments.

In order to act as a direct hedge against inflation, some governments have started to issue inflation-linked bonds, generally known as linkers. The United Kingdom began to issue linkers in 1981, and together with the United States and France, it accounts for almost 85% of global inflation-linked government bonds. Since the global financial crisis, inflation-linked bonds have expanded globally and spread to some emerging countries such as Brazil, Mexico, India, Turkey, and South Africa.

Government linkers and nominal/conventional bonds are similar in terms of maturities (five, ten, and twenty years) and coupon payments (annual, semi-annual, and quarterly). But both differ in terms of interest rates over the life of the

FIGURE 7.6

Interest rates on UK nominal and inflation-indexed 10-year government gilts 2004–2014

The chart shows averages of quarterly nominal interest rates on 10-year UK conventional and inflation-indexed government gilts for the period 2004Q1–2014Q4.

Source: United Kingdom Debt Management Office, "Gilt Market Index Ratio Data for Index-linked Gilts with a 3-month Indexation Lag," *https://www.dmo.gov.uk/data/ExportReport?reportCode=D10C.*

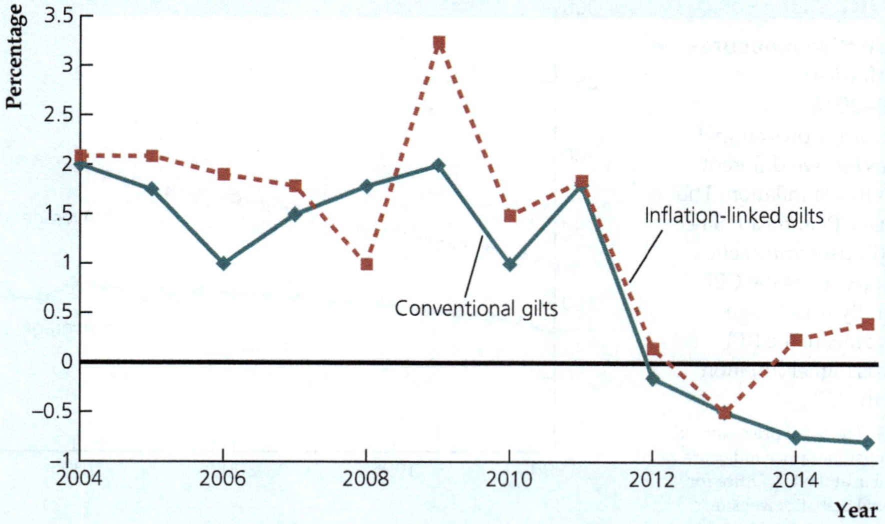

bond. While nominal bonds pay a given nominal interest rate, inflation-indexed bonds make a periodic coupon that is equal to the product of the daily inflation index and the nominal coupon rate. In this fashion, linkers hedge the real rate of return from inflation by adjusting both the interest payments and the principal amount of the bonds. On the other hand, the real interest rate on nominal bonds depends on the rate of inflation during the life of the bond. The expected real interest rate on the nominal bond is (recall Eq. 2.14) $r = i - \pi^e$, where i is the nominal interest rate and π^e is the expected rate of inflation during the life of the bond.

Figure 7.6 shows the average nominal interest rate on conventional UK 10-year government bonds, also known as gilts, and the average real interest rate for all inflation-linked gilts in issue over the last 10 years, based on a 3% inflation assumption. Since 2004, the real interest rate on UK linkers had trended down to less than 1% in 2007 but showed a temporary hike in 2008 in the midst of the global financial crisis.

If nominal conventional bonds and inflation-linked gilts were equally risky and equally liquid, then equilibrium in the asset market would imply that the expected real interest rate on nominal bonds, $i - \pi^e$, would equal the real interest rate on linkers, $r^{linkers}$. Setting $i - \pi^e$ equal to $r^{linkers}$ implies that $\pi^e = i - r^{linkers}$. Thus, the excess of the nominal interest rate over the inflation-linked gilt rate, $i - r^{linkers}$, which can be considered the *interest rate differential*, should theoretically provide a rough measure of expected inflation. However, this may not always be the case for two reasons. First, since linkers are less liquid (that is, they have fewer buyers and sellers), their interest rate is higher than that of traditional bonds sold in a more liquid market. Second, because buyers of conventional gilts are aware that they are shouldering a higher inflation risk in comparison to buyers of

(continued)

FIGURE 7.7

Alternative measures of inflation, 1990–2015

The chart shows annual values for two different measures of inflation: The annual CPI and RPI. Since the RPI uses arithmetic averages while the CPI generally uses the geometric mean, the RPI records higher inflation than the CPI.

Sources: The retail prices index and consumer price index are available at the UK Office for National Statistics website, *http://www.ons.gov.uk/*.

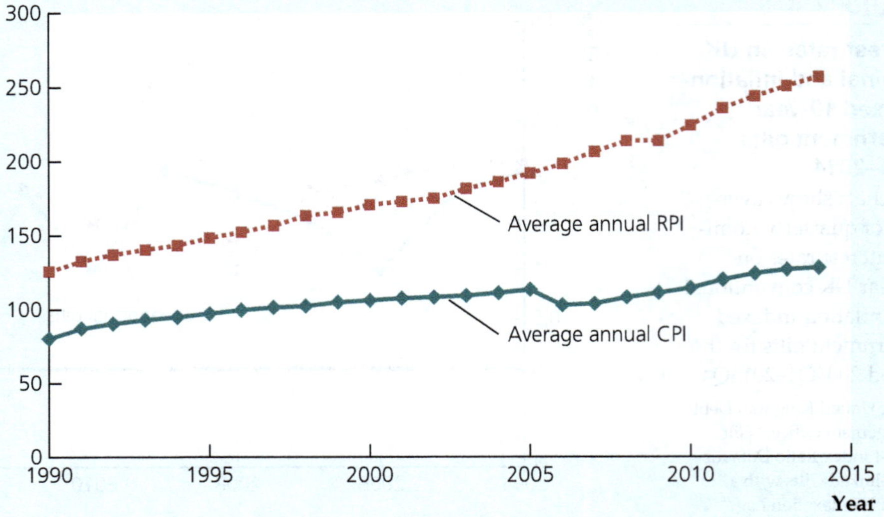

linkers, the *interest rate differential* is attributable to the risk factor and not to inflation per se. But these two effects would normally be small and work in opposite directions and, hence, have an overall small net effect.

But two words of caution must be highlighted. First, since bonds are always linked to a fixed inflation index, the preservation of purchasing power and the inflation protection that the investor attains is highly contingent on the components and calculation of the commodity basket that serves as the base for the price index. In the United States, the consumer price index (CPI) is used, while the United Kingdom uses the retail price index (RPI). The considerable differences in the RPI and CPI[19] (shown in Figure 7.7) have prompted heated discussions regarding the change to the CPI to index UK linkers.

Moreover, it must be noted that official inflation indices may not be highly accurate for indexing since they are not calculated on a daily but a monthly basis, with a time indexation lag of one to three months. Second, the European sovereign debt crisis has revealed that sovereign bankruptcy and high inflation often coexist, with the consequence that linkers may not offer adequate protection against inflation and default risks. As such, linkers in the United States, the United Kingdom, and Germany have been priced at negative real interest rates, making them less attractive. These two restraints indicate the importance of prudent risk and credit analysis of inflation-linked government gilts.

[19]The RPI is a UK home-grown measure dating back to the 1940s, whereas the CPI follows a European template drawn up in the 1990s. While the CPI includes all households, the RPI leaves out the richest 4% and low-income pensioners. The CPI and the RPI have substantially different patterns over the long term owing to the different treatment of council tax, insurance costs, ancillary rental costs, and interest costs, among others.

CHAPTER SUMMARY

1. Money is the set of assets that are widely used and accepted as payment, such as currency and checking accounts. Money functions as a medium of exchange, a unit of account, and a store of value.
2. The supply of money is set by the central bank—the Federal Reserve System in the United States. The central bank's official measures of money are called the monetary aggregates. M1 is made up primarily of currency and checking accounts and M2 includes a broader set of monetary assets.
3. A portfolio allocation decision is made by a holder of wealth when determining how much of each asset to hold. The characteristics of assets that most affect their desirability are expected return, risk, liquidity, and, for financial securities, time to maturity. The major assets that people hold are money, bonds, stocks, houses, and consumer durable goods.
4. Money demand is the total amount of money that people choose to hold in their portfolios. The principal macroeconomic variables that affect money demand are the price level, real income, and interest rates. Nominal money demand is proportional to the price level. Higher real income increases the number of transactions and thus raises real money demand. A higher interest rate on alternative, nonmonetary assets lowers real money demand by making the alternative assets more attractive relative to money. The money demand function measures the relationship between real money demand and these macroeconomic variables.
5. Velocity is the ratio of nominal GDP to the nominal money stock. The quantity theory of money is an early theory of money demand based on the assumption that velocity is constant, so that money demand is proportional to income. Historically, M2 velocity has been more stable than M1 velocity, although even M2 velocity isn't constant.
6. Under the simplifying assumption that assets can be grouped into two categories—money and nonmonetary assets—the asset market is in equilibrium if the quantity of money supplied equals the quantity of money demanded. When all markets are in equilibrium (the economy is at full employment), the level of output is determined by equilibrium in the labor market, the real interest rate is determined by equilibrium in the goods market, and the price level is determined by equilibrium in the asset market. The equilibrium price level is proportional to the nominal money supply.
7. The inflation rate equals the growth rate of the nominal money supply minus the growth rate of real money demand. The growth rate of real money demand in turn depends primarily on the real income growth rate. Expected inflation depends on expected growth rates of the nominal money supply and real income. For a given real interest rate, the nominal interest rate responds one-for-one to changes in expected inflation.

KEY TERMS

currency, p. 278
demand for money, p. 292
diversification, p. 291
expectations theory of the term structure, p. 286
expected returns, p. 285
income elasticity of money demand, p. 298
interest elasticity of money demand, p. 298
liquidity, p. 285
M1, p. 281
M2, p. 283
medium of exchange, p. 279
monetary aggregates, p. 280
money, p. 277
money demand function, p. 295
money supply, p. 283
open-market operations, p. 284
portfolio allocation decision, p. 284
quantity theory of money, p. 300
real balances, p. 295
risk, p. 285
risk premium, p. 285
store of value, p. 280
term premium, p. 286
time to maturity, p. 285
unit of account, p. 279
velocity, p. 299

KEY EQUATIONS

$$\frac{M^d}{P} = L(Y, r + \pi^e) \quad (7.3)$$

According to the money demand function, the real quantity of money demanded, M^d/P, depends on output and the nominal interest rate on alternative, nonmonetary assets. An increase in output, Y, raises the number of transactions people make and thus raises the demand for money. An increase in the nominal interest rate on nonmonetary assets, i (which equals the expected real interest rate, r, plus the expected rate of inflation, π^e) raises the attractiveness of alternative assets and thus reduces the demand for money.

$$V = \frac{\text{nominal GDP}}{\text{nominal money stock}} = \frac{PY}{M} \quad (7.4)$$

Velocity, V, is nominal GDP, or P times Y, divided by the nominal money stock, M. Velocity is assumed to be constant by the quantity theory of money.

$$\frac{M}{P} = L(Y, r + \pi^e) \quad (7.9)$$

The asset market equilibrium condition states that the real supply of money, M/P, and the real demand for money, $L(Y, r + \pi^e)$, are equal.

$$\pi = \frac{\Delta M}{M} - \eta_Y \frac{\Delta Y}{Y} \quad (7.12)$$

The inflation rate, π, equals the growth rate of the nominal money supply, $\Delta M/M$, minus the growth rate of real money demand. In long-run equilibrium with a constant nominal interest rate, the growth rate of real money demand equals the income elasticity of money demand, η_Y, times the growth rate of real income or output, $\Delta Y/Y$.

REVIEW QUESTIONS

1. Define *money*. How does the economist's use of this term differ from its everyday meaning?
2. What are the three functions of money? How does each function contribute to a more smoothly operating economy?
3. Who determines the nation's money supply? Explain how the money supply could be expanded or reduced in an economy in which all money is in the form of currency.
4. What are the four characteristics of assets that are most important to holders of wealth? How does money compare with other assets for each characteristic?
5. Describe what is meant by the expectations theory of the term structure of interest rates. Why isn't the expectations theory sufficient to describe the data on interest rates that we observe? What must be added to the expectations theory to form a more accurate theory?
6. List and discuss the macroeconomic variables that affect the aggregate demand for money.
7. What are the major components of M1? What are the major components of M2? Describe each component.
8. Why is equilibrium in the asset market described by the condition that real money supply equal real money demand? What aggregation assumption is needed to allow ignoring the markets for other assets?
9. What is the relationship between the price level and the nominal money supply? What is the relationship between inflation and the growth rate of the nominal money supply?
10. Give an example of a factor that would increase the public's expected rate of inflation. All else being equal, how would this increase in the expected inflation rate affect interest rates?

NUMERICAL PROBLEMS

1. Suppose the interest rate on a one-year bond today is 6% per year, the interest rate on a one-year bond one year from now is expected to be 4% per year, and the interest rate on a one-year bond two years from now is expected to be 3% per year. The term premium on a two-year bond is 0.5% per year and the term premium on a three-year bond is 1.0% per year. In equilibrium, what is the interest rate today on a two-year bond? On a three-year bond? What is the shape of the yield curve?
2. Money demand in an economy in which no interest is paid on money is

$$\frac{M^d}{P} = 500 + 0.2Y - 1000i.$$

a. Suppose that $P = 100$, $Y = 1000$, and $i = 0.10$. Find real money demand, nominal money demand, and velocity.

b. The price level doubles from $P = 100$ to $P = 200$. Find real money demand, nominal money demand, and velocity.

c. Starting from the values of the variables given in Part (*a*) and assuming that the money demand function as written holds, determine how velocity is affected by an increase in real income, by an increase in the nominal interest rate, and by an increase in the price level.

3. Jason has wealth of $100,000 that he invests entirely in money (a checking account) and government bonds. Jason instructs his broker to invest $50,000 in bonds, plus $5000 more in bonds for every percentage point that the interest rate on bonds exceeds the interest rate on his checking account.

a. Write an algebraic formula that gives Jason's demand for money as a function of bond and checking account interest rates.

b. Write an algebraic formula that gives Jason's demand for bonds. What is the sum of his demand for money and his demand for bonds?

c. Suppose that all holders of wealth in the economy are identical to Jason. Fixed asset supplies per person are $80,000 of bonds and $20,000 of checking accounts. Checking accounts pay no interest. What is the interest rate on bonds in asset market equilibrium?

4. Assume that the quantity theory of money holds and that velocity is constant at 5. Output is fixed at its full-employment value of 10,000, and the price level is 2.

a. Determine the real demand for money and the nominal demand for money.

b. In this same economy the government fixes the nominal money supply at 5000. With output fixed at its full-employment level and with the assumption that prices are flexible, what will be the new price level? What happens to the price level if the nominal money supply rises to 6000?

5. Consider an economy with a constant nominal money supply, a constant level of real output $Y = 100$, and a constant real interest rate $r = 0.10$. Suppose that the income elasticity of money demand is 0.5 and the interest elasticity of money demand is -0.1.

a. By what percentage does the equilibrium price level differ from its initial value if output increases to $Y = 106$ (and r remains at 0.10)? (*Hint:* Use Eq. 7.12.)

b. By what percentage does the equilibrium price level differ from its initial value if the real interest increases to $r = 0.11$ (and Y remains at 100)?

c. Suppose that the real interest rate increases to $r = 0.11$. What would real output have to be for the equilibrium price level to remain at its initial value?

6. Suppose that the real money demand function is

$$L(Y, r + \pi^e) = \frac{0.01Y}{r + \pi^e},$$

where Y is real output, r is the real interest rate, and π^e is the expected rate of inflation. Real output is constant over time at $Y = 150$. The real interest rate is fixed in the goods market at $r = 0.05$ per year.

a. Suppose that the nominal money supply is growing at the rate of 10% per year and that this growth rate is expected to persist forever. Currently, the nominal money supply is $M = 300$. What are the values of the real money supply and the current price level? (*Hint:* What is the value of the expected inflation rate that enters the money demand function?)

b. Suppose that the nominal money supply is $M = 300$. The central bank announces that from now on the nominal money supply will grow at the rate of 5% per year. If everyone believes this announcement, and if all markets are in equilibrium, what are the values of the real money supply and the current price level? Explain the effects on the real money supply and the current price level of a slowdown in the rate of money growth.

7. The income elasticity of money demand is 2/3 and the interest elasticity of money demand is -0.1. Real income is expected to grow by 4.5% over the next year, and the real interest rate is expected to remain constant over the next year. The rate of inflation has been zero for several years.

a. If the central bank wants zero inflation over the next year, what growth rate of the nominal money supply should it choose?

b. By how much will velocity change over the next year if the central bank follows the policy that achieves zero inflation?

ANALYTICAL PROBLEMS

1. What happens to M1 and M2 due to each of the following changes?
   a. You take $500 out of your checking account and put it into a passbook savings account.
   b. You take $1000 out of your checking account and buy traveler's checks.
   c. You take $1500 out of your money-market mutual fund and deposit it into your checking account.
   d. You cash in $2000 in savings bonds and invest the money in a certificate of deposit.
2. Figure 7.2 shows that, before the 1990s, M2 velocity generally rose over time. Suggest some explanations for this upward trend.
3. The prisoner-of-war camp described by Radford ("In Touch with Data and Research: Money in a Prisoner-of-War Camp") periodically received large shipments of cigarettes from the Red Cross or other sources.
   a. How did cigarette shipments affect the price level (the prices of goods in terms of cigarettes) in the POW camp?
   b. (More difficult) On some occasions the prisoners knew in advance when the cigarette shipments were to arrive. What happened to the demand for cigarette money and the price level in the camp in the days just before an anticipated shipment?
4. Assume that prices and wages adjust rapidly so that the markets for labor, goods, and assets are always in equilibrium. What are the effects of each of the following on output, the real interest rate, and the current price level?
   a. A temporary increase in government purchases.
   b. A reduction in expected inflation.
   c. A temporary increase in labor supply.
   d. An increase in the interest rate paid on money.

WORKING WITH MACROECONOMIC DATA

For data to use in these exercises, go to the Federal Reserve Bank of St. Louis FRED database at fred.stlouisfed.org.

1. Graph the current yield curve (see the section "Time to Maturity" in this chapter and the graph of the yield curve in Chapter 4, "In Touch with Data and Research: Interest Rates"), plotting the interest rate on bonds with different maturities against their time to maturity, using data from the Federal Reserve's H.15 release (*www.federalreserve.gov/releases/h15*). Use the Fed's "constant maturity" series of rates, which are designed for this purpose. Then look at the H.15 release from one year earlier and plot the yield curve for that date as well. What has happened to the term structure of interest rates over the past year? What economic events do you think have led to this change?
2. Graph the CPI inflation rate, M1 money growth, and M2 money growth for the United States, using annual data since 1959. (Find annual growth rates for December to December.) Also graph the three-year average rate of inflation and the three-year averages of M1 growth and M2 growth, starting with 1962. (The three-year average rate of inflation for, say, 1978 is the average of the inflation rates in 1976, 1977, and 1978. Similarly, the three-year average money growth rate for 1978 is the average of the money growth rates for 1976, 1977, and 1978.)

   Is the inflation rate more closely related to M1 growth or M2 growth? Is the relationship of inflation to money growth stronger in the short run (in annual data) or in the longer run (using three-year averages)? What has happened to the link between inflation and money growth since 1980?
3. Graph the three-month Treasury bill interest rate, the ten-year government bond interest rate, and the CPI inflation rate (based on the percentage change in the CPI from one year earlier) on the same figure, using data since 1961. Make sure that the units are comparable.
   a. In general, how are changes in interest rates related to changes in inflation? Why?
   b. Is the three-month rate or the ten-year rate more sensitive to current changes in inflation? Give an economic explanation.
4. Find and plot data since 1960 on the net worth as a percentage of disposable personal income of households and nonprofit organizations. In which periods was net wealth as a percentage of income generally rising? In what periods was it falling? By what percentage did it decline during the Great Recession from the fourth quarter of 2007 to the second quarter of 2009? (Note that net wealth data for nonprofit organizations is included with that of households for technical reasons but the net wealth of households is far larger than that of nonprofit organizations, so the data series mainly relates to households.)

8

Business Cycles

Since the Industrial Revolution, the economies of the United States and many other countries have grown tremendously. That growth has transformed economies and greatly improved living standards. Yet even in prosperous countries, economic expansion has been periodically interrupted by episodes of declining production and income and rising unemployment. Sometimes—fortunately, not often—these episodes have been severe and prolonged. But whether brief or more extended, declines in economic activity have been followed almost invariably by a resumption of economic growth.

This repeated sequence of economic expansion giving way to temporary decline followed by recovery, is known as the *business cycle*. The business cycle is a central concern in macroeconomics because business cycle fluctuations—the ups and downs in overall economic activity—are felt throughout the economy. When the economy is growing strongly, prosperity is shared by most of the nation's industries and their workers and owners of capital. When the economy weakens, many sectors of the economy experience declining sales and production, and workers are laid off or forced to work only part-time. Because the effects of business cycles are so widespread, and because economic downturns can cause great hardship, economists have tried to find the causes of these episodes and to determine what, if anything, can be done to counteract them. The two basic questions of (1) what causes business cycles and (2) how policymakers should respond to cyclical fluctuations are the main concern of Part 3 of this book.

The answers to these two questions remain highly controversial. Much of this controversy involves the proponents of the classical and Keynesian approaches to macroeconomics, introduced in Chapter 1. In brief, classical economists view business cycles as generally representing the economy's best response to disturbances in production or spending. Thus classical economists do not see much, if any, need for government action to counteract these fluctuations. In contrast, Keynesian economists argue that, because wages and prices adjust slowly, disturbances in production or spending may drive the economy away from its most desirable level of output and employment for long periods of time. According to the Keynesian view, government should intervene to smooth business cycle fluctuations.

We explore the debate between classicals and Keynesians, and the implications of that debate for economic analysis and macroeconomic policy, in Chapters 9–11. In this chapter we provide essential background for that discussion by presenting the basic features of the business cycle. We begin with a definition and a brief history of the business cycle in the United States. We then turn to a more detailed discussion of business cycle characteristics, or "business cycle facts." We conclude the chapter with a brief preview of the alternative approaches to the analysis of business cycles.

Learning Objectives

8.1 Define and describe the business cycle.

8.2 Summarize the history of the American business cycle.

8.3 Describe the behavior of various variables over the course of business cycles.

8.4 Use aggregate demand and aggregate supply to describe the impact on business cycles of various shocks.

8.1 What Is a Business Cycle?

Define and describe the business cycle.

Countries have experienced ups and downs in overall economic activity since they began to industrialize. Economists have measured and studied these fluctuations for more than a century. Marx and Engels referred to "commercial crises," an early term for business cycles, in their Communist Manifesto in 1848. In the United States, the National Bureau of Economic Research (NBER), a private nonprofit organization of economists founded in 1920, pioneered business cycle research. The NBER developed and continues to update the **business cycle chronology**, a detailed history of business cycles in the United States and other countries. The NBER has also sponsored many studies of the business cycle: One landmark study was the 1946 book *Measuring Business Cycles*, by Arthur Burns (who served as Federal Reserve chairman from 1970 until 1978) and Wesley Mitchell (a principal founder of the NBER). This work was among the first to document and analyze the empirical facts about business cycles. It begins with the following definition:

> Business cycles are a type of fluctuation found in the aggregate economic activity of nations that organize their work mainly in business enterprises. A cycle consists of expansions occurring at about the same time in many economic activities, followed by similarly general recessions, contractions, and revivals which merge into the expansion phase of the next cycle; this sequence of changes is recurrent but not periodic; in duration business cycles vary from more than one year to ten or twelve years.[1]

Five points in this definition should be clarified and emphasized.

1. *Aggregate economic activity.* Business cycles are defined broadly as fluctuations of "aggregate economic activity" rather than as fluctuations in a single, specific economic variable such as real GDP. Although real GDP may be the single variable that most closely measures aggregate economic activity, Burns and Mitchell also thought it important to look at other indicators of activity, such as employment and financial market variables.

2. *Expansions and contractions.* Figure 8.1—a diagram of a typical business cycle—helps explain what Burns and Mitchell meant by expansions and contractions. The dashed line shows the average, or normal, growth path of aggregate economic activity, as determined by the factors we considered in Chapter 6. The solid curve shows the rises and falls of actual economic activity. The period of time during which aggregate economic activity is falling is a **contraction** or **recession**. If the recession is particularly severe, it becomes a **depression**. After reaching the low point of the contraction, the **trough** (T), aggregate economic activity begins to increase. The period of time during which aggregate economic activity grows is an **expansion** or a **boom**. After reaching the high point of the expansion, the **peak** (P), aggregate economic activity begins to decline again. The entire sequence of decline followed by recovery, measured from peak to peak or trough to trough, is a **business cycle**.

Figure 8.1 suggests that business cycles are purely temporary deviations from the economy's normal growth path. However, part of the output losses and gains that occur during a business cycle may become permanent.

Peaks and troughs in the business cycle are known collectively as **turning points**. One goal of business cycle research is to identify when turning points

[1]Burns and Mitchell, *Measuring Business Cycles*, New York: National Bureau of Economic Research, 1946, p. 1.

FIGURE 8.1

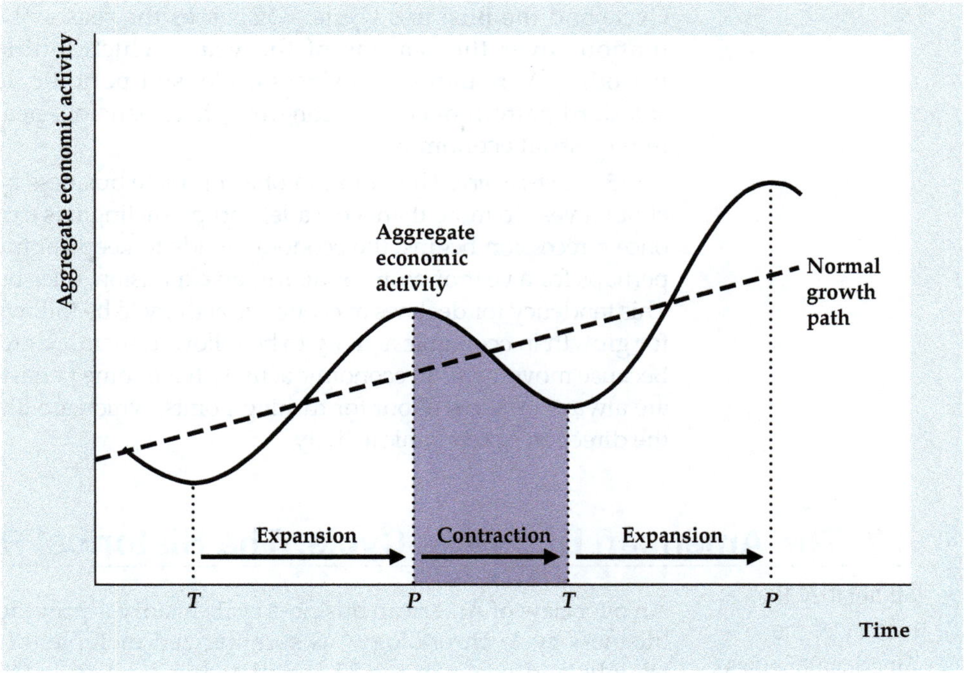

A business cycle
The solid curve graphs the behavior of aggregate economic activity over a typical business cycle. The dashed line shows the economy's normal growth path. During a contraction aggregate economic activity falls until it reaches a trough, *T*. The trough is followed by an expansion during which economic activity increases until it reaches a peak, *P*. A complete cycle is measured from peak to peak or trough to trough.

occur. Aggregate economic activity isn't measured directly by any single variable, so there's no simple formula that tells economists when a peak or trough has been reached.[2] In practice, a small group of economists who form the NBER's Business Cycle Dating Committee determine that date. The committee meets only when its members believe that a turning point may have occurred. By examining a variety of economic data, the committee determines whether a peak or trough has been reached and, if so, the month it happened. However, the committee's announcements usually come well after a peak or trough occurs, so their judgments are more useful for historical analysis of business cycles than as a guide to current policymaking.

3. *Comovement.* Business cycles do not occur in just a few sectors or in just a few economic variables. Instead, expansions or contractions "occur at about the same time in many economic activities." Thus, although some industries are more sensitive to the business cycle than others, output and employment in most industries tend to fall in recessions and rise in expansions. Many other economic variables, such as prices, productivity, investment, and government purchases, also have regular and predictable patterns of behavior over the course of the business cycle. The tendency of many economic variables to move together in a predictable way over the business cycle is called **comovement**.

4. *Recurrent but not periodic.* The business cycle isn't periodic, in that it does not occur at regular, predictable intervals and doesn't last for a fixed or predetermined length of time. ("In Touch with Data and Research: The Seasonal

---

[2]A conventional definition used by the media—that a recession has occurred when there are two consecutive quarters of negative real GDP growth—isn't widely accepted by economists. The reason that economists tend not to like this definition is that real GDP is only one of many possible indicators of economic activity.

Cycle and the Business Cycle," discusses the seasonal cycle—or economic fluctuations over the seasons of the year—which, unlike the business cycle, is periodic.) Although the business cycle isn't periodic, it is recurrent; that is, the standard pattern of contraction–trough–expansion–peak recurs again and again in industrial economies.

5. *Persistence.* The duration of a complete business cycle can vary greatly, from about a year to more than a decade, and predicting it is extremely difficult. However, once a recession begins, the economy tends to keep contracting for a period of time, perhaps for a year or more. Similarly, an expansion, once begun, usually lasts a while. This tendency for declines in economic activity to be followed by further declines, and for growth in economic activity to be followed by more growth, is called **persistence**. Because movements in economic activity have some persistence, economic forecasters are always on the lookout for turning points, which are likely to indicate a change in the direction of economic activity.

8.2 The American Business Cycle: The Historical Record

Summarize the history of the American business cycle.

An overview of American business cycle history is provided by the NBER's monthly business cycle chronology,[3] as summarized in Table 8.1. It gives the dates of the troughs and peaks of the 33 complete business cycles that the U.S. economy has experienced since 1854. Also shown is the number of months that each contraction and expansion lasted.

The Pre–World War I Period

The period between the Civil War (1861–1865) and World War I (1917–1918) was one of rapid economic growth in the United States. Nevertheless, as Table 8.1 shows, recessions were a serious problem during that time. Indeed, the longest contraction on record is the 65-month-long decline between October 1873 and March 1879, a contraction that was worldwide in scope and is referred to by economic historians as the Depression of the 1870s. Overall, during the 1854–1914 period the economy suffered 338 months of contraction, or nearly as many as the 382 months of expansion. In contrast, from the end of World War II in 1945 through June 2018, the number of months of expansion (750) outnumbered months of contraction (122) by more than six to one.

The Great Depression and World War II

The worst economic contraction in the history of the United States was the Great Depression of the 1930s. After a prosperous decade in the 1920s, aggregate economic activity reached a peak in August 1929, two months before the stock market crash in October 1929. Between the 1929 peak and the 1933 trough, real GDP fell by nearly 30%. During the same period the unemployment rate rose from about 3% to nearly 25%, with many of those lucky enough to have jobs only able to work part-time. To appreciate how severe the Great Depression was, compare it with the

[3]For a detailed discussion of the NBER chronologies, see Geoffrey H. Moore and Victor Zarnowitz, "The NBER's Business Cycle Chronologies," in Robert J. Gordon, ed., *The American Business Cycle: Continuity and Change*, Chicago: University of Chicago Press, 1986. The NBER chronology is available at the NBER's website, *www.nber.org*.

TABLE 8.1

NBER Business Cycle Turning Points and Durations of Post-1854 Business Cycles

Trough	Expansion (months from trough to peak)	Peak	Contraction (months from peak to next trough)
December 1854 (IV)	30	June 1857(II)	18
December 1858 (IV)	22	October 1860(III)	8
June 1861 (III)	46 (Civil War)	April 1865(I)	32
December 1867 (I)	18	June 1869(II)	18
December 1870 (IV)	34	October 1873(III)	65
March 1879 (I)	36	March 1882(I)	38
May 1885 (II)	22	March 1887(II)	13
April 1888 (I)	27	July 1890(III)	10
May 1891 (II)	20	January 1893(I)	17
June 1894 (II)	18	December 1895(IV)	18
June 1897 (II)	24	June 1899(III)	18
December 1900 (IV)	21	September 1902(IV)	23
August 1904 (III)	33	May 1907(II)	13
June 1908 (II)	19	January 1910(I)	24
January 1912 (IV)	12	January 1913(I)	23
December 1914 (IV)	44 (WWI)	August 1918(III)	7
March 1919 (I)	10	January 1920(I)	18
July 1921 (III)	22	May 1923(II)	14
July 1924 (III)	27	October 1926(III)	13
November 1927 (IV)	21	August 1929(III)	43 (Depression)
March 1933 (I)	50	May 1937(II)	13 (Depression)
June 1938 (II)	80 (WWII)	February 1945(I)	8
October 1945 (IV)	37	November 1948(IV)	11
October 1949 (IV)	45 (Korean War)	July 1953(II)	10
May 1954 (II)	39	August 1957(III)	8
April 1958 (II)	24	April 1960(II)	10
February 1961 (I)	106 (Vietnam War)	December 1969(IV)	11
November 1970 (IV)	36	November 1973(IV)	16
March 1975 (I)	58	January 1980(I)	6
July 1980 (III)	12	July 1981(III)	16
November 1982 (IV)	92	July 1990(III)	8
March 1991(I)	120	March 2001(I)	8
November 2001 (IV)	73	December 2007 (IV)	18
June 2009 (II)	128	February 2020 (IV)	2 (Pandemic)
April 2020 (II)	24*		

Source: Data from U.S. Business Cycle Expansions and Contractions. National Bureau of Economic Research, Inc., *www.nber.org/research/data/us-business-cycle-expansions-and-contractions*.

*As of April 2022, this expansion was 24 months old.

recession of 2007–2009, which was the longest recession and the recession with the largest drop in real GDP in the period since World War II. The 30% decline in real GDP from peak to trough during the Great Depression was far more severe than the 4.2% peak-to-trough decline in real GDP during the 2007–2009 recession. In addition, the 25% unemployment rate during the Great Depression was more than double the unemployment rate of 10% reached during the 2007–2009 recession.

Although no sector escaped the Great Depression, some were particularly hard hit. In the financial sector, stock prices continued to collapse after the crash. Depositors withdrew their money from banks, and borrowers, unable to repay their bank loans, were forced to default; as a result, thousands of banks were forced to go out of business or merge with other banks. In agriculture, farmers were bankrupted by low crop prices, and a prolonged drought in the Midwest turned thousands of farm families into homeless migrants. Investment, both business and residential, fell to extremely low levels, and a "trade war"—in which countries competed in erecting barriers to imports—virtually halted international trade.

Although most people think of the Great Depression as a single episode, technically it consisted of two business cycles, as Table 8.1 shows. The contraction phase of the first cycle lasted forty-three months, from August 1929 until March 1933, and was the most precipitous economic decline in U.S. history. After Franklin Roosevelt took office as President in March 1933 and instituted a set of policies known collectively as the New Deal, a strong expansion began and continued for 50 months, from March 1933 to May 1937. By 1937 real GDP was almost back to its 1929 level, although at 14% the unemployment rate remained high. Unemployment remained high in 1937 despite the recovery of real GDP because the number of people of working age had grown since 1929 and because increases in productivity allowed employment to grow more slowly than output.

The second cycle of the Great Depression began in May 1937 with a contraction phase that lasted more than a year. Despite a new recovery that began in June 1938, the unemployment rate was still more than 17% in 1939.

The Great Depression ended dramatically with the onset of World War II. Even before the Japanese attack on Pearl Harbor brought the United States into the war in December 1941, the economy was gearing up for increased armaments production. After the shock of Pearl Harbor, the United States prepared for total war. With production supervised by government boards and driven by the insatiable demands of the military for more guns, planes, and ships, real GDP almost doubled between 1939 and 1944. Unemployment dropped sharply, averaging less than 2% of the labor force in 1943–1945 and bottoming out at 1.2% in 1944.

Post–World War II U.S. Business Cycles

As World War II was ending in 1945, economists and policymakers were concerned that the economy would relapse into depression. As an expression of this concern, Congress passed the Employment Act of 1946, which required the government to fight recessions and depressions with any measures at its disposal. But instead of falling into a new depression as feared, the U.S. economy began to grow strongly.

Only a few relatively brief and mild recessions interrupted the economic expansion of the early postwar period. None of the five contractions that occurred between 1945 and 1970 lasted more than a year, whereas 18 of the 22 previous cyclical contractions in the NBER's monthly chronology had lasted a year or more. The largest drop in real GDP between 1945 and 1970 was 3.6% during the 1957–1958 recession, and throughout this period unemployment never exceeded 8.1% of the work force. Again, there was a correlation between economic expansion and war: The 1949–1953 expansion corresponded closely to the Korean War, and the latter part of the strong 1961–1969 expansion occurred during the military buildup to fight the Vietnam War.

Because no serious recession occurred between 1945 and 1970, some economists suggested that the business cycle had been "tamed," or even that it was "dead." This view was especially popular during the 106-month expansion of 1961–1969, which was widely attributed not only to high rates of military spending during the Vietnam War but also to the macroeconomic policies of Presidents John F. Kennedy and Lyndon B. Johnson. Some argued that policymakers should stop worrying about recessions and focus their attention on inflation, which had been gradually increasing over the 1960s.

Unfortunately, reports of the business cycle's death proved premature. Shortly after the Organization of Petroleum Exporting Countries (OPEC) succeeded in quadrupling oil prices in the fall of 1973, the U.S. economy and the economies of many other nations fell into a severe recession. In the 1973–1975 recession U.S. real GDP fell by 3.1% and the unemployment rate reached 9%—not a depression but a serious downturn nonetheless. Also disturbing was the fact that inflation, which had fallen during most previous recessions, shot up to unprecedented double-digit levels. Inflation continued to be a problem for the rest of the 1970s, even as the economy recovered from the 1973–1975 recession.

More evidence that the business cycle wasn't dead came with the sharp 1981–1982 recession. This contraction lasted sixteen months, the same length as the 1973–1975 decline, and the unemployment rate reached 11%, a postwar high. Many economists claim that the Fed knowingly created this recession to reduce inflation. Inflation did drop dramatically, from about 11% to less than 4% per year. The recovery from this recession was strong, however.

The "Long Boom"

After the severe 1981–1982 recession the U.S. economy began an extended period of economic growth and reduced volatility of major macroeconomic variables. The extended period of economic growth is often called the "long boom," which began in 1982 and ended with the recession of 2001. During this period of time there was only one recession, which began in July 1990 and ended in March 1991, eight months after the peak. Not only was the 1990–1991 recession short-lived, it was not severe (the unemployment rate peaked in mid 1992 at 7.7%—not particularly high for a recession). In the mid-1980s, during the early part of the Long Boom, the volatility of many major macroeconomic variables declined sharply. This period of reduced volatility, known as the Great Moderation, coincided with the remainder of the Long Boom and even beyond. (See the discussion of the Great Moderation in the section, "Have American Business Cycles Become Less Severe?")

The Great Recession

The long boom was ended by the 2001 recession, which was followed by six years of modest economic growth. Then in December 2007, the economy entered the longest and deepest recession to hit the United States since the Great Depression, a recession that has come to be known as the Great Recession. The Great Recession began with a housing crisis (see "In Touch with Data and Research: The Housing Crisis of 2007 to 2011," in Chapter 7), which was followed by a financial crisis that rivaled that of the Great Depression (see the Application "The Financial Crisis of 2008" in Chapter 14), as numerous financial institutions failed or required government assistance to save them. The unemployment rate rose above 10% for the first time since 1982, and the Federal Reserve reduced interest rates to near zero. The recession ended in June 2009, but in the years following, economic growth was fairly sluggish and the unemployment rate declined at a very slow pace despite the use of expansionary fiscal and monetary policies.

Have American Business Cycles Become Less Severe?

Macroeconomists believed that, over the long sweep of history, business cycles generally have become less severe. Obviously, no recession in the United States since World War II can begin to rival the severity of the Great Depression. Even putting aside the Great Depression, economists generally believed that business downturns before 1929 were longer and deeper than those since 1945. According to the NBER business cycle chronology (Table 8.1), for example, the average contraction before 1929 lasted nearly 21 months and the average expansion lasted slightly more than 25 months. Since 1945, contractions have shortened to an average of 11 months, and expansions have lengthened to an average of more than 50 months, even excluding the lengthy expansion of the 1990s. Standard measures of economic fluctuations, such as real GDP growth and the unemployment rate, also show considerably less volatility since 1945, relative to data available for the pre-1929 era.

Since World War II a major goal of economic policy has been to reduce the size and frequency of recessions. If researchers found—contrary to the generally accepted view—that business cycles had *not* moderated in the postwar period, serious doubt would be cast on the ability of economic policymakers to achieve this goal. For this reason, although the question of whether the business cycle has moderated over time may seem to be a matter of interest only to economic historians, this issue is of great practical importance.

Thus Christina Romer, who later served as Chair of the Council of Economic Advisers under President Obama, sparked a heated controversy by writing a series of articles in the 1980s denying the claim that the business cycle has moderated over time.[4] Romer's main point concerned the dubious quality of the pre–1929 data. Unlike today, in earlier periods the government didn't collect comprehensive data on economic variables such as GDP. Instead, economic historians, using whatever fragmentary information they could find, have had to estimate historical measures of these variables.

Romer argued that methods used for estimating historical data typically overstated the size of earlier cyclical fluctuations. For example, widely accepted estimates of pre–1929 GNP[5] were based on estimates of just the goods-producing sectors of the economy, which are volatile, while ignoring less-volatile sectors such as wholesale and retail distribution, transportation, and services. As a result, the volatility of GNP was overstated. Measured properly, GNP varied substantially less over time than the widely accepted statistics showed. Romer's arguments sparked additional research, though none proved decisively whether volatility truly declined after 1929. Nonetheless, the debate served the useful purpose of forcing a careful reexamination of the historical data.

Follow-on research showed that economic volatility declined in the mid 1980s and remained low until the financial crisis of 2008. Because the quality of the data is not an issue for the period following World War II, the decline in volatility in the

[4]The articles included "Is the Stabilization of the Postwar Economy a Figment of the Data?" *American Economic Review,* June 1986, pp. 314–334; "The Prewar Business Cycle Reconsidered: New Estimates of Gross National Product, 1869–1908," *Journal of Political Economy,* February 1989, pp. 1–37; and "The Cyclical Behavior of Individual Production Series, 1889–1984," *Quarterly Journal of Economics,* February 1991, pp. 1–31.

[5]As discussed in Chapter 2, until 1991 the U.S. national income and product accounts focused on GNP rather than GDP. As a result, studies of business cycle behavior have often focused on GNP rather than GDP.

mid 1980s, relative to the preceding forty years, probably reflects a genuine change in economic volatility rather than a change in how economic data are produced.

Other economic variables, including inflation, residential investment, output of durable goods, and output of structures, also appear to fluctuate less in the past 30 years than they did in the preceding 40 years. Research by James Stock of Harvard University and Mark Watson of Princeton University[6] shows that the volatility, as measured by the standard deviation of a variable, declined by 20% to 40% for many of the 21 variables they examine, including a decline of 33% for real GDP, 27% for employment, and 50% for inflation. Because the decline in volatility of macroeconomic variables has been so widespread, economists have dubbed this episode "the Great Moderation."[7]

To see what we mean by the Great Moderation, let's begin by looking at real GDP growth since 1952. In Figure 8.2, we have plotted the quarterly growth rate of real GDP (seasonally adjusted at an annual rate). You can see that from 1952 until about 1984, the growth rate changes significantly from quarter to quarter, but after 1984 it seems considerably more stable. In the Great Recession (2007–2009), the growth rate became more volatile but subsequently became very stable until the COVID recession of 2020.

Another graphical device that will help us to see the Great Moderation is a plot of the standard deviation of quarterly growth. The standard deviation of a variable is a measure of its volatility. Because we think the volatility has changed over time, we are going to calculate the standard deviation over five-year periods. The result is shown in Figure 8.3, where we plot the five-year standard deviations

FIGURE 8.2

GDP growth, 1952Q1–2021Q4

The chart shows the annualized quarterly growth rate of seasonally adjusted real GDP since the first quarter of 1952. The growth rate is more volatile before 1984 than after 1984.

Source: Authors' calculations from data on real GDP from Bureau of Economic Analysis, downloaded from the Federal Reserve Bank of St. Louis FRED database, *fred.stlouisfed.org/series/GDPC1*.

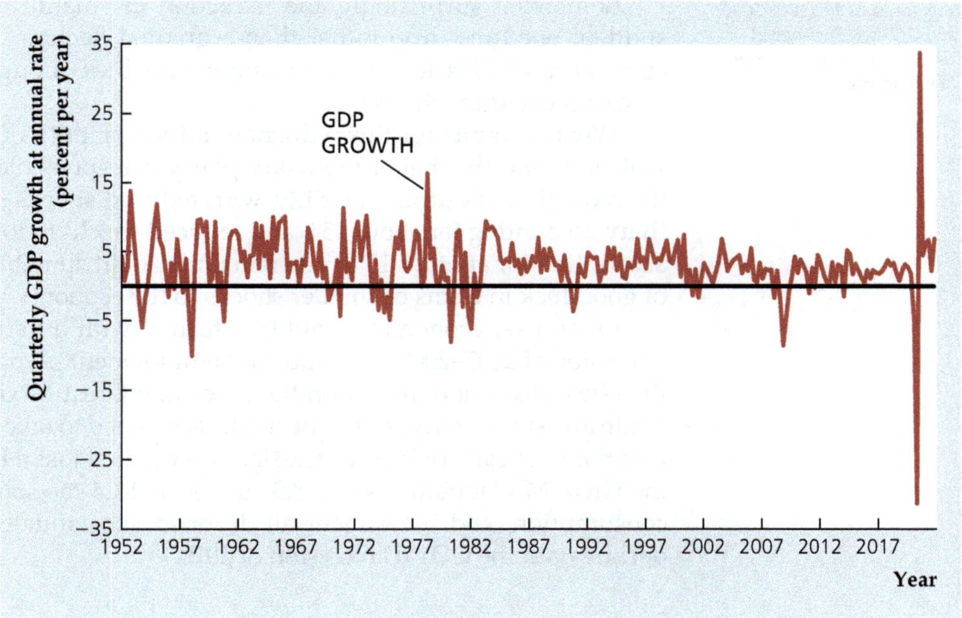

[6]"Has the Business Cycle Changed and Why?" *NBER Macroeconomics Annual 2002* (Cambridge, MA: MIT Press, 2002), pp. 159–218.

[7]See Ben S. Bernanke, "The Great Moderation." Speech at the Eastern Economic Association meetings, February 20, 2004, available at *www.federalreserve.gov/boarddocs/speeches/2004/20040220/default.htm*.

FIGURE 8.3

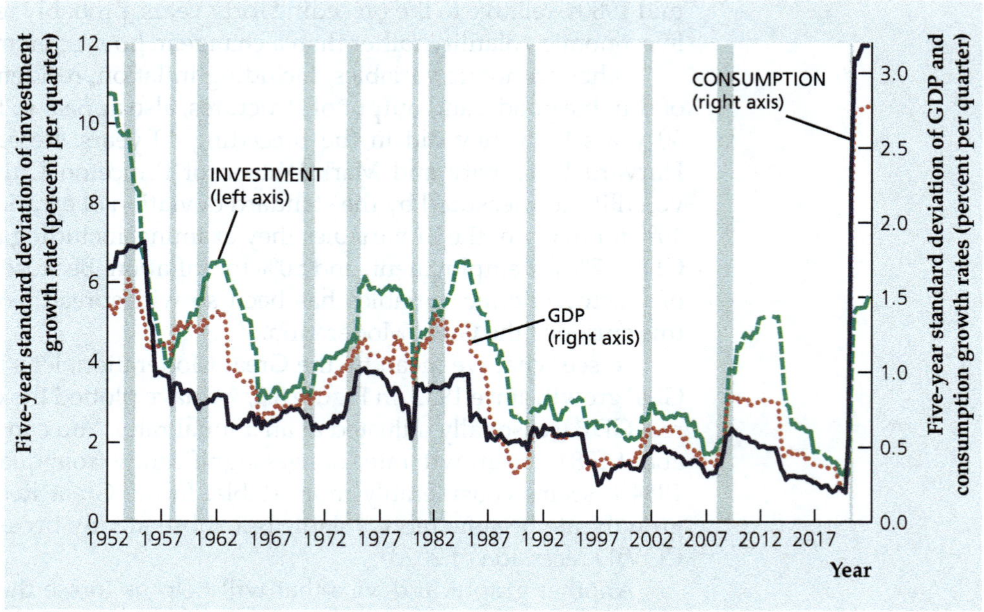

Volatility of GDP, consumption, and investment, 1952Q1–2021Q4

The chart shows the standard deviation of the quarterly growth rate of GDP, consumption, and investment, over five-year periods, from the first quarter of 1952 to the fourth quarter of 2021. The five-year standard deviation fell sharply in about 1984, but rose during the recession that began in 2007 and increased dramatically in the COVID recession in 2020.

Source: Authors' calculations from data on real GDP from Bureau of Economic Analysis, downloaded from the Federal Reserve Bank of St. Louis FRED database, *fred.stlouisfed.org/* series *GDPC1*, *PCECC96*, and *GPDIC1*. The shaded vertical bars indicate times of recessions.

of GDP, consumption, and investment. Note that each point shown on the graph represents the standard deviation of growth of that variable for the preceding five years. The graph shows a sharp decline in about 1984 in the five-year standard deviations of all three variables.

Somewhat surprisingly, the reduction in volatility seemed to come from a sudden, one-time drop rather than a gradual decline. The break seems to have come around 1984 for many economic variables, though for some variables the break occurred much later.

What accounts for this reduction in the volatility of the economy? Stock and Watson found that better monetary policy is responsible for about 20% to 30% of the reduction in output volatility, with reduced shocks to the economy's productivity accounting for about 15% and reduced shocks to food and commodity prices accounting for another 15%. The remainder is attributable to some unknown form of good luck in terms of smaller shocks to the economy.[8]

Of course, economic volatility returned with a vengeance during the Great Recession of 2007–2009, as output and employment plunged. Indeed, some blamed the Great Recession in part on the preceding Great Moderation, which may have made investors overly confident and thus inclined to take excessive risks. It appears that the financial crisis and recession represented just a temporary interruption in the Great Moderation. As Fig. 8.3 shows, in 2014 the standard deviations of GDP, consumption, and investment all dropped substantially, and they continued to decline until the COVID recession of 2020.

---

[8]Since the Stock and Watson paper was written, much additional research has been undertaken, with mixed results. For example, Shaghil Ahmed, Andrew Levin, and Beth Ann Wilson ("Recent Improvements in U.S. Macroeconomic Stability: Good Policy, Good Practices, or Good Luck?" *Review of Economics and Statistics*, 86 (2004), pp. 824–832) suggest that good luck played the biggest role, while others find a larger role for monetary policy, including Peter M. Summers ("What Caused the Great Moderation? Some Cross-Country Evidence," Federal Reserve Bank of Kansas City, *Economic Review*, Third Quarter 2005, pp. 5–32).

Application

Do Economic Expansions Die of Old Age?

Do economic expansions "run out of steam" or "die of old age"? That is, does the probability that an expansion will come to an end rise appreciably as an expansion ages, just as people are more likely to die as they reach old age?

Using a technique known as survival analysis, Glenn Rudebusch of the Federal Reserve Bank of San Francisco investigates the probability that an expansion of a given age will end in the next month and relates this probability to the age of the expansion.[9] He examines business cycles before World War II separately from business cycles after World War II. As shown in Figure 8.4, the postwar behavior of this probability differs from its prewar behavior in two important ways. First, an expansion of any given age was more likely to end within a month in the prewar period than in the postwar period; that is, the probabilities shown in Fig. 8.4 are higher in the prewar period than in the postwar period. Second, unlike the prewar expansions, for which the probability of ending within a month increases substantially with age, the postwar expansions show only a slight tendency for older expansions to be more likely than young expansions to end within a month. A prewar economic expansion is like a person: Over a given period of time, the older a person is, the more likely it is that he or she will die. However, postwar expansions look different: Older expansions are no more likely to die over a given period than younger expansions. As Rudebusch notes, "Accordingly, based only on age, an 80-month-old expansion has effectively the same chance of ending as a 40-month-old expansion."

In conclusion, it appears that the length of an economic expansion is not an indicator that the expansion is nearing its end.

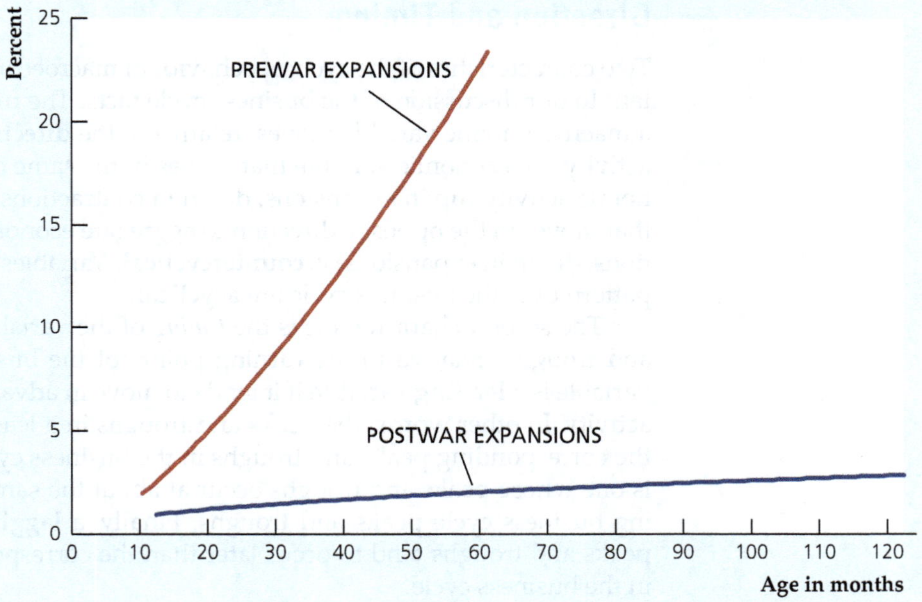

FIGURE 8.4

Probability that an expansion of a given age will end in the next month

The figure shows the probability that an economic expansion will end within a month, given the age of the expansion. The probabilities are very different before and after World War II.

Source: Data updated through May 2018 by Glenn Rudebusch, Federal Reserve Bank of San Francisco, based on article cited in footnote 9.

[9]See Glenn Rudebusch, "Will the Economic Recovery Die of Old Age?" Federal Reserve Bank of San Francisco *Economic Letter* 2016-03, February 8, 2016.

8.3 Business Cycle Facts

Describe the behavior of various variables over the course of business cycles.

Although no two business cycles are identical, all (or most) cycles have features in common. This point has been made strongly by a leading business cycle theorist, Nobel laureate Robert E. Lucas, Jr., of the University of Chicago:

> Though there is absolutely no theoretical reason to anticipate it, one is led by the facts to conclude that, with respect to the qualitative behavior of comovements among series [that is, economic variables], *business cycles are all alike.* To theoretically inclined economists, this conclusion should be attractive and challenging, for it suggests the possibility of a unified explanation of business cycles, grounded in the *general* laws governing market economies, rather than in political or institutional characteristics specific to particular countries or periods.[10]

Lucas's statement that business cycles are all alike (or more accurately, that they have many features in common) is based on examinations of comovements among economic variables over the business cycle. In this section, we study these comovements, which we call business cycle facts, for the post–World War II period in the United States. Knowing these business cycle facts is useful for interpreting economic data and evaluating the state of the economy. In addition, they provide guidance and discipline for developing economic theories of the business cycle. When we discuss alternative theories of the business cycle in Chapters 10 and 11, we evaluate the theories principally by determining how well they account for business cycle facts. To be successful, a theory of the business cycle must explain the cyclical behavior of not just a few variables, such as output and employment, but of a wide range of key economic variables.

The Cyclical Behavior of Economic Variables: Direction and Timing

Two characteristics of the cyclical behavior of macroeconomic variables are important to our discussion of the business cycle facts. The first is the *direction* in which a macroeconomic variable moves, relative to the direction of aggregate economic activity. An economic variable that moves in the same direction as aggregate economic activity (up in expansions, down in contractions) is **procyclical**. A variable that moves in the opposite direction to aggregate economic activity (up in contractions, down in expansions) is **countercyclical**. Variables that do not display a clear pattern over the business cycle are **acyclical**.

The second characteristic is the *timing* of the variable's turning points (peaks and troughs) relative to the turning points of the business cycle. An economic variable is a **leading variable** if it tends to move in advance of aggregate economic activity. In other words, the peaks and troughs in a leading variable occur before the corresponding peaks and troughs in the business cycle. A **coincident variable** is one whose peaks and troughs occur at about the same time as the corresponding business cycle peaks and troughs. Finally, a **lagging variable** is one whose peaks and troughs tend to occur later than the corresponding peaks and troughs in the business cycle.

---

[10]Robert E. Lucas, Jr., "Understanding Business Cycles," in K. Brunner and A. H. Meltzer, eds., *Carnegie-Rochester Conference Series on Public Policy*, 5 (Autumn 1977), p. 10.

The fact that some economic variables consistently lead the business cycle suggests that they might be used to forecast the future course of the economy. Some analysts have used downturns in the stock market to predict recessions, but such an indicator is not infallible. As Paul Samuelson noted: "Wall Street indexes predicted nine out of the last five recessions."[11]

In some cases, the cyclical timing of a variable is obvious from a graph of its behavior over the course of several business cycles; in other cases, elaborate statistical techniques are needed to determine timing. Conveniently, The Conference Board has analyzed the timing of dozens of economic variables. This information is published monthly in *Business Cycle Indicators,* along with the most recent data for these variables. For the most part, in this chapter we rely on The Conference Board's timing classifications.

Let's now examine the cyclical behavior of some key macroeconomic variables. We showed the historical behavior of several of these variables in Figs. 1.1–1.4. Those figures covered a long time period and were based on annual data. We can get a better view of short-run cyclical behavior by looking at quarterly or monthly data. The direction and timing of the variables considered are presented in Summary table 10.

Production

Because the level of production is a basic indicator of aggregate economic activity, peaks and troughs in production tend to occur at about the same time as peaks and troughs in aggregate economic activity. Thus production is a coincident and procyclical variable. Figure 8.5 shows the behavior of the industrial production

FIGURE 8.5

Cyclical behavior of the index of industrial production, 1947–2021

The index of industrial production, a broad measure of production in manufacturing, mining, and utilities, is procyclical and coincident.

Source: Board of Governors of the Federal Reserve System, downloaded from Federal Reserve Bank of St. Louis FRED database at *fred.stlouisfed.org/series/INDPRO.*

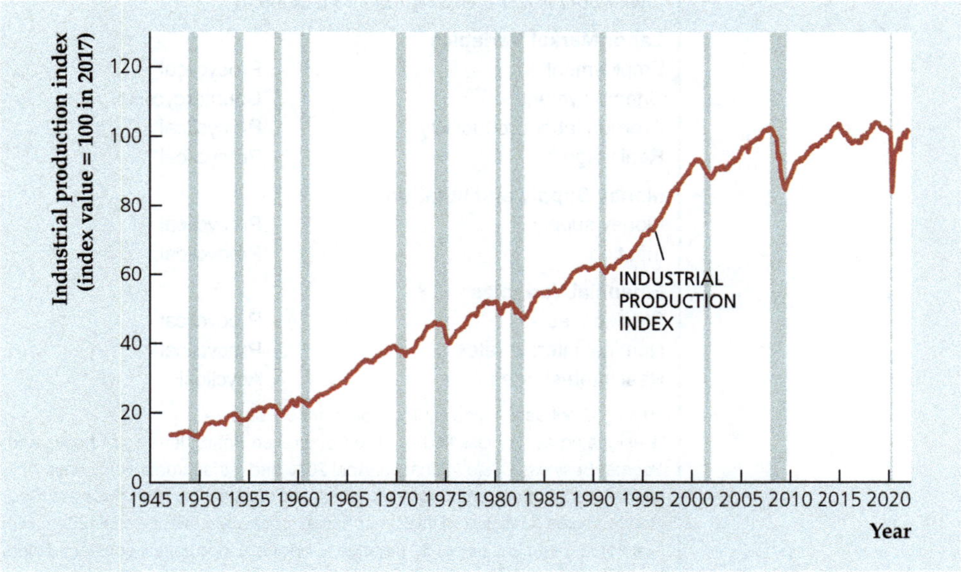

[11]*Newsweek* column, September 19, 1966, as quoted in John Bartlett, *Bartlett's Familiar Quotations,* Boston: Little Brown, 2002.

index in the United States since 1947. This index is a broad measure of production in manufacturing, mining, and utilities. The shaded vertical bars in Figs. 8.5–8.13, 8.15, and 8.16 indicate times of recessions, as determined by the NBER (see Table 8.1). The turning points in industrial production correspond closely to the turning points of the cycle.

Although almost all types of production rise in expansions and fall in recessions, the cyclical sensitivity of production in some sectors of the economy is greater than in others. Industries that produce relatively durable, or long-lasting, goods—houses, consumer durables (refrigerators, cars, washing machines), or capital goods (drill presses, computers, factories)—respond strongly to the business cycle, producing at high rates during expansions and at much lower rates during recessions. In contrast, industries that produce relatively nondurable or short-lived goods (foods, paper products) or services (education, insurance) are less sensitive to the business cycle.

SUMMARY 10

The Cyclical Behavior of Key Macroeconomic Variables (the Business Cycle Facts)

Variable	Direction	Timing
Production		
Industrial production	Procyclical	Coincident
Durable goods industries are more volatile than nondurable goods and services		
Expenditure		
Consumption	Procyclical	Coincident
Business fixed investment	Procyclical	Coincident
Residential investment	Procyclical	Leading
Inventory investment	Procyclical	Leading
Government purchases	Procyclical	—[a]
Investment is more volatile than consumption		
Labor Market Variables		
Employment	Procyclical	Coincident
Unemployment	Countercyclical	Unclassified[b]
Average labor productivity	Procyclical	Leading[a]
Real wage	Procyclical	—[a]
Money Supply and Inflation		
Money supply	Procyclical	Leading
Inflation	Procyclical	Lagging
Financial Variables		
Stock prices	Procyclical	Leading
Nominal interest rates	Procyclical	Lagging
Real interest rates	Acyclical	—[a]

[a]Timing is not designated by The Conference Board.

[b]Designated as "unclassified" by The Conference Board; leading at peaks and lagging at troughs.

Source: Business Cycle Indicators, April 2018. Industrial production: series 47 (industrial production); consumption: series 57 (manufacturing and trade sales, constant dollars); business fixed investment: series 86 (gross private nonresidential fixed investment); residential investment: series 28 (new private housing units started); inventory investment: series 30 (change in business inventories, constant dollars); employment: series 41 (employees on nonagricultural payrolls); unemployment: series 43 (civilian unemployment rate); money supply: series 106 (money supply M2, constant dollars); inflation: series 120 (CPI for services, change over six-month span); stock prices: series 19 (index of stock prices, 500 common stocks); nominal interest rates: series 119 (Federal funds rate), series 114 (discount rate on new 91-day Treasury bills), series 109 (average prime rate charged by banks).

Expenditure

For components of expenditure, as for types of production, durability is the key to determining sensitivity to the business cycle. Figure 8.6 shows the cyclical behavior of consumption of nondurable goods, consumption of services, consumption expenditures on durable goods, and investment. Investment is made up primarily of spending on durable goods and is strongly procyclical. In contrast, consumption of nondurable goods and consumption of services are both much smoother. Consumption expenditures on durable goods are more strongly procyclical than consumption expenditures on nondurable goods or consumption of services, but not as procyclical as investment expenditures. With respect to timing, consumption and investment are generally coincident with the business cycle, although individual components of fixed investment vary in their cyclical timing.[12]

One component of spending that seems to follow its own rules is inventory investment, or changes in business inventories (not shown), which often displays large fluctuations that aren't associated with business cycle peaks and troughs. In general, however, inventory investment is procyclical and leading. Even though goods kept in inventory need not be durable, inventory investment is also very volatile. Although, on average, inventory investment is a small part (about 1%) of total spending, sharp declines in inventory investment represented a large part of the total decline in spending in some recessions, most notably those of 1973–1975, 1981–1982, and 2001.

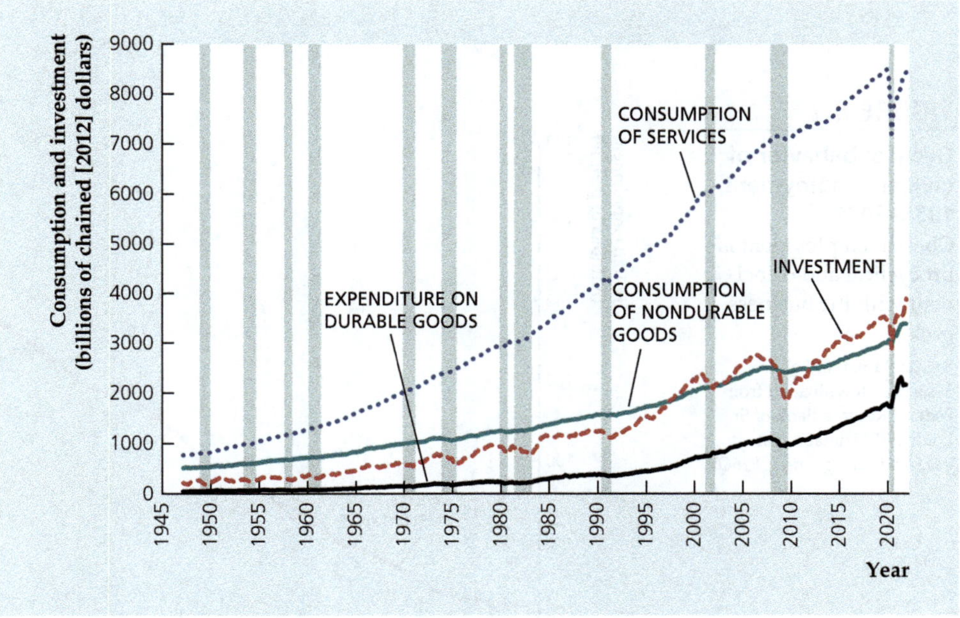

FIGURE 8.6

Cyclical behavior of consumption and investment, 1947–2021

Both consumption and investment are procyclical. However, investment is more sensitive than consumption to the business cycle, reflecting the fact that durable goods are a larger part of investment spending than they are of consumption spending. Similarly, expenditures on consumer durables are more sensitive to the business cycle than is consumption of nondurable goods or services.

Source: Authors' calculations based on data from U.S. Bureau of Economic Analysis, downloaded from Federal Reserve Bank of St. Louis FRED database at *fred.stlouisfed.org*. Durable goods: series *DDURRA3Q086SBEA* and *PCDG*; nondurable goods series *DNDGRA3Q086SBEA* and *PCND*; services series *DSERRA3Q086SBEA* and *PCESV*; investment series *GPDIC96*.

[12]Summary table 10 shows that residential investment leads the cycle.

Government purchases of goods and services generally are procyclical. Rapid military buildups, as during World War II, the Korean War, and the Vietnam War, are usually associated with economic expansions.

Employment and Unemployment

Business cycles are strongly felt in the labor market. In a recession, employment grows slowly or falls, many workers are laid off, and jobs become more difficult to find.

Figure 8.7 shows the number of civilians employed in the United States since 1955. Employment clearly is procyclical, as more people have jobs in booms than in recessions, and also is coincident with the cycle.

Figure 8.8 shows the civilian unemployment rate, which is the fraction of the civilian labor force (the number of people who are available for work and want to work) that is unemployed. The civilian unemployment rate is strongly countercyclical, rising sharply in contractions but falling more slowly in expansions. Although The Conference Board has studied the timing of unemployment, Summary table 10 shows that the timing of this variable is designated as "unclassified," owing to the absence of a clear pattern in the data. Figures 8.7 and 8.8 illustrate a worrisome change in the patterns of some recessions: namely in most of the recent recessions, employment growth stagnated and unemployment tended to rise for some time even after the recession's trough was reached. This pattern led observers to refer to the recovery periods following these recessions as "jobless recoveries." Fortunately, these recoveries eventually gained strength and the economy showed employment growth and a decline in the rate of unemployment.

FIGURE 8.7

Cyclical behavior of civilian employment, 1955–2021

Civilian employment is procyclical and coincident with the business cycle.

Source: Bureau of Labor Statistics, downloaded from Federal Reserve Bank of St. Louis FRED database at *fred.stlouisfed.org/series/CE16OV*.

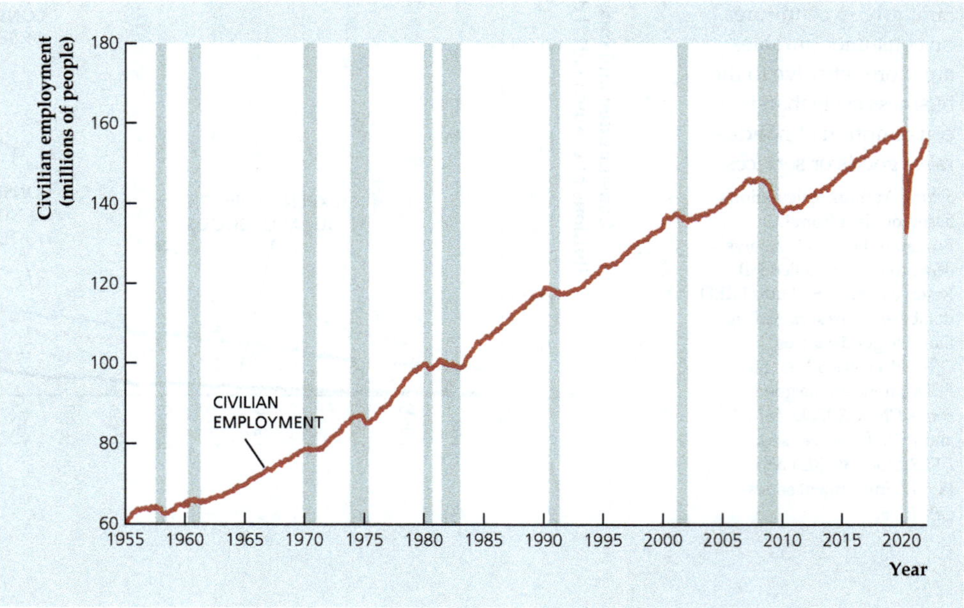

FIGURE 8.8

Cyclical behavior of the unemployment rate, 1955–2021

The unemployment rate is countercyclical and very sensitive to the business cycle. Its timing pattern relative to the cycle is unclassified, meaning that it has no definite tendency to lead, be coincident, or lag.

Source: Bureau of Labor Statistics, downloaded from Federal Reserve Bank of St. Louis FRED database at *fred.stlouisfed.org/series/UNRATE.*

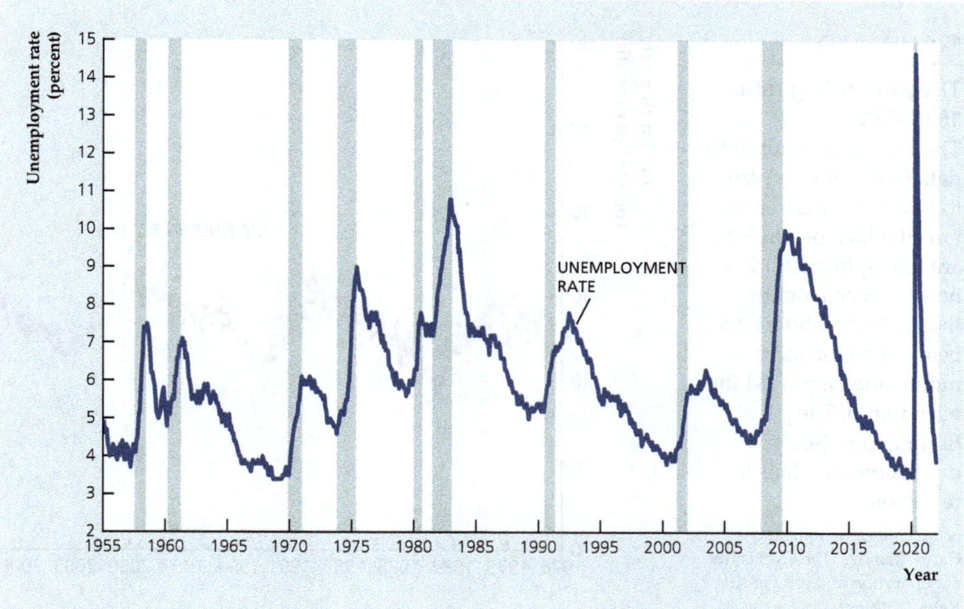

Application

The Job Finding Rate and the Job Loss Rate

In considering the cyclical movement of employment, we examined the total amount of employment in the economy. As we discussed in Chapter 3, in any given month, we can examine the probability that someone finds a job in that month or loses a job in that month. Those probabilities change over time, depending on whether the economy is in a recession or an expansion. For example, the probability that someone who is unemployed will find a job in the next month, which we call the **job finding rate**, declines during recessions and increases in expansions. As you might imagine, the probability that someone who is employed will lose their job in the next month, which we call the **job loss rate**, increases during recessions and decreases in expansions.[13]

Figure 8.9 shows the job finding rate over the course of the business cycle. Notice that the job finding rate generally rises during each economic expansion, and falls in recessions. The decline in recessions is a bit faster than the rise of the job finding rate in expansions. The job finding rate changes substantially over the business cycle. In the expansion of the 1980s, the job finding rate rose from a low of 18% in November 1982 to a peak of 33% in late 1989, an increase of 15 percentage points. In the expansion of the 1990s, the job finding rate rose from 21% in late 1991 to 35% in April 2000, an increase of 14 percentage points. And in

[13]This discussion is based on research by Shigeru Fujita and Garey Ramey, "The Cyclicality of Separation and Job Finding Rates," *International Economic Review* 50 (2009), pp. 415–430.

(*continued*)

FIGURE 8.9

The job finding rate, 1976–2021

The chart shows monthly data from January 1976 to December 2021 on the rate at which people who are unemployed find new jobs each month, that is, those who report being unemployed one month and employed the next month. The job finding rate rises in expansions and falls in recessions.

Source: Shigeru Fujita and Garey Ramey, "The Cyclicality of Separation and Job Finding Rates," *International Economic Review*, May 2009, pp. 415–430; data for January 1976 to January 1990 from Shigeru Fujita and data for February 1990 to December 2021 from Bureau of Labor Statistics website, *www.bls.gov/cps/cps_flows.htm*.

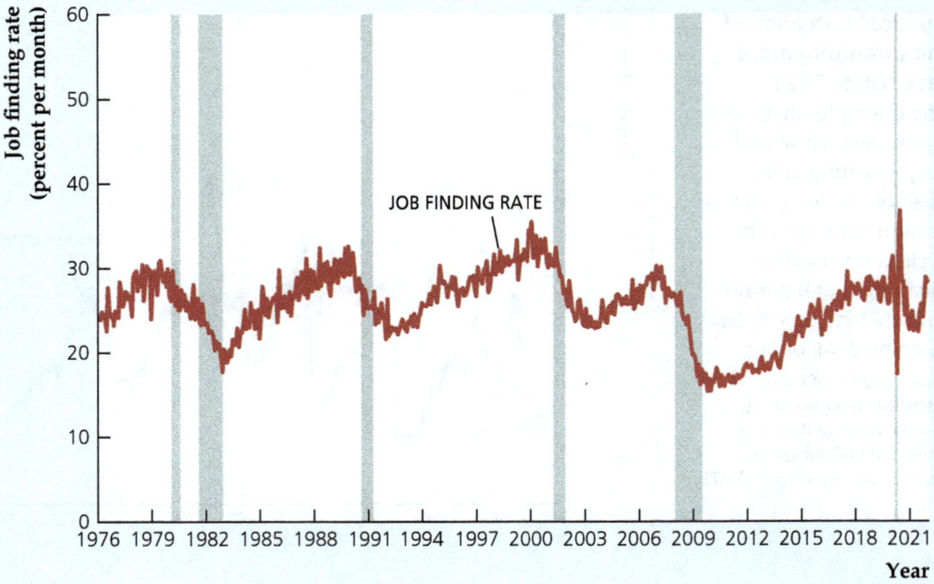

some recessions, such as the one in 2001, the decline in the job finding rate can be sharp, and it sometimes continues to decline even after the recession ends, as occurred following the 1990–1991 recession and the 2001 recession. A particularly disturbing feature of the 2007–2009 recession is the decline of the job finding rate to its lowest point since the data became available in 1976. The job finding rate was slower to rebound in the recovery that began in June 2009 than it did in the three previous recoveries. By mid-2015, 6 years into the recovery, the job finding rate remained well below the levels it reached at the same point in the previous four expansions. By 2018, which is 9 years after the recovery began, the job finding rate finally got back to the level it had been at before the recession.

Figure 8.10 shows the job loss rate, which is the probability that a person employed in one month becomes unemployed the next month.[14] The first thing to notice is that the job loss rate is very low compared with the job finding rate (the scales on Figs. 8.9 and 8.10 are different, so be sure to look at the percentages shown on the vertical axes of both graphs). The job loss rate averaged 1.5% from 1976 to February 2020. It appeared to be on a long steady decline over time in the 1980s and 1990s but did not decline much in the 2000s, and increased sharply in the 2007–2009 recession as well as the COVID recession in 2020. Fortunately, the job loss rate declined in the recovery that began in June 2009, fell below its historical average in October 2011 and continued to decline after that. After the COVID recession the job loss rate plummeted quickly and by 2021 was consistently below its long-run average.

[14]People who lose jobs in a given month may become unemployed or may move out of the labor force in the following month. We use the term *job loss* to indicate only the transition from being employed in one month to being unemployed in the following month.

FIGURE 8.10

The job loss rate, 1976–2021

The chart shows monthly data from January 1976 to December 2021 on the rate at which people who are employed lose their jobs each month, that is, those who report being employed one month and unemployed the next month. The job loss rate declines in expansions and rises in recessions.

Source: Same as for Figure 8.9.

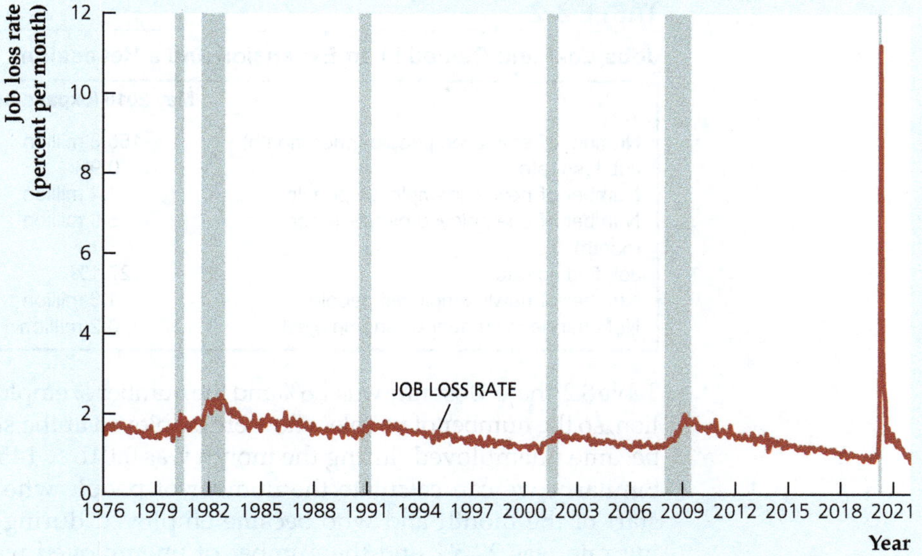

Over the course of the business cycle, the job loss rate generally declines in economic expansions and rises in recessions. Compared with the job finding rate, the changes in the job loss rate are small. So, at first glance, you might think that because the job finding rate falls substantially in recessions, while the job loss rate does not change much, changes in the job finding rate are primarily responsible for changes in the overall unemployment rate for the economy.

To investigate this issue, we will use the data in Table 8.2 to examine job losses and jobs found in an economic expansion and in a recession. First consider changes in employment status during May 2018. As shown in the first column of Table 8.2, in May 2018, the job loss rate was 0.9% and the number of employed workers was 155.3 million, so the number of people who were employed at the start of the month and who became unemployed during the month was 0.009×155.3 million $= 1.4$ million. Similarly, we can calculate the number of people who were unemployed at the start of the month and who became employed during the month. The job finding rate was 27.1% and the number of unemployed workers was 5.9 million, so the number of people who were unemployed at the start of the month and who became employed during the month was $0.271 \times 5.9 = 1.6$ million. With 1.4 million workers losing jobs and 1.6 million workers finding jobs, the number of unemployed people fell by 0.2 million during May 2018.[15]

In a recession, the decline in the job finding rate combined with the rise in the job loss rate together cause the number of employed workers to decline and the number of unemployed workers to rise. For example, consider changes in employment during October 2008, in the middle of the financial crisis. As shown in the second column of

[15]For simplicity, we have ignored people who have moved into or out of the labor force in our calculations.

(*continued*)

TABLE 8.2

Jobs Lost and Gained In an Expansion and a Recession

	May 2018 (expansion)	October 2008 (recession)
Number of employed people (prior month)	155.3 million	145.1 million
Job loss rate	0.9%	1.6%
Number of newly unemployed people	1.4 million	2.3 million
Number of unemployed people (prior month)	5.9 million	9.5 million
Job finding rate	27.1%	22.5%
Number of newly employed people	1.6 million	2.1 million
Net change in number of unemployed	−0.2 million	0.2 million

Table 8.2, the job loss rate was 1.6% and the number of employed workers was 145.1 million, so the number of people who were employed at the start of the month and who became unemployed during the month was 0.016×145.1 million $=$ 2.3 million. Similarly, we can calculate the number of people who were unemployed at the start of the month and who became employed during the month. The job finding rate was 22.5% and the number of unemployed workers was 9.5 million, so the number of people who were unemployed at the start of the month and who became employed during the month is 0.225×9.5 million $=$ 2.1 million. With 2.3 million workers losing jobs and only 2.1 million workers finding jobs, the number of unemployed people increased by 0.2 million.

Notice in these calculations that the number of people who are employed is much larger than the number of people who are unemployed. Thus, even though the job finding rate falls by more than the job loss rate rises in recessions, the job loss rate is multiplied by a much larger number than is the job finding rate. For example, during October 2008, the ratio of employed to unemployed was 15 to 1. So, smaller changes in the job loss rate may lead to larger changes in the number of unemployed workers than larger changes in the job finding rate.

In summary, economists have found interesting patterns to the changes in job losses and hiring over the course of the business cycle. The most surprising finding is that the job finding rate declines substantially more than the job loss rate rises during recessions. But since the job loss rate applies to many more people, the increased unemployment that arises during recessions can result as much, or even more, from increased job loss as from decreased job finding.

Average Labor Productivity and the Real Wage

Two other significant labor market variables are average labor productivity and the real wage. As discussed in Chapter 1, average labor productivity is output per unit of labor input. Figure 8.11 shows average labor productivity measured as total real output in the U.S. economy (excluding farms) divided by the total number of hours worked to produce that output. Average labor productivity tends to be procyclical: In booms workers produce more output during each hour of work than they do in recessions.[16] Although The Conference Board doesn't designate

[16]The Application in Chapter 3, "The Production Function of the U.S. Economy and U.S. Productivity Growth," made the point that total factor productivity A also tends to be procyclical.

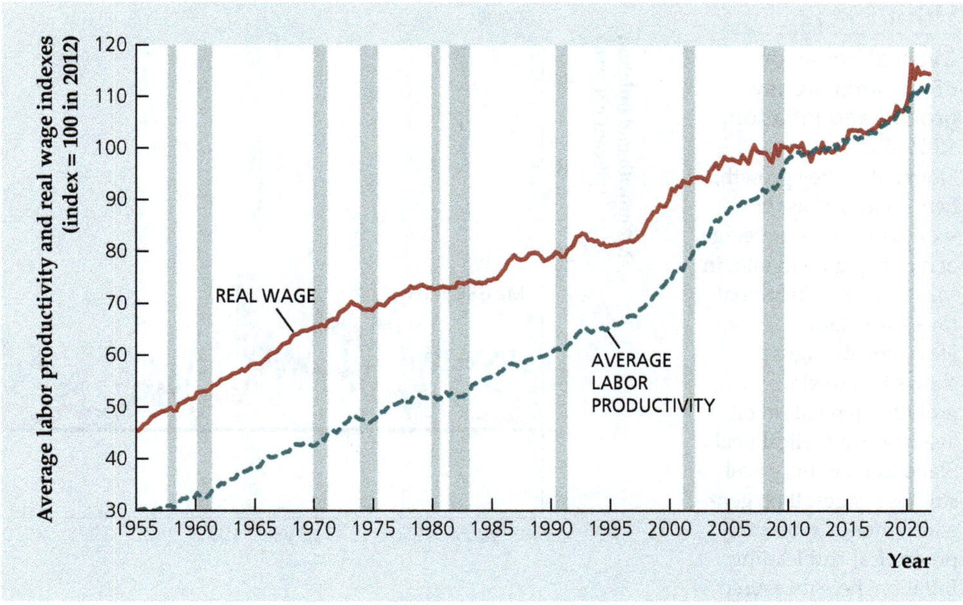

FIGURE 8.11

Cyclical behavior of average labor productivity and the real wage, 1955Q1–2021Q4

Average labor productivity, measured as real output per employee hour in the nonfarm business sector, is procyclical and leading. The economy-wide average real wage is mildly procyclical.

Source: Bureau of Labor Statistics, downloaded from Federal Reserve Bank of St. Louis FRED database at *fred.stlouisfed.org* series *OPHNFB* (productivity) and *COMPRNFB* (real wage).

the timing of this variable, studies show that average labor productivity tends to lead the business cycle.[17]

Recall from Chapter 3 that the real wage is the compensation received by workers per unit of time (such as an hour or a week) measured in real, or purchasing-power, terms. The real wage, as shown in Fig. 8.11, is an especially important variable in the study of business cycles because it is one of the main determinants of the amount of labor supplied by workers and demanded by firms. Most of the evidence points to the conclusion that real wages are mildly procyclical, but there is some controversy on this point.[18]

Money Growth and Inflation

Another variable whose cyclical behavior is somewhat controversial is the money supply. Figure 8.12 shows the behavior since 1960 of the growth in the M2 measure of the money supply.[19] Note that (nominal) money growth fluctuates a great

[17]See James H. Stock and Mark W. Watson, "Business Cycle Fluctuations in U.S. Macroeconomic Time Series," *Handbook of Macroeconomics*, Volume 1, Part A, pp. 3–64 (The Netherlands: Elsevier, 1999).

[18]Strong procyclicality for the real wage is claimed by Gary Solon, Robert Barsky, and Jonathan Parker, "Measuring the Cyclicality of Real Wages: How Important Is Composition Bias?" *Quarterly Journal of Economics*, February 1994, pp. 1–25. But their results are disputed by others, such as Paul J. Devereux, "The Cyclicality of Real Wages Within Employer-Employee Matches," *Industrial and Labor Relations Review*, July 2001, pp. 835–850.

[19]See Table 7.1 for a definition of M2. To reduce the effect of high month-to-month volatility in money growth, Fig. 8.12 presents a six-month moving average of money growth rates; that is, the reported growth rate in each month is actually the average of the growth rate in the current month and in the previous five months.

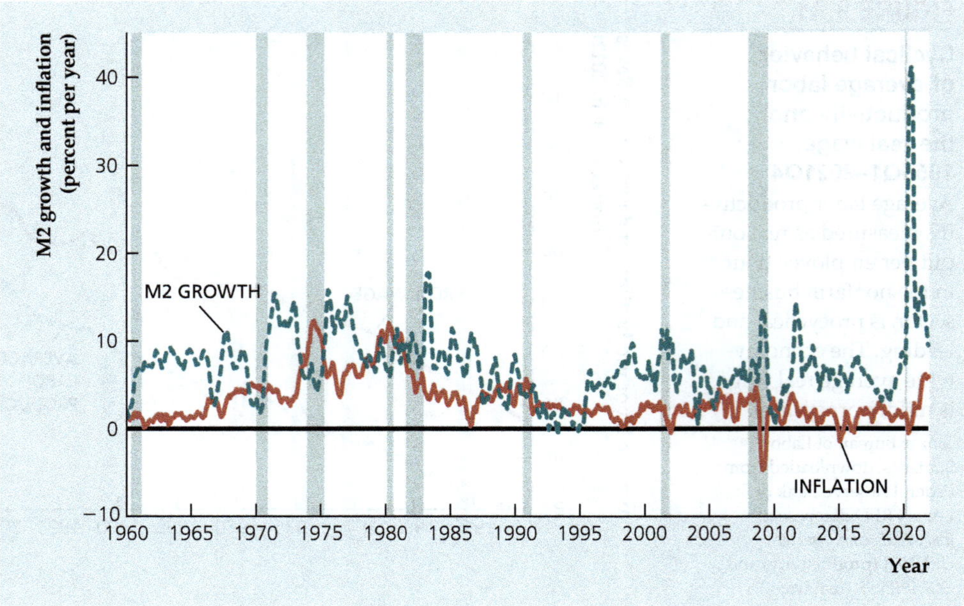

FIGURE 8.12

Cyclical behavior of nominal money growth and inflation, 1960–2021

Nominal money growth, here measured as the six-month moving average of monthly growth rates in M2 (expressed in annual rates), is volatile. However, the figure shows that money growth often falls at or just before a cyclical peak. Statistical and historical studies suggest that, generally, money growth is procyclical and leading. Inflation, here measured as the six-month moving average of monthly growth rates of the personal consumption expenditures price index (expressed in annual rates), is procyclical and lags the business cycle.

Source: Money supply: Board of Governors of the Federal Reserve System, downloaded from Federal Reserve Bank of St. Louis FRED database at *fred.stlouisfed.org* series *M2SL*; inflation: Bureau of Labor Statistics, downloaded from FRED database, series *PCEPI*.

deal and doesn't always display an obvious cyclical pattern. However, as Fig. 8.12 shows, money growth often falls sharply at or just before the onset of a recession. Moreover, many statistical and historical studies—including a classic work by Milton Friedman and Anna J. Schwartz[20] that used data back to 1867—demonstrate that money growth is procyclical and leads the cycle.

The cyclical behavior of inflation, also shown in Fig. 8.12, presents a somewhat clearer picture. Inflation is procyclical but with some lag. Inflation typically builds during an economic expansion, peaks slightly after the business cycle peak, and then falls until some time after the business cycle trough is reached. Atypically, inflation did not increase during the long boom of the 1990s. But inflation did rise substantially in the economic expansions in the 1960s and 1970s. More recently, inflation rose sharply in the aftermath of the COVID recession, following large increases in money-supply growth.

Financial Variables

Financial variables are another class of economic variables that are sensitive to the cycle. For example, stock prices are generally procyclical (stock prices rise in good economic times) and leading (stock prices usually fall in advance of a recession).

Nominal interest rates are procyclical and lagging. The nominal interest rate shown in Figure 8.13 is the rate on three-month Treasury bills. However, other

[20] *A Monetary History of the United States, 1867–1960*, Princeton, NJ: Princeton University Press for NBER, 1963. We discuss this study further in Chapter 10.

FIGURE 8.13

Cyclical behavior of the nominal interest rate, 1947–2021

The nominal interest rate, measured here as the interest rate on three-month Treasury bills, is procyclical and lagging.

Source: Federal Reserve Board of Governors, downloaded from Federal Reserve Bank of St. Louis FRED database at *fred.stlouisfed.org/series/TB3MS.*

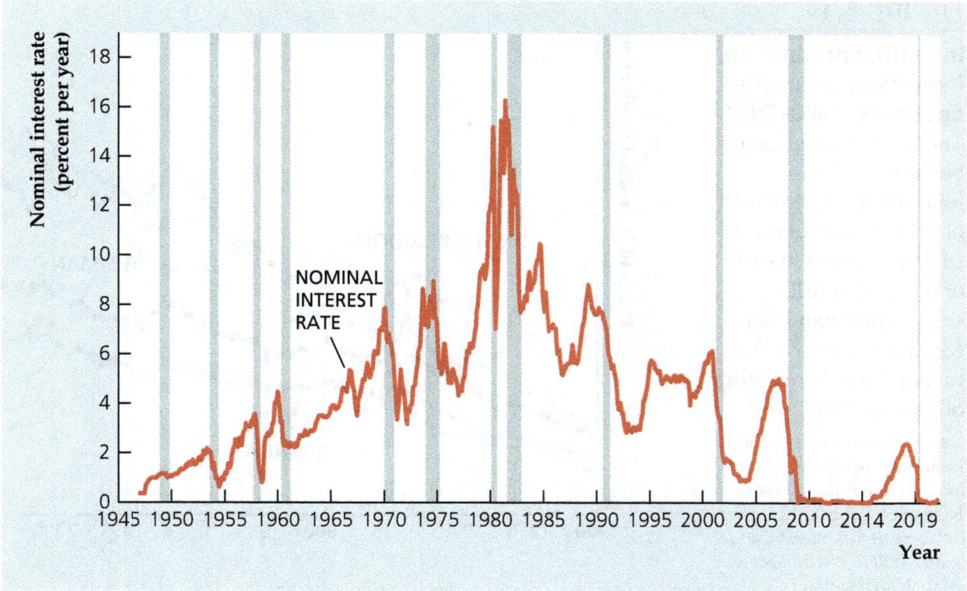

interest rates, such as the prime rate (charged by banks to their best customers) and the Federal funds rate (the interest rate on overnight loans made from one bank to another) also are procyclical and lagging. Note that nominal interest rates have the same general cyclical pattern as inflation; in Chapter 7 we discussed why nominal interest rates tend to move up and down with the inflation rate.

The real interest rate doesn't have an obvious cyclical pattern. For instance, the real interest rate actually was negative during the 1973–1975 recession but was very high during the 1981–1982 recession. (Annual values of the real interest rate are shown in Fig. 2.6.) The acyclicality of the real interest rate doesn't necessarily mean its movements are unimportant over the business cycle. Instead, the lack of a stable cyclical pattern may reflect the facts that individual business cycles have different causes and that these different sources of cycles have different effects on the real interest rate.

International Aspects of the Business Cycle

So far we have concentrated on business cycles in the United States. However, business cycles are by no means unique to the United States, having been regularly observed in all industrialized market economies. In most cases the cyclical behavior of key economic variables in these other economies is similar to that described for the United States.

The business cycle is an international phenomenon in another sense: Frequently, the major industrial economies undergo recessions and expansions at about the same time, suggesting that they share a common cycle. Figure 8.14 illustrates this

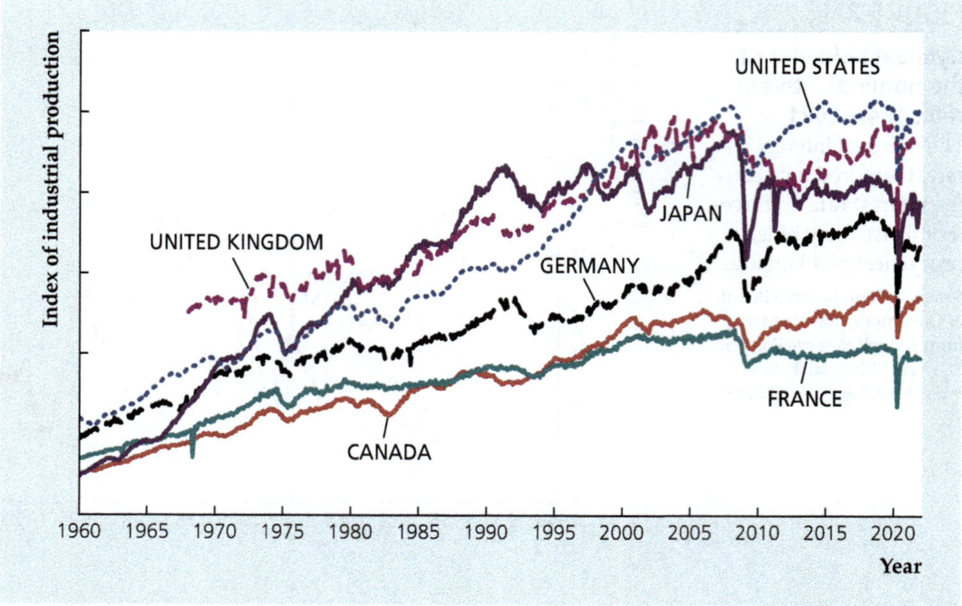

FIGURE 8.14

Industrial production indexes in six major countries, 1960–2021

The worldwide effect of business cycles is reflected in the similarity of the behavior of industrial production in each of the six countries shown. But individual countries also have fluctuations not shared with other countries.

Source: OECD Main Economic Indicators, April 2022, downloaded from Federal Reserve Bank of St. Louis FRED database at *fred.stlouisfed.org*, series *GBRPROINDMISMEI, DEUPROINDMISMEI, FRAPROINDMISMEI, JPNPROINDMISMEI, CANPROINDMISMEI, and USAPROINDMISMEI* (with scales adjusted for clarity).

Note: The scales for the industrial production indexes differ by country; for example, the figure does not imply that the United Kingdom's total industrial production is higher than that of Japan.

common cycle by showing the index of industrial production since 1960 for each of six major industrial countries. Note in particular the effects of worldwide recessions in about 1975, 1982, 1991, 2001, 2008, and 2020. Figure 8.14 also shows that each economy experiences many small fluctuations not shared by the others.

In Touch with Data and Research

Coincident and Leading Indexes

In this chapter, we discuss a large number of variables and describe how they behave as the economy goes through expansions and contractions. One difficulty faced by policymakers and economic analysts is how to sort through all of the different economic data and figure out where the economy stands overall; a more challenging problem is to forecast, in advance, when the economy will change course. To address these problems, economists have developed coincident and leading indexes. An index is a single number that combines data on a variety of economic variables. A *coincident index* is an index that is designed to have peaks and troughs that occur about the same time as the corresponding peaks and troughs in aggregate economic activity, and is useful for assessing whether the economy is currently in a recession or an expansion. A *leading index* is designed to have its peaks and troughs before the corresponding peaks and troughs in aggregate economic activity, and thus might be useful for forecasting turning points in the business cycle.

The first indexes were developed in the 1930s at the NBER by Wesley Mitchell and Arthur Burns,[21] whose important early work on business cycles was mentioned earlier in this chapter. Today, these original indexes (with some modification and updating) are produced by The Conference Board, and other indexes have been developed by other economists. In this box, we discuss two recently developed coincident indexes and The Conference Board's **index of leading economic indicators.**

The Chicago Fed National Activity Index (CFNAI) was developed in 2001 by economist Jonas Fisher of the Federal Reserve Bank of Chicago. This coincident index is based on 85 monthly economic variables in five categories: production and income, the labor market, consumption and housing, manufacturing and sales, and inventories and orders. The index is constructed so that it has an average value of 0 over time. Figure 8.15 shows the values of the CFNAI, averaged over the current and preceding two months, since March 1967. The graph includes recession bars, showing the dates of recessions as determined by the NBER. As the graph shows, the CFNAI turns significantly negative in recessions, falling much more in severe recessions (such as 1973–1975, 1981–1982, 2007–2009, and 2020) than in mild recessions (such as 1990–1991 and 2001).[22]

FIGURE 8.15

Chicago Fed National Activity Index, 1967–2021

The chart shows monthly data on the Chicago Fed National Activity Index (CFNAI), averaged over the current and preceding two months. The index tracks recessions closely, falling more in severe recessions than in mild recessions.

Source: Data from Federal Reserve Bank of Chicago, downloaded from Federal Reserve Bank of St. Louis FRED database, *fred.stlouisfed .org/series/CFNAIMA3.*

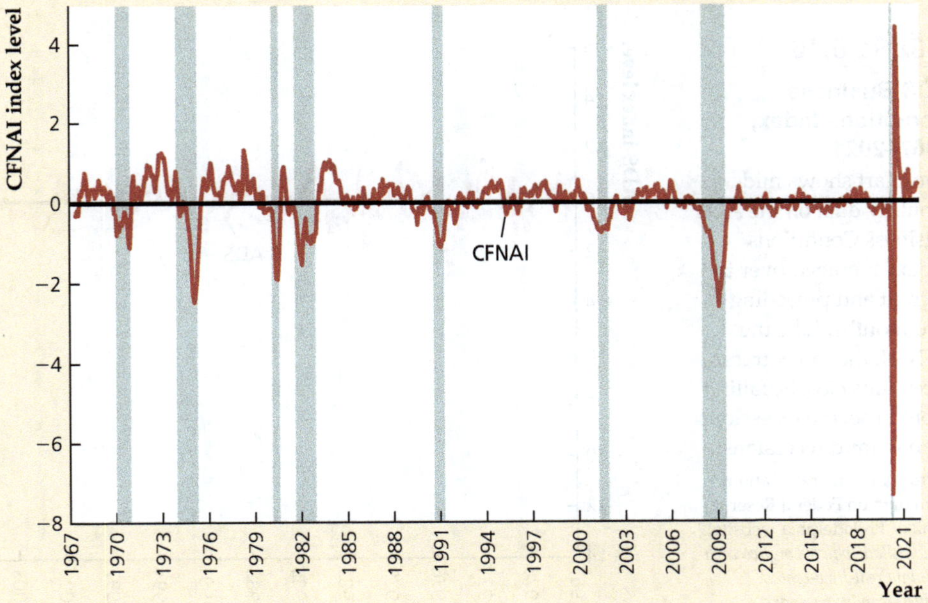

[21]*Statistical Indicators of Cyclical Revivals* (New York: National Bureau of Economic Research, 1938).

[22]For more details about the CFNAI, see the article by Charles L. Evans, Chin Te Liu, and Genevieve Pham-Kanter, "The 2001 Recession and the Chicago Fed National Activity Index: Identifying Business Cycle Turning Points," Federal Reserve Bank of Chicago Economic Perspectives, Third Quarter 2002, pp. 26–43; or read the discussion on the Chicago Fed's website at *www.chicagofed.org/economic_research_and_data/cfnai.cfm.*

(*continued*)

Another recently developed coincident index is the Aruoba-Diebold-Scotti (ADS) Business Conditions Index, which doesn't use as many variables as the CFNAI, but uses variables that have different frequencies: some quarterly data (real GDP), some monthly data (payroll employment, industrial production, personal income less transfer payments, and manufacturing and trade sales), and some weekly data (initial jobless claims). Like the CFNAI, the ADS index is constructed so that it has an average value of 0 over time. The developers of the index, S. Boragan Aruoba of the University of Maryland, Francis X. Diebold of the University of Pennsylvania, and Chiara Scotti of the Federal Reserve Board, sought an index that could be estimated to provide a measure of the state of the economy on a day-by-day basis. They implemented the index in partnership with the Federal Reserve Bank of Philadelphia, which updates the series once or twice each week. Figure 8.16 shows the values of the ADS index, averaged over the current and preceding two months.[23]

Comparing the two indexes, we can see that they are quite similar, despite using very different sets of data. Of course, it is not surprising that the two indexes are similar because they are both designed to measure the underlying state of aggregate economic activity. An advantage of the ADS index is that it is available very frequently (it gets updated once each week or more often). But the CFNAI

FIGURE 8.16

ADS Business Conditions Index, 1967–2021

The chart shows mid-monthly data on the ADS Business Conditions Index, averaged over the current and preceding two months. Like the CFNAI, the index tracks recessions closely, falling more in severe recessions than in mild recessions.

Source: Authors' calculations from data on Federal Reserve Bank of Philadelphia website, *www.philadelphiafed.org/research-and-data/real-time-center/business-conditions-index*.

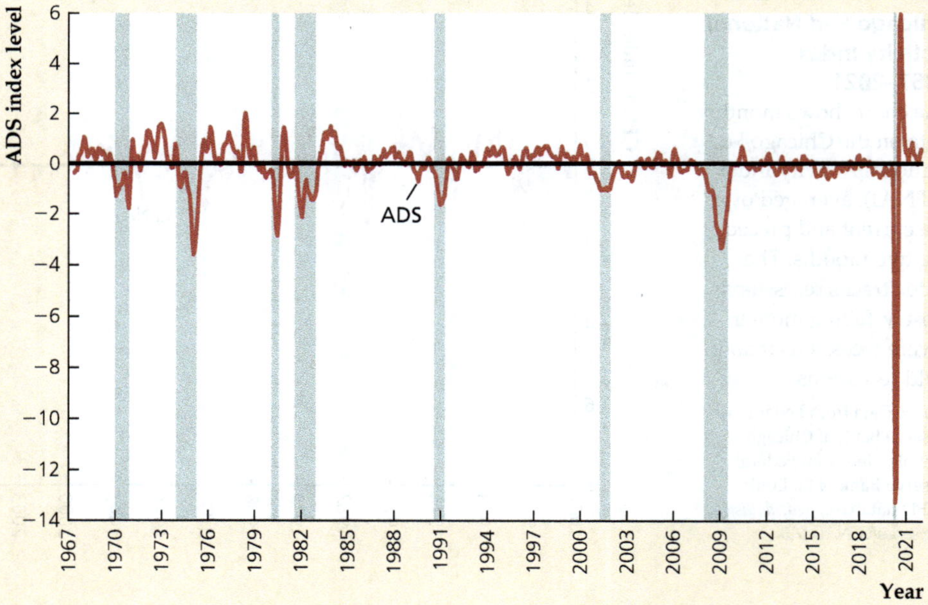

[23]For more on the ADS index, see S. Boragan Aruoba, Francis X. Diebold, and Chiara Scotti, "Real-Time Measurement of Business Conditions," *Journal of Business and Economic Statistics*, October 2009, pp. 417–427; the ADS index data are available at the Philadelphia Fed's website at *www.philadelphiafed.org/research-and-data/real-time-center/business-conditions-index*.

has a longer history of reliability in real time, since it was developed in 2001, whereas the ADS index just began to be produced in real time in 2009.

Unlike the CFNAI and the ADS index, which were designed to measure the current state of the economy, the composite index of leading economic indicators was designed to help anticipate or forecast turning points in aggregate economic activity. However, its record as a forecasting tool is mixed. When the index declines for two or three consecutive months, it warns that a recession is likely. However, its forecasting acumen in real time has not been very good because of the following problems:

1. Data on the components of the index are often revised when more complete data become available. Revisions change the value of the index and may even reverse a signal of a future recession.
2. The index is prone to giving false signals, predicting recessions that did not materialize.
3. The index does not provide any information on when a recession might arrive or how severe it might be.
4. Changes in the structure of the economy over time may cause some variables to become better predictors of the economy and others to become worse. For this reason, the index must be revised periodically, as the list of component indicators is changed.

Research by Francis X. Diebold and Glenn Rudebusch of the Federal Reserve Bank of San Francisco showed that the revisions were substantial.[24] The agency calculating the index (the Commerce Department or The Conference Board) often demonstrates the value of the index with a plot of the index over time, showing how it turns down just before every recession. But Diebold and Rudebusch showed that such a plot is illusory because the index plotted was not the one used at the time of each recession, but rather a revised index made many years after the fact. In real time, they concluded, the use of the index does not improve forecasts of industrial production.

For example, suppose you were examining the changes over time in the composite index of leading indicators, and used the rule of thumb that a decline in the index for three months in a row meant that a recession was likely in the next six months to one year. You would have noticed in December 1969 that the index had declined two months in a row; by January 1970 you would have seen the third monthly decline. In fact, the NBER declared that a recession had begun in December 1969, so the index did not give you any advance warning. Even worse, if you had been following the index in 1973 to 1974, you would have thought all was well until September 1974, when the index declined for the second month in a row, or October 1974, when the third monthly decline occurred. But the NBER declared that a recession had actually begun in November 1973, so the index was nearly a year late in calling the recession.

After missing a recession's onset so badly, the creators of the index naturally want to improve it. So, they may revise the index with different variables, give

[24]"Forecasting Output with the Composite Leading Index: A Real-Time Analysis." *Journal of the American Statistical Association*, September 1991, pp. 603–610.

(continued)

the variables different weights, or manipulate the statistics so that, if the new revised index had been available, it would have indicated that a recession were coming. For example, the revised index published in April 1979 would have given eight months of lead time before the recession that began in December 1969 and six months of lead time before the recession that began in November 1973. But of course, that index was not available to forecasters when it would have been useful—before the recessions began.

Because of the problems of the official composite index of leading indicators, James Stock and Mark Watson[25] set out to create some new indexes that would improve the value of such indexes in forecasting. They created several experimental leading indexes, with the hope that such indexes would prove better at helping economists forecast turning points in the business cycle. However, it appears that the next two recessions (those that began in 1990 and 2001) were sufficiently different from previous recessions that the experimental leading indexes did not suggest an appreciable probability of recession in either 1990 or 2001. In early 1990, the experimental recession index of Stock and Watson showed that the probability that a recession would occur in the next six months never exceeded 10%. Also, in late 2000 and early 2001, the index did not rise above 10%. So, although the Stock and Watson approach appeared promising in prospect, it did not deliver any improvement in forecasting recessions.

The inability of leading indicators to forecast recessions may simply mean that recessions are often unusual events, caused by large, unpredictable shocks such as disruptions in the world oil supply or a near-collapse of the financial system. If so, then the pursuit of the perfect index of leading indicators may prove to be frustrating.

[25]"New Indexes of Coincident and Leading Economic Indicators," in Olivier J. Blanchard and Stanley Fischer, eds., *NBER Macroeconomics Annual, 1989* (Cambridge, MA: MIT Press, 1989), pp. 351–394.

8.4 Business Cycle Analysis: A Preview

Use aggregate demand and aggregate supply to describe the impact on business cycles of various shocks.

The business cycle facts presented in this chapter would be useful even if we took them no further. For example, being familiar with the typical cyclical patterns of key macroeconomic variables may help forecasters project the course of these variables as the economy heads into a recession. Knowing the facts about cycles also is important for businesspeople making investment and hiring decisions and for financial investors trying to choose portfolios that provide the desired combinations of risk and return. However, macroeconomists are interested not only in *what* happens during business cycles but also in *why* it happens. This desire to understand cycles isn't just idle intellectual curiosity. For example, as we demonstrate in Chapters 9–11, the advice that macroeconomists give to policymakers about how to respond to a recession depends on what they think is causing the recession. Thus, with the business cycle facts as background, in the rest of Part 3 we describe the primary alternative explanations of business cycle fluctuations, as well as policy recommendations based on these explanations.

In Touch with Data and Research

The Seasonal Cycle and the Business Cycle

Did you know that GDP in most countries does not consistently grow at the same rate during the various seasons of the year? That may be because macroeconomic data published by governmental statistical agencies are usually seasonally adjusted. In other words, seasonal fluctuations that habitually occur are removed from the data. The possible rationale behind this is that, by disregarding seasonal fluctuations, users of data can concentrate on the more important long-term changes in the economy and business-cycle fluctuations. However, overlooking seasonal fluctuations may have serious repercussions: slow economic growth during certain months could leave some people unemployed for a considerable period of time, and this would go unreported on the annual macroeconomic published data. These fluctuations may be substantial for several nations, requiring policy makers to intervene during habitual seasonal slowdowns.

Classic examples of seasonal unemployment are the North African nations of Egypt and Tunisia, which heavily depend on tourism as a major contributor to GDP. Egypt suffers from a seasonal slowdown during the hot summer months, which prevents tourists from visiting a country home to almost 60% of the world's ancient monuments. Conversely, Tunisia is heavily dependent on shore tourism, which dwindles during the colder seasons. In both cases, economic booms are followed by deep recessions. The peak periods of these seasonal cycles account for more than 70% of GDP growth in a country such as Egypt. For the past few decades, economists have attempted to study seasonal fluctuations with the premise that the key variables affecting the business cycle characterize the seasonal cycle as well. Hence, interpretation of many of these stylized variables over the seasonal cycle is easier than their interpretation over the business cycle. In a famous study that triggered interest in this topic, Barsky and Miron concluded that the seasonal cycle in the U.S. economy depends on a number of factors, among which are higher purchases during the Christmas season and lower labor productivity in summer months.[26] Curiously, in the Middle East, seasonal cycles depend on substantially higher consumption during religious celebrations and the holy month of Ramadan, albeit with a considerable drop in labor productivity during the same period. Moreover, especially in the Gulf Cooperation Council (GCC) countries, which are heavily dependent on foreign labor, output drops as expatriates flee the scorching summer heat by going on their annual leave.

One must bear in mind that similar seasonal fluctuations may contribute to the overall business cycle in their own right. These factors must be taken into consideration so that government spending becomes procyclical. As discussed later in Chapter 10, classical economists say that business cycles are the best manner by which the economy responds to changes in the economic environment, so macroeconomic policy must not eliminate these responses.

---

[26]R.B. Barsky and J.A., Miron, "The Seasonal Cycle and the Business Cycle," *Journal of Political Economy* 97, no. 3, June 1989, pp. 503–535.

In general, theories of the business cycle have two main components. The first is a description of the types of factors that have major effects on the economy—wars, new inventions, harvest failures, and changes in government policy are examples. Economists often refer to these (typically unpredictable) forces hitting the economy as *shocks*. The other component of a business cycle theory is a *model* of how the economy responds to the various shocks. Think of the economy as a car moving down a poorly maintained highway: The shocks can be thought of as the potholes and bumps in the road; the model describes how the components of the car (its tires and shock absorbers) act to smooth out or amplify the effects of the shocks on the passengers.

The two principal business cycle theories that we discuss in this book are the *classical* and the *Keynesian* theories. Fortunately, to present and discuss these two theories we don't have to develop two completely different models. Instead, both can be considered within a general framework called the *aggregate demand–aggregate supply*, or *AD–AS, model*. To introduce some of the key differences between the classical and Keynesian approaches to business cycle analysis, in the rest of this chapter we preview the *AD–AS* model and how it is used to analyze business cycles.

Aggregate Demand and Aggregate Supply: A Brief Introduction

We develop and apply the *AD–AS* model, and a key building block of the *AD–AS* model, the *IS–LM* model, in Chapters 9–11. Here, we simply introduce and briefly explain the basic components of the *AD–AS* model. The *AD–AS* model has three components, as illustrated in Figure 8.17: (1) the aggregate demand curve, (2) the short-run aggregate supply curve, and (3) the long-run aggregate supply curve. Each curve represents a relationship between the aggregate price level, *P*, measured on the vertical axis in Fig. 8.17, and output, *Y*, measured along the horizontal axis.

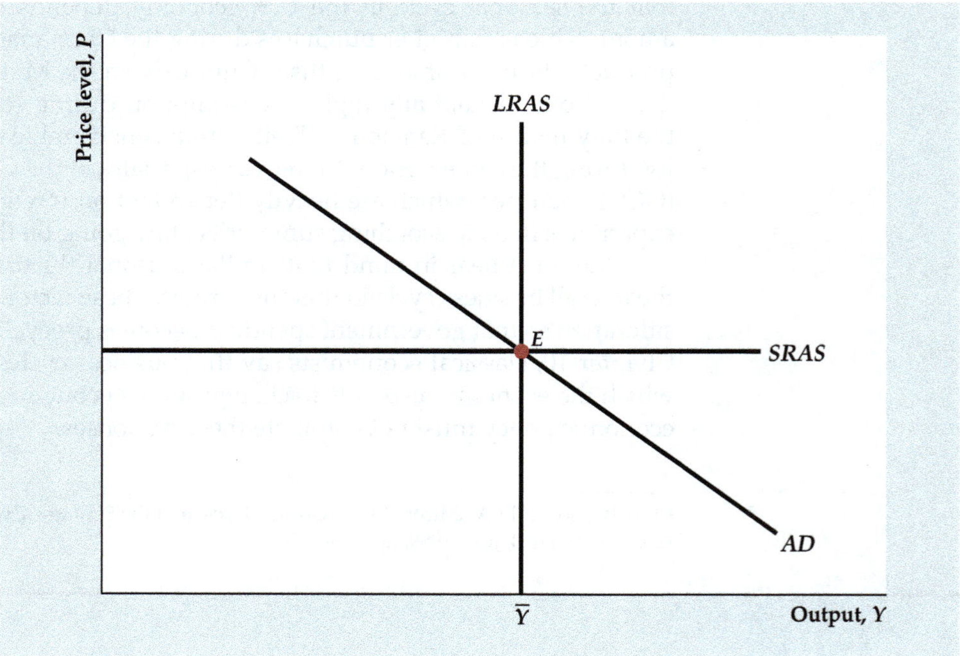

FIGURE 8.17

The aggregate demand–aggregate supply model

The aggregate demand (*AD*) curve slopes downward, reflecting the fact that the aggregate quantity of goods and services demanded, *Y*, falls when the price level, *P*, rises. The short-run aggregate supply (*SRAS*) curve is horizontal, reflecting the assumption that, in the short run, prices are fixed and firms simply produce whatever quantity is demanded. In the long run, firms produce their normal levels of output, so the long-run aggregate supply (*LRAS*) curve is vertical at the full-employment level of output, $\bar{Y}$. The economy's short-run equilibrium is at the point where the *AD* and *SRAS* curves intersect, and its long-run equilibrium is where the *AD* and *LRAS* curves intersect. In this example, the economy is in both short-run and long-run equilibrium at point *E*.

The *aggregate demand (AD) curve* shows for any price level, P, the total quantity of goods and services, Y, *demanded* by households, firms, and governments, which we call **aggregate demand**. The *AD* curve slopes downward in Fig. 8.17, implying that, when the general price level is higher, people demand fewer goods and services. We give the precise explanation for this downward slope in Chapter 9. The intuitive explanation for the downward slope of the *AD* curve—that when prices are higher people can afford to buy fewer goods—is *not* correct. The problem with the intuitive explanation is that, although an increase in the general price level does reflect an increase in the prices of most goods, it also implies an increase in the incomes of the people who produce and sell those goods. Thus to say that a higher price level reduces the quantities of goods and services that people can afford to buy is not correct because their incomes, as well as prices, have gone up.

The *AD* curve relates the amount of output demanded to the price level, if we hold other economic factors constant. However, for a specific price level, any change in the economy that increases the aggregate quantity of goods and services demanded will shift the *AD* curve to the right (and any change that decreases the quantity of goods and services demanded will shift the *AD* curve to the left). For example, a sharp rise in the stock market, by making consumers wealthier, would likely increase households' demand for goods and services, shifting the *AD* curve to the right. Similarly, the development of more efficient capital goods would increase firms' demand for new capital goods, again shifting the *AD* curve to the right. Government policies also can affect the *AD* curve. For example, a decline in government spending on military hardware reduces the aggregate quantity of goods and services demanded and shifts the *AD* curve to the left.

An aggregate supply curve indicates the amount of output producers are willing to *supply* at any particular price level, which we call **aggregate supply**. Two aggregate supply curves are shown in Fig. 8.17—one that holds in the short run and one that holds in the long run. The *short-run aggregate supply (SRAS) curve,* shown in Fig. 8.17, is a horizontal line. The horizontal *SRAS* curve captures the ideas that in the short run the price level is fixed and that firms are willing to supply any amount of output at that price. If the short run is a very short period of time, such as a day, this assumption is realistic. For instance, an ice cream store posts the price of ice cream in the morning and sells as much ice cream as is demanded at that price (up to its capacity to produce ice cream). During a single day, the owner typically won't raise the price of ice cream if the quantity demanded is unusually high; nor does the owner lower the price of ice cream if the quantity demanded is unusually low. The tendency of a producer to set a price for some time and then supply whatever is demanded at that price is represented by a horizontal *SRAS* curve.

However, suppose that the quantity of ice cream demanded remains high day after day, to the point that the owner is straining to produce enough ice cream to meet demand. In this case, the owner may raise her price to reduce the quantity of ice cream demanded to a more manageable level. The owner will keep raising the price of ice cream as long as the quantity demanded exceeds normal production capacity. In the long run, the price of ice cream will be whatever it has to be to equate the quantity demanded to the owner's normal level of output. Similarly, in the long run, all other firms in the economy will adjust their prices as necessary so as to be able to produce their normal level of output. As discussed in Chapter 3, the normal level of production for the economy as a whole is called the full-employment level of output, denoted $\bar{Y}$. In the long run, then, when prices fully adjust, the aggregate quantity of output supplied will simply equal the full-employment level of output, $\bar{Y}$. Thus the *long-run aggregate supply (LRAS) curve* is vertical, as shown in Fig. 8.17, at the point that output supplied, Y, equals $\bar{Y}$.

Figure 8.17 represents an economy that is simultaneously in short-run and long-run equilibrium. The short-run equilibrium is represented by the intersection of the *AD* and *SRAS* curves, shown as point *E*. The long-run equilibrium is represented by the intersection of the *AD* and *LRAS* curves, also shown as point *E*. However, when some change occurs in the economy, the short-run equilibrium can differ from the long-run equilibrium.

Aggregate Demand Shocks. Recall that a theory of business cycles has to include a description of the shocks hitting the economy. The *AD–AS* framework identifies shocks by their initial effects—on aggregate demand or aggregate supply. An *aggregate demand shock* is a change in the economy that shifts the *AD* curve. For example, a negative aggregate demand shock would occur if consumers became more pessimistic about the future and thus reduced their current consumption spending, shifting the *AD* curve to the left.

To analyze the effect of an aggregate demand shock, let's suppose that the economy initially is in both short-run and long-run equilibrium at point *E* in Figure 8.18. We assume that, because consumers become more pessimistic, the aggregate demand curve shifts down and to the left from AD^1 to AD^2. In this case, the new short-run equilibrium (the intersection of AD^2 and *SRAS*) is at point *F*, where output has fallen to Y_2 and the price level remains unchanged at P_1. Thus the decline in household consumption demand causes a recession, with output falling below its normal level. However, the economy will not stay at point *F* forever because firms won't be content to keep producing below their normal capacity.

FIGURE 8.18

An adverse aggregate demand shock

An adverse aggregate demand shock reduces the aggregate quantity of goods and services demanded at a given price level; an example is that consumers become more pessimistic and thus reduce their spending. This shock is represented by a shift to the left of the aggregate demand curve from AD^1 to AD^2. In the short run, the economy moves to point *F*. At this short-run equilibrium, output has fallen to Y_2 and the price level is unchanged. Eventually, price adjustment causes the economy to move to the new long-run equilibrium at point *H*, where output returns to its full-employment level, $\bar{Y}$, and the price level falls to P_2. In the strict classical view, the economy moves almost immediately to point *H*, so the adverse aggregate demand shock essentially has no effect on output in both the short run and the long run. Keynesians argue that the adjustment process takes longer, so that the adverse aggregate demand shock may lead to a sustained decline in output.

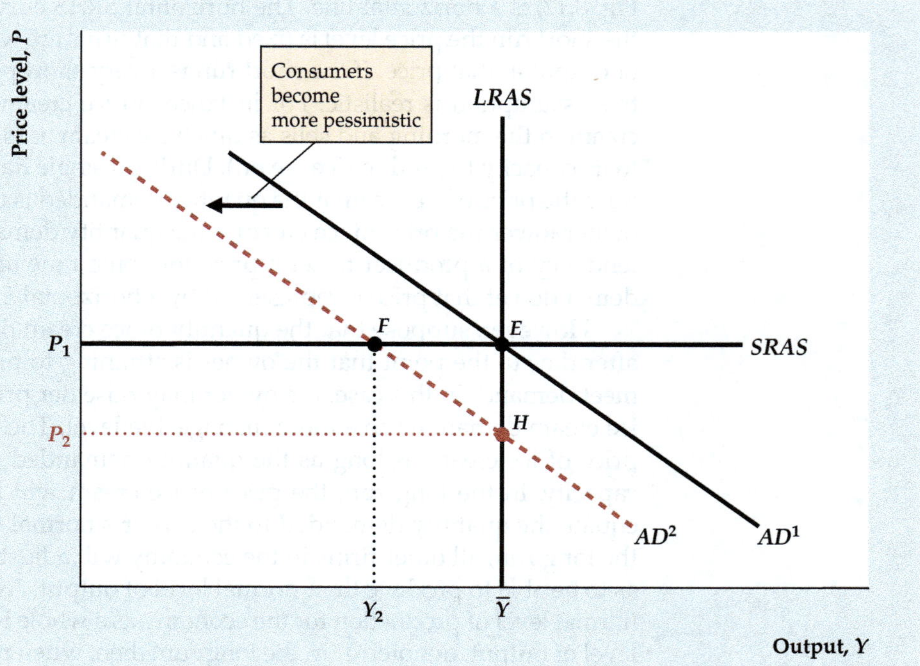

Eventually firms will respond to lower demand by adjusting their prices—in this case downward—until the economy reaches its new long-run equilibrium at point H, the intersection of AD^2 and $LRAS$. At point H, output is at its original level, $\bar{Y}$, but the price level has fallen to P_2.

Our analysis shows that an adverse aggregate demand shock, which shifts the AD curve down, will cause output to fall in the short run but not in the long run. How long does it take for the economy to reach the long run? This question is crucial to economic analysis and is one to which classical economists and Keynesian economists have different answers. Their answers help explain why classicals and Keynesians have different views about the appropriate role of government policy in fighting recessions.

The classical answer is that prices adjust quite rapidly to imbalances in quantities supplied and demanded so that the economy gets to its long-run equilibrium quickly—in a few months or less. Thus a recession caused by a downward shift of the AD curve is likely to end rather quickly, as the price level falls and the economy reaches the original level of output $\bar{Y}$. In the strictest versions of the classical model, the economy is assumed to reach its long-run equilibrium essentially immediately, implying that the short-run aggregate supply curve is irrelevant and that the economy always operates on the long-run aggregate supply *(LRAS)* curve. Because the adjustment takes place quickly, classical economists argue that little is gained by the government actively trying to fight recessions. Note that this conclusion is consistent with the "invisible hand" argument described in Chapter 1, according to which the free market and unconstrained price adjustments are sufficient to achieve good economic results.

In contrast to the classical view, Keynesian economists argue that prices (and wages, which are the price of labor) do not necessarily adjust quickly in response to shocks. Hence the return of the economy to its long-run equilibrium may be slow, taking perhaps years rather than months. In other words, although Keynesians agree with classicals that the economy's level of output will eventually return from its recessionary level (represented by Y_2 in Fig. 8.18) to its full-employment level, $\bar{Y}$, they believe that this process may be slow. Because they lack confidence in the self-correcting powers of the economy, Keynesians tend to see an important role for the government in fighting recessions. For example, Keynes himself originally argued that government could fight recessions by increasing purchases of goods and services. In terms of Fig. 8.18, an increase in government purchases could in principle shift the AD curve up and to the right, from AD^2 back to AD^1, restoring the economy to full employment.

Aggregate Supply Shocks. Because classical economists believe that aggregate demand shocks don't cause sustained fluctuations in output, they generally view aggregate supply shocks as the major force behind changes in output and employment. An *aggregate supply shock* is a change in the economy that causes the long-run aggregate supply ($LRAS$) curve to shift. The position of the $LRAS$ curve depends only on the full-employment level of output, $\bar{Y}$, so aggregate supply shocks can also be thought of as factors—such as changes in productivity or labor supply, for example—that lead to changes in $\bar{Y}$.

Figure 8.19 illustrates the effects of an adverse supply shock—that is, a shock that reduces the full-employment level of output (an example would be a severe drought that greatly reduces crop yields). Suppose that the economy is initially in long-run equilibrium at point E in Fig. 8.19, where the initial long-run aggregate

FIGURE 8.19

An adverse aggregate supply shock

An adverse aggregate supply shock, such as a drought, reduces the full-employment level of output from $\bar{Y}_1$ to $\bar{Y}_2$. Equivalently, the shock shifts the long-run aggregate supply curve to the left, from $LRAS^1$ to $LRAS^2$. As a result of the adverse supply shock, the long-run equilibrium moves from point E to point F. In the new long-run equilibrium, output has fallen from $\bar{Y}_1$ to $\bar{Y}_2$ and the price level has increased from P_1 to P_2.

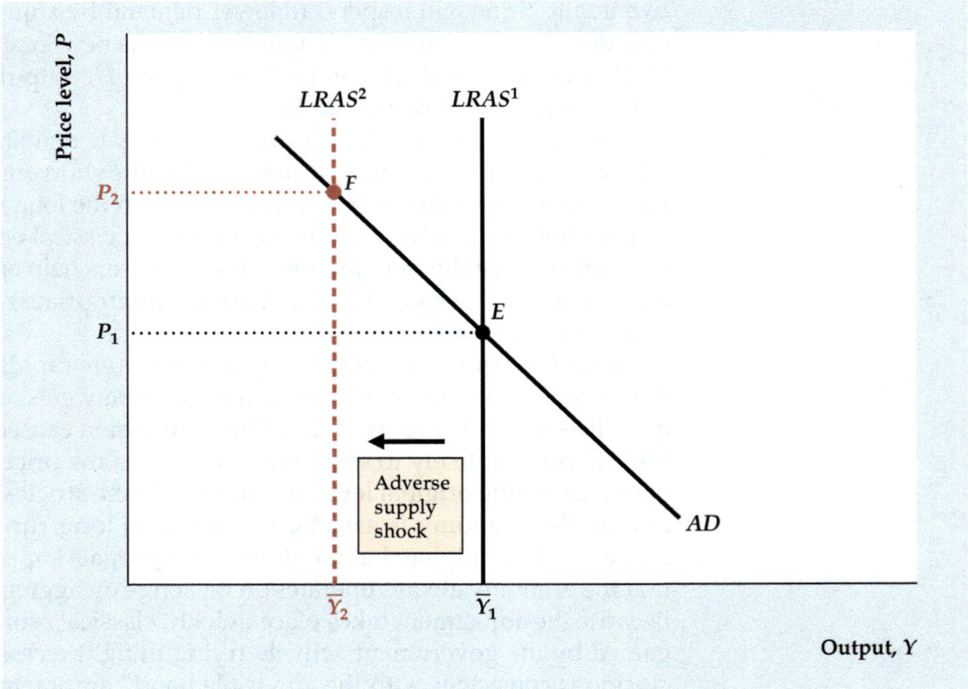

supply curve, $LRAS^1$, intersects the aggregate demand curve, AD. Now imagine that the adverse supply shock hits, reducing full-employment output from $\bar{Y}_1$ to $\bar{Y}_2$ and causing the long-run aggregate supply curve to shift to the left from $LRAS^1$ to $LRAS^2$. The new long-run equilibrium occurs at point F, where the level of output is lower than at point E. According to the classical view, the economy moves quickly from point E to point F and then remains at point F. The drop in output as the economy moves from point E to point F is a recession. Note that the new price level, P_2, is higher than the initial price level, P_1, so adverse supply shocks cause prices to rise during recessions. We return to this implication for the price level and discuss its relation to the business cycle facts in Chapter 10.

Although classical economists first emphasized supply shocks, Keynesian economists also recognize the importance of supply shocks in accounting for business cycle fluctuations in output. Keynesians agree that an adverse supply shock will reduce output and increase the price level in the long run. In Chapter 11, we discuss the Keynesian view of the process by which the economy moves from the short run to the long run in response to a supply shock.

CHAPTER SUMMARY

1. A business cycle consists of a period of declining aggregate economic activity (a contraction or recession) followed by a period of rising economic activity (an expansion or a boom). The low point of the contraction is called the *trough*, and the high point of the expansion is called the *peak*. Business cycles have been observed in market economies since the beginning of industrialization.
2. The tendency of many economic variables to move together in regular and predictable ways over the course of the cycle is called comovement. We refer to the typical cyclical patterns of key macroeconomic variables as the "business cycle facts."
3. The fluctuations in aggregate economic activity that constitute business cycles are recurrent, having been observed again and again in industrialized market economies. However, they aren't periodic, in that they don't occur at regular or predictable intervals. Business cycle fluctuations also are persistent, which means that once a recession or expansion begins, it usually lasts for a while.
4. Many economists believe that the U.S. economy before 1929 had longer recessions and more cyclical volatility than the post–World War II economy. However, data problems prevent precise measurements of how much more cyclical the pre–1929 economy was. The Great Depression that began in 1929 and didn't end until the onset of World War II was the most severe cyclical decline in U.S. history. The reduced severity of recessions after World War II led to premature declarations that the cycle was "dead." However, the U.S. economy suffered severe recessions in 1973–1975 and 1981–1982, after which the U.S. economy enjoyed a long period of steady growth and tranquility of the business cycle. The "long boom" began in 1982 and ended in 2001, with only one mild recession (1990–1991). The Great Moderation was a period of reduced volatility of GDP and other macroeconomic variables that began in the mid 1980s. Volatility increased during the Great Recession of 2007–2009 and rose even more during the COVID recession of 2020.
5. The direction of a variable relative to the business cycle can be procyclical, countercyclical, or acyclical. A procyclical variable moves in the same direction as aggregate economic activity, rising in booms and falling in recessions. A countercyclical variable moves in the opposite direction to aggregate economic activity, falling in booms and rising in recessions. An acyclical variable has no clear cyclical pattern.
6. The timing of a variable relative to the business cycle may be coincident, leading, or lagging. A coincident variable's peaks and troughs occur at about the same time as peaks and troughs in aggregate economic activity. Peaks and troughs in a leading variable come before, and peaks and troughs in a lagging variable come after, the corresponding peaks and troughs in aggregate economic activity.
7. The cyclical direction and timing of major macroeconomic variables—the business cycle facts—are described in Summary table 10. In brief, production, consumption, and investment are procyclical and coincident. Investment is much more volatile over the business cycle than consumption is. Employment is procyclical, but the unemployment rate is countercyclical. Average labor productivity and the real wage are procyclical, although according to most studies the real wage is only mildly so. Money and stock prices are procyclical and lead the cycle. Inflation and nominal interest rates are procyclical and lagging. The real interest rate is acyclical.
8. A theory of business cycles consists of (1) a description of shocks that affect the economy and (2) a model, such as the aggregate demand–aggregate supply (*AD–AS*) model, that describes how the economy responds to these shocks. In the *AD–AS* model, shocks to the aggregate demand (*AD*) curve cause output to change in the short run, but output returns to its full-employment level, $\bar{Y}$, in the long run. Shocks to the aggregate supply curve can affect output both in the long run and the short run.
9. Classical economists argue that the economy reaches its long-run equilibrium quickly because prices adjust rapidly. This view implies that aggregate demand shocks have only very short-lived effects on real variables such as output; instead, classical economists emphasize aggregate supply shocks as the source of business cycles. Classicals also see little role for government policies to fight recessions. Keynesian economists, in contrast, believe that it takes a long time for the economy to reach long-run equilibrium. They conclude, therefore, that aggregate demand shocks can affect output for substantial periods of time. Furthermore, they believe that government policies may be useful in speeding the economy's return to full employment.

KEY TERMS

Acyclical, p. 326
aggregate demand, p. 345
aggregate supply, p. 345
boom, p. 316
business cycle, p. 316
business cycle chronology, p. 316
coincident variable, p. 326
comovement, p. 317
contraction, p. 316
countercyclical, p. 326
depression, p. 316
expansion, p. 316
index of leading economic indicators, p. 339
job finding rate, p. 331
job loss rate, p. 331
lagging variable, p. 326
leading variable, p. 326
peak, p. 316
persistence, p. 318
procyclical, p. 326
recession, p. 316
trough, p. 316
turning points, p. 316

REVIEW QUESTIONS

1. Draw a diagram showing the phases and turning points of a business cycle. Using the diagram, illustrate the concepts of recurrence and persistence.
2. What is *comovement?* How is comovement related to the business cycle facts presented in this chapter?
3. If you were a member of the NBER business-cycle dating committee, would you declare that the U.S. economy is now in a recession? Why? Describe the major variables that you would look at to determine whether the economy is in a recession or not, and what features of the data you would look for.
4. What terms are used to describe the way a variable moves when aggregate economic activity is rising or falling? What terms are used to describe the timing of cyclical changes in economic variables?
5. If you knew that the economy was falling into a recession, what would you expect to happen to production during the next few quarters? To investment? To average labor productivity? To the real wage? To the unemployment rate?
6. When a recession occurs, do economists expect it to be temporary? Or is there some degree of permanence? What is the empirical evidence for this?
7. What are the two components of a theory of business cycles?
8. How do Keynesians and classicals differ in their beliefs about how long it takes the economy to reach long-run equilibrium? What implications do these differences in beliefs have for Keynesian and classical views about the usefulness of antirecessionary policies? About the types of shocks that cause most recessions?

ANALYTICAL PROBLEMS

1. Figure 8.1 shows that business cycle peaks and troughs are identified with peaks and troughs in the level of aggregate economic activity, which is consistent with current NBER methodology. However, for business cycles before 1927, the NBER identified business cycle peaks and troughs with peaks and troughs in *detrended* aggregate economic activity (aggregate economic activity minus the "normal growth path" shown in Fig. 8.1). Show that this alternative methodology implies that peaks occur earlier and that troughs occur later than you would find when using the current methodology. Compared to the current methodology, does the alternative methodology increase or decrease the computed length of contractions and expansions? How might this change in measurement account for the differences in the average measured lengths of expansions and contractions since World War II compared to the period before World War I?[27]

[27]For further discussion of these issues, see Christina D. Romer, "Remeasuring Business Cycles," *Journal of Economic History*, September 1994, pp. 573–609; and Randall E. Parker and Philip Rothman, "Further Evidence on the Stabilization of Postwar Economic Fluctuations," *Journal of Macroeconomics*, Spring 1996, pp. 289–298. Romer was the first to emphasize the potential importance of the change in business cycle dating methodology.

2. Consumer expenditures on durable goods such as cars and furniture, as well as purchases of new houses, fall much more than expenditures on nondurable goods and services during most recessions. Why do you think that is?

3. Output, total hours worked, and average labor productivity all are procyclical.

   a. Which variable, output or total hours worked, increases by a larger percentage in expansions and falls by a larger percentage in recessions? (*Hint:* Average labor productivity = output ÷ total hours worked, so that the percentage change in average labor productivity equals the percentage change in output minus the percentage change in total hours worked.)

   b. How is the procyclical behavior of average labor productivity related to Okun's law, discussed in Chapter 3?

4. During the period 1973–1975, the United States experienced a deep recession with a simultaneous sharp rise in the price level. Would you conclude that the recession was the result of a supply shock or a demand shock? Illustrate, using *AD–AS* analysis.

5. It is sometimes argued that economic growth that is "too rapid" will be associated with inflation. Use *AD–AS* analysis to show how this statement might be true. When this claim is made, what type of shock is implicitly assumed to be hitting the economy?

▶ WORKING WITH MACROECONOMIC DATA

For data to use in these exercises, go to the Federal Reserve Bank of St. Louis FRED database at fred.stlouisfed.org.

1. An economic variable is persistent if declines in the variable tend to be followed by more declines, and increases by more increases. This question asks you to study the persistence of the civilian unemployment rate.

   Using data since 1961, identify all quarters in which the unemployment rate changed by at least 0.2 percentage points from the previous quarter (either up or down). How many of these changes by 0.2 percentage points or more were followed in the subsequent quarter by (1) another change in the same direction, (2) a change in the opposite direction, or (3) no change? Based on your count, would you say that the unemployment rate is a persistent variable?

2. How does each of the following variables behave over the business cycle? Develop graphs to show your results and give economic explanations.

   a. Real imports

   b. Federal government receipts

   c. Housing starts

   d. Capacity utilization rate, manufacturing

   e. Average weekly hours, manufacturing

3. It has been argued that the stock market predicts recessions. Using quarterly data since 1961, plot the real value of the stock market index (the Wilshire 5000 index in the last month of the quarter divided by the GDP deflator). Do you find the stock market to be a good economic forecaster?

4. Graph the levels of real GDP for the United States, Canada, and Germany (data can be found at *www.oecd.org* under Statistics and then under National Accounts). Are U.S. and Canadian business cycles closely related? U.S. and German business cycles?

5. In the FRED database, find a variable that is available in both a seasonally adjusted form and a not seasonally adjusted form. Plot both over time and describe how large the seasonal variation in the variable is.

9

The *IS–LM/AD–AS* Model: A General Framework for Macroeconomic Analysis

Learning Objectives

9.1 Discuss factors that affect the full-employment (*FE*) line.

9.2 Discuss factors that affect the *IS* curve, which represents equilibrium in the goods market.

9.3 Discuss factors that affect the *LM* curve, which represents equilibrium in the asset market.

9.4 Describe the conditions necessary for general equilibrium using the *IS–LM* model.

9.5 Discuss the role of price adjustment in achieving general equilibrium.

9.6 Explain the fundamentals and implications of the *AD–AS* model.

The main goal of Chapter 8 was to *describe* business cycles by presenting the business cycle facts. This and the following two chapters attempt to *explain* business cycles and how policymakers should respond to them. First, we must develop a macroeconomic model that we can use to analyze cyclical fluctuations and the effects of policy changes on the economy. By examining the labor market in Chapter 3, the goods market in Chapter 4, and the asset market in Chapter 7, we already have identified the three components of a complete macroeconomic model. Now we put these three components together into a single framework that allows us to analyze them simultaneously. This chapter, then, consolidates our previous analyses to provide the theoretical structure for the rest of the book.

The basic macroeconomic model developed in this chapter is known as the *IS–LM* model. (As we discuss later, this name originates in two of its basic equilibrium conditions: that desired investment, I, must equal desired saving, S, and that money demanded, L, must equal money supplied, M/P.) The *IS–LM* model was developed in 1937 by Nobel laureate Sir John Hicks,[1] who intended it as a graphical representation of the ideas presented by Keynes in his famous 1936 book *The General Theory of Employment, Interest, and Money.* Reflecting Keynes's belief that wages and prices don't adjust quickly to clear markets (see Section 1.3), in his original *IS–LM* model Hicks assumed that the price level was fixed, at least temporarily. Since Hicks, several generations of economists have worked to refine the *IS–LM* model, and it has been widely applied in analyses of cyclical fluctuations and macroeconomic policy, and in forecasting.

Because of its origins, the *IS–LM* model is commonly identified with the Keynesian approach to business cycle analysis. Classical economists—who believe that wages and prices move rapidly to clear markets—would reject Hicks's *IS–LM* model because of his assumption that the price level is fixed. However, the conventional *IS–LM* model may be easily adapted to allow for rapidly adjusting wages and prices. Thus the *IS–LM* framework, although originally developed by Keynesians, also may be used to present and discuss the classical approach to business cycle analysis. In addition, the *IS–LM* model is

[1]Hicks outlined the *IS–LM* framework in an article titled "Mr. Keynes and the Classics: A Suggested Interpretation," *Econometrica*, April 1937, pp. 137–159.

equivalent to the *AD–AS* model that we previewed in Section 8.4. We show how the *AD–AS* model is derived from the *IS–LM* model and illustrate how the *AD–AS* model can be used with either a classical or a Keynesian perspective.

Using the *IS–LM* model (and the equivalent *AD–AS* model) as a framework for both classical and Keynesian analyses has several practical benefits: First, it avoids the need to learn two different models. Second, utilizing a single framework emphasizes the large areas of agreement between the Keynesian and classical approaches while showing clearly how the two approaches differ. Moreover, because versions of the *IS–LM* model (and its concepts and terminology) are so often applied in analyses of the economy and macroeconomic policy, studying this framework will help you understand and participate more fully in current economic debates.

We use a graphical approach to develop the *IS–LM* model. Appendix 9.B presents the identical analysis in algebraic form. If you have difficulty understanding why the curves used in the graphical analysis have the slopes they do or why they shift, you may find the algebra in the appendix helpful.

To keep things as simple as possible, in this chapter we assume that the economy is closed. In Chapter 13 we show how to extend the analysis to allow for a foreign sector.

9.1 The *FE* Line: Equilibrium in the Labor Market

Discuss factors that affect the full-employment (*FE*) line.

In previous chapters, we discussed the three main markets of the economy: the labor market, the goods market, and the asset market. We also identified some of the links among these markets, but now we want to be more precise about how they fit into a complete macroeconomic system.

Let's turn first to the labor market and recall from Chapter 3 the concepts of the full-employment level of employment and full-employment output. The *full-employment level of employment*, $\bar{N}$, is the equilibrium level of employment reached after wages and prices have fully adjusted. *Full-employment output*, $\bar{Y}$, is the amount of output produced when employment is at its full-employment level, for the current level of the capital stock and the production function. Algebraically, full-employment output, $\bar{Y}$, equals $AF(K, \bar{N})$, where K is the capital stock, A is productivity, and F is the production function (see Eq. 3.4).

Our ultimate goal is a diagram that has the real interest rate on the vertical axis and output on the horizontal axis. In such a diagram equilibrium in the labor market is represented by the **full-employment line**, or *FE*, in Figure 9.1. The *FE* line is vertical at $Y = \bar{Y}$ because, when the labor market is in equilibrium, output equals its full-employment level, regardless of the interest rate.[2]

Factors That Shift the *FE* Line

The full-employment level of output is determined by the full-employment level of employment and the current levels of capital and productivity. Any change that affects the full-employment level of output, $\bar{Y}$, will cause the *FE* line to shift.

[2]The real interest rate affects investment and thus the amount of capital that firms will have in the future, but it doesn't affect the current capital stock and hence does not affect current full-employment output.

FIGURE 9.1

The *FE* line
The full-employment (*FE*) line represents labor market equilibrium. When the labor market is in equilibrium, employment equals its full-employment level, $\bar{N}$, and output equals its full-employment level, $\bar{Y}$, regardless of the value of the real interest rate. Thus the *FE* line is vertical at $Y = \bar{Y}$.

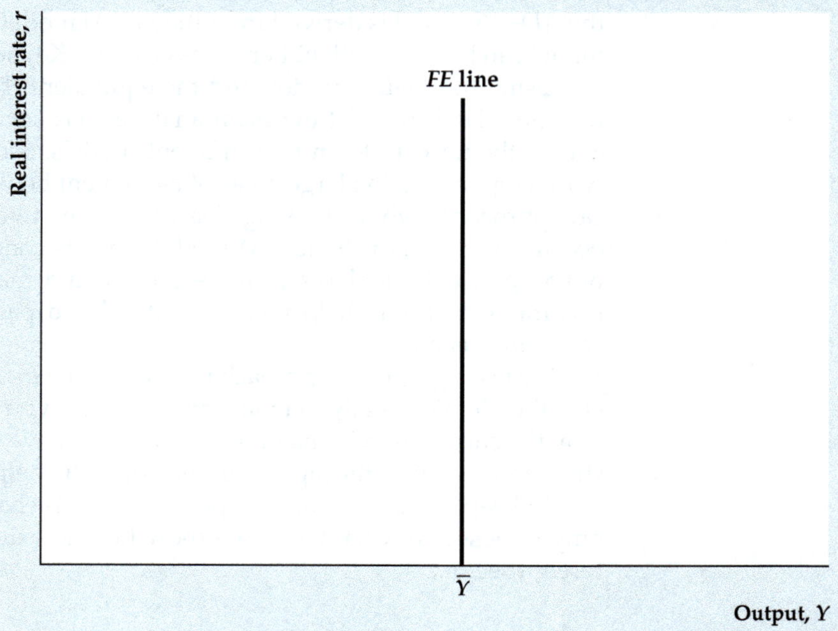

Recall that full-employment output, $\bar{Y}$, increases—and thus the *FE* line shifts to the right—when labor supply increases (which raises equilibrium employment $\bar{N}$), when the capital stock increases, or when there is a beneficial supply shock. Similarly, a drop in labor supply or capital stock or an adverse supply shock lowers full-employment output, $\bar{Y}$, and shifts the *FE* line to the left. Summary table 11 lists the factors that shift the *FE* line.

SUMMARY 11

Factors That Shift the Full-Employment (*FE*) Line

A(n)	Shifts the *FE* line	Reason
Beneficial supply shock	Right	1. More output can be produced for the same amount of capital and labor. 2. If the *MPN* rises, labor demand increases and raises employment. Full-employment output increases for both reasons.
Increase in labor supply	Right	Equilibrium employment rises, raising full-employment output.
Increase in the capital stock	Right	More output can be produced with the same amount of labor. In addition, increased capital may increase the *MPN*, which increases labor demand and equilibrium employment.

9.2 The *IS* Curve: Equilibrium in the Goods Market

Discuss factors that affect the *IS* curve, which represents equilibrium in the goods market.

The second of the three markets in our model is the goods market. Recall from Chapter 4 that the goods market is in equilibrium when desired investment and desired national saving are equal or, equivalently, when the aggregate quantity of goods supplied equals the aggregate quantity of goods demanded. Recall that adjustments in the real interest rate help bring about equilibrium in the goods market.

In a diagram with the real interest rate on the vertical axis and real output on the horizontal axis, equilibrium in the goods market is described by a curve called the *IS* curve. For any level of output (or income), Y, the ***IS* curve** shows the real interest rate, r, for which the goods market is in equilibrium. The *IS* curve is so named because at all points on the curve desired investment, I^d, equals desired national saving, S^d.

Figure 9.2 shows the derivation of the *IS* curve from the saving–investment diagram introduced in Chapter 4 (see Key Diagram 3). Figure 9.2(a) shows the saving–investment diagram drawn for two arbitrarily chosen levels of output, 4000 and 5000. Corresponding to each level is a saving curve, with the value of output indicated in parentheses next to it. Each saving curve slopes upward because an increase in the real interest rate causes households to increase their desired level of saving. An increase in current output (income) leads to more desired saving at any real interest rate, so the saving (S) curve for $Y = 5000$ lies to the right of the saving (S) curve for $Y = 4000$.

Also shown in Fig. 9.2(a) is an investment curve. Recall from Chapter 4 that the investment curve slopes downward. It slopes downward because an increase in the real interest rate increases the user cost of capital, which reduces the desired capital stock and hence desired investment. Desired investment isn't affected by current output, so the investment curve is the same whether $Y = 4000$ or $Y = 5000$.

Each level of output implies a different market-clearing real interest rate. When output is 4000, goods market equilibrium is at point D and the market-clearing real interest rate is 7%. When output is 5000, goods market equilibrium occurs at point F and the market-clearing real interest rate is 5%.

Figure 9.2(b) shows the *IS* curve for this economy, with output on the horizontal axis and the real interest rate on the vertical axis. For any level of output, the *IS* curve shows the real interest rate that clears the goods market. Thus $Y = 4000$ and $r = 7\%$ at point D on the *IS* curve. (Note that point D in Fig. 9.2b corresponds to point D in Fig. 9.2a.) Similarly, when output is 5000, the real interest rate that clears the goods market is 5%. This combination of output and the real interest rate occurs at point F on the *IS* curve in Fig. 9.2(b), which corresponds to point F in Fig. 9.2(a). In general, because a rise in output increases desired national saving, thereby reducing the real interest rate that clears the goods market, the *IS* curve slopes downward.

The slope of the *IS* curve may also be interpreted in terms of the alternative (but equivalent) version of the goods market equilibrium condition, which states that in equilibrium the aggregate quantity of goods demanded must equal the aggregate quantity of goods supplied. To illustrate, let's suppose that the economy is initially at point F in Fig. 9.2(b). The aggregate quantities of goods supplied and

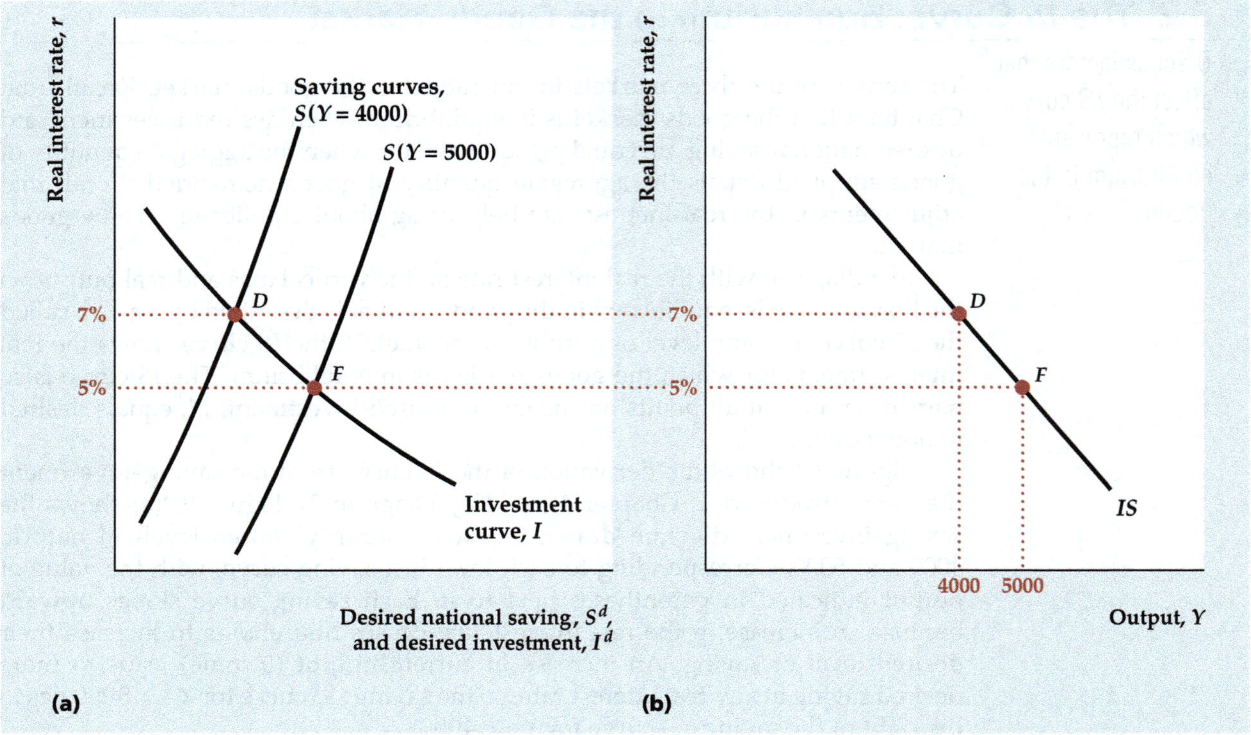

FIGURE 9.2

Deriving the *IS* curve

(a) The graph shows the goods market equilibrium for two different levels of output: 4000 and 5000 (the output corresponding to each saving curve is indicated in parentheses next to the curve). Higher levels of output (income) increase desired national saving and shift the saving curve to the right. When output is 4000, the real interest rate that clears the goods market is 7% (point *D*). When output is 5000, the market-clearing real interest rate is 5% (point *F*).

(b) For each level of output the *IS* curve shows the corresponding real interest rate that clears the goods market. Thus each point on the *IS* curve corresponds to an equilibrium point in the goods market. As in (a), when output is 4000, the real interest rate that clears the goods market is 7% (point *D*); when output is 5000, the market-clearing real interest rate is 5% (point *F*). Because higher output raises saving and leads to a lower market-clearing real interest rate, the *IS* curve slopes downward.

demanded are equal at point *F* because *F* lies on the *IS* curve, which means that the goods market is in equilibrium at that point.[3]

Now suppose that for some reason the real interest rate r rises from 5% to 7%. Recall from Chapter 4 that an increase in the real interest rate reduces both desired consumption, C^d (because people desire to save more when the real interest rate rises), and desired investment, I^d, thereby reducing the aggregate quantity of goods demanded. If output, Y, remained at its initial level of 5000, the increase in the real interest rate would imply that more goods were being supplied than demanded. For the goods market to reach equilibrium at the higher real interest rate, the quantity of goods supplied has to fall. At point *D* in Fig. 9.2(b), output

[3]We have just shown that desired national saving equals desired investment at point *F*, or $S^d = I^d$. Substituting the definition of desired national saving, $Y - C^d - G$, for S^d in the condition that desired national saving equals desired investment shows also that $Y = C^d + I^d + G$ at *F*.

has fallen enough (from 5000 to 4000) that the quantities of goods supplied and demanded are equal, and the goods market has returned to equilibrium.[4] Again, higher real interest rates are associated with less output in goods market equilibrium, so the *IS* curve slopes downward.

Factors That Shift the *IS* Curve

For any level of output, the *IS* curve shows the real interest rate needed to clear the goods market. With output held constant, any economic disturbance or policy change that changes the value of the goods-market-clearing real interest rate will cause the *IS* curve to shift. More specifically, for constant output, *any change in the economy that reduces desired national saving relative to desired investment will increase the real interest rate that clears the goods market and thus shift the* IS *curve up and to the right.* Similarly, for constant output, changes that increase desired saving relative to desired investment, thereby reducing the market-clearing real interest rate, shift the *IS* curve down and to the left. Factors that shift the *IS* curve are described in Summary table 12.

SUMMARY 12

Factors That Shift the *IS* Curve

An increase in	Shifts the *IS* curve	Reason
Expected future output	Up and to the right	Desired saving falls (desired consumption rises), raising the real interest rate that clears the goods market.
Wealth	Up and to the right	Desired saving falls (desired consumption rises), raising the real interest rate that clears the goods market.
Government purchases, *G*	Up and to the right	Desired saving falls (demand for goods rises), raising the real interest rate that clears the goods market.
Taxes, *T*	No change or down and to the left	No change, if consumers take into account an offsetting future tax cut and do not change consumption (Ricardian equivalence); down and to the left, if consumers don't take into account a future tax cut and reduce desired consumption, increasing desired national saving and lowering the real interest rate that clears the goods market.
Expected future TFP	Up and to the right	Desired investment and desired consumption increase, raising the real interest rate that clears the goods market.
Effective tax rate on capital	Down and to the left	Desired investment falls, lowering the real interest rate that clears the goods market.

[4]Although a drop in output, Y, obviously reduces the quantity of goods supplied, it also reduces the quantity of goods demanded. The reason is that a drop in output is also a drop in income, which reduces desired consumption. However, although a drop in output of one dollar reduces the supply of output by one dollar, a drop in income of one dollar reduces desired consumption, C^d, by less than one dollar (that is, the marginal propensity to consume, defined in Chapter 4, is less than 1). Thus a drop in output, Y, reduces goods supplied more than goods demanded and therefore reduces the excess supply of goods.

We can use a change in current government purchases to illustrate *IS* curve shifts in general. The effects of a temporary increase in government purchases on the *IS* curve are shown in Figure 9.3. Figure 9.3(a) shows the saving–investment diagram, with an initial saving curve, S^1, and an initial investment curve, I. The S^1 curve represents saving when output (income) is fixed at $Y = 4500$. Figure 9.3(b) shows the initial *IS* curve, IS^1. The initial goods market equilibrium when output, Y, equals 4500 is represented by point E in both (a) and (b). At E, the initial market-clearing real interest rate is 6%.

Now suppose that the government increases its current purchases of goods, G. Desired investment at any level of the real interest rate isn't affected by the increase in government purchases, so the investment curve doesn't shift. However, as discussed in Chapter 4, a temporary increase in government purchases reduces desired national saving, $Y - C^d - G$ (see Summary table 5 in Chapter 4), so the saving curve shifts to the left from S^1 to S^2 in Fig. 9.3(a). As a result of the reduction in desired national saving, the real interest rate that clears the goods market when output equals 4500 increases from 6% to 7% (point F in Fig. 9.3a).

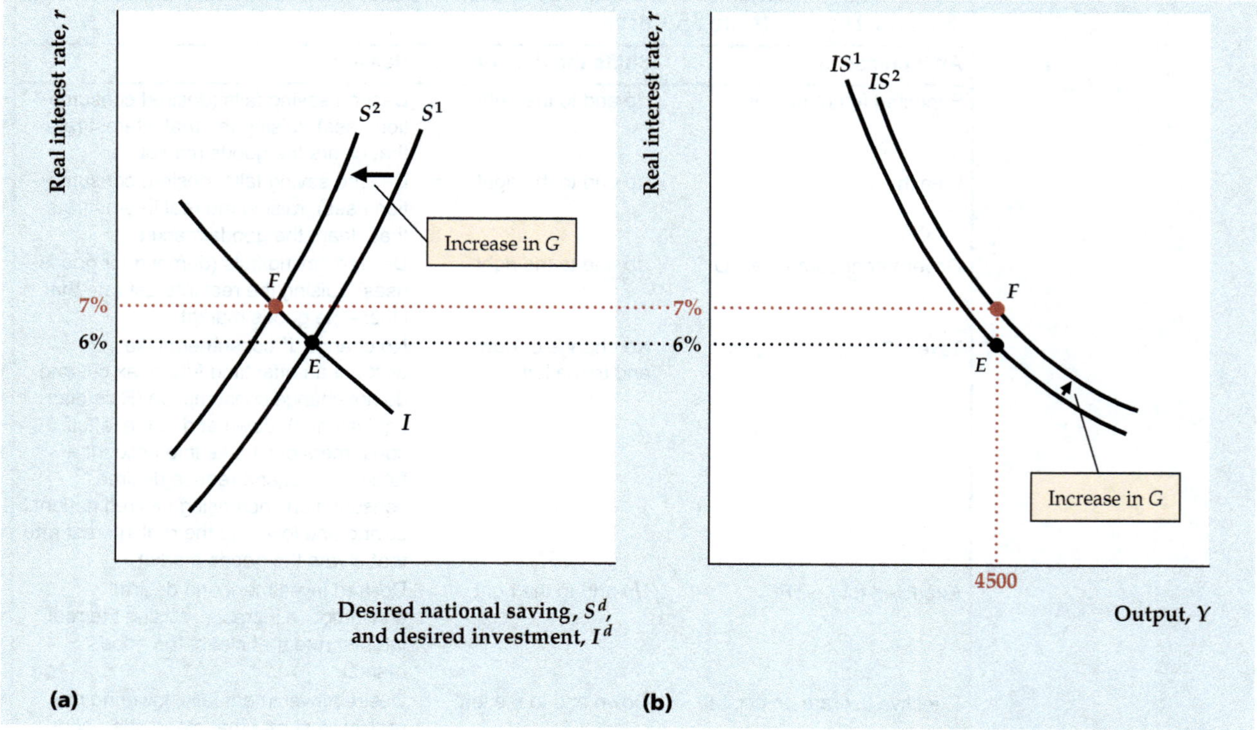

FIGURE 9.3

Effect on the *IS* curve of a temporary increase in government purchases

(a) The saving–investment diagram shows the effects of a temporary increase in government purchases, G, with output, Y, constant at 4500. The increase in G reduces desired national saving and shifts the saving curve to the left, from S^1 to S^2. The goods market equilibrium point moves from point E to point F, and the real interest rate rises from 6% to 7%.

(b) The increase in G raises the real interest rate that clears the goods market for any level of output. Thus the *IS* curve shifts up and to the right from IS^1 to IS^2. In this example, with output held constant at 4500, an increase in government purchases raises the real interest rate that clears the goods market from 6% (point E) to 7% (point F).

The effect on the *IS* curve is shown in Fig. 9.3(b). With output constant at 4500, the real interest rate that clears the goods market increases from 6% to 7%, as shown by the shift from point *E* to point *F*. The new *IS* curve, IS^2, passes through *F* and lies above and to the right of the initial *IS* curve, IS^1. Thus a temporary increase in government purchases shifts the *IS* curve up and to the right.

So far our discussion of *IS* curve shifts has focused on the goods market equilibrium condition that desired national saving must equal desired investment. However, factors that shift the *IS* curve may also be described in terms of the alternative (but equivalent) goods market equilibrium condition—that the aggregate quantities of goods demanded and supplied are equal. In particular, for a given level of output, *any change that increases the aggregate demand for goods shifts the* IS *curve up and to the right.*

This rule works because, for the initial level of output, an increase in the aggregate demand for goods causes the quantity of goods demanded to exceed the quantity supplied. Goods market equilibrium can be restored at the same level of output by an increase in the real interest rate, which reduces desired consumption, C^d, and desired investment, I^d. For any level of output, an increase in aggregate demand for goods raises the real interest rate that clears the goods market, so we conclude that an increase in the aggregate demand for goods shifts the *IS* curve up and to the right.

To illustrate this alternative way of thinking about shifts in the *IS* curve, we again use the example of a temporary increase in government purchases. Note that an increase in government purchases, *G*, directly raises the demand for goods, $C^d + I^d + G$, leading to an excess demand for goods at the initial level of output. The excess demand for goods can be eliminated and goods market equilibrium at the initial level of output restored by an increase in the real interest rate, which reduces C^d and I^d. Because a higher real interest rate is required for goods market equilibrium when government purchases increase, an increase in *G* causes the *IS* curve to shift up and to the right.

9.3 The *LM* Curve: Asset Market Equilibrium

Discuss factors that affect the *LM* curve, which represents equilibrium in the asset market.

The third and final market in our macroeconomic model is the asset market, presented in Chapter 7. The asset market is in equilibrium when the quantities of assets demanded by holders of wealth for their portfolios equal the supplies of those assets in the economy. In reality, there are many different assets, both real (houses, consumer durables, office buildings) and financial (checking accounts, government bonds). Recall, however, that we aggregated all assets into two categories—money and nonmonetary assets. We assumed that the nominal supply of money is *M* and that money pays a fixed nominal interest rate, i^m. Similarly, we assumed that the nominal supply of nonmonetary assets is *NM* and that these assets pay a nominal interest rate, *i*, and (given expected inflation, π^e) an expected real interest rate, *r*.

With this aggregation assumption, we showed that the asset market equilibrium condition reduces to the requirement that the quantities of money supplied and demanded be equal. In this section we show that asset market equilibrium can be represented by the *LM* curve. However, to discuss how the asset market comes into equilibrium—a task that we didn't complete in Chapter 7—we first introduce an important relationship used every day by traders in financial markets: the relationship between the *price* of a nonmonetary asset and the *interest rate* on that asset.

The Interest Rate and the Price of a Nonmonetary Asset

The price of a nonmonetary asset, such as a government bond, is what a buyer has to pay for it. Its price is closely related to the interest rate that it pays (sometimes called its *yield*). To illustrate this relationship with an example, let's consider a bond that matures in one year. At maturity, we assume, the bondholder will redeem it and receive $10,000; the bond doesn't pay any interest before it matures.[5] Suppose that this bond can be purchased now for $9615. At this price, over the coming year the bond will increase in value by $385 ($10,000 − $9615), or approximately 4% of its current price of $9615. Therefore the nominal interest rate on the bond, or its yield, is 4% per year.

Now suppose that for some reason the current price of a $10,000 bond that matures in one year drops to $9524. The increase in the bond's value over the coming year will be $476 ($10,000 − $9524), or approximately 5% of the purchase price of $9524. Therefore, when the current price of the bond falls to $9524, the nominal interest rate on the bond increases to 5% per year. More generally, for the promised schedule of payments on a bond or other nonmonetary asset, the higher the price of the asset, the lower the nominal interest rate that the asset pays. Thus a media report that, in yesterday's trading, the bond market "strengthened" (bond prices rose), is equivalent to saying that nominal interest rates fell.

We have just indicated why the price of a nonmonetary asset and its nominal interest rate are negatively related. For a given expected rate of inflation, π^e, movements in the nominal interest rate are matched by equal movements in the real interest rate, so the price of a nonmonetary asset and its *real* interest rate are also inversely related. This relationship is a key to deriving the *LM* curve and explaining how the asset market comes into equilibrium.

The Equality of Money Demanded and Money Supplied

To derive the *LM* curve, which represents asset market equilibrium, we recall that the asset market is in equilibrium only if the quantity of money demanded equals the currently available money supply. We depict the equality of money supplied and demanded using the *money supply–money demand diagram,* shown in Figure 9.4(a). The real interest rate is on the vertical axis and money, measured in real terms, is on the horizontal axis.[6] The *MS* line shows the economy's real money supply, M/P. The nominal money supply, M, is set by the central bank. Thus for a given price level, P, the real money supply, M/P, is a fixed number and the *MS* line is vertical. For example, if $M = 2000$ and $P = 2$, the *MS* line is vertical at $M/P = 1000$.

Real money demand at two different levels of income, Y, is shown by the two *MD* curves in Fig. 9.4(a). Recall from Chapter 7 that for a given value of the expected rate of inflation, π^e, a higher real interest rate, r, increases the relative attractiveness of nonmonetary assets and causes holders of wealth to demand less money. Thus the money demand curves slope downward. The money demand curve, *MD*, for $Y = 4000$ shows the real demand for money when output is 4000;

[5]A bond that doesn't pay any interest before maturity is called a *discount bond* or a *zero-coupon bond.*

[6]Asset market equilibrium may be expressed as either nominal money supplied equals nominal money demanded, or as real money supplied equals real money demanded. As in Chapter 7, we work with the condition expressed in real terms.

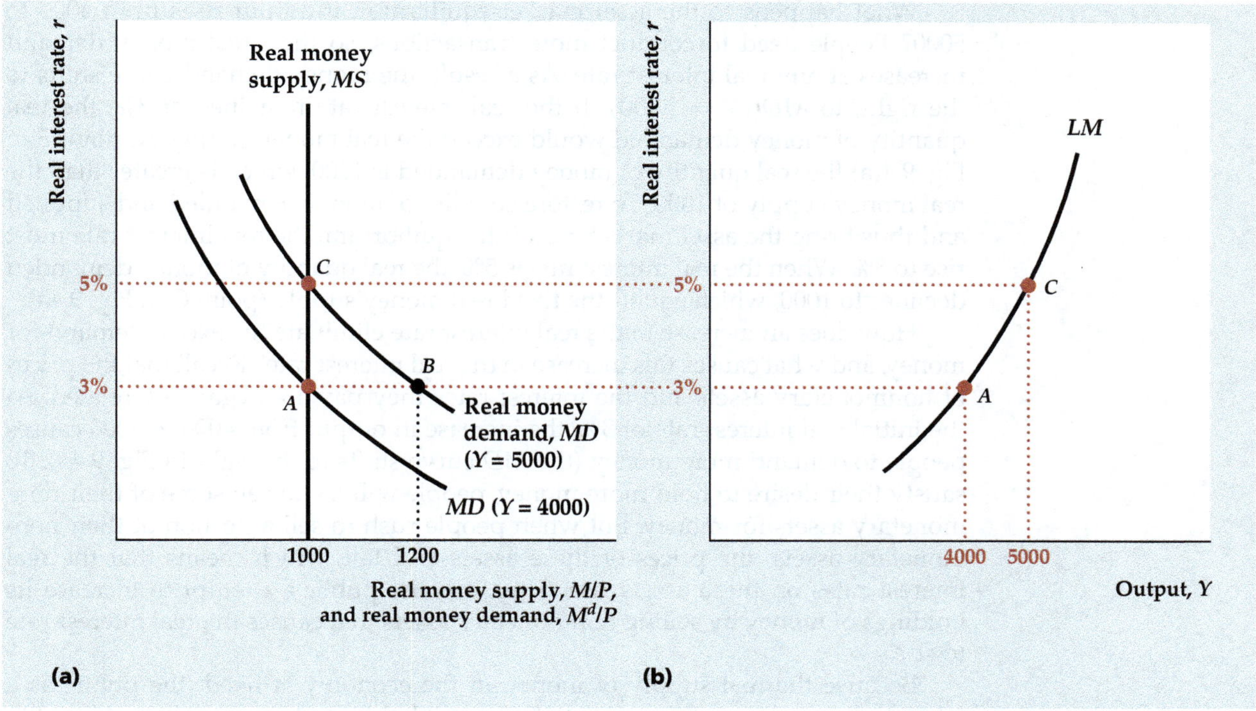

FIGURE 9.4

Deriving the *LM* curve

(a) The curves show real money demand and real money supply. Real money supply is fixed at 1000. When output is 4000, the real money demand curve is $MD\ (Y = 4000)$; the real interest rate that clears the asset market is 3% (point *A*). When output is 5000, more money is demanded at the same real interest rate, so the real money demand curve shifts to the right to $MD\ (Y = 5000)$. In this case the real interest rate that clears the asset market is 5% (point C).

(b) The graph shows the corresponding *LM* curve. For each level of output, the *LM* curve shows the real interest rate that clears the asset market. Thus when output is 4000, the *LM* curve shows that the real interest rate that clears the asset market is 3% (point *A*). When output is 5000, the *LM* curve shows a market-clearing real interest rate of 5% (point C). Because higher output raises money demand, and thus raises the real interest rate that clears the asset market, the *LM* curve slopes upward.

similarly, the *MD* curve for $Y = 5000$ shows the real demand for money when output is 5000. Because an increase in income increases the amount of money demanded at any real interest rate, the money demand curve for $Y = 5000$ is farther to the right than the money demand curve for $Y = 4000$.

Graphically, asset market equilibrium occurs at the intersection of the money supply and money demand curves, where the real quantities of money supplied and demanded are equal. For example, when output is 4000, so that the money demand curve is $MD\ (Y = 4000)$, the money demand and money supply curves intersect at point *A* in Fig. 9.4(a). The real interest rate at *A* is 3%. Thus when output is 4000, the real interest rate that clears the asset market (equalizes the quantities of money supplied and demanded) is 3%. At a real interest rate of 3% and an output of 4000, the real quantity of money demanded by holders of wealth is 1000, which equals the real money supply made available by the central bank at the given price level.

What happens to the asset market equilibrium if output rises from 4000 to 5000? People need to conduct more transactions, so their real money demand increases at any real interest rate. As a result, the money demand curve shifts to the right, to $MD\ (Y = 5000)$. If the real interest rate remained at 3%, the real quantity of money demanded would exceed the real money supply. At point *B* in Fig. 9.4(a) the real quantity of money demanded is 1200, which is greater than the real money supply of 1000. To restore equality of money demanded and supplied and thus bring the asset market back into equilibrium, the real interest rate must rise to 5%. When the real interest rate is 5%, the real quantity of money demanded declines to 1000, which equals the fixed real money supply (point *C* in Fig. 9.4a).

How does an increase in the real interest rate eliminate the excess demand for money, and what causes this increase in the real interest rate? Recall that the prices of nonmonetary assets and the interest rates they pay are negatively related. At the initial real interest rate of 3%, the increase in output from 4000 to 5000 causes people to demand more money (the *MD* curve shifts to the right in Fig. 9.4a). To satisfy their desire to hold more money, people will try to sell some of their nonmonetary assets for money. But when people rush to sell a portion of their nonmonetary assets, the prices of these assets will fall, which means that the real interest rates on these assets rise. Thus it is the public's attempt to increase its holdings of money by selling nonmonetary assets that causes the real interest rate to rise.

Because the real supply of money in the economy is fixed, the public as a whole cannot increase the amount of money it holds. As long as people attempt to do so by selling nonmonetary assets, the real interest rate will continue to rise. But the increase in the real interest rate paid by nonmonetary assets makes those assets more attractive relative to money, reducing the real quantity of money demanded (here the movement is *along* the *MD* curve for $Y = 5000$, from point *B* to point *C* in Fig. 9.4a). The real interest rate will rise until the real quantity of money demanded again equals the fixed supply of money and restores asset market equilibrium. The new asset market equilibrium is at *C*, where the real interest rate has risen from 3% to 5%.

The preceding example shows that when output rises, increasing real money demand, a higher real interest rate is needed to maintain equilibrium in the asset market. In general, the relationship between output and the real interest rate that clears the asset market is expressed graphically by the *LM* curve. For any level of output, the ***LM* curve** shows the real interest rate for which the asset market is in equilibrium, with equal quantities of money supplied and demanded. The term *LM* comes from the asset market equilibrium condition that the real quantity of money demanded, as determined by the real money demand function, *L*, must equal the real money supply, M/P.

The *LM* curve corresponding to our numerical example is shown in Fig. 9.4(b), with the real interest rate, *r*, on the vertical axis and output, *Y*, on the horizontal axis. Points *A* and *C* lie on the *LM* curve. At *A*, which corresponds to point *A* in the money supply–money demand diagram of Fig. 9.4(a), output, *Y*, is 4000 and the real interest rate, *r*, is 3%. Because *A* lies on the *LM* curve, when output is 4000 the real interest rate that clears the asset market is 3%. Similarly, because *C* lies on the *LM* curve, when output is 5000 the real interest rate that equalizes money supplied and demanded is 5%; this output–real interest rate combination corresponds to the asset market equilibrium at point *C* in Fig. 9.4(a).

Figure 9.4(b) illustrates the general point that the *LM* curve always slopes upward from left to right. It does so because increases in output, by raising money demand, also raise the real interest rate on nonmonetary assets needed to clear the asset market.

Factors That Shift the *LM* Curve

In deriving the *LM* curve we varied output but held constant other factors, such as the price level, that affect the real interest rate that clears the asset market. Changes in any of these other factors will cause the *LM* curve to shift. In particular, for constant output, *any change that reduces real money supply relative to real money demand will increase the real interest rate that clears the asset market and cause the* LM *curve to shift up and to the left.* Similarly, for constant output, anything that raises real money supply relative to real money demand will reduce the real interest rate that clears the asset market and shift the *LM* curve down and to the right. Here we discuss in general terms how changes in real money supply or demand affect the *LM* curve. Summary table 13 describes the factors that shift the *LM* curve.

Changes in the Real Money Supply. An increase in the real money supply M/P will reduce the real interest rate that clears the asset market and shift the *LM* curve down and to the right. Figure 9.5 illustrates this point and extends our previous numerical example.

Figure 9.5(a) contains the money supply–money demand diagram. Initially, suppose that the real money supply M/P is 1000 and output is 4000, so the money demand curve is $MD\ (Y = 4000)$. Then equilibrium in the asset market occurs at

SUMMARY 13

Factors That Shift the *LM* Curve

An increase in	Shifts the *LM* curve	Reason
Nominal money supply, M	Down and to the right	Real money supply increases, lowering the real interest rate that clears the asset market (equates money supplied and money demanded).
Price level, P	Up and to the left	Real money supply falls, raising the real interest rate that clears the asset market.
Expected inflation, π^e	Down and to the right	Demand for money falls, lowering the real interest rate that clears the asset market.
Nominal interest rate on money, i^m	Up and to the left	Demand for money increases, raising the real interest rate that clears the asset market.

In addition, for constant output, any factor that increases real money demand raises the real interest rate that clears the asset market and shifts the *LM* curve up and to the left. Other factors that increase real money demand (see Summary table 9 in Chapter 7) include

- an increase in wealth;
- an increase in the risk of alternative assets relative to the risk of holding money;
- a decline in the liquidity of alternative assets; and
- a decline in the efficiency of payment technologies.

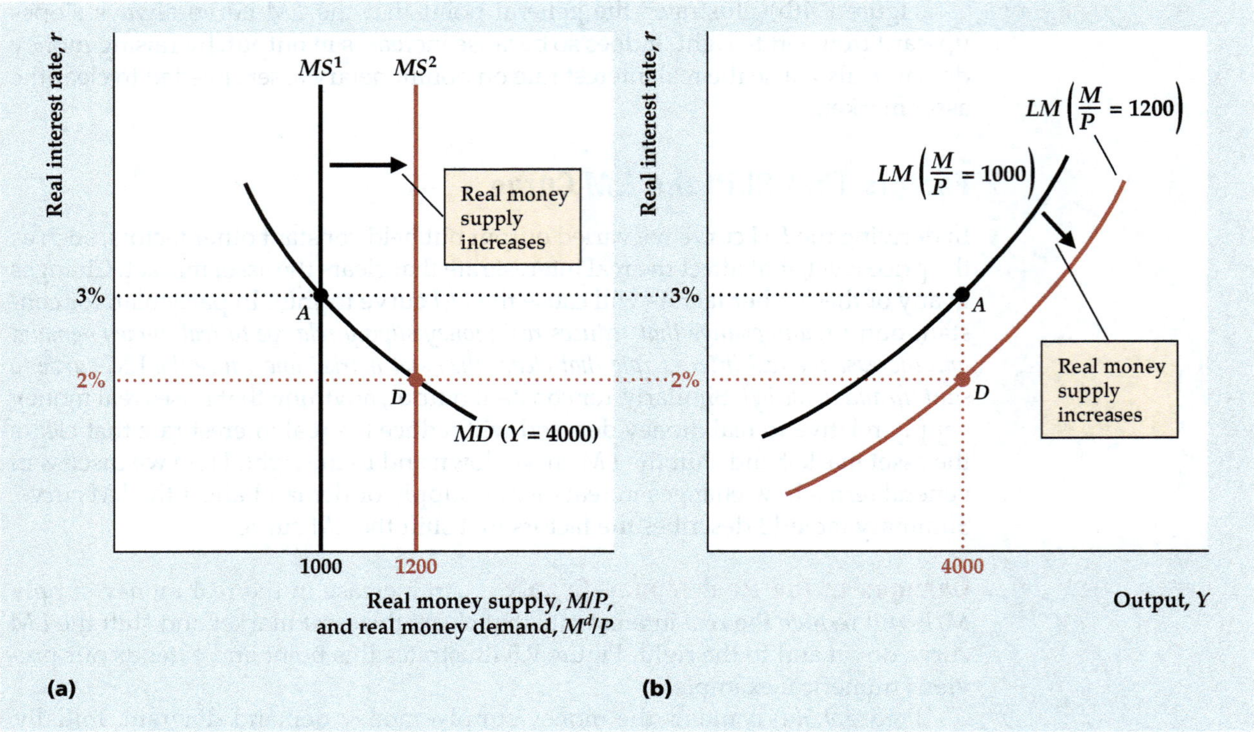

FIGURE 9.5

An increase in the real money supply shifts the *LM* curve down and to the right

(a) An increase in the real supply of money shifts the money supply curve to the right, from MS^1 to MS^2. For a constant level of output, the real interest rate that clears the asset market falls. If output is fixed at 4000, for example, the money demand curve is $MD\ (Y = 4000)$ and the real interest rate that clears the asset market falls from 3% (point *A*) to 2% (point *D*).

(b) The graph shows the effect of the increase in real money supply on the *LM* curve. For any level of output, the increase in the real money supply causes the real interest rate that clears the asset market to fall. So, for example, when output is 4000, the increase in the real money supply causes the real interest rate that clears the asset market to fall from 3% (point *A*) to 2% (point *D*). Thus the *LM* curve shifts down and to the right, from $LM\ (M/P = 1000)$ to $LM\ (M/P = 1200)$.

point *A* with a market-clearing real interest rate of 3%. The *LM* curve corresponding to the real money supply of 1000 is shown as $LM\ (M/P = 1000)$ in Fig. 9.5(b). At point *A* on this *LM* curve, as at point *A* in the money supply–money demand diagram in Fig. 9.5(a), output is 4000 and the real interest rate is 3%. Because *A* lies on the initial *LM* curve, when output is 4000 and the money supply is 1000, the real interest rate that clears the asset market is 3%.

Now suppose that, with output constant at 4000, the real money supply rises from 1000 to 1200. This increase in the real money supply causes the vertical money supply curve to shift to the right, from MS^1 to MS^2 in Fig. 9.5(a). The asset market equilibrium point is now point *D*, where, with output remaining at 4000, the market-clearing real interest rate has fallen to 2%.

Why has the real interest rate that clears the asset market fallen? At the initial real interest rate of 3%, there is an excess supply of money—that is, holders of wealth have more money in their portfolios than they want to hold and, consequently, they have a smaller share of their wealth than they would like in nonmonetary assets. To eliminate this imbalance in their portfolios, holders of wealth will want to use some of their money to buy nonmonetary assets. However, when holders of wealth as a group try to purchase nonmonetary assets, the price of nonmonetary assets is bid up and hence the real interest rate paid on these assets declines. As the real interest rate falls, nonmonetary assets become less attractive relative to money. The real interest rate continues to fall until it reaches 2% at point D in Fig. 9.5(a), where the excess supply of money and the excess demand for nonmonetary assets are eliminated and the asset market is back in equilibrium.

The effect of the increase in the real money supply on the *LM* curve is illustrated in Fig. 9.5(b). With output constant at 4000, the increase in the real money supply lowers the real interest rate that clears the asset market, from 3% to 2%. Thus point D, where $Y = 4000$ and $r = 2\%$, is now a point of asset market equilibrium, and point A no longer is. More generally, for any level of output, an increase in the real money supply lowers the real interest rate that clears the asset market. Therefore the entire *LM* curve shifts down and to the right. The new *LM* curve, for $M/P = 1200$, passes through the new equilibrium point D and lies below the old *LM* curve, for $M/P = 1000$.

Thus with fixed output, an increase in the real money supply lowers the real interest rate that clears the asset market and causes the *LM* curve to shift down and to the right. A similar analysis would show that a drop in the real money supply causes the *LM* curve to shift up and to the left.

What might cause the real money supply to increase? In general, because the real money supply equals M/P, it will increase whenever the nominal money supply, M, which is controlled by the central bank, increases proportionately more than the price level increases.

Changes in Real Money Demand. A change in any variable that affects real money demand, other than output or the real interest rate, will also shift the *LM* curve. More specifically, with output constant, an increase in real money demand raises the real interest rate that clears the asset market and thus shifts the *LM* curve up and to the left. Analogously, with output constant, a drop in real money demand shifts the *LM* curve down and to the right.

Figure 9.6 shows a graphical analysis of an increase in money demand similar to that for a change in money supply shown in Fig. 9.5. As before, the money supply–money demand diagram is shown on the left, Fig. 9.6(a). Output is constant at 4000, and the real money supply again is 1000. The initial money demand curve is MD^1. The initial asset market equilibrium point is at A, where the money demand curve, MD^1, and the money supply curve, MS, intersect. At initial equilibrium, point A, the real interest rate that clears the asset market is 3%.

Now suppose that, for a fixed level of output, a change occurs in the economy that increases real money demand. For example, if banks decided to increase the interest rate paid on money, i^m, the public would want to hold more money at the same levels of output and the real interest rate. Graphically, the increase in money demand shifts the money demand curve to the right, from MD^1 to MD^2 in Fig. 9.6(a). At the initial real interest rate of 3%, the real quantity of money demanded is 1300, which exceeds the available supply of 1000; so 3% is no longer the value of the real interest rate that clears the asset market.

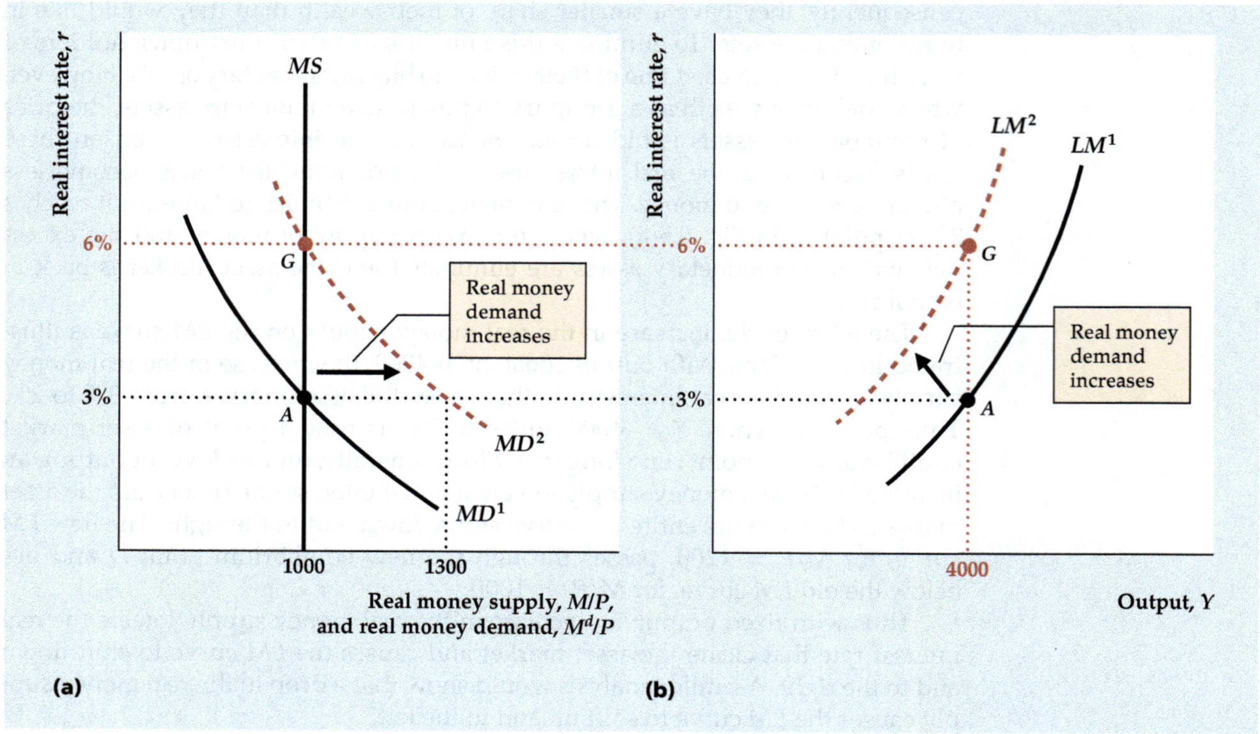

FIGURE 9.6

An increase in real money demand shifts the *LM* curve up and to the left

(a) With output constant at 4000 and the real money supply at 1000, an increase in the interest rate paid on money raises real money demand. The money demand curve shifts to the right, from MD^1 to MD^2, and the real interest rate that clears the asset market rises from 3% (point *A*) to 6% (point *G*).

(b) The graph shows the effect of the increase in real money demand on the *LM* curve. When output is 4000, the increase in real money demand raises the real interest rate that clears the asset market from 3% (point *A*) to 6% (point *G*). More generally, for any level of output, the increase in real money demand raises the real interest rate that clears the asset market. Thus the *LM* curve shifts up and to the left, from LM^1 to LM^2.

How will the real interest rate that clears the asset market change after the increase in money demand? If holders of wealth want to hold more money, they will exchange nonmonetary assets for money. Increased sales of nonmonetary assets will drive down their price and thus raise the real interest rate that they pay. The real interest rate will rise, reducing the attractiveness of holding money, until the public is satisfied to hold the available real money supply (1000). The real interest rate rises from its initial value of 3% at *A* to 6% at *G*.

Figure 9.6(b) shows the effect of the increase in money demand on the *LM* curve. The initial *LM* curve, LM^1, passes through point *A*, showing that when output is 4000, the real interest rate that clears the asset market is 3%. (Point *A* in Fig. 9.6b corresponds to point *A* in Fig. 9.6a.) Following the increase in money demand, with output fixed at 4000, the market-clearing real interest rate rises to 6%. Thus the new *LM* curve must pass through point *G* (corresponding to point *G* in Fig. 9.6a), where $Y = 4000$ and $r = 6\%$. The new *LM* curve, LM^2, is higher than LM^1 because the real interest rate that clears the asset market is now higher for any level of output.

9.4 General Equilibrium in the Complete *IS–LM* Model

Describe the conditions necessary for general equilibrium using the *IS–LM* model.

The next step is to put the labor market, the goods market, and the asset market together and examine the equilibrium of the economy as a whole. A situation in which all markets in an economy are simultaneously in equilibrium is called a **general equilibrium**. Figure 9.7 shows the complete *IS–LM* model, illustrating how the general equilibrium of the economy is determined. Shown are

- the full-employment, or *FE*, line, along which the labor market is in equilibrium;
- the *IS* curve, along which the goods market is in equilibrium; and
- the *LM* curve, along which the asset market is in equilibrium.

The three curves intersect at point *E*, indicating that all three markets are in equilibrium at that point. Therefore *E* represents a general equilibrium and, because it is the only point that lies on all three curves, the only general equilibrium for this economy.

Although point *E* obviously is a general equilibrium point, not so clear is which forces, if any, act to bring the economy to that point. To put it another way, although the *IS* curve and *FE* line must intersect somewhere, we haven't explained why the *LM* curve must pass through that same point. In Section 9.5 we discuss the economic forces that lead the economy to general equilibrium. There we show that (1) the general equilibrium of the economy always occurs at the intersection of the *IS* curve and the *FE* line; and (2) adjustments of the price level cause the *LM* curve to shift until it passes through the general equilibrium point defined by the intersection of the *IS* curve and the *FE* line. Before discussing the details of this adjustment process, however, let's consider an example that illustrates the use of the complete *IS–LM* model.

FIGURE 9.7

General equilibrium in the *IS–LM* model
The economy is in general equilibrium when quantities supplied equal quantities demanded in every market. The general equilibrium point, *E*, lies on the *IS* curve, the *LM* curve, and the *FE* line. Thus at *E*, and only at *E*, the goods market, the asset market, and the labor market are simultaneously in equilibrium.

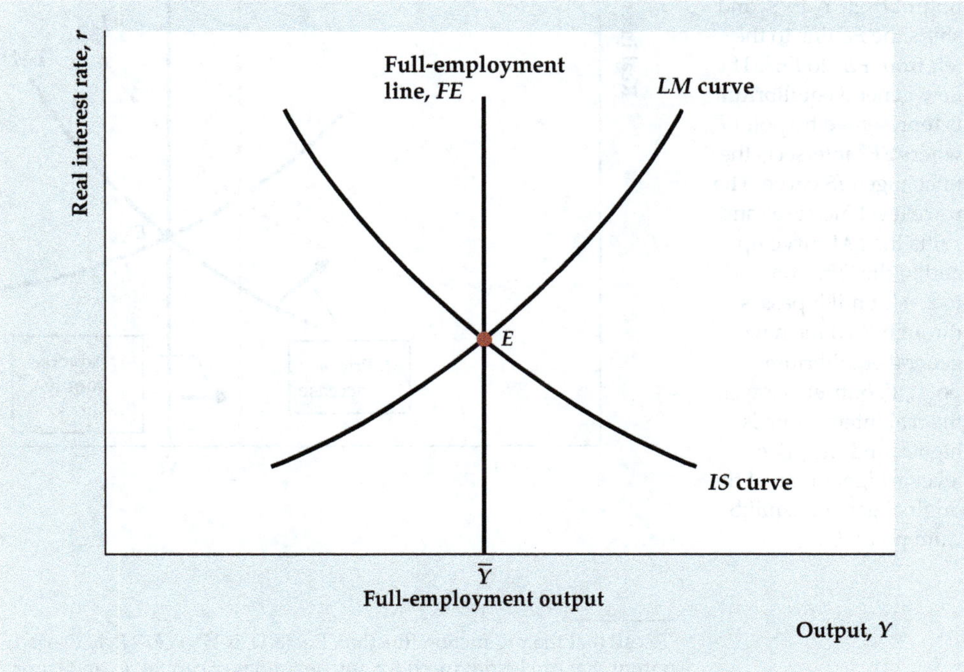

Applying the *IS–LM* Framework: A Temporary Adverse Supply Shock

An economic shock relevant to business cycle analysis is an adverse supply shock. Specifically, suppose that (because of bad weather or a temporary increase in oil prices) the productivity parameter, A, in the production function drops temporarily.[7] We can use the *IS–LM* model to analyze the effects of this shock on the general equilibrium of the economy and the general equilibrium values of economic variables such as the real wage, employment, output, the real interest rate, the price level, consumption, and investment.

Suppose that the economy is initially in general equilibrium at point E in Figure 9.8, where the initial *FE* line, FE^1, *IS* curve, and *LM* curve, LM^1, for this economy intersect. To determine the effects of a temporary supply shock on the general equilibrium of this economy, we must consider how the temporary drop in productivity A affects the positions of the *FE* line and the *IS* and *LM* curves.

The *FE* line describes equilibrium in the labor market. Hence to find the effect of the supply shock on the *FE* line we must first look at how the shock affects labor supply and labor demand. In Chapter 3 we demonstrated that an adverse supply shock reduces the marginal product of labor and thus shifts the labor demand curve down (see Fig. 3.10). Because the supply shock is temporary, we assume that it doesn't affect workers' wealth or expected future wages and so doesn't affect labor supply. As a result of the decline in labor demand, the equilibrium values of the real wage and employment, $\bar{N}$, fall.

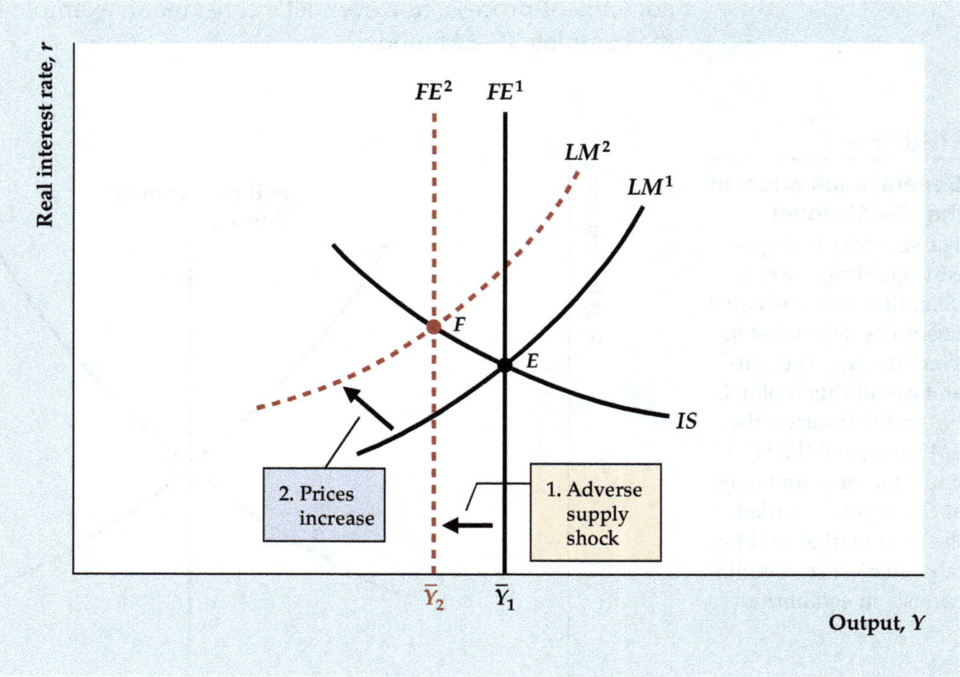

FIGURE 9.8

Effects of a temporary adverse supply shock

Initially, the economy is in general equilibrium at point E, with output at its full-employment level, $\bar{Y}_1$. A temporary adverse supply shock reduces full-employment output from $\bar{Y}_1$ to $\bar{Y}_2$ and shifts the *FE* line to the left from FE^1 to FE^2. The new general equilibrium is represented by point F, where FE^2 intersects the unchanged *IS* curve. The price level increases and shifts the *LM* curve up and to the left, from LM^1 to LM^2, until it passes through F. At the new general equilibrium point, F, output is lower, the real interest rate is higher, and the price level is higher than at the original general equilibrium point, E.

[7]Recall that the production function, Eq. (3.1), is $Y = AF(K,N)$, so a drop in A reduces the amount of output that can be produced for any quantities of capital, K, and labor, N.

The *FE* line shifts only to the degree that full-employment output, $\bar{Y}$, changes. Does $\bar{Y}$ change? Yes. Recall from Chapter 3 that an adverse supply shock reduces full-employment output, $\bar{Y}$, which equals $AF(K,\bar{N})$, for two reasons: (1) As we just mentioned, the supply shock reduces the equilibrium level of employment, $\bar{N}$, which lowers the amount of output that can be produced; and (2) the drop in productivity A directly reduces the amount of output produced by any combination of capital and labor. The reduction in $\bar{Y}$ is represented by a shift to the left of the *FE* line, from FE^1 to FE^2 in Fig. 9.8.

Now consider the effects of the temporary adverse supply shock on the *IS* curve. Recall that we derived the *IS* curve by changing the level of current output in the saving–investment diagram (Fig. 9.2) and finding for each level of current output the real interest rate for which desired saving equals desired investment. A *temporary* adverse supply shock reduces current output but doesn't change any other factor affecting desired saving or investment (such as wealth, expected future income, or the future marginal product of capital). Therefore a temporary supply shock is just the sort of change in current output that we used to trace out the *IS* curve. We conclude that a temporary adverse supply shock is a movement *along* the *IS* curve, *not a shift* of the *IS* curve, leaving it unchanged.[8]

Finally, we consider the *LM* curve. A temporary supply shock has no direct effect on the demand or supply of money and thus doesn't shift the *LM* curve.

We now look for the new general equilibrium of the economy. In Fig. 9.8, there is no point at which FE^2 (the new *FE* line), *IS*, and LM^1 all intersect. As we mentioned—and demonstrate in Section 9.5—when the *FE* line, the *IS* curve, and the *LM* curve don't intersect at a common point, the *LM* curve shifts until it passes through the intersection of the *FE* line and *IS* curve. This shift in the *LM* curve is caused by a change in the price level, *P*, which changes the real money supply, M/P, and thus affects the equilibrium of the asset market. As Fig. 9.8 shows, to restore general equilibrium at point *F*, the *LM* curve must shift up and to the left, from LM^1 to LM^2. For it to do so, the real money supply M/P must fall (see Summary table 13) and thus the price level, *P*, must rise. We infer (although we haven't yet given an economic explanation) that an adverse supply shock will cause the price level to rise.

What is the effect of a temporary supply shock on the inflation rate, as distinct from the price level? As the inflation rate is the growth rate of the price level, during the period in which prices are rising to their new, higher level, a burst of inflation will occur. However, after the price level stabilizes at its higher value (and is no longer rising), inflation will subside. Thus a temporary supply shock should cause a temporary, rather than a permanent, increase in the rate of inflation.

Let's pause and review our results.

1. As we had already shown in Chapter 3, a temporary adverse supply shock lowers the equilibrium values of the real wage and employment.
2. Comparing the new general equilibrium, point *F*, to the old general equilibrium, point *E*, in Fig. 9.8, we see that the supply shock lowers output and raises the real interest rate.

[8]Analytical Problem 2 at the end of the chapter examines the effect of a permanent adverse supply shock and identifies factors that shift the *IS* curve in that case.

3. The supply shock raises the price level and causes a temporary burst of inflation.
4. Because in the new general equilibrium the real interest rate is higher and output is lower, consumption must be lower than before the supply shock. The higher real interest rate also implies that investment must be lower after the shock.

In the Application "The Oil Price Shock of 2008," we check out how well our model explains the historical behavior of the economy. Note that economic models, such as the *IS–LM* model, also are used extensively in forecasting economic conditions ("In Touch with Data and Research: Econometric Models and Macroeconomic Forecasts for Monetary Policy Analysis").

Application

The Oil Price Shock of 2008

In 2008, oil prices swung wildly. In the first half of the year, oil prices (measured by the price of a barrel of West Texas Intermediate Grade Crude Oil) rose from $96 on January 1 (and had been as low as $51 in January 2007) to a peak of $145 in July. A supply shock of this magnitude would normally have an adverse effect on output, employment, and investment, of course. But when combined with the housing crisis and financial crisis that developed in 2008, the declines in output, employment, and investment were extremely steep as the economy entered the greatest recession since the Great Depression of the 1930s.

Our theory predicts that an adverse supply shock like the oil price shock of 2008 will cause real interest rates to rise. However, to combat the housing crisis and later the financial crisis that year, the Federal Reserve reduced nominal interest rates dramatically, especially when the financial crisis worsened in September 2008. As a result, real interest rates also declined, and in many cases became negative.

As the financial crisis spread across the globe, worldwide demand for oil fell sharply and the price of oil declined from $145 in July to $30 in mid-December. Thus the adverse supply shock became a beneficial supply shock. But of course, the damage to the economy from the housing crisis and financial crisis dominated the beneficial effects of lower oil prices.

In Touch with Data and Research

Econometric Models and Macroeconomic Forecasts for Monetary Policy Analysis

The *IS–LM* model developed in this chapter is a relatively simple example of a macroeconomic model. Much more complicated models of the economy (many, though not all of them, based on the *IS–LM* framework) are used in applied macroeconomic research and analysis.

A common use of macroeconomic models is to help economists forecast the course of the economy. In general, using a macroeconomic model to obtain quantitative economic forecasts involves three steps. First, numerical values for the *parameters* of the model (such as the income elasticity of money demand) must be obtained. In econometric models, these values are estimated through statistical analyses of the data. Second, projections must be made of the likely behavior of relevant *exogenous* variables, or variables whose values are not determined within the model. Examples of exogenous variables include policy variables (such as government spending and the money supply), oil prices, and changes in productivity. Third, based on the expected path of the exogenous variables and the model parameters, the model can be solved (usually on a computer) to give forecasts of variables determined within the model (such as output, employment, and interest rates). Variables determined within the model are *endogenous* variables.[9]

Although a relatively simple model like the *IS–LM* model developed in this chapter could be used to create real forecasts, the results probably would not be very good. Because real-world economies are complex, macroeconomic models actually used in forecasting tend to be much more detailed than the *IS–LM* model presented here. For example, the Federal Reserve Board has long had such a model in place for analyzing the economy and for developing forecasts for use in monetary policy.

In 1996, the Federal Reserve Board produced a new model for policy analysis and forecasting, known as the FRB/US model, and has been continually upgrading the model since then. FRB/US was based on a previous model known as the MPS model, which was developed closely from the theoretical *IS–LM* model but with hundreds of equations representing different industries and sectors of the economy. The new FRB/US model differed from the old MPS model in a number of ways: It featured a much better ability to handle people's expectations about the future values of inflation and other variables, improved modeling of people's and firms' reactions to economic shocks, and used newer statistical techniques to estimate the model. The model is also available for anyone to use on the Federal Reserve Board's website at *www.federalreserve.gov/econres/us-models-about.htm*.

The staff economists at the Federal Reserve Board now use the model as a workhorse for policy analysis. They apply results from the model to analyze alternative monetary policy scenarios—for example, what would happen to the economy over the next two years if the Fed raised the federal funds interest rate to 3%, compared with a scenario in which the rate were set at a lower level, such as 0.25%. This analysis gives policymakers an idea of how policy affects the economy and what are the likely outcomes of policy choices.

The model contains three main sectors of the economy, just as the *IS–LM* model does: households, firms, and financial markets. Households supply labor, as we discussed in Section 3.3, and decide how much to consume and save, as we saw in Section 4.1 and Appendix 4.A. Firms maximize their profits, choosing appropriate levels of investment, as we discussed in Section 4.2, and demand labor, as we saw in Section 3.2. Firms' and households' demand and supply of financial assets determine equilibrium in the financial markets, as we discussed in Chapter 7. The model is solved with general equilibrium concepts, as we showed

[9]This discussion of exogenous and endogenous variables elaborates on the discussion of these types of variables in Chapter 6.

(continued)

in Sections 3.4 for labor markets, 4.3 for goods markets, and 7.4 for asset markets. Overall economic growth is governed by the principles discussed in Chapter 6. Other assumptions of the model are based on new Keynesian theory, as we will discuss in Chapter 11.

Although the model is quite detailed, no macro model is able to provide accurate forecasts without some human judgment. So, to produce the forecasts that the Fed uses internally in its Tealbook (formerly Greenbook) publication, the FRB/US model forecasts are analyzed by the staff at the Federal Reserve Board and are often modified somewhat before being presented to monetary policymakers. The judgment of the staff economists who are experts in various sectors of the economy is an important input into the Tealbook forecasts. Research suggests that this method of producing forecasts produces better results than private-sector forecasts, especially when forecasting inflation.[10]

[10]See Christina Romer and David Romer, "Federal Reserve Information and the Behavior of Interest Rates," *American Economic Review* (June 2000), pp. 429–457; and Christopher Sims, "The Role of Models and Probabilities in the Monetary Policy Process," *Brookings Papers on Economic Activity* (2:2002), pp. 1–62.

9.5 Price Adjustment and the Attainment of General Equilibrium

Discuss the role of price adjustment in achieving general equilibrium.

We now explain the economic forces that lead the price level to change and shift the *LM* curve until it passes through the intersection of the *IS* curve and the *FE* line. In discussing the role of price adjustments in bringing the economy back to general equilibrium, we also show the basic difference between the two main approaches to business cycle analysis, classical and Keynesian.

To illustrate the adjustment process, let's use the complete *IS–LM* model to consider what happens to the economy if the nominal money supply increases. This analysis allows us to discuss monetary policy (the control of the money supply) and to introduce some ongoing controversies about the effects of monetary policy on the economy.

The Effects of a Monetary Expansion

Suppose that the central bank decides to raise the nominal money supply, M, by 10%. For now we hold the price level, P, constant so that the real money supply, M/P, also increases by 10%. What effects will this monetary expansion have on the economy? Figure 9.9 helps us answer this question with the complete *IS–LM* model.

The two parts of Fig. 9.9 show the sequence of events involved in the analysis. For simplicity, suppose that the economy initially is in general equilibrium so that in Fig. 9.9(a) the *IS* curve, the *FE* line, and the initial *LM* curve, LM^1, all pass through the general equilibrium point, E. At E output equals its full-employment value of 1000, and the real interest rate is 5%. Both the *IS* and *LM* curves pass through E, so we know that 5% is the market-clearing real interest rate in both the goods and asset markets. For the moment the price level, P, is fixed at its initial level of 100.

The 10% increase in the real supply of money, M/P, doesn't shift the *IS* curve or the *FE* line because, with output and the real interest rate held constant, a

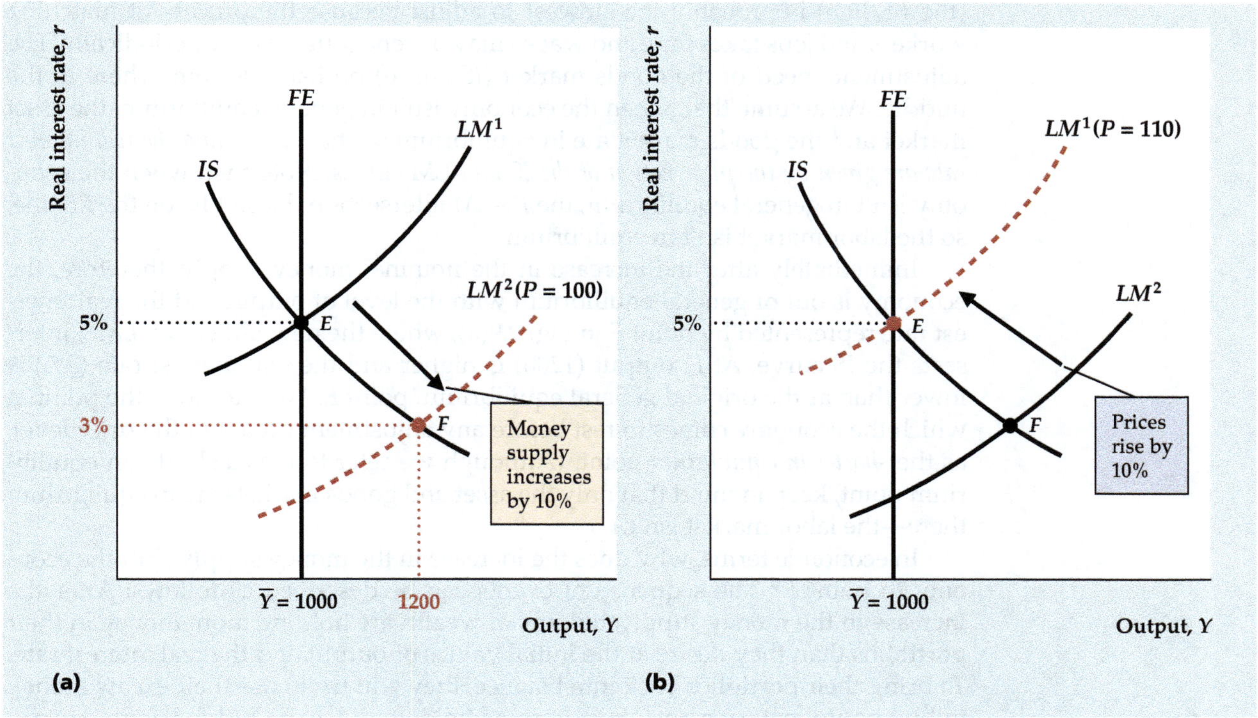

FIGURE 9.9

Effects of a monetary expansion

(a) The economy is in general equilibrium at point *E*. Output equals the full-employment level of 1000, the real interest rate is 5%, and the price level is 100. With the price level fixed, a 10% increase in the nominal money supply, *M*, raises the real money supply, M/P, and shifts the *LM* curve down and to the right from LM^1 to LM^2. At point *F*, the intersection of the *IS* curve and the new *LM* curve, LM^2, the real interest rate has fallen to 3%, which raises the aggregate demand for goods. If firms produce extra output to meet the increase in aggregate demand, output rises to 1200 (higher than full-employment output of 1000).

(b) Because aggregate demand exceeds full-employment output at point *F*, firms raise prices. A 10% rise in *P*, from 100 to 110, restores the real money supply to its original level and shifts the *LM* curve back to its original position at LM^1. This returns the economy to point *E*, where output again is at its full-employment level of 1000, but the price level has risen 10% from 100 to 110.

change in M/P doesn't affect desired national saving, desired investment, labor demand, labor supply, or productivity. However, Fig. 9.5 showed that an increase in the real money supply does shift the *LM* curve down and to the right, which we show here as a shift of the *LM* curve from LM^1 to LM^2, in Fig. 9.9(a). The *LM* curve shifts down and to the right because, at any level of output, an increase in the money supply lowers the real interest rate needed to clear the asset market.

Note that, after the *LM* curve has shifted down to LM^2, there is no point in Fig. 9.9(a) at which all three curves intersect. In other words, the goods market, the labor market, and the asset market no longer are simultaneously in equilibrium. We now must make some assumptions about how the economy behaves when it isn't in general equilibrium.

Of the three markets in the *IS–LM* model, the asset market (represented by the *LM* curve) undoubtedly adjusts the most quickly because financial markets can respond within minutes to changes in economic conditions. The labor market (the *FE* line) is probably the slowest to adjust because the process of matching workers and jobs takes time and wages may be renegotiated only periodically. The adjustment speed of the goods market (*IS* curve) probably is somewhere in the middle. We assume that, when the economy isn't in general equilibrium, the asset market and the goods market are in equilibrium so that *output and the real interest rate are given by the intersection of the* IS *and* LM *curves.* Note that, when the economy isn't in general equilibrium, the *IS–LM* intersection doesn't lie on the *FE* line, so the labor market isn't in equilibrium.

Immediately after the increase in the nominal money supply, therefore, the economy is out of general equilibrium with the level of output and the real interest rate represented by point *F* in Fig. 9.9(a), where the new *LM* curve, LM^2, intersects the *IS* curve. At *F*, output (1200) is higher and the real interest rate (3%) is lower than at the original general equilibrium, point *E*. We refer to *F*, the point at which the economy comes to rest before any adjustment occurs in the price level, as the *short-run equilibrium* point. (Although we refer to *F* as a short-run equilibrium point, keep in mind that only the asset and goods markets are in equilibrium there—the labor market isn't.)

In economic terms, why does the increase in the money supply shift the economy to point *F*? The sequence of events can be described as follows: After the increase in the money supply, holders of wealth are holding more money in their portfolios than they desire at the initial values of output and the real interest rate. To bring their portfolios back into balance, they will try to use their excess money to buy nonmonetary assets. However, as holders of wealth bid for nonmonetary assets, they put upward pressure on the prices of those assets, which reduces their interest rate. Thus after an increase in the money supply, wealth-holders' attempts to achieve their desired mix of money and nonmonetary assets cause the interest rate to fall.

The drop in the real interest rate isn't the end of the story, however. Because the lower real interest rate increases the demand by households for consumption, C^d, and the demand by firms for investment, I^d, the aggregate demand for goods rises. Here we make a fundamental assumption, to which we return shortly: When demanders increase their spending on goods, firms are willing (at least temporarily) to produce enough to meet the extra demand for their output. After the decline in the real interest rate raises the aggregate demand for goods, therefore, we assume that firms respond by increasing production, leading to higher output at the short-run equilibrium point, *F*.

To summarize, with the price level constant, an increase in the nominal money supply takes the economy to the short-run equilibrium point, *F*, in Fig. 9.9(a), at which the real interest rate is lower and output is higher than at the initial general equilibrium point, *E*. We made two assumptions: (1) When the economy isn't in general equilibrium, the economy's short-run equilibrium occurs at the intersection of the *IS* and *LM* curves; and (2) when the aggregate demand for goods rises, firms are willing (at least temporarily) to produce enough extra output to meet the expanded demand.

The Adjustment of the Price Level. So far we have simply taken the price level, *P*, as fixed. In reality, prices respond to conditions of supply and demand in the economy. The price level, *P*, refers to the price of output (goods), so to think about how prices are likely to adjust in this example, let's reconsider the effects of the increase in the money supply on the goods market.

In Fig. 9.9(a), the short-run equilibrium point, F, lies on the *IS* curve, implying that the goods market is in equilibrium at that point with equal aggregate quantities of goods supplied and demanded. Recall our assumption that firms are willing to meet any increases in aggregate demand by producing more. In that sense, then, the aggregate quantity of goods supplied equals the aggregate quantity of goods demanded. However, in another sense the goods market is *not* in equilibrium at point F. The problem is that, to meet the aggregate demand for goods at F, firms have to produce more output than their full-employment level of output, $\bar{Y}$. Full-employment output, $\bar{Y}$, is the level of output that maximizes firms' profits because that level of output corresponds to the profit-maximizing level of employment (Chapter 3). Therefore, in meeting the higher level of aggregate demand, firms are producing more output than they would like. In the sense that, at point F, the production of goods by firms is *not* the level of output that maximizes their profits, the goods market isn't truly in equilibrium.

At point F the aggregate demand for goods exceeds firms' desired supply of output, $\bar{Y}$, so we can expect firms to begin raising their prices, causing the price level, P, to rise. With the nominal money supply, M, set by the central bank, an increase in the price level, P, lowers the real money supply, M/P, which in turn causes the *LM* curve to shift up and to the left. Indeed, as long as the aggregate quantity of goods demanded exceeds what firms want to supply, prices will keep rising. Thus the *LM* curve will keep shifting up and to the left until the aggregate quantity of goods demanded equals full-employment output. Aggregate demand equals full-employment output only when the *LM* curve has returned to its initial position, LM^1 in Fig. 9.9(b), where it passes through the original general equilibrium point, E. At E all three markets of the economy again are in equilibrium, with output at its full-employment level.

Compare Fig. 9.9(b) to the initial situation in Fig. 9.9(a) and note that after the adjustment of the price level the 10% increase in the nominal money supply has had no effect on output or the real interest rate. Employment also is unchanged from its initial value, as the economy has returned to its original level of output. However, as a result of the 10% increase in the nominal money supply, the price level is 10% higher (so that $P = 110$). How do we know that the price level changes by exactly 10%? To return the *LM* curve to its original position, the increase in the price level had to return the real money supply, M/P, to its original value. Because the nominal money supply, M, was raised by 10%, to return M/P to its original value, the price level, P, had to rise by 10% as well. Thus the change in the nominal money supply causes the price level to change proportionally. This result is the same result obtained in Chapter 7 (see Eq. 7.10), where we assumed that all markets are in equilibrium.

Note that, because in general equilibrium the price level has risen by 10% but real economic variables are unaffected, all nominal economic variables must also rise by 10%. In particular, for the real wage to have the same value after prices have risen by 10% as it did before, the nominal wage must rise by 10%. Thus the return of the economy to general equilibrium requires adjustment of the nominal wage (the price of labor) as well as the price of goods.

Trend Money Growth and Inflation. In Fig 9.9 we analyzed the effects of a one-time 10% increase in the nominal money supply, followed by a one-time 10% adjustment in the price level. In reality, in most countries the money supply and the price level grow continuously. Our framework easily handles this situation. Suppose that in some country both the nominal money supply, M, and the price level, P, are growing steadily at 7% per year, which implies that the real money supply, M/P, is constant. The *LM* curve depends on the real money supply, M/P, so in this situation the *LM* curve won't shift, even though the nominal money supply and prices are rising.

Now suppose that for one year the money supply of this country is increased an additional 3%—for a total of 10%—while prices rise 7%. Then the real money supply, M/P, grows by 3% (10% minus 7%), and the *LM* curve shifts down and to the right. Similarly, if for one year the nominal money supply increased by only 4%, with inflation still at 7% per year, the *LM* curve would shift up and to the left, reflecting the 3% drop $(-3\% = 4\% - 7\%)$ in the real money supply.

This example illustrates that changes in M or P *relative to the expected or trend rate of growth of money and inflation* (7% in this example) shift the *LM* curve. Thus when we analyze the effects of "an increase in the money supply," we have in mind an increase in the money supply relative to the expected, or trend, rate of money growth (for example, a rise from 7% to 10% growth for one year); by a "decrease in the money supply," we mean a drop relative to a trend rate (such as a decline from 7% to 4% growth in money). Similarly, if we say something like "the price level falls to restore general equilibrium," we don't necessarily mean that the price level literally falls but only that it rises by less than its trend or expected rate of growth would suggest.

Classical Versus Keynesian Versions of the *IS–LM* Model

Our diagrammatic analysis of the effects of a change in the money supply highlights two questions that are central to the debate between the classical and Keynesian approaches to macroeconomics: (1) How rapidly does the economy reach general equilibrium? and (2) What are the effects of monetary policy on the economy? We previewed the first of these questions in Section 8.4, using the *AD–AS* model. Now we examine both questions, using the *IS–LM* model.

Price Adjustment and the Self-Correcting Economy. In our analysis of the effects of a monetary expansion, we showed that *the economy is brought into general equilibrium by adjustment of the price level.* In graphical terms, if the intersection of the *IS* and *LM* curves lies to the right of the *FE* line—so that the aggregate quantity of goods demanded exceeds full-employment output, as at point F in Fig. 9.9(a)—the price level will rise. The increase in P shifts the *LM* curve up and to the left, reducing the quantity of goods demanded, until all three curves intersect at the general equilibrium point, as in Fig. 9.9(b). Similarly, if the *IS–LM* intersection lies to the left of the full-employment line—so that desired spending on goods is below firms' profit-maximizing level of output—firms will cut prices. A decrease in the price level raises the real money supply and shifts the *LM* curve down and to the right, until all three curves again intersect, returning the economy to general equilibrium. In summary, in a short-run equilibrium, output and the real interest rate are endogenous variables in the model, and the price level is fixed and thus exogenous. In general equilibrium, all three variables (output, the real interest rate, and the price level) are endogenous and determined by the model.

There is little disagreement about the idea that, after some sort of economic disturbance, price level adjustments will eventually restore the economy to general equilibrium. However, as discussed in Section 8.4, the *speed* at which this process takes place is a controversial issue in macroeconomics. Under the classical assumption that prices are flexible, the adjustment process is rapid. When prices are flexible, the economy is effectively self-correcting, automatically returning to full employment after a shock moves it away from general equilibrium.[11] Indeed, if firms respond to increased demand by raising prices rather than by temporarily producing more (as we earlier assumed), the adjustment process would be almost immediate.

According to the opposing Keynesian view, however, sluggish adjustment of prices (and of wages, the price of labor) might prevent general equilibrium from being attained for a much longer period, perhaps even several years. While the economy is not in general equilibrium, Keynesians argue, output is determined by the level of aggregate demand, represented by the intersection of the *IS* and *LM* curves; the economy is not on the *FE* line, and the labor market is not in equilibrium. This assumption of sluggish price adjustment, and the consequent disequilibrium in the labor market, distinguishes the Keynesian version of the *IS–LM* model from the classical version.

Monetary Neutrality. Closely related to the issue of how fast the economy reaches general equilibrium is the question of how a change in the nominal money supply affects the economy. We showed that, after the economy reaches its general equilibrium, an increase in the nominal money supply has no effect on real variables such as output, employment, or the real interest rate but raises the price level. Economists say that there is **monetary neutrality,** or simply that money is neutral, if a change in the nominal money supply changes the price level proportionally but has no effect on real variables. Our analysis shows that, after the complete adjustment of prices, money is neutral in the *IS–LM* model.

The practical relevance of monetary neutrality is much debated by classicals and Keynesians. The basic issue again is the speed of price adjustment. In the classical view a monetary expansion is rapidly transmitted into prices and has, at most, a transitory effect on real variables; that is, the economy moves quickly from the general-equilibrium situation shown in Fig. 9.9(a) to the general-equilibrium situation shown in Fig. 9.9(b), spending little time out of general equilibrium at point *F* in Fig. 9.9(a). Keynesians agree that money is neutral after prices fully adjust but believe that, because of slow price adjustment, the economy may spend a long time in disequilibrium. During this period the increased money supply causes output and employment to rise and the real interest rate to fall (compare point *F* to point *E* in Fig. 9.9a).

In brief, Keynesians believe in monetary neutrality in the long run (after prices adjust) but not in the short run. Classicals are more accepting of the view that money is neutral even in the relatively short run. We return to the issue of monetary neutrality when we develop the classical and Keynesian models of the business cycle in more detail in Chapters 10 and 11.

9.6 Aggregate Demand and Aggregate Supply

Explain the fundamentals and implications of the *AD–AS* model.

The *IS–LM* model introduced in this chapter is a complete model representing the general equilibrium of the economy. In this section we use the *IS–LM* model to develop the aggregate demand–aggregate supply (*AD–AS*) model, which we previewed in Chapter 8. The *AD–AS* model appears to be different from the *IS–LM*

[11]The proposition that a free-market economy with flexible prices is automatically self-correcting is consistent with Adam Smith's invisible-hand idea , discussed in Chapter 1.

model, but in fact the two models are equivalent. They are based on the same assumptions about economic behavior and price adjustment, and they give the same answers when used to analyze the effects of various shocks on the economy. Why then do we bother to present both models? The reason is that, depending on the issue being addressed, one way of representing the economy may be more convenient than the other. The *IS–LM* model relates the real interest rate to output, and the *AD–AS* model relates the price level to output. Thus the *IS–LM* model is more useful for examining the effect of various shocks on the real interest rate and on variables, such as saving and investment, that depend on the real interest rate. In Chapter 13, for example, when we discuss international borrowing and lending in open economies, the behavior of the real interest rate is crucial; therefore, in that chapter we emphasize the *IS–LM* approach. However, for issues related to the price level or inflation, the *AD–AS* model is more convenient to use. For example, we rely on the *AD–AS* framework in Chapter 12 when we describe the relationship between inflation and unemployment. Keep in mind, though, that the choice of the *IS–LM* framework or the *AD–AS* framework is a matter of convenience; the two models express the same basic macroeconomic theory.

The Aggregate Demand Curve

The **aggregate demand curve** shows the relation between the aggregate quantity of goods demanded, $C^d + I^d + G$, and the price level, P. The aggregate demand curve slopes downward, as does the demand curve for a single product (apples, for example). Despite the superficial similarity between the *AD* curve and the demand curve for a specific good, however, there is an important difference between these two types of curves. The demand curve for apples relates the demand for apples to the price of apples *relative to the prices of other goods.* In contrast, the *AD* curve relates the aggregate quantity of output demanded to the *general price level.* If the prices of all goods increase by 10%, the price level, P, also increases by 10%, even though all relative prices of goods remain unchanged. Nevertheless, the increase in the price level reduces the aggregate quantity of goods demanded.

The reason that an increase in the price level, P, reduces the aggregate quantity of output demanded is illustrated in Figure 9.10. Recall that, for a *given price level,* the aggregate quantity of output that households, firms, and the government choose to demand is where the *IS* curve and the *LM* curve intersect. Suppose that the nominal money supply is M and that the initial price level is P_1. Then the real money supply is M/P_1, and the initial *LM* curve is LM^1 in Fig. 9.10(a). The *IS* and LM^1 curves intersect at point E, where the amount of output that households, firms, and the government want to buy is Y_1. Thus we conclude that, when the price level is P_1, the aggregate amount of output demanded is Y_1.

Now suppose that the price level increases to P_2. With a nominal money supply of M, this increase in the price level reduces the real money supply from M/P_1 to M/P_2. Recall (Summary table 13) that a decrease in the real money supply shifts the *LM* curve up and to the left, to LM^2. The *IS* and LM^2 curves intersect at point F, where the aggregate quantity of output demanded is Y_2. Thus the increase in the price level from P_1 to P_2 reduces the aggregate quantity of output demanded from Y_1 to Y_2.

This negative relation between the price level and the aggregate quantity of output demanded is shown as the downward-sloping *AD* curve in Fig. 9.10(b).

FIGURE 9.10

Derivation of the aggregate demand curve

For a given price level, the aggregate quantity of output demanded is determined where the *IS* and *LM* curves intersect. If the price level, *P*, is P_1 and the initial *LM* curve is LM^1, the initial aggregate quantity of output demanded is Y_1, corresponding to point *E* in both (a) and (b). To derive the aggregate demand curve, we examine what happens to the quantity of output demanded when the price level changes.
(a) An increase in the price level from P_1 to P_2 reduces the real money supply and shifts the *LM* curve up and to the left, from LM^1 to LM^2. Therefore the aggregate quantity of output demanded, represented by the intersection of the *IS* and *LM* curves, falls from Y_1 to Y_2.
(b) The increase in the price level from P_1 to P_2 reduces the aggregate quantity of output demanded from Y_1 at point *E* to Y_2 at point *F*, so the aggregate demand curve slopes downward.

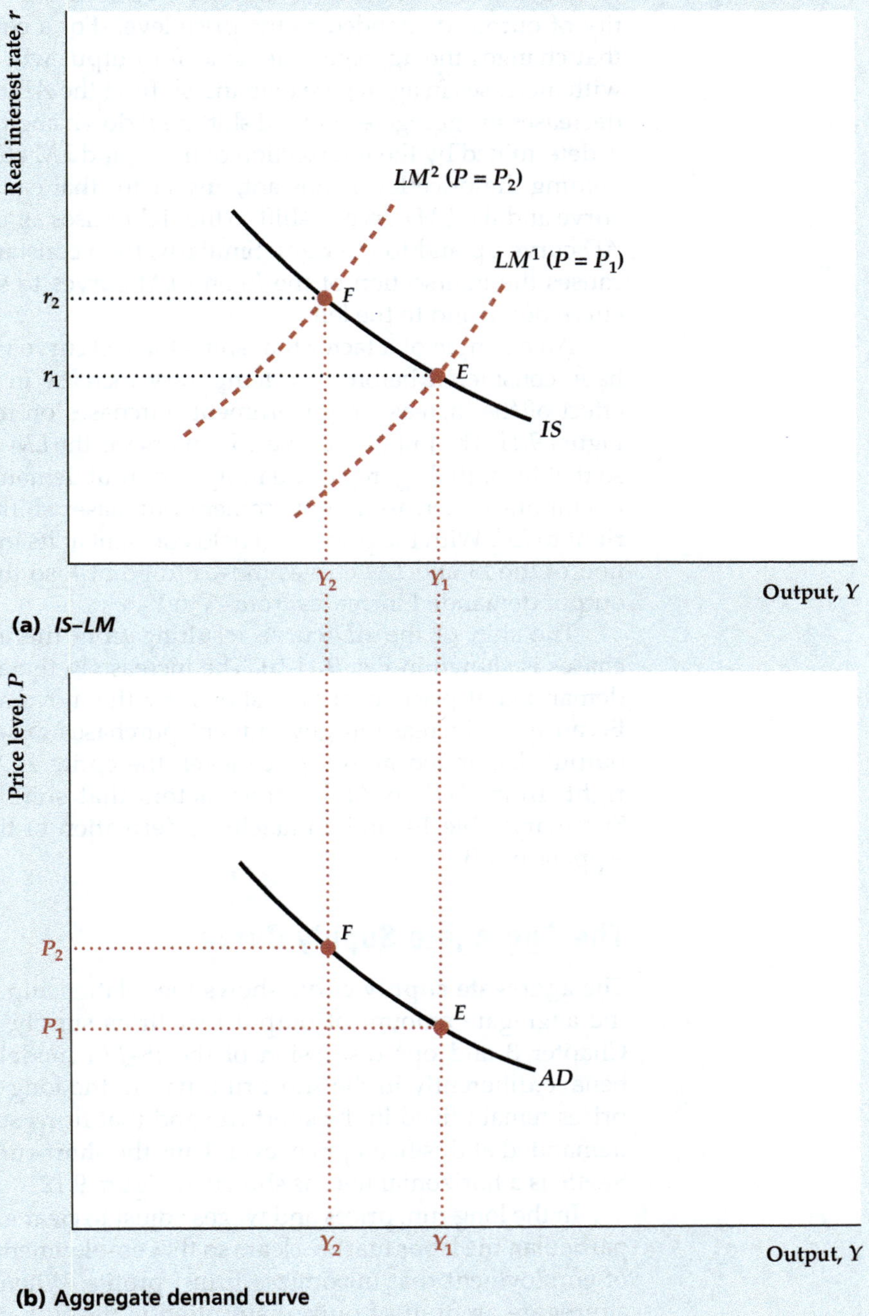

Points *E* and *F* in Fig. 9.10(b) correspond to points *E* and *F* in Fig. 9.10(a), respectively. The *AD* curve slopes downward because an increase in the price level reduces the real money supply, which shifts the *LM* curve up and to the left; the reduction in the real money supply increases the real interest rate, which reduces the demand for goods by households and firms.

Factors That Shift the *AD* Curve. The *AD* curve relates the aggregate quantity of output demanded to the price level. For a constant price level, any factor that changes the aggregate demand for output will cause the *AD* curve to shift, with increases in aggregate demand shifting the *AD* curve up and to the right and decreases in aggregate demand shifting it down and to the left. Aggregate demand is determined by the intersection of the *IS* and *LM* curves, so we can also say that, holding the price level constant, any factor that causes the intersection of the *IS* curve and the *LM* curve to shift to the right raises aggregate demand and shifts the *AD* curve up and to the right. Similarly, for a constant price level, any factor that causes the intersection of the *IS* and *LM* curves to shift to the left shifts the *AD* curve down and to the left.

An example of a factor that shifts the *AD* curve up and to the right, which we have considered before, is a temporary increase in government purchases. The effect of the increase in government purchases on the *AD* curve is illustrated in Figure 9.11. The initial *IS* curve, IS^1, intersects the *LM* curve at point *E* in Fig. 9.11(a) so that the initial aggregate quantity of output demanded is Y_1. As we have shown, a temporary increase in government purchases shifts the *IS* curve up and to the right to IS^2. With the price level held constant at its initial value of P_1, the intersection of the *IS* and *LM* curves moves to point *F* so that the aggregate quantity of output demanded increases from Y_1 to Y_2.

The shift of the *AD* curve resulting from the increase in government purchases is shown in Fig. 9.11(b). The increase in the aggregate quantity of output demanded at price level P_1 is shown by the movement from point *E* to point *F*. Because the increase in government purchases raises the aggregate quantity of output demanded at any price level, the entire *AD* curve shifts up and to the right, from AD^1 to AD^2. Other factors that shift the *AD* curve are listed in Summary table 14, and an algebraic derivation of the *AD* curve is presented in Appendix 9.B.

The Aggregate Supply Curve

The **aggregate supply curve** shows the relationship between the price level and the aggregate amount of output that firms supply. Recall from the preview in Chapter 8 and our discussion of the *IS–LM* model that firms are assumed to behave differently in the short run than in the long run. The assumption is that prices remain fixed in the short run and that firms supply the quantity of output demanded at this fixed price level. Thus the **short-run aggregate supply curve**, or *SRAS*, is a horizontal line, as shown in Figure 9.12.

In the long run, prices and wages adjust to clear all markets in the economy. In particular, the labor market clears so that employment equals $\bar{N}$, which is the level of employment that maximizes firms' profits. When employment equals $\bar{N}$, the aggregate amount of output supplied is the full-employment level, $\bar{Y}$, which equals $AF(K,\bar{N})$, regardless of the price level. In the long run, firms supply $\bar{Y}$ at any price level, so the **long-run aggregate supply curve**, or *LRAS*, is a vertical line at $Y = \bar{Y}$, as shown in Fig. 9.12.

Factors That Shift the Aggregate Supply Curves. Any factor that increases the full-employment level of output, $\bar{Y}$, shifts the long-run aggregate supply (*LRAS*) curve to the right, and any factor that reduces $\bar{Y}$ shifts the *LRAS* curve to

FIGURE 9.11

The effect of an increase in government purchases on the aggregate demand curve

(a) An increase in government purchases shifts the *IS* curve up and to the right, from IS^1 to IS^2. At price level P_1, the aggregate quantity of output demanded increases from Y_1 to Y_2, as shown by the shift of the *IS–LM* intersection from point *E* to point *F*. **(b)** Because the aggregate quantity of output demanded rises at any price level, the *AD* curve shifts up and to the right. Points *E* and *F* in (b) correspond to points *E* and *F* in (a), respectively.

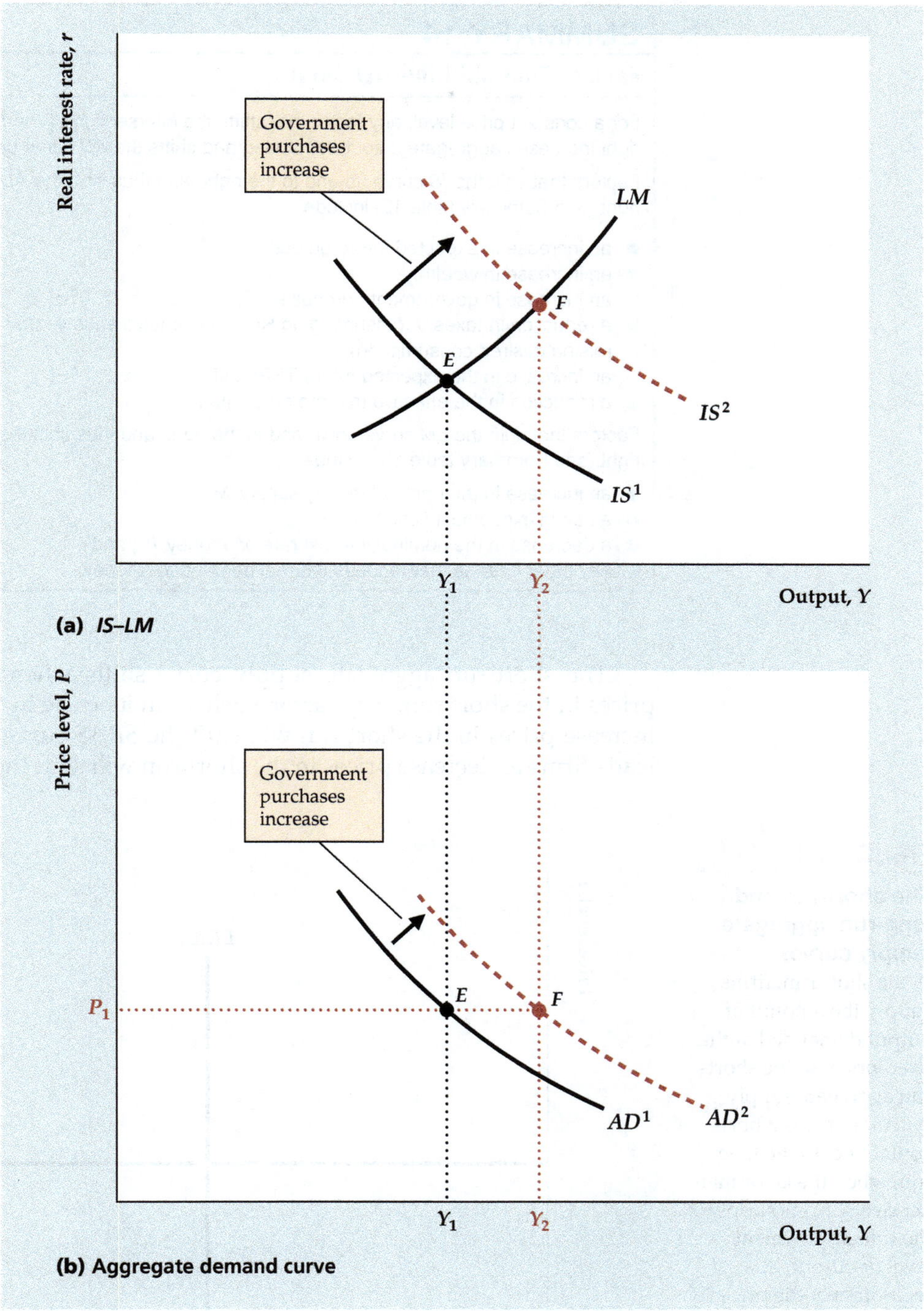

the left. Thus any change that shifts the *FE* line to the right in the *IS–LM* diagram also shifts the *LRAS* curve to the right. For instance, an increase in the labor force raises the full-employment levels of employment and output, shifting the *LRAS* curve to the right.

SUMMARY 14

Factors That Shift the *AD* Curve

For a constant price level, any factor that shifts the intersection of the *IS* and *LM* curves to the right increases aggregate output demanded and shifts the *AD* curve up and to the right.

Factors that shift the *IS* curve up and to the right, and thus shift the *AD* curve up and to the right (see Summary table 12) include

- an increase in expected future output;
- an increase in wealth;
- an increase in government purchases, *G*;
- a reduction in taxes, *T* (assuming no Ricardian equivalence so that consumers respond by raising desired consumption);
- an increase in the expected future TFP; and
- a reduction in the effective tax rate on capital.

Factors that shift the *LM* curve down and to the right, and thus shift the *AD* curve up and to the right (see Summary table 13) include

- an increase in the nominal money supply, *M*;
- a rise in expected inflation, π^e;
- a decrease in the nominal interest rate on money, i^m; and
- any other change that reduces the real demand for money.

The short-run aggregate supply curve shifts whenever firms change their prices in the short run. Any factor, such as an increase in costs, that leads firms to increase prices in the short run will shift the *SRAS* curve up, and any factor that leads firms to decrease prices in the short run will shift the *SRAS* curve down.

FIGURE 9.12

The short-run and long-run aggregate supply curves

In the short run, firms supply the amount of output demanded at the fixed price, so the short-run aggregate supply (*SRAS*) curve is a horizontal line. In the long run, when the labor market clears, firms supply the full-employment level of output, $\bar{Y}$, regardless of the price level. Thus the long-run aggregate supply (*LRAS*) curve is a vertical line at $Y = \bar{Y}$.

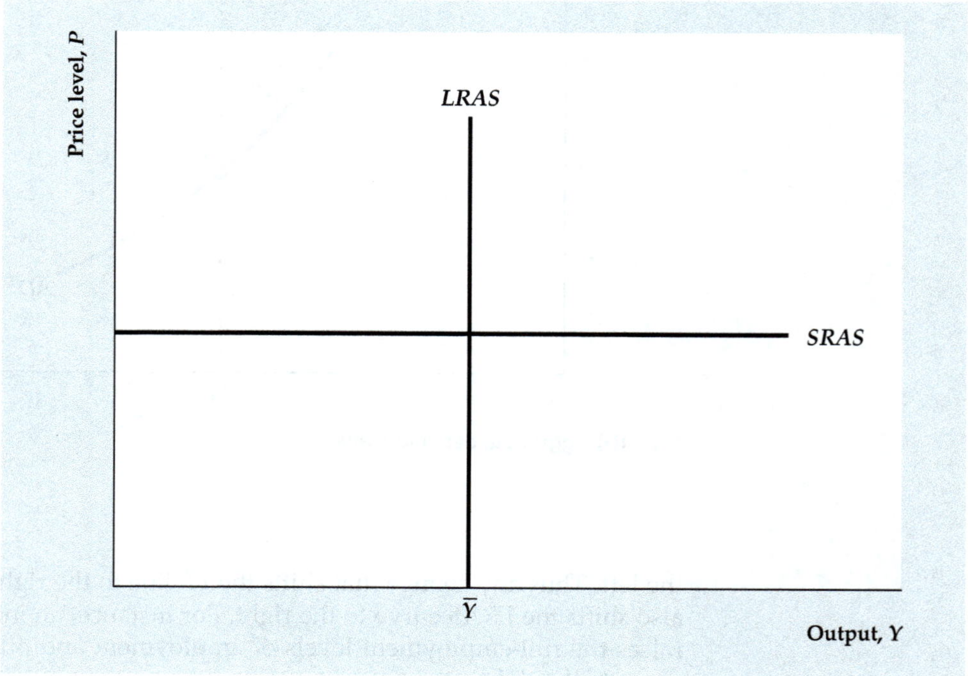

Equilibrium in the *AD–AS* Model

When we previewed the *AD–AS* model in Section 8.4, we introduced the distinction between short-run equilibrium (equilibrium when the price level is fixed) and long-run equilibrium (equilibrium when the price level has fully adjusted). Short-run equilibrium is represented by the intersection of the *AD* and *SRAS* curves, as at point *E* in Figure 9.13(a). Notice that in this figure there is no common point of intersection of all three curves. Long-run equilibrium is represented by the intersection of the *AD* and *LRAS* curves, which is at point *F* in Fig. 9.13(b). The economy is also in short-run equilibrium at point *F* because point *F* is also at the intersection of the *AD* and *SRAS* curves. When the economy is in long-run equilibrium, output equals its full-employment level, $\bar{Y}$. Long-run equilibrium is the same as general equilibrium because in long-run equilibrium all markets clear.

When the economy reaches general, or long-run, equilibrium, all three curves—*AD, SRAS,* and *LRAS*—intersect at a common point, as in Fig. 9.13(b). This condition isn't a coincidence. As with the *IS* curve, the *LM* curve, and the *FE* line, strong economic forces lead the economy to arrive eventually at a common point of intersection of the three curves. Indeed, the forces leading the *AD, SRAS,* and *LRAS* curves to intersect at a common point are the same as the forces leading the *IS* curve, the *LM* curve, and *FE* line to intersect at a common point. To illustrate, we use the *AD–AS* framework to examine the effects on the economy of an increase in the money supply, which we previously analyzed with the *IS–LM* model.

Monetary Neutrality in the *AD–AS* Model

Suppose that the economy is initially in equilibrium at point *E* in Figure 9.14, where the level of output is $\bar{Y}$ and the price level is P_1, and that the money supply then increases by 10%. In the *IS–LM* model an increase in the money supply shifts the *LM* curve down and to the right, raising the aggregate quantity of output demanded at any particular price level. Thus an increase in the money supply also shifts the *AD* curve up and to the right, from AD^1 to AD^2.

Moreover, *when the money supply rises by 10%, points on the new* AD *curve are those for which the price level is 10% higher at each level of output demanded.* To see why, compare points *E* and *H*. Because *H* lies on AD^2 and *E* lies on AD^1, the nominal money supply, *M*, is 10% higher at *H* than at *E*. However, the aggregate quantity of output demanded is the same $(\bar{Y})$ at *H* and *E*. The aggregate quantity of output demanded can be the same at *H* and *E* only if the real money supply, M/P, which determines the position of the *LM* curve and hence the aggregate quantity of output demanded, is the same at *H* and *E*. With the nominal money supply 10% higher at *H*, for the real money supply to be the same at the two points the price level at *H* must be 10% higher than at *E*. Therefore P_2 is 10% higher than P_1. Indeed, for every level of output, the price level is 10% higher on AD^2 than on AD^1.

In the short run, the price level remains fixed, and the increase in the nominal money supply shifts the aggregate demand curve from AD^1 to AD^2. Thus the short-run equilibrium moves from point *E* to point *F* (which corresponds to movement from point *E* to point *F* in the *IS–LM* diagram in Fig. 9.9a). Thus in the short

FIGURE 9.13

Equilibrium in the *AD–AS* model

(a) Short-run equilibrium is represented by the intersection of the *AD* and *SRAS* curves at point *E*. At short-run equilibrium, the price level is fixed at P_1 and firms meet demand at those prices. **(b)** Long-run equilibrium, which occurs after the price level has fully adjusted (declined) from P_1 to P_2, is represented by the intersection of the *AD* and *LRAS* curves at point *F*. Long-run equilibrium is the same as general equilibrium because in long-run equilibrium all markets clear.

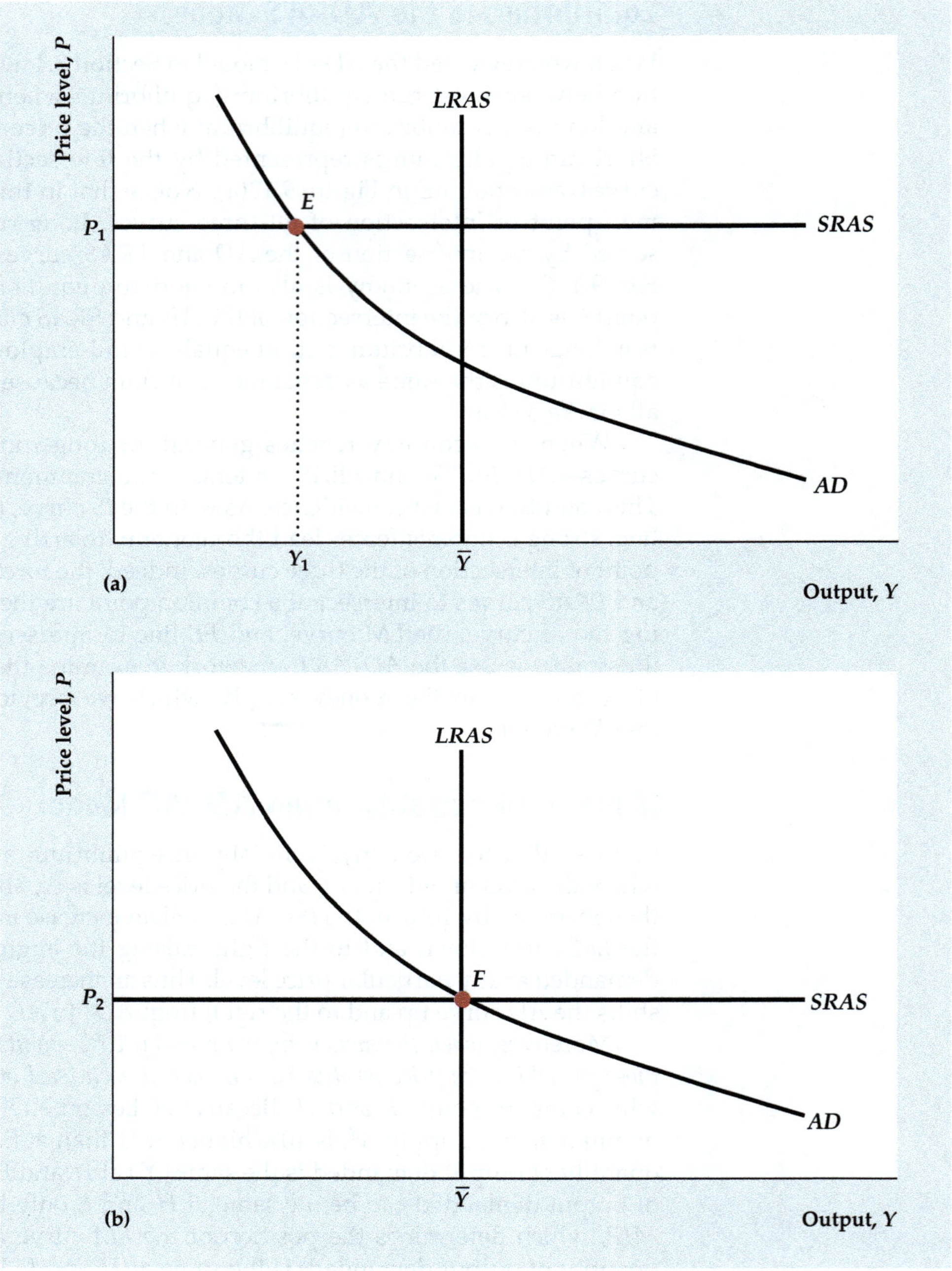

run the increase in the nominal money supply increases output from $\bar{Y}$ to Y_2, causing an economic boom.

However, the economy won't remain at point *F* indefinitely. Because the amount of output, Y_2, is higher than the profit-maximizing level of output, $\bar{Y}$, firms will eventually increase their prices. Rising prices cause the short-run

FIGURE 9.14

Monetary neutrality in the *AD–AS* framework

If we start from general equilibrium at point *E*, a 10% increase in the nominal money supply shifts the *AD* curve up and to the right from AD^1 to AD^2. The points on the new *AD* curve are those for which the price level is 10% higher at each level of output demanded because a 10% increase in the price level is needed to keep the real money supply, and thus the aggregate quantity of output demanded, unchanged. In the new short-run equilibrium at point *F*, the price level is unchanged, and output is higher than its full-employment level. In the new long-run equilibrium at point *H*, output is unchanged at $\bar{Y}$, and the price level P_2 is 10% higher than the initial price level P_1. Thus money is neutral in the long run.

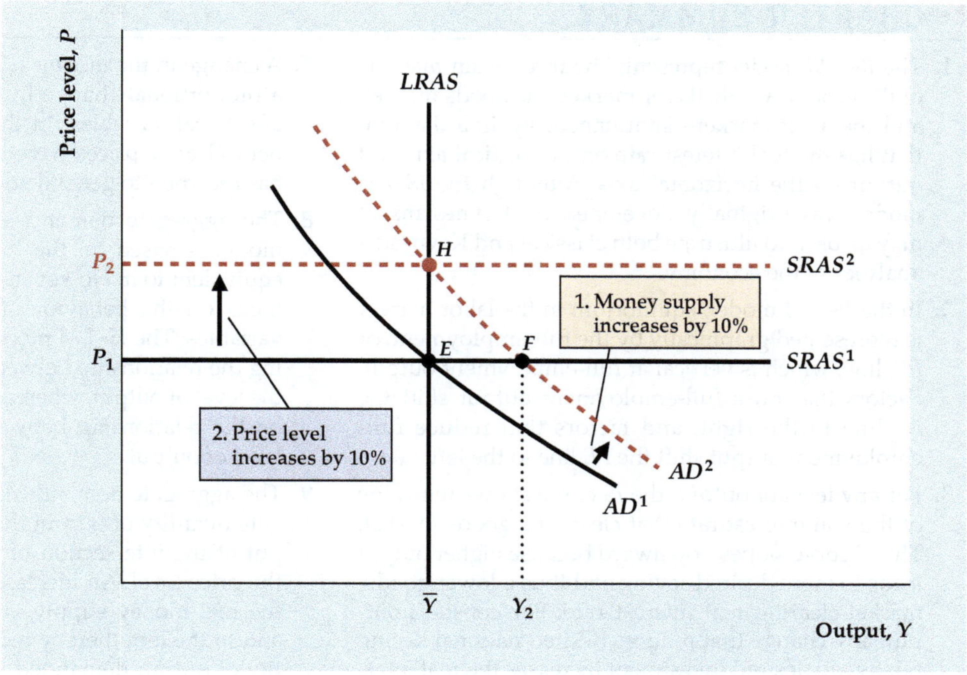

aggregate supply curve to shift up from $SRAS^1$. Firms will increase their prices until the quantity of output demanded falls to the profit-maximizing level of output, $\bar{Y}$. The new long-run equilibrium is represented by point *H*, where the *AD* curve, the *LRAS* curve, and the new short-run aggregate supply curve, or $SRAS^2$, all intersect. In the new long-run equilibrium, the price level has increased by 10%, which is the same amount that the nominal money supply has increased. Output is the same in the new long-run equilibrium at point *H* as at point *E*. Thus we conclude that money is neutral in the long run, as we did when using the *IS–LM* model.

Our analysis highlights the distinction between the short-run and long-run effects of an increase in the money supply, but it leaves open the crucial question of how long it takes the economy to reach long-run equilibrium. As we have emphasized in both Chapter 8 and this chapter, classical and Keynesian economists have very different answers to this question. Classical economists argue that the economy reaches its long-run equilibrium quickly. Indeed, in its strictest form, the classical view is that the economy reaches long-run equilibrium almost immediately, so that the long-run aggregate supply (*LRAS*) curve is the only aggregate supply curve that matters [the short-run aggregate supply (*SRAS*) curve is irrelevant]. However, Keynesians argue that the economy may take years to reach long-run equilibrium and that in the meantime output will differ from its full-employment level. We elaborate on these points of view in Chapter 10, which is devoted to the classical model, and in Chapter 11, which is devoted to the Keynesian model.

CHAPTER SUMMARY

1. The *IS–LM* model represents the three main markets of the economy—the labor market, the goods market, and the asset market—simultaneously, in a diagram that has the real interest rate on the vertical axis and output on the horizontal axis. Although the *IS–LM* model was originally developed by Keynesians, it may be used to illustrate both classical and Keynesian analyses of the economy.
2. In the *IS–LM* model, equilibrium in the labor market is represented graphically by the full-employment, or *FE*, line, which is vertical at full-employment output. Factors that raise full-employment output shift the *FE* line to the right, and factors that reduce full-employment output shift the *FE* line to the left.
3. For any level of output, the *IS* curve shows the value of the real interest rate that clears the goods market. The *IS* curve slopes downward because higher output leads to more desired saving and thus a lower goods-market-clearing real interest rate. For constant output, any change that reduces desired national saving relative to desired investment increases the real interest rate that clears the goods market and shifts the *IS* curve up and to the right. Equivalently, for constant output, any change that increases the aggregate demand for goods increases the real interest rate that clears the goods market and shifts the *IS* curve up and to the right.
4. For any level of output, the *LM* curve identifies the real interest rate that equates the quantities of money supplied and demanded and thus clears the asset market. The *LM* curve slopes upward because an increase in output raises money demand, implying that a higher real interest rate is needed to clear the asset market. With output fixed, any change that reduces the money supply relative to money demand increases the real interest rate that clears the asset market and causes the *LM* curve to shift up and to the left.
5. General equilibrium in the macroeconomy occurs when all markets are in equilibrium. Graphically, the general equilibrium point is where the *IS* curve, the *FE* line, and the *LM* curve intersect. Price level adjustments push the economy toward general equilibrium. Specifically, changes in the price level, P, change the real money supply, M/P, which causes the *LM* curve to shift until it passes through the point at which the *FE* line and the *IS* curve intersect.
6. A temporary adverse supply shock causes the general equilibrium levels of the real wage, employment, output, consumption, and investment to fall, and the general equilibrium levels of the real interest rate and price level to increase.
7. A change in the money supply is neutral if it leads to a proportional change in the price level but doesn't affect real variables. In the *IS–LM* model, money is neutral after prices have adjusted and the economy has returned to general equilibrium.
8. The aggregate demand–aggregate supply (*AD–AS*) model is based on the *IS–LM* model and in fact is equivalent to it. However, the two models allow us to focus on the behavior of different macroeconomic variables: The *IS–LM* model is most useful for studying the relationship between the real interest rate and the level of output, whereas the *AD–AS* model focuses on the relationship between the price level and the level of output.
9. The aggregate demand (*AD*) curve relates the aggregate quantity of output demanded—the level of output at the intersection of the *IS* and *LM* curves—to the price level. An increase in the price level reduces the real money supply and shifts the *LM* curve up and to the left, thereby reducing the aggregate quantity of output demanded. Because an increase in the price level reduces the aggregate quantity of goods demanded, the aggregate demand curve slopes downward. Factors that increase the aggregate quantity of output demanded at a given price level, such as increases in government purchases or the money supply, shift the *AD* curve up and to the right.
10. The aggregate supply curve relates the quantity of output supplied to the price level. In the short run, the price level is fixed and firms supply whatever level of output is demanded, so the short-run aggregate supply (*SRAS*) curve is horizontal. In the long run, after prices and wages have fully adjusted and all markets are in equilibrium, firms produce the profit-maximizing level of output. Hence, in the long run, aggregate output, Y, equals its full-employment level, $\bar{Y}$. In the long run, firms supply $\bar{Y}$ regardless of the price level, so the long-run aggregate supply (*LRAS*) curve is a vertical line at $Y = \bar{Y}$.
11. Classical macroeconomists argue that prices and wages adjust rapidly in response to changes in supply or demand. This argument implies that, following shocks or changes in policy, the economy quickly reaches its general equilibrium, represented by the *IS–LM–FE* intersection or, equivalently, by the intersection of the *AD* and *LRAS* curves. In contrast, Keynesian macroeconomists argue that prices and wages adjust slowly enough that the economy can remain away from its general equilibrium (long-run equilibrium) for a prolonged period of time. Keynesians agree with classicals, however, that eventually prices

and wages fully adjust so that the economy reaches its general equilibrium.

12. Classicals and Keynesians agree that money is neutral in the long run, after the economy has reached its general equilibrium. Because classicals believe that long-run equilibrium is reached quickly, they dismiss the short-run equilibrium in which money is not neutral as essentially irrelevant. Keynesians, who believe that it may take several years for the economy to reach general equilibrium, ascribe much more importance to the short-run period in which money is not neutral.

KEY DIAGRAM 6

The *IS–LM* model

The *IS–LM* model shows general equilibrium in the goods, asset, and labor markets. It can be used to analyze the effects of economic shocks on output, the real interest rate, the price level, and other macroeconomic variables.

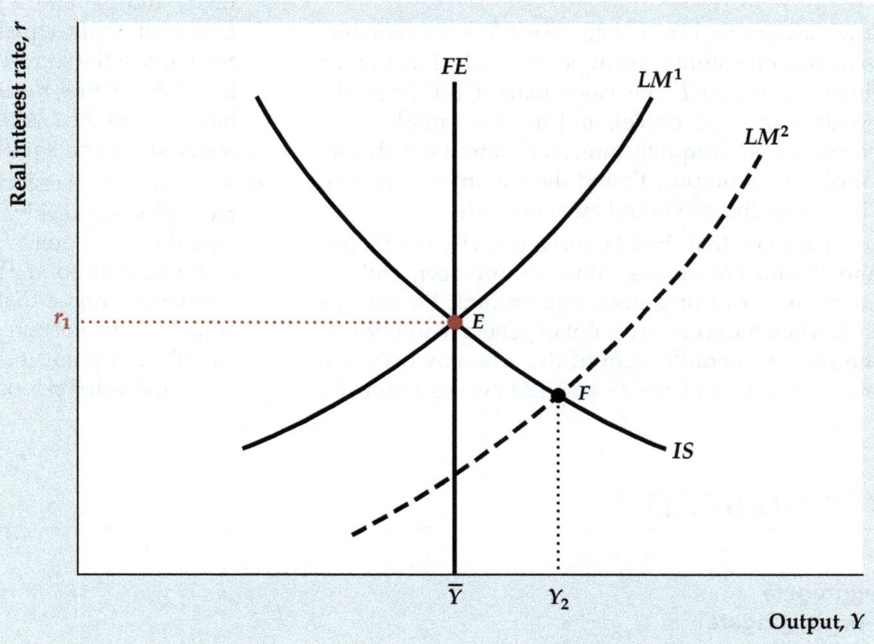

Diagram Elements

- The real interest rate, r, is on the vertical axis, and output, Y, is on the horizontal axis.
- The full-employment line, *FE*, is vertical at full-employment output. Full-employment output, $\bar{Y}$, is the level of output that firms supply when wages and prices have fully adjusted, so employment is at its full-employment level, $\bar{N}$. Full-employment output is determined by the equation $\bar{Y} = AF(K, \bar{N})$.
- For any level of output, Y, the *IS* curve gives the real interest rate, r, that clears the goods market—or, in other words, the rate that equalizes desired national saving, S^d, and desired investment, I^d. Because higher output raises desired saving and lowers the real interest rate that clears the goods market, the *IS* curve slopes downward. Equivalently, the *IS* curve gives combinations of output, Y, and the real interest rate, r, that equalize the aggregate quantities of goods supplied and demanded, $Y = C^d + I^d + G$.
- For given values of the price level and output, the *LM* curve gives the real interest rate that clears the asset market, making the real money supply, M/P, and the real quantity of money demanded, $L(Y, r + \pi^e)$, equal. Because an increase in income raises real money demand, which raises the real interest rate that clears the asset market, the *LM* curve slopes upward.

Factors That Shift the Curves

- Any factor that raises full-employment output shifts the *FE* line to the right. See Summary table 11.
- For constant output, any change that reduces desired national saving relative to desired investment increases the real interest rate that clears the goods market and shifts the *IS* curve up and to the right. Equivalently,

any change that increases the aggregate demand for goods at a specific level of income raises the real interest rate that clears the goods market and shifts the *IS* curve up and to the right. See Summary table 12.

- For constant output, any change that reduces real money supply relative to real money demand increases the real interest rate that clears the asset market and shifts the *LM* curve up and to the left. See Summary table 13.

Analysis

- If we assume that the *LM* curve is LM^1, the economy is in general equilibrium at point *E*, which lies on all three curves. At *E* the labor market (*FE* line), the goods market (*IS* curve), and the asset market (*LM* curve) are all in equilibrium. At *E* output equals full-employment output, $\bar{Y}$; and the real interest rate, r_1, clears both the goods and asset markets.
- If we assume that the *LM* curve is LM^2, the *FE* line and *IS* and *LM* curves don't all intersect, and the economy is out of general equilibrium. We assume that, when the economy is out of general equilibrium, the short-run equilibrium of the economy occurs at the intersection of the *IS* and *LM* curves (point *F*), where the goods and asset markets are in equilibrium but the labor market isn't. If we assume that (at least temporarily) firms produce enough output to meet the increased aggregate demand at *F*, in short-run equilibrium the economy's output is Y_2.
- At the short-run equilibrium point, *F*, output, Y_2, is greater than firms' profit-maximizing level of output, $\bar{Y}$. Because aggregate demand at *F* exceeds what firms want to produce, they raise prices. An increase in the price level, *P*, lowers the real money supply, *M*/*P*, and shifts the *LM* curve up and to the left, to LM^1, and general equilibrium is reached at *E*. At *E* output again equals full-employment output, $\bar{Y}$. Similarly, if the short-run equilibrium had been to the left of the *FE* line, declines in the price level, *P*, would have shifted the *LM* curve down and to the right and restored general equilibrium at *E*.
- According to classical economists, the price adjustment process quickly restores the economy to general equilibrium at point *E*, so the economy spends little or no time at point *F*, away from full employment. Keynesians argue that prices and wages are slow to adjust, so the economy may remain at the short-run equilibrium point, *F*, with output different from $\bar{Y}$, for an extended period of time.

▶ KEY DIAGRAM 7

The aggregate demand–aggregate supply model
The *AD–AS* model shows the determination of the price level and output. In the short run, before prices adjust, equilibrium occurs at the intersection of the *AD* and *SRAS* curves. In the long run, equilibrium occurs at the intersection of the *AD* and *LRAS* curves.

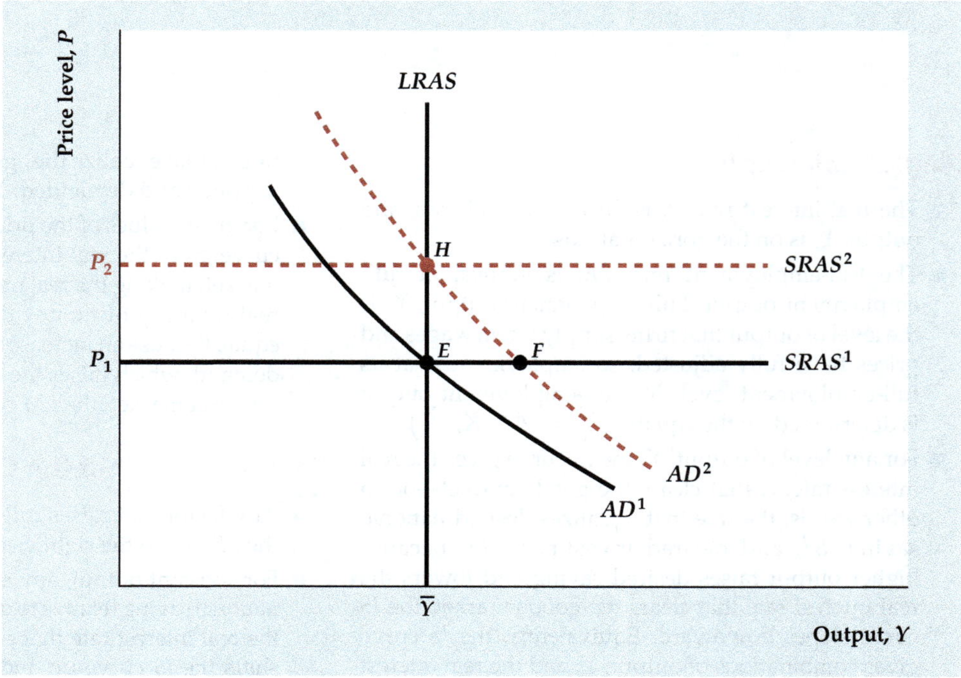

Diagram Elements

- The price level, P, is on the vertical axis, and the level of output, Y, is on the horizontal axis.
- The aggregate demand (AD) curve shows the aggregate quantity of output demanded at each price level. The aggregate amount of output demanded is determined by the intersection of the *IS* and *LM* curves (see Fig. 9.10). An increase in the price level, P, reduces the real money supply, shifting the *LM* curve up and to the left, and reduces the aggregate quantity of output demanded. Thus the *AD* curve slopes downward.
- The aggregate supply curves show the relationship between the price level and the aggregate quantity of output supplied in the short run and in the long run. In the short run, the price level is fixed, and firms supply whatever level of output is demanded. Thus the short-run aggregate supply (*SRAS*) curve is horizontal. In the long run, firms produce the amount of output that maximizes their profits, which is the full-employment level of output, $\bar{Y}$. Because aggregate output in the long run equals $\bar{Y}$ regardless of the price level, P, the long-run aggregate supply (*LRAS*) curve is a vertical line at $Y = \bar{Y}$.

Factors That Shift the Curves

- The aggregate quantity of output demanded is determined by the intersection of the *IS* and the *LM* curves. At a constant price level, any factor that shifts the *IS–LM* intersection to the right increases the aggregate quantity of goods demanded and thus also shifts the *AD* curve up and to the right. Factors that shift the *AD* curve are listed in Summary table 14.
- Any factor, such as an increase in the costs of production, that leads firms to increase prices in the short-run will shift the short-run aggregate supply (*SRAS*) curve up. Any factor that increases the full-employment level of output, $\bar{Y}$, shifts the long-run aggregate supply (*LRAS*) curve to the right. Factors that increase $\bar{Y}$ are listed in Summary table 11.

Analysis

- The economy's short-run equilibrium is represented by the intersection of the *AD* and *SRAS* curves, as at point E. The long-run equilibrium of the economy is represented by the intersection of the *AD* curve and *LRAS* curve, also at point E. In the long run, output equals its full-employment level, $\bar{Y}$.
- The short-run equilibrium can temporarily differ from the long-run equilibrium as a result of shocks or policy changes that affect the economy. For instance, an increase in the nominal money supply shifts the aggregate demand curve up and to the right from AD^1 to AD^2. The new short-run equilibrium is represented by point F, where output is higher than its full-employment level, $\bar{Y}$. At point F, firms produce an amount of output that is greater than the profit-maximizing level, and they begin to increase prices. In the new long-run equilibrium at point H, output is at its full-employment level and the price level is higher than its initial value, P_1. Because the new price level is P_2, the short-run aggregate supply curve shifts up to $SRAS^2$, which is a horizontal line at $P = P_2$.

▶ KEY TERMS

aggregate demand curve, p. 378
aggregate supply curve, p. 380
full-employment line, p. 353
general equilibrium, p. 367
***IS* curve**, p. 355
***LM* curve**, p. 362
long-run aggregate supply curve, p. 380
monetary neutrality, p. 377
short-run aggregate supply curve, p. 380

▶ REVIEW QUESTIONS

1. What determines the position of the *FE* line? Give two examples of changes in the economy that would shift the *FE* line to the right.
2. What relationship does the *IS* curve capture? Derive the *IS* curve graphically and show why it slopes as it does. Give two examples of changes in the economy that would cause the *IS* curve to shift down and to the left.
3. What relationship does the *LM* curve capture? Derive the *LM* curve graphically and show why it slopes as it does. Give two examples of changes in the economy that would cause the *LM* curve to shift down and to the right.
4. For constant output, if the real money supply exceeds the real quantity of money demanded, what will happen to the real interest rate that clears the asset market?

In describing the adjustment of the real interest rate, use the relationship that exists between the price of a nonmonetary asset and the interest rate that it pays.

5. Define *general equilibrium* and show the general equilibrium point in the *IS–LM* diagram. If the economy isn't in general equilibrium, what determines output and the real interest rate? What economic forces act to bring the economy back to general equilibrium?

6. Define *monetary neutrality*. Show that, after prices adjust completely, money is neutral in the *IS–LM* model. What are the classical and Keynesian views about whether money is neutral in the short run? In the long run?

7. What two variables are related by the aggregate demand (*AD*) curve? Why does the *AD* curve slope downward? Give two examples of changes in the economy that shift the *AD* curve up and to the right and explain why the shifts occur.

8. Describe the short-run aggregate supply (*SRAS*) curve and the long-run aggregate supply (*LRAS*) curve. Why is one of these curves horizontal and the other vertical?

9. Use the *AD–AS* framework to analyze whether money is neutral in the short run and whether it is neutral in the long run.

NUMERICAL PROBLEMS

1. Desired consumption and investment are

$$C^d = 4000 - 4000r + 0.20Y;$$
$$I^d = 2400 - 4000r.$$

As usual, Y is output and r is the real interest rate. Government purchases, G, are 2000.

a. Find an equation relating desired national saving, S^d, to r and Y.

b. What value of the real interest rate clears the goods market when $Y = 10{,}000$? Use both forms of the goods market equilibrium condition. What value of the real interest rate clears the goods market when $Y = 10{,}200$? Graph the *IS* curve.

c. Government purchases rise to 2400. How does this increase change the equation for national saving in part (*a*)? What value of the real interest rate clears the goods market when $Y = 10{,}000$? Use both forms of the goods market equilibrium condition. How is the *IS* curve affected by the increase in G?

2. In a particular economy the real money demand function is

$$\frac{M^d}{P} = 3000 + 0.1Y - 10{,}000i.$$

Assume that $M = 6000$, $P = 2.0$, and $\pi^e = 0.02$.

a. What is the real interest rate, r, that clears the asset market when $Y = 8000$? When $Y = 9000$? Graph the *LM* curve.

b. Repeat part (*a*) for $M = 6600$. How does the *LM* curve in this case compare with the *LM* curve in part (*a*)?

c. Use $M = 6000$ again and repeat part (*a*) for $\pi^e = 0.03$. Compare the *LM* curve in this case with the one in part (*a*).

3. An economy has full-employment output of 1000. Desired consumption and desired investment are

$$C^d = 200 + 0.8(Y - T) - 500r;$$
$$I^d = 200 - 500r.$$

Government purchases are 196, and taxes are

$$T = 20 + 0.25Y.$$

Money demand is

$$\frac{M^d}{P} = 0.5Y - 250(r + \pi^e),$$

where the expected rate of inflation, π^e, is 0.10. The nominal supply of money $M = 9890$.

a. What are the general equilibrium values of the real interest rate, price level, consumption, and investment?

b. Suppose that government purchases are increased to $G = 216$. What are the new general equilibrium values of the real interest rate, price level, consumption, and investment?

4. The production function in an economy is

$$Y = A(5N - 0.0025N^2),$$

where A is productivity. With this production function, the marginal product of labor is

$$MPN = 5A - 0.005AN.$$

Suppose that $A = 2$. The labor supply curve is

$$NS = 55 + 10(1 - t)w,$$

where NS is the amount of labor supplied, w is the real wage, and t is the tax rate on wage income, which is 0.5.

Desired consumption and investment are

$$C^d = 300 + 0.8(Y - T) - 200r;$$
$$I^d = 258.5 - 250r.$$

Taxes and government purchases are

$$T = 20 + 0.5Y;$$
$$G = 50.$$

Money demand is

$$\frac{M^d}{P} = 0.5Y - 250(r + \pi^e).$$

The expected rate of inflation, π^e, is 0.02, and the nominal money supply M is 9150.

a. What are the general equilibrium levels of the real wage, employment, and output?

b. For any level of output, Y, find an equation that gives the real interest rate, r, that clears the goods market; this equation describes the *IS* curve. (*Hint:* Write the goods market equilibrium condition and solve for r in terms of Y and other variables.) What are the general equilibrium values of the real interest rate, consumption, and investment?

c. For any level of output, Y, find an equation that gives the real interest rate that clears the asset market; this equation describes the *LM* curve. [*Hint:* As in part (*b*), write the appropriate equilibrium condition and solve for r in terms of Y and other variables.] What is the general equilibrium value of the price level?

d. Suppose that government purchases increase to $G = 72.5$. Now what are the general equilibrium values of the real wage, employment, output, the real interest rate, consumption, investment, and price level?

5. Consider the following economy:

Desired consumption	$C^d = 1275 + 0.5(Y - T) - 200r.$
Desired investment	$I^d = 900 - 200r.$
Real money demand	$L = 0.5Y - 200i.$
Full-employment output	$\bar{Y} = 4600.$
Expected inflation	$\pi^e = 0.$

a. Suppose that $T = G = 450$ and that $M = 9000$. Find an equation describing the *IS* curve. (*Hint:* Set desired national saving and desired investment equal, and solve for the relationship between r and Y.) Find an equation describing the *LM* curve. (*Hint:* Set real money supply and real money demand equal, and again solve for the relationship between r and Y, given P.) Finally, find an equation for the aggregate demand curve. (*Hint:* Use the *IS* and *LM* equations to find a relationship between Y and P.) What are the general equilibrium values of output, consumption, investment, the real interest rate, and price level?

b. Suppose that $T = G = 450$ and that $M = 4500$. What is the equation for the aggregate demand curve now? What are the general equilibrium values of output, consumption, investment, the real interest rate, and price level? Assume that full-employment output $\bar{Y}$ is fixed.

c. Repeat part (*b*) for $T = G = 330$ and $M = 9000$.

6. (Appendix 9.B) This question asks you to use the formulas in Appendix 9.B to find the general equilibrium values of variables for the economy described in Numerical Problem 4. Assume that $G = 50$.

a. Use the data from Numerical Problem 4 to find the numerical values of the parameters A, f_1, f_2, n_0, n_w, c_0, c_Y, c_r, t_0, t, i_0, i_r, ℓ_0, ℓ_Y, and ℓ_r defined in Appendix 9.B.

b. Substitute the values of these behavioral parameters into the relevant equations in Appendix 9.B to compute the general equilibrium values of the real wage, employment, output, the real interest rate, and the price level.

c. Assume that government purchases, G, increase to 72.5, and repeat part (*b*).

ANALYTICAL PROBLEMS

1. For each of the following changes, what happens to the real interest rate and output in the very short run, before the price level has adjusted to restore general equilibrium?

a. Wealth declines.

b. The money supply declines.

c. The future marginal productivity of capital declines.

d. Expected inflation rises.

e. Future income rises.

2. Use the *IS–LM* model to analyze the general equilibrium effects of a permanent increase in the price of oil (a permanent adverse supply shock) on current output, employment, the real wage, national saving, consumption, investment, the real interest rate, and the price level. Assume that, besides reducing the current productivity of capital and labor, the permanent supply shock lowers both the expected future *MPK* and households' expected future incomes. (Assume that the rightward shift in labor supply is smaller than the leftward shift in labor demand.) Show that, if the real interest rate rises at all, it will rise less than in the case of a temporary supply shock that has an equal effect on current output.

3. Suppose that the price level is fixed in the short run so that the economy doesn't reach general equilibrium immediately after a change in the economy. For each of the following changes, what are the short-run effects on the real interest rate and output? Assume that, when the economy is in disequilibrium, only the labor market is out of equilibrium; assume also that for a short period firms are willing to produce enough output to meet the aggregate demand for output.
   a. A decrease in the expected rate of inflation.
   b. An increase in consumer optimism that increases desired consumption at each level of income and the real interest rate.
   c. A temporary increase in government purchases.
   d. An increase in lump-sum taxes, with no change in government purchases (consider both the case in which Ricardian equivalence holds and the case in which it doesn't).
   e. A scientific breakthrough that increases the expected future *MPK.*

4. (Appendix 9.B) In some macroeconomic models, desired investment depends on both the current level of output and the real interest rate. One possible reason that desired investment may depend on output is that, when current production and sales are high, firms may expect continued strong demand for their products in the future, which leads them to want to expand capacity.

   Algebraically, we can allow for a link between desired investment and current output by replacing Eq. (9.B.10) with

$$I^d = i_0 - i_r r + i_Y Y,$$

   where i_Y is a positive number. Use this alternative equation for desired investment to derive the algebraic expressions for the general equilibrium values of employment, the real wage, output, the real interest rate, and the price level.

5. (Appendix 9.B) Recall from Chapter 7 that an increase in i^m, the nominal interest rate on money, increases the demand for money. To capture that effect, let's replace Eq. (9.B.17) with

$$\frac{M^d}{P} = \ell_0 + \ell_Y Y - \ell_r(r + \pi^e - i^m).$$

   How does this modification change the solutions for the general equilibrium values of the variables discussed in Appendix 9.B, including employment, the real wage, output, the real interest rate, and the price level?

Appendix

9.A

Worked-Out Numerical Exercise for Solving the *IS–LM/AD–AS* Model

To help you work through the algebra needed for numerical problems in this chapter, here is a worked-out numerical exercise as an example for solving the *IS–LM* model:

Consider an economy that is described by the following equations:

$$C^d = 300 + 0.75(Y - T) - 300r$$
$$T = 100 + 0.2Y$$
$$I^d = 200 - 200r$$
$$L = 0.5Y - 500i$$
$$\bar{Y} = 2500;\ G = 600;\ M = 133{,}200;\ \pi^e = 0.05;\ P_{sr} = 120.$$

In the short run, the price level is fixed at P_{sr}. Find the short-run and long-run equilibrium values of Y, P, r, C, I, and i.

To solve this problem, we will follow these steps:

Step 1. Find the equation for the *IS* curve by using the goods market equilibrium condition, $Y = C^d + I^d + G$. Substitute the equation for T into the equation for C^d from above. Then substitute the resulting equation and the equation for I^d from above, along with the value of G, into $Y = C^d + I^d + G$ to obtain: $Y = \{300 + 0.75[Y - (100 + 0.2Y)] - 300r\} + [200 - 200r] + 600$. Rearrange this equation as an equation for r in terms of Y: $Y = [300 + 0.75Y - 75 - 0.15Y - 300r] + [200 - 200r] + 600$, so $0.4Y = [300 - 75 + 200 + 600] - (300 + 200)r$, so $500r = 1025 - 0.4Y$. Therefore, $r = 1025/500 - (0.4/500)Y$, so $r = 2.05 - 0.0008Y$. This is the *IS* curve.

Step 2. Find the equation for the *LM* curve by using the asset market equilibrium condition.

a. First, find the equation for the *LM* curve with an unspecified value of the price level. The asset market equilibrium condition equates real money supply to real money demand. Real money demand is given by $L = 0.5Y - 500i = 0.5Y - 500(r + \pi^e) = 0.5Y - 500(r + 0.05)$, and real money supply is $M/P = 133{,}200/P$. In asset market equilibrium, $133{,}200/P = 0.5Y - 500(r + 0.05)$, so $500r = 0.5Y - 25 - 133{,}200/P$. Therefore, $r = (0.5/500)Y - (25/500) - (133{,}200/500)P = 0.001Y - 0.05 - 266.4/P$. This is the equation of the *LM* curve for an unspecified value of P.

b. Then find the equation for the *LM* curve when $P = P_{sr}$. Set $P = P_{sr} = 120$ in the *LM* curve to obtain $r = 0.001Y - 0.05 - 266.4/120$, so $r = 0.001Y - 0.05 - 2.22$. Therefore, $r = 0.001Y - 2.27$. This is the equation of the *LM* curve when $P = P_{sr}$.

Step 3. Find the short-run equilibrium.

a. Find the intersection of the *IS* and *LM* curves to find the short-run equilibrium values of Y and r. We have written the equations of the *IS* and *LM* curves so that the left side of each equation is simply r. Setting the right side of the *IS* curve equal to the right side of the *LM* curve yields $2.05 - 0.0008Y = 0.001Y - 2.27$, so $4.32 = 0.0018Y$. Therefore, $Y = 4.32/0.0018 = 2400$. Now use the value of Y in either the *IS* or the *LM* curve. In the *IS* curve, $r = 2.05 - 0.0008Y = 2.05 - (0.0008 \times 2400) = 2.05 - 1.92 = 0.13$. In the *LM* curve, $r = 0.001Y - 2.27 = (0.001 \times 2400) - 2.27 = 2.40 - 2.27 = 0.13$.

b. Plug these equilibrium values of Y and r into other equations to find equilibrium values for T, C, I, and i.

$$T = 100 + 0.2Y = 100 + (0.2 \times 2400), \text{ so } T = 580.$$

$$C = 300 + 0.75(Y - T) - 300r = 300 + [0.75(2400 - 580)] - (300 \times 0.13)$$
$$= 300 + 1365 - 39 = 1626.$$
$$I = 200 - 200r = 200 - (200 \times 0.13) = 200 - 26 = 174.$$

(Note that $C + I + G = 1626 + 174 + 600 = 2400$, which equals Y.)

$$i = r + \pi^e = 0.13 + 0.05 = 0.18.$$

Step 4. Find the long-run equilibrium.

a. Use the fact that in long-run equilibrium, $Y = \bar{Y}$. Plug the equilibrium level of output into the *IS* equation to find the equilibrium real interest rate. Use $\bar{Y} = 2500$ and the *IS* equation, $r = 2.05 - 0.0008Y$, to obtain $r = 2.05 - (0.0008 \times 25000) = 2.05 - 2.00 = 0.05$.

b. Plug the equilibrium values of Y and r into other equations to find equilibrium values for T, C, I, and i.

$$T = 100 + 0.2Y = 100 + (0.2 \times 2500), \text{ so } T = 600.$$
$$C = 300 + 0.75(Y - T) - 300r = 300 + [0.75(2500 - 600)] - (300 \times 0.05)$$
$$= 300 + 1425 - 15 = 1710.$$
$$I = 200 - 200r = 200 - (200 \times 0.05) = 200 - 10 = 190.$$

(Note that $C + I + G = 1710 + 190 + 600 = 2500$, which equals Y.)

$$i = r + \pi^e = 0.05 + 0.05 = 0.10.$$

c. Plug the equilibrium values of Y and i into the money demand equation to obtain the value of real money demand L. Then find the value of P that equates real money supply, M/P, with real money demand, L. The money demand curve is $L = 0.5Y - 500i = (0.5 \times 2500) - (500 \times 0.10) = 1250 - 50 = 1200$. Setting real money supply equal to real money demand gives $133{,}200/P = 1200$, so $P = 133{,}200/1200 = 111$.

Step 5. Find the equation for the *AD* curve by using the *IS* and *LM* curves. Use the form of the *LM* curve for an unspecified value of P.

The *IS* and *LM* curves are both written so that r appears alone on the left side, so the right sides of both can be equated to obtain:

$$2.05 - 0.0008Y = 0.001Y - 0.05 - 266.4/P, \text{ so } 0.0018Y = 2.10 + 266.4/P.$$

Dividing this equation through by 0.0018 yields $Y = 2.10/0.0018 + (266.4/0.0018)/P$, so $Y = 1166\frac{2}{3} + 148{,}000/P$. This is the *AD* curve.

Step 6. Illustrate the use of the *AD* curve and short-run and long-run aggregate supply curves. In the short run, the *SRAS* curve is $P = P_{sr} = 120$, which means it is a horizontal line. The short-run equilibrium occurs at the intersection of the *AD* and *SRAS* curves. Plug $P = 120$ into the *AD* curve to obtain $Y = 1166\frac{2}{3} + 148{,}000/120 = 1166\frac{2}{3} + 1233\frac{1}{3}$. Therefore $Y = 2400$, the same result we found in Step 3.

In the long run, output equals its full-employment level, so the *LRAS* curve is $Y = \bar{Y} = 2500$, which means it is a vertical line. The long-run equilibrium occurs at the intersection of the *AD* and *LRAS* curves. Plug $Y = \bar{Y} = 2500$, into the *AD* curve to obtain $2500 = Y = 1166\frac{2}{3} + 148{,}000/P$, so $1333\frac{1}{3} = 148{,}000/P$, which implies $P = 148{,}000/1333\frac{1}{3} = 111$, the same result we found in Step 4.

Appendix 9.B

Algebraic Versions of the *IS–LM/AD–AS* Model

In this appendix we present algebraic versions of the *IS–LM* and *AD–AS* models. For each of the three markets—labor, goods, and assets—we first present equations that describe demand and supply in that market, then find the market equilibrium. After considering each market separately, we solve for the general equilibrium of the complete *IS–LM* model. We use the *IS–LM* model to derive the aggregate demand (*AD*) curve and then introduce the short-run and long-run aggregate supply curves to derive the short-run and long-run equilibria.

The Labor Market

The demand for labor is based on the marginal product of labor, as determined by the production function. Recall from Chapter 3 (Eq. 3.1) that the production function can be written as $Y = AF(K, N)$, where Y is output, K is the capital stock, N is labor input, and A is productivity. Holding the capital stock K fixed, we can write the production function with output Y as a function only of labor input N and productivity A. A useful specific production function is

$$Y = A\left(f_1N - \frac{1}{2}f_2N^2\right), \quad \textbf{(9.B.1)}$$

where f_1 and f_2 are positive numbers.

The marginal product of labor, *MPN*, is the slope of the production function. The slope of the production function in Eq. (9.B.1) at any level of employment N equals[1] $A(f_1 - f_2N)$, so the marginal product of labor is

$$MPN = A(f_1 - f_2N). \quad \textbf{(9.B.2)}$$

Firms hire labor to the point at which the marginal product of labor equals the real wage. Thus the relation between the real wage, w, and the amount of labor demanded, *ND*, is

$$w = A(f_1 - f_2ND). \quad \textbf{(9.B.3)}$$

The supply of labor is an increasing function of the current, after-tax real wage. If t is the tax rate on wage income (we assume that $0 \leq t < 1$) so that $(1 - t)w$ is the after-tax real wage, a simple form of the labor supply curve is

$$NS = n_0 + n_w(1 - t)w, \quad \textbf{(9.B.4)}$$

[1]Students who know calculus can derive the slope of the production function by taking the derivative of Eq. (9.B.1) with respect to N.

where *NS* is the amount of labor supplied, and n_w is a positive number. Factors other than the after-tax real wage that affect labor supply, such as wealth or the working-age population, are captured by the constant term n_0 in Eq. (9.B.4).

Equilibrium in the Labor Market

In equilibrium, the amounts of labor demanded, *ND*, and supplied, *NS*, are equal; their common value is the full-employment level of employment, $\bar{N}$. If we substitute $\bar{N}$ for *NS* and *ND* in Eqs. (9.B.3) and (9.B.4), we have two linear equations in the two variables $\bar{N}$ and w. Solving these equations for w and $\bar{N}$ yields[2]

$$w = A\left[\frac{f_1 - f_2 n_0}{1 + (1 - t)Af_2 n_w}\right] \quad \textbf{(9.B.5)}$$

and

$$\bar{N} = \frac{n_0 + (1 - t)Af_1 n_w}{1 + (1 - t)Af_2 n_w}. \quad \textbf{(9.B.6)}$$

Using the full-employment level of employment, $\bar{N}$, in Eq. (9.B.6), we obtain the full-employment level of output, $\bar{Y}$, by substituting $\bar{N}$ into the production function (9.B.1):

$$\bar{Y} = A\left[f_1\bar{N} - \frac{1}{2}f_2\bar{N}^2\right], \quad FE \text{ line} \quad \textbf{(9.B.7)}$$

The value of full-employment output in Eq. (9.B.7) is the horizontal intercept of the *FE* line.

We use these equations to analyze the effects on the labor market of changes in productivity and labor supply. First consider an increase in productivity *A*. Equation (9.B.5) shows that an increase in *A* leads to an increase in the equilibrium real wage (an increase in *A* raises the ratio $A/[1 + (1 - t)Af_2n_w]$). Although not directly evident from Eq. (9.B.6), an increase in *A* also increases $\bar{N}$.[3] To see why, note first that an increase in *A* doesn't affect the labor supply curve, Eq. (9.B.4). Second, an increase in *A* raises the real wage. Hence the implication is that an increase in *A* raises the equilibrium amount of labor supplied and thus also the full-employment level of employment, $\bar{N}$. Because an increase in *A* raises $\bar{N}$, it must also raise full-employment output, $\bar{Y}$ (see Eq. 9.B.7), and shift the *FE* line to the right.

Now consider an increase in the amount of labor supplied at each level of the after-tax real wage, represented algebraically as an increase in n_0 in Eq. (9.B.4). Equations (9.B.5) and (9.B.6) show that an increase in n_0 reduces the equilibrium real wage and increases employment, $\bar{N}$. Because an increase in labor supply raises $\bar{N}$, it also raises full-employment output, $\bar{Y}$, and shifts the *FE* line to the right.

---

[2]We assume that the constants f_1, f_2, and n_0 are such that $f_1 - f_2n_0 > 0$. This assumption is needed to guarantee that the marginal product of labor and the equilibrium real wage are positive.

[3]Students who know calculus can compute the derivative of $\bar{N}$ with respect to *A* in Eq. (9.B.6) and will find that the sign of this derivative is positive if and only if $f_1 - f_2n_0 > 0$. As we have assumed that $f_1 - f_2n_0 > 0$ (see preceding footnote), an increase in A does indeed increase $\bar{N}$.

The Goods Market

To find equilibrium in the goods market, we start with equations describing desired consumption and desired investment. Desired consumption is

$$C^d = c_0 + c_Y\,(Y - T) - c_r r, \qquad \textbf{(9.B.8)}$$

where $Y - T$ is disposable income (income Y minus taxes T), r is the real interest rate, and c_0, c_Y, and c_r are positive numbers. The number c_Y in Eq. (9.B.8) is the marginal propensity to consume, as defined in Chapter 4; because people consume only part of an increase in disposable income, saving the rest, a reasonable assumption is that $0 < c_Y < 1$. According to Eq. (9.B.8), an increase in disposable income causes desired consumption to increase, and an increase in the real interest rate causes desired consumption to fall (and desired saving to rise). Other factors that affect desired consumption, such as wealth or expected future income, are included in the constant term c_0.[4]

Taxes in Eq. (9.B.8) are

$$T = t_0 + tY, \qquad \textbf{(9.B.9)}$$

where t is the tax rate on income (the same tax rate that is levied on wages) and t_0 is a lump-sum tax. As mentioned earlier, $0 \leq t < 1$, so an increase in income, Y, increases total taxes, T, and also increases disposable income, $Y - T$.

Desired investment is

$$I^d = i_0 - i_r r, \qquad \textbf{(9.B.10)}$$

where i_0 and i_r are positive numbers. Equation (9.B.10) indicates that desired investment falls when the real interest rate rises. Other factors affecting desired investment, such as the expected future marginal product of capital, are included in the constant term i_0.

Equilibrium in the Goods Market

The goods market equilibrium condition in a closed economy is given by Eq. (4.7), which we repeat here:

$$Y = C^d + I^d + G. \qquad \textbf{(9.B.11)}$$

Equation (9.B.11) is equivalent to the goods market equilibrium condition, $S^d = I^d$, which could be used equally well here.

If we substitute the equations for desired consumption (Eq. 9.B.8, with taxes T as given by Eq. 9.B.9) and desired investment (Eq. 9.B.10) into the goods market equilibrium condition (Eq. 9.B.11), we get

$$Y = c_0 + c_Y(Y - t_0 - tY) - c_r r + i_0 - i_r r + G. \qquad \textbf{(9.B.12)}$$

[4]Because an increase in taxes, T, reduces desired consumption in Eq. (9.B.8), this formulation of desired consumption appears, at first glance, to be inconsistent with the Ricardian equivalence proposition discussed in Chapter 4. However, essential to the idea of Ricardian equivalence is that consumers expect an increase in current taxes, T, to be accompanied by lower taxes in the future. This decrease in expected future taxes would increase desired consumption, which would be captured in Eq. (9.B.8) as an increase in c_0. According to the Ricardian equivalence proposition, after an increase in T with no change in current or planned government purchases, an increase in c_0 would exactly offset the reduction in $c_Y(Y - T)$ so that desired consumption would be unchanged.

Collecting the terms that multiply Y on the left side yields

$$[1 - (1 - t)c_Y]Y = c_0 + i_0 + G - c_Y t_0 - (c_r + i_r)r. \quad \textbf{(9.B.13)}$$

Equation (9.B.13) relates output, Y, to the real interest rate, r, that clears the goods market. This relationship between Y and r defines the *IS* curve. Because the *IS* curve is graphed with r on the vertical axis and Y on the horizontal axis, we rewrite Eq. (9.B.13) with r on the left side and Y on the right side. Solving Eq. (9.B.13) for r gives

$$r = \alpha_{IS} - \beta_{IS}Y, \quad \textit{IS curve.} \quad \textbf{(9.B.14)}$$

In Eq. (9.B.14), α_{IS} and β_{IS} are positive numbers defined as

$$\alpha_{IS} = \frac{c_0 + i_0 + G - c_Y t_0}{c_r + i_r} \quad \textbf{(9.B.15)}$$

and

$$\beta_{IS} = \frac{1 - (1 - t)c_Y}{c_r + i_r}. \quad \textbf{(9.B.16)}$$

Equation (9.B.14) yields the graph of the *IS* curve. In Eq. (9.B.14), the coefficient of Y, or $-\beta_{IS}$, is the slope of the *IS* curve; because this slope is negative, the *IS* curve slopes downward. Changes in the constant term α_{IS} in Eq. (9.B.14), which is defined in Eq. (9.B.15), shift the *IS* curve. Anything that increases α_{IS}—such as (1) an increase in consumer optimism that increases desired consumption by increasing c_0; (2) an increase in the expected future marginal product of capital, MPK^f, that raises desired investment by raising i_0; or (3) an increase in government purchases, G—shifts the *IS* curve up and to the right. Similarly, anything that decreases α_{IS} shifts the *IS* curve down and to the left.

The Asset Market

In general, the real demand for money depends on real income, Y, and the nominal interest rate on nonmonetary assets, i, which in turn equals the expected real interest rate, r, plus the expected rate of inflation, π^e. We assume that the money demand function takes the form

$$\frac{M^d}{P} = \ell_0 + \ell_Y Y - \ell_r(r + \pi^e), \quad \textbf{(9.B.17)}$$

where M^d is the nominal demand for money, P is the price level, and ℓ_Y and ℓ_r are positive numbers. The constant term ℓ_0 includes factors other than output and the interest rate that affect money demand, such as the liquidity of alternative assets. The real supply of money equals the nominal supply of money, M, which is determined by the central bank, divided by the price level, P.

Equilibrium in the Asset Market

As we showed in Chapter 7, if we assume that there are only two types of assets (money and nonmonetary assets), the asset market is in equilibrium when the real quantity of money demanded equals the real money supply, M/P. Using the money demand function in Eq. (9.B.17), we write the asset market equilibrium condition as

$$\frac{M}{P} = \ell_0 + \ell_Y Y - \ell_r(r + \pi^e). \quad \textbf{(9.B.18)}$$

For fixed levels of the nominal money supply, M, price level, P, and expected rate of inflation, π^e, Eq. (9.B.18) relates output, Y, and the real interest rate, r, that clears the asset market. Thus Eq. (9.B.18) defines the *LM* curve. To get Eq. (9.B.18) into a form that is easier to interpret graphically, we rewrite the equation with r alone on the left side:

$$r = \alpha_{LM} - \left(\frac{1}{\ell_r}\right)\left(\frac{M}{P}\right) + \beta_{LM}Y, \quad \textit{LM curve} \tag{9.B.19}$$

where

$$\alpha_{LM} = \left(\frac{\ell_0}{\ell_r}\right) - \pi^e \tag{9.B.20}$$

and

$$\beta_{LM} = \left(\frac{\ell_Y}{\ell_r}\right). \tag{9.B.21}$$

The graph of Eq. (9.B.19) is the *LM* curve. In Eq. (9.B.19), the coefficient of Y, or β_{LM}, is the slope of the *LM* curve; because this coefficient is positive, the *LM* curve slopes upward. Variables that change the intercept of the equation in Eq. (9.B.19), $\alpha_{LM} - (1/\ell_r)(M/P)$, shift the *LM* curve. An increase in the real money supply, M/P, reduces this intercept and thus shifts the *LM* curve down and to the right. An increase in the expected rate of inflation π^e reduces α_{LM} and shifts the *LM* curve down and to the right. An increase in real money demand arising from (for example) reduced liquidity of alternative assets raises ℓ_0, which raises α_{LM} and shifts the *LM* curve up and to the left.

General Equilibrium in the *IS–LM* Model

From the supply-and-demand relationships and equilibrium conditions in each market, we can calculate the general equilibrium values for the most important macroeconomic variables. We have already solved for the general equilibrium levels of the real wage, employment, and output in the labor market: The real wage is given by Eq. (9.B.5); employment equals its full-employment level, $\bar{N}$, given by Eq. (9.B.6); and, in general equilibrium, output equals its full-employment level, $\bar{Y}$, as given by Eq. (9.B.7).

Turning to the goods market, we obtain the general equilibrium real interest rate by substituting $\bar{Y}$ for Y in Eq. (9.B.14):

$$r = \alpha_{IS} - \beta_{IS}\bar{Y}. \tag{9.B.22}$$

Having output, Y, and the real interest rate, r (determined by Eq. 9.B.22), we use Eqs. (9.B.9), (9.B.8), and (9.B.10) to find the general equilibrium values of taxes, T, consumption, C, and investment, I, respectively.

The final important macroeconomic variable whose equilibrium value needs to be determined is the price level, P. To find the equilibrium price level, we work with the asset market equilibrium condition, Eq. (9.B.18). In Eq. (9.B.18), we substitute full-employment output, $\bar{Y}$, for Y and use Eq. (9.B.22) to substitute the equilibrium value of the real interest rate for r. Solving Eq. (9.B.18) for the price level gives

$$P = \frac{M}{\ell_0 + \ell_Y\bar{Y} - \ell_r(\alpha_{IS} - \beta_{IS}\bar{Y} + \pi^e)}. \tag{9.B.23}$$

Equation (9.B.23) confirms that the equilibrium price level, P, is proportional to the nominal money supply, M.

We can use these equations to analyze the effects of an adverse productivity shock on the general equilibrium, as in the text. We have already shown that an increase in the productivity parameter, A, increases the equilibrium real wage, the full-employment level of employment, and the full-employment level of output. Thus an adverse productivity shock (a reduction in A) reduces the general equilibrium levels of the real wage, employment, and output. Equation (9.B.22) indicates that an adverse productivity shock because it reduces $\bar{Y}$, must increase the equilibrium real interest rate. Lower output and a higher real interest rate imply that both consumption and investment must decline (Eqs. 9.B.8 and 9.B.10). Finally, the decrease in $\bar{Y}$ resulting from an adverse productivity shock reduces the denominator of the right side of Eq. (9.B.23), so the price level, P, must rise. All these results are the same as those found by graphical analysis.

The *AD–AS* Model

Building on the algebraic version of the *IS–LM* model just derived, we now derive an algebraic version of the *AD–AS* model presented in this chapter. We present algebraic versions of the aggregate demand (*AD*) curve, the short-run aggregate supply (*SRAS*) curve, and the long-run aggregate supply (*LRAS*) curve and then solve for short-run and long-run equilibria.

The Aggregate Demand Curve

Aggregate output demanded at any price level, P, is the amount of output corresponding to the intersection of the *IS* and *LM* curves. We find the value of Y at the intersection of the *IS* and *LM* curves by setting the right sides of Eqs. (9.B.14) and (9.B.19) equal and solving for Y:

$$Y = \frac{\alpha_{IS} - \alpha_{LM} + (1/\ell_r)(M/P)}{\beta_{IS} + \beta_{LM}}. \qquad \textbf{(9.B.24)}$$

Equation (9.B.24) is the aggregate demand curve. For constant nominal money supply, M, Eq. (9.B.24) shows that the aggregate quantity of goods demanded, Y, is a decreasing function of the price level, P, so that the *AD* curve slopes downward. Note that the numerator of the right side of Eq. (9.B.24) is the intercept of the *IS* curve minus the intercept of the *LM* curve. Thus for a constant price level, any change that shifts the *IS* curve up and to the right (such as an increase in the government purchases) or shifts the *LM* curve down and to the right (such as an increase in the nominal money supply) increases aggregate output demanded and shifts the *AD* curve up and to the right.

The Aggregate Supply Curve

In the short run, firms supply the output demanded at the fixed price level, which we denote P_{sr}. Thus the short-run aggregate supply (*SRAS*) curve is a horizontal line:

$$P = P_{sr}, \quad SRAS. \qquad \textbf{(9.B.25)}$$

The long-run aggregate supply curve is a vertical line at the full-employment level of output, $\bar{Y}$, or

$$Y = \bar{Y}, \quad LRAS. \tag{9.B.26}$$

Short-Run and Long-Run Equilibrium

The short-run equilibrium of the economy is represented by the intersection of the aggregate demand (*AD*) curve and the short-run aggregate supply (*SRAS*) curve. We find the quantity of output in short-run equilibrium simply by substituting the equation of the *SRAS* curve (Eq. 9.B.25) into the equation of the *AD* curve (Eq. 9.B.24) to obtain

$$Y = \frac{\alpha_{IS} - \alpha_{LM} + (1/\ell_r)(M/P_{sr})}{\beta_{IS} + \beta_{LM}}. \tag{9.B.27}$$

The long-run equilibrium of the economy, which is reached when the labor, goods, and asset markets are all in equilibrium, is represented by the intersection of the aggregate demand curve and the long-run aggregate supply curve. Thus $Y = \bar{Y}$ in long-run equilibrium, from the *LRAS* curve in Eq. (9.B.26). We find the price level in long-run equilibrium by setting the right sides of the equation of the *AD* curve (Eq. 9.B.24) and the equation of the *LRAS* curve (Eq. 9.B.26) equal and solving for P to obtain

$$P = \frac{M}{\ell_r[\alpha_{LM} - \alpha_{IS} + (\beta_{IS} + \beta_{LM})\bar{Y}]}. \tag{9.B.28}$$

The long-run equilibrium price level in Eq. (9.B.28) is the same as that at the *IS–LM–FE* intersection in Eq. (9.B.23). You can verify that the price level is the same in both equations by substituting the definitions of α_{LM} and β_{LM} from Eqs. (9.B.20) and (9.B.21), respectively, into Eq. (9.B.28).

10

Classical Business Cycle Analysis: Market-Clearing Macroeconomics

Learning Objectives

10.1 Summarize the real business cycle theory and describe how well it accounts for the business cycle facts.

10.2 Discuss the effects of fiscal policy shocks in the classical model.

10.3 Discuss unemployment in the classical model.

10.4 Explain the roles of money and monetary policy in the classical model.

10.5 Summarize the fundamentals and implications of the misperceptions theory.

Economists generally agree about the basic business cycle facts outlined in Chapter 8. They know that economic growth isn't necessarily smooth and that occasionally there are periods of recession in which output declines and unemployment rises. They know that recessions typically are followed by periods of recovery in which the economy grows more strongly than normal. And they also know a great deal about how other macroeconomic variables—such as productivity, interest rates, and inflation—behave during recessions.

Recall that recessions and booms in the economy raise two basic questions: (1) What are the underlying economic causes of these business cycles? and (2) What, if anything, should government policymakers do about them? Unfortunately, economists agree less about the answers to these two questions than about the basic business cycle facts.

The main disagreements about the causes and cures of recessions are between two broad groups of macroeconomists, the classicals and the Keynesians. As discussed first in Chapter 1 and again in Chapters 8 and 9, classicals and Keynesians—although agreeing on many points—differ primarily in their views on how rapidly prices and wages adjust to restore general equilibrium after an economic shock. Classical macroeconomists assume that prices and wages adjust quickly to equate quantities supplied and demanded in each market; as a result, they argue, a market economy is largely "self-correcting," with a strong tendency to return to general equilibrium on its own when it is disturbed by an economic shock or a change in public policy. Keynesians usually agree that prices and wages *eventually* change as needed to clear markets; however, they believe that *in the short run* price and wage adjustment is likely to be incomplete. That is, in the short run, quantities supplied and demanded need not be equal and the economy may remain out of general equilibrium. Although this difference in views may seem purely theoretical, it has a practical implication: Because Keynesians are skeptical about the economy's ability to reach equilibrium rapidly on its own, they are much more inclined than are classicals to recommend that government act to raise output and employment during recessions and to moderate economic growth during booms.

In this chapter and Chapter 11 we develop and compare the classical and Keynesian theories of the business cycle and the policy recommendations of the two groups, beginning with the classical perspective in this chapter. Conveniently, both the classical and Keynesian analyses can be expressed in terms of a common analytical framework, the *IS–LM/AD–AS* model. In this chapter we use the classical (or market-clearing) version of the *IS–LM/AD–AS* model, composed of the *IS–LM/AD–AS* model and the assumption that prices and wages adjust rapidly. The assumption that prices and wages adjust rapidly implies that the economy always is in or near general equilibrium and therefore that variables such as output and employment always are close to their general equilibrium levels.

In comparing the principal competing theories of the business cycle, we are particularly interested in how well the various theories explain the business cycle facts. The classical theory is consistent with many of the most important facts about the cycle. However, one business cycle fact that challenges the classical theory is the observation that changes in the money stock lead the cycle. Recall the implication of the classical assumption that wages and prices adjust quickly to clear markets, so that the economy reaches long-run equilibrium quickly. Money is neutral, which means that changes in the money supply do not affect output and other real variables. However, most economists interpret the fact that money leads the cycle as evidence that money is not neutral in all situations. If money isn't neutral, we must either modify the basic classical model to account for monetary nonneutrality or abandon the classical model in favor of alternative theories (such as the Keynesian approach) that are consistent with nonneutrality. In Section 10.5 we extend the classical model to allow for nonneutrality of money. We then examine the implications of this extended classical approach for macroeconomic policy.

10.1 The Real Business Cycle Theory

Summarize the real business cycle theory and describe how well it accounts for the business cycle facts.

We have identified two basic questions of business cycle analysis: What causes business cycles? and What can (or should) be done about them? Let's examine the classical answers to these questions, beginning with what causes business cycles.

Recall from Section 8.4 that a complete theory of the business cycle must have two components. The first is a description of the types of shocks or disturbances believed to affect the economy the most. Examples of economic disturbances emphasized by various theories of the business cycle include supply shocks, changes in monetary or fiscal policy, and changes in consumer spending. The second component is a model that describes how key macroeconomic variables, such as output, employment, and prices, respond to economic shocks. Classical economists prefer to build their models from microeconomic foundations, describing how people maximize their utility and how firms maximize profits. Thus their preferred models are quite complex and we cannot represent them easily in this textbook. However, the main results of their detailed models are similar to those from the market-clearing version of the *IS–LM* model, so in this text we will use that model to represent the views of classical macroeconomists. In addition, the issue of which shocks are crucial in driving cyclical fluctuations remains.

An influential group of classical macroeconomists, led by Nobel laureates Edward Prescott of Arizona State University and the Federal Reserve Bank of Minneapolis and Finn Kydland of the University of California at Santa Barbara, developed a theory that takes a strong stand on the sources of shocks that cause cyclical fluctuations. This theory, the **real business cycle theory** (or RBC theory), argues that real shocks to the economy are the primary cause of business cycles.[1] **Real shocks** are disturbances to the "real side" of the economy, such as shocks that affect the production function, the size of the labor force, the real quantity of government purchases, and the spending and saving decisions of consumers. Economists contrast real shocks with **nominal shocks**, or shocks to money supply or money demand. In terms of the *IS–LM* model, real shocks directly affect the *IS* curve or the *FE* line, whereas nominal shocks directly affect only the *LM* curve.

Although many types of real shocks could contribute to the business cycle, RBC economists give the largest role to production function shocks—what we've called *supply shocks* and what the RBC economists usually refer to as **productivity shocks**. Productivity shocks include the development of new products or production methods, the introduction of new management techniques, changes in the quality of capital or labor, changes in the availability of raw materials or energy, unusually good or unusually bad weather, changes in government regulations affecting production, and any other factor affecting productivity. According to RBC economists, most economic booms result from beneficial productivity shocks, and most recessions are caused by adverse productivity shocks.

The Recessionary Impact of an Adverse Productivity Shock. Does the RBC economists' idea that adverse productivity shocks lead to recessions (and, similarly, that beneficial productivity shocks lead to booms) make sense? We examined the theoretical effects on the economy of a temporary adverse productivity shock in Chapters 3, 8, and 9.[2] In Chapter 3 we showed that an adverse productivity shock (or supply shock), such as an increase in the price of oil, reduces the marginal product of labor (*MPN*) and the demand for labor at any real wage. As a result, the equilibrium values of the real wage and employment both fall (see Fig. 3.10). The equilibrium level of output (the full-employment level of output $\bar{Y}$) also falls, both because equilibrium employment declines and because the adverse productivity shock reduces the amount of output that can be produced by any amount of capital and labor.

We later used the complete *IS–LM* model (Fig. 9.8) to explore the general equilibrium effects of a temporary adverse productivity shock. We confirmed our earlier conclusion that an adverse productivity shock lowers the general equilibrium levels of the real wage, employment, and output. In addition, we showed that an adverse productivity shock raises the real interest rate, depresses consumption and investment, and raises the price level.

Broadly, then, our earlier analyses of the effects of an adverse productivity shock support the RBC economists' claim that such shocks are recessionary, in that they lead to declines in output. Similar analyses show that a beneficial productivity shock leads to a rise in output (a boom). Note that, in the RBC approach, output declines in recessions and rises in booms because the general equilibrium (or full-employment) level of output has changed and because rapid price adjustment ensures that actual output always equals full-employment output. As classical economists, RBC economists would reject the Keynesian view (which we will discuss in Chapter 11) that

[1]For a more detailed introduction to real business cycles, see Charles Plosser, "Understanding Real Business Cycles," *Journal of Economic Perspectives*, Summer 1989, pp. 51–78; and Robert G. King and Sergio Rebelo, "Resuscitating Real Business Cycles," in J. Taylor and M. Woodford, eds., *Handbook of Macroeconomics*, Elsevier, 1999.

[2]RBC economists analyze permanent as well as temporary productivity shocks; we focus on the case with temporary shocks because it is the slightly easier case.

recessions and booms are periods of disequilibrium, during which actual output is below or above its general equilibrium level for a protracted period of time.

Real Business Cycle Theory and the Business Cycle Facts. Although the RBC theory—which combines the classical, or market-clearing, version of the *IS–LM* model with the assumption that productivity shocks are the dominant form of economic disturbance—is relatively simple, it is consistent with many of the basic business cycle facts. First, under the assumption that the economy is being continuously buffeted by productivity shocks, the RBC approach predicts recurrent fluctuations in aggregate output, which actually occur. Second, the RBC theory correctly predicts that employment will move procyclically—that is, in the same direction as output. Third, the RBC theory predicts that real wages will be higher during booms than during recessions (procyclical real wages), as also occurs.

A fourth business cycle fact explained by the RBC theory is that average labor productivity is procyclical; that is, output per worker is higher during booms than during recessions. This fact is consistent with the RBC economists' assumption that booms are periods of beneficial productivity shocks, which tend to raise labor productivity, whereas recessions are the results of adverse productivity shocks, which tend to reduce labor productivity. The RBC economists point out that without productivity shocks—allowing the production function to remain stable over time—average labor productivity wouldn't be procyclical. With no productivity shocks, the expansion of employment that occurs during booms would tend to reduce average labor productivity because of the principle of diminishing marginal productivity of labor. Similarly, without productivity shocks, recessions would be periods of relatively higher labor productivity, instead of lower productivity as observed. Thus RBC economists regard the procyclical nature of average labor productivity as strong evidence supporting their approach.

A business cycle fact that does not seem to be consistent with the simple RBC theory is that inflation tends to slow during or immediately after a recession. The theory predicts that an adverse productivity shock will both cause a recession and increase the general price level. Thus according to the RBC approach, periods of recession should also be periods of inflation, contrary to the business cycle fact.

Some RBC economists have responded by taking issue with the conventional view that inflation is procyclical. For example, in a study of the period 1954–1989, RBC proponents Kydland and Prescott[3] showed that the finding of procyclical inflation is somewhat sensitive to the statistical methods used to calculate the trends in inflation and output. Using a different method of calculating these trends, Kydland and Prescott found evidence that, when aggregate output has been above its long-run trend, the price level has tended to be below its long-run trend, a result more nearly consistent with the RBC prediction about the cyclical behavior of prices. Kydland and Prescott suggested that standard views about the procyclicality of prices and inflation are based mostly on the experience of the economy between the two world wars (1918–1941), when the economy had a different structure and was subject to different types of shocks than the more recent economy. For example, many economists believe that the Great Depression—the most important macroeconomic event between the two world wars—resulted from a sequence of large, adverse aggregate demand shocks. As we illustrated in Fig. 8.18, an adverse

[3]"Business Cycles: Real Facts and a Monetary Myth," *Quarterly Review*, Federal Reserve Bank of Minneapolis, Spring 1990, pp. 3–18.

aggregate demand shock shifts the *AD* curve down and to the left, leading first to a decline in output and then to a decline in prices; this pattern is consistent with the conventional business cycle fact that inflation is procyclical and lagging. Kydland and Prescott argue, however, that since World War II large adverse supply shocks have caused the price level to rise while output fell. Most notably, inflation surged during the recessions that followed the oil price shocks of 1973–1974 and 1979–1980. The issue of the cyclical behavior of prices remains controversial, however.

Application

Calibrating the Business Cycle

If we put aside the debate about price level behavior, the RBC theory can account for some of the business cycle facts, including the procyclical behavior of employment, productivity, and real wages. However, real business cycle economists argue that an adequate theory of the business cycle should be *quantitative* as well as *qualitative*. In other words, in addition to predicting generally how key macroeconomic variables move throughout the business cycle, the theory should predict numerically the size of economic fluctuations and the strength of relationships among the variables.

To examine the quantitative implications of their theories, RBC economists developed a method called *calibration*. The idea is to work out a detailed numerical example of a more general theory. The results are then compared to macroeconomic data to see whether model and reality broadly agree.

The first step in calibration is to write down a model of the economy—such as the classical version of the *IS–LM* model—except that specific functions replace general functions. For example, instead of representing the production function in general terms as

$$Y = AF(K, N),$$

the person doing the calibration uses a specific algebraic form for the production function, such as[4]

$$Y = AK^{a}N^{1-a},$$

where a is a number between 0 and 1. Similarly, specific functions are used to describe the behavior of consumers and workers.

Next, the specific functions chosen are made even more specific by expressing them in numerical terms. For example, for $a = 0.3$, the production function becomes

$$Y = AK^{0.3}N^{0.7}.$$

In the same way, specific numbers are assigned to the functions describing the behavior of consumers and workers. Where do these numbers come from? Generally, they are *not* estimated from macroeconomic data but are based on other sources.

For example, the numbers assigned to the functions in the model may come from previous studies of the production function or of the saving behavior of individuals and families.

[4]This production function is the Cobb–Douglas production function (Chapter 3). As we noted, although it is relatively simple, it fits U.S. data quite well.

(*continued*)

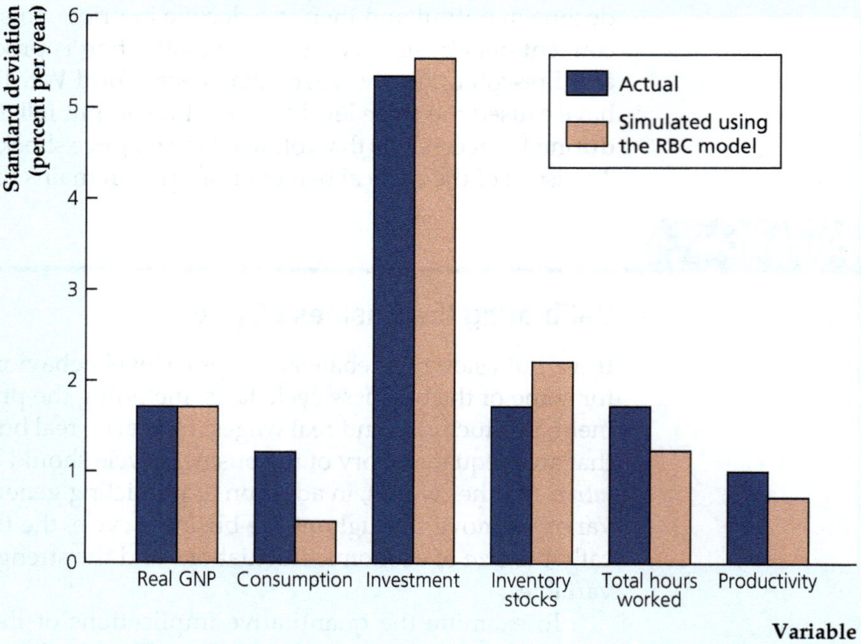

FIGURE 10.1

Actual versus simulated volatilities of key macroeconomic variables

The figure compares the actual volatilities of key macroeconomic variables observed in post–World War II U.S. data with the volatilities of the same variables predicted by computer simulations of Edward Prescott's calibrated RBC model. Prescott set the size of the random productivity shocks in his simulations so that the simulated volatility of GNP would match the actually observed volatility of GNP exactly. For these random productivity shocks, the simulated volatilities of the other five macroeconomic variables (with the possible exception of consumption) match the observed volatilities fairly well.

The third step, which must be carried out on a computer, is to find out how the numerically specified model behaves when it is hit by random shocks, such as productivity shocks. The shocks are created on the computer with a random number generator, with the size and persistence of the shocks (unlike the numbers assigned to the specific functions) being chosen to fit the actual macroeconomic data. For these shocks, the computer tracks the behavior of the model over many periods and reports the implied behavior of key macroeconomic variables such as output, employment, consumption, and investment. The results from these simulations are then compared to the behavior of the actual economy to determine how well the model fits reality.

Edward Prescott[5] performed an early and influential calibration exercise. He used a model similar to the RBC model we present here, the main difference being that our version of the RBC model is essentially a two-period model (the present and the future), and Prescott's model allowed for many periods. The results of his computer simulations are shown in Figures 10.1 and 10.2.

Figure 10.1 compares the actually observed volatilities of six macroeconomic variables, as calculated from post–World War II U.S. data, with the volatilities predicted by Prescott's calibrated RBC model.[6] Prescott set the size of the random productivity shocks in his simulations so that the volatility of GNP in his model would match the actual volatility in U.S. GNP.[7] That choice explains why the

[5]"Theory Ahead of Business Cycle Measurement," *Carnegie-Rochester Conference Series on Public Policy*, Volume 25, Autumn 1986, pp. 11–39. Reprinted in *Quarterly Review*, Federal Reserve Bank of Minneapolis, Fall 1986, pp. 9–22.

[6]The measure of volatility used is called the *standard deviation*. The higher the standard deviation, the more volatile the variable being measured.

[7]At the time of Prescott's study, the national income and product accounts of the United States focused on GNP rather than GDP, so Prescott also focused on GNP.

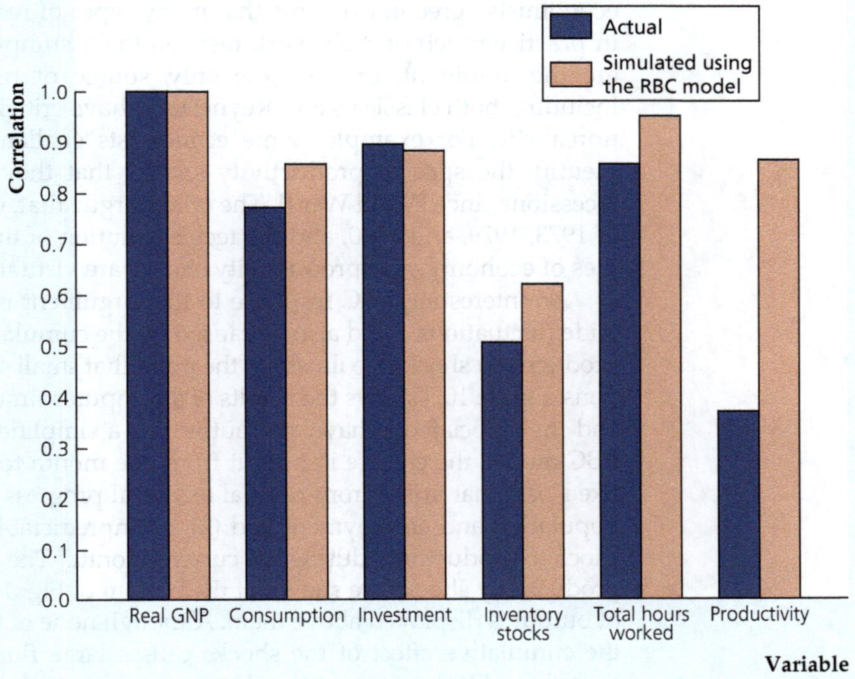

FIGURE 10.2

Actual versus simulated correlations of key macroeconomic variables with GNP

How closely a variable moves with GNP over the business cycle is measured by its correlation with GNP, with higher correlations implying a closer relationship. The figure compares the correlations of key variables with GNP that were actually observed in the post–World War II U.S. economy with the correlations predicted by computer simulations of Prescott's calibrated RBC model. Except for productivity, whose predicted correlation with GNP is too high, the simulations predicted correlations of macroeconomic variables with GNP that closely resemble the actual correlations of these variables with GNP.

actual and simulated volatilities of GNP are equal in Fig. 10.1. But he did nothing to guarantee that the simulation would match the actual volatilities of the other five variables. Note, however, that the simulated and actual volatilities for the other variables in most cases are quite close.

Figure 10.2 compares the actual economy with Prescott's calibrated model in another respect: how closely important macroeconomic variables move with GNP over the business cycle. The statistical measure of how closely variables move together is called *correlation*. If a variable's correlation with GNP is positive, the variable tends to move in the same direction as GNP over the business cycle (that is, the variable is procyclical). A correlation with GNP of 1.0 indicates that the variable's movements track the movements of GNP perfectly (thus the correlation of GNP with itself is 1.0), and a correlation with GNP of 0 indicates no relationship to GNP. Correlations with GNP between 0 and 1.0 reflect relationships with GNP of intermediate strength. Figure 10.2 shows that Prescott's model generally accounts well for the strength of the relationships between some of the variables and GNP, although the correlation of productivity and GNP predicted by Prescott's model is noticeably larger than the actual correlation.

The degree to which relatively simple calibrated RBC models can match the actual data is impressive. In addition, the results of calibration exercises help guide further development of the model. For example, the version of the RBC model discussed here has been modified to improve the match between the actual and predicted correlations of productivity with GNP.

Are Productivity Shocks the Only Source of Recessions? Although RBC economists agree in principle that many types of real shocks buffet the economy, in practice much of their work rests on the assumption that productivity shocks are the dominant, or even the only, source of recessions. Many economists, including both classicals and Keynesians, have criticized this assumption as being unrealistic. For example, some economists challenged the RBC economists to identify the specific productivity shocks that they believe caused each of the recessions since World War II. The critics argue that, except for the oil price shocks of 1973, 1979, and 1990, and the tech revolution of the late 1990s, historical examples of economywide productivity shocks are virtually nonexistent.

An interesting RBC response to that argument is that, in principle, economywide fluctuations could also be caused by the cumulative effects of a series of small productivity shocks. To illustrate the point that small shocks can cause large fluctuations, Figure 10.3 shows the results of a computer simulation of productivity shocks and the associated behavior of output for a simplified RBC model. In this simple RBC model, the change in output from one month to the next has two parts: (1) A fixed part that arises from normal technical progress or from a normal increase in population and employment and (2) an unpredictable part that reflects a random shock to productivity during the current month.[8] The random, computer-generated productivity shocks are shown at the bottom of Fig. 10.3, and the implied behavior of output is displayed above them. Although none of the individual shocks is large, the cumulative effect of the shocks causes large fluctuations in output that look something like business cycles. Hence business cycles may be the result of productivity shocks, even though identifying specific, large shocks is difficult.

Does the Solow Residual Measure Technology Shocks? Because productivity shocks are the primary source of business cycle fluctuations in RBC models, RBC economists have attempted to measure the size of these shocks. The most common measure of productivity shocks is known as the **Solow residual**, which is an empirical measure of total factor productivity, A. The Solow residual is named after the originator of modern growth theory, Robert Solow,[9] who used this measure in the 1950s.

Recall from Chapter 3 that, to measure total factor productivity A, we need data on output, Y, and the inputs of capital, K, and labor, N. In addition, we need to use a specific algebraic form for the production function. Then we have

$$\text{Solow residual} = \frac{Y}{K^a N^{1-a}} = A. \qquad \textbf{(10.1)}$$

The Solow residual is called a "residual" because it is the part of output that cannot be directly explained by measured capital and labor inputs.

When the Solow residual is computed from actual U.S. data, using Eq. (10.1), it turns out to be strongly procyclical, rising in economic expansions and falling in recessions. This procyclical behavior is consistent with the premise of RBC theory that cyclical fluctuations in aggregate output are driven largely by productivity shocks.

---

[8]Specifically, the model is $Y_t = 1.0025\, Y_{t-1} + e_t$, where Y_t is output in month t, Y_{t-1} is output in the previous month, and e_t is the random productivity shock in month t. The productivity shocks are randomly chosen numbers between -1.0 and 1.0. A similar example is given in Numerical Problem 6 at the end of this chapter.

[9]"Technical Change and the Aggregate Production Function," *Review of Economics and Statistics*, 1957, pp. 312–320. In Chapter 6 we described Solow's contributions to growth theory.

FIGURE 10.3

Small shocks and large cycles

A computer simulation of a simple RBC model is used to find the relationship between computer-generated random productivity shocks (shown at the bottom of the figure) and aggregate output (shown in the middle of the figure). Even though all of the productivity shocks are small, the simulation produces large cyclical fluctuations in aggregate output. Thus large productivity shocks aren't necessary to generate large cyclical fluctuations.

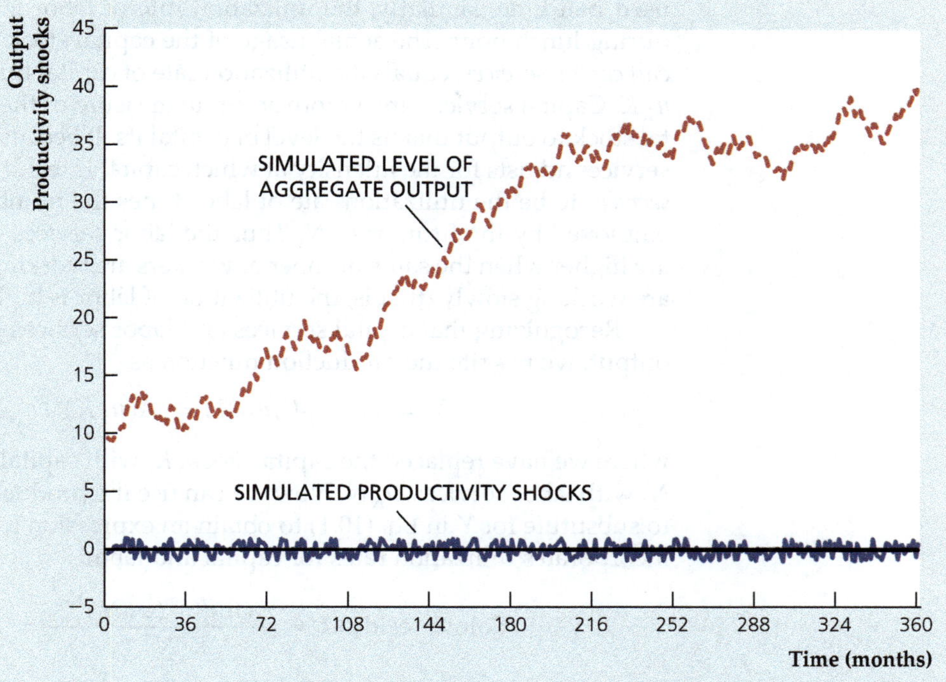

However, some economists have questioned whether the Solow residual should be interpreted solely as a measure of technology, as early RBC proponents tended to do. If changes in the Solow residual reflect only changes in the technologies available to an economy, its value should be unrelated to factors such as government purchases or monetary policy that don't directly affect scientific and technological progress (at least in the short run). However, statistical studies reveal that the Solow residual is in fact correlated with factors such as government expenditures, suggesting that movements in the Solow residual may also reflect the impacts of other factors.[10]

To understand why measured productivity can vary, even if the actual technology used in production doesn't change, we need to recognize that capital and labor sometimes are used more intensively than at other times and that more intensive use of inputs leads to higher output. For instance, a robotic car assembly tool used full-time contributes more to production than an otherwise identical tool used half-time. Similarly, workers working rapidly (for example, restaurant workers during a busy lunch hour) will produce more output and revenue than the same number of workers working more slowly (the same restaurant workers during the afternoon lull). To capture the idea that capital and labor resources can be used more or less intensively at different times, we define the *utilization rate of capital*, u_K, and the *utilization rate of labor*, u_N. The utilization rate of a factor measures the intensity at which it is being used. For example, the utilization rate of capital for the printing press run full-time would be twice as high as for the printing press

[10]Changes in technology might well be correlated with changes in government spending on research and development (R&D). However, the Solow residual is also highly correlated with non-R&D government spending and with lags too short to be accounted for by the effects of spending on the rate of invention.

used half-time; similarly, the utilization rate of labor is higher in the restaurant during lunch hour. The actual usage of the capital stock in production, which we call *capital services*, equals the utilization rate of capital times the stock of capital, or $u_K K$. Capital services are a more accurate measure of the contribution of the capital stock to output than is the level of capital itself because the definition of capital services adjusts for the intensity at which capital is used. Similarly, we define *labor services* to be the utilization rate of labor times the number of workers (or hours) employed by the firm, or $u_N N$. Thus the labor services received by an employer are higher when the same number of workers are working rapidly than when they are working slowly (that is, the utilization of labor is higher).

Recognizing that capital services and labor services go into the production of output, we rewrite the production function as

$$Y = AF(u_K K, u_N N) = A(u_K K)^a (u_N N)^{1-a}, \tag{10.2}$$

where we have replaced the capital stock, K, with capital services, $u_K K$, and labor, N, with labor services, $u_N N$. Now we can use the production function in Eq. (10.2) to substitute for Y in Eq. (10.1) to obtain an expression for the Solow residual that incorporates utilization rates for capital and labor:

$$\text{Solow residual} = \frac{A(u_K K)^a (u_N N)^{1-a}}{K^a N^{1-a}} = A u_K{}^a u_N{}^{1-a}. \tag{10.3}$$

Equation (10.3) shows that the Solow residual, as conventionally measured, includes not only parameter A (which reflects technology and perhaps other factors affecting productivity) but also utilization rates of capital and labor, u_K and u_N. Thus even if technology were unchanging, the calculated Solow residual would be procyclical if the utilization rates of capital and labor were procyclical.

There is evidence that utilization is procyclical (so that capital and labor are worked harder in boom periods than in economic slumps). For example, Craig Burnside of Duke University, and Martin Eichenbaum and Sergio Rebelo[11], both of Northwestern University, studied the cyclical behavior of capital utilization by using data on the amount of electricity used by producers. Their rationale for using data on electricity is that additional electricity is needed to increase capital utilization, whether the increased utilization is achieved by operating capital for an increased number of hours per day or by increasing the speed at which the capital is operated. This study revealed that electricity used per unit of capital rises in economic upturns, leading the authors to conclude that capital utilization is strongly procyclical. In addition, this study showed that a measure of technology, analogous to the term A in Eq. (10.2), is much less procyclical than is the Solow residual.

Measuring the cyclical behavior of labor utilization is more difficult, but various studies have found evidence that the utilization rate of labor is also procyclical. For example, Jon Fay and James Medoff[12] of Harvard University sent questionnaires to large manufacturing enterprises, asking about employment and production during the most recent downturn experienced at each plant. Fay and Medoff found that during a downturn the average plant surveyed cut production by 31% and cut its total use of blue-collar hours to 23% below the normal level.

---

[11]"Capital Utilization and Returns to Scale," in B. Bernanke and J. Rotemberg, eds., *NBER Macroeconomics Annual*, 1995.

[12]"Labor and Output Over the Business Cycle," *American Economic Review*, September 1985, pp. 638–655.

Plant managers estimated that total hours could have been reduced by an additional 6% of the normal level without further reducing output. Of this 6% of normal hours, about half (3% of normal hours) were typically assigned to various types of useful work, including equipment maintenance and overhaul, painting, cleaning, reworking output, and training. The remaining 3% of normal hours were assigned to "make-work" and other unproductive activities. These numbers suggest that firms utilize labor less intensively during recessions.

The tendency to use workers less intensively in recessions than in expansions has been referred to as labor hoarding. **Labor hoarding** occurs when, because of the costs of firing and hiring workers, firms retain some workers in a recession that they would otherwise lay off. Firms keep these workers on the payroll to avoid the costs of laying off workers and then rehiring them or hiring and training new workers when the economy revives. Hoarded labor either works less hard during the recession (there is less to do) or is put to work doing tasks, such as maintaining equipment, that aren't measured as part of the firm's output. When the economy revives, the hoarded labor goes back to working in the normal way. In much the same way, it may not pay the restaurant owner to send her workers home between the lunch and dinner rush hours, with the result that restaurant workers are less productive during the slow afternoon period. This lower rate of productivity during recessions (or during the afternoon slow period, in the restaurant) doesn't reflect changes in the available technology, but only changes in the rate at which firms utilize capital and labor. Hence you should be cautious about interpreting cyclical changes in the Solow residual (equivalently, total factor productivity, A) as solely reflecting changes in technology.

Although changes in technology or the utilization rates of capital and labor might cause aggregate cyclical fluctuations, history suggests that shocks other than productivity shocks also affect the economy; wars and the corresponding military buildups are but one obvious example. Thus many classical economists favor a broader definition of classical business cycle theory that allows for both productivity and other types of shocks to have an impact on the economy. Because the models they use allow for shocks other than "real" productivity shocks, the models are not called RBC models but rather dynamic, stochastic, general equilibrium (DSGE) models, as they model behavior over time (dynamic), allow for shocks to the economy (stochastic), and are based on general equilibrium concepts.

The macroeconomic effects of shocks other than productivity shocks can be analyzed with the classical *IS–LM* model. Let's use it to examine the effects of fiscal policy shocks.

10.2 Fiscal Policy Shocks in the Classical Model

Discuss the effects of fiscal policy shocks in the classical model.

Another type of shock that can be a source of business cycles in the classical model is a change in fiscal policy, such as an increase or decrease in real government purchases of goods and services.[13] Examples of shocks to government purchases include military buildups and the initiation of large road-building or other public

[13]Another important example of a change in fiscal policy is a change in the structure of the tax code. Classical economists argue that the greatest effects of tax changes are those that affect people's incentives to work, save, and invest, and thus affect full-employment output. However, because most classical economists accept the Ricardian equivalence proposition, they wouldn't expect lump-sum changes in taxes without accompanying changes in government purchases to have much effect on the economy.

works programs. Because government purchases are procyclical—and in particular, because national output tends to be above normal during wars and at other times when military spending is high—we need to explore how shocks to government purchases affect aggregate output and employment.

Let's consider what happens when the government purchases more goods, as it would, for example, when the country is at war. (Think of the increase in government purchases as temporary. Analytical Problem 2 at the end of the chapter asks you to work out what happens if the increase in government purchases is permanent.)

Figure 10.4 illustrates the effects of an increase in government purchases in the classical *IS–LM* model. Before the fiscal policy change, the economy's general equilibrium is represented by point *E* in both (a) and (b). To follow what happens after purchases rise, we start with the labor market in Fig. 10.4(a). The change in fiscal policy doesn't affect the production function or the marginal product of labor (the *MPN* curve), so the labor demand curve doesn't shift.

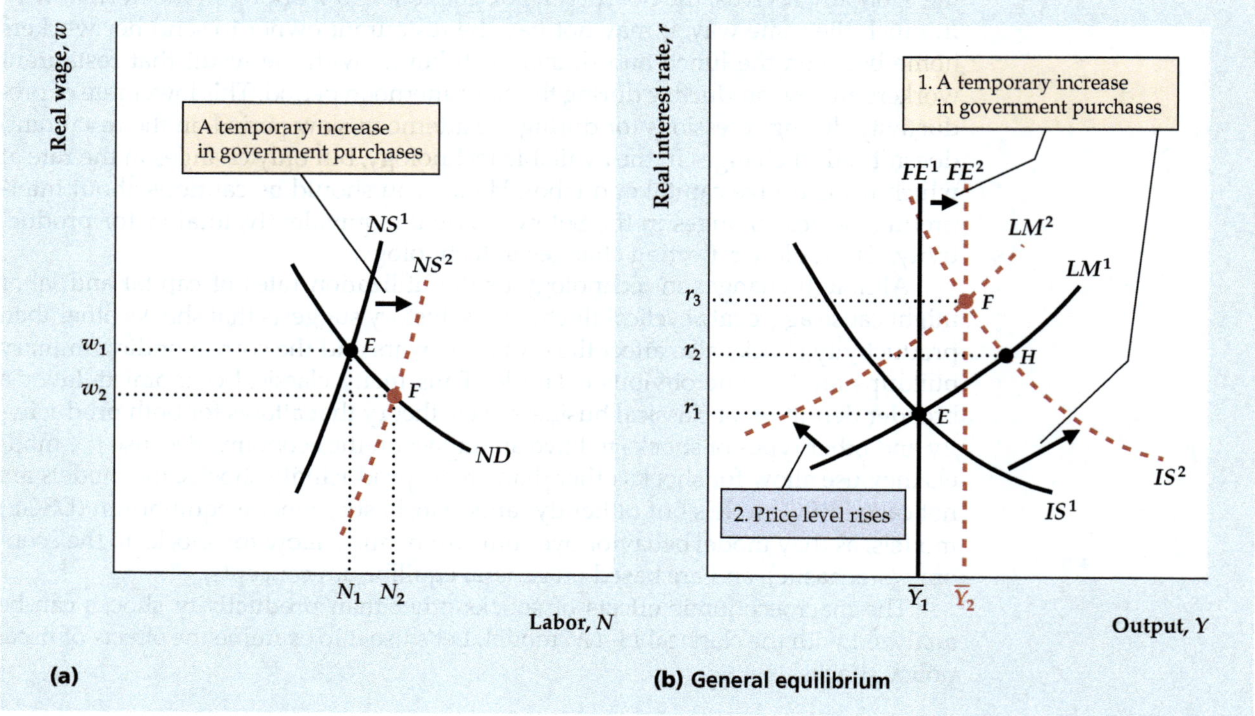

FIGURE 10.4

Effects of a temporary increase in government purchases

Initial equilibrium is at point *E* in both (a) and (b).

(a) A temporary increase in government purchases raises workers' current or future taxes. Because workers feel poorer, they supply more labor and the labor supply curve shifts to the right, from NS^1 to NS^2. The shift in the labor supply curve reduces the real wage and increases employment, as indicated by point *F*.

(b) The increase in employment raises full-employment output and shifts the *FE* line to the right, from FE^1 to FE^2. The increase in government purchases also reduces desired national saving and shifts the *IS* curve up and to the right, from IS^1 to IS^2. Because the intersection of IS^2 and LM^1 is to the right of FE^2, the aggregate quantity of output demanded is higher than the full-employment level of output, $\bar{Y}_2$, so the price level rises. The rise in the price level reduces the real money supply and shifts the *LM* curve up and to the left, from LM^1 to LM^2, until the new general equilibrium is reached at point *F*. The effect of the increase in government purchases is to increase output, the real interest rate, and the price level.

However, classical economists argue that an increase in government purchases will affect labor supply by reducing workers' wealth. People are made less wealthy because, if the government increases the amount of the nation's output that it takes for military purposes, less output will be left for private consumption and investment. This negative impact of increased government purchases on private wealth is most obvious if the government pays for its increased military spending by raising current taxes.[14] However, even if the government doesn't raise current taxes to pay for the extra military spending and borrows the funds it needs, taxes will still have to be raised in the future to pay the principal and interest on this extra government borrowing. So, whether or not taxes are currently raised, under the classical assumption that output is always at its full-employment level, an increase in government military spending effectively makes people poorer.

In Chapter 3 we showed that a decrease in wealth increases labor supply because someone who is poorer can afford less leisure. Thus according to the classical analysis, an increase in government purchases—which makes people financially worse off—should lead to an increase in aggregate labor supply.[15] The increase in government purchases causes the labor supply curve to shift to the right, from NS^1 to NS^2 in Fig. 10.4(a). Following the shift of the labor supply curve, the equilibrium in the labor market shifts from point E to point F, with employment increasing and the real wage decreasing.[16]

The effects of the increase in government purchases in the classical *IS–LM* framework are shown in Fig. 10.4(b). First, note that, because equilibrium employment increases, full-employment output, $\bar{Y}$, also increases. Thus the *FE* line shifts to the right, from FE^1 to FE^2.

In addition to shifting the *FE* line to the right, the fiscal policy change shifts the *IS* curve. Recall that, at any level of output, a temporary increase in government purchases reduces desired national saving and raises the real interest rate that clears the goods market. Thus the *IS* curve shifts up and to the right, from IS^1 to IS^2. (See also Summary table 12 in Chapter 9.) The *LM* curve isn't directly affected by the change in fiscal policy.

The new *IS* curve, IS^2, the initial *LM* curve, LM^1, and the new *FE* line, FE^2, have no common point of intersection. For general equilibrium to be restored, prices must adjust, shifting the *LM* curve until it passes through the intersection of IS^2 and FE^2 (point F). Will prices rise or fall? The answer to this question is ambiguous because the fiscal policy change has increased both the aggregate demand for goods (by reducing desired saving and shifting the *IS* curve up and to the right) and the full-employment level of output (by increasing labor supply and shifting the *FE* line to the right). If we assume that the effect on labor supply and full-employment output of the increase in government purchases isn't too large (probably a reasonable assumption), after the fiscal policy change the

[14]For simplicity, we assume that the tax increase is a lump sum. A tax increase that isn't a lump sum—for example, one that changes the effective tax rate on capital—has complicating effects.

[15]In theory, the effect on labor supply of an increase in government purchases should be the strongest for spending, such as military spending, that extracts resources without providing any direct benefits to the private sector. Government purchases that effectively replace private consumption expenditures—for example, purchases of medical services, roads, or playgrounds—should in principle have a smaller negative impact on people's economic well-being and thus a smaller positive effect on labor supply.

[16]Note that this labor supply effect was omitted from our discussion of the impact of increased government purchases in Chapter 4, as illustrated in Fig. 4.9.

aggregate quantity of goods demanded is likely to exceed full-employment output. In Fig. 10.4(b) the aggregate quantity of goods demanded (point H at the intersection of IS^2 and LM^1) exceeds full-employment output, $\bar{Y}_2$. Thus the price level must rise, shifting the LM curve up and to the left and causing the economy to return to general equilibrium at F. At F both output and the real interest rate are higher than at the initial equilibrium point, E.

Therefore the increase in government purchases increases output, employment, the real interest rate, and the price level. Because the increase in employment is the result of an increase in labor supply rather than an increase in labor demand, real wages fall when government purchases rise. Because of diminishing marginal productivity of labor, the increase in employment also implies a decline in average labor productivity when government purchases rise.

That fiscal shocks play some role in business cycles seems reasonable, which is itself justification for including them in the model. However, including fiscal shocks along with productivity shocks in the RBC model has the additional advantage of improving the match between model and data. We previously noted that government purchases are procyclical, which is consistent with the preceding analysis. Another advantage of adding fiscal shocks to a model that also contains productivity shocks is that it improves the model's ability to explain the behavior of labor productivity.

Refer back to Fig. 10.2 to recall a weakness of the RBC model with only productivity shocks: It predicts that average labor productivity and GNP are highly correlated. In fact, RBC theory predicts a correlation that is more than twice the actual correlation. However, as we have just shown, a classical business cycle model with shocks to government purchases predicts a negative correlation between labor productivity and GNP because a positive shock to government purchases raises output but lowers average productivity. A classical business cycle model that includes *both* shocks to productivity and shocks to government purchases can match the empirically observed correlation of productivity and GNP well, without reducing the fit of the model in other respects.[17] Thus adding fiscal shocks to the real business cycle model seems to improve its ability to explain the actual behavior of the economy.

Should Fiscal Policy Be Used to Dampen the Cycle? Our analysis shows that changes in government purchases can have real effects on the economy. Changes in the tax laws can also have real effects on the economy in the classical model, although these effects are more complicated and depend mainly on the nature of the tax, the type of income or revenue that is taxed, and so on. Potentially, then, changes in fiscal policy could be used to offset cyclical fluctuations and stabilize output and employment; for example, the government could increase its purchases during recessions. This observation leads to the second of the two questions posed in the introduction to the chapter: Should policymakers use fiscal policy to smooth business cycle fluctuations?

Recall that classical economists generally oppose active attempts to dampen cyclical fluctuations because of Adam Smith's invisible-hand argument that free markets produce efficient outcomes without government intervention. The classical

[17]See Lawrence Christiano and Martin Eichenbaum, "Current Real-Business-Cycle Theories and Aggregate Labor-Market Fluctuations," *American Economic Review*, June 1992, pp. 430–450. The analysis of this paper is technically complex, but it gives a flavor of research in classical business cycle analysis.

view holds that prices and wages adjust fairly rapidly to bring the economy into general equilibrium, allowing little scope for the government to improve the macroeconomy's response to economic disturbances. Therefore, although in principle fiscal policy could be used to fight recessions and reduce output fluctuations, classical economists advise against using this approach. Instead, classicals argue that not interfering in the economy's adjustment to disturbances is better.

This skepticism about the value of active antirecessionary policies does not mean that classical economists don't regard recessions as a serious problem. If an adverse productivity shock causes a recession, for example, real wages, employment, and output all fall, which means that many people experience economic hardship. But would offsetting the recession by, for example, increasing government purchases help? In the classical analysis, a rise in government purchases increases output by raising the amount of labor supplied, and the amount of labor supplied is increased by making workers poorer (as a result of higher current or future taxes). Thus under the classical assumption that the economy is always in general equilibrium, increasing government purchases for the sole purpose of increasing output and employment makes people worse off rather than better off. Classical economists conclude that government purchases should be increased only if the benefits of the expanded government program—in terms of improved military security or public services, for example—exceed the costs to taxpayers. Classicals apply this criterion for useful government spending—that the benefits should exceed the costs—whether or not the economy is currently in recession.

So far we have assumed that, because fiscal policy affects the equilibrium levels of employment and output, the government is capable of using fiscal policy to achieve the levels of employment and output it chooses. However, a variety of *lags* in the process may prevent fiscal policy from being effective. It may take time to realize that policy is needed, known as the *recognition lag*. The lawmaking process can lead to a *legislative lag* between the time that a fiscal policy change is proposed and the time that it is enacted. Additional lags occur in implementing the new policies *(implementation lag)* and in the response of the economy to the policy changes (*impact lag*). Because of these lags, fiscal policy changes contemplated today should be based on where the economy will be several quarters in the future; unfortunately, forecasting the future of the economy is an inexact art at best.[18] Beyond the problems of forecasting, policymakers also face uncertainties about how and by how much to modify their policies to get the desired output and employment effects. Classical economists cite these practical difficulties as another reason for not using fiscal policy to fight recessions.

10.3 Unemployment in the Classical Model

Discuss unemployment in the classical model.

A major weakness of the classical model is that it doesn't explain why unemployment rises during business downturns. Indeed, in the simple classical, or supply- and-demand, model of the labor market, unemployment is literally zero: Anyone who wants to work at the market-clearing wage can find a job. Of course, in reality unemployment is never zero. Furthermore, the sharp increases in

[18]Note that these lags also apply to monetary policy, as we discuss in Chapter 14, except that there is not a legislative lag for monetary policy.

unemployment that occur during recessions are a principal reason that policymakers and the public are so concerned about economic downturns.

Classical economists are perfectly aware of this issue, and they have developed more sophisticated versions of the classical business cycle model to account for unemployment. The main modification they make to the simple supply-and-demand model of the labor market is to drop the model's implicit assumption that all workers and jobs are the same. Rather than all being the same, workers in the real world have different abilities, skills, and interests, among other things; jobs entail different skill requirements, work environments, locations, and other characteristics. Because workers and jobs both vary in so many ways, matching workers to jobs isn't instantaneous and free but time-consuming and costly. The fact that someone who has lost a job or has just entered the labor force must spend time and effort to find a new job helps explain why there always are some unemployed people.

Some classical economists suggest that differences among workers and among jobs explain not only why the unemployment rate is always greater than zero, but also why unemployment rises so sharply in recessions. They argue that productivity shocks and other macroeconomic disturbances that cause recessions also often increase the degree of mismatch between workers and firms.[19] Thus a major adverse productivity shock might affect the various industries and regions within the country differently, with jobs being destroyed in some sectors but new opportunities emerging in others. An oil price shock, for example, would eliminate jobs in energy-intensive industries but create new opportunities in industries that supply energy or are light energy users.

Following such a shock, workers in industries and regions where labor demand has fallen will be induced to search elsewhere for jobs, which raises the frictional component of unemployment. Some of these workers will find that their skills don't match the requirements of industries with growing labor demand; these workers may become chronically unemployed, raising structural unemployment.[20] With many unemployed workers looking for jobs, and because creating new jobs takes a while, the time necessary to find a new job is likely to increase. For all these reasons, an adverse productivity shock may raise unemployment as well as reduce output and employment. Note that this predicted rise in frictional and structural unemployment during recessions is the same as an increase in the natural rate of unemployment (the sum of frictional and structural unemployment rates).

What is the evidence of worker–job mismatch and unemployment? The process of job creation and job destruction in U.S. manufacturing has been studied in some detail by Steven Davis of the University of Chicago and John Haltiwanger[21] of the University of Maryland. Using data for 160,000 manufacturing plants, the authors showed that, during the 1973–1986 period, about 11% of all existing manufacturing jobs disappeared, on average, each year, reflecting plant closings and cutbacks. During a typical year, about 81% of these lost jobs were replaced by newly created jobs elsewhere in the manufacturing sector (so that, overall, employment in manufacturing shrank over the period). Thus Davis and Haltiwanger confirmed that a great deal of "churning" of jobs and workers occurs in the economy.

---

[19]This idea was proposed in David Lilien, "Sectoral Shifts and Cyclical Unemployment," *Journal of Political Economy,* August 1982, pp. 777–793.

[20]See Chapter 3 for definitions and discussion of frictional and structural unemployment.

[21]"Gross Job Creation, Gross Job Destruction, and Employment Reallocation," *Quarterly Journal of Economics,* August 1992, pp. 819–864.

They also showed that much of this churning reflected closing of old plants and opening of new ones *within the same industries,* rather than a general decline in some industries and growth in others. Thus reallocation of workers within industries seems to be as important as movement of workers between industries as a source of unemployment.

Figure 10.5 shows the rates of job creation and destruction in U.S. nonfarm private businesses for the years 1978–2019.[22] You can see that during or immediately following recession years, such as 1981–1982, 1990–1991, 2001, and 2007–2009, more jobs were destroyed than created—although a significant number of new jobs were created even in recession years, reflecting shifts of workers among firms and industries. The biggest excess of job destruction over job creation came in the aftermath of the 2007–2009 recession. The rate of job destruction exceeded the rate of job creation by almost 5 percentage points in 2009 and remained nearly 2 percentage points higher than the job creation rate in 2010 before finally falling below the job creation rate in 2011.

It seems clear that increased mismatches between workers and jobs can't account for *all* the increase in unemployment that occurs during recessions. Much of that increase is in the form of temporary layoffs; rather than search for new jobs, many workers who are temporarily laid off simply wait until they are called back

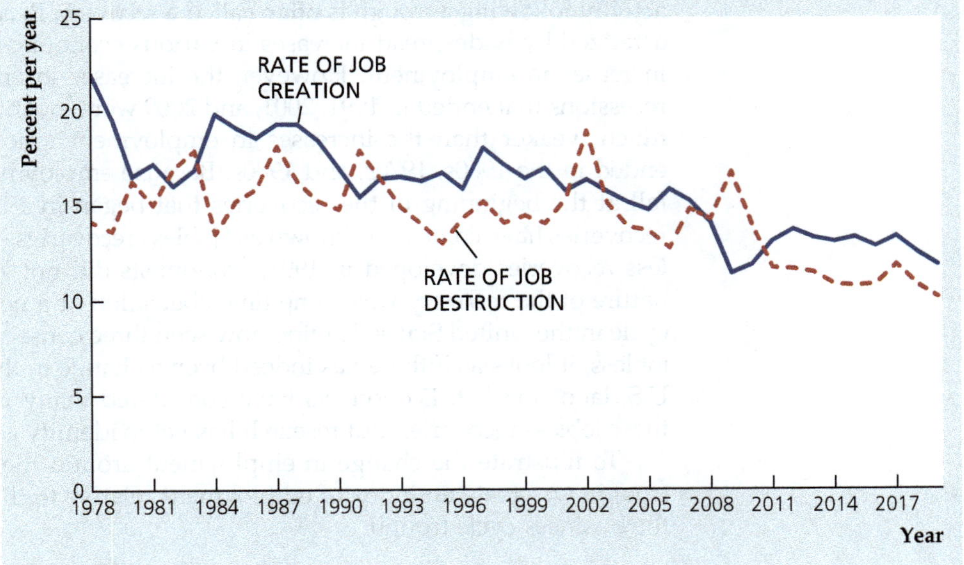

FIGURE 10.5

Rates of job creation and job destruction in U.S. private, nonfarm businesses, 1978–2019

The graph shows the rates of job creation and job destruction in the U.S. nonfarm private business sector between 1978 and 2019. Job creation is the number of new jobs created during the year in expanding firms as a percentage of existing jobs. Job destruction is the number of jobs lost during the year as a result of closing or downsizing plants, as a percentage of existing jobs.

Source: Data from U.S. Census Bureau, Business Dynamic Statistics, www.census.gov/data/datasets/time-series/econ/bds/bds-datasets.html.

[22]The data shown in Fig. 10.5 are published by the Census Bureau, based on the methods developed by Davis and Haltiwanger in the paper cited in footnote 21. Job creation and destruction data are based on data collected from business firms; job creation is net new jobs from expanding establishments and job destruction is the net loss of jobs from contracting establishments. By comparison, the data in Figs. 8.9 and 8.10 on the job finding rate and the job loss rate are based on data on individuals and show the probability that a given worker found or lost a job in a given month. Thus there may be substantial differences between job creation and job finding, as well as between job destruction and job loss.

by their old firm. Moreover, if recessions were times of increased mismatch in the labor market, more postings of vacancies and help-wanted ads during recessions would be expected; in fact, both vacancies and new job openings fall in recessions.[23] Despite these objections, however, economists generally agree that the dynamic reallocation of workers from shrinking to growing sectors is an important source of unemployment.

Modifying the classical model to allow for unemployment doesn't change the classical view that fiscal policy should not be actively used to combat recessions. Classical economists point out that raising the aggregate demand for goods (by increasing government purchases, for example) doesn't directly address the problem of unemployment arising from the mismatch that exists at the microeconomic level between workers and jobs. A better approach, in the classical view, is to eliminate barriers to labor market adjustment, such as high legal minimum wages that price low-skilled workers out of the labor market or burdensome regulations that raise businesses' costs of employing additional workers.

Jobless Recoveries

The economy reaches a business-cycle trough when aggregate economic activity stops falling and begins to increase. Because aggregate economic activity is rising after having fallen for a number of months, the increase in aggregate economic activity following a trough is often called a recovery. Recoveries are typically characterized by widespread increases in various economic activities, often including increases in employment. However, the increases in employment following the recessions that ended in 1991, 2001, and 2009 were much slower to materialize and much weaker than the increases in employment following the recessions that ended in the 1960s, 1970s, and 1980s. Because employment actually continued to fall at the beginning of the recoveries that began in 1991, 2001, and 2009, these recoveries have come to be known as "jobless recoveries." When the first of the jobless recoveries developed in 1991, economists did not know whether the jobless nature of the recovery was a one-time aberration or a new feature of the business cycle in the United States. Having now seen three consecutive recoveries that were jobless, it looks as if there has indeed been a change in the cyclical behavior of the U.S. labor market. Economists have considered many potential explanations for these jobless recoveries, but research has yet to identify a convincing explanation.

To illustrate the change in employment around the time of a business-cycle trough, we create an index of employment relative to the level of employment at the business-cycle trough:

$$\text{Index in given month} = 100 \times \frac{\text{employment in given month}}{\text{employment in trough month}}.$$

Thus the index in the trough month is simply 100. If the employment in a given month is 5% higher than in the trough month, the index has a value of 105. Similarly, an index value of 98 indicates that employment in the given month is 2% smaller than employment in the trough month.

[23]See Katharine Abraham and Lawrence Katz, "Cyclical Unemployment: Sectoral Shifts or Aggregate Disturbances?" *Journal of Political Economy*, June 1986, pp. 507–522.

Figure 10.6 is a graphical device that allows us to compare employment behavior around various business-cycle troughs. The horizontal axis shows the number of months before or after a business-cycle trough. The month of the trough is month 0 and is highlighted by the vertical line in the figure. A month that is 4 months after the trough is shown as month 4 on the horizontal axis; similarly, month −8 is 8 months before the trough. The vertical axis shows the value of the relative employment index defined above. As we have noted, for all business-cycle troughs, the value of the index is 100 in month 0, which is the month of the trough. The line labeled "Previous 5 troughs" shows the average value of the index relative to the business-cycle troughs in February 1961, November 1970, March 1975, July 1980, and November 1982. The graph also shows separate lines for the trough dates in March 1991, November 2001, and June 2009. Because the COVID recession of 2020 led to dramatically unusual swings in employment, we do not show that recession in the graph.

Figure 10.6 clearly shows the jobless nature of the three most recent recoveries. In all three cases, payroll employment continued to fall for months after the business-cycle trough, unlike in the previous five recoveries, which showed employment growth as soon as recovery began. One explanation offered for the jobless recoveries following the 1990–1991 and 2001 recessions was simply that those recessions were mild. That explanation argued that if a recession is mild, the recovery will be weak because there is not much to recover from. But the 2007–2009 recession was very deep, as you can tell by the large decline in the index of payroll employment during the recession, which declined from a value above 105 two years before the trough date. And this very deep recession was also accompanied by a very weak recovery in employment.

Another explanation is that increased labor productivity allows GDP to grow even as employment is declining. Generally, productivity growth is beneficial to the economy, as it raises incomes. But in the short run, according to Federal Reserve Chairman Ben Bernanke in 2003, "given erratic growth in final demand,

FIGURE 10.6

Payroll employment relative to business-cycle trough

The chart shows monthly values for an index of monthly payroll employment calculated as 100 × (employment in given month)/(employment in trough month). The values of this index are shown for each month from 24 months before the business-cycle trough (shown as date −24) to 24 months after the business-cycle trough (shown as date 24). The index is scaled so that its value is 100 at business-cycle troughs, which are shown by the vertical line.

Sources: Authors' calculations based on data from Bureau of Labor Statistics, downloaded from Federal Reserve Bank of St. Louis FRED database at *fred.stlouisfed.org/series/PAYEMS*.

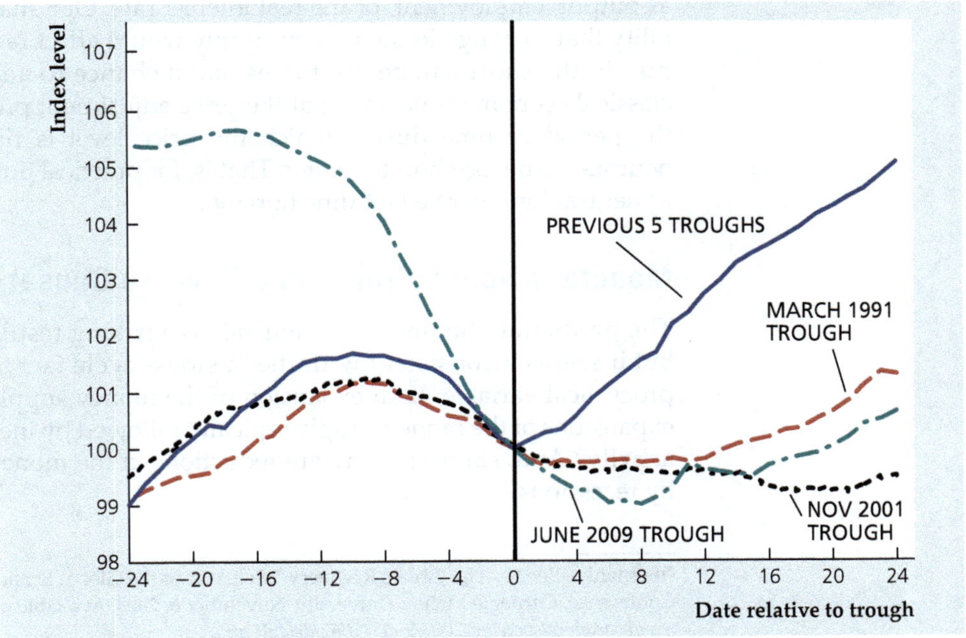

[productivity] has also enabled firms to meet the demand for their output without hiring new workers. Thus in the short run, productivity gains, coupled with growth in aggregate demand that has been insufficient to match the expansion in aggregate supply, have contributed to the slowness of the recovery of the labor market."[24] While this explanation has some appeal, it does not explain why the three most recent recoveries were jobless while the previous five recoveries exhibited job growth from the start.

10.4 Money in the Classical Model

Explain the roles of money and monetary policy in the classical model.

So far we have focused on real shocks to the economy, such as productivity shocks and changes in government purchases. However, many macroeconomists believe that nominal shocks—shocks to money supply and money demand—also affect the business cycle. In the rest of the chapter we discuss the role of money and monetary policy in the classical approach to the business cycle.

Monetary Policy and the Economy

Monetary policy refers to the central bank's decisions about how much money to supply to the economy (Chapter 7). Recall that the central bank (the Federal Reserve in the United States) can control the money supply through open market operations, in which it sells government bonds to the public in exchange for money (to reduce the money supply) or uses newly created money to buy bonds from the public (to increase the money supply).

In Chapter 9 we examined the effects of changes in the money supply, using the *IS–LM* model (Fig. 9.9) and the *AD–AS* model (Fig. 9.14). With both models we found that, after prices fully adjust, changes in the money supply are neutral: A change in the nominal money supply, M, causes the price level, P, to change proportionally, but a change in the money supply has no effect on real variables, such as output, employment, or the real interest rate. Our analysis left open the possibility that a change in the money supply would affect real variables, such as output, in the short run before prices had a chance to adjust. However, because classical economists believe that the price adjustment process is rapid, they view the period of time during which the price level is fixed—and money is not neutral—to be too short to matter. That is, for practical purposes, they view money as neutral for any relevant time horizon.

Monetary Nonneutrality and Reverse Causation

The prediction that money is neutral is a striking result of the classical model, but it seems inconsistent with the business cycle fact that money is a leading, procyclical variable. If an expansion of the money supply has no effect, why are expansions of the money supply typically followed by increased rates of economic activity? And, similarly, why are reductions in the money supply often followed by recessions?

[24]Bernanke, Ben S. "The Jobless Recovery." Remarks at the Global Economic and Investment Outlook Conference, Carnegie Mellon University, November 6, 2003. Available on-line at *www.federalreserve.gov/boarddocs/speeches/2003/200311062/default.htm.*

Some classical economists have responded to these questions by pointing out that, although increases in the money supply tend to *precede* expansions in output, this fact doesn't necessarily prove that economic expansions are caused by those increases. After all, just because people put storm windows on their houses before winter begins doesn't mean that winter is caused by putting on storm windows. Rather, people put storm windows on their houses because they know that winter is coming.

Many classical economists, including RBC economists in particular, argue that the link between money growth and economic expansion is like the link between putting on storm windows and the onset of winter, a relationship they call reverse causation. Specifically, **reverse causation** means that expected future increases in output cause increases in the current money supply and that expected future decreases in output cause decreases in the current money supply, rather than the other way around. Reverse causation explains how money could be a procyclical and leading variable even if the classical model is correct and changes in the money supply are neutral and have no real effects.[25]

Reverse causation might arise in any of several ways. One possibility (which you are asked to explore in more detail in Analytical Problem 5 at the end of the chapter) is based on the idea that money demand depends on both expected future output and current output. Suppose that a firm's managers expect business to pick up considerably in the next few quarters. To prepare for this expected increase in output, the firm may need to increase its current transactions (for example, to purchase raw materials, hire workers, and so on) and thus it will demand more money now. If many firms do so, the aggregate demand for money may rise in advance of the actual increase in output.

Now suppose that the Fed observes this increase in the demand for money. If the Fed does nothing, leaving the money supply unchanged, the increase in money demand will cause the equilibrium value of the price level to fall. As one of the Fed's objectives is stable prices, it won't like this outcome; to keep prices stable, instead of doing nothing, the Fed should provide enough extra money to the economy to meet the higher money demand. But if the Fed does so, the money supply will rise in advance of the increase in output, consistent with the business cycle fact—even though money is neutral.

Undoubtedly, reverse causation explains at least some of the tendency of money to lead output. However, this explanation doesn't rule out the possibility that changes in the money supply also sometimes cause changes in output so that money is nonneutral. That is, a combination of reverse causation and monetary nonneutrality could account for the procyclical behavior of money.

The Nonneutrality of Money: Additional Evidence

Because of reverse causation, the leading and procyclical behavior of money can't by itself establish that money is nonneutral. To settle the issue of whether money is neutral, we need additional evidence. One useful source is a historical analysis of monetary policy. The classic study is Milton Friedman and Anna J. Schwartz's,

[25]Robert King and Charles Plosser, "Money, Credit, and Prices in a Real Business Cycle," *American Economic Review,* June 1984, pp. 363–380, explains reverse causation and presents supporting evidence for the idea.

A Monetary History of the United States, 1867–1960.[26] Using a variety of sources, including Federal Reserve policy statements and the journals and correspondence of monetary policymakers, Friedman and Schwartz carefully described and analyzed the causes of money supply fluctuations and the interrelation of money and other economic variables. They concluded (p. 676):

Throughout the near-century examined in detail we have found that:

1. Changes in the behavior of the money stock have been closely associated with changes in economic activity, [nominal] income, and prices.
2. The interrelation between monetary and economic change has been highly stable.
3. Monetary changes have often had an independent origin; they have not been simply a reflection of changes in economic activity.

The first two conclusions restate the basic business cycle fact that money is procyclical. The third conclusion states that reverse causation can't explain the entire relationship between money and real income or output. Friedman and Schwartz focused on historical episodes in which changes in the supply of money were not (they argued) responses to macroeconomic conditions but instead resulted from other factors such as gold discoveries (which affected money supplies under the gold standard), changes in monetary institutions, or changes in the leadership of the Federal Reserve. In the majority of these cases, "independent" changes in money growth were followed by changes in the same direction in real output. This evidence suggests that money isn't neutral.

Christina Romer and David Romer[27] of the University of California at Berkeley reviewed and updated the Friedman-Schwartz analysis. Although they disputed some of Friedman and Schwartz's interpretations, they generally agreed with the conclusion that money isn't neutral. In particular, they argued that since 1960 half a dozen additional episodes of monetary nonneutrality have occurred. Probably the most famous one occurred in 1979, when Federal Reserve Chairman Paul Volcker announced that money supply procedures would change and that the money growth rate would be reduced to fight inflation. A minor recession in 1980 and a severe downturn in 1981–1982 followed Volcker's change in monetary policy. An economic boom followed relaxation of the Fed's anti-inflationary monetary policy in 1982.

Because of the Friedman-Schwartz evidence and episodes such as the 1979–1982 Volcker policy (and a similar experience in Great Britain at the same time), most economists now believe that money is not neutral. If we accept that evidence, contrary to the prediction of the classical model, we are left with two choices: Either we must adopt a different framework for macroeconomic analysis, or we must modify the classical model. In Section 10.5 we take the second approach and consider how monetary nonneutrality can be explained in a classical model.

[26]Princeton, NJ: Princeton University Press for NBER, 1963.

[27]"Does Monetary Policy Matter? A New Test in the Spirit of Friedman and Schwartz," in Olivier Blanchard and Stanley Fischer, eds., NBER *Macroeconomics Annual*, Cambridge, MA: MIT Press, 1989.

10.5 The Misperceptions Theory and the Nonneutrality of Money

Summarize the fundamentals and implications of the misperceptions theory.

According to the classical model, prices do not remain fixed for any substantial period of time, so the horizontal short-run aggregate supply curve developed in Chapter 9 is irrelevant. The only relevant aggregate supply curve is the long-run aggregate supply curve, which is vertical. As we showed in Fig. 9.14, changes in the money supply cause the *AD* curve to shift; because the aggregate supply curve is vertical, however, the effect of the *AD* shift is simply to change prices without changing the level of output. Thus money is neutral in the classical model.

For money to be nonneutral, the relevant aggregate supply curve must not be vertical. In this section, we extend the classical model to incorporate the assumption that producers have imperfect information about the general price level and thus sometimes misinterpret changes in the general price level as changes in the relative prices of the goods that they produce. We demonstrate that the assumption that producers may misperceive the aggregate price level—the *misperceptions theory*—implies a short-run aggregate supply curve that isn't vertical. Unlike the short-run aggregate supply curve developed in Chapter 9, however, the short-run aggregate supply curve based on the misperceptions theory doesn't require the assumption that prices are slow to adjust. Even though prices may adjust instantaneously, the short-run aggregate supply curve slopes upward, so money is nonneutral in the short run.

The misperceptions theory was originally proposed by Nobel laureate Milton Friedman and then was rigorously formulated by another Nobel laureate, Robert E. Lucas, Jr., of the University of Chicago.[28] According to the **misperceptions theory**, *the aggregate quantity of output supplied rises above the full-employment level,* $\bar{Y}$, *when the aggregate price level,* P, *is higher than expected.* Thus for any expected price level, the aggregate supply curve relating the price level and the aggregate quantity of output supplied slopes upward.

If you took a course in the principles of economics, you learned that supply curves generally slope upward, with higher prices leading to increased production. However, just as the demand curves for individual goods differ from the aggregate demand curve, the supply curves for individual goods differ from the aggregate supply curve. An ordinary supply curve relates the supply of some good to the price of that good *relative to other prices.* In contrast, the aggregate supply curve relates the aggregate amount of output produced to the *general price level.* Changes in the general price level can occur while the relative prices of individual goods remain unchanged.

To understand the misperceptions theory and why it implies an upward-sloping aggregate supply curve, let's think about an individual producer of a particular good, say bread. For simplicity, consider a bakery owned and operated by one person, a baker. The baker devotes all his labor to making bread and earns all his income from selling bread. Thus the price of bread is effectively the baker's nominal wage, and the price of bread relative to the general price level is the baker's real wage. When the relative price of bread increases, the baker responds to this increase in his current real wage by working more and producing more bread. Similarly, when the

[28]See Friedman, "The Role of Monetary Policy," *American Economic Review,* March 1968, pp. 1–17. Lucas's formalization of Friedman's theory was first presented in Lucas's article, "Expectations and the Neutrality of Money," *Journal of Economic Theory,* April 1972, pp. 103–124.

price of bread falls relative to the other prices in the economy, the baker's current real wage falls and he decreases the amount of bread he produces.

But how does an individual baker know whether the relative price of bread has changed? To calculate the relative price of bread, the baker needs to know both the nominal price of bread and the general price level. The baker knows the nominal price of bread because he sells bread every day and observes the price directly. However, the baker probably is not as well informed about the general price level because he observes the prices of the many goods and services he might want to buy less frequently than he observes the price of bread. Thus in calculating the relative price of bread, the baker can't use the actual current price level. The best he can do is to use his previously formed expectation of the current price level to estimate the actual price level.

Suppose that before he observes the current market price of bread, the baker expected an overall inflation rate of 5%. How will he react if he then observes that the price of bread increases by 5%? The baker reasons as follows: I expected the overall rate of inflation to be 5%, and now I know that the price of bread has increased by 5%. This 5% increase in the price of bread is consistent with what I had expected. My best estimate is that all prices increased by 5%, and thus I think that the relative price of bread is unchanged. There is no reason to change my output.

The baker's logic applies equally to suppliers of output in the aggregate. Suppose that all suppliers expected the nominal price level to increase by 5% and that in fact all prices do increase by 5%. Then each supplier will estimate that its relative price hasn't changed and won't change its output. Hence, if expected inflation is 5%, an actual increase in prices of 5% won't affect aggregate output.

For a change in the nominal price of bread to affect the quantity of bread produced, the increase in the nominal price of bread must differ from the *expected* increase in the general price level. For example, suppose that the baker expected the general price level to increase by 5% but then observes that the price of bread rises by 8%. The baker then estimates that the relative price of bread has increased so that the real wage he or she earns from baking is higher. In response to the perceived increase in the relative price, he or she increases the production of bread.

Again, the same logic applies to the economy in the aggregate. Suppose that everyone expects the general price level to increase by 5%, but instead it actually increases by 8%, with the prices of all goods increasing by 8%. Now all producers will estimate that the relative prices of the goods they make have increased, and hence the production of all goods will increase. Thus a greater than expected increase of the price level will tend to raise output. Similarly, if the price level actually increases by only 2% when all producers expected a 5% increase, producers will think that the relative prices of their own goods have declined; in response, all suppliers reduce their output.

Thus according to the misperceptions theory, the amount of output that producers choose to supply depends on the actual general price level compared to the expected general price level. When the price level exceeds what was expected, producers are fooled into thinking that the relative prices of their own goods have risen, and they increase their output. Similarly, when the price level is lower than expected, producers believe that the relative prices of their goods have fallen, and they reduce their output. This relation between output and prices is captured by the equation

$$Y = \bar{Y} + b(P - P^e), \tag{10.4}$$

where b is a positive number that describes how strongly output responds when the actual price level exceeds the expected price level. Equation (10.4) summarizes the misperceptions theory by showing that output, Y, exceeds full-employment output, $\bar{Y}$, when the price level, P, exceeds the expected price level, P^e.

To obtain an aggregate supply curve from the misperceptions theory, we graph Eq. (10.4) in Figure 10.7. Given full-employment output, $\bar{Y}$, and the expected price level, P^e, the aggregate supply curve slopes upward, illustrating the relation between the amount of output supplied, Y, and the actual price level, P. Because an increase in the price level of ΔP increases the amount of the output supplied by $\Delta Y = b\Delta P$, the slope of the aggregate supply curve is $\Delta P/\Delta Y = 1/b$. Thus the aggregate supply curve is steep if b is small and is relatively flat if b is large.

Point E helps us locate the aggregate supply curve. At E the price level, P, equals the expected price level, P^e, so that (from Eq. 10.4) the amount of output supplied equals full-employment output, $\bar{Y}$. When the actual price level is higher than expected ($P > P^e$), the aggregate supply curve shows that the amount of output supplied is greater than $\bar{Y}$; when the price level is lower than expected ($P < P^e$), output is less than $\bar{Y}$.

The aggregate curve in Fig. 10.7 is called the short-run aggregate supply (*SRAS*) curve because it applies only to the short period of time that P^e remains unchanged. When P^e rises, the *SRAS* curve shifts up because a higher value of P is needed to satisfy Eq. (10.4) for given values of Y and $\bar{Y}$. When P^e falls, the *SRAS* curve shifts down. In the long run, people learn what is actually happening to prices, and the expected price level adjusts to the actual price level ($P = P^e$). When the actual price level equals the expected price level, no misperceptions remain and producers supply the full-employment level of output. In terms of Eq. (10.4), in the long run P equals P^e, and output, Y, equals full-employment

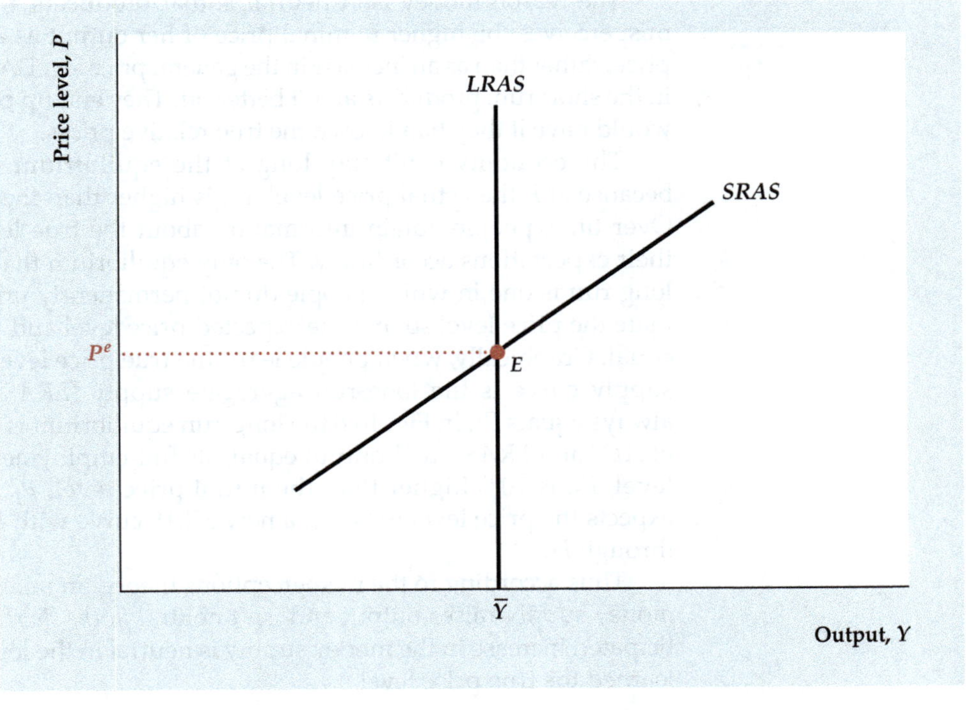

FIGURE 10.7

The aggregate supply curve in the misperceptions theory

The misperceptions theory holds that, for a given value of the expected price level, P^e, an increase in the actual price level, P, fools producers into increasing output. This relationship between output and the price level is shown by the short-run aggregate supply (*SRAS*) curve. Along the *SRAS* curve, output equals $\bar{Y}$ when prices equal their expected level ($P = P^e$, at point E), output exceeds $\bar{Y}$ when the price level is higher than expected ($P > P^e$), and output is less than $\bar{Y}$ when the price level is lower than expected ($P < P^e$). In the long run, the expected price level equals the actual price level so that output equals $\bar{Y}$. Thus the long-run aggregate supply (*LRAS*) curve is vertical at $Y = \bar{Y}$.

output, $\bar{Y}$. In the long run, then, the supply of output doesn't depend on the price level. Thus as in Chapters 8 and 9, the long-run aggregate supply (*LRAS*) curve is vertical at the point where output equals $\bar{Y}$.

Monetary Policy and the Misperceptions Theory

Let's now reexamine the neutrality of money in the extended version of the classical model based on the misperceptions theory. This framework highlights an important distinction between anticipated and unanticipated changes in the money supply: Unanticipated changes in the nominal money supply have real effects, but anticipated changes are neutral and have no real effects.

Unanticipated Changes in the Money Supply. Suppose that the economy is initially in general equilibrium at point *E* in Figure 10.8, where AD^1 intersects $SRAS^1$. Here, output equals the full-employment level, $\bar{Y}$, and the price level and the expected price level both equal P_1. Suppose that everyone expects the money supply and the price level to remain constant but that the Fed unexpectedly and without publicity increases the money supply by 10%. A 10% increase in the money supply shifts the *AD* curve up and to the right, from AD^1 to AD^2, such that for a given *Y*, the price level on AD^2 is 10% higher than the price level on AD^1. With the expected price level equal to P_1, the *SRAS* curve remains unchanged, still passing through point *E*.

The increase in aggregate demand bids up the price level to the new equilibrium level, P_2, where AD^2 intersects $SRAS^1$ (point *F*). In the new short-run equilibrium at *F*, the actual price level exceeds the expected price level and output exceeds $\bar{Y}$. Because the increase in the money supply leads to a rise in output, money isn't neutral in this analysis.

The reason money isn't neutral is that producers are fooled. Each producer misperceives the higher nominal price of her output as an increase in its relative price, rather than as an increase in the general price level. Although output increases in the short run, producers aren't better off. They end up producing more than they would have if they had known the true relative prices.

The economy can't stay long at the equilibrium represented by point *F* because at *F* the actual price level, P_2, is higher than the expected price level, P_1. Over time, people obtain information about the true level of prices and adjust their expectations accordingly. The only equilibrium that can be sustained in the long run is one in which people do not permanently underestimate or overestimate the price level so that the expected price level and the actual price level are equal. Graphically, when people learn the true price level, the relevant aggregate supply curve is the long-run aggregate supply (*LRAS*) curve, along which *P* always equals P^e. In Fig. 10.8 the long-run equilibrium is point *H*, the intersection of AD^2 and *LRAS*. At *H* output equals its full-employment level, $\bar{Y}$, and the price level, P_3, is 10% higher than the initial price level, P_1. Because everyone now expects the price level to be P_3, a new *SRAS* curve with $P^e = P_3$, $SRAS^2$, passes through *H*.

Thus according to the misperceptions theory, an unanticipated increase in the money supply raises output and isn't neutral *in the short run*. However, an unanticipated increase in the money supply is neutral in the long run, after people have learned the true price level.

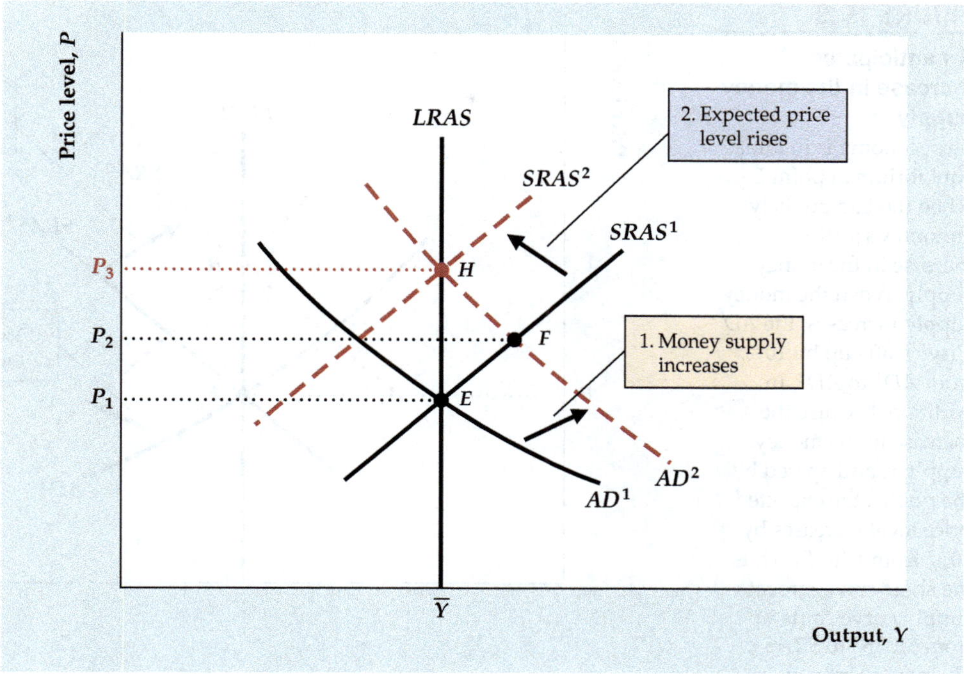

FIGURE 10.8

An unanticipated increase in the money supply

If we start from the initial equilibrium at point *E*, an unanticipated 10% increase in the money supply shifts the *AD* curve up and to the right, from AD^1 to AD^2, such that for a given *Y*, the price level on AD^2 is 10% higher than the price level on AD^1. The short-run equilibrium is located at point *F*, the intersection of AD^2 and the short-run aggregate supply curve $SRAS^1$, where prices and output are both higher than at point *E*. Thus an unanticipated change in the money supply isn't neutral in the short run. In the long run, people learn the true price level and the equilibrium shifts to point *H*, the intersection of AD^2 and the long-run aggregate supply curve *LRAS*. In the long-run equilibrium at *H*, the price level has risen by 10% but output returns to its full-employment level, $\bar{Y}$, so that money is neutral in the long run. As expectations of the price level rise from P_1 to P_3, the *SRAS* curve also shifts up until it passes through *H*.

Anticipated Changes in the Money Supply. In the extended classical model based on the misperceptions theory, the effects of an anticipated money supply increase are different from the effects of a surprise money supply increase. Figure 10.9 illustrates the effects of an anticipated money supply increase. Again, the initial general equilibrium point is at *E*, where output equals its full-employment level and the actual and expected price levels both equal P_1, just as in Fig. 10.8. Suppose that the Federal Reserve announces that it is going to increase the money supply by 10% and that the public believes this announcement.

As we have shown, a 10% increase in the money supply shifts the *AD* curve, from AD^1 to AD^2, where for each output level *Y*, the price level *P* on AD^2 is 10% higher than on AD^1. However, in this case the *SRAS* curve also shifts up. The reason is that the public's expected price level rises as soon as people learn of the increase in the money supply. Suppose that people expect—correctly—that the price level will also rise by 10% so that P^e rises by 10%, from P_1 to P_3. Then the new *SRAS* curve, $SRAS^2$, passes through point *H* in Fig. 10.9, where *Y* equals $\bar{Y}$ and both the actual and expected price levels equal P_3. The new equilibrium also is at *H*, where AD^2 and $SRAS^2$ intersect. At the new equilibrium, output equals its full-employment level, and prices are 10% higher than they were initially. The anticipated increase in the money supply hasn't affected output but has raised prices proportionally. Similarly, an anticipated drop in the money supply would lower prices but not affect output or other real variables. Thus *anticipated changes in the money supply are neutral in the short run as well as in the long run.* The reason is that, if producers know that increases in the nominal prices of their products are the result of an increase in the money supply and do not reflect a change in relative prices, they won't be fooled into increasing production when prices rise.

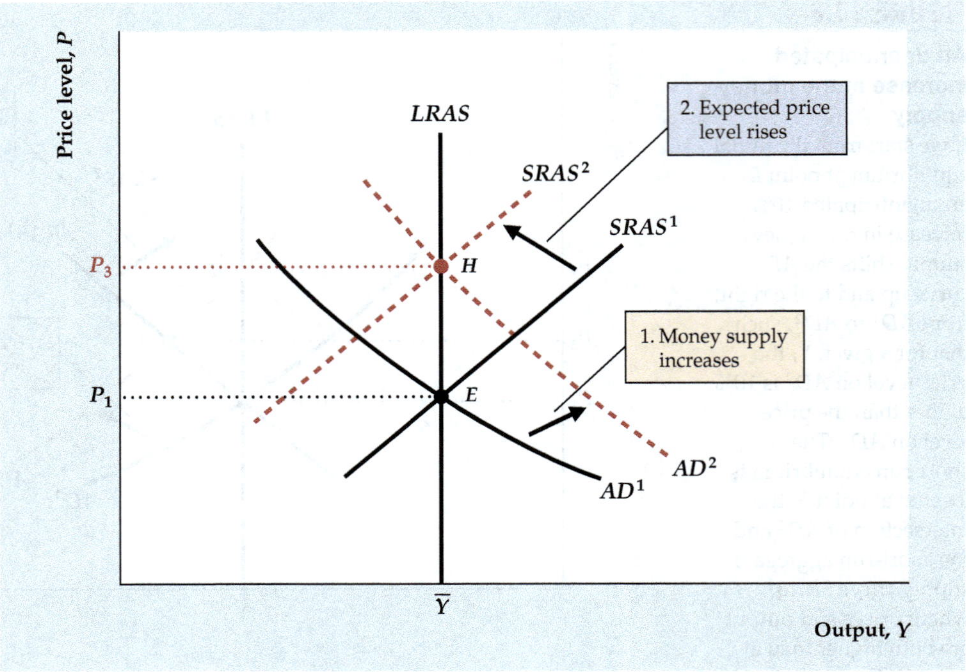

FIGURE 10.9

An anticipated increase in the money supply

The economy is in initial equilibrium at point *E* when the Fed publicly announces a 10% increase in the money supply. When the money supply increases, the *AD* curve shifts up by 10%, from AD^1 to AD^2. In addition, because the increase in the money supply is anticipated by the public, the expected price level increases by 10%, from P_1 to P_3. Thus the short-run aggregate supply curve shifts up from $SRAS^1$ to $SRAS^2$. The new short-run equilibrium, which is the same as the long-run equilibrium, is at point *H*. At *H* output is unchanged at $\bar{Y}$ and the price level is 10% higher than in the initial equilibrium at *E*. Thus an anticipated increase in the money supply is neutral in the short run as well as in the long run.

Rational Expectations and the Role of Monetary Policy

In the extended classical model based on the misperceptions theory, *unanticipated* changes in the money supply affect output, but *anticipated* changes in the money supply are neutral. Thus if the Federal Reserve wanted to use monetary policy to affect output, it seemingly should use only unanticipated changes in the money supply. So, for example, when the economy is in recession, the Fed would try to use surprise increases in the money supply to raise output; when the economy is booming, the Fed would try to use surprise decreases in the money supply to slow the economy.

A serious problem for this strategy is the presence of private economic forecasters and "Fed watchers" in financial markets. These people spend a good deal of time and effort trying to forecast macroeconomic variables such as the money supply and the price level, and their forecasts are well publicized. If the Fed began a pattern of raising the money supply in recessions and reducing it in booms, forecasters and Fed watchers would quickly understand and report this fact. As a result, the Fed's manipulations of the money supply would no longer be unanticipated, and the changes in the money supply would have no effect other than possibly causing instability in the price level. More generally, according to the misperceptions theory, to achieve any systematic change in the behavior of output, the Fed must conduct monetary policy in a way that systematically fools the public. But there are strong incentives in the financial markets and elsewhere for people to try to figure out what the Fed is doing. Thus most economists believe that attempts by the Fed to surprise the public in a systematic way cannot be successful.

The idea that the Federal Reserve cannot systematically surprise the public is part of a larger hypothesis that the public has rational expectations. The hypothesis of **rational expectations** states that the public's forecasts of various economic variables, including the money supply, the price level, and GDP, are based on reasoned and intelligent examination of available economic data.[29] (The evidence for rational expectations is discussed in "In Touch with Data and Research: Are Price Forecasts Rational?") If the public has rational expectations, it will eventually understand the Federal Reserve's general pattern of behavior. If expectations are rational, purely random changes in the money supply may be unanticipated and thus nonneutral. However, because the Fed won't be able to surprise the public systematically, it can't use monetary policy to stabilize output. Thus even if smoothing business cycles were desirable, according to the combination of the misperceptions theory and rational expectations, the Fed can't systematically use monetary policy to do so.

Propagating the Effects of Unanticipated Changes in the Money Supply. The misperceptions theory implies that unanticipated changes in the money supply are nonneutral because individual producers are temporarily fooled about the price level. However, money supply data are available weekly and price level data are reported monthly, suggesting that any misperceptions about monetary policy or the price level—and thus any real effects of money supply changes—should be quickly eliminated.

To explain how changes in the money supply can have real effects that last more than a few weeks, classical economists stress the role of propagation mechanisms. A **propagation mechanism** is an aspect of the economy that allows short-lived shocks to have relatively long-term effects on the economy.

An important example of a propagation mechanism is the behavior of inventories. Consider a manufacturing firm that has both a normal level of monthly sales and a normal amount of finished goods in inventory that it tries to maintain. Suppose that an unanticipated rise in the money supply increases aggregate demand and raises prices above their expected level. Because increasing production sharply in a short period of time is costly, the firm will respond to the increase in demand partly by producing more goods and partly by selling some finished goods from inventory, thus depleting its inventory stocks below their normal level.

Next month suppose that everyone learns the true price level and that the firm's rate of sales returns to its normal level. Despite the fact that the monetary shock has passed, the firm may continue to produce for a while at a higher than normal rate. The reason for the continued high level of production is that besides meeting its normal demand, the firm wants to replenish its inventory stock. The need to rebuild inventories illustrates a propagation mechanism that allows a short-lived shock (a monetary shock, in this case) to have a longer-term effect on the economy.

---

[29]The idea of rational expectations was first discussed by John F. Muth in his classic 1961 paper, "Rational Expectations and the Theory of Price Movements," *Econometrica*, July 1961, pp. 315–335. However, this idea wasn't widely used in macroeconomics until the new classical "revolution" of the early 1970s.

In Touch with Data and Research

Are Price Forecasts Rational?

Most classical economists assume that people have rational expectations about economic variables; that is, people make intelligent use of available information in forecasting variables that affect their economic decisions. The rational expectations assumption has important implications. For example, as we have demonstrated, if monetary nonneutrality is the result of temporary misperceptions of the price level and people have rational expectations about prices, monetary policy is not able to affect the real economy systematically.

The rational expectations assumption is attractive to economists—including many Keynesian as well as classical economists—because it fits well economists' presumption that people intelligently pursue their economic self-interests. If people's expectations aren't rational, the economic plans that individuals make won't generally be as good as they could be. But the theoretical attractiveness of rational expectations obviously isn't enough; economists would like to know whether people really do have rational expectations about important economic variables.

The rational expectations idea can be tested with data from surveys, in which people are asked their opinions about the future of the economy. To illustrate how such a test would be conducted, suppose that we have data from a survey in which people were asked to make a prediction of the price level one year in the future. Imagine that this survey is repeated each year for several years. Now suppose that, for each individual in the survey, we define

P_t^e = the individual's forecast, made in year $t - 1$, of the price level in year t.

Suppose also that we let P_t represent the price level that actually occurs in year t. Then the individual's forecast error for year t is the difference between the actual price level and the individual's forecast:

$$P_t - P_t^e = \text{the individual's forecast error in year } t.$$

If people have rational expectations, these forecast errors should be unpredictable random numbers. However, if forecast errors are consistently positive or negative—meaning that people systematically tend to underpredict or overpredict the price level—expectations are not rational. If forecast errors have a systematic pattern—for example, if people tend to overpredict the price level when prices have been rising in the recent past—again, expectations are not rational.

Early statistical studies of price level forecasts made by consumers, journalists, professional economists, and others tended to reject the rational expectations theory. These studies, which were conducted in the late 1970s and early 1980s, followed the period in which inflation reached unprecedented levels, in part because of the major increases in oil prices and expansionary monetary policy in 1973–1974 and in 1979. It is perhaps not surprising that people found forecasting price changes to be unusually difficult during such a volatile period.

Later studies of price level forecasts have been more favorable to the rational expectations theory. Michael Keane and David Runkle[30] of the Federal Reserve

[30]"Are Economic Forecasts Rational?" *Quarterly Review*, Federal Reserve Bank of Minneapolis, Spring 1989, pp. 26–33.

Bank of Minneapolis studied the price level forecasts of a panel of professional forecasters that has been surveyed by the American Statistical Association and the National Bureau of Economic Research since 1968. They found no evidence to refute the hypothesis that the professional forecasters had rational expectations. In another article, Dean Croushore[31] of the University of Richmond analyzed a variety of forecasts made not only by economists and forecasters but also by members of the general public, as reported in surveys of consumers. Croushore found that the forecasts of each of these groups were broadly consistent with rational expectations, although there appeared to be some tendency for expectations to lag behind reality in periods when inflation rose or fell sharply.

[31]"Inflation Forecasts: How Good Are They?" *Business Review*, Federal Reserve Bank of Philadelphia, May/June 1996, pp. 15–25.

CHAPTER SUMMARY

1. Classical business cycle analysis uses the classical *IS–LM* model along with the assumption that wages and prices adjust quickly to bring the economy into general equilibrium.
2. The real business cycle (RBC) theory is a version of the classical theory that emphasizes productivity shocks (shocks to the production function) as the source of business cycle fluctuations. In the classical *IS–LM* model, a temporary decline in productivity reduces the real wage, employment, and output, while raising the real interest rate and the price level. The RBC theory can account for the observed procyclical behavior of employment, real wages, and labor productivity. However, the prediction of the RBC theory that prices are countercyclical is viewed by some as a failing.
3. The Solow residual is an empirical measure of total factor productivity, A, in the production function. It increases as a result of technical progress that increases the amount of output that can be produced with the same amounts of labor and capital services (inputs). The Solow residual also changes as a result of changes in the utilization rates of capital and labor. It is procyclical at least partly because the utilization rates of capital and labor are procyclical. The procyclical behavior of the utilization rate of labor may reflect labor hoarding, which occurs when firms continue to employ workers during recessions but use them less intensively or on tasks, such as maintenance, that don't contribute directly to measured output.
4. Classical business cycle analysis allows for other shocks to the economy besides changes in productivity, including changes in fiscal policy. According to the classical *IS–LM* model, an increase in government purchases raises employment, output, the real interest rate, and the price level. Including both fiscal and productivity shocks in the classical model improves its ability to fit the data. Although fiscal policy can affect employment and output, classical economists argue that it should not be used to smooth the business cycle because the invisible hand leads the economy to an efficient outcome without government interference. Instead, decisions about government purchases should be based on comparisons of costs and benefits.
5. In the basic classical model (which includes RBC theory), money is neutral, which means that changes in the nominal money supply change the price level proportionally but do not affect real variables such as output, employment, and the real interest rate.
6. The basic classical model can account for the procyclical and leading behavior of money if there is reverse causation—that is, if anticipated changes in output lead to changes in the money supply in the same direction. For example, if firms increase their money demand in anticipation of future output increases, and if the Fed (to keep the price level stable) supplies enough extra money to meet the increase in money demand, increases in the money stock precede increases in output. This result holds even though changes in the money stock don't *cause* subsequent changes in output.
7. Examination of historical monetary policy actions suggests that money isn't neutral. Friedman and Schwartz identified occasions when the money supply changed for independent reasons, such as gold discoveries or changes in monetary institutions, and changes in output followed these changes in the money supply in the same direction. Later experiences, such as the severe economic slowdown that followed Federal Reserve Chairman Volcker's decision to reduce money growth in 1979, also provide evidence for the view that money isn't neutral.
8. The misperceptions theory is based on the idea that producers have imprecise information about the current price level. According to the misperceptions theory, the amount of output supplied equals the full-employment level of output, $\bar{Y}$, only if the actual price level equals the expected price level. When the price level is higher than expected, suppliers are fooled into thinking that the relative prices of the goods they supply have risen, so they supply a quantity of output that exceeds $\bar{Y}$. Similarly, when the price level is lower than expected, the quantity of output supplied is less than $\bar{Y}$.
9. The short-run aggregate supply (*SRAS*) curve based on the misperceptions theory slopes upward in describing the relationship between output and the actual price level, with the expected price level held constant. In the long run, the price level equals the expected price level so that the supply of output equals $\bar{Y}$; thus the long-run aggregate supply (*LRAS*) curve is a vertical line at the point where output equals $\bar{Y}$.
10. With the upward-sloping *SRAS* curve based on the misperceptions theory, an *unanticipated* increase in the money supply increases output (and is thus nonneutral) in the short run. However, because the long-run aggregate supply curve is vertical, an unanticipated increase in the money supply doesn't affect

output (and so is neutral) in the long run. An *anticipated* increase in the money supply causes price expectations to adjust immediately and leads to no misperceptions about the price level; thus an anticipated increase in the money supply is neutral in both the short and long runs.

11. According to the extended classical model based on the misperceptions theory, only surprise changes in the money supply can affect output. If the public has rational expectations about macroeconomic variables, including the money supply, the Fed cannot systematically surprise the public because the public will understand and anticipate the Fed's pattern of behavior. Thus classical economists argue that the Fed cannot systematically use changes in the money supply to affect output.

▶ KEY DIAGRAM 8

The misperceptions version of the *AD–AS* model

The misperceptions version of the *AD–AS* model shows how the aggregate demand for output and the aggregate supply of output interact to determine the price level and output in a classical model in which producers misperceive the aggregate price level.

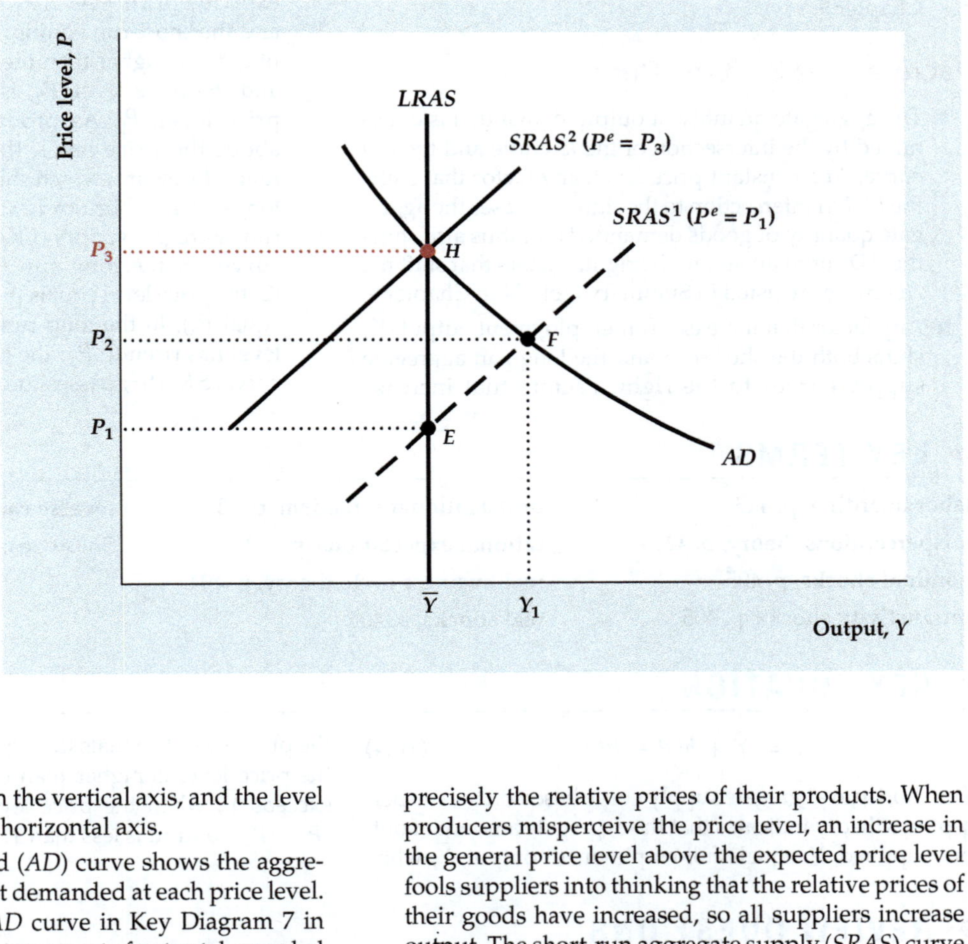

Diagram Elements

- The price level, P, is on the vertical axis, and the level of output, Y, is on the horizontal axis.
- The aggregate demand (*AD*) curve shows the aggregate quantity of output demanded at each price level. It is identical to the *AD* curve in Key Diagram 7 in Chapter 9. The aggregate amount of output demanded is determined by the intersection of the *IS* and *LM* curves (see Fig. 9.10). An increase in the price level, P, reduces the real money supply, shifting the *LM* curve up and to the left and reducing the aggregate quantity of output demanded. Thus the *AD* curve slopes downward.
- The misperceptions theory is based on the assumption that producers have imperfect information about the general price level and hence don't know precisely the relative prices of their products. When producers misperceive the price level, an increase in the general price level above the expected price level fools suppliers into thinking that the relative prices of their goods have increased, so all suppliers increase output. The short-run aggregate supply (*SRAS*) curve shows the aggregate quantity of output supplied at each price level, with the expected price level held constant. Because an increase in the price level fools producers into supplying more output, the short-run aggregate supply curve slopes upward, as shown by $SRAS^1$.
- The short-run aggregate supply curve, $SRAS^1$, is drawn so that the expected price level, P^e, equals P_1. When the actual price level equals the expected price

level, producers aren't fooled and so supply the full-employment level of output, $\bar{Y}$. Therefore at point E, where the actual price level equals the expected price level (both equal P_1), the short-run aggregate supply curve, $SRAS^1$, shows that producers supply $\bar{Y}$.

- In the long run, producers learn about the price level and adjust their expectations until the actual price level equals the expected price level. Producers then supply the full-employment level of output, $\bar{Y}$, regardless of the price level. Thus the long-run aggregate supply (*LRAS*) curve is vertical at $Y = \bar{Y}$, just as in the basic *AD–AS* model in Key Diagram 7 in Chapter 9.

Factors That Shift the Curves

- The aggregate quantity of output demanded is determined by the intersection of the *IS* curve and the *LM* curve. At a constant price level, any factor that shifts the *IS–LM* intersection to the right increases the aggregate quantity of goods demanded and thus also shifts the *AD* curve up and to the right. Factors that shift the *AD* curve are listed in Summary table 14 in Chapter 9.
- Any factor that increases full-employment output, $\bar{Y}$, shifts both the short-run and the long-run aggregate supply curves to the right. Factors that increase full-employment output are listed in Summary table 11 in Chapter 9. An increase in government purchases because it induces workers to supply more labor, also shifts the short-run and long-run aggregate supply curves to the right in the classical model.
- An increase in the expected price level shifts the short-run aggregate supply curve up.

Analysis

- The short-run equilibrium is at the intersection of the *AD* curve and the *SRAS* curve. For example, if the expected price level is P_1, the *SRAS* curve is $SRAS^1$, and the short-run equilibrium is at point F. At F output, Y_1, is higher than the full-employment level, $\bar{Y}$, and the price level, P_2, is higher than the expected price level, P_1. As producers obtain information about the price level, the expected price level is revised upward, which shifts the *SRAS* curve up. The long-run equilibrium is at point H, where the long-run aggregate supply (*LRAS*) curve intersects the *AD* curve. In the long run (1) output equals $\bar{Y}$, and (2) the price level equals the expected price level (both equal P_3). In the long run, when the expected price level has risen to P_3, the short-run aggregate supply curve, $SRAS^2$, passes through H.

KEY TERMS

labor hoarding, p. 413
misperceptions theory, p. 425
nominal shocks, p. 405
productivity shocks, p. 405
propagation mechanism, p. 431
rational expectations, p. 431
real business cycle theory, p. 404
real shocks, p. 405
reverse causation, p. 423
Solow residual, p. 410

KEY EQUATION

$$Y = \bar{Y} + b(P - P^e) \qquad \textbf{(10.4)}$$

The short-run aggregate supply curve based on the misperceptions theory indicates that the aggregate amount of output supplied, Y, equals full-employment output, $\bar{Y}$, when the price level, P, equals the expected price level, P^e. When the price level is higher than expected ($P > P^e$), output exceeds $\bar{Y}$; when the price level is lower than expected ($P < P^e$), output is less than $\bar{Y}$.

REVIEW QUESTIONS

1. Which school of economists, classical or Keynesian, supports government intervention in the face of economic shock? Explain your answer based on the underlying assumptions.
2. What are the two main components of any theory of the business cycle? Describe these two components for the real business cycle theory.
3. Define *real shock* and *nominal shock*. Give an example of each. What type of real shock do real business cycle economists consider the most important source of cyclical fluctuations?
4. What major business cycle facts does the RBC theory explain successfully? Does it explain any business cycle facts less well?
5. What is the Solow residual and how does it behave over the business cycle? What factors cause the Solow residual to change?
6. During a recession, some workers would urge the government to increase its purchases temporarily (for example, by building roads) so as to increase employment and raise wages. If you were a classical economist, would you agree with this statement?

Explain your answer in terms of the labor market, the *FE–IS–LM* model, and the practical difficulties associated with this approach.

7. An expansion of economic activities is observed to be followed by an increase in money supply. How would classical economists explain this—does the latter cause the former or vice versa? Explain.

8. According to the misperceptions theory, what effect does an increase in the price level have on the amount of output supplied by producers? Explain. Does it matter whether the increase in the price level was expected?

9. In the classical model, money is neutral in both the short run and the long run. Explain how the introduction of price misperception and unanticipated change in monetary policy to the classical model changes the result of money neutrality.

10. Define *rational expectations*. According to the classical model, what implications do rational expectations have for the ability of the central bank to use monetary policy to smooth business cycles?

NUMERICAL PROBLEMS

1. In a certain economy, the production function is

$$Y = A(150N - N^2),$$

where Y is the output, A is productivity, and N is the total hours worked. The marginal product of labor associated with this production function is

$$MPN = A(150 - 2N).$$

Initially, $A = 1.0$, but a beneficial productivity shock raises A to 1.2.

a. The supply of labor is

$$NS = 40 + 0.2w,$$

where w is the real wage. Find the equilibrium levels of output, hours worked, and the real wage before and after the productivity shock. Recall (Chapter 3) that the *MPN* curve is the same as the labor demand curve, with the real wage replacing the *MPN*.

b. Repeat part (*a*) if the labor supply is

$$NS = 20 + 0.6w.$$

c. How does the positive productivity shock shift the *ND* curve? What does the slope of the *NS* curve mean? Given the same productivity shock, how do the different slopes of the labor supply curve in parts *(a)* and *(b)* affect the wages? Show your results graphically. Based on your graph, explain how the slopes of the *NS* curve affect the procyclical behavior of wages.

2. A simplified model of the economy of Finland is described as follows:

Desired consumption	$C^d = 100 + 0.5(Y - T) - 50r.$
Desired investment	$I^d = 150 - 50r.$
Real money demand	$L = 0.5Y - 100i.$
Full-employment output	$\bar{Y} =$ €700 trillion.
Expected inflation	$\pi^e = 0.02.$

In this economy, the government always has a balanced budget, so $T = G$, where T is total taxes collected.

a. Suppose that $M = 1400$ and $G = 280$. Use the classical *IS–LM* model to find the equilibrium values of output, the real interest rate, the price level, consumption, and investment. (*Hint:* In the classical model, output always equals its full employment level.)

b. The money supply rises to 1540. Repeat part (*a*). Is money neutral?

c. With the money supply back at 1400, government purchases and taxes rise to 350. Repeat part (*a*). Assume for simplicity that $\bar{Y}$ is fixed (unaffected by *G*). Is fiscal policy neutral in this case? Explain.

3. Consider the following economy.

Desired consumption	$C^d = 200 + 0.4(Y - T) - 400r.$
Desired investment	$I^d = 300 - 400r.$
Real money demand	$L = 0.6Y - 400i.$
Full-employment output	$\bar{Y} = 900.$
Expected inflation	$\pi^e = 0.$

a. Suppose that $T = G = 175$ and that $M = 11{,}165$. Find an equation describing the *IS* curve. Find an equation describing the *LM* curve. Finally, find an equation for the aggregate demand curve. What are the equilibrium values of output, consumption, investment, the real interest rate, and the price level? Assume that there are no misperceptions about the price level.

b. Suppose that $T = G = 240$ and that $M = 11{,}165$. What is the equation for the aggregate demand curve now? What are the equilibrium values of output, consumption, investment, the real interest rate, and the price level? Assume that full employment output, $\bar{Y}$, is fixed.

c. Repeat part (*b*) for $T = G = 175$ and $M = 13{,}195$.

4. An economy has the following *AD* and *AS* curves.

AD curve	$Y = 400 + 25(M/P)$.
AS curve	$Y = Y_f + 15(P - P^e)$.

Here, $Y_f = 500$ and $M = 160$.

a. Suppose that $P^e = 40$. What are the equilibrium values of the price level, P, and output, Y? (*Hint:* The solutions for P in this part and in part (*b*) are multiples of 5.)

b. Money supply (M) increases unexpectedly to 500. Since the increase is unanticipated, P^e remains at 40. What are the equilibrium values of the price level, P, and output, Y?

c. The Fed announces that the money supply will be increased to $M = 500$, which the public believes. Now what are the equilibrium values of the price level, P, the expected price level, P^e, and output, Y?

5. Output in an economy is given by the production function $Y = AK^{0.3}N^{0.7}$, where Y is output, A measures productivity, the capital stock, K, is fixed at 30, and employment N is fixed at 100. Output equals 100 in the year 2021 and equals 105 in 2022.

a. Find the Solow residual in the years 2021 and 2022, and its growth rate between those two years.

b. What is the relationship between the growth in the Solow residual between 2021 and 2022 and the growth in productivity (as measured by the parameter A) in the same years? Assume that the rates of utilization of capital and labor remain unchanged.

c. Repeat part (*b*) under the assumption that utilization of labor increases by 3% between 2021 and 2022. You will have to modify the production function along the lines of Eq. (10.2).

d. Repeat part (*b*) under the assumption that the utilization rates of both labor and capital increase by 3% between 2021 and 2022.

6. Try the following experiment: Flip a coin fifty times, keeping track of the results. Think of each "heads" as a small positive shock that increases output by one unit; similarly, think of each "tails" as a small negative shock that reduces output by one unit. Let the initial value of output, Y, be 50, and graph the level of output over time as it is hit by the "positive" and "negative" shocks (coin flips). For example, if your first four flips are three heads and a tail, output takes the values 51, 52, 53, 52. After fifty flips, have your small shocks produced any large cycles in output?

7. In a particular economy the labor force (the sum of employed and unemployed workers) is fixed at 100 million. In this economy, each month 1% of the workers who were employed at the beginning of the month lose their jobs, and 19% of the workers who were unemployed at the beginning of the month find new jobs.

a. The January unemployment rate is 5%. For the rates of job loss and job finding given, what will the unemployment rate be in February? In March?

b. In April an adverse productivity shock raises the job loss rate to 3% of those employed. The job loss rate returns to 1% in May, while the job finding rate remains unchanged at 19% throughout. Find the unemployment rate for April, May, June, and July.

8. (Appendix 10.B) Consider the following economy:

IS curve	$r = 2.47 - 0.0004Y$.
Real money demand	$L = 0.5Y - 500(r + \pi^e)$.
Short-run aggregate supply	$Y = \bar{Y} + 100(P - P^e)$.

Here, r is the real interest rate, Y is output, and P is the price level. Assume that expected inflation, π^e, is 0, nominal money supply, M, is 88,950, and full-employment output, $\bar{Y}$, is 6000.

a. Use the notation of Appendixes 9.B and 10.B. What are the values of the parameters α_{IS}, β_{IS}, α_{LM}, β_{LM}, ℓ_r, and b? (*Hint:* Solve for asset market equilibrium to obtain the coefficients of the *LM* equation.)

b. What is the equation of the aggregate demand curve?

c. Suppose that the expected price level, P^e, is 29.15. What are the short-run equilibrium values of the price level, P, and output, Y?

d. What are the long-run equilibrium values of the price level, P, and output, Y?

ANALYTICAL PROBLEMS

1. Suppose firms invest in a new artificial intelligence program that develops high caliber robots that can handle large amounts of data and deliver instructions to workers.

a. Explain how the investment plan affects the *IS*, *LM*, and *AD* curves.

b. Suppose the workers' productivities and expected incomes are unaffected. How will this affect the *AS* curve with and without this assumption?

c. For simplicity, we keep the assumption in part (*b*). Use your answers in (*a*) and (*b*) to discuss the real interest rate, employment, real wages, nominal wages, consumption, investment, and the price level.

d. Based on the misperceptions theory, modify the above *AS–AD* graph to show the short-run equilibrium.

2. Use the classical *IS–LM* model to analyze the effects of a permanent increase in government purchases of 100 per year (in real terms). The increase in purchases is financed by a permanent increase in lump-sum taxes of 100 per year.
   a. Begin by finding the effects of the fiscal change on the labor market. How does the effect of the permanent increase in government purchases of 100 compare with the effect of a temporary increase in purchases of 100?
   b. Because the tax increase is permanent, assume that at any constant levels of output and the real interest rate, consumers respond by reducing their consumption each period by the full amount of the tax increase. Under this assumption, how does the permanent increase in government purchases affect desired national saving and the *IS* curve?
   c. Use the classical *IS–LM* model to find the effects of the permanent increase in government purchases and taxes on output, the real interest rate, and the price level in the current period. What happens if consumers reduce their current consumption by less than 100 at every level of output and the real interest rate?
3. Consider a business cycle theory that combines the classical *IS–LM* model with the assumption that temporary changes in government purchases are the main source of cyclical fluctuations. How well would this theory explain the observed cyclical behavior of each of the following variables? Give reasons for your answers.
   a. Employment
   b. The real wage
   c. Average labor productivity
   d. Investment
   e. The price level
4. Starting from a situation with no government spending and no taxes, the government introduces a foreign aid program (in which domestically produced goods are shipped abroad) and pays for it with a temporary 10% tax on current wages. Future wages are untaxed.

   What effects will the temporary wage tax have on labor supply? Use the classical *IS–LM* model to find the effects of the fiscal change on output, employment, the (before-tax) real wage, the real interest rate, and the price level.
5. This problem asks you to work out in more detail the example of reverse causation described in the text. Suppose that firms that expect to increase production in the future have to increase their current transactions (for example, they may need to purchase more raw materials). For this reason, current real money demand rises when expected future output rises.
   a. Under the assumption that real money demand depends on expected future output, use the classical *IS–LM* model to find the effects of an increase in expected future output on the current price level. For simplicity, assume that any effects of the increase in expected future output on the labor market or on desired saving and investment are small and can be ignored.
   b. Suppose that the Fed wants to stabilize the current price level. How will the Fed respond to the increase in expected future output? Explain why the Fed's response is an example of reverse causation.

▶ WORKING WITH MACROECONOMIC DATA

For data to use in these exercises, go to the Federal Reserve Bank of St. Louis FRED database at fred.stlouisfed.org.

1. According to the real business cycle theory, productivity shocks are an important source of business cycles. Using the Cobb–Douglas production function (for example, Eq. 3.2) and annual data since 1961, calculate and graph U.S. total factor productivity. Use real GDP for Y, the capital stock from the source listed in Table 3.1 for K, and civilian employment for N. Look for periods marked by sharp changes up or down in productivity. How well do these changes match up with the dates of business cycle peaks and troughs? (See Chapter 8.)
2. This question asks you to study whether unanticipated declines in the money stock tend to raise interest rates and lead to recessions, as implied by the misperceptions theory.
   a. Using quarterly data from 1960 to the present, define unanticipated money growth in each quarter to be the rate of M2 growth (expressed as an annual rate) from the preceding quarter to the current quarter, minus average M2 growth over the preceding four quarters. (Average M2 growth over the preceding four quarters is a simple approximation of expected money growth.) Plot unanticipated money growth since 1960. What happens to

unanticipated money growth before the recessions in the 1960s, 1970s, and 1980s?

b. On a separate figure, graph unanticipated money growth along with the nominal three-month Treasury bill interest rate. In the 1960s, what happens to the nominal interest rate when there is a sharp upward spike in unanticipated money growth?

c. On a separate figure, graph unanticipated money growth against the real three-month Treasury bill interest rate (the nominal rate minus the inflation rate). What is the relationship between unanticipated money growth and the real interest rate in the 1973–1975 recession?

3. Are people's inflation forecasts rational? To investigate this question, go to the website of the Federal Reserve Bank of Philadelphia at *www.philadelphiafed.org*. Find the webpages for Research and Data and look for data from the Survey of Professional Forecasters on forecasts of CPI inflation. Then, go to FRED and get actual data on the CPI. Make a plot showing the forecast of inflation at a given date on the horizontal axis against the actual inflation rate on the vertical axis. If forecasts are rational, what pattern should you see in the data? What pattern do you observe in your plot? Does the evidence support the idea that people's inflation forecasts are rational?

4. The University of Michigan has conducted an extensive survey of consumers since 1978, including a question on consumers' forecasts of inflation. Gather data on inflation expectations from the Michigan survey using FRED. First, plot those forecasts along with forecasts from the Survey of Professional Forecasters for CPI inflation (see the previous problem for the location of the data). Is one set of inflation expectations consistently different from the other? Next, compare the two sets of forecasts with the actual data on the CPI. Make a time-series plot of both forecasts and the actual value. Which survey seems to be more accurate? Does the evidence support the idea that people's inflation forecasts are rational?

Appendix

10.A

Worked-Out Numerical Exercise for Solving the Classical *AD–AS* Model with Misperceptions

Consider an economy that is described by the following equations:

$$AD \text{ curve: } Y = 1166\tfrac{2}{3} + 148{,}000/P.$$

$$SRAS \text{ curve: } Y = \bar{Y} + 10(P - P^e).$$

$$\bar{Y} = 2500;\ P^e = 130.$$

The *AD* curve is identical to the *AD* curve derived in Appendix 9.A, Step 5. So, we could have started with the functions for consumption, taxes, investment, and money demand, as well as the money supply from Appendix 9.A, and derived this *AD* curve.

The short-run equilibrium is found by the intersection of the *AD* curve and the *SRAS* curve: $1166\tfrac{2}{3} + 148{,}000/P = Y = \bar{Y} + 10(P - P^e)$. Substituting 2500 for $\bar{Y}$ and 130 for P^e yields $1166\tfrac{2}{3} + 148{,}000/P = 2500 + 10(P - 130)$, which implies $1166\tfrac{2}{3} + 148{,}000/P = 1200 + 10P$. Therefore $10P + 33\tfrac{1}{3} - 148{,}000/P = 0$.

Now multiply both sides of this equation by P and divide both sides by 10 to obtain the quadratic equation $P^2 + 3\tfrac{1}{3}P - 14{,}800 = 0$.

This quadratic equation has two solutions (known as roots): $P = 120$ and $P = -123\tfrac{1}{3}$. [*Hint:* You can find these roots either by using the formula for the roots of a quadratic equation[1] or by factoring the quadratic equation to obtain $(P - 120)(P + 123\tfrac{1}{3}) = 0$.] The positive root, $P = 120$, is the price level in short-run equilibrium. The level of output in short-run equilibrium can be found by plugging $P = 120$ into either the *AD* curve or the *SRAS* curve. In the *AD* curve, $Y = 1166\tfrac{2}{3} + 148{,}000/P = 1166\tfrac{2}{3} + 148{,}000/120 = 1166\tfrac{2}{3} + 1233\tfrac{1}{3}$, so $Y = 2400$. In the *SRAS* curve, $Y = \bar{Y} + 10(P - P^e) = 2500 + 10(120 - 130) = 2500 - 100$, so $Y = 2400$.

In the long run, there are no misperceptions, so the long-run equilibrium is the same as we found in Appendix 9.A, where $Y = 2500$ and $P = 111$.

[1]The roots of a general quadratic equation $AX^2 + BX + C = 0$ are given by $X = \left(-B \pm \sqrt{B^2 - 4AC}\right)/2A$.

Appendix
10.B

An Algebraic Version of the Classical *AD–AS* Model with Misperceptions

Building on the algebraic version of the *AD–AS* model developed in Appendix 9.B, in this appendix we derive an algebraic version of the classical *AD–AS* model with misperceptions. We present algebraic versions of the aggregate demand (*AD*) curve and the aggregate supply (*AS*) curve and then solve for the general equilibrium.

The Aggregate Demand Curve

Because misperceptions by producers don't affect the demand for goods, the aggregate demand curve is the same as in Appendix 9.B. Recall from Eq. (9.B.24) that the equation of the aggregate demand (*AD*) curve is

$$Y = \frac{\alpha_{IS} - \alpha_{LM} + (1/\ell_r)(M/P)}{\beta_{IS} + \beta_{LM}}, \qquad \textbf{(10.B.1)}$$

where the coefficients of the *IS* curve, α_{IS} and β_{IS}, are given by Eqs. (9.B.15) and (9.B.16), respectively, the coefficients of the *LM* curve, α_{LM} and β_{LM}, are given by Eqs. (9.B.20) and (9.B.21), respectively, and ℓ_r is the coefficient of the nominal interest rate in the money demand equation, Eq. (9.B.17).

The Aggregate Supply Curve

The short-run aggregate supply curve based on the misperceptions theory is represented by Eq. (10.4), which, for convenience, we repeat here:

$$Y = \bar{Y} + b(P - P^e), \qquad \textbf{(10.B.2)}$$

where b is a positive number.

General Equilibrium

For a given expected price level, P^e, the short-run equilibrium value of the price level is determined by the intersection of the aggregate demand curve (Eq. 10.B.1) and the short-run aggregate supply curve (Eq. 10.B.2). Setting the right sides of Eqs. (10.B.1) and (10.B.2) equal and multiplying both sides of the resulting equation by $P(\beta_{IS} + \beta_{LM})$ and rearranging yields a quadratic equation for the price level P:

$$a_2P^2 + a_1P - a_0 = 0, \qquad \textbf{(10.B.3)}$$

where

$$a_2 = (\beta_{IS} + \beta_{LM})b;$$
$$a_1 = (\beta_{IS} + \beta_{LM})(\bar{Y} - bP^e) - \alpha_{IS} + \alpha_{LM};$$
$$a_0 = \frac{M}{\ell_r}.$$

The coefficients a_2 and a_0 are positive, and the coefficient a_1 could be positive, negative, or zero. Because both a_2 and a_0 are positive, the solution of Eq. (10.B.3) yields one positive value of P and one negative value of P. The price level can't be negative, so the short-run equilibrium price level is the positive solution of this equation. Using the standard quadratic formula, we find the positive solution of Eq. (10.B.3) to be

$$P = \frac{-a_1 + \sqrt{a_1^2 + 4a_2a_0}}{2a_2}. \quad \textbf{(10.B.4)}$$

We obtain the short-run equilibrium level of output by substituting the value of the price level from Eq. (10.B.4) into either the aggregate demand curve Eq. (10.B.1) or the aggregate supply curve Eq. (10.B.2).

Note that an increase in the nominal money supply, M, increases the constant a_0 and thus according to Eq. (10.B.4), it increases the equilibrium price level. Because an increase in M doesn't affect the aggregate supply curve but does increase the equilibrium price level, Eq. (10.B.2) shows that it increases output.

We focused on short-run equilibrium in this appendix. In the long run, the actual price level equals the expected price level so that, according to Eq. (10.B.2), output equals its full-employment level, $\bar{Y}$. In the long run, the economy reaches the general equilibrium described in Appendix 9.B.

11

Keynesianism: The Macroeconomics of Wage and Price Rigidity

Learning Objectives

11.1 Summarize the Keynesian explanations for real-wage rigidity.

11.2 Describe the causes and effects of price stickiness according to the Keynesian model.

11.3 Analyze the effects of monetary and fiscal policy in the Keynesian model.

11.4 Explain Keynesian theories about business cycles and macroeconomic stabilization.

In Chapter 10 we presented the classical, or market-clearing, approach to business cycle analysis. In the classical approach wages and prices are assumed to adjust quickly so that markets are almost always in equilibrium. Classical economists argue that business cycles represent the economy's best response to disturbances, such as productivity shocks, so there is little justification for government attempts to smooth the cycle.

In contrast to the classicals, Keynesians are less optimistic about the ability of free-market economies to respond quickly and efficiently to shocks. One of the central ideas of Keynesianism is that wages and prices are "rigid" or "sticky" and do *not* adjust quickly to market-clearing levels. Wage and price rigidity implies that the economy can be away from its general equilibrium for significant periods of time. Thus a deep recession is not an optimal response of the free market to outside shocks; rather, it is a disequilibrium situation in which high unemployment reflects an excess of labor supplied over labor demanded. Keynesians believe that the government should act to eliminate—or at least minimize—these periods of low output and high unemployment. Keynesians view *equilibrium* as a situation in which there is no upward or downward pressure on wages.

As wage and price rigidity is the basis for Keynesian theory and policy recommendations, understanding the potential causes of rigidity is important. A telling criticism that the classicals aimed at the Keynesians in the early 1970s was that the Keynesians simply assumed that wages and prices are rigid, without giving a good economic explanation of why these rigidities occur. After all, argued the classicals, wages and prices are not simply "given" to the economy but are the results of decisions made by millions of individuals and firms. If excessively high wages are causing unemployment, why don't unemployed workers offer to work for lower wages until firms are willing to hire them? If prices aren't at the levels at which quantities supplied equal quantities demanded, why don't firms just change their prices? In effect, the classicals challenged the Keynesians to show how wage and price rigidity could be consistent with the idea—basic to almost all of economics—that individuals and firms are economically rational; that is, they do the best they can for themselves when making economic decisions.

Keynesian researchers accepted this challenge and have made progress in explaining wage and price rigidity in terms consistent with economic rationality. In the first part of this chapter we discuss some leading Keynesian explanations for wage and price rigidity. We then show how slow adjustment of wages and prices can be incorporated into the *IS–LM* model, converting it from a classical model to a Keynesian model. Using this model, we discuss the Keynesian answers to the two central questions about business cycles—namely, What causes business cycles? and What should policymakers do about them?

11.1 Real-Wage Rigidity

Summarize the Keynesian explanations for real-wage rigidity.

Because Keynesian analysis and policy prescriptions depend so greatly on the assumption that wages and prices do not move rapidly to clear markets, we begin by discussing in some detail the possible economic reasons for slow or incomplete adjustment. In this section we focus on the rigidity of real wages, and in Section 11.2 we look at the slow adjustment of prices.

The main reason that Keynesians bring wage rigidity into their analysis is their dissatisfaction with the classical explanation of unemployment. Recall that classicals believe that most unemployment, including the increases in unemployment that occur during recessions, arises from mismatches between workers and jobs (frictional or structural unemployment). Keynesians don't dispute that mismatch is a major source of unemployment, but they are skeptical that it explains all unemployment.

Keynesians are particularly unwilling to accept the classical idea that recessions are periods of increased mismatch between workers and jobs. If higher unemployment during downturns reflected increased mismatch, Keynesians argue, recessions should be periods of particularly active search by workers for jobs and by firms for new employees. However, surveys suggest that unemployed workers spend relatively little time searching for work (many are simply waiting, hoping to be recalled to their old jobs), and help-wanted advertising and vacancy postings by firms fall rather than rise during recessions. Rather than times of increased worker–job mismatch, Keynesians believe that recessions are periods of generally low demand for both output and workers throughout the economy.

To explain the existence of unemployment without relying solely on worker–job mismatch, Keynesians argue for rejecting the classical assumption that real wages adjust relatively quickly to equate the quantities of labor supplied and demanded. In particular, if the real wage is above the level that clears the labor market, unemployment (an excess of labor supplied over labor demanded) will result. From the Keynesian perspective, the idea that the real wage moves "too little" to keep the quantity of labor demanded equal to the quantity of labor supplied is called **real-wage rigidity**.

Some Reasons for Real-Wage Rigidity

For a rigid real wage to be the source of unemployment, the real wage that firms are paying must be higher than the market-clearing real wage, at which quantities of labor supplied and demanded are equal. But if the real wage is higher than necessary to attract workers, why don't firms save labor costs by simply reducing the wage that they pay, as suggested by the classical analysis?

Various explanations have been offered for why real wages might be rigid, even in the face of an excess supply of labor. One possibility is that there are legal and institutional factors that keep wages high, such as the minimum-wage law and union contracts. However, most U.S. workers are neither union members (less than 11% of workers were union members in 2017) nor minimum-wage earners (about 2.3% of all hourly paid workers in 2017), so these barriers to wage cutting can't be the main reason for real-wage rigidity.[1] Furthermore, the minimum wage in the United States is specified in nominal terms so that workers who are paid the minimum wage would have rigid nominal wages rather than rigid real wages. (Union contracts may help explain real-wage rigidity in Western European and other countries in which a higher proportion of workers are unionized.)

Another explanation for why a firm might pay a higher real wage than it "has" to is that this policy might reduce the firm's **turnover costs**, or the costs associated with firing existing workers or hiring and training new workers. By paying a high wage, the firm can keep more of its current workers, which saves the firm the cost of hiring and training replacements. Similarly, by developing a reputation for paying well, the firm can assure itself of more and better applicants for any position that it may have to fill.

A third reason that firms might pay real wages above market-clearing levels is that workers who are paid well may have greater incentives to work hard and effectively. If highly paid workers are more productive, the firm may profit from paying its employees well, even though it could attract all the workers it needs at a lower real wage. The idea that a worker's productivity depends on the real wage received, and that therefore firms may pay wages above the market-clearing level, is the essence of the **efficiency wage model**. Because this model of wage determination has played a key role in Keynesian analyses and because it has several interesting aspects, we focus on it for the remainder of this section.

The Efficiency Wage Model

If workers who are better-paid are more productive, firms may gain by paying wages higher than the minimum necessary to attract workers. But why might a worker's productivity depend on the real wage received? The answer has both "carrot" and "stick" aspects.

The *carrot*, or positive incentive, is based on the idea that workers who feel well treated will work harder and more efficiently. George Akerlof,[2] a Nobel laureate at the University of California at Berkeley, argued that workers who believe that their employer is treating them fairly—say, by paying higher wages than required to retain them and by not cutting wages in slack times—will in turn want to treat the employer fairly by doing a good job. Akerlof called this motivation the *gift exchange motive* because it's similar to the one that leads people to exchange gifts.

The *stick*, or threat, aspect of why a firm would pay a higher wage than necessary has been analyzed in an economic model called the "shirking" model of wage determination.[3] According to the *shirking model*, if workers are paid only the minimum amount needed to attract them to particular jobs, they won't be too concerned about the possibility of being fired if they don't perform well. After all, if jobs pay the minimum amount necessary to induce workers to take jobs, the

[1]Note that the BLS updates data on union membership annually at *www.bls.gov/news.release/union2.toc.htm* and updates data on minimum wage workers annually at *www.bls.gov/opub/reports/minimumwage/2017/home.htm*.

[2]See George Akerlof, "Labor Contracts as Partial Gift Exchange," *Quarterly Journal of Economics*, November 1982, pp. 543–569.

[3]See Carl Shapiro and Joseph E. Stiglitz, "Equilibrium Unemployment as a Worker Discipline Device," *American Economic Review*, June 1984, pp. 433–444.

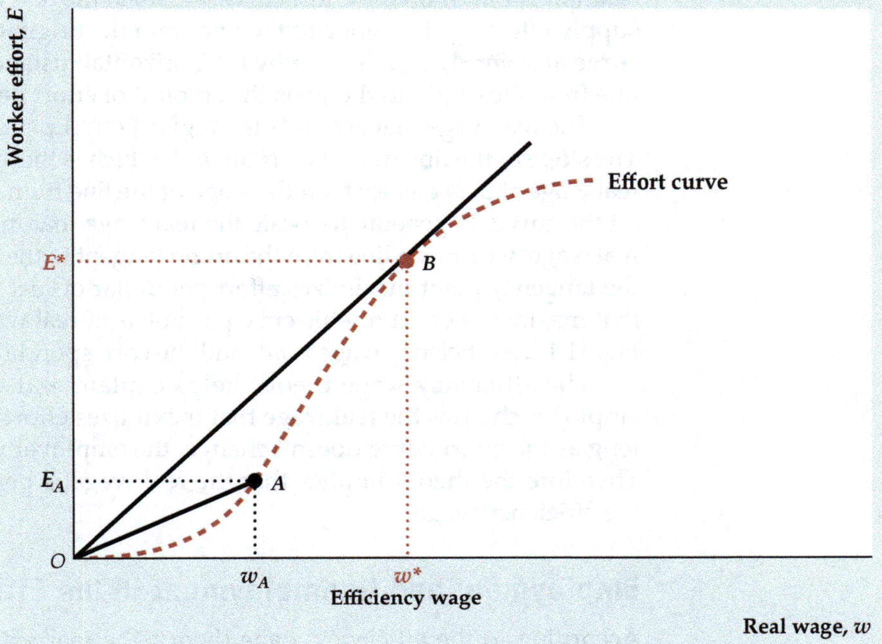

FIGURE 11.1

Determination of the efficiency wage

The effort curve shows the relation between worker effort, E, and the real wage workers receive, w. A higher real wage leads to more effort, but above a certain point higher wages are unable to spur effort much, so the effort curve is S-shaped. For any point on the curve, the amount of effort per dollar of real wage is the slope of the line from the origin to that point. At point A, effort per dollar of real wage is E_A/w_A. The highest level of effort per dollar of real wage is at point B, where the line from the origin is tangent to the curve. The real wage rate at B is the efficiency wage, w^*, and the corresponding level of effort is E^*.

workers aren't much happier with jobs than without jobs. In this case workers will be more inclined to take it easy at work and shirk their duties, and employers will have to bear the cost either of the shirking or of paying supervisors to make sure that the work gets done. In contrast, workers receiving higher wages will place a greater value on keeping their jobs (it's not that easy to find other jobs as good) and will work hard to avoid being fired for shirking.

The gift exchange idea and the shirking model both imply that workers' effort on the job depends on the real wages they receive. Graphically, the relationship between the real wage and the level of effort is shown by the **effort curve** in Figure 11.1. The real wage, w, is measured along the horizontal axis, and the level of effort, E, is measured along the vertical axis. The effort curve passes through points O, A, and B. When real wages are higher, workers choose to work harder, for either carrot or stick reasons; therefore the effort curve slopes upward. We assume that the effort curve is S-shaped. At the lowest levels of the real wage, workers make hardly any effort, and effort rises only slowly as the real wage increases. At higher levels of the real wage, effort rises sharply, as shown by the steeply rising portion of the curve. The curve flattens at very high levels of the real wage because there is some maximum level of effort that workers really can't exceed no matter how motivated they are.

Wage Determination in the Efficiency Wage Model

The effort curve shows that effort depends on the real wage, but what determines the real wage? To make as much profit as possible, *firms will choose the level of the real wage that gets the most effort from workers for each dollar of real wages paid.* The amount of effort per dollar of real wages equals the amount of effort, E, divided by the real wage, w. The ratio of E to w can be found graphically from Fig. 11.1. Consider, for example, point A on the effort curve, at which the real wage w_A induces workers to supply effort E_A. The slope of the line from the origin to A equals the height of the curve at point A, E_A, divided by the horizontal distance, w_A. Thus the slope of the line from the origin to A equals the amount of effort per dollar of real wages at A.

The real wage that achieves the highest effort per dollar of wages is at point B. The slope of the line from the origin to B, which is the amount of effort per dollar of real wage at B, is greater than the slope of the line from the origin to any other point on the curve. In general, to locate the real wage that maximizes effort per dollar of real wage, we draw a line from the origin tangent to the effort curve; the real wage at the tangency point maximizes effort per dollar of real wage. We call the real wage that maximizes effort or efficiency per dollar of real wages the **efficiency wage.** In Fig. 11.1 the efficiency wage is w^*, and the corresponding level of effort is E^*.

The efficiency wage theory helps explain real-wage rigidity. Because the employer chooses the real wage that maximizes effort received per dollar paid, as long as the effort curve doesn't change, the employer won't change the real wage. Therefore the theory implies that the real wage is permanently rigid and equals the efficiency wage.

Employment and Unemployment in the Efficiency Wage Model

According to the efficiency wage theory, the real wage is rigid at the level that maximizes effort per dollar of wages paid. We now consider how the levels of employment and unemployment in the labor market are determined.

The workings of the labor market when there is an efficiency wage are shown in Figure 11.2. The efficiency wage, w^*, is indicated by a horizontal line. Because the efficiency wage is determined solely by the effort curve, for the purpose of analyzing the labor market we can take w^* to be fixed. Similarly, we can take the level of effort, E^*, induced by the efficiency wage, w^*, as fixed at this stage of the analysis.

The upward-sloping curve is the standard labor supply curve, *NS*. As in the classical model, this curve shows the number of hours of work that people would like to supply at each level of the real wage.[4]

The downward-sloping curve is the demand curve for labor in the efficiency wage model. Recall from Chapter 3 that the amount of labor demanded by a firm depends on the marginal product of labor, or *MPN*. Specifically, the labor demand curve is identical to the *MPN* curve, which in turn relates the marginal product of labor, *MPN*, to the quantity of labor input, *N*, being used. The *MPN* curve—and hence the labor demand curve—slopes down because of the diminishing marginal productivity of labor.

In the classical model, the marginal product of labor depends only on the production function and the capital stock. A complication of the efficiency wage model is that the amount of output produced by an extra worker (or hour of work) also depends on the worker's effort. Fortunately, as we noted, the efficiency wage, w^*, and the effort level induced by that wage, E^*, are fixed at this stage of the analysis. Thus the labor demand curve in Fig. 11.2, ND^*, reflects the marginal product of labor *when worker effort is held fixed at* E^*. As in the classical case, an increase in productivity or in the capital stock shifts the labor demand curve, ND^*,

[4]For simplicity, we assume that the number of hours of labor that people want to supply doesn't depend on the effort they must exert while on the job.

FIGURE 11.2

Excess supply of labor in the efficiency wage model

When the efficiency wage, w^*, is paid, the firm's demand for labor is $\bar{N}$, represented by point A. However, the amount of labor that workers want to supply at a real wage of w^* is NS_1. The excess supply of labor equals distance AB. We assume that the efficiency wage, w^*, is higher than the market-clearing wage, w_E, that would prevail if the supply of labor equaled the demand for labor at point E.

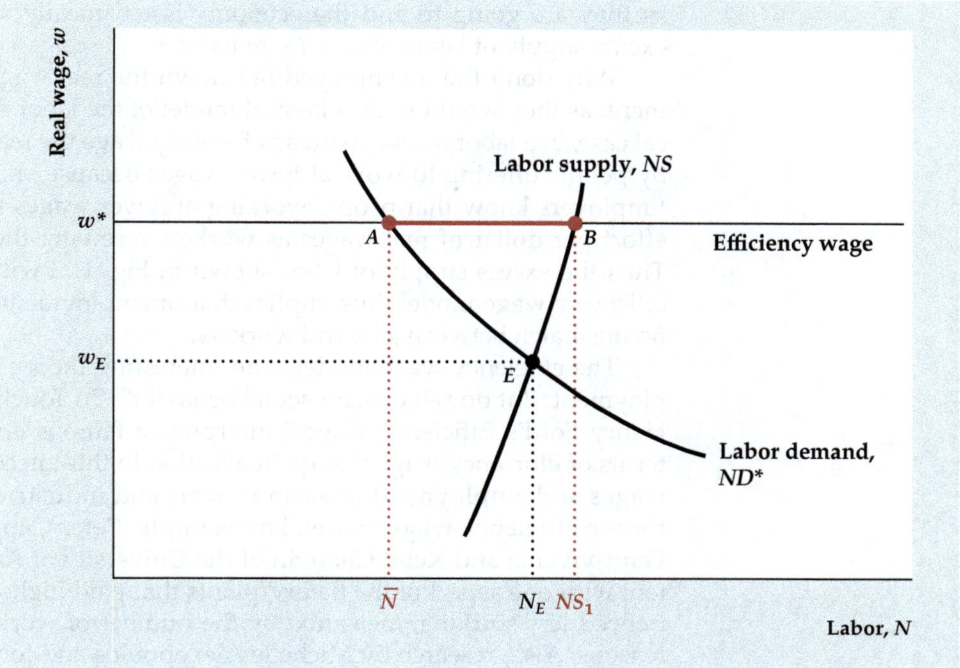

to the right. In addition, any change in the effort curve that leads to an increase in the optimal level of effort E^* would raise the MPN, and the labor demand curve, ND^*, again would shift to the right.

Now we can put the elements of Fig. 11.2 together to show how employment is determined. Point A on the labor demand curve, ND^*, indicates that, when the real wage is fixed at w^*, firms want to employ $\bar{N}$ hours of labor. Point B on the labor supply curve indicates that, when the real wage is fixed at w^*, workers want to supply NS_1 hours of labor, which is greater than the amount demanded by firms. At the efficiency wage, the quantity of labor supplied is greater than the quantity demanded,[5] so the level of employment is determined by the labor demand of firms and hence equals $\bar{N}$. The demand-determined level of employment is labeled $\bar{N}$ because it represents the full-employment level of employment for this model; that is, $\bar{N}$ is the level of employment reached after full adjustment of wages and prices. (Note that the value of $\bar{N}$ in the efficiency wage model differs from the full-employment level of employment in the classical model of the labor market, which would correspond to N_E in Fig. 11.2.) Because the efficiency wage is rigid at w^*, in the absence of shocks the level of employment in this economy remains at $\bar{N}$ indefinitely.

Perhaps the most interesting aspect of Fig. 11.2 is that it provides a new explanation of unemployment. It shows that, even when wages have adjusted as much

[5]The result that there is an excess supply of labor requires the assumption that the efficiency wage, w^*, is higher than the real wage that would clear the labor market, shown as w_E in Fig. 11.2. We always assume that the efficiency wage is higher than the market-clearing wage; if it weren't, firms would have to pay the market-clearing wage to attract workers.

as they are going to and the economy is technically at "full employment," an excess supply of labor, $NS_1 - \bar{N}$, remains.[6]

Why don't the unemployed bid down the real wage and thus gain employment, as they would in the classical model of the labor market? Unlike the classical case, in a labor market with an efficiency wage the real wage can't be bid down by people offering to work at lower wages because employers won't hire them. Employers know that people working at lower wages will not put out as much effort per dollar of real wages as workers receiving the higher efficiency wage. Thus the excess supply of labor shown in Fig. 11.2 will persist indefinitely. The efficiency wage model thus implies that unemployment will exist even if there is no mismatch between jobs and workers.

The efficiency wage model is an interesting theory of real wages and unemployment. But does it explain actual behavior? "In Touch with Data and Research: Henry Ford's Efficiency Wage," interprets a famous episode in labor history in terms of efficiency wage theory. In addition to this anecdotal evidence, studies of wages and employment in various firms and industries provide some support for the efficiency wage model. For example, Peter Cappelli of the University of Pennsylvania and Keith Chauvin of the University of Kansas[7] found that, consistent with one aspect of the theory, plants that paid higher wages to workers experienced less shirking, measured by the number of workers fired for disciplinary reasons. Also, research by Michelle Alexopoulos and Jon Cohen of the University of Toronto[8] showed that when wages became compressed in Sweden in the 1970s, workers' effort declined dramatically.

A criticism of the efficiency wage model presented here is that it predicts that the real wage is literally fixed (for no change in the effort curve). Of course, this result is too extreme because the real wage does change over time (and over the business cycle, as demonstrated in Chapter 8). However, the basic model can be extended to allow for changes in the effort curve that bring changes in the efficiency wage over time. For example, a reasonable assumption would be that workers are more concerned about losing their jobs during recessions, when finding a new job is more difficult, than during booms. Under this assumption, the real wage necessary to obtain any specific level of effort will be lower during recessions; hence the efficiency wage paid in recessions also may be lower. This extension may help the efficiency wage model match the business cycle fact that real wages are lower in recessions than in booms (procyclical real wages).

Efficiency Wages and the *FE* Line

In the Keynesian version of the *IS–LM* model, as in the classical version, the *FE* line is vertical, at a level of output that equals the full-employment level of output, $\bar{Y}$. If we assume that employers pay efficiency wages, full-employment output, $\bar{Y}$, in turn is the output produced when employment is at the full-employment level of employment, $\bar{N}$, as shown in Fig. 11.2, and the level of worker effort is E^*.

[6]Because the unemployment represented by the excess supply of labor persists even when the economy is at full employment, it is considered part of structural unemployment.

[7]"An Interplant Test of the Efficiency Wage Hypothesis," *Quarterly Journal of Economics*, August 1991, pp. 769–787.

[8]"Centralized Wage Bargaining and Structural Change in Sweden," *European Review of Economic History*, December 2003, pp. 331–366.

In Touch with Data and Research

Henry Ford's Efficiency Wage

During 1908–1914 Henry Ford instituted at Ford Motor Company a radically new way of producing automobiles.[9] Prior to Ford's innovations, automobile components weren't produced to uniform specifications. Instead, cars had to be assembled one by one by skilled craftsmen, who could make the parts fit even if sizes or shapes were off by fractions of an inch. Ford introduced a system of assemblyline production in which a standardized product, the Model T automobile, was produced from precisely made, interchangeable components. The production process also was broken into numerous small, simple steps, replacing the skilled craftsmen who had built cars from start to finish with unskilled workers who performed only a few operations over and over.

The high speed at which Ford ran the assembly line and the repetitiveness of the work were hard on the workers. As one laborer said, "If I keep putting on Nut No. 86 for about 86 more days, I will be Nut No. 86 in the Pontiac bughouse."[10] As a result, worker turnover was high, with the typical worker lasting only a few months on the job. Absenteeism also was high—about 10% on any given day—and morale was low. Worker slowdowns and even sabotage occurred.

In January 1914 Ford announced that the company would begin paying $5 a day to workers who met certain criteria, one being that the worker had been with the company at least six months. Five dollars a day was more than double the normal wage for production workers at the time. Although the motivation for Ford's announcement has been debated, its effect was stunning: Thousands of workers lined up outside the plant, hoping for jobs. Within the plant the number of people quitting dropped by 87%, absenteeism dropped by 75%, and productivity rose by 30% or more. The productivity increases helped increase Ford's profits, despite the higher wage bill and a cut in the price of a Model T.

Many results of Ford's $5 day can be predicted by the efficiency wage model, including improved efficiency and higher profits. As other automakers adopted Ford's technological innovations, they also adopted his wage policies. By 1928, before unions were important in the industry, auto industry wages were almost 40% higher than those in the rest of manufacturing.

---

[9]The source for this box is Daniel M. G. Raff and Lawrence H. Summers, "Did Henry Ford Pay Efficiency Wages?" *Journal of Labor Economics*, October 1987, pp. S57–S86.

[10]This quote is originally from Stephen Meyer, *The Five-Dollar Day: Labor Management and Social Control in the Ford Motor Company, 1908–1921*, Albany: State University of New York Press, 1981.

As in the classical model, anything that changes full-employment output, $\bar{Y}$, shifts the *FE* line. The classical model emphasizes two factors that shift the *FE* line: changes in the supply of labor and changes in productivity. In the efficiency wage model, however, labor supply doesn't affect employment, so *changes in labor supply don't affect the* FE *line in the Keynesian model* with efficiency wages. A change in productivity, however, does affect the *FE* line in the Keynesian model, as in the classical model. A drop in productivity reduces full-employment output, $\bar{Y}$, and shifts the *FE* line to the left, for two reasons. First, by reducing the marginal product of labor at any given level of employment, a drop in productivity reduces the demand for labor at any fixed real wage. With the real wage fixed at w^*, the full-employment level of employment, $\bar{N}$, falls. Second, a drop in productivity reduces the amount of output that can be produced with any particular amount of capital, labor, and effort.

11.2 Price Stickiness

Describe the causes and effects of price stickiness according to the Keynesian model.

The rigidity created by efficiency wages is a real rigidity in that the real wage, rather than the nominal wage, remains fixed. Keynesian theories also emphasize *nominal* rigidities that occur when a price or wage is fixed in nominal, or dollar, terms and doesn't readily change in response to changes in supply or demand. Keynesians often refer to rigidity of nominal prices—a tendency of prices to adjust only slowly to changes in the economy—as **price stickiness**.

We explained in Section 11.1 that Keynesians introduced real-wage rigidity because of their dissatisfaction with the classical explanation of unemployment. Similarly, the assumption of price stickiness addresses what Keynesians believe is another significant weakness of the basic classical model: the classical prediction that money is neutral.

Recall that, in the basic classical model without misperceptions, the assumption that wages and prices adjust quickly implies that money is neutral. If money is neutral, an increase or decrease in the money supply changes the price level by the same proportion but has no effect on real variables, such as output, employment, or the real interest rate. However, recall also that empirical studies—including analyses of historical episodes—have led most economists to conclude that money probably is not neutral in the real world.

One approach to accounting for monetary nonneutrality (pursued in Chapter 10) is to extend the classical model by assuming that workers and firms have imperfect information about the current price level (the misperceptions theory). However, Keynesians favor an alternative explanation of monetary nonneutrality: Prices are sticky; that is, they don't adjust quickly. If prices are sticky, the price level can't adjust immediately to offset changes in the money supply, and money isn't neutral. Thus, for Keynesians, the importance of price stickiness is that it helps explain monetary nonneutrality.

Although we focus on nominal-price rigidity in this section, a long Keynesian tradition emphasizes nominal-wage rigidity instead of nominal-price rigidity. We discuss an alternative version of the Keynesian model that rests on the assumption of nominal-wage rigidity in Appendix 11.A. This alternative model has similar implications to the Keynesian model with price rigidity—in particular, that money is not neutral.

Sources of Price Stickiness: Monopolistic Competition and Menu Costs

To say that price stickiness gives rise to monetary nonneutrality doesn't completely explain nonneutrality because it raises another question: Why are prices sticky? The Keynesian explanation for the existence of price rigidity relies on two main ideas: (1) Most firms actively set the prices of their products rather than taking the prices of their output as given by the market; and (2) when firms change prices, they incur a cost, known as a menu cost.

Monopolistic Competition. Talking about price stickiness in a highly competitive, organized market—such as the market for corn or the stock exchange—wouldn't make much sense. In these markets, prices adjust rapidly to reflect changes in supply or demand. Principal reasons for price flexibility in these competitive, highly organized markets include standardization of the product being traded (one bushel of corn of a certain grade, or one share of Microsoft stock, is much like any other) and the large number of actual or potential market participants. These two factors make it worthwhile to organize a centralized market (such as the New York Stock Exchange) in which prices can react swiftly to changes in supply and demand. These same two factors also promote keen competition among buyers and sellers, which greatly reduces the ability of any individual to affect prices.

Most participants in the corn market or stock market think of themselves as price takers. A **price taker** is a market participant who takes the market price as given. For example, a small farmer correctly perceives that the market price of corn is beyond one's control. In contrast, a **price setter** has some power to set prices.

Markets having fewer participants and less standardized products than the corn or stock markets may exhibit price-setting rather than price-taking behavior. For example, consider the market for movies in a medium-sized city. This market may be fairly competitive, with many different movie theaters, each trying to attract customers from other theaters, and so on. Although the market for movies is competitive, it isn't competitive to the same degree as the corn market. If a farmer tried to raise the price of a bushel of corn by 5¢ above the market price, the farmer would sell no corn; but a movie theater that raised its ticket prices by 5¢ above its competitors' prices wouldn't lose all its customers. Because the movie theater's product isn't completely standardized (it is showing a different movie than other theaters, its location is better for some people, it has different candy bars in the concession stand, a larger screen, or more comfortable seats, and so on), the theater has some price-setting discretion. It is a price setter, not a price taker.

Generally, a situation in which all buyers and sellers are price takers (such as the market for corn) is called **perfect competition**. In contrast, a situation in which there is some competition, but in which a smaller number of sellers and imperfect standardization of the product allow individual producers to act as price setters, is called **monopolistic competition**.

Perfect competition is the model underlying the classical view of price determination, and, as we have said, price rigidity or stickiness is extremely unlikely in a perfectly competitive market. Keynesians agree that price rigidity wouldn't occur in a perfectly competitive market but point out that a relatively small part of the economy is perfectly competitive. Keynesians argue that price rigidity is possible, even likely, in a monopolistically competitive market.

To illustrate the issues, let's return to the example of the competing movie theaters. If the market for movie tickets were perfectly competitive, how would tickets be priced? Presumably, there would be some central meeting place where buyers and sellers of tickets would congregate. Market organizers would call out "bids" (prices at which they are willing to buy) and "asks" (prices at which they are willing to sell). Prices would fluctuate continuously as new information hit the market, causing supplies and demands to change. For example, great reviews on websites such as Rotten Tomatoes and IMDb would instantly drive up the price of tickets to that movie, but news of a prospective shortage of babysitters would cause all movie ticket prices to fall.

Obviously, though, this scheme isn't how movie tickets are priced. Actual pricing by most theaters has the following three characteristics, which are also common to most price-setting markets:

1. Rather than accept the price of movies as completely determined by the market, a movie theater *sets* the price of tickets (or a schedule of prices), in *nominal* terms, and maintains the nominal price for some period of time.
2. At least within some range, the theater *meets the demand* that is forthcoming at the fixed nominal price. By "meets the demand" we mean that the theater will sell as many tickets as people want to buy at its fixed price, to the point that all its seats are filled.
3. The theater readjusts its price from time to time, generally when its costs or the level of demand changes significantly.

Can this type of pricing behavior maximize profits? Keynesian theory suggests that it can, if costs are associated with changing nominal prices, and if the market is monopolistically competitive.

Menu Costs and Price Setting. The classic example of a cost of changing prices is the cost that a restaurant faces when it has to reprint its menu to show changes in the prices of its offerings. Hence the cost of changing prices is called a **menu cost**. More general examples of menu costs (which can apply to any kind of firm) include costs of remarking merchandise, reprinting price lists and catalogues, and informing potential customers. Clearly, if firms incur costs when changing prices, they will change prices less often than they would otherwise, which creates a certain amount of price rigidity.

A potential problem with the menu cost explanation for price rigidity is that these costs seem to be rather small. How, then, can they be responsible for an amount of nominal rigidity that could have macroeconomic significance?

Here is the first point at which the monopolistic competition assumption is important. For a firm in a perfectly competitive market, getting the price "a little bit wrong" has serious consequences: The farmer who prices his corn 5¢ a bushel above the market price sells no corn. Therefore the existence of a menu cost wouldn't prevent the farmer from pricing his product at precisely the correct level. However, the demand for the output of a monopolistically competitive firm responds much less sharply to changes in its price; the movie theater doesn't lose many of its customers if its ticket price is 5¢ higher than its competitors'. Thus as long as the monopolistic competitor's price is in the right general range, the loss of profits from not getting the price exactly right isn't too great. If the loss in profits is less than the cost of changing prices—the menu costs—the firm won't change its price.

Over time, the production function and the demand curve the firm faces will undergo a variety of shocks so that eventually the profit-maximizing price for a firm may be significantly different from the preset price. When the profits lost by having the "wrong" price clearly exceed the cost of changing the price, the firm will change its nominal price. Thus movie theaters periodically raise their ticket and popcorn prices to reflect general inflation and other changes in market conditions.

Empirical Evidence on Price Stickiness. Several studies have examined the degree of rigidity or stickiness in actual prices.

To investigate whether firms perceive their own prices as being sticky or not, Alan Blinder[11] of Princeton University, assisted by a team of Princeton graduate students, interviewed the managers of 200 randomly selected firms about their pricing behavior. Almost half (49.5%) of managers interviewed said that their firms changed prices once a year or less. Only 22% of the firms changed prices more than four times per year. Besides probing into pricing behavior, Blinder and his students also asked firm managers *why* they tend to change prices infrequently. Direct costs of changing prices (menu costs) did appear to play a role for many firms. Nevertheless, many managers stressed as a reason for price stickiness their concern that, if they changed their own prices, their competitors would not necessarily follow suit. Managers were particularly reluctant to be the first in their market to raise prices, fearing that they would lose customers to their rivals. For this reason, many firms reported delaying price changes until it was evident throughout the industry that changes in costs or demand made price adjustment necessary.

In another study of price stickiness Anil Kashyap,[12] of the University of Chicago, examined the prices of twelve individual items listed in the catalogues of L.L. Bean, Orvis, and Recreational Equipment, Inc., over a 35-year period. Changing the prices listed in a new catalogue is virtually costless, yet Kashyap found that the nominal prices of many goods remained fixed in successive issues of the catalogue.

However, evidence based on a larger data set suggests that price stickiness may not be as pervasive as earlier studies indicated. In their 2004 paper, Mark Bils of the University of Rochester and Peter Klenow of Stanford University[13] found that the average time between price changes among 350 categories of goods (whose prices were recorded by the Bureau of Labor Statistics for use in calculating the Consumer Price Index) was just 4.3 months, suggesting that prices are changed much more frequently than reported by Blinder and by Kashyap. Prices of some goods and services, such as men's haircuts, taxicab fares, and newspapers, change very rarely and are clearly sticky. But prices of other goods and services, including food and gasoline, change very frequently.

The results by Bils and Klenow thus suggest that some prices are not too sticky, and these findings could cast doubt on the price stickiness view. Even though some prices may adjust frequently, many economists continue to use price stickiness in their models because the causes of the price changes are important. For instance, when firms run sales, they reduce their prices at the beginning of the sale and increase prices at the end of the sale. A study by Emi Nakamura and Jon Steinsson[14] of Columbia University found that if one looks at all changes in prices, including the changes that occur during sales, the median time between price changes is about 4.6 months, which is close to the finding in Bils and Klenow. However, when Nakamura and Steinsson exclude price changes associated with sales, they find

[11]"On Sticky Prices: Academic Theories Meet the Real World," in N. G. Mankiw, ed., *Monetary Policy*, University of Chicago Press, 1994.

[12]"Sticky Prices: New Evidence from Retail Catalogs," *Quarterly Journal of Economics*, February 1995, pp. 245–274.

[13]"Some Evidence on the Importance of Sticky Prices," *Journal of Political Economy*, October 2004, pp. 947–985.

[14]"Five Facts about Prices: A Reevaluation of Menu Cost Models," *Quarterly Journal of Economics*, November 2008, pp. 1415–1464.

that the median length of time between price changes more than doubles to 11 months, which is consistent with stickiness in non-sales prices. Another reason that economists continue to use the assumption of price stickiness in their models is that many of the price changes are caused by shifts in demand or supply in a particular industry. For example, day-to-day news about the supply of oil causes gasoline prices to change. But the assumption about price stickiness is going to be relevant in our macroeconomic model for how prices respond to changes in monetary policy and how prices change to restore general equilibrium, not how they respond to supply and demand shocks in their own industry. Research by Jean Boivin of HEC-Montreal, Marc Giannoni of the Federal Reserve Bank of Dallas, and Ilian Mihov of INSEAD[15] shows that in response to monetary policy, prices of many goods are very sticky, whereas those same prices respond quickly in response to shocks to supply and demand that affect the relative price of the good compared with other goods. Thus in our macroeconomic model, the assumption of sticky prices is a useful one, even in the face of the Bils and Klenow evidence.

Meeting the Demand at the Fixed Nominal Price. When prices are sticky, firms react to changes in demand by changing the amount of production rather than by changing prices. According to Keynesians, why are firms willing to meet demand at a fixed nominal price? To answer this question, we again rely on the assumption of monopolistic competition. We've stated that a monopolistically competitive firm can raise its price some without risk of losing all its customers. The profit-maximizing strategy for a monopolistically competitive firm is to charge a price higher than its **marginal cost**, or the cost of producing an additional unit of output. The excess of the price over the marginal cost is the **markup**. For example, if a firm charges a price 15% above its marginal cost, the firm has a markup of 15%. More generally, if the firm charges a constant markup of η over marginal cost, the following markup rule describes its price:

$$P = (1 + \eta)MC, \tag{11.1}$$

where P is the nominal price charged by the firm and MC is the nominal marginal cost.[16]

When the firm sets its price according to Eq. (11.1), it has an idea of how many units it will sell. Now suppose that, to the firm's surprise, customers demand several more units than the firm expected to sell at that price. Will it be profitable for the firm to meet the demand at this price?

The answer is "yes." Because the price the firm receives for each extra unit exceeds its cost of producing that extra unit (its marginal cost), the firm's profits increase when it sells additional units at the fixed price. Thus as long as the marginal cost remains below the fixed price of its product, the firm gladly supplies

[15] "Sticky Prices and Monetary Policy: Evidence from Disaggregated U.S. Data," *American Economic Review*, March 2009, pp. 350–384.

[16] Technical note: For a monopolistically competitive firm that faces a fixed wage and a demand curve with a constant price elasticity, the constant-markup rule in Eq. (11.1) will maximize profit. Also, in this case the labor demand curve is proportional to (rather than equal to) the marginal product of labor curve. Specifically, to maximize profits the firm equates the MPN to $(1 + \eta)w^*$, where w^* is the efficiency wage, rather than equating the MPN to w^* itself. This qualification doesn't affect any conclusions presented in this chapter.

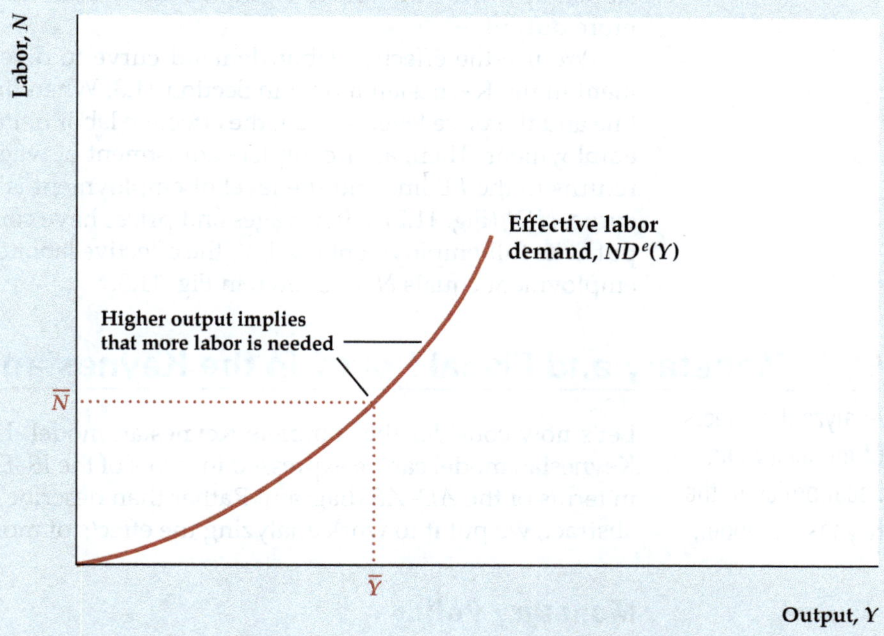

FIGURE 11.3

The effective labor demand curve

When a firm meets the demand for its output, it employs just the amount of labor needed to produce the quantity of output demanded. Because more labor is required to produce more output, firms must employ more labor when the demand for output is higher. This relationship between the amount of output demanded and the amount of labor employed is the effective labor demand curve. The effective labor demand curve is the same as the production function relating output and labor, except that labor is plotted on the vertical axis and output is plotted on the horizontal axis.

more units at this fixed price. Furthermore, if the firm is paying an efficiency wage, it can easily hire more workers to produce the units needed to meet the demand because there is an excess supply of labor.

The macroeconomic importance of firms' meeting demand at the fixed nominal price is that *the economy can produce an amount of output that is not on the full-employment line.* Recall that the *FE* line shows the amount of output that firms would produce after complete adjustment of all wages and prices. However, with nominal-price stickiness the prices of goods do not adjust rapidly to their general equilibrium values. During the period in which prices haven't yet completely adjusted, the amount of output produced need not be on the *FE* line. Instead, as long as marginal cost is below the fixed price, monopolistically competitive firms will produce the level of output demanded.

Effective Labor Demand. When a firm meets the demand for its output at a specific price, it may produce a different amount of output and employ a different amount of labor than it had planned. How much labor will a firm actually employ when it meets the demand? The answer is given by the effective labor demand curve, $ND^e(Y)$, shown in Figure 11.3. For any amount of output, Y, the **effective labor demand curve** indicates how much labor is needed to produce that output, with productivity, the capital stock, and effort held constant.

We already have a concept that expresses the relationship between the amount of labor used and the amount of output produced: the production function. Indeed, the effective labor demand curve in Fig. 11.3 is simply a graph of the production function relating output and labor input, except that output, Y, is measured on the horizontal axis and labor, N, is measured on the vertical axis. (This reversal of the axes is convenient later.) The effective labor demand curve slopes upward from left to right because a firm needs more labor to produce more output.

We use the effective labor demand curve to determine the level of employment in the Keynesian model in Section 11.3. When the economy is not on the *FE* line and the price level is fixed, the effective labor demand curve gives the level of employment. Then, after complete adjustment of wages and prices, the economy returns to the *FE* line and the level of employment is given by the labor demand curve, ND^* (Fig. 11.2). After wages and prices have completely adjusted, with output at its full-employment level, $\bar{Y}$, the effective labor demand curve indicates that employment equals $\bar{N}$, as shown in Fig. 11.3.

11.3 Monetary and Fiscal Policy in the Keynesian Model

Analyze the effects of monetary and fiscal policy in the Keynesian model.

Let's now consider the complete Keynesian model. Like the classical model, the Keynesian model can be expressed in terms of the *IS–LM* diagram or, alternatively, in terms of the *AD–AS* diagram. Rather than describe the Keynesian model in the abstract, we put it to work analyzing the effects of monetary and fiscal policy.

Monetary Policy

The main reason for introducing nominal-price stickiness into the Keynesian model was to explain monetary nonneutrality. We examine the link between price stickiness and monetary nonneutrality first in the Keynesian *IS–LM* framework and then in the Keynesian version of the *AD–AS* model.

Monetary Policy in the Keynesian *IS–LM* Model. The Keynesian version of the *IS–LM* model is quite similar to the *IS–LM* model discussed in Chapters 9 and 10. In particular, the *IS* curve and the *LM* curve are the same as in our earlier analyses. The *FE* line in the Keynesian model also is similar to the *FE* line used earlier. The Keynesian *FE* line is vertical at the full-employment level of output, $\bar{Y}$, which in turn depends on the full-employment level of employment determined in the labor market. However, the Keynesian and classical *FE* lines differ in two respects. First, in the Keynesian model the full-employment level of employment is determined at the intersection of the labor demand curve and the efficiency wage line, not at the point where the quantities of labor demanded and supplied are equal, as in the classical model. Second, because labor supply doesn't affect employment in the efficiency wage model, changes in labor supply don't affect the Keynesian *FE* line, although changes in labor supply do affect the classical *FE* line.

Because of price stickiness, in the Keynesian model the economy doesn't have to be in general equilibrium in the short run. However, in the long run when prices adjust, the economy reaches its general equilibrium at the intersection of the *IS* curve, the *LM* curve, and the *FE* line, as in the classical model.

According to Keynesians, what happens to the economy in the short run if sticky prices prevent it from reaching general equilibrium? Keynesians assume that the asset market clears quickly and that the level of output is determined by aggregate demand. Thus according to Keynesians, *the economy always lies at the intersection of the* IS *and* LM *curves.* However, because monopolistically competitive firms are willing to meet the demand for goods at fixed levels of prices, output can differ from full-employment output and the economy may not be on the

FE line in the short run. When the economy is off the *FE* line, firms use just enough labor to produce the output needed to meet demand. Under the assumption that the efficiency wage is higher than the market-clearing real wage, there are always unemployed workers who want to work, and firms are able to change employment as needed to meet the demand for output without changing the wage.

Figure 11.4 analyzes the effect of an increase in the nominal money supply in the Keynesian *IS–LM* model. We assume that the economy starts at its general equilibrium point, *E*. Recall that an increase in the money supply shifts the *LM* curve down and to the right, from LM^1 to LM^2 (Fig. 11.4a). Because an increase in

FIGURE 11.4

An increase in the money supply

(a) If we start from an initial general equilibrium at point *E*, an increase in the money supply shifts the *LM* curve down and to the right, from LM^1 to LM^2; the *IS* curve and the *FE* line remain unchanged. Because prices are fixed and firms meet the demand for output in the short run, the economy moves to point *F*, which is to the right of the *FE* line. Output rises to Y_2 and the real interest rate falls.
(b) Because firms produce more output, employment rises to N_2, as shown by the effective labor demand curve. In the long run, the price level rises in the same proportion as the money supply, the real money supply returns to its initial level, and the *LM* curve returns to its initial position, LM^1, in (a). The economy returns to *E* in both (a) and (b), and money is neutral in the long run.

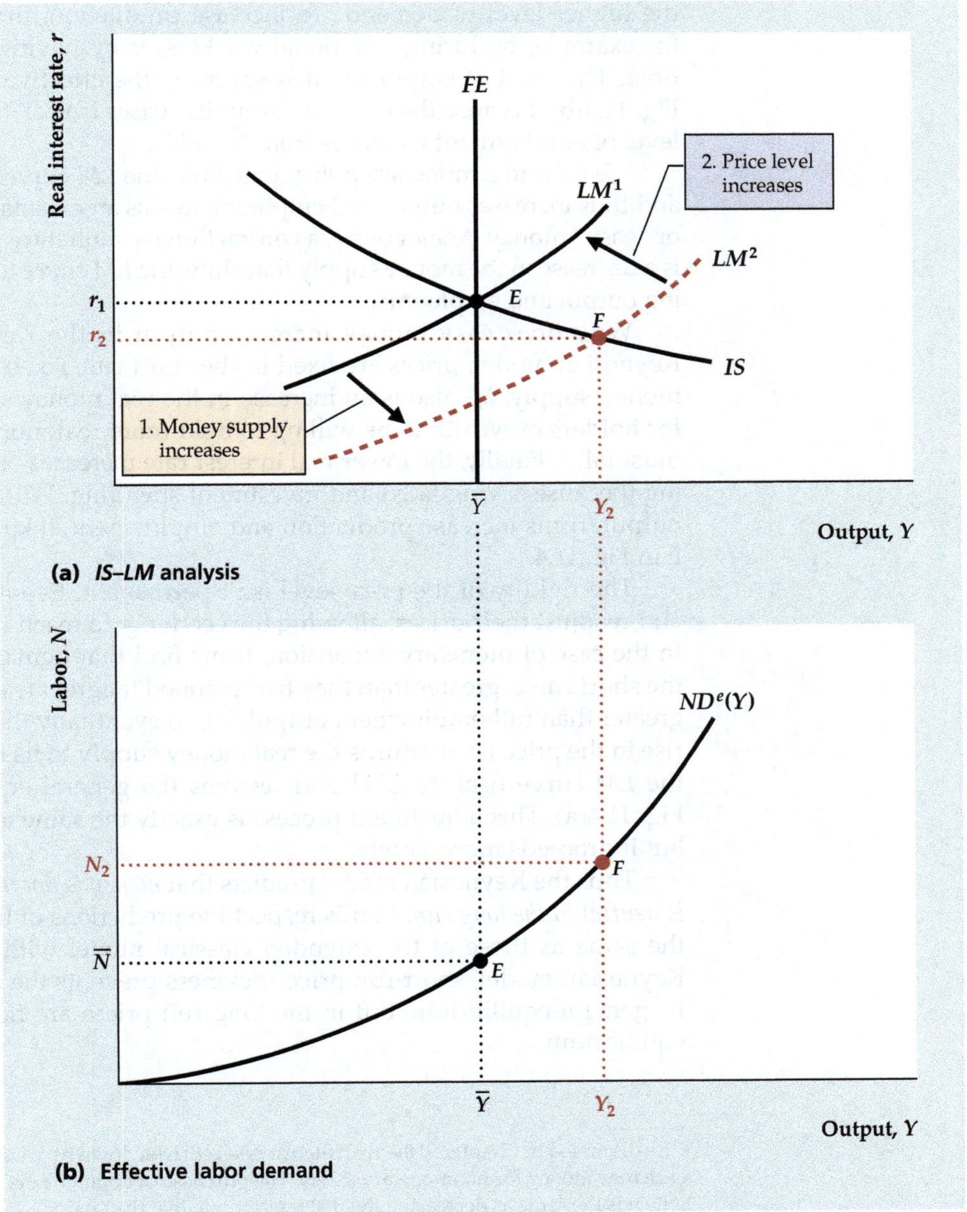

the money supply doesn't directly affect the goods or labor markets, the *IS* curve and the *FE* line are unaffected. So far this analysis is like that of the classical model.

Unlike the classical model, however, the Keynesian model is based on the assumption that prices are temporarily fixed (because of menu costs) so that the general equilibrium at *E* isn't restored immediately. Instead, the short-run equilibrium of the economy—that is, the resting point of the economy at the fixed price level—lies at the intersection of *IS* and LM^2 (point *F*), where output rises to Y_2 and the real interest rate falls to r_2.

Because the *IS–LM* intersection at point *F* is to the right of the *FE* line, aggregate output demanded, Y_2, is greater than the full-employment level of output, $\bar{Y}$. Monopolistically competitive firms facing menu costs don't raise their prices in the short run, as competitive firms do. Instead they increase production to Y_2 to satisfy the higher level of demand. To increase production, firms raise employment—for example, by hiring additional workers or by having employees work overtime. The level of employment is given by the effective labor demand curve in Fig. 11.4(b). Because the level of output increases from $\bar{Y}$ to Y_2 in the short run, the level of employment increases from $\bar{N}$ to N_2.

We refer to a monetary policy that shifts the *LM* curve down and to the right—and thus increases output and employment—as an **expansionary monetary policy**, or "easy" money. Analogously, a **contractionary monetary policy**, or "tight" money, is a decrease in the money supply that shifts the *LM* curve up and to the left, decreasing output and employment.

Why does easy money increase output in the Keynesian model? In the Keynesian model, prices are fixed in the short run, so an increase in the nominal money supply, *M*, also is an increase in the real money supply, M/P. Recall that, for holders of wealth to be willing to hold more real money, the real interest rate must fall.[17] Finally, the lower real interest rate increases both consumption spending (because saving falls) and investment spending. With more demand for their output, firms increase production and employment, taking the economy to point *F* in Fig. 11.4.

The rigidity of the price level isn't permanent. Eventually, firms will review and readjust their prices, allowing the economy to reach its long-run equilibrium. In the case of monetary expansion, firms find that demand for their products in the short run is greater than they had planned (aggregate output demanded, Y_2, is greater than full-employment output, $\bar{Y}$), so eventually they raise their prices. The rise in the price level returns the real money supply to its initial level, which shifts the *LM* curve back to LM^1 and restores the general equilibrium at point *E* in Fig. 11.4(a). This adjustment process is exactly the same as in the classical model, but it proceeds more slowly.

Thus the Keynesian model predicts that *money is not neutral in the short run but is neutral in the long run.* In this respect the predictions of the Keynesian model are the same as those of the extended classical model with misperceptions. In the Keynesian model, short-run price stickiness prevents the economy from reaching its general equilibrium, but in the long run prices are flexible, ensuring general equilibrium.

---

[17]As discussed in Chapter 9, the real interest rate is driven down by wealth-holders' attempts to exchange money for nonmonetary assets. The purchase of nonmonetary assets drives up their prices, which is the same as decreasing the real interest rate that they pay.

Monetary Policy in the Keynesian *AD–AS* Model. We can also analyze the effect of monetary policy on real output and the price level by using the Keynesian version of the *AD–AS* model. In fact, we have already performed this analysis in Fig. 9.14, where we used the *AD–AS* model to examine the effects of a 10% increase in the nominal money supply. Although we didn't identify that analysis as specifically Keynesian or classical, it can be readily given a Keynesian interpretation.

The distinguishing feature that determines whether an analysis is Keynesian or classical is the speed of price adjustment. As we emphasized in Chapter 10, classical economists argue that prices adjust quickly so that the economy reaches its long-run equilibrium quickly. In the extreme version of the classical model, the long-run equilibrium is reached virtually immediately, and the short-run aggregate supply (*SRAS*) curve is irrelevant. However, in the Keynesian model, monopolistically competitive firms that face menu costs keep their prices fixed for a while, producing the amount of output demanded at the fixed price level. This behavior is represented by a horizontal short-run aggregate supply curve such as $SRAS^1$ in Fig. 9.14. If we assume that firms maintain fixed prices and simply meet the demand for output for a substantial period of time, so that the departure from long-run equilibrium lasts for months or perhaps even years, the analysis illustrated in Fig. 9.14 reflects the Keynesian approach.

Let's briefly review that analysis from an explicitly Keynesian perspective. Figure 9.14 depicts the effects of a 10% increase in the nominal money supply on an economy that is initially in both short-run and long-run equilibrium (at point *E*). The increase in the nominal money supply causes the *AD* curve to shift up from AD^1 to AD^2. In fact, as we explained in Chapter 9, the 10% increase in the nominal money supply shifts the *AD* curve up by 10% at each level of output. The initial effect of this shift in the *AD* curve is to move the economy to a short-run equilibrium at point *F*, where output is higher than its full-employment level, $\bar{Y}$. Because of menu costs, firms don't immediately react to increased demand by raising prices, but instead increase production to meet the higher demand. Thus at point *F*, firms are producing more output than the amount that would maximize their profits in the absence of menu costs. Because output is temporarily higher than its full-employment level, we conclude that in the Keynesian model money isn't neutral in the short run. Eventually, however, firms will increase their prices to bring the quantity of output demanded back to the profit-maximizing level of output. In the long-run equilibrium, represented by point *H* in Fig. 9.14, output equals the full-employment level, $\bar{Y}$, and the price level, P_2, is 10% higher than the initial price level, P_1. In long-run equilibrium the expansion of the money supply affects only nominal quantities, such as the price level, not real quantities, such as output or employment, so we conclude that in the Keynesian model (as in the classical model) money is neutral in the long run.

Fiscal Policy

The Keynesian model was initially developed during the Great Depression as economists struggled to explain the worldwide economic collapse and find policies to help the economy return to normal. The early Keynesians stressed that fiscal policy—the government's decisions about government purchases and taxes—can significantly affect output and employment levels. Let's look at the Keynesians' conclusion that both increased government purchases and lower taxes can be used to raise output and employment.

The Effect of Increased Government Purchases. The Keynesian analysis of how increased government purchases affect the economy is shown in Figure 11.5. Again, we assume that the economy starts from full employment (later we discuss what happens if the economy starts from a recession). Point E represents the initial equilibrium in both (a) and (b). As before, a temporary increase in government purchases increases the demand for goods and reduces desired national saving at any level of the real interest rate, so that the IS curve shifts up and to the right, from IS^1 to IS^2 (see Summary table 12 in Chapter 9). In the short run, before prices can adjust, the economy moves to point F in Fig. 11.5(a), where the new IS curve, IS^2, and LM^1 intersect. At F both output

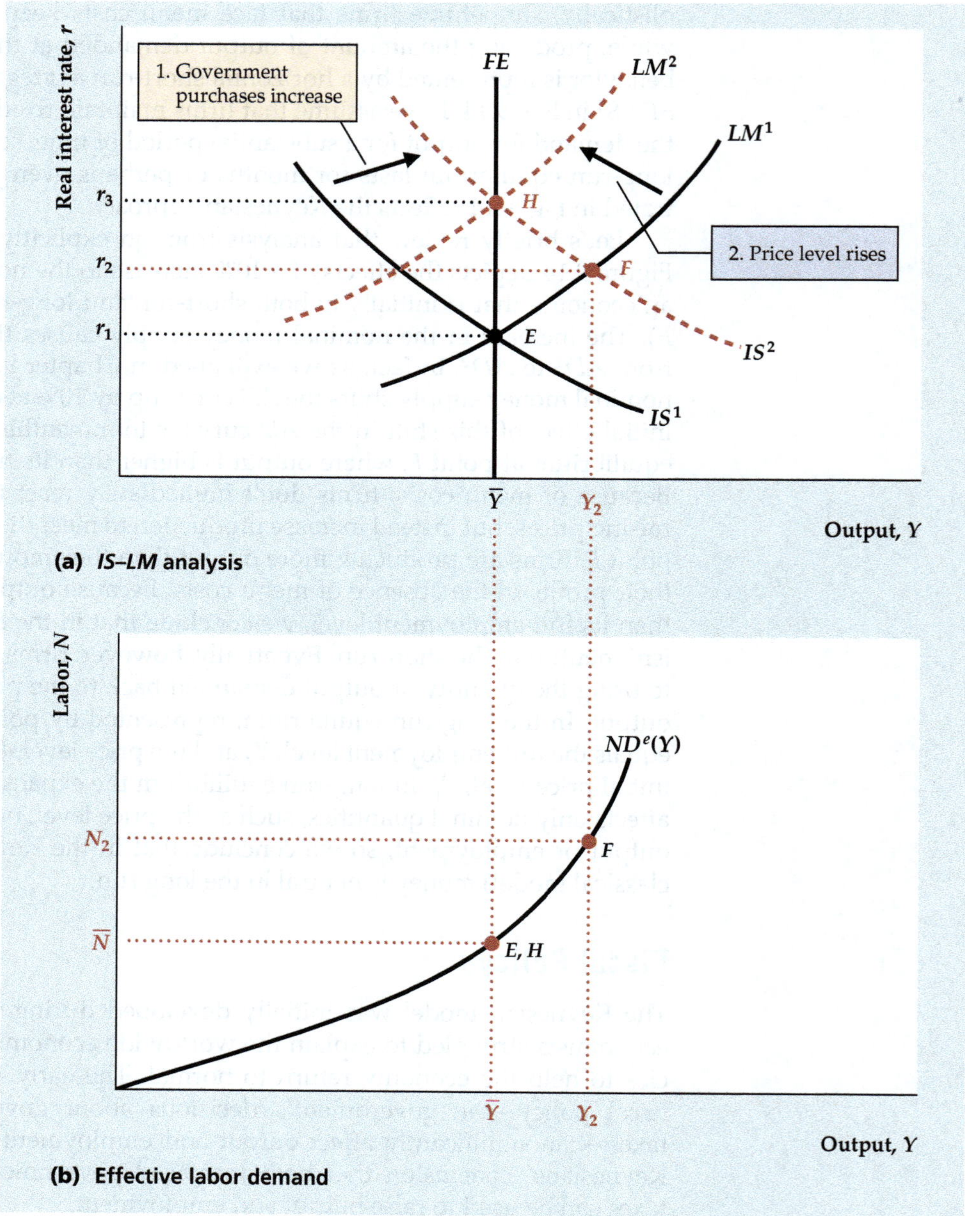

FIGURE 11.5

A temporary increase in government purchases

(a) If we start from the general equilibrium at point E, a temporary increase in government purchases reduces desired national saving and shifts the IS curve up and to the right, from IS^1 to IS^2. The short-run equilibrium is at point F, with output increasing to Y_2 and the real interest rate rising to r_2.

(b) As firms increase production to meet the demand, employment increases from $\bar{N}$ to N_2, as shown by the effective labor demand curve. However, the economy doesn't remain at point F. Because aggregate output demanded exceeds $\bar{Y}$ in the short run, the price level increases, reducing the real money supply and shifting the LM curve up and to the left, from LM^1 to LM^2. In the long run, with equilibrium at point H, output returns to $\bar{Y}$ and employment returns to $\bar{N}$, but the real interest rate rises further to r_3.

and the real interest rate have increased. Because firms meet the higher demand at the fixed price level, employment also rises, as shown by the movement from point *E* to point *F* along the effective labor demand curve in Fig. 11.5(b). A fiscal policy change, such as this one, that shifts the *IS* curve up and to the right and raises output and employment is an expansionary change. Similarly, a fiscal policy change (such as a reduction in government purchases) that shifts the *IS* curve down and to the left and reduces output and employment is a contractionary change.

In discussing the effects of increased government purchases or other types of spending, Keynesians often use the multiplier concept. The **multiplier** associated with any particular type of spending is the short-run change in total output resulting from a one-unit change in that type of spending. So, for example, if the increase in government purchases analyzed in Fig. 11.5 is ΔG and the resulting short-run increase in output between points *E* and *F* in Fig. 11.5 is ΔY, the multiplier associated with government purchases is $\Delta Y/\Delta G$. Keynesians usually argue that the fiscal policy multiplier is greater than 1, so that if government purchases rise by \$1 billion, output will rise by more than \$1 billion. We derive an algebraic expression for the government purchases multiplier in Appendix 11.C.

Recall that the classical version of the *IS–LM* model also predicts that a temporary increase in government purchases increases output, but in a different way. The classical analysis focuses on the fact that increased government purchases require higher current or future taxes to pay for the extra spending. Higher taxes make workers (who are taxpayers) effectively poorer, which induces them to supply more labor. This increase in labor supply shifts the *FE* line to the right and causes output to rise in the classical model. In contrast, the *FE* line in the Keynesian model doesn't depend on labor supply (because of efficiency wages) and thus is unaffected by the increase in government purchases. Instead, the increase in government purchases affects output by raising aggregate demand (that is, by shifting the *IS–LM* intersection to the right). Output increases above its full-employment level in the short run as firms satisfy extra demand at the initial price level.

The effect of increased government purchases on output in the Keynesian model lasts only as long as needed for the price level to adjust. (However, many Keynesians believe that price adjustment is sufficiently slow that this effect could be felt for several years.) In the long run, when firms adjust their prices, the *LM* curve moves up and to the left, from LM^1 to LM^2 in Fig. 11.5(a), and the economy reaches general equilibrium at point *H*, with output again at $\bar{Y}$. Thus an increase in government purchases doesn't raise output in the long run.

The effects of increased government purchases also appear in the Keynesian *AD–AS* framework (Figure 11.6). Increased government purchases shift the *IS* curve up and to the right and raise the aggregate demand for output at any given price level. Thus as a result of expansionary fiscal policy, the aggregate demand curve shifts to the right, from AD^1 to AD^2. The increase in aggregate demand raises output above $\bar{Y}$, as shown by the shift from the initial equilibrium at point *E* to the short-run equilibrium at point *F*. At *F* the aggregate demand for output is greater than full-employment output, so firms eventually raise their prices. In the long run the economy reaches the full-employment general equilibrium at point *H*, with output again at $\bar{Y}$ and with a higher price level. These results are identical to those we obtained using the Keynesian *IS–LM* framework.

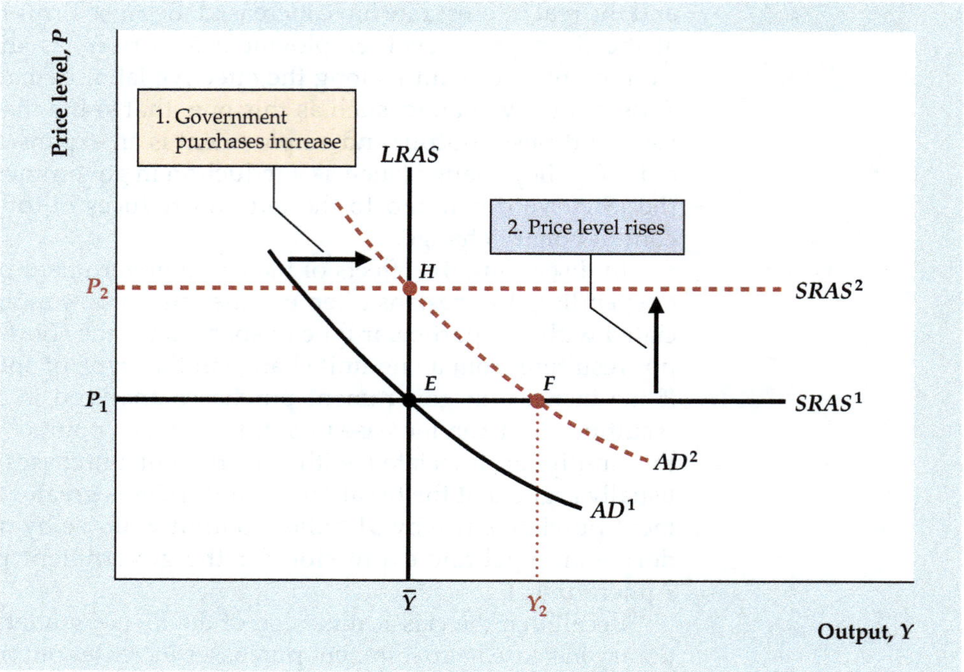

FIGURE 11.6

An increase in government purchases in the Keynesian *AD–AS* framework

An increase in government purchases raises aggregate demand for output at any price level (see Fig. 11.5). Thus the aggregate demand curve shifts to the right, from AD^1 to AD^2. In the short run the increase in aggregate demand increases output to Y_2 (point *F*) but doesn't affect the price level because prices are sticky in the short run. Because aggregate output demanded, Y_2, exceeds $\bar{Y}$ at *F*, firms eventually raise their prices. The long-run equilibrium is at *H*, where AD^2 intersects the *LRAS* curve. At *H*, output has returned to $\bar{Y}$ and the price level has risen from P_1 to P_2. The higher price level raises the short-run aggregate supply curve, from $SRAS^1$ to $SRAS^2$.

The Effect of Lower Taxes. Keynesians generally believe that, like an increase in government purchases, a lump-sum reduction in current taxes is expansionary. In other words, they expect that a tax cut will shift the *IS* curve up and to the right, raising output and employment in the short run. Similarly, they expect a tax increase to be contractionary, shifting the *IS* curve down and to the left.

Why does a tax cut affect the *IS* curve, according to Keynesians? The argument is that if consumers receive a tax cut, they will spend part of it on increased consumption. For any output, *Y*, and level of government purchases, *G*, an increase in desired consumption arising from a tax cut will lower desired national saving, $Y - C^d - G$. A drop in desired saving raises the real interest rate that clears the goods market and shifts the *IS* curve up.[18]

If a tax cut raises desired consumption and shifts the *IS* curve up, as Keynesians claim, the effects on the economy are similar to the effects of increased government purchases (Figs. 11.5 and 11.6). In the short run, a tax cut raises aggregate demand and thus output and employment at the initial price level. In the long run, after complete price adjustment, the economy returns to full employment with a higher real interest rate than in the initial general equilibrium. The only difference between the tax cut and the increase in government purchases is that, instead of raising the portion of full-employment output devoted to government purchases, a tax cut raises the portion of full-employment output devoted to consumption.

[18]In arguing that a tax cut raises desired consumption and lowers desired national saving, Keynesian economists reject the Ricardian equivalence proposition (Chapter 4), which states that a lump-sum tax cut should *not* affect consumption or national saving. We discuss Ricardian equivalence further in Chapter 15.

11.4 The Keynesian Theory of Business Cycles and Macroeconomic Stabilization

Explain Keynesian theories about business cycles and macroeconomic stabilization.

Recall that there are two basic questions about business cycles that a macroeconomic theory should try to answer: (1) What causes recurrent fluctuations in the economy? and (2) What, if anything, should policymakers try to do about cycles? We are now ready to give the Keynesian answers to these two questions.

Keynesian Business Cycle Theory

An explanation of the business cycle requires not only a macroeconomic model but also some assumptions about the types of shocks hitting the economy. For example, RBC economists believe that productivity shocks, which directly shift the *FE* line, are the most important type of macroeconomic shock.

In contrast to RBC economists, most Keynesians believe that aggregate demand shocks are the primary source of business cycle fluctuations. **Aggregate demand shocks** are shocks to the economy that shift *either* the *IS* curve or the *LM* curve and thus affect the aggregate demand for output. Examples of aggregate demand shocks affecting the *IS* curve are changes in fiscal policy, changes in desired investment arising from changes in expected future TFP,[19] and changes in consumer confidence about the future that affect desired saving. Examples of aggregate demand shocks affecting the *LM* curve are changes in the demand for money or changes in the money supply. The Keynesian version of the *IS–LM* model, combined with the view that most shocks are aggregate demand shocks, constitutes the Keynesian theory of business cycles.

Figure 11.7 uses the Keynesian model to illustrate a recession caused by an aggregate demand shock. Suppose that consumers become pessimistic about the long-term future of the economy and thus reduce their current desired consumption; equivalently, they raise their current desired saving. For any level of income, an increase in desired saving lowers the real interest rate that clears the goods market and thus shifts the *IS* curve down, from IS^1 to IS^2. The economy goes into recession at point *F*, and, as prices don't adjust immediately to restore full employment, it remains in recession for some period of time with output below its full-employment level. Because firms face below-normal levels of demand, they also cut employment.

Note that a decline in investment spending (reflecting, for example, pessimism of business investors) or reduced government purchases would have similar recessionary effects as the decline in consumer spending analyzed in Fig. 11.7. Alternatively, a shift up and to the left of the *LM* curve (because of either increased money demand or reduced money supply) also could cause a recession in the Keynesian framework; in this case, high real interest rates caused by the "shortage" of money would cause the declines in consumer spending and investment. Thus Keynesians attribute recessions to "not enough demand" for goods, in contrast to classical economists who attribute recessions to "not enough supply."

[19]A change in expected future *TFP* might also be thought of as a technological shock because it involves a change in the future production function. However, because a change in future *TFP* shifts the *IS* curve but doesn't affect the current *FE* line, Keynesians classify it as an aggregate demand shock.

FIGURE 11.7

A recession arising from an aggregate demand shock

The figure illustrates how an adverse aggregate demand shock can cause a recession in the Keynesian model. The economy starts at general equilibrium at point E. A decline in consumer confidence about the future of the economy reduces desired consumption and raises desired saving so that the IS curve shifts down, from IS^1 to IS^2. The economy falls into recession at point F, with output below its full-employment level, $\bar{Y}$.

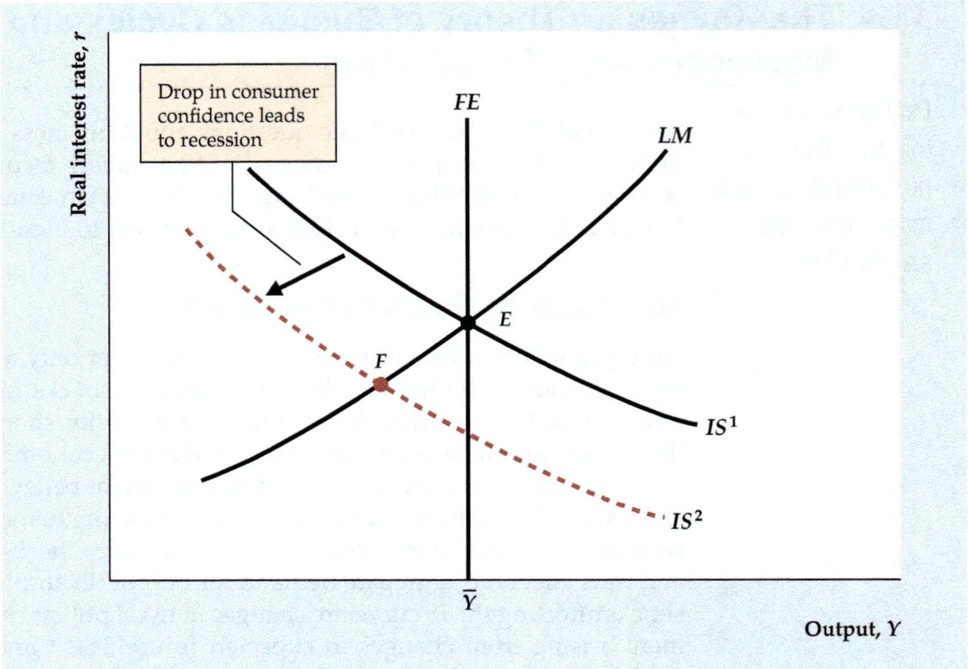

Like the real business cycle theory, the Keynesian theory of cycles can account for several of the business cycle facts: (1) In response to occasional aggregate demand shocks, the theory predicts recurrent fluctuations in output; (2) the theory correctly implies that employment will fluctuate in the same direction as output; and (3) because it predicts that shocks to the money supply will be nonneutral, the theory is consistent with the business cycle fact that money is procyclical and leading.

A business cycle fact that we previously emphasized (Chapter 8) is that spending on investment goods and other durable goods is strongly procyclical and volatile. This cyclical behavior of durable goods spending can be explained by the Keynesian theory if shocks to durable goods demand are themselves a main source of cycles. The demand for durable goods would be a source of cyclical fluctuations if, for example, investors frequently reassessed their expectations of the future *MPK*. Keynes himself thought that waves of investor optimism and pessimism, which he called "animal spirits," were a significant source of cyclical fluctuations. A rise in the demand for investment goods or consumer durables (at fixed levels of output and the real interest rate) is expansionary because it shifts the *IS* curve up and to the right. Investment will also be procyclical in the Keynesian model whenever cycles are caused by fluctuations in the *LM* curve; for example, an increase in the money supply, which shifts the *LM* curve down and to the right, both increases output and (by reducing the real interest rate) increases investment.

Another important business cycle fact that is consistent with the Keynesian theory is the observation that inflation tends to slow during or just after recessions (inflation is procyclical and lagging). In the Keynesian view, as Fig. 11.7 illustrates, during a recession, aggregate output demanded is less than the full-employment level of output. Thus when firms do adjust their prices, they will be likely to cut them to increase their sales. According to the Keynesian model, because demand pressure is low during recessions, inflation will tend to subside when the economy is weak.

Procyclical Labor Productivity and Labor Hoarding. Although the Keynesian model is consistent with many of the business cycle facts, one fact—that labor productivity is procyclical—presents problems for this approach. Recall that procyclical labor productivity is consistent with the real business cycle assumption that cycles are caused by productivity shocks—that recessions are times when productivity is unusually low and booms are times when productivity is unusually high. Unlike the RBC economists, however, Keynesians assume that demand shocks rather than supply (productivity) shocks cause most cyclical fluctuations.

Because supply shocks are shifts of the production function, the Keynesian assumption that supply shocks usually are unimportant is the same as saying that the production function is fairly stable over the business cycle. But if the production function is stable, increases in employment during booms should *reduce* average labor productivity because of the diminishing marginal productivity of labor. Thus the Keynesian model predicts that average labor productivity is countercyclical, contrary to the business cycle fact.

To explain the procyclical behavior of average labor productivity, Keynesians have modified their models to include labor hoarding. As discussed in Section 10.1, labor hoarding occurs if firms retain, or "hoard," labor in a recession rather than laying off or firing workers. The reason that firms might hoard labor during a recession is to avoid the costs of letting workers go and then having to rehire them or hire and train new workers when the recession ends. Thus hoarded labor may be used less intensively (for example, store clerks may wait on fewer customers in a day) or be assigned to activities such as painting, cleaning, maintaining equipment, and training. If labor is utilized less intensively during a recession, or workers spend time on activities such as maintenance that don't directly contribute to measured output, labor productivity may fall during a recession even though the production function is stable. Thus labor hoarding provides a way of explaining the procyclical behavior of average labor productivity without assuming that recessions and expansions are caused by productivity shocks.

Macroeconomic Stabilization

From the Keynesian explanation of why business cycles occur, we turn to the Keynesian view on how policymakers should respond to recessions and booms. Briefly, Keynesians—unlike classical economists—generally favor policy actions to "stabilize" the economy by eliminating large fluctuations in output and employment. Keynesian support of more active policy measures follows from the theory's characterization of business cycle expansions and contractions as periods in which the economy is temporarily away from its general equilibrium (or not at the *IS–LM–FE* intersection). According to Keynesians, recessions are particularly undesirable because in a recession, employment may be far below the amount of labor that workers want to supply, which leads to hardships for the unemployed and to output that is "too low." Keynesians therefore argue that average economic well-being would be increased if governments tried to reduce cyclical fluctuations, especially recessions.

The Keynesian analysis of monetary and fiscal policies suggests that these policies could be used to smooth the business cycle. To understand how, consider

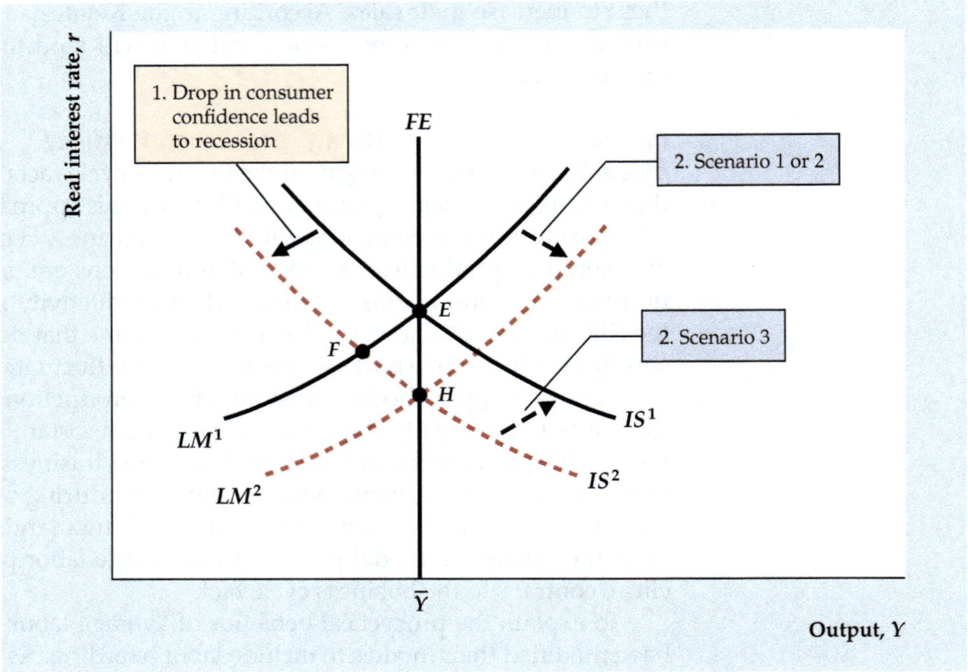

FIGURE 11.8

Stabilization policy in the Keynesian model

From point E the economy is driven into a recession at point F by a drop in consumer confidence and spending, which shifts the IS curve down, from IS^1 to IS^2. If the government took no action, in the long run price adjustment would shift the LM curve from LM^1 to LM^2 and restore general equilibrium at point H (Scenario 1). Alternatively, the government could try to offset the recession through stabilization policy. For example, the Fed could increase the money supply, which would shift the LM curve directly from LM^1 to LM^2, speeding the recovery in output (Scenario 2). Another possibility is a fiscal expansion, such as an increase in government purchases, which would shift the IS curve from IS^2 back to IS^1, again restoring full employment at E (Scenario 3). Compared to a strategy of doing nothing, expansionary monetary or fiscal policy helps the economy recover more quickly but leads to a higher price level in the long run.

Figure 11.8. Suppose that the economy, initially in general equilibrium at point E, has been driven into recession at point F. Various types of shocks could have caused this recession. In Fig. 11.7, for example, we considered a drop in consumer confidence about the future of the economy. A drop in confidence would reduce current desired consumption and increase current desired saving, thereby shifting the IS curve down from IS^1 to IS^2. This sort of change in consumer attitudes may have contributed to the 1990–1991 recession.

How might policymakers respond to this recession? We consider three possible scenarios: (1) no change in monetary or fiscal policy, (2) an increase in the money supply, and (3) an increase in government purchases.

- *Scenario 1: No change in macroeconomic policy.* One policy option is to do nothing. With no government intervention, the economy eventually will correct itself. At point F in Fig. 11.8, aggregate output demanded is below the full-employment level of output $\bar{Y}$. Therefore, over time, prices will begin to fall, increasing the real money supply and shifting the LM curve down and to the right. In the long run, price declines shift the LM curve from LM^1 to LM^2, restoring the economy to general equilibrium at point H. However, a disadvantage of this strategy is that, during the (possibly lengthy) price adjustment process, output and employment remain below their full-employment levels.
- *Scenario 2: An increase in the money supply.* Instead of waiting for the economy to reach general equilibrium through price adjustment, the Fed could increase the money supply, which also would shift the LM curve from LM^1 to LM^2 in Fig. 11.8. If prices adjust slowly, this expansionary policy would move the economy to general equilibrium at point H more quickly than would doing nothing.

- *Scenario 3: An increase in government purchases.* An alternative policy of raising government purchases will shift the *IS* curve up and to the right, from IS^2 to IS^1. This policy also takes the economy to full employment, although at point *E* in Fig. 11.8 rather than at point *H*.

In all three scenarios, the economy eventually returns to full employment. However, the use of monetary or fiscal policy to achieve full employment leads to two important differences from the scenario in which no policy action is taken. First, if the government uses monetary or fiscal expansion to end the recession, the economy returns directly to full employment; if policy isn't changed, the economy remains in recession in the short run, returning to full employment only when prices have fully adjusted. Second, if there is no policy change (Scenario 1), in the long run the price level falls, which increases the real money supply, shifts the *LM* curve down and to the right, and restores full employment at point *H*. In contrast, when monetary or fiscal policy is used to restore full employment (Scenarios 2 and 3), the downward adjustment of the price level doesn't occur because expansionary policy directly returns aggregate demand to the full-employment level. (The real money supply, *M/P*, increases by the same amount in Scenario 1 and Scenario 2, but the increase in *M/P* is achieved by a reduction in *P* in Scenario 1 and by an increase in *M*, with unchanged *P*, in Scenario 2.) Thus according to the Keynesian analysis, using expansionary monetary or fiscal policy has the advantage of bringing the economy back to full employment more quickly but the disadvantage of leading to a higher price level than if no policy action is undertaken.

Usually, either monetary or fiscal policy can be used to bring the economy back to full employment. Does it matter which policy is used? Yes, there is at least one basic difference between the outcomes of the two policies: Monetary and fiscal policies affect the composition of spending (the amount of output that is devoted to consumption, the amount to investment, and so on) differently. In Fig. 11.8, although total output is the same at the alternative general equilibrium points *E* and *H*, at *E* (reached by an increase in government purchases) government purchases are higher than at *H* (reached by an increase in the money supply). Because government purchases are higher at *E*, the remaining components of spending—in a closed economy, consumption and investment—must be lower at *E* than at *H*. Relative to a monetary expansion, an increase in government purchases crowds out consumption and investment by raising the real interest rate, which is higher at *E* than at *H*. In addition, increased government purchases imply higher current or future tax burdens, which also reduces consumption relative to what it would be with monetary expansion.

Difficulties of Macroeconomic Stabilization. The use of monetary and fiscal policies to smooth or moderate the business cycle is called **macroeconomic stabilization**. Using macroeconomic policies to try to smooth the cycle is also sometimes called **aggregate demand management** because monetary and fiscal policies shift the aggregate demand curve. Macroeconomic stabilization was a popular concept in the heyday of Keynesian economics in the 1960s, and it still influences policy discussions. Unfortunately, even putting aside the debates between classicals and Keynesians about whether smoothing the business cycle is desirable, actual macroeconomic stabilization has been much less successful than the simple Keynesian theory suggests.

As discussed in connection with fiscal policy (Section 10.2), attempts to stabilize the economy run into some technical problems. First, because the ability to measure and analyze the economy is imperfect, gauging how far the economy is from full employment at any particular time is difficult. Second, the amount that output will increase in response to a monetary or fiscal expansion isn't known exactly. These uncertainties make assessing how much of a monetary or fiscal change is needed to restore full employment difficult. Finally, even knowing the size of the policy change needed still wouldn't provide enough information. Because macroeconomic policies take time to implement (the implementation lag discussed in Chapter 10) and more time to affect the economy (the impact lag discussed in Chapter 10), their optimal use requires knowledge of where the economy will be six months or a year from now. But such knowledge is, at best, very imprecise.

Because of these problems, aggregate demand management has been likened to trying to hit a moving target in a heavy fog. These problems haven't persuaded most Keynesians to abandon stabilization policy; however, many Keynesians agree that policymakers should concentrate on fighting major recessions and not try to fine-tune the economy by smoothing every bump and wiggle in output and employment.

Supply Shocks in the Keynesian Model

Until the 1970s, the Keynesian business cycle theory focused almost exclusively on aggregate demand shocks as the source of business cycle fluctuations. Because aggregate demand shocks lead to procyclical movements in inflation, however, the Keynesian theory failed to account for the stagflation—high inflation together with a recession—that hit the U.S. economy during the 1973–1975 recession, which was induced by a quadrupling of oil prices in 1973.

This experience led to much criticism of the traditional theory by both economists and policymakers, so Keynesians recast the theory to allow for both supply and demand shocks. Although Keynesians wouldn't go so far as to agree with RBC economists that supply (productivity) shocks are a factor in most recessions, they now concede that there have been occasional episodes—the oil price shocks of the 1970s being the leading examples—in which supply shocks have played a primary role in an economic downturn. (See "In Touch with Data and Research: DSGE Models and the Classical–Keynesian Debate," for further discussion of agreement and disagreement between Keynesians and classicals.)

Figure 11.9 shows a Keynesian analysis of the effects of a sharp temporary increase in the price of oil (a similar analysis would apply to other supply shocks, such as a drought). As we showed in Chapter 3, if firms respond to an increase in the price of oil by using less energy, the amount of output that can be produced with the same amount of capital and labor falls. Thus the increase in the price of oil is an adverse supply shock, which reduces the full-employment level of output and shifts the *FE* line to the left, from FE^1 to FE^2. After complete wage and price adjustment, which occurs virtually immediately in the basic classical model but only in the long run in the Keynesian model, output falls to its new full-employment level, $\bar{Y}_2$. Thus in the long run (after full wage and price adjustment), the Keynesian analysis and the classical analysis of a supply shock are the same.

However, the Keynesian analysis of the short-run effects of an oil price shock is slightly different from the classical analysis. To understand the short-term effects of the oil price shock in the Keynesian model, first think about the effects of the increase in the oil price on the general price level. Recall that firms facing menu

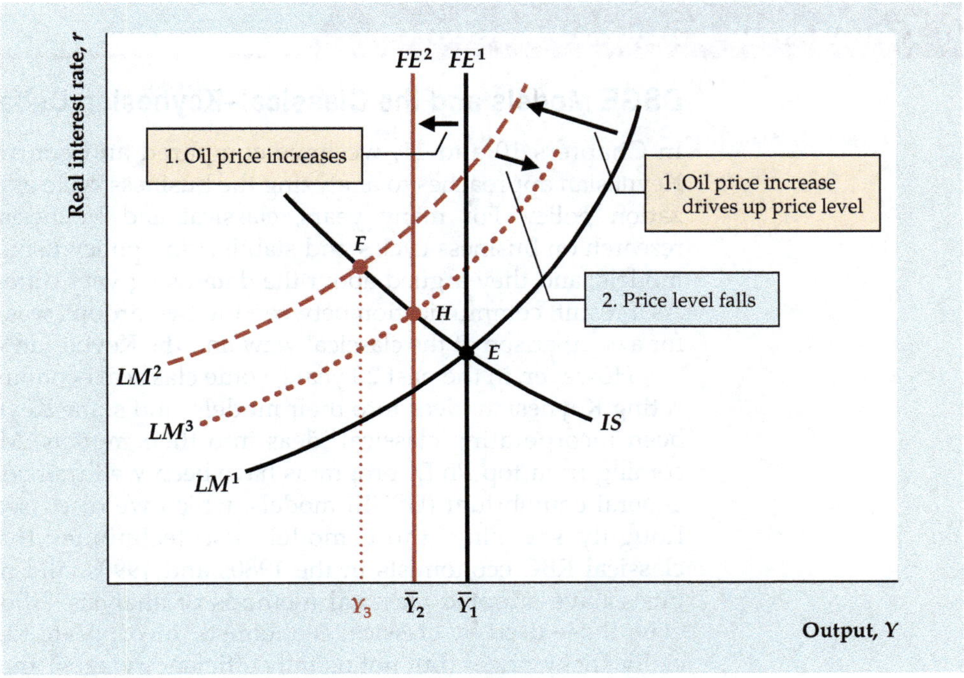

FIGURE 11.9

An oil price shock in the Keynesian model

An increase in the price of oil is an adverse supply shock that reduces full-employment output from $\bar{Y}_1$ to $\bar{Y}_2$ and thus shifts the *FE* line to the left. In addition, the increase in the price of oil increases prices in sectors that depend heavily on oil, whereas prices in other sectors remain fixed in the short run. Thus the average price level rises, which reduces the real money supply, *M*/*P*, and shifts the *LM* curve up and to the left, from LM^1 to LM^2. In the short run, the economy moves to point *F*, with output falling below the new, lower value of full-employment output and the real interest rate increasing. Because the aggregate quantity of goods demanded at *F* is less than the full-employment level of output, $\bar{Y}_2$, in the long run the price level falls, partially offsetting the initial increase in prices. The drop in the price level causes the *LM* curve to shift down and to the right, from LM^2 to LM^3, moving the economy to full-employment equilibrium at point *H*.

costs will not change their prices if the "right" prices are only a little different from the preset prices. However, if the right prices are substantially different from the preset prices, so that firms would lose considerable profits by maintaining the preset prices, they will change their prices. In the case of a large increase in the price of oil, firms whose costs are strongly affected by the price of oil—including gas stations, suppliers of home heating oil, and airlines, for example—find that the right prices for their products are substantially higher than the preset prices. These oil-dependent firms increase their prices quickly, whereas firms in other sectors maintain their preset prices in the short run. Thus there is price stickiness in the sense that not all prices adjust to their equilibrium values, and yet the average price level rises in the short run.

Because a sharp increase in the price of oil raises the price level, *P*, in the short run, it also reduces the real money supply, *M*/*P*. A decline in the real money supply shifts the *LM* curve up and to the left, from LM^1 to LM^2 in Fig. 11.9. As drawn, the intersection of the *LM* curve and the *IS* curve is located to the left of the new *FE* line, although this outcome isn't logically necessary. The short-run equilibrium is at point *F*, where LM^2 intersects the *IS* curve. Because *F* is to the left of the *FE* line, the economy is in a recession at *F*, with output (at Y_3) below the new value of full-employment output, $\bar{Y}_2$. In the short run, the economy experiences stagflation, with both a drop in output and a burst of inflation. Note that, according to this analysis, the short-run decline in output has two components: (1) the drop in full-employment output from $\bar{Y}_1$ to $\bar{Y}_2$ and (2) the drop in output below the new full-employment level arising from the shift up and to the left of the *LM* curve (the difference between $\bar{Y}_2$ and Y_3).

Supply shocks of the type analyzed in Fig. 11.9 pose tremendous difficulties for Keynesian stabilization policies. First, monetary or fiscal policy can do little

In Touch with Data and Research

DSGE Models and the Classical–Keynesian Debate

In Chapters 10 and 11, we have compared and contrasted the classical and Keynesian approaches to analyzing the business cycle and to determining stabilization policy. For many years, classical and Keynesian economists pursued research on business cycles and stabilization policy using very different types of models, and they argued about the data using very different empirical methods. As a result, communication between the two groups was difficult. (See Table 11.1 for a comparison of the classical view and the Keynesian view.)

However, in the past 20 years, some classical economists have been incorporating Keynesian ideas into their models, and some Keynesian economists have been incorporating classical ideas into their models. Many young economists coming from top Ph.D. programs have been well trained in dynamic, stochastic, general equilibrium (DSGE) models, which we discussed briefly in Chapter 10. Roughly speaking, those models use techniques that were developed by classical RBC economists in the 1980s and 1990s, and many Keynesian economists have adopted classical methods of analysis.[20] But many of the models, even those used by classical economists, incorporate Keynesian features, especially sticky prices (but not usually efficiency wages) and imperfect competition among firms. As a result, classical and Keynesian economists are now speaking the same language and can communicate with each other more clearly, and research on macroeconomic ideas is advancing more smoothly. Their research is increasingly being used to influence policymakers, as DSGE models incorporating sticky prices and financial factors are increasingly used by central banks for applied policy analysis.

[20]See, for example, Michael Woodford, *Interest and Prices: Foundations of a Theory of Monetary Policy* (Princeton, NJ: Princeton University Press, 2003).

about the portion of the decline in output resulting from the shift of the *FE* line; attempts to expand the economy beyond the new full-employment output level, $\bar{Y}_2$, will increase output only temporarily and worsen inflation. In contrast, the portion of the output decline arising from the shift up and to the left of the *LM* curve (the difference between $\bar{Y}_2$ and Y_3) represents an output level below the full-employment level and could, in principle, be eliminated by expansionary monetary or fiscal policies that raise output to $\bar{Y}_2$. However, by using expansionary policies at point *F*, rather than doing nothing, the government risks worsening the already-high rate of inflation. Hence, in the face of a shock that induces stagflation like the one shown in Fig. 11.9, macroeconomic policy can neither avoid a sharp decline in output nor restore output even to its new, lower full-employment level without potentially worsening inflation.

TABLE 11.1

Comparing the Keynesian View with the Classical View

Category	Classical View	Keynesian View
How fast does the price level adjust to restore general equilibrium?	Quickly	Slowly
What type of model is appropriate?	A model with microeconomic foundations	An aggregate model
Are supply shocks important?	They are the most important shocks	Aggregate demand shocks are more important
What is the role for government intervention in the economy?	Government intervention is usually unwarranted	Government intervention is vital
Do inflation and inflation expectations matter?	Yes, they matter	No, they do not matter much
What type of model is best?	A dynamic model	A static model is fine
What model of unemployment is appropriate?	A matching model of unemployment	A disequilibrium model of unemployment
Where is the equilibrium in the labor market?	Where the labor supply curve intersects the labor demand curve	Where the efficiency wage hits the labor demand curve
Does a shift in labor supply affect the *FE* line?	Yes	No

CHAPTER SUMMARY

1. Keynesians are skeptical that a mismatch between workers and jobs can explain all unemployment. They argue that some unemployment is caused by real wages that are rigid and above the level at which the quantities of labor demanded and supplied are equal.
2. One explanation for real-wage rigidity is based on the efficiency wage model, which assumes that workers work harder in response to an increase in the real wage. Firms can attain the highest level of profit by paying the real wage, known as the *efficiency wage*, that elicits the most worker effort per dollar of wages. If the effort curve relating effort provided by workers to the real wage doesn't change, the efficiency wage, and hence the real wage actually paid, is rigid.
3. At the efficiency wage, firms demand the level of employment, $\bar{N}$, at which the marginal product of labor equals the efficiency wage. If the efficiency wage is above the market-clearing real wage, employment is determined by labor demand. The difference between the quantity of labor supplied and the quantity of labor demanded at the efficiency wage represents unemployment.
4. Full-employment output, $\bar{Y}$, is the output that can be produced when employment is at its full-employment level, $\bar{N}$, and worker effort is at the level induced by the efficiency wage. The *FE* line in the Keynesian *IS–LM* model is vertical where output equals its full-employment level. In the Keynesian model, full-employment output and the *FE* line are affected by productivity shocks but not by changes in labor supply because changes in labor supply don't affect employment in the efficiency wage model.
5. Keynesians attribute the nonneutrality of money to price stickiness, which means that some firms may not change their prices in the short run even though the demand for or supply of their product has changed. Price stickiness is contrary to the assumption of the basic classical model that prices and wages are completely flexible.
6. Price stickiness can arise from the profit-maximizing behavior of monopolistically competitive firms that face menu costs, or costs of changing prices. Such firms are price setters rather than price takers, and once they set their prices they meet customer demand at that fixed price. These firms readjust prices only occasionally, generally when costs or demand have changed significantly.
7. In the Keynesian model with sticky prices, output is determined in the short run at the intersection of the *IS* and *LM* curves. The economy can be off the *FE* line in the short run because firms are willing to meet demand at predetermined prices. The level of employment in the short run is given by the effective labor demand curve, which shows the amount of labor needed to produce any given amount of output. In the long run, after prices and wages have completely adjusted, the *LM* curve has shifted to restore general equilibrium with full employment.
8. The short-run and long-run equilibria in the Keynesian model can also be analyzed with the *AD–AS* model. The short-run equilibrium is represented by the intersection of the downward-sloping aggregate demand (*AD*) curve and the horizontal short-run aggregate supply (*SRAS*) curve. In short-run equilibrium, monopolistically competitive firms produce whatever level of output is demanded at the fixed price level. Eventually, however, the price level adjusts and the economy reaches its long-run equilibrium, represented by the intersection of the *AD* curve and the vertical long-run aggregate supply (*LRAS*) curve. In long-run equilibrium, output equals its full-employment level, $\bar{Y}$.
9. In the Keynesian model, an increase in the money supply shifts the *LM* curve down and to the right, raising output and lowering the real interest rate in the short run. Thus money isn't neutral in the short run. In the long run, however, money is neutral; monetary expansion raises the price level proportionally but has no real effects.
10. In the Keynesian model, an increase in government purchases or a cut in taxes shifts the *IS* curve up and to the right, raising output and the real interest rate in the short run. In the long run, output returns to the full-employment level but the real interest rate increases. Fiscal policy isn't neutral in the long run because it affects the composition of output among consumption, investment, and government purchases.
11. Keynesians attribute most business cycles to aggregate demand shocks. These shocks hit the *IS* curve (changes in government purchases, desired consumption, or desired investment) or the *LM* curve (changes in money supply or money demand). Keynesian business cycle theory, which has traditionally emphasized the importance of aggregate demand shocks, can account for the procyclical behavior of employment, money, inflation, and investment. To explain the procyclical behavior of average labor productivity, the Keynesian theory must include the additional assumption that firms hoard labor—that is, they employ more workers than necessary during recessions.
12. Macroeconomic stabilization, also called aggregate demand management, is the use of monetary or fiscal

policy to try to eliminate recessions and keep the economy at full employment. The Keynesian theory suggests that macroeconomic stabilization is both desirable and possible. However, practical problems include the difficulty of measuring and forecasting the state of the economy and determining how much monetary and fiscal stimulus is needed at any particular time. Keynesian antirecessionary policies also lead to a higher price level than would occur in the absence of policy changes.

13. Following the oil price shocks of the 1970s, the Keynesian theory was modified to allow for supply shocks. Supply shocks lead to stagflation (a combination of inflation and recession) and pose great difficulties for stabilization policy.

KEY TERMS

aggregate demand management, p. 469
aggregate demand shocks, p. 465
contractionary monetary policy, p. 460
effective labor demand curve, p. 457
efficiency wage, p. 448
efficiency wage model, p. 446
effort curve, p. 447
expansionary monetary policy, p. 460
macroeconomic stabilization, p. 469
marginal cost, p. 456
markup, p. 456
menu cost, p. 454
monopolistic competition, p. 453
multiplier, p. 463
perfect competition, p. 453
price setter, p. 453
price stickiness, p. 452
price taker, p. 453
real-wage rigidity, p. 445
turnover costs, p. 446

REVIEW QUESTIONS

1. Define *efficiency wage*. What assumption about worker behavior underlies the efficiency wage theory? Why does it predict that the real wage will remain rigid even if there is an excess supply of labor?
2. How does the full-employment level of employment, $\bar{N}$, defined in the Keynesian model differ from that defined in the classical model? How might a productivity shock affect $\bar{N}$ for the classical model but not for the Keynesian model?
3. How do the assumptions of prices in the Keynesian and classical models have different implications on monetary policy?
4. Define *menu cost*. Why might small menu costs lead to price stickiness in monopolistically competitive markets but not in perfectly competitive markets? Why can a monopolistically competitive firm profitably meet demand at its fixed price when actual demand is greater than the firm anticipated?
5. What does the Keynesian model predict about monetary neutrality (both in the short run and in the long run)? Compare the Keynesian predictions about neutrality with those of the basic classical model and the extended classical model with misperceptions.
6. In the Keynesian model, how do increased government purchases affect output and the real interest rate in the short run? In the long run? How do increased government purchases affect the composition of output in the long run?
7. Describe three alternative responses available to policymakers when the economy is in recession. What are the advantages and disadvantages of each strategy? Be sure to discuss the effects on employment, the price level, and the composition of output. What are some of the practical difficulties in using macroeconomic stabilization policies to fight recessions?
8. Use the Keynesian model to explain the procyclical behavior of employment, money, inflation, and investment.
9. Why does the classical model perform better than the Keynesian model in explaining the business cycle fact of procyclical labor productivity? How can the concept of labor hoarding help Keynesians improve their model's prediction?
10. According to the Keynesian analysis, in what two ways does an adverse supply shock reduce output? What problems do supply shocks create for Keynesian stabilization policies?

NUMERICAL PROBLEMS

1. A firm identifies the following relationship between the real wage it pays and the effort made by workers:

Real Wage	Effort
2	1
3	6
4	17
5	22
6	27
7	28

The marginal product of labor for this firm is

$$MPN = \frac{E(60 - N)}{27},$$

where E is the effort level and N is the number of workers employed. If the firm can pay only one of the wage levels shown above, which should it choose? How many workers will it employ? If the firm launches a morale boosting plan and the effort exerted by workers increases by 10 at the given wage level, will the firm stay at the same wage level as before? How many workers will it employ after the plan?

2. An economy is described by the following equations:

Desired consumption	$C^d = 130 + 0.5(Y - T) - 500r$.
Desired investment	$I^d = 100 - 500r$.
Government purchases	$G = 100$.
Taxes	$T = 100$.
Real money demand	$L = 0.5Y - 1000r$.
Money supply	$M = 1320$.
Full-employment output	$\bar{Y} = 500$.

Note that the expected rate of inflation is assumed to equal zero so that money demand depends directly on the real interest rate, which equals the nominal interest rate.

a. Write the equations for the *IS* and *LM* curves. (These equations express the relationship between r and Y when the goods and asset markets, respectively, are in equilibrium.)

b. Calculate the full-employment values of output, the real interest rate, the price level, consumption, and investment.

c. Suppose that, because of investor optimism about the future marginal product of capital, the investment function becomes

$$I^d = 200 - 500r.$$

Assuming that the economy was initially at full employment, what are the new values of output, the real interest rate, the price level, consumption, and investment in the short run? In the long run? Show your results graphically.

3. Consider the following Keynesian closed economy:

Consumption	$C = 388 + 0.4(Y - T) - 600r$.
Investment	$I = 352 - 400r$.
Government purchases	$G = 280$.
Taxes	$T = 300$.
Full-employment output	$\bar{Y} = 1400$.
Money supply	$M = 12{,}600$.
Real money demand	$L = 1750 + 0.75Y - 8750(r + \pi^e)$.
Expected inflation	$\pi^e = 0.02$.

a. What is the equation of the *IS* curve?

b. Suppose that the price level is fixed at $P_{sr} = 7$ in the short run. What is the equation of the *LM* curve in the short run, while the price level remains fixed?

c. What are the short-run equilibrium values of output, the real interest rate, consumption, and investment?

d. What are the long-run equilibrium values of output, the real interest rate, consumption, investment, and the price level?

e. What is the value of velocity in long-run equilibrium?

f. Suppose that the government wants to increase its purchases to $G = 350$ and to achieve a long-run equilibrium with investment, I, equal to 320, and the price level, P, equal to 6. What level of taxes, T, and money supply, M, will achieve this long-run equilibrium? The following questions will guide you to the answer. (1) What value of the real interest rate leads to $I = 320$? (2) What is the value of consumption in long-run equilibrium when $I = 320$ and $G = 350$? (3) What value of taxes, T, will lead to the level of consumption, C, in part (2), thereby achieving $I = 320$ and $G = 350$ in long-run equilibrium? (4) What value of the nominal money supply, M, will lead to a price level of 6 in long-run equilibrium with $I = 320$ and $G = 350$? (Note: continue to assume that $\pi^e = 0.02$.)

4. An economy is described by the following equations:

Desired consumption $C^d = 300 + 0.5(Y - T) - 300r$.

Desired investment $I^d = 100 - 100r$.

Government purchases $G = 100$.

Taxes $T = 100$.

Real money demand $L = 0.5Y - 200r$.

Money supply $M = 6300$.

Full-employment output $\bar{Y} = 700$.

Note that the expected rate of inflation is assumed to equal zero so that money demand depends directly on the real interest rate, which equals the nominal interest rate.

a. Write the equation for the aggregate demand curve. (*Hint:* Find the equations describing the goods market and asset market equilibria. Use these two equations to eliminate the real interest rate. For any given price level, the equation of the aggregate demand curve gives the level of output that satisfies both goods market and asset market equilibria.)

b. Suppose that $P = 15$. What are the short-run equilibrium values of output, the real interest rate, consumption, and investment?

c. What are the long-run equilibrium values of output, the real interest rate, consumption, investment, and the price level?

5. (Appendix 11.A) Consider an economy in which all workers are covered by contracts that specify the nominal wage and give the employer the right to choose the amount of employment. The production function is

$$Y = 20\sqrt{N},$$

and the corresponding marginal product of labor is

$$MPN = \frac{10}{\sqrt{N}}.$$

Suppose that the nominal wage is $W = 20$.

a. Derive an equation that relates the real wage to the amount of labor demanded by firms (the labor demand curve).

b. For the nominal wage of 20, what is the relationship between the price level and the amount of labor demanded by firms?

c. What is the relationship between the price level and the amount of output supplied by firms? Graph this relationship.

Now suppose that the *IS* and *LM* curves of the economy (the goods market and asset market equilibrium conditions) are described by the following equations:

IS curve $Y = 120 - 500r$.

LM curve $M/P = 0.5Y - 500r$.

d. The money supply *M* is 300. Use the *IS* and *LM* equations to derive a relationship between output, *Y*, and the price level, *P*. This relationship is the equation for the aggregate demand curve. Graph it on the same axis as the relationship between the price level and the amount of output supplied by firms (the aggregate supply curve) from part (*c*).

e. What are the equilibrium values of the price level, output, employment, real wage, and real interest rate?

f. Suppose that the money supply, *M*, is 135. What are the equilibrium values of the price level, output, employment, real wage, and real interest rate?

6. (Appendix 11.C) Consider the following economy.

Desired consumption $C^d = 325 + 0.5(Y - T) - 500r$.

Desired investment $I^d = 200 - 500r$.

Government purchases $G = 150$.

Taxes $T = 150$.

Real money demand $L = 0.5Y - 1000r$.

Money supply $M = 6000$.

Full-employment output $\bar{Y} = 1000$.

Note that the expected rate of inflation is assumed to equal zero so that money demand depends directly on the real interest rate, which equals the nominal interest rate.

a. Calculate the full-employment values of the real interest rate, the price level, consumption, and investment.

b. What are the values of α_{IS}, β_{IS}, α_{LM}, β_{LM}, and ℓ_r for this economy? (You'll have to refer back to Appendix 9.B for definitions of these coefficients.)

c. Suppose that the price level is fixed at $P_{sr} = 15$. What are the short-run equilibrium values of output and the real interest rate?

d. With the price level still fixed at $P_{sr} = 15$, suppose that government purchases increase from $G = 150$ to $G = 250$. What are the new values of α_{IS} and the short-run equilibrium level of output?

e. Use Eq. (11.C.5) to compute the government purchases multiplier. Use your answer to compute the short-run change in *Y* resulting from an increase in government purchases from $G = 150$ to $G = 250$. How does your answer here compare to your answer in part (*d*)?

ANALYTICAL PROBLEMS

1. Examine the effect of each of the following on output, the real interest rate, employment, and the price level in the short run and the long run. Use the Keynesian *IS–LM* graph to explain your answer.
   a. A government builds more public housing, and construction firms invest more in machinery to speed up their housing construction.
   b. The young generation has to save more to buy apartments in the future.
   c. Firms move their offices and factories to other countries as a civil war begins in their home country.
   d. More tourists and local consumers visit new theme parks and increase their spending.
2. Examine the effect of each of the following on output, the real interest rate, employment, and the price level in the short run and the long run. Use the Keynesian *IS–LM* graph to explain your answer.
   a. After a financial crisis, people lose confidence in the financial market and prefer to hold more cash.
   b. People use Bitcoin rather than money since more shops now accept it for transactions and banks accept it for deposits.
   c. A nuclear power accident destroys factories and pollutes agricultural products, driving up price levels.
   d. A new holiday scheme raises the morale and productivity of workers.
3. Suppose that the Fed has a policy of increasing the money supply when it observes that the economy is in recession. However, suppose that about six months are needed for an increase in the money supply to affect aggregate demand, which is about the same amount of time needed for firms to review and reset their prices. What effects will the Fed's policy have on output and price stability? Does your answer change if (*a*) the Fed has some ability to forecast recessions or (*b*) price adjustment takes longer than six months?
4. Classical economists argue that using fiscal policy to fight a recession doesn't make workers better off. Suppose, however, that the Keynesian model is correct. Relative to a policy of doing nothing, does an increase in government purchases that brings the economy to full employment make workers better off? In answering the question, discuss the effects of the fiscal expansion on the real wage, employment, consumption, and current and future taxes. How does your answer depend on (a) the direct benefits of the government spending program and (b) the speed with which prices adjust in the absence of fiscal stimulus?
5. Some labor economists argue that it is useful to think of the labor market as being divided into two sectors: a primary sector, where "good" (high-paying, long-term) jobs are located, and a secondary sector, which has "bad" (low-paying, short-term) jobs. Suppose that the primary sector has a high marginal product of labor and that (because effort is costly for firms to monitor) firms pay an efficiency wage. The secondary sector has a low marginal product of labor and no efficiency wage; instead, the real wage in the secondary sector adjusts so that the quantities of labor demanded and supplied are equal in that sector. Workers are alike, and all would prefer to work in the primary sector. However, workers who can't find jobs in the primary sector work in the secondary sector.

   What are the effects of each of the following on the real wage, employment, and output in both sectors?
   a. Expansionary monetary policy increases the demand for primary sector output.
   b. Immigration increases the labor force.
   c. The effort curve changes so that a higher real wage is needed to elicit the greatest effort per dollar in the primary sector. Effort exerted at the higher real wage is the same as before the change in the effort curve.
   d. There is a temporary productivity improvement in the primary sector.
   e. There is a temporary productivity improvement in the secondary sector.

WORKING WITH MACROECONOMIC DATA

For data to use in these exercises, go to the Federal Reserve Bank of St. Louis FRED database at fred.stlouisfed.org.

1. Keynesian theory predicts that expansionary fiscal policy—either higher spending or lower taxes—will raise the real interest rate.

   Using data since 1960, graph the Federal government budget deficit, the state-local government budget deficit (both relative to GDP), and the real interest rate (three-month Treasury bill rate minus the CPI inflation rate over the preceding twelve-month period).

Do you see a link between deficits and real interest rates? In what period does the relationship seem clearest? Do your answers change when the ten-year government bond interest rate is used instead of the three-month rate?

2. Because of price stickiness, the Keynesian model predicts that an increase in the growth rate of money will lead to higher inflation only after some lag, when firms begin to adjust their prices. Using data since 1960, graph the inflation rate and the rate of growth of M2. Prior to 1980, is it true that increases in money growth only affected inflation with a lag? What has happened since 1980?

   Keynesians argue that financial innovations, such as the introduction of money market deposit accounts at banks, led to a large increase in the demand for M2 in the early 1980s. If this claim is true, how does it help explain the relationship between money growth and inflation that you observe after 1980?

3. *Working with Macroeconomic Data* Exercise 1, Chapter 10, asked you to look at the cyclical behavior of total factor productivity. If you have not completed that problem, do it now and compare productivity changes with changes in the producer price index for fuels and related products and power. How would Keynesian interpretations differ from those offered by classical macroeconomics?

4. The theory of macroeconomic stabilization policy in this chapter provides a playbook for monetary policy. When the economy is weak, the Federal Reserve eases monetary policy by increasing the money supply and reducing the real interest rate. When the economy is strong and inflation is rising, the Federal Reserve tightens monetary policy by reducing the money supply and raising the real interest rate. To test whether the Federal Reserve has followed this playbook, get data from FRED on the federal funds interest rate and on expected inflation from the University of Michigan survey of consumers. From those two data series, calculate and plot the real interest rate since 1990. Does the real interest rate usually decline in recessions? Does the real interest rate usually rise as economic expansions are under way?

Appendix 11.A

Labor Contracts and Nominal-Wage Rigidity

In the Keynesian theory, the nonneutrality of money is a consequence of nominal rigidity. In this chapter we emphasized nominal-*price* rigidity. An alternative nominal rigidity that could account for the nonneutrality of money, which many Keynesians emphasize, is nominal-*wage* rigidity. Nominal-wage rigidity could reflect long-term labor contracts between firms and unions in which wages are set in nominal terms (the case we study here). In terms of the *AD–AS* framework the difference between nominal-price rigidity and nominal-wage rigidity is that nominal-price rigidity implies a horizontal short-run aggregate supply curve, whereas nominal-wage rigidity implies a short-run aggregate supply curve that slopes upward. However, this difference doesn't really affect the results obtained from the Keynesian model. In particular, in the Keynesian model with nominal-wage rigidity, money remains nonneutral in the short run and neutral in the long run.

The Short-Run Aggregate Supply Curve with Labor Contracts

In the United States most labor contracts specify employment conditions and nominal wages for a period of three to five years. Although labor contracts specify the nominal wage rate, they usually don't specify the total amount of employment. Instead, employers unilaterally decide how many hours will be worked and whether workers will be laid off. These factors imply that the short-run aggregate supply curve slopes upward.

We can see why the short-run aggregate supply curve slopes upward when labor contracts prespecify the nominal wage by considering what happens when the price level increases. With the nominal wage, W, already determined by the contract, an increase in the price level, P, reduces the real wage, w, or W/P. In response to the drop in the real wage, firms demand more labor. Because firms unilaterally choose the level of employment, the increase in the amount of labor demanded leads to an increase in employment and therefore an increase in output. Thus an increase in the price level leads to an increase in the amount of output supplied, as shown by the *SRAS* curves in Figure 11.A.1.

Nonneutrality of Money

Money is nonneutral in the short run in the model with long-term labor contracts, as illustrated in Fig. 11.A.1. The initial general equilibrium is at point E, where the initial aggregate demand curve, AD^1, intersects the short-run aggregate supply curve, $SRAS^1$. A 10% increase in the money supply shifts the AD curve up to AD^2. (For any level of output the price level is 10% higher on AD^2 than on AD^1.) In the short run, the increase in the money supply raises the price level to P_2 and

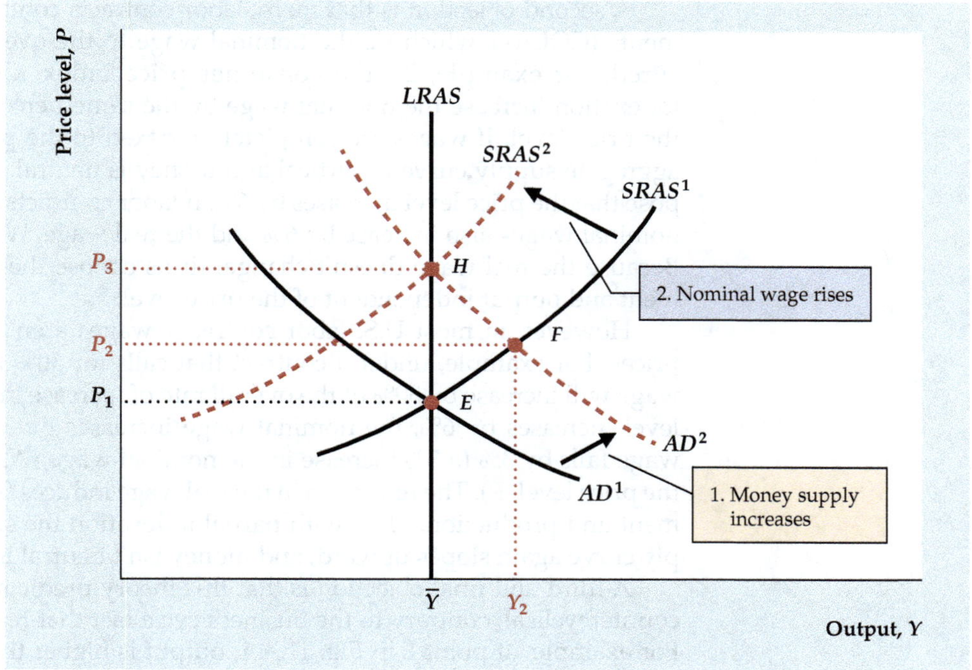

FIGURE 11.A.1

Monetary nonneutrality with long-term contracts

With labor contracts that fix the nominal wage in the short run, an increase in the price level lowers the real wage and induces firms to employ more labor and produce more output. Thus the short-run aggregate supply curve *SRAS*¹ slopes upward. When nominal wages are rigid, money isn't neutral. From the initial equilibrium point, *E*, a 10% increase in the money supply shifts the *AD* curve up, from *AD*¹ to *AD*². In the short run, both output and the price level increase, as shown by point *F*. Over time, contracts are renegotiated and nominal wages rise to match the increase in prices. As wages rise, the short-run aggregate supply curve shifts up, from *SRAS*¹ to *SRAS*², so that general equilibrium is restored at *H*. At *H* both the price level, *P*, and the nominal wage, *W*, have risen by 10%, so the real wage is the same as it was initially, and firms supply the full-employment level of output, $\bar{Y}$.

output to Y_2 at point *F*. Output at *F* is higher than its full-employment level because the rise in prices lowers the real wage, which leads firms to employ more labor and produce more output.

At the short-run equilibrium point, *F*, however, workers will be dissatisfied because their real wages are lower than they had expected. Over time, as contracts are renewed or renegotiated, nominal wages will rise to offset the increase in prices. At any price level, a rise in the nominal wage also raises the real wage, inducing firms to employ less labor and produce less output. Thus rising nominal wages cause the short-run aggregate supply curve to shift up and to the left, from *SRAS*¹ to *SRAS*². Eventually, general equilibrium is restored at point *H*.

In the long run at point *H*, the price level rises to P_3, which is 10% higher than its initial value, P_1. At *H* the nominal wage, *W*, has also increased by 10% so that the real wage, W/P, has returned to its initial value. With the real wage back at its original value, firms employ the same amount of labor and produce the same amount of output $(\bar{Y})$ as they did at the initial equilibrium point, *E*. Thus as in the Keynesian model based on efficiency wages and price stickiness, in the Keynesian model with nominal-wage rigidity, money is neutral in the long run but not in the short run.

Although nominal-wage rigidity arising from labor contracts can explain short-run monetary nonneutrality, some economists object to this explanation. One objection is that about one-ninth of workers in the United States are unionized and covered by long-term labor contracts. However, many nonunion workers receive wages similar to those set in union contracts. For example, although most nonunion workers don't have formal wage contracts, they may have "implicit contracts" with their employers, or informal unwritten arrangements for comparable wages.

A second objection is that many labor contracts contain cost-of-living adjustments (COLAs), which tie the nominal wage to the overall price level, as measured, for example, by the consumer price index. Contracts with *complete* indexation increase the nominal wage by the same percentage as the increase in the price level. If wages are completely indexed to the price level, the short-run aggregate supply curve is vertical and money is neutral. To show why, let's suppose that the price level increases by 6%. If labor contracts are completely indexed, nominal wages also increase by 6% and the real wage, W/P, remains unchanged. Because the real wage doesn't change, firms choose the same levels of employment and output independent of the price level.

However, in most U.S. labor contracts, wages aren't completely indexed to prices. For example, under a contract that calls for 50% indexation, the nominal wage will increase by 50% of the overall rate of increase in prices. Thus if the price level increases by 6%, the nominal wage increases by 3%. As a result, the real wage falls by 3% (a 3% increase in the nominal wage, W, minus a 6% increase in the price level, P). The reduction in the real wage induces firms to increase employment and production. Thus with partial indexation the short-run aggregate supply curve again slopes upward, and money isn't neutral in the short run.

A third and final objection is that this theory predicts that real wages will be countercyclical, contrary to the business cycle fact that real wages are procyclical. For example, at point F in Fig. 11.A.1, output is higher than the full-employment level, but the real wage is lower than at full employment (indeed, the low real wage induces firms to produce the extra output). Thus the theory holds that real wages will fall in booms—that is, the real wage is countercyclical—which is inconsistent with the evidence.

However, perhaps both supply shocks and aggregate demand shocks affect real wages. For the real business cycle theory we showed that, if productivity shocks cause cyclical fluctuations, the real wage should be procyclical, perhaps strongly so. A combination of supply shocks (which cause the real wage to move procyclically) and aggregate demand shocks (which, as in Fig. 11.A.1, cause the real wage to move countercyclically) might average out to a real wage that is at least mildly procyclical. Some evidence for this view was provided in a study by Scott Sumner of Bentley College and Stephen Silver[1] of Virginia Military Institute, which shows that the real wage has been procyclical during periods dominated by supply shocks but has been countercyclical during periods in which aggregate demand shocks were more important.

[1]"Real Wages, Employment and the Phillips Curve," *Journal of Political Economy*, June 1989, pp. 706–720.

Appendix 11.B

Worked-Out Numerical Exercise for Calculating the Multiplier in a Keynesian Model

This appendix illustrates the model from Appendix 9.A with a numerical exercise to show how to calculate the government purchases multiplier. In that problem, the economy is given by the following equations:

$$C^d = 300 + 0.75(Y - T) - 300r$$
$$T = 100 + 0.2Y$$
$$I^d = 200 - 200r$$
$$L = 0.5Y - 500i$$

$$\bar{Y} = 2500;\ G = 600;\ M = 133{,}200;\ \pi^e = 0.05;\ P_{sr} = 120.$$

In Appendix 9.A, we found the short-run and long-run equilibrium values of Y, P, r, T, C, I, and i. Now we want to calculate the government purchases multiplier in the short run if government purchases rises from 600 to 690. (Of course, in the long run, the multiplier is zero because output will be at its full-employment level, and increases in government purchases do not affect the full-employment level of output in the Keynesian model.) To do this, we use the short-run equilibrium results from Appendix 9.A and then repeat our procedure with the higher level of government purchases to see how output is affected. From that, we can calculate the multiplier, which is the change in output divided by the change in government purchases.

In Appendix 9.A, we found that in the short run, $Y = 2400$. With an increase in government purchases, in the short run, the *IS* curve will change, but the *LM* curve will be the same as before, $r = 0.001Y - 2.27$.

First, we find the equation for the *IS* curve by using the goods market equilibrium condition. The goods market equilibrium condition is $Y = C^d + I^d + G$. Substitute the equation for T into the equation for C^d from above. Then substitute the resulting equation and the equation for I^d from above, along with the value of G, into $Y = C^d + I^d + G$ to obtain: $Y = \{300 + 0.75[Y - (100 + 0.2Y)] - 300r\} + [200 - 200r] + 690$. Rearrange this equation as an equation for r in terms of Y: $Y = \{300 + 0.75Y - [(0.75 \times 100) + (0.75 \times 0.2Y)] - 300r\} + [200 - 200r] + 690$, so $Y = [300 + 0.75Y - 75 - 0.15Y - 300r] + [200 - 200r] + 690$, so $0.4Y = [300 - 75 + 200 + 690] - (300 + 200)r$, so $500r = 1115 - 0.4Y$. Therefore, $r = (1115/500) - (0.4/500)Y$, so $r = 2.23 - 0.0008Y$. This is the *IS* curve.

Next, we find the intersection of the *IS* and *LM* curves to calculate the short-run equilibrium values of Y and r. We have written the equations of the *IS* and *LM* curves so that the left side of each equation is simply r. Setting the right side of the *IS* equation equal to the right side of the *LM* equation yields $2.23 - 0.0008Y = 0.001Y - 2.27$, so $4.5 = 0.0018Y$. Therefore, $Y = 4.5/0.0018 = 2500$.

The multiplier is the change in output divided by the change in government purchases, which is $(2500 - 2400)/(690 - 600) = 10/9 = 1\frac{1}{9}$. In this example, output rises by 100 when government purchases rises by 90.

Equation (11.C.5) in Appendix 11.C shows that the multiplier equals

$$\Delta Y/\Delta G = 1/[(c_r + i_r)(\beta_{IS} + \beta_{LM})].$$

Filling in the data, we find that $\Delta Y/\Delta G = 1/[(c_r + i_r)(\beta_{IS} + \beta_{LM})] = 1/[(300 + 200)(0.0008 + 0.001)] = 1/(500 \times 0.0018) = 1/0.9 = 1\frac{1}{9}$, exactly as we found above.

Appendix 11.C

The Multiplier in the Keynesian Model

In Chapter 11 we defined the multiplier associated with any particular type of spending as the short-run change in total output resulting from a one-unit change in that type of spending. Here we use the analysis in Appendix 9.B to derive the multiplier associated with government purchases G. We proceed in three steps: First, we calculate the effect on α_{IS} (the intercept of the *IS* curve in Eq. 9.B.14) of an increase in G. Then we calculate the effect on the short-run equilibrium value of Y, shown by Eq. (9.B.27), of an increase in α_{IS}. Finally, we combine these two effects to calculate the effect on output, Y, of an increase in G.

To calculate the effect on α_{IS} of an increase in G, we repeat the definition of α_{IS}, Eq. (9.B.15):

$$\alpha_{IS} = \frac{c_0 + i_0 + G - c_Y t_0}{c_r + i_r}, \tag{11.C.1}$$

where c_0, i_0, c_Y, c_r, i_r, and t_0 are parameters that determine desired consumption and desired investment (see Appendix 9.B). If G increases by ΔG, then α_{IS} increases by $\Delta G/(c_r + i_r)$, so

$$\Delta\alpha_{IS} = \frac{\Delta G}{c_r + i_r}. \tag{11.C.2}$$

Next, recall from Eq. (9.B.27) that, in the short run when $P = P_{sr}$, the level of output is

$$Y = \frac{\alpha_{IS} - \alpha_{LM} + (1/\ell_r)(M/P_{sr})}{\beta_{IS} + \beta_{LM}}. \tag{11.C.3}$$

Observe from Eq. (11.C.3) that, if α_{IS} increases by $\Delta\alpha_{IS}$, output, Y, increases by $\Delta\alpha_{IS}/(\beta_{IS} + \beta_{LM})$, or

$$\Delta Y = \frac{\Delta\alpha_{IS}}{\beta_{IS} + \beta_{LM}}. \tag{11.C.4}$$

Finally, if we substitute the right side of Eq. (11.C.2) for $\Delta\alpha_{IS}$ on the right side of Eq. (11.C.4) and then divide both sides of the resulting equation by ΔG, we obtain

$$\frac{\Delta Y}{\Delta G} = \frac{1}{(c_r + i_r)(\beta_{IS} + \beta_{LM})}. \tag{11.C.5}$$

The right side of Eq. (11.C.5) is the increase in short-run equilibrium output, Y, that occurs for each one-unit increase in government purchases, G. In other words, it is the government purchases multiplier. Similar calculations show that changes in desired consumption or desired investment (as reflected in the terms c_0 and i_0) have the same multiplier as government purchases.

Because c_r, i_r, β_{IS}, and β_{LM} all are positive, the multiplier is positive. However, depending on the specific values of those parameters, the multiplier may be greater or less than 1. A case in which the multiplier is likely to be large occurs when the *LM* curve is horizontal (that is, when the slope of the *LM* curve, β_{LM}, is 0). If the *LM* curve is horizontal, shifts in the *IS* curve induced by changes in spending have relatively large effects on output. Recall that Eq. (9.B.16) gives the (negative of the) slope of the *IS* curve, β_{IS}, as $[1 - (1 - t)c_Y]/(c_r + i_r)$. Making this substitution and setting the slope of the *LM* curve, β_{LM}, at 0 yield a simple form of the multiplier:

$$\frac{\Delta Y}{\Delta G} = \frac{1}{1 - (1 - t)c_Y}. \tag{11.C.6}$$

For example, suppose that the marginal propensity to consume, c_Y, is 0.8 and that the tax rate, t, is 0.25. Then the multiplier defined in Eq. (11.C.6) is $1/[1 - (0.75)(0.8)] = 1/0.4$, or 2.5. If the *LM* curve is very steep, by contrast—that is, β_{LM} is large—then the multiplier could be quite small, as you can see from Eq. (11.C.5).

12

Unemployment and Inflation

In the past several chapters we focused on the concepts of the business cycle, macroeconomic stabilization, and classical and Keynesian approaches to business cycle analysis. Although these concepts are central to today's macroeconomics, actual policy discussions rarely involve such abstract terms. Policy debates tend to focus on highly publicized economic statistics such as inflation and unemployment. To make a stronger connection between business cycle theories and policy debates, we now take a closer look at unemployment and inflation, first together and then separately.

Unemployment and inflation—sometimes referred to as the "twin evils" of macroeconomics—are among the most difficult and politically sensitive economic issues that policymakers face. High rates of unemployment and inflation generate intense public concern because their effects are direct and visible: Almost everyone is affected by rising prices, and few workers can be confident that they will never lose their jobs.

Moreover, there is a long-standing idea in macroeconomics that unemployment and inflation are somehow related. In the first part of this chapter we discuss in some detail the concept of the Phillips curve—an empirical relationship between inflation and unemployment. According to the Phillips curve, inflation tends to be low when unemployment is high and high when unemployment is low. The Phillips curve relationship raises some important questions about how the economy works and how macroeconomic policies should be used.

We then look at unemployment and inflation separately. We examine the costs that each imposes on society and consider the options that policymakers have for dealing with these problems.

This chapter begins Part 4 of the book, the purpose of which is to explore macroeconomic policymaking in detail. Following the discussion of inflation and unemployment in this chapter, in Chapter 13 we address the issue of how economic openness—as reflected in the trading and financial links among countries—affects macroeconomic policy. In Chapter 14 we take a closer look at institutions and debates related to the making of monetary policy and in Chapter 15 we provide a similar overview of fiscal policy.

Learning Objectives

12.1 Describe the Phillips curve relationship between unemployment and inflation.

12.2 Discuss whether the Phillips curve offers a "menu" of inflation-unemployment combinations from which policymakers can choose.

12.3 Identify the costs of unemployment and discuss the natural rate of unemployment.

12.4 Discuss the types and costs of inflation.

12.5 Discuss the challenges and costs of reducing inflation.

12.1 Unemployment and Inflation: Is There a Trade-Off?

Describe the Phillips curve relationship between unemployment and inflation.

Newspaper editorials and public discussions about economic policy often refer to the "trade-off" between inflation and unemployment. The idea is that, to reduce inflation, the economy must tolerate high unemployment, or alternatively that, to reduce unemployment, more inflation must be accepted. This section examines the idea of an inflation–unemployment trade-off and its implications for macroeconomic policy.

The origin of the idea of a trade-off between inflation and unemployment was a 1958 article by economist A. W. Phillips.[1] Phillips examined 97 years of British data on unemployment and nominal wage growth and found that, historically, unemployment tended to be low in years when nominal wages grew rapidly and high in years when nominal wages grew slowly. Economists who built on Phillips's work shifted its focus slightly by looking at the link between unemployment and inflation—that is, the growth rate of prices—rather than the link between unemployment and the growth rate of wages. During the late 1950s and the 1960s, many statistical studies examined inflation and unemployment data for numerous countries and time periods, in many cases finding a negative relationship between the two variables. This negative empirical relationship between unemployment and inflation is known as the **Phillips curve.**

A striking example of a Phillips curve, shown in Figure 12.1, occurred in the United States during the 1960s. The U.S. economy expanded throughout most of the 1960s, with unemployment falling and inflation rising steadily. In Fig. 12.1, the inflation rate is measured on the vertical axis, and the unemployment rate is measured on the horizontal axis. Note that years, such as 1961, that had high unemployment also had low inflation, and that years, such as 1969, that had high inflation also had low unemployment. The data produce an almost perfect downward-sloping relation between inflation and unemployment—that is, a Phillips curve. The experience of the United States in the 1960s, which came after Phillips's article

FIGURE 12.1

The Phillips curve and the U.S. economy during the 1960s

During the 1960s, U.S. rates of inflation and unemployment seemed to lie along a Phillips curve. Inflation rose and unemployment fell fairly steadily during this decade, and policymakers apparently had decided to live with higher inflation so as to reduce unemployment.

Source: Bureau of Labor Statistics, downloaded from Federal Reserve Bank of St. Louis FRED database at *fred.stlouisfed.org*, series *CPIAUCSL* and *UNRATE*.

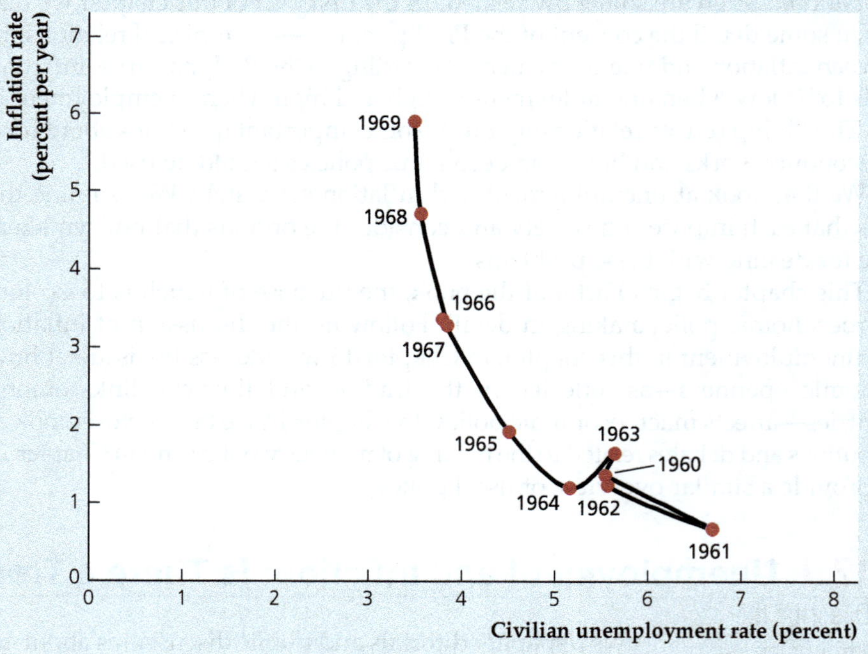

[1]"The Relation Between Unemployment and the Rate of Change of Money Wage Rates in the United Kingdom, 1861–1957," *Economica*, November 1958, pp. 283–299.

had been published and widely disseminated, was viewed by many as a confirmation of his basic finding.

The policy implications of these findings were much debated. Initially, the Phillips curve seemed to offer policymakers a "menu" of combinations of inflation and unemployment from which they could choose. Indeed, during the 1960s some economists argued that, by accepting a modest amount of inflation, macroeconomic policymakers could keep the unemployment rate low indefinitely. This belief seemed to be borne out during the 1960s, when rising inflation was accompanied by falling unemployment.

In the following decades, however, this relationship between inflation and unemployment failed to hold: Figure 12.2 shows inflation and unemployment for the period 1970–2021. During those years, unlike the 1960s, there seemed to be no reliable relationship between unemployment and inflation. From the perspective of the Phillips curve the most puzzling period was the mid-1970s, during which the country experienced high inflation and high unemployment simultaneously (stagflation). In 1975, for example, unemployment reached 8.5% of the labor force and the annual inflation rate was 7.1%. High unemployment, together with high inflation, is inconsistent with the Phillips curve.

The original empirical results of Phillips and others who extended his work, together with the unexpected experience of the U.S. economy after 1970, raise at least three important questions:

- Why was the original Phillips curve relationship between inflation and unemployment frequently observed historically, as in the cases of Great Britain in the century before 1958 and the United States in the 1960s?
- Why did the simple negative relationship between inflation and unemployment that seemed to exist during the 1960s in the United States vanish after

FIGURE 12.2

Inflation and unemployment in the United States, 1970–2021

The figure shows the combinations of inflation and unemployment experienced in the United States each year since 1970. Unlike during the 1960s (see Fig. 12.1), after 1970 a clear negative relationship between inflation and unemployment in the United States didn't seem to exist.

Source: Same as for Fig. 12.1.

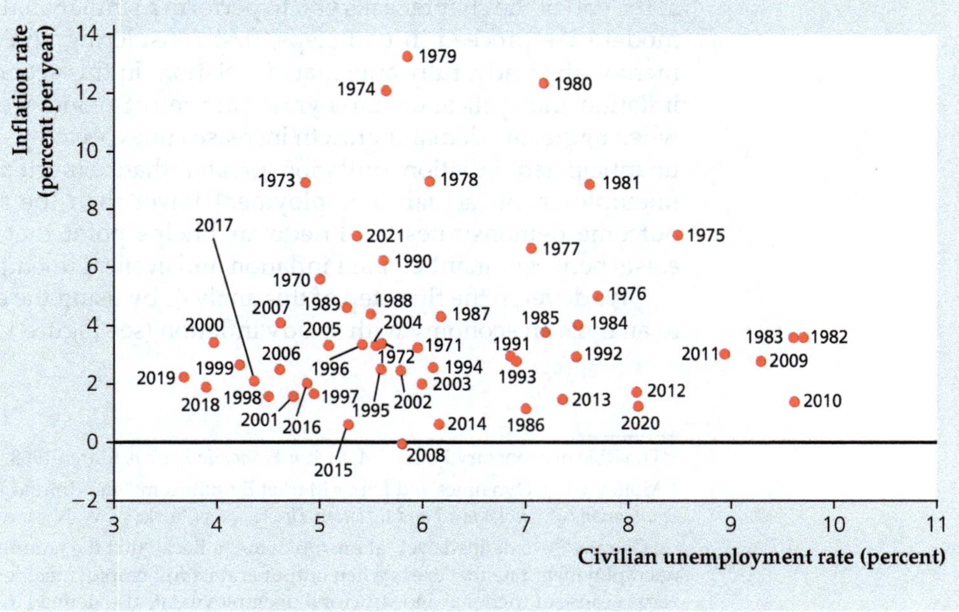

1970? In other words, was there in fact no systematic relationship between inflation and unemployment in the U.S. economy after 1970?

- Does the Phillips curve actually provide a menu of choices from which policymakers can choose? For example, by electing to maintain a high inflation rate can policymakers guarantee a *permanently* low rate of unemployment?

Economic theory provides reasonable answers to these questions; in particular, it explains the collapse of the Phillips curve after 1970. Interestingly, the key economic analysis of the Phillips curve—which predicted that this relationship would not be stable—was done during the 1960s, *before* the Phillips curve had actually broken down. Thus we have at least one example of economic theorists predicting an important development in the economy that policymakers and the public didn't anticipate.

The Expectations-Augmented Phillips Curve

Although the Phillips curve seemed to describe adequately the unemployment–inflation relationship in the United States in the 1960s, during the second half of the decade some economists, notably Nobel Laureates Milton Friedman[2] of the University of Chicago and Edmund Phelps[3] of Columbia University, questioned the logic of the Phillips curve. Friedman and Phelps argued—purely on the basis of economic theory—that there should not be a stable negative relationship between inflation and unemployment. Instead, a negative relationship should exist between **unanticipated inflation** (the difference between the actual and expected inflation rates) and *cyclical* unemployment (the difference between the actual and natural unemployment ratesdefined in Chapter 3).[4] Although these distinctions appear to be merely technical, they are crucial in understanding the relationship between the actual rates of inflation and unemployment.

Before discussing the significance of their analyses, we need to explain how Friedman and Phelps arrived at their conclusions. To do so we use the extended classical model, which includes the misperceptions theory. (Analytical Problem 3 at the end of the chapter asks you to perform a similar analysis using the Keynesian model.) We proceed in two steps, first considering an economy at full employment with steady, fully anticipated inflation. In this economy, both unanticipated inflation and cyclical unemployment are zero. Second, we consider what happens when aggregate demand growth increases unexpectedly. In this case both positive unanticipated inflation (inflation greater than expected) and negative cyclical unemployment (actual unemployment lower than the natural rate) occur. This outcome demonstrates the Friedman–Phelps point that a negative relationship exists between unanticipated inflation and cyclical unemployment.

We develop the first step of this analysis by using the extended classical model to analyze an economy with steady inflation (see Figure 12.3). We assume that this

[2]"The Role of Monetary Policy," *American Economic Review*, March 1968, pp. 1–17.

[3]"Money Wage Dynamics and Labor Market Equilibrium," in Edmund Phelps, ed., *Microeconomic Foundations of Employment and Inflation Theory*, New York: W. W. Norton, 1970, pp. 124–166.

[4]In Chapter 3 we defined cyclical unemployment. Recall that the natural rate of unemployment is the unemployment rate that exists when output is at its full-employment level. The natural rate exceeds zero because of frictional and structural unemployment, also defined in Chapter 3.

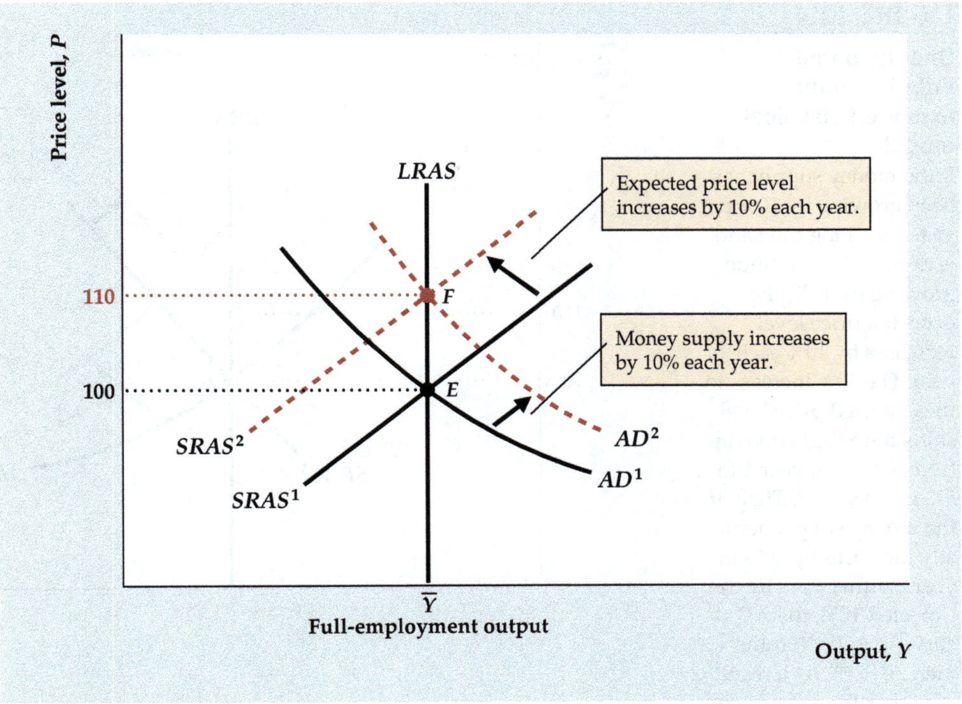

FIGURE 12.3

Ongoing inflation in the extended classical model

If the money supply grows by 10% every year, the *AD* curve shifts up by 10% every year, from AD^1 in year 1 to AD^2 in year 2, and so on. If the money supply has been growing by 10% per year for some time and the rate of inflation has been 10% for some time, the expected rate of inflation also is 10%. Thus the expected price level also grows by 10% each year, from 100 in year 1 to 110 in year 2, and so on. The 10% annual increase in the expected price level shifts the *SRAS* curve up by 10% each year, for example, from $SRAS^1$ in year 1 to $SRAS^2$ in year 2. The economy remains in full-employment equilibrium at the intersection of the *AD* curve and the *SRAS* curve in each year (point *E* in year 1 and point *F* in year 2), with output at $\bar{Y}$, unemployment at the natural rate of unemployment, $\bar{u}$, and inflation and expected inflation both at 10% per year.

economy is in full-employment equilibrium in which the money supply has been growing at 10% per year for many years and is expected to continue to grow at this rate indefinitely. With the money supply growing by 10% per year, the aggregate demand curve shifts up by 10% each year, from AD^1 in year 1 to AD^2 in year 2, and so on. For simplicity we assume that full-employment output, $\bar{Y}$, is constant, but relaxing that assumption wouldn't affect our basic conclusions.

In Fig. 12.3 the short-run aggregate supply (*SRAS*) curve shifts up by 10% each year. Why? With the growth in money supply fully anticipated, there are no misperceptions. Instead, people expect the price level to rise by 10% per year (a 10% inflation rate), which in turn causes the *SRAS* curve to shift up by 10% per year. With no misperceptions, the economy remains at full employment with output at $\bar{Y}$. For example, when the expected price level is 100 in year 1, the short-run aggregate supply curve is $SRAS^1$. At point *E* the price level is 100 (the same as the expected price level) and output is $\bar{Y}$. In year 2 the expected price level is 110, and the short-run aggregate supply curve is $SRAS^2$. In year 2 equilibrium occurs at point *F*, again with output of $\bar{Y}$ and equal expected and actual price levels. Each year, both the *AD* curve and the *SRAS* curve shift up by 10%, increasing the actual price level and expected price level by 10% and maintaining output at its full-employment level.

What happens to unemployment in this economy? Because output is continuously at its full-employment level, $\bar{Y}$, unemployment remains at the natural rate, $\bar{u}$. With unemployment at its natural rate, cyclical unemployment is zero. Hence this economy has zero unanticipated inflation *and* zero cyclical unemployment.

Against this backdrop of 10% monetary growth and 10% inflation, suppose now that in year 2 the money supply grows by 20% rather than by the expected 10% (Figure 12.4). In this case, instead of being 10% higher than AD^1 (as shown

FIGURE 12.4

Unanticipated inflation in the extended classical model

If the money supply has been growing by 10% per year for a long time and is expected to continue growing by 10%, the expected price level increases by 10% each year. The 10% increase in the expected price level shifts the *SRAS* curve up from $SRAS^1$ in year 1 to $SRAS^2$ in year 2. Then, if the money supply actually increases by 20% in year 2 rather than by the expected 10%, the *AD* curve is $AD^{2,\text{new}}$ rather than $AD^{2,\text{old}}$. As a result of higher-than-expected money growth, output increases above $\bar{Y}$ in year 2 and the price level increases to 115, at point *G*. Because the price level rises by 15% rather than the expected 10%, unanticipated inflation is 5% in year 2. This unanticipated inflation is associated with output higher than $\bar{Y}$ and unemployment below the natural rate, $\bar{u}$ (negative cyclical unemployment).

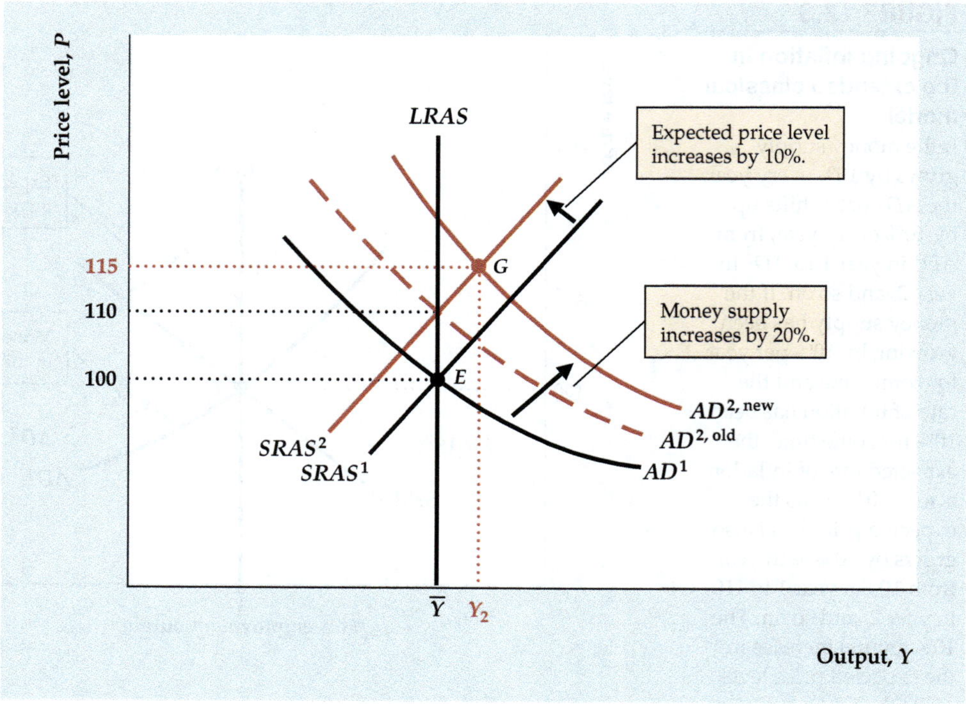

by $AD^{2,\text{old}}$), the aggregate demand curve in year 2 will be 20% higher than AD^1 (as shown by $AD^{2,\text{new}}$). If this increase in the rate of monetary growth is *unanticipated* at the beginning of year 2, the expected price level in year 2 remains at 110, and the short-run aggregate supply curve is $SRAS^2$, as before. The short-run equilibrium in year 2 is at point *G*, the intersection of the $AD^{2,\text{new}}$ and $SRAS^2$ curves. At *G* the price level is 115, so the actual rate of inflation in year 2 is 15%. Because the expected rate of inflation was 10%, the 15% inflation rate implies unanticipated inflation of 5% in year 2. Furthermore, because output is above its full-employment level, $\bar{Y}$, at *G*, the actual unemployment rate is below the natural rate and cyclical unemployment is negative.

Why is output above its full-employment level in year 2? Note that in year 2 the 15% rate of inflation is less than the 20% rate of money growth but greater than the 10% expected rate of inflation. Because the price level grows by less than does the nominal money supply in year 2, the real money supply, M/P, increases, lowering the real interest rate and raising the aggregate quantity of goods demanded above $\bar{Y}$. At the same time, because the price level grows by more than expected, the aggregate quantity of goods supplied also is greater than $\bar{Y}$, as producers are fooled into thinking that the relative prices of their products have increased.

Producers can't be fooled about price behavior indefinitely, however. In the long run, producers learn the true price level, the economy returns to full employment, and the inflation rate again equals the expected inflation rate, as in Fig. 12.3. In the meantime, however, as long as actual output is higher than full-employment output, $\bar{Y}$, and actual unemployment is below the natural rate, $\bar{u}$, the actual price level must be higher than the expected price level. Indeed, according to the misperceptions theory, output can be higher than $\bar{Y}$ only when prices are higher than expected (and therefore when inflation is also higher than expected).

Thus in this economy, when the public correctly predicts aggregate demand growth and inflation, unanticipated inflation is zero, actual unemployment equals the natural rate, and cyclical unemployment is zero (Fig. 12.3). However, if aggregate demand growth unexpectedly speeds up, the economy faces a period of positive unanticipated inflation and negative cyclical unemployment (Fig. 12.4). Similarly, an unexpected slowdown in aggregate demand growth could occur, causing the *AD* curve to rise more slowly than expected; for a time unanticipated inflation would be negative (actual inflation less than expected) and cyclical unemployment would be positive (actual unemployment greater than the natural rate).

The relationship between unanticipated inflation and cyclical unemployment implied by this analysis is

$$\pi - \pi^e = -h(u - \bar{u}),$$

where

$\pi - \pi^e$ = unanticipated inflation (the difference between actual inflation, π, and expected inflation, π^e);

$u - \bar{u}$ = cyclical unemployment (the difference between the actual unemployment rate, u, and the natural unemployment rate, $\bar{u}$);

h = a positive number that measures the slope of the relationship between unanticipated inflation and cyclical unemployment.

The preceding equation expresses mathematically the idea that unanticipated inflation will be positive when cyclical unemployment is negative, negative when cyclical unemployment is positive, and zero when cyclical unemployment is zero.[5] If we add π^e to both sides of the equation, it becomes

$$\pi = \pi^e - h(u - \bar{u}). \quad \textbf{(12.1)}$$

Equation (12.1) describes the expectations-augmented Phillips curve. According to the **expectations-augmented Phillips curve**, actual inflation, π, exceeds expected inflation, π^e, if the actual unemployment rate, u, is less than the natural rate, $\bar{u}$; actual inflation is less than expected inflation if the unemployment rate exceeds the natural rate.

The Shifting Phillips Curve

Let's return to the original Phillips curve, which links the levels of inflation and unemployment in the economy. The insight gained from the Friedman–Phelps analysis is that the relationship illustrated by the Phillips curve depends on the expected rate of inflation and the natural rate of unemployment. If either factor changes, the Phillips curve will shift. To reflect this idea, we call the curve relating the inflation rate to the unemployment rate for a given natural rate of unemployment and expected rate of inflation a **short-run Phillips curve**.

[5]The equation also implies that the relationship between unanticipated inflation and cyclical unemployment is linear, but this formulation is for convenience only. The relationship of the two variables might as easily be a curve as a line.

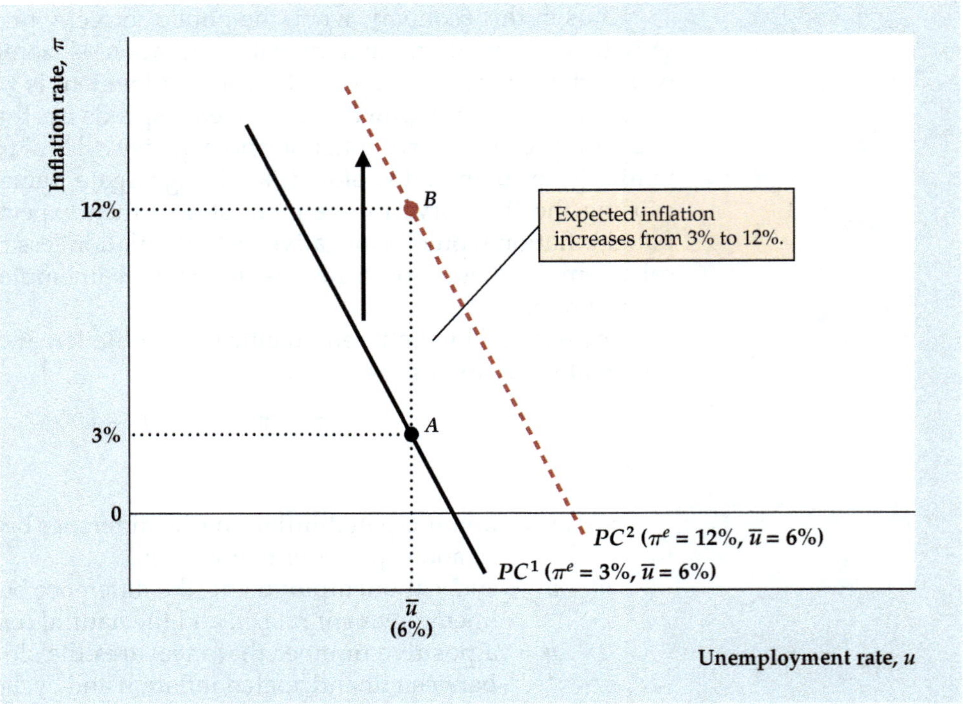

FIGURE 12.5

The shifting short-run Phillips curve: an increase in expected inflation

The Friedman–Phelps theory implies that there is a different short-run Phillips curve for every expected inflation rate. For example, PC^1 is the short-run Phillips curve when the expected rate of inflation is 3%. To verify this claim, note from Eq. (12.1) that, when the actual unemployment rate equals the natural rate, $\bar{u}$ (6% here), the actual inflation rate equals the expected inflation rate. At point *A*, the unemployment rate equals the natural rate and the inflation rate equals 3% on PC^1, so the expected inflation rate is 3% on PC^1. Similarly, at point *B* on PC^2, where the unemployment rate equals its natural rate, the inflation rate is 12%, so the expected inflation rate is 12% along PC^2. Thus an increase in the expected inflation rate from 3% to 12% shifts the short-run Phillips curve up and to the right, from PC^1 to PC^2.

Changes in the Expected Rate of Inflation. Figure 12.5 shows how a change in the expected inflation rate affects the relationship between inflation and unemployment, according to the Friedman–Phelps theory. The curve PC^1 is the short-run Phillips curve for an expected rate of inflation of 3% and a natural rate of unemployment of 6%. What identifies the expected rate of inflation as 3% along PC^1? Equation (12.1) indicates that, when the actual unemployment rate equals the natural rate (6% in this example), the actual inflation rate equals the expected inflation rate. Thus to determine the expected inflation rate on a short-run Phillips curve, we find the inflation rate at the point where the actual unemployment rate equals the natural rate. For instance, at point *A* on curve PC^1, the unemployment rate equals the natural rate, and the actual and expected rates of inflation both equal 3%. As long as the expected inflation rate remains at 3% (and the natural unemployment rate remains at 6%), the short-run Phillips curve PC^1 will describe the relationship between inflation and unemployment.

Now suppose that the expected rate of inflation increases from 3% to 12%. Figure 12.5 shows that this 9 percentage point increase in the expected rate of inflation shifts the short-run Phillips curve up by 9 percentage points at each level of the unemployment rate, from PC^1 to PC^2. When the actual unemployment rate equals the natural rate on PC^2 (at point *B*), the inflation rate is 12%, confirming that the expected inflation rate is 12% along PC^2. Comparing PC^2 and PC^1 reveals that an increase in the expected inflation rate shifts the short-run Phillips curve relationship between inflation and unemployment up and to the right.

Changes in the Natural Rate of Unemployment. The Phillips curve relationship between inflation and unemployment also is shifted by changes in the natural unemployment rate, as illustrated by Figure 12.6. The short-run Phillips curve

FIGURE 12.6

The shifting short-run Phillips curve: an increase in the natural unemployment rate

According to the Friedman–Phelps theory, an increase in the natural unemployment rate shifts the short-run Phillips curve up and to the right. At point *A* on PC^1, the actual inflation rate and the expected inflation rate are equal at 3%, so the natural unemployment rate equals the actual unemployment rate at *A*, or 6%. Thus PC^1 is the short-run Phillips curve when the natural unemployment rate is 6% and the expected inflation rate is 3%, as in Fig. 12.5. If the natural unemployment rate increases to 7%, with expected inflation unchanged, the short-run Phillips curve shifts to PC^3. At point C on PC^3, both expected and actual inflation equal 3%, so the natural unemployment rate equals the actual unemployment rate at C, or 7%.

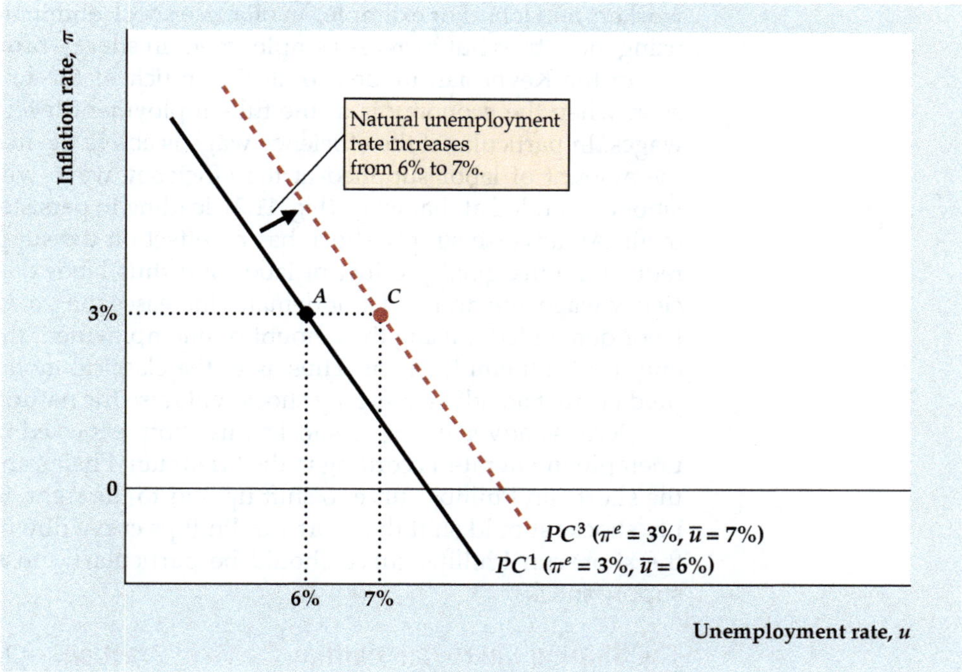

PC^1 shows a natural unemployment rate at 6% and an expected inflation rate at 3% (PC^1 in Fig. 12.6 is the same as PC^1 in Fig. 12.5). Now suppose that the natural unemployment rate increases to 7% but that the expected inflation rate remains unchanged at 3%. As Fig. 12.6 shows, the increase in the natural unemployment rate causes the short-run Phillips curve to shift, from PC^1 to PC^3.

To confirm that the natural unemployment rate corresponding to short-run Phillips curve PC^3 in Fig. 12.6 is 7%, look at point C on PC^3: At C, where the actual and expected inflation rates are equal, the unemployment rate is 7%. Thus the natural unemployment rate associated with short-run Phillips curve PC^3 is 7%. This example illustrates that—like an increase in expected inflation—an increase in the natural unemployment rate causes the short-run Phillips curve relationship between inflation and unemployment to shift up and to the right.

Supply Shocks and the Phillips Curve. The Friedman–Phelps theory holds that changes in either expected inflation or the natural unemployment rate will shift the short-run Phillips curve. One type of economic disturbance that is likely to affect both factors is a supply shock. Recall that an adverse supply shock causes a burst of inflation, which may lead people to expect higher inflation.[6] An adverse supply shock also tends to increase the natural unemployment rate, although the reasons for this effect are different in the classical and Keynesian models.

Recall that, from the classical perspective, an adverse supply shock raises the natural rate of unemployment by increasing the degree of mismatch between

[6]The inflationary impact of a supply shock will be reinforced if, in an attempt to moderate the rise in unemployment caused by the shock, the central bank increases the money supply.

workers and jobs. For example, an oil price shock eliminates jobs in heavy-energy-using industries but increases employment in energy-providing industries.

In the Keynesian model, recall that much of the unemployment that exists even when the economy is at the full-employment level is blamed on rigid real wages. In particular, if the efficiency wage is above the market-clearing real wage, the amount of labor supplied at the efficiency wage will exceed the amount of labor demanded at that wage (Fig. 11.2), leading to persistent structural unemployment. An adverse supply shock has no effect on the supply of labor,[7] but it does reduce the marginal product of labor and thus labor demand. With a rigid efficiency wage, the drop in labor demand increases the excess of labor supplied over labor demanded, raising the amount of unemployment that exists when the economy is at full employment. Thus as in the classical model, the Keynesian model predicts that an adverse supply shock will raise the natural unemployment rate.

Because adverse supply shocks raise both expected inflation and the natural unemployment rate, according to the Friedman–Phelps analysis they should cause the short-run Phillips curve to shift up and to the right. Similarly, beneficial supply shocks should shift the short-run Phillips curve down and to the left. Overall, the short-run Phillips curve should be particularly unstable during periods of supply shocks.

The Shifting Short-Run Phillips Curve in Practice. Our analysis of the shifting short-run Phillips curve (Figs. 12.5 and 12.6) helps answer the basic questions about the Phillips curve raised previously in the chapter. The first question was: Why did the original Phillips curve relationship between inflation and unemployment apply to many historical cases, including the United States during the 1960s? The Friedman–Phelps analysis shows that a negative relationship between the levels of inflation and unemployment holds *as long as expected inflation and the natural unemployment rate are approximately constant.* As shown in Fig. 12.9 later in this chapter, the natural unemployment rate changes relatively slowly, and during the 1960s it changed very little. Expected inflation probably was also nearly constant in the United States in the 1960s because at that time people were used to low and stable inflation and inflation remained low for most of the decade. Thus not surprisingly, the U.S. inflation and unemployment data for the 1960s seem to lie along a single Phillips curve (Fig. 12.1).

The second question was: Why did the Phillips curve relationship, so apparent in the United States in the 1960s, seem to disappear after 1970 (Fig. 12.2)? The answer suggested by the Friedman–Phelps analysis is that, in the period after 1970, the expected inflation rate and the natural unemployment rate varied considerably more than they had in the 1960s, causing the Phillips curve relationship to shift erratically.

Contributing to the shifts of the Phillips curve after 1970 were the two large supply shocks associated with sharp increases in the price of oil that hit the U.S. economy in 1973–1974 and 1979–1980. Recall that adverse supply shocks are likely to increase both expected inflation and the natural rate of unemployment, shifting the Phillips curve up and to the right.

Beyond the direct effects of supply shocks, other forces may have increased the variability of expected inflation and the natural unemployment rate after 1970.

[7]This statement is strictly true only for a temporary adverse supply shock. A permanent adverse supply shock, if it reduces expected future wages, would increase labor supply and thus cause an even larger rise in the natural rate of unemployment.

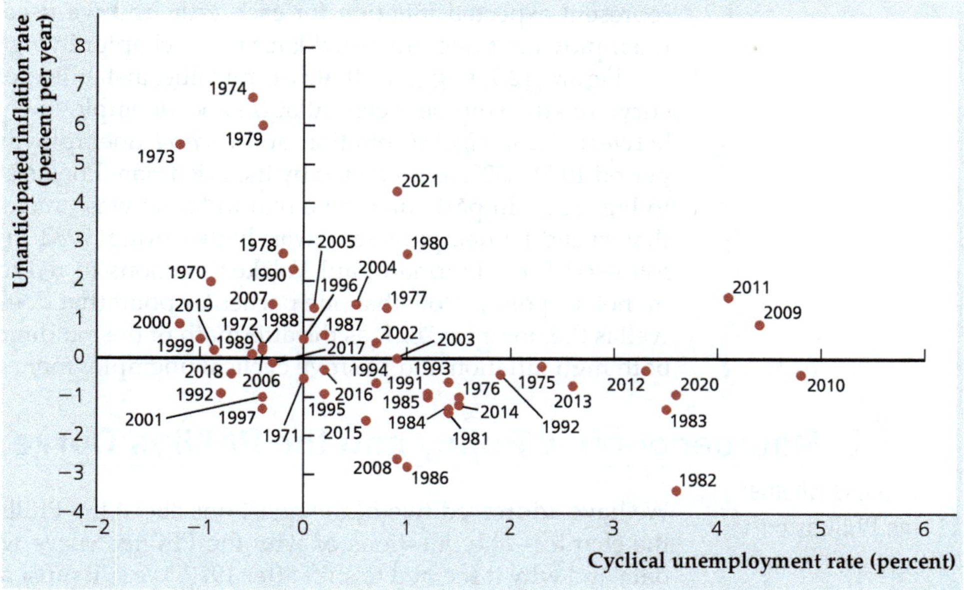

FIGURE 12.7

The expectations-augmented Phillips curve in the United States, 1970–2021

The expectations-augmented Phillips curve is a negative relationship between unanticipated inflation and cyclical unemployment. Shown is this relationship for the years 1970–2021 in the United States. Unanticipated inflation equals actual minus expected inflation, where expected inflation in any year is the forecast of CPI inflation from the Livingston Survey. Cyclical unemployment for each year is actual unemployment minus an estimate of the natural unemployment rate for that year (see Fig. 12.9). Note that years in which unanticipated inflation is high usually are years in which cyclical unemployment is low.

Source: Bureau of Labor Statistics, downloaded from Federal Reserve Bank of St. Louis FRED database at *fred.stlouisfed.org*, series *CPIAUCSL* (inflation) and *UNRATE* (unemployment rate); expected inflation: Federal Reserve Bank of Philadelphia Livingston Survey at *www.philadelphiafed.org/surveys-and-data/real-time-data-research/livingston-survey*; natural rate of unemployment: Congressional Budget Office, downloaded from FRED database, series *NROU*.

As we discuss later in the chapter, the natural unemployment rate first rose during the 1970s, then fell during the 1980s and 1990s, before leveling off for the first several years of the 2000s, and then rising after the onset of the Great Recession in 2007.

Expected inflation probably varied more after 1970 because actual inflation varied more (see Fig. 2.4, for the U.S. inflation rate for 1960–2021). After being relatively low for a long time, inflation—driven by monetary and fiscal policies that had probably been over-expansionary for several years—emerged as a problem at the end of the 1960s.[8] The 1970s were a period of high and erratic inflation, the result of the oil price shocks and macroeconomic policies that again were probably too expansionary, especially in the latter part of the decade. In contrast, following the tough anti-inflationary policies of the Federal Reserve during 1979–1982, inflation returned to a relatively low level during the 1980s. To the extent that expected inflation followed the path of actual inflation—high and erratic in the 1970s, low in the 1980s—our analysis suggests that the Phillips curve relationship between inflation and unemployment wouldn't have been stable over the period.

Does the unstable Phillips curve during 1970–2021 imply that there was no systematic relationship between inflation and unemployment during that period? The answer is "no." According to the Friedman–Phelps analysis, a negative relationship between *unanticipated* inflation and *cyclical* unemployment should appear in the data, even if expected inflation and the natural unemployment rate are changing. Measures of unanticipated inflation and cyclical unemployment for each year during the period 1970–2021 are shown in Figure 12.7. These measures are approximate because we can't directly observe either expected inflation (needed to calculate unanticipated inflation) or the natural unemployment rate (needed to find cyclical unemployment). We used the forecast of Consumer Price Index (CPI) inflation from the Federal Reserve Bank of Philadelphia's Livingston Survey to

[8]Two sources of fiscal expansion during the 1960s were military expenditures associated with the Vietnam War and increased social spending for the Great Society programs.

represent expected inflation for each year, and we used estimates of the natural unemployment rate presented later in the chapter in Fig. 12.9.

Figure 12.7 suggests that, despite the instability of the traditional Phillips curve relationship between inflation and unemployment, a negative relationship between *unanticipated* inflation and *cyclical* unemployment did exist during the period 1970–2021, as predicted by the Friedman–Phelps analysis (compare Fig. 12.7 to Fig. 12.2). In particular, note that inflation was much lower than expected and that cyclical unemployment was high during 1982 and 1983, both years that followed Fed Chairman Paul Volcker's actions to reduce inflation through tight monetary policy. Note that one particular point that does not fit the Phillips curve well is the point for 2021, as the aftermath of the pandemic recession in 2020 led to both high inflation and positive cyclical unemployment.

12.2 Macroeconomic Policy and the Phillips Curve

Discuss whether the Phillips curve offers a "menu" of inflation-unemployment combinations from which policymakers can choose.

We have addressed two of the questions about the Phillips curve raised earlier in the chapter—the questions of why the Phillips curve was observed in historical data and why it seemed to shift after 1970. We still must answer the third question: Can the Phillips curve be thought of as a "menu" of inflation–unemployment combinations from which policymakers can choose? For example, can policymakers reduce the unemployment rate by increasing the rate of inflation (moving up and to the left along the Phillips curve)?

According to the expectations-augmented Phillips curve, unemployment will fall below the natural rate only when inflation is unanticipated. So the question becomes: Can macroeconomic policy be used systematically to create unanticipated inflation?

Classical and Keynesian economists disagree on the answer to this question. Classicals argue that wages and prices adjust quickly in response to new economic information, including information about changes in government policies. Furthermore, classicals believe that people have rational expectations, meaning that they make intelligent forecasts of future policy changes. Because prices and price-level expectations respond quickly to new information, the government can't keep actual inflation above expected inflation—as would be needed to drive unemployment below the natural rate—except perhaps for a very short time. According to classicals, policies (such as more rapid monetary expansion) that increase the growth rate of aggregate demand act primarily to raise actual *and* expected inflation and so do not lead to a sustained reduction in unemployment. Because any systematic attempt to affect the unemployment rate will be thwarted by the rapid adjustment of inflation expectations, classicals conclude that the Phillips curve does *not* represent a usable trade-off for policymakers. ("In Touch with Data and Research: The Lucas Critique," explores a general lesson for policymakers of the shifting Phillips curve.)

In contrast, Keynesians contend that policymakers do have some ability—in the short run, at least—to create unanticipated inflation and thus to bring unemployment below the natural rate.[9] Although many Keynesians accept the notion

[9]As we discussed in Chapter 11, Keynesian economists also believe that macroeconomic policy can be used to return the unemployment rate to its natural level if the economy starts out in a recession or a boom.

In Touch with Data and Research

The Lucas Critique

Suppose that a particular tennis player, RN, has consistently won the French Open tournament, which is played on a clay surface, for the last five years. However, you notice that RN has not won any tournaments played on other surfaces. Based on this knowledge, placing a bet on RN winning the next French Open would seem safe. Now, consider a hypothetical situation where, aiming to decrease on-court injuries, the organizers decide to change all the surfaces to grass. Clearly, it would be foolhardy to place a huge bet on RN winning the next tournament under this new arrangement. Simply put, when the tournament rules change, people's expectations and subsequent behavior change as well.

How important are expectations and behavior for effective policymaking when it comes to the macroeconomy? In 1976, Robert E. Lucas of the University of Chicago published a seminal paper[10] critiquing the use of econometric models such as the Phillips curve for policymaking and policy evaluation. In what has become known as the *Lucas Critique*, he argued that agents' expectations of the policy process were unlikely to remain stable when policymakers changed their behavior. In other words, when new policies are implemented or expected, economic behavior is affected, and an assumption that the historical relationships will remain the same is likely to be misplaced.

The observation of what seemed to be a historic trade-off between inflation and unemployment led some policymakers to believe that unemployment could be permanently reduced by increasing inflation. However, *expected* changes in inflation will shift the Phillips curve rather than move along it, so the short-run Phillips curve breaks down. New economic policies, like the tournament's replacement of the playing surface in the hypothetical example above, can change the economic landscape, which in turn influences expectations, behaviors, and outcomes.

The Lucas critique thus emphasizes the need for caution when anticipating the effectiveness of policies, because rational agents tend to anticipate the consequences of new policies and will adapt their behaviors in ways that will affect the effectiveness of those policies. It is therefore important that economists and policymakers consider the potential impact of policy change on behavior—this is particularly important when new policies are being introduced. Notably, the Lucas critique has been influential in helping to reorientate macroeconomic research toward models with explicit considerations of expectations and taste.

[10]"Econometric Policy Evaluation: A Critique," in K. Brunner and A. H. Meltzer, eds., *Carnegie-Rochester Conference Series on Public Policy* 1, 1976, pp. 19–46.

that people have rational expectations, they argue that the expected rate of inflation that should be included in the expectations-augmented Phillips curve is the forecast of inflation made at the time that the oldest sticky prices in the economy were set. Because of price stickiness, when policymakers cause aggregate demand to rise above the expected level, time is needed for prices to fully reflect this new information. In the meantime, some prices reflect older information, and the rate of inflation is higher than the expected inflation rate based on this older information. In response to increased inflation, therefore, unemployment may remain below the natural rate for a while.

The Long-Run Phillips Curve

Although classicals and Keynesians disagree about whether the Phillips curve relationship can be exploited to reduce unemployment temporarily, they agree that policymakers can't keep the unemployment rate *permanently* below the natural rate by maintaining a high rate of inflation. Expectations about inflation eventually will adjust so that the expected and actual inflation rates are equal, or $\pi^e = \pi$. The expectations-augmented Phillips curve (Eq. 12.1) implies that, when $\pi^e = \pi$, the actual unemployment rate, u, equals the natural unemployment rate, $\bar{u}$. Thus the actual unemployment rate equals the natural rate in the long run regardless of the inflation rate maintained.

The long-run relationship of unemployment and inflation is shown by the **long-run Phillips curve.** In the long run, because unemployment equals the natural rate regardless of the inflation rate, the long-run Phillips curve is a vertical line at $u = \bar{u}$, as shown in Figure 12.8.

The vertical long-run Phillips curve is related to the long-run neutrality of money , discussed in Chapters 10 and 11. Classicals and Keynesians agree that changes in the money supply will have no long-run effects on real variables, including unemployment. The vertical long-run Phillips curve carries the notion of monetary neutrality one step further by indicating that changes in the *growth rate* of money, which lead to changes in the inflation rate, also have no real effects in the long run.

FIGURE 12.8

The long-run Phillips curve

People won't permanently overestimate or underestimate the rate of inflation, so in the long run the expected and actual inflation rates are equal and the actual unemployment rate equals the natural unemployment rate. Because actual unemployment equals the natural rate in the long run, regardless of the inflation rate, the long-run Phillips curve is vertical.

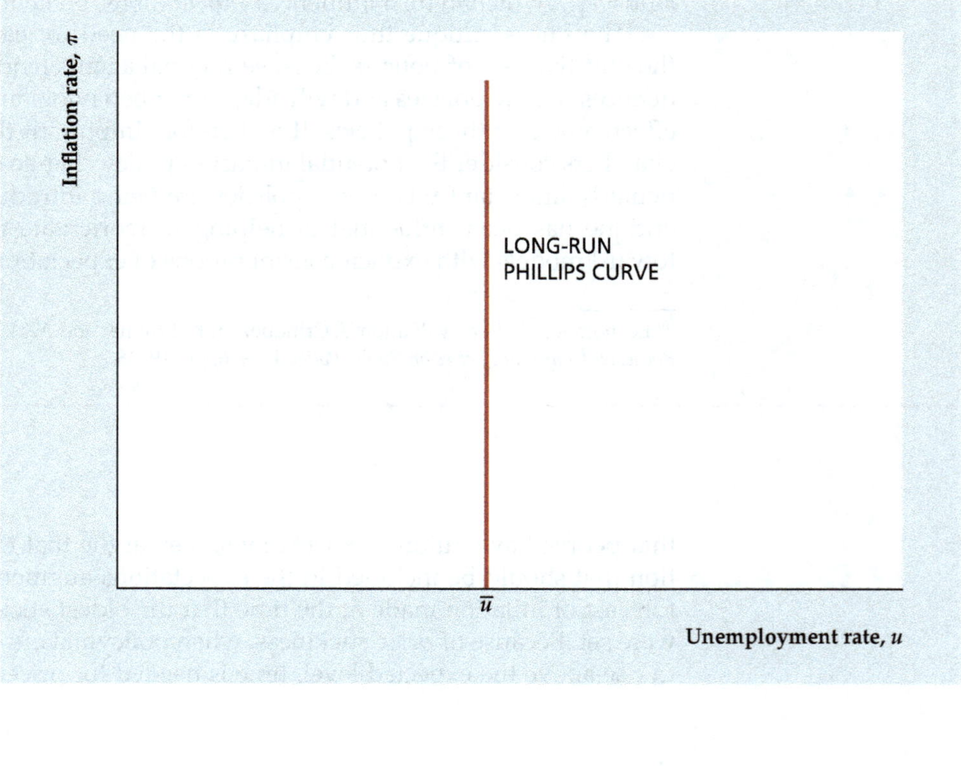

12.3 The Problem of Unemployment

Identify the costs of unemployment and discuss the natural rate of unemployment.

In the rest of the chapter we look more closely at unemployment and inflation, beginning with unemployment in this section. We start by discussing the costs of unemployment, then consider the factors that determine the long-run unemployment level, and conclude by exploring some ways in which macroeconomic policy can address unemployment.

The Costs of Unemployment

There are two principal costs of unemployment. The first is the loss of output that occurs because fewer people are productively employed. This cost is borne disproportionately by workers who are unemployed themselves, in terms of the income they lose because they are out of work. However, because the unemployed may stop paying taxes and instead receive unemployment insurance benefits or other government payments, society (in this case, the taxpayer) also bears some of the output cost of unemployment.

How big is the output cost of unemployment? One estimate is provided by Okun's law (see Eq. 3.5), which states that each percentage point of *cyclical* unemployment is associated with a loss equal to 2% of full-employment output. Thus, if full-employment output is $20,000 billion, Okun's law indicates that each percentage point of unemployment sustained for one year reduces output by $400 billion. The loss of output predicted by Okun's law reflects not only the direct impact of increased unemployment, but also other labor market changes that occur during recessions, such as shorter workweeks, reduced labor force participation, and lower productivity. (Numerical Problem 10 in Chapter 3 illustrates these effects.)

The other substantial cost of unemployment is the personal or psychological cost faced by workers who are unemployed and their families and close associates. This cost is especially important for workers suffering long spells of unemployment and for the chronically unemployed. Workers without steady employment for long periods lose job skills and self-esteem, experience significant declines in earnings that may last a long time, and suffer from stress-related health problems.[11]

Severe recessions—such as the recessions of 1980 and 1981–1982, which are sometimes regarded as a "double-dip" recessionary episode, and the Great Recession of 2007–2009—exacerbate the problems from unemployment. In a study of severe recessions, Dirk Krueger of the University of Pennsylvania, Kurt Mitman of Stockholm University, and Fabrizio Perri of the Federal Reserve Bank of Minneapolis found that the average cost of losing one's job in the Great Recession varied inversely with wealth.[12] Measuring losses using the present value of lifetime consumption (PVLC , defined in the Appendix to Chapter 4), job loss caused the PVLC to decline about 5% for households with low wealth but only about 3% for wealthier households. Even workers who kept their jobs suffered a decline in their PVLC because of lower wages, lower returns to capital, and an increased probability of future unemployment. Severe recessions are more persistent than brief recessions, leading to these large costs over a lifetime.

---

[11]See Ben S. Bernanke, "Recent Developments in the Labor Market," speech for the National Association of Business Economists, March 26, 2012, available online at *www.federalreserve.gov/newsevents/speech/bernanke20120326a.htm*.

[12]"On the Distribution of the Welfare Losses of Large Recessions," Chapter 6 in Bo Honoré, Ariel Pakes, Monika Piazzesi, and Larry Samuelson, eds., *Advances in Economics and Econometrics*, vol. 2. Cambridge: Cambridge University Press, 2017.

A second major cost of severe recessions arises from long-term unemployment. When a recession is severe, the probability of a worker who is unemployed finding a job declines. In addition, the longer the worker is unemployed, the lower is the probability that the worker will find a job in any given month. Also, expected future earnings of workers decline the longer they are unemployed.[13]

The costs of unemployment may also vary across people in different demographic groups. The 2007–2009 recession affected men, Black and Hispanic workers, young workers, and those with low levels of education more than it did those in other demographic groups.[14]

The costs of unemployment are real and serious, but two offsetting factors should be noted. First, to the extent that workers who are unemployed engage in economically productive activities such as searching for a job or acquiring new skills, the loss of output arising from current unemployment may be compensated for by increased output in the future. In particular, frictional unemployment—the result of workers and firms seeking appropriate matches—raises future productivity and output and thus may impose little net economic cost, or even lead to an economic gain.

A second offsetting factor is that unemployed people have more leisure time—to spend with family and friends, work around the house, and so on. However, the benefits of extra leisure time decrease as the amount of leisure increases, and most workers who are unemployed wouldn't feel that increased leisure was adequate compensation for their lost income.

The Long-Term Behavior of the Unemployment Rate

Classical and Keynesian economists agree that, although the actual unemployment rate may deviate from the natural unemployment rate in the short run, in the long run the actual rate equals the natural rate. Thus understanding the behavior of unemployment in all but the short run requires identifying the determinants of the natural rate of unemployment. In Chapter 3 we discussed the reasons for the natural unemployment rate always being greater than zero; here we focus more narrowly on the reasons for changes in the natural rate in the United States.

The Changing Natural Rate. The natural unemployment rate corresponds to full-employment output. Unfortunately, because we can't be sure when the economy is at full employment, we can't directly observe the natural rate and so must estimate it. Inevitably, therefore, there is some uncertainty about the value of the natural rate at any particular time. Figure 12.9 shows estimated values of the natural unemployment rate, published by the Congressional Budget Office, along with the actual unemployment rate, for the period 1960–2021.

Giving a fully satisfactory explanation of the rise and fall in the natural rate of unemployment is difficult, but part of the story seems to have been the result of demographic changes. The proportion of workers from differing demographic groups (based on age, gender, race, or ethnicity) changes gradually over time.

---

[13]For more details, see Katharine G. Abraham, John C. Haltiwanger, Kristin Sandusky, and James Spletzer, "The Consequences of Long Term Unemployment: Evidence from Matched Employer-Employee Data," Working Paper 16-40, Center for Economic Studies, U.S. Census Bureau, 2016.

[14]See Hilary Hoynes, Douglas L. Miller, and Jessamyn Schaller, "Who Suffers in Recessions?" Journal of Economic Perspectives, Summer 2012, pp. 27–48.

FIGURE 12.9

Actual and natural unemployment rates in the United States, 1960–2021

The figure shows the actual unemployment rate and an estimate of the natural rate of unemployment in the United States for the period 1960–2021. The difference between the actual and natural unemployment rates is the cyclical unemployment rate. Note that the natural rate of unemployment rose from the 1960s until the late 1970s and declined from 1980 to 1999. It remained fairly constant around 5.0% for a few years after then but began declining in the mid-2010s.

Sources: Actual unemployment rate, Bureau of Labor Statistics, downloaded from Federal Reserve Bank of St. Louis FRED database at *fred .stlouisfed.org*, series *UNRATE*; natural rate of unemployment: Congressional Budget Office, downloaded from FRED database, series *NROU*.

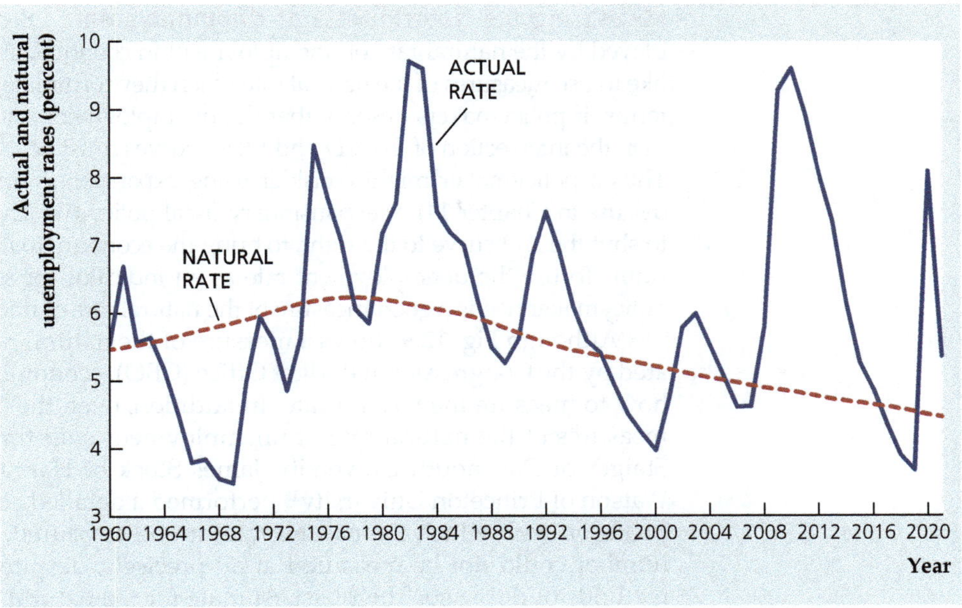

Because some groups have higher unemployment rates than others, the natural rate of unemployment changes over time. For example, in the 1960s, as women entered the labor force in greater numbers, the natural rate of unemployment rose because women's average unemployment rate was higher than men's.[15] Teenagers have particularly high unemployment rates both because they move in and out of the labor force frequently while in school and because many teenagers work at low-skill jobs that do not provide long-term employment.

From World War II through about 1978, teenagers and women made up an increasingly large portion of the labor force in the United States. This shift in the composition of the labor force toward groups that have traditionally experienced higher unemployment rates may have raised the overall unemployment rate during that period, particularly in the 1960s and 1970s. In contrast, since about 1978, demographic factors tended to reduce the natural rate of unemployment. One factor is the decline in the share of young people in the labor force—a trend that reflects the aging of the population as a whole. Indeed, the percentage of the U.S. labor force aged 16 to 24 fell from 25% in 1980 to 16% in 1998 and to 13% in 2021. A study by Robert Shimer[16] of the University of Chicago concluded that the declining share of younger workers, who are prone to periods of unemployment, can account for the bulk of the decline in the natural rate of unemployment in the United States in the 1980s and 1990s.

---

[15]However, since the early 1980s, the average unemployment rates for men and women have been about the same, so changes in the proportion of women in the labor force would no longer change the natural rate of unemployment.

[16]Robert Shimer, "Why Is the U.S. Unemployment Rate So Much Lower?" in B. Bernanke and J. Rotemberg, eds., NBER *Macroeconomics Annual*, 1998.

Measuring the Natural Rate of Unemployment. Because of the prominent role played by the natural rate of unemployment in economic theory, policymakers would like to use measures of the natural rate when they formulate economic policy. In simple terms, if policymakers observe that the unemployment rate is above the natural rate, then the intersection of the *AD* and *SRAS* curves must be to the left of the *LRAS* curve. Thus a policymaker might consider using expansionary monetary policy (which we discuss in Chapter 14) or expansionary fiscal policy (which we discuss in Chapter 15) to shift the *AD* curve to the right, to bring the economy to its full-employment equilibrium. To use the unemployment rate as an indicator for setting policy, however, the policymaker needs a good measure of the natural rate of unemployment.

Although Fig. 12.9 shows a measure of the natural rate of unemployment created by the Congressional Budget Office (CBO), economists widely disagree about how to measure the natural rate. In addition, even the CBO has often revised its measures of the natural rate of unemployment over time.[17] Economists Douglas Staiger of Dartmouth University, James Stock of Harvard University, and Mark Watson of Princeton University[18] performed a detailed econometric analysis of the precision with which the natural rate can be measured. They concluded that the number could not be measured at all precisely, despite trying many alternative methods of doing so. Their best estimate for the natural rate of unemployment in 1994, for example, is that it equaled 5¾%, but that there was so much uncertainty about the number that they were 95% confident that it was between 4.8% and 6.6%. That interval is far too large to be of much use to policymakers.

In the face of this evidence, researchers in the late 1990s pondered what policymakers should do. Given uncertainty about the natural rate of unemployment, policymakers may want to be less aggressive with policy changes than they would be if they knew the value of the natural rate more precisely.[19] Some researchers have even blamed the rise of inflation in the 1970s on the Federal Reserve's failure to estimate the natural rate of unemployment properly.[20] Policymakers face the problem, though, that measures of full-employment output may be even more imprecise. So, although economic theory relies on the concepts of full-employment output and the natural rate of unemployment, policymaking is difficult because economists cannot measure these concepts in a precise manner.

12.4 The Problem of Inflation

Discuss the types and costs of inflation.

In August 1971 President Richard M. Nixon instituted a set of wage and price controls in an attempt to reduce U.S. inflation. These strong measures were taken even though the inflation rate was only 5% at the time. During the late 1970s, when the U.S. inflation rate approached "double-digits," surveys of voters found

[17]To appreciate how dramatically the CBO has revised its numbers, see the article by Sharon Kozicki, "How Do Data Revisions Affect the Evaluation and Conduct of Monetary Policy?" Federal Reserve Bank of Kansas City, *Economic Review*, First Quarter 2004, pp. 5–38.

[18]"The NAIRU, Unemployment and Monetary Policy," *Journal of Economic Perspectives*, Winter 1997, pp. 33–49.

[19]For example, see Volker Wieland, "Monetary Policy and Uncertainty about the Natural Unemployment Rate: Brainard-Style Conservatism versus Experimental Activism," *B.E. Journal of Macroeconomics: Advances in Macroeconomics*, vol. 6, no. 1, 2006.

[20]See Athanasios Orphanides and John Williams, "The Decline of Activist Stabilization Policy: Natural Rate Misperceptions, Learning, and Expectations," *Journal of Economic Dynamics and Control*, November 2005, pp. 1927–1950.

that they thought inflation was "public enemy number one"; one victim of the public's fear of inflation was President Jimmy Carter, who lost his reelection bid to Ronald Reagan in 1980 in part because of his perceived inability to control inflation. In this section we look at inflation, beginning with a discussion of inflation costs and then turning to the question of what can be done to control inflation.

The Costs of Inflation

The costs of inflation depend primarily on whether consumers, investors, workers, and firms are able to predict the inflation before it occurs. To illustrate this point, we discuss two extreme cases: an inflation that everyone is able to predict and an inflation that comes as a complete surprise.

Perfectly Anticipated Inflation. Let's first consider the case of an inflation that is perfectly anticipated by the public. Imagine, for example, that everyone knew that the inflation rate would be 4% per year. To keep things simple, assume no change in relative prices so that the prices of all individual goods and services also are rising at the rate of 4% per year.

Why then does a fully anticipated inflation impose any costs? The prices you pay for groceries, movie tickets, and other goods would increase by 4% per year but so would your nominal wage or the nominal value of the goods or services you produce. Because your nominal income is rising along with prices, your purchasing power isn't hurt by the perfectly anticipated inflation.[21]

What about the money that you hold in your savings account? Although inflation reduces the purchasing power of money, perfectly anticipated inflation wouldn't hurt the value of your savings account. The reason is that the nominal interest rate would adjust to offset the drop in the purchasing power of money. For instance, with a zero inflation rate and a nominal interest rate on savings deposits of 3%, the real interest rate also is 3% per year. If inflation rises to a perfectly anticipated rate of 4% per year, an increase in the nominal interest rate to 7% per year will leave the real interest rate unchanged at 3%. Because both savers and banks care only about the real interest rate, when inflation rises to 4% banks should be willing to offer 7% nominal interest, and savers should be willing to accept that nominal return. Thus neither banks nor savers are hurt by an anticipated increase in inflation.[22]

The suggestion that perfectly anticipated inflation imposes no economic costs isn't quite correct: Inflation erodes the value of currency, which leads people to keep less currency on hand—for example, by going to the bank or the automatic teller machine to make withdrawals every week instead of twice a month. Similarly, inflation may induce firms to reduce their cash holdings by introducing computerized cash management systems or adding staff to the accounting department. The costs in time and effort incurred by people and firms who are trying to minimize their holdings of cash are called **shoe leather costs**. For modest inflation

[21]It may be true that, psychologically, people think of increases in their wages arising from ongoing inflation as being earned and thus "fair" but increases in the prices they pay because of inflation as "unfair." This is a confusion, although one that may have real political consequences if it causes the public to demand strong action on inflation.

[22]This argument ignores the fact that interest is taxed on a nominal basis. If the after-tax real interest rate is to be kept constant, the nominal interest rate will have to rise by somewhat more than the increase in inflation. See Table 4.1 on the expected real after-tax interest rate.

rates, shoe leather costs are small but not completely trivial. For example, the shoe leather costs of a 10% perfectly anticipated inflation have been estimated to be about 0.3% of GDP, which is more than $50 billion per year in the United States.[23]

A second cost of perfectly anticipated inflation arises from menu costs, or the costs of changing nominal prices. When there is inflation and prices are continually rising, sellers of goods and services must use resources to change nominal prices. For instance, mail-order firms have to print and mail catalogues frequently to report the increases in prices. Although some firms face substantial menu costs, for the economy as a whole these costs probably are small. Furthermore, technological progress, such as the introduction of electronic scanners in supermarkets, reduces the cost of changing prices.

Unanticipated Inflation. Much of the public's aversion to inflation is aversion to unanticipated inflation—inflation that is different from the rate expected. For example, if everyone expects the inflation rate to be 4% per year, but it actually is 6% per year, unanticipated inflation is 2% per year.

What is the effect of 6% inflation if (1) you expected 4% inflation and (2) your savings account pays 7% interest? When inflation is 6% per year instead of 4% per year, the actual real interest rate on your savings account is only 1% per year (the nominal interest rate of 7% minus the inflation rate of 6%) instead of the 3% per year that you expected. By earning a lower actual real interest rate, you lose as a result of the unanticipated inflation. However, your loss is the bank's gain because the bank pays a lower real interest rate than it expected. Note that the roles would have been reversed if the actual inflation rate had been lower than expected; in that case the real interest rate that you earn, and that the bank has to pay, would be higher than anticipated.

Similarly, suppose that your nominal salary is set in advance. If inflation is higher than expected, the real value of your salary is less than you expected, and your loss is your employer's gain. If inflation is lower than expected, however, you benefit and your employer loses.

These examples show that a primary effect of unanticipated inflation is to transfer wealth from one person or firm to another. People who lend or save at fixed interest rates (creditors) and those with incomes set in nominal terms are hurt by unanticipated inflation, whereas people who borrow at fixed interest rates (debtors) or who must make fixed nominal payments are helped by unanticipated inflation.

For the economy as a whole, a transfer of wealth from one group to another isn't a net loss of resources and hence doesn't represent a true cost. However, from the viewpoints of individual people and firms in the economy, the *risk* of gaining or losing wealth as a result of unanticipated inflation is unwelcome. Because most people don't like risk, the possibility of significant gains or losses arising from unexpected inflation makes people feel worse off and hence is a cost of unanticipated inflation. Furthermore, any resources that people use in forecasting inflation and trying to protect themselves against the risks of unanticipated inflation represent an additional cost. However, some of these costs of unanticipated inflation can be eliminated by contracts that are indexed to the price level, as we discuss in "In Touch with Data and Research: Indexed Contracts."

---

[23]See Stanley Fischer, "Towards an Understanding of the Costs of Inflation: II," in K. Brunner and A. Meltzer, eds., *Carnegie-Rochester Conference Series on Public Policy*, vol. 15, Autumn 1981.

In Touch with Data and Research

Indexed Contracts

In principle, much of the risk of gains and losses associated with unanticipated inflation can be eliminated by using contracts in which payments are indexed to inflation. If a bank wanted to offer a guaranteed 3% real interest rate on savings accounts, for instance, it could index the nominal interest rate to the rate of inflation by offering to pay a nominal interest rate equal to 3% plus whatever the rate of inflation turns out to be. Then if the actual inflation rate is 6%, the bank would end up paying a nominal interest rate of 9%—giving the depositor the promised 3% real interest rate. Similarly, other financial contracts, such as loans, mortgages, and bonds, can be indexed to protect the real rate of return against unanticipated inflation. Wage payments set by labor contracts can also be indexed to protect workers and employers against unanticipated inflation. (We discussed the macroeconomic effects of wage indexation in Appendix 11.A.)

How widespread is indexing? Most financial contracts in the United States are not indexed to the rate of inflation, although payments on some long-term financial contracts (adjustable-rate mortgages, for example) are indexed to nominal interest rates such as the prime rate charged by banks or the Treasury bill interest rate. Because nominal interest rates move roughly in step with inflation, these long-term financial contracts are to some extent indexed to inflation. Some labor contracts in the United States are indexed to the rate of inflation through provisions called cost-of-living adjustments, or COLAs. They provide for some increase in nominal wages if inflation is higher than expected, but usually a 1% increase in unanticipated inflation results in somewhat less than a 1% adjustment of wages. In January 1997 the U.S. Treasury began to sell bonds indexed to the rate of inflation, which are known as Treasury Inflation-Protected Securities (TIPS).

In countries that have experienced high and unpredictable inflation rates, indexed contracts are common. A case in point is Israel, which had a CPI inflation rate of 445% per year in 1984. At that time, more than 80% of liquid financial assets in Israel were indexed: For example, long-term government bonds were indexed to the CPI, and banks offered short-term deposits whose purchasing power was tied to that of the U.S. dollar. However, the fraction of financial assets that were indexed decreased after the Israeli hyperinflation ended in the second half of 1985, and continued to decrease as Israeli inflation fell to single digits.[24]

[24]See Stanley Fischer, "Israeli Inflation and Indexation," in J. Williamson, ed., *Inflation and Indexation: Argentina, Brazil, and Israel*, Institute for International Economics, 1985, reprinted in Stanley Fischer, *Indexing, Inflation, and Economic Policy*, Cambridge, MA: MIT Press, 1986; and Zalman F. Shiffer, "Adjusting to High Inflation: The Israeli Experience," Federal Reserve Bank of St. Louis *Review*, May 1986, pp. 18–29.

Another cost of unanticipated inflation relates to the fact that prices serve as signals in a market economy. For example, if wheat becomes more expensive than corn, that is a signal to consumers to switch from wheat to corn and to farmers to produce more wheat and less corn. However, the prices that act as signals in the economy are *relative* prices, such as the price of wheat relative to the price of corn. Knowing that wheat is so many dollars per bushel doesn't help the consumer and farmer make good economic decisions unless they also know the price of corn. When inflation is unanticipated, particularly if it is erratic, people may confuse changes in prices arising from changes in the general price level with changes in prices arising from shifts in the supply or demand for individual goods. Because the signals provided by prices may be distorted by unanticipated inflation, the market economy works less efficiently. In addition, when there is a great deal of uncertainty about the true inflation rate, people must spend time and effort learning about different prices, by comparison shopping, for example.

The Costs of Hyperinflation. **Hyperinflation** occurs when the inflation rate is extremely high for a sustained period of time.[25] For example, during a 12-month period beginning in August 1945, the average rate of inflation in Hungary was 19,800% *per month.*[26] In the more recent hyperinflation in Zimbabwe, the annual rate of inflation was 1017% in 2006, 10,453% in 2007, and soared to 55.6 billion percent in 2008, before dropping to 6.5% in 2009.[27] The costs of inflation during these hyperinflations were much greater than the costs associated with moderate inflation. For example, when prices are increasing at such mind-boggling rates, the incentives to minimize holdings of currency are powerful and the resulting shoe leather costs are enormous. In severe hyperinflations, workers are paid much more frequently—perhaps even more than once a day—and they rush out to spend their money (or to convert their money into some other form, such as a foreign currency) before prices rise even further. The time and energy devoted to getting rid of currency as fast as possible wastes resources and disrupts production.

One early casualty of hyperinflations is the government's ability to collect taxes. In a hyperinflation, taxpayers have an incentive to delay paying their taxes as long as possible. Because tax bills usually are set in nominal terms, the longer the taxpayer delays, the less the real value of that obligation is. The real value of taxes collected by the government falls sharply during hyperinflations, with destructive effects on the government's finances and its ability to provide public services.

Finally, the disruptive effect of inflation on market efficiency that we discussed earlier becomes most severe in the case of a hyperinflation. If prices change so often that they cease to be reliable indicators of the supply and demand for different goods and services, the invisible hand of the free market can't allocate resources efficiently.

Can Inflation Be Too Low? Our discussion of the costs of inflation has focused on the case of inflation that is too high. What about the case in which inflation is very low, or prices are actually falling, a situation known as *deflation*? Should central banks be concerned?

In fact, very low *inflation*, and especially deflation, can be harmful for the economy. For example, just as unanticipated inflation helps those who borrow at fixed interest rates, unexpected *deflation* hurts borrowers. Indeed, sufficiently severe unexpected deflation—as occurred in the United States during the 1930s, when

---

[25]Philip Cagan, in his classic study of hyperinflation ("The Monetary Dynamics of Hyperinflation," in Milton Friedman, ed., *Studies in the Quantity Theory of Money*, Chicago: University of Chicago Press, 1956), defined a hyperinflation as beginning in the month in which the rate of inflation first exceeds 50% *per month.*

[26]*Ibid.*, Table 1.

[27]See the World Bank's Data and Statistics for Zimbabwe at *siteresources.worldbank.org/INTZIMBABWE/Resources/zimbabawe_Monitor_tables.xlsx.*

prices for a time fell by about 10% per year—can lead to widespread bankruptcies and financial distress, as borrowers' nominal incomes fall relative to their contractual debt payments.

Like anticipated inflation, anticipated deflation also has costs. For example, if nominal wages are sticky (and, in particular, if they do not easily adjust downward), deflation will raise real wages over time, by lowering the prices of the things workers buy. That's good for those who remain employed, but it can also create more unemployment if the real wage rises above the level implied by the balancing of supply and demand in the labor market. Like anticipated inflation, anticipated deflation can also reduce the efficiency of markets because people find it more difficult to determine the relative prices of the goods and services they buy and sell.

An important cost of anticipated deflation arises from the fact that nominal interest rates generally cannot fall below zero. Suppose, for example, that prices are falling at 2% per year ($\pi = -2\%$ per year). Then the lowest possible value for the *real* interest rate that the central bank can achieve is 2%, equal to a zero nominal interest rate less the inflation rate of minus 2% per year; in equation form, $r = i - \pi = 0 - (-2) = 2\%$ per year. If the real interest rate required to restore full employment is less than 2% per year, but a 2% per year deflation is ongoing, the central bank will not be able to cut the real interest rate by as much as the economy needs, even by cutting the nominal interest rate all the way to zero. (In contrast, if inflation were positive 2% per year, by cutting the nominal interest rate to zero the central bank could achieve a real interest rate of minus 2% per year, since $r = i - \pi = 0 - 2 = -2\%$ per year.) In Chapter 14, we discuss issues related to the zero lower bound on the nominal interest rate (and point out a few cases in which the nominal interest rate has been slightly negative in some countries).

If both high inflation and very low inflation have costs, what inflation rate should the central bank aim for? Today, many central banks around the world aim for an inflation rate of about 2% per year, which is a relatively low rate (thereby minimizing the costs of inflation that is too high) but which also reduces the risk that an unexpected shock will drive the economy into deflation. In addition, some evidence suggests that, for technical reasons, official measures of inflation in the United States somewhat overstate the true inflation rate; accordingly, if the Fed targets 2% inflation, it is actually targeting a true inflation rate that is somewhat lower , as we discussed in Chapter 2, "In Touch with Data and Research: Does CPI Inflation Overstate Increases in the Cost of Living?"

12.5 Fighting Inflation: The Role of Inflationary Expectations

Discuss the challenges and costs of reducing inflation.

Basically, inflation occurs when the aggregate quantity of goods demanded at any particular price level is rising more quickly than the aggregate quantity of goods supplied at that price level. (Figure 12.3 illustrates such a situation.) Many factors can cause rapid increases in the aggregate quantity of goods demanded relative to the aggregate quantity supplied. Among these sources of inflation are increases in consumption or investment spending, expansionary fiscal policies, and adverse supply shocks. However, as discussed in Chapter 7, in general the only factor that can create *sustained* rises in aggregate demand, and thus ongoing inflation, is a high rate of money growth.

If rapid money growth is inflationary, why do central banks permit rapid monetary expansion? As mentioned in Chapter 7 (and discussed in more detail in

Chapter 15), in developing or war-torn countries, governments may not be able to raise enough revenue by taxing or borrowing, so they print money to finance their spending. However, in industrialized countries not engaged in or recovering from a war, governments usually are able either to tax or borrow enough to cover their expenditures. In these countries, rapid money growth usually is the result of attempts to use expansionary monetary policy to fight recessions, not balanced by tighter monetary policies in periods when output is above its full-employment level.

Because ongoing inflation generally is the result of rapid money growth, the prescription for stopping inflation appears to be simple: Reduce the rate of money growth. Unfortunately, the process of **disinflation**—the reduction of the inflation rate—by slowing money growth may lead to recession. In terms of the expectations-augmented Phillips curve, Eq. (12.1), if macroeconomic policy succeeds in reducing inflation below the expected rate, unemployment will rise above the natural rate. Unemployment will remain above the natural rate until expected inflation falls to the new, lower actual inflation rate.

Is there some way to reduce inflation without incurring serious unemployment costs? The expectations-augmented Phillips curve suggests one possibility: If the public's expected rate of inflation could be lowered as actual inflation was being brought down, unemployment wouldn't have to rise above the natural rate. (You should confirm that, in Eq. 12.1, if actual inflation, π, and expected inflation, π^e, fall by the same amount, cyclical unemployment, $u - \bar{u}$, doesn't increase.) That is, if *expected* inflation can be reduced, the original Phillips curve relating inflation and unemployment can be shifted down and to the left, reducing the rate of inflation associated with any level of unemployment.

But how can policymakers reduce the public's inflationary expectations? In the rest of this section we discuss some suggested approaches for reducing both inflation and inflationary expectations.

Rapid Versus Gradual Disinflation. Some classical economists have proposed that disinflation should be implemented quickly by a rapid and decisive reduction in the growth rate of the money supply—a strategy sometimes referred to as **cold turkey**. Because a cold-turkey disinflation is dramatic and highly visible to the public, proponents of this policy argue that it will quickly and substantially reduce inflationary expectations, particularly if the policy is announced well in advance. If expected inflation falls sufficiently, the expectations-augmented Phillips curve implies that the unemployment costs of the disinflation will be minimal.

However, most Keynesian economists disagree with the idea that rapid disinflation can be achieved without significant costs in terms of increased cyclical unemployment. They argue that, because of factors such as menu costs and nominal wage contracts, several years may be required for prices and wages to adjust to a disinflationary policy; during the adjustment period cyclical unemployment could be high. Furthermore, Keynesians point out that the cold-turkey strategy may not lower inflation expectations because people may expect the government to abandon the policy if the resulting unemployment reaches politically intolerable levels.

Because they fear the possible unemployment consequences of the cold-turkey strategy, many Keynesians recommend a policy of **gradualism**, or reducing the rate of money growth and inflation gradually over a period of years. Keynesians argue that a gradual approach, which gives prices, wages, and expectations more time to adjust to the disinflation, will raise the unemployment rate by less than the cold-turkey strategy—although the period during which unemployment exceeds the natural rate may be longer. They further argue that, because the policy will be viewed as sustainable politically, gradualism may be as effective as the cold-turkey approach at reducing inflationary expectations. The results of one study comparing cold turkey and gradualism are discussed below.

In Touch with Data and Research

The Sacrifice Ratio

To reduce inflation, tight monetary and fiscal policies must be used to slow the growth rate of aggregate demand. However, if these policies aren't perfectly anticipated, they will also cause output and employment to fall below their full-employment levels—at least for a time. This loss of output and jobs is an important cost that must be weighed against the benefits of inflation-reducing policies.

Economists sometimes use the sacrifice ratio to measure the cost of lowering the inflation rate. The **sacrifice ratio** is the amount of output lost when the inflation rate is reduced by 1 percentage point. For example, according to a study by Laurence Ball of Johns Hopkins University,[28] during the disinflation of the early 1980s the inflation rate in the United States fell by 8.83 percentage points (from a rate of 12.10% per year to 3.27% per year). For the 15 quarters of this disinflation, Ball estimated the total loss in output caused by inflation-reducing policies to be 16.18% of one year's potential GDP. Dividing the output loss of 16.18% of potential GDP by the 8.83 percentage point reduction in inflation yields a sacrifice ratio of 1.83 for this episode. We can interpret this result as saying that each percentage point by which U.S. inflation was reduced during the early 1980s cost the country 1.83% of a year's potential GDP.

Using quarterly data for nine countries, Ball calculated the sacrifice ratio for 28 disinflations that occurred during the 1960s, 1970s, and 1980s. The accompanying table reports the average sacrifice ratio he found for each country and demonstrates that the output cost of reducing inflation may vary considerably. The average sacrifice ratio ranges from less than 1.0 in France, the United Kingdom, and Japan to almost 3.0 in Germany. In other words, reducing inflation in Germany was three times as expensive, in terms of lost output, as it was in those other industrialized countries. What accounts for these differences?

Average Sacrifice Ratios by Country	
Australia	1.00
Canada	1.50
France	0.75
Germany	2.92
Italy	1.74
Japan	0.93
Switzerland	1.57
United Kingdom	0.79
United States	2.39

[28]"What Determines the Sacrifice Ratio?" in N. Gregory Mankiw, ed., *Monetary Policy*, Chicago: University of Chicago Press, 1994, pp. 155–188.

(*continued*)

By comparing the characteristics of the different countries in his sample, Ball found that one factor affecting the sacrifice ratio is the flexibility of the labor market. Countries in which wages adjust relatively slowly to changes in labor supply and demand—owing, for example, to heavy government regulation of the labor market—tend to have higher sacrifice ratios. This finding makes sense because countries with inflexible labor markets should take longer to reach long-run equilibrium following an unexpected slowing of the growth of aggregate demand. Ball also found that rapid disinflations tend to have lower sacrifice ratios than do slow disinflations, which is a bit of evidence in favor of the cold-turkey approach rather than gradualism.

Ball's results are interesting but should be interpreted with some caution. One problem is that determining exactly how much output loss can be attributed to a particular set of anti-inflationary policies isn't easy. For example, to calculate the output loss owing to disinflation we have to estimate the amount of output if there had been no disinflation, which is difficult. If the output loss calculation is wrong, the sacrifice ratio calculation will also be wrong. Factors such as supply shocks, which affect both output and inflation, can also distort the calculation of sacrifice ratios. Thus at best, the sacrifice ratio is a rough measure of the costs of reducing inflation.

Wage and Price Controls. Frustrated by the costs and difficulties of reducing inflation by reducing money growth, policymakers in some countries have taken a more direct approach and imposed wage and price controls—legal limits on the ability of firms to raise wages or prices. Supporters of wage–price controls (or of *incomes policies*, as wage–price controls are also called) argue that by using the force of law to stop price increases the government can "break the back" of inflationary expectations, allowing the disinflation to proceed without serious unemployment consequences.

Critics of price controls make two points. First, price controls are likely to cause shortages. In a free market the ever-changing forces of supply and demand lead to changes in relative prices, with the prices of some products rising more rapidly than the prices of others. If price controls prevent the price of a product from rising to the level at which quantity supplied equals quantity demanded, there will be excess demand for the product—that is, a shortage. These shortages and the disruptions they cause are a major cost of price controls.

Second, critics dispute that wage–price controls have a major effect on the public's inflation expectations. Although controls stop inflation for the moment, because they cause shortages and disrupt the economy they eventually have to be removed. Knowing that the controls are temporary, people may expect even greater inflation in the future.

The most recent U.S. experience with price controls occurred in the early 1970s. President Nixon imposed price controls from August 1971 to April 1974 in an attempt to prevent inflation from rising higher than 5%. But shortages arose for many goods, including chicken broilers, lumber, and various steel products. And when the price controls were lifted, prices returned to the levels they would have attained had the controls never been put in place.

One factor that may affect expectations of inflation during the period of controls is how the government handles monetary and fiscal policy. If macroeconomic policies allow aggregate demand to continue to grow rapidly, people may expect renewed inflation when the controls are lifted (see Analytical Problem 5 at the end of the chapter). This failure to reduce aggregate demand growth appears to have been the problem with the Nixon wage–price controls that began in 1971. But if controls are accompanied by tight monetary and fiscal policy, the idea that inflation will not resume when controls are lifted is more plausible.

Credibility and Reputation. Classicals and Keynesians agree that, for disinflation to be achieved without high unemployment costs, reducing the public's expected inflation rate is important. Perhaps the most important factor determining how quickly expected inflation adjusts is the credibility, or believability, of the government's announced disinflationary policy. If the government (in the person of the President or the chairman of the Federal Reserve, for example) announces a policy to reduce the inflation rate—and if workers, consumers, and firms believe that the government means what it says—expected inflation should drop fairly rapidly.

How can a government improve its credibility with the public? One desirable way would be for the government to develop a reputation for carrying through on its promises; then when it announces a disinflation program, people would likely take this announcement seriously. Unfortunately, time is needed to develop such a reputation, and changes in administration may lead to relatively frequent changes in the people who make policy decisions.

Another strategy is to organize policymaking institutions in ways that create credibility with the public. For example, a strong and independent central bank, run by someone with well-known anti-inflation views, may have credibility with the public when it announces a disinflationary policy. However, if the central bank is controlled directly by the executive branch—and is therefore exposed to intense political pressure when unemployment rises—an announced disinflationary program is likely to be less credible. We explore the relationship among institutional structure, government credibility, and inflation expectations in greater detail in Chapter 14.

The U.S. Disinflation of the 1980s and 1990s

Theories about disinflation were put to the test in the 1980s and 1990s in the United States. Beginning in 1979 under Paul Volcker and continuing in 1987 under Alan Greenspan, the Federal Reserve sought to eliminate inflation as a major source of economic instability. From 1979 to 1982, Chairman Volcker reduced inflation from double-digit levels to about 4%. From 1982 on, Volcker and then Greenspan gradually reduced the inflation rate. Their goal was to keep inflation from being a major consideration in the minds of consumers and investors. They wanted inflation to be at such a low and stable rate that it would no longer worry people and they would have confidence that it would never rise substantially again.

One way to judge the success of the Federal Reserve is to examine people's inflation expectations. To do so, we use inflation forecasts from the Survey of Professional Forecasters, collected by the Federal Reserve Bank of Philadelphia, as

FIGURE 12.10

Expected inflation rate, 1971Q1–2021Q4

The figure shows quarterly values for the expected inflation rate over the coming four quarters beginning with the date shown on the horizontal axis, for the period from the first quarter of 1971 to the fourth quarter of 2021. Expected inflation displayed large movements in the 1970s and 1980s before declining gradually in the 1990s. Expected inflation remained below 2.5% in the 2000s through mid-2021 and then began to rise as inflation in the second half of 2021 increased sharply.

Sources: Survey of Professional Forecasters, Federal Reserve Bank of Philadelphia, available at *www.philadelphiafed.org/research-and-data/real-time-center/survey-of-professional-forecasters.*

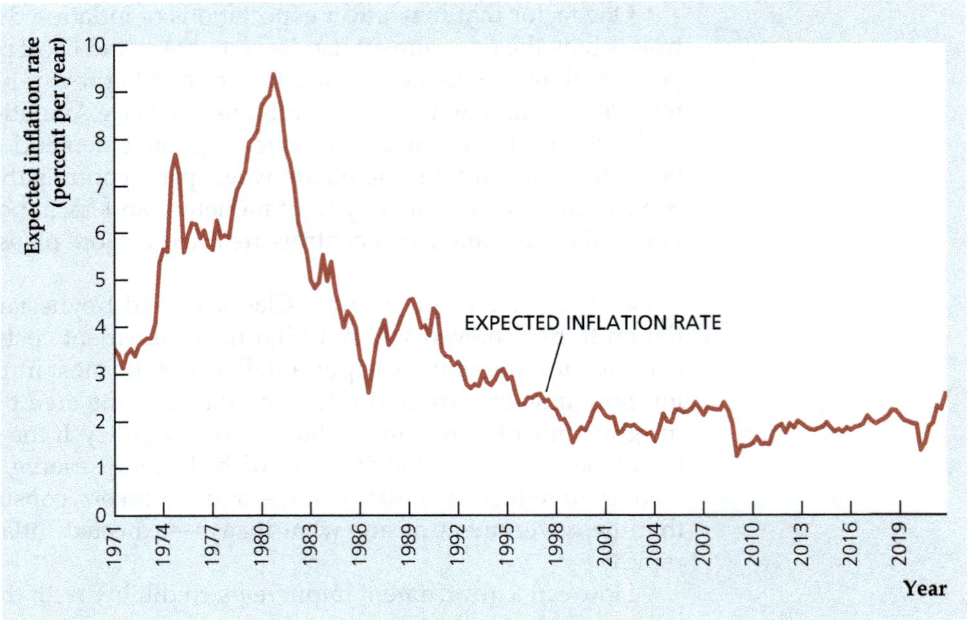

shown in Figure 12.10. The graph shows sharp swings up and down prior to about 1990. After that, the expected inflation rate follows a gradual downward trend until about 1998 and has been fairly stable since then.

The Fed's disinflation process, beginning in 1979, was at first a bit unstable, perhaps because the Fed had failed to curb inflation during the 1970s and the newly appointed Fed chairman, Paul Volcker, had not yet established his credibility. As a result, inflation expectations did not decline immediately when inflation fell. Over the decade, as people came to accept the Fed's desire to reduce inflation, the Fed gained credibility. The period since 1990, characterized by gradualism, was accompanied by a slow, steady drop in inflation expectations. By the time Greenspan left office in 2006 and Ben Bernanke took over, the Fed's credibility was well established. The fact that inflation expectations barely increased in the period from 2004 to 2008, despite large increases in oil prices, suggested that the Fed's reputation and credibility were well established. To solidify its reputation, in January 2012 the Fed took the additional step of announcing an explicit long-run inflation target of 2%, as measured by the price index for personal consumption expenditures. In 2020, the Fed announced a policy of flexible average inflation targeting, in which it would allow inflation to temporarily rise above 2% to make up for periods when inflation was below 2%. This policy change may have backfired when inflation began rising significantly in 2021.

CHAPTER SUMMARY

1. Following the famous 1958 article by A. W. Phillips, empirical studies often showed that inflation is high when unemployment is low and low when unemployment is high. This negative empirical relationship between inflation and unemployment is called the Phillips curve. Inflation and unemployment in the United States conformed to the Phillips curve during the 1960s but not during the 1970s and 1980s.

2. Economic theory suggests that, in general, the negative relationship between inflation and unemployment should not be stable. Instead, in an economy in which there are unanticipated changes in the growth rate of aggregate demand, there should be a negative relationship between *unanticipated* inflation and *cyclical* unemployment. In particular, when actual and expected inflation are equal (so that unanticipated inflation is zero), the actual unemployment rate will equal the natural unemployment rate (so that cyclical unemployment is zero). This negative relationship between unanticipated inflation and cyclical unemployment is called the expectations-augmented Phillips curve.

3. According to the theory of the expectations-augmented Phillips curve, a stable negative relationship between inflation and unemployment (a Phillips curve) will be observed only if expected inflation and the natural unemployment rate are constant. An increase in expected inflation or an increase in the natural unemployment rate shifts the short-run Phillips curve up and to the right. Adverse supply shocks typically increase both expected inflation and the natural unemployment rate and thus shift the short-run Phillips curve up and to the right. Major supply shocks during the 1970s, a rising natural unemployment rate, and highly variable expected inflation rates explain why the Phillips curve shifted erratically in the United States after about 1970.

4. According to the expectations-augmented Phillips curve, macroeconomic policy can reduce unemployment below the natural rate only by surprising the public with higher-than-expected inflation. Classical economists argue that, because of rational expectations and rapid price adjustment, policy cannot be used systematically to create inflation higher than expected; thus policymakers cannot usefully exploit the Phillips curve relationship by trading higher inflation for lower unemployment. Keynesians believe that, because not all prices adjust rapidly to reflect new information, policymakers are able to create surprise inflation temporarily and thus trade off inflation and unemployment in the short run.

5. Classicals and Keynesians agree that, in the long run, expected and actual inflation rates are equal. Thus in the long run the actual unemployment rate equals the natural rate, regardless of the inflation rate. Reflecting the fact that there is no long-run trade-off between inflation and unemployment, the long-run Phillips curve is vertical at the natural unemployment rate.

6. The costs of unemployment include output lost when fewer people are working and the personal or psychological costs for workers who are unemployed, their families, and close associates.

7. In the long run the unemployment rate is determined by the natural unemployment rate. According to some estimates, the natural unemployment rate in the United States rose during the 1960s and 1970s but has since declined. Demographic changes in the labor force help to explain many of these changes. However, although policymakers would like to have a precise estimate of the natural rate of unemployment, economists have been unable to measure it very precisely.

8. The costs of inflation depend on whether the inflation was anticipated or unanticipated. The costs of anticipated inflation, which (except in extreme inflations) are relatively minor, include shoe leather costs (resources used by individuals and firms to reduce their holdings of currency) and menu costs (costs of changing posted prices during an inflation). Unanticipated inflation causes unpredictable transfers of wealth among individuals and firms. The risk of unpredictable gains and losses, and the resources that people expend in trying to reduce this risk, are costs of unanticipated inflation. Unanticipated inflation may also reduce the efficiency of the market system by making it more difficult for people to observe relative prices.

9. Disinflation is a reduction in the rate of inflation. Attempts to disinflate by slowing money growth will cause cyclical unemployment to rise if actual inflation falls below expected inflation. To reduce the unemployment cost of disinflation, the public's expected inflation rate should be brought down along with the actual inflation rate. Strategies for reducing expected inflation include rapid and decisive reduction in the growth rate of the money supply (the cold-turkey approach), wage and price controls, and taking measures to improve the credibility of government policy announcements.

10. The disinflation that occurred in the United States in the 1980s and 1990s was costly at first because expected inflation did not decline immediately. But as time passed and the Federal Reserve gained credibility, inflation expectations declined, along with inflation.

KEY TERMS

cold turkey, p. 510
disinflation, p. 510
expectations-augmented Phillips curve, p. 493
gradualism, p. 510
hyperinflation, p. 508
long-run Phillips curve, p. 500
Phillips curve, p. 488
sacrifice ratio, p. 511
shoe leather costs, p. 505
short-run Phillips curve, p. 493
unanticipated inflation, p. 490

KEY EQUATION

$$\pi = \pi^e - h(u - \bar{u}) \quad \textbf{(12.1)}$$

The expectations-augmented Phillips curve states that unanticipated inflation, $\pi - \pi^e$, is negatively related to cyclical unemployment, $u - \bar{u}$. The expectations-augmented Phillips curve also implies that inflation, π, is negatively related to unemployment, u, only if the expected inflation rate, π^e, and the natural unemployment rate, $\bar{u}$, are constant. Changes in the expected inflation rate or in the natural unemployment rate cause the relationship between inflation and unemployment—the short-run Phillips curve—to shift.

REVIEW QUESTIONS

1. What is the Phillips curve? Does the Phillips curve relationship hold for U.S. data? Explain.
2. How does the expectations-augmented Phillips curve differ from the original Phillips curve? According to the theory of the expectations-augmented Phillips curve, under what conditions should the short-run Phillips curve relationship appear in the data?
3. In a particular economy, recent labor statistics show that unemployment has fallen. Its economic advisor explains that economic expansion and falling inflation may persist if oil prices continue to fall. Can you justify her argument in terms of the Phillips curve?
4. Can policymakers exploit the Phillips curve relationship by trading more inflation for less unemployment in the short run? In the long run? Explain both the classical and Keynesian points of view.
5. Why do policymakers want to keep inflation low? Who suffers when there is cyclical unemployment?
6. Two changes are observed in a labor market: firms are quicker to hire and fire workers, and the mismatch across industrial sectors increases. Will these raise the natural unemployment rate? If yes, what government policies would you suggest to lower it?
7. Give two costs of anticipated inflation and two costs of unanticipated inflation. How is the magnitude of each affected if, instead of a moderate inflation, hyperinflation occurs?
8. How does the sacrifice ratio measure the costs of disinflation? Use the expectations-augmented Phillips curve to explain how expectations can reduce the costs of disinflation.
9. Discuss at least two strategies for reducing expected inflation rapidly. What are the pros and cons of these strategies?
10. Why does the Federal Reserve work hard to establish its credibility? What benefits might the public gain if the Federal Reserve has a great deal of credibility?

NUMERICAL PROBLEMS

1. Consider the following extended classical economy (in which the misperceptions theory holds):

AD	$Y = 300 + 10(M/P)$.
SRAS	$Y = \bar{Y} + P - P^e$.
Okun's law	$(Y - \bar{Y})/\bar{Y} = -2(u - \bar{u})$.
Full-employment output	$\bar{Y} = 500$.
Natural unemployment rate	$\bar{u} = 0.06$.

a. Suppose that the money supply $M = 1000$ and that the expected price level $P^e = 50$. What are the short-run equilibrium values of output, Y, the price level, P, and the unemployment rate, u? What are the long-run equilibrium values of these three variables?

b. Now suppose that an unanticipated increase raises the nominal money supply to $M = 1260$. What are the new short-run equilibrium values of output, Y, the price level, P, and the unemployment rate, u? What are the new long-run equilibrium values of these three variables? In general, are your results consistent with an expectations-augmented Phillips curve?

2. In a certain economy the expectations-augmented Phillips curve is

$$\pi = \pi^e - 2(u - \bar{u}) \text{ and } \bar{u} = 0.06.$$

a. Graph the Phillips curve of this economy for an expected inflation rate of 0.10. If the Fed chooses to keep the actual inflation rate at 0.10, what will be the unemployment rate?

b. An aggregate demand shock (resulting from increased military spending) raises expected inflation to 0.12 (the natural unemployment rate is unaffected). Graph the new Phillips curve and compare it to the curve you drew in part *(a)*. What happens to the unemployment rate if the Fed holds actual inflation at 0.10? What happens to the Phillips curve and the unemployment rate if the Fed announces that it will hold inflation at 0.10 after the aggregate demand shock, and this announcement is fully believed by the public?

c. Suppose that a supply shock (a drought) raises expected inflation to 0.12 *and* raises the natural unemployment rate to 0.08. Repeat part *(b)*.

3. An economy is described by the following equations:

AD	$Y = 4000 + 2(M/P)$.
SRAS	$Y = \bar{Y} + 100(P - P^e)$.
Okun's law	$(Y - \bar{Y})/\bar{Y} = -2(u - \bar{u})$.

In this economy full-employment output $\bar{Y}$ equals 6000 and the natural unemployment rate $\bar{u}$ equals 0.05.

a. Suppose that the nominal money supply has long been constant at $M = 4000$ and is expected by the public to remain constant forever. What are the equilibrium values of the price level, P, the expected price level, P^e, expected inflation, π^e, output, Y, and the unemployment rate, u?

b. A totally unexpected increase in the money supply occurs, raising it from 4000 to 4488. What are the short-run equilibrium values of the price level, expected price level, output, and unemployment rate? What are the values of cyclical unemployment and unanticipated inflation?

c. What is the slope of the expectations-augmented Phillips curve (equal to $-h$ in Eq. 12.1) in this economy?

4. Consider an economy in long-run equilibrium with an inflation rate, π, of 12% (0.12) per year and a natural unemployment rate, $\bar{u}$, of 6% (0.06). The expectations-augmented Phillips curve is

$$\pi = \pi^e - 2(u - \bar{u}).$$

Assume that Okun's law holds so that a 1 percentage point increase in the cyclical unemployment rate maintained for one year reduces GDP by 2% of full-employment output.

a. Consider a two-year disinflation. In the first year $\pi = 0.04$ and $\pi^e = 0.08$. In the second year $\pi = 0.04$ and $\pi^e = 0.04$. In the first year, what is the unemployment rate? By what percentage does output fall short of full-employment output? In the second year, what is the unemployment rate? By what percentage does output fall short of full-employment output? What is the sacrifice ratio for this disinflation?

b. Now consider a four-year disinflation according to the following table:

Year	1	2	3	4
π	0.08	0.04	0.04	0.04
π^e	0.10	0.08	0.06	0.04

What is the unemployment rate in each of the four years? By what percentage does output fall short of full-employment output each year? What is the sacrifice ratio for this disinflation?

ANALYTICAL PROBLEMS

1. Suppose that the government provides more job training programs and job search services so as to help workers improve productivity and find jobs.

a. What will be the effect on the natural unemployment rate? How does this affect the expectations-augmented Phillips curve and the long-run Phillips curve?

b. Do you think that continuous expansionary monetary policy can have the same effects as in your answer to *(a)*? Explain your answer.

2. Two extended classical economies (in which the misperceptions theory holds) differ only in one respect: In economy A money growth and inflation have been low and stable for many years, but in economy B money growth and inflation have fluctuated erratically between very low and very high levels. When producers in economy B observe changes in the prices of the goods they produce, from past experience they usually attribute these changes to fluctuations in the overall price level rather than to changes in the relative prices of their goods.

Will the slope of the short-run aggregate supply curve for economy B be higher or lower than the slope of the curve for economy A? What about the slope of the Phillips curve?

3. In this problem you are asked to show that the expectations-augmented Phillips curve (derived in the text using the extended classical model) can be derived using the Keynesian model.

Consider a Keynesian economy in which full-employment output is constant, and in which the nominal money supply has been growing at 10% per year for some time and is expected to keep growing at that rate in the future. To avoid some technical complications, suppose that, instead of growing continuously over time, the money supply is increased by 10% each December 31 and then held constant until the next December 31. Monopolistically competitive firms reset their prices on December 31 of each year at the level that they expect will allow them to sell the full-employment level of output during the coming year. Inflation is measured as the percentage change in prices between January 1 and December 31 of each year.

a. Show how the *AD* curve, *SRAS* curve, output, the price level, and the expected price level evolve over time in this economy. What are the values of unanticipated inflation and cyclical unemployment?

b. Now suppose that on June 30, 2023, the money supply is unexpectedly raised by an additional 5%. However, the central bank announces—and firms believe—that this extra increase in the money supply is a one-time-only increase and that next December 31 the central bank will return to its policy of increasing the money supply by 10%. (Thus the total increase in the money supply between January 1, 2023, and December 31, 2023, is approximately 15%.) Firms don't change prices until December 31, as usual, but when they do they respond fully to the new information about money supply growth.

What are the actual and unanticipated inflation rates during 2023? Is cyclical unemployment positive, negative, or zero (on average) during 2023? Relate your results to the expectations-augmented Phillips curve.

4. Some economists have suggested that someday we will live in a "cashless society" in which all businesses (including stores) and banks will be linked to a centralized accounting system. In this system you will be able to pay for purchases directly from your bank account or phone without using cash. What are the costs of anticipated inflation in a cashless society? What are the costs of unanticipated inflation?

5. To fight an ongoing 10% inflation, the government makes raising wages or prices illegal. However, the government continues to increase the money supply (and hence aggregate demand) by 10% per year. The economy starts at full-employment output, which remains constant.

a. Using the Keynesian *AD–AS* framework, show the effects of the government's policies on the economy. Assume that firms meet the demand at the fixed price level.

b. After several years in which the controls have kept prices from rising, the government declares victory over inflation and removes the controls. What happens?

6. How would each of the following likely affect the natural unemployment rate?

a. A new law prohibits people from seeking employment before age eighteen.

b. A new Internet service, *Findwork.com*, makes it easy for people to check on the availability of jobs around the country.

c. The length of time that workers who are unemployed can receive government benefits increases from six months to one year.

d. A shift in the public's buying habits greatly expands the demand for sophisticated consumer electronics while reducing the demand for traditional consumer goods and services, such as clothing and restaurant meals.

e. Tight monetary policy, introduced to get the inflation rate down, drives the economy into a recession.

▶ WORKING WITH MACROECONOMIC DATA

For data to use in these exercises, go to the Federal Reserve Bank of St. Louis FRED database at fred.stlouisfed.org.

1. Using annual data since 1956, create scatter plots of the following variables:

a. CPI inflation rate (December to December) against the average unemployment rate for the year.

b. CPI inflation rate against the cyclical unemployment rate. (The cyclical unemployment rate is the actual unemployment rate minus the natural unemployment rate, which is variable *NROU* in the FRED database.)

c. Change in the CPI inflation rate from the previous year against the cyclical unemployment rate.

Discuss your results in light of the theory of the Phillips curve.

2. In this exercise, you are going to examine the historical data on Okun's Law, which we used in our discussion of the costs of unemployment. The level form of Okun's Law in Eq. (3.5) states that the output gap, $\frac{\bar{Y} - Y}{\bar{Y}}$, equals cyclical unemployment, $u - \bar{u}$, multiplied by 2. First, get the Congressional Budget Office's quarterly estimates of the natural rate of unemployment (FRED series *NROU*) and real potential GDP (FRED series GDPPOT) from the FRED database. Second, collect quarterly data on real GDP from the FRED database in each quarter beginning in 1960, and then use it with the CBO potential output data series to calculate the output gap at each date. Third, download the quarterly average of monthly data on the unemployment rate from the FRED database beginning in 1960. Use those quarterly data and the CBO's natural rate series to calculate cyclical unemployment. Fourth, draw a graph of the output gap (on the vertical axis) versus cyclical unemployment (on the horizontal axis). Also, on the same set of axes, draw a straight line through the origin with a slope of 2. Do the data points lie close to this line?

3. For each month since January 1960, calculate the share of total unemployment accounted for by people unemployed for 15 weeks or more. How is this ratio related to the business cycle (for peak and trough dates, see Table 8.1), and to the overall unemployment rate? What are the implications of these results for a policymaker who wants to assess the costs of a recession?

4. Download data from FRED on inflation expectations from the University of Michigan survey of consumers. In Excel, plot the change in the expected inflation rate from 12 months earlier. In which periods did expected inflation decline by more than one percentage point over the 12 months? In which periods did expected inflation rise by more than one percentage point over the 12 months? Are the months of significant declines or increases in expected inflation associated with a particular stage of the business cycle?

13

Exchange Rates, Business Cycles, and Macroeconomic Policy in the Open Economy

Learning Objectives

13.1 Describe real and nominal exchange rates, how they are related, and how they change over time.

13.2 Use a supply-and-demand framework to explain how exchange rates are determined.

13.3 Use the relationship between exchange rates and international trade to develop an open-economy *IS–LM* model.

13.4 Discuss the international effects of domestic macroeconomic policies.

13.5 Evaluate the strengths and weaknesses of different types of exchange rate systems.

In Chapters 9–12 we focused on a closed economy, or one that doesn't interact with other economies. For some purposes, ignoring the foreign sector simplifies the analysis. But the reality is that today, more than ever, we live in a highly interdependent world economic system.

There are two primary aspects of the interdependence of the world's economies. The first is international trade in goods and services, which has increased steadily in volume since World War II. Today, firms produce goods and services with an eye on foreign *and* domestic markets, and they obtain many raw materials from distant sources. Expanded international trade has increased productivity by allowing economies to specialize in producing the goods and services best suited to their natural and human resources. However, expanded trade also implies that national economies are more dependent on what happens in other countries. For example, because Japan sells so much of its output to the United States, a U.S. recession or macroeconomic policy change may affect the Japanese economy as well. In the fourth quarter of 2008, during the financial crisis, U.S. GDP declined 8% (at an annual rate), causing a sharp decline in imports from Japan, which contributed to a 12% decline (at an annual rate) in Japan's GDP.

The second is the worldwide integration of financial markets, which allows borrowers to obtain funds and savers to look for their best lending opportunities almost anywhere in the world, not just in their own countries. By allowing saving to flow to the highest-return uses regardless of where savers and investors happen to live, the integration of world financial markets increases worldwide productivity, as does the development of an integrated world trading system. But financial market linkages, like trade linkages, increase the sensitivity of individual economies to developments abroad. For example, because of closely connected financial markets, macroeconomic policies that change the real interest rate in one country may affect real interest rates and economic activity in other countries. When U.S. real interest rates declined sharply and turned negative during the financial crisis in 2008, real interest rates in many other countries declined similarly as well.

In this chapter, we build on earlier analyses of the open economy (Chapter 5) and cyclical fluctuations (Chapters 8–11) to examine the macroeconomic implications of trading and financial links among countries. We are particularly concerned in this chapter with how economic openness affects fiscal and monetary policies and how macroeconomic policy changes affect the economies of a country's trading partners. We begin our discussion by introducing two new variables that play central roles in the international economy: the nominal exchange rate and the real exchange rate.

13.1 Exchange Rates

Describe real and nominal exchange rates, how they are related, and how they change over time.

In discussing exchange rates, we must distinguish between nominal and real exchange rates. Briefly stated, the nominal exchange rate is the answer to the question: How many units of a foreign *currency* can I get in exchange for one unit of my domestic *currency?* The real exchange rate is the answer to the question: How many units of the foreign *good* can I get in exchange for one unit of my domestic *good?*

Nominal Exchange Rates

Most countries have their own national currencies: The U.S. dollar, the Japanese yen, the British pound, and the Swiss franc are but a few well-known currencies. (Exceptions include a number of European countries, which use the euro as their common currency, and Ecuador, which uses U.S. dollars as its official currency.) If someone in one country wants to buy goods, services, or assets from someone in another country, normally the person buying will first have to trade for the seller's currency to make the payment to complete the transaction.

The rate at which two currencies can be traded is the nominal exchange rate between the two currencies. For example, if the nominal exchange rate between the U.S. dollar and the Japanese yen is 120 yen per dollar, a dollar can buy 120 yen (ignoring transaction costs) in the **foreign exchange market**, which is the market for international currencies. Equivalently, 120 yen can buy 1 dollar in the foreign exchange market. More precisely, the **nominal exchange rate** between two currencies, e_{nom}, is the number of units of foreign currency that can be purchased with one unit of the domestic currency. For residents of the United States the domestic currency is the U.S. dollar, and the nominal exchange rate between the U.S. dollar and the Japanese yen is expressed as $e_{\text{nom}} = 120$ yen per dollar. The nominal exchange rate often is simply called the **exchange rate**, so whenever someone mentions the exchange rate without specifying real or nominal, the reference is taken to mean the *nominal* exchange rate.

The dollar–yen exchange rate isn't constant. The dollar might trade for 120 yen one day, but the next day it might rise in value to 122 yen or fall in value to 118 yen. Such changes in the exchange rate are normal under a flexible-exchange-rate system, the type of system in which many of the world's major currencies (including the dollar and the yen) are currently traded. In a **flexible-exchange-rate system**, or **floating-exchange-rate system**, exchange rates are not officially fixed but are determined by conditions of supply and demand in the foreign exchange market. Under a flexible-exchange-rate system, exchange rates move continuously and respond quickly to any economic or political news that might influence the supplies and demands for various currencies. "In Touch with Data and Research: Exchange Rates," discusses exchange rate data.

The values of currencies haven't always been determined by a flexible-exchange-rate system. In the past, some type of **fixed-exchange-rate system** under which exchange rates were set at officially determined levels, often operated. Usually, these official rates were maintained by the commitment of nations' central banks to buy and sell their own currencies at the fixed exchange rate. For example, under the international gold standard system that operated in the late 1800s and early 1900s, the central bank of each country maintained the value of its currency in terms of gold by agreeing to buy or sell gold in exchange for currency at a fixed rate of exchange. The gold standard was suspended during World War I, was temporarily restored in the late 1920s, and then collapsed during the economic and financial crises of the 1930s.

A more recent example of a fixed-exchange-rate system was the Bretton Woods system, named after the town in New Hampshire where the 1944 conference establishing the system was held. Under the Bretton Woods system, the values of various currencies were fixed in terms of the U.S. dollar, and the value of the dollar was set at $35 per ounce of gold. The Bretton Woods system functioned until the early 1970s, when inflation in the United States made keeping the price of gold from rising above $35 per ounce virtually impossible. Since the breakdown of the Bretton Woods system, no fixed-exchange-rate system has encompassed all the world's major currencies. In particular, U.S. policymakers haven't attempted to maintain a fixed value for the dollar.

Although no worldwide system of fixed exchange rates currently exists, fixed exchange rates haven't disappeared entirely. Many individual countries, especially smaller ones, attempt to fix their exchange rates against a major currency. For example, several African countries tie their currencies to the euro, and from 1991 to 2002, Argentina used a system under which its currency, the peso, traded one-for-one with the U.S. dollar. By fixing their exchange rates, countries hope to stabilize their own currencies and reduce the sharp swings in import and export prices that may result from exchange rate fluctuations. We discuss fixed exchange rates in Section 13.5.

In Touch with Data and Research

Exchange Rates

Exchange rates are determined in foreign exchange markets, in which the currencies of different countries are traded. Principal foreign exchange markets are located in New York, London, Tokyo, and other financial centers. Because foreign exchange markets are in widely separated time zones, at least one of the markets is open at almost any time of the day, so trading in currencies essentially takes place around the clock.

Exchange rates among major currencies often are reported daily on radio and television, and daily quotations of exchange rates are printed in major newspapers and financial dailies. The exchange rates in the accompanying table were reported on the FXEmpire website, *www.fxempire.com/currencies*, on May 5, 2022, and apply to transactions on that day.

Three exchange rates relative to the U.S. dollar are reported in the table for each country: a spot rate and two forward rates. All are expressed as units of foreign currency per U.S. dollar. The spot rate is the rate at which foreign currency can be traded immediately for U.S. dollars. For instance, the spot exchange rate for Great Britain, 0.8088, means that on May 5, 2022, one U.S. dollar could buy 0.8088 pounds for immediate delivery.

Forward exchange rates are prices at which you can agree now to buy foreign currency at a specified date in the future. For example, on May 5, 2022, you could have arranged to buy or sell Japanese yen 90 days later at an exchange rate of 130.39 yen per dollar. Note that for the pound and the euro, the 90-day forward exchange rate was lower than the spot exchange rate and the 180-day forward exchange rate was lower than the 90-day forward exchange rate. This pattern of falling forward rates indicates that, as of May 5, 2022, participants in the foreign exchange market expected the value of the dollar relative to the pound and the euro to decrease over the following six months.

Exchange Rate Against U.S. Dollar

Country	Spot	90-day forward	180-day forward
Great Britain (pounds per U.S. dollar)	0.8088	0.8083	0.8071
Euro Area (euros per U.S. dollar)	0.9514	0.9468	0.9407
Japan (yen per U.S. dollar)	130.39	130.39	130.38

Real Exchange Rates

The nominal exchange rate doesn't tell you all you need to know about the purchasing power of a currency. If you were told, for example, that the nominal exchange rate between the U.S. dollar and the Japanese yen is 110 yen per dollar, but you didn't know anything else about the U.S. or Japanese economies, you might be tempted to conclude that someone from Kansas City could visit Tokyo very cheaply—after all, 110 yen for just 1 dollar seems like a good deal. But even at 110 yen per dollar, Japan is an expensive place to visit. The reason is that, although 1 dollar can buy a lot of yen, it also takes a lot of yen (thousands or hundreds of thousands) to buy everyday goods in Japan.

Suppose, for example, that you want to compare the price of hamburgers in Tokyo and Kansas City. Knowing that the exchange rate is 110 yen per dollar doesn't help much. But if you also know that a hamburger costs 2 dollars in Kansas City and 1100 yen in Tokyo, you can compare the price of a hamburger in the two cities by asking how many dollars are needed to buy a hamburger in Japan. Because a hamburger costs 1100 yen in Tokyo, and 110 yen cost 1 dollar, the price of a hamburger in Tokyo is 10 dollars (calculated by dividing the price of a Japanese hamburger, ¥1100, by ¥110/$1, to obtain $10 per hamburger). The price of a U.S. hamburger relative to a Japanese hamburger is therefore ($2 per U.S. hamburger)/($10 per Japanese hamburger) = 0.20 Japanese hamburgers per U.S. hamburger. The Japanese hamburger is expensive in the sense that (in this example) one U.S. hamburger equals only one-fifth of a Japanese hamburger.

The price of domestic goods relative to foreign goods—equivalently, the number of foreign goods someone gets in exchange for one domestic good—is called the **real exchange rate**. In the hamburger example the real exchange rate between the United States and Japan is 0.20 Japanese hamburgers per U.S. hamburger.

In general, the real exchange rate is related to the nominal exchange rate and to prices in both countries. To write this relation we use the following symbols:

e_{nom} = the nominal exchange rate (110 yen per dollar);

P_{For} = the price of foreign goods, measured in the foreign currency (1100 yen per Japanese hamburger);

P = the price of domestic goods, measured in the domestic currency (2 dollars per U.S. hamburger).

The real exchange rate, e, is the number of foreign goods (Japanese hamburgers) that can be obtained in exchange for one unit of the domestic good (U.S. hamburgers). The general formula for the real exchange rate is

$$\begin{aligned} e &= \frac{e_{\text{nom}}P}{P_{\text{For}}} \\ &= \frac{(\yen 110/\$1)(\$2/\text{U.S. hamburger})}{\yen 1100/\text{Japanese hamburger}} \qquad (13.1) \\ &= 0.20 \text{ Japanese hamburgers per U.S. hamburger.} \end{aligned}$$

In defining the real exchange rate as the number of foreign goods that can be obtained for each domestic good, we assume that each country produces a single, unique good. (Think of France producing only bottles of wine and Saudi Arabia producing only barrels of oil; then the French real exchange rate with respect to Saudi Arabia is the number of barrels of oil that can be purchased for one bottle of wine.) The assumption that each country produces a single good (which is different from the good produced by any other country) simplifies the theoretical analysis in this chapter.[1]

Of course, in reality, countries produce thousands of different goods, so real exchange rates must be based on price indexes (such as the GDP deflator) to measure P and P_{For}. Thus the real exchange rate isn't actually the rate of exchange between two specific goods but instead is the rate of exchange between a typical basket of goods in one country and a typical basket of goods in the other country. Changes in the real exchange rate over time indicate that, on average, the goods of the country whose real exchange rate is rising are becoming more expensive relative to the goods of the other country.

Appreciation and Depreciation

When the nominal exchange rate, e_{nom}, falls so that, say, a dollar buys fewer units of foreign currency, we say that the dollar has undergone a **nominal depreciation**. This is the same as saying that the dollar has become "weaker." If the dollar's nominal exchange rate, e_{nom}, rises, the dollar has had a **nominal appreciation**. When the dollar appreciates, it can buy more units of foreign currency and thus has become

[1]The assumption that different countries produce different goods is a change from Chapter 5, where we implicitly assumed that all countries produce an identical good that can be used for all purposes (consumption, investment, and so on). The assumption that all countries produce the same good implied that, in the analysis of that chapter, the real exchange rate was always 1.

SUMMARY 15

Terminology for Changes in Exchange Rates

Type of exchange rate system	Exchange rate increases (currency strengthens)	Exchange rate decreases (currency weakens)
Flexible exchange rates	Appreciation	Depreciation
Fixed exchange rates	Revaluation	Devaluation

"stronger."[2] The terms appreciation and depreciation are associated with flexible exchange rates. Under a fixed-exchange-rate system, in which exchange rates are changed only by official government action, different terms are used. Instead of a depreciation, a weakening of the currency is called a **devaluation**. A strengthening of the currency under fixed exchange rates is called a **revaluation** rather than an appreciation. These terms are listed for convenience in Summary table 15.

An increase in the real exchange rate, e, is called a **real appreciation**. With a real appreciation, the same quantity of domestic goods can be traded for more of the foreign good than before because e, the price of domestic goods relative to the price of foreign goods, has risen. A drop in the real exchange rate, which decreases the quantity of foreign goods that can be purchased with the same quantity of domestic goods, is called a **real depreciation**.

Purchasing Power Parity

How are nominal exchange rates and real exchange rates related? A simple hypothetical case that allows us to think about this question is when all countries produce the same good (or same set of goods) and goods are freely traded among countries. In this case, no one would trade domestic goods for foreign goods except on a one-for-one basis, so (ignoring transportation costs) the real exchange rate, e, would always equal 1. If $e = 1$, we can use Eq. (13.1) to write

$$P = \frac{P_{\text{For}}}{e_{\text{nom}}}. \tag{13.2}$$

Equation (13.2) says that the price of the domestic good must equal the price of the foreign good when the price of the foreign good is expressed in terms of the domestic currency. (To express the foreign price in terms of the domestic currency, divide by the exchange rate.) The idea that similar foreign and domestic goods, or baskets of goods, should have the same price in terms of the same currency is called **purchasing power parity (PPP)**. Equivalently, as implied by Eq. (13.2), purchasing power parity says that the nominal exchange rate should equal the foreign price level divided by the domestic price level, so that

$$e_{\text{nom}} = \frac{P_{\text{For}}}{P}.$$

[2]You will sometimes see the exchange rate defined as the number of units of domestic currency per unit of foreign currency, which is the reciprocal of how we have defined it. For example, the exchange rate between the British pound and the U.S. dollar is typically quoted in this form (for example, \$1.60 per pound). Under this alternative definition an appreciation of the dollar corresponds to a drop in the nominal exchange rate. The two ways of defining the exchange rate are equally valid as long as consistency is maintained. We have chosen to define the exchange rate as the number of units of foreign currency per unit of home currency because it is easier to remember that an appreciation (when the value of the dollar goes up) is associated with a rise in the exchange rate.

In Touch with Data and Research

McParity

If *PPP* holds, similar goods produced in different countries should cost about the same when their prices are expressed in a common currency—say, U.S. dollars. As a test of this hypothesis, *The Economist* magazine has long recorded the prices of Big Mac hamburgers in different countries. In the table below, the first column of data shows dollar prices of Big Macs in selected countries as reported in *The Economist's* February 2, 2022, issue.

Big Macs aren't exactly the same product the world over. For example, in Denmark, ketchup costs about 25 cents extra, instead of being included in the price as in the United States and Canada. Nevertheless, the prices suggest that *PPP* holds only approximately at best for Big Macs. Dollar-equivalent Big Mac prices range from a low of $1.74 in Russia to a high of $6.98 in Switzerland.

Even though *PPP* fails to hold exactly, Big Mac prices in different countries still might be expected to come gradually closer together. Such a convergence could occur, for example, if the currencies in countries in which Big Macs are relatively expensive depreciated relative to the currencies of the countries in which Big Macs are cheap. Such a calculation would suggest that the Swiss franc is likely to depreciate in value relative to the dollar (because Big Macs are most expensive there). In contrast, the Big Mac index suggests that all of the other currencies shown in the table may appreciate against the dollar. Even though an undervalued currency may appreciate, we don't know *when* it might appreciate. It could take a number of years for the currency to appreciate, so forecasting movements in exchange rates based on *PPP* is difficult at best.

Big Mac Prices Around the World

	Dollar price	GDP adjusted
United States	$5.81	0%
Argentina	4.29	20
Brazil	4.31	23
Canada	5.32	7
China	3.83	5
Euro area	4.95	4
Great Britain	4.82	−1
India	2.55	−23
Japan	3.38	−30
Mexico	3.34	−6
Russia	1.74	−52
South Korea	3.82	−16
Switzerland	6.98	3

Source: The Economist magazine, www.economist.com/big-mac-index

With only one country's dollar price above the U.S. price, is something incorrect about the theory of purchasing power parity? Many economists now believe the PPP theory is not very useful and have worked on other versions of the theory. One version, now used by *The Economist* magazine in its comparison of Big Mac prices, is that the wages paid to workers who produce Big Macs in different countries are directly related to each country's GDP per capita. As a result, Big Mac prices are higher in countries with higher real GDP per capita. The data confirm that result.

So *The Economist* now also shows the percentage deviations of a country's Big Mac dollar price after adjusting for differences in GDP per capita.[3] In the table, these percentage deviations are shown in the column headed "GDP adjusted."

The results show that once an adjustment for GDP per capita is made, about half of the countries have a Big Mac price that is higher than expected, and the other half have a Big Mac price that is lower than expected. After making this adjustment, the Big Mac price in Switzerland, which was the only country with a dollar price higher than the U.S. price, is only 3% higher than expected, whereas the price in Brazil is 23% higher than expected. The lowest adjusted price is Russia, at 52% less than expected. So, this alternative view of PPP seems to fit the data a bit better than the original PPP theory does.

[3]Formally, this is done by running an econometric regression of Big Mac dollar prices for each country on the country's real GDP per capita and then calculating the residual.

There is some empirical evidence that *PPP* holds in the very long run, but (as "In Touch with Data and Research: McParity" suggests) over shorter periods *PPP* does not describe exchange rate behavior very well. The failure of *PPP* in the short to medium run occurs for various reasons. For example, countries produce different baskets of goods and services, not the same goods as assumed for *PPP*; some types of goods and services are not internationally traded; and transportation costs and legal barriers to trade may prevent the prices of traded goods and services from being equalized in different countries.

To find a relationship between real and nominal exchange rates that holds more generally, we can use the definition of the real exchange rate in Eq. (13.1), $e = e_{\text{nom}}P/P_{\text{For}}$, to calculate $\Delta e/e$, the percentage change in the real exchange rate. Because the real exchange rate is expressed as a ratio, its percentage change equals the percentage change in the numerator minus the percentage change in the denominator.[4] The percentage change in the numerator of the expression for the real exchange rate[5] is $\Delta e_{\text{nom}}/e_{\text{nom}} + \Delta P/P$, and the percentage change in the denominator is $\Delta P_{\text{For}}/P_{\text{For}}$. Thus the percentage change in the real exchange rate is

$$\frac{\Delta e}{e} = \frac{\Delta e_{\text{nom}}}{e_{\text{nom}}} + \frac{\Delta P}{P} - \frac{\Delta P_{\text{For}}}{P_{\text{For}}}.$$

In the preceding equation the term $\Delta P/P$, the percentage change in the domestic price level, is the same as the domestic rate of inflation, π, and the term $\Delta P_{\text{For}}/P_{\text{For}}$, the percentage change in the foreign price level, is the same as the foreign rate of inflation, π_{For}. Making these substitutions and rearranging the equation, we rewrite this equation as

$$\frac{\Delta e_{\text{nom}}}{e_{\text{nom}}} = \frac{\Delta e}{e} + \pi_{\text{For}} - \pi. \tag{13.3}$$

Equation (13.3) is purely definitional and thus must always be satisfied. It states that the rate of nominal exchange rate appreciation, $\Delta e_{\text{nom}}/e_{\text{nom}}$, equals the

[4]Appendix A, Section A.7, describes how to calculate growth rates of products and ratios.

[5]This result is obtained by using the rule that the percentage change in a product XY is the percentage change in X plus the percentage change in Y. See Appendix A, Section A.7.

rate of real exchange rate appreciation, $\Delta e/e$, plus the excess of foreign inflation over domestic inflation, $\pi_{For} - \pi$. Hence two factors contribute to strengthening a currency (a nominal appreciation): (1) an increase in the relative price of a country's exports (a real appreciation), which might occur if, for example, foreign demand for those exports rises; and (2) a rate of domestic inflation, π, lower than that of the country's trading partners, π_{For}.

A special case of Eq. (13.3) occurs when the real exchange rate is constant, so that

$$\frac{\Delta e_{nom}}{e_{nom}} = \pi_{For} - \pi.$$

In this case, the preceding equation expresses a relationship called relative purchasing power parity. According to **relative purchasing power parity**, the rate of appreciation of the nominal exchange rate equals the foreign inflation rate minus the domestic inflation rate. Relative purchasing power parity usually works well for high-inflation countries because in those countries, differences in relative inflation rates are usually much larger than changes in the real exchange rate.

The Real Exchange Rate and Net Exports

We've defined the real exchange rate, but so far we haven't indicated why it is important in macroeconomic analysis. One reason that policymakers and the public care about the real exchange rate is that it represents the rate at which domestic goods and services can be traded for those produced abroad. An increase in the real exchange rate—also sometimes referred to as the **terms of trade**—is good for a country in the sense that its citizens are able to obtain more foreign goods and services in exchange for a given amount of domestic production.

A second reason is that the real exchange rate affects a country's net exports, or exports less imports. Changes in net exports in turn have a direct impact on the domestic industries that produce for export or that compete with imported goods in the domestic market. In addition, as we discuss later in the chapter, changes in net exports affect a country's overall level of economic activity and are a primary channel through which business cycle disturbances and macroeconomic policy changes are transmitted internationally.

What is the link between the real exchange rate and net exports? A basic determinant of the demand for any good or service—say, coffee or taxi rides—is the price of that good or service relative to alternatives. If the price of coffee is too high, some people will switch to tea; if taxi fares rise, more people will take the bus. Similarly, the real exchange rate—the price of domestic goods relative to foreign goods—helps determine the demand for domestic goods both in home and foreign markets.

Suppose that the real exchange rate is high, so that a unit of the domestic good can buy relatively many units of the foreign good. For example, let's say that a domestically produced car costs twice as much as a comparable foreign car (both prices are measured in terms of the same currency). Domestic residents will then find that foreign cars are less expensive than domestic cars, so (all else being equal) their demand for imported autos will be high. Foreign residents, in contrast, will find that the domestic country's cars are more expensive than their own, so they will want to purchase relatively few of the domestic country's exports. With few cars being sold abroad and many cars being imported, the country's net exports of cars will be low, probably even negative.

Conversely, suppose that the real exchange rate is low; for example, imagine that a domestically produced automobile costs only half what a comparable foreign car costs. Then, all else being equal, the domestic country will be able to export relatively large quantities of cars and will import relatively few, so that its net exports of cars will be high.

The general conclusion, then, is that *the higher the real exchange rate is, the lower a country's net exports will be,* holding constant other factors affecting export and import demand. The reason for this result is the same reason that higher prices reduce the amount of coffee people drink or the number of taxi rides they take. Because the real exchange rate is the relative price of a country's goods and services, an increase in the real exchange rate induces both foreigners and domestic residents to consume less domestic production and more goods and services produced abroad, which lowers net exports.

The J Curve. Although the conclusion that (holding other factors constant) a higher real exchange rate depresses net exports is generally valid, there is one important qualification: Depending on how quickly importers and exporters respond to changes in relative prices, the effect of a change in the real exchange rate on net exports may be weak in the short run and may even go the "wrong" way.

To understand why, consider a country that imports most of its oil and suddenly faces a sharp increase in world oil prices. Because the country's domestic goods now can buy less of the foreign good (oil), the country's real exchange rate has fallen. In the long run, this decline in the real exchange rate may increase the country's net exports because high oil prices will lead domestic residents to reduce oil imports and the relative cheapness of domestic goods will stimulate exports (to oil-producing countries, for example). In the short run, however, switching to other fuels and increasing domestic oil production are difficult, so the number of barrels of oil imported may drop only slightly. For this reason, and because the real cost of each barrel of oil (in terms of the domestic good) has risen, for some period of time after the oil price increase the country's total real cost of imports (measured in terms of the domestic good) may rise. Thus in the short run, a decline in the real exchange rate might be associated with a *drop* rather than a rise in net exports, contrary to our earlier conclusion. (Numerical Problem 2 at the end of the chapter provides an example of how a real depreciation can cause net exports to fall.)

Figure 13.1 shows the typical response pattern of a country's net exports to a drop in the real exchange rate (a real depreciation). The economy initially has negative net exports when the real exchange rate depreciates. In the short run, the real depreciation reduces rather than increases net exports because the drop in the real exchange rate forces the country to pay more for its imports. Over time, however, as the lower real exchange rate leads to larger export quantities and smaller import quantities, net exports begin to rise (even taking into account the higher relative cost of imports). Eventually, the country's net exports rise relative to the initial situation. This typical response pattern of net exports to a real depreciation is called the **J curve** because the graph of net exports against time looks like the letter J lying on its back.

The macroeconomic analyses in this chapter are based on the assumption that the time period is long enough that (all else being equal) a real depreciation increases net exports and that a real appreciation reduces net exports. Keep in mind, though, that this assumption may not be valid for shorter periods—and in some cases, even for several years—as the following application demonstrates.

FIGURE 13.1

The J curve

The J curve shows the response pattern of net exports to a real depreciation. Here, net exports are negative at time zero, when the real exchange rate depreciates. In the short run, net exports become more negative, as the decline in the real exchange rate raises the real cost of imports (measured in terms of the export good). Over time, however, increased exports and reduced quantities of imports more than compensate for the increased cost of imports, and net exports rise above their initial level.

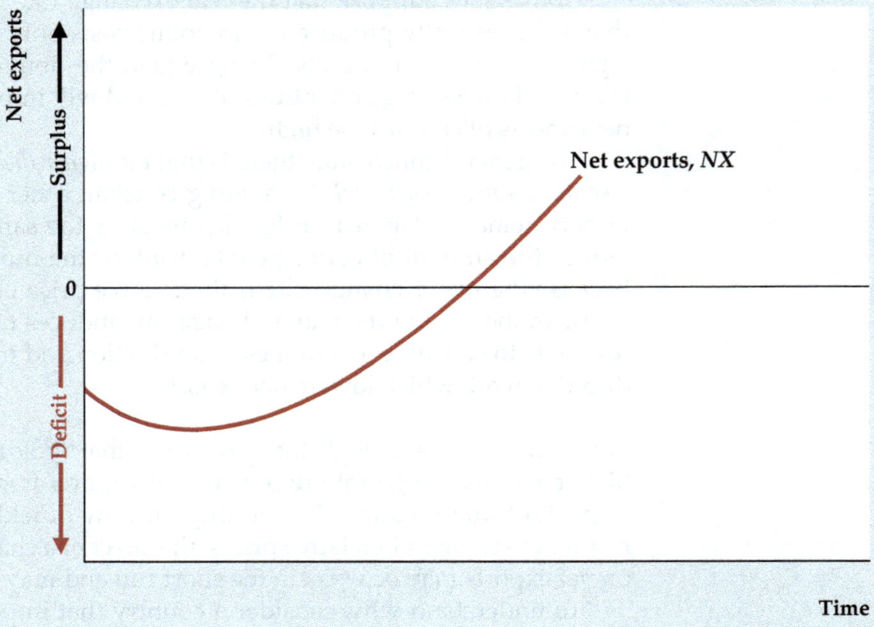

Application

The Value of the Dollar and U.S. Net Exports

In the early 1970s, the major industrialized countries of the world switched from fixed to flexible exchange rates. Figure 13.2 shows the U.S. real exchange rate (the "real value of the dollar") and real U.S. net exports since 1973. Because the U.S. real exchange rate is the relative price of U.S. goods, the real value of the dollar and U.S. net exports should move in opposite directions (assuming that changes in the real exchange rate are the primary source of changes in net exports).

An apparent confirmation that the real exchange rate and net exports move in opposite directions occurred during the early 1980s. From 1980 to 1985, the real value of the dollar increased by about 50%. This sharp increase was followed, with a brief delay, by a large decline in U.S. net exports. At the time, many U.S. firms complained that the strong dollar was pricing their products out of foreign markets and, by making imported goods cheap for U.S. consumers, also reducing their sales at home.

After peaking in March 1985, the real value of the dollar fell sharply for almost three years. Despite this precipitous decline, U.S. net exports continued to fall until late in 1987, when they finally began to rise. During the two and a half years in which U.S. net exports continued to decline despite the rapid depreciation of the dollar, the public and policymakers expressed increasing skepticism about economists' predictions that the depreciation would lead to more net exports. Initially, economists responded by saying that, because of the J curve, there would be some delay between the depreciation of the dollar and the improvement in net exports. By 1987, however, even the strongest believers in the J curve had begun to wonder whether net exports would ever begin to rise. Finally, U.S. real net exports did recover substantially, although they remained negative.

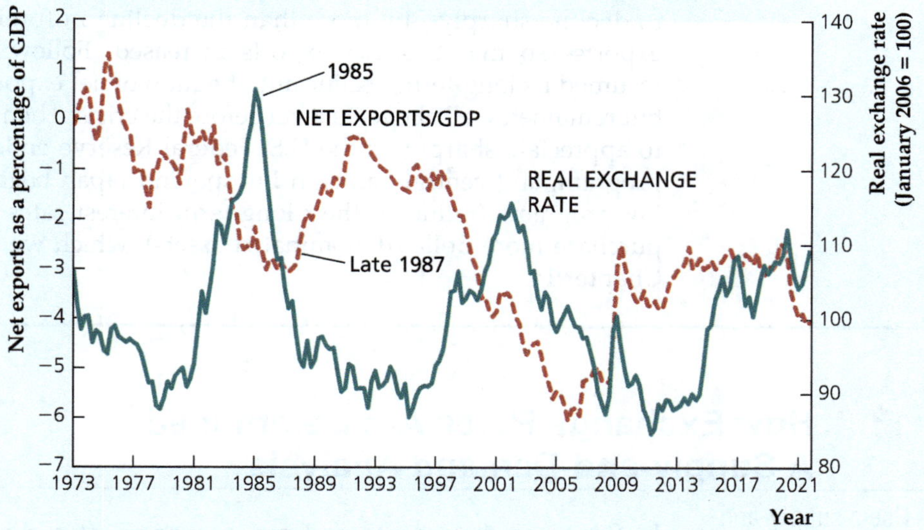

FIGURE 13.2

U.S. net exports as a percentage of GDP and the real exchange rate, 1973Q1–2021Q4

U.S. net exports as a percentage of GDP from the first quarter of 1973 to the fourth quarter of 2021 are measured along the left vertical axis, and the U.S. real exchange rate (the real value of the dollar) is measured along the right vertical axis. The sharp increase in the real exchange rate in the first half of the 1980s was accompanied by a decline in U.S. net exports. The decline of the dollar after 1985 stimulated U.S. net exports, but with a delay that probably reflected the J-curve effect.

Sources: Real exchange rate: U.S. real broad dollar index, Federal Reserve Board of Governors, downloaded from Federal Reserve Bank of St. Louis FRED database, *fred.stlouisfed.org*, series *TWEXBPA* and *RTWEXBGS*, spliced together at 2006Q1; net exports as a percentage of GDP, from FRED database, series *NETEXP* and *GDP*.

What took so long? One explanation suggests that, because the dollar was so strong in the first half of the 1980s (which made U.S. goods very expensive relative to foreign goods), U.S. firms lost many of their foreign customers. Once these foreign customers were lost, regaining them or adding new foreign customers was difficult, especially as many U.S. exporters reduced production capacity and cut back foreign sales operations when the value of the dollar was high. Similarly, the strong dollar gave foreign producers, including some that hadn't previously sold their output to the United States, a chance to make inroads into the U.S. domestic market. Having established sales networks and customer relationships in the United States, these foreign companies were better able than before to compete with U.S. firms when the dollar began its decline in 1985. The idea that the strong dollar permanently increased the penetration of the U.S. market by foreign producers, while similarly reducing the capability of U.S. firms to sell in foreign markets, has been called the "beachhead effect."[6]

The U.S. real exchange rate and U.S. net exports moved in opposite directions again from 1997 to 2001, as the dollar strengthened and net exports fell sharply. In part this decline in net exports reflected the higher value of the dollar. However, the major factor in this episode was probably the slow growth or outright recession experienced by most U.S. trading partners during this period. As incomes abroad stagnated or declined, the demand for U.S. exports fell with them. We discuss the effects of national income on imports and exports in the next section.

After reaching a peak in early 2002, the dollar weakened for the next six years. It took some time for net exports relative to GDP to reverse course and begin rising, but this ratio finally began to rise in 2006 and continued doing so until 2008. Then, in the financial crisis of 2008, investors' loss of confidence throughout the world led them to buy dollar-denominated assets for safety, causing the dollar to appreciate sharply. At the same time, the fall in U.S. income caused imports

[6]Empirical support for the beachhead effect is presented in Richard E. Baldwin, "Hysteresis in Import Prices: The Beachhead Effect," *American Economic Review*, September 1988, pp. 773–785.

(*continued*)

to decline sharply—by more than the decline in foreign income reduced U.S. exports—so that U.S. net exports increased. Following the crisis, the dollar resumed its long-term decline and the ratio of net exports to GDP fell somewhat, but remained well above its level before the crisis. Then, in 2014, the dollar began to appreciate sharply, as the U.S. Federal Reserve ended its quantitative easing program, and central banks in Europe and Japan began large quantitative easing programs (reducing their long-term interest rates and leading investors to purchase more dollar-denominated assets), which we discuss in more detail in Chapter 14.

13.2 How Exchange Rates Are Determined: A Supply-and-Demand Analysis

Use a supply-and-demand framework to explain how exchange rates are determined.

In flexible-exchange-rate systems, exchange rates change constantly. In fixed-exchange-rate systems, by definition, exchange rates are stable most of the time; even under a fixed-rate system, large devaluations or revaluations aren't uncommon. What economic forces cause a nation's exchange rate to rise or fall? In this section we address this question by using supply and demand to analyze the determination of exchange rates in a flexible-exchange-rate system. (We return to fixed exchange rates in Section 13.5.)

For clarity, our supply-and-demand analysis focuses on the nominal exchange rate rather than the real exchange rate. However, recall from Eq. (13.1) that, for given levels of domestic and foreign prices, the real exchange rate and the nominal exchange rate are proportional. Because we hold price levels constant in this section, *all our conclusions about the nominal exchange rate apply equally to the real exchange rate.*

The nominal exchange rate, e_{nom}, is the value of a currency—say, the dollar. The value of the dollar, like that of any asset, is determined by supply and demand in the relevant market. For dollars, the relevant market is the foreign exchange market, where banks and currency traders continuously trade dollars for other currencies.

Figure 13.3 shows the supply and demand for dollars. The horizontal axis measures the quantity of dollars supplied or demanded, and the vertical axis measures the value of the dollar in terms of other currencies, or the nominal exchange rate, e_{nom}. The supply curve for dollars, S, shows the number of dollars that people want to supply to the foreign exchange market at each "price" (nominal exchange rate). To supply dollars to the foreign exchange market means to offer to exchange dollars for some other currency. When the dollar's value in terms of other currencies is high, people are more willing to supply dollars to the market; thus the supply curve slopes upward. Similarly, the demand curve for dollars, D, shows the quantity of dollars that people want to buy in the foreign exchange market at each exchange rate. When the dollar is more expensive in terms of other currencies, people demand fewer dollars, so the demand curve slopes downward. The equilibrium value of the dollar at point E is e^1_{nom}, the exchange rate at which the quantity of dollars supplied and the quantity of dollars demanded are equal.

Figure 13.3 helps explain the forces that determine the value of the dollar, or any other currency. To go any further, though, we must ask why people decide to demand or supply dollars. Unlike apples or haircuts, dollars aren't demanded

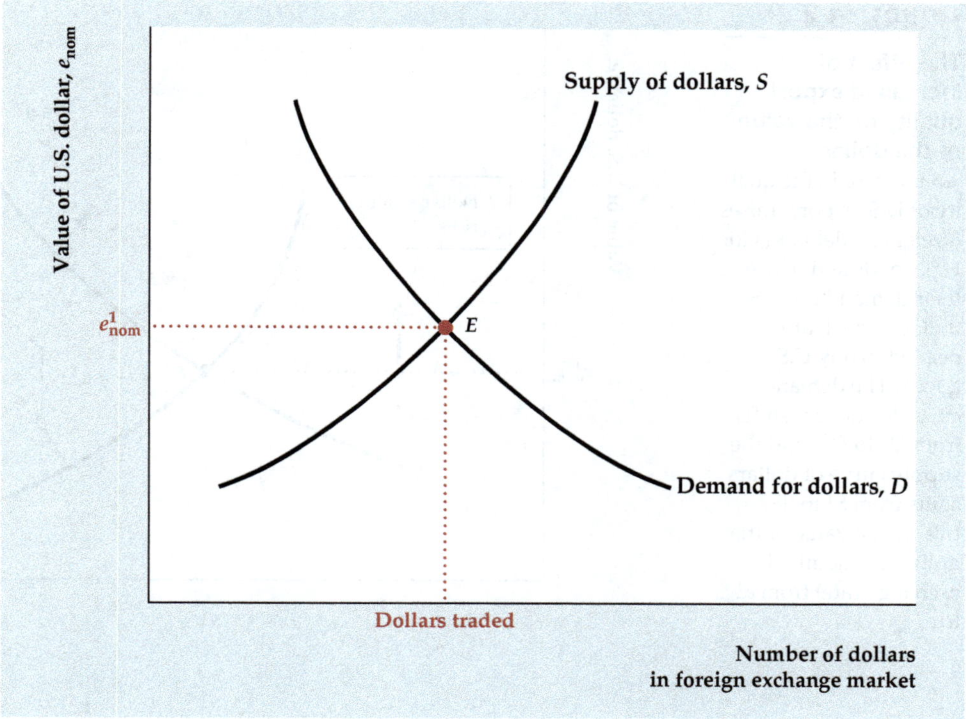

FIGURE 13.3

The supply of and demand for the dollar
The figure shows the determination of the value of the dollar in the foreign exchange market. The supply curve for dollars, S, indicates the number of dollars that people are willing to sell in the foreign exchange market at each value of the U.S. nominal exchange rate, e_{nom}. The demand curve for dollars, D, shows the number of dollars that people want to buy at each nominal exchange rate. At equilibrium, point E, the value of the dollar, e^1_{nom}, is the nominal exchange rate at which the quantity of dollars supplied equals the quantity of dollars demanded.

because people value them in themselves; rather, people value dollars because of what they can buy. Specifically, foreign individuals or firms demand dollars in the foreign exchange market for two reasons:

1. to be able to buy U.S. goods and services (U.S. exports), and
2. to be able to buy U.S. real and financial assets (U.S. financial inflows).

Note that the two types of transactions for which foreigners need dollars (to purchase U.S. exports and U.S. assets) correspond to the two major components of the balance of payments accounts: the current account and the financial account.[7]

Similarly, U.S. residents supply dollars to the foreign exchange market, thereby acquiring foreign currencies, for two reasons:

1. to be able to buy foreign goods and services (U.S. imports), and
2. to be able to buy real and financial assets in foreign countries (U.S. financial outflows).

[7]We defined and discussed the current account and the financial account in Chapter 5. Throughout this chapter we ignore the capital account, the third component of the balance of payments, because it is so small. The idea that foreigners must hold dollars to buy U.S. goods or assets isn't completely accurate because many transactions between the United States and foreigners are done without anyone ever literally holding any dollars or the foreign currency. Nevertheless, this way of thinking about the determination of exchange rates is fairly simple and gives the same answers as would a more complex analysis.

FIGURE 13.4

The effect of increased export quality on the value of the dollar

An increase in the quality of U.S. exports raises foreigners' demands for U.S. goods and hence their demand for U.S. dollars, which are needed to buy U.S. goods. The demand curve for dollars shifts from D^1 to D^2, and the supply curve of dollars shifts from S^1 to S^2, raising the value of the dollar (the nominal exchange rate) from e^1_{nom} to e^2_{nom}.

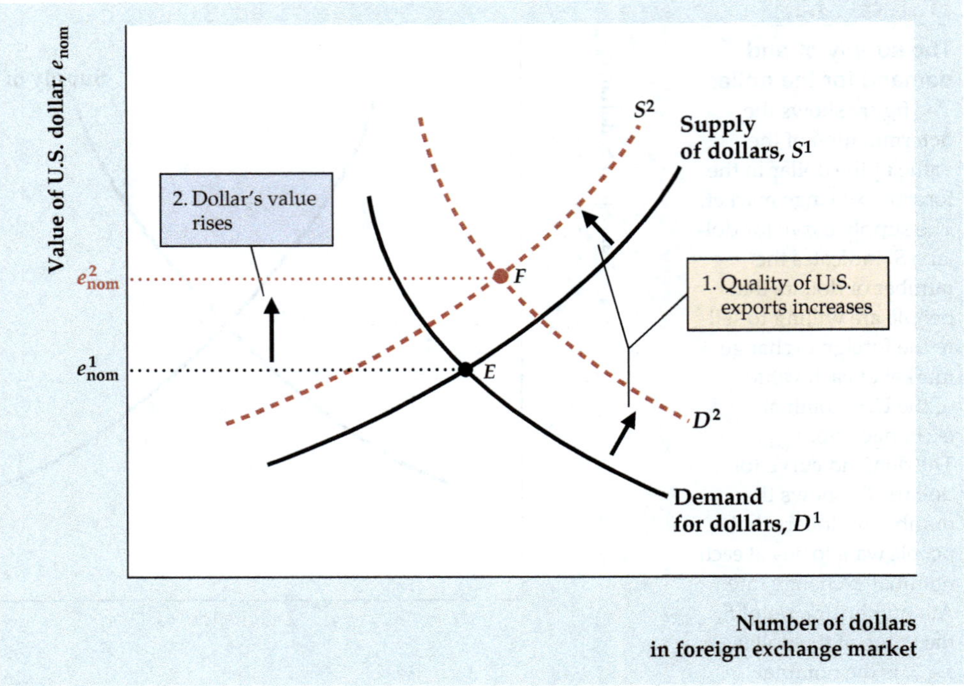

Thus factors that increase foreigners' demand for U.S. exports and assets will also increase the foreign-exchange-market demand for dollars, raising the dollar exchange rate. Likewise, the value of the dollar will rise if U.S. residents' demand for foreign goods and assets declines, so they supply fewer dollars to the foreign exchange market.

For example, suppose that U.S. goods improve in quality so that foreigners demand more of them. This increase in the demand for U.S. exports would translate into an increase in the demand for U.S. dollars. In Figure 13.4 the demand curve for dollars shifts to the right, from D^1 to D^2. An improvement in the quality of U.S. goods may also lead U.S. residents to substitute U.S. goods for foreign goods, thereby reducing U.S. imports, and reducing the supply of dollars in the foreign exchange market at each real exchange rate, shifting the supply curve of dollars from S^1 to S^2. As a result, the equilibrium value of the dollar rises from e^1_{nom} to e^2_{nom}. All else being equal, then, improvements in the quality of U.S. goods would lead to an appreciation of the dollar.

Macroeconomic Determinants of the Exchange Rate and Net Export Demand

In our previous *IS–LM* analyses we emphasized two key macroeconomic variables: real output (income), Y, and the real interest rate, r. In anticipation of the open-economy version of the *IS–LM* model presented in Section 13.3, we now consider how changes in real output or the real interest rate (either at home or abroad) are linked to the exchange rate and net exports. Again, because we are holding domestic and foreign price levels constant, the results we discuss here apply equally to the nominal exchange rate and the real exchange rate.

Effects of Changes in Output (Income). Imagine that domestic output (equivalently, domestic income), Y, increases but that other factors (such as the real interest rate) remain unchanged. How would the increase in Y affect the exchange rate and net exports?

To consider the effect on net exports first is easier. We know that spending by consumers depends in part on their current incomes. When domestic income rises, consumers will spend more on all goods and services, *including imports*. Thus when domestic output (income) rises, net exports (exports minus imports) must fall, other factors held constant.[8]

To determine the effect of increased domestic output on the exchange rate, recall that, to increase their purchases of imports, domestic residents must obtain foreign currencies. Equivalently, domestic residents must supply more domestic currency to the foreign exchange market. An increased supply of domestic currency causes its value to fall; that is, the exchange rate depreciates.

We can also analyze the effects of an increase in the real output of the country's trading partners, Y_{For} (foreign output or income). An increase in Y_{For} leads foreign consumers to increase their spending on all goods and services, including the exports of the domestic country. Thus an increase in the income of Germany and Japan, for example, would increase those nations' demand for U.S. exports and raise U.S. net exports. The increase in foreign demand for U.S. goods also would increase foreigners' demand for U.S. dollars, raising the value of the dollar. Note that the effects of changes in foreign income are the opposite of the effects of changes in domestic income.

Effects of Changes in Real Interest Rates. A second key macroeconomic variable to be considered is the real interest rate. Imagine that the domestic country's real interest rate, r, rises, with other factors (including the foreign real interest rate) held constant.[9] In this case, the country's real and financial assets will become more attractive to both domestic and foreign savers seeking the highest return on their funds. Because domestic currency can be used to buy domestic assets, a rise in the domestic real interest rate also increases the demand for and reduces the supply of domestic currency. An increased demand and decreased supply of domestic currency in turn leads to exchange rate appreciation.

A rise in the domestic real interest rate, r, has no *direct* effect on net exports, but it does have an *indirect* effect through the exchange rate. An increase in r raises the exchange rate so that domestic exports become more expensive and imports

---

[8]The conclusion that an increase in output reduces net exports seems to contradict a result obtained in Chapter 5— that an increase in output owing to a beneficial supply shock raises net exports. There is no contradiction because a supply shock doesn't hold variables other than output constant as we are assuming here. See Analytical Problem 4 at the end of the chapter.

[9]Note that, by holding the foreign real interest rate constant, we no longer assume (as we did in Chapter 5) that the domestic and foreign countries face the same world real interest rate. In general, real interest rates in different countries need not be the same when countries produce different goods, as we assume in this chapter. The reason is that real interest rates in different countries measure different things. For example, the Japanese real interest rate measures the growth of an asset's purchasing power in terms of Japanese goods, whereas the German real interest rate measures the growth of an asset's purchasing power in terms of German goods. If the Japanese–German real exchange rate is changing, the two real interest rates need not be the same.

from abroad become cheaper. Thus other factors being constant, an increase in r reduces the domestic country's net exports.

The effects of a change in the foreign real interest rate, r_{For}, are the opposite of the effects of a change in the domestic real interest rate. If the foreign real interest rate rises, for example, foreign assets will become more attractive to domestic and foreign savers. To get the foreign currency needed to buy foreign assets, domestic savers will supply domestic currency to the foreign exchange market. Foreign savers will also demand less domestic currency. The increased supply and decreased demand for domestic currency will lead to a depreciation of the exchange rate. The depreciation of the exchange rate caused by the rise in r_{For} in turn raises the domestic country's net exports.

Summary tables 16 and 17 list the effects of the various macroeconomic factors on the exchange rate and net exports.

SUMMARY 16

Determinants of the Exchange Rate (Real or Nominal)

An increase in	Causes the exchange rate to	Reason
Domestic output (income), Y	Fall	Higher domestic output raises demand for imports and increases supply of domestic currency.
Foreign output (income), Y_{For}	Rise	Higher foreign output raises demand for exports and increases demand for domestic currency.
Domestic real interest rate, r	Rise	Higher real interest rate makes domestic assets more attractive and increases demand and decreases supply of domestic currency.
Foreign real interest rate, r_{For}	Fall	Higher foreign real interest rate makes foreign assets more attractive and increases supply and decreases demand for domestic currency.
World demand for domestic goods	Rise	Higher demand for domestic goods increases foreign demand for domestic currency and reduces supply of domestic currency in foreign exchange market.

SUMMARY 17

Determinants of Net Exports

An increase in	Causes net exports to	Reason
Domestic output (income), Y	Fall	Higher domestic output raises demand for imports.
Foreign output (income), Y_{For}	Rise	Higher foreign output raises foreign demand for exports.
Domestic real interest rate, r	Fall	Higher real interest rate appreciates the real exchange rate and makes domestic goods more expensive relative to foreign goods.
Foreign real interest rate, r_{For}	Rise	Higher foreign real interest rate depreciates the real exchange rate and makes domestic goods cheaper relative to foreign goods.
World demand for domestic goods	Rise	Higher demand for domestic goods directly increases net exports.

13.3 The *IS–LM* Model for an Open Economy

Use the relationship between exchange rates and international trade to develop an open-economy *IS–LM* model.

Now we're ready to explore how exchange rates and international trade interact with the behavior of the economy as a whole. To do so, we extend the *IS–LM* model to allow for trade and lending among nations. An algebraic version of this analysis is presented in Appendix 13.B. We use the *IS–LM* diagram rather than the *AD–AS* diagram because we want to focus on the real interest rate, which plays a key role in determining exchange rates and the flows of goods and assets.

Recall that the components of the *IS–LM* model are the *IS* curve, which describes goods market equilibrium; the *LM* curve, which describes asset market equilibrium; and the *FE* line, which describes labor market equilibrium. Nothing discussed in this chapter affects our analysis of the supply of or demand for money in the domestic asset market; so, in developing the open-economy *IS–LM* model, we use the same *LM* curve that we used for the closed-economy model. Similarly, the labor market and the production function aren't directly affected by international factors, so the *FE* line also is unchanged.[10]

However, because net exports are part of the demand for goods, we have to modify the *IS* curve to describe the open economy. Three main points need to be made about the *IS* curve in the open economy:

1. Although the open-economy *IS* curve is derived somewhat differently than the closed-economy *IS* curve, it is a downward-sloping relationship between output and the real interest rate, as the closed-economy *IS* curve is.
2. All factors that shift the *IS* curve in the closed economy shift the *IS* curve in the open economy in the same way.
3. In an open economy, factors that change net exports also shift the *IS* curve. Specifically, for given values of domestic output and the domestic real interest rate, factors that raise a country's net exports shift the open-economy *IS* curve up and to the right; factors that lower a country's net exports shift the *IS* curve down and to the left.

After discussing each point, we use the open-economy *IS–LM* model to analyze the international transmission of business cycles and the operation of macroeconomic policies in an open economy.

The Open-Economy *IS* Curve

For any level of output the *IS* curve gives the real interest rate that brings the goods market into equilibrium. In a closed economy, the goods market equilibrium condition is that desired national saving, S^d, must equal desired investment, I^d, or $S^d - I^d = 0$. In an open economy, as we showed in Chapter 5, the goods market equilibrium condition is that desired saving, S^d, must equal desired investment, I^d, plus net exports, *NX*. Writing the goods market equilibrium condition for an open economy, we have

$$S^d - I^d = NX. \tag{13.4}$$

[10]A case in which the *FE* line does depend on international considerations is when some raw materials (such as oil) are imported. In this book we have modeled oil price shocks as productivity shocks, which captures the main domestic macroeconomic effects. A full analysis that includes all the international aspects of an oil price shock is complex, so we don't present it here.

To interpret Eq. (13.4), recall that $S^d - I^d$, the excess of national saving over investment, is the amount that domestic residents desire to lend abroad. Recall also that net exports, NX (which, if net factor payments and net unilateral transfers are zero, is the same as the current account balance), equals the amount that foreigners want to borrow from domestic savers. Thus Eq. (13.4) indicates that, for the goods market to be in equilibrium, the amount that domestic residents desire to lend to foreigners must equal the amount that foreigners desire to borrow from domestic residents.

Equivalently, we can write the goods market equilibrium condition as

$$Y = C^d + I^d + G + NX. \quad \textbf{(13.5)}$$

We obtained Eq. (13.5) from Eq. (13.4) by replacing desired saving, S^d, with its definition, $Y - C^d - G$, and rearranging. Equation (13.5) states that the goods market is in equilibrium when the supply of goods, Y, equals the demand for goods, $C^d + I^d + G + NX$. Note that in an open economy the total demand for goods includes spending on net exports.

Figure 13.5 illustrates goods market equilibrium in an open economy. The horizontal axis measures desired saving minus desired investment, $S^d - I^d$, and net exports, NX. Note that the horizontal axis includes both positive and negative values. The vertical axis measures the domestic real interest rate, r.

The upward-sloping curve, $S^d - I^d$, shows the difference between desired national saving and desired investment for each value of the real interest rate, r. This curve slopes upward because, with output held constant, an increase in the real interest rate raises desired national saving and reduces desired investment, raising the country's desired foreign lending.

The downward-sloping curve, NX, in Fig. 13.5, shows the relationship between the country's net exports and the domestic real interest rate, other factors held constant. As discussed in Section 13.2, a rise in the real interest rate appreciates the

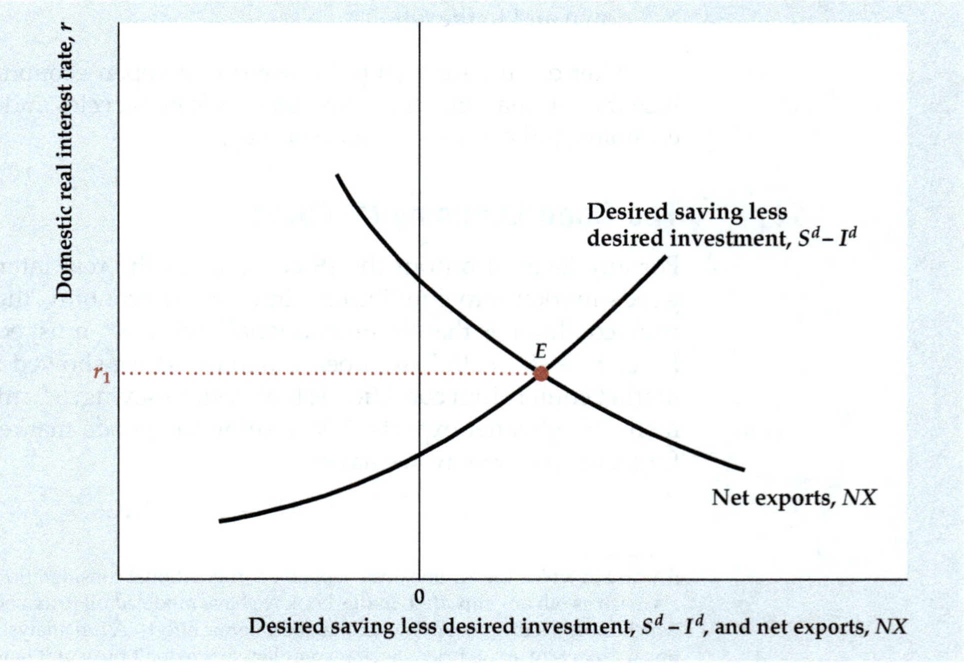

FIGURE 13.5

Goods market equilibrium in an open economy

The upward-sloping curve shows desired saving, S^d, less desired investment, I^d. This curve slopes upward because a higher domestic real interest rate increases the excess of desired saving over desired investment. The NX curve relates net exports to the domestic real interest rate. This curve slopes downward because a higher domestic real interest rate causes the real exchange rate to appreciate, reducing net exports. Goods market equilibrium occurs at point E, where the excess of desired saving over desired investment equals net exports (equivalently, where desired lending abroad equals desired borrowing by foreigners). The real interest rate that clears the goods market is r_1.

exchange rate, which in turn reduces net exports (see Summary table 17). Hence the NX curve slopes downward.

Goods market equilibrium requires that the excess of desired saving over desired investment equal net exports (Eq. 13.4). This condition is satisfied at the intersection of the $S^d - I^d$ and NX curves at point E. Thus the domestic real interest rate that clears the goods market is the interest rate at E, or r_1.

To derive the open-economy IS curve, we need to know what happens to the real interest rate that clears the goods market when the current level of domestic output rises (see Figure 13.6). Suppose that domestic output initially equals Y_1 and that goods market equilibrium is at point E, with a real interest rate of r_1. Now suppose that output rises to Y_2. An increase in current output raises desired national saving but doesn't affect desired investment, so the excess of desired saving over desired investment rises at any real interest rate. Thus the curve measuring the excess of desired saving over desired investment shifts to the right, from $(S^d - I^d)^1$ to $(S^d - I^d)^2$ in Fig. 13.6(a).

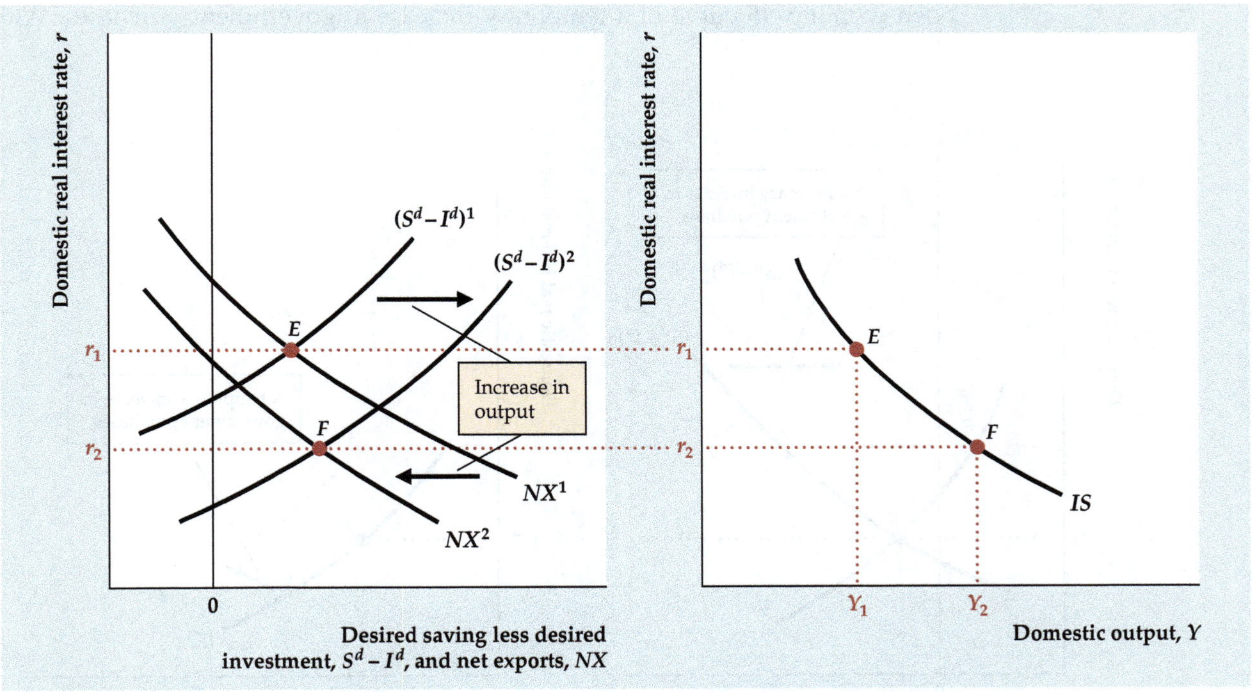

(a) Goods market equilibrium

(b) Open-economy IS curve

FIGURE 13.6

Derivation of the *IS* curve in an open economy

The initial equilibrium in the goods market is represented by point E in both (a) and (b).

(a) At point E, domestic output is Y_1 and the domestic real interest rate is r_1. An increase in domestic output from Y_1 to Y_2 raises desired national saving at each real interest rate and doesn't affect desired investment. Therefore the $S^d - I^d$ curve shifts to the right, from $(S^d - I^d)^1$ to $(S^d - I^d)^2$. The increase in output also raises domestic spending on imports, reducing net exports and causing the NX curve to shift to the left, from NX^1 to NX^2. At the new equilibrium point, F, the real interest rate is r_2.

(b) Because an increase in output from Y_1 to Y_2 lowers the real interest rate that clears the goods market from r_1 to r_2, the IS curve slopes downward.

What about the *NX* curve? An increase in domestic income causes domestic consumers to spend more on imported goods, which (other factors held constant) reduces net exports (Summary table 17). Thus, when output rises from Y_1 to Y_2, net exports fall, and the *NX* curve shifts to the left, from NX^1 to NX^2.

After the increase in output from Y_1 to Y_2, the new goods market equilibrium is at point *F* in Fig. 13.6(a), with the real interest rate at r_2. The *IS* curve in Fig. 13.6(b) shows that, when output equals Y_1, the real interest rate that clears the goods market is r_1; and that when output equals Y_2, the real interest rate that clears the goods market is r_2. Because higher current output lowers the real interest rate that clears the goods market, the open-economy *IS* curve slopes downward, as for a closed economy.

Factors That Shift the Open-Economy *IS* Curve

As in a closed economy, in an open economy any factor that raises the real interest rate that clears the goods market at a constant level of output shifts the *IS* curve up. This point is illustrated in Figure 13.7 which shows the effects on the open-economy *IS* curve of a temporary increase in government purchases. With

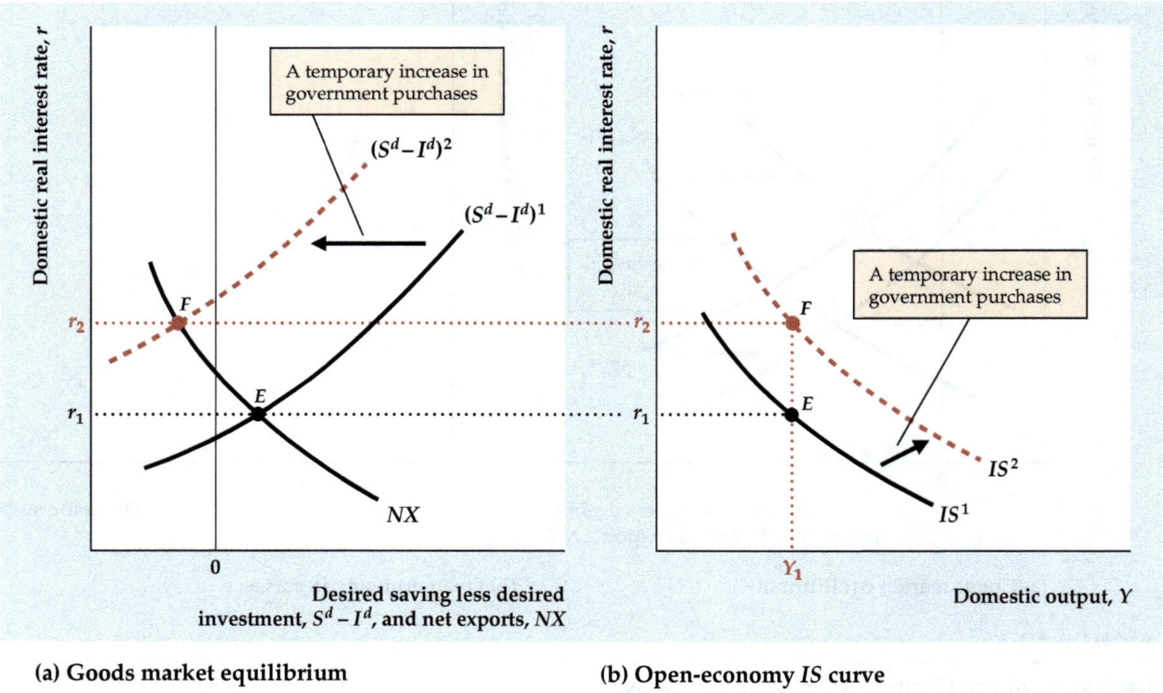

FIGURE 13.7

Effect of an increase in government purchases on the open-economy *IS* curve

Initial equilibrium is at point *E*, where output is Y_1 and the real interest rate is r_1, in both (a) and (b).
(a) A temporary increase in government purchases lowers desired national saving at every level of output and the real interest rate. Thus the $S^d - I^d$ curve shifts to the left, from $(S^d - I^d)^1$ to $(S^d - I^d)^2$.
(b) For output Y_1, the real interest rate that clears the goods market increases to r_2, at point *F* in both (a) and (b). Because the real interest rate that clears the goods market has risen, the *IS* curve shifts up and to the right, from IS^1 to IS^2.

output held constant at Y_1, the initial equilibrium is at point E, where the real interest rate is r_1. A temporary increase in government purchases lowers desired national saving at every level of output and the real interest rate. Thus the $S^d - I^d$ curve shifts to the left, from $(S^d - I^d)^1$ to $(S^d - I^d)^2$, as shown in Fig. 13.7(a). The new goods market equilibrium is at point F, where the real interest rate is r_2.

Figure 13.7(b) shows the effect on the *IS* curve. For output Y_1, the increase in government purchases raises the real interest rate that clears the goods market from r_1 to r_2. Thus the *IS* curve shifts up and to the right, from IS^1 to IS^2.

In general, any factor that shifts the closed-economy *IS* curve up does so by reducing desired national saving relative to desired investment. Because a change that reduces desired national saving relative to desired investment shifts the $S^d - I^d$ curve to the left (Fig. 13.7a), such a change also shifts the open-economy *IS* curve up.

In addition to the standard factors that shift the *IS* curve in a closed economy, some new factors affect the position of the *IS* curve in an open economy. In particular, anything that raises a country's net exports, given domestic output and the domestic real interest rate, will shift the open-economy *IS* curve up. This point is illustrated in Figure 13.8.

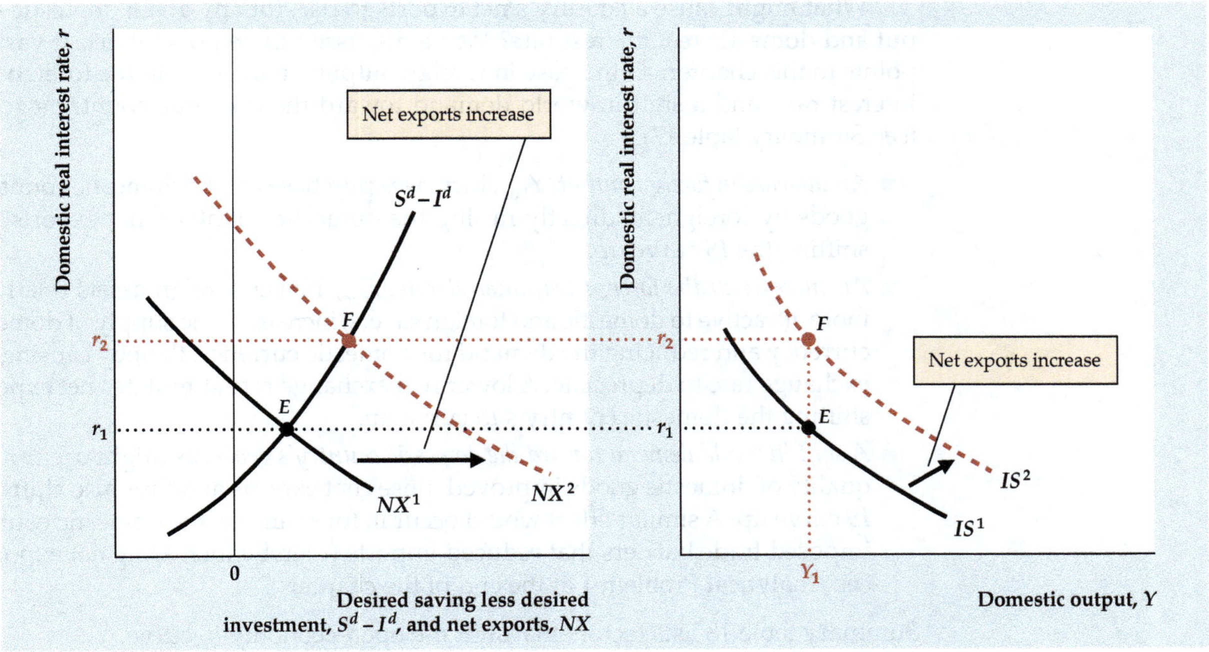

(a) Goods market equilibrium **(b) Open-economy *IS* curve**

FIGURE 13.8

Effect of an increase in net exports on the open-economy *IS* curve

In both (a) and (b), at the initial equilibrium point, E, output is Y_1 and the real interest rate that clears the goods market is r_1.
(a) If some change raises the country's net exports at any given domestic output and domestic real interest rate, the NX curve shifts to the right, from NX^1 to NX^2.
(b) For output Y_1, the real interest rate that clears the goods market has risen from r_1 to r_2, at point F in both (a) and (b). Thus the *IS* curve shifts up and to the right, from IS^1 to IS^2.

SUMMARY 18

International Factors That Shift the *IS* Curve

An increase in	Shifts the *IS* curve	Reason
Foreign output, Y_{For}	Up	Higher foreign output raises demand for home country exports.
Foreign real interest rate, r_{For}	Up	Higher foreign real interest rate depreciates the real exchange rate and raises net exports.
Demand for domestic goods relative to foreign goods	Up	Higher demand for domestic goods raises net exports.

At the initial equilibrium point, E, in both Figs. 13.8(a) and (b), domestic output is Y_1 and the domestic real interest rate is r_1. Now suppose that some change raises the country's net exports at any level of domestic output and the domestic real interest rate. This increase in net exports is shown as a shift to the right of the NX curve in Fig. 13.8(a), from NX^1 to NX^2. At the new goods market equilibrium point, F, the real interest rate has risen to r_2. Because the real interest rate that clears the goods market has risen for constant output, the IS curve shifts up and to the right, as shown in Fig. 13.8(b), from IS^1 to IS^2.

What might cause a country's net exports to rise, for any given domestic output and domestic real interest rate? We've discussed three possibilities at various points in this chapter: an increase in foreign output, an increase in the foreign real interest rate, and a shift in world demand toward the domestic country's goods (see Summary table 17).

- *An increase in foreign output,* Y_{For}, increases purchases of the domestic country's goods by foreigners, directly raising the domestic country's net exports and shifting the IS curve up.
- *An increase in the foreign real interest rate,* r_{For}, makes foreign assets relatively more attractive to domestic and foreign savers, increasing the supply of domestic currency and reducing the demand for domestic currency, thereby causing the exchange rate to depreciate. A lower real exchange rate stimulates net exports, shifting the domestic country's IS curve up.
- *A shift in world demand toward the domestic country's goods,* as might occur if the quality of domestic goods improved, raises net exports and thus also shifts the IS curve up. A similar effect would occur if, for example, the domestic country imposed trade barriers that reduced imports (thereby increasing net exports); see Analytical Problem 1 at the end of the chapter.

Summary table 18 lists factors that shift the open-economy IS curve.

The International Transmission of Business Cycles

In the introduction to this chapter we discussed briefly how trade and financial links among countries transmit cyclical fluctuations across borders. The analysis here shows that the impact of foreign economic conditions on the real exchange rate and net exports is one of the principal ways by which cycles are transmitted internationally.

For example, consider the impact of a recession in the United States on an economy for which the United States is a major export market—say, Japan. In terms of the *IS–LM* model, a decline in U.S. output lowers the demand for Japanese net exports, which shifts the Japanese *IS* curve down. In the Keynesian version of the model, this downward shift of the *IS* curve throws the Japanese economy into a recession, with output below its full-employment level, until price adjustment restores full employment (see, for example, Fig. 11.7). Japanese output also is predicted to fall in the classical model with misperceptions because the drop in net exports implies a decline in the Japanese aggregate demand (*AD*) curve and the short-run aggregate supply (*SRAS*) curve slopes upward. However, in the basic classical model without misperceptions, output remains at its full-employment level so the decline in net exports wouldn't affect Japanese output.

Similarly, a country's domestic economy can be sensitive to shifts in international tastes for various goods. For example, a shift in demand away from Japanese goods—induced perhaps by trade restrictions against Japanese products—would shift the Japanese *IS* curve down, with the same contractionary effects as the decrease in foreign (U.S.) output had.

13.4 Macroeconomic Policy in an Open Economy with Flexible Exchange Rates

Discuss the international effects of domestic macroeconomic policies.

A primary reason for developing the *IS–LM* model for the open economy is to determine how borrowing and trading links among countries affect fiscal and monetary policies. When exchange rates are flexible, the effects of macroeconomic policy on domestic variables such as output and the real interest rate are largely unchanged when foreign trade is added. However, adding foreign trade raises two new questions: (1) How do fiscal and monetary policy affect a country's real exchange rate and net exports? and (2) How do the macroeconomic policies of one country affect the economies of other countries? With the open-economy *IS–LM* model, we can answer both questions.

To examine the international effects of various domestic macroeconomic policies, we proceed as follows:

1. We use the *IS–LM* diagram for the domestic economy to determine the effects of the policies on domestic output and the domestic real interest rate. This step is the same as in our analyses of closed economies in Chapters 9–11.
2. We apply the results of Section 13.2 (see in particular Summary table 16 and Summary table 17) to determine how changes in domestic output and the domestic real interest rate affect the exchange rate and net exports.
3. We use the *IS–LM* diagram for the foreign economy to determine the effects of the domestic policies on foreign output and the foreign real interest rate. Domestic policies that change the demand for the foreign country's net exports will shift the foreign *IS* curve.

A Fiscal Expansion

To consider the effects of fiscal policy in an open economy, let's look again at a temporary increase in domestic government purchases. In analyzing this policy change we use the classical version of the *IS–LM* model (with no misperceptions) but also discuss the results that would be obtained in the Keynesian framework.

Figure 13.9 shows two *IS–LM* diagrams, one for the domestic country (where the fiscal policy change is taking place) and one for the foreign country, representing the domestic country's major trading partners. Suppose that the original equilibrium is at point *E* in Fig. 13.9(a). As usual, the increase in government purchases shifts the domestic *IS* curve up and to the right, from IS^1 to IS^2. In addition, in the

FIGURE 13.9

Effects of an increase in domestic government purchases

(a) In the classical *IS–LM* model, an increase in domestic government purchases shifts the domestic *IS* curve up and to the right, from IS^1 to IS^2. It also shifts the domestic *FE* line to the right, from FE^1 to FE^2. Therefore domestic output and the domestic real interest rate both increase. These increases reduce net exports but have an ambiguous effect on the real exchange rate. The results are similar in the Keynesian model.
(b) Because the domestic country's exports are the foreign country's imports, and vice versa, the decrease in the domestic country's net exports is equivalent to a rise in the foreign country's net exports. This increase shifts the foreign *IS* curve up, from IS^1_{For} to IS^2_{For}. In the classical model, prices adjust rapidly, shifting the *LM* curve from LM^1_{For} to LM^2_{For}. The new equilibrium is at point *F*, where the foreign real interest rate and price level are higher but foreign output is unchanged. In the Keynesian model, price stickiness would cause a temporary increase in foreign output at *H* before price adjustment restores general equilibrium at *F*.

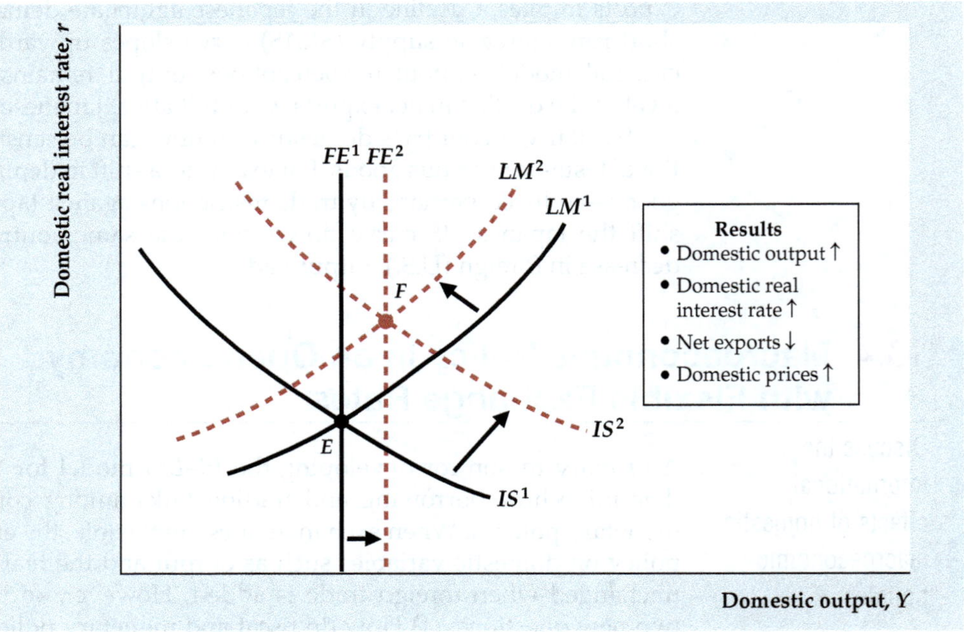

(a) Domestic country

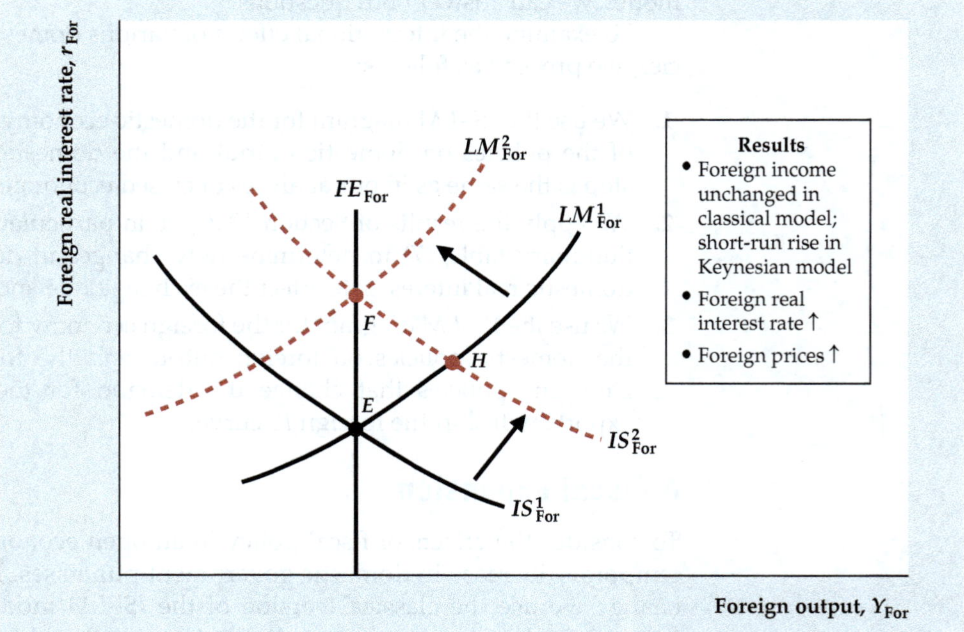

(b) Foreign country

classical model the *FE* line shifts to the right, from FE^1 to FE^2. The reason for this shift is that the increase in government purchases raises present or future tax burdens; because higher taxes make workers poorer, they increase their labor supply, which raises full-employment output. The new equilibrium is represented by point *F*, the intersection of IS^2 and FE^2. The domestic price level rises, shifting the domestic *LM* curve up and to the left, from LM^1 to LM^2, until it passes through *F*. Comparing point *F* with point *E* reveals that the increase in government purchases increases both output, *Y*, and the real interest rate, *r*, in the domestic country. So far the analysis is identical to the classical analysis for a closed economy (Chapter 10). Note also that fiscal expansion raises output and the real interest rate—the same results that we would get from the Keynesian model.

To examine the role of international trade, we first consider the effects on the exchange rate of the increases in domestic output and the domestic real interest rate. Recall that an increase in output, *Y*, causes domestic residents to demand more imports and thus to supply more currency to the foreign exchange market. The increase in domestic output therefore depreciates the exchange rate. However, the rise in the domestic real interest rate makes domestic assets more attractive, causing foreign savers to demand the domestic currency and domestic savers to supply less domestic currency to the foreign exchange market and causing the exchange rate to appreciate. The overall effect of the increase in government purchases on the exchange rate is ambiguous: We can't be sure whether the increase in government purchases will raise or lower the exchange rate.

The effect of the fiscal expansion on the country's net export demand isn't ambiguous. Recall that the increase in domestic output (which raises domestic consumers' demand for imports) and the increase in the real interest rate (which tends to appreciate the exchange rate) both cause net exports to fall. Thus the overall effect of the fiscal expansion clearly is to move the country's trade balance toward deficit. This result is consistent with the analysis of the "twin deficits" (the government budget deficit and the trade deficit) in Chapter 5.

In an interconnected world, the effects of macroeconomic policies in one country aren't limited to that country but also are felt abroad. Based on the analysis we've just finished, taking the extra step and finding out how the domestic fiscal expansion affects the economies of the domestic country's trading partners isn't difficult.

The effects of the domestic fiscal expansion on the rest of the world—represented by the foreign country *IS–LM* diagram in Fig. 13.9(b)—are transmitted through the change in net exports. Because the domestic country's imports are the foreign country's exports, and vice versa, the decline in net exports of the domestic country is equivalent to an increase in net exports for the foreign country. Thus the foreign country's *IS* curve shifts up, from IS^1_{For} to IS^2_{For}.

In the classical *IS–LM* model, the upward shift of the foreign *IS* curve doesn't affect foreign output; instead the price level rises immediately to restore general equilibrium (the *LM* curve shifts up from LM^1_{For} to LM^2_{For}). The foreign economy ends up at point *F*, with the real interest rate and the price level higher than they were initially.

If prices were sticky, as in the Keynesian model, the effects of the shift of the foreign country's *IS* curve would be slightly different. If prices don't adjust in the short run, the shift of the *IS* curve implies that the foreign economy would have temporarily higher output at the intersection of the *IS* and *LM* curves at point *H* in Fig. 13.9(b); only after firms adjust their prices would the economy arrive at point *F*. Otherwise, the implications of the classical and Keynesian analyses are the same.[11]

Therefore, in the open-economy versions of both the classical and Keynesian models, a temporary increase in government purchases raises domestic income and the domestic real interest rate, as in a closed economy. In addition, net exports fall; thus increased government purchases reduce, or crowd out, both investment and net exports. The effect on the real exchange rate is ambiguous: It can either rise or fall. In the foreign economy the real interest rate and the price level rise. In the Keynesian version of the model, foreign output also rises, but only in the short run.

A Monetary Contraction

We can also use the open-economy *IS–LM* model to study the effects of monetary policy when exchange rates are flexible. For the Keynesian version of the *IS–LM* model we analyze the effects of a drop in the money supply in both the short and long run. Because the effects of monetary policy are the same in the basic classical model (without misperceptions) and the long-run Keynesian model, our analysis applies to the classical model as well.

Short-Run Effects on the Domestic and Foreign Economies. The effects of a monetary contraction are shown in Figure 13.10, which shows *IS–LM* diagrams corresponding to both the domestic and foreign countries. Suppose that the initial equilibrium is represented by point *E* and that a decrease in the money supply shifts the domestic *LM* curve up and to the left, from LM^1 to LM^2, in Fig. 13.10(a). In the Keynesian model, the price level is rigid in the short run, so the short-run equilibrium is at point *F*, the intersection of the *IS* and LM^2 curves. Comparing points *F* and *E* reveals that in the short run domestic output falls and the domestic real interest rate rises. This result is the same as for the closed economy.

After the monetary contraction, the exchange rate appreciates in the short run, for two reasons. First, the drop in domestic income reduces the domestic demand for imports, leading domestic consumers to demand less foreign currency to buy imported goods. Second, the rise in the domestic real interest rate makes domestic assets relatively more attractive to foreign and domestic savers, increasing foreign savers' demand for the domestic currency and reducing domestic savers' supply of domestic currency to the foreign exchange market.

What happens to the country's net exports? Here there are two competing effects: (1) The drop in domestic income created by the monetary contraction reduces the domestic demand for foreign goods and thus tends to increase the country's net exports; but (2) the rise in the real interest rate, which leads to exchange rate appreciation, tends to reduce net exports. The theory doesn't indicate for certain which way net exports will change. In our earlier discussion of the J curve, however, we noted that the effects of changes in the real exchange rate on net exports may be weak in the short run. Based on that analysis, we assume that *in the short run exchange rate effects on net exports are weaker than the effects of changes in domestic income* so that overall the country's net exports will increase.

---

[11]In principle, we could continue the analysis by discussing how changes in foreign output and real interest rates in turn affect the domestic economy. However, these so-called *feedback effects* are generally small and thus don't reverse any of our conclusions, so we omit this discussion.

The next question is: How does the domestic monetary contraction affect the economies of the country's trading partners? The effects on the typical foreign economy are illustrated by Fig. 13.10(b). If the domestic country's net exports are increased by the monetary contraction, the foreign country's net exports must

FIGURE 13.10

Effects of a decrease in the domestic money supply

(a) A decrease in the domestic money supply shifts the domestic *LM* curve up, from LM^1 to LM^2. The short-run equilibrium in the Keynesian model is at point *F*, the intersection of the *IS* and LM^2 curves. The decline in the money supply reduces domestic output and increases the domestic real interest rate. The drop in domestic output and the rise in the real interest rate cause the real exchange rate to appreciate. The effect on net exports is potentially ambiguous; if we assume that the effect on net exports of the drop in domestic income is stronger than the effect of the appreciation of the exchange rate, net exports increase as domestic residents demand fewer goods from abroad.

(b) Because the domestic country's net exports increase, the foreign country's net exports fall and the foreign *IS* curve shifts down, from IS^1_{For} to IS^2_{For}. Thus output and the real interest rate fall in the foreign country in the short run. In the long run domestic prices fall and both economies return to equilibrium at point *E*. Thus in the long run money is neutral.

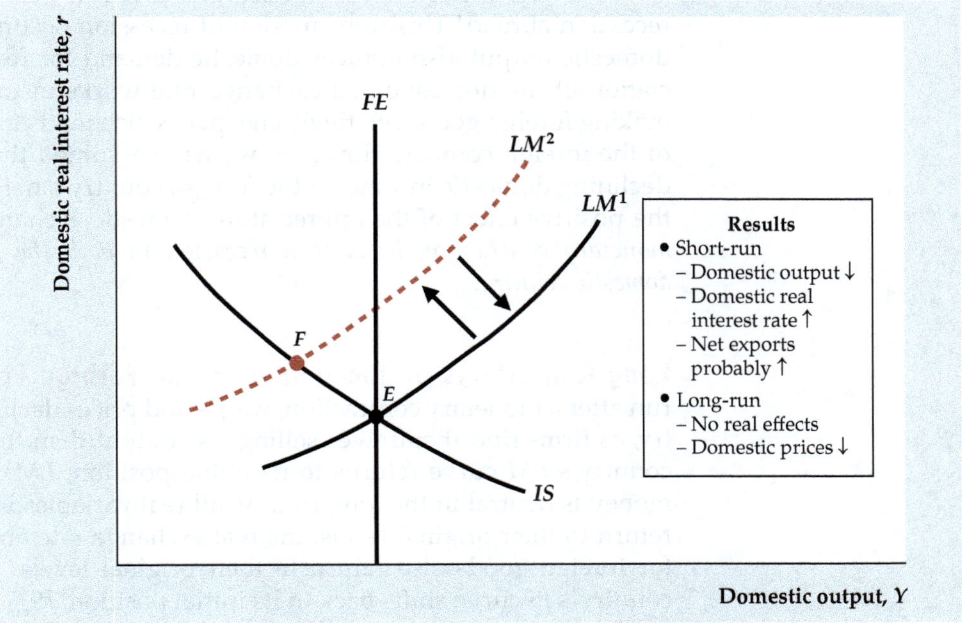

(a) Domestic country

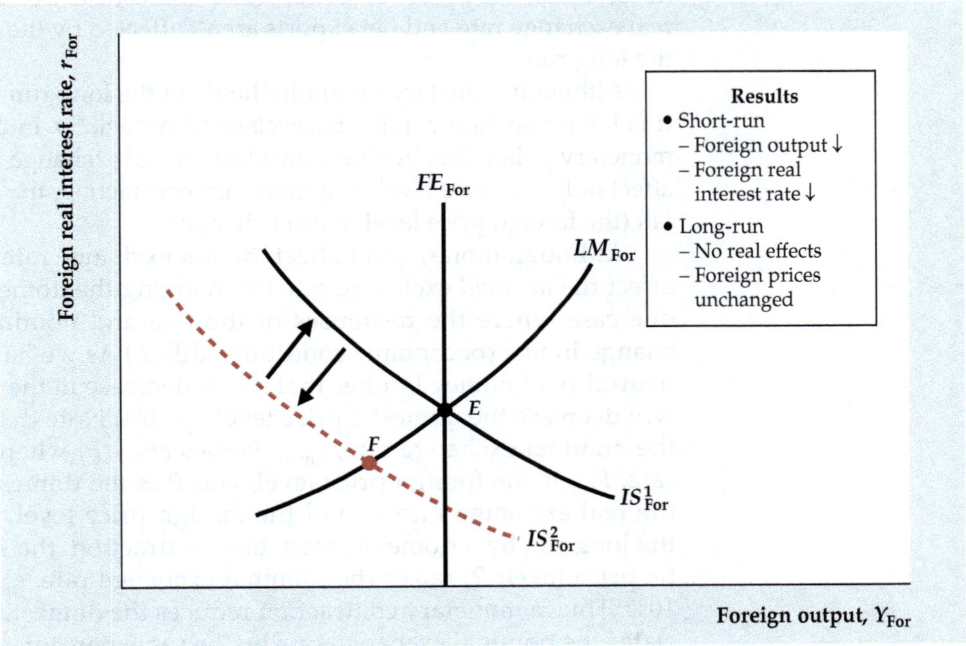

(b) Foreign country

decrease because the domestic country's exports are the foreign country's imports. Thus the *IS* curve of the foreign country shifts down and to the left, from IS^1_{For} to IS^2_{For}. The short-run equilibrium is at point *F*, where the IS^2_{For} and LM_{For} curves intersect. Output in the foreign country declines, and the foreign real interest rate falls.

These results show that a domestic monetary contraction also leads to a recession abroad. This transmission of recession occurs because the decline in domestic output also reduces domestic demand for foreign goods. The appreciation of the domestic real exchange rate works in the opposite direction by making foreign goods relatively cheaper, which tends to increase the net exports of the foreign country. However, we have assumed that the negative effect of declining domestic income on the foreign country's net exports is stronger than the positive effect of the appreciating domestic exchange rate. Thus *a domestic monetary contraction leads to a recession in both the foreign country and the domestic country.*

Long-Run Effects on the Domestic and Foreign Economies. In the long run after a monetary contraction, wages and prices decline in the domestic country, as firms find themselves selling less output than they desire. The domestic country's *LM* curve returns to its initial position, LM^1 in Fig. 13.10(a), so that money is neutral in the long run. As all real variables in the domestic economy return to their original levels, the real exchange rate and the domestic demand for foreign goods also return to their original levels. As a result, the foreign country's *IS* curve shifts back to its initial position, IS^1_{For} in Fig. 13.10(b), and the foreign country's economy also returns to its initial equilibrium point, *E*. At *E*, all foreign macroeconomic variables (including the price level) are at their original levels. Hence in the long run the change in the domestic money supply doesn't affect any real variables, either domestically or abroad. In particular, the real exchange rate and net exports aren't affected by the monetary contraction in the long run.

Although monetary neutrality holds in the long run in the Keynesian model, it holds immediately in the basic classical model. So, in the basic classical model, monetary policy changes have no effect on real exchange rates or trade flows; they affect only the price level. In a monetary contraction, the domestic price level will fall (the foreign price level doesn't change).

Although money can't affect the *real* exchange rate in the long run, it does affect the *nominal* exchange rate by changing the domestic price level. (This is one case where the responses of the real and nominal exchange rates to a change in macroeconomic conditions differ.) As we have shown, the long-run neutrality of money implies that a 10% decrease in the nominal money supply will decrease the domestic price level by 10%. Note that Eq. (13.1) implies that the nominal exchange rate, e_{nom}, equals eP_{For}/P, where *e* is the real exchange rate, P_{For} is the foreign price level, and *P* is the domestic price level. Because the real exchange rate, *e*, and the foreign price level, P_{For}, are unchanged in the long run by a domestic monetary contraction, the 10% drop in the domestic price level, *P*, raises the nominal exchange rate, e_{nom}, by (approximately) 10%. Thus a monetary contraction reduces the domestic price level and appreciates the nominal exchange rate by the same percentage as the drop in money supply.

13.5 Fixed Exchange Rates

Evaluate the strengths and weaknesses of different types of exchange rate systems.

The United States has had a flexible exchange rate since abandonment of the Bretton Woods system of fixed exchange rates during the early 1970s. However, fixed-exchange-rate systems—in which exchange rates are officially set by international agreement—have been important historically and are still used by many countries. Let's now consider fixed-exchange-rate systems and address two questions: (1) How does the use of a fixed-exchange-rate system affect an economy and macroeconomic policy? and (2) Ultimately, which is the better system, flexible or fixed exchange rates?

Fixing the Exchange Rate

In contrast to flexible-exchange-rate systems—where exchange rates are determined by supply and demand in foreign exchange markets—in a fixed-exchange-rate system the value of the nominal exchange rate is officially set by the government, perhaps in consultation or agreement with other countries.[12]

A potential problem with fixed-exchange-rate systems is that the value of the exchange rate set by the government may not be the exchange rate determined by the supply and demand for currency. Figure 13.11 shows a situation in which the official exchange rate, $\bar{e}_{nom}$, is higher than the **fundamental value of the exchange rate,** e^1_{nom}, or the value that would be determined by free market forces without government

FIGURE 13.11

An overvalued exchange rate

The figure shows a situation in which the officially fixed nominal exchange rate, $\bar{e}_{nom}$, is higher than the fundamental value of the exchange rate, e^1_{nom}, as determined by supply and demand in the foreign exchange market. In this situation the exchange rate is said to be overvalued. The country's central bank can maintain the exchange rate at the official rate by using its reserves to purchase its own currency in the foreign exchange market, in the amount of *AB* in each period. This loss of reserves also is referred to as the country's balance of payments deficit.

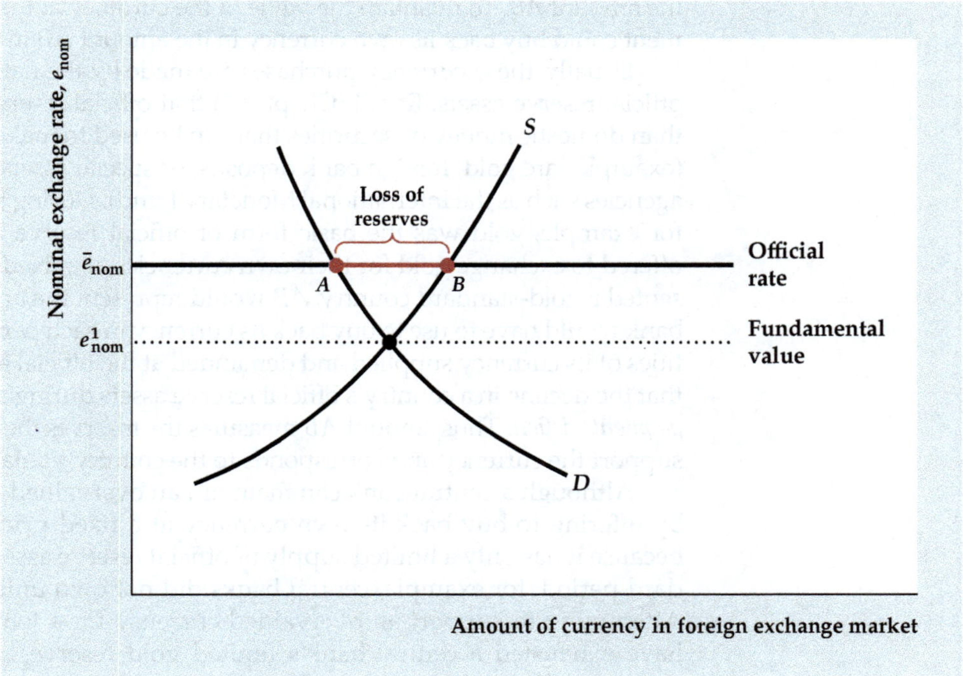

[12]In some fixed-exchange-rate systems, the exchange rate is allowed to fluctuate within a narrow, prespecified band. For simplicity, we will assume in this section that the exchange rate is fixed at a single value.

intervention. When an exchange rate is higher than its fundamental value, it is an **overvalued exchange rate** (often referred to as an overvalued currency).

How can a country deal with a situation in which its official exchange rate is different from the fundamental value of its exchange rate? There are several possible strategies: First, the country can simply change the official value of its exchange rate so that it equals, or is close to, its fundamental value. For example, in the case of overvaluation shown in Fig. 13.11, the country could simply devalue (lower) its nominal fixed exchange rate from $\bar{e}_{nom}$ to e^1_{nom}. However, although occasional devaluations or revaluations can be expected under fixed-exchange-rate systems, if a country continuously adjusts its exchange rate it might as well switch to a flexible-rate system.

Second, the government could restrict international transactions—for example, by limiting or taxing imports or financial outflows. Such policies reduce the supply of the domestic currency to the foreign exchange market, thus raising the fundamental value of the exchange rate toward its fixed value. Some countries go even further and prohibit people from trading the domestic currency for foreign currencies without government approval; a currency that can't be freely traded for other currencies is said to be an **inconvertible currency**. However, direct government intervention in international transactions has many economic costs, including reduced access to foreign goods and credit.

Third, the government itself may become a demander or supplier of its currency in the foreign exchange market, an approach used by most of the industrialized countries having fixed exchange rates. For example, in the case of overvaluation shown in Fig. 13.11, the supply of the country's currency to the foreign exchange market (point *B*) exceeds private demand for the currency (point *A*) at the official exchange rate by the amount *AB*. To maintain the value of the currency at the official rate, the government could buy back its own currency in the amount *AB* in each period.

Usually, these currency purchases are made by the nation's central bank, using official reserve assets. Recall (Chapter 5) that official reserve assets are assets other than domestic money or securities that can be used to make international payments (examples are gold, foreign bank deposits, or special assets created by international agencies such as the International Monetary Fund). During the gold standard period, for example, gold was the basic form of official reserve asset, and central banks offered to exchange gold for their own currencies at a fixed price. If Fig. 13.11 represented a gold-standard country, *AB* would represent the amount of gold the central bank would have to use to buy back its currency in each period to equalize the quantities of its currency supplied and demanded at the official exchange rate. Recall also that the decline in a country's official reserve assets during a year equals its *balance of payments deficit*. Thus amount *AB* measures the reserves the central bank must use to support the currency and corresponds to the country's balance of payments deficit.

Although a central bank can maintain an overvalued exchange rate for a time by offering to buy back its own currency at a fixed price, it can't do so forever because it has only a limited supply of official reserve assets. During the gold standard period, for example, central banks did not own unlimited amounts of gold. Attempting to support an overvalued currency for a long period of time would have exhausted a central bank's limited gold reserves, leaving the country no choice but to devalue its currency.

A central bank's attempts to support an overvalued currency can be ended quickly and dramatically by a speculative run. A **speculative run**, also called a *speculative attack*, occurs when financial investors begin to fear that an overvalued currency may soon be devalued, reducing the value of assets denominated in that

FIGURE 13.12

A speculative run on an overvalued currency

Initially, the supply curve of the domestic currency is S_1, and to maintain the fixed exchange rate, the central bank must use amount *AB* of its reserves each period to purchase its own currency in the foreign exchange market. A speculative run occurs when holders of domestic assets begin to fear a devaluation, which would reduce the values of their assets (measured in terms of foreign currency). Panicky sales of domestic-currency assets lead to more domestic currency being supplied to the foreign exchange market, which shifts the supply curve of the domestic currency to the right, from S^1 to S^2. The central bank must now purchase its currency and lose reserves in the amount *AC*. This more rapid loss of reserves may force the central bank to stop supporting the overvalued currency and to devalue it, confirming the market's expectations.

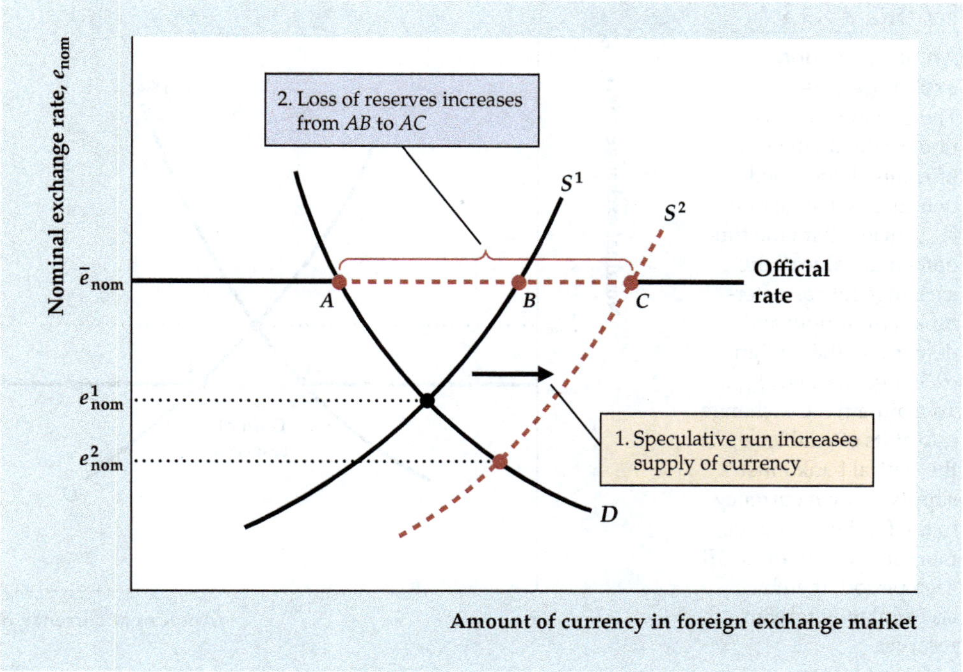

currency relative to assets denominated in other currencies. To avoid losses, financial investors frantically sell assets denominated in the overvalued currency. The panicky sales of domestic assets associated with a speculative run on a currency shift the supply curve for that currency sharply to the right (see Figure 13.12), increasing the gap between the quantities supplied and demanded of the currency from amount *AB* to amount *AC*. This widening gap increases the rate at which the central bank has to spend its official reserve assets to maintain the overvalued exchange rate, speeding devaluation and confirming the financial investors' expectations.

Without strong restrictions on international trade and finance (themselves economically costly), we conclude that an overvalued exchange rate isn't sustainable for long. If the exchange rate is overvalued, the country must either devalue its currency or make some policy change to raise the fundamental value of the exchange rate. We show in the next section that the basic tool for changing the fundamental value of the exchange rate is monetary policy.

We've focused on overvaluation, but an exchange rate also could be undervalued. As illustrated in Figure 13.13, an **undervalued exchange rate** (or undervalued currency) exists if the officially fixed value is less than the value determined by supply and demand in the foreign exchange market. In this case, instead of buying its own currency, the central bank sells its currency to the foreign exchange market and accumulates reserves in the amount *AB* each period. With no limit to the quantity of reserve assets (gold, for example) a central bank could accumulate, an undervalued exchange rate could apparently be maintained indefinitely. However, a country with an undervalued exchange rate can accumulate reserves only at the expense of trading partners who have overvalued exchange rates and are therefore losing reserves. Because the country's trading partners can't continue to lose reserves indefinitely, eventually they may put political pressure on the country to bring the fundamental value of its exchange rate back in line with the official rate.

FIGURE 13.13

An undervalued exchange rate

The exchange rate is undervalued when the officially determined nominal exchange rate, $\bar{e}_{nom}$, is less than the fundamental value of the exchange rate as determined by supply and demand in the foreign exchange market, e^1_{nom}. To maintain the exchange rate at its official level, the central bank must supply its own currency to the foreign exchange market in the amount AB each period, thereby accumulating foreign reserves.

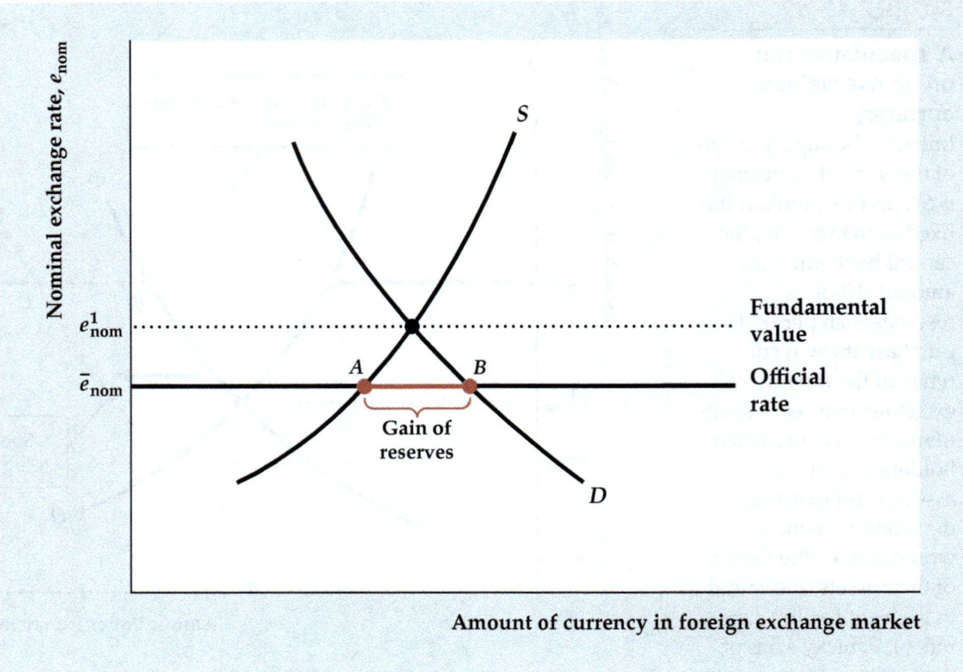

Monetary Policy and the Fixed Exchange Rate

Suppose that a country wants to eliminate currency overvaluation by raising the fundamental value of its nominal exchange rate until it equals the fixed value of the exchange rate. How can it achieve this goal? Economists have long recognized that the best way for a country to do so is through contraction of its money supply.

To demonstrate why a monetary contraction raises the fundamental value of the nominal exchange rate, we first rewrite Eq. (13.1), which defined the relationship of the real and nominal exchange rates:

$$e_{nom} = \frac{eP_{For}}{P}. \tag{13.6}$$

Equation (13.6) states that, for any foreign price level, P_{For}, the nominal exchange rate, e_{nom}, is proportional to the real exchange rate, e, and inversely proportional to the domestic price level, P.

In our earlier discussion of monetary policy in the Keynesian model with flexible exchange rates, we showed that a monetary contraction causes the real exchange rate to appreciate in the short run by reducing domestic output and increasing the real interest rate. Because short-run domestic and foreign price levels are fixed in the Keynesian model, Eq. (13.6) indicates that the short-run appreciation of the real exchange rate also implies a short-run appreciation of the nominal exchange rate. In the long run money is neutral; hence a monetary contraction has no effect on the real exchange rate, but it does cause the domestic price level to fall. In the long run the domestic price level, P, falls but the real exchange rate, e, is unaffected, so Eq. (13.6) implies that the nominal exchange rate rises (appreciates) both in the long run and the short run. Thus in both the short and long runs a monetary contraction increases the fundamental value of the nominal exchange rate, or the value of the nominal exchange rate determined by supply and demand in the foreign exchange market.[13] Conversely, a monetary easing reduces the fundamental value of the nominal exchange rate in both the short run and long run.

Figure 13.14 illustrates the relationship between the nominal exchange rate and the money supply in a country with a fixed exchange rate.[14] The downward-sloping curve shows the relationship of the money supply to the fundamental value of the nominal exchange rate. This curve slopes downward because, other factors being equal, an increase in the money supply reduces the fundamental value of the nominal exchange rate. The horizontal line in Fig. 13.14 is the officially determined exchange rate. M_1 on the horizontal axis is the value of the money supply that equalizes the fundamental value of the exchange rate and its officially fixed value. If the money supply is more than M_1, the country has an overvaluation problem (the fundamental value of the exchange rate is below the official value), and if the money supply is less than M_1, the country has an undervaluation problem.

Figure 13.14 suggests that, in a fixed-exchange-rate system, individual countries typically are *not* free to expand their money supplies to try to raise output and employment. Instead, the money supply is governed by the condition that the official and fundamental values of the exchange rate be the same. If the country represented in Fig. 13.14 wanted to expand its money supply to fight a recession, for example, it could do so only by creating an overvaluation problem (most likely

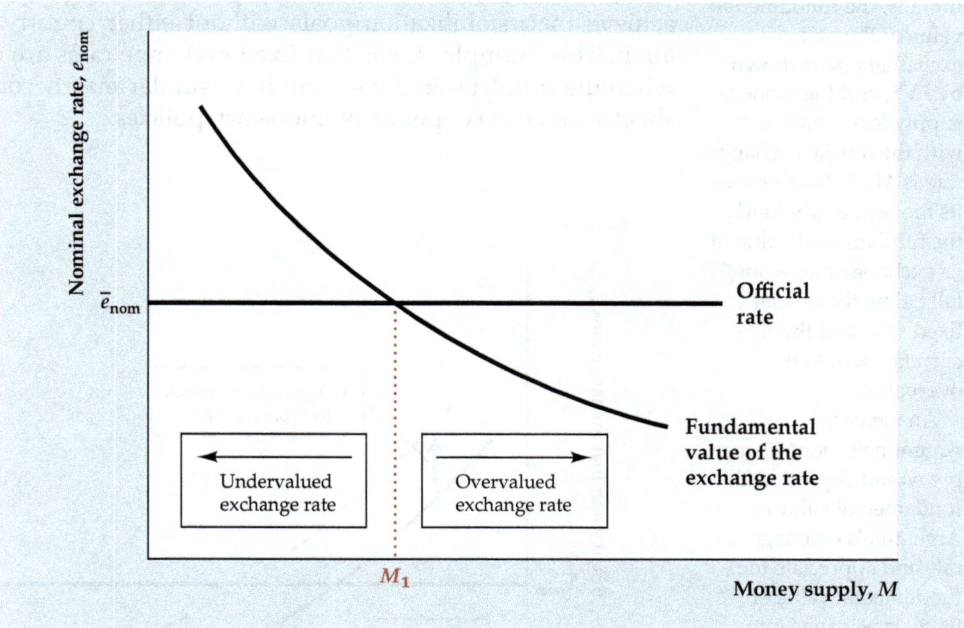

FIGURE 13.14

Determination of the money supply under fixed exchange rates

The downward-sloping fundamental value curve shows that a higher domestic money supply causes a lower fundamental value of the exchange rate. The horizontal line shows the officially fixed nominal exchange rate. Only when the country's money supply equals M_1 does the fundamental value of the exchange rate equal the official rate. If the central bank increased the money supply above M_1, the exchange rate would become overvalued. A money supply below M_1 would result in an undervalued currency.

[13]Because money is always neutral in the basic classical model, a monetary contraction increases the fundamental value of the nominal exchange rate in the basic classical model as well.

[14]The country's money supply is the amount of money in circulation domestically , as in previous chapters. It is *not* the supply of currency to foreign exchange markets, which depends only on domestic residents' demands for foreign goods and assets.

leading to a future devaluation) or by devaluing its currency immediately. Under fixed exchange rates, then, a central bank cannot use monetary policy to pursue macroeconomic stabilization goals.

Although one member of a group of countries in a fixed-exchange-rate system generally isn't free to use monetary policy by itself, the group *as a whole* may be able to do so, *if* the members coordinate their policies. For example, suppose that Argentina and Brazil have a fixed exchange rate between their two currencies and that, because of a recession in both countries, both want to expand their money supplies. If Brazil attempts a monetary expansion on its own, from M_1 to M_2 in Figure 13.15, its exchange rate will become overvalued (its fundamental value, at the intersection of M_2 and FV^1, would be lower than the official exchange rate). As a result, the central bank of Brazil would lose reserves, ultimately forcing Brazil to undo its attempted expansion.

Suppose, however, that Argentina goes ahead with its own money supply expansion. If Brazil's money supply remains constant, an increase in Argentina's money supply reduces the fundamental value of Argentina's (nominal) exchange rate, which is equivalent to raising the fundamental value of Brazil's exchange rate at any level of its money supply, as shown in Fig. 13.15. The fundamental value curve in Fig. 13.15 shifts up, from FV^1 to FV^2. Now Brazil can expand its money supply, from M_1 to M_2, without creating an overvaluation problem (the fundamental value of the Brazilian exchange rate at the intersection of M_2 and FV^2 is the same as the official exchange rate). Thus, if Argentina and Brazil cooperate by changing their money supplies in the same proportion, both countries can achieve their stabilization goals without either country experiencing overvaluation. This example shows that fixed exchange rates are most likely to work well when the countries in the system have similar macroeconomic goals, face similar shocks, and can cooperate on monetary policies.

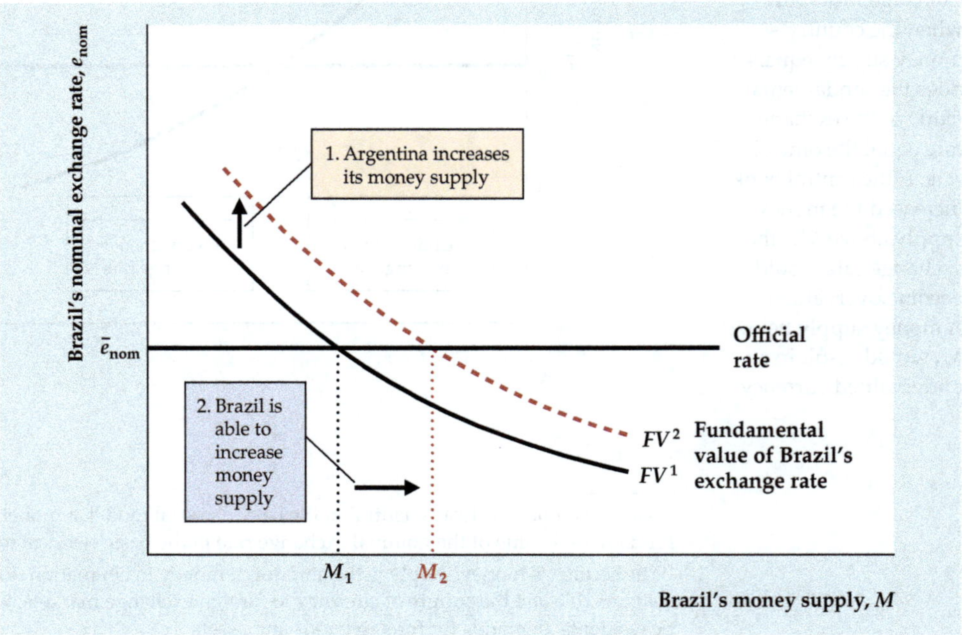

FIGURE 13.15

Coordinated monetary expansion

Initially, the fundamental value of Brazil's exchange rate is shown by FV^1, and the money supply level consistent with the official exchange rate is M_1. If Brazil raises its money supply to M_2, the fundamental value of its exchange rate would fall below the official fixed rate, and Brazil's currency would be overvalued.

An increase in Argentina's money supply would depreciate the fundamental value of Argentina's exchange rate and appreciate the fundamental value of Brazil's exchange rate. The curve showing the fundamental value of Brazil's exchange rate shifts up, from FV^1 to FV^2. Brazil can now increase its money supply to M_2 without creating an overvaluation problem.

Fixed Versus Flexible Exchange Rates

We have discussed the overvaluation and undervaluation problems that can arise in fixed-exchange-rate systems. However, flexible-exchange-rate systems have problems of their own, primarily the volatility of exchange rates, which introduces uncertainty for people and businesses in their transactions with other countries. Each type of system has its problems, so which is preferable?

Proponents of fixed-exchange-rate systems stress two major benefits. First, relative to a situation in which exchange rates fluctuate continuously, fixed exchange rates (if they are stable and not subject to frequent changes or speculative crises) may make trading goods and assets among countries easier and less costly. Thus a system of fixed rates may promote economic and financial integration and improve economic efficiency. Second, fixed exchange rates may improve monetary policy "discipline," in the sense that countries with fixed exchange rates typically are less able to carry out highly expansionary monetary policies; the result may be lower inflation in the long run.

The other side of the monetary discipline argument is that fixed exchange rates take away a country's ability to use monetary policy flexibly to deal with recessions.[15] This inability is particularly serious if the different countries in the fixed-exchange-rate system have different policy goals and face different types of economic shocks. Thus, for instance, one country may want to expand its money supply to fight a recession while another country does not want to increase its money supply. This divergence in monetary policies between the two countries would put downward pressure on the exchange rate of the country that increases its money supply, and thus would strain the fixed exchange rate between the two countries.

Which system is better depends on the circumstances. Fixed exchange rates among a group of countries are useful when large benefits can be gained from increased trade and integration and when the countries in the system coordinate their monetary policies closely. Countries that value the ability to use monetary policy independently—perhaps because they face different macroeconomic shocks than other countries or hold different views about the relative costs of unemployment and inflation—should use a floating exchange rate.

Currency Unions

An alternative to fixing exchange rates is for a group of countries to form a **currency union**, under which they agree to share a common currency. Members of a currency union also typically cooperate economically and politically. The agreement among the original thirteen colonies, enshrined in the U.S. Constitution, to abandon their individual currencies and create a single currency, is an early example of a currency union. The Application "European Monetary Unification," discusses a contemporary currency union.

An effective currency union usually requires more than just cooperation of national central banks. For a currency union to work, the common monetary policy must be controlled by a single institution. Because countries are typically

[15]Keynesians consider this inflexibility to be a cost, but classicals don't.

reluctant to give up their own currencies and monetary policies, currency unions have been rare. However, if politically feasible, a currency union has at least two advantages over fixed exchange rates. First, the costs of trading goods and assets among countries are even lower with a single currency than under fixed exchange rates. Second, if national currencies are eliminated in favor of the common currency, speculative attacks on the national currencies obviously can no longer occur.

However, a currency union shares the major disadvantage of a fixed-exchange-rate system: It requires all of its members to pursue a common monetary policy. Thus, if one member of a currency union is in a recession while another is concerned about inflation, the common monetary policy can't deal with both countries' problems simultaneously. In contrast, under flexible exchange rates, each country could set its own monetary policy independently.

Under what circumstances does forming a currency union make economic sense? Economist Robert Mundell of Columbia University defined an **optimum currency area** as any geographic region for which the benefits of having a common currency exceed the costs.[16] So, to put the question another way, why might one region be an optimum currency area while another is not?

Researchers have identified four general criteria that help determine whether a group of countries (or other political units) forms an optimum currency area:

1. Countries within an optimum currency area *trade extensively* with each other (and may hope for even further economic integration). A common currency makes trade across borders easier and is therefore most beneficial when trade is extensive.
2. Countries within an optimum currency area should have *similar business cycle patterns*. Because a common currency forces countries to have the same monetary policy, conflicts are minimized if booms and recessions in the various countries are closely linked and tend to occur at about the same time.

Even if countries have similar business cycle patterns, those patterns won't be exactly the same. Countries in an optimum currency area therefore need other ways to collectively adjust to economic shocks. The need for economic flexibility is reflected in the third and fourth criteria for an optimum currency area:

3. Countries within an optimum currency area will have high levels of *capital and labor mobility*; in other words, there are few barriers to flows of investment or of workers across borders. With high levels of mobility, resources can flow to countries within the optimum currency area where their marginal products are highest from regions where their marginal products are lowest; and
4. The fiscal systems within an optimum currency area will allow for the possibility of *fiscal transfers*, through which the countries or regions within the optimum currency area who are doing relatively better can help countries or regions that are doing worse (and which do not have the possibility of using an independent monetary policy to address their problems).

[16] See Robert A. Mundell, "A Theory of Optimum Currency Areas," *American Economic Review*, September 1961, pp. 657–665.

Application

Is Either the United States or Europe an Optimum Currency Area?

Based on our discussion of an optimum currency area, a natural question to ask is whether either the United States or Europe meets the criteria proposed by Mundell to qualify as an optimum currency area. All 50 states in the United States use the dollar, whereas 19 European countries share the use of the euro. But should they?

The United States has had a common currency since Alexander Hamilton integrated our fiscal and monetary systems. Looking at the evidence, it appears that the United States meets all four criteria for being an optimum currency area. Trade across states is quite extensive. Business cycles tend to hit the country as a whole, although there can be significant differences among states or regions. For example, in the recent recession the states—the "sand states"[17]—that had bigger increases in house prices before the recession tended to do worse as those prices collapsed. Capital and labor mobility are quite high as well. There are extensive fiscal transfers. Taxpayers in rich states indirectly subsidize poor states, as there is much less federal government spending in rich states than they pay in federal taxes. For example, in 2005 federal spending in Mississippi, which had the lowest per-capita income in the country, was $2.02 per $1 of federal taxes paid, and federal spending in Connecticut, which had the highest per-capita income in the country, was just $0.69 per $1 of federal taxes paid.[18] Also, the federal government rather than the states is responsible for Social Security, Medicare, and defense spending.

What about Europe? As in the United States, there is much trade within Europe. However, recently we have seen recessions hit Spain, Italy, and Greece much harder than Germany. Labor and capital are legally free to move between countries but language and cultural barriers mean that workers are less mobile. For example, workers are less likely to move from Greece to Germany than from Illinois to Texas. Fiscal transfers in Europe occur but are much more limited than in the United States because each country retains control of its own spending and taxation decisions. Thus Europe is less obviously an optimum currency area than the United States is, and a number of economists (such as Milton Friedman) pointed this out in advance of European monetary unification (see the Application "European Monetary Unification," for more on this topic).

Some of the problems of the euro predicted by the theory of optimum currency areas seem to have occurred. There were large differences in the recessions in different countries. For example, Germany's unemployment rate peaked at 8% in 2009, whereas the unemployment rate in the remaining countries using the euro averaged more than 14% as recently as 2013. As a result, Germany resisted aggressive monetary policy by the European Central Bank because it was not appropriate for Germany, which meant that monetary policy was too tight for other countries after the financial crisis. Countries such as Greece, Portugal, Ireland, Spain, and Italy all had major fiscal problems that prevented them from using fiscal policy as

[17] The sand states are Arizona, California, Florida, and Nevada.

[18] Tax Foundation 2007 report, *Federal Taxes Paid Versus Federal Spending Received by State, 1981–2005.*

(continued)

a substitute for monetary policy. Germany did not need and did not want more expansionary fiscal policy, and so fiscal policy in the euro zone was also relatively tight. The high unemployment rates persisted in many other countries, such as Spain, where the unemployment rate in June 2015 was 22.5% for all workers and 49.2% for young workers (younger than age 25). Thus labor mobility evidently did not do much to help reduce unemployment.

Although the United Kingdom was not part of the euro currency union, it did belong to the European Union (EU), in which the countries in Europe agreed to a number of common practices for immigration, open borders between each other, zero tariffs, and many common rules for business firms. In 2016, voters in the United Kingdom voted to leave the European Union. The consequences were significant because of the trade integration that had occurred between the UK and EU as well as the integration of businesses across the region. In completing its exit from the European Union in 2018, the UK was required to pay a significant penalty for leaving the union, and many businesses (especially in the banking sector) moved people out of London and into other parts of Europe. UK voters wanted out of the union because they thought the gains from increased trade with the rest of Europe did not exceed the costs that came from subscribing to rules on immigration and labor markets that were determined by the EU and not the UK. The withdrawal from the EU was not significant enough, however, to cause recessions in either the UK or the EU. But the withdrawal of the UK from the EU heightened worries about what might happen to the euro currency area if a country withdrew from using the euro currency.

These stresses in Europe have raised the question of whether the euro zone will survive. Even if it survives, will any of the countries that currently use the euro discontinue their use of the euro? One reason to think the euro will survive is the political motivations behind the euro project, especially the desire to enhance European political cooperation and integration. Another reason is that the transition back to individual currencies would be technically complicated and risky. How would new currencies be introduced? What would be done about existing contracts written in euros? So the future of the euro remains an open question.

Application

European Monetary Unification

In December 1991 at a summit meeting in Maastricht in the Netherlands, the member countries of the European Community (EC) adopted the Treaty on European Union, usually called the Maastricht Treaty. This treaty took effect in November 1993, after being ratified (with some resistance) by popular votes in the member countries. The motivation for the treaty was both economic and political. European countries felt that greater economic and political cooperation would lead to faster economic growth and help end the nationalism that contributed to World Wars I and II. One of the most important provisions of the treaty was that those member countries meeting certain criteria (including the achievement of low inflation rates and small government budget deficits) would adopt a common currency, to be called the euro. The common currency came into being on January 1, 1999. Eleven countries, with a collective population and GDP similar to those of the United States, joined the new currency union.[19]

The common monetary policy for the euro countries is determined by the Governing Council of the European Central Bank (ECB), a multinational institution located in Frankfurt, Germany. The Council includes six members of an Executive Board, appointed through a collective decision of the member countries, plus the governors of the national central banks of the member countries. Except through their representation on the Council, the national central banks, such as Germany's Bundesbank and the Bank of France, gave up their power to make monetary policy for their countries.

Although the European Central Bank was set up to be similar to the Federal Reserve in the United States, two important differences remain. First, U.S. banks are supervised by the Federal Reserve and other U.S. government banking regulators, whereas in Europe each individual country supervised its own banks until recently. Second, in the United States, a single federal government engages in fiscal policy, determining taxes and government spending; in Europe each of the 19 countries runs its own fiscal policy and there is no central control. Both of these differences became important as the euro system went through a series of crises that began in 2008.[20] One major improvement in the European banking system occurred in late 2014, when the European Central Bank was given regulatory authority over the largest banks in Europe.

The financial crisis that struck the United States beginning in 2008 had a strong impact all over the world, including Europe. Banks in both the United States and Europe lost large sums when their holdings of mortgage-related securities declined in value. Both the Federal Reserve in the United States and the European Central Bank responded to the crisis by reducing interest rates sharply and by increasing funds available to the economy. However, the two central banks differed in their handling of banks. In the United States, banks first received injections of capital from the U.S. government and later were required to raise additional capital from the private sector because the U.S. government and the Federal Reserve could issue regulations that covered every U.S. bank. However, banks in Europe were not recapitalized and remained weak because the European Central Bank had no control over the banking system, and national governments provided loans to banks in their own countries but did not require them to increase their capital. Because banks in many countries in Europe were weak, they did not lend very much. As a result, the economies of these countries did not grow very fast; thus the financial crisis directly led to a slowdown of the economies in Europe.

---

[19]Eight additional countries have subsequently joined the union, so now 19 countries have adopted the euro.

[20]For a broad overview of the problems in Europe, see Martin S. Feldstein, "The Euro and European Economic Conditions," National Bureau of Economic Research Working Paper No. 17617, November 2011; Jay C. Shambaugh, "The Euro's Three Crises," *Brookings Papers on Economic Activity*, Spring 2012, online at *www.brookings.edu/bpea-articles/the-euros-three-crises/*; and Philip R. Lane, "The European Sovereign Debt Crisis," *Journal of Economic Perspectives*, Summer 2012, pp. 49–68.

(*continued*)

When the euro monetary union was begun, the countries in the union were required to keep their government deficits smaller than 3% of their GDP. However, beginning in the mid-2000s, a number of the European countries began to violate the deficit requirement and run deficits larger than 3% of GDP. At first, financial markets ignored the growing deficits of these countries, but by spring 2010 investors began to recognize the danger that some countries (especially Greece, Spain, and Italy) might not be able to repay their loans. Interest rates began to rise in those countries relative to interest rates on bonds in the rest of Europe. As more information about the fiscal policy in various European countries was revealed, investors became concerned and began withdrawing funds from those countries. In addition, weaknesses at banks in those countries led to a downward spiral: the government had to provide loans to the weak banks, which in turn meant a higher government budget deficit, which caused interest rates to rise, which caused the banks to weaken further, and so on. In addition, many of the banks in Europe own bonds issued by countries that might not repay them, so a default in those countries would exacerbate the problems at banks. Thus the banking problems and the government deficit problems are intertwined.

Some countries in Europe, especially Germany, had low debt and relatively stronger banks, so their economies performed relatively well and they ran current account surpluses. Other countries had severe problems in their banks and have issued too much government debt; their interest rates rose and they ran current account deficits. If the countries were not tied together with the same currency, the exchange rate could adjust to help bring about balance: for example, the German currency could rise in value relative to the Greek currency, changing relative prices of goods, and helping to restore equilibrium. But because they share a common currency, the exchange rate cannot adjust.

CHAPTER SUMMARY

1. The nominal exchange rate is the number of units of foreign currency that can be obtained for one unit of domestic currency. The real exchange rate is the number of units of foreign goods that can be obtained for one unit of the domestic good. The idea that similar foreign and domestic goods should have the same prices in terms of the same currency is called purchasing power parity (*PPP*).
2. There are two major types of exchange rate systems: flexible- or floating-exchange-rate systems, in which the value of the nominal exchange rate is determined by market forces; and fixed-exchange-rate systems, in which the value of the exchange rate is officially set by a government or group of governments. In a flexible-exchange-rate system, an exchange rate increase is called an appreciation, and an exchange rate decrease is called a depreciation.
3. The real exchange rate is important because it affects net exports, or exports minus imports. Other factors held constant, a decline in the real exchange rate makes domestic goods cheaper relative to foreign goods and thus tends to increase net exports in the long run. Because a drop in the real exchange rate raises the cost of imports, however, it may cause net exports to fall in the short run before physical flows of exports and imports have had time to adjust. The characteristic pattern of the response of net exports to a drop in the real exchange rate—falling net exports in the short run but rising net exports in the long run—is called the J curve.
4. In a flexible-exchange-rate system, the value of the (nominal) exchange rate is determined by supply and demand in the foreign exchange market. Foreigners demand the domestic currency to buy domestic goods and assets. Domestic residents supply the domestic currency to obtain the foreign currency needed to buy foreign goods and assets.
5. Other factors held constant, an increase in domestic output leads domestic residents to demand more imports, reducing the country's net exports and depreciating its exchange rate. An increase in the domestic real interest rate makes domestic assets more attractive, increasing the demand for the domestic currency and appreciating the exchange rate; the higher exchange rate in turn reduces net exports. The effects of changes in foreign output and the foreign real interest rate on the domestic country's net exports and exchange rate are the opposite of the effects of changes in domestic output and the domestic real interest rate.
6. The *IS–LM* model for an open economy is similar to that for the closed economy. The principal difference is that, in the open-economy *IS–LM* model, factors (other than output or the real interest rate) that increase a country's net exports cause the *IS* curve to shift up. Among the factors that increase net exports are a rise in foreign output, an increase in the foreign real interest rate, and a shift in world demand toward the domestic country's goods. Economic shocks or policy changes are transmitted from one country to another by changes in net exports that lead to *IS* curve shifts.
7. In an open economy with flexible exchange rates, a fiscal expansion increases domestic output, domestic prices, and the domestic real interest rate, as in a closed economy. The effect on the exchange rate is ambiguous. The increase in output raises the demand for imported goods, which weakens the exchange rate, but the higher real interest rate makes domestic assets more attractive, which strengthens the exchange rate. Because increased output raises the demand for imports, net exports fall. The fiscal expansion is transmitted to the foreign country by the increase in demand for the foreign country's exports.
8. In an open economy with flexible exchange rates, changes in the money supply are neutral in the basic classical model. Changes in the money supply also are neutral in the long run in the Keynesian model. In the short run in the Keynesian model, however, a decrease in the domestic money supply reduces domestic output and raises the domestic real interest rate, causing the current real exchange rate to appreciate. Net exports by the domestic country increase, if the effect of lower output (which increases net exports) is stronger than the effect of the rise in the real exchange rate (which tends to reduce net exports). The monetary contraction is transmitted to the foreign country by the effect on the foreign country's net exports, which decline.
9. In a fixed-exchange-rate system, nominal exchange rates are officially determined. If the officially determined exchange rate is greater than the fundamental value of the exchange rate as determined by supply and demand in the foreign exchange market, the exchange rate is said to be overvalued. The central bank can maintain the exchange rate at an overvalued level for a time by using official reserves (such as gold or foreign-currency bank deposits) to buy its own currency in the foreign exchange market. A country that tries to maintain an overvalued exchange rate for too long will run out of reserves and be forced to devalue its currency. If financial

investors expect a devaluation, they may sell large quantities of domestic assets (a speculative run). A speculative run increases the supply of the domestic currency in the foreign exchange market and increases the rate at which the central bank must pay out its reserves.

10. To raise the fundamental value of its exchange rate, the central bank can tighten monetary policy. There is only one value of the domestic money supply at which the fundamental value of the exchange rate equals its officially fixed rate. With fixed exchange rates, individual countries aren't free to use expansionary monetary policies to fight recessions because such policies result in an overvalued exchange rate. However, a group of countries in a fixed-exchange-rate system can use expansionary monetary policies effectively if they coordinate their policies.

11. The advantages of a fixed-exchange-rate system are that it may promote economic and financial integration among countries and that it imposes discipline on the monetary policies of individual countries. A fixed-exchange-rate system won't work well if member countries have different macroeconomic policy goals or face different macroeconomic disturbances and thus are unable or unwilling to coordinate their monetary policies.

KEY TERMS

currency union, p. 555
devaluation, p. 525
exchange rate, p. 521
fixed-exchange-rate system, p. 521
flexible-exchange-rate system, p. 521
floating-exchange-rate system, p. 521
foreign exchange market, p. 521
fundamental value of the exchange rate, p. 549
inconvertible currency, p. 550
J curve, p. 529
nominal appreciation, p. 524
nominal depreciation, p. 524
nominal exchange rate, p. 521
optimum currency area, p. 556
overvalued exchange rate, p. 550
purchasing power parity (PPP), p. 525
real appreciation, p. 525
real depreciation, p. 525
real exchange rate, p. 523
relative purchasing power parity, p. 528
revaluation, p. 525
speculative run, p. 550
terms of trade, p. 528
undervalued exchange rate, p. 551

KEY EQUATIONS

$$e = \frac{e_{nom}P}{P_{For}} \qquad (13.1)$$

The real exchange rate, e, or the number of foreign goods that can be obtained for one domestic good, is defined in terms of the nominal exchange rate, e_{nom} (the amount of foreign currency that can be obtained for one unit of domestic currency), the domestic price level, P, and the foreign price level, P_{For}.

$$\frac{\Delta e_{nom}}{e_{nom}} = \frac{\Delta e}{e} + \pi_{For} - \pi \qquad (13.3)$$

The percentage change in the nominal exchange rate, $\Delta e_{nom}/e_{nom}$, equals the percentage change in the real exchange rate, $\Delta e/e$, plus the excess of the foreign rate of inflation over the domestic rate of inflation, $\pi_{For} - \pi$.

$$S^d - I^d = NX \qquad (13.4)$$

In an open economy, goods market equilibrium (the *IS* curve) requires that the excess of desired national saving over desired investment equal net exports. Equation (13.4) is equivalent to the condition that output, Y, must equal the aggregate demand for goods, $C^d + I^d + G + NX$, Eq. (13.5).

REVIEW QUESTIONS

1. Define *nominal exchange rate* and *real exchange rate*. How are changes in the real exchange rate and the nominal exchange rate related?
2. What are the two main types of exchange-rate systems? Currently, which type of system determines the values of the major currencies, such as the dollar, yen, and euro?
3. Define *purchasing power parity*, or *PPP*. Does *PPP* work well empirically? Explain.
4. What is the J curve? What explains the behavior of net exports represented by the J curve?
5. Why is the real exchange rate important in macroeconomic analysis? How does it affect net exports? Explain and give an example.

6. After seven years of decreasing and steadily low interest rates, the Federal Reserve Bank decided in December 2015 to make a policy change and increase the Federal Fund Rate. Assuming that all other factors are held constant, which effects would this change in real interest rates have had on the U.S. economy?
7. What are the factors that influence the open economy *IS* curve? How did China benefit from opening its economy?
8. How are net exports affected by expansionary fiscal policy? By expansionary monetary policy? What is the potential ambiguity in determining these effects?
9. What effects does expansionary monetary policy have on the nominal exchange rate in both the short and long run? Explain.
10. What is the *fundamental value* of a currency? What does it mean to say that a currency is *overvalued*? Why is an overvalued currency a problem? What can a country do about an overvalued currency?
11. Find a country that has fixed its exchange rate to a foreign currency. Describe its advantages and disadvantages for the economy.
12. Discuss the relative advantages and disadvantages of flexible exchange rates, fixed exchange rates, and a currency union.

NUMERICAL PROBLEMS

1. West Bubble makes ordinary soap bars that are sold for 5 guilders each. East Bubble makes deluxe soap bars that are sold for 100 florins each. The real exchange rate between West and East Bubble is two ordinary soap bars per deluxe soap bar.
   a. What is the nominal exchange rate between the two countries?
   b. During the following year West Bubble has 10% domestic inflation and East Bubble has 20% domestic inflation. Two ordinary soap bars are still traded for a deluxe soap bar. At the end of the year what has happened to the nominal exchange rate? Which country has had a nominal appreciation? Which has had a nominal depreciation?
2. Japan produces and exports only cameras, and Saudi Arabia produces and exports only barrels of oil. Initially, Japan exports 40 cameras to Saudi Arabia and imports 64 barrels of oil. The real exchange rate is 4 barrels of oil per camera. Neither country has any other trading partners.
   a. Initially, what is the real value of Japan's net exports, measured in terms of its domestic good? (*Hint:* You have to use the real exchange rate to express Japan's oil imports in terms of an equivalent number of cameras. Then calculate Japan's net exports as the number of cameras exported minus the real value of its imports in terms of cameras.)
   b. The real exchange rate falls to 3 barrels of oil per camera. Although the decline in the real exchange rate makes oil more expensive in terms of cameras, in the short run there is relatively little change in the quantities of exports and imports, as Japan's exports rise to 42 cameras and its imports fall to 60 barrels of oil. What has happened to the real value of Japan's net exports?
   c. In the longer run, quantities of exports and imports adjust more to the drop in the real exchange rate from 4 to 3, and Japan's exports rise to 45 cameras and its imports of oil fall to 54 barrels. What are Japan's real net exports now?
   d. Relate your answers to parts (*b*) and (*c*) to the J-curve concept.
3. Consider the following classical economy:

Desired consumption	$C^d = 300 + 0.5Y - 200r.$
Desired investment	$I^d = 200 - 300r.$
Government purchases	$G = 100.$
Net exports	$NX = 150 - 0.1Y - 0.5e.$
Real exchange rate	$e = 20 + 600r.$
Full-employment output	$\bar{Y} = 900.$

   a. What are the equilibrium values of the real interest rate, real exchange rate, consumption, investment, and net exports?
   b. Now suppose that full-employment output increases to 940. What are the equilibrium values of the real interest rate, real exchange rate, consumption, investment, and net exports?

c. Suppose that full-employment output remains at 940 and that government purchases increase to 132. What are the equilibrium values of the real interest rate, real exchange rate, consumption, investment, and net exports?

4. Consider the following Keynesian economy:

Desired consumption	$C^d = 200 + 0.6\,(Y - T) - 200r.$
Desired investment	$I^d = 300 - 300r.$
Taxes	$T = 20 + 0.2Y.$
Government purchases	$G = 152.$
Net exports	$NX = 150 - 0.08Y - 500r.$
Money demand	$L = 0.5Y - 200r.$
Money supply	$M = 924.$
Full-employment output	$\bar{Y} = 1000.$

a. What are the general equilibrium (that is, long-run) values of output, the real interest rate, consumption, investment, net exports, and the price level?

b. Starting from full employment, government purchases are increased by 62, to 214. What are the effects of this change on output, the real interest rate, consumption, investment, net exports, and the price level in the short run? In the long run?

c. With government purchases at their initial value of 152, net exports increase by 62 at any income and real interest rate so that $NX = 212 - 0.08Y - 500r$. What are the effects of this change on output, the real interest rate, consumption, investment, net exports, and the price level in the short run? In the long run? Compare your answer to that for part (*b*).

5. Consider the following classical economy:

$$AD \quad Y = 400 + 50\,M/P.$$

$$AS \quad Y = \bar{Y} = 1000.$$

This economy produces only wine, its output is measured in terms of wine, and its currency is francs. It trades with a country that produces only cheese, and the currency of that country is crowns. The real exchange rate, *e*, equals 5 wedges of cheese per bottle of wine. The foreign price level is 20 crowns per wedge of cheese, and the domestic money supply is 48 francs.

a. What is the domestic price level? What is the fundamental value of the (nominal) exchange rate?

b. Suppose that the domestic country fixes its exchange rate at 50 crowns per franc. Is its currency overvalued, undervalued, or neither? What will happen to the domestic central bank's stock of official reserve assets if it maintains the exchange rate at 50 crowns per franc?

c. Suppose that the domestic country wants a money supply level that equalizes the fundamental value of the exchange rate and the fixed rate of 50 crowns per franc. What level of the domestic money supply achieves this goal? (*Hint:* For the given real exchange rate and foreign price level, what domestic price level is consistent with the official rate? What domestic money supply level will yield this price level?)

6. (Appendix 13.B)

a. For the economy described in Numerical Problem 4, find the values of all the parameters of Eqs. (13.B.1), (13.B.2), and (13.B.3). Use Eqs. (13.B.8) and (13.B.9) to derive the open-economy *IS* curve for this economy.

b. Derive the *LM* curve for this economy.

c. Find output, the real interest rate, and the price level when the economy is in general equilibrium.

d. Derive the *AD* curve for this economy. Suppose that net exports increase by 62 at any given level of domestic output and the domestic interest rate. How is the *AD* curve affected?

e. Find the effect of the increase in net exports on output in this economy, assuming that the price level is fixed at the general equilibrium value you found in part (*c*). (*Hint:* This assumption is equivalent to assuming that the *SRAS* curve is horizontal.)

ANALYTICAL PROBLEMS

1. Recessions often lead to calls for protectionist measures to preserve domestic jobs. Suppose that a country that is in a recession imposes restrictions that sharply reduce the amount of goods imported by the country.

a. Using the Keynesian *IS–LM* model, analyze the effects of import restrictions on the domestic country's employment, output, real interest rate, and real exchange rate, keeping in mind that the country is initially in a recession.

b. What are the effects of the country's action on foreign employment, output, real interest rate, and real exchange rate? What happens if the foreign country retaliates by imposing restrictions on goods exported by the domestic country?

c. Suppose that the domestic economy is at full employment when it imposes restrictions on imports. Using the basic classical model without misperceptions, find the effects on the country's employment, output, real interest rate, and real exchange rate.

2. After the financial crisis reached Europe in 2008, a lot of EU citizens sold their euro investments and converted the money into Swiss francs or gold. Why did they do this? What impact did this have on the exchange rates of the euro and Swiss franc and the price of gold? Use the classical *IS–LM* model to describe the effects on the European economy and the Swiss economy.

3. The Greek government-debt crisis started in late 2009 and forced the European Union and the European Central Bank (ECB) to adapt their policies in order to save Greece from bankruptcy.

a. What was the effect of the problems in Greece and other struggling eurozone countries on the exchange rate of the euro and the eurozone's economy?

b. Which monetary policy instruments did the ECB use to stabilize the economy and create demand?

c. Suppose that Greece left the eurozone and introduced the Greek drachma again. Describe some advantages and disadvantages of this.

4. Use a diagram like that in Fig. 13.7a to analyze the effect on a country's net exports of a beneficial supply shock that temporarily raises full-employment output by 100 per person. Assume that the basic classical model applies so that income is always at its full-employment level.

a. Suppose that, in response to the temporary increase in income, the residents of the country do not change the amount they desire to spend at any real interest rate (on either domestic or foreign goods). What is the effect of the supply shock on the country's net exports? (*Hint:* What is the effect of the increase in income on the curve representing desired saving minus desired investment? What is the effect on the curve representing net exports?)

b. Now suppose that, in response to a temporary increase in income, the residents of the country increase their desired spending at any real interest rate by 100 per person. A portion of this increased spending is for foreign-produced goods. What is the effect on the country's net exports?

c. More difficult: If the increase in income is temporary, would the spending behavior assumed in part (*a*) or the spending behavior assumed in part (*b*) be more likely to occur? Based on your answer, do the results of this problem confirm or contradict the prediction of the model in Chapter 5 of the response of net exports to a supply shock? Explain.

5. Consider the theoretical impact of a trade war, with increased tariffs imposed by all major countries in the world. Suppose that the trade war's main effect is to reduce the benefits of comparative advantage, so that countries no longer specialize in goods as much as before and that therefore the production function shifts down because of the loss of the gains from trade. How is this likely to affect the curves in the *IS–LM* model? (*Hint:* You might begin the analysis by assuming that the trade war affects both imports and exports equally, so that there is no impact on net exports.) First, analyze the long-run impact of the trade war in a classical model, assuming that labor supply is not affected. Second, consider the short-run impact in a Keynesian model, in which the tariffs initially cause reduced investment by firms in exporting industries and reduced consumption by consumers facing lower expected future earnings.

▶ WORKING WITH MACROECONOMIC DATA

For data to use in these exercises, go to the Federal Reserve Bank of St. Louis FRED database at fred.stlouisfed.org.

1. The Bretton Woods fixed-exchange-rate system was terminated in 1972, and the main currencies of the world now follow a flexible exchange rate system governed by market forces.

a. Graph the eurozone's nominal exchange rate and real effective exchange rates from 1994 to the present. What are your observations when comparing the two curves? Would you say that fluctuations in the real exchange rate arise primarily from fluctuations in the nominal exchange rate or from changes in domestic and foreign price levels?

b. Higher real interest rates ought to strengthen the domestic currency (all else being equal) by making the domestic currency's assets more attractive. Graph the interest rate of government securities for the eurozone and compare it to the first graph on nominal and real effective exchange rates. Do you see the hypothesized relationship between the real interest rate and the exchange rates?

2. Using quarterly data since 1994, graph Japan's real exchange rate against its net exports as a fraction of GDP. Also create a scatterplot of these two variables and add a trend line for each. Is the theoretically predicted relationship of the real exchange rate and net exports visible in the figures?

3. Plot the exchange rate of the Hong Kong dollar relative to the U.S. dollar from January 1981 to the present. Was the Hong Kong dollar generally appreciating or depreciating relative to the U.S. dollar between 1981 and late 1983? What happened after 1983? Research and find an explanation for the value of the exchange rate after 1983.

4. Plot data on the exchange rate between the dollar and the euro, along with the FRED series for the trade-weighted broad exchange rate for the United States. How do the patterns of the two exchange rates differ? (*Hint:* Consider plotting the inverse of the exchange rate between the dollar and euro to see the relationship.)

Appendix 13.A

Worked-Out Numerical Exercise for the Open-Economy *IS–LM* Model

To help you work through the algebra needed for numerical problems in this chapter, here is a worked-out numerical exercise as an example for solving the open-economy *IS–LM* model.

Consider an economy that is described by the following equations:

$$C^d = 140 + 0.8(Y - T) - 200r$$

$$T = 400 + 0.1Y$$

$$I^d = 1000 - 700r$$

$$NX = 50 - 0.07Y + 0.15Y_{For} - 100r + 400r_{For}$$

$$L = 0.5Y - 1000i$$

$$\bar{Y} = 5000; G = 400; M = 489{,}900; \pi^e = 0.17; Y_{For} = 4000; r_{For} = 0.2; P_{sr} = 213.$$

Find the short-run and long-run equilibrium values of Y, P, r, T, C, I, NX, and i. To solve this problem, we follow these steps:

Step 1: Find the equation for the *IS* curve by using the goods market equilibrium condition. The goods market equilibrium condition is $Y = C^d + I^d + G + NX$. Substitute the equation for T into the equation for C^d from above. Then substitute the resulting equation and the equations for I^d and NX from above along with the values of G, Y_{For}, and r_{For} into $Y = C^d + I^d + G + NX$ to obtain:

$$Y = \{140 + 0.8[Y - (400 + 0.1Y)] - 200r\} + [1000 - 700r] + 400 + [50 - 0.07Y + (0.15 \times 4000) - 100r + (400 \times 0.2)].$$

Rearrange this equation as an equation for r in terms of Y:

$$Y = \{140 + 0.8Y - [(0.8 \times 400) + (0.8 \times 0.1Y)] - 200r\} + [1000 - 700r] + 400 + [50 - 0.07Y + 600 - 100r + 80],$$

so

$$Y = [140 + 0.8Y - 320 - 0.08Y - 200r] + [1000 - 700r] + 400 + [50 - 0.07Y + 600 - 100r + 80],$$

so

$$0.35Y = [140 - 320 + 1000 + 400 + 50 + 600 + 80] - (200 + 700 + 100)r,$$

so

$$1000r = 1950 - 0.35Y.$$

Therefore, $r = 1950/1000 - (0.35/1000)Y$, so

$$r = 1.95 - 0.00035Y.$$

This equation is the *IS* curve.

Step 2: Find the equation for the *LM* curve by using the asset market equilibrium condition.

a. First find the equation for the *LM* curve with an unspecified value of the price level. The asset market equilibrium condition equates real money supply to real money demand. Real money demand is given by $L = 0.5Y - 1000i = 0.5Y - 1000(r + \pi^e) = 0.5Y - 1000(r + 0.17)$, and real money supply is $M/P = 489{,}900/P$. In asset market equilibrium, $489{,}900/P = 0.5Y - 1000(r + 0.17)$, so $1000r = 0.5Y - 170 - 489{,}900/P$. Therefore, $r = (0.5/1000)Y - (170/1000) - (489{,}900/1000)/P$, so $r = 0.0005Y - 0.17 - 489.9/P$. This equation is the equation of the *LM* curve for an unspecified value of *P*.

b. Then find the equation for the *LM* curve when $P = P_{sr}$. Set $P = P_{sr} = 213$ in the *LM* curve to obtain $r = 0.0005Y - 0.17 - 489.9\ /\ 213$, so $r = 0.0005Y - 0.17 - 2.30$. Therefore, $r = 0.0005Y - 2.47$. This equation is the equation of the *LM* curve when $P = P_{sr}$.

Step 3: Find the short-run equilibrium.

a. Find the intersection of the *IS* and *LM* curves to find the short-run equilibrium values of *Y* and *r*. We have written the equations of the *IS* and *LM* curves so that the left side of each equation is simply *r*. Setting the right side of the *IS* curve equal to the right side of the *LM* curve yields $1.95 - 0.00035Y = 0.0005Y - 2.47$, so $4.42 = 0.00085Y$. Therefore, $Y = 4.42/0.00085 = 5200$. Now use the value of *Y* in either the *IS* or the *LM* curve. In the *IS* curve: $r = 1.95 - 0.00035Y = 1.95 - (0.00035 \times 5200) = 1.95 - 1.82 = 0.13$. In the *LM* curve: $r = 0.0005Y - 2.47 = (0.0005 \times 5200) - 2.47 = 2.60 - 2.47 = 0.13$.

b. Plug these equilibrium values of *Y* and *r* into other equations to find equilibrium values for *T*, *C*, *I*, *NX*, and *i*.

$T = 400 + 0.1Y = 400 + (0.1 \times 5200)$, so $T = 920$.

$C = 140 + 0.8(Y - T) - 200r = 140 + 0.8(5200 - 920) - (200 \times 0.13) = 140 + 3424 - 26 = 3538.$

$I = 1000 - 700r = 1000 - (700 \times 0.13) = 1000 - 91 = 909.$

$NX = 50 - 0.07Y + 0.15Y_{\text{For}} - 100r + 400r_{\text{For}} = 50 - (0.07 \times 5200) + (0.15 \times 4000) - (100 \times 0.13) + (400 \times 0.2) = 50 - 364 + 600 - 13 + 80 = 353.$

(Note that $C + I + G + NX = 3538 + 909 + 400 + 353 = 5200$, which equals *Y*.)

$$i = r + \pi^e = 0.13 + 0.17 = 0.3.$$

Step 4: Find the long-run equilibrium.

a. Use the fact that in long-run equilibrium, $Y = \bar{Y}$. Plug the equilibrium level of output into the *IS* equation to find the equilibrium real interest rate. Use $\bar{Y} = 5000$ and the *IS* equation, $r = 1.95 - 0.00035Y$, to obtain $r = 1.95 - (0.00035 \times 5000) = 1.95 - 1.75 = 0.20$.

b. Plug the equilibrium values of Y and r into other equations to find equilibrium values for T, C, I, NX, and i.

$$T = 400 + 0.1Y = 400 + (0.1 \times 5000), \text{ so } T = 900.$$

$$C = 140 + 0.8(Y - T) - 200r = 140 + 0.8(5000 - 900) - (200 \times 0.2) = 140 + 3280 - 40 = 3380.$$

$$I = 1000 - 700r = 1000 - (700 \times 0.2) = 1000 - 140 = 860.$$

$$NX = 50 - 0.07Y + 0.15Y_{\text{For}} - 100r + 400r_{\text{For}} = 50 - (0.07 \times 5000) + (0.15 \times 4000) - (100 \times 0.2) + (400 \times 0.2) = 50 - 350 + 600 - 20 + 80 = 360.$$

(Note that $C + I + G + NX = 3380 + 860 + 400 + 360 = 5000$, which equals Y.)

$$i = r + \pi^e = 0.20 + 0.17 = 0.37.$$

c. Plug the equilibrium values of Y and i into the money demand equation to obtain the value of real money demand, L. Then find the value of P that equates real money supply, M/P, with real money demand, L.

The money demand curve is $L = 0.5Y - 1000i = (0.5 \times 5000) - (1000 \times 0.37) = 2500 - 370 = 2130$. Setting real money supply equal to real money demand gives $489{,}900/P = 2130$, so $P = 489{,}900/2130 = 230$.

Here is an additional problem for calculating the real exchange rate and the nominal exchange rate in the economy above:

Problem: Suppose the real exchange rate e is given by $e = 67 - 0.005Y + 0.002Y_{\text{For}} + 100r - 300r_{\text{For}}$ and the foreign price level is $P_{\text{For}} = 115$ units of foreign currency per foreign good. Calculate the values of the real exchange rate and the nominal exchange rate for the long-run equilibrium given this information.

Solution: Plugging in the long-run equilibrium values of Y and r and the values of Y_{For} and r_{For} yields $e = 67 - (0.005 \times 5000) + (0.002 \times 4000) + (100 \times 0.2) - (300 \times 0.2) = 67 - 25 + 8 + 20 - 60 = 10$ foreign goods per domestic good. The nominal exchange rate, e_{nom}, is $e_{\text{nom}} = e \times P_{\text{For}}/P =$ (10 foreign goods per domestic good)$\times$(115 units of foreign currency per foreign good)/(230 units of domestic currency per domestic good), so $e_{\text{nom}} = 5$ units of foreign currency per unit of domestic currency.

Appendix 13.B

An Algebraic Version of the Open-Economy *IS–LM* Model

The *IS–LM* model for the open economy is basically the same as the closed-economy *IS–LM* model derived in Appendix 9.B, with the exception that the goods market equilibrium condition (the *IS* curve) is expanded to include net exports. The *LM* curve and the *FE* line are unchanged from previous analyses.

To derive the *IS* curve for the open economy, we begin with the equations describing desired consumption and desired investment, Eqs. (9.B.8) and (9.B.10):

$$C^d = c_0 + c_Y[Y - (t_0 + tY)] - c_r r, \qquad \textbf{(13.B.1)}$$

$$I^d = i_0 - i_r r. \qquad \textbf{(13.B.2)}$$

Equation (13.B.1) shows that desired consumption depends positively on disposable income, $Y - T$, and negatively on the real interest rate, r. (In Eq. 13.B.1 we used Eq. 9.B.9 to substitute for taxes, T.) Equation (13.B.2) states that desired investment depends negatively on the real interest rate, r. Other factors influencing desired consumption and desired investment are included in the constant terms c_0 and i_0, respectively.

In an open economy net exports also are a source of demand for domestic output. We assume that net exports are

$$NX = x_0 - x_Y Y + x_{YF} Y_{For} - x_r r + x_{rF} r_{For}, \qquad \textbf{(13.B.3)}$$

where x_0, x_Y, x_{YF}, x_r, and x_{rF} are positive numbers. According to Eq. (13.B.3), a country's net exports depend negatively on domestic income, Y (increased domestic income raises spending on imports), and positively on foreign income, Y_{For} (increased foreign income raises spending on exports). Net exports also depend negatively on the domestic real interest rate, r (a higher real interest rate appreciates the real exchange rate, making domestic goods relatively more expensive), and positively on the foreign real interest rate, r_{For} (a higher foreign real interest rate depreciates the domestic country's real exchange rate). Other factors influencing net exports, such as the qualities of domestic and foreign goods, are reflected in the constant term x_0 in Eq. (13.B.3).

The goods market equilibrium condition for an open economy, Eq. (13.5), is

$$Y = C^d + I^d + G + NX. \qquad \textbf{(13.B.4)}$$

The alternative version of the open-economy goods market equilibrium condition, $S^d = I^d + NX$, which is emphasized in the text, could be used equally well.

If we substitute the equations for desired consumption, Eq. (13.B.1), desired investment, Eq. (13.B.2), and net exports, Eq. (13.B.3), into the goods market equilibrium condition, Eq. (13.B.4), we get

$$Y = c_0 + c_Y(Y - t_0 - tY) - c_r r + i_0 - i_r r + G + x_0 - x_Y Y + x_{YF} Y_{For} - x_r r + x_{rF} r_{For}. \quad \textbf{(13.B.5)}$$

Collecting the terms that multiply Y on the left side yields

$$[1 - (1 - t)c_Y + x_Y]Y = c_0 + i_0 + G - c_Y t_0 + x_0 + x_{YF} Y_{For} + x_{rF} r_{For} - (c_r + i_r + x_r)r. \quad \textbf{(13.B.6)}$$

Equation (13.B.6) relates output, Y, to the real interest rate, r, that clears the goods market and thus defines the open-economy *IS* curve. To put Eq. (13.B.6) in a form that is easier to interpret graphically, we rewrite it with r on the left side and Y on the right side to obtain

$$r = \alpha'_{IS} - \beta'_{IS} Y, \quad \text{open-economy } IS \text{ curve.} \quad \textbf{(13.B.7)}$$

Here, α'_{IS} and β'_{IS} are positive numbers defined as

$$\alpha'_{IS} = \frac{c_0 + i_0 + G - c_Y t_0 + x_0 + x_{YF} Y_{For} + x_{rF} r_{For}}{c_r + i_r + x_r}, \quad \textbf{(13.B.8)}$$

and

$$\beta'_{IS} = \frac{1 - (1 - t)c_Y + x_Y}{c_r + i_r + x_r}. \quad \textbf{(13.B.9)}$$

If there are no net exports, so that $x_0 = x_Y = x_{YF} = x_r = x_{rF} = 0$, the coefficients α'_{IS} and β'_{IS} reduce to the coefficients of the closed-economy *IS* curve, α_{IS} and β_{IS} (compare Eqs. 13.B.8 and 13.B.9 to Eqs. 9.B.15 and 9.B.16).

We use the open-economy *IS* curve equation, Eq. (13.B.7), to confirm the three points made about the curve in the text. First, it slopes downward (the slope of the *IS* curve is $-\beta'_{IS}$, which is negative). Second, any factor that shifts the closed-economy *IS* curve also shifts the open-economy *IS* curve (any factor that changes the intercept α_{IS} also changes the intercept α'_{IS} in the same direction). Finally, for a given output and real interest rate, any factor that increases net exports shifts the open-economy *IS* curve up. That is, an increase in Y_{For} or r_{For}, or some other change that increases the demand for net exports as reflected in an increase in x_0, raises the intercept term α'_{IS} and thus shifts the *IS* curve up.

General equilibrium in the open-economy *IS–LM* model is determined as in the closed-economy model, except that the open-economy *IS* curve (Eq. 13.B.7) replaces the closed-economy *IS* curve (Eq. 9.B.14). Similarly, classical and Keynesian *AD–AS* analyses in the open economy are the same as in the closed economy (Appendix 9.B), except that the coefficients α_{IS} and β_{IS} in the equation for the aggregate demand curve, Eq. (9.B.24), are replaced by their open-economy analogues, α'_{IS} and β'_{IS}.

For values of output, Y, the real interest rate, r, and the price level, P, determined by the open-economy *IS–LM* or *AD–AS* model, exchange rates can be determined from

$$e = e_0 - e_Y Y + e_{YF} Y_{For} + e_r r - e_{rF} r_{For}, \quad \textbf{(13.B.10)}$$

where e_0, e_Y, e_{YF}, e_r, and e_{rF} are positive numbers, and

$$e_{\text{nom}} = \frac{eP_{\text{For}}}{P}. \tag{13.B.11}$$

According to Eq. (13.B.10), an increase in foreign income, Y_{For}, or the domestic real interest rate, r—either of which raises the demand for the domestic currency in the foreign exchange market—appreciates the real exchange rate, e. Also, an increase in domestic income, Y, or the foreign real interest rate, r_{For}—either of which increases the supply of domestic currency in the foreign exchange market—depreciates the real exchange rate. Equation (13.B.11), which is the same as Eq. (13.6), states that the nominal exchange rate, e_{nom}, depends on the real exchange rate, e, and the foreign and domestic price levels, P_{For} and P.

To illustrate the use of Eqs. (13.B.10) and (13.B.11), let's consider the effects of a monetary expansion in the Keynesian model. In the short run an increase in the money supply raises domestic output, Y, lowers the domestic real interest rate, r, and leaves the domestic price level, P, unchanged. For these changes, Eqs. (13.B.10) and (13.B.11)—holding constant foreign output, Y_{For}, and the foreign real interest rate, r_{For}—imply a lower real exchange rate, e, and a lower nominal exchange rate, e_{nom} (both a real and a nominal depreciation). In the long run money is neutral, so Y and r return to their original levels. Equation (13.B.10) indicates therefore that the real exchange rate, e, also returns to its original value in the long run. However, a monetary expansion leads to a long-run increase in the domestic price level, P. Hence Eq. (13.B.11) shows that the nominal exchange rate, e_{nom}, also depreciates in the long run.

14

Monetary Policy and the Federal Reserve System

Learning Objectives

14.1 Explain how the nation's money supply is determined.

14.2 Describe the policy tools used by the Federal Reserve to control the money supply.

14.3 Explain the Fed's setting of monetary policy targets.

14.4 Discuss the difficulties of making monetary policy.

14.5 Discuss whether monetary policy should be conducted by rules or discretion.

Monetary policy—the government's decisions about how much money to supply to the economy—is one of the two principal tools available for affecting macroeconomic behavior. (The other, fiscal policy, is discussed in Chapter 15.) Monetary policy decisions have widespread implications for the economy. The macroeconomic models that we have presented predict that changes in the money supply will affect nominal variables such as the price level and the nominal exchange rate. In addition, theories that allow for nonneutrality (including the extended classical theory with misperceptions and the Keynesian theory) imply that, in the short run, monetary policy also affects real variables such as real GDP, the real interest rate, and the unemployment rate. Because monetary policy has such pervasive economic effects, the central bank's announcements and actions are closely monitored by the media, financial market participants, and the general public.

In this chapter we look more closely at monetary policy, concentrating first on the basic question of how the nation's money supply is determined. We demonstrate that, although a nation's central bank (the Federal Reserve System in the United States) can exert strong influence over the level of the money supply, the money supply also is affected by the banking system's behavior and the public's decisions. We then explain why the Federal Reserve and many other central banks now target interest rates rather than the money supply.

In the second part of the chapter, we explore the question: How should the central bank conduct monetary policy? Not surprisingly, because of classical and Keynesian differences over the effects of monetary policy and the desirability of trying to smooth the business cycle (Chapters 10 and 11), the question is controversial. Keynesians usually argue that monetary authorities should have considerable latitude to try to offset cyclical fluctuations. Opposing the Keynesian view, both classical economists and a group of economists called *monetarists* believe that monetary policy shouldn't be left to the discretion of the central bank but instead should be governed by simple rules. Although establishing rules for monetary policy might seem to tie policymakers' hands unnecessarily, monetarists and classicals argue that the use of rules would lead to a more stable and less inflationary economy in the long run. After examining the arguments for and against the use of rules, we discuss the effectiveness of rules-based monetary policies in the United States and other countries. We also discuss how the debate about rules is related to questions of how monetary policymaking institutions should be designed. For example, should the central bank be largely independent from the rest of the government, or should it be more directly controlled by the executive and legislative branches?

14.1 Principles of Money Supply Determination

Explain how the nation's money supply is determined.

How is the nation's money supply determined? So far we have assumed that the money supply, M, is controlled directly by the central bank. Although this assumption is a useful simplification, it isn't literally true. The central bank's control of the money supply is only indirect and depends to some extent on the structure of the economy.

Most generally, three groups affect the money supply: the central bank, depository institutions, and the public.

1. In nearly all countries the **central bank** is the government institution responsible for monetary policy.[1] Examples of central banks are the Federal Reserve System in the United States, the European Central Bank, and the Bank of Japan.
2. **Depository institutions** are privately owned banks and thrift institutions (such as savings and loan associations) that accept deposits from and make loans directly to the public. We refer to depository institutions as banks, for short.
3. The public includes every person or firm (except banks) that holds money, either as currency and coin or as deposits in banks—in other words, virtually the whole private economy outside the banking system.

Let's consider a simplified example of the U.S. economy, where the currency is dollars and the central bank is the Federal Reserve (the "Fed," for short), though our discussion in this section is more general and could apply to almost any currency and any central bank.

Suppose the Fed's balance sheet looks like this:

Federal Reserve Bank

Assets		**Liabilities**	
Securities	\$ 900	Currency held by nonbank public	\$ 700
Gold	100	Vault cash held by banks	100
		Reserve deposits	200
Total assets	**\$1000**	**Total liabilities**	**\$1000**

On the left side of the balance sheet are the Fed's assets—what it owns or is owed. In this case, the assets are securities and gold. Typically, securities are U.S. Treasury bills, notes, and bonds, which are liabilities of the U.S. Treasury and assets of the Fed, just as, say, U.S. Treasury bonds held by an investor are liabilities of the U.S. Treasury and assets of the investor. During the recent financial crisis, the Fed broadened the scope of the securities on its balance sheet to include mortgage-backed securities and loans to financial firms. On the right side of the balance sheet are the Fed's liabilities—what it owes to others. Currency issued by the Fed and held either by the nonbank public or in vaults of private-sector banks is a debt obligation of the Fed and is thus entered as a liability in the Fed's balance sheet. Reserve deposits are deposit accounts at the Fed that are owned by banks. These deposits are liabilities of the Fed and assets of private-sector banks. The sum of reserve deposits and currency (including both currency held by the nonbank public and vault cash held by banks) is

[1]Most industrialized countries established central banks in the nineteenth century or early twentieth century. Prior to the establishment of central banks, national treasury departments often were responsible for currency issue and other matters pertaining to the money supply.

called the **monetary base**, or, equivalently, **high-powered money**. The monetary base in this example is $1000.

Next, consider the balance sheets of banks in the private sector. We will combine all the banks together. Suppose their consolidated balance sheet looks like this:

Consolidated Balance Sheet of Banks			
Assets		**Liabilities**	
Vault cash	$ 100	Deposits	$3000
Reserve deposits	200		
Loans	2700		
Total assets	**$3000**	**Total liabilities**	**$3000**

The banks' assets consist of vault cash of $100 (the same $100 that appears as a liability on the Fed's balance sheet), reserve deposits of $200 (the same $200 that appears as a liability on the Fed's balance sheet), plus loans of $2700 that banks have extended to the nonbank public. The banks' liabilities consist of $3000 of deposits held by the nonbank public. For instance, if you have a checking account at your local bank, that checking account is one of your assets and it appears on your bank's balance sheet as a liability.

Liquid assets held by banks to meet the demands for withdrawals by depositors or to pay the checks drawn on depositors' accounts are called **bank reserves**. Bank reserves comprise currency held by banks in their vaults and deposits held by banks at the Fed, so bank reserves in this example total $300 ($100 of vault cash plus $200 of reserve deposits). Until 2008, banks in the United States did not earn any interest on their reserves: Currency held as vault cash, of course, does not earn interest, and the Fed did not pay interest on reserve deposits that banks held at the Fed. But in October 2008, the Fed began to pay interest on reserves, as we discuss in more detail in Section 14.2. When banks have creditworthy customers seeking to borrow money from them, they can generally earn more income by lending some of their assets to these borrowers rather than holding all of their assets as reserves. Because banks lend out some of their deposits, the reserves held by a bank equal only a fraction of its outstanding deposits. In our example, the **reserve–deposit ratio**, or reserves divided by deposits, equals 10% because reserves equal $300 and deposits equal $3000. A banking system in which the reserve–deposit ratio is less than 1 is called **fractional reserve banking.** The alternative to fractional reserve banking is **100% reserve banking**, in which bank reserves equal 100% of deposits. Under 100% reserve banking, banks are nothing more than a safekeeping service for the public's currency. If the central bank pays zero or very low interest on reserve deposits, the only way that banks could cover their expenses and make a profit under 100% reserve banking would be to charge depositors a fee for holding their money for them (that is, to pay negative interest on deposits).

Open-Market Transactions

Suppose the Fed wanted to increase the amount of money in the economy. It could do so by buying securities from private investors in the bond market. For example, suppose that the Fed buys $100 of securities from an investor who has a bank account at Barclays Bank. The Fed receives $100 in securities from the investor and pays for these securities by increasing Barclays Bank's deposit account at the Fed by $100. Barclays Bank then increases the investor's account balance at Barclays

Bank by $100. As a result of this transaction, the securities on the left side of the Fed's balance sheet increase by $100 to $1000 and banks' reserve deposits on the right side of the Fed's balance sheet increase by $100 to $300. On the asset side of the consolidated balance sheet of banks, reserve deposits rise by $100, and on the liabilities side, deposits rise by $100 to capture the additional $100 in the investor's deposit account. After all of these transactions, the Fed's and the banks' balance sheets are as follows:

Federal Reserve Bank

Assets		**Liabilities**	
Securities	$1000	Currency held by nonbank public	$ 700
Gold	100	Vault cash held by banks	100
		Reserve deposits	300
Total assets	**$1100**	**Total liabilities**	**$1100**

Consolidated Balance Sheet of Banks

Assets		**Liabilities**	
Vault cash	$ 100	Deposits	$3100
Reserve deposits	300		
Loans	2700		
Total assets	**$3100**	**Total liabilities**	**$3100**

As the bankers examine their balance sheets, they note that their reserves (vault cash plus reserve deposits) are $400, whereas their deposits equal $3100. If the banks want to maintain a reserve–deposit ratio of 10% (which was its value before the purchase of bonds by the Fed), they would need only 0.1 × $3100, or $310 of reserves. Since they have $400 in reserves, they can lend $400 − $310 = $90 to earn additional interest.

Suppose that Barclays Bank lends $90 to Anne, who uses the loan to buy some goods from Paul. Paul then deposits the $90 in his bank. (We are assuming at this point that Paul wants to hold all the additional funds as bank deposits.) The $90 loan to Anne will increase the loans on the banks' balance sheet by $90 to $2790, and when Paul deposits the $90 in his bank, the banks' deposits increase by $90 to $3190. (The reserves of the banking system are not changed, as the $90 is essentially transferred from Anne's bank to Paul's bank.) At this point the consolidated balance sheet of all the banks is:

Consolidated Balance Sheet of Banks

Assets		**Liabilities**	
Vault cash	$ 100	Deposits	$3190
Reserve deposits	300		
Loans	2790		
Total assets	**$3190**	**Total liabilities**	**$3190**

The process doesn't stop here. Looking at their balance sheets after this latest round of loans and deposits, the bankers find that their reserves ($400) still exceed 10% of their deposits, or 0.10 × $3190 = $319. So yet another round of loans and deposits of loaned funds will occur.

This process of **multiple expansion of loans and deposits**, in which fractional reserve banking increases an economy's loans and deposits, will stop only when the reserves of the banking system equal 10% of its deposits. The reserves of the banks always equal $400 at the end of each round,[2] so the process will stop when total bank deposits equal $400/0.10, or $4000. At this final point the consolidated balance sheet of the banks is:

Consolidated Balance Sheet of Banks			
Assets		**Liabilities**	
Vault cash	$ 100	Deposits	$4000
Reserve deposits	300		
Loans	3600		
Total assets	**$4000**	**Total liabilities**	**$4000**

At this final stage, the ratio of reserves to deposits equals the ratio desired by banks (10%). No further expansion of loans and deposits will occur after this point.

Notice that the purchase of $100 in securities by the Fed led to additional deposits in the banking system of $1000 and additional loans of $900. Recall (Chapter 7) that a purchase of assets by the central bank is called an **open-market purchase**.[3] It increases the monetary base and thus the money supply. A sale of assets to the public by the central bank is called an **open-market sale**. It reduces the monetary base and the money supply. Open-market purchases and sales collectively are called *open-market operations*. Open-market operations are the most direct way for central banks to change their national money supplies.

Bank Runs

Fractional reserve banking works on the assumption that outflows and inflows of reserves will roughly balance, and in particular that a large fraction of a bank's depositors will never want to withdraw their funds at the same time. If a large number of depositors attempt to withdraw currency simultaneously (more than 10% of the bank's deposits in the example shown earlier in the section "Open Market Transactions"), the bank will run out of reserves and be unable to meet all its depositors' demands for cash.

Historically in the United States, there have been episodes in which rumors circulated that a particular bank had made some bad loans and was at risk of becoming bankrupt. On the principle of "better safe than sorry," the bank's depositors lined up to withdraw their money. From the depositors' perspective, withdrawal avoided the risk that the bank would fail and not be able to pay off depositors in full. A large-scale, panicky withdrawal of deposits from a bank is called a **bank run**. Even if the rumors about the bank's loans proved untrue, a large enough run could exhaust the bank's reserves and force it to close.[4]

To prevent future bank runs from occurring, the Federal Deposit Insurance Corporation (FDIC) was established in 1933 to provide deposit insurance. Deposit insurance guarantees that depositors will not lose the money they hold in an insured bank account (up to some limit) even if the bank were to go bankrupt. As

[2]The reserves held by the banking system remain unchanged at $400 at the end of each round because, in this example, we have assumed that the proceeds of any loan are fully redeposited in the banking system so that the public does not increase its holdings of currency.

[3]The term *open-market* means that the central bank's transactions take place in regular asset markets in which government securities dealers compete with each other to trade securities with the central bank.

[4]To stop a run, a bank had to convince customers that it was "sound"—financially solvent—and had plenty of funds available. This was Jimmy Stewart's strategy in the movie *It's A Wonderful Life*.

a result, depositors would have no incentive to start a bank run. The FDIC obtains the funds needed to provide such insurance by charging an insurance premium to banks. Further, the Federal government effectively stands behind the FDIC, so that if in a crisis the FDIC fund were to become exhausted, the government would provide any funds needed to prevent losses to depositors on insured deposits, as it did in the late 1980s and early 1990s. As a result of deposit insurance, when the financial crisis hit in 2008,[5] people poured money *into* banks, where their money was insured, instead of out of banks, as occurred during the Great Depression.

14.2 Monetary Control in the United States

Describe the policy tools used by the Federal Reserve to control the money supply.

The principles of money supply determination we described in Section 14.1 apply fairly generally to central banks and banking systems. In this section we focus on specific institutional details of the central bank in the United States, which is the Federal Reserve System.

The Federal Reserve System

The central bank of the United States is called the Federal Reserve System, or the Fed for short. It was created by the Federal Reserve Act in 1913 and began operation in 1914. One of Congress's primary motives in establishing the Fed was the hope that a central bank would help eliminate the severe financial crises (combinations of stock market crashes, business failures, and banking panics) that had periodically afflicted the United States before World War I. Ironically, the most severe financial crisis in U.S. history occurred in 1930–1933, barely a decade and a half after the creation of the Fed.

The Federal Reserve Act established a system of twelve regional Federal Reserve Banks, each associated with a geographical area called a Federal Reserve district. The locations of the twelve Federal Reserve Banks are shown in Figure 14.1. Technically, the regional Federal Reserve Banks are owned by the private banks within the district that are members of the Federal Reserve System. All federally chartered private banks are members of the Federal Reserve System, and state-chartered banks may join. Whether an individual bank is a member of the system has ceased to mean much, however, because Congress passed legislation in 1980 extending the responsibilities and privileges of member banks to all banks. Before 1980 member banks faced stricter regulatory requirements than nonmembers but also had access to some useful services (such as check-clearing services).

The leadership of the Federal Reserve System is provided by the **Board of Governors of the Federal Reserve System** (also called the Federal Reserve Board), located in Washington, D.C. The board consists of seven governors, appointed by the President of the United States to staggered 14-year terms, with one of the governors beginning a new term every other year. The President appoints one board member to be the chairman of the Board of Governors for a term of four years. Besides having considerable influence over monetary policy, the chairman is an important figure in financial markets (the Fed has partial responsibility for

[5]During the financial crisis, the Federal government increased the FDIC limit on insured deposits to $250,000 from $100,000, which was the FDIC limit before the crisis. In addition, certain accounts had no limit on the amount covered by deposit insurance from October 2008 to December 2010 under the FDIC's Temporary Liquidity Guarantee Program.

FIGURE 14.1

Location of the Federal Reserve Banks

The twelve regional Federal Reserve Banks are located in twelve major cities in the United States. The Board of Governors of the Federal Reserve System is located in Washington, D.C.

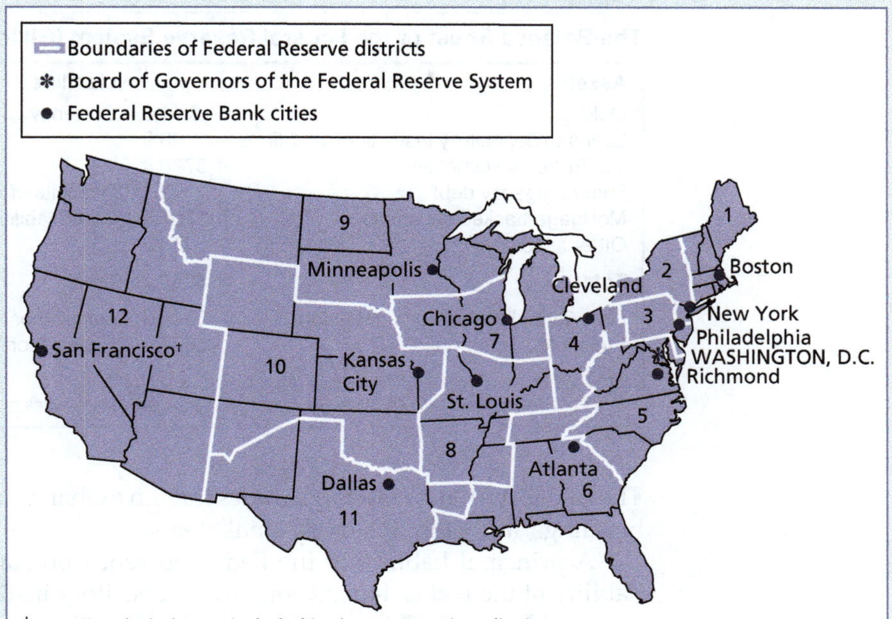

†Hawaii and Alaska are included in the San Francisco district.

regulating securities markets and the banking sector) and often is consulted by Congress and the President on matters of national economic policy.

Decisions about monetary policy are the responsibility of the **Federal Open Market Committee (FOMC)**. The FOMC consists of the seven governors, the president of the Federal Reserve Bank of New York, and four of the presidents of the other regional Federal Reserve Banks, who serve on the FOMC on a rotating basis.[6] The FOMC meets about eight times a year to review the state of the economy and to plan the conduct of monetary policy. The FOMC can meet more frequently (in person or by conference call) if developments in the economy seem to warrant discussion. FOMC decisions to tighten or ease monetary policy are announced immediately after the meeting and are closely monitored by the press, public, and financial markets.

The Federal Reserve's Balance Sheet

The balance sheet of the Federal Reserve System (all Federal Reserve Banks taken together) as of June 2022 is shown in Table 14.1. The Fed's largest asset is its holdings of U.S. Treasury securities, or government bonds. The bonds are assets of the Fed and liabilities of the U.S. Treasury. It also owns gold and makes loans, which count as Fed assets. During the financial crisis of 2008, the Fed began purchasing a variety of assets other than Treasury securities, including bonds issued by Federal agencies and mortgage-backed securities. During the pandemic in 2020, the Fed began making loans to business firms through the Paycheck Protection Program.

[6]The other seven presidents of Federal Reserve Banks attend each FOMC meeting and participate fully in the discussions but do not vote on the policy action.

TABLE 14.1

The Balance Sheet of the Federal Reserve System (Billions of Dollars)

Assets		Liabilities	
Gold	$ 11.0	Currency	2278.9
Loans to depository institutions and firms	20.9		
US Treasury securities	5770.4		
Federal agency debt	2.3	Deposits of depository institutions	3322.0
Mortgage-backed securities	2707.4	Other liabilities and net worth	3364.3
Other assets	453.2		
Total	**8965.2**	**Total**	**8965.2**
Less Other liabilities and net worth	3364.3	*Less* Other liabilities and net worth	3364.3
Equals Monetary base	5600.9	*Equals* Monetary base	5600.9

Note: Numbers may not add to totals shown owing to rounding.
Source: Federal Reserve Statistical Release H.4.1. Data are for the week ending June 1, 2022.

The category "Other assets" includes foreign exchange, the value of Federal Reserve buildings, and other relatively small items.

A principal liability of the Fed is currency outstanding. The other principal liability of the Fed is deposits made by depository institutions, such as banks, savings and loan associations, and mutual savings banks. In accepting deposits from depository institutions, the Fed acts as the "banks' bank." Depository institutions make deposits at the Fed because it is a convenient way of holding reserves.

Open-Market Operations

If the Fed wants to change the money supply, one of its primary tools is open-market operations. To increase the money supply, for example, the Fed could conduct an open-market purchase, in which it would buy U.S. Treasury securities from government securities dealers. As we discussed in Section 14.1, this open-market purchase would increase the monetary base, and the money supply would increase as well. To decrease the money supply, the Fed could conduct an open-market sale, in which it would sell U.S. Treasury securities to government securities dealers, which would reduce the monetary base.

When the Fed engages in open-market operations, the transactions affect the interest rate in the market for bank reserves. A bank can borrow reserves from other banks that have extra reserves. These borrowed funds are called federal funds, or fed funds, and the interest rate charged on these loans is the **federal funds rate**, also called the **fed funds rate**. Despite its name, the fed funds rate is not an interest rate charged by the Fed; it is the interest rate charged on loans from one bank to another. Figure 14.2 shows how the fed funds rate has changed over time from 1979 to 2022. Generally, the fed funds rate moves in line with other short-term interest rates, such as the three-month Treasury bill interest rate shown in the graph. But the fed funds rate is particularly important, as we discuss in the next section, because the Fed often chooses to target it in conducting monetary policy.

Reserve Requirements

Although open-market operations are the main way that the Fed affects the money supply, it has three other methods available: changes in reserve requirements, discount window lending, and changes in the interest rate the Fed pays on reserve deposits held by banks.

FIGURE 14.2

The federal funds rate and three-month Treasury bill interest rate, 1979–2022

Banks can borrow reserves from other banks and pay the federal funds rate. The Fed often implements monetary policy by using open-market operations to affect the fed funds rate. The fed funds rate moves in a similar fashion with other short-term interest rates, such as the three-month Treasury bill interest rate shown here.

Source: Federal Reserve Board of Governors, downloaded from FRED database, Federal Reserve Bank of St. Louis, *fred.stlouisfed.org*, series *FEDFUNDS* (fed funds rate) and *TB3MS* (three-month Treasury bill interest rate).

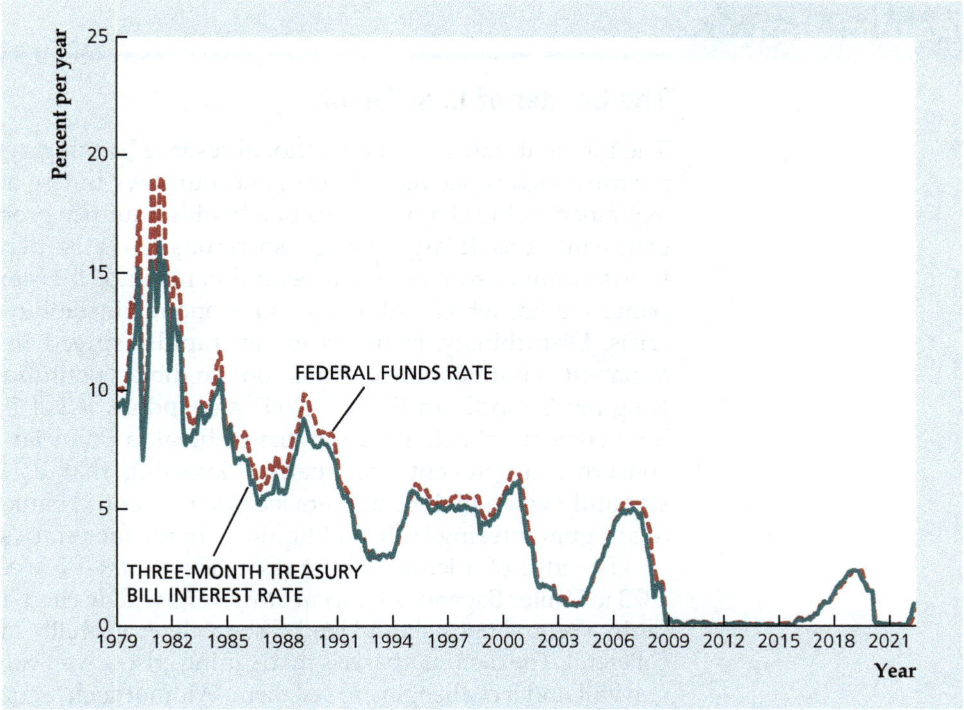

The Fed has the authority to require banks to keep reserves (either on deposit at the Fed or in the form of vault cash) of a certain percentage of the amount of the transactions deposits held at the bank. The Fed could influence the money supply by changing this reserve requirement, but seldom does so because changes in reserve requirements have a large impact on banks' profitability and the money supply. As a result, the Fed prefers to use its other instruments. From 1992 to 2020, the Fed did not change reserve requirements at all. In March 2020, the Fed set reserve requirements to zero, though it still has the authority and infrastructure to set a positive reserve requirement in the future.

Discount Window Lending

A principal reason that the Fed was created was to try to reduce severe financial crises. The Fed was supposed to accomplish this goal mainly by acting as a "lender of last resort"—that is, by standing ready to lend reserves to banks that need cash to meet depositors' demands or reserve requirements. For example, during the financial crisis in 2008, the Fed lent $400 billion to banks through the discount window. The Fed's lending of reserves to banks is called **discount window lending**, and the interest rate it charges for lending reserves is called the **discount rate**. For more on the function of a central bank as a lender of last resort, see the Application "The Lender of Last Resort."

When the Fed lends reserves to banks through the discount window, it changes the monetary base. For example, if banks borrow $1 billion from the Fed and deposit these borrowings in their reserve accounts at the Fed, the Fed's balance sheet is affected in two ways: (1) on the asset side, loans to depository institutions rise by $1 billion; and (2) on the liability side, deposits held by depository institutions also rise by $1 billion, increasing the monetary base by $1 billion. Thus

Application

The Lender of Last Resort

The inherent nature of the fractional reserve banking system carries the potential for mismatches between inflows and outflows unless adequate care is taken. As explained in the chapter, news of a bank's liquidity problems, even if untrue, can start bank runs. If large enough, such runs can cause depositors to withdraw their funds simultaneously. When several banks face the same problem concurrently, panic sets in, which culminates in economic instability and a systemic banking crisis. Disturbingly, some crises can rapidly spread to other countries with no apparent vulnerabilities. Runs on credible institutions such as the United Kingdom's Northern Rock in 2007 and India's ICICI Bank in 2008 demonstrate how customers' actions can make or break a financial institution over liquidity concerns. To prevent such panics, knowing that banks will continue to run smoothly when their customers feel secure, central banks stand as the *lender of last resort*, guaranteeing sufficient liquidity in the monetary system.

The idea of a lender of last resort is not new—it was discussed as far back as 1873 in Walter Bagehot's *Lombard Street*.[7] His widely cited dictum is that, in a financial crisis, a central bank should lend cash freely at a penalty rate in exchange for "good" collateral. The dictum's basis is that, during crises, even banks with marketable collateral will find it challenging to sell them. Without such assurances of liquidity support, even solvent banks will have no option but to sell their marketable assets at highly deflated prices, thereby further depleting their financial base and worsening the crisis. It may be difficult to distinguish bankruptcy from illiquidity, but the broad spirit of Bagehot's principle is that a central bank should do what is necessary to curb a crisis while protecting itself against losses to the maximum extent possible. Being higher than normal, penalty interest rates should deter unnecessary use of the mechanism.

There are recent examples of central banks taking a firm stance as lenders of last resort and thereby averting exacerbated bank runs. In September 2007, rumors of a crisis surrounding Northern Rock resulted in queues at many of its 76 branches, and the firm's shares plunged by more than 40%. Depositors' confidence was only restored when Chancellor Alistair Darling agreed to guarantee all deposits held by Northern Rock and the Bank of England said it would inject £10 billion into the money markets. In September 2008, ICICI Bank, India's largest private-sector bank, also faced runs across the country on the basis of rumors that it might fail. The Reserve Bank of India had to step in as the lender of last resort, issuing a statement that there was enough liquidity at ICICI Bank and that they had arranged for the provision of adequate cash to guarantee customers' deposits.

[7]Walter Bagehot, *Lombard Street*, London: Henry S. King & Co., 1873.

an increase in borrowing from the discount window raises the monetary base, and a decrease in discount window borrowing lowers the monetary base.

Changes in the discount rates can be used by the Fed to influence the money supply.[8] An increase in the discount rate makes borrowing at the discount window more costly. If banks reduce their borrowing in response to the higher discount rates, the monetary base falls.

[8]There are actually two different discount rates. The primary credit discount rate applies to banks in good condition. The secondary credit discount rate is higher than the primary credit discount rate and is charged to banks that are in worse condition; such banks will also be subject to careful supervision by the Fed.

Interest Rate on Reserves

In October 2008, the Federal Reserve began to pay interest on banks' reserve deposits at the Fed. The rationale is that banks had been expending resources trying to keep their reserves as low as possible, which was distorting the market for reserves and causing the federal funds rate to be volatile. Banks had developed a system of sweep accounts, in which they swept funds from accounts that were subject to reserve requirements into accounts on which no reserves needed to be held, but this is a costly use of resources with little societal benefit. The payment of interest on reserves gives banks the incentive not to expend substantial resources just to avoid holding reserves.

Not only did the move to paying interest on reserves lead banks to hold substantially more reserves, it also gave the Fed an additional tool to use to affect the money supply. By raising the interest rate on reserves, the Fed can encourage banks to hold additional reserves, thus reducing the money supply. Alternatively, if the Fed wants to increase the money supply, it can do so by reducing the interest rate it pays on reserves. Although this tool for adjusting the money supply is relatively new, it has become the main policy tool employed by the Fed, as we discuss further in Section 14.4.[9]

New Monetary Policy Tools Developed in the Great Recession

In the first months of the housing crisis (see "In Touch with Data and Research: The Housing Crisis of 2007 to 2011," in Chapter 7), many analysts thought that the decline in house prices would lead to some losses at banks and other financial institutions and might propel the economy into a recession (as it did), but no one foresaw the sudden collapse of the financial system that would occur in the fall of 2008. The result was an episode that we now call the Great Recession because its impact on the U.S. and global economies was immense, though not as destructive as the Great Depression of the 1930s.

The economy deteriorated rapidly during the Great Recession. Real GDP fell 2.1% (at an annual rate) in the third quarter of 2008, 8.4% in the fourth quarter, and 4.4% in the first quarter of 2009. Overall, the length and depth of the recession made it more severe than the recessions of 1973–1975 and 1981–1982, but not nearly as bad as the Great Depression in the 1930s. The economy recovered very slowly from the recession, even after it ended in June 2009. Three years after the recession was over, the unemployment rate remained above 8% and economic growth was stagnant. The unemployment rate began to decline more rapidly from 2013 to 2015, though GDP growth remained below its historical average in those years.

The Zero Lower Bound. During and after the recession, the Fed used a variety of new policy tools to help the economy recover and to stabilize financial markets. The Fed faced a major obstacle: the **zero lower bound** on interest rates. By the end of 2008, monetary policymakers were unable to reduce the interest rate further to stimulate the economy because the interest rate was at its lower bound of zero. The nominal interest rate cannot decline below zero because a nominal interest

[9]See Glenn D. Rudebusch, "The Fed's Exit Strategy for Monetary Policy," Federal Reserve Bank of San Francisco Economic Letter 2010–18, June 14, 2010; and David Bowman, Etienne Gagnon, and Mike Leahy, "Interest on Excess Reserves as a Monetary Policy Instrument: The Experience of Foreign Central Banks," Federal Reserve Board of Governors, International Finance Discussion Papers Number 996, March 2010.

rate below zero would make it more profitable for an investor to hold cash rather than to make a loan, although there are exceptions, as we discuss in the Application "Is There Really a Zero Lower Bound?" This situation is called a **liquidity trap**, which was also faced by Japan in the 1990s. In a liquidity trap, any additional money supplied by the central bank is held by banks or the public, with no decline in interest rates or increase in spending. Japan's policymakers failed to solve the liquidity trap, and their economy suffered from deflation (declining prices) and very slow growth for more than two decades.

To get the U.S. economy out of the liquidity trap, and to avoid the problems caused by the zero lower bound, the Fed took a number of unusual policy measures from 2009 to 2014, including affecting interest rate expectations and expanding the size of the central bank balance sheet.[10]

One method for dealing with the zero bound is for the central bank to take action to change people's expectations of future interest rates. To affect interest-rate expectations, the Fed used a policy of **forward guidance**, in which it signaled to the market how long it thought interest rates would remain low. The idea is that if people base their consumption and investment decisions on long-term interest rates but the central bank can affect only short-term interest rates, then the central bank may not have much impact on consumption and investment. But if the central bank tells people that it expects to keep short-term interest rates very low for a long time, then long-term interest rates may decline relative to what they would be if people thought the central bank would raise short-term interest rates in the near future. By announcing that it expects to keep short-term interest rates very low, the central bank hopes to reduce long-term interest rates, thereby flattening the yield curve (see "In Touch with Data and Research: Interest Rates," in Chapter 4 and the discussion in the section "Time to Maturity" in Chapter 7).

Application

Is There Really a Zero Lower Bound?

To stimulate their economies, central banks usually employ expansionary monetary policies by lowering short-term interest rates. Following the global financial crisis, many central banks aggressively cut nominal interest rates to zero or very close to zero. But can interest rates can fall to sub-zero?

Although sub-zero nominal interest rates seem counterintuitive, in recent years, some central banks have indeed implemented negative official interest rates, such as in 2012, when Danmarks Nationalbank, the central bank of Denmark, ran an experiment with one of the longest-lasting negative nominal interest rates. Others entering negative territory include Sweden, Switzerland, Japan, and the euro area. In fact, nominal interest rates on different types of securities have, over time, fallen near or marginally below zero for varying periods.

Negative nominal interest rates suggest that lenders will pay borrowers to keep their money rather than receive interest. There must, therefore, be other

[10]Interestingly, former Fed Chairman Ben S. Bernanke had developed the ideas for these steps in 2004, two years before he became Fed chairman. See Ben S. Bernanke and Vincent R. Reinhart, "Conducting Monetary Policy at Very Low Short-Term Interest Rates," speech at the meetings of the American Economic Association, San Diego, California, January 3, 2004, and at the International Center for Monetary and Banking Studies Lecture, Geneva, Switzerland, January 14, 2004; available at *www.federalreserve.gov/boarddocs/speeches/2004*.

enticing attributes that lenders value. These may include security, insurance, convenience, and often, confidentiality.

Evidence from countries where sub-zero interest rates have been implemented shows that banks have been reluctant to charge ordinary customers to hold money in their own accounts. They note that competition is fierce, and households are ready to move their money to another bank. However, it's a different story for big companies and wealthy customers. In 2019, Denmark's Jyske Bank introduced negative interest rates for customers with cash balances over $1.1million, charging them 0.6% per annum to hold their money. In January 2021, Swiss bank UBS announced clients with cash balances above CHF 250,000 would be charged a 0.75% fee that from July 2021 onward. Above a certain limit, consumers' attitude toward negative rates change. But in Germany, where some banks impose charges on deposits above €100,000, some depositors have resorted to keeping their money in vaults.

What are the implications for mortgage holders? Some European banks have offered attractive deals. In 2019, Jyske Bank offered a 10-year loan with a −0.5% annual rate. In 2021, Finland's Nordea Bank offered 20-year mortgages at 0%. Such attractive deals may only work in mortgage markets where banks act as intermediaries and charge higher product fees to make their profit.

However, most lenders have embedded clauses stipulating that their mortgages have a "floor" (typically 0%) below which mortgage rates cannot fall, as customers of UK mortgage lender Cheltenham and Gloucester, with mortgage interest rates indexed at 1.01% below the base rate, were reminded in 2009. Thus, though it is possible for nominal interest rates go sub-zero for savers, there is a tolerance limit. For mortgages, however, the zero bound is stricter.[11]

The Fed implemented forward guidance in March 2009, when it announced that it expected interest rates to remain low for an "extended period." In August 2011, the Fed stated that it expected interest rates to remain "exceptionally low" at least through mid-2013. That statement was modified in January 2012 to say that the Fed expected interest rates to remain low at least through the end of 2014. Beginning in December 2012, the Fed described its forward guidance in a different manner, referring to outcomes for the unemployment rate and inflation rather than focusing on a particular date. For example, in December 2012, the Fed stated that "the Committee decided to keep the target range for the federal funds rate at 0% to 1/4% and currently anticipates that this exceptionally low range for the federal funds rate will be appropriate at least as long as the unemployment rate remains above $6\frac{1}{2}$%, inflation between one and two years ahead is projected to be no more than a half percentage point above the Committee's 2% longer-run goal, and longer-term inflation expectations continue to be well anchored."[12]

Another method a central bank can use to get around problems caused by the zero lower bound is to increase its total holdings of assets, known as **quantitative easing**. Under quantitative easing, the Fed buys bonds in the open market. The sellers of the bonds deposit the proceeds from the sale in their banks, which adds to banks' reserves. Higher bank reserves increase high-powered money and the

[11]Kevin Peachey, "What Low Interest Rates Mean for You," *BBC News*, March 5, 2009, *http://news.bbc.co.uk/1/hi/business/7924201.stm.*

[12]See Federal Reserve issues FOMC statement, 2012 at *www.federalreserve.gov/newsevents/pressreleases/monetary20121212a.htm.*

money supply. Quantitative easing also works by affecting long-term interest rates. The Fed's purchases of longer-term securities also tend to push down the interest rates on those securities, which provides stimulus to spending; for example, by lowering mortgage interest rates to encourage home purchases.[13] Rather than focusing on targeting the federal funds rate, the Fed changes its focus to the quantity of the monetary base or bank reserves, as it did in the 1979–1982 period. Japan used this method of "quantitative easing" in 2002–2003 to prevent its deflation from worsening and to bring inflation back to near zero in 2004. In a system of quantitative easing, the central bank buys financial assets and increases the size of its balance sheet, which it can do even when short-term interest rates are near zero.

In the aftermath of the financial crisis, the Fed also altered the types of assets that it owns. Prior to the financial crisis, the Fed mainly owned short-term Treasury securities. During the crisis and in the following years, the Fed transformed its balance sheet to hold more long-term Treasury securities and both debt and mortgage-backed securities issued by agencies known as Fannie Mae and Freddie Mac. (Those agencies were designed to help improve the efficiency of the housing market, though both went bankrupt in the financial crisis and were taken over by the Federal government.) The rationale for buying long-term Treasury securities is to reduce long-term interest rates, spurring an increase in consumption and investment. The rationale for buying agency debt and mortgage-backed securities is to reduce interest rates in the mortgage markets and help the housing market recover.

In September 2011, the Fed began a concerted effort to sell short-term Treasury securities and buy long-term Treasury securities in the market, in a program that came to be called Operation Twist (formally, it is the Maturity Extension Program) because doing so might raise short-term interest rates and lower long-term interest rates, causing the yield curve (see "In Touch with Data and Research: Interest Rates" in Chapter 4) to "twist," that is, to rise at short maturities and to fall at long maturities. Again, the goal was to lower long-term interest rates to stimulate consumption and investment. Long-term interest rates indeed declined as the operation took place, though the impact on consumption and investment was not clear. As we discussed in Chapter 4, consumption and investment spending may be more sensitive to income and economic conditions than they are to the real interest rate.

Figure 14.3 shows the Fed's balance sheet, specifically, the Fed's overall holdings of various assets, which include traditional security holdings (mainly short-term Treasury securities) in the orange shaded area, long-term Treasury securities in the green shaded area, loans to banks and financial markets in the blue shaded area, and agency (Fannie Mae and Freddie Mac) debt and mortgage-backed securities in the purple shaded area. Before the financial crisis in 2007 and early 2008, the size of the Fed's balance sheet was about $0.9 trillion. In spring 2008, as the financial crisis began to emerge, the Fed began lending funds to various financial institutions to prevent the financial crisis from spreading. In Fig. 14.3, you can see how the Fed increased its lending by about $0.4 trillion, offsetting that by selling Treasury securities to keep its total balance sheet unchanged. Then, as the financial crisis unfolded in September and October 2008, the Fed made many additional loans, increasing the size of its balance sheet to more than $2 trillion. By

---

[13]In the aftermath of the financial crisis, even though short-term interest rates, such as the federal funds rate, were at or near zero, longer-term rates, like mortgage rates, remained above zero. Thus, even though the Fed couldn't lower the fed funds rate any further, through asset purchases it was able to lower longer-term rates.

FIGURE 14.3

The asset side of the Fed's balance sheet, 2007–2022

The Fed increased the size of its balance sheet substantially in the Great Recession, increasing its ownership of financial assets from less than $1 trillion before the crisis to almost $3 trillion by the end of 2011 and to $4.5 trillion in 2014. When the financial crisis began, the Fed made emergency loans and supplied liquidity to financial markets, causing its balance sheet to more than double in size. As those loans were repaid, the Fed began buying long-term Treasury securities and agency debt and mortgage-backed securities. The Fed undertook similar actions in the pandemic of 2020.

Source: Federal Reserve Board of Governors website at *www.federalreserve.gov/monetarypolicy/bst_recenttrends.htm* and Federal Reserve Bank of Cleveland website at *www.clevelandfed.org/our-research/indicators-and-data/~/media/files/webcharts/crediteasing/crediteasingbalancesheet.xls.*

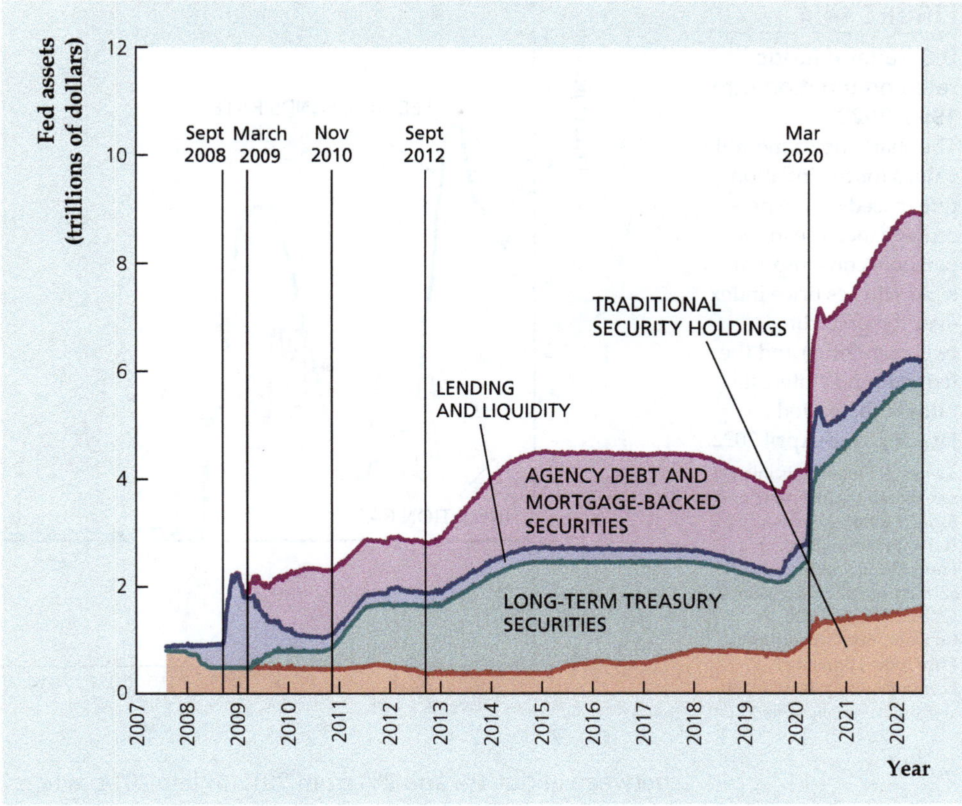

December 2008, the fed funds rate was below 0.25% and the United States had effectively hit the zero lower bound, as Figure 14.4 shows. Policymakers were worried about deflation, as the inflation rate turned negative for several months.

Quantitative easing during the recovery from the Great Recession occurred in phases. The first phase began in late 2008. The Fed's balance sheet exceeded $2 trillion, but the increase in the Fed's balance sheet was temporary because it arose from emergency lending that would be mostly paid off within a year. However, the Fed determined that as its loans to banks and financial markets were repaid, it would engage in quantitative easing by purchasing Treasury securities and mortgage-backed securities to keep its balance sheet from shrinking, as Fig. 14.3 shows. As the blue area showing the Fed's lending shrank from early 2009 to mid-2009, the Fed bought mortgage-backed securities and Treasury securities, so that its balance sheet remained about $2 trillion. In March 2009, the Fed announced a further expansion of its balance sheet, which reached $2.3 trillion by June 2010. The economy continued to grow slowly and the unemployment rate remained high, so the Fed announced in November 2010 that it would increase its balance sheet by another $0.6 trillion by mid-2011; the balance sheet indeed topped out at $2.9 trillion by the end of 2011. In September 2012, the Fed began another round of quantitative easing, which brought the Fed's assets up to almost $4.5 trillion by the end of 2014.

One benefit of quantitative easing is that it pushed the inflation rate up and prevented deflation. As Fig. 14.4 shows, the inflation rate increased from negative values to about 2% on average in 2010 and 2011. Thus the U.S. economy did not suffer from deflation, as Japan had done two decades earlier. Inflation remained

FIGURE 14.4

U.S. federal funds rate and inflation rate, 1998–2022

The chart shows monthly values for the inflation rate (based on the percentage increase in the personal consumption expenditures price index over the preceding twelve months) and the federal funds interest rate for the period January 1998–April 2022.

Sources: Federal funds interest rate: Board of Governors of the Federal Reserve System, Federal Reserve Bank of St. Louis FRED database, available at *fred.stlouisfed.org/series/FEDFUNDS*; Personal Consumption Expenditures Price Index, Bureau of Economic Analysis, available at *fred.stlouisfed.org/series/PCEPI*.

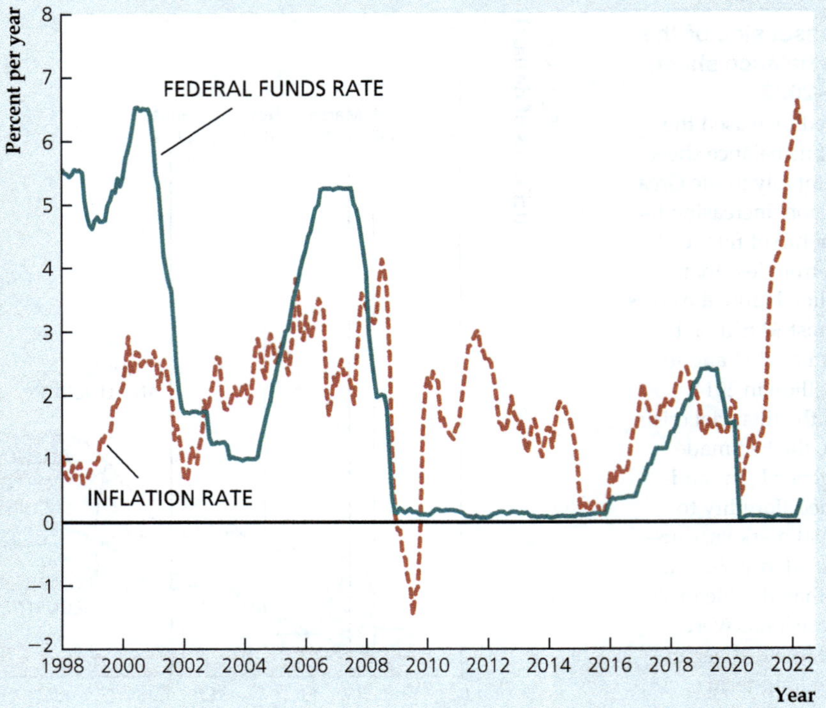

between about 1% and 2% from 2012 to late 2014, when it fell sharply because of a significant decline in energy prices.

The Federal Reserve began to raise the federal funds interest rate in December 2015 and continued to do so in a very gradual fashion for the next several years. At the same time, the inflation rate remained below 2% for most of that period.

Application

The Financial Crisis of 2008: Some Implications for the Global Economy

As shown in Figure 14.4, the U.S. federal funds rate underwent significant reductions around 2000, which encouraged bank lending. The massive credit expansion fueled mortgage uptake in subprime markets, encouraging new financial instruments including multilayered, mortgage-backed securities. Increasing the federal funds rate after 2004 rattled the housing boom, causing numerous defaults in low-quality mortgages and bursting the bubble. In August 2007, BNP Paribas, a leading global financial services firm, announced that it was ceasing activity in three hedge funds that specialized in U.S. mortgage debt. Lehman Brothers' unexpected bankruptcy in September 2008 further intensified a massive liquidity preference and credit evaporation, prompting huge increases in perceived counterparty risk. Their involvement with several hedge funds and financial institutions led to multiple bank failures in the United States, and the solvent nature of many financial institutions became suspect. As the effects hit the real economy, consumer spending and investment plummeted, causing a leftward shift in the *IS* curve.

High interdependencies among global financial markets meant that the crisis spread to the financial sectors of other countries. At the crisis' onset, advanced economies suffered considerably from financial strains and the deterioration of housing markets. In 2008's last quarter, the annualized rate of GDP contraction topped 10% in some high-income countries. Significant damage was inflicted through financial channels in emerging markets in Europe and the Commonwealth of Independent States, which had been relying heavily on capital inflows to fuel growth. Even countries that did not seem to have problems with their financial systems started experiencing significant decreases in industrial production in addition to adverse changes in capital flows, commodity prices, interest rates, remittances, risk premiums, and trade opportunities.

In Brazil, the annualized rate of GDP and industrial production fell by about 11% and 30%, respectively, in 2008's last quarter. In Africa, sharp falls in commodity prices hit the resource-rich countries hard. The tightening of global credit conditions reduced foreign direct investment and reversed portfolio flows especially hit emerging and frontier markets. Countries relying heavily on manufacturing exports were hammered by falling export market demand. Japan's GDP shrunk by over 10% on an annualized basis in the two quarters following Lehman Brothers' bankruptcy. Plummeting demand for durable goods and a decline in investment activity in emerging economies hurt manufacturing exports. The rapid fall in confidence among consumers and businesses, rising uncertainty, weakening labor markets, tighter financial conditions, and rising spare capacity weakened domestic demand. In other parts of Asia, the manufacturing-oriented economies also plummeted and, by the end of 2008, experienced industrial production declines of about 25% compared with 2007 levels. Only China, Indonesia, and India escaped severe recessions, mainly because of a large policy stimulus and, in the case of India, less dependence on exports.

Governments around the world quickly realized drastic action was needed to reverse the *IS* shift; however, responses differed. Governments in developed countries reduced policy rates to almost 0%, and when that did not achieve desired results, they decided to inject liquidity through asset purchases. In Europe, the strict fiscal deficit restrictions enshrined in the Maastricht Treaty were temporarily loosened. The UK also allowed fiscal flexibility to help economic recovery. China increased public investment expenditure, mainly in infrastructure, by over $500 billion. Brazil prioritized fiscal policy expansion, and by late 2008, the authorities had approved a fiscal stimulus package comprising tax reductions, public investment, and unemployment benefits and minimum wage increases. It was only in January 2009, after industrial production had plummeted by 16.4% in December 2008 compared to December 2007, did interest rates reduction begin. Many blamed this delay for the GDP decline from 5.1% to −0.7% in 2009. Although fiscal expansions helped job creation, they also ballooned countries' sovereign debt.[14]

Monetary Policy in Response to the Pandemic of 2020

When the global pandemic began in 2020, as we discussed in Chapter 4 in the "Application: The Impact of the Pandemic Recession of 2020 on Consumption," governments all over the world provided income support for workers who were unable to work. The Federal Reserve also employed tools from the financial crisis, including quantitative easing, funding for financial institutions through liquidity facilities, and reducing nominal interest rates near zero. In addition, the Federal Reserve employed several new tools.

A unique aspect of the Fed's new tools in the pandemic was direct lending to business firms, whereas most previous Fed lending was only to financial institutions.

[14]See International Monetary Fund, *World Economic Outlook* (Washington DC: IMF, 2009), p. 85.

The Fed made some loans to business firms through the Main Street Business Lending Program, which was designed to support lending to medium-sized businesses. The Fed also created the Primary Market Corporate Credit Facility (PMCCF), which supported large businesses that wished to issue new bonds and loans, and the Secondary Market Corporate Credit Facility (SMCCF), which provided additional liquidity for outstanding corporate bonds of large businesses. The main idea behind these lending programs was to keep businesses afloat when much of the demand for their products declined and when their workers were unable to work because of the pandemic. The lending facilities for corporations, municipalities, and medium-sized businesses were authorized by Congress, which provided funds to protect the Fed from any losses.

Perhaps the most important new tool, however, was the Paycheck Protection Program. In this program, the Small Business Administration worked with local banks to make loans to keep small businesses open. The Fed supported the program by making loans to those banks making the PPP loans.

Later in 2020, as the pandemic continued, the Fed announced a new system of flexible average inflation targeting. The official announcement noted that when inflation has been averaging below 2% for some time, the Fed would allow inflation to run above 2% to make up for that. For a while, it appeared that the Fed's new policy could be helpful in stimulating the economy without worrying about inflation rising too much. But, as Figure 14.4 shows, the Fed's focus on stimulating the economy at the same time that other income support policies by the federal government were in place, along with supply shocks, led inflation to rise substantially. Supply shocks included the snarling of supply chains, unavailability of critical parts (like semiconductors needed for auto production), and reduced labor supply as many workers delayed coming back to work and some older workers retired early. Also, Russia's war on Ukraine contributed to large increases in the prices of oil, wheat, and other foodstuffs. By the time the Fed realized its mistake, the inflation rate had become unacceptably high, leading the Fed to have to raise interest rates substantially.

14.3 Setting Monetary Policy Targets

Explain the Fed's setting of monetary policy targets.

We described the tools of monetary policy in Section 14.2. But how do policymakers use these tools in practice? In this section, we show the main considerations for setting monetary policy.

Targeting the Federal Funds Rate

In conducting monetary policy, the Fed has certain goals, or ultimate targets, such as price stability and stable economic growth. In trying to reach these goals, the Fed can use the monetary policy tools, or **instruments**, that we've discussed: reserve requirements, the discount rate, the interest rate on reserves, and especially open-market operations. The problem the Fed faces is how to use the instruments that it controls directly, particularly open-market operations, to achieve its goals. Because there are several steps between open-market operations and the ultimate behavior of prices and economic activity—and because these steps often can't be predicted accurately—the Fed uses intermediate targets to guide monetary policy. **Intermediate targets**, also sometimes called *indicators*, are macroeconomic variables that the Fed cannot control directly but can influence fairly predictably, and that in turn are related to the goals the Fed is trying to achieve.

Historically, the most frequently used intermediate targets have been monetary aggregates, such as M1 and M2, and short-term interest rates, such as the fed funds rate. By using open-market operations, the Fed can directly control the level of the monetary base, which influences the monetary aggregates. Fluctuations in the money supply in turn affect interest rates, at least temporarily, by causing the *LM* curve to shift. Neither monetary aggregates nor short-term interest rates are important determinants of economic welfare in and of themselves, but both influence the state of the macroeconomy. Because monetary aggregates and short-term interest rates are affected in a predictable way by the Fed's policies and because both in turn affect the economy, these variables qualify as intermediate targets.

At various times the Fed has guided monetary policy by attempting to keep either monetary growth rates or short-term interest rates in or near pre-established target ranges. Note that, although the Fed may be able to stabilize one or the other of these variables, it cannot target both simultaneously. For example, suppose that the Fed were trying to target both the money supply and the fed funds rate and that the pre-established target ranges called for an increase in both variables. How could the Fed meet these targets simultaneously? If it raised the monetary base to raise the money supply, in the short run the increase in money supply would shift the *LM* curve down and to the right, which would lower rather than raise the fed funds rate. Alternatively, if the Fed lowered the monetary base to try to increase the fed funds rate, the money supply would fall instead of rising, as required. Thus, in general, the Fed cannot simultaneously meet targets for *both* interest rates and the money supply, unless those targets are set to be consistent with each other.

In recent years the Fed has typically downplayed monetary aggregates and focused on stabilizing the fed funds rate at a target level. Figure 14.5 shows a

FIGURE 14.5

Interest rate targeting

The figure shows an economy that is buffeted by nominal shocks. Changes in the money supply or money demand cause the *LM* curve to shift between LM^2 and LM^3 and cause aggregate demand to move erratically between Y_2 and Y_3. A Fed policy of keeping the real interest rate at r_1, by raising the monetary base whenever the interest rate exceeds r_1 and lowering the base whenever the interest rate falls below r_1, will keep the economy at full employment at *E*.

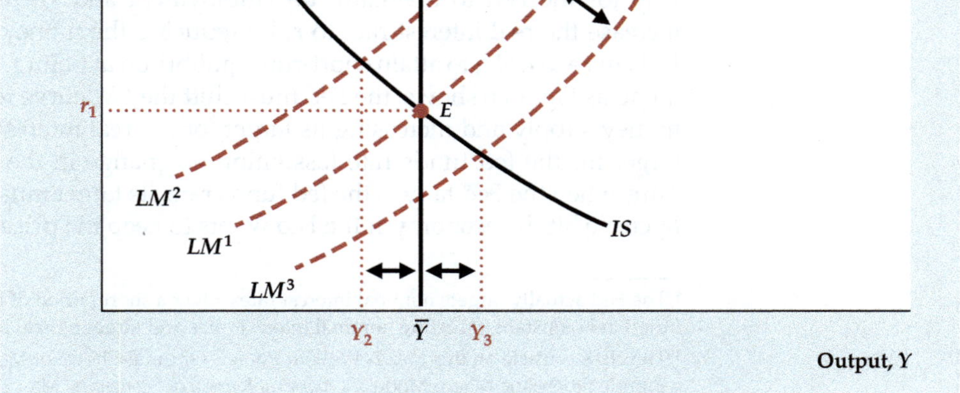

situation in which this strategy is useful. When the *LM* curve is LM^1, the economy is at full-employment equilibrium at point *E*, with output at $\bar{Y}$ and a real interest rate of r_1. Suppose that most of the shocks hitting the economy are nominal shocks, including shocks to money supply and to money demand. Without intervention by the Fed, these nominal shocks cause the *LM* curve to shift between LM^2 and LM^3, leading aggregate demand to shift erratically between Y_2 and Y_3. In either the extended classical model with misperceptions or the Keynesian model, random shifts in aggregate demand cause undesirable cyclical fluctuations in the economy.

The Fed could reduce the instability caused by nominal shocks by using monetary policy to hold the real interest rate at r_1.[15] In other words, whenever the *LM* curve shifted up to LM^2, the Fed could increase the money supply to restore the *LM* curve to LM^1; similarly, shifts of the *LM* curve to LM^3 could be offset by reductions in the money supply to return the *LM* curve to LM^1. In this case stabilizing the intermediate target, the interest rate, also would stabilize output at its full-employment level. For interest rate targeting to be a good strategy, however, nominal shocks, that is, shocks to the *LM* curve, must be the main source of instability.

When the Fed decided to target the fed funds rate in the late 1980s, some economists worried that the central bank was returning to a flawed policy that contributed to the large rise in inflation in the 1960s and 1970s. But Fed policymakers argued that the policy flaw was not the use of the fed funds rate as an intermediate target per se, but the Fed's failure to change its target for the fed funds rate in a timely manner.

Suppose, for example, that a shock hits the economy that shifts the *IS* curve to the right; a sudden increase in foreign demand for exported goods is one possibility. How should the Fed respond? Figure 14.6 illustrates this situation. In the graph, suppose that before the shock, the economy is in general equilibrium at point *E*, where the initial *IS* curve, IS^1, intersects the initial *LM* curve, LM^1, so the initial equilibrium real interest rate is r_1 and the level of output is $\bar{Y}$. The increase in export demand causes the *IS* curve to shift up and to the right to IS^2. If the Fed were to keep the *LM* curve unchanged at LM^1, then, as shown by point *F*, output would rise to Y_2 and the real interest rate would rise to r_2 in the short run, and the price level would rise in the long run. If the Fed were instead to maintain the real interest rate at r_1 by increasing the money supply and shifting the *LM* curve to LM^2, then, as shown by point *H*, output would increase to Y_3 in the short run and the price level would rise to restore equilibrium in the long run. Thus maintaining a constant nominal money supply and keeping the *LM* curve unchanged will lead to more stable output than would maintaining the real interest rate unchanged at r_1.[16] The only way for the Fed to maintain full employment and keep prices from rising is to increase the real interest rate to r_3 by reducing the money supply and shifting the *LM* curve to LM^3, to attain short-run equilibrium at point *J*. To maintain full employment, as Fig. 14.6 shows, the Fed must shift the *LM* curve to the left by reducing the money supply and increasing its target for the real interest rate, thus increasing its target for the fed funds rate (assuming no change in the expected inflation rate). Thus when the Fed targets the fed funds rate, its target must change as shocks to the *IS* curve hit the economy, if the Fed wants to keep the price level from changing.

---

[15]The Fed actually targets nominal interest rates. Over a short period of time, in which expected inflation is constant, targeting nominal interest rates and targeting real interest rates are the same.

[16]The classic article on this idea is William Poole, "Optimal Choice of Monetary Policy Instruments in a Simple Stochastic Macro Model," *Quarterly Journal of Economics*, May 1970, pp. 197–216.

FIGURE 14.6

Interest rate targeting when an *IS* shock occurs

The figure shows an economy that starts at point *E* and experiences a shock that shifts the *IS* curve up and to the right. A Fed policy of not changing the *LM* curve leads to higher output at Y_2 and a higher real interest rate at r_2 in the short run (point *F*), and the price level would rise in the long run. A Fed policy of maintaining the real interest rate at r_1 by increasing the money supply causes the *LM* curve to shift to LM^2, increasing output to Y_3 in the short run (point *H*) and raising the price level in the long run. A Fed policy of raising the real interest rate to r_3 by reducing the money supply and shifting the *LM* curve to LM^3 is the only way to maintain full employment (point *J*) in the short run and not increase the price level in the long run.

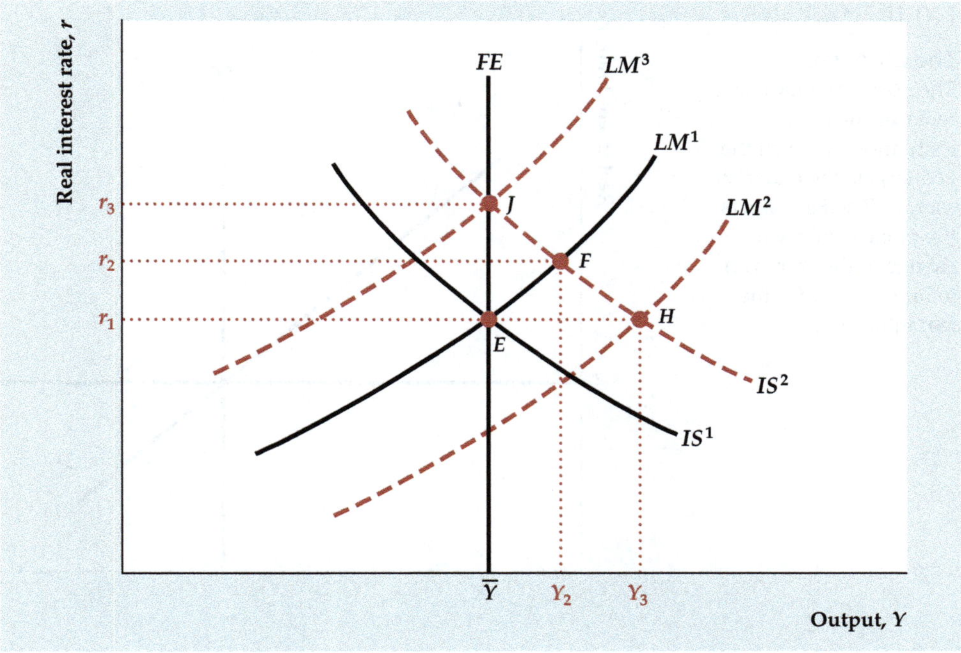

To summarize, our analysis in Figs. 14.5 and 14.6 shows that when there are shocks to the *LM* curve, the Fed can stabilize the economy by setting a fixed real interest rate. But if there are shocks to the *IS* curve, the Fed needs to modify its target for the interest rate, or else its policy is destabilizing.

If the Fed targets the real interest rate, then it is useful to modify the *LM* curve. Rather than having the *LM* slope upward as in our previous graphs, we could instead directly show the Fed's policy as represented by a horizontal line in the *IS–LM* diagram (Figure 14.7), which we will call the *LR* curve. In the graph, the target real interest rate is denoted r^T. The Fed uses open-market operations to hit this target real interest rate on a day-to-day basis and allows the money supply to change to whatever level is necessary to attain this target.

In setting monetary policy using the *LR* curve, the Fed now must think about what real interest rate is desirable for the economy rather than what nominal money supply is needed. Consider the Fed's response to a shock to the *IS* curve, which we considered in Fig. 14.6. In that situation, we noted that the Fed should modify its target for the real federal funds rate to keep the economy at its full-employment equilibrium without causing a change in the price level in the long run. Thus the Fed must be flexible in setting its real federal funds rate target, r^T, constantly monitoring the economy to see if the *IS* curve might have shifted. To see how the Fed can change its fed funds target to promote economic stability and low inflation, see the section on the Taylor Rule.

One advantage of targeting the real interest rate and using the *LR* curve is that shocks to money demand are automatically offset. An increase in money demand caused by some shock to the economy is automatically matched by an increase in money supply, and the real interest rate remains unchanged. In addition, if the target real interest rate is raised when inflation rises, inflation can be kept low and stable.[17]

[17]See David Romer, "Keynesian Macroeconomics Without the *LM* Curve," *Journal of Economic Perspectives*, Spring 2000, pp. 149–169.

FIGURE 14.7

The *LR* curve

The horizontal *LR* curve replaces the *LM* curve in a situation in which the Fed targets the real interest rate. The Fed allows the money supply to change in the short run to hit its target for the real interest rate.

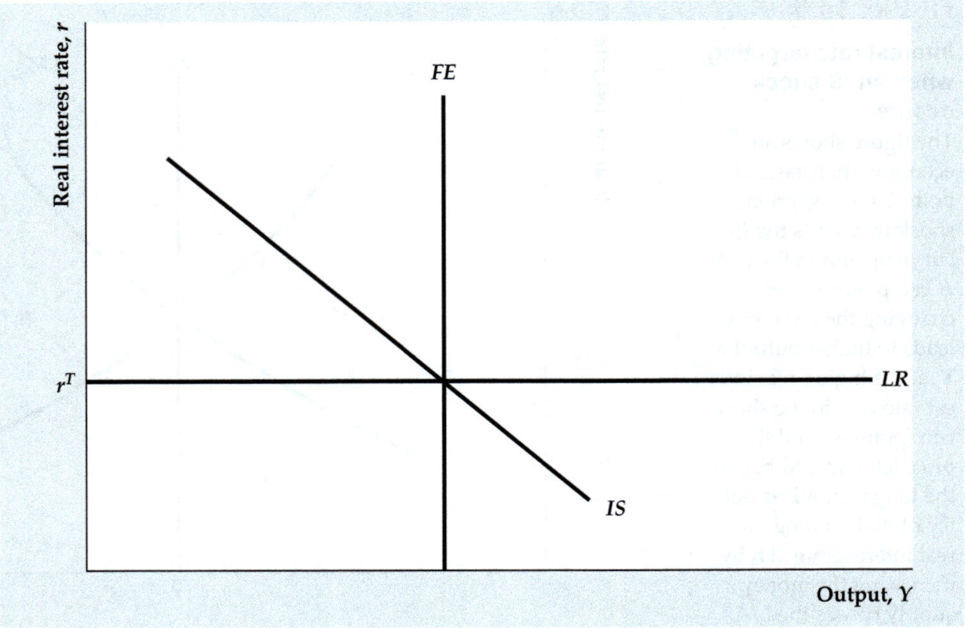

Monetary Policy with Abundant Reserves

In the aftermath of the financial crisis, the Fed changed its method of engaging in monetary policy on a day-to-day basis. Because quantitative easing had increased the supply of reserves to a very high level, the federal funds rate was determined more by the interest rate on reserves rather than the supply and demand for reserves. This new abundant-reserves regime is illustrated in Figure 14.8.

In Fig. 14.8, the primary credit discount rate is *d*. The fed funds rate would not rise above *d* because if it did, banks in good condition that want additional reserves would borrow reserves from the Fed at the primary credit discount rate rather than borrow from other banks in the fed funds market. Therefore, the demand for fed funds by banks in good condition would fall to zero if the fed funds rate were even a tiny amount higher than the primary credit discount rate, *d*.

In the figure, *IORB* is the rate of interest on reserve balances. If the fed funds rate were to fall below *IORB*, then banks could earn virtually unlimited arbitrage profits by borrowing reserves at the fed funds rate and earning the *IORB* rate on those reserves. The possibility of virtually unlimited arbitrage profits for banks if the fed funds rate were to fall below *IORB* makes the demand for reserves infinitely elastic when the fed funds rate equals the *IORB* rate; thus, the demand curve become horizontal when the fed funds rate equals the *IORB* rate.[18]

[18]The potential arbitrage described in the text requires that borrowers in the fed funds market have the opportunity to earn the *IORB* rate. However, because a few institutions, such as Fannie Mae and Freddie Mac, can lend funds in the fed funds market but cannot earn interest on reserves, the fed funds rate has often been slightly below the *IORB* rate. In addition, the Fed has been engaging in overnight reverse repurchase agreements with institutions such as money-market mutual funds, so that some of the base money created by the Fed ends up in institutions other than banks. But despite these minor technical issues, Fig. 14.8 illustrates the main features of the market for reserves.

FIGURE 14.8

The Reserves Market with Abundant Reserves.
When bank reserves are abundant, the supply of reserves, *S*, intersects the demand for reserves, *D*, on the horizontal portion of the demand curve at the interest rate on reserves. As a result, the equilibrium federal funds rate equals the interest rate on reserves.

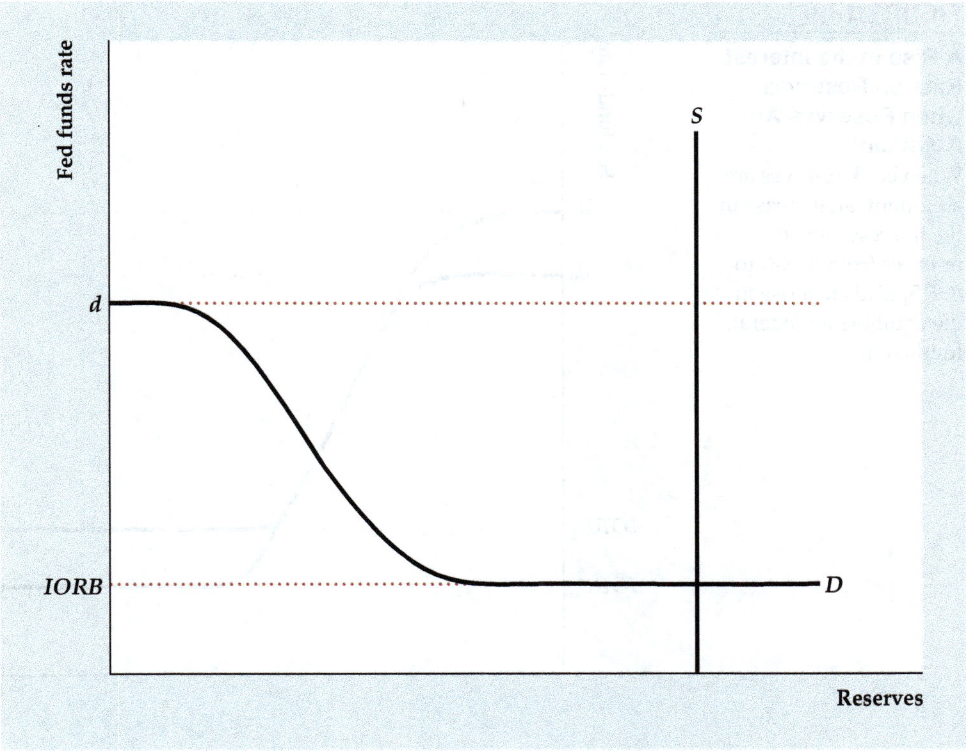

The vertical line labeled *S* is the supply curve of reserves, which is determined by the Fed. The Fed chooses the monetary base, *MB*, and knows the amount of currency, *C*, in circulation. The supply of reserves equals $MB - C$. Given that *d* is the maximum level of the fed funds rate and *IORB* is the minimum level, banks' demand for reserves is given by the curve labeled *D*. Prior to 2008, the relevant portion of the demand curve was the downward-sloping part. But after the Fed engaged in quantitative easing in a major way, the *S* line moved so far to the right that it intersected the *D* curve on its horizontal segment, where the fed funds rate equals *IORB*.

With the equilibrium in the economy like that depicted in Fig. 14.8, small movements of the supply curve do not affect the fed funds rate. So, if the Fed engages in quantitative easing to move the supply curve to the right, there is no change to the fed funds rate, but the open-market purchases of long-term bonds may affect the market for long-term securities, so long-term interest rates may decline. Similarly, quantitative tightening, in which the Fed sells securities in the open market, have no impact on short-term interest rates, but might raise long-term interest rates.

If the Fed wants to raise interest rates in the situation shown in Fig. 14.8, it can do so by raising the *IORB* rate, as Figure 14.9 shows. The original equilibrium is at point A, with the fed funds rate equal to $IORB_0$ and the amount of reserves at R^*. The Fed increases the interest rate on reserves from $IORB_0$ to $IORB_1$. Usually, the Fed raises the discount rate at the same time that it raises the interest rate on reserves, so this is shown by a rise in the discount rate from d_0 to d_1. In equilibrium, the quantity of reserves in the market remains unchanged at R^* and the federal funds rate rises to $IORB_1$.

When the Fed raises the interest rate on reserves, it often reduces the supply of reserves at the same time, which would be depicted as a shift to the left of the

FIGURE 14.9

A Rise in the Interest Rate on Reserves when Reserves Are Abundant

When bank reserves are abundant, an increase in the interest rate on reserves from $IORB_0$ to $IORB_1$ leads to a rise in the equilibrium federal funds rate.

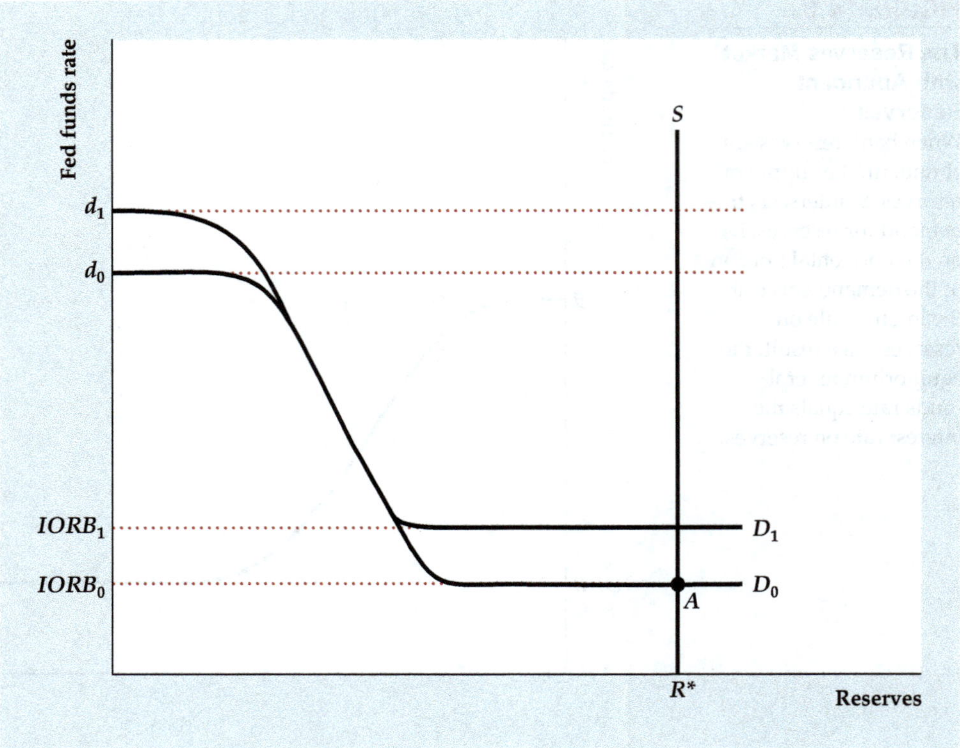

supply curve, *S*. Doing so would not have any impact on the federal funds rate (as long as the equilibrium between demand and supply of reserves remains on the horizontal part of the demand curve) but would reduce the equilibrium amount of reserves. To keep things simple, we have not shown this effect in Fig. 14.9, but that is an easy effect to add to the diagram.

14.4 Making Monetary Policy in Practice

Discuss the difficulties of making monetary policy.

The *IS–LM* or *AD–AS* analysis of monetary policy suggests that using monetary policy to affect output and prices is a relatively simple matter: All that the Fed needs to do is change the money supply enough to shift the *LM* curve or the *AD* curve to the desired point. In reality, however, making monetary policy is a complex, ongoing process. Two important practical issues that policymakers have to deal with are the lags in the effects of monetary policy on the economy and how to deal with uncertainty about the state of the economy, economic models, and expectations.

Lags in the Effects of Monetary Policy

If changes in the money supply led to immediate changes in output or prices, using monetary policy to stabilize the economy would be relatively easy. The Fed would simply have to adjust its policy instruments until the economy attained full employment with stable prices. Unfortunately, most empirical evidence suggests that changes in monetary policy take a fairly long time to affect the economy, which is the impact lag that we discussed in the section "Should Fiscal Policy Be Used to Dampen the Cycle?" in Chapter 10.

FIGURE 14.10

Responses of output, prices, and the fed funds rate to a monetary policy shock

Shown are the estimated changes in the fed funds rate, real GDP, and the GDP deflator during the first 48 months following an unanticipated tightening of monetary policy by the Fed. The fed funds rate and other interest rates respond quickly to monetary policy changes, but output (real GDP) and the price level (the GDP deflator) respond much more slowly. The long impact lags in the responses of output and prices illustrate the difficulty of using monetary policy to stabilize the economy.

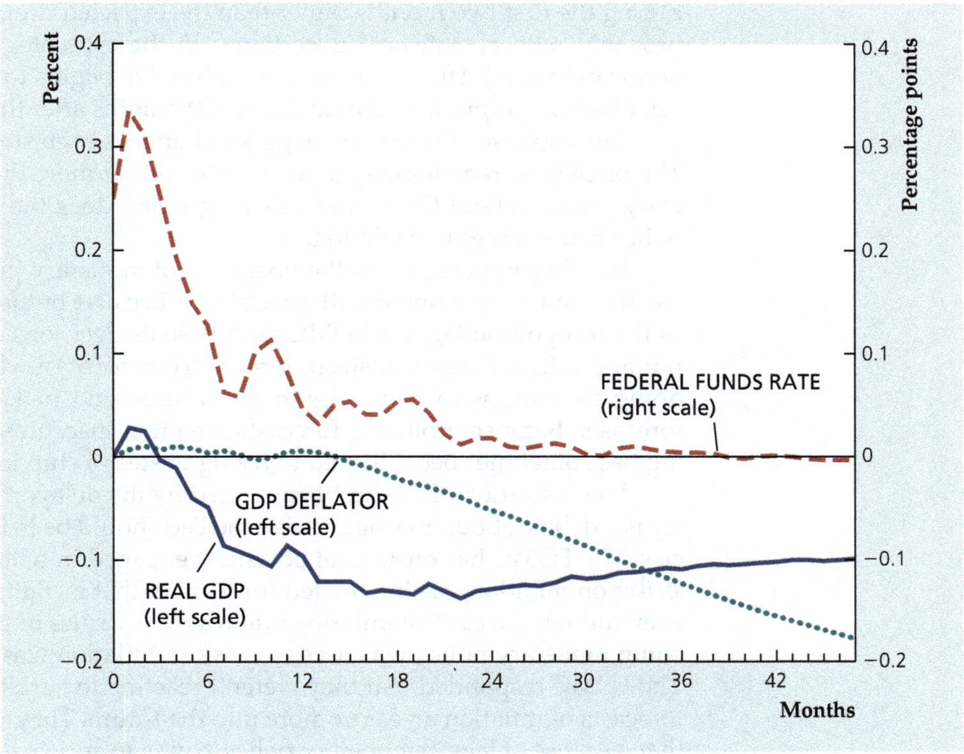

Some empirical estimates of how long it takes monetary policy to work are presented in Figure 14.10, adapted from an article by former Federal Reserve Chairman Ben Bernanke and Mark Gertler[19] of New York University. Shown are the estimated behaviors of three important variables during the first 48 months after an unanticipated tightening of monetary policy by the Fed. The variables shown are the fed funds rate (described in Section 14.2), real GDP (a measure of output), and the GDP deflator (a measure of the price level).[20] The left vertical axis measures the *changes* in real GDP and the GDP deflator that occur after the policy change, in percent; the right vertical axis measures the change in the federal funds rate that occurs after the policy change, in percentage points.

Note that interest rates (here, the fed funds rate) react quickly to monetary policy changes. Following a tightening of monetary policy, the fed funds rate rises by more than 0.3 percentage point (for example, from 5.0% to 5.3%) within a month. However, the effect of the policy change on interest rates is transitory; the fed funds rate starts falling quickly, and six to twelve months after the monetary policy tightening it has nearly returned to its original value.

In contrast, output and (especially) the price level take much longer to respond to the change in monetary policy. Real GDP barely responds to the policy change during the first four months or so. (Figure 14.10 actually shows a slight rise in GDP

[19]"Inside the Black Box: The Credit Channel of Monetary Policy Transmission," *Journal of Economic Perspectives*, Fall 1995, pp. 27–48. Bernanke was a professor at Princeton University when this article was written.

[20]Official data on real GDP and the GDP deflator are available only quarterly. For their study, Bernanke and Gertler used statistical interpolation methods to construct monthly series for these two variables.

during the first two months rather than the expected drop; this "wrong" response probably reflects statistical uncertainty in the estimates rather than actual economic behavior.) After about four months GDP begins to decline sharply, but the full effect on output isn't felt until 16 to 20 months after the initial policy change.

The response of prices to the policy change is even slower than that of output. The price level remains essentially unaffected for more than a year after the monetary policy action! Only after this long delay does the tightening of monetary policy cause prices to begin to fall.

The long impact lags in the operation of monetary policy make it difficult to use this policy instrument with precision.[21] Because of the long impact lag as well as the recognition lag, the FOMC can't base its decisions on current levels of output and inflation alone. Instead, it must try to forecast what the economy will be doing six months to two years in the future—and make policy based on those forecasts. Because economic forecasts are often inaccurate, monetary policymaking has sometimes been likened to trying to steer a ship in a dense fog.

An illustration of the problems raised by the delayed effects of monetary policy is a debate about how aggressive the Fed should be in its anti-inflationary policies. The FOMC has on several occasions engaged in what were called *preemptive strikes* on inflation, raising the fed funds rate (that is, tightening monetary policy) even though the current inflation rate was low. Critics of the Fed asked why tightening monetary policy was necessary when inflation wasn't currently a problem. The FOMC responded that they weren't reacting to current inflation but rather to forecasts of inflation a year or more into the future. They were correct in asserting that, because of lags in monetary policy, trying to anticipate future inflation, rather than reacting only to current inflation, is necessary. Because of the difficulties in forecasting inflation, however, there was plenty of room for debate about how tight monetary policy needed to be to prevent future inflation.

Conducting Monetary Policy Under Uncertainty

In practice, conducting monetary policy is much more difficult than our models suggest because policymakers face uncertainty in three dimensions: (1) They are uncertain about the current state of the economy; (2) their models of the economy are incomplete; and (3) they are unsure about how the expectations of the public will be affected by economic shocks and policy actions.[22]

Policymakers try to discern the overall state of the economy by examining data on hundreds of different economic variables, which often give conflicting signals about the current strength of the economy. Complicating the matter further, data are often revised, and the initial releases of the data are much less accurate than later releases of the data.[23] Recent research has shown that one way to get a handle on the current state of the economy is to combine the information

[21]Indeed, as we discuss shortly, a group of economists called *monetarists* has argued that these long lags make monetary policy next to worthless as a tool for stabilizing the economy.

[22]This discussion of uncertainty and policy is based on a speech by former Fed Chairman Ben S. Bernanke, "Monetary Policy and Uncertainty," October 19, 2007, available online at *www.federalreserve.gov/newsevents/speech/bernanke20071019a.htm*. The speech includes references to the research behind the results discussed in this section.

[23]For a review of research on policymaking when data may be revised, see Dean Croushore, "Frontiers of Real-Time Data Analysis," *Journal of Economic Literature*, March 2011, pp. 72–100.

from many different variables in a dynamic factor model such as the CFNAI or ADS index , as we saw in Chapter 8, "In Touch with Data and Research: Coincident and Leading Indexes."[24]

A second source of uncertainty that affects policymaking is uncertainty about the structure of the economy. Is the economy best described by the classical model or the Keynesian model, and which variation of each is the best? What are the slopes and locations of each of the curves in each model? What are the levels of full-employment output and the natural rate of unemployment?[25] No one knows the answers to these questions precisely. In the face of such uncertainty about the structure of the economy, early research suggested that policymakers should respond less to shocks to the economy than if they knew the structure of the economy for sure.[26] However, research suggests that if there is a possibility of a particularly bad outcome, such as a deflation leading to a severe recession, then stronger action by monetary policy is warranted. Another aspect of uncertainty about the structure of the economy is uncertainty about the predominant source of shocks to the economy. For instance, in Fig. 14.5, we showed that in the face of nominal shocks to the economy, which cause the *LM* curve to shift, the central bank can stabilize output by targeting the interest rate. On the other hand, as we showed in Fig. 14.6, if shocks cause shifts of the *IS* curve, then output will be more stable if the Fed maintains an unchanged nominal money supply than if it maintains an unchanged interest rate. In fact, the economy is hit by both types of shocks. The Taylor Rule (discussed later in this chapter) is a flexible interest rate target that is designed to provide good outcomes under a wide variety of circumstances and in response to various types of shocks.

A third major source of uncertainty facing policymakers comes from the impact of economic shocks and policy changes on people's expectations. In the rational-expectations revolution in the 1980s, macroeconomists learned that people's expectations have a major effect on the economy's response to shocks and to policy, as we discussed in Section 10.5 "The Misperceptions Theory and the Nonneutrality of Money" in Chapter 10. Recent research has shown that if the public is not sure of the central bank's motives, then the central bank should work hard to keep the inflation rate as stable as possible, so that people's expectations can become anchored. In addition, the research suggests that there are large benefits to informing people about the central bank's plans and forecasts. This idea has been put into practice recently by the Federal Reserve, which has explained its actions much more clearly than previously, by providing more detailed minutes of its meetings, announcing its own forecasts four times a year, and holding press conferences after FOMC meetings four times per year.

Uncertainty makes monetary policymaking much more difficult than it would be if we knew everything about the economy. As Fed Chairman Ben Bernanke noted in a 2007 speech, "Uncertainty—about the state of the economy, the economy's structure, and the inferences that the public will draw from policy actions or

---

[24]For more on the development of these models, see James Stock and Mark Watson, "Forecasting Using Principal Components from a Large Number of Predictors," *Journal of the American Statistical Association*, December 2002, pp. 1167–1179.

[25]See the section "The Long-Term Behavior of the Unemployment Rate" in Chapter 12, for a discussion of the difficulty of measuring the natural rate of unemployment.

[26]See William C. Brainard, "Uncertainty and the Effectiveness of Policy," *American Economic Review*, May 1967, pp. 411–425.

economic developments—is a pervasive feature of monetary policy making .... Most fundamentally, our discussions of the pervasive uncertainty that we face as policymakers is a powerful reminder of the need for humility about our ability to forecast and manage the future course of the economy."[27]

14.5 The Conduct of Monetary Policy: Rules Versus Discretion

Discuss whether monetary policy should be conducted by rules or discretion.

How should monetary policy be used? On some aspects of this question, there is broad agreement. Most classicals and Keynesians agree that money is neutral in the long run so that changes in money growth affect inflation but not real variables in the long run. Therefore most would accept that the main long-run goal of monetary policy should be to maintain a low and stable inflation rate. However, there is much less agreement about the effects of monetary policy and its appropriate use in the short run (Chapters 10 and 11). Most Keynesians believe that monetary policy can and should be used to smooth the business cycle, but most classicals don't. In this section we revisit the debate about the appropriate use of monetary policy by addressing a long-standing question in macroeconomics: Should monetary policy be conducted according to fixed rules or at the discretion of the central bank?

The use of rules in monetary policy has been advocated primarily by a group of economists called monetarists, and also by classical macroeconomists. Supporters of **rules** believe that monetary policy should be essentially automatic. In particular, in its control of the money supply, the central bank should be required to follow a set of simple, prespecified, and publicly announced rules. Many such rules can be imagined. For example, the Fed might be instructed to increase the monetary base by 1% each quarter. An alternative rule, which has been used historically, is to require the central bank to conduct monetary policy to keep the price of gold at a predetermined level (this rule was the essence of the gold standard). One might also imagine a rule that permits the Fed to respond to the state of the economy, as we will discuss shortly.

Although the exact form of the rule chosen isn't crucial, supporters of the rule-based approach emphasize that the monetary rule should be simple; there can't be dozens of exceptions and conditions. Furthermore, the rule should be stated in terms of variables that the Fed can control directly or nearly directly. Because the Fed can control the monetary base precisely, a prespecified growth rate for the monetary base is acceptable as a rule. But as the Fed's control over, say, the national unemployment rate is indirect and imperfect, an instruction to the Fed to "keep the unemployment rate at 4%" isn't acceptable to advocates of a rule-guided monetary policy.

The opposite of the rules approach, which has been supported by most (though not all) Keynesian economists, is called **discretion**. The idea behind discretion is that the central bank should be free to conduct monetary policy in any way that it believes will advance the ultimate objectives of low and stable inflation, high economic growth, and low unemployment. In particular, the central bank should continuously monitor the economy and, using the advice of economic experts, should change the money supply as needed to best achieve its goals. Because a strategy of discretion involves active responses by the central bank to changes in economic circumstances, such a strategy sometimes is called **activist**.

---

[27]Ben S. Bernanke, "Monetary Policy and Uncertainty," October 19, 2007, available online at *www.federalreserve.gov/newsevents/speech/bernanke20071019a.htm*.

From this description of rules and discretion, you may have trouble understanding why many economists advocate the use of rules. After all, why should anyone arbitrarily and unnecessarily tie the hands of the central bank? The idea that giving the central bank the option of responding to changing economic conditions as it sees fit is always better than putting monetary policy in a straitjacket dictated by rules is the essence of the Keynesian case for discretion.

This basic argument for discretion is attractive, but a strong case also may be made for rules. Next we discuss the traditional monetarist argument for rules. We then consider a relatively new argument for rules: that the use of rules increases the credibility of the central bank.

The Monetarist Case for Rules

Monetarism emphasizes the importance of monetary factors in the macroeconomy. Although monetarists have included numerous outstanding economists, the dominant figure and leader of the group was Milton Friedman. For many years, Friedman argued that monetary policy should be conducted by rules, and this idea has become an important part of monetarist doctrine.[28]

Friedman's argument for rules may be broken down into a series of propositions.

> **Proposition 1.** Monetary policy has powerful short-run effects on the real economy. In the longer run, however, changes in the money supply have their primary effect on the price level.

Friedman's research on U.S. monetary history (with Anna Schwartz) provided some of the earliest and best evidence that changes in the money supply can be nonneutral in the short run (Chapter 10). Friedman and other monetarists believe that fluctuations in the money supply historically have been one of the most significant—if not the most significant—sources of business cycle fluctuations. On long-run neutrality, Friedman (along with Edmund Phelps) was one of the first to argue that, because prices eventually adjust to changes in the money supply, the effect of money on real variables can be only temporary (Chapter 12).

> **Proposition 2.** Despite the powerful short-run effect of money on the economy, there is little scope for using monetary policy actively to try to smooth business cycles.

Friedman backed this proposition with several points (several of which we discussed in connection with macroeconomic policy more generally in earlier chapters). First, time is needed for the central bank and other agencies to gather and process information about the current state of the economy. These information lags may make it difficult for the central bank to determine whether the economy actually is in a recession and whether a change in policy is appropriate.

Second, there is considerable uncertainty about how much effect a change in the money supply will have on the economy and how long the effect will take to occur (see Fig. 14.10). Friedman has emphasized that there are *long and variable lags* between monetary policy actions and their economic results. That is, not only does monetary policy take a relatively long time to work, but the amount of time it takes to work is unpredictable and can vary from episode to episode.

---

[28]Friedman's 1959 book *A Program for Monetary Stability*, New York: Fordham University Press, presents a clear early statement of his views.

Third, wage and price adjustment, although not instantaneous, occurs rapidly enough that, by the time the Fed recognizes that the economy is in a recession and increases the money supply, the economy may already be heading out of the recession. If the expansion in the money supply stimulates the economy with a lag of about a year, the stimulus may take effect when output has already recovered and the economy is in a boom. In this case the monetary expansion will cause the economy to overshoot full employment and cause prices to rise. Thus the monetary increase, intended to fight the recession, may actually be destabilizing (causing more variability of output than there would have been otherwise), as well as inflationary.

> **Proposition 3.** Even if there is some scope for using monetary policy to smooth business cycles, the Fed cannot be relied on to do so effectively.

One reason that Friedman didn't trust the Fed to manage an activist monetary policy effectively was political. He believed that despite its supposed independence, the Fed is susceptible to short-run political pressures from the President and others in the administration. For example, the Fed might be pressured to stimulate the economy during an election year. If timed reasonably well, an election-year monetary expansion could expand output and employment just before voters go to the polls, with the inflationary effects of the policy not being felt until after the incumbents were safely reelected.

More fundamentally, though, Friedman's distrust of the Fed arose from his interpretation of macroeconomic history. From his work with Anna Schwartz, Friedman concluded that for whatever reason—incompetence, shortsightedness, or bad luck—monetary policy historically has been a greater source of economic instability than stability. The primary example cited by Friedman is the 1929–1933 period, when the Fed was unable or unwilling to stop the money supply from falling by one-third in the wake of widespread runs on banks. Friedman and Schwartz argued that this monetary contraction was one of the main causes of the Great Depression. Thus Friedman concluded that eliminating monetary policy as a source of instability would substantially improve macroeconomic performance.

How could the Fed be removed as a source of instability? This question led to Friedman's policy recommendation, the last proposition.

> **Proposition 4.** The Fed should choose a specific monetary aggregate (such as M1 or M2) and commit itself to making that aggregate grow at a fixed percentage rate, year in and year out.

For Friedman, the crucial step in eliminating the Fed as a source of instability was to get it to give up activist, or discretionary, monetary policy and to commit itself—publicly and in advance—to following some rule. Although the exact choice of a rule isn't critical, Friedman believed that a constant-money-growth rule would be a good choice for two reasons. First, the Fed has considerable influence, though not complete control, over the rate of money growth. Thus if money growth deviated significantly from its target, the Fed couldn't easily blame the deviation on forces beyond its control. Second, Friedman argued that steady money growth would lead to smaller cyclical fluctuations than the supposedly "countercyclical" monetary policies utilized historically. He concluded that a constant money growth rate would provide a "stable monetary background" that would allow economic growth to proceed without concern about monetary instability.

Friedman didn't advocate a sudden shift from discretionary monetary policy to a low, constant rate of money growth. Instead, he envisioned a transition period in which the Fed, by gradual preannounced steps, would steadily reduce the growth rate of money. Ultimately, the growth rate of the monetary aggregate selected would be consistent with an inflation rate near zero. Importantly, after the constant growth rate has been attained, the Fed wouldn't respond to modest economic downturns by increasing money growth but would continue to follow the policy of maintaining a fixed rate of money growth. However, in some of his writings Friedman appeared to leave open the possibility that the monetary rule could be temporarily suspended in the face of major economic crises, such as a depression.

Rules and Central Bank Credibility

Much of the monetarist argument for rules rests on pessimism about the competence or political reliability of the Federal Reserve. Economists who are more optimistic about the ability of the government to intervene effectively in the economy (which includes many Keynesians) question the monetarist case for rules. A "policy optimist" could argue as follows:

> Monetary policy may have performed badly in the past. However, as time passes, we learn more about the economy and the use of policy gets better. For example, U.S. monetary policy clearly was handled better after World War II than during the Great Depression. Imposing rigid rules just as we are beginning to learn how to use activist policy properly would be foolish. As to the issue of political reliability, that problem affects fiscal policymakers and indeed all our branches of government. We just have to trust in the democratic process to ensure that policymakers will take actions that for the most part are in the best interests of the country.

For policy optimists this reply to the monetarist case for rules seems perfectly satisfactory. During the past three decades, however, a new argument for rules has been developed that applies even if the central bank knows exactly how monetary changes affect the economy and is completely public-spirited. Thus the new argument for rules is a challenge even to policy optimists. It holds that the use of monetary rules can improve the **credibility** of the central bank, or the degree to which the public believes central bank announcements about future policy, and that the credibility of the central bank influences how well monetary policy works.

One reason that the central bank's credibility matters is that people's expectations of the central bank's actions affect their behavior. For example, suppose that the central bank announces that it intends to maintain a stable price level by maintaining a stable money supply. If firms increase prices and the aggregate price level increases, the real money supply will fall, causing the *LM* curve to shift up and to the left. As a result output and employment will fall. If firms collectively believe the Fed will try to fight the drop in output and employment by increasing the nominal money supply—contrary to its stated intentions to maintain a stable money supply—they will go ahead and raise prices. However, if firms collectively believe that the central bank will abide by its stated intention to maintain a stable money supply, they will not increase their prices because they realize that the central bank will allow the drop in output and employment to occur and the firms will have to reduce prices in the future anyway. Thus, if the central bank's statement that it intends to maintain stable prices and money is credible, firms won't raise prices; however, if the central bank's statement lacks credibility, prices will rise.

Rules, Commitment, and Credibility. We have seen why central bank credibility is important. If a central bank is credible, it can maintain stable prices even if business firms threaten to raise prices. But how can a central bank achieve credibility?

One possibility is for the central bank to develop a reputation for carrying out its promises. Suppose that in the preceding example firms raise their prices, fully expecting the Fed to increase the money supply. However, the Fed holds the money supply constant, causing a recession. The next time, the firms may take the Fed's promises more seriously.

The problem with this strategy is that it may involve serious costs while the reputation is being established: The economy suffers a recession while the central bank establishes its reputation. Is there some less costly way to achieve credibility?

Advocates of rules suggest that, by forcing the central bank to keep its promises, rules may substitute for reputation in establishing credibility. Suppose that there is an ironclad rule—ideally, enforced by some outside agency—that the Fed must maintain a constant growth rate of the money supply. Observing the existence of this rule, the firms might well believe that money supply growth is going to be steady no matter what, and price stability can be achieved. Note that if it increases credibility, a rule improves central bank performance even if the central bank is competent and public-spirited. Hence this reason for monetary policy rules is different from the monetarists' argument presented earlier.

How do advocates of discretion respond to the credibility argument for rules? Keynesians argue that there may be a trade-off between credibility and flexibility. For a rule to establish credibility, it must be virtually impossible to change—otherwise, no one will believe that the Fed will stick to it. In the extreme, the monetary growth rule would be added as an amendment to the Constitution, which could then be changed only at great cost and with long delays. But if a rule is completely unbreakable, what happens (ask the Keynesians) if some unexpected crisis arises—for example, a new depression? In that case the inability of the Fed to take corrective action—that is, its lack of flexibility—could prove disastrous. Therefore, Keynesians argue, establishing a rule ironclad enough to create credibility for the central bank would, by eliminating policy flexibility, also create unacceptable risks.

The Taylor Rule

Advocates of the use of rules in monetary policy believe that the Fed should be required to follow a set of simple, prespecified, and publicly announced rules when setting policy instruments. Nothing in the concept of rules, however, necessarily prohibits the Fed from responding to the state of the economy, as long as those responses are built into the rule itself. An example of a monetary policy rule that allows the Fed to take economic conditions into account is the so-called **Taylor rule**, introduced by John Taylor[29] of Stanford University. The Taylor rule is given by

$$i = \pi + 0.02 + 0.5y + 0.5(\pi - 0.02), \qquad \textbf{(14.1)}$$

where

i = the nominal fed funds rate (the Fed's intermediate target);

π = the rate of inflation over the previous four quarters;

$y = (Y - \bar{Y})/\bar{Y}$ = the percentage deviation of output from full-employment output.

[29]"Discretion Versus Policy Rules in Practice," *Carnegie-Rochester Conference Series on Public Policy*, 1993, pp. 195–214.

The Taylor rule requires that the *real* fed funds rate, $i - \pi$, respond to (1) the difference between output and full-employment output and (2) the difference between inflation and its target, here taken to be 2%, or 0.02. The Taylor rule fits in with the idea we discussed in Section 14.3 that many central banks target the real interest rate rather than the real money supply, as an intermediate target. Notice that if output is at its full-employment level and inflation is at its 2% target, the Taylor rule has the Fed setting the real fed funds rate at 2%, which is approximately its long-run average level. If the economy is "overheating," with output above its full-employment level and inflation above its target, the Taylor rule would have the Fed tighten monetary policy by raising the real fed funds rate above 2%. Conversely, if the economy shows weakness, with output below its full-employment level and inflation below its target, the Taylor rule indicates that the real fed funds rate should be reduced below 2%, thereby easing monetary policy. Both responses are consistent with standard Fed practice. Indeed, Taylor showed that, historically, his relatively simple rule describes actual Fed behavior quite accurately.

Since Taylor first wrote about the rule in 1993, economists all over the world have studied its properties, and it has become common to assume that a central bank follows some type of rule that is similar to the Taylor rule. In practice, economists at central banks often show what policy should be used to follow the Taylor rule and then make an argument for why they might want to deviate from the rule. Recently, Taylor himself has suggested an even stronger role for his rule, advocating legislation requiring the Fed to follow the rule and to justify to Congress any deviations from the rule. Such a requirement would face many operational difficulties, however, such as defining the output gap in real time and dealing with the fact that the rule would sometimes require a negative nominal interest rate, which would be difficult to achieve.

Figure 14.11 illustrates the actual federal funds rate over time and what the federal funds rate would have been if the original Taylor rule had been followed.[30] The Fed set the federal funds rate well below the level suggested by the Taylor rule in the late 1960s and throughout the 1970s. In that period, the inflation rate rose from about 1% in 1963 to more than 10% by 1975, averaging 2.4% in the 1960s and 6.7% in the 1970s. In the 1980s, the Fed set the federal funds rate above the level suggested by the Taylor rule, causing inflation to decline from 10% in 1981 to 3.5% in 1989; it averaged 4.5% over the decade. In the 1990s, the federal funds rate was set close to or slightly above the level suggested by the Taylor rule, and the inflation rate averaged just 2.1% over the decade. From 2000 to 2020, the federal funds rate was frequently lower than the level suggested by the Taylor rule, though the inflation rate averaged 2.0%. But inflation began rising in 2021, and the Federal Reserve was very slow in raising interest rates and tightening monetary policy, as Figure 14.4 shows. The Taylor rule suggested that the federal funds rate should have been nearly 10% by the end of 2021, while the Fed kept the rate near zero.

For the past 50 years, the Taylor rule seems to have performed about as expected. When the Fed has set the federal funds rate below the level suggested by the Taylor rule, inflation has often risen, and when the fed funds rate has been above the level suggested by the Taylor rule, inflation has often fallen. One

[30]The line marked "Taylor rule" in Fig. 14.11 is based on the data available today and not exactly what the Fed would have done in real time if it followed the Taylor rule because of data revisions and the fact that today we know more about what the level of full-employment output was in the past.

FIGURE 14.11

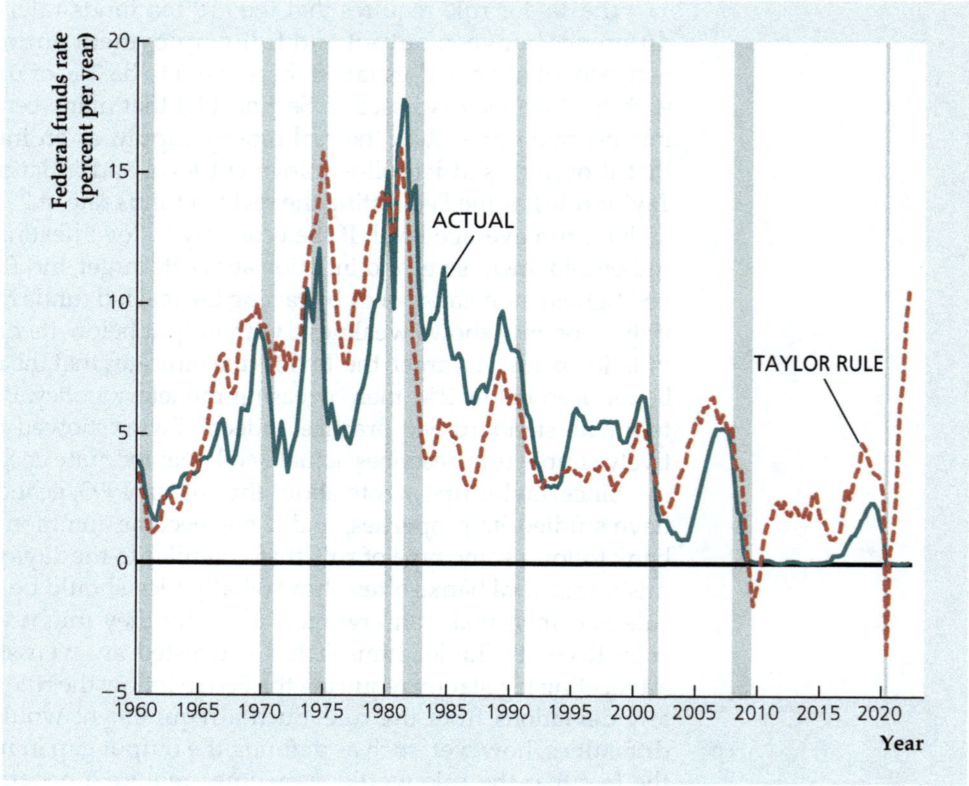

Taylor rule and actual federal funds rate, 1960–2022

The Fed set the federal funds rate well below the level suggested by the Taylor rule in the late 1960s and 1970s, leading to increased inflation. In the 1980s, the Fed set the federal funds rate above the level suggested by the Taylor rule, causing inflation to decline. In the 1990s, the federal funds rate was set fairly close to that suggested by the rule. In the 2000s, the federal funds rate has mainly been lower than the level suggested by the Taylor rule. The shaded bars in the figure represent recessions.

Source: Author's calculations based on Eq. (14.1) and data from 1960 to the first quarter of 2022, downloaded from Federal Reserve Bank of St. Louis FRED database, *fred.stlouisfed.org*. GDP price index and nominal output from Bureau of Economic Analysis, FRED variables *GDPCTPI* and *GDP*, respectively. Full-employment output from Congressional Budget Office, FRED variable *GDPPOT*. Federal funds rate from Federal Reserve Board of Governors, FRED variable *FEDFUNDS*.

exception has been from 2000 to 2020, when inflation did not rise, even though the Fed seems to have set the federal funds rate below the level suggested by the Taylor rule for a substantial part of the period. Clearly, in the financial crisis of 2008, with a potentially catastrophic breakdown in credit markets, the Fed could justify its actions. But even in the early 2000s, when the economy was in a recession followed by a period of slow growth, the Fed indicated concerns about the possibility of deflation, which justified keeping the federal funds rate below the level suggested by the Taylor rule. However, inflation began rising sharply in 2021, consistent with the fed funds rate being far below that suggested by the Taylor rule.

The Taylor rule in Eq. (14.1) has been the subject of extensive research in the past 20 years. Economists have discovered that the rule may work better if formulated in terms of forecasts for the future values of inflation and the deviation of output from full-employment output rather than looking at past inflation and the current level of output relative to full-employment output. Economists have also experimented with different coefficients on the terms of the rule (alternatives to Taylor's initial 0.5 coefficients on the output term and the inflation term) and examined targets other than 2% inflation. Experience with the Taylor rule has shown that uncertainty about the output term in the Taylor rule is large because output is revised significantly at times and because the level of potential output is sometimes very different than what policymakers and economists thought it was in real time.[31] Nonetheless, for central banks all over the world, the Taylor rule has become a focal point of policy discussions.

---

[31]See Athanasios Orphanides. "Monetary Policy Rules Based on Real-Time Data," *American Economic Review*, September 2001, pp. 964–985.

Other Ways to Achieve Central Bank Credibility

Besides announcing targets for money growth or inflation, are there other ways to increase the central bank's credibility and thus improve the performance of monetary policy?

One way to increase a central bank's credibility is by enhancing its reputation as an inflation fighter. A central bank's reputation can be improved when it announces specific goals and shows that it can meet them. Another way to enhance the central bank's reputation is by appointing a tough central banker. For example, the President could appoint a Fed chairman who strongly dislikes inflation and who people believe is willing to accept increased unemployment if necessary to bring inflation down. Thus when President Jimmy Carter faced a serious inflation problem in 1979, he appointed Paul Volcker—an imposing individual with a strong anti-inflation reputation—to be chairman of the Fed. In appointing a "tough" central banker, Carter hoped to convince the financial markets and the public that he was serious about reducing inflation. Volcker succeeded in getting rid of inflation, but because unemployment

Application

Inflation Targeting

By the early 1980s, most countries in the Organization for Economic Co-operation and Development (OECD) were already announcing some form of money or credit target to convince markets of their commitment to control inflation. However, the focus was on "intermediate targets" such as the quantity of money or credit, rather than inflation. Although price stability is acknowledged as the long-run goal of monetary policy, there is no consensus on how monetary policy can be conducted to achieve it. A widely used monetary policy regime in recent times is *inflation targeting (IT)*.[32] A credible inflation target becomes a nominal anchor, providing conditions that make the price level uniquely determined. This is necessary for price stability and helps tie down inflation expectations directly.

By committing to inflation targeting, countries make an explicit commitment to meet a specified inflation rate (or range) within a certain time frame. Specific elements include (a) regular public announcements of medium-term numerical targets, or ranges, for inflation, with a reduced role for intermediate targets such as money growth; (b) an institutional commitment to price stability as the primary, long-run monetary policy goal and to achievement of the inflation target; and (c) accountability of the central bank for meeting the target.

New Zealand became the first country to formally adopt inflation targeting as we now know it when The Reserve Bank of New Zealand Act, 1989, came into effect in February 1990. The policy arose from widespread dissatisfaction with the economy's performance over the decade, especially in 1984, when inflation averaged over 10% and economic growth rate was abysmal. Since 1990, several central banks from every

[32]See B.S. Bernanke, and F.S. Mishkin, "Inflation Targeting: A New Framework for Monetary Policy?" *Journal of Economic Perspectives* 11, no. 2, 1997, pp. 97–116 for a comprehensive discussion.

(continued)

continent have adopted inflation targeting, including Canada (1991), the United Kingdom (1992), Sweden (1993), Finland (1993), Australia (1994), Spain (1994), South Africa (2000), India (2015), and Ghana (2007). Some advanced economies' central banks such as the European Central Bank and the U.S. Federal Reserve, though not officially "inflation targeters," adopt many elements of inflation targeting and pursue a modified inflation targeting approach. Some countries, including Finland and Spain, gave up their own targets with their adoption of the euro.

Advocates of inflation targeting argue that commitment to an explicit numerical target increases central banks' accountability and potentially increases the likelihood that they will focus on long-run policies while resisting pressures to pursue short-run expansionary policies that are inconsistent with the long-run goal of price stability. Critics, however, caution that the central banks' focus on inflation targeting may allow unsustainable speculative bubbles and other economic distortions to thrive unchecked until it is too late, when the inflation trickles down from asset prices to retail consumer prices, as was the case in the 2008 financial crisis.[33] Moreover, inflation is known to respond to policy with a long lag.

For inflation targeting to succeed, fiscal policy considerations should not dictate monetary policy. Although inflation-targeting central banks may not be entirely independent of governments' influence, they must have the freedom to decide the instruments to use to achieve the target. They must commit to not target other indicators, such as wages, employment levels, or the exchange rate. In many countries, these commitments are difficult, and unsurprisingly, many consistently fall outside their target bands.

[33]See Willem Buiter and Paolo Pesenti, "Rational Speculative Bubbles in an Exchange Rate Target Zone," *NBER Working Paper 3467, 1990, https://www.nber.org/papers/w3467.*

rose significantly in the process, his appointment didn't completely solve the credibility problem.[34] But after inflation came down sharply under Volcker and declined even more under Alan Greenspan, the Fed's reputation increased significantly. People began to expect the Fed to keep inflation low. Thus, even with the financial crisis in 2008 and the increase in the monetary base from 2008 to 2014, the Fed's reputation was so strong that long-term inflation expectations did not change very much.

Another strategy for improving a central bank's credibility is to increase the independence of the central bank from the other parts of the government—for example, by limiting the legal ability of the executive and legislative branches to interfere in monetary policy decisions. The rationale is that a more independent central bank will be less subject to short-term political pressures to try to expand output and employment (say, before an election) and will be more strongly committed to maintaining a low long-run inflation rate. Because the public will recognize that an independent central bank is less subject to political pressures, announcements made by the central bank should be more credible.

[34]The point that appointing a tough central banker may improve central bank credibility was made by Kenneth Rogoff, "The Optimal Degree of Commitment to an Intermediate Monetary Target," *Quarterly Journal of Economics,* November 1985, pp. 1169–1189. Keynesians might argue that Volcker was credible but that long-lived stickiness in wages and prices led unemployment to increase in 1981–1982 anyway.

CHAPTER SUMMARY

1. Three groups help determine the money supply: the central bank, private-sector banks, and the general public. The central bank sets the monetary base, which is the quantity of central bank liabilities that can be used as money. The monetary base equals the sum of bank reserves (deposits by banks at the central bank plus currency in the vaults of banks) and currency held by the nonbank public.
2. The central bank can affect the size of the monetary base and thus the money supply through open-market operations. An open-market sale (in which central bank assets are sold for currency or bank reserves) reduces the monetary base. An open-market purchase (in which the central bank uses money to buy assets, such as government securities, from the public) increases the monetary base.
3. The central bank of the United States is called the Federal Reserve System, or the Fed. The leadership of the Fed is the Board of Governors, which in turn is headed by the chairman of the Federal Reserve. The Federal Open Market Committee (FOMC) meets about eight times each year to set monetary policy.
4. The Fed affects the U.S. money supply through open-market operations, discount window lending, changes in the interest rate on reserves, and changes in reserve requirements. To deal with the zero lower bound in the financial crisis of 2008, the Fed developed new tools, including forward guidance and quantitative easing.
5. The Fed uses intermediate targets such as the money supply or short-term interest rates (primarily the fed funds rate) to guide monetary policy. Stabilizing interest rates is a useful strategy when fluctuations in money supply or demand would otherwise cause the *LM* curve to shift randomly back and forth.
6. The Federal Reserve and many other central banks choose to target interest rates in setting policy. This method can be analyzed either in the traditional *IS-LM* model, or in a modified model with a horizontal *LR* curve replacing the *LM* curve.
7. In a monetary-policy regime with abundant reserves, the Fed primarily changes the federal funds rate by changing the interest rate on reserves.
8. Setting monetary policy is difficult because of uncertainty about the state of the economy, about the structure of the economy, and about how people's expectations will respond to economic shocks or policy actions.
9. In the Great Recession that accompanied the financial crisis of 2008, the Fed found itself in a liquidity trap, having hit the zero lower bound on short-term interest rates. In response, the Fed used new policies, including forward guidance and quantitative easing.
10. Monetary policy may be conducted either by rules or by discretion. Under rules, the central bank is required to follow a simple predetermined rule for monetary policy, such as a requirement for constant money growth. Under discretion, the central bank is expected to monitor the economy and use monetary policy actively to maintain full employment and to keep inflation low. Discretion for monetary policy is usually favored by Keynesians, who argue that it gives the Fed maximum flexibility to stabilize the economy.
11. Monetarists, led by Milton Friedman, argue that, because of information problems and lags between the implementation of policy changes and their effects, the scope for using monetary policy to stabilize the economy is small. Furthermore, they argue, the Fed cannot be relied on to use active monetary policy wisely and in the public interest. Monetarists advocate a constant-growth-rate rule for the money supply to discipline the Fed and keep monetary fluctuations from destabilizing the economy.
12. An additional argument for rules is that they increase central bank credibility. Supporters of rules claim that the use of ironclad rules will cause the public to believe the central bank if it says (for example) that money supply growth will be reduced, with the implication that inflation can be reduced without a large increase in unemployment.
13. The Taylor rule suggests that a central bank targets interest rates based on the deviation of inflation from its target and the deviation of output from its full-employment level.
14. Inflation targeting has been adopted by a number of countries. This approach allows the central bank some discretion in the short run but commits the bank to achieving a preannounced target for inflation in the longer run.
15. Possible ways to enhance a central bank's credibility are to appoint a central banker who is "tough" on inflation and to increase the central bank's independence from other parts of the government.

KEY TERMS

activist, p. 600
bank reserves, p. 575
bank run, p. 577
Board of Governors of the Federal Reserve System, p. 578
central bank, p. 574
credibility, p. 603
depository institutions, p. 574
discount rate, p. 581
discount window lending, p. 581
discretion, p. 600
Federal Open Market Committee (FOMC), p. 579
federal funds rate, p. 580
fed funds rate, p. 580
forward guidance, p. 584
fractional reserve banking, p. 575
high-powered money, p. 575
instruments, p. 590
intermediate targets, p. 590
liquidity trap, p. 584
monetarism, p. 601
monetary base, p. 575
multiple expansion of loans and deposits, p. 576
100% reserve banking, p. 575
open-market purchase, p. 577
open-market sale, p. 577
quantitative easing, p. 585
reserve–deposit ratio, p. 575
rules, p. 600
Taylor rule, p. 604
zero lower bound, p. 583

KEY EQUATIONS

$$i = \pi + 0.02 + 0.5y + 0.5(\pi - 0.02) \quad \textbf{(14.1)}$$

The Taylor rule describes how the Fed targets the nominal federal funds rate, i, depending on the inflation rate, π, the long-run average real federal funds rate (0.02), the deviation of output from full-employment output, y, and the deviation of inflation from its target (0.02).

REVIEW QUESTIONS

1. Define *monetary base*. How does the monetary base differ from the money supply?
2. What is the effect on the monetary base of an open-market purchase of U.S. Treasury securities? What is the effect on the money supply?
3. What is the reserve–deposit ratio, and how does it affect bank runs?
4. Besides open-market operations, what other means does the Federal Reserve have for controlling the money supply? Explain how these alternative methods work.
5. Besides open-market operations, what other means does a central bank like the European Central Bank use to control the money supply? Explain how these alternative methods work.
6. Describe how the federal funds rate is determined in a regime of abundant reserves.
7. Describe the main sources of uncertainty that affect monetary policymakers and give an example of each.
8. Define the main tools the Fed used in the Great Recession to avoid problems caused by the zero lower bound.
9. "It is plain to see that discretion is a better way to run monetary policy than following a rule because a policy of discretion gives the central bank the ability to react to news about the economy." What is the monetarist response to this statement? What is the more recent argument for using rules rather than discretion?
10. Describe the Taylor rule. What are the variables that determine the recommended interest rate according to the rule? How has the rule performed historically?
11. How does the use of inflation targeting improve central bank credibility? What is the main disadvantage of inflation targeting?

NUMERICAL PROBLEMS

1. The monetary base is $1,000,000. The public always holds half its money supply as currency and half as deposits. Banks hold 20% of deposits in the form of reserves. Starting with the initial creation of the monetary base that accompanies the purchase by the central bank of $1,000,000 worth of securities from the public, show the consolidated balance sheet of the banks after they first receive deposits, after a first round of loans and redeposits, and after a second round of loans and redeposits. (*Hint:* Don't forget that the public keeps only half its money in the form of bank deposits.)

Show the balance sheets of the central bank, the banking system, and the public at the end of the process of multiple expansion of loans and deposits. What is the final value of the money supply?

2. Suppose the current price level in the United Kingdom is 128.40, and one year ago the price level was 126. Output is currently £2900, and potential output is £3000 (both in billions of 2015 pounds).

a. What value of the key interest rate would the Bank of England (BoE) choose if it followed the Taylor rule given by Eq. (14.6)?

b. Suppose that one year later, the price level has declined by 0.4%, output has declined by 1.3%, and potential output has increased 3%. In this new situation, what value of the key interest rate would the BoE choose if it followed the Taylor rule? What is the problem with setting the key interest rate to follow the Taylor rule in this case?

ANALYTICAL PROBLEMS

1. How would the following monetary decisions of the European Central Bank influence individuals?

a. A decrease in interest rates

b. An asset purchase program to support struggling member-states

c. A target inflation rate of 2%

d. A fixed exchange rate to the U.S. dollar

e. An abolition of cash

2. Since 1989, many central banks have adopted inflation targeting as a strategy for conducting monetary policy. What is inflation targeting? What influence do the following decisions have on inflation?

a. An increase in interest rates

b. Reduction of income taxes

c. Government support programs for small and medium-sized enterprises

d. Government demand for better infrastructure

e. Tightened lending criteria for private loans

3. Describe the following measures of monetary policy the Fed used to fight the Great Recession starting in 2007. What effect did they have on the U.S. economy?

a. Zero lower bound and forward guidance

b. Credit easing

c. Quantitative easing

d. Increased limit for coverage on deposits from $100,000 to $250,000

4. Why do many governments have policies against negotiating with hostage-taking terrorists? Under what conditions, if any, are such policies likely to reduce hostage taking? Discuss the analogy to monetary rules.

WORKING WITH MACROECONOMIC DATA

For data to use in these exercises, go to the Federal Reserve Bank of St. Louis FRED database at fred.stlouisfed.org.

1. During much of the postwar period, the Fed attempted to stabilize nominal interest rates. However, during 1979–1982 the Fed under Paul Volcker greatly reduced its emphasis on interest rate stabilization to focus on fighting inflation.

Calculate and graph the quarter-to-quarter change in the three-month Treasury bill rate since 1961. What happened to the volatility of interest rates in the 1979–1982 period? What has happened to the volatility of interest rates since 1982? Does your answer change if your measure of the interest rate is the ten-year government bond rate?

2. As discussed in the text, if money demand is unstable, the Fed may prefer to target interest rates rather than the money supply itself. When the Fed follows an interest-rate-targeting policy, "Fed watchers" in financial markets and the media typically look to changes in short-term interest rates rather than changes in the money supply to gauge the Fed's intentions.

Graph the three-month Treasury bill interest rate and the unemployment rate, using monthly data since 1961. If changes in monetary policy are reflected primarily by changes in the short-term interest rate, what relationship would you expect to see between these two variables? Does this relationship hold up in the data?

3. Plot monthly data, beginning in 1990, on the U.S. monetary base and excess reserves of depository institutions. How would you characterize the relationship between the two variables before and after the financial crisis in the fall of 2008? What explains this changing relationship?

15

Government Spending and Its Financing

At every level of government, from the town hall to the White House, fiscal policy—government decisions about how much to spend, what to spend for, and how to finance its spending—is of central importance. Politicians and the public understand that the government's fiscal choices have a direct impact on the "bread and butter" issues of how much they pay in taxes and what government benefits and services they receive. Equally important are the effects of fiscal policy on the economy. In recent years, people have become more aware of the macroeconomic effects of fiscal policy as the economic implications of government budget deficits and surpluses, tax reform, Social Security reform, government bailouts, and other aspects of fiscal policy have been extensively debated.

In this chapter we take a close look at fiscal policy and its macroeconomic effects. To provide some background, we begin with definitions and facts about the government's budget. We then discuss some basic fiscal policy issues, including the effects of government spending and taxes on economic activity, the burden of government debt, and the link between budget deficits and inflation.

Learning Objectives

15.1 Use the measures of government outlays and taxes to measure government surpluses and deficits.

15.2 Describe how government spending and taxing decisions affect the macroeconomy.

15.3 Discuss the economic effects of government deficits and debt.

15.4 Explain the link between deficits and inflation.

15.1 The Government Budget: Some Facts and Figures

Use the measures of government outlays and taxes to measure government surpluses and deficits.

Before getting into the analytical issues of fiscal policy, we set the stage by looking at the components of the government budget and their recent trends. We discuss three main aspects of the budget: (1) spending, or outlays; (2) tax revenues, or receipts; and (3) the budget surplus or deficit. Our discussion reviews and builds on Chapter 2, in which we introduced basic budget concepts.

Government Outlays

Government outlays, the total spending by the government during a period of time, are classified into three primary categories: government purchases, transfer payments, and net interest payments.

1. *Government purchases* (*G*) are government expenditures on currently produced goods and services, including capital goods. Government spending on capital goods, or *government investment*, accounts for about one-sixth of government purchases of goods and services. The remaining five-sixths of government purchases are *government consumption expenditures.*
2. *Transfer payments* (*TR*) are payments made to individuals for which the government does not receive *current* goods or services in exchange. Examples of transfers are Social Security benefit payments, military and civil service pensions, unemployment insurance, welfare payments (Temporary Assistance for Needy Families), and Medicare.[1]
3. *Net interest payments* (*INT*) are the interest paid to the holders of government bonds less the interest received by the government—for example, on outstanding government loans to students or farmers.

In addition there is a minor category called *subsidies less surpluses of government enterprises.* Subsidies are government payments that are intended to affect the production or prices of various goods. Examples are price support payments to farmers and fare subsidies for mass transit systems. The surpluses of government enterprises represent the profits of government-run enterprises such as the Tennessee Valley Authority (an electricity producer). This category of outlays is relatively small, so for simplicity we will ignore it.

In the United States, total government outlays (Federal, state, and local) were about 37% of GDP over the past five years. Figure 15.1 shows the trends since 1940 in the three main categories of government outlays, as well as total government outlays, expressed as a percentage of GDP. The most obvious feature of Fig. 15.1

FIGURE 15.1

Government outlays: Federal, state, and local, 1940–2021

The figure shows the behavior since 1940 of the three major components of government outlays, as well as total government outlays, for all levels of government combined and measured as a percentage of GDP. Government purchases rose most sharply during World War II (1941–1945) and the Korean War (1951–1953). Transfer payments have risen steadily as a share of GDP and then jumped sharply in the pandemic of 2020–2021. Interest payments rose most sharply during World War II and in the 1980s.

Sources: National Income and Product Accounts, Bureau of Economic Analysis, *www.bea.gov*. GDP: Table 1.1.5; components of government outlays: Table 3.1. For detailed updates and projections of the Federal budget by the Congressional Budget Office, see *www.cbo.gov*.

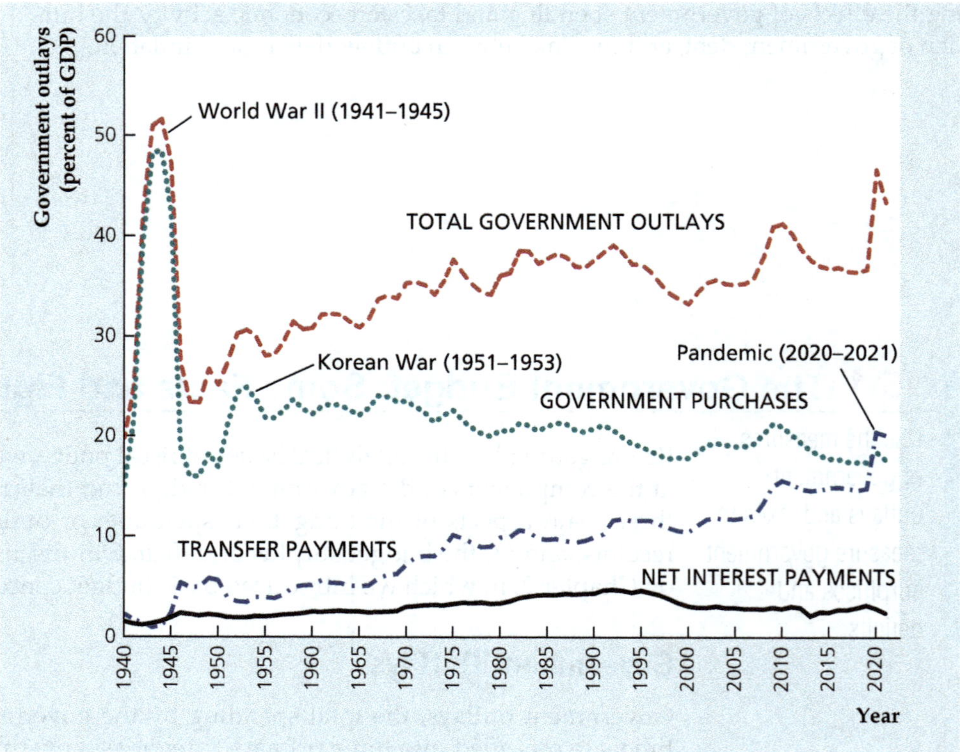

[1]Although government outlays for Medicare and Medicaid are used to pay for current medical services, they are treated as transfer payments to individuals who then purchase these services.

is the enormous increase in government purchases during World War II: In 1943 and 1944, when the war effort was at its peak, government purchases exceeded 45% of GDP. The impact of the Korean War (1951–1953) also is evident, though less dramatic. The share of GDP devoted to government purchases drifted gradually downward from about 23% of GDP in the late 1960s to around 17% of GDP in the late 1990s and then rose during the financial crisis of 2008 and its aftermath before declining again to about 17% in recent years.

Figure 15.1 also shows that transfer payments rose steadily as a share of GDP from the early 1950s until the early 1980s, doubling their share of GDP during that thirty-year period. Transfers averaged about 12% of GDP in the 2000s before the financial crisis in 2008 and averaged about 15% from 2008 until the pandemic in 2020–2021, when they rose sharply. The long-term increase in transfer payments is the result of the creation of new social programs (such as Medicare and Medicaid in 1965), the expansion of benefits under existing programs (such as Social Security, which is discussed later in the chapter in the Application "Social Security in the United Kingdom: How Can It Be Fixed?"), and the increased number of people covered by the various programs.

Finally, Fig. 15.1 shows how net interest payments—interest payments, for short—have evolved. Because interest payments are much smaller than the other two categories of government outlays, they appear to fluctuate less. However, interest payments rose sharply as a percentage of GDP in two periods. First, interest payments doubled from 1.2% of GDP in 1941 to 2.4% of GDP in 1946, reflecting the large amount of government borrowing done to finance the war effort during World War II. Second, interest payments as a share of GDP increased significantly during the 1980s, rising from 3.2% in 1979 to 4.2% in 1989. This increase reflected both increased borrowing by the government and the generally high level of interest rates during the 1980s. Net interest payments as a share of GDP declined in the 1990s because interest rates fell and the government budget moved into surplus and fell further in the 2000s as interest rates declined even more.

How does the rate of government expenditure in the United States compare with rates in other countries with similar living standards? Because official accounting rules for measuring the government budget vary widely among countries, the answer isn't as straightforward as you might think. Nevertheless, Table 15.1 compares the ratios of government spending to GDP for 18 countries in the Organization for Economic Cooperation and Development (OECD). The United States has the fourth lowest rate of total government spending as a percentage of GDP; the lowest is Ireland at just 25.0%. The low rate of government spending in the United States relative to most of the other countries largely reflects the more extensive government-financed social welfare programs (such as national health insurance) in those countries.

Taxes

On the revenue side of the government's budget are tax receipts. There are four principal categories of tax receipts: personal taxes, contributions for social insurance, taxes on production and imports, and corporate taxes. Figure 15.2 shows the history of revenues from these four major categories of taxes in the United States, all expressed as a percentage of GDP. The share of taxes in GDP grew dramatically from 15.7% of GDP in 1940 to 28.3% of GDP in 2000, declined to 23.5% in 2011, and was 25% to 27% from 2013 to 2021.

TABLE 15.1

Government Spending in 18 OECD Countries, Percentage of GDP, 2021

Country	
United States	45.1
Japan	43.0
Germany	51.6
France	59.1
Italy	55.6
United Kingdom	47.3
Canada	46.0
Australia	40.2
Austria	56.0
Belgium	54.9
Denmark	51.0
Finland	54.9
Greece	56.9
Iceland	49.3
Ireland	25.0
Netherlands	46.4
Spain	50.6
Sweden	49.6

Source: OECD Economic Outlook, Annex Table 29, *www.oecd.org/economy/outlook/EO111_Fiscal-balances-and-Public-Indebteness.xlsx.*

The largest category of tax receipts is *personal taxes,* which are primarily personal income taxes and property taxes. Income taxes were first introduced at the Federal level in the United States (at very low rates and for only the richest people) during the Civil War. However, this tax faced a series of legal challenges, and eventually the Supreme Court declared the income tax unconstitutional. In 1913, the Sixteenth Amendment to the Constitution gave Congress the right to impose an income tax. Used lightly at first, this tax is now a major source of revenue for government.

Personal taxes took their biggest jump during World War II, rising from 1.7% of GDP in 1940 to 8.5% of GDP in 1945. The general upward drift in personal tax receipts from 1945 to 2000 was interrupted by several tax cut bills, notably the Kennedy–Johnson tax cut of 1964 and the Reagan tax cut of 1981. Personal taxes rose as a result of the deficit-reduction efforts of President Bill Clinton and then declined with President George W. Bush's tax cuts in the 2000s.

Figure 15.2 shows that a large share of the increase in tax receipts since World War II reflects the increase in a second category of taxes, *contributions for social insurance* (primarily Social Security taxes). Social insurance contributions usually are levied as a fixed percentage of a worker's salary, up to a ceiling; income above that ceiling isn't taxed.[2] In most cases the worker's contributions are matched by the employer so that the deduction appearing on the worker's paycheck reflects only half the total tax levied. Increases in social insurance contributions are the result of increases both in the contribution rate and higher ceilings on the amount of income subject to the tax.

A third category of tax receipts is *taxes on production and imports,* mainly sales taxes. These taxes declined as a share of GDP during World War II and haven't shown any significant long-term increase or decrease since.

[2]Note that there is no ceiling for Medicare taxes.

FIGURE 15.2

Taxes: Federal, state, and local, 1940–2021
Shown is the history of revenues collected from various types of taxes, for all levels of government combined and measured as a percentage of GDP. Total taxes drifted upward from 1940 to 2000 but have declined since then. Most of the earlier increase in taxes was accounted for by increases in contributions for social insurance and in personal taxes.

Sources: National Income and Product Accounts, Bureau of Economic Analysis, *www.bea.gov/itable/national-gdp-and-personal-income*. GDP: Table 1.1.5; components of government receipts: Table 3.1.

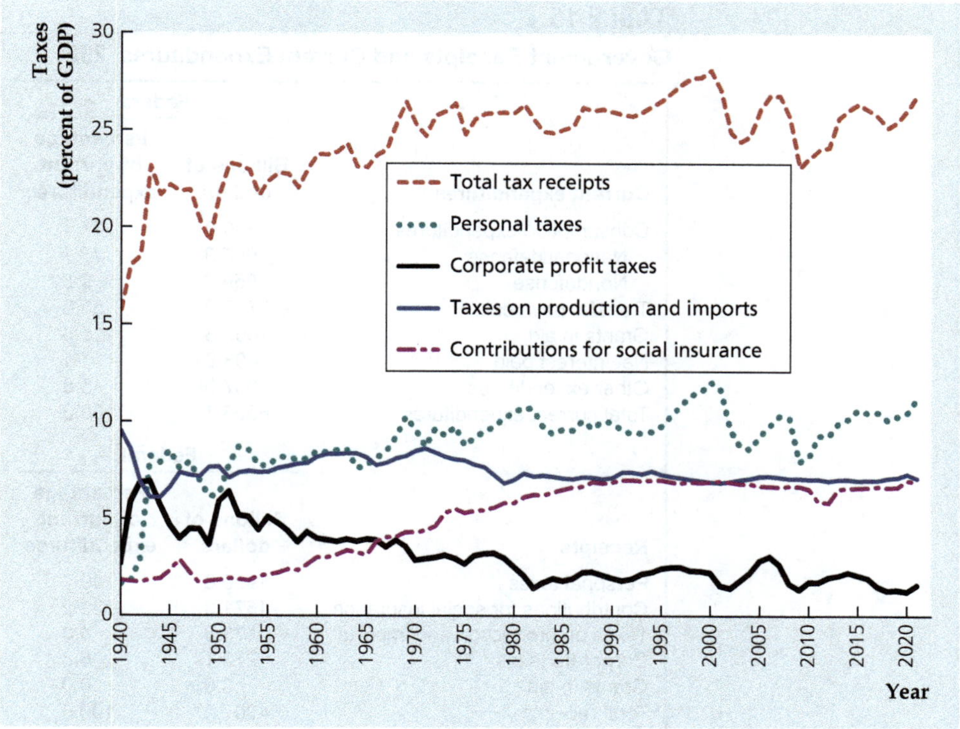

A final category of tax receipts is *corporate taxes*, particularly corporate profit taxes. Figure 15.2 shows that corporate taxes rose sharply during World War II and the Korean War and then drifted gradually downward as a share of GDP from the mid-1950s until the mid-1980s. Corporate tax receipts have accounted for 1% to 2% of GDP in recent years.

The Composition of Outlays and Taxes: The Federal Government Versus State and Local Governments. The components of government spending shown in Fig. 15.1 and the components of taxes shown in Fig. 15.2 lump together Federal, state, and local governments. For most purposes of macroeconomic analysis, combining Federal, state, and local fiscal policy is the most sensible choice. The macroeconomic effect of a new highway-building program, for example, shouldn't depend on whether the new highways are financed from the Federal, state, or local budgets—or from a combination of those budgets. In this respect the tendency of many news stories about fiscal policy to focus exclusively on the Federal government's budget can be misleading.

Nevertheless, it is useful to know that in the United States, Federal government budgets have a much different composition, on both the expenditure and the revenue sides, than those of state and local governments. A summary of the major components of both the Federal and the combined state and local government budgets for 2021 is given in Table 15.2. Note in particular the following points:

1. *Government consumption expenditures.* Over 60% of state and local current expenditures (expenditures excluding investment) is for consumption expenditures. In contrast, less than 20% of Federal current expenditures is for consumption

TABLE 15.2

Government Receipts and Current Expenditures, 2021

	Federal		State and local	
Current expenditures	**Billions of dollars**	**Percentage of current expenditures**	**Billions of dollars**	**Percentage of current expenditures**
Consumption expenditures	1205.0	17.4	2045.4	63.1
National defense	*905.3*	*13.1*	*0.0*	*0.0*
Nondefense	*659.7*	*9.5*	*2045.4*	*63.1*
Transfer payments	3717.9	53.8	902.0	27.8
Grants in aid	1093.8	15.8	0.0	0.0
Net interest paid	493.9	7.1	291.8	9.0
Other expenditures*	397.5	5.8	3.1	0.1
Total current expenditures	6908.1	100.0	3242.3	100.0

	Federal		State and local	
Receipts	**Billions of dollars**	**Percentage of current expenditures**	**Billions of dollars**	**Percentage of receipts**
Personal taxes	1990.0	49.7	595.2	18.2
Contributions for social insurance	1571.3	39.2	22.1	0.7
Taxes on production and imports	173.8	4.3	1467.4	44.8
Corporate taxes	272.1	6.8	97.0	3.0
Grants in aid	0.0	0.0	1093.8	33.4
Total receipts	4007.2	100.0	3275.5	100.0
Current deficit (current expenditures less receipts; negative if surplus)	2900.9		–33.2	
Primary current deficit (negative if surplus)	2407.0		–325.0	

**Subsidies* less surpluses of government enterprises, taxes from the rest of the world, dividends, rents and royalties, and transfer receipts

Note: Components may not add exactly to totals owing to rounding.
Source: BEA Web site, *www.bea.gov/itable/national-gdp-and-personal-income*, NIPA Tables 3.2, 3.3, and 3.9.5.

expenditures, and about three-fourths of this amount is for national defense. *About 75% of government consumption expenditures on nondefense goods and services in the United States comes from state and local governments.*

2. *Transfer payments.* The Federal budget is more heavily weighted toward transfer payments (particularly, benefits from Social Security and related programs) than state and local budgets are.
3. *Grants in aid.* Grants in aid are payments made by the Federal government to state and local governments to help support various education, transportation, and welfare programs. Grants in aid appear as a current expenditure for the Federal government and as a receipt for state and local governments. In 2021, these grants made up about one-third of state and local government receipts.
4. *Net interest paid.* Because of the large quantity of Federal government bonds outstanding, net interest payments are an important component of Federal spending. In contrast, net interest payments for state and local governments

are smaller and sometimes *negative,* which occurs when state and local governments (which hold substantial amounts of Federal government bonds) receive more interest than they pay out.

5. *Composition of taxes.* More than 80% of Federal government receipts come from personal taxes (primarily the Federal income tax) and contributions for social insurance. Less than 10% of Federal revenues are from corporate taxes, and less than 5% are from taxes on production and imports such as sales taxes. In contrast, taxes on production and imports account for about half of state and local revenues. About one-fifth of state and local revenues come from personal taxes (both income taxes and property taxes) and contributions for social insurance. As already mentioned, state and local governments also count as revenue the grants in aid they receive from the Federal government.

Deficits and Surpluses

Government outlays need not equal tax revenues in each period. In Chapter 2 we showed that, when government outlays exceed revenues, there is a government budget deficit (or simply a deficit); when revenues exceed outlays, there is a government budget surplus. For ease of reference, we write the definition of the deficit as

$$\begin{aligned} \text{deficit} &= \text{outlays} - \text{tax revenues} \\ &= (\text{government purchases} + \text{transfers} + \text{net interest}) - \text{tax revenues} \\ &= (G + TR + INT) - T. \end{aligned} \tag{15.1}$$

A second deficit concept, called the **primary government budget deficit**, excludes net interest from government outlays:

$$\begin{aligned} \text{primary deficit} &= \text{outlays} - \text{net interest} - \text{tax revenues} \\ &= (\text{government purchases} + \text{transfers}) - \text{tax revenues} \\ &= (G + TR) - T. \end{aligned} \tag{15.2}$$

The primary deficit is the amount by which government purchases and transfers exceed tax revenues; the primary deficit plus net interest payments equals the deficit. Figure 15.3 illustrates the relationship between the two concepts.

Why have two deficit concepts? The reason is that each answers a different question. The standard or total budget deficit answers the question: How much does the government currently have to borrow to pay for its total outlays? When measured in nominal terms, the deficit during any year is the number of additional dollars that the government must borrow during that year.

The primary deficit answers the question: Can the government afford its *current* programs? If the primary deficit is zero, the government is collecting just enough tax revenue to pay for its current purchases of goods and services and its current social programs (as reflected by transfer payments). If the primary deficit is greater than zero, current government purchases and social programs cost more than current tax revenue can pay for. Net interest payments are ignored in the primary deficit because they represent not current program costs but costs of past expenditures financed by government borrowing.

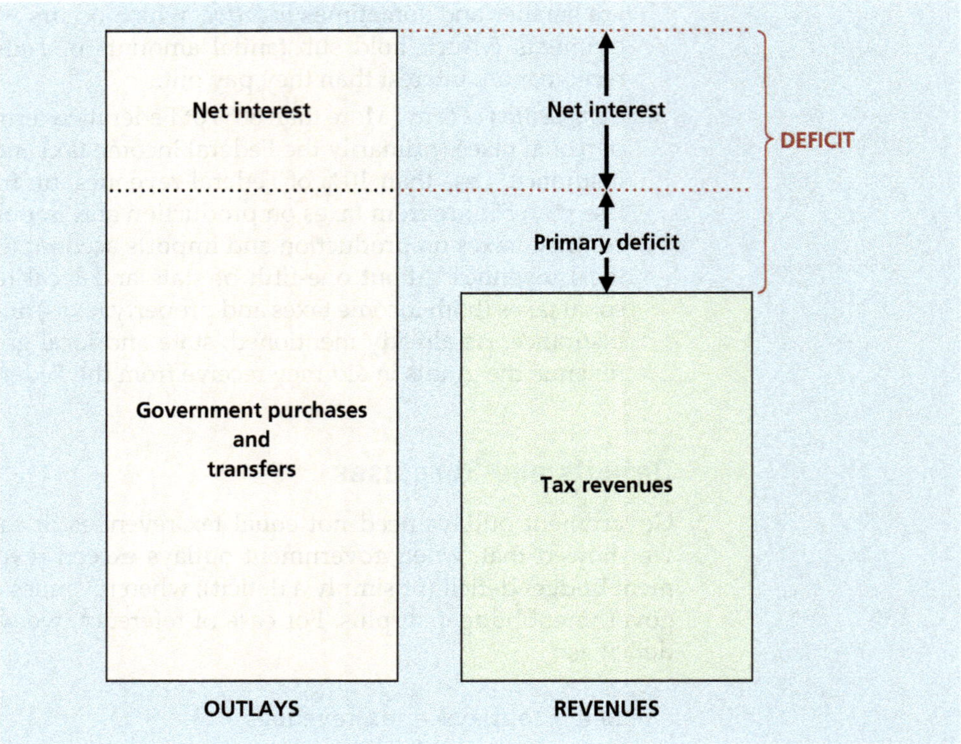

FIGURE 15.3

The relationship between the total budget deficit and the primary deficit

The standard measure of the total government budget deficit is the amount by which government outlays exceed tax revenues. The primary deficit is the amount by which government purchases plus transfers exceed tax revenues. The total budget deficit equals the primary deficit plus net interest payments.

The separation of government purchases into government investment and government consumption expenditures introduces another set of deficit concepts: the *current deficit* and the *primary current deficit*. The current deficit is equivalent to the deficit in Eq. (15.1), with outlays replaced by current expenditures, which are all government outlays except government investment. The primary current deficit is the current deficit minus interest payments. Table 15.2 shows the current deficit and the primary current deficit for 2021.

Figure 15.4 shows the current deficit and primary current deficit for all levels of government combined as a percentage of GDP since 1940. Again, the World War II period stands out; the government financed only part of the war effort with taxes and thus ran large primary and overall deficits.[3] Large deficits (using both concepts) also occurred in the mid-1970s and again in the early 1980s. Although the primary deficit actually became a primary surplus for several years in the 1980s and 1990s, large interest payments kept the overall deficit large until the late 1990s, when the overall budget went into surplus. Tax cuts in the early 2000s eliminated the large primary current surplus of the late 1990s. The Federal government increased spending during the Great Recession from 2007 to 2009, leading to large current deficits and primary current deficits for several years. From 2013 to 2017, the current deficit was 4% to 5% of GDP, while the primary current deficit was 1% to 2% of GDP. The tax cut of 2017, led to an increase in both deficits substantially as a share of GDP in 2018 and 2019.

[3]Much of the increased government spending in World War II was on government investment, which is not counted in the current deficit. As a result, the overall deficit, defined in Eq. (15.1), was even higher than the current deficit and exceeded 20% of GDP, as you can see by comparing Fig. 15.1 with Fig. 15.2.

FIGURE 15.4

Current deficit and primary current deficit: Federal, state, and local, 1940–2021
Shown are the current government budget deficit and the primary current deficit, both measured as a percentage of GDP, since 1940. The government ran large primary current deficits during World War II, after the financial crisis in 2008 and during the pandemic in 2020. The widening gap between the current deficit and the current primary deficit between 1975 and 1991 reflects increasing interest payments on the government's accumulated debt.

Sources: National Income and Product Accounts, Bureau of Economic Analysis, *www.bea.gov/itable/national-gdp-and-personal-income*. GDP: Table 1.1.5; current deficit: Table 3.1; primary current deficit: authors' calculations from data on deficit and net interest paid in Table 3.1.

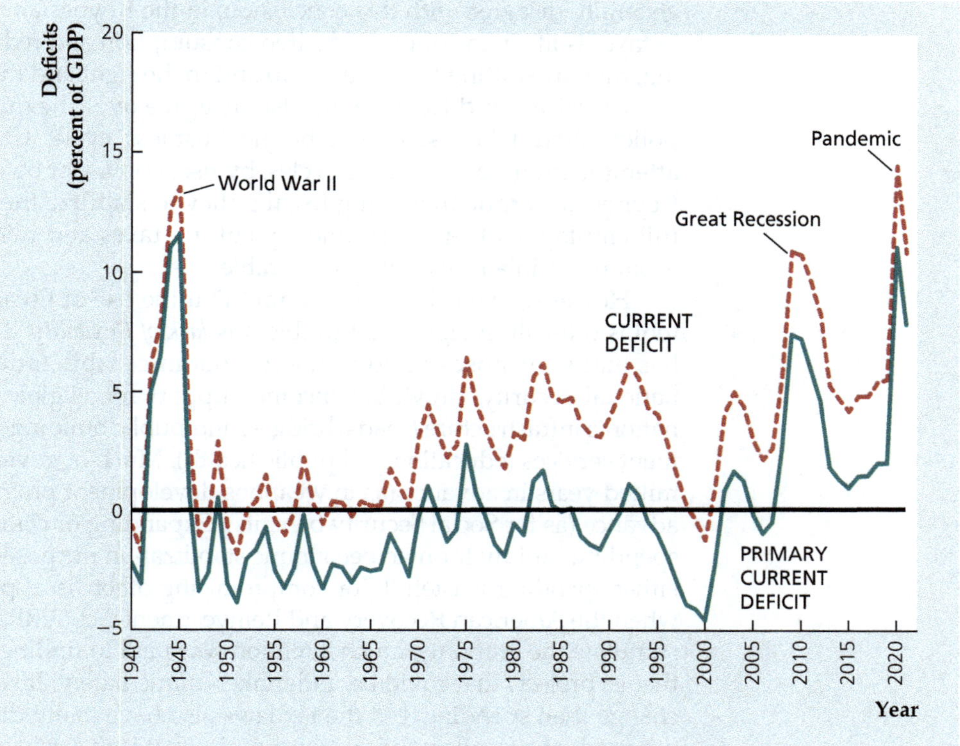

15.2 Government Spending, Taxes, and the Macroeconomy

Describe how government spending and taxing decisions affect the macroeconomy.

How does fiscal policy affect the performance of the macroeconomy? Economists emphasize three main ways by which government spending and taxing decisions influence macroeconomic variables such as output, employment, and prices: (1) aggregate demand, (2) government capital formation, and (3) incentives.

Fiscal Policy and Aggregate Demand

Fiscal policy can affect economic activity by influencing the total amount of spending in the economy, or aggregate demand. Recall that aggregate demand is represented by the intersection of the *IS* and *LM* curves. In either the classical or the Keynesian *IS–LM* model, a temporary increase in government purchases reduces desired national saving and shifts the *IS* curve up and to the right, thereby raising aggregate demand.

Classical and Keynesian economists have different beliefs about the effect of tax changes on aggregate demand. Classicals usually accept the Ricardian equivalence proposition, which says that lump-sum tax changes do not affect desired national saving and thus have no impact on the *IS* curve or aggregate demand.[4] Keynesians

[4]We introduced Ricardian equivalence in Chapter 4. We discuss this idea further in Section 15.3.

generally disagree with this conclusion; in the Keynesian view, a cut (for example) in taxes is likely to stimulate desired consumption and reduce desired national saving, thereby shifting the *IS* curve up and to the right and raising aggregate demand.

Classicals and Keynesians also disagree over the question of whether fiscal policy should be used to fight the business cycle. Classicals generally reject attempts to smooth business cycles, by fiscal policy or by other means. In contrast, Keynesians argue that using fiscal policy to stabilize the economy and maintain full employment—for example, by cutting taxes and raising spending when the economy is in a recession—is desirable.

However, even Keynesians admit that the use of fiscal policy as a stabilization tool is difficult. A significant problem is *lack of flexibility.* The government's budget has many purposes besides macroeconomic stabilization, such as maintaining national security, providing income support for eligible groups, developing the nation's infrastructure (roads, bridges, and public buildings), and supplying government services (education and public health). Much of government spending is committed years in advance (as in weapons development programs) or even decades in advance (as for Social Security benefits). Expanding or contracting total government spending rapidly for macroeconomic stabilization purposes thus is difficult without either spending wastefully or compromising other fiscal policy goals. For instance, when the American Recovery and Reinvestment Act (ARRA) was enacted in 2009 to stimulate the economy, much attention was paid to finding "shovel-ready" projects, that is, projects that could be undertaken immediately. Taxes are somewhat easier to change than spending, but the tax laws also have many different goals and may be the result of a fragile political compromise that isn't easily altered.

Compounding the problem of inflexibility is the problem of *long time lags* that result from the slow-moving political process by which fiscal policy is made. From the time a spending or tax proposal is made until it goes into effect is rarely less than 18 months. This lag makes effective countercyclical use of fiscal policy difficult because (for example), by the time an antirecession fiscal measure actually had an impact on the economy, the recession might already be over.

Automatic Stabilizers and the Full-Employment Deficit. One way to get around the problems of fiscal policy inflexibility and long lags that impede the use of countercyclical fiscal policies is to build automatic stabilizers into the budget. **Automatic stabilizers** are provisions in the budget that cause government spending to rise or taxes to fall automatically—without legislative action—when GDP falls. Similarly, when GDP rises, automatic stabilizers cause spending to fall or taxes to rise without any need for direct legislative action.

A good example of an automatic stabilizer is unemployment insurance. When the economy goes into a recession and unemployment rises, more people receive unemployment benefits, which are paid automatically without further action by Congress. Thus the unemployment insurance component of transfers rises during recessions, making fiscal policy automatically more expansionary.[5]

Quantitatively, the most important automatic stabilizer is the income tax system. When the economy goes into a recession, people's incomes fall, and they pay less income tax. This "automatic tax cut" helps cushion the drop in disposable income and (according to Keynesians) prevents aggregate demand from falling as far as it might otherwise. Likewise, when people's incomes rise during a boom,

[5]This statement is based on the Keynesian view that an increase in transfers—which is equivalent to a reduction in taxes—raises aggregate demand.

the government collects more income tax revenue, which helps restrain the increase in aggregate demand. Keynesians argue that this automatic fiscal policy is a major reason for the increased stability of the economy since World War II.

A side effect of automatic stabilizers is that government budget deficits tend to increase in recessions because government spending automatically rises and taxes automatically fall when GDP declines. Similarly, the deficit tends to fall in booms. To distinguish changes in the deficit caused by recessions or booms from changes caused by other factors, some economists advocate the use of a deficit measure called the full-employment deficit. The **full-employment deficit** indicates what the government budget deficit *would be*—given the tax and spending policies currently in force—if the economy were operating at its full-employment level.[6] Because it eliminates the effects of automatic stabilizers, the full-employment deficit measure is affected primarily by changes in fiscal policy reflected in new legislation. In particular, expansionary fiscal changes—such as increases in government spending programs or (in the Keynesian model) reduced tax rates—raise the full-employment budget deficit, whereas contractionary fiscal changes reduce the full-employment deficit.

Figure 15.5 shows the actual and full-employment budget deficits (as percentages of full-employment output) of the Federal government since 1965. Note that the actual budget deficit substantially exceeded the full-employment budget deficit during or slightly after the recessions of 1973–1975, 1981–1982, 1990–1991, 2001, and 2007–2009 when output was below its full-employment level. The difference between the two deficit measures reflects the importance of automatic stabilizers in the budget.

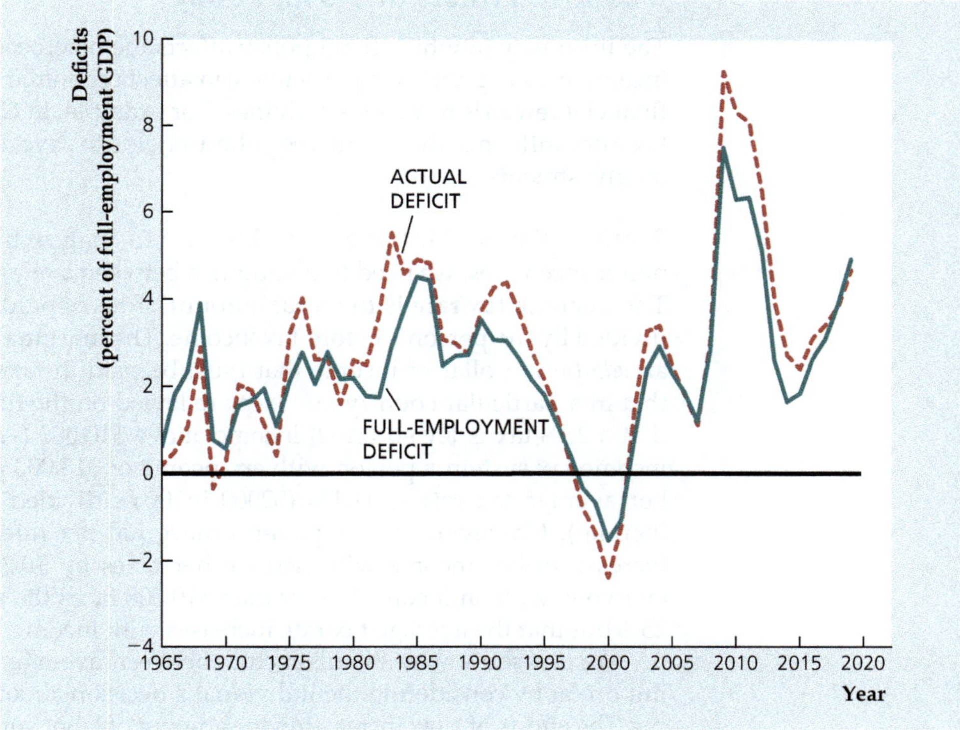

FIGURE 15.5

Full-employment and actual budget deficits, 1965–2019

The actual and full-employment Federal budget deficits are shown as percentages of full-employment output. The actual budget deficit exceeded the full-employment deficit by substantial amounts during or slightly after the 1973–1975, 1981–1982, 1990–1991, 2001, and 2007–2009 recessions, reflecting the importance of automatic stabilizers. Data are not shown for the pandemic period of 2020–2021 because the CBO did not estimate the full-employment deficit during the pandemic.

Source: Congressional Budget Office, *www.cbo.gov/system/files?file=2020-02/51139-2020-02-automaticstabilizers.xlsx*.

[6]In practice, the calculation of full-employment deficits is based on the Keynesian assumption that recessions reflect deviations from full employment rather than the classical assumption that (in the absence of misperceptions) recessions reflect changes in full-employment output.

Government Capital Formation

The health of the economy depends not only on *how much* the government spends but also on *how* it spends its resources. For example, as discussed in Chapter 6, the quantity and quality of public infrastructure—roads, schools, public hospitals, and the like—are potentially important for the rate of economic growth. Thus the formation of **government capital**—long-lived physical assets owned by the government—is one way that fiscal policy affects the macroeconomy. The government budget affects not only physical capital formation but also human capital formation. At least part of government expenditures on health, nutrition, and education are an investment, in the sense that they will lead to a more productive work force in the future.

The official figures for government capital investment focus on physical capital formation and exclude human capital formation. In 2021 Federal government investment expenditures were $360 billion (about 23% of Federal purchases of goods and services), with 55% of investment spending for national defense and 45% for nondefense government capital. State and local government investment was $442.3 billion (about one-sixth of state and local government purchases of goods and services). The composition of government investment by state and local governments differs from that by the Federal government. Most Federal government investment is in the form of intellectual property products (such as research and development) rather than equipment or structures, but about three-quarters of state and local government investment is for structures.

Incentive Effects of Fiscal Policy

The third way in which fiscal policy affects the macroeconomy is by its effects on incentives. Tax policies in particular can affect economic behavior by changing the financial rewards to various activities. For example, in Chapter 4 we showed how tax rates influence the incentives of households to save and of firms to make capital investments.

Average Versus Marginal Tax Rates. To analyze the effects of taxes on economic incentives, we need to distinguish between average and marginal tax rates. The **average tax rate** is the total amount of taxes paid by a person (or a firm), divided by the person's before-tax income. The **marginal tax rate** is the fraction of an *additional* dollar of income that must be paid in taxes. For example, suppose that in a particular country no taxes are levied on the first $10,000 of income and that a 25% tax is levied on all income above $10,000 (see Table 15.3). Under this income tax system a person with an income of $18,000 pays a tax of $2000. Thus her average tax rate is 11.1% ($2000 in taxes divided by $18,000 in before-tax income). However, this taxpayer's marginal tax rate is 25% because a $1.00 increase in her income will increase her taxes by $0.25. Table 15.3 shows that everyone with an income higher than $10,000 faces the same marginal tax rate of 25% but that the average tax rate increases with income.

We can show why the distinction between average and marginal tax rates is important by considering the individual's decision about how much labor to supply. The effects of a tax increase on the amount of labor supplied depend strongly on whether average or marginal taxes are being increased. Economic theory predicts that an increase in the average tax rate, with the marginal tax rate held constant, will *increase* the amount of labor supplied at any (before-tax) real wage. In contrast,

TABLE 15.3

Marginal and Average Tax Rates: An Example (Total Tax = 25% of Income More Than $10,000)

Income	Income–$10,000	Tax	Average tax rate	Marginal tax rate
$ 18,000	$ 8,000	$ 2,000	11.1%	25%
50,000	40,000	10,000	20.0%	25%
100,000	90,000	22,500	22.5%	25%

the theory predicts that an increase in the marginal tax rate, with the average tax rate held constant, will *decrease* the amount of labor supplied at any real wage.

To explain these conclusions, let's first consider the effects of a change in the average tax rate. Returning to our example from Table 15.3, imagine that the marginal tax rate stays at 25% but that now all income over $8000 (rather than all income more than $10,000) is subject to a 25% tax. The taxpayer with an income of $18,000 finds that her tax bill has risen from $2000 to $2500, or $0.25(\$18{,}000 - \$8000)$, so her average tax rate has risen from 11.1% to 13.9%, or $2500/$18,000. As a result, the taxpayer is $500 poorer. Because she is effectively less wealthy, she will increase the amount of labor she supplies at any real wage (see Summary table 4 in Chapter 3). Hence an increase in the average tax rate, holding the marginal tax rate fixed, shifts the labor supply curve (in a diagram with the before-tax real wage on the vertical axis) to the right.[7]

Now consider the effects of an increase in the marginal tax rate, with the average tax rate constant. Suppose that the marginal tax rate on income increases from 25% to 40% and the rise is accompanied by other changes in the tax law that keep the average tax rate—and thus the total amount of taxes paid by the typical taxpayer—the same. To be specific, suppose that the portion of income not subject to tax is increased from $10,000 to $13,000. Then for the taxpayer earning $18,000, total taxes are $2000, or $0.40(\$18{,}000 - \$13{,}000)$, and the average tax rate of 11.1%, or $2000/$18,000, is the same as it was under the original tax law.[8]

With the average tax rate unchanged, the taxpayer's wealth is unaffected, and so there is no change in labor supply stemming from a change in wealth. However, the increase in the marginal tax rate implies that the taxpayer's after-tax reward for each extra hour worked declines. For example, if her wage is $20 per hour before taxes, at the original marginal tax rate of 25%, her actual take-home pay for each extra hour of work is $15 ($20 minus 25% of $20, or $5, in taxes). At the new marginal tax rate of 40%, the taxpayer's take-home pay for each extra hour of work is only $12 ($20 in before-tax wages minus $8 in taxes). Because extra hours of work no longer carry as much reward in terms of real income earned, at any specific before-tax real wage the taxpayer is likely to work fewer hours and enjoy more leisure instead. Thus, if the average tax rate is held fixed, an increase in the marginal tax rate causes the labor supply curve to shift to the left.[9]

[7]In terms of the analysis of Chapter 3, the increase in the average tax rate has a pure income effect on labor supply.

[8]Although the average tax rate is unchanged for the taxpayer earning $18,000, the average tax rate increases for taxpayers earning more than $18,000 and decreases for taxpayers earning less than $18,000.

[9]In terms of the discussion in Chapter 3, a change in the marginal tax rate with no change in the average tax rate has a pure substitution effect on labor supply.

The Tax Act of 2017 reduced marginal tax rates for most taxpayers in 2018, but these reductions were legislated to be temporary. The decline in marginal tax rates was designed to encourage economic activity, and our theory says this should cause labor supply curves to shift to the right. Econometric estimates of the effect suggested that the decline in the marginal tax rates might have increased GDP growth by about 0.9 percentage points in 2019 but not much after that.[10] The tax changes in 2017 also reduced business taxation, which might have a longer-lasting impact on output through increased incentives for investment, leading to a higher capital stock. However, measuring the actual impact of these tax changes was difficult because of the pandemic's effects in 2020 and 2021.

Tax-Induced Distortions and Tax Rate Smoothing. Because taxes affect economic incentives, they change the pattern of economic behavior. If the invisible hand of free markets is working properly, the pattern of economic activity in the absence of taxes is the most efficient, so changes in behavior caused by taxes reduce economic welfare. Tax-induced deviations from efficient, free-market outcomes are called **distortions**.

To illustrate the idea of a distortion, let's go back to the example of the worker whose before-tax real wage is \$20. Because profit-maximizing employers demand labor up to the point that the marginal product of labor equals the real wage, the real output produced by an extra hour of the worker's labor (her marginal product) also is \$20. Now suppose that the worker is willing to sacrifice leisure to work an extra hour if she receives at least \$14 in additional real earnings. Because the value of what the worker can produce in an extra hour of labor exceeds the value that she places on an extra hour of leisure, her working the extra hour is economically efficient.

In an economy without taxes, this efficient outcome occurs because the worker is willing to work the extra hour for the extra \$20 in real wages. She would also be willing to work the extra hour if the marginal tax rate on earnings was 25% because at a marginal tax rate of 25% her after-tax real wage is \$15, which exceeds the \$14 real wage minimum that she is willing to accept. However, if the marginal tax rate rises to 40%, so that the worker's after-tax wage falls to only \$12, she would decide that it isn't worth her while to work the extra hour, even though for her to do so would have been economically efficient. The difference between the number of hours the worker would have worked had there been no tax on wages and the number of hours she actually works when there is a tax reflects the distorting effect of the tax. The higher the tax rate is, the greater the distortion is likely to be.

Because doing without taxes entirely isn't possible, the problem for fiscal policymakers is how to raise needed government revenues while keeping distortions relatively small. Because high tax rates are particularly costly in terms of economic efficiency, economists argue that keeping tax rates roughly constant at a moderate level is preferable to alternate periods of very low and very high tax rates. For example, if the government's spending plans require it to levy a tax rate that over a number of years averages 20%, most economists would advise the government *not* to set the tax rate at 30% half the time and 10% the other half. The reason is the large distortions that the 30% tax rate would cause in the years that it was effective. A better strategy is to hold the tax rate constant at 20%. A policy of maintaining stable tax rates so as to minimize distortions is called **tax rate smoothing**.

[10]See Robert J. Barro and Jason Furman, "The Macroeconomic Effects of the 2017 Tax Reform," *Brookings Papers on Economic Activity, www.brookings.edu/bpea-articles/macroeconomic-effects-of-the-2017-tax-reform/.*

Application

Supply-Side Economics

Economic incentives play a significant role in influencing economic agents' decisions. Intuitively, the higher the benefits associated with an activity, the higher the incentive. Although economic output is the outcome of the interaction of aggregate supply (*AS*) and aggregate demand (*AD*), **supply-side economics** focuses on *AS* and is based on the idea that efficient supply of goods and services within the economy is a main driver of long-term growth. Broadly, it is concerned with the determinants of potential output, or productive capacity, and changes. Originating in the United States in the mid-1970s, the term gained prominence in the 1980s under UK prime minister Margaret Thatcher and U.S. president Ronald Reagan. As an intertemporal approach, supply-side economics focuses on the effects of today's actions over time and on the effects of expected action on today's behavior.

One of the main means of incentivizing economic agents to increase supply is through tax policy, and "supply-siders" argue that labor supply, productivity, savings, and investments respond positively to tax incentives through their significant effect on these variables. Supply-side economics is often visually represented by the so-called *Laffer curve*, which charts the theoretical relationship between tax rates and tax revenue. The curve, created by the U.S. economist Arthur Laffer, argues that beyond a certain tax level, lowering tax rates improves tax revenue through higher economic growth. The basis is that at a constant tax-rate of t and labor income Y, tax revenue ($R = tY$) is increased when t is reduced as it incentivizes a bigger increase in Y. The Laffer curve (Figure 15.6) is motivated by three intuitive observations. First, when $t = 0\%$, $R = 0$, (shown at point O). Second, when $t = 100\%$, there will be no incentive to work (discounting totally altruistic considerations) and labor income will be zero; therefore, $R = 0$ (shown at point B). Third, for $0\% < t < 100\%$, workers will supply labor, earn incomes, and pay income taxes, resulting in positive tax revenue ($R > 0$). Since $R = 0$ for $t = 0\%$ and $t = 100\%$ and tax revenue is positive for $0\% < t < 100\%$, the Laffer curve will have to peak at some point, t^*, which provides government with the highest tax revenue, R^*. In countries where supply-siders push for marginal tax-rate reductions, their argument is that t is on the right-side of t^*, so reductions in t will increase R. Put differently, below t^*, the marginal tax revenue raised decreases as t increases, until it reaches t^* (point A, where the slope of the Laffer curve becomes zero). Beyond t^*, any tax-rate increases reduce tax revenue.

Based on the above explanation, the importance of getting t^* right cannot be overstated. However, most of the empirical evidence advanced to support the supply-siders' position concerns U.S. economic policy. An obvious problem with any empirical test of the Laffer curve's effects in most countries is the paucity of data available.

To test the Laffer curve's relevance on a broader scale, the Fiscal Affairs Department of the IMF conducted a project in 1984 analyzing the relevance to developing countries of the tax policy recommendations of supply-side economics made in the context of developed countries. The results were, at best, mixed. Ebrill, analyzing 1970s data for Jamaica and India, concludes that, although there is some evidence of tax revenue buoyancy in Jamaica, the opposite was found

(*continued*)

FIGURE 15.6

The Laffer curve

At tax rates of 0% and 100%, the government collects no tax revenue. Beginning with a tax rate of 0%, increasing the tax rate leads to increased tax revenue. But as the tax rate continues to rise, tax revenue grows less and less as people work less. For tax rates above t^*, a higher tax rate leads to lower tax revenues.

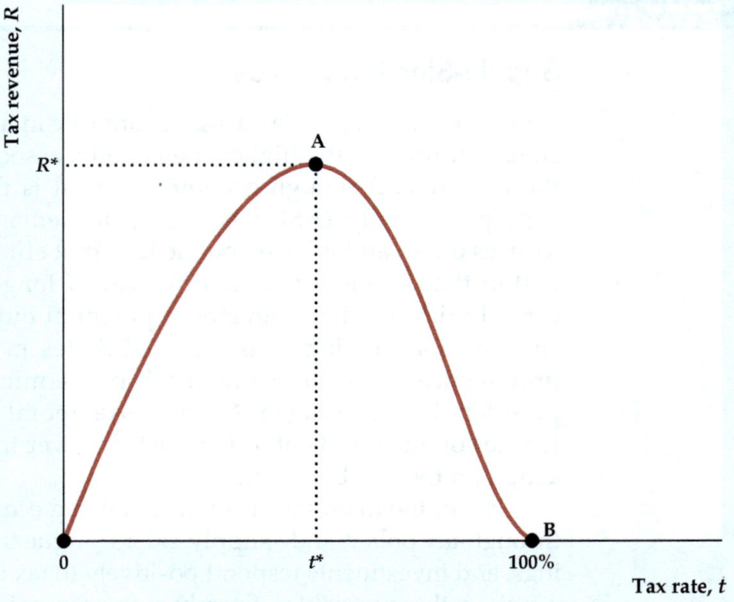

in India.[11] For India, the "revenue performance" of the highest income group was rather poor even though this group, which included taxpayers that had the greatest marginal tax-rate reduction (20.75 percentage points), should have exhibited the most pronounced Laffer-type effects. Analyzing Korean data, Ohchul Kwon, an American economist, concluded that the behavior of tax revenues over time as tax rates were increased was not inconsistent with the existence of a Laffer curve.[12] Kwon showed that when the marginal tax rate increased from 4.3% in 1972 to 17.8% in 1974, tax revenue rose at increasing rates from 6.3% to 56.3%. However, as the marginal tax rate increased from 17.8% in 1974 to 22.3% in 1976, tax revenue increased at decreased rates from 56.3% to 49.5%.

Proponents argue that supply-side policies can help reduce inflationary pressures in the long term because of efficiency and productivity gains in the product and labor markets; it can also help create real jobs and sustainable growth through their positive effect on labor productivity and competitiveness. However, such policies must be implemented cautiously. In 2022, shortly after taking office, former UK prime minister Liz Truss rashly implemented a broad set of supply-side fiscal policies, including significant tax cuts and spending plans. However, markets reacted unfavorably, leading to a sudden and sharp devaluation of the British pound to historically low levels, accompanied by mounting inflation. Critics argue that relying on supply alone does not create demand. Moreover, it can take a long time to work its way through the economy. Yet supply-side economics remains an important policymaking tool, even as identifying the optimal tax-rate remains a non-trivial task, as does knowing which income groups should get tax reductions to increase tax revenues.

[11]For more details, Liam P. Ebrill, "Evidence on the Laffer Curve: The Cases of Jamaica and India," *Supply-Side Tax Policy*, June 15, 1987, International Monetary Fund, https://www.elibrary.imf.org/view/book/9780939934911/ch007.xml.

[12]Ohchul Kwon, "Taxes, Tax Revenues, and the Laffer Curve for a Developing Country Like Korea," *International Tax Journal* 10, no. 4, pp. 269–72.

Has the Federal government had a policy of tax rate smoothing? Statistical studies typically have found that Federal tax rates are affected by political and other factors and hence aren't as smooth as is necessary to minimize distortions.[13] Nevertheless, the idea of tax smoothing is still useful. For example, what explains the U.S. government's huge deficit during World War II (Fig. 15.4)? The alternative to deficit financing of the war would have been a large wartime increase in tax rates, coupled with a drop in tax rates when the war was over. But high tax rates during the war would have distorted the economy when productive efficiency was especially important. By financing the war largely through borrowing, the government effectively spread the needed tax increase over a long period of time (as the debt was repaid) rather than raising current taxes by a large amount. This action is consistent with the idea of tax smoothing.

15.3 Government Deficits and Debt

Discuss the economic effects of government deficits and debt.

The single number in the Federal government's budget that is the focus of most public attention is the size of the budget deficit or surplus. During the 1980s and early 1990s, large deficits led to vigorous public debate about the potential impact of big deficits on the economy, and this debate was reignited following the recent financial crisis that began in 2009, as the budget deficit averaged almost 9% of GDP from 2009 to 2011. In the rest of this chapter we discuss the government budget deficit, the government debt, and their effects on the economy.

The Growth of the Government Debt

There is an important distinction between the government budget deficit and the government debt (also called the national debt). The government budget *deficit* (a flow variable) is the difference between expenditures and tax revenues in any fiscal year. The **government debt** (a stock variable) is the total value of government bonds outstanding at any particular time. Because the excess of government expenditures over revenues equals the amount of new borrowing that the government must do—that is, the amount of new government debt that it must issue—any year's deficit (measured in dollar, or nominal, terms) equals the change in the debt in that year. We can express the relationship between government debt and the budget deficit by

$$\Delta B = \text{nominal government budget deficit}, \tag{15.3}$$

where ΔB is the change in the nominal value of government bonds outstanding.

In a period of persistently large budget deficits, such as that experienced by the United States in the 1980s and early and mid-1990s, and again after 2002, the nominal value of the government's debt will grow quickly. For example, between 1980 and 2021, Federal government debt held by the public grew by over 30 times

[13]David Bizer and Steven Durlauf, "Testing the Positive Theory of Government Finance," *Journal of Monetary Economics*, August 1990, pp. 123–141.

in nominal terms, from $712 billion in 1980 to $22,284 billion in 2021.[14] Taking inflation into account, the real value of government debt outstanding increased more than 11-fold during this period.

Because countries with a high GDP have relatively more resources available to pay the principal and interest on the government's bonds, a useful measure of government indebtedness is the quantity of government debt outstanding divided by the GDP, or the *debt–GDP ratio.* Figure 15.7 shows the history of the debt–GDP ratio in the United States since 1939. The upper curve shows the debt–GDP ratio when the measure of total government debt outstanding includes both government bonds held by the public and government bonds held by government agencies and the Federal Reserve. The lower curve includes in the measure of debt outstanding only the government debt held by the public, which, strictly speaking, includes the Federal Reserve.

The most striking feature of Fig. 15.7 is the large increase in the debt–GDP ratio that occurred during World War II when the government sold bonds to finance the war effort. By the end of the war, the debt–GDP ratio exceeded 100%, implying that the value of government debt outstanding was greater than a year's GDP. Over the following 35 years the government steadily reduced its indebtedness relative to GDP. Beginning in about 1980, though, greater budget deficits caused the debt–GDP ratio to rise, which it did throughout the decade. Despite

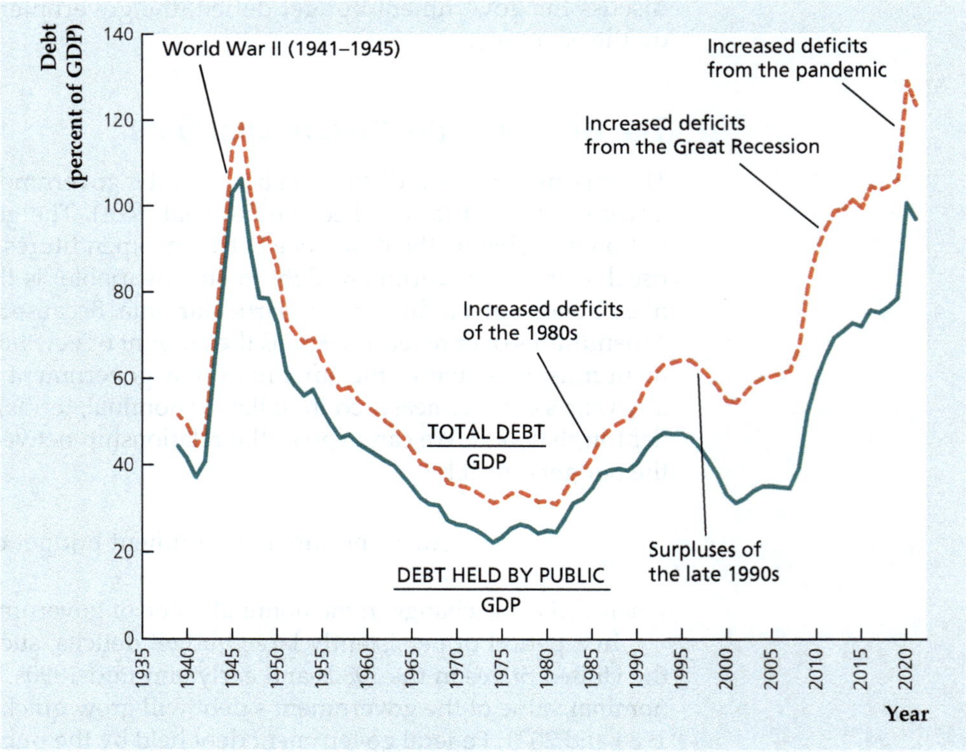

FIGURE 15.7

Ratio of Federal debt to GDP, 1939–2021

The upper curve shows the ratio of total government debt—including government bonds held by government agencies and the Federal Reserve—to GDP. The lower curve shows the ratio of government bonds held by the public to GDP. The debt–GDP ratio rose dramatically during World War II, fell steadily for the next 35 years, and then rose again from 1980 until the mid-1990s. The surpluses of the late 1990s reduced the debt–GDP ratio considerably, though large deficits beginning in 2002 increased this ratio.

Source: Economic Report of the President, downloaded from Federal Reserve Bank of St. Louis FRED database, variables *FYGFDPUB* (publicly held debt), *FYGFD* (gross debt), *GDP* (GDP).

[14]*Economic Report of the President*, downloaded from Federal Reserve Bank of St. Louis FRED database, variable *FYGFDPUB*.

this increase, by 1995 the ratio of Federal debt to GDP was still only about half its size at the end of World War II. In the late 1990s, rapid economic growth caused tax revenues to increase substantially, leading to government budget surpluses that reduced the debt–GDP ratio considerably. The debt–GDP ratio began to increase in 2002 as large Federal budget deficits emerged and it grew even more dramatically in the Great Recession, as the Federal government increased spending to try to stimulate the economy and because automatic stabilizers kicked in, increasing transfers and reducing taxes.

We can describe changes in the debt–GDP ratio over time by the following formula (derived in Appendix 15. A at the end of the chapter):

$$\frac{\text{change in}}{\text{debt-GDP ratio}} = \frac{\text{deficit}}{\text{nominal GDP}} - \left(\frac{\text{total debt}}{\text{nominal GDP}} \times \frac{\text{growth rate of}}{\text{nominal GDP}}\right) \quad (15.4)$$

Equation (15.4) emphasizes two factors that cause the debt–GDP ratio to rise quickly:

- a high deficit relative to GDP and
- a slow rate of GDP growth.

Equation (15.4) helps account for the pattern of the debt–GDP ratio shown in Fig. 15.7. The sharp increase during World War II was the result of large deficits. In contrast, for the three and a half decades after World War II, the Federal government's deficit was small and GDP growth was rapid, so the debt–GDP ratio declined. The debt–GDP ratio increased during the 1980s and early 1990s because the Federal deficit was high. Large surpluses helped reduce the debt–GDP ratio in the late 1990s, but large deficits beginning in 2002 and increasing during the Great Recession have reversed the decline in the debt–GDP ratio. The pandemic in 2020 propelled the ratio of debt held by the public to GDP to over 100% for the first time since 1946, and it is projected to keep increasing in the future.[15] One factor affecting the debt–GDP ratio is the Social Security system, discussed in the Application "Social Security in the United Kingdom: How Can It Be Fixed?"

Application

Social Security in the United Kingdom: How Can It Be fixed?

Established in the first half of the twentieth century, the United Kingdom's social security benefits system is based predominantly on the *contributory* principle. As part of the post–Second World War welfare state, the National Insurance (NI) system, first introduced in 1912, was extended significantly. Under this scheme, eligibility for benefits was to be primarily based on NI contributions. It was hoped at the time that means-testing would not have to play a significant role. Since the 1970s, however, the proportion of total working-age social security spending based on means-tested benefits and tax credits targeted at low-income households has risen significantly.

(continued)

[15]See the projections by the Congressional Budget Office at *www.cbo.gov*.

Over time, using the social security system, different governments in the United Kingdom have aimed to alleviate poverty; maintain and replace incomes during unemployment, sickness, and bereavement; promote income redistribution; help in meeting additional costs such as for disabilities, housing, and childcare; and provide compensations for industrial injuries or diseases. Wider social aims have also been pursued. These include encouraging labor market participation, providing income support and economic stimulus in downturns, and changing behaviors to encourage claimants to take responsibility for budgeting (such as by providing Universal Credit as a single monthly payment).

The responsibilities of the Department for Work and Pensions (DWP) include overseeing the benefits system, delivering the State Pension, and a range of working-age, disability, and sickness benefits to around 20 million claimants. The DWP is responsible for spending more than any other department, that is, about £220 billion in 2020–21. However, another government department, Her Majesty's Revenue and Customs, is responsible for tax credits as well as Child Benefits. Moreover, local authorities are responsible for administering Housing Benefits, and since April 2013, local authorities in England have also been responsible for their own Council Tax Reduction schemes and local welfare assistance schemes (Scotland and Wales continue to maintain the national scheme).

As shown in Figure 15.8, the United Kingdom's social security spending consistently surpasses social security contributions, and there is no indication that the gap is narrowing, which raises questions about its sustainability. The UK Poverty 2022 report[16] by the Joseph Rowntree Foundation (JRF) found that 13.4 million people were in poverty in 2020–21, including 3.9 million children, and it concludes that the current welfare system is unfit for its purpose. The report argues that many of the welfare benefits are income-related and explicitly only available to low-income families, so lapses in the welfare system will only worsen poverty. The administration of the United Kingdom's benefits system is complex. Social Assistance payments—including Universal Credit, Income Support, Income-based Jobseeker's Allowance (JSA), Income-related Employment and

FIGURE 15.8

Social Security Spending and Contributions as a Percentage of GDP, 1980–2021

The figure shows annual values for the cost of providing benefits and the tax revenue collected by the Social Security system each year from 1990 to 2021 and the projected payout and tax revenue from 2022 to 2100. Benefits payments have begun to rise sharply compared with tax revenue, a development that is creating financial problems for the system.

Sources: OECD, "Social Spending (Indicator)," 2023, *doi: 10.1787/7497563b-en;* and OECD, "Social Security Contributions (Indicator)," 2023, *doi: 10.1787/3ebfe901-en.*

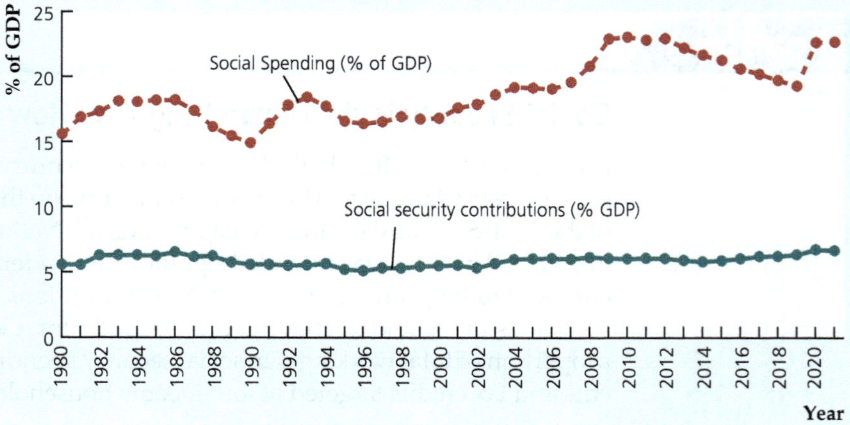

[16]Joseph Rowntree Foundation, "UK Poverty 2022: The Essential Guide to Understanding Poverty in the UK," January 18, 2022, https://www.jrf.org.uk/report/uk-poverty-2022.

Support Allowance (ESA), Pension Credit, Housing Benefits, and Working Tax Credit—are all means-tested and meant for people who have limited incomes and capital. Contributory benefits (Social Insurance), which require some eligibility criteria, such as prior contributions to National Insurance, include State Pensions, Employment Support Allowances and Jobseeker's Allowances. Finally, there are noncontributory benefits such as Child Benefits, Disability Living Allowance, Personal Independence Payments, and Carer's Allowances.

Under recent reforms, measures are being implemented to simplify the welfare system, reduce wastage, and improve efficiency. For example, Universal Credit is replacing the following benefits: Child Tax Credit, Housing Benefit, Income Support, JSA, ESA, and Working Tax Credits. The contributory JSA/ESA is also being replaced with a New Style JSA/ESA, which is paid to eligible claimants who are unable to work due to ill health or disability. Paid fortnightly, claimants of this New Style JSA/ESA together with the Universal Credit will have their Universal Credit payment reduced by the New Style ESA amount. The Social Security Advisory Committee (SSAC), under its statutory remit to provide independent advice, has made several recommendations in its October 2022 report,[17] the overarching one being that the government should develop a clearly articulated long-term vision for the role of contributory benefits for people of working age who are not in paid work.

Are sustainability concerns warranted? Current trends and reforms suggest a recognition that the efficiency of the social security system needs to be improved. The system remains deeply woven into the fabric of the United Kingdom's culture and continues to enjoy political support, but ongoing reforms aimed at improving efficiency suggest that, despite its challenges, the system will remain viable.

The Burden of the Government Debt on Future Generations

People often express concern that the trillions of dollars of Federal government debt will impose a crushing financial burden on their children and grandchildren, who will someday be taxed to pay off these debts. In this view, high rates of government borrowing amount to "robbing the future" to pay for government spending that is too high or taxes that are too low in the present. In addition, some researchers have associated high levels of government debt relative to GDP with lower GDP growth.[18]

Until recently, it was reasonable to argue that most U.S. government bonds are owned by U.S. citizens. Therefore, although our descendants someday may face heavy taxes to pay the interest and principal of the government debt, these future taxpayers also will inherit outstanding government bonds and thus will be the *recipients* of most of those interest and principal payments. In that case, one could

[17]Social Security Advisory Committee, "SSAC Occasional Paper 26: The Future of Working Age Contributory Benefits for Those Not in Paid Work," GOV.UK, October 24, 2022, *(https://www.gov.uk/government/publications/ssac-occasional-paper-26-the-future-of-working-age-contributory-benefits-for-those-not-in-paid-work).*

[18]See Carmen M. Reinhart, Vincent R. Reinhart, and Kenneth S. Rogoff, "Debt Overhangs: Past and Present," *Journal of Economic Perspectives*, Summer 2012, pp. 69–86; and Thomas Herndon, Michael Ash, and Robert Pollin, "Does High Public Debt Consistently Stifle Economic Growth? A Critique of Reinhart and Rogoff," University of Massachusetts Amherst, Political Economy Research Institute working paper, April 2013.

argue that to a substantial degree, we owe the government debt to ourselves, so the debt isn't a burden in the same sense that it would be if it were owed entirely to outsiders. However, over the past 25 years, investors, institutions, and governments in other countries—most notably, China—have bought large amounts of U.S. government debt. Since 2001, foreigners have owned more than 30% of all publicly owned U.S. government debt. So, the argument that the debt is not a burden because we owe it to ourselves is no longer valid.

Although the popular view of the burden of the government debt is faulty, economists have pointed out several ways in which the government debt can become a burden on future generations. First, if tax rates have to be raised substantially in the future to pay off the debt, the resulting distortions could cause the economy to function less efficiently and impose costs on future generations.

Second, most people hold small amounts of government bonds or no government bonds at all (except perhaps indirectly, as through pension funds). In the future, people who hold few or no bonds may have to pay more in taxes to pay off the government debt than they receive in interest and principal payments; people holding large quantities of bonds may receive more in interest and principal than they pay in increased taxes. Bondholders are richer on average than nonbondholders, so the need to service the government debt might lead to a transfer of resources from the relatively poor to the relatively rich. However, this transfer could be offset by other tax and transfer policies—for example, by raising taxes on high-income people.

The third argument is probably the most significant: Many economists claim that government deficits reduce national saving; that is, when the government runs a deficit, the economy accumulates less domestic capital and fewer foreign assets than it would have if the deficit had been lower. If this argument is correct, deficits will lower the standard of living for our children and grandchildren, both because they will inherit a smaller capital stock and because they will have to pay more interest to (or receive less interest from) foreigners than they otherwise would have. This reduction in the future standard of living would constitute a true burden of the government debt.

Crucial to this argument, however, is the idea that government budget deficits reduce national saving. As we have mentioned at several points in this book (notably in Chapter 4), the question of whether budget deficits affect national saving is highly controversial. We devote most of the rest of this section to further discussion of this issue.

Budget Deficits and National Saving: Ricardian Equivalence Revisited

Under what circumstances will an increased government budget deficit cause national saving to fall? Virtually all economists agree that an increase in the deficit caused by a rise in government purchases—say, to fight a war—reduces national saving and imposes a real burden on the economy. However, whether a deficit caused by a cut in current taxes or an increase in current transfers reduces national saving is much less clear. Recall that advocates of Ricardian equivalence argue that tax cuts or increases in transfers will not affect national saving, whereas its opponents disagree.

Ricardian Equivalence: An Example. To illustrate Ricardian equivalence let's suppose that, holding its current and planned future purchases constant, the government cuts this year's taxes by $100 per person. (Assuming that the tax cut is a lump sum allows us to ignore incentive effects.) What impact will this reduction in taxes have on national saving? In answering this question, we first recall the definition of national saving (Eq. 2.8):

$$S = Y - C - G. \qquad \textbf{(15.5)}$$

Equation (15.5) states that national saving, S, equals output, Y, less consumption, C, and government purchases, G.[19] If we assume that government purchases, G, are constant and that output, Y, is fixed at its full-employment level, we know from Eq. (15.5) that the tax cut will reduce national saving, S, only if it causes consumption, C, to rise. Advocates of Ricardian equivalence assert that, if current and planned future government purchases are unchanged, a tax cut will *not* affect consumption and thus won't affect national saving.

Why wouldn't a tax cut that raises after-tax incomes cause people to consume more? The answer is that—if current and planned future government purchases don't change—a tax cut today must be accompanied by an offsetting increase in expected future taxes. To see why, note that if current taxes are reduced by $100 per person without any change in government purchases, the government must borrow an additional $100 per person by selling bonds. Suppose that the bonds are one-year bonds that pay a real interest rate, r. In the following year, when the government repays the principal ($100 per person) and interest ($\$100 \times r$ per person) on the bonds, it will have to collect an additional $\$100(1 + r)$ per person in taxes. Thus, when the public learns of the current tax cut of $100 per person, they should also expect their taxes to increase by $\$100(1 + r)$ per person next year.[20]

Because the current tax cut is balanced by an increase in expected future taxes, it doesn't make taxpayers any better off in the long run despite raising their current after-tax incomes. Indeed, after the tax cut, *taxpayers' abilities to consume today and in the future are the same as they were originally.* That is, if no one consumes more in response to the tax cut—so that each person saves the entire $100 increase in after-tax income—in the following year the $100 per person of additional saving will grow to $\$100(1 + r)$ per person. This additional $\$100(1 + r)$ per person is precisely the amount needed to pay the extra taxes that will be levied in the future, leaving people able to consume as much in the future as they had originally planned. Because people aren't made better off by the tax cut (which must be coupled with a future tax increase), they have no reason to consume more today. Thus national saving should be unaffected by the tax cut, as supporters of Ricardian equivalence claim.

Ricardian Equivalence Across Generations. The argument for Ricardian equivalence rests on the assumption that current government borrowing will be repaid within the lifetimes of people who are alive today. In other words, any tax cuts received today are offset by the higher taxes that people must pay later. But what if some of the debt the government is accumulating will be repaid not by the people who receive the tax cut but by their children or grandchildren? In that case, wouldn't people react to a tax cut by consuming more?

---

[19]We assume that net factor payments from abroad, *NFP*, are zero.

[20]The government might put the tax increase off for two, three, or more years. Nevertheless, the general conclusion that the current tax cut must be offset by future tax increases would be unchanged.

Harvard economist Robert Barro[21] has shown that, in theory, Ricardian equivalence may still apply even if the current generation receives the tax cut and future generations bear the burden of repaying the government's debt. To state Barro's argument in its simplest form, let's imagine an economy in which every generation has the same number of people and suppose that the current generation receives a tax cut of \$100 per person. With government purchases held constant, this tax cut increases the government's borrowing and outstanding debt by \$100 per person. However, people currently alive are not taxed to repay this debt; instead, this obligation is deferred until the next generation. To repay the government's increased debt, the next generation's taxes (in real terms) will be raised by $\$100(1 + \rho)$ per person, where $1 + \rho$ is the real value of a dollar borrowed today at the time the debt is repaid.[22]

Seemingly, the current generation of people, who receive the tax cut, should increase their consumption because the reduction in their taxes isn't expected to be balanced by an increase in taxes during their lifetimes. However, Barro argued that people in the current generation shouldn't increase their consumption in response to a tax cut if they care about the well-being of the next generation. Of course, people do care about the well-being of their children, as is reflected in part in the economic resources devoted to children, including funds spent on children's health and education, gifts, and inheritances.

How does the concern of this generation for the next affect the response of people to a tax cut? A member of the current generation who receives a tax cut—call him Joel—might be inclined to increase his own consumption, all else being equal. But, Barro argues, Joel should realize that, for each dollar of tax cut he receives today, his child Joel Junior will have to pay $1 + \rho$ dollars of extra taxes in the future. Can Joel do anything on his own to help out Joel Junior? The answer is yes. Suppose that, instead of consuming his \$100 tax cut, Joel saves the \$100 and uses the extra savings to increase Joel Junior's inheritance. By the time the next generation is required to pay the government debt, Joel Junior's extra inheritance plus accumulated interest will be $\$100(1 + \rho)$, or just enough to cover the increase in Joel Junior's taxes. Thus by saving his tax cut and adding these savings to his planned bequest, Joel can keep both his own consumption and Joel Junior's consumption the same as they would have been if the tax cut had never occurred.

Furthermore, Barro points out, Joel *should* save all his tax cut for Joel Junior's benefit. Why? If Joel consumes even part of his tax cut, he won't leave enough extra inheritance to allow Joel Junior to pay the expected increase in his taxes, and so Joel Junior will have to consume less than he could have if there had been no tax cut for Joel. But if Joel wanted to increase his own consumption at Joel Junior's expense, he could have done so without changes in the tax laws—for example, by contributing less to Joel Junior's college tuition payments or by planning to leave a smaller inheritance. That Joel didn't take these actions shows that he was satisfied with the division of consumption between himself and Joel Junior that he had planned before the tax cut was enacted; there is no reason that the tax cut should cause this original consumption plan to change. Therefore if Joel and other members of the current generation don't consume more in response to a tax cut, Ricardian equivalence should hold even when debt repayment is deferred to the next generation.

---

[21]"Are Government Bonds Net Wealth?" *Journal of Political Economy*, November/December 1974, pp. 1095–1117.

[22]For example, if the debt is to be repaid in 30 years and r is the one-year real interest rate, then $1 + \rho = (1 + r)^{30}$.

This analysis can be extended to allow for multiple generations and in other ways. These extensions don't change the main point, which is that, if taxpayers understand that they are ultimately responsible for the government's debt, they shouldn't change their consumption in response to changes in taxes or transfers that are unaccompanied by changes in planned government purchases. As a result, deficits created by tax cuts shouldn't reduce national saving and therefore shouldn't burden future generations.

Departures from Ricardian Equivalence

The arguments for Ricardian equivalence are logically sound, and this idea has greatly influenced economists' thinking about deficits. Although 40 years ago most economists would have taken for granted that a tax cut would substantially increase consumption, today there is much less agreement about this claim. Although Ricardian equivalence seemed to fail spectacularly in the 1980s in the United States—when high government budget deficits were accompanied by extremely low rates of national saving—data covering longer periods of time suggest little relationship between budget deficits and national saving rates in the United States. In some other countries, such as Canada and Israel, Ricardian equivalence seems to have worked quite well at times.[23]

Our judgment is that tax cuts that lead to increased government borrowing probably affect consumption and national saving, although the effect may be small. We base this conclusion both on the experience of the United States during the 1980s and on the fact that there are some theoretical reasons to expect Ricardian equivalence not to hold exactly. The main arguments against Ricardian equivalence are the possible existence of borrowing constraints, consumers' shortsightedness, the failure of some people to leave bequests, and the non-lump-sum nature of most tax changes.

1. *Borrowing constraints.* Many people would be willing to consume more if they could find lenders who would extend them credit. However, consumers often face limits, known as *borrowing constraints,* on the amounts that they can borrow. A person who wants to consume more, but who is unable to borrow to do so, will be eager to take advantage of a tax cut to increase consumption. Thus the existence of borrowing constraints may cause Ricardian equivalence to fail.
2. *Shortsightedness.* In the view of some economists, many people are shortsighted and don't understand that as taxpayers they are ultimately responsible for the government's debt. For example, some people may determine their consumption by simple "rules of thumb," such as the rule that a family should spend fixed percentages of its current after-tax income on food, clothing, housing, and so on, without regard for how its income is likely to change in the future. If people are shortsighted, they may respond to a tax cut by consuming more, contrary to the prediction of Ricardian equivalence. However, Ricardians could reply that ultrasophisticated analyses of fiscal policy by consumers aren't necessary for Ricardian equivalence to be approximately correct. For example, if people know generally that big government deficits mean

[23]For surveys of the evidence by a supporter and an opponent of Ricardian equivalence, respectively, see Robert Barro, "The Ricardian Approach to Budget Deficits," *Journal of Economic Perspectives,* Spring 1989, pp. 37–54; and B. Douglas Bernheim, "Ricardian Equivalence: An Evaluation of Theory and Evidence," in Stanley Fischer, ed., NBER *Macroeconomics Annual,* Cambridge, MA: MIT Press, 1987.

future problems for the economy (without knowing exactly why), they may be reluctant to spend from a tax cut that causes the deficit to balloon, consistent with the Ricardian prediction.

3. *Failure to leave bequests.* If people don't leave bequests, perhaps because they don't care or think about the long-run economic welfare of their children, they will increase their consumption if their taxes are cut, and Ricardian equivalence won't hold. Some people may not leave bequests because they expect their children to be richer than they are and thus not need any bequest. If people continue to hold this belief after they receive a tax cut, they will increase their consumption and again Ricardian equivalence will fail.
4. *Non-lump-sum taxes.* In theory, Ricardian equivalence holds only for lump-sum tax changes, with each person's change in taxes being a fixed amount that doesn't depend on the person's economic decisions, such as how much to work or save. As discussed in Section 15.2, when taxes are not lump-sum, the level and timing of taxes will affect incentives and thus economic behavior. Thus non-lump-sum tax cuts will have real effects on the economy, in contrast to the simple Ricardian view.

We emphasize, though, that with non-lump-sum taxes, the incentive effects of a tax cut on consumption and saving behavior will depend heavily on the tax structure and on which taxes are cut. For example, a temporary cut in sales taxes would likely stimulate consumption, but a reduction in the tax rate on interest earned on savings accounts might increase saving. Thus we cannot always conclude that, just because taxes aren't lump-sum, a tax cut will increase consumption. That conclusion has to rest primarily on the other three arguments against Ricardian equivalence that we presented.

In Touch with Data and Research

Measuring the Impact of Government Purchases on the Economy

The United Kingdom's Coronavirus Job Retention Scheme, in effect between March 1, 2020, and September 30, 2021, provided grants to employers so they could retain and continue to pay staff during coronavirus-related lockdowns by furloughing employees at up to 80% of their wages. Official government sources reported that 11.7 million jobs were furloughed at a cost of £70 billion, part of an estimated £122 billion put into a form of reverse taxation by HM Revenue and Customs and involving the Self-employed Income Support Scheme. The 2020–2021 fiscal year's government spending reached £1.096 trillion—the first time £1 trillion has ever been surpassed—with a one-year increase of 23.5%.

Although few would argue against the Scheme's usefulness, economists with classical and Keynesian leanings have been debating the effects of the government's purchases on aggregate economic activity, with no clear consensus emerging. As consumer spending typically accounts for over 60% of the United Kingdom's aggregate demand, its response is an important determinant of the fiscal multiplier's size. The standard real business cycle (RBC) and the *IS–LM* models offer different qualitative predictions. While the *IS–LM* model predicts that consumption should rise, thereby amplifying the effects of increased government spending on output, the RBC model generally predicts a decline in consumption in response. The different impacts of the two models derive from assumptions about how consumers behave in each case. The RBC model assumes Ricardian households, whose consumption decisions at any point in time are based on an across-time budget constraint; in other words, Ricardian equivalence holds. In the *IS–LM* model, however, consumers behave in a non-Ricardian fashion, with consumption being a function of current disposable income and not of their lifetime resources. To illustrate this using the *IS–LM* model, a temporary increase in government purchases shifts the *IS* curve up (and right) (as discussed in Section 9.2, "The *IS* Curve: Equilibrium in the Goods Market") resulting in a new *IS–LM* intersection to the right of the former. When prices remain fixed in the short run, as in the Keynesian version of the model, the new intersection implies a short-run output increase.

However, when prices are assumed to adjust quickly, the *LM* curve shifts up (and left), thereby offsetting the rightward *IS* curve shift. It is also worth noting that, as discussed in Section 10.2 ("Fiscal Policy Shocks in the Classical Model"), an increase in government spending may be the equivalent of a rise in workers' current or future taxes, with the result that they see themselves as poorer and hence supply more labor, thereby increasing output. In effect, both classical and Keynesian approaches can be used to explain how temporary increases in government spending can lead to higher output, albeit through different mechanisms.

The fiscal multiplier is estimated by determining the short-run national output changes due to a unit change in government spending. However, researchers have noted the difficulty in assigning causality to specific government spending because of other potential shocks that also affect the economy. Further, the choice of the appropriate variable is important. Research by Riera-Crichton, Vegh, and Vuletin (2012) underscores this need. Their analysis, using a novel value-added tax rate dataset and the corresponding cyclically adjusted revenue measured at a quarterly frequency for 14 industrialized countries between 1980 and 2009, strongly supports using tax rates as the true measure of a tax policy.[24] Further, some studies have found that fiscal multipliers could be different during recessions compared to booms, as there would be less crowding when supply constraints are not binding. Auerbach and Gorodnichenko (2012), for example, found that spending multipliers are significantly higher during recessions.[25] As discussed in Section 14.2 ("Monetary Control in the United States"), the size of the fiscal multiplier can be impacted by the monetary policy response. Research by Boubaker and colleagues (2018) found that, for the big four eurozone economies (France, Germany, Italy, and Spain), the government spending multiplier is above 1.8 when associated with a long-term commitment to keeping the nominal interest rate at the zero lower bound.[26]

As for the United Kingdom, the Office of Budget Responsibility's *Economic and Fiscal Outlook* reported fiscal multipliers ranging from 0.15 to 1.00 across several fiscal policy activities for 2020–21.[27] Overall, evidence from the extant literature indicates that care needs to be taken in estimating fiscal multipliers.

[24] D. Riera-Crichton, C. Vegh, and G. Vuletin, "Tax Multipliers: Pitfalls in Measurement and Identification," NBER Working Paper Series, No. 18497, 2012.

[25] A. Auerbach, Y. Gorodnichenko, "Measuring Output Responses to Fiscal Policy," *American Economic Journal: Economic Policy*, 4(2), 2012, pp. 1–27.

[26] Sabri Boubaker, Duc Khuong Nguyen, and Nikos Paltalidis, "Fiscal Policy Interventions at the Zero Lower Bound," *Journal of Economic Dynamics and Control* 93, August 2018, pp. 297–314, https://doi.org/10.1016/j.jedc.2018.01.048.

[27] Office for Budget Responsibility, *Economic and Fiscal Outlook*, March 2022, https://obr.uk/docs/dlm_uploads/CCS0222366764-001_OBR-EFO-March-2022_Web-Accessible-2.pdf.

15.4 Deficits and Inflation

Explain the link between deficits and inflation.

In this final section of the chapter we discuss one more concern that has been expressed about government budget deficits: that deficits are inflationary. We show that the principal link between deficits and inflation is that in some circumstances deficits lead to higher rates of growth in the money supply and that high rates of money growth in turn cause inflation.

The Deficit and the Money Supply

Inflation—a rising price level—results when aggregate demand increases more quickly than does aggregate supply. In terms of the *AD–AS* framework, suppose that the long-run aggregate supply curve (which reflects the productive capacity of the economy) is fixed. Then for the price level to rise, the aggregate demand curve must rise over time.

Both the classical and Keynesian models of the economy imply that deficits can cause aggregate demand to rise more quickly than aggregate supply, leading to an increase in the price level. In both models a deficit owing to increased government purchases reduces desired national saving, shifting the *IS* curve up and to the right and causing aggregate demand to rise. This increase in aggregate demand causes the price level to rise.[28] If we assume (as Keynesians usually do) that Ricardian equivalence doesn't hold, a budget deficit resulting from a cut in taxes or an increase in transfers also reduces desired national saving, increases aggregate demand, and raises the price level. Thus deficits resulting from expansionary fiscal policies (increased spending or reduced taxes) will be associated with inflation.

However, an increase in government purchases or a cut in taxes causes only a one-time increase in aggregate demand. Therefore, although we expect expansionary fiscal policies to lead to a one-time increase in the price level (that is, a temporary burst in inflation), we don't expect an increase in government purchases or a cut in taxes to cause a *sustained* increase in inflation. In general, the only factor that can sustain an increase in aggregate demand, leading to continuing inflation, is sustained growth in the money supply. Indeed, high rates of inflation are almost invariably linked to high rates of national money growth (recall the Application "Money Growth and Inflation in European Countries in Transition," in Chapter 7). The key question therefore is: Can government budget deficits lead to ongoing increases in the money supply?

The answer is "yes." The link is the printing of money to finance government spending when the government cannot (or does not want to) finance all of its spending by taxes or borrowing from the public. In the extreme case, imagine a government that wants to spend \$10 billion (say, on submarines) but has no ability to tax or borrow from the public. One option is for this government to print \$10 billion worth of currency and use this currency to pay for the submarines. The revenue that a government raises by printing money is called **seignorage**. Any government with the authority to issue money can use seignorage; governments that do not have the authority to issue money, such as state governments in the United States, can't use seignorage.

[28]The classical analysis predicts that an increase in government purchases will cause aggregate supply to rise as well, but we have assumed that the supply effect is smaller than the demand effect.

Actually, governments that want to finance their deficits through seignorage don't simply print new currency but use an indirect procedure. First, the Treasury authorizes government borrowing equal to the amount of the budget deficit ($10 billion in our example), and a corresponding quantity of new government bonds is printed and sold. Thus the deficit still equals the change in the outstanding government debt (Eq. 15.3). However, the new government bonds aren't sold to the public. Instead, the Treasury asks (or requires) the central bank to purchase the $10 billion in new bonds. The central bank pays for its purchases of new bonds by printing $10 billion in new currency,[29] which it gives to the Treasury in exchange for the bonds. This newly issued currency enters general circulation when the government spends it on its various outlays (the submarines). Note that the purchase of bonds by the central bank increases the monetary base by the amount of the purchase (see Chapter 14), as when the central bank purchases government bonds on the open market.

The precise relationship between the size of the deficit and the increase in the monetary base is

$$\text{deficit} = \Delta B = \Delta B^p + \Delta B^{cb} = \Delta B^p + \Delta BASE. \qquad \textbf{(15.6)}$$

Equation (15.6) states that the (nominal) government budget deficit equals the total increase in (nominal) government debt outstanding, ΔB, which can be broken into additional government debt held by the public, ΔB^p, and by the central bank, ΔB^{cb}. The increase in government debt held by the central bank in turn equals the increase in the monetary base, $\Delta BASE$. The increase in the monetary base equals the amount of seignorage collected by the government.

The final link between the budget deficit and the money supply has to do with the relationship between the money supply and the monetary base. To make the link as simple as possible, we consider an all-currency economy. Specifically, in an all-currency economy there are no banks, and all money is held in the form of currency. In an all-currency economy, the money supply equals the amount of currency outstanding (because there are no deposits) and the monetary base equals the amount of currency outstanding (because there are no bank reserves), so the money supply and the monetary base are equal. Therefore, in an all-currency economy, Eq. (15.6) implies that

$$\text{deficit} = \Delta B = \Delta B^p + \Delta B^{cb} = \Delta B^p + \Delta M, \qquad \textbf{(15.7)}$$

where $\Delta BASE = \Delta M$.

Why would governments use seignorage to finance their deficits, knowing that continued money creation ultimately leads to inflation? Under normal conditions developed countries rarely use seignorage. For example, in recent years (preceding the financial crisis of 2008) the monetary base in the United States increased on average by about $40 billion per year, which equals about 2% of Federal government receipts. Heavy reliance on seignorage usually occurs in war-torn or developing countries, in which military or social conditions dictate levels of government spending well above what the country can raise in taxes or borrow from the public.

[29]The new money created by the central bank could also be in the form of deposits at the central bank; the ultimate effect is the same.

Real Seignorage Collection and Inflation

The amount of real revenue that the government collects from seignorage is closely related to the inflation rate. To examine this link let's consider an all-currency economy in which real output and the real interest rate are fixed and the rates of money growth and inflation are constant. In such an economy the real quantity of money demanded is constant[30] and hence, in equilibrium, the real money supply must also be constant. Because the real money supply M/P doesn't change, the growth rate of the nominal money supply $\Delta M/M$ must equal the growth rate of the price level, or the rate of inflation π:

$$\pi = \frac{\Delta M}{M}. \tag{15.8}$$

Equation (15.8) expresses the close link between an economy's inflation rate and money growth rate.

How much seignorage is the government collecting in this economy? The *nominal* value of seignorage in any period is the increase in the amount of money in circulation ΔM. Multiplying both sides of Eq. (15.8) by M and rearranging gives an equation for the nominal value of seignorage:

$$\Delta M = \pi M. \tag{15.9}$$

Real seignorage revenue, R, is the real value of the newly created money, which equals nominal seignorage revenue, ΔM, divided by the price level, P. Dividing both sides of Eq. (15.9) by the price level P gives

$$R = \frac{\Delta M}{P} = \pi \frac{M}{P}. \tag{15.10}$$

Equation (15.10) states that the government's real seignorage revenue, R, equals the inflation rate, π, times the real money supply, M/P.

Equation (15.10) illustrates why economists sometimes call seignorage the **inflation tax**. In general, for any type of tax, tax revenue equals the tax rate multiplied by the tax base (whatever is being taxed). In the case of the inflation tax, the tax base is the real money supply and the tax rate is the rate of inflation. Multiplying the tax base (the real money supply) by the tax rate (the rate of inflation) gives the total inflation tax revenue.

How does the government collect the inflation tax and who pays this tax? The government collects the inflation tax by printing money (or by having the central bank issue new money) and using the newly created money to purchase goods and services. The inflation tax is paid by any member of the public who holds money because inflation erodes the purchasing power of money. For example, when the inflation rate is 10% per year, a person who holds currency for a year loses 10% of the purchasing power of that money and thus effectively pays a 10% tax on the real money holdings.

---

[30]Real money demand depends on real output and the nominal interest rate (we assume that the interest rate paid on money is fixed). Output is constant, and because the real interest rate and the inflation rate are constant, the nominal interest rate is constant as well. Thus the real quantity of money demanded is constant.

Suppose that a government finds that the seignorage being collected doesn't cover its spending and begins to increase the money supply faster. Will this increase in the money growth rate cause the real seignorage collected by the government to rise? Somewhat surprisingly, it may not. As Eq. (15.10) shows, the real seignorage collected by the government is the product of two terms—the rate of inflation (the tax rate) and the real money supply (the tax base). By raising the money growth rate, the government can increase the inflation rate. However, at a constant real interest rate, a higher rate of inflation will raise the nominal interest rate, causing people to reduce the real quantity of money held. Thus whether real seignorage revenue increases when the money growth rate increases depends on whether the rise in inflation, π, outweighs the decline in real money holdings, M/P.[31]

This point is illustrated by Figure 15.9, which shows the determination of real seignorage revenue at an assumed constant real interest rate of 3%. The real quantity of money is measured along the horizontal axes, and the nominal interest rate is measured along the vertical axes. The downward-sloping *MD* curves show the real demand for money; they slope downward because an increase in the nominal interest rate reduces the real quantity of money demanded.

In Fig. 15.9(a) the actual and expected rate of inflation is 8%, so that (for a real interest rate of 3%) the nominal interest rate is 11%. When the nominal interest rate is 11%, the real quantity of money that people are willing to hold is \$150 billion (point *H*). Using Eq. (15.10), we find that the real value of seignorage revenue is $0.08 \times$ \$150 billion, or \$12 billion. Real seignorage revenue is represented graphically by the area of the shaded rectangle. The rectangle's height equals the inflation rate (8%) and the rectangle's width equals the real quantity of money held by the public (\$150 billion).

Figure 15.9(b) shows the real amount of seignorage revenue at two different inflation rates. The real interest rate (3%) and the money demand curve in Fig. 15.9(b) are identical to those in Fig. 15.9(a). When the rate of inflation is 1% per year, the nominal interest rate is 4%, and the real quantity of money that the public holds is \$400 billion. Real seignorage revenue is $0.01 \times$ \$400 billion $=$ \$4 billion, or the area of rectangle *ABCD*. Alternatively, when the rate of inflation is 15% per year, the nominal interest rate is 18% per year, and the real value of the public's money holdings is \$50 billion. Real seignorage revenue in this case is \$7.5 billion, or the area of rectangle *AEFG*.

Comparing Fig. 15.9(a) and Fig. 15.9(b) reveals that real seignorage revenue is higher when inflation is 8% per year than when inflation is either 1% per year or 15% per year. Figure 15.10 shows the relationship between the inflation rate and seignorage revenue. At low inflation rates an increase in the inflation rate increases real seignorage revenue. However, at high inflation rates an increase in inflation reduces real seignorage revenue. In Fig. 15.10 the maximum possible real seignorage revenue is \$12 billion, which is achieved at the intermediate level of inflation of 8% per year.

What happens if the government tries to raise more seignorage revenue than the maximum possible amount? If it does so, inflation will rise but the real value

[31]The opposing effects on seignorage revenue of an increase in the inflation rate and the resulting reduction in real money holdings is similar to the opposing effects, discussed in the Application "Supply-Side Economics," on labor income tax revenue of a reduction in the labor income tax rate and the resulting increase in labor income.

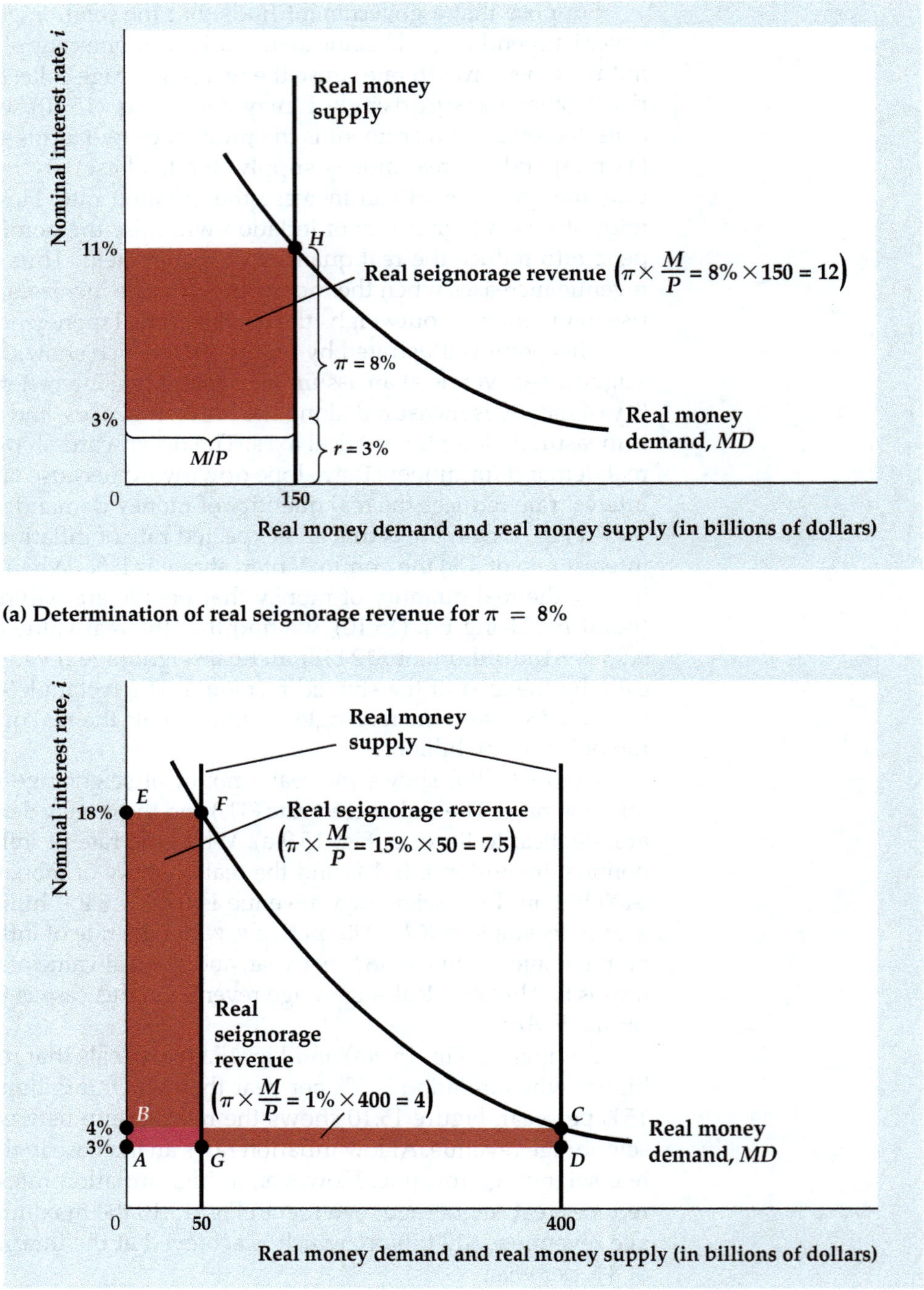

(a) Determination of real seignorage revenue for $\pi = 8\%$

(b) Determination of real seignorage revenue for $\pi = 1\%$ and $\pi = 15\%$

FIGURE 15.9

The determination of real seignorage revenue

(a) The downward-sloping curve, *MD*, is the money demand function for a given level of real income. The real interest rate is assumed to be 3%. When the rate of inflation is 8%, the nominal interest rate is 11%, and the real quantity of money held by the public is \$150 billion (point *H*). Real seignorage revenue collected by the government, represented by the area of the shaded rectangle, equals the rate of inflation (8%) times the real money stock (\$150 billion), or \$12 billion.
(b) The money demand function, *MD*, is the same as in (a), and the real interest rate remains at 3%. When the inflation rate is 1%, the nominal interest rate is 4%, and the real quantity of money held by the public is \$400 billion. In this case real seignorage revenue equals the area of the rectangle, *ABCD*, or \$4 billion. When the rate of inflation is 15%, the nominal interest rate is 18%, and the real money stock held by the public is \$50 billion. Real seignorage revenue in this case equals the area of the rectangle *AEFG*, or \$7.5 billion.

of the government's seignorage will fall as real money holdings fall. If the government continues to increase the rate of money creation, the economy will experience a high rate of inflation or even hyperinflation. Inflation will continue until the government reduces the rate of money creation either by balancing its budget or by finding some other way to finance its deficit.

FIGURE 15.10

The relation of real seignorage revenue to the rate of inflation
Continuing the example of Fig. 15.9, this figure shows the relation of real seignorage revenue, R, measured on the vertical axis, to the rate of inflation, π, measured on the horizontal axis. From Fig. 15.9(a), when inflation is 8% per year, real seignorage revenue is \$12 billion. From Fig. 15.9(b), real seignorage is \$4 billion when inflation is 1% and \$7.5 billion when inflation is 15%. At low rates of inflation, an increase in inflation increases seignorage revenue. At high rates of inflation, increased inflation can cause seignorage revenue to fall. In this example the maximum amount of seignorage revenue the government can obtain is \$12 billion, which occurs when the inflation rate is 8%.

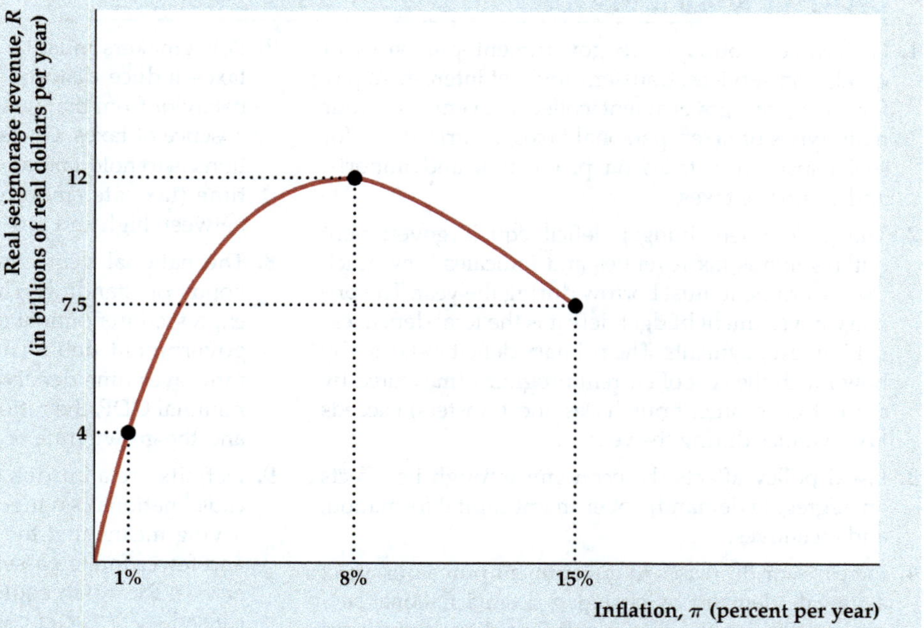

In some hyperinflations, governments desperate for revenue raise the rate of money creation well above the level that maximizes real seignorage. For example, in the extreme hyperinflation that hit Germany after World War I, rapid money creation drove the rate of inflation to 322% *per month.* In contrast, in his classic study of the German hyperinflation, Philip Cagan[32] of Columbia University calculated that the constant rate of inflation that would have maximized the German government's real seignorage revenue was "only" 20% per month.

[32]"The Monetary Dynamics of Hyperinflation," in Milton Friedman, ed., *Studies in the Quantity Theory of Money*, Chicago: University of Chicago Press, 1956.

CHAPTER SUMMARY

1. Government outlays are government purchases of goods and services, transfers, and net interest. To pay for them, the government collects revenue by four main types of taxes: personal taxes, contributions for social insurance, taxes on production and imports, and corporate taxes.

2. The government budget deficit equals government outlays minus tax revenues and indicates how much the government must borrow during the year. The primary government budget deficit is the total deficit less net interest payments. The primary deficit indicates by how much the cost of current programs (measured by current government purchases and transfers) exceeds tax revenues during the year.

3. Fiscal policy affects the economy through its effects on aggregate demand, government capital formation, and incentives.

4. Increases or decreases in government purchases affect aggregate demand by changing desired national saving and shifting the *IS* curve. If Ricardian equivalence doesn't hold, as Keynesians usually argue, changes in taxes also affect desired national saving, the *IS* curve, and aggregate demand. Automatic stabilizers in the government's budget allow spending to rise or taxes to fall automatically in a recession, which helps cushion the drop in aggregate demand during a recession. The full-employment deficit is what the deficit would be—given current government spending programs and tax laws—if the economy were at full employment. Because of automatic stabilizers that increase spending and reduce taxes in recessions, the actual deficit rises above the full-employment deficit in recessions.

5. Government capital formation contributes to the productive capacity of the economy. Government capital formation includes both investment in physical capital (roads, schools) and investment in human capital (education, child nutrition). Official measures of government investment include only investment in physical capital.

6. The average tax rate is the fraction of total income paid in taxes, and the marginal tax rate is the fraction of an additional dollar of income that must be paid in taxes. Changes in average tax rates and changes in marginal tax rates have different effects on economic behavior. For example, an increase in the average tax rate (with no change in the marginal tax rate) increases labor supply, but an increase in the marginal tax rate (with no change in the average tax rate) decreases labor supply.

7. Policymakers must be concerned about the fact that taxes induce distortions, or deviations in economic behavior from that which would have occurred in the absence of taxes. One strategy for minimizing distortions is to hold tax rates approximately constant over time (tax rate smoothing), rather than alternating between high and low tax rates.

8. The national debt equals the value of government bonds outstanding. The government budget deficit, expressed in nominal terms, equals the change in the government debt. The behavior of the debt–GDP ratio over time depends on the ratio of the deficit to nominal GDP, the ratio of total debt to nominal GDP, and the growth rate of nominal GDP.

9. Deficits are a burden on future generations if they cause national saving to fall because lower national saving means that the country will have less capital and fewer foreign assets than it would have had otherwise. Ricardian equivalence indicates that a deficit caused by a tax cut won't affect consumption and therefore won't affect national saving. In the Ricardian view, a tax cut doesn't affect consumption because the increase in consumers' current income arising from the tax cut is offset by the prospect of increased taxes in the future, leaving consumers no better off. In theory, Ricardian equivalence still holds if the government debt isn't repaid by the current generation, provided that people care about the well-being of their descendants and thus choose not to consume more at their descendants' expense.

10. Ricardian equivalence may not hold—and thus tax cuts may affect national saving—if (1) borrowing constraints prevent some people from consuming as much as they want to; (2) people are shortsighted and don't take expected future changes in taxes into account in their planning; (3) people do not leave bequests; or (4) taxes aren't lump-sum. The empirical evidence on Ricardian equivalence is mixed.

11. Deficits are linked to inflation when a government finances its deficits by printing money. The amount of revenue that the government raises by printing money is called seignorage. The real value of seignorage equals the inflation rate times the real money supply. Increasing the inflation rate doesn't always increase the government's real seignorage because higher inflation causes the public to hold a smaller real quantity of money. Attempts to push the collection of seignorage above its maximum can lead to hyperinflation.

KEY TERMS

automatic stabilizers, p. 622
average tax rate, p. 624
distortions, p. 626
full-employment deficit, p. 623
government capital, p. 624
government debt, p. 629
inflation tax, p. 642
marginal tax rate, p. 624
primary government budget deficit, p. 619
seignorage, p. 640
supply-side economics, p. 627
tax rate smoothing, p. 626

KEY EQUATIONS

$$\Delta B = \text{nominal government budget deficit} \quad \textbf{(15.3)}$$

The change in the nominal value of the government debt equals the nominal government budget deficit.

$$\text{change in debt-GDP ratio} = \frac{\text{deficit}}{\text{nominal GDP}} - \left(\frac{\text{total debt}}{\text{nominal GDP}} \times \text{growth rate of nominal GDP}\right) \quad \textbf{(15.4)}$$

The change in the ratio of government debt outstanding to GDP depends on the ratio of the deficit to nominal GDP, the ratio of total debt to nominal GDP, and the growth rate of nominal GDP.

$$\text{deficit} = \Delta B = \Delta B^p + \Delta B^{cb} = \Delta B^p + \Delta M \quad \textbf{(15.7)}$$

The government budget deficit equals the increase in the stock of government debt outstanding, B, which in turn equals the sum of additional holdings of government debt by the public, B^p, and by the central bank, B^{cb}. The increase in debt held by the central bank equals the increase in the monetary base, which in an all-currency economy is the same as the increase in the money supply, M.

$$R = \frac{\Delta M}{P} = \pi \frac{M}{P}. \quad \textbf{(15.10)}$$

In an all-currency economy, real seignorage revenue, R, equals the increase in the money supply, ΔM, divided by the price level, P. This ratio in turn equals the inflation rate (the tax rate on money) multiplied by the real money supply (the tax base).

REVIEW QUESTIONS

1. What are the major components of government outlays? What are the major sources of government revenues? How does the composition of the Federal government's outlays and revenues differ from that of state and local governments?
2. Explain the difference between the overall government budget deficit, the current deficit, and the primary current deficit. Why are three deficit concepts needed?
3. Who bears the burden of government debt? Explain why. Under what circumstances is there no burden to be borne?
4. What are the three main ways that fiscal policy affects the macroeconomy? Explain briefly how each channel of policy works.
5. Define *automatic stabilizer* and give an example. For proponents of antirecessionary fiscal policies, what advantage do automatic stabilizers have over other types of taxing and spending policies?
6. Give a numerical example that shows the difference between the average tax rate and the marginal tax rate on a person's income. For a constant before-tax real wage, which type of tax rate most directly affects how wealthy a person feels? Which type of tax rate affects the reward for working an extra hour?
7. How is real seignorage revenue related to inflation? How does the quantity of real seignorage revenue change as inflation rises from zero to a positive level, to still higher levels?
8. In what ways is the government debt a potential burden on future generations? What is the relationship between Ricardian equivalence and the idea that government debt is a burden?
9. Discuss four reasons why the Ricardian equivalence proposition isn't likely to hold exactly.
10. Define *inflation tax* (also called *seignorage*). How does the government collect this tax, and who pays it? Can the government always increase its real revenues from the inflation tax by increasing money growth and inflation?

NUMERICAL PROBLEMS

1. The following budget data are for a country having both a central government and provincial governments:

Central purchases of goods and services	200
Provincial purchases of goods and services	150
Central transfer payments	100
Provincial transfer payments	50
Grants in aid (central to provincial)	100
Central tax receipts	450
Provincial tax receipts	100
Interest received from private sector by central government	10
Interest received from private sector by provincial governments	10
Total central government debt	1000
Total provincial government debt	0
Central government debt held by provincial governments	200
Nominal interest rate	10%

Calculate the overall and primary deficits for the central government, the provincial governments, and the combined governments.

2. At the beginning of year one, there is no government debt outstanding. The government runs a $100 billion deficit in year one. Interest at a nominal rate of 10% must be paid starting in year two. Assume nominal GDP in year one is $2 trillion, and the nominal growth rate of GDP is 4%. Assume the government balances its primary budget in the future and the interest rate and growth rate do not change.

a. What will be the government deficit in years two, three, four, and five?

b. What will be the value of government bonds outstanding at the end of the fifth year?

c. What will be the debt-GDP ratio at the end of year five?

3. Because of automatic stabilizers, various components of the government's budget depend on the level of output, Y. The following are the main components of that budget:

Tax revenues	$1000 + 0.1Y$
Transfers	$800 - 0.05Y$
Government purchases	1800
Interest payments	100

Full-employment output is 10,000. Find the full-employment budget deficit and the actual budget deficit for

a. $Y = 12,000$. *b.* $Y = 10,000$. *c.* $Y = 8000$.

In general, how does the relationship between the actual deficit and the full-employment deficit depend on the state of the economy?

4. Suppose that the income tax law exempts income of less than $8000 from the tax, taxes income between $8000 and $20,000 at a 25% rate, and taxes income greater than $20,000 at a 30% rate.

a. Find the average tax rate and the marginal tax rate for someone earning $16,000 and for someone earning $30,000.

b. The tax law is changed so that income of less than $6000 is untaxed, income from $6000 to $20,000 is taxed at 20%, and income of more than $20,000 continues to be taxed at 30%. Repeat part (*a*).

c. How will the tax law change in part (*b*) affect the labor supply of the person initially earning $16,000? How will it affect the labor supply of the person initially earning $30,000?

5. Suppose that all workers value their leisure at 90 goods per day. The production function relating output per day, Y, to the number of people working per day, N, is

$$Y = 250N - 0.5N^2.$$

Corresponding to this production function, the marginal product of labor is

$$MPN = 250 - N.$$

a. Assume that there are no taxes. What are the equilibrium values of the real wage, employment, N, and output, Y? (*Hint:* In equilibrium the real wage will equal both the marginal product of labor and the value of a day's leisure to workers.)

b. A 25% tax is levied on wage income. What are the equilibrium values of the real wage, employment, and output? In terms of lost output, what is the distortion cost of this tax?

c. Suppose that the tax on wages rises to 50%. What are the equilibrium values of the real wage, employment, and output? In terms of lost output, what is the distortion cost of this higher tax rate? Compare the distortion caused by a 50% tax rate with that caused by a 25% tax rate. Is the distortion caused by a 50% tax rate twice as large, more than twice as large, or less than twice as large as that caused by a 25% tax rate? How does your answer relate to the idea of tax smoothing?

6. Find the largest nominal deficit that the government can run without raising the debt–GDP ratio, under each of the following sets of assumptions:

a. Nominal GDP growth is 10% and outstanding nominal debt is 1000.

b. Real GDP is 5000 and remains constant, nominal GDP is initially 10,000, inflation is 5%, and the debt-GDP ratio is 0.6.

7. In this problem you are asked to analyze the question: By issuing new bonds and using the proceeds to pay the principal and interest on its old bonds, can government avoid ever repaying its debts?

a. Suppose that nominal GDP is $1 billion and the government has $100 million of bonds outstanding. The bonds are one-year bonds that pay a 7% nominal interest rate. The growth rate of nominal GDP is 5% per year. Beginning now the government runs a zero primary deficit forever and pays principal and interest on its existing debt by issuing new bonds. What is the current debt–GDP ratio? What will this ratio be after 1, 2, 5, and 10 years? Suppose that, if the debt–GDP ratio exceeds 10, the public refuses to buy additional government bonds. Will the debt–GDP ratio ever reach that level? Will the government someday have to run a primary surplus to repay its debts, or can it avoid repayment forever? Why?

b. Repeat part (*a*) for nominal GDP growth of 8% per year and a nominal interest rate on government bonds of 7% per year.

8. Real money demand in an all-currency economy with fixed real output and real interest rate, and constant inflation rate and money growth rate is

$$L = 0.2Y - 500i,$$

where Y is real income and i is the nominal interest rate. In equilibrium, real money demand, L, equals real money supply, M/P. Suppose that Y is 1000 and the real interest rate, r, is 0.04.

a. Draw a graph with real seignorage revenue on the vertical axis and inflation on the horizontal axis. Show the values of seignorage for inflation rates of 0, 0.02, 0.04, 0.06, . . . , 0.30.

b. What inflation rate maximizes seignorage?

c. What is the maximum amount of seignorage revenue?

d. Repeat Parts (*a*)–(*c*) for $Y = 1000$ and $r = 0.08$.

9. Consider an economy in which the money supply consists of both currency and deposits. The growth rate of the monetary base, the growth rate of the money supply, inflation, and expected inflation all are constant at 10% per year. Output and the real interest rate are constant. Monetary data for this economy as of January 1, 2019, are as follows:

Currency held by nonbank public	$200
Bank reserves	$50
Monetary base	$250
Deposits	$600
Money supply	$800

a. What is the nominal value of seignorage over the year? (*Hint:* How much monetary base is created during the year?)

b. Suppose that deposits and bank reserves pay no interest, and that banks lend deposits not held as reserves at the market rate of interest. Who pays the inflation tax (measured in nominal terms), and how much do they pay? (*Hint:* The inflation tax paid by banks in this example is negative.)

c. Suppose that deposits pay a market rate of interest. Who pays the inflation tax, and how much do they pay?

ANALYTICAL PROBLEMS

1. Why is some state and local spending paid for by grants in aid from the Federal government instead of entirely through taxes levied by states and localities on residents? What are the advantages and disadvantages of a system of grants in aid?

2. Both transfer programs and taxes affect incentives. Consider a program designed to help the poor that promises each aid recipient a minimum income of $10,000. That is, if the recipient earns less than $10,000, the program supplements his income by enough to bring him up to $10,000.

Explain why this program would adversely affect incentives for low-wage recipients. (*Hint:* Show that this program is equivalent to giving the recipient $10,000 and then taxing his labor income at a high marginal rate.) Describe a transfer program that contains better incentives. Would that program have any disadvantages? If so, what would they be?

3. *a* Use the fact that the nominal deficit equals the nominal primary deficit plus nominal interest payments on government debt to rewrite Equation (15.4) showing the change in the debt–GDP ratio as a function of the ratio of the primary deficit to GDP, the ratio of debt to GDP, and the difference between the growth rate of nominal GDP and the nominal interest rate.

b. Show that, if the primary deficit is zero, the change in the debt–GDP ratio equals the product of (1) the debt–GDP ratio and (2) the excess of the real interest rate over the growth rate of real GDP.

4. A constitutional amendment has been proposed that would force Congress to balance the budget each year (that is, outlays must equal revenues in each year). Discuss some advantages and disadvantages of such an amendment. How would a balanced-budget amendment affect the following, if in the absence of such an amendment the Federal government would run a large deficit?

a. The use of automatic stabilizers.

b. The ability of Congress to "smooth" taxes over time.

c. The ability of Congress to make capital investments.

WORKING WITH MACROECONOMIC DATA

For data to use in these exercises, go to the Federal Reserve Bank of St. Louis FRED database at fred.stlouisfed.org.

1. Using quarterly data since 1959, graph Federal government expenditures and receipts as a percentage of GDP. Separately, graph state and local government expenditures and receipts as a percentage of GDP. Compare the two graphs. How do Federal and state/local governments compare in terms of (a) growth of total spending and taxes over time and (b) the tendency to run deficits?
2. Using quarterly data since 1948, graph the Federal deficit as a percentage of GDP. What is the cyclical behavior of the Federal deficit?

   Repeat this exercise for the deficits of state and local governments. Are state and local deficits more or less cyclically sensitive than Federal deficits?
3. Go to the website of the Congressional Budget Office (*www.cbo.gov*) and find projections for the government budget deficit for the coming five years. Compare the size of the deficit and the full-employment deficit (which the CBO calls the budget deficit without automatic stabilizers) relative to potential GDP in those years, and compare your results to the history shown in Fig. 15.5. What macroeconomic or political factors have caused the changes you observe in the deficit measures?
4. In Section 15.4, we discuss the potential relationship between government deficits and inflation. In this question, you will investigate the data on government debt as a share of GDP and the monetary base as a share of GDP. First, find data on the amount of U.S. Federal government debt held by the public as a share of GDP. Then find data on the monetary base and divide it by GDP, noting that the monetary base is available at a monthly frequency and GDP is available at a quarterly frequency, so you will need to create a quarterly series for the monetary base. One way to create such a quarterly series is to compute quarterly averages of the monthly monetary base series. (FRED does this automatically.) Plot the debt-to-GDP data and the monetary base-to-GDP data on the same graph. Does there appear to be a relationship between the two variables? How did the relationship change in the Great Recession of 2007–2009? Can you explain this change, given what you learned about the financial crisis in Chapter 14?

Appendix 15.A

The Debt–GDP Ratio

In this appendix we derive Eq. (15.4), which shows how the debt–GDP ratio evolves. If we let Q represent the ratio of government debt to GDP, by definition

$$Q = \frac{B}{PY}, \tag{15.A.1}$$

where B is the nominal value of government bonds outstanding (government debt), P is the price level, and Y is real GDP (so that PY is nominal GDP). A useful rule is that the percentage change in any ratio equals the percentage change in the numerator minus the percentage change in the denominator (Appendix A, Section A.7). Applying this rule to Eq. (15.A.1) gives

$$\frac{\Delta Q}{Q} = \frac{\Delta B}{B} - \frac{\Delta(PY)}{PY}. \tag{15.A.2}$$

Now multiply the left side of Eq. (15.A.2) by Q and multiply the right side by B/PY, as is legitimate because $Q = B/PY$ by Eq. (15.A.1). This gives

$$\frac{\Delta Q}{Q} \times Q = \left(\frac{\Delta B}{B} \times \frac{B}{PY}\right) - \left(\frac{\Delta(PY)}{PY} \times \frac{B}{PY}\right).$$

Simplifying this expression gives

$$\Delta Q = \frac{\Delta B}{PY} - \left(\frac{B}{PY} \times \frac{\Delta(PY)}{PY}\right), \tag{15.A.3}$$

which in words means the change in the ratio of government debt to GDP = deficit/GDP minus (debt/GDP times the growth rate of nominal GDP). Eq. (15.A.3) is identical to Eq. (15.4).

Appendix A

Some Useful Analytical Tools

In this appendix we review some basic algebraic and graphical tools used in this book.

A.1 Functions and Graphs

A function is a relationship among two or more variables. For an economic illustration of a function, suppose that in a certain firm each worker employed can produce five units of output per day. Let

N = the number of workers employed by the firm;
Y = total daily output of the firm.

In this example, the relationship of output, Y, to the number of workers, N, is

$$Y = 5N. \qquad \textbf{(A.1)}$$

Equation (A.1) is an example of a function relating the variable Y to the variable N. Using this function, for any number of workers, N, we can calculate the total amount of output, Y, that the firm can produce each day. For example, if $N = 3$, then $Y = 15$.

Functions can be described graphically as well as algebraically. The graph of the function $Y = 5N$, for values of N between 0 and 16, is shown in Fig. A.1. Output, Y, is shown on the vertical axis, and the number of workers, N, is shown on the horizontal axis. Points on the line $0AB$ satisfy Eq. (A.1). For example, at point A, $N = 4$ and $Y = 20$, a combination of N and Y that satisfies Eq. (A.1). Similarly, at point B, $N = 12.5$ and $Y = 62.5$, which also satisfies the relationship $Y = 5N$. Note that (at B, for example) the relationship between Y and N allows the variables to have values that are not whole numbers. Allowing fractional values of N and Y is reasonable because workers can work part-time or overtime, and a unit of output may be only partially completed during a day.

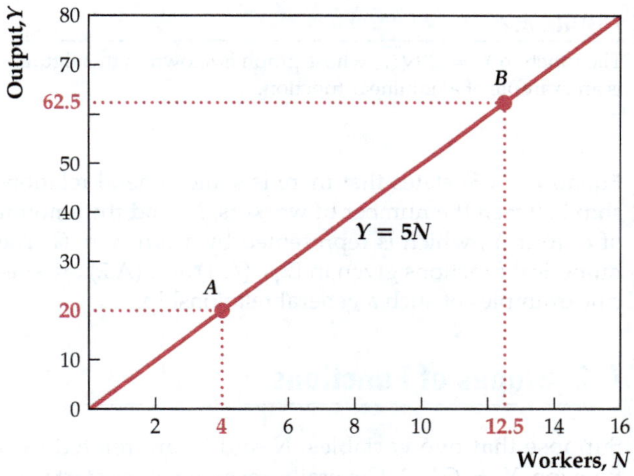

FIGURE A.1

Points on the line $0AB$ satisfy the relationship $Y = 5N$. Because the graph of the function $Y = 5N$ is a straight line, this function is called a linear function.

Functions such as $Y = 5N$ whose graph is a straight line are called *linear functions.* Functions whose graph is not a line are called *nonlinear.* An example of a nonlinear function is

$$Y = 20\sqrt{N}. \qquad \textbf{(A.2)}$$

The graph of the nonlinear function $Y = 20\sqrt{N}$ is shown in Fig. A.2. All points on the curve satisfy Eq. (A.2). For example, at point C, $N = 4$ and $Y = 20\sqrt{4} = 40$. At point D, $N = 9$ and $Y = 20\sqrt{9} = 60$.

Both examples of functions given so far are specific numerical relationships. We can also write functions in more general terms, using letters or symbols. For example, we might write

$$Y = G(N). \qquad \textbf{(A.3)}$$

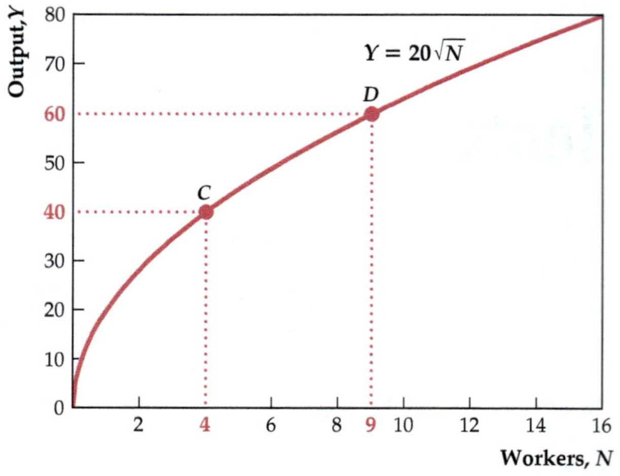

FIGURE A.2

The function $Y = 20\sqrt{N}$, whose graph is shown in this figure, is an example of a nonlinear function.

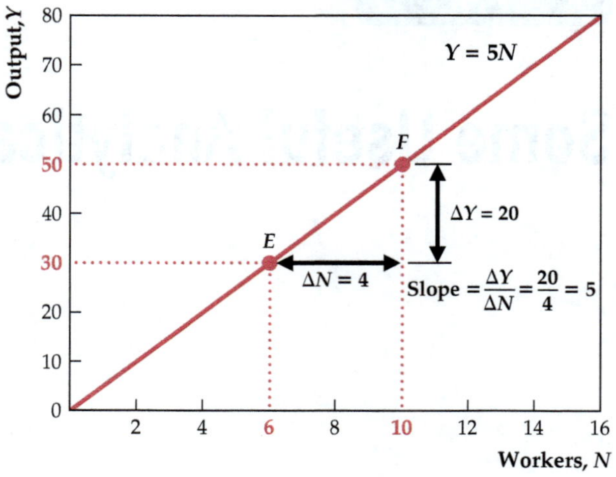

FIGURE A.3

The slope of a function equals the change in the variable on the vertical axis (Y) divided by the change in the variable on the horizontal axis (N). For example, between points E and F, the increase in N, ΔN, equals 4 and the increase in Y, ΔY, equals 20. Therefore the slope of the function between E and F, $\Delta Y/\Delta N$, equals 5. In general, the slope of a linear function is constant, so the slope of this function between any two points is 5.

Equation (A.3) states that there is some general relationship between the number of workers, N, and the amount of output, Y, which is represented by a function, G. The numerical functions given in Eqs. (A.1) and (A.2) are specific examples of such a general relationship.

A.2 Slopes of Functions

Suppose that two variables, N and Y, are related by a function, $Y = G(N)$. Generally speaking, if we start from some given combination of N and Y that satisfies the function G, the slope of the function G at that point indicates by how much Y changes when N changes by one unit.

To define the slope more precisely, we suppose that the current value of N is a specific number, N_1, so that the current value of Y equals $G(N_1)$. Now consider what happens if N is increased by an amount ΔN (ΔN is read "the change in N"). Output, Y, depends on N; therefore if N changes, Y may also change. The value of N is now $N_1 + \Delta N$, so the value of Y after N increases is $G(N_1 + \Delta N)$. The *change* in Y is

$$\Delta Y = G(N_1 + \Delta N) - G(N_1).$$

The slope of the function G, for an increase in N from N_1 to $N_1 + \Delta N$, is

$$\text{slope} = \frac{\Delta Y}{\Delta N} = \frac{G(N_1 + \Delta N) - G(N_1)}{(N_1 + \Delta N) - N_1}. \qquad \textbf{(A.4)}$$

Note that if $\Delta N = 1$, the slope equals ΔY, the change in Y.

Figures A.3 and A.4 show graphically how to determine slopes for the two functions discussed in the preceding section. Figure A.3 shows the graph of the function $Y = 5N$ (as in Fig. A.1). Suppose that we start from point E in Fig. A.3, where $N = 6$ and $Y = 30$. If N is increased by 4 (for example), we move to point F on the graph, where $N = 10$ and $Y = 50$. Between E and F, $\Delta N = 10 - 6 = 4$ and $\Delta Y = 50 - 30 = 20$, so the slope $\Delta Y/\Delta N = 20/4 = 5$.

In general, the slope of a linear function is the same at all points. You can prove this result for the linear function $Y = 5N$ by showing that for any change ΔN, $\Delta Y = 5\Delta N$. So for this particular linear function, the slope $\Delta Y/\Delta N$ always equals 5, a constant number.

For a nonlinear function, such as $Y = 20\sqrt{N}$, the slope isn't constant but depends on both the initial value of N and the size of the change in N. These results are illustrated in Fig. A.4, which displays the graph of the function $Y = 20\sqrt{N}$ (as in Fig. A.2). Suppose that we are initially at point G, where $N = 1$ and $Y = 20$, and we increase N by 8 units. After the increase in N we are at point D, where $N = 9$ and $Y = 20\sqrt{9} = 60$. Between G and D, $\Delta N = 9 - 1 = 8$ and $\Delta Y = 60 - 20 = 40$. Thus the slope of the function between G and D is $40/8 = 5$. Geometrically, the slope of the function between G and D equals the slope of the straight line between G and D.

Starting once again from point G in Fig. A.4, if we instead increase N by 3 units, we come to point C, where $N = 4$ and $Y = 20\sqrt{4} = 40$. In this case $\Delta N = 3$ and $\Delta Y = 40 - 20 = 20$, so the slope between G and C is $20/3 = 6\frac{2}{3}$, which isn't the same as the slope of 5 that

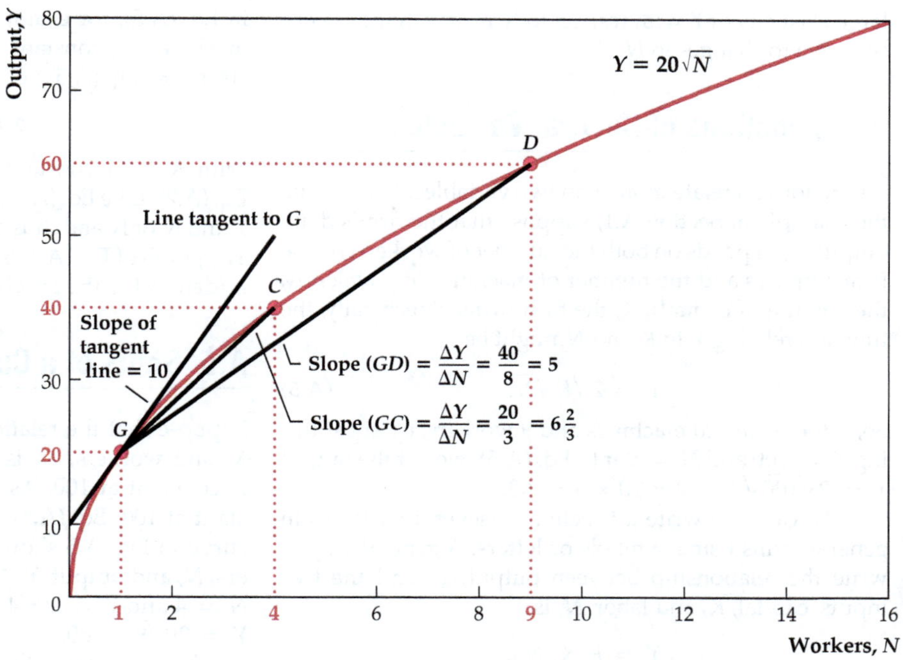

FIGURE A.4

Between points G and D, the change in N, ΔN is 8 and the change in Y, ΔY, is 40, so the slope of the function between points G and D is $\Delta Y/\Delta N = 40/8 = 5$. This slope is the same as the slope of the line GD. Similarly, the slope of the function between points G and C is $\Delta Y/\Delta N = 20/3 = 6\frac{2}{3}$. The slope of the line tangent to point G, which equals 10, approximates the slope of the function for very small changes in N. Generally, when we refer to the slope of a nonlinear function at a specific point, we mean the slope of the line tangent to the function at that point.

we calculated earlier when we increased N by 8 units. Geometrically, the slope of the line between G and C is greater than the slope of the line between G and D; that is, line GC is steeper than line GD.

In Fig. A.4 we have also drawn a line that touches but does not cross the graph of the function at point G; this line is *tangent* to the graph of the function at point G. If you start from point G and find the slope of the function for different values of ΔN, you will discover that the smaller the value of ΔN is, the closer the slope will be to the slope of the tangent line. For example, if you compare the slope of line GD (for which $\Delta N = 8$) with the slope of line GC (for which $\Delta N = 3$), you will see that of the two the slope of line GC is closer to the slope of the line tangent to point G. For values of ΔN even smaller than 3, the slope would be still closer to the slope of the tangent line.

These observations lead to an important result: *For small values of* ΔN *the slope of a function at any point is closely approximated by the slope of the line tangent to the function at that point.* Unless specified otherwise, in this book when we refer to the slope of a nonlinear function, we mean the slope of the line tangent to the function at the specified point. Thus in Fig. A.4, the slope of the function at point G means the slope of the line tangent to the function at point G, which happens to be 10.[1]

The numerical example illustrated in Fig. A.4 shows that the slope of a nonlinear function depends on the size of the increase in ΔN being considered. The slope of a nonlinear function also depends on the point at which the slope is being measured. In Fig. A.4 note that the slope of a line drawn tangent to point D, for example, would be less than the slope of a line drawn tangent to point G. Thus the slope of this particular function (measured with respect to small changes in N) is greater at G than at D.

A.3 Elasticities

Like slopes, elasticities indicate how much one variable responds when a second variable changes. Suppose again that there is a function relating Y to N, so that when N changes, Y changes as well. The *elasticity* of Y with respect to N is defined to be the percentage change in Y, $\Delta Y/Y$, divided by the percentage change in N, $\Delta N/N$. Writing the formula, we have

$$\text{elasticity of } Y \text{ with respect to } N = \frac{\Delta Y/Y}{\Delta N/N}.$$

Because the slope of a function is $\Delta Y/\Delta N$, we can also write the elasticity of Y with respect to N as the slope times (N/Y).

If the elasticity of Y with respect to N is large, a 1% change in N causes a large percentage change in Y. Thus a

[1]Showing that the slope of the line tangent to point G equals 10 requires basic calculus. The derivative of the function $Y = 20\sqrt{N}$, which is the same as the slope, is $dY/dN = 10/\sqrt{N}$. Evaluating this derivative at $N = 1$ yields a slope of 10.

large elasticity of Y with respect to N means that Y is very sensitive to changes in N.

A.4 Functions of Several Variables

A function can relate more than two variables. To continue the example of Section A.1, suppose that the firm's daily output, Y, depends on both the number of workers, N, the firm employs and the number of machines (equivalently, the amount of capital), K, the firm owns. Specifically, the function relating Y to K and N might be

$$Y = 2\sqrt{K}\sqrt{N}. \qquad \textbf{(A.5)}$$

So, if there are 100 machines and 9 workers, by substituting $K = 100$ and $N = 9$ into Eq. (A.5), we get the output $Y = 2\sqrt{100}\sqrt{9} = 2 \times 10 \times 3 = 60$.

We can also write a function of several variables in general terms using symbols or letters. A general way to write the relationship between output, Y, and the two inputs, capital, K, and labor, N, is

$$Y = F(K, N).$$

This equation is a slight simplification of a relationship called the production function, which we introduce in Chapter 3.

The graph of a function relating three variables requires three dimensions. As a convenient way to graph such a function on a two-dimensional page, we hold one of the right-side variables constant. To graph the function in Eq. (A.5), for example, we might hold the number of machines, K, constant at a value of 100. If we substitute 100 for K, Eq. (A.5) becomes

$$Y = 2\sqrt{100}\sqrt{N} = 20\sqrt{N}. \qquad \textbf{(A.6)}$$

With K held constant at 100, Eq. (A.6) is identical to Eq. (A.2). Like Eq. (A.2), Eq. (A.6) is a relationship between Y and N only and thus can be graphed in two dimensions. The graph of Eq. (A.6), shown as the solid curve in Fig. A.5, is identical to the graph of Eq. (A.2) in Fig. A.2.

A.5 Shifts of a Curve

Suppose that the relationship of output, Y, to machines, K, and workers, N, is given by Eq. (A.5) and we hold K constant at 100. As in Section A.4, with K held constant at 100, Eq. (A.5) reduces to Eq. (A.6) and the solid curve in Fig. A.5 shows the relationship between workers, N, and output, Y. At point C in Fig. A.5, for example, $N = 4$ and $Y = 20\sqrt{4} = 40$. At point D, where $N = 9$, $Y = 20\sqrt{9} = 60$.

Now suppose that the firm purchases additional machines, raising the number of machines, K, from 100 to 225. If we substitute this new value for K, Eq. (A.5) becomes

$$Y = 2\sqrt{225}\sqrt{N} = 30\sqrt{N}. \qquad \textbf{(A.7)}$$

Equation (A.7) is shown graphically as the dashed curve in Fig. A.5. Note that the increase in K has shifted the curve up. Because of the increase in the number of

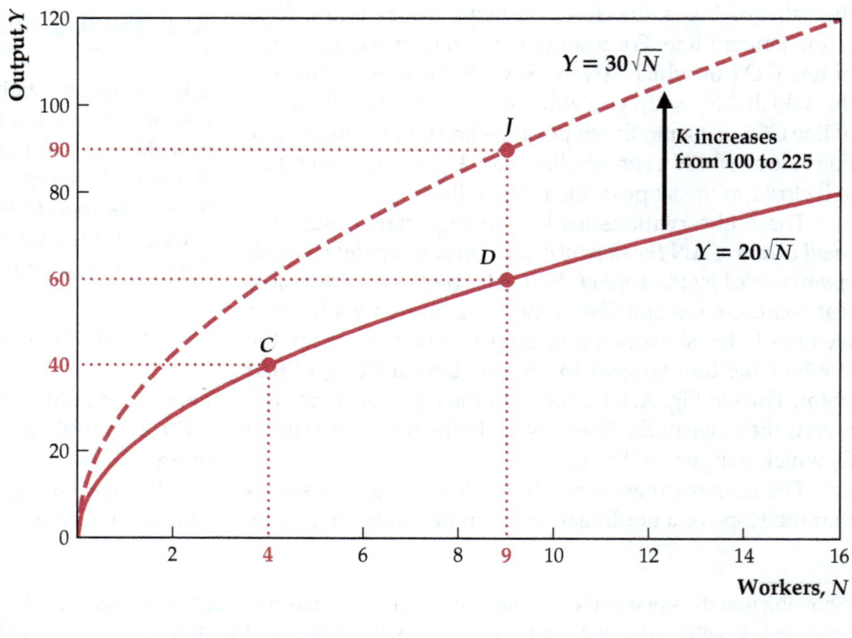

FIGURE A.5

Suppose that output, Y, depends on capital, K, and workers, N, according to the function in Eq. (A.5). If we hold K fixed at 100, the relationship between Y and N is shown by the solid curve. If K rises to 225, so that more output can be produced with a given number of workers, the curve showing the relationship between Y and N shifts up, from the solid curve to the dashed curve. In general, a change in any right-side variable that doesn't appear on an axis of the graph causes the curve to shift.

machines, the amount of daily output, Y, that can be produced for any given number of workers, N, has risen. For example, initially when N equaled 9, output, Y, equaled 60 (point D in Fig. A.5). After the increase in K, if $N = 9$, then $Y = 30\sqrt{9} = 90$ (point J in Fig. A.5).

This example illustrates some important general points about the graphs of functions of several variables.

1. To graph a function of several variables in two dimensions, we hold all but one of the right-side variables constant.

2. The one right-side variable that isn't held constant (N in this example) appears on the horizontal axis. Changes in this variable don't shift the graph of the function. Instead, changes in the variable on the horizontal axis represent movements *along* the curve that represents the function.

3. The right-side variables held constant for the purpose of drawing the graph (K in this example) don't appear on either axis of the graph. If the value of one of these variables is changed, the entire curve shifts. In this example, for any number of workers, N, the increase in machines, K, means that more output, Y, can be produced. Thus the curve shifts up, from the solid curve to the dashed curve in Fig. A.5.

A.6 Exponents

Powers of numbers or variables can be expressed by using superscripts called *exponents*. In the following examples, 2 and 4 are the exponents:

$$5^2 = 5 \times 5, \text{and } Z^4 = Z \times Z \times Z \times Z.$$

For any numbers Z, a, and b, exponents obey the following rules:

$$Z^a \times Z^b = Z^{a+b}, \text{and } (Z^a)^b = Z^{ab}.$$

An illustration of the first rule is $5^2 \times 5^3 = (5 \times 5) \times (5 \times 5 \times 5) = 5^5$ An illustration of the second rule is $(5^3)^2 = (5^3) \times (5^3) = (5 \times 5 \times 5) \times (5 \times 5 \times 5) = 5^6$.

Exponents don't have to be whole numbers. For example, $5^{0.5}$ represents the square root of 5. To understand why, note that by the second of the two rules for exponents, $(5^{0.5})^2 = 5^{(0.5)2} = 5^1 = 5$. That is, the square of $5^{0.5}$ is 5. Similarly, for any number Z and any nonzero integer q, $Z^{1/q}$ is the qth root of Z. Thus $5^{0.25}$ means the fourth root of 5, for example. Using exponents, we can rewrite Eq. (A.5) as

$$Y = 2K^{0.5}N^{0.5},$$

where $K^{0.5} = \sqrt{K}$ and $N^{0.5} = \sqrt{N}$.

In general, consider any number that can be expressed as a ratio of two nonzero integers, p and q. Using the rules of exponents, we have

$$Z^{p/q} = (Z^p)^{1/q} = q\text{th root of } Z^p.$$

Thus for example, as 0.7 equals 7/10, $N^{0.7}$ equals the tenth root of N^7. For values of N greater than 1, $N^{0.7}$ is a number larger than the square root of N, $N^{0.5}$, but smaller than N itself.

Exponents also may be zero or negative. In general, the following two relationships hold:

$$Z^0 = 1, \text{and } Z^{-a} = \frac{1}{Z^a}.$$

Here is a useful way to relate exponents and elasticities: Suppose that two variables, Y and N, are related by a function of the form

$$Y = kN^a, \tag{A.8}$$

where a is a number and k can be either a number or a function of variables other than N. Then the elasticity of Y with respect to N (see Section A.3) equals a.

A.7 Growth Rate Formulas

Let X and Z be any two variables, not necessarily related by a function, that are changing over time. Let $\Delta X/X$ and $\Delta Z/Z$ represent the growth rates (percentage changes) of X and Z, respectively. Then the following rules provide useful approximations (proofs of the various rules are included for reference).

Rule 1: The growth rate of the product of X and Z equals the growth rate of X plus the growth rate of Z.

Proof: Suppose that X increases by ΔX and Z increases by ΔZ. Then the absolute increase in the product of X and Z is $(X + \Delta X)(Z + \Delta Z) - XZ$, and the growth rate of the product of X and Z is

$$\begin{aligned}\text{growth rate of } (XZ) &= \frac{(X + \Delta X)(Z + \Delta Z) - XZ}{XZ} \\ &= \frac{(\Delta X)Z + (\Delta Z)X + \Delta X\Delta Z}{XZ} \\ &= \frac{\Delta X}{X} + \frac{\Delta Z}{Z} + \frac{\Delta X\Delta Z}{XZ}.\end{aligned} \tag{A.9}$$

The last term on the right side of Eq. (A.9), $(\Delta X\Delta Z)/XZ$, equals the growth rate of X, $\Delta X/X$, times the growth rate of Z, $\Delta Z/Z$. This term is generally small; for example, if the growth rates of X and Z are both 5% (0.05), the product of the two growth rates is only 0.25% (0.0025). If we assume that this last term is small enough to ignore,

Eq. (A.9) indicates that the growth rate of the product XZ equals the growth rate of X, $\Delta X/X$, plus the growth rate of Z, $\Delta Z/Z$.

Rule 2: The growth rate of the ratio of X to Z is the growth rate of X minus the growth rate of Z.

Proof: Let W be the ratio of X to Z, so $W = X/Z$. Then $X = ZW$. By Rule 1, as X equals the product of Z and W, the growth rate of X equals the growth rate of Z plus the growth rate of W:

$$\frac{\Delta X}{X} = \frac{\Delta Z}{Z} + \frac{\Delta W}{W}.$$

Rearranging this equation to put $\Delta W/W$ on the left side and recalling that $\Delta W/W$ equals the growth rate of (X/Z), we have

$$\text{growth rate of } (X/Z) = \frac{\Delta X}{X} - \frac{\Delta Z}{Z}. \quad \textbf{(A.10)}$$

Rule 3: Suppose that Y is a variable that is a function of two other variables, X and Z. Then

$$\frac{\Delta Y}{Y} = \eta_{Y,X}\frac{\Delta X}{X} + \eta_{Y,Z}\frac{\Delta Z}{Z}, \quad \textbf{(A.11)}$$

where $\eta_{Y,X}$ is the elasticity of Y with respect to X and $\eta_{Y,Z}$ is the elasticity of Y with respect to Z.

Proof (informal): Suppose that only X changes so that $\Delta Z/Z = 0$. Then Eq. (A.11) becomes the definition of an elasticity, $\eta_{Y,X} = (\Delta Y/Y)/(\Delta X/X)$, as in Section A.3. Similarly, if only Z changes, Eq. (A.11) becomes $\eta_{Y,Z} = (\Delta Y/Y)/(\Delta Z/Z)$, which is the definition of the elasticity of Y with respect to Z. If both X and Z change, Eq. (A.11) indicates that the overall effect on Y is approximately equal to the sum of the individual effects on Y of the change in X and the change in Z.

Rule 4: The growth rate of X raised to the power a, or X^a, is a times the growth rate of X,

$$\text{growth rate of } (X^a) = a\frac{\Delta X}{X}. \quad \textbf{(A.12)}$$

Proof: Let $Y = X^a$. Applying the rule from Eq. (A.8) and setting $k = 1$, we find that the elasticity of Y with respect to X equals a. Therefore, by Eq. (A.11), the growth rate of Y equals a times the growth rate of X. Because $Y = X^a$, the growth rate of Y is the same as the growth rate of X^a, which proves the relationship in Eq. (A.12).

Example: The real interest rate. To apply the growth rate formulas, we derive the equation that relates the real interest rate to the nominal interest rate and the inflation rate, Eq. (2.13).

The real value of any asset—say, a savings account—equals the nominal or dollar value of the asset divided by the price level:

$$\text{real asset value} = \frac{\text{nominal asset value}}{\text{price level}}. \quad \textbf{(A.13)}$$

The real value of an asset is the ratio of the nominal asset value to the price level, so, according to Rule 2, the *growth rate* of the real asset value is approximately equal to the *growth rate* of the nominal asset value minus the *growth rate* of the price level. The growth rate of the real value of an interest-bearing asset equals the real interest rate earned by that asset; the growth rate of the nominal value of an interest-bearing asset is the nominal interest rate for that asset; and the growth rate of the price level is the inflation rate. Therefore Rule 2 implies the relationship

$$\text{real interest rate} = \text{nominal interest rate} - \text{inflation rate},$$

which is the relationship given in Eq. (2.13).

Problems

1. Graph the function $Y = 3X + 5$ for $0 \leq X \leq 5$. What is the slope of this function?
2. Graph the function $Y = X^2 + 2$ for $0 \leq X \leq 5$. Starting from the point at which $X = 1$, find the slope of the function for $\Delta X = 1$ and $\Delta X = -1$. What is the slope of the line tangent to the function at $X = 1$? (See Problem 3.)
3. For the function $Y = X^2 + 2$, use Eq. (A.4) to write a general expression for the slope. This expression for the slope will depend on the initial value of X, X_1, and on the change in X, ΔX. For values of ΔX sufficiently small that the term (ΔX^2) can be ignored, show that the slope depends only on the initial value of X, X_1. What is the slope of the function (which is the same as the slope of the tangent line) when $X_1 = 1$?
4. Suppose that the amount of output, Y, that a firm can produce depends on its amount of capital, K, and the number of workers employed, N, according to the function

$$Y = K^{0.3}N^{0.7}.$$

   a. Suppose that $N = 100$. Give the function that relates Y to K and graph this relationship for $0 \leq K \leq 50$. (You need calculate only enough values of Y to get a rough idea of the shape of the function.)

b. What happens to the function relating Y and K and to the graph of the relationship if N rises to 200? If N falls to 50? Give an economic interpretation.

c. For the function relating Y to K and N, find the elasticity of Y with respect to K and the elasticity of Y with respect to N.

5. Use a calculator to find each of the following:

a. $5^{0.3}$

b. $5^{0.3}5^{0.2}$

c. $(5^{0.25})^2$

d. $(5^{0.5}5^{0.3})^2\,5^{0.4}$

e. $5^{0.2}/5^{0.5}$

f. $5^{-0.5}$

6. *a.* Nominal GDP equals real GDP times the GDP deflator (see Section 2.4). Suppose that nominal GDP growth is 12% and real GDP growth is 4%. What is inflation (the rate of growth of the GDP deflator)?

b. The "velocity of money," V, is defined by the equation

$$V = \frac{PY}{M},$$

where P is the price level, Y is real output, and M is the money supply (see Eq. 7.4). In a particular year velocity is constant, money growth is 10%, and inflation (the rate of growth of the price level) is 7%. What is real output growth?

c. Output, Y, is related to capital, K, and the number of workers, N, by the function

$$Y = 10K^{0.3}N^{0.7}.$$

In a particular year the capital stock grows by 2% and the number of workers grows by 1%. By how much does output grow?

Glossary

(The number in parentheses after the glossary term is the chapter in which that term first appears or is most extensively discussed.)

absorption: (5) total spending by domestic residents, firms, and governments, equal to $C + I + G$.

activist: (14) describes a policy strategy that involves active responses by the central bank to changes in economic circumstances. See *discretion*.

acyclical: (8) not displaying a regular pattern of behavior over the business cycle. See *procyclical, countercyclical*.

aggregate demand: (8) the total amount of goods and services demanded by households, businesses, and governments.

aggregate demand (AD) curve: (9) in a diagram with output on the horizontal axis and the price level on the vertical axis, the downward-sloping relation between the price level and the economy-wide demand for output.

aggregate demand for labor: (3) the sum of the labor demands of all employers in an economy.

aggregate demand management: (11) the use of monetary and fiscal policies, which shift the aggregate demand curve, to try to smooth out the business cycle; also known as *macroeconomic stabilization* or *stabilization policy*.

aggregate demand shocks: (11) shocks to the economy that shift the IS curve or the LM curve and thus affect the aggregate demand for output.

aggregate supply: (8) the total amount of output that producers as a whole are willing to supply at any particular price level.

aggregate supply (AS) curve: (9) in a diagram with output on the horizontal axis and the price level on the vertical axis, the relation between the price level and the total amount of output that firms supply.

aggregate supply of labor: (3) the sum of the labor supplied by everyone in the economy.

aggregation: (1) the process of adding individual economic variables to obtain economy-wide totals.

appreciation: (13) see *nominal appreciation, real appreciation*.

automatic stabilizers: (15) provisions in the government's budget that automatically cause government spending to rise or taxes to fall when GDP falls.

average labor productivity: (1) the amount of output produced per unit of labor input (per worker or per hour of work).

average tax rate: (15) the total amount of taxes paid divided by the taxpayer's income.

balance of payments: (5) the net increase (domestic less foreign) in a country's official reserve assets.

balance of payments accounts: (5) the record of a country's international transactions, consisting of the current account and the financial account.

bank reserves: (14) liquid assets held by banks to meet the demands for withdrawals by depositors or to pay the checks drawn on depositors' accounts.

bank run: (14) a large-scale withdrawal of deposits from a bank, caused by depositors' fear that the bank may go bankrupt and not pay depositors in full.

Board of Governors of the Federal Reserve System: (14) a group of seven governors, appointed by the President of the United States to staggered 14-year terms, that provides the leadership of the Federal Reserve System.

boom: (8) in a business cycle, the period of time during which aggregate economic activity grows; also known as an *expansion*.

borrowing constraint: (4) a restriction imposed by lenders on the amount that someone can borrow. If a borrowing constraint causes an individual to borrow less than he or she would choose to borrow in the absence of the constraint, the borrowing constraint is binding; otherwise it is nonbinding.

budget constraint: (4) a relation that shows how much current and future consumption a consumer can afford given the consumer's initial wealth, current and future income, and the interest rate.

budget deficit: (2) government outlays minus government receipts. See *government outlays, government receipts*.

budget line: (4) the graph of the consumer's budget constraint; the budget line shows graphically the combinations of current and future consumption a consumer can afford given the consumer's initial wealth, current and future income, and the interest rate.

budget surplus: (2) government receipts minus government outlays. See *government outlays, government receipts, government saving*.

business cycle: (8) a decline in aggregate economic activity (a contraction or recession) to a low point (a trough), followed by a recovery of activity (an expansion or boom) to a high point (a peak). A complete business cycle can be measured from peak to peak or from trough to trough.

business cycle chronology: (8) a history of the dates of business cycle peaks and troughs.

capital good: (2) a good that is produced, is used to produce other goods, and—unlike an intermediate good—is not used up in the same period in which it is produced.

capital–labor ratio: (6) the amount of capital per worker, equal to the capital stock divided by the number of workers.

central bank: (14) the governmental institution responsible for monetary policy, such as the Federal Reserve System in the United States and the Bank of Japan in Japan.

chronically unemployed: (3) workers who are unemployed a large fraction of the time.

classical approach: (1) an approach to macroeconomics based on the assumption that wages and prices adjust quickly to equate quantities supplied and demanded in each market. Classical economists generally argue that free markets are a good way to organize the economy and that the scope for government intervention in the economy—for example, to smooth out the business cycle—should be limited.

closed economy: (1) a national economy that does not have trading or financial relationships with the rest of the world.

coincident variable: (8) a variable with peaks and troughs that occur at about the same time as the corresponding business cycle peaks and troughs. See *lagging variable, leading variable*.

cold turkey: (12) a rapid and decisive reduction in the growth rate of the money supply aimed at reducing the rate of inflation; contrast with *gradualism*.

comovement: (8) the tendency of many economic variables to move together in a predictable way over the business cycle.

consumer price index: (2) a price index calculated as the current cost of a basket of consumer goods and services divided by the cost of the basket in the base period.

consumption: (2) spending by domestic households on final goods and services.

consumption-smoothing motive: (4) the preference of most people for a relatively constant or stable pattern of consumption over time, as opposed to having high consumption at some times and low consumption at others.

contraction: (8) in a business cycle, the period of time during which aggregate economic activity is falling; also known as a recession.

contractionary monetary policy: (11) a monetary or fiscal policy that reduces aggregate demand.

countercyclical: (8) tending to move in the opposite direction of aggregate economic activity over the business cycle (up in contractions, down in expansions). See *procyclical, acyclical*.

credibility: (14) the degree to which the public believes the central bank's announcements about future policy.

currency: (7) paper money and coin issued by the government; cash.

currency union: (13) a group of countries that agree to share a common currency.

current account: (5) the record of a country's international trade in currently produced goods and services.

current account balance: (2, 5) payments received from abroad in exchange for currently produced goods and services (including factor services and unilateral transfers), minus the analogous payments made to foreigners by the domestic economy.

cyclical unemployment: (3) the excess of the actual unemployment rate over the natural rate of unemployment; equivalently, unemployment that occurs when output is below its full-employment level.

deflation: (1) a situation in which the prices of most goods and services are falling over time.

demand for money: (7) the quantity of monetary assets, such as cash and checking accounts, that people choose to hold in their portfolios.

depository institutions: (14) privately owned banks and thrift institutions (such as savings and loans) that accept deposits from and make loans directly to the public.

depreciation: 1. (2) the amount of capital that wears out during a given period of time. 2. (13) a decline in the exchange rate; see *nominal depreciation, real depreciation*.

depression: (8) a particularly severe and prolonged downturn in economic activity.

desired capital stock: (4) the amount of capital that allows a firm to earn the highest possible expected profit.

devaluation: (13) a reduction in the value of a currency by official government action under a fixed-exchange-rate system.

diminishing marginal productivity: (3) a feature of production functions that implies that, the more a particular factor of production is used, the less extra output can be gained by increasing the use of that factor still further (with the usage of other factors of production held constant). For example, for a given capital stock, adding an extra worker increases output more when employment is initially low than when it is initially high.

discount rate: (14) the interest rate charged by the Fed when it lends reserves to banks.

discount window lending: (14) the lending of reserves to banks by the Fed.

discouraged workers: (3) people who stop searching for jobs because they have become discouraged by lack of success at finding a job; discouraged workers are not included in the official unemployment rate.

discretion: (14) the freedom of the central bank to conduct monetary policy in any way that it believes will advance the ultimate objectives of low and stable inflation, high economic growth, and low unemployment; in contrast to *rules*.

disinflation: (12) a fall in the rate of inflation.

distortions: (15) tax-induced deviations in economic behavior from the efficient, free-market outcome.

diversification: (7) the idea that spreading out investment in different assets can reduce an investor's overall risk.

duration: (3) the length of time that an unemployment spell lasts.

economic model: (1) a simplified description of some aspect of the economy, usually expressed in mathematical form.

economic theory: (1) a set of ideas about the economy that have been organized in a logical framework.

effective labor demand curve: (11) in a diagram with output on the horizontal axis and the quantity of labor on the vertical axis, an upward-sloping curve that shows how much labor is needed to produce a given amount of output, with productivity, the capital stock, and effort held constant.

effective tax rate (on capital): (4) a single measure of the tax burden on capital that summarizes the many provisions of the tax code that affect investment.

efficiency wage: (11) the real wage that maximizes worker effort or efficiency per dollar of real wages received.

efficiency wage model: (11) a model of the labor market in which, because workers exert more effort when they receive a higher real wage, profit-maximizing employers choose to pay a real wage that is higher than the real wage that clears the labor market; the efficiency wage model can be used to help explain real-wage rigidity and the existence of unemployment.

effort curve: (11) the relation between the level of effort put forth by workers and the real wage; its positive slope indicates that a higher real wage induces workers to exert greater effort.

empirical analysis: (1) a comparison of the implications of an economic theory or model with real-world data.

employment ratio: (3) the fraction of the adult population that is employed.

endogenous growth theory: (6) a branch of growth theory that tries to explain productivity growth (hence, the growth rate of output) within the context of a model of economic growth.

endogenous variable: (6) a variable determined by a model.

equilibrium: 1. (1) a situation in which the quantities demanded and supplied are equal in a market or a set of markets. 2. (11) in the labor market, the absence of any upward or downward pressure on wages.

equilibrium condition: (6) an equation that is satisfied in equilibrium.

exchange rate: (13) the number of units of foreign currency that can be purchased with one unit of the home currency; also known as the *nominal exchange rate.*

exogenous variable: (6) a variable that is given, or determined outside a model.

expansion: (8) in a business cycle, the period of time during which aggregate economic activity is rising; also known as a *boom.*

expansionary monetary policy: (11) a monetary policy that increases aggregate demand.

expectations-augmented Phillips curve: (12) an inverse relation between unanticipated inflation and cyclical unemployment.

expectations theory of the term structure: (7) the idea that investors compare the expected rates of return on a long-term bond and on a sequence of short-term bonds over the same horizon as the long-term bond; in equilibrium, the expected rate of return on an N-year bond equals the average of the expected rates of return on one-year bonds during the current year and the N-1 succeeding years.

expected real after-tax interest rate: (4) the nominal after-tax rate of return (equal to the nominal interest rate times 1 minus the tax rate) minus the expected rate of inflation; equals the expected increase in the real value of an asset after payment of taxes on interest income.

expected real interest rate: (2) the nominal interest rate minus the expected rate of inflation; equals the expected increase in the real value of an asset.

expected returns: (7) the rates of return on real or financial assets that financial investors expect to earn on average.

expenditure approach: (2) a procedure for measuring economic activity by adding the amount spent by all purchasers of final goods and services.

factors of production: (3) inputs to the production process, such as capital goods, labor, raw materials, and energy.

FE line: (9) see *full-employment line.*

Federal Open Market Committee (FOMC): (14) a twelve-member committee (consisting of the seven governors of the Federal Reserve Board, the president of the Federal Reserve Bank of New York, and four of the presidents of the other regional Federal Reserve Banks) that decides the course of U.S. monetary policy.

federal funds rate: (14) the interest rate charged on reserves that one bank lends to another; also known as *fed funds rate*.

fed funds rate: (14) the interest rate charged on reserves that one bank lends to another; also known as federal funds rate.

final goods and services: (2) goods and services that are the end products of the productive process, in contrast to *intermediate goods and services*.

financial account: (5) the record of a country's flow of assets into or out of the country (other than assets transferred unilaterally).

financial account balance: (5) equals the value of financial inflows minus the value of financial outflows.

financial inflow: (5) an entry in a country's financial account that arises when a resident of the country sells an asset to someone in another country.

financial outflow: (5) an entry in a country's financial account that arises when a resident of the country buys an asset from abroad.

fiscal policy: (1) policy concerning the level and composition of government spending and taxation.

fixed-exchange-rate system: (13) a system in which exchange rates are set at officially determined levels and are changed only by direct governmental action.

flexible-exchange-rate system: (13) a system in which exchange rates are not officially fixed but are determined by conditions of supply and demand in the foreign exchange market; also known as a *floating-exchange-rate system*.

floating-exchange-rate system: (13) see *flexible-exchange-rate system*.

flow variable: (2) a variable that is measured per unit of time; an example is GDP, which is measured as output per year or quarter. See *stock variable*.

foreign direct investment: (5) the purchase or construction of capital goods by a foreign business firm; for example, a Japanese auto company builds a new plant in the United States.

foreign exchange market: (13) the market in which the currencies of different nations are traded.

forward guidance: (14) a tool that the Fed can use to influence long-term interest rates by signaling its expectations about future short-term interest rates.

fractional reserve banking: (14) a banking system in which banks hold reserves equal to a fraction of their deposits so that the reserve–deposit ratio is less than 1.

frictional unemployment: (3) the unemployment that arises as the result of the matching process in which workers search for suitable jobs and firms search for suitable workers.

full-employment deficit: (15) what the government budget deficit *would be*, given the tax and spending policies currently in force, if the economy were operating at its full-employment level.

full-employment level of employment: (3) the equilibrium level of employment, achieved after wages and prices fully adjust.

full-employment (FE) line: (9) in a diagram with output on the horizontal axis and the real interest rate on the vertical axis, a vertical line at full-employment output. Points on the *FE* line correspond to points of equilibrium in the labor market.

full-employment output: (3) the level of output that firms supply when wages and prices in the economy have fully adjusted to their equilibrium levels.

fundamental identity of national income accounting: (2) the accounting identity that states that total production, total income, and total expenditure during a given period are equal.

fundamental value of the exchange rate: (13) the value of the exchange rate that would be determined by the forces of supply and demand in the foreign exchange market, in the absence of government intervention.

GDP: (2) see *gross domestic product*.

GDP deflator: (2) a measure of the price level, calculated as the ratio of current nominal GDP to current real GDP.

general equilibrium: (9) a situation in which all markets in an economy are simultaneously in equilibrium.

GNP: (2) see *gross national product*.

Golden Rule capital–labor ratio: (6) the level of the capital–labor ratio that maximizes consumption per worker in the steady state.

government capital: (15) long-lived physical assets owned by the government, such as roads and public schools.

government debt: (15) the total value of government bonds outstanding at any given time.

government outlays: (2) the government's purchases of goods and services plus transfers and interest payments; also known as *government expenditures*.

government purchases: (2) spending by the government on currently produced goods and services.

government receipts: (2) taxes and other revenues collected by the government.

government saving: (2) net government income minus government purchases; equivalently, the government's tax receipts minus its outlays; equal to the government budget surplus.

gradualism: (12) a prescription for disinflation that involves reducing the rate of monetary growth and the rate of inflation gradually over a period of several years; contrast with *cold turkey*.

gross domestic product (GDP): (2) the market value of final goods and services newly produced within a nation's borders during a fixed period of time.

gross investment: (4) the total purchase or construction of new capital goods.

gross national product (GNP): (2) the market value of final goods and services newly produced by domestically owned factors of production during a fixed period of time.

growth accounting: (6) a method for breaking down total output growth into parts attributable to growth of capital, labor, and productivity.

growth accounting equation: (6) the production function written in growth rate form; it states that the growth rate of output is the sum of (1) the growth rate of productivity, (2) the elasticity of output with respect to capital times the growth rate of capital, and (3) the elasticity of output with respect to labor times the growth rate of labor.

high-powered money: (14) the liabilities of the central bank, consisting of bank reserves and currency held by the nonbank public, that are usable as money; also known as *monetary base*.

human capital: (6) the productive knowledge, skills, and training of individuals.

hyperinflation: (12) a situation in which the rate of inflation is extremely high for a sustained period of time; one suggested definition is a 50% or higher monthly rate of inflation.

income approach: (2) a procedure for measuring economic activity by adding all income received, including taxes and after-tax profits.

income effect: (4) a change in economic behavior (such as the amount a person saves or works) in response to a change in income or wealth; graphically, a change in behavior induced by a parallel shift in the budget line.

income effect of a higher real wage: (3) the tendency of workers to supply less labor when the real wage increases, as a result of the fact that a higher real wage makes workers wealthier.

income effect of the real interest rate on saving: (4) the tendency of savers to consume more and save less in response to an increase in the real interest rate because they are made wealthier; the tendency of borrowers to consume less and save more in response to an increase in the real interest rate because they are made less wealthy.

income elasticity of money demand: (7) the percentage change in money demand resulting from a 1% increase in real income.

income–expenditure identity: (2) the accounting identity that states that total income (product) equals the sum of the four types of expenditure: consumption, investment, government purchases, and net exports.

inconvertible currency: (13) a currency that cannot be traded freely for other currencies, usually because of government-imposed restrictions.

index of leading economic indicators: (8) a weighted average of economic variables that lead the business cycle, used for forecasting future business activity.

indicators: (14) see *intermediate targets*.

indifference curve: (4) shows graphically the combinations of current and future consumption that yield any given level of utility.

inflation: (1) a situation in which the prices of most goods and services are rising over time.

inflation tax: (15) the resources raised by the government by issuing money and creating inflation; also known as *seignorage*.

instruments: (14) the policy tools that the Fed can use to influence the economy; they include reserve requirements, the discount rate, the interest rate on reserves, and, especially, open-market operations.

interest elasticity of money demand: (7) the percentage change in money demand resulting from a 1% increase (different from a 1 percentage point increase) in the interest rate.

interest rate: (2) the rate of return promised by a borrower to a lender.

intermediate goods and services: (2) goods and services that are used up in the production of other goods and services in the same period that they themselves were produced; an example is wheat used up in making bread.

intermediate targets: (14) macroeconomic variables that the Fed cannot control directly but can influence fairly predictably and that, in turn, are related to the ultimate goals the Fed is trying to achieve; also known as *indicators*. Examples of intermediate targets are the growth rates of monetary aggregates and short-term interest rates.

inventories: (2) stocks of unsold finished goods, goods in process, and production materials held by firms.

investment: (2) spending for new capital goods, called *fixed investment*, and increases in firms' inventory holdings, called *inventory investment*. See *gross investment, net investment*.

invisible hand: (1) the idea (proposed by Adam Smith) that, if there are free markets and individuals conduct their economic affairs in their own best interests, the economy as a whole will work well.

***IS* curve:** (9) in a diagram with output on the horizontal axis and the real interest rate on the vertical axis, a downward-sloping curve that shows the value of the real interest rate that clears the goods market for any given value of output. At any point on the *IS* curve, desired national saving equals desired investment (in a closed economy); equivalently, the aggregate quantity of goods demanded equals the aggregate quantity of goods supplied.

J curve: (13) the typical time pattern of the response of net exports to a depreciation of the real exchange rate, in which net exports initially decline but then increase.

job finding rate: (8) the probability that someone who is unemployed will find a job in the next month.

job loss rate: (8) the probability that someone who is employed will lose his or her job in the next month.

Keynesian approach: (1) an approach to macroeconomics based on the assumption that wages and prices may not adjust quickly to equate quantities supplied and demanded in each market. Keynesian economists are more likely than classical economists to argue that government intervention in the economy—for example, to smooth out the business cycle—may be desirable.

labor force: (3) the number of people willing to work, including unemployed people actively searching for work, as well as employed workers.

labor hoarding: (10) a situation that occurs if, because of the costs of firing and hiring workers, firms continue to employ some workers in a recession that they otherwise would have laid off.

lagging variable: (8) a variable with peaks and troughs that tend to occur later than the corresponding peaks and troughs in the business cycle. See *coincident variable, leading variable.*

large open economy: (5) an economy that trades with other economies and is large enough to affect the world real interest rate.

leading variable: (8) a variable with peaks and troughs that tend to occur earlier than the corresponding peaks and troughs in the business cycle. See *coincident variable, lagging variable.*

leisure: (3) all off-the-job activities, including eating, sleeping, recreation, and household chores.

life-cycle model: (4) a multi-period version of the basic two-period model of consumer behavior that focuses on the patterns of income, consumption, and saving over the various stages of an individual's life.

liquidity: (7) the ease and quickness with which an asset can be exchanged for goods, services, or other assets.

liquidity trap: (14) a situation in which any additional money supplied by the central bank is held by banks or the public, with no decline in interest rates or increase in spending.

***LM* curve:** (9) in a diagram with output on the horizontal axis and the real interest rate on the vertical axis, an upward-sloping curve that shows the value of the real interest rate that clears the asset market for any given value of output. At any point on the *LM* curve, the quantities of money supplied and demanded are equal.

long-run aggregate supply (*LRAS*) curve: (9) in a diagram with output on the horizontal axis and the price level on the vertical axis, a vertical line at full-employment output; indicates that in the long run the supply of output does not depend on the price level.

long-run Phillips curve: (12) in a diagram with unemployment on the horizontal axis and inflation on the vertical axis, a vertical line at the natural rate of unemployment; indicates that in the long run the unemployment rate equals the natural rate, independent of the rate of inflation.

lump-sum tax cut: (4) a tax cut in which every taxpayer's taxes are reduced by the same amount.

M1: (7) a monetary aggregate that includes currency and travelers' checks held by the public, demand deposits (non-interest–bearing checking accounts), and other checkable deposits.

M2: (7) a monetary aggregate that includes everything in M1 and a number of other assets that are somewhat less moneylike, such as savings deposits, small-denomination (under $100,000) time deposits, noninstitutional holdings of money market mutual funds (MMMFs), and money market deposit accounts (MMDAs).

macroeconomics: (1) the study of the structure and performance of national economies and of the policies that governments use to try to affect economic performance.

macroeconomic stabilization: (11) the use of monetary and fiscal policies to moderate cyclical fluctuations and maintain low inflation; also known as *aggregate demand management* or *stabilization policy*.

marginal cost: (11) the cost of producing an additional unit of output.

marginal product of capital (*MPK*): (3) the amount of output produced by an additional unit of capital.

marginal product of labor (*MPN*): (3) the amount of output produced by an additional unit of labor.

marginal propensity to consume (*MPC*): (4) the amount by which desired consumption rises when current income rises by one unit.

marginal revenue product of labor (*MRPN*): (3) the extra revenue obtained by a firm when it employs an additional unit of labor and sells the resulting increase in output; for competitive firms, equal to the price of output times the marginal product of labor.

marginal tax rate: (15) the fraction of an additional dollar of income that must be paid in taxes.

markup: (11) the difference between the price charged for a good and its marginal cost of production, expressed as a percentage of marginal cost.

medium of exchange: (7) an asset used in making transactions.

menu cost: (11) the cost of changing prices—for example, the cost of printing a new menu or remarking merchandise.

misperceptions theory: (10) predicts that, because of producers' inability to observe directly the general price level, the aggregate quantity of output supplied rises above the full-employment level when the aggregate price level is higher than expected; hence the short-run aggregate supply curve is upward-sloping.

monetarism: (14) a school of macroeconomic thought that emphasizes the importance of monetary factors in the macroeconomy, but which opposes the active use of monetary policy to stabilize the economy.

monetary aggregates: (7) the official measures of the money supply, such as M1 and M2. See *M1, M2*.

monetary base: (14) the liabilities of the central bank, consisting of bank reserves and currency held by the nonbank public, that are usable as money; also known as *high-powered money*.

monetary neutrality: (9) characterizes an economy in which changes in the nominal money supply change the price level proportionally but have no effect on real variables. The basic classical model predicts neutrality; the classical model with misperceptions and the Keynesian model predict that neutrality holds in the long run but not in the short run.

monetary policy: (1) policies determining the level and rate of growth of the nation's money supply, which are under the control of a government institution known as the *central bank* (the Federal Reserve System in the United States).

money: (7) assets that are widely used and accepted as payment.

money demand function: (7) the function that relates the real demand for money to output and the interest rate paid by nonmonetary assets.

money supply: (7) the total amount of money available in an economy, consisting of currency held by the nonbank public and deposits; also known as the *money stock*.

monopolistic competition: (11) a market situation in which some competition exists but in which a relatively small number of sellers and imperfect standardization of the product allow individual producers to act as price setters rather than as price takers.

multiple expansion of loans and deposits: (14) in a fractional reserve banking system, the process in which banks lend out some of their deposits, the loaned funds are ultimately redeposited in the banking system, and the new deposits are lent out again; as a result of the multiple-expansion process, the money supply can greatly exceed the monetary base.

multiplier: (11) for any particular type of spending, the short-run change in output resulting from a one-unit change in that type of spending.

national income: (2) the amount of income available to distribute among producers, equal to the sum of employee compensation, proprietors' income, rental income of persons, corporate profits, net interest, taxes on production and imports, business current transfer payments, and current surplus of government enterprises. Also measured as gross domestic product plus net factor payments less depreciation and statistical discrepancy.

national income accounts: (2) an accounting framework used in measuring current economic activity.

national saving: (2) the saving of the economy as a whole, including both private saving (business and household) and government saving.

national wealth: (2) the total wealth of the residents of a country, consisting of the country's domestic physical assets (such as its stock of capital goods and land) and its net foreign assets.

natural rate of unemployment: (3) the rate of unemployment that exists when the economy's output is at its full-employment level; consists of frictional unemployment and structural unemployment.

net exports: (2) exports of goods and services minus imports of goods and services.

net factor payments from abroad (NFP): (2) income paid to domestic factors of production by the rest of the world minus income paid to foreign factors of production by the domestic economy.

net foreign assets: (2) a country's foreign assets (for example, foreign stocks, bonds, and factories owned by domestic residents) minus its foreign liabilities (domestic physical and financial assets owned by foreigners).

net government income: (2) the part of GDP that is not at the disposal of the private sector. It equals taxes paid by the private sector minus payments from the government to the private sector (transfers and interest payments on the government debt).

net investment: (4) the change in the capital stock over the year, equal to gross investment minus depreciation of existing capital.

net national product (NNP): (2) GNP minus depreciation.

no-borrowing, no-lending point: (4) on the budget line, the point at which current consumption equals current income plus initial wealth; if the consumer chooses the consumption combination corresponding to this point, he or she neither borrows nor carries over resources into the future.

nominal appreciation: (13) an increase in the nominal exchange rate in a flexible-exchange-rate system.

nominal depreciation: (13) a decrease in the nominal exchange rate in a flexible-exchange-rate system.

nominal exchange rate: (13) the number of units of foreign currency that can be purchased with one unit of the home currency; also known as the *exchange rate*.

nominal GDP: (2) the value of an economy's final output measured using current market prices; also known as *current-dollar GDP*.

nominal interest rate: (2) the rate at which the nominal value of an interest-bearing asset increases over time; equivalent to the market interest rate.

nominal shock: (10) a shock to money supply or money demand, which causes the *LM* curve to shift.

nominal variables: (2) variables measured in terms of current market prices.

normative analysis: (1) an analysis of policy that tries to determine whether a certain policy should be used; involves both analysis of the consequences of the policy and value judgments about the desirability of those consequences. See *positive analysis*.

official reserve assets: (5) assets held by central banks, other than domestic money or securities, that can be used in making international payments; examples are gold, foreign bank deposits, and special assets created by the International Monetary Fund.

Okun's law: (3) a rule of thumb that says that output falls by 2% for each percentage point increase in the unemployment rate.

100% reserve banking: (14) a banking system in which banks hold reserves equal to 100% of their deposits.

open economy: (1) a national economy that has significant trading and financial relationships with other national economies.

open-market operation: (7) an open-market purchase or sale of assets by the central bank, used to affect the money supply. See *open-market purchase, open-market sale*.

open-market purchase: (14) a purchase of assets (such as Treasury securities) from the public by the central bank, used to increase the money supply.

open-market sale: (14) a sale of assets (such as Treasury securities) to the public by the central bank, used to reduce the money supply.

optimum currency area: (13) a geographic region for which the benefits of having a common currency exceed the costs.

overvalued exchange rate: (13) in a fixed-exchange-rate system, an exchange rate that is higher than its fundamental value. See *fundamental value of the exchange rate*.

participation rate: (3) the fraction of adults who are in the labor force.

peak: (8) in a business cycle, the point in time when economic activity stops increasing and begins to decline.

perfect competition: (11) a market situation in which there is a standardized good and many buyers and sellers so that all buyers and sellers are price takers.

permanent income theory: (4) a theory that states that consumption depends on the present value of lifetime resources, with the implication that consumption responds much less to temporary than to permanent changes in income.

persistence: (8) the tendency for declines in economic activity to be followed by further declines and for growth in economic activity to be followed by more growth.

Phillips curve: (12) a downward-sloping relationship between the inflation rate and the unemployment rate; theory suggests that a Phillips curve will be observed in the data only in periods in which expected inflation and the natural rate of unemployment are relatively stable. See *expectations-augmented Phillips curve, short-run Phillips curve, long-run Phillips curve*.

portfolio allocation decision: (7) a wealth holder's decision about which assets and how much of each asset to hold.

positive analysis: (1) an analysis of the economic consequences of a policy that doesn't address the question of whether those consequences are desirable. See *normative analysis*.

present value: (4) the value of a future payment in terms of today's dollars; equal to the amount of money that must be invested today at a given interest rate to be worth the specified payment at the specified date in the future.

present value of lifetime consumption (*PVLC*): (4) the present value of current and future consumption, which equals *PVLR* according to the budget constraint.

present value of lifetime resources (*PVLR*): (4) the present value of current and expected future income plus initial wealth; corresponds to the horizontal intercept of the budget line.

price index: (2) a measure of the average level of prices for some specified set of goods and services, relative to the prices of a specified base period.

price setter: (11) a market participant with some power to set prices; see *monopolistic competition*.

price stickiness: (11) in Keynesian theory, the tendency of prices to adjust only slowly to changes in the economy; also known as *price rigidity*.

price taker: (11) a market participant who takes the market price as given; see *perfect competition*.

primary government budget deficit: (15) a measure of the deficit that excludes government interest payments from total outlays; equal to government purchases of goods and services plus transfers minus tax revenues.

private disposable income: (2) the income of the private sector (households and businesses taken together) after payment of taxes and receipt of transfer payments and interest from the government.

private saving: (2) the saving of the private sector (households and businesses), equal to private disposable income minus consumption.

procyclical: (8) tending to move in the same direction as aggregate economic activity over the business cycle (up in expansions, down in contractions). See *acyclical, countercyclical*.

product approach: (2) a procedure for measuring economic activity by adding the market values of goods and services produced, excluding any goods and services used up in intermediate stages of production; equivalently, by summing the value added of all producers.

production function: (3) a function that shows the amount of output that can be produced (by a firm or by an entire economy) by using any given quantities of capital and labor.

productivity: (3) a measure of the overall effectiveness with which the economy uses capital and labor to produce output; also known as *total factor productivity*.

productivity shock: (10) a change in an economy's production function; equivalently, a change in the amount of output that can be produced using given quantities of capital and labor; also known as a *supply shock*.

propagation mechanism: (10) an aspect of the economy, such as the behavior of inventories, that allows short-lived shocks to have longer-term effects on the economy.

purchasing power parity (PPP): (13) the idea that similar foreign and domestic goods, or baskets of goods, should have the same price in terms of the same currency.

quantitative easing: (14) a tool used by the Fed in which it increases its total holdings of assets by buying securities in the open market.

quantity theory of money: (7) a theory that asserts that nominal money demand is proportional to nominal GDP so that velocity is constant.

rational expectations: (10) expectations about the values of economic variables that are based on reasoned and intelligent examination of available economic data; although they may make forecast errors, people with rational expectations cannot be *systematically* surprised by changes in macroeconomic policy or in the economy.

real appreciation: (13) an increase in the real exchange rate, which increases the quantity of foreign goods that can be purchased with a given quantity of domestic goods.

real balances: (7) the real amount of money held by the public, measured as the nominal amount of money divided by the price level.

real business cycle (RBC) theory: (10) a version of the classical theory that assumes that productivity shocks (supply shocks) are the primary source of cyclical fluctuations.

real depreciation: (13) a fall in the real exchange rate, which decreases the quantity of foreign goods that can be purchased with a given quantity of domestic goods.

real exchange rate: (13) the quantity of foreign goods that can be obtained in exchange for one domestic good; also known as the *terms of trade*.

real GDP: (2) the market value of an economy's final output measured in terms of the prices that prevailed during some fixed base period; also known as *constant-dollar GDP*.

real interest rate: (2) the rate at which the real value or purchasing power of an interest-bearing asset increases over time; equal to the nominal interest rate minus the rate of inflation.

real shocks: (10) disturbances to the "real side" of the economy, such as shocks that affect the production function, the size of the labor force, the real quantity of government purchases, or the spending and saving decisions of consumers; real shocks affect the *IS* curve or the *FE* line.

real variable: (2) a variable measured in terms of the prices of a fixed base year; a measure intended to represent physical quantities produced or used.

real wage: (3) the real value (measured in terms of goods) of what firms must pay per unit of labor input that they employ; equal to the nominal (dollar) wage divided by the price level.

real-wage rigidity: (11) from the Keynesian perspective, the apparent tendency of real wages to move too little over the business cycle to keep the quantity of labor supplied equal to the quantity of labor demanded.

recession: (8) in a business cycle, the period of time during which aggregate economic activity is falling; also known as a *contraction*.

relative purchasing power parity: (13) the idea that the rate of appreciation of the nominal exchange rate equals the foreign inflation rate minus the domestic inflation rate.

reserve–deposit ratio: (14) the ratio of reserves held by banks to the public's deposits in banks.

reserves: 1. (14) see *bank reserves*. 2. (5) see *official reserve assets*.

revaluation: (13) an increase in the value of a currency by official government action under a fixed-exchange-rate system.

reverse causation: (10) the tendency of expected future changes in output to cause changes in the current money supply in the same direction; used by real business cycle theorists to explain why the money supply leads the cycle.

Ricardian equivalence proposition: (4) the proposition that changes in the government budget deficit caused entirely by changes in (lump-sum) tax collections have no effect on the economy.

risk: (7) the possibility that the actual return received on an asset will be substantially different from the expected return.

risk premium: (7) the amount by which the expected return on a risky asset exceeds the return on an otherwise comparable safe asset.

rules: (14) a set of simple, prespecified, and publicly announced guidelines for conducting monetary policy; in contrast to *discretion*.

sacrifice ratio: (12) the amount of output lost when the inflation rate is reduced by one percentage point.

saving: (2) current income minus spending on current needs.

seignorage: (15) government revenue raised by printing money; also known as the *inflation tax*.

shoe leather costs: (12) the costs incurred in the process of economizing on holdings of cash—for example, in more frequent trips to the bank.

short-run aggregate supply (*SRAS*) curve: (9) in a diagram with output on the horizontal axis and the price level on the vertical axis, the relationship between the price level and the amount of output supplied that applies in the short run. In the short run, prices remain fixed and producers produce the quantity of output demanded at the fixed price level, so the *SRAS* curve is horizontal. In the extended classical model based on the misperceptions theory, the *SRAS* curve slopes upward, as producers are fooled into supplying more output when the price level is higher than expected; the short run in this model is the period of time during which the expected price level remains unchanged.

short-run Phillips curve: (12) the curve relating the inflation rate to the unemployment rate for a given natural rate of unemployment and a given expected rate of inflation.

small open economy: (5) an economy that trades with other economies but is too small to affect the world real interest rate.

Solow residual: (10) an empirical measure of total factor productivity.

speculative run: (13) a situation in which financial investors, fearing the imminent devaluation of a currency in a fixed-exchange-rate system, rush to sell assets denominated in that currency.

spell of unemployment: (3) see *unemployment spell*.

stagflation: (1) the simultaneous existence of both high unemployment (stagnation) and high inflation, as occurred in the United States in the mid 1970s.

statistical discrepancy: 1. (2) arises because of errors of measurement and incomplete reporting. 2. (5) the amount that would have to be added to the sum of the current account balance and financial account balance for this sum to reach its theoretical value of zero.

steady state: (6) a situation in which the economy's output per worker, consumption per worker, and capital stock per worker are constant over time.

stock variable: (2) an economic quantity that is defined at a specific time; examples are wealth or the money supply. See *flow variable*.

store of value: (7) a means of holding wealth over time.

structural unemployment: (3) long-term and chronic unemployment arising from imbalances between the skills and other characteristics of workers in the market and the needs of employers.

substitution effect of a higher real wage: (3) the tendency of workers to substitute work for leisure, and thus supply more labor, in response to an increase in the reward for working when the real wage increases.

substitution effect of the real interest rate on saving: (4) the tendency of consumers to save more, and thereby substitute future consumption for current consumption, in response to a higher reward for saving.

supply shock: (3) a change in an economy's production function—that is, in the amount of output that can be produced by using given quantities of capital and labor; also known as a *productivity shock*.

supply-side economics: (15) a school of economic thought based on the premise that all aspects of economic behavior—such as labor supply, saving, and investment—respond strongly to economic incentives, and, in particular, to incentives provided by the tax code.

tax-adjusted user cost of capital: (4) indicates how large the before-tax expected future marginal product of capital must be to make a proposed investment profitable; equivalently, the (unadjusted) user cost of capital divided by 1 minus the effective tax rate.

tax rate smoothing: (15) a policy of maintaining stable tax rates over time so as to minimize the distortions created by the tax code. See *distortions*.

Taylor rule: (14) a guideline for monetary policy, it relates the real Fed funds rate to the difference between output and full-employment output and the difference between inflation and its target.

terms of trade: (13) the quantity of foreign goods that can be obtained in exchange for one domestic good; also known as the *real exchange rate*.

term premium: (7) the higher interest rate paid to holders of long-term bonds to compensate them for the added risk compared with short-term bonds, so that the interest rate on long-term bonds exceeds that suggested by the expectations theory of the term structure.

time to maturity: (7) the amount of time until an asset matures and the investors receive their principal.

total factor productivity: (3) a measure of the overall effectiveness with which the economy uses capital and labor to produce output; also known as *productivity*.

trade deficit: (1) a nation's excess of imports over exports.

trade surplus: (1) a nation's excess of exports over imports.

transfers: (2) payments by the government, excluding interest payments and payments made in exchange for current goods or services; examples of transfers are Social Security and Medicare benefits, unemployment insurance, and welfare payments.

trough: (8) in a business cycle, the time when economic activity stops falling and begins rising.

turning points: (8) peaks or troughs in the business cycle.

turnover costs: (11) the costs associated with firing existing workers or hiring and training new workers.

unanticipated inflation: (12) the actual rate of inflation minus the rate of inflation that was expected to occur.

underground economy: (2) the portion of the economy that includes both legal activities hidden from government record keepers and illegal activities.

undervalued exchange rate: (13) in a fixed-exchange-rate system, an exchange rate that is lower than its fundamental value. See *fundamental value of the exchange rate*.

unemployment: (1) the number of people who are available for work and actively seeking work but cannot find jobs.

unemployment rate: (3) the fraction of the labor force that is unemployed.

unemployment spell: (3) the period of time that an individual is continuously unemployed.

unilateral transfers: (5) payments made from one country to another that do not correspond to the purchase of any good, service, or asset; examples are foreign aid and gifts by domestic residents to foreigners.

unit of account: (7) the basic unit for measuring economic value (dollars, for example).

user cost of capital: (4) the expected real cost of using a unit of capital for a specified period of time; equal to the depreciation cost plus the interest cost.

uses-of-saving identity: (2) the accounting identity that states that private saving equals the sum of investment, the government deficit, and the current account balance.

utility: (4) an individual's economic satisfaction or well-being.

value added: (2) for any producer, the value of output minus the value of purchased inputs.

velocity: (7) the number of times the money stock "turns over" each period; calculated as nominal GDP divided by the nominal money supply.

wealth: (2) the assets minus the liabilities of an individual, firm, or country; also known as *net worth*.

world real interest rate: (5) the real interest rate that prevails in the international capital market in which individuals, businesses, and governments borrow and lend across national borders.

zero lower bound: (14) a situation in which the nominal interest rate is zero and cannot decline further because a nominal interest rate below zero would make it more profitable for an investor to hold cash rather than make a loan.

Name Index

Note: Page numbers followed by *n* indicate footnotes.

Subject Index

Note: Page numbers in **boldface** type indicate pages where terms are defined; page numbers followed by *n* indicate footnotes.